MW00857172

The New International Commentary on the New Testament

General Editors

NED B. STONEHOUSE
(1946-1962)

F. F. BRUCE
(1962-1990)

GORDON D. FEE
(1990-   )

The Second Epistle
to the
CORINTHIANS

PAUL BARNETT

WILLIAM B. EERDMANS PUBLISHING COMPANY
GRAND RAPIDS, MICHIGAN / CAMBRIDGE, U.K.

© 1997 Wm. B. Eerdmans Publishing Co.
255 Jefferson Ave. S.E., Grand Rapids, Michigan 49503 /
P.O. Box 163, Cambridge CB3 9PU U.K.
All rights reserved

Printed in the United States of America

04 03 02 01 00 99 98   7 6 5 4 3 2 1

Library of Congress Cataloging-in-Publication Data

Barnett, Paul (Paul William)
The Second Epistle to the Corinthians / Paul Barnett.
p.   cm.
— (The new international commentary on the New Testament)
Includes bibliographical references and indexes.
ISBN 0-8028-2300-9 (cloth: alk. paper)
1. Bible. N.T. Corinthians, 2nd — Commentaries.
I. Title.   II. Series.
BS2675.3.B29   1997
227′.3077 — dc21   96-49755
                                    CIP

Scripture taken from the HOLY BIBLE: NEW INTERNATIONAL VERSION®. NIV®. Copyright
© 1973, 1978, 1984 by International Bible Society. Used by permission of Zondervan Publishing
House.

FOR
ANITA BARNETT
in gratitude
for
much sacrifice
in apostolic-style
"long-suffering"

CONTENTS

EDITOR'S PREFACE

It has now been nearly thirty-five years since the original commentary on 2 Corinthians, written by Philip Edgcumbe Hughes, appeared in this series. This was a significant volume in the original series not only because it received deserved critical acclaim but also because it set a new standard for the series (acknowledged by the editor, Ned Stonehouse). Though now dated in many ways, it will, and should, continue to be consulted. Nonetheless, the proliferation of Pauline studies, including works on 2 Corinthians, has meant that this volume, too, needed to be replaced so as to bring the busy pastor and student up to date on the interpretation and theology of this very important Pauline letter.

This task has now been brought to a happy conclusion by the Rt. Rev. Dr. Paul Barnett, Anglican bishop of North Sydney, New South Wales, Australia. Dr. Barnett took his first degree in classics and history at the University of Sydney. His Ph.D. was awarded in 1978 by the University of London for a thesis entitled "The Jewish Sign Prophets in Their Theological and Political Setting." In addition to spending many years in the parish ministry, he held teaching posts at Robert Menzies College (Macquarie University) and the University of Sydney before being elevated to bishop in 1990.

Besides his obvious exegetical skills, Dr. Barnett thus brings two other specialties to the writing of this commentary: first, his expertise in the history of the first Christian century, including Roman history and sociology as well as intertestamental and first-century Judaism; second, the fact that he is bishop, which has given him a special interest in the pastoral dimension of this letter, which the reader will find highlighted throughout. Although it was not by design, it turns out to be a pleasant coincidence that the replacement volume is thus written by an Anglican clergyman from Australia, just as was Dr. Hughes (although the latter was only born in Australia and spent most of his life elsewhere).

As with several other replacement volumes in the series, the New International Version has been used as the basis of comment, although the reader will quickly recognize that the commentary rests ultimately on the Greek text itself.

This is a welcome addition to the series.

GORDON D. FEE

AUTHOR'S PREFACE

This commentary began its life as Bible studies at student and missionary conventions in the 1970s. Although many commentaries had been devoted to 2 Corinthians, it was at that time relatively closed to the general reader, apart from some well-known passages. This seemed regrettable because its total message is so powerful and relevant. Those Bible studies issued in a commentary in the Bible Speaks Today, whose editor is the celebrated John R. W. Stott.

During the 1980s it was my privilege to work as an academic colleague of Professor E. A. Judge at Macquarie University. Clustered around Edwin Judge, who is an authority on the cultural world of the apostle Paul, were a number of younger scholars who have produced innovative studies, including works on Paul's Second Letter to the Corinthians. The exciting ethos of this great scholar served to keep alive my own long-standing interest in the letter.

An invitation to write for this series brought me into relationship with its distinguished editor, Gordon D. Fee. Fee's knowledge of the Corinthian correspondence is of the highest order, and his commentary on the First Letter set new standards for this and all other commentaries in this series. Certainly Fee's goal — that texts be allowed to speak within the context of their paragraphs and extended passages,[1] all within the historical setting of the letter — has also been mine. I have deeply appreciated Dr. Fee's advice and encouragement; whatever shortcomings may be found in this exposition are entirely mine.

There is an extensive bibliography on Second Corinthians, including commentaries, monographs, and articles. This letter is a scholar's favorite, even if it remains less well known to general readers than some of Paul's other letters. It has not been possible to refer to more than a selection of the

---

1. I have paid particular attention to connectives, or, on occasion, lack of connectives, as pointing out the flow of Paul's argument within and between passages.

scholarly works in the footnotes of this book. Of the commentaries I consulted, those by Plummer, Barrett, Bultmann, Hughes, Martin and Furnish exerted the greatest influence on me. Furnish's commentary in particular is nearly exhaustive, thorough, and full of insight. The first part of Margaret Thrall's International Critical Commentary volume appeared too late for much more than a survey of her very detailed presentation; the second volume is yet to appear. An "Index of Authors" is found at the end of this commentary, and a "Select Bibliography" of much-cited works, including commentaries, appears near the beginning.

For the sake of historical context Dr. Fee placed 2 Corinthians in chronological order in listing Paul's letters. I have followed his general procedure by citing in order letters of Paul known to have been written prior to 2 Corinthians. Thus I have given as his first letters 1 and 2 Thessalonians, followed by 1 Corinthians. Unlike Dr. Fee, I tend to favor an early date for Galatians, but since this is a matter of scholarly debate that has minimal bearing on issues in 2 Corinthians, I have listed that letter with others that are known to come after 2 Corinthians. It has been interesting to trace Paul's use of vocabulary in 2 Corinthians through the three letters that are known to have preceded it.

In working closely with his text I have repeatedly been overwhelmed by the subtlety and sensitivity of the one on whose letter I have been privileged to spend so much time. Though long departed, he still ministers to us through these remarkable, God-breathed words.

I express my gratitude to Bishop Donald Robinson, Drs. Chris Forbes, Bruce Harris, and Peter O'Brien, and Miss Evonne Paddison for their kind advice on many points. The laborious work of indexing was done by Pat Geidans and Tim and Sarah Watson.

Above all, I place on record my deep thanks to my wife Anita, whose side I would all too often leave in the early hours of the morning to spend time with one whom she humorously called "your Corinthian woman." Without her prayerful, cheerful, and ongoing encouragement it would have been virtually impossible to see this work through to the end.

PAUL BARNETT

ABBREVIATIONS

For text-critical symbols see the Introduction to Erwin Nestle and Kurt Aland, *Novum Testamentum Graece* (26th ed.).

AB	Anchor Bible
'Abod. Zar.	'Aboda Zara
AJP	American Journal of Philology
ANRW	H. Temporini, ed., Aufstieg und Niedergang der römischen Welt
Apoc. Bar.	Apocalypse of Baruch
Apoc. Paul	Apocalypse of Paul
Asc. Isa.	The Ascension of Isaiah
As. Moses	Assumption of Moses
ASV	American Standard Version
ATR	Anglican Theological Review
AusBR	Australian Biblical Review
BA	Biblical Archaeologist
BAGD	W. Bauer, W. F. Arndt, F. W. Gingrich, and F. W. Danker, Greek-English Lexicon of the NT (2d ed.; Chicago, 1979)
BAR	Biblical Archaeology Review
BDB	F. Brown, S. R. Driver, and C. A. Briggs, Hebrew and English Lexicon of the OT
BDF	F. Blass, A. Debrunner and R. W. Funk, A Greek Grammar of the NT (Chicago, 1961)
BEvT	Beiträge zur evangelischen Theologie
Ber.	Berakoth
Bib	Biblica
BJRL	Bulletin of the John Rylands Library
BJS	Brown Judaic Studies
BR	Biblical Research

BSac	*Bibliotheca Sacra*
BT	*Bible Translator*
BTB	*Biblical Theology Bulletin*
BTD	Beiträge zum theologischen Dialog
Burton	E. W. Burton, *Syntax of the Moods and Tenses of NT Greek* (Chicago, 1893)
BZ	*Biblische Zeitschrift*
c.	*circa*
CBC	Cambridge Bible Commentary
CBQ	*Catholic Biblical Quarterly*
cf.	confer, compare
DPL	R. P. Martin, G. F. Hawthorne, and D. Reid, eds., *Dictionary of Paul and His Letters*
Ditt. *Syl.*	W. Dittenberger, ed., *Sylloge Inscriptionum Graecorum*
EBC	Expositor's Bible Commentary
EBib	Etudes Bibliques
EDNT	*Exegetical Dictionary of the NT*
EGT	*Expositor's Greek Testament*
Esdr	*Esdras*
ET	English translation
ETL	*Ephemerides theologicae lovanienses*
Eusebius	
Hist. Eccl.	*Historia Ecclesiastica*
EvQ	*Evangelical Quarterly*
ExpT	*Expository Times*
Gk.	Greek
GNB	Good News Bible
Ḥag.	*Ḥagiga*
HBT	*Horizons in Biblical Theology*
Heb.	Hebrew
HTR	*Harvard Theological Review*
ICC	International Critical Commentary
IDB	G. A. Buttrick, ed., *Interpreter's Dictionary of the Bible*
Int	*Interpretation*
ITQ	*Irish Theological Quarterly*
JAC	Jahrbuch für Antike und Christentum
JB	Jerusalem Bible
JBL	*Journal of Biblical Literature*
JBR	*Journal of the Bible and Religion*
JETS	*Journal of the Evangelical Theological Society*
JJS	*Journal of Jewish Studies*
Jos. and As.	Joseph and Asenath

Josephus
    Ag. Ap.   *Against Apion*
    Ant.   *Jewish Antiquities*
    J.W.   *Jewish War*
JSNT   *Journal for the Study of the NT*
JSNTSS   *Journal for the Study of the NT* Supplementary Series
JSOT   *Journal for the Study of the OT*
JSS   *Journal of Semitic Studies*
JTS   *Journal of Theological Studies*
Jub.   Book of Jubilees
Justin
    Apol.   *Apology*
    Dial.   *Dialogue with Trypho*
Ketub.   *Ketubot*
KJV   King James Version
lit.   literally
LCL   Loeb Classical Library
LSJ   Liddell-Scott-Jones, *Greek-English Lexicon* (Oxford)
LXX   The Septuagint
Macc   Maccabees
Mak.   *Makkot*
Metzger   B. A. Metzger, *A Textual Commentary on the Greek NT* (London, 1971)
MeyerK   H. A. W. Meyer, Kritisch-exegetischer Kommentar über das Neue Testament
mg.   margin
Midr. Num.   *Midrash on Numbers*
Midr. Pss.   *Midrash on Psalms*
Midr. Qol.   *Midrash on Qoheleth* (Ecclesiastes)
MM   J. H. Moulton and G. Milligan, *The Vocabulary of the Greek Testament* (1930)
MNTC   Moffatt NT Commentary
Moule   Moule, C. F. D., *Idiom Book of NT Greek* (Cambridge, 1953)
MS(S)   manuscripts
n. (nn.)   note (notes)
NASB   New American Standard Bible
NCBC   New Century Bible Commentary
NEB   New English Bible
New Docs.   G. H. R. Horsley, *New Documents Illustrating Early Christianity* (Macquarie University)
NICNT   New International Commentary on the NT

NIDNTT	C. Brown, ed., *The New International Dictionary of NT Theology*
NIV	New International Version
NovT	*Novum Testamentum*
NovTSup	Supplements to *Novum Testamentum*
NT	New Testament
NTS	*NT Studies*
NTTS	NT Tools and Studies
OT	The Old Testament
OTP	J. H. Charlesworth, ed., *The OT Pseudepigrapha*
p. (pp.)	page(s)
PG	*Patrologia Graeca*
P.Oxy.	*The Oxyrhynchus Papyri* (London, 1899–)
Ps. Sol.	*Psalms of Solomon*
PW	G. Wissowa, ed., *Paulys Real-Encyclopädie der classischen Altertumswissenschaft* and supplementary volumes
q.v.	*quod vide,* which see
RB	*Revue Biblique*
RTR	*Reformed Theological Review*
RevExp	*Review and Expositor*
Robertson	A. T. Robertson, *A Grammar of the Greek NT in the Light of Historical Research* (Nashville, 1934)
RSV	Revised Standard Version
RV	Revised Version
Šabb.	*Šabbat*
Sanh.	*Sanhedrin*
SBLDS	Society of Biblical Literature Dissertation Series
SBLSP	Society of Biblical Literature Seminar Papers
SBT	Studies in Biblical Theology
ScrB	*Scripture Bulletin*
SE	*Studia Evangelica*
Sib. Or.	*Sibylline Oracles*
Sir	Sirach
SJT	*Scottish Journal of Theology*
SNTSMS	Society for NT Studies Monograph Series
ST	*Studia Theologica*
Str-B	H. Strack and P. Billerbeck, *Kommentar zum Neuen Testament*
b. Taʿan.	*b. Taʿanit*
T. Abr.	*Testament of Abraham*
T. Benj.	*The Testament of Benjamin*

T. Dan	*The Testament of Dan*
T. Job	*The Testament of Job*
T. Jud.	*The Testament of Judah*
T. Lev.	*The Testament of Levi*
T. Naph.	*The Testament of Naphtali*
T. Reub.	*The Testament of Reuben*
T. Sim.	*The Testament of Simeon*
TDNT	G. Kittel and G. Friedrich, eds., *Theological Dictionary of the NT*
TLZ	*Theologische Literaturzeitung*
TNTC	Tyndale NT Commentaries
Tob	Tobit
TR	Textus Receptus
TS	*Theological Studies*
trans.	translation, or translated by
TynB	*Tyndale Bulletin*
TZ	*Theologische Zeitschrift*
UBS³	United Bible Societies *Greek NT* (3d ed.)
v. (vv.)	verse(s)
VC	*Vigiliae Christianae*
Wis	Wisdom of Solomon
WTJ	*Westminister Theological Journal*
WBC	Word Biblical Commentary
WC	Westminster Commentaries
WUNT	Wissenschaftliche Untersuchungen zum Neuen Testament
Yebam.	*Yebamoth*
Zerwick	M. Zerwick and M. Grosvenor, *A Grammatical Analysis of the Greek New Testament* (Rome, 1966)
ZKNT	Zahn's Kommentar zum Neuen Testament
ZNW	*Zeitschrift für die neutestamentliche Wissenschaft*

SELECT BIBLIOGRAPHY

I. COMMENTARIES

Alford, H. *The Greek NT* 2 (3d ed.; London, 1957).

Allo, P. E. B. *Saint Paul: seconde épître aux Corinthiens* (EBib; Paris, 1956).

Bachmann, P. *Der zweite Brief des Paulus an der Korinther* (ZKNT; Leipzig, 1918).

Barrett, C. K. *A Commentary on the Second Epistle to the Corinthians* (London, 1973).

Beasley-Murray, G. R. "2 Corinthians," The Broadman Bible Commentary, vol. 11 (Nashville, 1971).

Bruce, F. F. *1 and 2 Corinthians* (NCBC; Grand Rapids, 1971).

Bultmann, R. *The Second Letter to the Corinthians,* (ET Minneapolis, 1985).

Calvin, J. *Romans–Galatians* (Wilmington, n.d.).

Collange, J.-F. *Enigmes de la deuxième épître de Paul aux Corinthiens: Etude exegétique de 2 Cor. 2:14–7:4* (SNTSMS 18; Cambridge, 1972).

Denney, J. *The Second Epistle to the Corinthians* (Expositor's Bible; London, 1894).

Furnish, V. P. *II Corinthians* (AB 32A; New York, 1984).

Goudge, H. L. *The Second Epistle to the Corinthians* (WC; London, 1927).

Harris, M. J. "2 Corinthians," in The Expositor's Bible Commentary (ed. F. E. Gaebelein; Grand Rapids, 1976).

Héring, J. *The Second Epistle of Saint Paul to the Corinthians* (ET London, 1967).

Hughes, P. E. *Paul's Second Epistle to the Corinthians* (NICNT; Grand Rapids, 1961).

Kruse, C. *The Second Epistle of Paul to the Corinthians* (TNTC; Leicester, 1987).

Martin, R. P. *2 Corinthians* (WBC 40; Waco, 1986).

Menzies, A. *The Second Epistle of the Apostle Paul to the Corinthians* (London, 1912).

Plummer, A. *A Critical and Exegetical Commentary on the Second Epistle of Paul to the Corinthians* (ICC; Edinburgh, 1915).

Rendall, G. H., *The Epistles of Paul to the Corinthians* (London, 1909).

Strachan, R. H. *The Second Letter of Paul to the Corinthians* (MNTC; London, 1935).

Tasker, R. V. G. *The Second Epistle of Paul to the Corinthians* (TNTC; London, 1958).

Thrall, M. E. *The First and Second Letters of Paul to the Corinthians* (CBC; Cambridge, 1965).

Wendland, H. D. *Der Briefe an die Korinther* (BTD 7; Göttingen, 1964).

Windisch, H. *Der zweite Korintherbrief* (MeyerK 6; Göttingen, 1924).

II. OTHER SIGNIFICANT BOOKS

Abraham, W. J. *The Logic of Evangelism* (Grand Rapids, 1989).

Akurgal, A. *Ancient Civilizations and Ruins of Turkey* (Istanbul, 1985).

Barrett, C. K. *Essays on Paul* (London, 1982).

————. *NT Background: Selected Documents* (London, 1987).

Barton, C. A. *The Sorrows of the Ancient Romans,* (Princeton, 1993).

Batey, R. A. *NT Nuptial Imagery* (Leiden, 1971).

Beker, J. C. *Paul the Apostle: The Triumph of God in Life and Thought* (Philadelphia, 1980).

Belleville, L. L. *Reflections of Glory. Paul's Polemical Use of the Moses Doxa Tradition in 2 Corinthians 3.1-18* (JSNTSS 52; Sheffield, 1991).

Betz, H. D. *Der Apostel Paulus und die sokratische Tradition* (Tübingen, 1972).

————. *Paul's Apology, 2 Corinthians 10–13 and the Socratic Tradition* (Berkeley, 1975).

————. *2 Corinthians 8 and 9* (Philadelphia, 1985).

Bruce, F. F. *Paul, Apostle of the Heart Set Free* (Grand Rapids, 1977).

————. *The Epistle of Paul to the Galatians* (Exeter, 1982).

————. *The Pauline Circle* (Grand Rapids, 1985).

Brunner, E. *The Mediator* (London, 1963).

Capes, D. *Old Testament Yahweh Texts in Paul's Christology* (WUNT 2/47; Tübingen, 1992).

Carcopino, J. *Daily Life in Ancient Rome* (Harmondsworth, 1967).

Carson, D. A. *From Triumphalism to Maturity* (Leicester, 1984).

Charlesworth, J. H. *Jesus within Judaism* (London, 1988).

Cornell, T., and J. Matthews. *Atlas of the Roman World* (Oxford, 1982).

Collins, J. N. *Diakonia: Reinterpretation of Ancient Sources* (Oxford, 1990).

Cranfield, C. E. B. *Romans* (ICC; Edinburgh, 1979).

Cullmann, O. *Christ and Time* (London, 1962).

Cuss, S. D. *The Imperial Cult and Honorary Terms in the NT* (Fribourg, 1974).

Deissmann, A. *Light from the Ancient East* (ET London, 1909).

———. *Bible Studies* (ET Edinburgh, 1909).

Delling, G. *Worship in the NT* (Philadelphia, 1962).

Denney, J. *The Death of Christ* (London, 1960).

Dunn, J. D. G. *Christology in the Making* (London, 1980).

Ellis, E. E. *Paul's Use of the OT* (Edinburgh, 1957).

Everding, H. E. *The Living God: A Study in the Function and Meaning of Biblical Terminology* (Unpub. Th.D. diss., Harvard University, 1968).

Fee, G. D. *The First Epistle to the Corinthians* (NICNT; Grand Rapids, 1987).

———. *God's Empowering Presence* (Peabody, Mass., 1994).

———. *Paul's Letter to the Philippians* (NICNT; Grand Rapids, 1995).

Fitzgerald, J. T. *Cracks in Earthen Vessels: An Examination of the Catalogues of Hardships in the Corinthian Correspondence* (SBLDS 99; Atlanta, 1988).

Gärtner, B. *The Temple and the Community in Qumran and the NT* (SNTSMS 1; Cambridge, 1965).

Gardner, P. D. *The Gifts of God and the Authentication of a Christian: An Exegetical Study of 1 Corinthians 8:1–11:1* (New York, 1994).

Georgi, D. *The Opponents of Paul in Second Corinthians* (ET Philadelphia, 1986).

Hafemann, S. J. *Suffering and Ministry in the Spirit* (Grand Rapids, 1990).

Hanhart, K. *The Intermediate State in the NT* (Franeker, 1966).

Hanson, A. T. *The Image of the Invisible God* (London, 1982).

———. *Jesus Christ in the OT* (London, 1965).

———. *The Paradox of the Cross in the Thought of St Paul* (Sheffield, 1987).

———. *Studies in the Pastoral Epistles* (London, 1968).

———. *Studies in Paul's Technique and Theology* (Grand Rapids, 1974).

Hays, R. B. *Echoes of Scripture in the Letters of Paul* (New Haven, 1989).

Hemer, C. J. *The Book of Acts in the Setting of Hellenistic History* (Tübingen, 1989).

Hengel, M. *Between Jesus and Paul* (London, 1983).

———. *The "Hellenization" of Judaea in the First Century after Christ* (London, 1989).

———. *Pre-Christian Paul* (London, 1991).

———. *The Son of God* (London, 1976).

Hock, R. F. *The Social Context of Paul's Ministry* (Philadelphia, 1980).

Hurtado, L. W. *One God, One Lord* (Philadelphia, 1988).

Judge, E. A. *The Social Pattern of the Christian Groups in the First Century* (London, 1960).

Kennedy, G. *Classical Rhetoric and Its Christian and Secular Tradition from Ancient to Modern Times* (London, 1980).

————. *NT Interpretation through Rhetorical Criticism* (Chapel Hill, N.C., 1984).

Kent, J. H. *Corinth VIII/3. The Inscriptions,* 1926-1950 (Princeton, n.d.).

Kim, C.-H. *Form and Structure of the Familiar Greek Letter of Recommendation* (SBLDS 4; Missoula, 1972).

Kim, S. *The Origin of Paul's Gospel* (Grand Rapids, 1982).

————. *The Son of Man as the Son of God* (Grand Rapids, 1985).

Kümmel, W. G. *Introduction to the NT* (ET London, 1975).

Ladd, G. E. *The Pattern of NT Truth* (Grand Rapids, 1968).

Longenecker, R. L. *The Christology of Early Jewish Christianity* (Grand Rapids, 1981).

McGrath, A. *Bridge Building* (Leicester, 1992).

McKay, K. L, *A New Syntax of the Verb in NT Greek: An Aspectival Approach* (New York, 1994).

McRay, J. *Archaeology and the NT* (Grand Rapids, 1991).

Malherbe, A. J. *Social Aspects of Early Christianity* (Philadelphia, 1983).

Manson, T. W. *On Paul and John* (SBT 38; London, 1963).

Marmorstein, A. *The Old Rabbinic Doctrine of God* (New York, 1968).

Marshall, I. H. *The Origin of NT Christology* (Leicester, 1977).

Marshall, P. *Enmity in Corinth: Social Conventions in Paul's Relations with the Corinthians* (Tübingen, 1987).

Martin, R. P. *Reconciliation. A Study of Paul's Theology* (Atlanta, 1981).

————. *The Spirit and the Congregation* (Grand Rapids, 1984).

Meeks, W. A. *The First Urban Christians: The Social World of the Apostle Paul* (New Haven, 1983).

Morrice, W. G. *Joy in the NT* (Exeter, 1984).

Moule, C. F. D. *The Origin of Christology* (London, 1977).

————. *The Phenomenon of the NT* (London, 1967).

Moulton, J. H. *A Grammar of NT Greek:* Vol. 1: *Prolegomena* (Edinburgh, 1908).

Murphy-O'Connor, J. *St Paul's Corinth,* (Wilmington, 1983).

————. *The Theology of the Second Letter to the Corinthians* (Cambridge, 1991).

Nickle, K. *The Collection: A Study of Paul's Strategy* (SBT 48; London, 1966).

O'Brien, P. T. *Introductory Thanksgivings in the Letters of Paul* (NovTSup 9; Leiden, 1977).

————. *Commentary on Philippians* (NIGTC; Grand Rapids, 1991).

————. *Consumed by Passion* (Sydney, 1993).

Packer, J. I. *Knowing God* (London, 1973).

Papahatzis, N. *Ancient Corinth: The Museums of Corinth, Isthmia and Sicyon* (Athens, 1977).

Petrakos, B. *National Museum* (Athens, 1981).

Pierce, C. A. *Conscience in the NT* (SBT; London, 1955).

Porter, S. E. Καταλλάσσω *in Ancient Greek Literature, with Reference to the Pauline Writings* (Cordoba, 1994).

Ramsey, A. M. *The Glory of God and the Transfiguration of Christ* (London, 1949).

Renwick, D. A. *Paul, the Temple and the Presence of God* (BJS 224; Atlanta, 1991).

Reumann, J., et al., *Righteousness in the NT* (Philadelphia, 1982).

Robertson, A. T. *A Grammar of the Greek NT in the Light of Historical Research* (London, 1919).

Robinson, J. A. T. *The Body: A Study in Pauline Theology* (SBT 5; London, 1952).

Rowland, C. *The Open Heaven: A Study of Apocalyptic in Judaism and Early Christianity* (London, 1982)

Sanders, E. P. *Paul and Palestinian Judaism* (Philadelphia, 1979).

————. *Paul, the Law and the Jewish People* (Philadelphia, 1983).

Schmithals, W. *Gnosticism in Corinth* (Nashville, 1971).

Scholem, G. *Jewish Gnosticism, Merkabah Mysticism and Talmudic Tradition* (New York, 1960).

Schreiner, T. R. *The Law and Its Fulfilment* (Grand Rapids, 1992).

Scott, J. M. *Adoption As Sons of God* (WUNT 48; Tübingen, 1992).

Schürer, E. *The History of the Jewish People in the Age of Jesus Christ (175 B.C.–A.D. 135),* vol. 1 (rev. and ed. G. Vermes and F. Millar; Edinburgh, 1973).

Schütz, J. H. *Paul and the Anatomy of Apostolic Authority* (SNTSMS 26; Cambridge, 1975).

Sherwin-White, A. N. *Roman Society and Roman Law in the NT* (Oxford, 1965).

Snaith, N. H. *The Distinctive Ideas of the OT* (London, 1944).

Stowers, S. K. *Letter Writing in Greco-Roman Antiquity* (Philadelphia, 1986).

Strack, H. L., and G. Stemberger. *Introduction to the Talmud and Midrash* (Minneapolis, 1992).

Sumney, J. L. *Identifying Paul's Opponents: The Question of Method in 2 Corinthians* (Sheffield, 1990).

Tannehill, R. *Dying and Rising with Jesus* (Berlin, 1967).

Theissen, G. *Psychological Aspects of Pauline Theology* (ET Edinburgh, 1987).

—————. *Essays on Corinth: The Social Setting of Pauline Christianity* (Edinburgh, 1982).

Thielman, F. *From Plight to Solution* (Leiden, 1989).

Thrall, M. E. *Greek Particles in the NT* (NTTS 3; Leiden, 1962).

Turner, N. *Grammatical Insights into the NT* (Edinburgh, 1965).

Vliet, H. van. *No Single Testimony: A Study on the Adopting of the Law of Deut 19:15 par. into the NT* (Utrecht, 1958).

Warfield, B. B. *The Inspiration and Authority of the Bible* (Philadelphia, 1948).

White, J. L. *Light from Ancient Letters* (Philadelphia, 1986).

Witherington, B. *Jesus, Paul and the End of the World* (Downers Grove, 1992).

Wilken, R. L. *The Christians as the Romans Saw Them* (New Haven, 1984).

Young, F., and D. F. Ford. *Meaning and Truth in 2 Corinthians* (London, 1987).

Yadin, Y. *Bar-Kokhba* (London, 1978).

III. ARTICLES

Agnew, F. W. "The Origin of the NT Apostle-Concept: A Review of Research," *JBL* 105/1 (1986) 75-96.

Aus, R. "Paul's Travel Plans to Spain and the 'Full Number of the Gentiles' of Rom 11:25," *NovT* 21 (1979) 232-62.

Baird, W. "Letters of Recommendation. A Study of 2 Cor. 3:1-3," *JBL* 80 (1961) 166-72.

Barnett, P. "Opposition in Corinth," *JSNT* 22 (1984) 3-17.

Barrett, C. K. "Paul's Opponents in II Corinthians," *NTS* 17 (1971) 233-54.

Bates, W. H. "The Integrity of 2 Corinthians," *NTS* 12 (1965/66) 56-69.

Bauckham, R. J. "The Worship of Jesus in Apocalyptic Christianity," *NTS* 27 (1980-81) 322-41.

Beale, G. K. "The OT Background of Reconciliation in 2 Corinthians 5–7 and Its Bearing on the Literary Problem of 2 Corinthians 6:14–7:1," *NTS* 35/4 (1989) 550-81.

Belleville, L. A. "Gospel and Kerygma in 2 Corinthians," in *Gospel in Paul: Studies on Corinthians, Galatians and Romans* (FS R. Longenecker; ed. L. A. Jervis and P. Richardson; Sheffield, 1995) 110-33.

Benoit, P. "Qûmran et le Nouveau Testament." *NTS* 7 (1961), 258-64.

Berger, K. "Apostelbrief und apostolische Rede / Zum Formular frühchristlicher Briefe," *ZNW* 65 (1974) 191-207.

Betz, H. D. "2 Corinthians 6:14–7:1: An Anti-Pauline Fragment?" *JBL* 92 (1973) 88-108.

Bishop, E. F. F. "Does Aretas Belong in 2 Corinthians or Galatians?" *ExpT* 64 (1953) 188-89.

———. "In Famine and in Drought," *EvQ* 38 (1966) 169-71.

Bjerkelund, B. J. "*Parakalō:* Form, Funktion und Sinn der *Parakalō*-Sätze in den paulinischen Briefen," *Bibliotheca Theologica Norvegica,* vol. 1 (Oslo, 1967) 164-67.

Bornkamm, G. "The History of the Origin of the So-Called Second Letter to the Corinthians," *NTS* 8 (1962) 260.

Bowers, W. P. "Fulfilling the Gospel," *JETS* 30 (1987) 185-98.

Branick, V. P. "Apocalyptic Paul," *CBQ* 47 (1985) 664-75.

Buck, C. H. "The Collection for the Saints," *HTR* 43 (1950) 1-29.

Carrez, M. "Le 'Nous' en 2 Corinthiens," *NTS* 26 (1980) 474-86.

Carson, D. A. "The Purpose of Signs and Wonders in the NT," in *Power Religion* (ed. M. S. Horton; Chicago, 1992) 89-118.

Catchpole, D. R. "Paul, James and the Apostolic Decree," *NTS* 23 (1977) 436-39.

Clark, K. W. "The Meaning of ἐνεργέω and καταργέω in the NT," *JBL* 54 (1935) 93-101.

Conzelmann, H. "Korinth und die Mädchen der Aphrodite: Zur Religionsgeschichte der Stadt Korinth," in *Theologie als Schriftauslegund: Aufsätze zum neuen Testament* (BEvT 65; 1974) 152-66.

Craig, W. L. "Paul's Dilemma in 2 Corinthians 5:1-10: A 'Catch 22,' " *NTS* 34 (1988) 145-47.

Cranfield, C. E. B. "Changes in Person and Number in Paul's Epistles," in *Paul and Paulinism* (FS C. K. Barrett; ed. M. D. Hooker and S. G. Wilson; London, 1982) 280-89.

Dinkler, E. "Die Taufterminologie in 2 Kor. i21f.," in *Neotestamentica et Patristica* (FS Oscar Cullmann; ed. W. C. van Unnik; NovT Sup 6; Leiden, 1962) 173-91.

Dodd, C. H. "The Mind of Paul: Change and Development," in *NT Studies* (Manchester, 1953).

Duff, P. B. "Metaphor, Motif and Meaning: The Rhetorical Strategy Behind the Image 'Led in Triumph' in 2 Cor 2:14," *CBQ* 53 (1991) 79-92.

Dumbrell, W. J. "Paul's Use of Exodus 34 in 2 Corinthians 3," in *God Who Is Rich in Mercy* (FS for D. B. Knox; ed. P. T. O'Brien and D. G. Peterson; Sydney, 1986) 179-94.

Dunn, J. D. G. "The Relationship between Paul and Jerusalem according to Galatians 1 and 2," *NTS* 28 (1982) 461-78.

———. "Paul's Understanding of the Death of Jesus," in *Reconciliation and Hope* (ed. R. Banks; Grand Rapids, 1974) 140-41.

———. "2 Corinthians III.17 — 'The Lord Is the Spirit,' " *JTS* 21, n.s. 2 (1970) 309-20.

Dupont, J. "Le Chrétien, miroir de la grâce divine, d'après 2 Cor. 3:18," *RB* 46 (1949) 393-411.

Ellis, E. E. "A Note on Pauline Hermeneutics," *NTS* 2 (1955-56).

———. "Paul and His Co-Workers," *NTS* 17 (1971) 437-53.

———. "Paul and His Opponents," in *Christianity, Judaism and Other Greco-Roman Cults* (ed. J. Neusner; Leiden, 1975) 264-98.

———. "II Corinthians v.1-10 in Pauline Eschatology," *NTS* 6 (1959-60) 211-24.

Fallon, F. T. "Self-Sufficiency or God's Sufficiency: 2 Corinthians 2:16," *HTR* 76.3 (1983) 369-74.

Fee, G. D. " 'Another Gospel Which You Did Not Embrace': 2 Corinthians 11:4 and the Theology of 1 and 2 Corinthians," in *Gospel in Paul: Studies on Corinthians, Galatians and Romans* (FS R. Longenecker; ed. L. A. Jervis and P. Richardson; Sheffield, 1995) 110-33.

———. "II Corinthians vi.14–vii.1 and Food Offered to Idols," *NTS* 23 (1977) 140-61.

———. "ΧΑΡΙΣ in II Corinthians 1:15: Apostolic Parousia and Paul-Corinth Chronology," *NTS* 24 (1978) 533-38.

Fitzmyer, J. A. "Glory Reflected on the Face of Jesus Christ [2 Cor 3:7–4:6] and a Palestinian Motif," *TS* 42 (1981) 630-44.

———. "Qumran and the Interpolated Paragraph in 2 Corinthians 6:14-17," *CBQ* 23 (1961) 271-80.

Forbes, C. B. "Comparison, Self-Praise and Irony: Paul's Boasting and the Conventions of Hellenistic Rhetoric," *NTS* 32 (1986) 1-30.

France, R. T. "The Worship of Jesus," in *Christ the Lord* (ed. H. H. Rowdon; Leicester, 1982).

Francis, D. P. "The Holy Spirit. A Statistical Enquiry," *ExpTim* 96 (1985) 136ff.

Fraser, J. W. "Paul's Knowledge of Jesus 5.16 Once More," *NTS* 17 (1971) 293-313.

Fung, R. Y.-K. "Justification by Faith in 1 and 2 Corinthians," in *Pauline Studies* (ed. D. A. Hagner and M. J. Harris; Grand Rapids, 1980) 247-61.

Furnish, V. P. "The Archaeology of Paul's Corinth," *BAR* 14/3 (1988) 15-27.

Glasson, T. F. "2 Corinthians v.1-10 versus Platonism," *SJT* 43 (1990) 145-55.

Gundry, R. H. "Grace, Works, and Staying Saved in Paul," *Bib* 66 (1985) 1-38.

———. "The Moral Frustration of Paul before His Conversion," in *Pauline Studies* (ed. D. A. Hagner and M. J. Harris; Grand Rapids, 1980) 228-45.

Hafemann, S. J. "The Glory and Veil of Moses in 2 Cor 3:7-14: An Example of Paul's Contextual Exegesis of the OT — A Proposal," *HBT* 14/1 (1992) 31-49.

———. " 'Self-Commendation' and Apostolic Legitimacy in 2 Corinthians: A Pauline Dialectic," *NTS* 36 (1990) 66-88.

Hanson, A. T. "The Midrash in II Corinthians 3: A Reconsideration," *JSNT* 9 (1980) 12-18.

Harris, M. J. "2 Corinthians 5:1-10: Watershed in Paul's Eschatology?" *TynB* 22 (1971) 32-57.

Hay, D. M. "The Shaping of Theology in 2 Corinthians: Convictions, Doubts, and Warrants," *SBLSP* 29 (1990), ed. D. J. Lull, 257-72.

Heiny, S. B. "The Motive for the Metaphor," *SBLSP* 26 (1987) 1-21.

Hemer, C. J. "Alexandrian Troas," *TynB* 26 (1975) 79-112.

———. "A Note on 2 Corinthians 1:9," *TynB* 23 (1972) 103-7.

———. "Observations on Pauline Chronology," in *Pauline Studies* (ed. D. A. Hagner and M. J. Harris; Grand Rapids, 1980) 6-9.

Hendrickson, G. L. "Ancient Reading," *The Classical Journal* 25 (1929) 182-96.

Hickling, C. J. "Is Second Corinthians a Source of Early Church History?" *ZNW* 66 (1975) 284-87.

———. "The Sequence of Thought in II Corinthians, Chapter Three," *NTS* 21 (1975) 380-95.

Howe, E. M. "Interpretations of Paul in the Acts of Paul and Thecla," in *Pauline Studies* (FS F. F. Bruce; ed. D. A. Hagner and M. J. Harris; Grand Rapids, 1980) 33-49.

Humphreys, C. J., and W. G. Waddington. "Dating the Crucifixion," *Nature* 306 (1983) 743-46.

Judge, E. A. "The Conflict of Educational Aims in NT Thought," *Journal of Christian Education* 9 (1966) 32-45.

———. "Cultural Conformity and Innovation in Paul," *TynB* 35 (1984) 20-22.

———. "Paul's Boasting in Relation to Contemporary Professional Practice," *AusBr* 16 (1968) 37-50.

———. "St Paul and Classical Society," *JAC* 15 (1972) 19-36.

Käsemann, E. "Die Legitimität des Apostels," *ZNW* 41 (1942) 33-71.

Keyes, C. W. "The Greek Letter of Introduction," *AJP* 56 (1935) 28-44.

Kreitzer, L. K. "A Numismatic Clue to Acts 19:23-41: The Ephesian Cistophori of Claudius and Agrippina," *JSNT* 30 (1987) 59-70.

Kruse, C. "The Offender and the Offence in 2 Corinthians 2:5 and 7:12," *EvQ* 88 (1988) 129-39.

Lambrecht, J. "Philological and Exegetical Notes on 2 Cor 1:4," *Bijdragen* 46 (1985) 261-69.

———. "Structure and Line of Thought in 2 Cor 2, 14-4, 6," *Bib* 64/3 (1983) 344-80.

————. "Transformation in 2 Cor 3:18," *Bib* 64 (1983) 243-49.

Lane, W. L. "Covenant: The Key to Paul's Conflict with Corinth," *TynB* 33 (1982) 3-29.

Lindars, B. "The Sound of the Trumpet: Paul and Eschatology," *BJRL* 67/2 (1985) 766-82.

Longenecker, R. N. "The Forms, Function and Authority of the NT Letters," in *Scripture and Truth* (ed. D. Carson and J. Woodbridge; Leicester, 1983) 101-14.

McCant, J. "Paul's Thorn of Rejected Apostleship," *NTS* 34/4 (1988) 550-72.

McDonald, J. I. H. "Paul and the Preaching Ministry: A Reconsideration of 2 Cor. 2:14-17 in Its Context," *JSNT* 17 (1983) 35-50.

McLean, B. H. "The Absence of Atoning Sacrifice in Paul's Soteriology," *NTS* 38/4 (1992) 531-53.

Malherbe, A. J. "Antisthenes and Odysseus and Paul at War," *HTR* 76 (1983) 143-73.

Manson T. W. "2 Corinthians 2:14-17": Suggestions towards an Exegesis," in *Studia Paulina* (FS J. de Zwaan; ed. J. N. Sevenster and W. C. van Unnik; Haarlem, 1953).

Marshall, I. H. "The Meaning of 'Reconciliation,'" in *Unity and Diversity in NT Theology* (FS G. E. Ladd; ed. R. A. Guelich; Grand Rapids, 1978).

————. "A Metaphor of Social Shame: θριαμβεύειν in 2 Cor. 2:14," *NovT* 25 (1983) 302-17.

Marshall, P. "Invective: Paul and His Enemies in Corinth," in *Perspectives on Language and Text* (FS F. I. Andersen; ed. E. Conrad and E. Newing; Winona Lake, 1987) 359-73.

Martin, R. P. "The Opponents of Paul in 2 Corinthians: An Old Issue Revisited," in *Tradition and Interpretation in the NT* (FS E. E. Ellis; ed. G. F. Hawthorne with O. Betz; Grand Rapids, 1987).

————. "The Setting of 2 Corinthians," *TynB* 37 (1986) 3-4.

————. "The Spirit in 2 Corinthians in the Light of "The Fellowship of the Spirit in 2 Corinthians 13:14," in *Eschatology and the NT* (ed. W. Hulitt Gloer; Peabody, Mass., 1988) 12-128.

————. "Theological Perspectives in 2 Corinthians," *SBLSP* 29 (1990), ed. D. J. Lull, 240-56.

Mitchell, M. M. "NT Envoys in the Context of Greco-Roman Diplomatic and Epistolary Conventions: The Example of Timothy and Titus," *JBL* III/4 (1992) 641-62.

Moule, C. F. D. "2 Cor. 3:18b," in *Neues Testament und Geschichte* (ed. H. Baltensweiler and B. Reicke; Tübingen, 1972) 232.

Murphy-O'Connor, J. "Another Jesus," *RB* 97 (1990) 238-51.

————. "Being at Home in the Body We Are in Exile from the Lord (2 Cor 5:6b)," *RB* 93/2 (1986) 214-21.

————. "Paul and Macedonia," *JSNT* 25 (1985) 99-103.

————. "Pneumatikoi in 2 Corinthians," *AusBR* 34 (1986) 42-58.

————. "What Paul Knew of Jesus," *ScrB* 12 (1982) 35-40.

O'Brien, P. T. "Justification in Paul and Some Crucial Issues of the Past Two Decades," in *Right with God* (ed. D. A. Carson; Grand Rapids, 1992) 69-95.

Olson, S. N. "Pauline Expressions of Confidence in His Addressees," *CBQ* 47 (1985) 282-95.

Oostendorp, D. W. *Another Jesus: A Gospel of Jewish-Christian Superiority in 2 Corinthians* (Kampen, 1967).

Osborne, R. E. "Paul and the Wild Beasts," *JBL* 85 (1965) 225-30.

Osei-Bonsu, J. "Does 2 Cor 5:1-10 Teach the Reception of the Resurrection Body at the Moment of Death?" *JSNT* 28 (1986) 81-101.

————. "Soul and Body in Life after Death: An Examination of the New Testament Evidence with Some Reference to Patristic Exegesis" (Unpub. Ph.D. thesis, University of Aberdeen, 1980).

Pallas, D., et al., "Inscriptions lyciennes trouveves a Solômos près de Corinthe," *Bulletin de Correspondence Hellénique* 83 (1959) 496-508.

Perriman, A. C. "Between Troas and Macedonia: 2 Cor 2:13-14," *ExpTim* 101/2 (1989) 39-41.

————. "Paul and the Parousia: 1 Corinthians 15:50-57 and 2 Corinthians 5:1-5," *NTS* 35 (1985) 512-21.

Pohill, J. B. "The Comfort and Power of the Gospel," *RevExp* (1989) 325-45.

Proudfoot, C. M. "Imitation or Realistic Participation," *Int* 17 (1963) 140-60.

Provence, T. E. "Who Is Sufficient for These Things," *NovT* 24.1 (1982) 54-81.

Richard, E. "Polemics, Old Testament and Theology: A Study in II Cor. III.1–IV.6," *RB* 88 (1981) 340-67.

Saenger, P. "Silent Reading: Its Impact on Late Medieval Script and Society," *Viator: Medieval and Renaissance Studies* 13 (1982) 367-414.

Snodgrass, K. R. "The Place of Romans 2 in the Theology of Paul," *NTS* 32 (1986) 72-83.

Spicq, C. "L'Image spotive de II Cor 4:7-9," *ETL* 13 (1937) 202-29.

Spittler, R. "The Limits of Ecstasy: An Exegesis of 2 Corinthians 12:1-10," in *Current Issues in Biblical and Patristic Interpretation* (ed. G. Hawthorne; Grand Rapids, 1975) 259-66.

Stoops, R. F. "Riot and Assembly: The Social Context of Acts 19:23-41," *JBL* 108 (1989) 73-91.

Stowers, S. K. "*Peri men gar* and the Integrity of 2 Corinthians 8 and 9," *NovT* 32 (1980) 340-48.

Sweet, J. P. M. "A House Not Made with Hands," in *Templum Amicitiae* (FS E. Bammel; ed. W. Horbury; Sheffield, 1991).

Talbert, C. H. "Money Management in Early Mediterranean Christianity: 2 Corinthians 8–9," *RevExp* 86 (1989) 359-70.

Taylor, N. H. "The Composition and Chronology of Second Corinthians," *JSNT* 44 (1991) 67-87.

Thrall, M. E. "The Problem of II Cor. VI.14–VII.1 in Some Recent Discussion," *NTS* 24 (1977) 132-38.

———. "2 Corinthians 1:12: ἁγιότητι and ἁπλότητι?" in *Studies in NT Language and Text* (FS G. D. Kilpatrick; ed. J. K. Elliott; NovTSup 44; Leiden, 1976).

———. "Super-Apostles, Servants of Christ, and Servants of Satan," *JSNT* 6 (1980) 42-57.

Travis, S. "Paul's Boasting in 2 Corinthians 10–12," *SE* 6 (1973) 527-32.

Unnik, W. C. van. "Reiseplane und Amen-sagen, Zusammenhang und Gedankenfolge in 2 Korinther i 15-25," in *Studia Paulina* (Haarlem, 1953).

———. "With Unveiled Face," *NovT* 2/3 (1963) 160-61.

Wagner, G. "Alliance de la lettre, alliance de l'esprit: essai d'analyse de 2 Corinthiens 2:14–3:18," *Etudes théologiques et religieuses* 60/1 (1985) 55-65.

Watson, N. M. "To Make Us Rely Not on Ourselves but on God Who Raises the Dead"— 2 Cor. 1,9b as the Heart of Paul's Theology," *Die Mitte des Neuen Testament* (FS E. Schweitzer; ed. U. Luz and H. Weder; Göttingen, 1983) 384-98.

Webb, W. J. "What Is the Unequal Yoke (ἑτεροζυγοῦντες) in 2 Corinthians 6:14?" *BSac* 594 (1992) 162-79.

———. "Who Are the Unbelievers (ἄπιστοι) in 2 Corinthians 6:14?" *BSac* 593 (1992) 27-44.

Wenham, D. "2 Corinthians 1:17, 18: Echo of a Dominical Logion," *NovT* 28 (1986) 271-80.

Westerholm, S. " 'Letter' and 'Spirit': The Foundation of Pauline *Ethics*," *NTS* 30 (1984) 229-48.

Williamson, L. "Led in Triumph: Paul's Use of *Thriambeuō*," *Int* 22 (1968) 317-32.

Wiseman, J. "Corinth and Rome I: 228 B.C.–A.D. 267," in *ANRW* VII/I, 438-538.

Wong, E. "The Lord Is the Spirit (2 Cor 3:17a)," *ETL* 61 (1985) 1.48-72.

Wright, N. T. "On Becoming the Righteousness of God," in *Pauline Theology* (ed. D. Hay; Minneapolis, 1993) 200-208.

———. "The Paul of History and the Apostle of Faith," *TynB* 29 (1978) 82-83.

————. "Reflected Glory: 2 Corinthians 3:18," in *The Glory of Christ in the New Testament* (in memory of G. B. Caird) (ed. L. D. Hurst and N. T. Wright; Oxford, 1987) 139-50.

Young, F. "Note on 2 Corinthians 1:17b," *JTS* 17/2 (1986) 404-15.

INTRODUCTION

I. CORINTH IN THE TIME OF PAUL

At the time of Paul's three visits (*c.* A.D. 50-56) Corinth was officially a Roman city.[1]

Ancient Corinth, symbolized by the remains of the Doric-columned temple of Apollo, rivaled Athens for supremacy as a Greek city-state and maritime power during the preclassical and classical eras (6th to 4th cents. B.C.). During the second century B.C., however, Corinth, with other states in the Peloponnese, sought protection from the invading Romans through membership in the Achaean league, but to no avail. In 146 B.C. a Roman army led by L. Mummius destroyed the city and killed or enslaved the population,[2] causing the extinction, according to Cicero, of "the light of all Greece."[3]

In 44 B.C. — almost a century before Paul's arrival — Julius Caesar, recognizing Corinth's strategic location, directed the creation of a Roman colony on the run-down site of the ancient city. It was named *Colonia Laus Iulia Corinthiensis* in his honor, and the process of repopulation was begun. Unlike other colonies, new Corinth was not settled with Roman army veterans but with poorer Romans,[4] many of whom were *libertini,* freed slaves, as well as with people from the eastern Mediterranean — Syrians, Egyptians, and Jews — who would have had some familiarity with *koine* Greek. The offense to other Greeks of the resettlement of Corinth with such inhabitants may be noted in the rather exaggerated remarks of a contemporary poet:

---

1. N. Papahatzis, *Ancient Corinth;* V. Furnish, "Archaeology," 15-27; J. McRay, *Archaeology,* 311-38.

2. Pausanias, *Description of Greece* 7.16.7-10; Strabo, *Geography* 8.6.23b.

3. Cicero, *On the Manilian Law* 5.

4. Appian, *Roman History* 8.20.136.

1

> What inhabitants, O luckless city, hast thou received,
>   and in place of whom?
> Alas for the great calamity of Greece! . . .
>   wholly abandoned to such a crowd of scoundrelly slaves. . . .[5]

This opinion is confirmed, to some degree, by Strabo's comment that the new inhabitants left no grave unransacked in their search for valuables from ancient Corinth, which they shipped to Rome.[6]

In this new city, built according to Roman town planning,[7] Latin was the official language.[8] Typical of Roman colonies elsewhere, Corinth was governed by four magistrates (two *duoviri* and two *aediles,* elected annually), along with other civic officials,[9] and a city council *(decurio)* composed of elected citizens and former magistrates. As capital of the province of Achaia, Corinth was the home of the Roman Proconsul, who in the time of Paul's first visit was L. Iunius Gallio (Acts 18:12).[10]

Such were the origins of the city to which Paul came a century later.[11]

In the meantime Roman Corinth had become at least as prosperous as the ancient city. Whatever the accidents of history, the wealth of Corinth was guaranteed by the city's unique position. Corinth was located on the narrow isthmus that joined the Peloponnese to the mainland and separated the Aegean Sea from the Ionian Sea by a mere 6,000 meters at the narrowest, a remarkable geographical feature upon which contemporary writers often remarked. Strabo observed:

> Corinth is called "wealthy" because of its commerce, since it is situated
> on the isthmus and is master of two harbours, of which one leads straight
> to Asia and the other to Italy: and it makes easy the exchange of merchan-

5. Crinagoras, *Greek Anthology* 9.284.

6. Strabo, *Geography* 8.6.23c.

7. According to A. Gellius, a second-century writer, Rome's colonies "have the appearance of miniatures, and are reproductions of Rome herself" (16.13.9).

8. J. H. Kent, *Corinth,* 7/3 (passim).

9. E.g., the Ἔραστος ὁ οἰκονόμος τῆς πόλεως who sends greetings to the believers in Rome (Rom 16:23). C. E. B. Cranfield, *Romans,* 2.807, doubts that this is the same Erastus commemorated in a paving stone in a plaza near the theatre: "[———] ERASTUS PRO AEDILIT[AT]E S[UA] P[ECUNIA] STRAVIT" ("Erastus, director for city works, laid this pavement at his own expense"). A "city treasurer" is distinct from a "city works director" (in Greek ἀγορανόμος). But the same Erastus may have held different magistracies.

10. This information is confirmed by a famous inscription from Delphi, on which see J. Murphy-O'Connor, *Corinth,* 173-76. In A.D. 15 Tiberius reclassified Achaia as an imperial province, but Claudius restored the province to the Senate in A.D. 44, a few years in advance of Paul's arrival.

11. For a comprehensive treatment see J. Wiseman, "Corinth and Rome," 438-538.

dise from both countries that are far distant from each other. . . . To land their cargoes there was a welcome alternative to the voyage to Maleae [a dangerous promontory at the bottom of the Peloponnese] for merchants from both Italy and Asia. And also the duties on what was exported by land from the Peloponnese as well as what was imported into it . . . to the Corinthians of later times still greater advantages were added, for also the Isthmian games, which were celebrated there, were wont to draw crowds of people.[12]

According to Strabo, the wealth of Corinth flowed from the exchange of merchandise, duties on goods transferred across the isthmus, and the crowds attracted to the Isthmian games. These games were held every two years, as compared with other games, which were held at four-year intervals.[13]

Other revenue was attracted by the constant two-way traffic of travelers whose route from Greece and western Asia to Italy took them through the port towns of Cenchreae and Lechaeum across the isthmus.[14] Since Corinth was the capital of Achaia, many ambassadors and other officials came to it to wait upon the Proconsul. Not least, Corinth was made prosperous by the much-sought-after art works fashioned in the uniquely blended local bronze for which the city was renowned.[15] Inevitably, wealthy Corinth became one of the most notable centers for banking and finance in the Roman world.[16]

The prosperity of Corinth and its constituent ports, so quickly acquired after its refounding, was manifested in a great array of splendid buildings and facilities — city walls, paved roads, harbor infrastructure, water supply, agora, shopping area, senate house, numerous temples, fountains and monuments, gymnasiums, baths, schools, administrative buildings, theatre, odeium, library,

---

12. Strabo, *Geography* 8.6.20. According to Pliny the Elder, it was "a peninsula inferior in celebrity to no region on earth" (*Natural History* 4.9). Cicero commented: "Placed in the narrowest part of Greece, as in a pass, it held on the land side the keys of the country and on the other side almost united, so narrow was the space between them, two seas open to navigation in diametrically opposed senses" (*On the Agrarian Law* 2.87); cf. Pausanias, *Description of Greece* 1.5; 2.3; Strabo, *Geography* 8.6.22a-22b; Dio Chrysostom, *Discourses* 8.6; A. Aristides, *Orations* 46.21.

13. According to A. Aristides, the Isthmian games were "the best and most famous festival — which assembles every two years and meets twice as often as the others" (*Orations* 46.31).

14. Philostratus tells how Apollonius "set sail [from Smyrna] . . . for Achaia . . . landed at Corinth . . . and embarked in the evening for Sicily" (*Life of Apollonius of Tyana* 7.10).

15. According to Pliny the Elder, "Corinthian bronze is valued before silver and even before gold" (*Natural History* 34.1).

16. Plutarch, *Moralia* 831A.

parks, and athletics fields — as described by professional tourists of the time, Strabo and Pausanias.[17] Remains of some of Corinth's illustrious past may still be seen today.

The wealth of new Corinth is spectacularly illustrated by an inscription commemorating one Lucius Castricius Regulus, an *aedile,* judicial prefect *(iure dicundo)* and *duovir* "who was [the first] to preside over the Isthmian games at the isthmus of *Colonia Laus Iulia Corinthiensis.* . . . He gave a banquet for all the inhabitants of the colony."[18]

There was, however, another side to Corinth. One traveler declined to enter the city proper, having learned of ". . . the sordidness of the rich there and the misery of the poor" and of a place ". . . abounding in luxuries but inhabited by people ungracious and unblessed by Aphrodite." He comments that while ". . . the women have Aphrodite, Guardian of the City, as their cult goddess, the men have Famine."[19]

The well-known notoriety of Corinth in sexual matters arises mostly from texts relating to old Corinth (i.e., the pre-Roman city two centuries before Paul's time) that are, in the opinion of some, based on misinformation from jealous Athens.[20] Recent commentators tend to play down the evil reputation of the city. Nonetheless, it would be surprising if new Corinth, as a recently founded, rapidly expanding and prosperous city, served by two seaports and with numerous short-term visitors, was not characterized by the sexual practices of the earlier era.

It is significant that Paul did not spend much time in the "university city," Athens, whose glory had long passed. Corinth was far bigger — modern estimates reach as high as a million people — and equally important, strategically located as it was to take advantage of the considerable volume of passing traffic. It can be no accident that Paul positioned himself in Thessalonica, Corinth, and Ephesus, for they were bustling cities and formed a strategic triangle in the Aegean region, enabling the gospel to be spread along the busiest trading routes in the world.

Roman Corinth was destroyed by earthquake in A.D. 521.

17. Strabo, *Geography* 8.6.21a; Pausanias, *Description of Greece* 1.7-2.2; 2.6-3.1; 3.5; cf. A. Aristides, *Orations* 46.27-28.

18. Cited in J. Murphy-O'Connor, *Corinth,* 14-15.

19. Alciphron, *Letters of Parasites* 3.60.

20. E.g., H. Conzelmann, "Korinth," 8.247-61.

II. PAUL AND CHRISTIANITY IN CORINTH

The apostle Paul came alone to Corinth from Athens in the autumn of A.D. 50.[21] His assistants Timothy and Silvanus, who were still occupied with the churches in Macedonia, arrived sometime later (1 Thess 3:1, 6; cf. Acts 18:5; 2 Cor 1:19).

Paul immediately attached himself to Aquila and Priscilla, who, along with other Jews, had been expelled from Rome in A.D. 49 by decree of the emperor Claudius.[22] He worked with them as a tentmaker[23] — a trade they shared — and he lived with them. It is probable, but not certain, that Aquila and Priscilla were already believers when they came to Corinth, and that they, with Paul, formed a nucleus of an *ekklēsia* in the city. They appear to have created a house church in other places as well (1 Cor 16:19; Rom 16:5).

The apostle spent a year and a half in this his first visit to the Achaian capital, a period that can be divided into two unequal parts.

At first he went to the synagogue[24] — composed of "Greeks," that is, "God-fearers,"[25] as well as Jews (Acts 18:4). There he argued that the OT scriptures had been fulfilled by the Messiah Jesus (Acts 18:4, 5; cf. 17:2-3; 1 Cor 15:3-4; 2 Cor 1:19). At this time the God-fearer Titius Justus (who is probably the "Gaius" referred to elsewhere as "host to the whole church"[26]) accepted Paul's message (Acts 18:7). If Stephanas, "the first fruits" of Paul's ministry in Achaia (1 Cor 16:15; cf. 1:16), was a Jew or a God-fearer, then he, too, would have been converted in the context of Paul's synagogue ministry. After Paul's expulsion from the synagogue, Crispus, the ruler of the synagogue, "believed in the Lord" (Acts 18:8; cf. 1 Cor 1:15). Shortly afterward members of the synagogue accused Paul before the newly arrived Pro-

21. C. J. Hemer, "Pauline Chronology," 6-9.

22. Acts 18:1; Suetonius, *Claudius* 25.4.

23. According to Acts 18:3; see R. F. Hock, *Social Context,* 34-35. Paul alludes to this in 1 Cor 4:12.

24. An inscription "[Syn]agogue of the Heb[rews]" on a lintel, together with a post bearing a seven-branched menorah, has been found in Corinth. Although that synagogue is datable to later centuries, it is possible that a synagogue from Paul's time was located on the same site. See Furnish, 26.

25. Acts 18:4. These were Gentiles who were attracted to the beliefs of Judaism and who, although not yet circumcised, attended the synagogue. In spite of being referred to in the Acts, their existence has been doubted by many scholars because of a lack of corroborating external evidence. The discovery of an inscription at Aphrodisias, datable to the 3d cent. A.D., has put the existence of the God-fearers on a much firmer foundation. See C. J. Hemer, *Acts in the Setting of Hellenistic History,* 444-47.

26. Rom 16:23; cf. 1 Cor 1:14. For the identification Titius Justus = Gaius, see F. F. Bruce, *Pauline Circle,* 97-98.

consul L. Iunius Gallio of promoting the worship of God contrary to the law, charges that Gallio dismissed.[27]

Paul's ministry to Gentiles, which was the second and longer ministry phase, appears to have been based in the house of Gaius. Regrettably we are unable to identify those who accepted Paul's message during this latter period. Other names are known to us — Chloe,[28] Fortunatus, Achaicus, Lucius, Jason, Sosipater, Erastus, Quartus, Tertius, and Phoebe from Cenchreae[29] — but we do not know whether they became believers while Paul was in Corinth or after his withdrawal.

From the passing references in the Acts and the letters of Paul we may reconstruct a partial picture of church life in Roman Corinth during the fifties.[30] We have an impression that, although Paul made the rhetorical disclaimer that "not many" of the believers were "wise by human standards . . . influential . . . of noble birth" (1 Cor 1:26), the reality was somewhat different. The tentmaking Jews Aquila and Priscilla are not merely humble artisans but, in all probability, traders who traveled to Rome, Corinth, and Ephesus (Acts 18:1-3, 18; 1 Cor. 16:19; Rom 16:3; 2 Tim 4:19). Gaius [Titius Justus?] was of sufficient means to own a villa large enough to accommodate the "whole church"[31] (Rom 16:23; cf. 1 Cor 14:23), while Crispus was "ruler" of the synagogue in Corinth, a sign of local eminence. Stephanas is said to have a "household,"[32] and it is probable that Fortunatus and Achaicus, whose names are bracketed with his, were freedmen who belonged to his retinue.[33] Chloe also has a "household" whose members travel from Corinth to Ephesus.[34] Phoebe is literally the "patroness"[35] of the church at Cenchreae — in all probability the hostess of the church — who is described in terms resembling

27. Acts 18:12-16. Gallio took up his twelve-month appointment as Proconsul July 1, A.D. 51.

28. 1 Cor 1:11. Chloe, however, may have been an Asian visiting Corinth.

29. 1 Cor 16:17; Rom 16:1-2; 16:22-23.

30. See generally G. Theissen, *Essays on Corinth,* 60-119; W. Meeks, *First Urban Christians,* 51-73.

31. See below, nn. 48 and 49.

32. Gk. οἶκος (1 Cor 1:16); οἰκία (1 Cor 16:15).

33. That the members of wealthy Stephanas's household devoted themselves to "the service (διακονία) of the saints" (1 Cor 16:15) should be taken as a statement of social inversion in keeping with the servant status of the Lord Jesus.

34. 1 Cor 1:11. Literally "those of Chloe" (τῶν Χλόης).

35. προστάτις (Rom 16:2). That she is also called "a servant (διάκονος) of the church in Cenchreae" (Rom 16:1) may be another example of the inverting of titles. Cf. Stephanas (n. 29). The mention of the names of women like Chloe and Phoebe without the names of husbands suggests that they were widowed, divorced, or women with the requisite number of children to act χώρις κυρίου according to the *ius liberorum*. See *New Docs.* 2.29-32.

Iunia Theodora, the noted Corinthian patroness of that era.[36] Erastus, the "city treasurer,"[37] is clearly a leading member of the Corinthian elite.

At the beginning of the twentieth century A. Deissmann believed that the early Christians were of the lower class, that is, peasants, slaves, and artisans.[38] More recently, however, E. A. Judge has shown that, "Far from being a socially depressed group, then, if the Corinthians are typical, the Christians were dominated by a socially pretentious section of the population of a big city."[39] Those whose names are preserved — because they offered leadership or hospitality or were able to travel from Corinth to Ephesus — appear to have been financially independent. The only people in Corinth whose names are to be found in the literature belonged to the middle class or above, or were among their retinues. There must have been many poorer people, however, since the Christian congregation at Corinth was large.[40] Moreover, as he commented earlier, "not many . . . were influential . . . of noble birth" (1 Cor 1:26).

The Roman names [Gaius?] Titius Justus, Crispus, Fortunatus, Achaicus, Erastus, Quartus, and Tertius are consistent with the Roman character of new Corinth. At the least, Fortunatus and Achaicus are names appropriate to freedmen,[41] and possibly the others as well. Chloe and Phoebe are names taken from Greek mythology, which may suggest that they were freedwomen named after Greek heroines. The Jews Aquila, Priscilla, and Lucius have Roman names, suggesting that they had been slaves who had been given their freedom and taken on the names of Roman masters.

This sample of names from the church appears to represent a reasonable cross section of Corinthian society as it emerges from the ancient sources. It was a community composed of former slaves and freedmen that was significantly Roman, but with eastern Mediterranean folk as well, people who had made good in a city that quickly became wealthy after its refounding. From Paul's Corinthian correspondence, supplemented by the Acts of the Apostles,

---

36. In the decree of the Lycian city of Telmessos Iunia Theodora is described as a "benefactress (εὐεργεσία) . . . [who] welcomes into her own house Lycian travellers . . . displaying her patronage (προστασία)." Paul declares that Phoebe has been "a προστάτις of many [at Cenchreae] and of myself as well." See further D. Pallas et al., "Inscriptions lyciennes," 496-508; E. A. Judge, "Cultural Conformity," 20-22.

37. ὁ οἰκονόμος τῆς πόλεως (Rom 16:23). This Erastus may also appear in the pavement inscription (see n. 9 above). While *aedile* was a more senior position than οἰκονόμος, it was common for public officials to hold different positions in the course of their career.

38. A. Deissmann, *Light,* 290-291.

39. E. A. Judge, *Social Pattern,* 60.

40. Gk. λαὸς . . . πολύς, according to the vision of Acts 18:10.

41. "Fortunate" and "Achaian" are names a master might give to a slave or freedman.

we have identified the names of men and women of substance — Jews and Gentiles — some of whom may have been freedmen (cf. 1 Cor 7:22). Yet Paul specifically refers also to the lower orders, to slaves and the poor within the circle of Corinthian believers (1 Cor 7:21-24; 11:21; cf. 8:10), and he may have identified himself with them (2 Cor 11:29).

This congregation drew a number of its members from the urban elite of wealthy Greco-Roman Corinth, where patron-client relationships were customary. E. A. Judge has drawn attention to a social phenomenon that he calls "status,"[42] a position of power arising from wealth rather than official position or "rank." Patronage occurred not only from those who held political appointment ("rank") but also at a domestic and social level from men and women of wealth ("status"). It was quite common for citizens of rank and status to provide hospitality and financial benefits to visiting rhetoricians who might come to Corinth to participate in the poetry-reading and public-speaking competition at the Isthmian games held every two years,[43] but doubtless at other times as well.

In refusing to accept such patronage by insisting on working (at a menial trade) to support himself,[44] Paul identified with the lower orders. This nonacceptance represented an unresolved tension between Paul and the Corinthians.[45] His studied refusal to exercise the techniques of the rhetorician while at Corinth was also a point of serious criticism.[46] Paul's rejection of patronage and his unwillingness to fulfill their expectations of a public speaker were, according to Judge, in deliberate repudiation of patronage based on "status."[47] He argues that while Paul called for subordination to those with rank, that is, to those who held an official position whether in society or the church, he rejected the conventions associated with status.

As converts were added to the community of believers in Corinth, they probably clustered around the villas of the wealthier members like Aquila, Stephanas, Crispus, Erastus, Chloe, and Phoebe (at Cenchreae), with Gaius providing his house for the meeting of "the whole church." These are the only names of household leaders known to us. It would be remarkable if there were not many more. From archaeological investigation of the few remains of Corinthian villas it appears that they could not accommodate more than fifty guests,[48] though the *insulae* of Roman Ephesus are more spacious by

42. E. A. Judge, "Cultural Conformity," 12ff.

43. Dio Chrysostom, *Discourses* 8.9; J. Murphy-O'Connor, *Corinth,* 14.

44. Paul may be referring to this at various points in his "sufferings" lists (see 6:5; 11:27).

45. 1 Cor 9:3-23; 2 Cor 11:7-11; 12:14-16a. See generally P. Marshall, *Enmity.*

46. 1 Cor 2:1-5; 2 Cor 10:10; Paul accepts the fact that in public speaking he is ἰδιώτης, i.e., nonprofessional (2 Cor 11:6).

47. E. A. Judge, "Cultural Conformity," 12ff.

48. J. Murphy-O'Connor, *Corinth,* 153-58.

far.[49] The seeds of the divisions that soon characterized the Christian community in Corinth (1 Cor 1:10-17; 4:6; 2 Cor 2:6) may have been sown in these semi-independent house churches. Not least, the wealthier members in whose houses subcongregations met would have given hospitality and patronage to other ministers who came to Corinth. From the First Letter to the Corinthians we know of Apollos, Cephas, and possibly the "brothers of the Lord" who visited the city (1 Cor 9:4-6),[50] and from the Second Letter, of the "false apostles" who received a welcome (2 Cor 11:4-5, 13-15). These house meetings would have been influenced by the views of their wealthy hosts and hostesses as well as by visiting ministers who would have stayed there as guests.

III. PAUL'S LATER RELATIONSHIPS WITH THE CORINTHIANS

The incoming Proconsul in succession to Gallio would have taken up his post on July 1, A.D. 52. It seems likely that Paul timed his withdrawal from Corinth to avoid facing further accusations from the Jewish community before a new governor.

Sometime in the summer of A.D. 52 Paul set out from Cenchreae to Judaea. On the way he stopped for a brief sojourn in Ephesus, in anticipation of an extended ministry there later (Acts 18:18-21). Arriving in Caesarea, he apparently visited the church in Jerusalem[51] before returning for a time to the original sending church at Antioch in Syria (Acts 18:22-23; cf. Acts 13:1-3). Paul then traveled overland from Antioch through Galatia and Phrygia, strengthening the disciples who had turned to the Lord during the first missionary journey (Acts 18:23; cf. Acts 13:13–14:24).

It was probably not earlier than the summer of A.D. 53 that Paul at last returned to the Aegean region for his three-year ministry in Ephesus (Acts 19:1; 20:31; cf. 19:8, 10), resuming once more his relationships with the Corinthians.

In the meantime the Corinthians had received a visit from another Christian leader, the gifted Alexandrian Jew Apollos (Acts 18:27–9:1). While there is no hint that Paul's relationship with Apollos was other than

49. A. Akurgal, *Turkey*, 378-82.
50. See F. Young and D. F. Ford, *Meaning*, 46-47.
51. Since it was customary to refer to going "up" to or "down" from Jerusalem, it is assumed that when "[Paul] went *up* to the church, and then went *down* to Antioch" (Acts 18:22) Jerusalem is being signaled.

cordial,[52] his coming to Corinth must have demonstrated to the Corinthians that Paul's was not the only expression of the gospel and that some, at least, probably regarded it as inferior to Apollos's.[53] Before long Corinth would be graced by a visit from no less a person than Cephas,[54] the leading disciple of the Lord, who had previously assumed the leadership of the Jerusalem church (1 Cor 9:5; cf. 1:12; 3:22).[55]

If the visit of Apollos raised the question of Paul's rhetorical abilities, the coming of Cephas prompted the even more fundamental question that would cloud all subsequent relationships with the Corinthians, namely, was Paul truly qualified to be an apostle?[56] The recent arrival of the "false apostles" reflected in 2 Corinthians will raise the issue of Paul's apostleship even more sharply.[57] Whatever the dynamics of the Corinthians' relationships with one another, the surviving correspondence is also characterized by questions associated with Paul's own relationships with them, and the basis of his relationships with them.

Paul's ministry at Ephesus was punctuated by periodic communications by both delegation and letter to and from Corinth that expose the emerging problems within that community and between that community and Paul.

First came the news (by letter or by personal report?) of the failure of some of the Corinthian believers to separate from people within the believing community who were sexually immoral.[58] Paul responded by a letter that has not survived (the "Previous Letter"). The Corinthians misinterpreted the letter to mean wholesale separation from wider Corinthian society.

---

52. From 1 Cor 16:12 we learn that Apollos returned to Ephesus when Paul was there and that Paul had encouraged him — unsuccessfully — to return to Corinth.

53. Paul's defensive remarks about his unrhetorical preaching (1 Cor 2:1-5) may be contrasted with Acts's glowing account of Apollos's style of speaking (ἀνὴρ λόγιος . . . δυνατὸς . . . ἐν ταῖς γραφαῖς . . . ζέων τῷ πνεύματι, Acts 18:24-25; τοῖς Ἰουδαίοις διακατηλέγχετο δημοσίᾳ, Acts 18:28).

54. Although the text does not explicitly say that Cephas had been to Corinth, Paul's way of referring to him makes little sense unless he had visited the city and was known to the Corinthians.

55. By the time of Paul's Aegean ministry, however, the Jerusalem church was led by James (Gal 2:9; Acts 15:13-21).

56. From the time of writing 1 Corinthians Paul becomes emphatic about his apostleship (9:1-3, 5; 15:8-11; cf. 4:9; 12:28, 29); cf. 1 and 2 Thessalonians, where he has little to say on the subject. Something appears to have occurred between the writing of 1 and 2 Thessalonians and 1 Corinthians. The questioning of Paul's apostolic qualifications by sections of the Jerusalem church as reflected in Galatians (1:1, 10-21; 2:7-9) may have been reported at Corinth by Cephas, and perhaps to some degree endorsed by him.

57. 2 Cor 2:17–3:2; 5:12-13; 10:12–12:13 passim).

58. 1 Cor 5:9-13. The consistent male gender references may suggest homosexual activity (but cf. 1 Cor 6:12-20, where men consorting with female prostitutes are mentioned).

10

At about the time of that letter[59] Paul sent Titus to Corinth to establish the collection for the Judaean churches (8:6, 10; 9:2; cf. 1 Cor 16:1-2).

Soon afterward the Corinthians wrote to Paul seeking clarification about a range of matters[60] relating to sexual conduct, local temple worship, food sacrificed to idols, speaking in tongues, and the collection for the saints in Judaea.[61] Their letter appears to have been brought by Stephanas, accompanied by Fortunatus and Achaicus (1 Cor 16:17).

At about the same time as the arrival of their letter, a delegation came from Chloe bringing news of the fragmentation of the Corinthian church into separate factions. This was to be the first problem Paul addressed in canonical 1 Corinthians (1 Cor 1:11). That letter also deals with reports of other serious difficulties, such as gross immorality, litigation among the members, irregularities at the plenary meeting of the congregation, and doubts about the resurrection of the dead.[62] It is not clear, however, which of these issues were raised by Chloe's delegation as opposed to those raised by Stephanas's group. Whatever the source, it is evident that matters had seriously deteriorated at Corinth since Paul had been there. Paul's dispatch of Timothy to Corinth at about that time (1 Cor 16:10; cf. 4:17) appears to have been for the unenviable task of explaining Paul's letter to them, as well as to provide Paul with a reliable report on the Corinthian problems (1 Cor 16:11-12).

In the First Letter Paul told the Corinthians that he wished to withdraw from the region soon (1 Cor 16:6). As the apostle to the Gentiles, he was keen to go to Rome, the capital of the Gentile world (Rom 1:13; cf. Acts 19:21). As a Jew, he would probably not have been free to do so until the death of Claudius; Claudius had expelled Jews from Rome in A.D. 49.[63] The death of Claudius in A.D. 54 cleared the way for Paul to come to Rome. As part of his withdrawal from the region he planned to stay in Ephesus until Pentecost (late spring, of A.D. 55?), travel through Macedonia (during summer and autumn), and spend the winter in Corinth before finally journeying to Judaea (1 Cor 16:6-8; Acts 19:21; cf. 2 Cor 1:16, early in 56?), accompanied by provincial delegates who would take the collection to Jerusalem (1 Cor 16:3-4).

Before he could leave Ephesus for Macedonia, however, more bad news arrived, almost certainly brought by Timothy on his return from Corinth after the delivery of 1 Corinthians (in early spring, A.D. 55 — with Titus?). So serious was this news that Paul himself now had to go immediately to Corinth, almost a year earlier than he had planned. The crisis in Corinth is

59. It is possible that Titus delivered the "Previous Letter."

60. For a different view, see G. D. Fee, *1 Corinthians,* 7, who sees the Corinthians' letter as a response to Paul's "Previous Letter."

61. Gk. περὶ δὲ ὧν ἐγράψατε (1 Cor 7:1); περὶ δέ (7:25; 8:1; 12:1; 16:1).

62. 1 Cor 5:1; 6:1; 11:2, 17-18; 14:26-36; 15:12.

63. See above, n. 22.

shrouded in mystery; the only sources of information are the passing references in canonical 2 Corinthians. Evidently there had been a significant falling away into "impurity, sexual sin and debauchery" (12:21; cf. 13:2). When Paul sought to rectify the situation, this led to "quarreling, jealousy, outbursts of anger, factions, slander, gossip, arrogance and disorder" (12:20). Paul also writes of a man "who caused grief . . . who did the wrong" and "the injured party" (also a male), the latter almost certainly Paul himself (2:5; 7:12).[64] Paul's second visit to Corinth was, he says, "painful," a source of "grief" to the Corinthians (2:1) and probably also to himself (2:1-4; cf. 12:21).

While present in Corinth at that time, Paul disclosed a change of plans (cf. 1 Cor 16:5-7). Doubtless due to his perception of the deterioration in the church as he found it, he felt he had to return to the Corinthians directly, then travel to Macedonia, and come to them again before making his final withdrawal from the Aegean region. The new plan meant that he would see them twice, whereas the original plan provided for only one final visit. Paul's announcement of these revised travel arrangements was to have serious consequences for his relationships with the Corinthians (1:15-24).

Upon his return to Ephesus,[65] however, Paul decided to abandon that plan and to revert to the original itinerary, which would take him from Ephesus through Macedonia to Corinth. This change meant that he would now visit the Corinthians only once (more), and later than he had said. Evidently, upon reflection, he decided that a return visit to the Corinthians in the near future would create further grief for them as well as for him (2:1-2; 1:6). Rather, he chose to write a letter, now lost to us, and known only by references in 2 Corinthians (2:3-4; 7:8-12), which we will refer to as the "Severe Letter." Having sent the letter, Paul experienced regret at its severity. Anxious months followed as he awaited a reply, first in Troas and then in Macedonia, which Titus, the bearer of the "Severe Letter," would bring back to him (cf. 2:12-13; 7:5-7). Paul may have feared that the "Severe Letter" would spell the end of his relationships with the Corinthians.

---

64. C. K. Barrett, *Essays,* 108-17.

65. The sequence is uncertain at a number of points: (1) The time of the dispatch of Timothy and Erastus to Macedonia. According to Acts 19:22 Paul sent Timothy and Erastus from Ephesus to Macedonia before the riot in Ephesus, but it is unclear whether this was before or after the "Painful Visit" to Corinth. (2) The time and place of the writing of the "Severe Letter." We do not know Paul's movements between the "Painful Visit" to Corinth (1:23; 2:1) and the crisis in Asia (1:8-11). Did he return directly from Corinth to Ephesus, or did he return via Macedonia? Did he write the "Severe Letter" before or after the deadly peril in Asia? If it was beforehand, was it from Macedonia or Asia? If it was afterward, did he write from Ephesus or en route to or at Troas? We are inclined to the view that the crisis in Asia forced Paul (1) to implement a long-held plan to preach in Macedonia via Troas (cf. Acts 19:21-22; 1 Cor 16:5; 2 Cor 1:16), and (2) to dispatch Titus to Corinth with the "Severe Letter," arranging to meet him either in Troas or Macedonia.

So Paul left Ephesus for Troas, the nearest port in Asia to Macedonia, where he had planned to engage in some evangelism (2:12). He would then proceed to Macedonia, where Timothy and Erastus had been sent on ahead (Acts 19:22). If Titus did not arrive in Troas by late autumn — when the weather closed the seas to sailing — Paul would meet him in Macedonia (Philippi?).

When Titus did not arrive at Troas by the agreed deadline, Paul sailed for Macedonia, where, we assume, he was reunited with Timothy[66] (1:1) and where, after more anxious waiting, Titus finally appeared (7:5-6). On his arrival Paul found the churches in Macedonia to be subject to "severe trial" so that Paul himself suffered "conflicts on the outside" (8:2; 7:5). It appears that Paul had extensive contact with the Macedonian churches (Philippi, Thessalonica, and Beroea) during this period (8:3-4, 18–9:5; Acts 20:2). Moreover, it is possible that before he made his way to Corinth he engaged briefly in mission work in the northwest of Macedonia toward the borders of Illyricum (Rom 15:19).

To the apostle's great relief Titus brought the good news that (the section of) the church that had failed to support Paul in public against his aggressor had now responded positively to the "Severe Letter" and had taken disciplinary action (7:7-16).

Not all the news, however, was encouraging: (1) Some took the view that Paul's vacillation over his travel plans confirmed him to be a "man of flesh" (1:12, 17), whose sequence of misfortunes marked him out as inadequate in ministry (2:14-16; 3:5, 6), having lacked the capacity to resolve the problems in Corinth during the second visit (10:2, 7; 12:20; 13:3).[67] (2) The collection, established by Titus during the previous year, had lapsed (8:6, 10; 9:2). (3) Despite his second letter (canonical 1 Corinthians) and the second ("painful") visit, a section of the church remained entangled in the cultic and immoral life of the city (6:14–7:1; 12:2–13:2). (4) The criticism that Paul supported himself and declined to receive money from the Corinthians was a continuing source of unhappiness (cf. 1 Cor 9:1-23), not least that he showed no sign of changing his policy (11:7-11; 12:13-16a). Some, however, thought that he did receive money, "craftily," through his coworkers, in order to gain some moral advantage (12:16b-18; cf. 4:2; 7:2). (5) The worst news, however, was that in recent times the Corinthian congregation had been infiltrated by a group of Jewish Christian "false apostles" whose influence threatened to destroy altogether Paul's relationship with the Corinthians (2:17–3:2; 5:11-13; 10:12–12:13). In the six years of Paul's association with them, this was by far the most serious problem that had arisen.

66. We do not know when or where Paul was reunited with Timothy in Macedonia. Based on Acts 19:22, it seems likely that Timothy (and Erastus) were sent on ahead of Paul for ministry purposes and to prepare for the eventual arrival of the apostle.

67. See below, IV.B. Historical Issues.

Titus's reunion with Paul in Macedonia, bringing this good and bad news, became the occasion for Paul to write the present letter, perhaps sometime in the winter of A.D. 55. Whereas the First Letter was his response to a cluster of questions in a letter and verbal reports from one or more delegations, the Second Letter was his response to Titus's news about a range of matters in Corinth. Above all, this letter would prepare the Corinthians for Paul's third and final visit (2:2-3; 9:4; 10:2; 11:9; 12:14, 20, 21; 13:1, 2, 7, 10).

Thus it appears that Paul finally arrived in Corinth at the beginning of A.D. 56, and, according to the Acts 20:3, spent three months there. It is generally agreed that Paul wrote his letter to the Romans while staying at Corinth, as he prepared to accompany the collection to Jerusalem (Rom 15:25-26). It is probable that this letter, his most carefully structured statement, arose out of the issues raised by his most recent problems with the Corinthians, as more hastily expressed in 2 Corinthians. Did Romans have its genesis in lectures given in Corinth in the light of the recent problems there?

Corinth was the planned point of departure for the collection, the place to which the delegates carrying the contributions from the churches of Macedonia, Asia, and Galatia would converge. From Corinth this group was to set out for Jerusalem, where Paul planned to arrive by Pentecost (late spring — Acts 20:2-3, 16). His original plan was to travel by ship (Acts 20:3-4), but this intention was thwarted by news of a Jewish plot to be activated while Paul and his companions were at sea. By a revised itinerary, Paul and the provincial delegates — including those from Achaia (Rom 15:26) — were forced to travel north to Macedonia and thence to Judaea via Asia.

Paul's relationships with the Corinthians may be summarized as follows (the dates are tentative):

A.D.

50-52   Paul in Corinth

52-53   Paul travels from Corinth to Ephesus, Caesarea, Jerusalem, Antioch in Syria, and Galatia/Phrygia, and finally arrives at Ephesus.

53-55   Paul in Ephesus

News from Corinth; Paul writes "Previous Letter"

Titus in Corinth to establish the collection (2 Cor 8:6, 10; 9:2; cf. 12:17-18)

News from Chloe's people and from Stephanas bringing the letter from Corinth; Paul writes 1 Corinthians (borne by Timothy, Stephanas et al.?)

55   Timothy returns to Ephesus; Paul's second ("painful") visit to Corinth

IV. ISSUES IN 2 CORINTHIANS[68]

A. Literary

2 Corinthians is very different from the letters between which it was written, 1 Corinthians and Romans. Whereas each of those letters is, in its own way, systematic and orderly, 2 Corinthians is, on the face of it, uneven and digressive. It is no surprise, therefore, that many scholars have suggested that 2 Corinthians is really a collection of letters put together later as a single letter.[69]

In particular, it is widely held that chapters 10–13 were written by Paul separately from and later than chapters 1–9.[70] Doubt has also been cast whether 2:14–6:10 and chapters 8–9 are original to chapters 1–9. Many scholars also believe that 6:14–7:1 is a non-Pauline fragment that has been inserted into the text. Some have identified 6:14–7:1 as from the lost "Previous Letter" and chapters 10–13 as the lost "Severe Letter." Further, a number of scholars regard chapter 9 as a replica of chapter 8 and not continuous with it. Clearly

---

68. My discussion is limited to issues taken up by this commentary.

69. For a summary of the history of opinion on the unity of 2 Corinthians as well as a comprehensive review of the arguments for and against the integrity of the disputed sections see Furnish, 30-41 and Martin, xl-lii. Scholars who support the unity of 2 Corinthians include W. G. Kümmel, *Introduction,* 287-93; W. H. Bates, "Integrity," 56-69; F. Young and D. F. Ford, *Meaning,* 36-44. For arguments supporting a diversity of constituent source-letters, see Taylor, "Composition and Chronology," 67-87.

70. In recent times many scholars (e.g., Furnish, Martin) have taken the view that chapters 10–13 were written separately from, *but not much later than,* chapters 1–9. On this hypothesis the two parts are effectively treated as one letter. While this is not the view taken in this commentary, it is more acceptable than an older view that saw chapters 10–13 as the lost "Severe Letter," written prior to chapters 1–9.

there is widespread conviction that the letter as received originated as a series of letters subsequently amalgamated into our 2 Corinthians.

Before commenting on these views, I should make clear that, as it stands, 2 Corinthians consists of six sections of uneven length.

1. From 1:1 to 2:13 Paul recounts his movements in Asia, defending himself for writing the "Severe Letter" rather than returning directly to Corinth.
2. In 2:14–6:13, the longest section of the letter, Paul describes and defends his ministry under the new covenant.
3. Somewhat abruptly (6:14–7:4) he admonishes the Corinthians to separate themselves from unbelievers.
4. Resuming his account of his movements (7:5-16), he describes his joyous reunion with Titus in Macedonia and expresses thanks that the Corinthians have taken to heart the "Severe Letter."
5. Continuing to bring the Corinthians up to date, he appeals to them to complete the collection in view of the coming of Titus and the two Macedonian delegates (8:1–9:15), observing that the poor Macedonian churches have contributed generously to it.
6. Finally (10:1–13:14), Paul exhorts the Corinthians to prepare for his impending third and final visit. Within this section his interaction with various sources of criticism and opposition may be discerned, in particular, from the "false apostles."

This commentary is written from the conviction that, despite its apparently uneven and disordered character, 2 Corinthians possesses an intrinsic unity.[71]

In broad terms the subject matter of 2 Corinthians is consistent with Paul's historical situation in the period between his second and third visits to Corinth. Second Corinthians, as outlined above, is a window into Paul's soul and expresses his feelings about the Corinthians as he prepares to make his final visit to them. Thus, in terms of the above summary, (i) he answers their criticisms of his spiritual integrity, (ii) he defends his ministry in the new covenant against those who question his "sufficiency," (iii) he admonishes them to separate themselves from Corinthian temple worship, (iv) he rejoices in their acceptance of his discipline through the "Severe Letter," (v) he exhorts

---

71. As was its predecessor in this series (Hughes, xxi-xxv). There is no textual or patristic evidence to suggest various partition theories. This is not a strong point in favor of unity, however, since there is little certain external attestation for 2 Corinthians prior to the middle of the second century (see Furnish, 29-30) and all known copies of Paul's letters are from the time when they were gathered into one corpus.

them to complete the collection, and (vi) he urges them to correct false attitudes to him as they prepare for his third visit. Viewed in this way, the letter is written against the background of an unsuccessful second visit in the light of new difficulties that have now arisen (especially the arrival of the Jewish Christian "false apostles") with the intent to make the Corinthians ready for Paul's last visit, when he and they can be reconciled before he finally leaves the Aegean region.

1. The Unity of Chapters 10–13 with Chapters 1–9[72]

There are several reasons for viewing these sections as belonging to one letter.

First, rhetorical criticism has pointed to a similarity of format between a number of Paul's letters, including 2 Corinthians, and certain literature of the period.[73] Scholars have drawn attention to a letter from Demosthenes (384-322 B.C.) in exile to Athens (*Ep.* 2), that is really a speech in his defense written in epistolary form[74] and whose structural outline broadly resembles 2 Corinthians. It should be noted that 2 Corinthians, like other NT literature and indeed all literature from the period, was written to be read *aloud* to the audience to whom it was sent.[75]

In "apologetic" epistles the *exordium (prooimion)* raises the issues that

---

72. Furnish, 30-32, gives the following reasons for regarding chapters 10–13 as originally separate from chapters 1–9: (1) In the earlier section Paul writes in an expository, generally encouraging manner, whereas in the later section his style is polemical and passionate, mindful of the lure of the false apostles. (But the long section chapters 10–13 is "framed" by words of encouragement, 10:1-2 and 13:5-10.) (2) The later chapters are full of admonitions in view of his oft-repeated intention to come to them; the earlier chapters have no reference to an impending visit (but see 2:2-3; 9:4). (3) There is incongruity between the appeal to conclude the collection (chap. 9) and the sharp polemic that immediately follows it. (But 10:1-2 is couched in specifically encouraging words, which virtually repeat 5:20.) (4) Chapters 1–9 imply only one earlier visit by Titus (7:4), whereas the later chapters imply a second visit (12:18a [but see on 8:6, 10, 18, 22; 9:2]). (5) There is a predominance of first person plurals in chapters 1–9 but of first person singulars in chapters 10–13. (But first person plurals occur not infrequently in these later chapters — see 10:2-8, 11-18; 12:18b-19; 13:4b, 6b-9; the absence of the first person plural pronoun from the "Fool's Speech" [11:1–12:13] is rhetorically consistent with the intensely person nature of that "Speech.") A case for the unity of the Letter, based in part on the insights of rhetorical criticism, is set forth in F. Young and D. F. Ford, *Meaning*, 27-44.

73. H. D. Betz, *Paulus und die sokratische Tradition;* G. Kennedy, *Classical Rhetoric* and *Rhetorical Criticism;* A. Malherbe, *Social Aspects;* F. Young and D. F. Ford, *Meaning,* 36-44.

74. The point is not affected by the possibility that *Epistle* 2 is not a genuine work of Demosthenes, as some suggest.

75. P. Saenger, "Silent Reading," 367-414. Cf. G. L. Hendrickson, "Ancient Reading," 182-96.

17

will be developed, but in subtle ways, seeking the sympathetic attention of the audience. The *narrative (diēgēsis)* — which is not invariably included in such works — recounts the events leading to the court case whose decision is being contested. The *proof (pistis),* which is the heart of the speech, cites witnesses for the defense who refute the charge, introducing emotional argument to arouse pity or character witnesses to support the probity of the accused. The concluding *peroration,* in contrast to the quiet *exordium,* is emotional in tone, geared to arouse anger at the injustice of the case.

I am not suggesting that Paul was familiar with the writings of Demosthenes, but rather that he was acquainted with popular rhetorical conventions reflected in that author and others like Dionysius of Halicarnassus or Quintilian, who were closer to Paul's times.[76] Furthermore, I am insinuating that these conventions had become sufficiently commonplace that ordinary folk, not classically educated, were unconsciously aware of them.

Paul begins, as in the classical *exordium,* with thanksgiving and mutual encouragement (1:1-11). The *narrative* begins within the *exordium* with the apostle's account of his trials in Asia (1:8-11) and periodically surfaces in various travel details (2:3-13; 7:5-16; 8:1-6, 16-23; 9:2-5; 11:22–12:10). The *proofs,* by which he answers various accusations, are closely connected with the *narrative* at a number of points. Broadly speaking, Paul is defending his personal integrity in his actions (1:12-18, 23–2:11) and his "sufficiency" in ministry against the perception of weakness (2:14–4:15). Finally, the *peroration* is an emotional recapitulation of the argument of the letter, appealing for a verdict in favor of the writer (chaps. 10–13), in particular within the main part of the "Fool's Speech" (11:21–12:13). Paul reproaches them for failing to "commend" his ministry (12:11).

Pseudo-Demetrius, an analyst of ancient letter writing from Paul's general era, lists twenty-one types of letters, of which the eighteenth is described as: "The apologetic . . . one which brings against charges the opposite arguments with proof."[77] Paul specifically acknowledges the "apologetic" nature of his letter, even if apology did not exhaust his intentions in writing to the Corinthians (12:19, *q.v.*). If we accept 2 Corinthians as an "apologetic" letter, the powerfully rhetorical chapters 10 through 13 need not be considered as a separate letter but as a *peroration,* gathering up previously mentioned elements and making a final emotional appeal to the hearers. Certainly those final chapters contain rhetorical elements like *comparison* and *boasting* that have many parallels in the literature of the period.[78] Not least, the letter throughout is marked by powerful appeals addressed directly to the Corinthi-

---

76. Cf. F. Young and D. F. Ford, *Meaning,* 37-39.
77. Quoted in F. Young and D. F. Ford, *Meaning,* 39-40.
78. E. A. Judge, "Boasting," 37-50; C. B. Forbes, "Comparison," 1-30.

ans (5:20–6:2; 6:11–7:1; 10:1-2; 12:11-13; 13:5-11). Paul the pastor also uses tones of warm confidence within critical "bridge" passages where he moves from one difficult topic to another (7:2-4; 7:13-16; 10:1-2), and he concludes the letter on a very positive, confidence-inspiring note (13:5-14).

Second, throughout the letter Paul foreshadows his pending final visit. To be sure, these references come thick and fast in the later chapters (10:2, 6; 11:9; 12:14, 20, 21; 13:1, 2, 10). But they are also to be found in the early chapters (2:1, 3), as well as in the middle chapters (9:4). In each case Paul is alluding to some attitude to correct or action to take before he comes: (1) That the Corinthians and Paul should be reconciled over the man who had wronged Paul (2:1, 3). (2) That the Corinthians should complete the collection so as to avoid shame when he and the Macedonians arrive (9:4). (3) That the Corinthians turn from their cultic/sexual practices (also 12:20, 21; 13:1, 2, 10). (4) That the Corinthians accept that Paul will continue financially to support himself in ministry despite pressure from the Corinthians and the intruders (11:9, 12; 12:14). The observation that the references to the future visit are found in all parts of the letter contributes to the case for its unity.

There is, in fact, an overarching logic to Paul's argument throughout the letter. Having explained and defended past behavior (1:1–2:13) and having expounded the new covenant ministry (2:14–7:4), he encourages the Corinthians about their response retrospectively to the "Severe Letter" (7:5-16) and prospectively to the collection (chaps. 8–9). In the last section (10:1–13:14), in view of his pending visit, he responds to the charge that he is powerful only by letter (10:2-10), arguing, however, that his power is realized and recognized in weakness (12:7-10), indicating thereby that, as a "minister of Christ," he is "better" than the "superlative" apostles (11:23). Seen in this light, 2 Corinthians, as it now stands (and thus originally written), is all of a piece.

Third, we find distinctive vocabulary distributed throughout the letter that is said to have originated independently.

a. In chapters 1–9 Paul refers to "the ministry that brings righteousness," to "this ministry . . . the ministry," and to himself as "a minister of God" (3:9; 4:1; 6:3, 4). In chapters 10–13, which most interpreters regard as not belonging to the earlier chapters, however, he pointedly speaks of the newcomers as "ministers [of Satan who] masquerade as ministers of righteousness" (11:15; cf. 1:23). Since Paul nowhere else in his letters juxtaposes "ministry"/"minister" with "righteousness,"[79] these references, which contrast two "ministries of righteousness," support the notion of the unity of the two main parts of the letter.

---

79. Gk. ἡ διακονία τῆς δικαιοσύνης (3:9); διάκονοι δικαιοσύνης (11:15).

19

b. A keyword in this letter is "commend"[80]; it appears to originate in the debate over Paul's ministry as compared to that of the newcomers. "Commend" does not occur in a letter written by Paul prior to 2 Corinthians. This word occurs throughout the letter (3:1; 4:2; 5:12; 6:4; 10:12, 18; 12:11), in both of the parts that are said to have arisen separately. In particular, his "I ought to have been commended by you," his plaintive climax to the "Fool's Speech" (12:11), ties that part of the letter to all that has gone before.

c. Words rarely used by Paul, which appear together in 4:2 ("we do not use *deception,* nor do we *distort* the word of God"), recur in a closely related parallel in 12:16 (*"crafty* fellow that I am, I caught you by *trickery"*).[81] In no other place in Paul's writings do these words appear together.

d. Paul's combination "I appeal . . . I beg" (10:1, 2) matches closely his earlier exhortation "God making his appeal . . . we implore you" (5:20).[82] In no other letter does Paul connect these two verbs.

e. "Confidence,"[83] another word rarely used by Paul, occurs in chapter 10, as well as in the earlier chapters (1:15; 3:4; 8:22; 10:2).

f. The phrase "before God in Christ we speak"[84] is found in 2:17 and 12:19; it occurs nowhere else in Paul's writings.

Repetition of vocabulary is also found within the four "sufferings" passages scattered throughout 2 Corinthians (1:7-11; 4:8-10; 6:4-10; 11:23–12:10), the fourth of which occurs within chapters 10–13. "Sufferings" passages in themselves do not conclusively prove the unity of 2 Corinthians since there are similar passages in other Pauline letters.[85] Vocabulary common to these passages, however, is evidence for the overarching unity of 2 Corinthians. For example, the Greek words from the first passage, "surpassing . . . power," reappear in the second as "surpassing power" and are repeated in the fourth passage as "surpassingly great revelations" contrasted with "power . . . in weakness."[86]

There are other verbal linkages. The closely related Greek words that are translated "crushed"/"distresses"/"difficulties"[87] appear in the second, third, and fourth lists. No fewer than seven words are common to the third

---

80. Gk. συνίστημι.

81. Gk. ἐν πανουργίᾳ μηδὲ δολοῦντες . . . (4:2); ὑπάρχων πανοῦργος δόλῳ (12:16).

82. Gk. παρακαλῶ . . . δέομαι (10:1, 2); παρακαλοῦντος . . . δεόμεθα (5:20).

83. Gk. πεποίθησις occurs in Eph 3:12; Phil 3:4, but it is not to be found in any letter earlier than 2 Corinthians.

84. Gk. κατέναντι θεοῦ ἐν Χριστῷ λαλοῦμεν.

85. E.g., Rom 8:35-39; 1 Cor 4:8-11.

86. Gk. καθ' ὑπερβολὴν ὑπὲρ δύναμιν (1:8); ἡ ὑπερβολὴ τῆς δυνάμεως (4:7); τῇ ὑπερβολῇ τῶν ἀποκαλύψεων . . . ἡ . . . δύναμις ἐν ἀσθενείᾳ (12:7, 9).

87. Gk. στενοχωρέω/στενοχωρία (4:8; 6:4; 6:4; 12:10).

and fourth lists.[88] This argument is more powerful still because four of these seven words do not appear elsewhere in Paul's writings.[89] Other linguistic considerations add cumulatively to an impression of epistolary unity.[90]

Fourth, a reference late in the letter (12:19) appears to be a summary of the *whole* letter, including the "apologetic" early chapters:

> Have you been thinking all along that we have been defending ourselves to you? We have been speaking in the sight of God as those in Christ; and everything is for your strengthening.

For the reasons following it is likely that Paul has in mind the entire letter to this point and not merely the immediate context relating to financial matters: (1) His reference to "have you been thinking *all along*" and to *"everything,"* (2) his "we have been defending ourselves to you" (which calls to mind his initial defense of his actions — 1:3–2:13), and (3) his "double oath," "before God in Christ we speak" replicates exactly an earlier passage (2:17). Because Paul appears to be reviewing the letter as a whole, the partition theory is rendered unlikely.

Fifth, the reasons given for partitioning the supposedly independent letters are capable of other interpretations.[91] The argument for the separation of chapters 10–13 — the most serious case — rests principally on Paul's assertion in 12:18 that he *"sent* our brother with [Titus]" to Corinth, whereas in 8:18, 22 Paul is *"sending* with [Titus] the brother . . . and our brother." On this basis it is argued that 12:18 belongs to a letter written later than the earlier letter, to which 8:18, 22 is said to have belonged.

Each of the earlier aorist references "with [Titus] we *are sending* the brother" (8:18) and "with [Titus and the brother] we *are sending* our brother" (8:22) appears in its context to be an epistolary aorist,[92] and is so taken by the translations.[93] On the other hand, the latter aorist "I *sent* the brother with Titus" (12:18) is to be understood in a historic, as opposed to an epistolary, sense. But it is by no means clear to us to which "sending" Paul is here referring, though it would have been to the writer and the original readers.

88. Gk. διάκονος (6:4; 11:23); ἀνάγκη (6:4; 12:10); πληγή (6:5; 11:23); φυλακή (6:5; 11:23); κόπος (6:5; 11:23); ἀγρυπνία (6:5; 11:27); νηστεία (6:5; 11:27).

89. Gk. πληγή, φυλακή, ἀγρυπνία, and νηστεία.

90. E.g., (1) his address to them as "brothers" within chapters 10–13 (13:11) is matched within chapters 1–9 (1:8; 8:1), and (2) his final admonition (παρακαλεῖσθε — 13:11) yields only one specific parallel in chapters 10–13 (10:1), but several in chapters 1–9 (2:8; 5:20; 6:1).

91. F. Young and D. F. Ford, *Meaning,* 28-36.

92. Where the form is aorist but the meaning is present, "we are sending" (cf. also Col 4:8; Phil. 2:28). See further K. L. McKay, *Verb,* 48-49.

93. As, e.g., by the RSV, NRSV, NIV, NEB, and JB, but not by the NASB.

We know of three occasions on which Paul "sent" Titus to Corinth: (1) to establish the collection in Corinth sometime in the previous calendar year (8:6, 10; 9:2), (2) to deliver the "Severe Letter" (2:13; 7:6), and (3) to deliver the present letter (8:16, 18, 22). The reference to "the brother" (12:18; cf. 8:16, 18) probably points to Titus's visit (3) referred to earlier (8:16, 18, 22).[94]

The use of the aorist "sent" in 12:18 does not demand a visit earlier than the writing of 12:18. The aorist as aspectively understood does not require a past meaning so much as a completed meaning.[95] From Paul's and the Corinthians' viewpoint the aorist "I sent" could be understood to refer to the visit that is in prospect at 8:18, 22, when, it is supposed, the present letter was brought to the Corinthians (8:6), but which is now a completed reality in the context of 12:18. An epistolary understanding of the aorists in 8:18, 22 and a historic understanding of the aorist in 12:18, which is grammatically cogent, are arguments for the unity of chapters 1–9 with 10–13.

What, then, may be said to explain the change in tone from joy and confidence in chapter 7 and encouragement in chapters 8 and 9 to the irony in chapters 10–13?

The joy and confidence expressed at the end of chapter 7 needs to be understood in terms of Paul's pastoral method.[96] His positive expressions about the Corinthians are not absolute but relative, circumscribed by (1) his thankfulness that the "Severe Letter" has been effective in achieving its major objective, that is, their expression of loyalty to Paul in disciplining of the wrongdoer (7:12), and (2) his preparation of the Corinthian mind for his appeal that the Corinthians complete the collection by the hand of Titus whom Paul is sending back to them for that very purpose and which he will immediately raise with them (8:6; cf. 7:13b-16).

---

94. Paul distinguishes between an eminent brother ("the brother") and a lesser or more junior colleague ("our brother"). A close and prominent association existed between Titus and "the brother"; Paul sends "the brother" *with* Titus (8:18; 12:18), whereas he sends "our brother" *with them* (i.e., with Titus and "the brother" — 8:22). The lack of reference to "our brother" in 12:18 is inconsequential, given the prominence *together* of Titus and "the brother," and is no evidence of a separate visit. Nonetheless, it is possible that this eminent "brother" may have accompanied Titus at visit (1), when the collection was first proposed. The words "Did I take advantage of you through any of *those whom* I sent to you" (12:17) point to (1) a plurality of persons whom (2) Paul *had* sent (ἀπέσταλκα — perfect tense).

95. According to K. L. McKay, *Verb,* 30: "The aorist . . . is the aspect normally used for expressing an activity simply as an act or event, an action pure and otherwise undefined, in its totality. . . . In narrative contexts referring to past time the aorist indicative normally has past reference, but in other contexts it is just as likely to have a timeless (or even present or future time) implication. . . . Any apparent time reference is always due to the context and not to the aorist aspect itself."

96. See S. N. Olson, "Confidence," 282-95.

Moreover, the change of tone is well accounted for if 2 Corinthians is regarded as an "apologetic" letter whose later chapters are a peroration where more intense rhetoric was customary.[97] But, as we have noted earlier, this peroration is based on the foundation of confidence and encouragement in chapters 7–9.

Those who see chapters 10–13 as fundamentally different from chapters 1–9, but whose approach is generally conservative, tend to resolve the problem in several ways. On the one hand, they suppose that Paul received news of a deteriorating situation in Corinth during the writing of the letter, which dramatically affected the character of chapters 10–13.[98] (But would Paul have sent a letter the first part of which would now be redundant?) On the other hand, they suggest that chapters 10–13 were written as a separate letter not too long after the dispatch of the letter represented by chapters 1–9. By this explanation chapters 10–13 were editorially attached to the earlier letter as a kind of canonical appendix at some later time.[99] (But it may be questioned whether in copying his manuscripts the early Christians would have felt at liberty to discard the concluding sentences of one and the opening sentence of another of Paul's letters.)

2. The Unity of Passages within Chapters 1–9

We will now consider briefly passages within chapters 1–9 held to have originated separately.[100]

a. The long passage 2:14–7:4 is deemed to be extraneous on account of the references to Macedonia ("So . . . I went on to Macedonia" — 2:13; "When we came into Macedonia" — 7:5). But this proves too much. It is less likely that someone else has inserted a long, seemingly unrelated, passage between two references to Macedonia, the second of which does not easily follow the first, than that Paul himself, conscious of a long digression, has reintroduced "Macedonia" to signal that he has resumed his recapitulation of events.

b. Because 6:14–7:1 has a large number of *hapax legomena* and appears to interrupt the line of Paul's argument, many have regarded it as a non-Pauline insertion. Verbal parallels with Qumran literature have led some scholars to argue for its origin in the writings of the Dead Sea sect.[101] But the passage

97. See F. Young and D. F. Ford, *Meaning,* 37-39.
98. So, e.g., D. A. Carson, *Triumphalism,* 15-16.
99. This view is held by many recent commentators, e.g., Barrett, Bruce, Furnish, Martin and Kruse.
100. For greater detail see comments on the specific passages.
101. See J. A. Fitzmyer, "Interpolated Paragraph," 271-80.

is a powerful call for separation from Gentile temple worship and may reasonably be seen as a logical continuation of Paul's exhortations in 1 Corinthians.[102] The listing of OT texts, some of which were employed at Qumran, to drive home his point may only illustrate a dependence on the OT shared by the apostle and the sectaries. The demand that the Corinthians break with Gentile practice, so far from interrupting Paul's line of thought on the subject of the new covenant, is actually a pointed appeal to them that forms a fitting climax to the whole passage begun at 2:14.

c. Some commentators have argued that since chapters 8 and 9 cover the same ground, one of them arose independently and was inserted later.[103] In 9:1 Paul says that he has no need to write about this matter, though the previous chapter is devoted to it. But given Paul's defensiveness toward the Corinthians about matters dealing with money,[104] it is quite understandable that he would retrace his argument to establish his policy. Repetition was a well-known rhetorical device in the writings of ancient authors.[105]

In summary, whether in regard to the major question of the unity of chapters 10–13 with chapters 1–9 or the lesser questions of unity within chapters 1–9, there are several good reasons for upholding the unity of 2 Corinthians and no conclusive arguments for rejecting it.

In our view 2 Corinthians is not a pastiche of letters of independent origin. Rather, the letter was always a unity, written in the cultural mode of an apologetic letter and controlled from beginning to end by the following simple aims:

a. To explain and defend (1) Paul's actions since he was last with the Corinthians, that is, that he wrote to them but did not return to them directly (1:1–2:13; 7:2-16), and (2) his refusal to accept payment, while appearing to accept payment through his colleagues (7:2; 11:7-11; 12:13-18).

b. To explain and defend his new covenant ministry as nontriumphalist (2:14), yet, despite its sufferings, effective (3:6), the evidence of which is the presence among them of the Spirit of the living God (3:3, 6, 8, 18; 5:5).

---

102. G. D. Fee, "II Corinthians vi.14–vii.1," 140-61; G. K. Beale, "Reconciliation," 550-81.

103. Classically stated in H. D. Betz, *2 Corinthians 8 and 9.* For a grammatically argued case for the unity of these chapters, see S. K. Stowers, *"Peri men gar,"* 230-348. See also S. N. Olson, "Confidence," 282-95, who argues that, in line with epistolary convention, Paul's expresses "confidence" so as to encourage the readers' response along the line of his "confidence." Such expressions occur particularly within chapters 7–9 (e.g., 7:14-16; 9:1-5), adding weight to the suggestion that those chapters lay the foundation for the powerful admonitions of the final chapters that prepare the ground for the apostle's final visit. See, further, the extended note at the beginning of chapter 8.

104. 1 Cor 9:3-18; 2 Cor 11:7-9; 12:16-18; cf. 4:2; 7:2.

105. F. Young and D. F. Ford, *Meaning,* 34-35.

c. To encourage them to resolve various difficulties in advance of his final visit (13:10): (1) the finalization of the collection (8:1–9:5), (2) the repentance of those still involved in sexual immorality/cultic practice (12:20–13:3; 6:14–7:1), and (3) the rejection of the intruding "false apostles" (10:12–12:13).

d. As a pastoral opportunist, to teach the Corinthians a number of important doctrines while dealing with matters of immediate concern.[106]

3. Cultural Diversity within 2 Corinthians

Within this letter, as in no other by Paul, one may see evidence of the diverse cultural influences on the writer. Consistent with his assertion that he is a "Hebrew" (11:22), we note echoes from the liturgy of the synagogue in various benedictions (e.g., 1:3-11, 20; 11:31), thanksgivings (e.g., 2:14; 9:15), and asseverations arising from the OT (e.g., 1:12, 23; 11:10). Paul peppers his text with quotations from and allusions to the OT (e.g., 3:3-6, 16; 4:13; 5:12, 17; 6:1-2, 14–7:1; 9:6-8, 9-10; 10:17; 11:2; 13:1). The vocabulary and thought of Isaiah 40–55 appear to underlie 5:14–7:1. Both the well-developed midrash on Moses' veil based on a passage from the Pentateuch (3:7-18) and the dualistic apocalypse arising from the division of the ages (4:16–5:10), hinged around the general resurrection (4:14; cf. 1:14; 5:10),[107] arise from the religious culture of contemporary Judaism.

On the other hand, increased awareness of the Greco-Roman culture of the period indicates that Paul was familiar with, and prepared to express himself in terms of, that culture. It has been long understood that 2 Corinthians is written in educated *koinē* in the format of a Hellenistic letter. More recently, however, similarities in Pauline epistolary layout and expression have been detected in (1) Hellenistic forensic political speeches, with, for example, their *exordia* (cf. 1:12-15) and *encomia* (cf. 1:15ff.), and (2) the so-called *peristaseis,* whereby lists of sufferings and achievements, often stated contrastively (cf. 4:8-9; 6:3-10; 11:23-33; 12:7-10), are given.[108] The contrasts — negative and positive (2:17; 11:22-23a; cf. 10:12) — between himself and his opponents and the catalogues of weaknesses that serve to disclose a God-given power to overcome them (4:8-9; 6:3-10; 11:23b–12:10), and which legitimate his ministry in the face of rivalry, appear to have numbers of parallels within Hellenism, including Hellenistic Judaism. Attention has also been drawn to

---

106. See below, IV.C. Theological Issues.

107. On the significant place of apocalyptic in the thought of the apostle see J. C. Beker, *Paul the Apostle,* 143-63; B. Lindars, "Sound of the Trumpet," 766-82.

108. See, e.g., F. Young and D. F. Ford, *Meaning;* J. T. Fitzgerald, *Earthen Vessels,* 148-201.

Paul's use of paradox,[109] metaphor,[110] invective,[111] and comparison.[112] The "Fool's Speech" (11:1–12:13) probably remains the most striking example of Hellenistic cultural influence in regard to "boasting," which, however, he subverts by his use of irony.

The veil-midrash (chap. 3), on the one hand, and the "Fool's Speech" (chaps. 11–12), on the other, serve to symbolize that Paul was both Hebrew and Hellenist. By birth, upbringing, and profession he was a Hellenistic Jew of intense commitment to the pharisaic ideal. More fundamentally, however, the thorough christological permeation of these forms — whether the Hebraic midrash or the Hellenistic "Fool's Speech" — reveals the profound degree by which the Hellenistic Jew, Saul of Tarsus, had been converted in heart and mind to Jesus as Messiah and to his Spirit who had now come to them.

B. Historical

Second Corinthians is no abstract piece of theology, as if written in a vacuum.[113] Rather, it is Paul's response to reports brought by Titus to him in Macedonia about the state of the church in Corinth, in particular the attitudes of the Corinthians to him at that time. When he refers to "the daily pressure of my concern for all the churches" (11:23), he is likely thinking primarily of the chaotic state of that church from whom he has recently heard and which he must visit next, the church in Corinth.

Above all, 2 Corinthians mirrors the current unhappiness of the Corinthians toward Paul. His defensive tone throughout (cf. 12:19) indicates that he faced a cluster of negative attitudes.

Attempts to reconstruct the contemporary *Sitz im Leben* of the Corinthian church, however, though worth the effort, are bedeviled by several problems: (1) While Paul frequently addresses the Corinthians globally, he nowhere identifies or addresses directly particular individuals or groups who oppose him, though he does occasionally refer to them in the third person (2:17–3:1; 5:12; 10:2, 7, 10; 10:12–12:13 passim).[114] (2) Only rarely do we

---

109. See Martin, 242-43.
110. See F. Young and D. F. Ford, *Meaning,* chap. 6.
111. See P. Marshall, "Invective," 359-73.
112. See C. B. Forbes, "Comparison," 1-30.
113. C. J. Hickling, "Source of Early Church History?" 284-87 and "Sequence," 380-95, rejects the view that Paul's theology in 2 Corinthians is a response to alternative theologies (of the Corinthians and Paul's rivals). For a reply see R. P. Martin, "Setting of 2 Corinthians," 3-4.
114. Some references are to outsiders (2:17–3:1; 10:12–12:13 passim); others are unclear (5:12; 10:2, 7, 10).

hear Corinthian words against or about him (10:10); we are driven to deduce their complaints from his rebuttals. "Mirror" exegesis is a limited tool. (3) His pastoral/theological method, whereby he deals with matters topically (e.g., the new covenant ministry — 2:14–7:4), makes it difficult to know precisely who is being addressed within the particular passages.

1. Issues Addressed in 2 Corinthians

Broadly speaking, the issues Paul addresses in 2 Corinthians fall into three categories: (1) those problems evident in the the church discernible in 1 Corinthians that continued to be problems and are reflected in 2 Corinthians, (2) those matters associated with the Second Visit and the follow-up "Severe Letter," and (3) more recent problems.

a. Problems That Continued from First Corinthians[115]

Although specific evidence is lacking, the factionalism evident in the First Letter probably did not cease, but continued to be a characteristic of the Corinthian congregation. Paul specified that factionalism (1) in terms of rich versus poor at the Lord's Supper (1 Cor 11:18-19), and (2) in relationship to particular leaders ("each one of you says, 'I am of Paul,' or 'I am of Apollos,' or 'I am of Cephas,' or 'I am of Christ.' Is Christ divided?" — 1 Cor 1:12, 13). Doubtlessly these various leaders — Paul and Apollos, who had visited Corinth — and, in all probability, Cephas too — continued to have their supporters in Corinth. There was, as noted above, only a brief period between the two canonical letters. When the direct references to "divisions" and "factions" in the First Letter (*schismata* and *haireseis* — 1 Cor 11:18-19) are read with the apostle's warnings and encouragements (1 Cor 3:1-4, 16-17; 12:25), they give a picture of partisanship within the Corinthian congregation.

Hints of discrete groups are to be found in the Second Letter. The "majority" who punished the offender implies a minority who did not (2:6), and a division between the two. "Those who sinned earlier and *all the others*" (13:2) suggests a definable group that, in some way, is against those who have remained pure. In the Second Letter the present need for unity within the church is appealed for by a verb ("be restored"[116] — 13:11; cf. 13:9, "What we pray for is your restoration") that, significantly, is found in the First Letter where Paul begins to admonish them about their factionalism (1 Cor 1:10).

---

115. For a list of matters raised in 1 Corinthians that may be identified in 2 Corinthians, see F. Young and D. F. Ford, *Meaning,* 55-57.

116. Gk. καταρτίζεσθε. This verb is found in Paul only at 1 Thess 3:10 and Gal 6:1; the noun does not appear elsewhere in the NT.

Particular matters raised in the First Letter that remained matters of contention in the church include (1) unhappiness (among wealthier members?) over Paul's refusal to be supported financially (1 Cor 9:15-18; 2 Cor 11:7-12; 12:13-16), and (2) criticism (from the pro-Apollos group?) over his inadequacy in rhetoric (1 Cor 2:1-5; 2 Cor 10:10; 11:5).

The difficulties between Paul and the Corinthians implicit in these issues appear to have been intensified by later events, namely, (1) his own perceived failures (during the second visit, his nonreappearance in Corinth, and his dispatch of a letter instead), and (2) the arrival of the "false apostles."

b. Problems Associated with the "Painful" Visit and the "Severe Letter"

A significant, though unspecified, problem arose in Corinth between the writing of the First and the Second Letters that necessitated the Second ("Painful") Visit, which in turn required the writing of the (lost) "Severe Letter." What was that problem? In my view Paul's reason for making his second visit may be deduced from the final section of the Second Letter (10:1-11; 12:14–13:14), where he warns about matters to be set right before he arrives for the third time, namely, that a number of the Corinthians have not repented of the sexually related practices of "impurity, sexual sin and debauchery."[117] It is clear that not all the Corinthians were involved. He refers to "many who have sinned earlier" and "those who sinned earlier and all the others" (12:21; 13:2).

This suggests that these were the matters about which he had issued severe warnings during that visit (13:2). It is probable, therefore, that the reason Paul made his second visit to Corinth was to deal with a crisis of unrepented sexual immorality within the Corinthian church. It appears that the persistent sexual immorality, that characterized certain believers from the beginnings of the church in Corinth has put the spiritual survival of those believers in jeopardy.[118]

Likewise, Paul's powerful call for separation from temple worship and idolatry (6:14–7:1) may well repeat a similar admonition made during the second visit, and which still awaits repentance by (a section of?) the Corinthian church at the time of writing 2 Corinthians. As with sexual immorality, the Corinthian believers had long-term problems with Gentile cultic worship

---

117. Gk. ἀκαθαρσία, πορνεία, ἀσελγεία (12:21).

118. Continuing sexual immorality by Corinthian Christians may be traced from the time of the lost "Previous Letter" (1 Cor 5:9-11) through 1 Corinthians (1 Cor 6:15-20), the second visit (2 Cor 12:21; 13:2), and the "Severe Letter" (probably); it is still unresolved in prospect of the third visit (2 Cor 12:21; 13:2).

(1 Cor 8:4-10; 10:7-22). Temple worship and sexual immorality were often culturally connected in Greco-Roman cities of the period.[119] Failure to disengage from the one would have meant ongoing involvement with the other.

In his attempts to deal with these problems Paul was apparently subjected to a personal attack during that second visit. This is almost probably what he means when he speaks of a man "who did the wrong" (7:12), a man who has "caused grief" to Paul (2:5), and "the wronged party" (7:12).[120] The majority of the Corinthians, though theoretically siding with Paul, did not take practical disciplinary action against the offender at the time, so that Paul left Corinth humiliated. They failed to indicate their active support for Paul against the wrongdoer until the arrival of the "Severe Letter" (2:9; 7:12). This assault on Paul may have been provoked by Paul's insistence that some Corinthians utterly abandon their gross sexual immorality. The minority (2:6),[121] who have not given their support to Paul at the time of the writing of 2 Corinthians, may be the ones he calls "all the others" who are associated with the unrepentant sexual offenders whom Paul admonishes in the light of his prospective third visit (13:2). His fear that the third visit will provoke "quarreling, jealousy, outbursts of anger, factions, slander, gossip, arrogance and disorder" (12:20) appears to be based upon his memory that precisely these things occurred when he attempted to resolve the immorality issue at the last visit.

While a majority of the members agreed with Paul, their support was passive (2:9; 7:12). It is reasonable to conclude that the Corinthians felt some disappointment with Paul's apparent indecisiveness during his second visit. His approach to the sexually immoral — and perhaps to the aggressor — had been not at all what people living in Roman Corinth might have expected. He came neither with the legal might of a Roman magistrate nor in the power of a charismatic personality but "in the meekness and gentleness of Christ" (10:1), as one who "grieved" and who "humbled" himself "before" the congregation (12:21). But this seemed to speak only of weakness (10:2-6), not strength.

---

119. Cf. the imperatives φεύγετε τὴν πορνείαν and φεύγετε ἀπὸ τῆς εἰδωλολατρίας (1 Cor 6:18 and 10:14). The two — idolatry and immorality — are juxtaposed (1 Cor 10:7-8); see G. D. Fee, *1 Corinthians*, 455-56.

120. Gk. ὁ ἀδίκησας/ὁ ἀδικηθείς (7:12; cf. 2:5-10). Traditionally this offender has been identified as the "incestuous man" whom Paul exhorted the Corinthians to discipline in 1 Cor 5:1-5, 12-13 (e.g., Hughes, 59-64). For a more recent statement of this position see C. Kruse, "Offender," 129-39. However, the evidence for this identification is inconclusive. See Furnish, 164-66, for a detailed response to the traditional view and 166-68 for his defense of the proposal that the offender had slandered Paul (or someone close to him). See further on 2:5-11 and 7:12.

121. His reference to "by the majority" (ὑπὸ τῶν πλειόνων) (2:6) implies a "minority."

Further, his failure to return to them in the immediate future in a follow-up visit, as he had promised (1:15-16, 23), and his dispatch instead of a letter, appear to have had very damaging consequences that Titus had the painful duty to convey to the apostle when they were finally reunited in Macedonia (7:6-7).

Beyond that, however, it seems that particular collectives within the wider church community were sharply critical of Paul's actions.[122] Those long-term critics of his inadequacy in rhetoric and in physical presence (10:10; cf. 11:5) — a pro-Apollos group? (cf. 1 Cor 1:12; 2:1-5) — appear to have been incensed at his nonarrival and the arrival instead of a letter, which was "frightening" (10:9), which caused them much "sorrow" (2:4; 7:8-9), and which was, in part, obscure (1:13-14).

Moreover, Paul appears to be under constraint to answer the criticism that in failing to reappear he has acted out of "fleshly wisdom" (1:12), that he made his plans "according to the flesh" (1:17), and that, while recently in Corinth he had "wage[d] his warfare according to the flesh" (10:3) and "ha[d] weapons" that were "fleshly" (10:3). The criticisms that Paul's ministry had proved to be "flesh" occur in a passage where Paul writes defensively, "If any one is confident that he is of Christ, let him remind himself that as he is of Christ, so are we" (10:7, RSV).[123] When he reacts later, "Since you desire proof that Christ is speaking in me . . ." (13:2), it is possible that some (most?) thought they were "of Christ," but that Paul had, by his recent visit, shown that he was not "of Christ" but, in fact, a man of "flesh," one whose "bodily presence is weak and his speech beneath contempt" (10:10).[124]

But such an opinion of Paul — though now accentuated — may not have been novel. The First Letter reveals the belief that, over against Paul, the Corinthians — in his words — "*already* have all they wish, *already* are rich" and, without Paul, "rule as kings" and, again — against him — are "wise . . . powerful . . . honored" (1 Cor 4:8, 10; cf. 14:36).[125] While a heightened eschatology appears to have been characteristic of the church as

122. While upholding the value of attempting the reconstruction of the situation in Corinth J. L. Sumney, *Identifying Paul's Opponents,* 81, 82, warns against reconstructions based on *possibilities.* "Reconstructions which can only expose possibilities . . . prove nothing. Probability must be established from work on the primary document, which does not presuppose reconstruction. . . . An interpretation controlled by a reconstruction must be classified as conjectural."

123. In 10:1-11 Paul is dealing with long-standing attitudes toward him. He begins to discuss the newcomers only from 11:12 on. The reference "of Christ" does not relate to the new ministers who question Paul's credentials, but to long-term criticisms of him among the Corinthians.

124. Gk. ἡ δὲ παρουσία τοῦ σώματος ἀσθενὴς καὶ ὁ λόγος ἐξουθενημένος.

125. See J. Murphy-O'Connor, "Pneumatikoi," 42-58, for the proposition that Paul is addressing Judaizers in 2:14–3:6 and Philo-influenced *pneumatikoi* in 4:1-6. His *Theology,* 12-15, sets forth a profile of the *pneumatikoi* as in 1 Corinthians.

a whole, it is possible that those who say, "We are 'of Christ'" (1:12), may have been particularly associated with that eschatology. Those who had such an outlook may have been confirmed in their low estimate of Paul by his ineffectual approach to the moral crisis in the church during the second visit and by his subsequent failure to stick to his plans to return to them (". . . you desire proof that *Christ* is speaking in me" — 13:3). They felt that he was a fundamentally "weak" person (10:10; cf. 11:21–13:4 passim), altogether lacking in "competence" (3:5; cf. 2:16). He seemed to have been subject to an endless list of misfortunes and difficulties (cf. 4:8-9). Surely his morale is low, even to the point of giving up his ministry (4:1, 16).

c. Three New Problems

In addition to the problems that had arisen during and since the "Painful Visit," Titus also brought reports of worrying new developments.

(1) The first of these — the cessation of the collection for the "saints" (in Jerusalem) — was probably a direct consequence of Paul's loss of standing in Corinth through the "Painful Visit" and the "Severe Letter" (see B.1.b. above). Paul had established the collection in Corinth during Titus's visit the previous calendar year (see on 8:6, 10; 9:2), a visit that probably raised issues that Paul must answer in 1 Corinthians (see 1 Cor 16:1-2). Later, having dispatched Titus with the "Severe Letter," Paul left Ephesus, arriving eventually in Macedonia. In his ministry to the Macedonian churches he had informed them, on a false assumption, and now to his embarrassment, that the Corinthians were "ready" with their collection (9:2). Paul addresses this major problem in chapters 8 and 9.

(2) A further problem was also in relation to financial matters. It was a sharpened version, now bitterly felt, of a complaint that went back to the first visit (1 Cor 9:3-18), namely, his unwillingness to accept financial support from the Corinthians, in breach of existing conventions governing the patronage of visiting teachers. To make matters worse, the newly arrived Jewish-Christian ministers of Christ were prepared to accept payment (cf. 11:20), something we infer the newcomers were not slow to exploit against Paul (cf. 11:12). To the Corinthians it was a "sin" that Paul "lowered" himself to work to support himself (11:7), declining their payment, a "wrong" (12:13) he inflicted on them.[126] They felt slighted that he had accepted money from the Macedonians but not from them (11:8-9).

There was also a new twist to this matter. Some Corinthians now believed that his refusal to accept money during the first (and second?) visit

126. See, further, E. A. Judge, "Social Conformity," 15-16; P. Marshall, *Enmity,* 218-58.

was motivated by guile, that he was hiding behind a mask of altruism. Paul was now accused of being a "crafty" man acting out of "cunning"[127] who had taken moral advantage of the Corinthians (12:16-18; cf. 4:2; 7:2). Some pointed to his coworkers' accepting support as evidence that, after all, Paul did receive money from the Corinthians, despite his disclaimers (12:16b-18). This is why he must reassure them that he will not be a "burden" when he comes for the third time (11:9; 12:14-18), that he does not seek their possessions (12:14), and that his coworkers had not taken advantage of them on previous occasions (12:17-18).

(3) Arguably the most important problem reported by Titus to Paul relates to the newly arrived "false apostles" in Corinth.

Scholars have devoted considerable effort to identifying these opponents. So critical is the question of their identity that C. K. Barrett declared it to be "one of the crucial questions for the understanding of the New Testament and the origins of Christianity."[128]

---

127. Note the vocabulary of "trickery" — ὑπάρχων πανοῦργος δόλῳ — in 12:16 (cf. μὴ περιπατοῦντες ἐν πανουργίᾳ — 4:2; ὡς ἐξ εἰλικρινείας — 2:17).

128. C. K. Barrett, "Opponents," 233. For a general survey of Paul's opponents see E. E. Ellis, "Opponents," 264-98. For a more recent survey of this question see R. P. Martin, "Opponents." Broadly speaking, the identity of the opponents in 2 Corinthians has been classified in three ways.

1. Judaizers. This view argues that the newcomers to Corinth were Palestinian Jews bent on bringing the Gentile Corinthians within the framework of Judaism. It has been classically expressed by F. C. Baur and repeated with refinements by C. K. Barrett, "Opponents," and R. P. Martin, "Opponents."

2. Gnostics. Diametrically opposed to the Baur thesis is the opinion that the opponents were "Gnostic pneumatics" who minimized the earthly Jesus in favor of a heavenly Lord and who pushed Paul's doctrine of grace to antinomian extremes. They despise Paul's inferior gnosis (11:6) and self-confessed weakness (10:10) and present themselves as offering a higher gnosis supported by miraculous and visionary "signs." An early advocate of this theory was W. Lütgert, who saw the opponents' backgound in liberal diaspora Judaism. Lütgert, in turn, influenced the more recent expositions of Bultmann and Schmithals.

3. "Divine Men" (Gk. θεῖοι ἄνδρες). Georgi (Opponents) developed the hypothesis that Paul's opponents claimed — on the basis of their gifts and signs — to be "divine men" in succession to Jesus and Moses, who were both charismatic, wonder-working figures. Their confident claims and strong demands made on the Corinthians were part of their legitimacy as θεῖοι ἄνδρες, which they insisted upon over against the manifest weaknesses of Paul. A variation of this theory may be found in that of G. Friedrich, who holds that the models to which the newcomers pointed were not drawn from the Hellenistic world but from early Christianity, namely, Stephen and Philip, the miracle-working Hellenist leaders of Acts 6.

Closely linked is the question whether or not the "false apostles"[129] and the "superlative" apostles[130] are to be distinguished or equated. F. C. Baur argued that the "false apostles" were newly arrived ministers in Corinth, whereas the "superlative" apostles were the Jerusalem apostles from whom they had come.[131] The view taken here is that the differentiation of the two is arbitrary, the transition from the former (11:1-4) to the latter (11:5) being too abrupt to make sense.

Moreover, the one explicit reference to "false apostles" is sandwiched between the two references to "superlative" *(hyperlian)* apostles (11:5; 12:12)[132] in that part of the letter (chaps. 10–12) where Paul makes extensive use of the preposition *hyper* ("better") as an ironical instrument against the pretentious claims of the "false apostles." Paul uses words prefixed with *hyper* to attack the "false apostles" — for their missionary intrusiveness (*over*-extending themselves[133]) into lands *beyond*,[134] for their boast of *abundance* of revelations,[135] and the resulting *super*elation.[136] To expose their boastfulness Paul himself boasts ironically of being a "better" *(hyper)* minister of Christ in terms of the sufferings that he catalogues (11:23ff.). The close association of *hyper* words with "false apostles" makes it likely that the "superlative" *(hyperlian)* apostles and the "false apostles" were the same people.

2. The "False Apostles"

a. Their Identity

Who, then, were these "false apostles"? It is evident from 2 Corinthians that they were a group ("many" — 2:17; 11:18; cf. 10:12) of men (probably)[137]

---

129. Gk. οἱ ψευδαπόστολοι — 11:11-13.

130. Gk. οἱ ὑπερλίαν ἀπόστολοι — 11:5; 12:11.

131. Thus also C. K. Barrett, "Opponents," 233-54; M. E. Thrall, "Super-Apostles," 42-57. For a contrary view see P. W. Barnett, "Opposition," 3-17. On the relationship between Paul and the Jerusalem church see J. D. G. Dunn, "Relationship," 461-78.

132. In relation to the second reference to ὑπερλίαν ἀπόστολοι (12:11, 12), Paul uses the aorist tense of the verb "I was not inferior (ὑστέρησα) [to them]." This verb, being singular, pinpoints Paul's sojourn in Corinth. Thus his contrast appears to be between himself and those who have been in Corinth (e.g., the "false apostles"), rather than among those apostolic leaders of the church in Jerusalem.

133. Gk. ὑπερεκτείνω — 10:14.

134. Gk. τὰ ὑπερέκεινα — 10:16.

135. Gk. τῇ ὑπερβολῇ τῶν ἀποκαλύψεων — 12:6. This is inferred from the tone of Paul's apologetic in this passage.

136. Gk. ὑπεραίρομαι — 12:7.

137. Gk. οἱ καπηλεύοντες — 2:17; τοιοῦτοι — 11:13.

who had "come" to Corinth (11:4-5) from outside ("letters of commendation" — 3:1) and who had trespassed into Paul's "field" of ministry (10:15-16), where they and their message had been "received" (11:4, 20).

The key to their identity is to be found in Paul's questions in 11:22-23a:

Hebrews	are they?	So am I.
Israelites	are they?	So am I.
Seed of Abraham	are they?	So am I.
Ministers of Christ	are they?	I am better.

Like Paul these men are "Hebrews" and "Israelites," physical descendants from the patriarchal fountainhead, Abraham. They are Jews.

That they have come to the Greco-Roman metropolis Corinth makes it almost certain that they were Greek-speaking Jews, as Paul also was. A significant level of competence in Greek is implied.[138]

Where have they come from? His allusions to "the limits God has apportioned us, to reach even to you" and "not overextending ourselves" and "our field among you" (10:12-16, RSV) appear to be to the Jerusalem Concordat whereby it was agreed that the Antioch delegates Saul and Barnabas should "go" to the Gentiles and the "pillar" apostles of Jerusalem, James, Cephas, and John, to the circumcised (Gal 2:7-9). Granted that a connection between these passages makes it likely that the newcomers were from Jerusalem, is it possible that they could have possessed the linguistic fluency sufficient for a ministry in Corinth? It is now understood that Palestine was Hellenized[139] to such a degree that these "Hebrews . . . Israelites" may well have been capable of displaying proficiency in the rhetorical arts of "boasting" and "comparison" that are mirrored by Paul's rebuttals within this letter (see on 10:12). Paul will not concede inferiority to these men in the fundamentals of apostleship, but he does in language (11:5-6; cf. 10:10).

But what of their interest in paranormal ecstasy, visions, and revelations (and miracles — 12:12?), on which they depended (5:11-13; 12:1-6), in part at least, for their acceptance in Corinth? Are these things compatible with Jews

138. So M. Hengel, *Pre-Christian Paul,* 60.

139. Information is now available, however, that changes our conception of first-century Judaea. Clearly it was not the unrelievedly Pharisaic-Judaic enclave it was once thought to be. M. Hengel, *"Hellenization,"* 10, has argued on the basis of funerary inscriptions that there may have been as many as 16,000 Greek-speaking Jews in Jerusalem out of an estimated population of 100,000. He reasons that many of these must have enjoyed a high level of classical education. It is quite conceivable, therefore, that the "Hebrews" who came to Corinth spoke polished Greek and possessed skills in rhetoric. Saul/Paul himself was not altogether without abilities in these areas, to say nothing of his coworker Silas/Silvanus, the Jewish-Christian prophet of Jerusalem to whom is attributed the stylishly written 1 Peter (Acts 15:32; 2 Cor 1:19; 1 Pet 5:12).

from Judaea? Judaea in the period A.D. 44-66 was subject to political disintegration, revolutionary activism, and apocalyptic fervor expressed in prophetic inspiration and miraculous signs (see, e.g., Josephus, *J.W.* 2.258-59). It is quite possible that Judaea at this time represented the kind of religious environment from which these "ministers of Christ" with their "visions and revelations of the Lord" (12:1) could have come. Mirrored elsewhere in Paul's own writing is the Jewish preoccupation with miracles: "Jews demand signs . . ." (1 Cor 1:22).

We conclude that these newly arrived ministers are Jews, Greek-speaking Jews, Jews from Judaea who also recognized Jesus to be the Christ (they were "ministers of Christ" — 11:23).

b. Their Mission

If these men are "ministers of Christ" (11:23a), what was their "ministry," their mission? A few verses earlier Paul called them "ministers of righteousness," which, when read with the contrast between the "ministries"[140] of the "old covenant" (i.e., of Moses) and the "new covenant" (i.e., of Christ/righteousness and the Spirit), suggests that their purpose in coming to Corinth was to "minister" the "righteousness" associated with Moses and the law ("on tablets of stone . . . the letter" — 3:3, 6), as opposed to the "righteousness" issuing in "reconciliation with God" based on Christ's death (3:9; 5:21), which was the "ministry" of Paul (3:6; cf. 2:17–3:4; 5:18, 19, 20).

Since their "ministry" was predicated on "tablets of stone," that is, on the law of "Moses" (3:6-7), we take it that these "ministers of righteousness" were "Judaizers"[141] and that their version of the "righteousness of God" lay at the heart of their message and was their chief point of difference with the apostle to the Gentiles.

It is not altogether clear in what terms and with what nuances the intruders presented their message about "Moses." As those who were both "ministers of Christ" (11:23a) and "of the written code" (3:6), did they preach as their gospel that "Moses" along with Christ was foundational to faith, that Christ belonged to the covenant of Moses with no discontinuity? Alternatively, did they claim that having begun with Christ, the believer was perfected by "Moses"?[142]

---

140. See 3:3, 7, 8, 9.

141. "Judaizers" in the sense traditionally understood, namely, those who sought to persuade Gentile Christians to live like Jews. Strictly speaking, Ἰουδαΐζω means "to live as a Jew" (Gal 2:14).

142. As apparently was being urged upon the Galatians (see Gal 3:3). The questions related to "getting in" and "staying in" have been raised by E. P. Sanders, *Paul and Palestinian Judaism* and *Paul, the Law and the Jewish People*. For a major review of Sanders's views see R. H. Gundry, "Grace," 1-38.

Paul's use of the word "righteousness" may assist us to understand the mission/message of these "ministers of Christ." The single appearance of "righteousness" to this point in a letter written to a Greek church (1 Cor 1:30)[143] suggests that the issues associated with "righteousness" had not been raised in Macedonia or Achaia until the writing of 2 Corinthians in *c.* 55.[144] Paul's use of the word appears to have been conditioned by its use by his opponents. Paul's understanding of "righteousness" is thoroughly spelled out in Romans (see the key text 1:17),[145] which, by general agreement, was written in Corinth not long after the writing of 2 Corinthians from Macedonia. Since it is likely that in Romans Paul is defining "righteousness" polemically against the same opponents, it would follow that their view of "righteousness" is mirrored in reverse in that letter. Although Paul makes no mention of circumcision in 2 Corinthians, it is quite possible that circumcision was part of the dispute at Corinth; it was prominent in Romans.[146]

Why did Paul refer to these "ministers of Christ" as "false apostles . . . deceitful workmen . . . ministers of Satan [in disguise]" (11:13-15)? The connected reference to "[disguised as] ministers of righteousness" insinuates that it was their alternative teaching on "righteousness" that provoked such strong language from the apostle. Was it because they appeared to promote "righteousness" through ceremonial/law-based behavior, which had the appearance, as it were, of "light," rather than through the "righteousness" of the one "who was made sin" (5:21), that message which was so offensive to Jews and foolish to Greeks (1 Cor 1:23)?

The problem was not that they denied Paul apostleship. Rather, it was that they claimed (1) the same apostolic basis as he (11:12), (2) in regard to which (see 10:12–12:13), however, they said they were "superior" *(hyper)* and he "inferior" *(hyster-).* Nonetheless, although these men come on a "Christian" mission, as "ministers of Christ," Paul saw them as *pseudo,* as "false apostles" (11:13) and "false brothers" (11:26) who put his life in danger and whose ministry would reap terrible consequences for them (11:15).

---

143. The dating of Galatians is problematic.

144. The noun, adjective, and verb are used extensively in Galatians, where the issues associated with Judaizing are prominent. Perhaps the appearance of this vocabulary — both by Paul and by his opponents? — points to a theological dispute rather than to an evolution in Paul's use of words, by which we might have been enabled chronologically to date his letters. The appearance of such vocabulary in Galatians does not mean that this letter was necessarily written around the time of 2 Corinthians and Romans.

145. Where "righteousness" (δικαιοσύνη) appears 49 times, and its cognates "justify" and "righteous" (δικαιόω, δίκαιος) occur numerous times.

146. Rom 2:25, 26, 27, 28, 29; 3:1, 30; 4:9, 10, 11 (twice); 15:8.

c. Their Attack on Paul

A number of elements that occur immediately in his apologetic excursus on new covenant ministry (2:14–7:4) call for explanation and may, in that regard, suggest certain lines of their attack on Paul. Even the casual reader is struck by the following: (1) his immediate and surprising presentation of himself in the humiliation of his sufferings (2:14), (2) his assertion of the greater glory of the new, as contrasted with the old, covenant (3:7-18), and (3) his concession that, to some, his gospel is "veiled" (4:4).

His connecting the themes of suffering, glory, and veiling, which simply appear, without introduction, does indeed raise questions in the mind of the reader.[147] Where do these themes come from and why is Paul discussing them?

Our reconstruction, which is of necessity conjectural, is as follows:

(1) On arrival in Corinth, the newcomers challenged Paul's teaching to the Corinthians on a number of matters, for example, his fulfillment eschatology (15:3-4) and his separation of those "baptized into Moses" (1 Cor 10:2; *"them"* — 10:6) from *"us . . .* upon whom the ends of the ages have come" (1 Cor 10:11). As Jews who were also Christians, they reject Paul's inference of the supersession of the old covenant, asserting it to be still operative.

On the other hand, Paul's claims to be an apostle are based on having "seen" the glorious Lord, the man of heaven (1 Cor 2:8; 9:1; 15:49). But this would surely demand that he be, in some sense, a "glorious" figure as Moses had been, who had seen the glory of the Lord at Mount Sinai. But, to the contrary, he is a weak, suffering figure, one lacking "glory."

(2) The newcomers argued that Moses' undiminished glory, as it was popularly believed to be,[148] is a sign of the continuing applicability of the Mosaic covenant. In their view Paul's preaching that the old dispensation had been fulfilled, thereby discontinuing it, is quite unacceptable.

(3) Paul's sufferings reveal him to be anything but "glorious"; therefore, his theology of "fulfillment" must be questioned. Paul is the living denial of what he preaches.

(4) Paul's focus on Jesus as a crucified Messiah effectively "veils" his gospel from Jewish audiences, for whom the notion of a humiliated Messiah was unimaginable (cf. 1 Cor 1:23; Mark 8:29-33).

Such a line of attack on Paul would go some distance toward explaining

---

147. See Thrall, 1.238-39, for a review of the many theories advanced to explain Paul's exposition in 3:1–4:6, including the view that Paul was responding to an existing exegesis of Exod 34:29-35.

148. Thrall, 1.244 n. 365, cites a Targum Fragment: "The splendor of [Moses'] face was not changed." See further Thrall, 1.243-44.

his theological emphases in the critical passage 2:14–4:12 with which he commences his apologia on new covenant ministry:

(1) In his humiliation in suffering Paul is "the aroma of Christ to God" (2:15), that is, he replicates the sacrificial death of Christ and so is acceptable and pleasing to God.

(2) Whereas the old covenant written on stone tables brought "condemnation" and "death," under the new covenant there is "righteousness" and "the Spirit" (3:7-11). Glorious as the old covenant had been, its glory had only been anticipatory; it is now deglorified by the greater and permanent glory that "ends" it, the glory of the new covenant.

(3) Paul, who on the Damascus Road saw this greater glory in the face of Jesus Christ the Lord, is the bearer and, through the preaching of the gospel, the mediator of that light to all who will receive it (4:4-6). Nonetheless, he is himself a frail vessel, a mere jar of clay (4:7). His missionary sufferings and God's deliverances from them replicate the dying, on the one hand, but also the resurrection of Jesus (4:8-12), on the other. His "death" is for the Corinthians' "life." But such frailty is not limited to Paul but is endemic to all who live in this age (4:16–5:10; cf. 12:19).

(4) Against their theology of Moses' glory as the touchstone of truth and Paul's self-evident lack of glory, Paul asserts a theology of the glory of the Crucified, in whom there is righteousness from God in place of condemnation and through whom has come the long-awaited life-giving and life-transforming Spirit of God (3:3-18; cf. 5:18-21).

(5) Moreover, the Crucified Messiah gives "cruciform shape" to a ministry that is offered in his name. The "ambassador of Christ" (5:20), like the One he represents, suffers in place of the suffering Christ for the sake of/in place of the people (12:10, 15) and is their "slave," giving himself in death for their life (4:5, 11-12), raising them, and making them rich, as Christ had done (6:10b; 11:7).

d. Their Alliances and Method

Fortuitously for them, these men appear to have arrived in Corinth after Paul's second visit, when his stocks were low.

But with whom did they stay? Who among the Corinthian assembly "received" these people (cf. 11:4)? Since they were "Hebrews . . . Israelites . . . Abraham's seed" (11:22), it is almost certain that their hosts would have been Jews, possibly those who said, "I am of Cephas" (1 Cor 1:12). Whoever they were, as Hellenistic Jews domiciled in the Greco-Roman city of Corinth, they would have been able to brief their guests both about the shortcomings of Paul and about the qualities the Corinthians valued in their ministers.

Quite possibly the newcomers exploited to their advantage the low Corinthian opinion of Paul at that time,[149] in several areas.

(1) As men who accept financial support for their ministry (11:20) they appear to have forged an alliance against Paul with those Corinthians who criticized Paul for not accepting payment. If Paul would receive payment, he would acknowledge their ministry to be on the same basis as his (see on 11:12).

(2) Less certainly, they have presented themselves as superior in public speaking and self-presentation, capitalizing on Paul's perceived inferiority in these areas (10:10; 11:5; cf. 1 Cor 2:1-5).

(3) Again, less certainly, their mystic/ecstatic "visions and revelations" (5:11-13; 12:1-4) may have resonated with the ecstatic *pneumatikoi* of Corinth (1 Cor 4:8, 10; 14:12, 36).

One thing is clear. For their part, these newcomers legitimated their "ministry" in Corinth — over against Paul — by "commending" themselves, by "boasting"[150] (10:12–12:13 passim) of their achievements, and by "classifying [and] contrasting"[151] (10:12) their strengths with his perceived weaknesses. They have "letters of commendation" (from Jerusalem?); Paul has none (3:1-3). They are "self-sufficient," "triumphant" figures; Paul is inadequate, a sorry figure as he limps from place to place in defeat (2:14–3:5; 4:1, 16). They are men of divine power ("beside" themselves — 5:13; "caught up . . . out of the body . . . into Paradise," where they see "visions" and hear "revelations" of what "cannot be told" — 12:1-5[152]), whereas Paul is mundane, a minister without power, worldly and weak (10:3-6; cf. 1:12, 17; 5:12-13). Possibly they performed "the signs of an apostle" (12:12), whereas Paul was unable even to heal himself (12:7-9). They are powerful in speech (11:5-6) and in wisdom, whereas he is "unskilled" in speech and in general "a fool" (11:1–12:13). In all things he is "inferior" (*hyster* — cf. 11:5; 12:11), whereas they are superior, "better" (*hyper* — 11:23).

To all of this "boasting" Paul responds with his "Fool's Speech" (11:1–12:13), in which he daringly accepts their characterization as "weak" and "inferior" and in which he ironically calls them "superlative" apostles

---

149. Barrett (251) thought that the newcomers had been "Corinthianized," an idea that J. Murphy-O'Connor extends to some degree by suggesting an alliance between the indigenous *pneumatikoi* and the newly arrived Judaizers (*Theology,* 48-49).

150. Gk. καυχᾶσθαι (5:12; 7:4; 9:2; 10:8, 13, 15, 16, 17; 11:12, 16, 18, 30; 12:1, 5, 6, 9).

151. Gk. ἐγκρῖναι . . . συγκρῖναι.

152. We infer that, when combined with 12:1-5, 5:13 points to the experiences of both Paul and the "superlative" apostles. The difference would be that for Paul this experience is to/for God, not man (5:13), and thus he is not permitted to speak what he has heard (12:4). Unlike them he does not seek to legitimate ministry from his experience.

(11:5; 12:11). They are, metaphorically speaking — in their own minds — "over-uplifted" (*hyperairōsthai* — 12:7), but according to him, it is in pride.

In all of this the Crucified One is in his mind. In his utter powerlessness in the face of his "thorn," reminiscent of the powerlessness of Jesus on the cross, Paul learns of the prevailing grace and power of Christ (12:7-9). He willingly accepts "weaknesses" such as the "thorn" because he does so *hyper Christou,* "on behalf of Christ" (12:10), and, *hyper . . . hymōn,* "for your sakes" (12:15).

C. Theological[153]

As noted earlier,[154] Paul appears to have three interlocking objectives in writing this letter: (1) to explain and defend his recent actions; (2) to exhort the Corinthians to rectify a number of matters ahead of his impending farewell visit; and (3) to take the opportunity to teach various doctrines as he pursues (1) and (2).

Clearly the theological objective was very important to Paul. After all, he could easily have dealt with (1) and (2) quite briefly. But it was important that the Corinthians understand the matters raised from a theological perspective. Moreover, it should not be forgotten that the letter is addressed to "all the saints in the whole of Achaia," not just to the Corinthians. It was his expectation that his letters would be copied and exchanged among the churches. Although they were provoked by particular circumstances in specific churches, the theological character of this and other letters by Paul indicates that his letters were to have a use beyond those immediate circumstances.

Paul's theology is encountered in the text of the letter, which I take to be one piece, a unity.[155] His doctrines are not found under the text but in the text. To be sure, the historical questions must be asked, and, to the extent that we can answer them, they contribute to our exegetical and therefore to our theological understanding. But in the end the locus of the theology is the text itself.

1. Three Theological Themes

Are there key themes within the overall theological exposition of the letter? Given the intense and complex apologetic and polemical elements in 2 Cor-

---

153. See *SBLSP 1990,* 29; R. P. Martin, "Theological Perspectives," 240-56; D. M. Hay, "The Shaping of Theology in 2 Cor," 257-72; F. Young and D. F. Ford, *Meaning,* 235-60; L. A. Belleville, "Gospel and Kerygma," 134-63.

154. See above, IV.A. Literary Issues.

155. See above, IV.A. Literary Issues.

inthians, it is no easy task to identify them. Nonetheless, we discern three bright strands running through the letter.

a. The Eschatological Centrality of Christ

Even the casual reader of this letter is immediately struck by the words appearing early in the book, "*in* him . . . *through* him" (1:19-20), which point to the centrality of Jesus Christ. *In* Jesus Christ, the Son of God, God fulfills all the promises of God under the old covenant (1:18-20), thereby bringing that covenant to its appointed "end" (3:7-11). *Through* Jesus Christ, the church, which has been gathered by the apostolic word centered in him, utters its "Amen" as it draws near to God in prayer and thanksgiving (1:20).

In a unique and cosmic event he has died and been raised for all, bringing the old order to an end (4:16-18; 5:17) and dividing history into "no longer" and "now" aeons (5:15-16). The "day of God's salvation" has dawned. The blessings of the end time — the righteousness of God, reconciliation with God, and the Holy Spirit, at least by "deposit" — have come into the present (1:20-22; 5:18–6:2).

Jesus Christ is called "Lord" and preached as "Lord" (4:5). On his great coming "day," all will be raised from the dead, all will be made manifest before his judge's tribunal (1:14; 4:14; 5:10). The church, like a virgin daughter, is pledged to her Lord for consummation on that day (11:2-3).

Yet in his gracious incarnation, "rich" though he was, he made himself poor to enrich the impoverished (8:9). In his death, without sin though he was, he so embraced sins as to bestow the righteousness of God on all who belong to him. In "meekness and gentleness" of life (10:1) Jesus Christ was a "slave" for his people, "handed over to death" for them (4:5, 11).

In Jesus Christ, God has gathered up the past and anticipated the future. All the promises of the past are fulfilled in him; all the blessings of the future are found in him. In the light of the eschatological centrality of Jesus Christ the message of the apostle to the wayward Corinthians is simple and direct, "Be reconciled to God . . ." *now,* because "now is the day of salvation" (5:20; 6:2).

Paul does not allow the reader's eyes to leave Jesus Christ.

b. The Apostolic Ministry in the New Covenant

But this call to be reconciled to God in this his eschatological "day" cannot be separated from the call to the Corinthians to acknowledge Paul as God's ambassador, spokesman, and coworker (5:20; 6:1, 11-13). When God reconciled "us" (i.e., his people) to himself through Christ, he also gave "us" (now referring to Paul as apostle) the ministry of reconciliation (5:18).

Paul's view of his ministry in this the day of God's salvation is a strand that runs through the letter from beginning to end. That doctrine is in direct response to the negative attitudes toward him in the church at Corinth at that time, whether by local detractors or newly arrived "superlative" apostles, as he calls them, or by alliances of both local and visiting opponents.

While the precise sources of the detractions and opposition are impossible to clarify at this distance, the broad criticisms are clear enough from Paul's answers to them, namely, that (1) he lacks resolution and integrity (1:17-22), (2) he is "inadequate" in ministry (cf. 2:16; 3:5-6), in particular, in his alleged ineffectiveness in disciplining moral offenders during the Second ("Painful") Visit (10:1-11; 13:1-3), (3) he is self-commended (3:1; 4:2; 5:12; 6:4; 10:12; 12:11), (4) he is "inferior" to the newly arrived Jewish missioners (10:12–12:13, especially 11:5; 12:11-13), and (5) he declined their financial support or, alternatively, deviously secured it through his coworkers (4:2; 7:2; 11:7-12; 12:13-18). His apologetic tone in relation to sufferings (i.e., 2:14; 4:7) and the various sufferings lists suggest that he must explain these. How can a gospel preached by a sufferer supersede Moses when Moses was and remains a glorious figure whereas Paul, who claims to have seen the glorious man from heaven, is not?

Paul's references to his ministry throughout the letter are conditioned by this barrage of detraction and criticism from Corinth.

(1) He is "an apostle of Christ by the will of God" (1:1), as the Corinthians should know; "the signs of the apostle were wrought among [them] . . . signs, wonders and mighty works" (12:12).

Undergirding this confidence is God's historic call of him as indicated by his use of verbs in the aorist tense to point to the moment of that call. It is God who has *made* Paul *competent*[156] as minister of a new covenant (3:6) and, in a probable reference to the Damascus event, he says that "God made his light *shine*[157] in our hearts" (4:6). Twice he writes of "the authority the Lord *gave*"[158] (10:8; 13:10). He speaks of "the field which God *assigned*"[159] (10:13).

In a number of passages Paul makes a studied connection between the present tense, reflecting his ongoing ministry, and the aorist tense, pointing to the moment when that ministry began. Having "been *convinced* [at or soon after the Damascus Christophany] that one died for all," Paul "*persuades* men . . . [*being*] compelled by Christ's love"[160] (5:14, 11). Again referring to his com-

---

156. Gk. ἱκάνωσεν.
157. Gk. ἔλαμψεν.
158. Gk. ἔδωκεν.
159. Gk. ἐμέρισεν.
160. Gk. ἀνθρώπους πείθομεν . . . ἡ . . . ἀγάπη τοῦ Χριστοῦ συνέχει ἡμᾶς, κρίναντες τοῦτο.

mission in the past, he writes, "God *gave* us the ministry of reconciliation . . . *committed* to us the message of reconciliation"[161] (5:18, 19). This he contrasts with his ongoing ministry "*representing* Christ . . . God *making* his appeal through us. We [*continue to*] implore you . . . *working* with God we [*continue to*] to urge you"[162] (5:20; 6:1). Three times Paul uses the present tense "we [*continue to*] speak"[163] to characterize an ongoing ministry that arose from God's unique and specific call to him to do so (2:17; 4:13; 12:19; cf. 13:3).

Mindful of the impact within him of the Damascus event, he solemnly asserts that "the truth of Christ is *in* [him]" (11:10), referring almost immediately, and by contrast, to "*false* apostles" who disguise themselves as "apostles of Christ" (11:13). Paul "speaks [the word of God] . . . from God" (2:17). He is a true apostle of Christ.

(2) It is not Paul, but the Lord (Christ), who commends his ministry (3:3; 10:18). Paul appeals to the Corinthians' experience of the Spirit of the living God in their hearts (3:3, 18; 5:5; 13:14), which is theirs in consequence of his preaching in their midst (1:19-22; cf. 11:4), whereby they are a "temple of the living God" (6:16). Since this is the Spirit promised in fulfillment of the new covenant (Jer 31:31-35; Ezek 36:26-27), this is now the era of the "ministry of the Spirit" (3:8) and Paul is a minister of the new covenant, "made competent" for it by God (3:5-6; cf. 2:16). That the Corinthians have the Spirit, that Jesus Christ is "in" them, a matter they can "prove" (13:5-6), is evidence that Paul is a minister of the new covenant. Paul is not "incompetent" in ministry, but "made competent" by God. The presence and activity of the Spirit in them shows that he is not self-commended, but commended by the Lord (10:18).

(3) But yes, he is "superior" to the "superlative" apostles, though in an astonishing way. Fools boast, and Paul will boast of the foolishness, even the madness, of — of all things! — "weaknesses." Many times in the letter (1:8-11; 4:8-11; 6:3-10), but especially in the "Fool's Speech" proper (11:23–12:10), he will point to afflictions and sufferings sustained in the course of his ministry. The repeated sufferings-catalogues *(peristaseis)* show that, unlike the "superlative" apostles, the true apostle of Christ displays no triumphalism (2:14). Nor was there any triumphalism in the Christ, who was "crucified in weakness" (13:4). Paul's sufferings replicate, extend into history, the "sufferings of Christ" (1:5; 2:15; 4:10-12; 12:10), showing that he is, in fact, a "better minister of Christ" than the "superlative" apostles (11:23).

---

161. Gk. τοῦ θεοῦ . . . <u>δόντος</u> ἡμῖν τὴν διακονίαν τῆς καταλλαγῆς . . . <u>θέμενος</u> ἐν ἡμῖν τὸν λόγον τῆς καταλλαγῆς.

162. Gk. πρεσβεύομεν . . . ὡς τοῦ θεοῦ παρακαλοῦντος . . . δεόμεθα . . . συνεργοῦντες . . . παρακαλοῦμεν . . .).

163. Gk. λαλοῦμεν.

The climax of those "weaknesses" was the "weakness" of the "thorn in the flesh . . . the messenger of Satan" (12:7-9). Paul had experienced a "vision and revelation" from the Lord, which had transported him to Paradise, where he had heard words that he was not permitted to utter (12:1-6). God's "gift" of this unidentified and protracted "weakness," however, pinned him to the earth in humility and dependence on the Lord to whom he prayed. The inference is clear. Through their "visions and revelations" the newcomers are uplifted in religious pride; they are, in Paul's grimly ironical words, "superlative" apostles. With the "thorn" unremoved, Paul exercises his ministry in humility and patience, lacking power of his own, utterly dependent on the Lord, who himself had been powerless at Golgotha. *God's* power is made perfect in weakness.

For Paul Christ in his sufferings is the model for ministry. It is "on account of Jesus"[164] that Paul is the Corinthians' "slave" (4:5), that he is continually "handed over to death" in the course of his ministry. It is "on behalf of"[165] Christ that he comes as an envoy, "on behalf of" Christ that he pleads, "Be reconciled to God" (5:20), and "on behalf of" Christ that he must be content with "weaknesses, insults, hardships, persecutions, difficulties" (12:10). Even his discipline of offenders in church is by the "meekness and gentleness of Christ" (10:1), although they took this to be "weakness" (10:10). As Jesus' ministry was nontriumphal, so, too, was Paul's. Paul replicated the life, but more particularly the death, of Jesus.

As the "minister" of the "Minister" (11:23; Mark 10:45), Paul "lowers" himself in arduous labor of self-support to "elevate" them in salvation (11:7), he is "spent for their souls" (12:15), and "though poor [he] makes many rich" (6:10). The "superlative" apostles, by contrast, are lords who enslave and exploit the people (11:20).

(4) Despite current allegations to the contrary, he is a man of holiness and godly sincerity (1:12; 2:17), he is true to his word (1:18), he has rejected deceit and guile (4:2), and he has not manipulated or cheated the Corinthians (7:2; 12:16-18). His life is an open book before God (12:19), and he trusts also before the Corinthians (4:2; 5:11), in the light of the coming judgment (1:14; 1:23; 2:17; 5:10).

The eschatological texts "Be reconciled to God . . . now" (5:20; 6:2) and "God has given to us the ministry of reconciliation . . . entrusted to us the message of reconciliation" are critical to this letter. It follows that the ministry and the message of reconciliation, as exercised by the apostle Paul, must be regarded as articles of faith, which the Corinthians — and all readers since — are challenged to acknowledge.

164. Gk. διὰ Ἰησοῦν.
165. Gk. ὑπὲρ Χριστοῦ.

c. The Hope of Glory

Whereas the doctrine of Paul the apostle as minister of the new covenant is a strand running through the entire letter, his teaching on the hope of the glory of God is contained within the excursus on apostolic ministry (2:14–7:4). It appears in two passages, 3:12–4:7 and 4:14, 16–5:10, both of which are universal in character and flow out of passages focused on Paul's ministry (2:14–3:11 and 4:7-13, 15).

(1) Paul sees the glory of God as "permanent" (3:11), the ultimate goal (3:18), and beyond the universal resurrection (4:14) and the universal judgment (5:10). This glory is eternal and weighty (4:17).

(2) By contrast, within this present aeon humans are blinded to God by the god of this aeon, and perishing (4:3-4). Each is a mere earthen vessel (4:7) whose outer form is withering away (4:16) under the impact of "affliction" (4:16), a mere "tent" to be dismantled at death (5:1).

(3) By the light of the gospel, however, God shines his light into human darkness, in the face of Jesus Christ (4:6). As one turns to the Lord, there is the inner illumination of understanding that anticipates the ultimate glory of God and the believer's conformity to the image of the Lord (3:16, 18). The present experience of glory corresponds with the present "deposit" of the Spirit, in anticipation and promise of his fullness in the end time (1:22; 5:5).

(4) Overwhelming though "such a hope" of future glory is, Paul does not minimize the dark realities of the present life. Those who are still "in the body" are not yet "at home with the Lord" (5:6, 8). The intervention of death prior to the onset of the end time will mean a time of nakedness, something that provokes a "burdened sighing." Beyond that the tribunal of Christ the judge faces every believer with its revelation of deeds done in the body and divine recompense for them (5:10).

(5) It is likely that Paul deliberately emphasizes the painful realities of the present to bring about an appropriate sobriety to the Corinthians. It appears that they had an overrealized spirituality, along with pride, based on the evident manifestations of the Spirit among them (1 Cor 1:7; 4:7-8; 14:36). Now, additionally, they have welcomed "superlative" apostles, who boast of "visions and revelations of the Lord" (11:5; 12:1, 11).

(6) It may be no coincidence that Paul's sober portrayal of ministry, as sketched above, corresponds to his candid presentation of the dark realities of mortal existence. Apostolic ministry is exercised in the power of God, but in the midst of weakness. But "weakness" is also every believer's experience (cf. 4:16–5:10). To be sure, the future is laden with glory, but the present is, frankly, painful, and death is not to be romanticized. Christ was raised and lives in power, but only subsequent to the weakness of death. Only after death is there life. There is power, the power of God, but it rests upon apostles and

people not in power, but in weakness. And there is glory, which is glimpsed now through hearing the gospel, but it is not yet fully realized. The children of God walk by faith, not by sight (5:7).

2. Theological Background in Isaiah 40–55

The critical eschatological text in the letter — 2 Cor 6:2 — is a quotation of Isa 49:8 (LXX), which belongs to an important passage within Isaiah 40–55, namely, Isa 49:8-13. When examined (in the LXX), the passage reveals a number of words — "salvation," "covenant," "comfort," "lowly" — that prove to be significant within the structure of 2 Corinthians.[166] Not only are individual words from this passage in Isaiah reproduced, but we also find some groupings of words in 2 Corinthians ("salvation" and "comfort" in 1:6; "comfort" and "lowly" in 7:6; cf. 10:1). This short passage in Isaiah appears to have been a quarry for a number of ideas employed by the apostle in this letter.

However, when Isa 49:8-13 is examined in the light of the wider background of Isaiah 40–66, it appears that Paul has been significantly influenced by themes found there in what he writes in 2 Corinthians.[167] The themes of "new creation" and "reconciliation," so prominent in 2 Cor 5:17-21, appear to arise out of Isaiah's twin themes "new creation" and "restoration."[168] While there is no verbal equivalent to "reconciliation" in the Isaianic passages, the prominent concept of "restoration" bears a similarity to it. Israel's exile in Isaiah approximates humanity's alienation from God. In Isaiah 43 the "new creation" and "restoration" are achieved by the "ransom" of people "in exchange" for Israel (Isa 43:3-4) and by Yahweh's "blotting out the sins" of his people (Isa 43:22-28), themes that are expressed — as fulfilled in Christ — in 2 Cor 5:17-21.

In 2 Cor 5:20–6:2, Paul views himself (and, we presume, the apostolic circle) as "Christ's ambassadors," "God's fellow-workers" exhorting the Corinthians to "be reconciled to God," and, in the knowledge that this is "the day of salvation," not "to receive God's grace in vain." But then, in a short space, the apostle also urges the Corinthians to be reconciled to *him,* "to open wide" their hearts to him (6:11-13). Between (6:3-10) these two exhortations — one related to God, the other to himself — Paul applies to himself as a

166. Gk. σωτηρία (1:6; 6:2; 7:10); διαθήκη (3:6, 14); παρακαλέω (1:4 [3 times], 6; 2:7, 8; 5:20; 6:1; 7:6, 7, 13; 8:6; 9:5; 10:1; 12:8; 13:1); ταπεινός (7:6; 10:1).

167. See G. K. Beale, "Background of Reconciliation," 550-81 (and literature cited); also W. L. Lane, "Covenant," 3-29.

168. See Isa 40:28-31; 41:17-20; 42:5-9; 44:21-23, 24-28; 45:1-8, 9-13, 18-20; 49:8-13; 51:1-3, 9-11, 12-16; 54:1-10; 55:6-13.

"minister of God" language evocative of the suffering "servant of Yahweh" found in Isaiah 40–55. As the apostle the Corinthians are close to rejecting, Paul reminds them that he is the divinely "sent" messenger who announces that "now" is "the time of God's favor" and that they must be reconciled to God through aligning themselves with the message brought by his apostle. The language of suffering as embodied in an apostle (6:3-10) serves to legitimate Paul's ministry because it was first fulfilled in the vicarious sufferings of the true Servant of the Lord, the Messiah, Jesus (5:14-21).

It seems likely that he meditated on Isaiah 40–55 in the light of the crisis in Corinth and, as it were, prophesied from it, exhorting the Corinthians — in particular the wayward groups — to align themselves with God's "day of salvation," which Paul had heralded.

D. Pastoral Ministry from Second Corinthians

Second Corinthians presents many inspiring texts and passages to the reader and teacher of God's Word. A quick survey reveals approximately eighty individual verses lending themselves to extended meditation and exposition, apart from the sixty or so constituent paragraphs of the letter. This letter is a rich lode for the edification of God's people.

But how are those who stand outside the ranks of the initial recipients of the letter to interpret and apply it to themselves?

In addressing this question two considerations should be kept in mind. One is Paul's own pastoral method by which he was not content merely to deal with immediate issues. This he could have done in a few pages. Rather, we see Paul taking those issues and allowing them to form the agenda for a treatise of theological weight, whose application, therefore, transcends the immediate and somewhat mundane problems in Corinth of the mid-fifties.

The other consideration is that the author was not writing merely to one group of readers, the troublesome assembly at Corinth, but together with its members, "all the saints in the whole of Achaia" (see on 1:1; cf. 1 Cor 1:2). If the letter addresses issues in terms beyond the immediate, it is also directed to a broader readership than the particular target group. That Paul intended his letters to be read and passed from church to church (cf. Col 4:16) signals that their purpose, though occasioned by particular factors, was not limited to or exhausted by those particulars.

How, then, should those outside the original addressees read, interpret, and apply this letter?

The preliminary question for every reader and congregation is: Does this writer have any claim over my thinking and behavior? If Paul's words lack a dominical authority, this letter is of only relative interest, with no power

47

in the conscience of individual or church. No issue in this letter is more important to resolve than this. The view taken here acknowledges the unique place of the apostle to the Gentiles, authorized as he was to edify the churches (10:8; 12:19; 13:10). This letter comes to us with the full weight of canonical Scripture.

Once the canonicity of this letter is recognized, the admonitions the apostle made to that church readily carry over to churches and their members in other places and times. Throughout history churches have struggled with their relationship with their secular environment, with a tendency to stray from revealed truth and a lifestyle in accord with it, resulting in fragmentation and division. Given this fact, it is helpful for us to place ourselves in the Corinthians' shoes and be reconciled to the God who has reconciled us to himself, who is faithful to covenantal promise, who comforts the downcast, and who raises the dead. It is also necessary to remain focused on Christ, in whom there is forgiveness and upon whom all hopes rest, and to be encouraged that the Spirit who seals believers is transforming us from glory to glory. May the churches seek the "mending" and the unity that come only through the grace of Christ, the love of God, and the fellowship of the Holy Spirit.

But 2 Corinthians will not permit a narrow congregationalism. The powerful appeal to complete the collection (chaps. 8–9) will not allow the Corinthians to regard themselves as the only island in the sea. Rather, they are to see themselves as part of an archipelago stretching across the world. It is, indeed, a test of their grasp of the gospel that they recognize the need for "equality" in material things among the far-flung people of God, despite the distances involved and the differences of theological emphasis and tradition between the churches of the Pauline mission and the churches of Judaea.

In one passage late in the letter Paul declares that he has not been defending himself, but speaking for the edification of the readers (12:19). It is likely that Paul is, in particular, pointing to passages about himself. Given the triumphalism of the "superlative" apostles and, indeed, the spiritual pride of the Corinthians, it is likely that Paul has in mind those passages about *himself* in which the *non*triumphalist, "slave"-like character of his ministry has been set forth (e.g., 2:14-16; 4:1-15; 6:3-13). Above all, there is Paul's own example, the model of one who might well have been inflated in pride through his extraordinary visions and revelations but who was forced to learn the lesson of humility and deep dependence on the Lord in the thorn that was not removed (12:1-10). Here is a rebuke for triumphalists and proud "Corinthians" of every generation.

A further matter for their edification is the triumph of the power of God in human weakness to which he has repeatedly referred. Here Paul applies to himself the motif of the death and resurrection of Christ. The message that he preached, focused on that death and resurrection, also gave shape to his own experience. His sufferings in ministry corresponded to those of Golgotha, and his deliverances to Christ's Easter victory over death. This motif recurs, whether in reference to the deadly perils in Asia from which he was delivered (1:8-10), various unspecified missionary sufferings from which he was rescued (4:7-11), or the unremoved "thorn for the flesh," in which, however, he was given power to persevere (12:7-11). Paul's defense of himself to the Corinthians, in terms of God's resurrectionlike deliverances from crosslike afflictions, is ultimately for the Corinthians' edification, and, indeed, ours. He is the God who raises the dead (1:9), who comforts the downcast (7:6).

What, then, of the more specialized reader whose vocation is missionary or pastor? Here we face the problem that 2 Corinthians is, in particular, the *apologia* for Paul's person and for his apostolic ministry. Apart from the chapters devoted to the collection (8–9), the other major passages (1:1–2:13; 2:14–7:16; 10:1–13:14), despite their diversity, are united by the common theme of Paul's defense and exposition of *his* apostolic ministry. Even the plural pronouns "we . . . us," with few exceptions,[169] are expressive not of coauthors Paul and Timothy (1:1), nor of fellow proclaimers Timothy and Silas (1:19), but of Paul alone, Paul as *apostle*.[170] Thus the "we" who are, for example, "Christ's ambassadors . . . God's fellow workers" (5:20; 6:1), who "preach . . . Jesus Christ as Lord" (4:5; cf. 11:4), to whom God gave "the ministry . . . the word of reconciliation" (5:18, 19), is *Paul*, who worked "the signs of an apostle . . . signs, wonders and miracles" when present in Corinth (12:12). It was in *Paul's* heart that God shone his light that his apostle might reveal Jesus Christ to others (4:6), and it was he to whom the Lord gave his authority to edify the churches (10:8; 12:19; 13:10). How, then — if at all — is the missionary or pastor able to apply to himself or herself passages that Paul originally related deliberately to himself?

The answer is that the ministry of the new covenant was not confined to the generation of the apostle, but *continues* until the Lord comes. To be sure, Paul as apostle stood uniquely as a pioneer of that ministry, following hard on the Lord who commissioned him en route to Damascus. As revelator Paul as apostle cannot be replicated, and his insistence on self-support in ministry was peculiar to him and for unique reasons. Few are called on to suffer as he did, establishing and caring for the churches.

---

169. 3:18; 4:16–5:10.

170. See on 1:1, where it is argued that, apart from a few exceptions (e.g., 3:18; 4:16–5:10), Paul's use of "we . . . us" in this letter is a literary plural whose singular subject is the apostle. This phenomenon occurs in a number of passages where he quickly lapses from plural to singular (e.g., 6:11-13; 7:2-4) or where a singular subject is logically demanded (e.g., "Our conscience testifies," 1:12).

True, God "appointed" Paul as "apostle . . . teacher of the Gentiles" (1 Tim 2:7; 2 Tim 1:11). But the apostolic message did not cease with Paul but was to be entrusted to others (2 Tim 2:2), so that the gospel torch is passed from generation to generation until the Lord comes.

Thus the greater part of his teachings about ministry stand as a model and an inspiration to subsequent generations of missionaries and pastors. His comments about ministry — that at its heart lie endurance and patience, sacrifice and service, love of the churches, fidelity to the gospel, sincerity before God, and, above all, a rejection of triumphalism with its accompanying pride — remain throughout the aeon to shape and direct the lives of the Lord's servants. Paul's ministry as sufferer and servant is precisely modeled on that of Jesus, and finds it legitimacy in the face of detraction and opposition for just that reason, as also must ours, if that is our calling. Thus 2 Corinthians may be bracketed with the Pastoral Letters in its applicability to the work of those whose vocation it is to serve God as his ministers.

E. Text for the Commentary

The text printed for this commentary is the New International Version. At many points, however, the author's own translation is set forth, particularly where some rhetorical emphasis occurs within the original text. The Greek text underlying this commentary is the *Greek New Testament* (4th rev. ed.; ed. K. Aland et al.; Stuttgart: United Bible Societies, 1993).

ANALYSIS OF 2 CORINTHIANS

The Second Epistle
to the
CORINTHIANS

Text, Exposition, and Notes

I. INTRODUCTION (1:1-11)

Paul commences his letter formally with a salutation (vv. 1-2) and a benediction (vv. 3-7). God's deliverance of Paul in Asia (vv. 8-11) is a concrete example of his comfort of the apostle more generally stated in the benediction. The salutation and benediction are not merely formal, however, but are closely connected with and lead into the next section (1:12–2:13), where Paul defends his decision to write to them (the lost "Severe Letter") instead of returning to them directly as, apparently, he had indicated during the recent "Painful Visit."

From the outset Paul is attempting to restore the now-strained relationships with the Corinthians. As an apostle, "by the will of God" (v. 1), he has the duty to comfort the saints in their affliction with the comfort he has received from God (vv. 4-5). Having stated that general principle, he specifically declares that God's comfort in his afflictions — including the extreme affliction in Asia (vv. 8-9) — is for the sake of the Corinthians (v. 6). Such is the intended spiritual unity between apostle and messianic people that, just as his comfort by God was for them, so, in response, their prayers are for him (v. 11).

This theme continues beyond the present section. He is their fellow worker for their joy, not the Lord of their faith (1:24). His expectation and concern is that the Corinthians will understand and take pride in him, as, indeed, he will take pride in them on the "day of Christ" (1:14). He reminds them that their experience of the Spirit of God resulted from his preaching of the Son of God among them (1:19, 22). He knows of the possibility that Satan will get the better of them, separating him from them (2:11). This mutuality between him and them depends in turn on a reestablished confidence in his

55

integrity (1:12-14). The restoration of unity between him and them is a major theme not only in this opening section of the letter but throughout his exposition of his new covenant ministry (2:14–7:4) and the passionate final chapters of the letter (chaps. 10–13).

References to God — his character and actions — unify the Introduction, and indeed the first sections of this letter. God is the Father of the Lord Jesus Christ and "our" Father, from whom grace and peace come (vv. 1-2). Paul's use of the present tense for God's actions implies a number of divine attributes. (1) God is a comforter who comforts the afflicted (1:4). (2) God who raises the dead has delivered and will deliver his servant (1:9-10). God is to be blessed (1:3) and thanked for answered prayer (v. 11). (3) God, who is faithful, guarantees their ongoing Christward confidence, following the preaching of the Son of God and the beginning of the activity of the Spirit among them, confirming that they have turned to the Lord (1:18, 19, 22; cf. 3:16, 17).

Paul also gives a number of divine reasons for suffering. Suffering is a nursery for the growth (1) of compassion (v. 4), (2) of encouragement, and (3) of intensified hope (vv. 9-10).

A. SALUTATION (1:1-2)

> 1 *Paul, an apostle of Christ Jesus[1] by the will of God, and Timothy our brother, To the church of God in Corinth, together with all the saints throughout Achaia:* 2 *Grace and peace to you from God our Father and the Lord Jesus Christ.*

Typically, letters from the Greco-Roman period begin: A to B: greeting, followed by C, either a prayer or thanksgiving to God/the gods for the addressee. For example:

> Ptolemaios to Kassianos his brother, very many greetings. Before everything I pray you are in good health.[2]

Paul follows this basic A, B, C format but also states (1) his office ("an apostle of Christ Jesus by the will of God") and the fact and name of a co-sender,[3]

---

1. The sequence Χριστοῦ Ἰησοῦ, as in p[46] ℵ B M P vg[mss] syr[bo] cop[sa], is preferred to Ἰησοῦ Χριστοῦ, as in A D G K L Ψ.

2. *New Docs.* 2.62. See generally S. K. Stowers, *Letter Writing;* J. L. White, *Ancient Letters;* and *New Docs.* 4.58-59.

3. See Furnish, 103-4, for this term; Timothy does not seem to be a coauthor of the letter itself.

titled ("and Timothy the brother"), and (2) modifies the prayer along the lines of salutations found in Jewish letters.

The addressees are both "the church . . . in Corinth" and believers throughout the constituent Roman province ("all the saints in the whole of Achaia"), giving the letter a broader character than would be the case if the readership were merely the local assembly of believers in the capital city.

His insertion of specifically Christian elements — "apostle *of Christ Jesus*," "Timothy *the brother*," "to the church *of God*," and "God *our Father* and *the Lord Jesus* Christ" — into this standard epistolary format serves immediately to confront readers ancient and modern with Christian distinctives.

God himself is dominant in the salutation (vv. 1-2), as well as in the introduction (vv. 1-11) as a whole. It is "by the will of God" that Paul is an apostle, who now writes to the "church of God." Significantly, God — the God of Israel — is declared to be not only "our Father" but also, as carried through into the benediction, "the Father of our Lord Jesus Christ" (v. 3).

1   The first sentence of the letter — the apostle's address to the church — with its implications of Paul's authority over the Corinthians, encapsulates the major issue of the letter as it will unfold.

In earlier letters[4] Paul does not mention "apostle" in the opening address but brackets Silvanus and Timothy with himself on equal terms and includes them with him as "apostles of Christ" (1 Thess 1:1; 2:6; 2 Thess 1:1). But from the time of the writing of 1 Corinthians — due to mounting questioning of his apostleship? — Paul declares himself to be an "apostle" in the salutation of his letters (cf. Gal 1:1; 1 Cor 1:1; Rom 1:1), and is careful to distance himself as an "apostle" from various coworkers (1 Cor 1:1; Col 1:1; but cf. Phil 1:1) — in this case, "Timothy our brother."[5] Timothy and

---

4. This depends on one's view of the place of Galatians in the sequence of Paul's letters. For argument supporting the earlier dating of Galatians see F. F. Bruce, *Galatians,* 1-18, and for the later dating, W. G. Kümmel, *Introduction,* 298-304, a view that is more generally accepted.

5. Timothy had visited Corinth at or soon after the dispatch of 1 Corinthians (1 Cor 4:17; 16:10) and was probably the source of the report back to Paul in Ephesus that made necessary the "Painful Visit." It may be significant that, on his return to Ephesus, Paul sent his "Severe Letter" with Titus, rather than with Timothy. Timothy, with Erastus, was sent on ahead of Paul to Macedonia (Acts 19:22), where, as this reference makes clear, he was reunited with Paul. See Martin, 2, for the view that Paul mentions Timothy as co-sender to assist in his rehabilitation in the eyes of the Corinthians. This is unlikely, however, since Timothy also appears as coauthor or co-sender in 1 and 2 Thessalonians, Philippians, and Colossians.

Silvanus are linked with Paul as preachers to the Corinthians, but only Paul is an apostle (1:19).[6]

Although Timothy's name is joined with Paul's, we do not sense that he participates with Paul in the vigorous and passionate interchange with the Corinthian readers that is the chief subject of the letter. Although the first person plural pronouns "we," "us," "our" are very common in the letter,[7] the various contexts tend either to be inconclusive in assessing the possible involvement of Timothy or imply rather strongly that Paul is using the plural of himself. Most likely Timothy is mentioned because he is a distinguished "brother" who happened to be present with Paul at the time of writing in Macedonia, rather than because Timothy is being actively included in what is being said — namely, the urgent relationship problems between Paul and the Corinthians. He is a co-sender rather than a coauthor.

There has been some debate over the social origins of the word "apostle,"[8] by which Paul usually introduces himself to his readers. The word

6. It appears that the central place of "Paul, an apostle . . ." in the Salutation in 1 and 2 Corinthians was broadly followed in subsequent letters. But Phil 1:1 — "Paul and Timothy, servants of Christ Jesus" — should be noted. Here we observe (1) that the word "apostle" does not appear, and (2) that Timothy's name is joined to Paul's. Col 1:1 is identical with 2 Cor 1:1.

7. Broadly speaking, the first person plural pronoun dominates chapters 1–9 (but singulars occur at 1:13b, 15-17, 23; 2:1-13; 5:11b; 6:13b; 7:3, 4, 7b-12, 14a, 16; 8:3, 8, 10a-15, 23b; 9:1-4), whereas the first person singular dominates chapters 10–13 (but plurals occur at 10:2b-8, 11-18; 11:4, 6; 12:18b-19, 21; 13:4b, 6b-9). See M. Carrez, "Le 'Nous,' " 474-86; C. E. B. Cranfield, "Changes in Person and Number," 280-89; S. J. Hafemann, *Suffering and Ministry,* 12-16; and Thrall, 1.105-7.

From the confusing use of the plural and singular in the letter, the following may be noted: (1) Paul tends to use the plural throughout the extended passage on the apostolic ministry (2:14–7:4 — but see 5:11b; 6:13b; 7:3, 4), and (2) he uses the singular through the more personal "Fool's Speech" (11:1–12:13).

In our view Paul's use of the plural in 2:14–7:4 and of the singular in 11:1–12:13 is consistent and calculated. His uses of the plural do not appear to include Timothy, here cited with Paul, or Timothy and Silas, who preached with him at Corinth, except where the context makes it clear. Rather, Paul generally uses the plural to refer to himself, whether by design (as in 2:14–7:4) or coincidentally. By way of exception, however, in 1:18-19 the plurals refer to the historical preaching in Corinth by Paul, Silas, and Timothy; and in 3:12-18, 4:14, 16–5:10; 5:18a, 21 the plurals refer to the new covenant people for whom Paul writes representatively.

See *New Docs.* 6.169-72 for the appearance of plural and singular pronouns within letters from the general period, as well as also for a statistical analysis of the generally high frequency of first person plural pronouns in Paul's letters. Of the first person verbs and pronouns in 2 Corinthians 55 percent are plural, which, however, is only slightly higher than the lowest incidence of 50 percent.

8. See F. H. Agnew, "Apostle," 75-96. Since Paul is — chronologically speaking — the earliest writer of the NT, and since he uses "apostle" more than any other NT author,

apostolos was used only infrequently in the Greek language prior to NT times.[9] When we notice that Paul uses the word thirty-five out of the eighty times it occurs in the NT, it is evident that *apostolos* was important to him.

Earlier doubts about Paul's apostleship by some of the Corinthians[10] have apparently now hardened into opposition. This is attributable to the recent arrival of self-professed "ministers" or "apostles" (11:23, 13) who have launched a countermission against Paul (2:17–3:1; 11:4, 12) and who are, according to them, "superior" in ministry to Paul (11:5, 23; 12:11). By his opening words "Paul, an apostle . . . by the will of God," he pointedly reminds the Corinthians that he is not an apostle by self-appointment but by divine appointment (cf. 10:8; 13:10).[11] Moreover, he is "an apostle *of Christ Jesus*"; his authority is derived. In the First Letter, he wrote, "Christ sent ("apostled" — *apesteilen*) me" (1 Cor 1:17; cf. 1 Thess 2:6). Later in the present letter Paul makes a close connection between the Corinthians being "reconciled to God" and having their hearts widely "open" to Paul (5:20; 6:12). To reject the authority of the one who is an apostle "by the will of God" comes close to rejecting the authority of God/Christ, though Paul does not explicitly say so (cf. Mark 9:37, 41 pars.).[12]

What would the citizens of a Greco-Roman city like Corinth have understood by Paul's address to them as "the church . . . in Corinth"? Today the word "church" carries many meanings — a building for religious worship, a congregation, a denomination, worldwide Christianity, the Christian faith — to mention only a few. But in Paul's day — as used by Luke in an everyday sense in Acts 19 — it bore the meaning of "an assembly," whether an occasional assembly (such as the "assembly" of Ephesians in the city theater — Acts 19:32, 41) or an official assembly (such as the "legal assembly" of the city of Ephesus — Acts 19:39). It is presumed that these Corinthian readers

---

all historical investigations of the origin, meaning, and significance of the word properly begin with his letters. Despite wide-ranging opinions of the origin of "apostle" within the NT, there is broad agreement that "apostle" is used in two main senses both of which appear in 2 Corinthians: (1) solemn ("apostle of Christ Jesus" — 1:1; cf. 11:5, 13; 12:11, 12), and (2) nontechnical ("messengers from the churches" — 8:23). See, further, J. A. Bühner, *EDNT* 1.142-46.

9. K. H. Rengstorf, *TDNT* 1.407-47. The opinion favored here, following J. B. Lightfoot and Rengstorf, is that "apostle" derives from *shaliah* (= "sent man," "surrogate"), referred to in the literature of Rabbinic Judaism (cf. John 13:16; Mark 6:30). According to Mishnah *Berakoth* 5:5, "a man's agent *(shaliah)* is as himself." The *shaliah*'s relationship with the sender is primary, the content of the commission secondary.

10. 1 Cor 9:1; cf. 15:8-9.

11. Cf. κλητὸς ἀπόστολος in Rom 1:1; 1 Cor 1:1.

12. While Paul's references to Jesus Christ usually mean no more than his name, his use of Christ or of Christ Jesus, as here, imply Jesus' messianic office or title. See further R. N. Longenecker, *Christology,* 63-82.

would have understood "church" as meaning the plenary assembly of believers — as opposed to the constituent house meetings — in Corinth (cf. 1 Cor 11:18-22; 14:23).[13]

Paul's own usage is almost certainly conditioned by the frequent use of "church" *(ekklēsia)* in the LXX for the gatherings of the people of God. These were usually great gatherings; for example, "All the tribes of Israel stood before the LORD in the assembly *(ekklēsia)* of the people of God" (Judg 20:2; cf. 1 Chron 23:8).[14] In the NT Stephen spoke of God's people as "the congregation *(ekklēsia)* in the desert" gathered to hear "living words" that Moses had received (Acts 7:38). The "church of God in Corinth" is to be thought of as the Israel of God gathered to hear God's word (cf. Gal 6:16; 1 Cor 14:23-25).[15]

But Paul qualifies "church" with the possessive "of God," adding "in Corinth." Literally rendered, Paul's original words are "the church of God, which has its being in Corinth."[16] Since, as Paul told the Thessalonians, their church was "in God our Father and the Lord Jesus Christ" (1 Thess 1:1; 2 Thess 1:1), we infer that the church is an eschatological reality that, though now hidden "in God," will be revealed at the parousia (cf. 2 Thess 2:1; Col 3:3). The local church is the anticipatory manifestation in history of the gathered, end-time people of God (cf. Matt 16:18; Heb 12:22).[17]

It is striking that Paul should address this divided community by such a phrase as "the church of God 'manifested' in Corinth." The very phrase "the church of God in Corinth" is laden with irony, intended or unintended. How could the church of *God* be in such a godless city[18] and be so divided a community of professed believers? It seems likely that there were a series of splinter groups with points of difference as great if not greater than points of agreement. One group was interested in the "judaizing" message of the "false apostles" (11:4), while another was involved in sexual immorality (12:21) and probably in worship in the local cults (6:14–7:1).[19] Nonetheless,

13. See further, Introduction, 8-9.

14. *Contra* Thrall, 1.89-93, who diminishes the theological connotations of the use of ἐκκλησία in LXX passages as a background for Pauline use. She finds the origin of the word as used by Paul in the Gentile mission of the Hellenists, who sought an alternative word to συναγωγή.

15. The verbs Paul characteristically uses with "church" — directly or indirectly — are συνάγω (1 Cor 5:4) and συνέρχομαι (1 Cor 11:17, 18, 20, 33, 34; 14:23, 26).

16. Gk. τῇ ἐκκλησίᾳ τοῦ θεοῦ τῇ οὔσῃ ἐν Κορίνθῳ (cf. 1 Cor 1:2). But see also Phil 1:1 — πᾶσιν τοῖς ἁγίοις . . . τοῖς οὖσιν ἐν Φιλίπποις, suggesting a close association of ideas between the *ekklēsia* of God in a particular place and the presence of the saints in a particular place.

17. *Contra* K. L. Schmidt, *TDNT* 3.506, who sees the church in Corinth as a local manifestation of the "one great church."

18. On Corinth the Roman city of Paul's day, see Introduction, 1-4.

19. See Introduction, 28-29.

Paul addresses them solemnly as an entity, as the *ekklēsia* of *God,* very probably to encourage them to become what God graciously saw them to be.[20]

Paul includes in his address "all the saints throughout Achaia." While the salutation of the First Letter implied the existence of believers outside Corinth, the Second Letter is explicit. This change may reflect the growth of the faith throughout the province of Achaia.[21] We know of some believers in Athens (Acts 17:34) and of a church in Cenchreae (Rom 16:1-2). It is quite probable that the gospel had spread to some of the towns adjacent to the great metropolis of Corinth, as well as north from Athens.[22] Paul's words imply that some lines of communication existed between the church of the metropolis and the outlying centers, suggesting the beginnings of the metropolitical "diocese" that would develop in the following centuries. The wider scope of Achaian addressees alerts us that this letter has broader theological purposes than the narrower immediate matters between Paul and the Corinthians that a merely Corinthian destination may imply.

The term "saints" *(hagioi)* should be bracketed with "the church of God" as Paul's attempt to impress upon the Corinthians their God-given status. *Hagios* is the LXX's rendering of *qds,* covenantal separation from evil, on the one hand, and dedication to God and his service, on the other.[23] Historically, it appears that the term "holy ones" ("saints") was first applied to the members of the Jerusalem church; Paul can apply this word to them with no need to explain it (8:4; 9:1; cf. 1 Cor 16:1). His deliberate application of the term to include Gentiles may be pointed, given the judaizing thrust in Corinth at that time. Be that as it may, in Paul's mind the churches of God were the inheritors of Israel's sacred vocation as God's "holy ones."[24] Paul's First Letter repeatedly told the Corinthians about the holiness they enjoyed in God's sight, which they were to display in practical living (e.g., 1 Cor 1:2, 30; 3:17; 6:11-12; 7:14). If the phrase "the church of God" told them of the unity they were expected to express, that they were deemed by God to be "saints" or "holy ones" was his call to live distinctively in Corinth as God's covenant people, separated from evil and dedicated to him (6:14–7:1; 12:21; 13:5-6).

---

20. Cf. 1 Cor 3:16-17, where Paul has to remind them that they *are* the "temple of God" (cf. 2 Cor 6:16). Therefore, they must act as if they are; the indicative always precedes the imperative in Paul's view.

21. The D-text of Acts 18:27 refers to "churches" in Achaia.

22. At the time the province of Achaia extended approximately 100 km. north of Athens. See T. Cornell and J. Matthews, *Atlas,* 146. Thrall, 1.87, thinks that Paul's reference to "the whole of Achaia" is either an exaggeration or has in mind a region smaller than the Roman province. She questions the applicability of sections of the letter to readers other than the Corinthians and those near at hand, e.g., the church at Cenchreae.

23. Cf. N. H. Snaith, *Distinctive Ideas,* 29-30.

24. Exod 19:5, 6; Lev 11:44, 45; 19:1, 2; Deut 7:6; 14:2; cf. 1 Pet 2:9-10.

2 The opening lines of Paul's letters follow the general format of Greco-Roman correspondence of the period. The difference, however, is to be discerned in his theological nuances. Whereas the Greco-Roman letters expressed a "greeting" followed by prayer for the readers, often addressed to the gods,[25] the first element in Paul's two-part prayer is "grace." This differs, too, from the Jewish prayer, "mercy and peace. . . ."[26] Paul prays that his readers will apprehend the "grace"[27] of God, his unconditioned covenantal love to his people (cf. 6:1; 8:9), and the "peace"[28] with him and with each other that issues from that "grace" (cf. 13:14). As striking as Paul's prayer is against its Gentile (and Jewish?) cultural environment, however, it has no special force in this letter, being found in identical form in 1 Cor 1:3, Rom 1:7, Gal 1:3, Eph 1:2, Phil 1:2, Col 1:2, and Phlm 3.

Although the Jewish reader would have been familiar with the epistolary greeting, "mercy and peace," there may have been some surprise at the words "*grace* and peace." There would have been astonishment (and offense?) that blessings associated with Yahweh, the covenantal God of Israel, should flow from "God our Father and the Lord Jesus Christ."[29] The designation of God as "our Father" together with the joining of that name "*and* the Lord Jesus Christ" in these opening lines of the letter testifies to the radical redefinition of Paul's conception of God, initially mediated to him from the OT through Pharisaism but then subjectively through his conversion to "the Lord Jesus Christ."[30]

Paul will have much to say about God in 2 Corinthians, including the first chapter. God is immediately identified as "Father," the Father of his people ("our Father"), and in the next verse as "Father of our Lord Jesus Christ." Here we see the profound influence of the teachings of Jesus about God as "Father,"[31] which pervade even the earliest literature of the NT (e.g., 1 Thess 1:1; 1 Cor 8:6; Gal 4:6; Jas 1:16; cf. 1 Pet 1:17; 1 John 3:1; Jude 1).

25. See n. 2, above.

26. It is striking that Paul begins with "grace." To be sure, Paul's prayer appears to have its origins in contemporary Jewish epistolary prayers, but these do not mention "grace." See, e.g., Baruch's letter to the exiles in which he prays "mercy and peace . . . unto the brethren carried into captivity" (quoted in 2 *Apoc. Bar.* 78:2; cf. Gal 6:16). See further K. Berger, "Apostelbrief," 191-207.

27. Gk. χάρις; see K. Berger, *EDNT* 3.457-60.

28. Gk. εἰρήνη; see V. Hasler, *EDNT* 1.394-97.

29. Jewish letters would offer a point of comparison for Paul's statement about God. According to *New Docs.* 3.142, however, very few personal letters between Jews of the period have survived. The semiofficial Bar Kokhba letters often begin, "A to B, peace," without any reference to God (see Y. Yadin, *Bar-Kokhba,* 124-39).

30. See F. Young and D. F. Ford, *Meaning,* 239-41.

31. See, e.g., Mark 12:36 pars., John 5:16-23, and throughout the Sermon on the Mount (Matt 5–7).

Joined with "God our Father" as the source of "grace and peace" is "the Lord Jesus Christ." "Lord" *(kyrios)* is the most common title for Jesus in the letters of Paul. Its probable derivation from an earlier Aramaic form may be seen in Paul's words: "If anyone does not love the Lord *(kyrios)* — a curse on him. *Marana tha"* (1 Cor 16:22). The Aramaic invocation *Marana tha* (= "Our Lord, come") was probably used in the earliest Jerusalem community of believers (cf. Rev 22:19), becoming in time, by translation, the much used *kyrios* of Paul's preaching to the Gentiles.

Kyrios is the word used for Yahweh in the LXX. While many scholars have challenged any connection between Jesus and Yahweh based on *kyrios,* pointing out that *kyrios,* especially when used in the vocative ("O Lord"), means no more than "sir" as a respectful form of address. Yet it appears that Paul does use *kyrios* to identify Jesus with Yahweh, as may be seen in the way he applies to Jesus a number of texts from the LXX that refer to *Kyrios* = Yahweh. For example,

LXX Psalm 46:5	**1 Thess 4:16**
God is gone up with a shout, the *kyrios*	The *kyrios* (Jesus) . . . will descend . . .
with the sound of the trumpet	with the sound of the trumpet

LXX Joel 2:32	**Rom 10:9, 13**
	If you confess . . . Jesus is *kyrios* . . . you will be saved. . . .
Whosoever will call on the name of the *kyrios* will be saved	For "every one who calls upon upon the name of the *kyrios* will be saved."

LXX Isaiah 45:22-23	**Philippians 2:10-11**
. . . I am God. . . . Before me every knee shall bow; by me every tongue shall swear.	At the name of Jesus every knee should bow . . . every tongue confess that Jesus Christ is *kyrios*.

Comparison between these and other texts[32] leaves little doubt that Jesus the *kyrios* was regarded by Paul in terms identical to or at least similar to Yahweh the *kyrios,* the God of Israel.

---

32. See further L. W. Hurtado, *One God, One Lord,* 93-128.

On the three occasions that Paul uses the phrase "Jesus [Christ] is *kyrios*" these words are "confessed" or "said" (Rom 10:9; 1 Cor 12:3; Phil 2:11). Since, as it appears, 1 Cor 12:3, 12-13 is a baptismal setting, the words "Jesus is *kyrios,*" wherever they occur in Paul's Letters, probably echo a new convert's public acknowledgment of the Lordship of Jesus made to a congregation in the context of baptism (cf. 1 Pet 3:15, 21-22).[33] Paul can sum up his apostolic proclamation as "Jesus Christ as Lord" (2 Cor 4:5; cf. 8:5), knowing the association of these words with the convert's baptism in the presence of the congregation.

Paul writes of the *kyrios* with great reverence as the one who "died and lived again, that he might be Lord both of the dead and the living" (Rom 14:9). When Paul speaks of Jesus' return he invariably speaks of him as the *kyrios* (e.g., 1 Thess 4:16-17). Yet he will speak of the earthly Jesus under the same title — for example, the brothers of the Lord, the cup of the Lord, the table of the Lord (1 Cor 9:5; 10:21). The commands of the Lord who is now risen bind believers (e.g., 1 Cor 7:10). The *kyrios* is the judge of all (e.g., 1 Cor 4:4; 2 Cor 5:10), the one before whom every knee shall bow and every tongue confess that he is Lord (Phil 2:11).

It is clear that the Pharisee Saul's theology of God has been transformed by his encounter with the Risen One, the *kyrios*. For Paul God is not to be understood independently of but through the revelation of the *kyrios* Jesus Christ in his poverty, his weakness, his being "made sin," but also in his resurrection and exaltation.[34] Although v. 2 does no more than repeat the conjunction of "our Father" *and* "the Lord Jesus Christ" found in earlier letters (cf. 2 Thess 1:2 and 1 Cor 1:3), it is quite possible that, in view of the repetition of the conjunction in the next verse, Paul is wishing to reinforce a view of God as "Father" against the alternative doctrines of "Jesus" and "righteousness," and indeed of God himself as enunciated by the "false apostles" (cf. 11:4, 15). God is revealed as "Father" by the incarnation, death, and exaltation of the *kyrios* Jesus Christ under the new covenant. Paul's view of God has been permanently redefined by the revelation of his Son in his incarnation, atonement, and exaltation.

33. On the other hand, it could be argued that 1 Cor 12:3 and 12–13 are focused on the Spirit, not on baptism (so G. D. Fee, *1 Corinthians*, 603-6). The confession is by the Spirit; the one body of believers results from their baptism by the one Spirit. Nonetheless, Paul's Spirit references in 1 Corinthians 12 appear to imply the structure and formality of a baptismal-liturgical setting.

34. See further F. Young and D. F. Ford, *Meaning*, 241.

B. BENEDICTION (1:3-7)

> 3 *Praise be to the God and Father of our Lord Jesus Christ, the Father of compassion and the God of all comfort, 4 who comforts us in all our troubles, so that we can comfort those in any trouble with the comfort we ourselves have received from God. 5 For just as the sufferings of Christ flow over into our lives, so also through Christ our comfort overflows. 6 ¹If we are distressed, it is for your comfort and salvation; if we are comforted, it is for your comfort, which produces in you patient endurance of the same sufferings we suffer. 7 And our hope for you is firm,² because we know that just as you share in our sufferings, so also you share in our comfort.*

The salutation completed, Paul the writer next offers a benediction of God. This tightly knit statement (1) begins with an ascription to God ("Blessed be God . . ." — v. 3a), (2) on account of God's ongoing comfort of his minister ("who comforts us in all our troubles" — vv. 4-5), a comfort that is (3) for the benefit of the Corinthians ("if we are distressed . . . if we are comforted, it is *for you*" — vv. 6-7), who (4) are likewise suffering ("the *same* sufferings we suffer" — v. 6), and (5) for whose patient endurance Paul is confident ("our hope for you is *firm*" — v. 7).

One wonders why Paul here offers a benediction of God[3] rather than his more customary thanksgiving for his readers?[4] It is to be noted that the thanksgiving is modeled on Hellenistic forms, whereas the benediction originates in the benediction of God within the OT as it came to be expressed in the Jewish liturgical tradition,[5] an example of which is given below.

The appearance here of a benediction rather than the more common thanksgiving is interpreted by some as an indication either of Paul's strained relationships with his readers or of his low view of their discipleship.[6] The

---

1. The reading followed by NIV is supported by p[46] ℵ A C P Ψ 0243 1739 1881 it[r] vg syr[p] cop[sa,bo]. Several texts omit parts of the second εἶτα clause, doubtless due to homoeoteleuton, while others seek to rectify this omission. See Metzger, 573-74.

2. The reading of words from παρακλήσεως to εἰδότες is followed by most authorities and makes good sense of the connection between v. 6 and v. 7. The major variant, B, appears to have arisen on account of homoeoteleuton (παρακλήσεως to παρακλήσεως, with words in between omitted).

3. Cf. Eph 1:3-10; also 1 Pet 1:3-9; Luke 1:68.

4. Rom 1:8-15; 1 Cor 1:4-9; Phil 1:3-11; Col 1:3-8; 1 Thess 1:2-10; 2 Thess 1:3-12; 2 Tim 1:3-7; Phlm 4-7.

5. So Furnish, 108, 116, citing many instances, e.g., Gen 14:20; 2 Chron 2:12; Ps 65:20.

6. Furnish, 116-17, cites but then rejects this explanation. According to Martin, 8, Paul employs a benediction for benefits that he and his readers *shared* rather than a

absence of a thanksgiving, however, should not be viewed as a criticism of the Corinthians, especially since the benediction leads directly into Paul's grateful account of God's deliverance of him in Asia, which concludes with his encouragement that their prayers for him will issue in *thanksgiving* (v. 11).

Rather, Paul's "blessing" of God at the beginning of the letter should be seen as expressing his heartfelt worship of God for recent mercies to him that he will expand upon later in the letter. As the repetition of the "sufferings-comfort" vocabulary from this passage in later passages[7] indicates, this benediction anticipates in particular (1) the recent deliverance from the "deadly peril" in Asia (1:8-11), and (2) the good news brought by Titus that the Corinthians had responded to his (lost) "Painful Letter" with genuine repentance (7:5-11). Beyond that — though in more general terms — Paul's account of his ministry under the new covenant (2:14–7:4) has many references to sufferings,[8] through which, however, God comforted his minister (2:14, 16; 3:6; 4:7-11; 6:3-5; 7:4; 12:7-9).

Closely related is Paul's emphasis on God that the benediction carries forward from the salutation (vv. 1-2) into the Escape from Asia (vv. 8-11) and beyond that into his Defense of Changed Travel Plans (1:15–2:2), where he writes of the faithfulness of God to his promises and to his people. Here God is characterized as the comforter of his minister and of his people in their sufferings (vv. 3-7).

References to sufferings, too, are prominent in this opening benediction. Is this because the Corinthians are urgently questioning why the apostle Paul sustains such a degree of pain and difficulty in the course of his ministry? Do his references to their sufferings ("the *same* suffering we suffer" — v. 6) suggest that these, too, were an issue for them? Paul's immediate introduction of the theme of suffering may be to put sufferings — his and theirs — into divine perspective.[9] This is hinted at in the phrase "the sufferings of Christ flow over into our lives" (v. 5). The apostle's sufferings listed in the letter

---

thanksgiving for God's work in the lives of the addressees. J. T. Fitzgerald's opinion (*Earthen Vessels,* 153-57) — based on the thesis of N. A. Dahl — that this benediction is self-congratulatory ("self-referential") may put the matter too strongly. Nonetheless, Paul does so bless God as to draw attention to himself, namely, in the twin realities of (1) his sufferings (θλίψεις· . . . παθήματα), and (2) God's comfort (παράκλησις) of him, elements in tandem that will repeat 4:8-9 and 11:23b–12:10. In the benediction Paul is "the comforted comforter" (155).

7. Gk. θλῖψις . . . θλῖψις (1:4 . . . 1:8); εὐλογητὸς ὁ θεὸς . . . ὁ παρακαλῶν . . . ὁ παρακαλῶν . . . ὁ θεὸς . . . διὰ τοῦτο παρακεκλήμεθα (1:3-4; 7:6, 13).

8. The keyword θλῖψις reappears in 4:17; 6:4; 7:4.

9. Perhaps this early introduction of the theme of his sufferings is deliberate, in view of the Corinthians' appreciation of triumphalism on the one hand, and their low view of Paul's apostleship on the other.

(2:14; 4:7-12; 6:3-10; 11:23–12:10) should be seen as replicating the "sufferings of Christ," by — as it were — a principle of divine inevitability. Just as the One whom God sent suffered in and for a world alienated from God (cf. 5:14-21), so, too, the apostle of the Sent One and the community of the Sent One experience the pain of rejection in that same world as they bear witness to Christ.

A further and connected theme of the benediction, the unity of people and apostle, may also reflect the need Paul felt to strengthen the bonds between himself and the Corinthians. His repeated "our" — "*our* Father . . . *our* Lord" (vv. 2, 3) — is picked up later in the chapter by his encouragement of their prayer for him (v. 11) and by *his* and *their* experience of the Spirit (1:21-22; cf. 4:14; 6:16).[10] These words express the reciprocity between apostle and people. As noted above, this unity is also to be seen in the sufferings that he and they share, in which, however, their God and Father, whom they know in common, comforts his people in Christ (vv. 4-5). God's comfort of his suffering apostle is for the special benefit of the Corinthians (v. 6), just as their prayer to God for him is for his deliverance (1:11).

In his salutation (vv. 1-2) Paul christianizes the form of address used in Greco-Roman (and Jewish) letters. In the next five sentences he takes another existing form, the synagogue benediction,[11] shaping it, too, along distinctively Christian lines. This can be readily seen by comparison with the first of the nineteen synagogue benedictions, which arose in the NT era:[12]

> Blessed art thou, O Lord our God and God of our fathers, God of Abraham, God of Isaac, and God of Jacob, great, mighty and fearful God, most high, who bestowest abundant grace and createst all things and rememberest the promises of grace to the fathers and bringest a Redeemer to their children's children for thy name's sake out of love. O King who bringest help and salvation and who art a shield. Blessed art thou, Lord, Shield of Abraham.[13]

In the hands of the now-converted Paul the "God of *our fathers*" is identified as "the God and Father of *our Lord Jesus Christ.*" The "promises to the

10. See also 4:14 ("'[God] will present *us* with *you*'") and 6:16 ("*we* are the temple of the living God"; cf. 1 Cor 3:16 — "*you* are God's temple?").

11. M. Hengel, *Pre-Christian Paul,* 55-67, argues that prior to his conversion Saul/Paul was a teacher in the Hellenistic synagogues in Jerusalem. If so, the liturgy that the Christian Paul adapted may have been the liturgy of the *Hellenistic* synagogue.

12. Although the benedictions may not have reached their present form until after A.D. 70, it is almost certain that benediction 1 as quoted was close to the prayer used in Paul's day.

13. Quoted in E. Schürer, *Jewish People,* 2.456.

fathers" have been kept (1:20), and the hoped-for "redeemer" has been proclaimed in Corinth (1:19). The radically changed language in Paul's benediction of God as compared to this Pharisaic benediction is, in itself, powerful testimony to his Damascus Road encounter.

The calculated christianization of salutation (vv. 1-2) and benediction (vv. 3-7) as representing, respectively, Greco-Roman culture and Jewish synagogue worship are evidence of the profound conversion of the Hellenistic Jew, Saul of Tarsus, to the Messiah Jesus.

The opening sentence of the benediction is not found in letters earlier than 2 Corinthians, though it is found in identical terms in Eph 1:3 and 1 Pet 1:3. Therefore, it is likely that these references derive from the present benediction, whose wording by Paul may have been provoked by the "judaizing" theology of the "false apostles." It was important for Paul to establish at the outset that God, the God of the fathers Abraham, Isaac, and Jacob, was "the . . . Father of our Lord Jesus Christ." Let those Corinthians who are yielding to judaizing influence understand that God is now eschatologically revealed and defined under the new covenant as the Father of Jesus, their Lord (cf. 1:19; 4:5; cf. 11:31).

Paul probably writes his benediction conscious that his letter will be read aloud to the congregation assembled for the worship of God, "where the liturgical language of invocation and praise has its natural place. . . . This may explain the heavy concentration on the prayer and praise-idiom in the opening parts of his letters."[14]

3 The opening verse of the benediction (vv. 3-7) commences with "praise be,"[15] an ascription often made to the God of Israel in the OT,[16] and within the Jewish liturgical tradition.[17] Strikingly, however, Paul directs this blessing to "the God" who is at the same time (1) "the Father of our Lord Jesus Christ"[18] and (2) "the Father of compassion and the God of all comfort." The latter establishes continuity with the known character of the God of the OT as currently worshiped in the synagogues (see below), but the former expresses the recent historic revelation of the inner being of God as Father of his Son, the Lord Jesus Christ.

---

14. Martin, 7.

15. Gk. εὐλογητός, "blessed be" (RSV). It should be noted that there is no verb; this may be "simply an exclamation, expressing what is already true of God" (Thrall, 1.100-101), i.e., "the blessed One."

16. See e.g., LXX Gen 14:20; 2 Kgdms 6:21; Ps 65:20; 67:36.

17. See Mishnah *Berakoth* (passim) and Qumran texts (e.g., 1QM 18:6-7).

18. Gk. ὁ θεὸς καὶ πατὴρ τοῦ κυρίου ἡμῶν Ἰησοῦ Χριστοῦ. The genitive τοῦ κυρίου ἡμῶν depends on both ὁ θεός and πατήρ, as suggested by the absence of a second definite article before πατήρ, serving also to tie together θεός and πατήρ. The κύριος is not independent of ὁ θεὸς καὶ πατήρ.

The verse has a chiastic (crisscross) structure:

Blessed be the God   the Father of mercies
                and   and
                Father of our Lord . . .   the God of all comfort.

The effect of this rhetorical device is to emphasize that the God who is here "praised" is both (1) Father of his Son, our Lord Jesus Christ, and (2) Father (= source) of mercies. The former part continues from "grace and peace from God our Father" of the verse preceding, whereas the latter part, "the God of all comfort," is preparatory for "who comforts us" in the verse following.

Also repeated from the previous verse is the emphasis "our" — "our Father . . . our Lord." Paul and the saints of Corinth share in common the one Father and the one Lord, his Son. The unity of the messianic community with its apostle and their reciprocity of relationships — important themes throughout the letter — are affirmed at the outset.

This benediction focusing on "the Father of our Lord" echoes back to God his own gospel word to us, with its dual emphasis on *"the Son of God"* and "Jesus Christ as *Lord,"* which appear within the letter as summaries of the message first brought to the Corinthians (1:19; 4:5). This reminds us of the close association between the apostles' *proclamation* and, subsequently, the believers' *confession* in the church (cf. Rom 10:9, 14-15). The word God speaks as gospel is returned to him by the church as the "blessing" of his name.

It is probable that "the God *and* Father of our Lord Jesus Christ" is to be understood as "God, *even* the Father," that is, as Paul's gloss on the synagogue benediction of God (cf. 11:31; Rom 15:6). The God of the patriarchs blessed by Paul the Jew is now blessed especially as "the Father of the Lord Jesus Christ" and "our Father" (v. 2). This is the first occasion within Paul's (extant) letters that he has adapted the synagogue liturgy in this way, and it may reflect his response to the judaizing pressure evident at Corinth at that time (cf. 11:22, 31).

"The Father of mercies" is an ascription of God found in synagogue prayers contemporary with Paul,[19] which in turn derives from the OT (e.g., Exod 34:6; Ps 25:6; 69:16). "Comfort" *(paraklēsis),* or perhaps better "encouragement" or "consolation," is the keyword in the benediction (occurring ten times), and is frequently used within the letter,[20] evoking OT images of the messianic age (Isa 40:1; 49:13; 51:3, 12, 19; 52:9; 61:2; 66:13). By NT

---

19. A. Marmorstein, *Old Rabbinic Doctrine of God,* 56.
20. As noun and verb: 2:7, 8; 5:20; 6:1; 7:4, 6, 7, 13; 8:4, 6, 17; 9:5; 10:1; 12:8, 18; 13:11. In many ways 2 Corinthians is a letter of encouragement; Paul often uses this language in various critical appeals to the Corinthians (see 5:20; 10:1; 13:11).

times Jews were looking for the "consolation [comforting] of Israel" (Luke 2:25; cf. Matt 5:4).[21] An environment of hostility against God's people, but also the firm promise of deliverance from that hostility, is implied by the notion of "comfort."

This cluster of references to "comfort" at the beginning of the letter, notwithstanding the implications of suffering, suggests that the twin notions of the messianic *age* and the messianic *people* are important themes (cf. 1:20; 3:3; 6:1-2) for Paul to impress upon the Corinthians at a time when, perhaps, the distinctive "newness" of the present dispensation is questioned by a judaizing influence. But the messianic "comfort" is mediated by the God who is "Father of our Lord Jesus Christ," his Son.

"The God of all comfort," like the "Father of mercies," originates in traditional synagogue piety: "May the Lord of consolations comfort you. Blessed be he, who comforts the mourners."[22] Such a view of God arises from many references in the Psalms.[23] Paul's insertion of the adjective "all" — implying "every kind of" or "immeasurable" — intensifies the believers' devotion to the God who is now revealed as Father.

This "God, *even* the Father of Christ," is the divine source from whom flow down his "compassion and all comfort." Such a conceptual model — which rests on the notion of the Father as source and the Lord Jesus Christ as channel — is found elsewhere in Paul's writings. For example,

> there is but one God, the Father,
> > *from* whom all things came . . .
> and . . . one Lord, Jesus Christ,
> > *through* whom all things came. (1 Cor 8:6)

Paul's is a vertical model, the Father being at the top — as it were — the blessings of "compassion and comfort," as well as of divine self-disclosure, flowing from him through and in his Son, our Lord, to his people. The prepositions "from" *(ek)* and "through" *(dia)*, though unstated in our passage,[24] are implicit in the imagery of God as the "Father [i.e., source] of compassion . . . comfort."

---

21. Cf. *2 Apoc. Bar.* 44:7; see further Str-B 2.124-26.

22. See *Ketubot* 8B, 27 in Str-B 3.494. Although this is a post-Christian citation, it is probably pre-Christian in origin, given the conservative patterns of liturgical transmission.

23. E.g., Ps 25:6 (LXX 24:6); 40:12 (LXX 39:12); 51:2 (LXX 50:2) 69:16 (LXX 68:16); 77:9 (LXX 76:9); 79:8 (LXX 78:8); 103:4 (LXX 102:4); 106:46 (LXX 105:46); 119:77, 156 (LXX 118:77, 156); 145:8-9 (LXX 144:8-9).

24. But see 1:5 — διὰ τοῦ Χριστοῦ περισσεύει καὶ ἡ παράκλησις ἡμῶν; NIV, "through Christ our comfort overflows."

The Lord Jesus Christ does not stand next to the Father as a co-regent, but beneath him as mediator to humankind of the blessings of God, and at the same time revelator of that God. The Lord who came to us and who is now over us put a human face to God, brought God to us as One whom we could readily recognize. The glory of God shines on the *face* of Jesus Christ (4:6).[25] Whatever else, the "great, mighty and fearful God" of the Jewish synagogue is forever to be known as "the Father of our Lord Jesus Christ."

4   From his ascription to God as the source of all comfort the benediction is now personalized in terms of Paul and the Corinthians. The God whom he blesses comforts Paul so that, in turn, Paul is enabled to comfort others — that is, the Corinthians — with the comfort he himself has received from God. In the succeeding clauses Paul will elaborate on the dark theme of suffering ("all our troubles") that he has introduced in this verse. But for the moment (in the two opening verses of the benediction) he wishes to concentrate on God and his comfort.

Once again (cf. v. 3) we find a chiastic structure, based on "God . . . us . . . we . . . God":[26]

[God] who			A
comforts	us	in all our affliction	B
	that we may be able		
to comfort		those who are in any affliction	B
with the			
comfort			
	with which we ourselves		
are comforted			
by God.			A

The chiasmus is complex and uneven, serving to direct our attention to "God

---

25. A similar vertical model is found in 1 Cor 11:3 (cf. 1 Cor 3:23; 15:28):

    The head of every man is Christ. . . .

and

    the head of Christ   is God. . . .

The vertical structure found in Paul's writings serves — without contradiction — the notion that the Father is the *source* of Christ (who is the *source* of both creation and redemption) as well as that the Father is *over* Christ, who is the Lord *over* humanity.

The vertical thought structure is reinforced later in the first chapter by: "through [Jesus Christ] the 'Amen' is spoken by us to (the glory of) God" (1:20, noting carefully the prepositions: δι' αὐτοῦ τὸ ἀμὴν τῷ θεῷ πρὸς δόξαν δι' ἡμῶν). Blessings and revelation flow from God through Christ to us; prayer and thanksgiving are offered by us through Christ to God.

26. Based on Gk. ὁ παρακαλῶν . . . ἡμᾶς . . . παρακαλούμεθα . . . θεός.

71

. . . us," the latter accentuated by the emphatic pronoun, "we *ourselves*[27] are comforted." There is also repetition: "*all* comfort . . . *all* affliction . . . *every* affliction"[28] — and striking contrast between "comfort" and "affliction," the vocabulary that dominates the benediction and that, in the case of "affliction," significantly carries over to the next passage ("affliction in Asia" — v. 8).

Though continuing an idiom influenced by the synagogue benediction (see on v. 3), Paul's use of the participial clause "God . . . who comforts" is also hymnic, calling to mind, for example, "the Lord . . . who forgives . . . who redeems . . . who crowns . . . who satisfies" (Ps. 103:2-5[29]). This grammatical idiom points to actions that God typically does, in this case "God . . . comforts." The God whom Paul blesses is dynamic in relationships; he is no heavenly abstraction (as was the *theos* of the Greeks).

Isaiah's report of God's command to him, "Comfort, comfort my people," with which Isaiah 40–55 commences (a passage upon which Paul depends heavily throughout the letter[30]) appears to be in Paul's mind. As noted in v. 3, the notion of "comfort" *(paraklēsis)* implies both (1) the sufferings of God's people in an alien environment, and (2) the hope of God's deliverance from those sufferings.

Who, then, are the "us . . . we" in this verse who receive and give the comfort of God: (1) Paul, speaking of himself as apostle in the plural? (2) Paul with his co-sender Timothy? or (3) believers in general? The first option appears to be the most likely. Paul's clear contrast "we"/"us . . . you" (vv. 6-7; cf. v. 11) suggests that Paul's "we"/"us" is a plural reference to himself in his apostolic ministry.

Paul's "in all our *afflictions*" introduces one of the keywords of the letter,[31] which, as noted above, is significantly repeated within the next passage (v. 8) as an example of "troubles." The vocabulary *(thlipsis/thlibein)* carries the idea of "pressure" felt inwardly resulting from difficult outward circumstances usually associated with Christian ministry and witness in the face of hostility. Both Paul and the Corinthians are subject to "trouble." In Paul's case "all our troubles," as spelled out in the catalogue of missionary suffering

27. Gk. παρακαλούμεθα αὐτοί.

28. Gk. πάσης . . . πάσῃ . . . πάσῃ. We note two uses of πᾶς in v. 4: (1) with the article ("*all* affliction"), and (2) without the article ("*every* affliction").

29. LXX Ps 102:2-5, τὸν Κύριον . . . τὸν εὐιλατεύοντα . . . τὸν ἰώμενον . . . τὸν λυτρούμενον . . . τὸν στεφανοῦντα . . . τὸν ἐμπιπλῶντα, "the Lord . . . who forgives . . . who heals . . . who redeems . . . who crowns . . . who satisfies . . ."; cf. LXX Ps 135:3ff.; 143:1; 146:6ff.

30. See Isa 40:1; 51:3, 12, 19 and Introduction, 46-47.

31. 1:4, 8; 2:4; 4:17; 6:4; 7:4; 8:2 (θλίψις); 1:6; 4:8; 7:5 (θλίβω). This vocabulary had been used in the LXX for the affliction of Israel as well as of righteous individuals. See H. Schlier, *TDNT* 3.140-43.

(11:23b–12:10), expresses a life marked by suffering;[32] in the Corinthians' "in every — that is, in various kinds of — affliction."[33] "Afflictions" are the portion of the messianic people, but so too, is the divine "comfort." The obvious linkage between "God . . . who comforts us in all our affliction" (v. 4) and "the afflictions we suffered in . . . Asia" (v. 8) gives this benediction its concrete character; there is nothing theoretical or remote here.

The corporate character of the messianic fellowship (= those who are "in Christ") clearly emerges from this. God comforted Paul by Titus, who had been comforted by the Corinthians (7:6-7), enabling Paul in turn (by means of these words in this letter) to comfort the Corinthians — and indeed members of other churches — with the comfort of God. The Corinthians had sustained pain through Paul's "Severe Letter" to them (7:7-11); now he comforts them. Thus God's "comfort" comes full circle among his people. The closeness and reciprocity of fellowship within, and between, congregations[34] as expressed here by Paul is rather pointed, given the Corinthians' coolness to him at that time. It also calls into question the individualism of modern Christianity and the sense of remoteness within and among many contemporary churches.

How does God comfort his people? Although the later reference reveals God's use of human intermediaries (7:6-7), in this verse there is no hint of such mediation. The exercise of "comfort" appears as a charisma, a concrete manifestation of the grace of God, a divine intervention. Paul declares that God's "comfort in affliction" is divinely purposeful — as indicated by the purpose construction[35] — "in order to enable" those comforted to comfort others.[36] Basic to this process is the sense of sympathy for others evoked by God's comfort of oneself in afflictions. God's comfort is to stir up compassion leading to the passing on to others of the comfort of God; it is not to terminate on the receiver.

32. The sufferings incurred in the course of his apostolic ministry are set out both in the First and Second Letters to the Corinthians (1 Cor 4:9-13; 2 Cor 1:8-11; 2:12-17; 4:7-11; 6:3-13; 11:21–12:10; cf. Rom 8:35-39; Phil 3:7-11; Col 1:24-29).

33. Gk. πάσῃ τῇ θλίψει . . . ἐν πάσῃ θλίψει. Typical of his usage elsewhere, Paul here employs the singular (but see 6:4; 1 Thess 3:3; Rom 5:3). Despite the fact that "in all our troubles" (NIV) sounds rather general, the reference should not be taken as indefinite but as concrete. See further BDF #275 (3).

34. Letters of introduction illustrate the fraternal nature of relations between congregations (Acts 15:23-29; 18:27; Rom 16:1; 2 Cor 8:22; Col 4:7-9) as, indeed, did the collection by the Gentile churches for the church in Jerusalem (1 Cor 16:1-3; 2 Cor 9:12-14; Rom 15:25-27).

35. Gk. εἰς τὸ δύνασθαι.

36. Some of Paul's remarks suggest that (sections of?) the Corinthian church questioned his spiritual power (cf. 1:12, 17; 2:16; 3:4-6; 10:2-7; 13:3). His assertion ὁ παρακαλῶν ἡμᾶς . . . εἰς τὸ δύνασθαι ἡμᾶς so early in the letter may be deliberate, to establish with them his ἱκανότης (3:4).

5 Paul now gives the reason for his statement (v. 4) that God has enabled him to comfort others with the comfort he has received from God. It is "because" the "comfort" of God overflows to him. This, however, is set in balance with another that is given first, namely, that sufferings overflow to him. Thus he now brings the sufferings theme to the fore. Just as the sufferings of Christ overflow to him, so, too — he is quick to say — the comfort of God overflows through Christ to him. Christ is the channel to the apostle not only of sufferings but also of divine comfort.

This verse flows out of its predecessor (as introduced by "because"), indicating the basis for his assertion. The assonant "even as . . . so also"[37] and the quasi-chiastic "sufferings . . . flow over/flow over . . . comfort" serve (1) to contrast "sufferings" with "comfort,"[38] and (2) to accentuate the notion of "overflowing," giving the sentence as read aloud in church a solemn ring.[39] "Christ" is central to Paul in this experience; he is the *source* from whom sufferings overflow to him and the *channel*[40] through whom the comfort (from God) overflows to him.

Basing their views on passages in the OT, Jews of the NT era believed that the triumphal messianic age would be preceded by "woes" or sufferings.[41] The "sufferings of Christ,"[42] therefore, "are not sufferings personally borne by the Messiah . . . but sufferings associated with him, 'messianic sufferings' ushering in the messianic age in a period of woe preceding eternal bliss."[43] The Messiah, when he appeared, however, would be a powerful and victorious figure.[44] Accordingly, a "suffering" Messiah — *crucified,* no less (and by the Gentiles!) — was, according to Paul, a "stumbling block to Jews" (1 Cor 1:23; cf. Mark 8:31-33), and presumably to the views of those other "ministers of Christ," the "false apostles" (11:13, 23). It may be that, in part, for this reason, Paul introduces "the sufferings of Christ/the Messiah" so early in the letter to rebut an alternative, Christ-triumphal theology of his newly arrived opponents. During the course of the letter Paul will expand

---

37. Gk. καθὼς . . . οὕτως.

38. Gk. τὰ παθήματα . . . ἡ παράκλησις.

39. Thrall, 1.104, suggests that the two occurrences of περισσεύει may be significant, pointing to the intensity of the experience of both the affliction and the comfort.

40. Gk. τὰ παθήματα τοῦ Χριστοῦ . . . διὰ τοῦ Χριστοῦ . . . ἡ παράκλησις.

41. Isa 26:17; 66:8; Jer 22:23; Hos 13:13; Mic 4:9-10; cf. 4 Ezra 14:16-17; *As. Moses* 10:4; *2 Apoc. Bar.* 10:10-35. We note, however, that the usual term in the LXX is not πάθημα but ὠδίν.

42. Gk. τὰ παθήματα τοῦ Χριστοῦ. See also Phil 3:10 (τὰ παθήματα αὐτοῦ), 1 Pet 1:11 (Χριστὸν παθήματα), 4:13 (τοῦ Χριστοῦ παθήμασιν), and 5:1 (Χριστοῦ παθημάτων). See also Heb 2:9, 10.

43. Barrett, 61-62.

44. See, e.g., *Pss. Sol.* 17:21-27; *Pal. Targ.* Gen. 49:10.

upon the "sufferings of Christ" as the One who was "made . . . to be sin," in whom "we become the righteousness of God" (5:14-21).[45] Moreover, and closely connected with this, we note Paul's portrayal of his own ministry as an "ambassador" of Christ (5:20; 6:3-10) and a "minister" of Christ (11:23–12:10) in antitriumphalist and indeed explicitly suffering terms (2:14; cf. 4:7-11).

It is evident that Jesus foresaw not only his own sufferings but also those of his disciples, in particular the Twelve. Jesus' thinking appears to have been influenced, on the one hand, by the passages in Isaiah that were prophetic of the sufferings of the "Servant" (Isa 42:1-4; 49:1-6; 50:4-9; 52:13–53:12) and, on the other, by the sufferings of "saints of the Most High" with whom the "Son of Man" is closely connected (Dan 7:21-22, 25). Jesus spoke prophetically of the suffering that awaited both him and them (Mark 8:31, 34-38; 9:31; 10:30, 32-34, 39 pars.). Using the images of shepherd/sheep (Mark 14:27; Zech 13:7-9) and vine/branches (John 15:1–16:5), Jesus described their closeness to him and the suffering he and they were to share. Jesus' teaching about his own "sufferings" has probably influenced Paul (Phil 3:10; Col 1:24) as well as other NT writers (1 Pet 1:11; 4:13; 5:1; Heb 2:9, 10).

"The sufferings of Christ," as suffered by Paul, in this context are to be identified with "all our afflictions . . . in every affliction" (v. 4), "we are afflicted" (v. 6), and "the same sufferings we also suffer" (v. 6). These "afflictions" arise directly from his missionary message and lifestyle, so abundantly set forth in this letter. Just as Christ suffered in his ministry and death from forces hostile to God, so, too, the apostle, in continuity with Christ, suffered in the course of his ministry and proclamation.[46]

Paul now matches "suffering" with "comfort," suggesting perhaps a symmetry corresponding with Christ's death and resurrection. This pairing of the gospel fundamentals (cf. 1 Cor 15:3-5) may be seen at other places within the letter, whether implicitly (cf. 2:16; 12:7-9) or explicitly (4:7-14; 5:15; 13:3-4). Just as Christ's "sufferings" in death overflow, so also resurrection "comfort" overflows through Christ. What does Paul mean by this? When later in the letter he writes, "God comforted us by the coming of Titus, and not only by his coming but also by the comfort you had given"

45. The divine necessity for the "sufferings ($\pi\alpha\theta\dot{\eta}\alpha\tau\alpha$) of Christ" are set out, e.g., in Luke 24:26, 46; Acts 3:18; 17:3 (where the verb $\pi\dot{\alpha}\sigma\chi\omega$ is used).

46. In her review of various options for the meaning of "the sufferings of Christ," Thrall, 1.107-10, does not fully canvass the above. Her preferred option is that "the sufferings of Christ" are "derived from a mystical fellowship with Christ grounded in baptism," as based on the parallel "the fellowship of his sufferings" (Phil 3:10). Paul's thrust in this passage, however, is not baptism but "afflictions" sustained in the course of ministry, as the passage immediately following (1:8-10) makes clear.

(7:6-7), it is clear that he has in mind the ministry of fellow Christians to one another.[47]

To this point (vv. 4-5) Paul has spoken of himself as the one to whom sufferings and comfort overflow. In the remaining clauses of the benediction he will declare how these affect the Corinthians.

6 As in the previous verse Paul begins with the "sufferings" theme, which he, too, now balances with a "comfort" reference. Paul is the receiver of suffering but also of comfort, which, as he stated in v. 4, is for their benefit. Therefore, "whether" distressed or, in consequence, "whether" comforted, it is for their comfort. That divinely originating comfort energizes patience in the Corinthians as they endure the same sufferings as the apostle. What began as benediction is now merging into explanation as Paul prepares to move to the specific matter for which he is blessing God, his deliverance from Asia (1:8-11).

Each of the contrastive parts of this sentence is introduced by "Whether"[48] and followed by "we are afflicted"/"comforted [it is] for your comfort. . . ."

> Whether we are afflicted
> > [it is] for your comfort and salvation;
> Whether we are comforted
> > [it is] for your comfort
> > > with which you are energized
> in the same sufferings
> > > that
> > we also suffer.

The line of thought is "cause and effect." "Affliction" to *Paul,* as in the first half of the sentence, brings "comfort and salvation" to *them.* But this is because, in his "affliction," Paul would be "comforted" by God, as in the second half of the sentence. Through his ministry to them — now by letter (see particularly 1:8-11; 7:5-16), later in person — Paul would mediate to the Corinthians the "comfort" that he had himself received from God (cf. v. 3).

Although the twin themes of "affliction" and "comfort" dominate this sentence, he also introduces the word "salvation," and with it a strongly eschatological note.[49] Without elaboration upon it, Paul is confident about the Corinthians' *salvation,* about which he also expresses "firm hope" in the next

---

47. This, however, does not exclude the insight of Thrall, 1.110, who points to "the bestowal of inward power in the midst of weakness (cf. 12:7-9)" and "changes in external situation . . . for preliminary victories over the hostile powers might be expected."

48. Gk. εἶτα δέ, though rendered by the NIV as "if," is more properly understood as "whether" (see BDF #454 [3]).

49. See, e.g., 1 Thess 5:8, 9; 1 Cor 5:5; Rom 1:16.

verse.[50] "Salvation" appears in the key passage, "Now is the time of salvation" (6:2), and is one of the critical words found in Isaiah 40–55, a significant ideas-"quarry" for Paul's exposition to the Corinthians.[51] Throughout the letter Paul is enjoining the Corinthians, by their attitudes and actions, to align themselves with God's eschatological action in history in this "the day of salvation" in which he has established a new covenant (3:6-16). While salvation flows from the death and resurrection of Christ, the apostle is the bearer of the gospel of that salvation to the world. Paul is afflicted "for their . . . salvation" in the sense that his vocation as an apostle is wrought with suffering (see further on 4:8-12) and also because they have received the gospel in the context of his sufferings. What they tend to despise in him is part and parcel of what brought life to them.

The "comfort and salvation" from the first half of the sentence are explained in the second by the phrase "comfort, which produces in you patient endurance," or, more literally, "comfort, which is *energized*[52] in, that is, *by*,[53] patient endurance *(hypomonē),*" the divine passive pointing to God as the source of that comfort. In this God's "day of salvation," God brings that salvation by means of the gospel (Rom 1:16) and energizes his servants for that salvation by means of "patient endurance" in the midst of "afflictions." This "patient endurance" is very important in the letter since it is one of the marks by which Paul commends himself as an authentic "minister of God" (6:4) and as an "apostle" of Christ (12:12).

This verse points to the commonality of suffering ("the *same* sufferings"),[54] that is, "the sufferings of Christ" in which the apostle and the wider community of believers participate. These sufferings are in historical continuation of "the sufferings of Christ" (see on v. 5). Paul does not expand upon the sufferings of the Corinthians in this letter, but it is reasonable to locate them at those occasions of social interface between members of the messianic community and the cultic worship and sexual practice of the civic life of Corinth (cf. 6:14–7:1; 12:20-21).[55] The Corinthians would have en-

50. Toward the end of the letter he declares, "Do you not recognize that Jesus Christ is in you. . . ?" (13:5).

51. See Introduction, 46-47.

52. Gk. τῆς ἐνεργουμένης; NIV, "produces." This word is often used by Paul to speak of God's effective "working" in behalf of his people. See K. W. Clark, "ἐνεργέω and καταργέω," 93-101. Although the form could be middle, it is more likely to be (divine) passive, signifying that they are being energized *by* God.

53. Gk. ἐν, here an instrumental use, "by" or "by means of."

54. C. M. Proudfoot, "Realistic Participation," 148, 156, argues for "a realistic union between Paul and the Corinthians in the body of Christ," but of an "inward" kind. But Paul would not need to tell them about it, were this his meaning.

55. Thrall, 1.111, regards it as unlikely that the Corinthians were then suffering persecution, but thinks that it may point to future suffering. The passage suggests that the Corinthians were subject to suffering (through persecution?).

dured similar social pressure as that sustained by other Greek congregations set within Greco-Roman cities such as the Thessalonians, the Philippians, and the Ephesians (see, i.e., Phil 1:27-30; 3:10; 1 Thess 2:14; cf. 1 Cor 16:9).[56]

Paul's "the same sufferings we suffer" may reflect his apologetic sensitivity to Corinthian criticism that he is weak and ineffectual[57] and, on that account, lacking legitimacy as an apostle of Christ. But if, as he reminds them, the Corinthians suffer in the "same" way, then their criticisms of him are implicitly answered. As he suffers, so, too, do they!

It is striking that Paul says that both the "distress" and the "comfort" he has experienced are "for" the Corinthians. Since this is the preposition *(hyper)* chiefly used of Christ's death for his people (5:14, 15 [twice], 21),[58] are we to infer, as some have,[59] that the sufferings of Paul "for" the churches in some way resemble and continue the sufferings of Christ "for" believers?

In this passage the *hyper/*"for" relates only indirectly to Paul's sufferings *for* them.[60] The sufferings bring God's comfort to Paul, and it is

56. Furnish's suggestion, 119-20, based on Phil 3:10-11 and Romans 6, that Christians somehow share these sufferings with Christ in his crucifixion from the time of their baptism into his death only to be comforted by his resurrection, does not appear to be the nuance here. Paul's lists of sufferings throughout the letter are not "mystical" but concrete, arising from the practical difficulty of the self-supporting apostle in a dangerous and hostile world. These he portrays in this passage as "the sufferings of Christ . . . the same sufferings."

57. Cf. 3:6; 10:1, 10; 11:5, 16-12:13 (passim).

58. But see Moule, 65, who takes ὑπέρ in the sense of "with a view to." The preposition ὑπέρ is used in a totally nonvicarious sense in the next verse.

59. See A. T. Hanson, *Paradox,* 141-43. Hanson's observations are to be challenged in two matters: (1) that the apostles' sufferings are redemptive, and (2) that the sufferings of the "apostolic community" (i.e., apostles and people) as a whole are redemptive. In regard to (1), Hanson states: ". . . in Paul's sufferings God in Christ is making contemporary the once-for-all redemptive work of Christ" (141). He goes so far as to say that "Paul regarded the sufferings and possible death of the apostles as possessing an atoning, reconciling, salvific value" (36). But, as argued in the text above, Paul's vicarious *(hyper)* language regarding his sufferings appears to be entirely metaphorical and analogous. As to (2), Hanson states that "the apostolic community . . . continues God's saving activity based on the once-for-all events of Jesus Christ's career" (36). However, Hanson's "apostolic community" reference tends to blur Paul's careful distinction between himself as an apostle and his churches. While Paul is seeking to strengthen the then strained relationships with the Corinthians, he does not fail to emphasize his own unique role as an apostle (see, e.g., 1:1; 2:14–3:6; 5:18–6:13; 10:7-11; 11:1-12; 12:11-13; 13:5-10). To be sure, Paul and the Corinthians participate in the "same sufferings [of Christ]," but he makes only passing reference to *their* sufferings.

60. For Paul's use of ὑπέρ language of himself in relationship to believers in other places, see Eph 3:1; Col 1:24.

this comfort that Paul mediates to the Corinthians and other believers. His sufferings are *for* them only in that sense.[61] Later in the letter he declares, "Death is at work in us, but life is at work in you," and, "All this" [= his sufferings — 4:7-11] is *for* your benefit" (4:12, 15; cf. 12:15).[62] In using this language Paul is recognizing the closeness of the relationships that exist within the people of the new covenant and himself as apostle and evangelist.[63] In the words of his earlier letter, if Paul became "the scum of the earth, the refuse of the world" (1 Cor 4:13), it was for the establishment and nurture of the churches. Apostolic ministry involved great personal cost to Paul. It is only in an analogous, not a vicarious or redemptive sense, however, that Paul uses this *hyper*-language in these passages of his sufferings. The sufferings of Christ for his people have an eternal and uniquely redemptive quality to them; Paul's sufferings "for" people were those of a minister or pastor. The Corinthians and other believers — with their shortcomings and sins — were "written" on Paul's heart (3:3; 6:12; 7:2), bringing him much suffering. Moreover, there is a reciprocity between apostle and people. Paul uses *hyper* not only of his sufferings "for" the Corinthians but also of the Corinthians' prayer, pride, zeal, and devotion "for" him (1:11; 5:12; 7:7, 12). Apostle and people together are "in Christ" corporately the messianic people.

7 Paul now reaches the end point and climax of the benediction. His "hope" for them, that is, for their "comfort and salvation" (v. 6),[64] is "firm." He knows that just as they share with Paul the same sufferings as he does, so, too, they will share with him the same comfort and salvation. He is confident that, as energized by God through patient endurance, they will continue a faithful congregation and community of Christians.

This "hope" is "firm" in the sense that it is assured or guaranteed.[65] Paul does not base his "firm hope" on sentiment or pious wish, but on God.

---

61. Any idea of redemptive or vicarious suffering by the apostle is ruled out by his earlier disclaimer, "Was Paul crucified *for* you?" (1 Cor 1:13). Note that the rhetorical question introduced by μή must be answered in the negative.

62. Gk. τὰ γὰρ πάντα δι᾽ ὑμᾶς, noting that the preposition is not ὑπέρ.

63. In the First Letter, apart from their primary ironic intent, Paul's words as quoted may imply that his various sufferings are for their benefit: *We* are fools . . . weak . . . in disrepute . . . *you* are strong . . . wise . . . in honor (1 Cor 4:10). Such foolishness, however, is διὰ Χριστόν.

64. "Comfort and salvation" (v. 6) repeats more briefly as "comfort" (v. 7b), but "salvation" is also to be understood; both are connected and eschatological gifts of God. Thrall, 1.112, however, locates the hope only in "comfort" and is uncertain whether it is future (citing RSV and JB) or present "comfort" (citing Barrett, Furnish, and Martin).

65. Gk. βεβαία, a commercial term meaning "guaranteed"; cf. the verb βεβαιόω in 1:21 (cf. 1 Cor 1:6, 8).

In v. 22, which should be read alongside v. 7, Paul notes that "it is *God* who makes both us [apostles] and you [Corinthians] *stand firm* in Christ."[66]

Paul "knows that"[67]

> as you are sharers of the sufferings,
> so also [you are sharers] of the comfort.[68]

A dynamic relationship exists between these "sufferings" and this "comfort," both of which the Corinthians and Paul "share." They, the people, and he, the apostle, are "sharers"[69] of the "same sufferings" (i.e., "the sufferings of Christ" — vv. 6, 5) on account of their confession of Christ in a hostile culture, that is, to the "world" alienated from God, in need of "reconciliation" to him (5:19). According to vv. 4-5 the "comfort" is not mediated directly to both parties, but given in the first instance to Paul, that he might "comfort" them, which he does through his ministry, both in person and by letter, including the present letter (see in particular 1:8-11; 7:5-16), and presumably also by his prospective final visit. Because they share with him in both the sufferings of persecution and in the comfort of God in those sufferings, Paul's hope for the survival of the Corinthians as a faithful church is firm.

A similar confidence is expressed in his twofold challenge near the end of the letter, "Examine yourselves . . . test yourselves" (see on 13:5). These are inspired not by doubt, but by his confidence that the Corinthians do, in fact, "hold the faith" and that "Jesus Christ is in [them]."

Paul's experience of suffering and comfort in the course of his ministry is replicated in every generation in the lives of godly missionaries and pastors in their interrelationships with their congregations. While both minister and people suffer as they bear witness to Christ in an alien culture, there remains a distinctive role and therefore a distinctive suffering to the Christian leader. As the comfort of God is experienced in the life of the leader, so it will be passed on through ministry to the people.

---

66. With ὁ δὲ βεβαιῶν ἡμᾶς . . . (1:21) compare ἡ ἐλπὶς ἡμῶν βεβαία (1:7).

67. Strictly speaking, the participle εἰδότες should be εἰδότων, agreeing with the preceding ἡμῶν. The "agreement" is conceptual — in his own mind he had written, "we, too, have hope." The nominative plural, which is taken causally, probably agrees with θλιβόμεθα, παρακαλούμεθα, and πάσχομεν in the previous two verses.

68. The assonant "as . . . so also" (ὡς . . . οὕτως) repeats the "even as . . . so also" (καθὼς . . . οὕτως) of v. 5; the two verses also have "sufferings . . . comfort" respectively in the first and second parts of the sentence.

69. Gk. κοινωνοί.

C. ESCAPE FROM ASIA (1:8-11)

> 8 *We do not want you to be uninformed, brothers, about the hardships we suffered in the province of Asia. We were under great pressure, far beyond our ability to endure, so that we despaired even of life.* 9 *Indeed, in our hearts we felt the sentence of death. But this happened that we might not rely on ourselves but on God, who raises the dead.* 10 *He has delivered us from such a deadly peril,*[1] *and he will deliver us. On him we have set our hope that he will continue to deliver us,*[2] 11 *as you help us*[3] *by your prayers. Then many will give thanks on our behalf for the gracious favor granted us in answer to the prayers of many.*

The main themes of the benediction (vv. 3-7) are carried forward into this passage: (1) the immediate repetition of "affliction" *(thlipsis)* (v. 8), which Paul applies to his near-death experience in Asia. (2) God as Father and comforter in the benediction appears now as deliverer of Paul from the *thlipsis* in Asia. (3) The firm "hope" he expressed for their continuance (v. 7) is repeated as his "hope" that God will deliver him from the perils that await him, ultimately by resurrection from the dead ("our hope," v. 7; "we have set our hope," v. 10).

The Escape from Asia stands in a very important relationship with the benediction. If the benediction (vv. 3-7) gives a generalized expression of Paul's deep gratitude to God for comforting him, this passage immediately gives one of the two concrete matters for which the apostle was at that time "blessing" his God and Father.[4] Paul's description of his plight is quite graphic ("under great pressure, far beyond our ability to endure, so that we despaired even of life. . . . we felt the sentence of death. . . . God . . . delivered us from so deadly a peril" — vv. 8-10). But this serves only to reveal the depth of his gratitude to God for his deliverance.

---

1. The plural form τηλικούτων θανάτων is found in the early p[46], whereas the singular τηλικούτου θανάτου has the support of a majority of MSS, including ℵ A B C D. The former is held to be idiomatically Pauline, the change to the singular thus attributable to a pedantic scribe (only one death is possible). The context of the passage, however, better suits the singular.

2. This, the more difficult reading (ἐρρύσατο . . . ῥύσεται . . . ῥύσεται, "has delivered, will deliver, will deliver"), rather than "has delivered, is delivering, will deliver" — past, present, and future — has the support of most ancient authorities (including p[46] ℵ B).

3. p[46c] ℵ A C D* and the flow of the text support ἡμῶν against p[46c] B D ὑμῶν.

4. The other was the determination of the Corinthians actively to discipline the offender (see 2:5-11; 7:5-12).

As noted above, the benediction (1:3-7) is Paul's christianized adaptation of the first of the Nineteen Benedictions, or perhaps of an earlier form of that benediction. It is noteworthy that the passage now following bears some similarity to the second of the Nineteen Benedictions:

> Lord, you are almighty, making the dead alive. You are mighty to help, sustaining the living out of grace, making the dead alive out of great mercy, supporting those who fall, healing the sick, freeing the captive and keeping your word to them who sleep in the dust. And who is like you, Lord of mighty deeds, and who is comparable to you, King, who causes death and life and help to spring forth? And you are faithful to make the dead alive. Blessed are you, Lord, who makes the dead alive.[5]

The echoes of "God, who raises the dead, [who] has delivered from such a death . . . and will deliver" (vv. 9-10) are striking. It is possible that Paul has deliberately alluded to these consecutive Synagogue Benedictions, (1) on the one hand to establish his continuity with the faith of his fathers, and yet (2) in such a way as to indicate fulfillment — and therefore discontinuity — through the Messiah Jesus, whom God raised from the dead (cf. 4:14).

Immediately picking up the benediction's keyword "affliction" (NIV "hardships"[6]), Paul declares that he wants the Corinthians to know of *the* grave "affliction" that he suffered in Asia. His untranslated "that"[7] serves as a bridge to his amplification of that "affliction," namely, that he had stared death in the face. But the God who raises the dead had delivered him from such a deadly peril. Confident that God would continue to deliver him, he encourages the Corinthians to work together with God in their intercessions for him so that, they, in turn, may offer their thanksgiving to God for his deliverance.

8 The conjunction "for"[8] that occurs almost immediately, and for the first time in 2 Corinthians, ties the passage following (vv. 8-11) with the benediction. It serves as an explanatory bridge from the general reference to "all our afflictions" in the benediction (v. 4) to the specific "our affliction in Asia" in this present passage. Having pointed to this concrete "affliction,"

---

5. Modernized from E. Schürer, *Jewish People,* 2.456.

6. Gk. θλίψις, a keyword in the letter, is used in the singular in a generic sense in the benediction as well as in this verse as the concrete example of "affliction," in the Escape from Asia (1:8). NIV's plural "hardships" misses that point.

7. Gk. ὅτι.

8. Gk. γάρ. Cf. the role of γάρ in 1 Cor 1:11, where it first occurs as in this letter, in the passage immediately following the thanksgiving/benediction, where Paul begins to elaborate upon matters he wishes his readers to understand.

the writer then (1) declares its severity ("we were under great pressure, far beyond our ability to endure"), and (2) discloses his personal reaction to it ("so that we despaired even of life").

"Brothers and sisters,"[9] Paul's term of address for the Corinthians, introduced at the first opportunity after the benediction, reappears in the Farewell (13:11) and, perhaps significantly, on only one other occasion in 2 Corinthians (8:1).

His disclosure formula "we do not want you to be uninformed," relating to "our affliction which occurred in Asia," indicates that new information is about to be given,[10] or, more probably, in this case, a new perspective about the seriousness of that "affliction."[11]

Paul wants the Corinthians to know that:

> we were weighed down far beyond our power
> so that we came to despair of life itself,
>> but we felt within ourselves
>> that we had received the sentence of death.

Paul's repeated use of the first person "we . . . our" serves to convey the intensity and the deeply personal nature of the "affliction in Asia" (see also on v. 9). Perhaps his account of the impact on him of this dreadful experience will mollify the Corinthian criticism that he had not come to them directly from Ephesus (see on vv. 15-17).

Although he gives no further details of this "affliction," Paul is most likely referring to the city-wide commotion in Ephesus[12] that brought to an

---

9. Gk. ἀδελφοί, taken as inclusive for "brothers and sisters." This stands in contrast to the extensive use of the word as applied to the Corinthians in 1 Corinthians. While the brotherhood of the messianic community is affirmed in 2 Corinthians, the emphasis in this letter is rather more *paternal* (6:13: "I speak as to my children"; 11:2: "I betrothed you to one husband"; cf. 12:14) and *authoritative* (10:8: "the authority the Lord gave"; cf. 13:10). This may reflect the strained relationships between Paul and the Corinthians.

10. Following a widespread epistolary tradition. See Rom 1:13; 11:25; 1 Cor 10:1; 1 Thess 4:13; cf. Rom 6:3; 7:1. See further Furnish, 112.

11. Although the Corinthians have not heard of this "affliction" from Paul since it happened after the writing of the "Severe Letter," his lack of details suggests some knowledge in Corinth. It is possible that the Ephesian Christians may have independently reported the incident to their Corinthian brothers and sisters, or that Titus and the Macedonian bearers of 2 Corinthians would tell them on arrival (see on 8:16-24). In our view Paul is here emphasizing the intensity rather than the fact of the "affliction."

12. Since Paul does not specify Ephesus, as he does elsewhere (1 Cor 15:32; 16:8), he could be pointing away from that place in this instance (so Thrall, 1.114). On the other hand, (1) Ephesus was the leading city of the province (despite uncertainty whether Ephesus or Pergamum was the capital), (2) we know that Paul was in Ephesus for a considerable period, and (3) we know of no other location for his ministry in Asia.

end his (two- to three-year) ministry there.[13] While some scholars doubt that Paul is here referring to the disturbance described in Acts 19:23–20:1,[14] the conjunction of sequence and place (Asia . . . Macedonia — 2 Cor 1:8; 2:13; Ephesus . . . Macedonia — Acts 19:1; 20:1) makes it likely that the two passages point to the one event. The silence of the Acts about the gravity of the occasion does not logically require these verses to refer to another incident. Given the well-known passion of the Ephesians for their goddess Artemis, it is likely that the Acts incident was extremely dangerous to Paul.[15]

There are dark hints of trouble in Ephesus even in the First Letter: "a great door for effective work has opened to me, and there are many who *oppose* me"[16] (1 Cor 16:9). Possibly this opposition, expressed metaphorically in Paul's "I fought with wild beasts in Ephesus" in the First Letter,[17] was part of a process that reached its climax in the "*thlipsis* suffered in Asia" mentioned in the Second Letter. The furor in Ephesus, which arose from the silversmith Demetrius's complaint that Paul's message that "man-made gods are not gods at all" (Acts 19:26) had discredited the goddess Artemis, the pride of Asia,[18] and diminished the trade in cult artifacts, is readily identifiable with Paul's grim account in these verses.

Paul's verb "we were weighed down,"[19] which literally means "weighed down" as by ballast in a ship, is qualified by two phrases, "far beyond" and "beyond [our] power,"[20] adding to the severity of the picture. These emotional words, which expand upon the "affliction" in the first part of the verse, are consistent with the more detached narrative of Acts, which, nonetheless, presumes a crisis so serious that Paul could not reappear publicly

---

13. Acts 19:8, 10; 20:31.

14. Various suggestions have been made about the unidentified *thlipsis* in Asia, namely, (1) depression provoked by the Corinthian attitude to him (Rendall), (2) a severe illness (Barrett), (3) an imprisonment (Furnish), (4) severe persecution, perhaps in the form of imprisonment (Thrall), and (5) the commotion inspired by the Ephesian silversmiths. See further Furnish, 122-23, and Thrall 1.115-17, for arguments for and against the above suggestions.

15. See n. 18 below.

16. See further L. J. Kreitzer, "Numismatic Clue," 59-70; R. F. Stoops, "Riot," 73-91.

17. 1 Cor 15:32. So G. D. Fee, *1 Corinthians*, 770-72. See also R. E. Osborne, "Paul and the Wild Beasts," 225-30.

18. Pausanias comments that "all cities recognise Ephesian Artemis, and some persons worship her privately above all the gods. . . ." He speaks of the "renown of the Ephesian Artemis" based on "the size of the temple, which is the largest building in the world, the prosperity of the city of Ephesus, and the distinction which the goddess there enjoys" (*Description of Greece* 4.31.8).

19. Gk. ἐβαρήθημεν. Cf. P.Tebt. 23.5 — καρ' ὑπερβολὴν βεβαρυμμένοι, "weighed down to an extraordinary degree" (cited in Thrall, 1.115 n. 235).

20. Gk. καθ' ὑπερβολὴν ὑπὲρ δύναμιν; NIV, "beyond our ability to endure."

in Ephesus, from which he was probably forced to withdraw in secrecy.[21] The words introduced here — "weighed," "far beyond," "beyond power" — like notes of a signature theme, will be heard throughout the letter.[22]

In consequence of this, or perhaps coincidental with it, Paul "despaired even of life," or, in terms of his more literal physical image, "was barred from life."[23] No stranger to extreme danger (see 11:23-27), the apostle here expresses his exceptionally dire circumstances. He stared death in the face and fully expected it to embrace him, a sentiment he repeats in v. 9a.

In all probability Paul is here reflecting upon the implacable opposition he experienced, whether from pagan culture in general in the various Greco-Roman cities of the region, or from the Artemis cult in particular, whether in Ephesus or elsewhere. He is aware that he has become a notorious figure wherever he is in the Aegean region.

9 Following closely on his despair of *life* (v. 8) Paul begins this verse by referring to the "sentence of *death*" that, he felt within himself, he had received. But this was for a purpose, that he might now rely on the God who raises the dead rather than on himself.

In the first part of v. 9 Paul describes the effect on him of the "affliction . . . in Asia":

. . . even to live,	v. 9
but [we] ourselves [felt[24]] within ourselves	v. 10
[that] we had received	
the sentence of death.	

The adversative "but"[25] sets in contrast the last words in the previous verse, "to *live*,"[26] and the first words in this verse, "the sentence[27] of *death*." The

---

21. Is this a further — though unexpressed — reason for Paul to bypass Ephesus during his final withdrawal? (See Acts 20:16.)

22. See the discussion on 4:7 (ὑπερβολὴ τῆς δυνάμεως); 4:17 (καθ᾽ ὑπερβολὴν εἰς ὑβερβολὴν . . . βάρος); 12:9 (δύναμις ἐν ἀσθενείᾳ).

23. Gk. ἐξαπορηθῆναι = ἐξ + α + πόρος — lit., "without a way," or "to be in despair."

24. The bracketed "[we] . . . [felt] . . . [that]" is not found in the original, but must be understood.

25. Gk. ἀλλά (NIV, "indeed"), which reinforces v. 9a ("sentence of death") as following v. 8b ("despair for life"), as argued by Furnish, 108. This is to be preferred to "but," where v. 9 ("trust . . . in the God who raises the dead") generally contrasts with v. 8 ("despair for life"), as suggested by Thrall, 1.118.

26. The use of τοῦ with the infinitive ζῆν follows an infinitive of hindering, ἐξαπορηθῆναι, giving a concessive sense, "even of life" (Burton, *Syntax,* 401).

27. Gk. ἀπόκριμα, which occurs only here in the NT, is to be taken as "official report" (so BAGD). *Contra* C. J. Hemer, "A Note on 2 Cor 1:9," 103-7, who argues that there is no basis in contemporary usage for a judicial metaphor for a death sentence, but

way to life was barred; death was in prospect. The perfect tense of the verb "we received"[28] probably means both that he felt the impact of that "death sentence" at the time and that he continues to feel it. Metaphorically speaking, he now feels like a condemned man awaiting execution. The powerful effect on Paul's emotions is conveyed by the connecting pronouns, literally, "ourselves within ourselves."[29]

But, as he explains in the second part,[30] the intensity of his suffering had been for a divine purpose, stated negatively, then positively ("that we might not . . . but [that we might]"[31]:

> that we might not rely on ourselves
> but on God
> who raises the dead.

The verb tenses are important. The permanent sense of being under a death sentence (as reflected by the perfect tense "received") is now matched by Paul's continuing confidence (as reflected by the periphrastic perfect) — "that [he] might . . . rely,"[32] not on himself but on God. Henceforth his will be an instinctive and implicit trust in God. Paul was a changed man as a consequence of this experience.

---

that ἀπόκριμα is best understood as a divine answer to the apostle's petition. Such an understanding does not fit easily into the apostle's argument at this point. For argument in favor of "death sentence" see Thrall, 1.118.

28. Gk. ἐσχήκαμεν; NIV, "felt." See discussion in Hughes, 21 n. 16, as to the force of the perfect tense used here, whether it is (1) a true perfect (i.e., with continuing effect) or (2) an aoristic perfect (i.e., a "one off" event). While inclining to (1), Hughes is cautious about a theory associated with it by Allo, that ἐσχήκαμεν points to the onset of a serious and periodically recurring fever, which is to be identified with Paul's "thorn" (12:7-9). Hughes notes that (2) is associated with a particular event (e.g., mob violence as at Lystra — Acts 14:9) that lay in the past, but that could happen again, but from which he is confident of God's deliverance. This verb is used in the same perfect tense in 2:13, where, however, it, too, could be either a "true perfect" or "aoristic." The view taken here is that while Paul has in mind a single event (i.e., the riot in Ephesus), the personal impact of that event on him continued, a nuance well captured by the RSV, "we felt we had received." It was as if a sentence had been passed against him and only awaited execution.

29. Gk. αὐτοὶ ἐν ἑαυτοῖς; NIV, "in our hearts."

30. N. M. Watson, "God Who Raises the Dead," 384-98, regards this as the most critical verse in Paul's writings. Be that as it may, the notion of God raising the dead, metaphorically understood, is a recurring motif within the letter (4:7-16; 7:5-6; 12:7-9).

31. Gk. ἵνα μὴ . . . ἐφ' ἑαυτοῖς ἀλλὰ ἐπὶ τῷ θεῷ . . . ; NIV, "that we might not [rely] on ourselves but on God. . . ."

32. Gk. πεποιθότες ὦμεν, a periphrastic perfect preceded by ἵνα ("to make us rely" — RSV). Whereas the perfect tense ἐσχήκαμεν expresses the ongoing awareness of a "death sentence," the words πεποιθότες ὦμεν express his present and ongoing reliance on God.

It is significant that God, about whom Paul has so much to say in his opening chapter,[33] is here qualified as "[the one] who raises the dead." The power to raise the dead was, and remains, the supreme demonstration of divine power (cf. Heb 11:19; Deut 32:39; LXX 1 Sam 2:6). Paul employs the present tense, "raises,"[34] because while God displayed that irresistible power when he raised Jesus from the dead (cf. 4:14), he continues to display that power — as seen in the deliverance of his servants from impossible circumstances (4:8-9; cf. v. 10) — and he will finally reveal that power in the resurrection of the end time (cf. 4:14; 5:1-10). Raising the dead is no abstract attribute but what God typically does (4:14; Rom 4:17; 2 Kings 5:7). As noted above, it may be no coincidence that, as he adapted the First Synagogue Benediction in his epistolary benediction, he now alludes to the Second Benediction,[35] whose subject is resurrection. Paul's own piety has been shaped by the synagogue, which he is unashamed to betray. Yet, the experience of the Risen One has permanently altered the structure of his thought.

But why, in the context of his reflections on his "affliction . . . in Asia," does he refer to "God who raises the dead"?

10 Paul now states the actions past, immediate future, and ultimate future of "the God who raises the dead." God has delivered Paul (from the affliction in Asia), will deliver him (from other afflictions), and will finally deliver him (from death). The sentence of death had closed Paul off from self-trust in order that he would, instead, trust in God (v. 9), which now, as a concluding remark to vv. 8-10, he expresses as hope in God's ultimate future deliverance.

Thus:

God who		raises the dead,	v. 9
who		delivered us from such a death	
also	will	deliver [us].	v. 10
Upon him		we have set our hope	
[who] will yet[36] deliver		us.[37]	

---

33. See generally F. Young and D. F. Ford, *Meaning*, 234-61.

34. Gk. ἐγείροντι is a "timeless present participle expressing a permanent attribute" (so Plummer, 18). Raising the dead, literally and metaphorically, is what God characteristically does.

35. In support of an allusion here to the Second Benediction see Barrett, 65; Furnish, 114; Thrall, 1.119.

36. The καί serves to underscore ἔτι, "he will *still* deliver."

37. The psalmist's personal reflections on this theme may have informed the apostle. Paul appears to echo the language of LXX Psalm 114 at a number of points: θλίψιν καὶ ὀδύνην εὗρον, "I found *affliction* and sorrow" (v. 3), ὦ κύριε ῥῦσαι τὴν ψυχήν μου, "O Lord, *deliver* my soul" (v. 4), ἐξείλετο τὴν ψυχήν μου ἐκ θανάτου, "he has delivered my soul from *death*" (v. 8). See also LXX Ps 32:19; Job 33:30; Prov 10:2; 23:14.

As with the benediction, where God is the subject of an activity typical to him ("the God of all comfort, who comforts . . ."), so here, "the God who raises the dead" has "delivered" Paul from the "affliction in Asia" (v. 8), that is, "from so great a death."[38] Regrettably we do not have the details as to how Paul was "delivered." Perhaps Priscilla and Aquila, who "risked their lives for [Paul],"[39] were the human instruments of his escape?

Paul's word repetition would have had an imposing aural effect on the original hearers: God "has delivered us, also will deliver us . . . and will yet deliver us."[40] Since by his nature God is and will always be a rescuer or redeemer ("God, who *raises* the dead"[41]), he "also will deliver" Paul from other "afflictions" — as he has recently done in Asia — and he will yet deliver Paul, ultimately, from death itself (see on 4:14; 5:8).

The God who raises the dead at the great eschatological "moments" of Easter and the Parousia is not, in the meantime, remote and removed from his servants in the day-to-day circumstances within mundane history. Chrysostom comments that "when God raises up again a man whose life is despaired of, and who has been brought to the very gates of hell, He shows nothing other than a resurrection, snatching from the very jaws of death the one who had fallen into them."[42] God must be seen as active within history both to "comfort" (v. 4) and to "deliver," overlapping realities to which Paul gives eloquent testimony elsewhere in 2 Corinthians (4:8-10; 11:23-32). Paul's escape from grave danger in Asia dramatizes the experience of God's "comfort," which, through his present words, he is sharing with the Corinthians (see on v. 6).

The note of trust in God rather than in oneself was prominent in the previous verse. Paul now reintroduces the note of "hope" in God (cf. v. 7). Paul has set and continues to "set [his] hope" toward the One who raises the dead, the perfect tense answering the corresponding conviction — also stated

---

38. Gk. τηλικούτου θανάτου — "from so great a death," the more literal translation, is preferable to "from such a deadly peril" (NIV). The adjective τηλικοῦτος is found in the LXX only in 1 Maccabees and, though rare in the NT, is used in contexts of significant events: "such a great salvation" (Heb 2:3); "ships . . . so great" (Jas 3:4); "an earthquake so great" (Rev 16:18). Although p[46] gives τηλικούτων θανάτων, the singular — which is found in most ancient texts — is to be preferred (see n. 1 above). Clearly, it is the *danger* of death that Paul has in mind; otherwise Paul had been miraculously brought back to life. The later reference ἐν θανάτοις πολλάκις (11:23) means "often in danger of death" (cf. RSV, "often near death").

39. Rom 16:4. It is probable that Priscilla and Aquila were in Ephesus at the time (Acts 18:24–19:1).

40. On the textual question, see n. 2 above.

41. Gk. τῷ θεῷ τῷ ἐγείροντι τοὺς νεκρούς (see n. 34).

42. Quoted by Hughes, 21.

in the perfect tense[43] — that he had "received" the death sentence (v. 9). Paul places his confidence in God for the future, both the mundane future and the supramundane or eschatological future. Since the God who raises the dead has delivered Paul in Asia, his servants may both rely on him in the present and hope in him in the future.

11 This verse, which is syntactically awkward,[44] picks up v. 9, where Paul wrote of the divine purpose that he should "not rely on" himself "but on God, who raises the dead." Now, as a complementary statement, he refers to the Corinthians, who are encouraged to pray for him that they, in turn, might give thanks for God's gracious answer to their prayer.

The verse continues from its predecessor:

> and he will deliver us . . .
>> he will yet deliver us,   v. 10
> while you also work together by your intercession for us.

The present participle "working together"[45] establishes a close connection between the powerfully active God who raises the dead, that is, delivers his people (vv. 9-10), and intercessory prayer. Striking is the portrayal of prayer as people "working together with one another," and perhaps also with God,[46] helping Paul, on his behalf.[47] To a divided community, as the Corinthians were, as well as a church somewhat alienated from their apostle, Paul's expression of the Corinthians working together with one another (and with

---

43. Gk. ἐσχήκαμεν . . . ἠλπίκαμεν are both perfect tense — "we received . . . we hope."

44. Many questions arise from this text the answers to which can only be tentative: (1) Does the initial genitive absolute indicate (a) an implied imperative ("you also must help" — RSV), (b) attendant circumstances ("as you help" — TEV), or (c) a conditional ("if you help" — Martin, 14). In terms of the context the genitive absolute appears to be used for (b) attendant circumstances, "as you help." (2) Why does he repeat, and what is the significance of, ἐκ πολλῶν . . . διὰ πολλῶν? The probability is that ἐκ πολλῶν points to "thanksgivings from many," whereas διὰ πολλῶν points to "through the prayers of many." (3) Which verb is to be supplied, and in which tense — present or future — for τὸ εἰς ἡμᾶς χάρισμα? It would make sense for the verb to be "granted" (i.e., ἐχαρίσθη — aorist passive) since it is cognate with χάρισμα. (4) What is the subject of εὐχαριστηθῇ? Most probably it is ἐκ πολλῶν προσώπων, "thanks offered by many people." See further on these questions Furnish, 115.

45. Gk. συνυπουργούντων — συν + ὑπ' + ουργεῖν, "join in serving," "cooperate" — but with whom? With Paul, in his prayers? With the prayers of Christians elsewhere? Or, more probably, with the prayers of one another in Corinth?

46. *Contra* Thrall, 1.122, who sees the Corinthian cooperation in prayer *with Paul* (as paralleled in Rom 15:30).

47. Gk. ὑπέρ occurs twice in v. 11. For discussion of the use of ὑπέρ in the relationship between the apostle and his churches see on vv. 6-7.

God?) for Paul is an encouragement to unity and reconciliation. Moreover, it points to the effectiveness of prayer.

Such intercession is purposeful, as signaled by "that"[48] at the head of the second part of the verse:

> that thanks may be offered
> for [God's] blessing[49]   to us
> through many prayers for us
> from many people.[50]

Flowing from intercession is thanksgiving to God. As "many" pray to the God on whom Paul relies for deliverance, so "many" in turn will "give thanks . . . for the blessing [i.e., ongoing deliverance] granted us." Because God raises the dead and delivers his people, he is to be prayed to for continued deliverance; because he graciously answers prayer for such deliverance, he will be thanked by those who pray. Paul's twofold reference to "many [Corinthians]" acknowledges that, while problems exist between Paul and the Corinthians, a majority have now declared their support for him against his aggressor (2:6; 7:12).

This verse is marked by strong imagery. "Prayers of many [people]" translates an unusual phrase that could also be taken as "the *faces* of many."[51] This may refer to the upturned faces of the people to their heavenly Father, first as they intercede and subsequently as they offer their thanks to him.

Paul's account of the Escape from Asia, which thematically flows on from and completes the Benediction (vv. 3-7) — itself providing the concrete example of God's "comfort" of the afflicted — is now ended, appropriately

48. Gk. ἵνα. So Thrall, 1.123 n. 306, *contra* P. T. O'Brien, *Introductory Thanks-givings,* 253 n. 122, who takes it in a consecutive sense.

49. Gk. τὸ εἰς ἡμᾶς χάρισμα. See G. D. Fee, *Presence,* 286, for the view that χάρισμα means "some concrete expression of grace received. In this case . . . the gracious activity of God on Paul's behalf is rescuing him from a deadly peril from which at one point he did not expect to recover."

50. Cf. Zerwick-Grosvenor's translation: "while you will help by your prayers for us, in order that many thanks will be offered on our behalf by (ἐκ) many persons for the favor (χάρισμα) granted us through (διά — in answer to their prayers?) many."

51. Gk. ἐκ πολλῶν προσώπων, and as so taken by numbers of commentators, including Plummer. In prayer, one "lifts up the face" (Ezra 9:6). Hughes, however, 23 n. 21, rejects the "from many faces" interpretation in favor of "from many persons," noting that MM find that in koine Greek προσώπον is practically equivalent to "person." Thrall, 1.124, rejects προσώπων = (1) "faces," or (2) "people," in favor of (3) actors in a play, each playing his part (as in Epictetus, *Dissertations* 1.29.45, 57). It is questionable, however, whether the former Pharisee would feel free to use the imagery of the theater in so positive a metaphor. On balance, προσώπων, "faces," metaphorically understood, is preferred. On προσώπον see generally K. Berger, *EDNT* 3.180-81.

by intercession and thanksgiving.[52] Such intercession has the declared intention further to bless God for his deliverance of Paul. Having secured his unity
with the Corinthians in God their Father by appeal to shared benediction and
intercession followed by thanksgiving, the apostle now moves into the delicate
matter of their criticisms of him.

II. PERSONAL DEFENSE (1:12–2:13)

Verse 12 marks the beginning of the body of the letter. Having addressed his
readers (1:1-2) and his benediction to God (1:3-7), in particular for his deliverance of Paul from deadly peril in Asia (1:8-11), Paul turns to respond to the
criticisms the Corinthians have against him.

Clearly Paul seeks above all to restore relationships between himself
and the Corinthian church. This he seeks to do by a carefully written defense
of his motives and actions. (1) He assures them in general terms that, based
on the witness of his conscience, he has acted toward them in "holiness
and sincerity" and that in the "day of the Lord Jesus" they will be able to
take pride in him, just as he will take pride in them (1:12-14). (2) He then
rejects the particular criticism that his changed travel plans reveal him to
be a man who makes his plans "lightly" and who had been disingenuous
in his assurances that he would return to them directly (1:15-17). (3) He
affirms that both his gospel word and his personal word are from the God
who is faithful to his promises and loyal to his people, whose ongoing
orientation to Christ he underwrites (1:18-22). (4) Paul now states why he
did not return directly to them: it was to spare them another "Painful Visit"
(1:23–2:1). (5) He had written the letter with "many tears," and, despite
their negative interpretation of it, it was motivated by his love for them, to
the end that when he returned to them it would not be an occasion of further
grief but of mutual joy (2:2-4). (6) Now that the majority have, in response
to the "Severe Letter," punished the offender, they must "forgive and
comfort" the man, as Paul has, lest Satan get the upper hand by using the
dispute as a way to divide the Corinthians from Paul their apostle (2:5-11).
(7) His account of his anguish at not finding Titus in Troas — where he
had come for ministry — and thus not knowing how the Corinthians had
responded to the "Severe Letter," further serves to assure them both of his
love for them and of the seriousness of the present difficulties between
them (2:12-13).

---

52. Thrall, 1.126, notes that in concluding this introductory eulogy, unlike others,
Paul is the one for whom thanks are offered, rather than the one offering thanks to God.

Thus in this section (1:11–2:13) Paul sets forth a sustained and carefully developed defense against their criticisms, which appear to have placed great strains on their relationship. The point is clear: Paul sought to restore good relations between the Corinthians and himself in view of an upcoming visit, which is here hinted at (2:3; see, too, 9:4; chaps. 10–13 passim).

A. PRELIMINARY DEFENSE (1:12-14)

12 *Now this is our boast: Our conscience testifies that we have conducted ourselves in the world, and especially in our relations with you, in the holiness[1] and sincerity that are from God. We have done so not according to worldly wisdom but according to God's grace. 13 For we do not write you anything you cannot read or understand. And I hope that, 14 as you have understood us in part, you will come to understand fully that you can boast of us just as we will boast of you in the day of the Lord Jesus.*

This short passage forms a bridge from the Introduction (vv. 1-11) to Paul's Personal Defense (1:15–2:11) and thus to the main body of the letter. Apologetic in character, it briefly and in general terms raises two connected issues, which will be dealt with immediately and at greater length (1:15–2:11): (1) Paul has, in fact, acted properly toward the Corinthians, and (2) his letters, including the present letter, are written intelligibly. By reestablishing his integrity in their eyes, Paul is seeking to strengthen the bonds of fellowship between himself and this church. So understood, these verses fulfill the function of an Exordium (Introduction) in speeches of that period.[2]

The initial "for" marks the beginning of a new passage.[3] Paul now

---

1. NIV follows $\mathfrak{p}^{46}$ $\aleph$* and many uncials in reading ἁγιότητι ("holiness") against ἁπλότητι ("single-mindedness"), which has less support in $\aleph^2$ D F G lat syr. For further discussion in favor of ἁγιότητι see further M. E. Thrall, "2 Corinthians 1:12," 366-72. In our view, however, ἁπλότητι is probably to be preferred as better suited to the context and, moreover, recurring in 2 Corinthians (8:2; 9:11, 13; 11:3), whereas ἁγιότης is not used elsewhere by Paul. See further Metzger, 575.

2. According to Aristotle, "But in speeches and epic poems the exordia provide a sample of the subject, in order that the hearers may know beforehand what it is about. . . . So then the most essential and special function of the exordium is to make clear what is the end or function of a speech" (*Rhetoric* 3.14.16). Insofar as vv. 12-14 serve as apologetic introduction to chapters 1–7 they may be regarded as an exordium.

3. Gk. γάρ; NIV, "now." This word does not depend on what has preceded; the passage is not structurally tied to the previous verse. Nonetheless, based on Rom 1:17 and Gal 1:10, where Address + another section (thanksgiving in Romans; rebuke in Galatians is followed by γάρ), it appears to be his practice to use γάρ to introduce the main matter

launches into the main argument of the letter. His desire to be reunited spiritually with the Corinthians is contingent on a reinstated confidence in his sincerity on their part. These verses are important, therefore, as a bridge to his *apologia* of his behavior and ministry, which will dominate the first seven chapters of the letter.

Structurally, these verses are "framed" by references to "boasting" at the beginning and at the end (v. 12 and v. 14[4]), a rhetorical device known as *inclusio*. Moreover, in v. 13 two similar-sounding words — *anaginōskete* ("read") and *epiginōskete* ("understand") — are paired.[5] This brief passage, begun and ended by references to "boasting" and with its play on similar-sounding words, would have had a significant impact on its original hearers.

A defensive tone is at once struck by the initial appearance of "boast," one of the word clusters that are critical to this letter. His appeal to "conscience" suggests that he is responding to negative opinion. The recurring "boast" vocabulary signals the degree of criticism and opposition in Corinth as reported to Paul, to which he feels bound to respond.

We see something of Paul's pastoral method here. He makes the (somewhat?) charitable assumption that the Corinthians really do have a true, if partial, appreciation of his character. He then expresses the hope that this understanding will develop further in light of what will be fully revealed to them about him at the "day of the Lord Jesus."

12 Based on his practice in other letters, his use of "for"[6] introduces the major concern of this letter, at least of the first seven chapters, Paul's defense of his past behavior. Thus he begins by assuring them of his spiritual integrity. His "boast," he tells them, *is* the testimony of his conscience, namely, *that* both in general and, more particularly toward them, he has conducted himself in single-mindedness and sincerity and not in worldly wisdom. Apparently Paul gave high priority to the reestablishment of their confidence in his probity.

Paul's "boast" is the affirmative witness of his own conscience, that he has "conducted"[7] himself properly both in the world and toward the

---

of the letter at this point. Less likely, however, is the view of Thrall, 1.129, who sees a possible connection with v. 11, in which Paul can seek the Corinthians' help in prayer because (γάρ) he can boast of his behavior.

4. Gk. ἡ γὰρ καύχησις ἡμῶν αὕτη ἐστίν ("for our boasting is this") . . . ὅτι καύχημα ὑμῶν ἐσμεν καθάπερ καὶ ὑμεῖς ἡμῶν ("because we are your boast, just as you are ours"). Note that καύχησις probably stresses the verbal idea ("boasting"), whereas καύχημα ("boast") is a concrete expression of the former, pointing to the eschatological conclusion in which each is the other's boast.

5. Gk. ἀναγινώσκετε . . . ἐπιγινώσκετε.

6. See preceding n. 3.

7. Gk. ἀνεστράφημεν. Greek usage underlies ἀναστρέφειν (cf. ἀναστροφή — Gal 1:13; Eph 4:22; 1 Tim 4:12). The parallel περιπατέω, "I walk" (4:2; 5:7; 10:2), however, is Hebraic.

Corinthians. This he states positively ("in single-mindedness and godly sincerity"), not negatively ("not in fleshly wisdom").

It seems likely from this verse that (sections of?) the Corinthian church believe Paul has not "conducted" himself properly toward them. Two matters were of concern to them. First, he failed to reappear in Corinth, as he had undertaken to do during his second visit. Instead he sent them a letter (1:17–2:1), a "Severe Letter" at that (7:8-9; 10:9-10). Second, his refusal to accept payment (see on 11:7-9) was thought to have been inspired by "craftiness"; it was not the lofty action it appeared to be (see on 12:19; cf. 4:2; 7:2). These perceptions have given Paul's critics in Corinth high moral ground from which to accuse him.

Paul's word "boast," which frames this passage (cf. v. 14), with its cognates, will occur many times within 2 Corinthians.[8] Though significant elsewhere in his writings, the "boasting" word group in 2 Corinthians exceeds all other Pauline references combined.[9] The word is part of a cultural landscape long forgotten, so that Paul's usage, which is so pointed, must be understood against that culture. Paul use of the "boasting" vocabulary within the letter either (1) mirrors the bragging of others about their achievements (see 11:10–12:9 passim), or (2) discloses his own quite opposite understanding, as seen throughout the letter, which is, essentially, that boasting can only be "in the Lord"[10] (10:17; 11:17; cf. Jer 9:23). As used here by Paul of himself, the word approximates "confidence" or "justifiable pride," rather than some kind of self-glorification. In Paul's appeal to the witness of his conscience he is specifically pointing, at the same time, to consistent observable behavior.

What is Paul's source of his "boasting"? It is, as in the next phrase, "the testimony of our conscience" (NRSV).[11] Paul has heard the charges of

---

8. Within 2 Corinthians the καυχάομαι — καύχησις — καύχημα word group appears at 1:12; 5:12; 7:4, 14; 8:24; 9:2, 3; 10:8, 13, 15, 16, 17; 11:10, 12, 16, 17, 18, 30; 12:1, 5, 6, 9. As is evident from the foregoing list, the "boasting" word group occurs with greatest frequency in chapters 10–13. See J. A. Zmijewski, *EDNT* 2.276-79; R. Bultmann, *TDNT* 3.645-54.

9. The members of the καυχάομαι — καύχησις — καύχημα word group appear only once in the Thessalonian correspondence (1 Thess 2:19), with ten occurrences in 1 Corinthians, so that the roots of Paul's usage should be sought in the First Letter, where it springs in particular from Jer 9:23-24. According to G. D. Fee, *1 Corinthians,* 84, there is "an interesting fluctuation between positive and pejorative usages in Paul; but there is no problem in finding the key. For him the watershed is the grace of God manifested in the death of Jesus for sinners, whereby God has eliminated every human pretension and all self-sufficiency. Every other form of 'boasting' is thereby abolished."

10. Thus argued in J. A. Zmijewski, *EDNT* 2.276-79.

11. Gk. συνείδησις, "conscience." Furnish's definition of συνείδησις as "critical self-evaluation" (127) is to be preferred to the usually negative attitude to oneself, as in C. A. Pierce, *Conscience* (60-65). According to Thrall, 1.131-32, it is "a neutral inward

the Corinthians against him, and his conscience has answered him that their accusations are without foundation. Paul measures his conscience by two criteria, apart from its own testimony: (1) the consciences of others to which he appeals in regard to his behavior (4:2; 5:11), and (2) God, in whose presence[12] he lives (4:2; 8:21; cf. 7:12), before whom[13] he speaks in ministry (2:17; 12:19) and whose potential future witness against him he faces (1:23; 5:10-11).[14] This latter witness, therefore, is not so much psychological as eschatological. Paul knows that in that "day" the Lord Jesus "will expose the secrets of people's hearts," including his own (1 Cor 4:5). Thus Paul's personal vindication of his own conscience is no light matter; it is done in the confidence of God's present and eschatological vindication of him.

The testimony of Paul's conscience is that he has "conducted" himself "in the world" and "especially in relation with you [Corinthians] in . . . single-mindedness and sincerity." As noted above, Paul does not speak of these qualities in the abstract; the Corinthians doubted him in regard to both. His assertion of the former is made against the suspicion that he has acted irresolutely, and of the latter that he has been crafty. By "single-mindedness" Paul means straightforwardness or candor, and by "sincerity,"[15] purity of motive. These attributes are not human virtues that arise from him. Each is "of God," that is, true of God and issuing from God in the course of his service of God.

The change in his plans Paul felt obliged to make suggested to them that he was guided by "fleshly wisdom"[16] rather than, as we infer he claims, the wisdom inspired by the Spirit. He is forced to respond to this kind of charge throughout the letter (1:17; 5:16; 10:2-3[17]). But this is not the case.

---

faculty of judgement . . . which evaluates conduct in an objective way, in accordance with given . . . norms. For Christian believers, these criteria will be Christian." See further *NIDNTT* 1.348-53.

12. Gk. ἐνώπιον.

13. Gk. κατέναντι.

14. On this see D. A. Renwick, *Presence of God,* 41-46.

15. These words appear elsewhere within the letter: ἁπλότης (8:2; 9:11, 13; 11:3) and εἰλικρίνεια (2:17; cf. 1 Cor 5:8). See n. 1 for comment on the alternative reading ἁγιότητι. This reading is preferred on internal grounds by, e.g., Thrall, 1.130-31, who argues that "holiness" is more appropriately "of God" than "single-mindedness." Given the overall context of the letter and the Corinthian suspicion that Paul lacked a sense of purpose, however, "single-mindedness" is the more likely reading.

16. Gk. σοφία σαρκική; NIV, "worldly wisdom." Since it is one of the keywords in 1 Corinthians (chaps. 1 and 2 passim) against them, the Corinthians may be playing σοφία back to the apostle.

17. Paul's consistent refutation of the charge that he has lived according to the σάρξ, "flesh" (see 1:17; 10:3-6; cf. 10:7; 13:3) may imply particular criticism of the church as a whole or of a group within the church (see Introduction, 30-31).

His rejoinder, "but in the grace of God," gives the true source of his decision making. This phrase is common in this letter and summarizes the totality of God's eschatological dealings with his people (cf. 4:15; 6:1; 8:1, 4, 6, 7, 9; 9:8, 14; 12:9; 13:14). Everything planned, and indeed every change of plans, has been in accord with Paul's total involvement in that great plan and activity of God, which he summarizes in the words "the grace of God."

As apostle and minister of the new covenant Paul has exercised himself in the God-given qualities of "single-mindedness and sincerity," and he has made and unmade plans according to "the grace of God." For the moment he will say no more; answers to the Corinthian criticisms will be given at greater length shortly (1:15–2:11).

13-14a The initial "for"[18] indicates that Paul now pursues further the matter of his "conduct" toward them (see v. 12), about which we infer that he feels constrained to defend himself. His immediate "we do not write anything to you" identifies their complaint, namely, that they cannot "understand" what he has written. This accusation denied, he expresses the hope that they will "understand" *him* "fully" instead of only partially.

To this point Paul has written three letters — the "Previous Letter," the canonical 1 Corinthians, and the "Severe Letter."[19] To which letter[20] is he referring? In all probability, they were particularly upset over the "Severe Letter" because (1) it was the most recent letter, (2) *it* came when he had led them to expect that *he* would come, and (3) they thought he had written that letter to "grieve" them (7:8). Their complaint may not be that his letters are hard to understand (cf. 2 Pet 3:16) — that would not warrant his present reply — rather, they may be saying that they are *deliberately* so written, perhaps to intimidate them (cf. 10:9-10). Whatever it was, Paul denies altogether any doubtful motivation in writing to them, whether in any earlier letter or in the present letter. Whether by letter or in person Paul makes it his aim to be readily understandable (cf. 4:2).

Paul connects similar-sounding words, *anaginōskete* and *epiginōskete* (cf. "comprehend" and "apprehend" as a partial analogy in English), as a rhetorical device. If the first, "read," applies to the hearing of what is read *aloud* to the gathered congregation, the second, "understand," applies to its

---

18. Gk. γάρ.

19. 1 Cor 5:9; 2 Cor 1:1; 2:3-4.

20. Paul may be referring to the "Previous Letter," which they had seriously misunderstood (see 1 Cor 5:8-11). Alternatively, they may have been referring to matters in 1 Corinthians, either the question of his payment (1 Cor 9:12-18), or his travel plans (1 Cor 16:5-7), whose clarity has been obscured by Paul's subsequent actions in receiving support from the Macedonians, on the one hand, and by his changed itineraries, on the other (see further Thrall, 1.133-34). In all probability, however, Paul is responding to the Corinthians' criticisms of his most recent correspondence, the "Severe Letter."

acceptance and implementation. (See 3:2, where "known" approximates "understood," being matched with "read," though in reverse order to v. 13.)

Paul will carry forward the idea of "understanding" what he has *written* (v. 13) to understanding *him,* his *own person* (v. 14). Consistent with his positive pastoral method, he expresses the "hope"[21] (i.e., "assured confidence") that, as the Corinthians have "understood" him "in part," they may come to understand him "fully." There may be a double entendre here. "Understand fully"[22] can mean both "in full" (i.e., as distinct from "in part") and, in "the day of the Lord Jesus" (at the "end") as distinct from at present ("now"). Paul's hopes — now strikingly expressed in the first person singular "I"[23] — are that their understanding of him here and now will increasingly be in conformity with the eschatological revelation of his single-mindedness and sincerity in relation to them (cf. 5:10). The present letter is written with that end in mind; no other letter of Paul is so open and personal as this

14b-d   Paul reintroduces "boast" to round off the passage (cf. v. 12), namely, that

> because   we   are   your boast
>   just as you   also will be ours,
>   in the day
>   of the Lord Jesus.

We may see a bold stroke in Paul's words. He began with his own boast, the ground for which was the witness of his conscience. Now he shifts the "boast" from his to *theirs* — and he is it!

With some pathos Paul declares that, although they are dubious of it, he is in fact the basis of their confidence. Their very salvation cannot be separated from his ministry to them. He has evangelized them (1:19), "fathered" them in the gospel (6:13; cf. 1 Cor 4:14-16), and will present them as a matchmaker presents a pure virgin to her husband, Christ (11:2; cf. 12:14-15). They owe their reconciliation with God to Paul's labors (5:18–6:1).

---

21. Gk. ἐλπίζω (cf. 1:7, 10). Cf. S. N. Olson, "Confidence," 282-95, who suggests that Paul's use of such vocabulary is in line with techniques of persuasion used by letter writers of the period. It is more likely, however, that Paul was a pastorally instinctive persuader than a calculated one.

22. Gk. ἕως τέλους ἐπιγνώσεσθε καθὼς καὶ ἐπέγνωτε ἡμᾶς ἀπὸ μέρους (cf. 1 Cor 13:9-12). Scholars are divided as to whether ἕως τέλους is eschatological (i.e., until the Parousia — so, e.g., Barrett 68-69) or comparative ("fully," i.e., in contrast with ἀπὸ μέρους, "partially" — so, e.g., Furnish, 128, who notes an example of this sense in LXX Ps 37:7). While the latter appears more likely, it is quite possible that Paul means both.

23. To this point in the letter Paul has used the plural pronoun. The sudden introduction of the singular here and in 1:15-17, 23; 2:1-11 may express Paul's intensity of feelings.

On the "day of the Lord Jesus" the Corinthians (and others believers) will be the visible object of the apostle's confidence. They will then be — what they already are to him — a tangible evidence of his ministry and a basis for his confidence as an apostle (cf. 1 Cor 9:2; Phil 4:1). But as surely as[24] they will be the basis of *his* confidence on that "day," so let them take "justifiable pride" ("boast") in his ministry to them *now*. They will indeed be proud of him then, among other things because he has conducted himself toward them in "holiness and sincerity . . . from God" (v. 12); so let them be confident in him now (cf. 5:12).

The "day of the Lord Jesus"[25] is an important eschatological "moment" and bears an important relationship with the "day of salvation" (6:2) that it concludes and consummates. The "day of salvation" was begun by the incarnation in history of the grace of God (6:1; cf. 8:9; 1:19), the historical inauguration of the new covenant (3:3-6), and the beginning of the apostolic preaching (1:18-20; 5:18-21; 12:12), accompanied by the gift of the Spirit to the messianic people (1:18-22). The "day of the Lord Jesus" is the occasion of the general resurrection (4:14) and the universal judgment (5:10), and issues in the union between the heavenly Lord and his betrothed, the church (11:2).

B. DEFENSE OF CHANGED TRAVEL PLANS (1:15–2:11)

Paul now expands upon the defense of his behavior offered in general terms in vv. 12-14. Moving to specifics, he first reminds the Corinthians of the revised itinerary he presented to them during the "Painful Visit" (vv. 15-17), to which then, apparently, unlike now, they raised no moral objections. He then goes on to explain why he did not proceed with that visit (1:23–2:2).

He interrupts this explanation, however, to make an important theological statement about the faithfulness of God (vv. 18-22). This digression serves two purposes: (1) It locates the motives and behavior of Paul, the servant of God, within the character and actions of the faithful God whom he serves. There is no hiatus between God and the actions of his "minister" (cf. 6:4). (2) Further, by its focus on the apostolic proclamation as the fulfillment of the divine promises (v. 20), Paul introduces the eschatological thread that he will take up later in the letter (i.e., 3:3-6), reaching its climax in the apostolic call to the Corinthians to be reconciled to God since the "day of salvation" has now come (5:14–6:2). By this striking theological statement, which is able to stand in its own right, the wayward groups within the messianic

---

24. Based on Gk. καθὼς . . . καθάπερ, "just as . . . even as."

25. "The day of the Lord Jesus" is the Christian counterpart of the OT "day of the LORD" (Amos 5:18; Joel 2:1, 11), a day of God's judgment.

community in Corinth are put on notice that they will soon be exhorted to align their attitudes and behavior with God's saving actions.

It seems likely that these verses are classifiable rhetorically as an "apologetic encomium." Whereas vv. 12-14 serve as an exordium in which the chief apologetic elements are introduced, these verses — as in forensic and apologetical political speeches of the period — set out to neutralize suspicion or prejudice.[1] This is not to suggest that Paul had detailed knowledge of the classical manuals of rhetoric. It is quite likely, however, that such conventions were part of a popular culture with which Paul was familiar.

1. Accusations Answered (1:15-17)

> 15 *Because I was confident of this, I planned to visit you first so that you might benefit[2] twice.* 16 *I planned to visit you on my way to Macedonia and to come back to you from Macedonia, and then to have you send me on my way to Judea.* 17 *When I planned this, did I do it lightly? Or do I make my plans in a worldly manner so that in the same breath I say, "Yes, yes" and "No, no"?*[3]

Continuing to use the first person, Paul reminds the Corinthians of the travel plan he gave them when most recently present with them, which he has since changed, necessitating the personal defense he now offers. Paul assures them that the revised plan, to come back to Corinth and from there to go to Macedonia and then return to Corinth, thus bestowing a double benefit on them, was not made lightly or insincerely.

15 Paul's "in *this* confidence," by which he "planned to come to [them] twice," was made in the "hope" (i.e., "expectation") that he was fully their "boast" (i.e., "pride" — vv. 13-14). He made that plan confident in the

---

1. See generally F. Young and D. F. Ford, *Meaning* 37-38. Following his comments on the Exordium, Aristotle remarks, "One way of removing prejudice is to make use of arguments by which one may clear himself from disagreeable suspicion . . ." (*Rhetoric* 3.15.1). This is what Paul seeks to do in 1:15–2:13; 7:5-16. For a persuasive exposition of this view see J. T. Fitzgerald, *Earthen Vessels,* 158-60.

2. Though not without some textual support, χαράν (אᶜ B L P copᵇᵒ) must yield to χάριν (supported by א* A C D G K vg syrᵖ·ʰ copˢᵃ arm) as the preferred reading because of the "more difficult reading" principle. Evidently a scribe sought to soften what might appear as arrogance on Paul's part. See further G. D. Fee, "ΧΑΡΙΣ," 533-38 (cf. n. 7). Furnish, 133, and Thrall, 1.137-38, give comprehensive surveys of the meaning of χάριν. Many translators and commentators render χάριν as "benefit," as in the NIV.

3. 𝔭⁴⁶ 424ᶜ vg Pelagius read simply "Yes and No," leading some to prefer the shorter reading, the longer being explained as assimilation from Matt 5:37; Jas 5:12. More probably, however, the shorter reading is an assimilation from vv. 18-19.

Corinthians' trust in him as their apostle, which, he implies, they do not now have. By inference he is asking: "If you were confident in my spiritual motives for *that* changed itinerary, why do you doubt my motives for *this* changed itinerary?" Is he hinting that their present lack of confidence is because they are peeved that the Macedonians are now getting the same or more attention from him than they?[4]

At the time of writing 1 Corinthians, during the previous calendar year, Paul outlined plans for a visit to Corinth, which would coincide with the Corinthians' finalization of the collection. He would leave Ephesus after Pentecost (spring), travel through Macedonia during summer and fall, and arrive in Corinth, where he would spend the winter before being sent on his way to Jerusalem (1 Cor 16:5-6).

As things turned out, however, he made an unscheduled visit to Corinth beforehand, which resulted in pain for both him and them (2:1). It was probably during this visit that he changed his plans, "confident" of the Corinthians' understanding of him (vv. 14, 15). At the time he felt the Corinthians would place a charitable interpretation on such a change, especially since it would have involved the "double benefit" of two visits to them.

Reflecting on that changed itinerary he now writes, "I planned to visit you first[5] so that you might benefit[6] twice," that is, by a second visit, on his return to them from Macedonia (as in v. 16). That plan deliberately provided for two visits, the implication being that the second visit would be for a longer period. Paul confidently and objectively believed his visits would bring spiritual benefits to the Corinthians[7] (as he likewise expected of his coming to Rome — see Rom 1:11; 15:29). It is because he expects his visits to bring blessing that he can rebut the accusation of making his plans for "worldly" motives (vv. 12, 17).

16 Paul now rehearses[8] the itinerary of the second plan. Corinth was to have been the pivot. He would, literally, "pass *through you* to

---

4. See 9:2-4; 11:9.

5. Gk. πρότερον, "first," probably qualifies "come" (so most commentators) rather than "planned." The next verse supports this option.

6. See n. 2 above on the preferred reading, χάριν over χαράν.

7. *Contra* G. D. Fee, "ΧΑΡΙΣ," 533-38, who sees the Corinthians as the sending church in each case, with the visits providing them with opportunities to show him kindness during these visits. In his view the "Painful Visit" itself became the first part of the revised plan. This would depend on the view that Paul then traveled on from Corinth to Macedonia rather than to Ephesus directly.

8. According to Furnish, 132-33, the καί introducing the verse is epexegetic, explaining by what follows the first and second benefit of the previous verse. This is preferred to Thrall, 1.139 n. 81, who regards the four infinitives of vv. 15-16 as dependent on ἐβουλόμην in v. 15.

Macedonia,[9] come again *to you* from Macedonia and be sent *by you*[10] to Judea."[11] Apparently this plan brought him pleasure in prospect, suggesting the anticipation of a profitable time among them. Paul is taking the opportunity to remind the Corinthians how central *("through you . . . to you . . . by you")* they had been in that plan,[12] the inference being that their failure to see him on the two occasions as planned was, in the final analysis, their fault and thus their loss (cf. 1:23; 2:1).

In this revised plan, as briefly summarized here, there is no mention of Paul's return to Ephesus, which in our view he did, with the full knowledge of the Corinthians,[13] and by the most direct route. After all, the visit from Ephesus to Corinth was unscheduled. Presumably he would need to return to the Asian metropolis before making his departure. On his return to Ephesus he faced the ordeal mentioned earlier (vv. 8-11), and, for reasons he will soon give (1:24–2:2), he abandoned the revised plan in favor of the original itinerary (1 Cor 16:5-6).[14]

17 Paul sharpens his defense. He had declared his desire to come to them first so as to visit them twice (vv. 15-16), a thought that he picks up in

---

9. Paul doubtless wished to revisit and consolidate the Macedonian congregations at Philippi, Thessalonica, and Beroea(?), which were located on (or near) the Egnatian Way. Possibly he wished to evangelize from them in a westerly direction toward Illyricum (cf. Rom 15:19). At the time he made those plans he had not expected the Macedonians to participate in the collection (cf. 2 Cor 8:1-4).

10. Gk. ὑφ' ὑμῶν προπεμφθῆναι; NIV, "have you send [me]," or, more literally, "to be sent on by you." This is probably a technical term for missionary "sending," perhaps involving last-minute hospitality, escort to shipping, letters of recommendation, and so on. (cf. 1 Cor 16:6; Tit 3:13; 3 John 6-8). Thrall's assertion (1.140) that Paul expected financial assistance on these various departures from Corinth depends on a technical meaning for προπεμφθῆναι along those lines (so BAGD προπέμπω). But given Paul's resolute refusal to accept money from the Corinthians, this is to be doubted. Hospitality and other help, however, may have been implied.

11. Cf. 1 Cor 16:3. In effect Paul would be sent off to Jerusalem, the spiritual capital of Judaea and the home of the mother church (cf. Gal 4:25-26). Caesarea Maritima, not Jerusalem, was at that time the political capital of Judaea. Paul's return to Judaea with the collection was preliminary to his visit to Rome, now made possible by the death of Claudius (A.D. 54), who had previously expelled Jews from Italy in A.D. 49.

12. Underlying Paul's emphasis on the central place of Corinth in those plans may have been his sensitivity to a long-standing Corinthian resentment of his cordial relationships with the Macedonian churches, especially over the fact that he was prepared to accept the gifts of the Macedonians but not those of the Corinthians (11:7-11; cf. 1 Cor 9:3-18).

13. To suggest that Paul purported to go to Macedonia with a view to returning directly to Corinth, without revealing his real intention to return to Ephesus, would have laid him open to the charge of outright duplicity. Presently, however, he is answering charges of unreliability and lighthearted and "fleshly" decision making (vv. 12, 17).

14. See Introduction, 12-15.

his initial, "therefore,[15] wishing this" (i.e., to come twice to them). Now he asks two pointed rhetorical questions,[16] each demanding a negative[17] answer.

They did not object then to a changed plan, presumably since it was to their advantage (see on v. 16). That they *now* make a series of complaints — as mirrored by his rhetorical questions — only highlights their moral inconsistency. Some apparently complain that he made his plans "lightly"[18] (impulsively?), others that he made them "according to the flesh"[19] — in other words, while his words[20] at the time were "Yes, yes" ("I am coming back soon"), he really meant "No, no"[21] ("I am not coming back until much later").

This last accusation, when considered alongside the suspicion that Paul wrote his letters for devious reasons (v. 13), suggests that these accusers had quite negative attitudes toward the apostle. Paul rejects outright the negative interpretations of his conduct implied by his answers in this verse. His rejection may be seen (1) by the assertiveness of the fourfold repetition of the personal pronoun "I," and (2) by a grammatical structuring of his question that allows only a negative answer to both questions.[22] His earlier protest stands; his

15. Gk. οὖν.

16. Rhetorical questions are common in this letter (see 2:2, 16b; 3:1a, b, 7-8; 1:7, 11a, 22a, c, e, 23a, 29a, b; 12:13a, 15b, 18b, c, d, 19a; 13:5c).

17. Both questions are introduced by the initial μήτι ἄρα, which Hughes, 34 n. 13, translates, "Did I really show fickleness? Of course not! Do I really purpose according to the flesh? Of course not!"

18. Gk. τῇ ἐλαφρίᾳ. Thrall, 1.140, draws attention to the definite article as pointing to something both parties know about. They say that he is unreliable and he knows that they are saying it!

19. Gk. κατὰ σάρκα; NIV, "in a worldly manner." However, κατὰ σάρκα (cf. ἐν σοφίᾳ σαρκικῇ — 1:12) implies behavior independent of the Spirit of God, that is, by purely human standards. The clause βουλεύομαι (NIV, "did I make my plans") κατὰ σάρκα could point to an accusation of (1) obstinacy, or more probably of (2) momentary expediency. In support of this, rather than of obstinacy, is their accusation of lack of single-mindedness and sincerity (v. 12), and of acting lightly and saying "Yes" one moment and "No" the next. For extended discussion favoring (2), see Thrall, 1.140-42.

20. Verse 17b is difficult to translate, being cast in few words. The ἵνα in ἃ βουλεύομαι κατὰ σάρκα βουλεύομαι ἵνα we take to be epexegetic ("what I planned I planned according to the flesh, *namely* . . ."). His παρ' ἐμοί probably means, "my words," i.e., "Yes, yes . . . No, no." The article τό before both ναὶ ναί and οὺ οὐ probably reproduces the actual words of those Corinthians who spoke them. However, F. Young, "Note on 2 Cor 1:17b," 404-15, argues that Paul is saying, rather, that the change of plans did not rest on himself (κατὰ σάρκα), but on God. Young renders v. 17b as: "Or do I make my plans at the human level so that 'yes' and 'no' rests in my hands?" In consequence Young dismisses the view of most scholars that vv. 18-22 are a digression.

21. To be noted is Jesus' warning against oath taking: ἔστω δὲ ὁ λόγος ὑμῶν ναὶ ναί, οὺ οὐ (Matt 5:37). For the view — improbable in our opinion — that Paul's words rest on a dominical oracle, see D. Wenham, "2 Cor 1:17, 18," 271-80.

22. The interrogative μήτι expects the answer, "No."

conscience bears witness to him that, by the grace of God, he has behaved in single-mindedness and sincerity toward them, not in *fleshly* wisdom but "according to God's grace" (see on v. 12). In making and unmaking his plans, as dictated by changing circumstances, he acts consistently with the God in whose overarching purposes he has been caught up.

2. Theological Basis of Paul's Integrity (1:18-22)

> 18 *But as surely as God is faithful, our message to you is not "Yes" and "No." 19 For the Son of God, Jesus Christ, who was preached among you by me and Silas and Timothy, was not "Yes" and "No," but in him it has always been "Yes." 20 For no matter how many promises God has made, they are "Yes" in Christ. And so through him the "Amen" is spoken by us to the glory of God. 21 Now it is God who makes both us and you stand firm in Christ. He anointed us, 22 set his seal of ownership on us, and put his Spirit in our hearts as a deposit, guaranteeing what is to come.*

No, despite their criticisms, as we infer them to be, he has not made his plans "lightly," nor "according to the flesh" (v. 17). In vv. 18-22 the apostle continues to defend himself against their objections to him, but now indirectly, by means of an apparent theological digression, asserting the faithfulness of God. This faithfulness of God is seen (1) in the unambiguous Son of God (God's eternal "Yes") as proclaimed by Paul (vv. 18-19), (2) in the fulfillment of the promises of God (v. 20), and (3) to his people by his ongoing guarantee of their Christward focus, in consequence of his gift to them of the Spirit (vv. 21-22).

Critical to this passage is Paul's play on the word "word" *(logos)*. Paul proclaimed that "word" — the Son of God, Jesus Christ — in Corinth, as from God, who is faithful (vv. 18-19). Their very existence came through that trustworthy "word" spoken by Paul, which, as they received it, brought the Spirit of God to them. His personal "word" in regard to his itinerary is no less trustworthy. By this Paul must mean trustworthy in its *motivation* and *intent;* strictly speaking, on the face of it, he did not fulfill it. (Nonetheless, he did fulfill the initial travel plan.)

Paul has seized the opportunity both to defend his integrity and to teach about matters on which he will elaborate further later in the letter: (1) the proclamation of Christ in fulfillment of the "promises" of God;[1] (2) God's gift of the Spirit to those who have receptively heard that word;[2] and (3) God's

---

1. Cf. 4:5; 11:2-4.
2. Cf. 3:3, 6; 11:4.

guarantee of the ongoing Christward orientation — together, that is, Paul's and theirs — of a Spirit-"christed" people.[3] Significantly, Paul will point to the Corinthians' experience of "the Spirit of the living God" (3:3) to legitimate himself as a "minister of the new covenant" (3:6; cf. 13:5). This short passage lays the foundation for that important theological apologetic for Paul's ministry.

18 Paul interrupts,[4] or, rather, *apparently* interrupts,[5] his defense against the charge of making his plans "lightly" or "according to the flesh" (v. 17) with the assertion "God is faithful."[6] This is followed by the statement "our word to you is not 'Yes' and 'No.'" This format — an assertion about God followed by Paul's assurance about his own integrity — possibly represents an oath formula.[7] This is the solemn witness of his conscience regarding the probity of his conduct toward them (v. 12).

Paul's use of *logos* ("word")[8] is carefully chosen, referring both to that "word" which was "preached"[9] in Corinth (v. 19) and to his personal "word" as given to the Corinthians in the now defunct revised travel plan (vv. 15-16). Paul, the minister of the God who is "faithful," asserts that his "word" — whether his kerygmatic "word" or his personal "word" — has not been "lightly" spoken, is not in the same breath "Yes" and "No."

In particular, the kerygmatic word — "the Son of God, Jesus Christ" (v. 19) — expresses the great truth, "God is faithful"; the many promises made under the old covenant are now seen to have been kept in the apostolic preaching of the Son of God (v. 20). The faithfulness of God is to be seen also in the consequences of the preaching of the Son of God, namely: (1) in God's gift of the Spirit to those who, like the Corinthians, have received that "word," and, in consequence, (2) in his guarantee of their ongoing Christward focus (vv. 21-22).

If the kerygmatic "word" was true to the God who is faithful to his promises and loyal to his covenant people, so, too, is Paul's personal "word" about his travel plans.[10] Paul, like the God with whom he is in partnership

---

3. Cf. 5:5.

4. By means of the Greek particle δέ.

5. This apparent digression actually serves to undergird Paul's personal apologetic, which he began in 1:12.

6. Gk. πιστὸς . . . ὁ θεός. A statement often made by Paul (1 Cor 1:9; 10:13; cf. 1 Thess 5:24; 2 Thess 3:3); see, too, e.g., Isa 49:7; Ps 89:38; Prov 14:5, 25.

7. So Furnish, 135, based on the statement about God followed by ὅτι, which is followed by a statement about Paul's integrity; see also Thrall, 1.143-44. It is less likely to be causal; "our word to you is not 'Yes and No'" *because* (ὅτι) "God is faithful."

8. Gk. λόγος; NIV, "message."

9. Gk. ὁ . . . κηρυχθείς. Elsewhere Paul uses λόγος for missionary preaching (1 Thess 1:6; 2:13; 1 Cor 1:18; 2:4).

10. An argument from the greater to the lesser. So W. C. van Unnik, "Reisepläne und Amen-sagen," 218. Paul did not, as a matter of fact, honor the promise in the terms in which he made it, for reasons given in 1:23–2:1. His bold identification of the word of

and whose spokesman he is (5:20–6:1), is faithful. He did not, as a matter of fact, say to the Corinthians, "Yes, I am coming back soon," when he really meant, "No, I am coming back later." He changed those plans, and for good reasons; but he did not lie when he was present with them in Corinth.

19 Paul has declared God to be "faithful" and solemnly asserted that his own "word" is not "Yes" and "No" (v. 18). On that basis — hence the connective "for"[11] — Paul asserts that the "word," "the Son of God, Jesus Christ," who was proclaimed by Paul and his associates in Corinth, was not ambiguous ("Yes" *and* "No").[12] On the contrary,[13] Christ — incarnate and exalted — is God's unambiguous and unretracted "Yes." Thus Paul picks up their criticism of him (his "word" is at the same time "Yes" and "No") and turns it into a powerful christological affirmation, namely, that Jesus Christ, the Son of God, stands as the abiding "Yes" of God.

> For
>
>> the Son of God, Jesus Christ,
>> who was proclaimed
>>
>>> among you
>>> through us
>>> through me, Silas and Timothy
>>>> was not "Yes and No"
>
>> but in him
>>
>>> is always "Yes."

We infer, then, that Paul's kerygmatic "word" and his personal "word" are inseparable; both express the faithfulness of God, whose minister Paul is. This is a bold claim, but it merely expresses in a different way his conviction that his apostleship is precisely in keeping with God's will (1:1; cf. 5:20–6:2).

The significance of that message is conveyed by the solemn verb "preached," or, better, "proclaimed as by a herald." Paul's choice of the

---

God with his own word must be seen as limited to his sincere *intention* as stated at that time and to his ultimate return, which, as it happened, was delayed (probably by an unforeseen dramatic turn of events in Ephesus). As God is not double-minded but single-minded in the making of his promises, so, too, is his servant Paul, despite the accusations of (some of?) the Corinthians.

11. Gk. γάρ.

12. The word order is significant: (1) The initial "of God . . . the Son" picks up the initial "God is faithful" of the previous verse; (2) "who among you through us" picks up "our word to you" of the previous verse. Paul (and his coworkers) as heralds of the Son of God are fundamental in the purposes of the God who is faithful.

13. Gk. ἀλλά; NIV, "but."

passive voice "preached"[14] may be deliberate in the present context. The message of the Son of God was, to be sure, preached by Paul, Silas, and Timothy; but Paul may be strongly implying here (as by the divine passive) that, in ultimate terms, the message was preached by God. In this case the God who preaches the gospel by Paul is also active in Paul's words regarding the recently made travel arrangements. From Paul's viewpoint all his words, whether preaching Christ or in ordinary conversation, are spoken in the presence of God (see on v. 12).

Here is a historical[15] reminiscence about the foundations of the church in the Achaian capital: this preaching in Corinth six years earlier was done "among you" and it was done "by us,"[16] that is, by Paul, Silas,[17] and Timothy[18] (Acts 18:1-11).

It was no inconsequential message indifferently delivered, or "peddled," as by his opponents (2:17; cf. 4:2). That message, which he now rehearses in summary form, focused on the "the Son of God, Jesus Christ" (cf. the intruders' "other" Jesus — 11:4).[19]

In his letters Paul refers to Jesus as the "Son of God" on five occasions, as "the Son" once, and as "his [God's] Son" eleven times.[20] (But, according to Thrall,[21] "The title ["the Son of God"] has more meaning than the numerical evidences might imply.")

---

14. Gk. κηρύχθεις, from κηρύσσω, "proclaim" (1:19; 4:5; 11:4). τὸ κήρυγμα, "the proclamation," and ὁ κήρυξ, "the proclaimer," are very important within the NT in regard to spreading the word of God, first by Jesus and then by the apostles. For the associations of the word group with the public proclamations of rulers from Greek classical times, see G. Friedrich, *TDNT* 3.683-94.

15. Cf. 1 Cor 15:1-2.

16. Gk. ἐν ὑμῖν δι' ἡμῶν. The NIV does not translate δι' ἡμῶν, "through us." Paul's words are immediately amplified by "through me and Silas and Timothy." Clearly the first person plural "us" in this verse points to the three preachers in Corinth. See on 1:1 for Paul's use of "we"/"us" throughout the the letter.

17. Silas (Aramaic for Hebrew "Saul," known also by the Latinized "Silvanus"). This is, doubtless, the Christian prophet from Jerusalem (Acts 15:22, 27, 32) who became the missionary companion of Paul in Syria, Asia Minor, Macedonia, and Achaia (Acts 15:40–18:5) and co-sender of 1 and 2 Thessalonians. He is probably the same person referred to by Peter, perhaps as his amanuensis (1 Pet 5:12).

18. Note the same sequence of names as in 1 Thess 1:1; 2 Thess 1:1. Seniority in the Lord is probably implied by the word order. Cf. Gal 2:1, 9; Acts 13:2, 13.

19. It may be significant that the first sentence or "title" of (probably) the first written Gospel, the Gospel of Mark, refers to "the gospel of Jesus Christ, the Son of God."

20. Only here does Paul refer to "the Son of God, Jesus Christ," and only twice to "the Son of God" (Rom 1:4; Gal 4:4), both of which appear to be repetitions of formulas. See further M. Hengel, *Son of God,* 7-15.

21. Thrall, 1.146. Thrall notes that it is as the Son of God that Christ performs God's salvific purposes. She also observes "an implicit likeness or even identity of

At the same time that Paul and his companions were proclaiming Jesus as "the Son of God" in Corinth, they were writing from Corinth to the Thessalonians that Jesus was "his [God's] Son" (1 Thess 1:1, 10). It is evident that such preaching of "the Son of God" did not begin in the fifties in Macedonia and Achaia. In the late thirties Paul was proclaiming the Son of God ("his Son") in the regions of Cilicia, something that came to the surprised attention of the churches in Judaea (Gal 1:16, 21-23). Earlier still he preached the Son of God in Damascus (Acts 9:20; cf. Gal 1:16). Against those who argue that the "Son of God" was a later Hellenistic adaptation of more Semitic modes of referring to Jesus, it should be noted that from the time of his conversion, that is, from the mid-thirties,[22] Saul proclaimed Jesus as "the Son of God."[23]

Nonetheless, "Son of God" was used within Judaism at this time as a way of referring to the Messiah.[24] It is evident that, while for Jesus this implied his messianic status, he used it more particularly to refer to his filial relationship with God.[25] Jesus addressed God as "*Abba,* Father" and referred to himself as "*the* Son" (Mark 13:32; 14:36; cf. 12:6).[26] In a notable statement later in the letter, Paul will speak of the incarnation of the preexistent one, in a manner consistent with his filial relationship with God (see on 8:9).

Paul's denial of his ambiguity (his "word" is "Yes" and "No") leads him powerfully to affirm the Son of God as God's everlasting and unretracted "Yes." Hints of incarnation may be found in the verbs used of the Son of God in the present verse. The Son of God, who had been proclaimed in Corinth, literally, "did not become[27] 'Yes' and 'No,' " but, putting it positively, "became," that is, "came." The use here of the aorist tense (completed action) pinpoints the historical intervention of God in Christ, the coming, death, and resurrection of Christ. This "coming" was not ambiguous or lacking in purpose ("Yes" and "No" at the same time), but deliberate and intentional, for the reconciliation of lost humankind to God (5:18-19, 21).

---

character" between God and the Son of God. God is faithful to his promises (v. 18); Christ puts into effect the divine promises.

22. Based on the calculation of the date of the first Easter as A.D. 33, as in C. J. Humphreys and W. G. Waddington, "Dating the Crucifixion," 743-46. See M. Hengel, *Between Jesus and Paul,* 30-48, for arguments in favor of the brevity of time between the first Easter and the conversion of Saul of Tarsus. Hengel, however, argues for A.D. 30 as the date of the first Easter.

23. See L. Hurtado, "Son of God," *DPL,* 900-906.

24. See Mark 14:61; Matt 16:16.

25. See M. Hengel, *Son of God,* 41-51.

26. See I. H. Marshall, *Christology,* 111-25; J. H. Charlesworth, *Jesus within Judaism,* 131ff.; S. Kim, *Son of Man,* 74-81.

27. Gk. ἐγένετο; NIV, "was." Cf. the aorist tense ἐγένετο, "became," in John 1:14: ὁ λόγος σὰρξ ἐγένετο.

Moreover, God has not had second thoughts about or gone back on what he has done in Christ. Christ "has become," that is, he remains,[28] God's "Yes." This points to his ongoing life as the exalted Lord who continues forever to bear the affirmation of God. Implicit in this verse is a broad christological statement. The Son of God became, first, by incarnation from preexistence the historic Jesus of Nazareth (8:9; cf. 10:1), the unambiguous instrument of divine reconciliation and righteousness (cf. 5:18-21), then, by exaltation to his now eternal status, the heavenly Lord who will be the judge of all (cf. 1:3, 14; 4:5; 5:10; 8:5).

Paul's preaching of the Son of God in Corinth expressed the consistency of the divine purpose,[29] but so, too, did his own "word" regarding his travel arrangements.

20 A further amplification[30] of the statement that "God is faithful" (v. 18) — and by implication that Paul also[31] is faithful — is now given. The divine fidelity is demonstrated in "the Son of God . . . preached" as the *fulfillment of promises* made under the old covenant.[32] "No matter how many[33] promises God has made," in particular to Abraham,[34] thereby establishing a pattern of prophetic promise that became the characteristic of the old covenant, "they are 'Yes' in Christ."

Few OT passages sum up God's faithfulness to his word so clearly as

> God is not a man, that he should lie,
>> nor a son of man, that he should change his mind.
> Does he speak and then not act?
> Does he promise and not fulfill? (Num 23:19)

28. Gk. γέγονεν (perfect tense); NIV, "has always been." To be noted is the force of the tenses of the verb γίνομαι, "I become," used in v. 19. Through incarnation/death Christ *"became"* (ἐγένετο — aorist; cf. "he was *made* sin" — 5:21; "he *became* poor" — 8:9), whereas through exaltation he *"has become* [Lord]" (γέγονεν — perfect).

29. Is this why Paul mentions himself, Silas, and Timothy as three witnesses to the reliability of the message, fulfilling OT legal requirements (Num 35:30; Deut 17:6; 19:15).

30. Gk. γάρ, as in v. 19. The entire verse is elliptical; neither half has a verb.

31. This is signaled by his δι' ἡμῶν. God is faithful, "through us" (v. 19), i.e., through our preaching of the One in whom God's purposes are reliably fulfilled and in whom they are not subsequently retracted. The apostolic activity is a sign of God's faithfulness.

32. E.g., Christ is the promised descendant of David (Rom 1:3; cf. Isa 11:1); he is the deliverer from Zion (Rom 11:26; cf. Isa 59:20); he is the seed of Abraham (Gal 3:16; Gen 12:7; 13:15; 17:7-8). According to Paul, he is the "Last Adam" (1 Cor 15:45) and the goal and end point of the Law (Rom 10:4).

33. Gk. ὅσαι.

34. See Gal 3:21 for the parallel "promises of God." In Rom 4:14 and Gal 3:17, 18 (but see 3:16, 21) the singular "promise" is also used, though chiefly directed to Abraham.

In Paul's brief statement set out in v. 19 he allows us to see the panorama of God's eschatological purposes expressed first as his word of promise and then by his "Yes" as the Son of God proclaimed by the apostles. Not only do the Corinthians need to be reminded that Paul is, like the God he serves, faithful to his promises, but sections of the Corinthian church need to return to the pathway of God's now-revealed eschatological purpose from which in recent days they have strayed ("you bear with . . . someone who preaches *another* Jesus").[35]

The prepositional phrases "in him" and "through him" point to the significance of Christ to the apostle Paul. Christ is the fulfillment of all the promises of God made under the old covenant, and thus of that covenant in its entirety; no promise remains unfulfilled. "In him" God has spoken his "Yes." His fulfillment is absolute, dimming whatever glory there had been in the old covenant (3:10). Those who are "toward" him have the Spirit (vv. 21-22); those who are "in him" have "become the righteousness of God" (5:21), and are "the new creation" (5:17). Now that God has pronounced his affirmation in Christ incarnate and exalted there can be no going back to the covenant that promised him, as the peddlers seek to do (3:7-11).

If Christ is God's "Yes," he is the church's "Amen," since "through him" the church prays to and praises God. Again we see a connection between the church's praise of God and apostolic proclamation (see on v. 3).[36] The words of the church's worship echo back to God that gospel word through which the church has its existence. Speaking for God and from God the apostle proclaimed the Son of God (cf. 2:12, 19; 4:5; 5:19-20; 6:1, 7; 11:7; 12:19), God's great "Yes"; the messianic assembly, gathered by that word, answers with its "Amen,"[37] to the glory of God[38] through Jesus Christ (cf. 1 Cor 14:16). Both from God's side and ours everything is centered on Jesus Christ; for this reason the prepositions *in* and *through* are important. God has kept his promises *in* Christ and we say the "Amen" to God *through* Jesus Christ.

---

35. Cf. 11:3-4; 12:21–13:5.

36. See R. P. Martin, *Spirit and the Congregation,* 71.

37. The Hebrew root *'mn,* often used to conclude a doxology in the OT (e.g., 1 Chron 16:36; Neh 8:6); see H. Schlier, *TDNT* 1.335-38. Liturgically the churches may have concluded prayer with "through Christ Jesus thy Son, Amen" (so C. F. D. Moule, *Phenomenon,* 54). It is quite likely that Jesus' frequent use of "Amen" to introduce weighty utterances — almost as the equivalent to an oath — has influenced the use of the liturgical "Amen" in the early churches (Moule, 68). According to Rev 3:14, Jesus is "the Amen, the faithful and true witness." The "Amen" was uttered in synagogue worship after benedictions, though not as a conclusion to prayers. See G. Delling, *Worship,* 71-75.

38. Gk. τῷ θεῷ πρὸς δόξαν, lit. "to God for glory." Possibly this is a further liturgical interjection following the "Amen." For parallel doxologies see Gal 1:5; Phil 4:20; 1 Tim 1:17; 2 Tim 4:18; Heb 13:21; 1 Pet 4:11; 2 Pet 3:18; Jude 25; Rev 1:6; 7:12.

Each of the extant letters to the Corinthians contains an echo of Paul's mission preaching in Corinth in *c.* A.D. 50. It is significant that in both cases the message of Jesus Christ is seen to be in fulfillment of the OT scriptures/promises. In the former letter, Paul repeats a received tradition that he handed on to the Corinthians, that Christ died for our sins, that he was buried, that he was raised the third day, and that he appeared alive on a number of occasions (1 Cor 15:3-8). In the latter, the proclamation was the Son of God, Jesus Christ.[39] That Paul can remind the readers of two versions of apostolic preaching should caution us that the message had more facets to it than some simple reconstructions suggest.

In short, Paul has argued in vv. 18-20 that as God is faithful, so, too, is Paul's "word." His personal "word" is subsumed within his kerygmatic "word." God's faithfulness is to be seen (1) in the Son of God preached in Corinth as God's unambiguous, unretracted, and now-eternal "Yes," and (2) in the fact of all the promises of God having been kept in the Son of God, as proclaimed by the apostles. Likewise "faithful" is the "word" of Paul, the minister of the God who speaks unambiguously (cf. 1:13) and who keeps his promises. Their very existence is predicated on it.

21-22 Paul continues the theme of faithfulness — God's faithfulness, in the first instance — but also his own, which he is defending in these verses.[40] The God who does not change his mind (v. 19) and who is faithful to his promises (v. 20), as seen in the apostolic proclamation of the Son of God in fulfillment of the promises of God, is also loyal to his covenant people.[41] The faithful God "makes both us [i.e., Paul, Silas, and Timothy] and you [i.e., the Corinthians] stand firm in Christ" (or, more literally, "Christward"[42]). God is the guarantor[43]

39. See 2:12; 4:5; 5:20; 8:5; 11:4 for further possible echoes of Paul's mission preaching in Corinth.

40. The reader faces the question whether Paul is here *primarily* defending his integrity and his apostolicity, or whether he is taking the opportunity to teach important truths about God and his dealings with his people. He appears to be doing both.

41. Once again in the first chapter of this letter we notice that God is the subject of important action to his people. "God . . . comforts" (1:3-4); "God, who raises the dead . . . has delivered . . . will deliver" (1:9-10); God is faithful . . . [to his] promises . . . they are "Yes" in Christ . . . who was preached (by God?) among you (1:19-20); God . . . makes . . . us stand firm in Christ . . . anointed us, set his seal . . . on us . . . given us his Spirit in our hearts . . . (1:21-22).

42. Gk. εἰς Χριστόν.

43. The commercial vocabulary in this verse was noticed by A. Deissmann, *Bible Studies,* 104-9. In Greek classical times a βεβαίωσις was a seller's guarantee to a buyer that as money had been paid the goods would be forthcoming, and the ἀρραβών, a deposit promising that full payment would be made. In this imagery, as adapted by Paul, God is the "guarantor," and God also pays the "deposit" (the Spirit). For further background use of this vocabulary in the LXX and in Attic texts, see Thrall, 1.153-54.

of a lifelong, and indeed of an eternity-long, relationship with Christ. The Corinthians' Christward focus results from the apostolic *kērygma* of the Son of God (v. 19), whose reception was accompanied by God's gift of the Spirit in their hearts.

Not to be missed is the plural "us with you Christward." Here is an ecclesial as well as an eschatological picture, with apostle and people *together* centered on him as well as looking to his coming. This Christward focus of both apostle and people arises from their knowledge of Christ — in Paul's case by the Damascus intervention, in the Corinthians' by their hearing of the word of God — in both cases accompanied by the coming of the Spirit, which has resulted in a Spirit-anointed, Christward community.[44] The proclamation of the One in whom all the promises of God are fulfilled, as received by the Corinthians, has brought the Spirit of God to them (vv. 19-20).

The tenses of the verbs in vv. 21-22 should be carefully noted.[45] God's ongoing action toward his people guaranteeing their Christward focus rests upon and is in contrast to a single complete action (which is here stated as three closely connected actions, each involving the Spirit).[46] That single complete action of God corresponds to the action of the apostolic proclamation of the Son of God in Corinth. Paul "preached" Christ, and the hearers were "anointed" by the Spirit.

In consequence, Christ having been "preached," God "guarantees us Christward" (present tense), *having* "(1) *anointed . . .* (2) *set* his seal . . . (3) *put* his Spirit in our hearts" (aorist — completed action — tense). God's ongoing "guarantee"[47] (a commercial term for an undertaking by a seller to a purchaser) of us toward Christ is in consequence of the gift of his Spirit accompanying the hearing of the message of the Son of God (cf. Gal 3:2). God currently "con-

---

44. In v. 21 Paul distinguishes himself ("we") from the Corinthians ("you"), whereas in v. 22 the "we . . . you" is amalgamated as "us . . . our" applying to both apostle and people, and thus to all believers (as also "we *all*" in [1] 3:18, and [2] 5:10 as the climax to the universally applicable passage, 4:16–5:10).

45. So, too, the sentence structure of v. 22 — in particular the two participial phrases introduced by "and" — should be noted. These participial phrases flow from and explain what it means to be "christed" by God (χρίσας — v. 21). The two uses of καί ("and") should not be understood as merely additional but (1) as ascensive in the first ("who having 'christed' *thereby also* sealed"), and (2) epexegetical, i.e., giving the content of the first in the second ("who sealed us, *that is, by* giving us the deposit of the Spirit"). See also G. D. Fee, *Presence,* 291.

46. The present participle βεβαιῶν is followed by three aorist participles: χρίσας . . . σφραγισάμενος . . . δούς.

47. Gk. βεβαιῶν; NIV, "makes . . . stand firm." See further H. Schlier, *TDNT* 1.600-603; A. Fuchs, *EDNT* 1.210-211. For eschatological associations of βεβαιῶν see Rom 15:8; 1 Cor 1:6, 8. According to Hughes, 39, ". . . the present tense [βεβαιῶν] showing that this is a *constant* experience, and the graphic "into" [εἰς] that it is a *progressive* experience . . . continuous, but is ever being intensified."

111

firms" Paul's gospel word and the Corinthians as Christ's people in giving them the Spirit (cf. 13:5-6). This point should not be lost on the Corinthians, who hold the activity of the Spirit among them in high regard (cf. 1 Cor 14:12). If they have the Spirit of God arising from Paul's preaching of Christ, as they do, why are they tending to reject him as a true minister of Christ (cf. 3:2-6)?

This endowment of the Spirit is the source of God's three closely connected actions within. The first — "God . . . christed us Christward" *(eis Christon . . . chrisas)*[48] — must be regarded as deliberate a play on words, signifying that God has "made us Christ's people," "a messianic community." Here Paul may be implicitly rebutting the alternative ministry of the Judaizers, as if to say that only through the *Christ* proclaimed by Paul (as opposed to the *Jesus* proclaimed by them) and the related experience of the Spirit have the Corinthians become Christ's people, the eschatological messianic community of the new covenant (3:3, 6, 8, 18; cf. 11:2, 4).

The second, "he set his seal of ownership on us,"[49] returns to and reinforces the commercial imagery associated with "he guarantees." The "seal" — often in wax — is a mark of ownership, but also a guarantee of authenticity. The "seal" is nothing less than the Spirit himself, by whom God has marked believers as his own ultimate possession.[50] As in Eph 1:13 and 4:30, the "seal" is here also eschatological. On the "day of redemption" God will take possession of those who are already sealed as his own.

The third, God "put his Spirit in our hearts as a deposit, guaranteeing what is to come,"[51] is another commercial image. As the first and lesser payment

---

48. Gk. χρίσας; NIV, "anointed." This verb is not found elsewhere in Paul; but cf. Luke 4:18; Acts 4:27; 10:38; Heb 1:9. On its scarcity of use in Paul, see G. D. Fee, *Presence,* 291-92. Here is an image that recalls OT traditions of the anointing of kings and priests (e.g., LXX Exod 29:7; Lev 8:12; 1 Kings 9:16; 15:1, 17; 16:12), and especially in Isaiah, of the anointing of the Messiah with the Spirit (e.g., Isa 61:1-3). The cognate noun χρίσμα occurs in 1 John 2:20, 27. According to Thrall, 1.155, "The Christ whom God consecrates as messianic king has with him his own community to reign with him. Believers are themselves 'christed' to share in the messianic kingdom."

49. Gk. σφραγισάμενος means to fix a seal of ownership on an object, e.g., a letter. It is used in this sense with the Spirit only in Eph 1:13; 4:30 (cf. Rom 4:11; 15:28; 1 Cor 9:2; 2 Tim. 2:19). See BAGD 2b; MM, 617; and discussions in G. Fitzer, *TDNT* 7.939ff. and *NIDNTT* 3.492.

50. Although Thrall, 1.156, does not equate the "seal" with baptism, she does argue that "since baptism is the rite of entry into the holy community . . . the moment of 'sealing' must be the occasion of baptism." However, this is an inference and a connection that Paul nowhere makes. Only by the time of Irenaeus and Tertullian does σφραγίς become the term for baptism; see Thrall, 1.157-58.

51. Gk. ἀρραβῶν. Cf. 5:5; Eph 1:14. Originally a Semitic loanword, ἀρραβῶν appears in the commercial papyri as a first installment of a guaranteed final payment. Chrysostom called it "a part of the whole." See further M. Barth, *Ephesians,* 96-97.

guaranteeing full settlement, the "deposit" underlines and makes even clearer the two-stage eschatological structure implicit in the previous metaphor, the "sealing." As the Spirit himself is the "seal," so, too, he is both the "deposit" and "what is to come," the full settlement (cf. 5:5, 7-8). Christian believers live between the ages. The inauguration of the age of the new covenant lies behind; the coming age lies ahead (1:14; 4:14, 16–5:10). The Spirit as God's "seal" and "deposit" is the evidence within us as individuals, and as congregations, that the old covenant has been fulfilled, but that the coming age is "not yet" (see on 5:2-5).

Paul's pastoral method here is positively to encourage the Corinthians, including those who are drifting off course, to continue as faithful believers. In this the "day of salvation" (see on 6:2), all God's promises have been kept in Christ. Let the Corinthians understand that God remains loyal toward them, underwriting their ongoing relationship with Christ and guaranteeing to give his Spirit fully at the end, of which that given in part at their initiation into Christ is a pledge.

A trinity of persons, based on function rather than ontology, with the persons — Christ, God, Spirit — mentioned in the same order as the famous "grace" of 13:14, should be noted.[52] The eschatological salvation here described results from God the Father's own initiative, implemented by his Son, as proclaimed by the apostles, the enduring "Yes" to all the promises of God. God himself upholds the lifelong orientation of a people toward Christ, guaranteeing their full participation in the eschatological blessings by the Spirit by whom he seals them as his own.

There is a juxtaposition in vv. 20-22 between promise and Spirit that occurs in other Pauline passages.[53] The fulfillment of the promises of God is not static but dynamic. In the Son of God preached by the apostles God pronounces his ongoing and lively "Yes" to his promises. As the confirmation of the promise is continuous, so, too, is the believers' experience of the Spirit. God actively underwrites their continuing relationship Christward as they continuously experience the eschatological blessings of the Spirit within their lives, in consequence of hearing the proclamation of the Son of God.

3. Reasons for the Change: Why Paul Did Not Return to Corinth (1:23–2:2)

> 23 *I call God as my witness that it was in order to spare you that I did not return to Corinth.* 24 *Not that we lord it over your faith, but we work with you for your joy, because it is by faith you stand firm.* 1 *So*[1]

---

52. Cf. 2 Thess 2:13; 1 Cor 6:11, 20 as examples from earlier letters.
53. Gal 3:14; 4:28-29 (cf. Luke 24:29; Acts 1:4; 2:33, 38-39).
1. Although δέ is well supported (e.g., ℵ A C D vg syrᴾ) because 2:1 is "neither

I made up my mind that I would not make another painful visit to you.
2 *For if I grieve you, who is left to make me glad but you whom I have grieved?*

To this point Paul has (1) made a defense of his conduct in general and toward them in particular (vv. 12-14), and (2) asserted that he did not change his itinerary "lightly" or "according to the flesh" (1:15-17). Rather, as the minister of the God who is faithful, since Paul's gospel "word," which has brought them the Spirit, has proved faithful to the promises of God, so, too, Paul's personal "word" has proved to be faithful (1:18-22). As Paul had earlier called on the "witness" of his conscience (1:12), so, too, he calls on the God who is faithful (1:18) as "witness" against him in regard to his defense of his changed travel plans: it was to spare them that he did not return directly to Corinth.

23 Reverting to the first person singular (see on 1:1), Paul reintroduces the notion of "witness." Whereas earlier it had been the "witness" of his conscience in regard to his conduct (1:12-14), it is now the "witness" of God, which he calls "against my life,"[2] that he is, indeed, speaking the truth about his motives in not coming back directly to Corinth. The gravity of his words indicates that Paul's absence from Corinth remained a matter of deep hurt.

Once again Paul sounds an eschatological note, pointing back to "the day of the Lord Jesus" mentioned earlier (1:14; cf. 4:14; 5:10), in the prospect of which his conscience bears him good "witness"[3] in the matters of which the Corinthians are accusing him (1:12). Thus, in the first part of the verse — in what is, in effect, an oath[4] — he calls God as "witness" against him on that "day" if he is not in fact speaking the truth.[5] The second part, introduced

a mere addition nor a contrasting statement" (Metzger, 576), γάρ is to be preferred on account of the quality and diversity of MSS (i.e., p[46] B it[r] syr[h,pal], cop[sa,bo]).

2. Gk. ἐπὶ τὴν ἐμὴν ψυχήν; NIV, "my [witness]." According to Hughes, "may my life be forfeit if I am not speaking the truth" (46 n. 32). For OT precedents see Ruth 1:17; 1 Sam 14:44; 2 Sam 3:35; 1 Kings 2:23. Thrall, 1.160, refers to this as "a self-execration of a comprehensive kind."

3. See also Rom 1:9; Phil 1:8; 1 Thess 2:5, 10. Note the repetition of "witness" from 1:12 to 1:23: τὸ μαρτύριον τῆς συνειδήσεως ἡμῶν (1:12); ἐγὼ δὲ μάρτυρα τὸν θεὸν ἐπικαλοῦμαι (1:23). Paul's notion of "conscience," which is related to "witness," is not so much psychological as eschatological (cf. 5:10). He is conscious that his life is lived out before God (κατέναντι θεοῦ — 2:17; 12:19; ἐνώπιον τοῦ θεοῦ — 4:2; 7:12) and before the consciences of others (4:2; 5:11).

4. The apostle may not have been aware of Jesus' attitude toward oaths, as in Matt 5:33-37 (cf. the prohibition of oaths among the Essenes in Josephus, *J.W.* 2.135).

5. This is but one of a series of occasions in 2 Corinthians when Paul must offer a solemn account of the genuineness of his motives in the face of Corinthian disbelief and doubt (cf. 2:17; 4:2; 5:11; 11:10, 31; 12:6, 19).

by "that,"[6] gives the oath's content: "it was to spare you I came not again[7] to Corinth."

What dark thoughts do the Corinthians harbor against Paul, which he must answer, as supported by a conscience to whose integrity God is "witness"? It is that in not returning (directly) to Corinth he has made his plans "lightly . . . in a worldly manner" (1:17). But the true reason why he did not come, he solemnly assures them, was to "spare" them (cf. 1 Cor 4:21; 7:28). He wanted to avoid disciplinary action against them as at the previous "Painful Visit," and he hopes such action may not be necessary when he makes his final visit (2:3; 12:21–13:3). In the verses following Paul will explain further why he wished to avoid a disciplinary confrontation.

In passing, we may detect an interesting — but entirely human — ambivalence on the part of the Corinthians toward Paul. On the one hand, it appears that many of them criticized Paul for his fickleness in changing his plans as well as for his apparent weakness in dealing with disciplinary problems (cf. 10:1-2; 13:3). On the other hand, they are peeved that he has not come back to them as they expected him to, critical perhaps that he favored the Macedonians against them. They appear to be dismissive of his actions toward them yet jealous that he is returning to them through Macedonia.

24 Paul's opening "Not that[8] . . . but" springs from the previous verse, offering a clarification before proceeding further lest the Corinthians misunderstand him.[9] Let them be clear, Paul does not and will not "lord it" over them. That is not his apostolic role in relationship to them. Rather, "we" (i.e., Paul, Silas, and Timothy — cf. 1:19) "are coworkers[10] for your joy."

But there is a problem.[11] How can Paul speak of "sparing" them and yet not be said to "lord it" over them? The language of "sparing"[12] refers to the apostolic discipline of the Corinthians (cf. 13:2). But even here there is the "meekness and gentleness of Christ" (10:1-2), a humbling of himself before them as he grieves over their sins (12:21). At no point in the apostolic ministry is the model of the servant abandoned for that of the lord (cf. 4:5). He is quite unlike the newly arrived ministers who "enslave[s] . . . exploit[s]

---

6. Gk. ὅτι.

7. Gk. οὐκέτι ἦλθον; NIV, "I did not return."

8. The ellipsis οὐκ ὅτι is taken as, "It is not that. . . ."

9. Gk. οὐχ ὅτι . . . ἀλλά. Cf. 7:9; 2 Thess 3:9; Phil 4:17; John 7:22; 12:6.

10. Gk. συνεργοί. Thrall, 1.161-62, demonstrates that this does not refer to (1) Paul in partnership with a church or the churches (he nowhere else uses the word in this manner), nor (2) Paul and God (there is no other reference here to God — but cf. 1 Cor 3:9). By elimination συνεργοί points to Paul's coevangelists Silas and Timothy in Corinth (1:19).

11. See Thrall, 1.161, for a review of other possible solutions to the apparent contradiction between v. 23 and v. 24.

12. Gk. φειδόμενος; NIV, "spare."

. . . take[s] advantage of . . ." them (11:20). Rather, his relationship with them is graciously paternal (6:13; 11:2; 12:14-15).

In repudiating any notion of "lord[ing] it over [their] faith," he cannot but add, "but it is by faith you stand" (cf. Rom 11:20). Here the emphasis is on the responsibility the Corinthians must take in their relation with God. Though Paul brought them the message focused on the Son of God (1:18-20), it is their part, not his, to make their church "stand," and that "by faith."

But what is here meant by "faith"? This word *(pistis)* and its cognates, so important elsewhere in Paul's letters, is used infrequently in 2 Corinthians and, with one exception, not in contexts that clearly determine the meaning. That exception is: "Examine yourself to see whether you are in *the* faith" (13:5), that is, the gospel of the Son of God, toward whom their faith is directed. But in v. 24 "the faith by which you stand" appears to be their activity of faith, their personally held faith in the Son of God (cf. 1:19), as implied in the first part of the sentence (*"your* faith").

Paul now introduces into the flow of the letter the twin themes of "joy" and "pain" (or, better, "grief").[13] The apostle works for their "joy" rather than their "pain." In Paul's usage, "joy" is an eschatological blessing (Rom 14:17) that is experienced now as a fruit of the Spirit (Gal 5:22). "Joy" is experienced in this dispensation even in the face of grievous difficulty (cf. 6:10; 7:4; 1 Thess 1:6). Thus Paul encourages his churches to "rejoice constantly" (cf. Phil 3:1; 4:4). In prospect of the eschatological blessings, therefore, Paul sees "joy," not "grief," as the proper outcome of his work for the churches, as he proceeds to say (2:1-2).

1 The initial "for"[14] resumes the argument from v. 23, that it was to forbear further discipline that he did not again come to Corinth. The recurrence from v. 23 of "come" and of "to Corinth" as "to you" indicates the closeness between that verse and this; v. 24 is parenthetical. Paul took the weighty decision ("I made up my mind"[15]) not to come again[16] to them "in grief."[17]

---

13. The NIV translates variously both the λύπ- word group (λύπη/λυπῶ — 2:1, 2, 3, 4, 5, 7; 7:10; 9:7) and the χάρ- word group (χαρά/χαίρω — 1:24; 2:3 [twice]; 6:10; 7:4, 7, 9, 13 [twice], 16; 8:2; 13:9, 11).

14. Gk. γάρ. See textual comment above.

15. Gk. ἔκρινα . . . ἐμαυτῷ, which is to be coordinated with "I wrote" (ἔγραψα — 2:4). He made up his mind that he would not come, so he wrote the letter instead, actions that were to have far-reaching consequences with the Corinthians (see on 1:12-17).

16. Gk. πάλιν. While it is possible that πάλιν may be read exclusively with ἐλθεῖν, "come again" (for some hypothetical earlier visit), it is better to read it with the whole clause and in particular with ἐν λύπῃ, "come again in grief." Paul wanted to avoid a repetition of that earlier visit, which had been grievous.

17. Gk. ἐν λύπῃ; NIV, "painful." For consistency I have used the vocabulary of "grief" wherever λυπ- words are found in 2:1-11 and 7:7-10.

116

It appears that he concluded that his relationships with the Corinthians could not survive another such visit. It is possible that his statement, "I decided not to come to you again," may have been intended in an absolute sense. Only the impact of the "Severe Letter," as delivered and explained by Titus, has made it possible for Paul to contemplate the forthcoming visit to Corinth, which is the underlying reason for writing the present letter (7:8-16; 13:10; cf. 2:3; 9:4).

The "grief" of the unscheduled visit arose from the unjust action of a Corinthian against Paul (2:5; 7:12), possibly associated with serious public quarreling and disorder (cf. 12:20-21). Therefore, he chose to write to them instead of coming,[18] admonishing them to adopt an active approach to disciplining Paul's aggressor, rather than their present passive one (2:6, 9; 7:11). Had they failed to do this, it may have meant the end of his relationships with them and their end as a Pauline church, as a community experiencing the "joy" of God.

2   Again he commences with "For,"[19] pointing back to "grief" of v. 1, which he picks up as "if I[20] *grieve* you. . . ." This he follows with the rhetorical question, "Then[21] who is to make me glad except the one who has been grieved by me?" Further discipline from him would bring "grief" to them, thus destroying their capacity to bring him the gladness appropriate to the relationship between a church and its apostle. His proper role is to mediate the comfort of God to them (1:4), not grief and sadness.

The Corinthians have responded positively to the "Severe Letter" (2:6), so that relationships between the church and their apostolic founder have been restored in this matter, at least to some degree. Once again Paul can speak warmly in terms of the reciprocal relationships between him and them referred to earlier (see on 1:6-7, 11). As he is a coworker (with his apostolic colleagues) with them (1:24; cf. 1:19), the source of their comfort (1:6), and the one who works with them for their "joy" (1:24), so they in turn "make him glad," as later he will be "comforted" by Titus, who had been comforted by them (7:7). But if he had "grieved" them (again), as he had done in the recent visit and as he would have done by returning directly to them (1:23; 2:1), who would there be to comfort him?[22] As their comfort

---

18. See further M. M. Mitchell, "Envoys," 641-62, for an exposition of the place in that culture of the sending of letters and envoys in place of a visit by the principal party.

19. Gk. γάρ.

20. Gk. ἐγώ — "I" emphatic. Note the interpersonal ἐγώ . . . ὑμεῖς, "If *I* grieve *you*. . . ."

21. Gk. καί, an unusual use as an apodosis to εἰ; "If . . . then. . . ." See Thrall, 1.166-67.

22. This understanding is to be preferred to that which identifies ὁ λυπούμενος as Paul's opponent (so Martin). The singular ὁ λυπούμενος agrees with τίς, both of which should be interpreted as referring to the Corinthians.

and joy arose from his ministry to them, so his comfort and gladness arose from them; such were the bonds of fellowship between Paul and his churches. Typical of Paul's pastoral method, once some positive response is evident, he is quick to affirm their good standing with him and their ministry to him.

Unlike many ministers throughout Christian history, Paul, for his part, makes every effort to unite and weld together God's people, rather than to divide them. Under the impulse of God's Spirit Paul sought to strengthen the bonds among God's people, whether between him and the Corinthians, or among the Corinthians themselves (13:9, 11), or between the Corinthians and the churches of Judaea and elsewhere (9:13-14). None knew better than he that fragmented relationships between the Corinthians and him meant allowing Satan to gain the upper hand (see on 2:11).

4. Why Paul Wrote instead of Returning (2:3-4)

> 3 *I wrote as I did so that when I came I should not be distressed[1] by those who ought to make me rejoice. I had confidence in all of you, that you would all share my joy.* 4 *For I wrote you out of great distress and anguish of heart and with many tears, not to grieve you but to let you know the depth of my love for you.*

In these verses Paul gives his *purpose* in (v. 3) and *reason* for[2] (v. 4) writing.

The initial (and untranslated) "and"[3] of v. 3 suggests continuity with the preceding verses. Paul decided that he would not come again in person and bring grief to them (2:1), since they are the ones who ought to bring him joy (2:2). *And* for that purpose — that he might have joy, not grief — he wrote instead of coming. The "for"[4] of the following verse introduces his reason for writing — not to grieve them, but that they might know the overflowing love he has for them. Thus vv. 3-4 develop further the elements of "grief" and "joy" introduced in 2:1-2.

More broadly, Paul is continuing his defense of his conduct toward the Corinthians (see 1:12). On the one hand, he did not return as promised (cf. 1:15-16) so as to spare them further discipline (1:23; 2:1). On the other hand,

---

1. The variant λύπην ἐπὶ λύπην (so D G 1739 et al.) is to be rejected as far less well attested and as attributable to scribal assimilation (to Phil 2:27?).
2. Purpose and explanation are conveyed respectively by ἵνα (v. 3) and γάρ (v. 4).
3. Gk. καί.
4. Gk. γάρ.

as he now declares, he sent them a letter instead (the so-called "Severe Letter," now lost to us[5]).

Had he come and so not spared them the discipline necessary to the situation (1:23; 2:1), it would have then resulted in a grievous outcome for him. Rather, he looked to them as a source of joy, which he felt, and which he confidently expected that they would share. A letter could make that possible, but a further visit at that time would not.

Contrary to their suspicion that he wrote that letter to confuse, grieve, or intimidate them (1:13; 7:8; 10:9), he now assures them that he wrote out of deep personal distress and with many tears (v. 4). It was not that they might be grieved but that they might know his overflowing love for them.

3 In the previous verse Paul states his decision not to come again in a disciplinary manner, so as not to grieve those who ought to make him rejoice (2:1-2). The untranslated opening "and"[6] signals specific connection with this line of thought.

Paul refers directly for the first time to having written the now-lost "Severe Letter." "I wrote[7] this very thing,"[8] he reminds them, with a negative intention, namely, "lest coming[9] I would have grief. . . ." Coming back to Corinth at that time would have meant "grief," but from a quarter "from whom [he] was owed joy."[10] But he wrote confident that, in time, the joy he felt would be their joy, too.

The distress from the Corinthians that he experienced during the second visit, which evidently weighed heavily with him (2:1, 5; cf. 7:12), he did not wish to undergo during a third visit (12:14; 13:1). Time alone would not heal his pain nor bring reconciliation with the Corinthians; the letter to which he now refers was necessary. That letter was addressed to "those who ought to have gladdened him," the Corinthians (see on v. 2; cf. 6:11-13; 7:2-3). Paul's continued use of the first person singular pronoun, which he has used from

---

5. *Contra* Hughes, 54-57, who with older commentators generally understands this to refer to 1 Corinthians. Following Furnish, 153-54, we take the aorist ἔγραψα here to be historic ("I wrote"), not epistolary ("I am writing"). The ἔγραψα looks back to ἔκρινα and onward to ἔγραψα in vv. 4 and 9, which in turn anticipates ἔγραψα in 7:12 (cf. 7:8). See Introduction, 28-31. The letter was probably written from Ephesus before Paul's journey to Troas (2:12) and taken by Titus to Corinth.

6. Gk. καί.

7. Gk. ἔγραψα (cf. 1:12; 2:4, 9; 7:12); τὸ γράφειν (cf. 9:1); γράφω (cf. 13:10). Here ἔγραψα is a "true aorist," i.e., like 2:4, 9; 7:12, it refers to an earlier letter.

8. Following Furnish, 154, we take τοῦτο αὐτό as a simple objective, "this very thing," over against Barrett, 87, who takes it in an adverbial sense, "[I wrote] to just this effect." An adverbial interpretation, however, would usually follow an intransitive verb.

9. Gk. ἵνα μὴ ἐλθών . . . ; NIV, "so that when I came. . . ."

10. Gk. ἀφ' ὧν ἔδει με χαίρειν; NIV, "by those who ought to make me rejoice."

1:15, with the exception of 1:18-22, 24, indicates the depth of his own feelings on this matter; the generally less personal plural pronouns "we . . . us" predominate throughout the first part of this letter (see on 1:1).

Paul carries forward into this passage the theme of "pain" from the previous passage (1:23–2:2). By using a variety of words — "painful," "grieve," "grief," "distress" — the NIV obscures the consistency of Paul's one noun/verb of common root in 2:1-7 (also 7:7-10), which would be more literally rendered "grief"/"grieve." [11] It should be noted that Paul sets "grief"/"grieve" alongside "joy"/"rejoice" in 2 Corinthians in what appears to be an eschatological pairing. [12] If "joy/rejoice" represents the end-time happiness that is now a fruit of the Spirit (Gal 5:22), [13] "grief"/"grieve" is the pain experienced in the present, particularly in regard to the discipline of an erring member (2:1, 2 [twice], 3, 4, 7; 7:8 [twice], 9, 10, 11) or to the sufferings he has generated, which have made the discipline necessary (2:5).

In a rather difficult second clause he writes of being "confident about you all" *that* his "joy is the joy of all of you." But is this the joy he felt when writing the earlier letter, or the joy he feels at the present time? The former would suit better the flow from the first clause of the verse, though it is difficult to know how he could have been so "confident" about the "joy" of the Corinthians in light of the anxiety hinted at over their prospective response to that letter (2:13; 7:5-7). The latter is consistent with his joyful reaction to the news of the Corinthian response to the "Severe Letter" received via Titus (7:13), which he may have felt would be shared by them now that the disciplinary problem has been resolved. Although this alternative would mark a dislocation of thought in relationship to the first part of the verse, it is probably to be preferred.

Thus we take "joy" to be that which Paul experienced upon receiving news of their response to the "Severe Letter" (7:4, 7, 9, 13, 16). But he is "confident" that his joy was shared by "all" of them, that reconciliation with them brought as much joy to them as it had to him. Whatever the pain suffered during the second visit, he is warmly encouraged that the "joy" he now feels will be shared by them when they read this letter and hear of his feelings toward them. Pastorally, this is — to some degree — Paul's way of reinforcing his readers in behaviors and attitudes they should have. [14]

---

11. The common root λύπ- is used in 2:1-7; 7:7-10, whether the word be λύπη or λυπῶ. Paul uses this vocabulary seventeen times in 2 Corinthians as compared to only five times in the remainder of his letters.

12. 2:3 (ἵνα μὴ ἐλθὼν λύπην σχῶ ἀφ' ὧν ἔδει με χαίρειν . . . ἡ ἐμὴ χαρά); 6:10 (ὡς λυπούμενοι ἀεὶ δὲ χαίροντες); 7:9 (νῦν χαίρω, οὐχ ὅτι ἐλυπήθητε . . .).

13. See on 1:24; 2:2.

14. S. N. Olson, "Confidence," 282-95, puts forth the view that, following epistolary convention, such expressions of confidence are really techniques to persuade the readers rather than sincere observations about the readers' attitudes. While there may be

Even though the source of the "grief" was the wrong done against Paul by a man in the Corinthian church (2:5-10; 7:12), the more serious problem was their failure positively to support the apostle (2:9; 7:12). He had expected them to be a source of "joy" when present with them, which they would indeed be on the last day (cf. Phil 4:1). The eschatological reality of "joy" was to be a present experience. The reason Paul wrote — and wrote confidently — instead of returning was to actualize that reality for himself. While Paul had his critics and detractors within the community of believers in Corinth, the greater majority (see on v. 6) were favorable toward the apostle, even though they had been reticent to take appropriate disciplinary action against the offender. But Paul wrote in confident expectation about the response of "all of you," a phrase he uses twice.[15]

4 Paul's "for[16] . . . I wrote" points back to and explains what he meant by "and I wrote *as* I did" (v. 3), namely, (1) the *circumstances* of writing — he wrote out of deep distress, and (2) his *intention* in writing — stated negatively and positively[17] — not that they might be grieved but that they might know the overflowing love he has for them.

Paul is remarkably candid in revealing his emotions at the time he wrote this now-lost letter. He mentions, first, "great distress," which may suggest that the context of writing was the "distress[18] . . . suffered in the province of Asia" (1:8). Moreover, he recalls his "anguish of heart" as well as the "many tears" accompanying the writing of the letter. Paul was torn between his love for the Corinthians and his desire that they uphold appropriate standards of godly behavior toward him. Perhaps he feared that their very future as an apostolic church was in jeopardy.

Despite his own deep feelings of pain, however, he did not write in order to "grieve" them. Just as he did not wish to be "grieved" by paying them the return visit as originally planned (2:1, 3; cf. 1:15-16), so, too, it was not his immediate intention to "grieve" them by his letter (but cf.

---

an element of truth in this suggestion, Paul is also seeking to reinforce and encourage the Corinthians to express the faith in appropriate ways, based on the reality of Christian eschatology being "already fulfilled" but "not yet fully experienced."

15. Gk. πάντας ὑμᾶς . . . πάντων ὑμῶν.

16. Another explanatory Gk. γάρ. Thrall, 1.170, suggests that the γάρ might serve further to substantiate the reason for writing rather than coming to Corinth. "If my letter caused grief, how much more a personal visit!"

17. Gk. οὐκ . . . ἀλλά.

18. Gk. θλίψις; NIV for 1:8, "hardships." θλίψις is also used in 2:4; NIV, "distress." However, θλίψις is not used in the verses between 1:8 and 2:4, supporting the proposal that the "Severe Letter" — which is first referred to in 2:3 (but cf. 1:13) — was written after Paul's near-death experience in Asia (1:8-10). But see Martin, 36, for the opposite view; he notes that θλίψις is a "natural partner" for συνοχή ("anguish"), as in 1 Thess 3:7; Rom 2:9.

7:8-11).[19] Rather, his purpose in writing was "to let [them] know the depth of [his] love[20] for [them]." Here is an insight into the mind of Paul the pastor. The Corinthians' failure actively to support him — when they should have — caused him deep sadness. In a manner that calls to mind Jesus' forgiveness of those who caused him pain at the time of the crucifixion (Luke 23:34), Paul responded with a deep expression of overflowing[21] love for those who had failed him. And, despite the pain, he wrote confident that, as the Corinthians received this letter, they would respond in such a way as to bring him "joy" (v. 3).

5. The Outcome of the Letter: The Corinthians Pass the Test (2:5-11)

> 5 *If anyone has caused grief, he has not so much grieved me as he has grieved all of you, to some extent — not to put it too severely.* 6 *The punishment inflicted on him by the majority is sufficient for him.* 7 *Now instead, you[1] ought to forgive and comfort him, so that he will not be overwhelmed by excessive sorrow.* 8 *I urge you, therefore, to reaffirm your love for him.* 9 *The reason I wrote you was to see if[2] you would stand the test and be obedient in everything.* 10 *If you forgive anyone, I also forgive him. And what I have forgiven — if there was anything to forgive — I have forgiven in the sight of Christ for your sake,* 11 *in order that Satan might not outwit us. For we are not unaware of his schemes.*

19. Following Martin, 36, it is important to distinguish between Paul's "immediate and direct purpose in writing . . . and the way such a letter was received." Possibly some Corinthians felt that his letter was motivated by malice toward them (cf. 1:13; 7:8; 10:9).

20. Gk. τὴν ἀγάπην, which for emphasis is brought forward to precede even the conjunction διά (so Thrall, 1.170). For other references to his love for them see 8:7; 11:11; 12:15.

21. Gk. περισσοτέρως; NIV, "depth." The elative or intensifying meaning of περισσοτέρως ("the more," "the most") carries the idea "how much love" (RSV, "the abundant love"; NEB, "the more than ordinary love"). The force of περισσοτέρως is to reinforce rather than to compare; Paul is not saying that he loved the Corinthians more than others.

1. The reading μᾶλλον ὑμᾶς is strongly supported (so 𝔭46 ℵ C K L P 081 vg syrh copssa,bo arm) and justified despite the absence of μᾶλλον in some authorities (e.g., A B syrp eth Jerome) or a reverse order in others (D G 33 itd,g goth Theodoret). The absence of μᾶλλον in the above authorities is accounted for by accidental omission.

2. The omission of εἰ by good authorities (𝔭46 436 2495) is explained by its connection with εἰς. Some authorities have ἤ (A B 33), possibly as a late variant of εἰ. The reading ὡς has negligible support, whereas εἰ is well supported (ℵ C D G etc. it vg syrp,h,pal copbo goth arm).

So how did the Corinthians react to the "Severe Letter," which arrived in Corinth instead of the apostle? Certainly, his failure to reappear at that time caused criticism (1:12, 15-17, 23), and there were those who were critical of the letter that came in his place (10:9-11; cf. 1:13; 7:8).

Nonetheless, somewhat to our surprise, in the light of his generally defensive words to this point, this passage reflects a generally positive reception of the letter on their part. Paul, too, may have been pleasantly surprised after the many weeks of anxious waiting that elapsed before hearing from Titus (2:12; 7:5-6).[3]

Paul carries forward in this section the theme of "grief/grieve" that dominated vv. 1-4. Although the "grief/grieve" vocabulary is not as prominent here as in vv. 1-4 (apart from v. 5 it appears only in v. 7), nonetheless it forms the background for the present passage.

This passage is concerned with the triangular relationships between (1) Paul, (2) a man ("someone") who had offended, and (3) the Corinthians. Paul begins by asserting that — with due qualifications — if "someone" has caused grief it is not ultimately to him, but to "you all" (v. 5). Then he declares what is to be done (vv. 6-8): (1) the punishment by the Corinthians has been sufficient, so that (2) they must now, instead, forgive and comfort him lest he be consumed with grief; wherefore (3) Paul encourages them to reaffirm their love to him. The "Severe Letter," like the present letter, was to the effect that the Corinthians "prove" their obedience to Paul, which in the present case means their restoration of the offender (v. 9). Although Paul does not want them to make more of this issue than is warranted, nonetheless they should know that Paul has forgiven and does forgive this man (v. 10). Paul's great concern is the reconciliation of the majority and the minority in Corinth to one another, and especially to him. A wedge driven between the Corinthians and Paul would allow Satan to have the upper hand (v. 11).

5 The introductory contrastive particle[4] (untranslated) indicates a correction Paul wishes to make against any possible misunderstanding. To be sure, he did not embark on a further visit lest he be grieved (v. 3). But he wants them to know that, at the former visit, the offending person who had grieved Paul had not grieved him alone, but "all of you" as well.

Paul's deceptively vague-sounding conditional ("If anyone[5] has caused

---

3. We may conjecture that Titus had skills of diplomacy that softened the impact of the letter in Corinth. For a fuller impression of the Corinthian response to Paul's "Severe Letter," the present passage must be read alongside relevant parts of that later chapter (7:8-16).

4. Gk. δέ.

5. The indefinite pronoun τις in the protasis is not general; a specific person is in mind (see vv. 6, 7, and 8).

grief") leads to a "not . . . but" contrast[6] between its effects on Paul and on the Corinthians ("he has not grieved *me* . . . but [he has grieved] . . . *you all*." Cautiously, too, he qualifies this by "to some extent[7] — not to put it too severely."[8] Paul is concerned to state the problem carefully, without exaggeration.

For the first time in 2 Corinthians the man ("him" — v. 8) who caused Paul the "grief" during the second visit comes into view. Who is he and what had he done? Although many commentators have identified him as the "incestuous man" of 1 Cor 5:1-5, 13,[9] there is no compelling reason to do so.[10] All that can be said with confidence is that he had "wronged" Paul during that visit (see 7:12; cf. 2:10). In our view he may have been connected with the sexual aberrations in Corinth that involved a number of people and that appear to have necessitated Paul's recent unscheduled visit (12:21–13:2). It is quite possible that the man also supported the practice of ongoing attendance at temples in the city (6:14–7:1), despite Paul's warnings in the First Letter (1 Cor 10:14-22). Culturally, sexual license and cultic worship in Greco-Roman cities went hand in hand. Perhaps this man resisted Paul's admonitions to the Corinthians during his second visit and was himself the major reason that visit was so painful for Paul?[11]

The "offender" and the "grief" he caused Paul were the chief reasons the apostle abandoned his plan to return directly to Corinth, sending the "Severe Letter" instead. Consistent with Paul's practice elsewhere, he does not name his opponent.[12]

6. Gk. οὐκ . . . ἀλλά.

7. The phrase ἀλλὰ ἀπὸ μέρους, which is also used in 1:14 (cf. Rom 11:25; 15:15, 24), is helpfully rendered "to some extent" by the NIV. Less satisfactorily, some commentators take the expression to refer to the uneven impact of the dispute upon the Corinthians (see further Furnish, 154). For a survey of various ways of dividing the apodosis see Thrall, 1.172-73.

8. Gk. ἵνα μὴ ἐπιβαρῶ is somewhat ambiguous. Taken transitively, ἐπιβαρῶ would mean "lay a burden on" (as in 1 Thess 2:9; 2 Thess 3:8); taken intransitively, as most interpreters understand it, it would mean "exaggerate."

9. So most commentators before modern times (but see also, e.g., Hughes, 59-65; C. Kruse, "Offender," 129-39). For a detailed rebuttal of this view, see Furnish, 164-66. Of the other views, there is some weight to Barrett's (89), that the offender had insulted Paul, calling into question his authority in the church. If Paul was not an apostle, then the church was no church; thus the whole congregation was "grieved" by his action. Rather more conjectural is Thrall's hypothesis that the man had misappropriated money from the collection so as to diminish Paul's control over the congregation (68-69, 171-72).

10. See on 7:12.

11. Furnish, 164, 166-68, helpfully suggests that the man's offense was slander against Paul (or someone close to him), which is not inconsistent with the suggestions made above.

12. Paul does not mention any Corinthian by name in 2 Corinthians.

Nonetheless, Paul is concerned in this sentence not to portray his recent difficulties in Corinth as a one-to-one struggle with the man who has caused him "grief." There is a sense in which the whole congregation ("you all" — also v. 3)[13] has suffered, and continues to suffer, "grief."[14] While the "majority" (v. 6) of the community now actively support Paul, there were no winners. The total fellowship was disadvantaged by the continuing division implied by the "majority" (v. 6) and the failure of the whole church to restore the man. Satan alone stood to get the upper hand unless harmony was restored between Paul and this church (see on v. 11).

6 The apostle now makes a pronouncement.[15] The punishment applied by the majority is "sufficient" for him, implying that it should now cease.

As later readers we discover that disciplinary action was eventually taken against the man who had wronged Paul. The "Severe Letter," as borne by Titus, has had its effect (cf. 7:11, 15). However, there is still a problem. If the Corinthians had proved slow actively to support Paul in disciplining the man, the difficulty implied by v. 6 is that the (majority of the) Corinthians have continued their discipline of him beyond a reasonable point.[16]

This verse also brings into clearer focus the alignments of the Corinthian community at that time. The "you all" of vv. 3 and 5 is contrasted with "the majority."[17] This group represents the greater proportion of the Corinthians, whose general support for Paul had been confirmed by their action against the man. But this fact implies the existence of a *minority* who remain on the side of the man against Paul in this dispute, despite his own change of heart. The close connection between "the majority" and "you all" (vv. 3, 5)[18] suggests that

---

13. Barrett, 89, suggests that the man was "not a member of the Corinthian church." But this runs contrary to the present call to restore him (vv. 7-8, 10). A more probable suggestion is that the man is a recent member who joined the church after Paul founded it and whose influence Paul must overturn, first by the emergency visit, then — more successfully — by the "Severe Letter" as borne by Titus.

14. The twice-repeated perfect λελύπηκεν indicates the present reality of the grief, as does the οὐκ ἐμὲ . . . ἀλλὰ . . . ὑμᾶς contrast.

15. The absence of any connecting particle (asyndeton) may indicate an important free-standing statement.

16. That the "punishment" is "sufficient" (ἱκανόν) implies a forensic context (cf. Acts 17:9), which, however, here points to the "sufficiency" of the duration of the "punishment" rather than of its severity.

17. Gk. πάντας ὑμᾶς . . . τῶν πλειόνων. See Thrall, 1.175-76, for a consideration but also a rejection of the view that "majority" here refers to a Qumran idiom meaning "the many," i.e., the community as a whole, so that no division along majority/minority lines is envisaged.

18. Gk. τῶν πλειόνων . . . πάντας ὑμᾶς. Possibly Paul's use of a vocabulary of "majority" implies a deliberative session of the Corinthian assembly, with some voting mechanism.

almost all supported Paul and that those who opposed him were few — at least in this matter!

But what is "the punishment" the Corinthians "inflicted" on the offender? There is no clear evidence of the meaning of Paul's original word.[19] Opinions range from excommunication, on one extreme, to a mild rebuke, on the other.[20] The paragraph as a whole, however, suggests some kind of formal action against the man upon which the congregation have decided and which they have now implemented. In all probability, this action would have meant his exclusion from the plenary meeting of the *ekklēsia*.

7 This verse, which closely follows and is consequent[21] upon its predecessor, calls for a course of action opposite[22] to what has recently been pursued. The Corinthians are to forgive and comfort the man; otherwise,[23] he will be "consumed"[24] by grief.

Paul considers it necessary to call a halt to the "punishment" — some form of congregational discipline, apparently — that a majority of the Corinthians have applied to the "offender," arising out of Paul's admonition in the "Severe Letter." The contrary policy he now calls for follows naturally from his statement that there has been "sufficient" discipline to the man (v. 6).

Specifically, Paul asks them both to "forgive and comfort" him. If the first action[25] is to release from their minds any anger or resentment they may have harbored toward the man, the second[26] is actively to assure and encourage him that he is now restored to their fellowship. Earlier, he recalls writing the "Severe Letter" so that the hurtfully apathetic Corinthians might

---

19. Gk. ἐπιτιμία. According to Furnish, 155, ἐπιτιμία can mean punishment as a specific penalty or criticism or reproof. Nonuse in the LXX and the NT prevents us from establishing Paul's meaning of the word with clarity in this passage. For analysis of the cognates ἐπιτιμάω and ἐπιτίμιον, and the possible light they cast on ἐπιτιμία, see Thrall, 1.171-72.

20. Thrall, 1.174, believes that ἐπιτιμία means "punishment," perhaps in the form of official and public rebuke with exclusion from congregational activities, in particular the Eucharist. See Furnish, 155, for a summary of opinions.

21. Gk. ὥστε.

22. The words τοὐναντίον (= τὸ ἐναντίον — cf. Gal 2:7; 1 Pet 3;9) μᾶλλον literally mean "on the contrary," "rather."

23. Gk. μή πως.

24. Gk. καταποθῇ; NIV, "overwhelmed." The compound indicates intensifying force: "swallow up" (see also 5:4; Matt 23:24; 1 Cor 15:54; Heb 11:29; 1 Pet 5:8; Rev 12:6).

25. Gk. χαρίσασθαι, "to be gracious or generous," here approximates ἀφιέναι, "to forgive" (NIV, "forgive"). See, too, 12:13; but cf., e.g., 1 Cor 2:12; Phil 1:29.

26. Gk. παρακαλέσαι; NIV, "comfort." The verb is used of the father in the parable seeking to conciliate the estranged older brother (Luke 15:28; cf. 1 Thess 2:11-12).

know the "depth of [his] love [for them]" (v. 4). Now Paul, the wronged party, urges upon the congregation to "forgive and comfort" the offender (cf. Gal 6:1). Thus, by his attitudes in these mundane, even petty matters, Paul reveals himself to be "in Christ," committed to a practical expression of the reconciliation that lies at the heart of the gospel he proclaims (cf. 5:18–6:2; 13:9, 11). Although Paul does not use the vocabulary of imitation, it is quite likely that he here sets himself forth as a type or paradigm of godly behavior for the Corinthians to follow (cf. 2 Thess 3:7, 9; 1 Cor 4:16; 11:1; Phil 3:17)

The actions Paul calls for have a goal, which he states negatively. It is that the man will not be overtaken by "excessive sorrow,"[27] which might perhaps lead him to abandon the faith.[28] This aim suggests that Titus, who has recently returned from Corinth, had observed just this possibility and reported it to Paul. We may reasonably conclude, therefore, that the disciplinary action against the man took the form of some kind of exclusion, whether from the fellowship altogether or from participation in the fellowship meal. If perpetuated, this exclusion could become absolute.

Once again Paul's pastoral concern emerges as he shows deep concern for the offender's welfare. Earlier, when he had sought their recognition of his apostolic authority (2:9; 7:12) in matters relating to sexual immorality (12:21; 13:2), he powerfully advocated the discipline of the man (2:4). Now, in the face of evidence of repentance (vv. 6-7), he urges forgiveness and reconciliation with equal vigor.[29] In both discipline and reconciliation Paul fulfills the word of the Lord (Luke 17:3: "If your brother sins, rebuke him, and if he repents, forgive him"), though his own words betray no precise knowledge of the words of Jesus.

8 Reinforcing the statement of the previous verse that they "forgive and comfort" the man, Paul urges the Corinthians, "therefore,[30] reaffirm your love for him." The encouragement of this verse, that they "love" him, amounts to the same thing as that stated in the previous verse, namely, that they "forgive and comfort" him. Failure to "forgive and comfort" (i.e., "love") the man will result in his being swallowed up in "grief" (v. 7). Thus this verse summarizes his pastoral advice begun at v. 6.

---

27. Gk. τῇ περισσοτέρᾳ λύπῃ. The article indicates "his" and the comparative "overmuch," rather than "greater than hitherto." Thus, "his very great sorrow."

28. Chrysostom (*PG* 61, col. 422) suggests that this sorrow may have led to suicide or moral indifference.

29. Hughes, 66-67, comments, ". . . it is no less a scandal to cut off the penitent sinner from all hope of re-entry into the comfort and security of the fellowship of the redeemed community than it is to permit flagrant wickedness to continue unpunished in the Body of Christ."

30. Gk. διό, a strong inferential, "and so. . . ."

127

He repeats the "comfort"[31] vocabulary from the previous sentence, as appropriate in a changed context. In this verse it carries the idea of "apostolic counsel,"[32] which, however, is not altogether removed from the "comfort" he enjoins the congregation to show to the offender (v. 7). By contrast with the warmly pastoral "I urge," or, better, "I encourage," the word "reaffirm"[33] is technical and legal in character, adding weight to the hypothesis that a congregational "hearing" would occur to "forgive and comfort" just as a "hearing" had apparently occurred at which the man was subject to some form of discipline.

But Paul is probably also picking up the "comfort" theme of the benediction (1:3-7). The God of all comfort comforts his servant Paul that he might comfort others, which he now seeks to do to the "offender" through the comfort of the Corinthians to the man.

The centrality of "love" in Christian behavior emerges in this context. Paul wrote his earlier letter to the Corinthians that they may know his love for them (2:4). Now he exhorts them to show their love to this man who had wronged Paul, and whom Paul had forgiven. This practical, all-too-human, situation provides the opportunity for all parties, apostle and people, to display love, the preeminent "fruit," the greater "gift" of the Spirit, "the way" of excellence, which is the mark of the Christian and the fulfillment of the "new commandment" of Jesus and "the law of Christ."[34]

9 Paul now returns to his purpose in writing the "Severe Letter," references to which were introduced in the previous section (cf. 2:2, 3). The explanatory "for"[35] introduces a statement of purpose,[36] "to this end *indeed*[37] I wrote." His real purpose in writing the "Severe Letter" was the same as in writing the present letter, namely, "that I might know the proof of you, that you are obedient in everything." He called for discipline of the man then; he calls for forgiveness of him now (vv. 6-8); but the principle is constant, that they "prove" themselves to be "obedient."

Paul reveals that his ultimate goal in writing to them was not, as they

---

31. Gk. παρακαλῶ; NIV, "I urge."

32. So, Furnish, 156, citing Rom 12:1; 15:30. For a study of Paul's use of verbs of petition in their cultural environment, see *New Docs.* 6.145-46.

33. Gk. κυρῶσαι; NIV, "reaffirm." This is a legal term, "decide in favor of" (BAGD; cf. Gal 3:15), whose starkness is seen by its following παρακαλῶ and in its object: to show *love!*

34. Cf. Gal 5:22; 1 Cor 12:31; John 13:34-35; Gal 6:2; 1 Cor 9:21; cf. Rom 13:8-10; Gal 5:14.

35. Gk. γάρ.

36. Gk. εἰς τοῦτο; cf. 1 Thess 3:3; Rom 14:9; 1 Tim 4:10; also 1 Pet 2:21; 3:9.

37. Gk. καί, which qualifies so as to intensify εἰς τοῦτο (not ἔγραψα). It was, *indeed,* to achieve this end that he wrote, "that I might know the proof of you. . . ."

may have thought, for the disciplining of the man who had wronged Paul. Rather, as the sentence structure indicates — in which the second phrase explains the first — it was that he might "know" the positive outcome of the "test" or "proof"[38] that this matter presented to them, namely, that they would prove to be "obedient in everything."

Thus their obedience was but the symbol or "proof" whereby Paul might "know" the greater reality that they acknowledged him to be their apostle (see on 7:12). He wrote because he could not bear to come to them again in "grief," that is, to discipline them (2:3). As they well knew, he did not come to them as they had expected. And perhaps he would not come to them in the future if they had failed to act against the man. That letter may have signaled the possible end of his relationship with them, a somber alternative in contrast to the "day of the Lord" when apostle and church would boast in each other (1:14). It may have been as serious as that. The grief created by the man, in the end, was not for him to suffer, but for them to do so (v. 5). Thus, he wrote the letter that they might know "the depth of [his] love" for them (2:4), so that in turn they might, by their discipline of the man who had wronged Paul, demonstrate their acceptance of his apostolic ministry and therefore their welcome of him on a future occasion, whenever that might be.[39] In the later passage (7:7-16), which must be read alongside this one, Paul speaks of the *Corinthians'* repentance (7:9), making no comment about the offender's change of heart.

There is no contradiction between the servant status of the apostle stated elsewhere (1:24; 4:5) and the obedience he had called for in the "Severe Letter."[40] It is part of the paradox of the apostolic office that the minister will serve the people, yet expect them to obey him. The object of their obedience, however, is not the fortification of Paul's ego but the edification of the church, which in the case of the Corinthians was in considerable difficulty (10:8; 12:19; 13:10; cf. 13:5).

10   Paul's introductory contrastive particle[41] reintroduces the theme of forgiveness, using the same keyword "forgive" (v. 7)[42] that appears three

---

38. Gk. δοκιμήν, indicating a proving of something that results from testing. This is an important word in this letter (see 8:2; 9:13; 13:5-7; cf. 8:8, 22; 13:5; cf. Phil 2:22). Although we possess no examples of this word earlier than Paul, he is unlikely to have been its creator. See further G. Schunack, *EDNT* 1.341-43.

39. Perhaps, though, Paul has contradicted himself to his readers; in v. 4 his declared reason for writing was to assure them of his love for them, and in 1:24 he disclaimed "lording" it over their faith. From his viewpoint as their "father" in the Lord, however, there would be no contradiction.

40. *Contra* Barrett, 92, who thinks that, in view of 1:24, the obedience is not in regard to Paul.

41. Gk. δέ.

42. Gk. χαρίζεσθε.

times in the present verse. Their forgiveness of the man has been matched by Paul's, which, however, is for the sake of the Corinthians.

Whereas previously Paul enjoined forgiveness for the good of the man ("lest he be consumed with grief"), he now does so for the good of the congregation ("for your sake"), namely, as amplified in the verse following, that Satan might not be allowed to take advantage of the situation.

Let the Corinthians understand that they are to forgive the offender because Paul has already forgiven and continues to forgive him.[43] He has shown the way, as the emphatic pronouns "*I* also . . . *I*"[44] indicate. He is, however, careful to get the balance right. On the one hand, he reinforces their need to forgive by telling them that he, too, has forgiven him. On the other hand, as the weak "[forgive] *anything,*"[45] twice repeated, seems to indicate, he is concerned not to overstate the case (see on v. 5). Perhaps Paul does not want the Corinthians to lose the right sense of proportion in the matter by enlarging the significance of this man in the eyes of the Corinthians.

Paul is here reinforcing the solidarity between the apostle and the churches ("you forgive . . . I also forgive"). While recent circumstances have driven Paul and the Corinthians, Paul is seeking throughout this letter to bring about reconciliation and restoration between him and them (see 1:6-7, 11, 14, 21, 23–2:4; 6:11-13; 7:2-4; 12:14-18).

By his words "I have forgiven in the sight of Christ" Paul appears to be hinting at a pastoral-disciplinary procedure, whose outlines are only dimly and incompletely visible from this historical distance. Proper process had to be observed; for example, two or three witnesses must give evidence (see 13:1) before "punishment [was] inflicted by [a] majority" (v. 6) or "love" was "reaffirmed" (v. 8).[46]

When read alongside his earlier admonitions for judging the "incestuous man," it appears that, though physically absent, Paul considered himself to be spiritually present when the congregation assembled to discipline the

---

43. Paul twice uses perfect tense κεχάρισμαι, which may indicate either (1) his ongoing forgiveness based on a past act of forgiveness, or, more probably, (2) that by the time they received the letter his forgiveness was already a reality. In this case they are "epistolary perfects" following the initial verb χαρίζεσθε, a present tense.

44. Gk. κἀγὼ . . . ἐγώ.

45. Gk. τι.

46. It is possible that disciplinary procedures in the Pauline churches arose out of the practices of the synagogues, but less likely that Qumran practices had been influential (G. D. Fee, *1 Corinthians,* 203 n. 33). Fee, 206, however, rejects any notion that the procedures in 1 Cor 5:3-5 reflect some kind of ecclesiastical tribunal; rather, he asserts that the actions taken were congregational, carried out in the context of the Spirit.

offender (1 Cor 5:3-5). Participation in judging or forgiving an offender also occurred when Paul was present with the church (see 12:21–13:2).[47]

In the present context, however, the purpose of their assembling, and his with them — though absent — was "to forgive and comfort" (v. 7). It is important that the Corinthians understand that when they at last formally meet "to forgive and comfort" the man, as Paul now asks them to do (v. 8), he has already forgiven the man. This is possible because it is done "in the sight of Christ" (lit. "in" the "face" or "presence"[48] of Christ). As they and he pass judgment "in the name of the Lord Jesus/with the power of our Lord Jesus" (1 Cor 5:4), so, too, they and he declare forgiveness "in the sight of Christ." Christ's twin eschatological works of reconciliation/righteousness and judgment (5:18-21; 5:10) appear to have been been the loci, respectively, of forgiveness and discipline within the Pauline churches.

11 The reason for forgiving the offender — in relationship to the welfare of the church as opposed to that of the man (vv. 7, 10) — is now given. It is that Satan[49] might not[50] "outwit us," or, perhaps, "get the upper hand."[51]

---

47. We assume that Paul's humility (cf. 10:1) when present in Corinth during the second visit, participating in a disciplinary assembly, failed to impress (some of) the Corinthians (10:2, 6, 10; 13:3-4), who were doubtless used to vigorous, if not ruthless, court procedures in Roman Corinth. See Introduction, 28-31.

48. Gk. ἐν πρυσώπῳ Χριστοῦ; NIV, "in the sight of Christ." πρόσωπον is used variously within 2 Corinthians — as "face" (3:7, 13, 18 and 11:20), as "persons" (1:11 plural), as "outward appearance" (5:12; 10:7), and as "personal presence," as opposed to absence (10:1). The phrase ἐν προσώπῳ Χριστοῦ, used in 4:6, according to its context, carries the meaning "face" rather than "person." In v. 10 ἐν προσώπῳ, which appears to be a semitism (cf. Prov 8:30), functions as a "prepositional adverb" like κατέναντι, ἔμπροσθεν, and ἐνώπιον (so Furnish, 157), which are used in eschatological references (see 5:10; 8:21; Gal 1:20). Nonetheless, while ἐν προσώπῳ Χριστοῦ appears to carry an eschatological nuance (cf. 1:14, 23), the context suggests that the eschatology relates to the forgiveness and reconciliation of the cross rather than the judgment of the last day. The phrase ἐν προσώπῳ Χριστοῦ has been variously interpreted, either as (1) "in the person of Christ" (i.e., as Christ's representative, as in 5:20; 12:10 — so Wettstein, cited in Thrall, 1.180), or (2) "in the presence of Christ" (i.e., eschatologically, with Christ as a witness — so Furnish, Thrall). Option (2) is be preferred on account of the context of forgiveness.

49. Gk. ὁ Σατανᾶς is transliterated from Heb. śāṭān and means "adversary" (see Job 1–2). It is the proper title of the devil, the great Adversary of God and his people. For other uses in 2 Corinthians, see 11:14; 12:7.

50. Gk. ἵνα μή.

51. Gk. πλεονεκτηθῶμεν; NIV, "outwit." Literally, the verb (πλέον = more + ἔχειν = to have) can mean "take advantage of," "cheat" or "rob." If taken in the sense of "rob" (cf. 1 Cor 5:10; 6:10), it could mean "lest [the church] be robbed" of those disaffected members who might withdraw (so Martin, 39). But Paul would hardly express this as "lest *we* be robbed." See other references in 2 Corinthians, where it is used in the sense of "take advantage of," "exploit" (7:2; 12:17, 18).

But what are we to understand by this? The meaning may be discerned in the stated possibility that "we," that is, Paul,[52] may be disadvantaged by Satan and his "schemes."[53] On this understanding Satan's "schemes" — of which Paul is "not unaware" — would separate the Corinthians from him.[54] The continued existence of a minority[55] who support the offender against the "majority" (v. 6) who now support Paul represents an ongoing opportunity for division with the potential for final separation of the Corinthians from Paul. The forgiveness and comfort of the man, however, will serve also to reconcile the minority with the majority and thus the *whole* congregation with Paul (cf. "you *all*" — vv. 3, 5). It will well serve Satan's purposes for the Corinthians to be separated from the authority and influence of the apostle Paul.

Paul, however, may also be applying pastorally to the Corinthians the related theological truth that believers have been "rescued from the dominion of darkness" (i.e., of Satan) and "brought into the kingdom of the Son [God] loves, in whom [there is] redemption, the forgiveness of sins" (Col 1:13-14). The Son, beloved of God, exercises his kingship among those who have been forgiven by God and who in turn forgive others. Failure to forgive members of that community is in line with Satan's "schemes" since it reintroduces the "dominion of darkness."

C. PAUL IN TROAS: TURMOIL IN MINISTRY (2:12-13)

It is open to question whether vv. 12-13 should be regarded as forming a closure to Paul's apologia for his failure to reappear in Corinth and his dispatch instead of the "Severe Letter." The reference to inner turmoil in Troas (v. 13) adds to, and is continuous with, problems in Ephesus ("Asia"), namely, the "deadly peril" from which God delivered him and the "great distress and

52. Following Hughes, 71, who takes the plural to refer here to Paul alone, and suggesting that he would say "we all" if the Corinthians were included. Paul's plural "we"/"us" is generally used as a literary plural in the first part of the letter (see on 1:1).

53. Gk. αὐτοῦ τὰ νοήματα. Furnish, 158, sees a subtle wordplay in αὐτοῦ τὰ νοήματα ἀγνοοῦμεν, "we are not unmindful of his mind," noting here an example of litotes, or understatement, for the sake of emphasis.

54. See Thrall, 1.181, for alternative views, that being disadvantaged by Satan means (1) dissension in the church, (2) spiritual danger to them and him through remaining unforgiving, or — her preference — (3) the loss of the offender from the congregation through his permanent alienation from the community. In my view, however, these alternatives do not address the question of the plural, "lest *we* [i.e., Paul] be disadvantaged. . . ."

55. However, Thrall, 1.181, views the minority not as supporting the previous stance of the offender but as in favor of "harsher measures" against him.

anguish" at writing the "Severe Letter" (1:10; 2:4).[1] That travel apologia, with further references to inner suffering, will be resumed in 7:5-6; the material between forms a defense of Paul's new covenant ministry. Moreover, the anxiety experienced in Troas relates to *them,* giving expression to the love he had for them when writing the "Severe Letter" (2:1-4).

On the other hand, vv. 12-13 also point forward, serving as the foundation on which his apologia for new covenant ministry is built, of which vv. 14-16 is the first part. In particular, Paul's coming to Troas "for the gospel" is the basis for his statements that he "spreads everywhere the . . . knowledge of [Christ]" (v. 14) and that, "unlike . . . many [he] does not peddle the word of God for profit" (v. 17).

Thus vv. 12-13 should be regarded as transitional, belonging to the end of 1:12–2:11 while forming an introduction to 2:14–7:4. It serves as a bridge[2] between all that has gone before and the apologia for his new covenant ministry that follows.

> 12 *Now when I went to Troas to preach the gospel of Christ and found that the Lord had opened a door for me,* 13 *I still had no peace of mind, because I did not find my brother Titus there. So I said good-bye to them and went on to Macedonia.*

In Paul's defense of his conduct to the Corinthians (see on 1:12) he has recapitulated various painful events that have occurred since he was last present with them — the affliction suffered in Asia (1:8-11), the decision not to come (back directly) to Corinth (2:1), and the writing of the letter, which he did out of great distress (2:4).

His "Now when I went to Troas" (2:12) is the next painful milestone on his apostolic journey (cf. 7:5 — "For when we came to Macedonia, this body had no rest"), in which God leads him in triumphal procession (2:14).

---

1. The sequence is not apparent. Our difficulty is that we do not know Paul's movements between the "Painful Visit" to Corinth (1:23; 2:1) and the crisis in Asia (1:8-11). Did he return directly from Corinth to Ephesus, or did he return via Macedonia? Did he make his decision to write before or after the deadly peril in Asia? If it was beforehand, was it from Macedonia or Asia? If it was after the crisis in Asia, did he write the letter to the Corinthians from Ephesus or from somewhere else en route to Troas? We are inclined to the view that the crisis in Asia forced Paul (1) to implement a long-held plan to preach in Macedonia via Troas (cf. 1 Cor 16:5; Acts 19:21-22; cf. 2 Cor 1:16), and (2) to dispatch Titus to Corinth with the "Severe Letter," arranging to meet him in Troas or, failing that, in Macedonia.

2. Parallels to this transitional technique may be seen in (1) 7:2-4, where, on the one hand, Paul concludes the excursus on new covenant ministry and, on the other, he lays the foundation for the next subject (7:5-16), and (2) 12:13, which concludes the "Fool's Speech" while introducing the next theme about not being a financial burden.

Troas proved to be painful because Paul went there for gospel ministry and a "door" of opportunity was "open." But he was so distressed because Titus had not arrived bringing news about the Corinthian response to the "Severe Letter" that he made his valedictory farewell and departed for Macedonia, his "plan B" rendezvous.

12 The contrastive particle *de*[3] ("Now" — NIV) marks the beginning of a new section. The first part of this verse is a statement of purpose ("I[4] went to Troas[5] to preach the gospel of Christ"), while the second gives the welcome circumstances ("and the Lord . . . opened a door[6] for me").

Paul now resumes the narrative of his travels since being forced from Asia (1:8-10). He did not feel able to return to Corinth until the man who had wronged him (2:5; 7:12) had been disciplined by the church, according to Paul's demand in the (lost) "Severe Letter" (2:3-11; 7:12). The closure of Achaia to further ministry for the moment apparently caused Paul to direct his attention to Troas and beyond there to Macedonia (see 1 Cor 16:5; 2 Cor 1:15-16; Acts 19:22; 20:2). Thus he set out from Ephesus for Troas, the main exit port on the northern coast of western Asia, from which to travel to

---

3. Gk. δέ.

4. Paul uses the singular "I"/"me" in vv. 12-13, as he has in general to this point to explain controversial actions to the Corinthians (1:15-17, 23–2:4; 7:8-16). At the same time, of course, it is a natural way to differentiate himself from Titus, whose arrival he was expecting. However, apart from the "Fool's Speech" (11:1–12:13), more typically he employs the plural "we"/"us" throughout the letter (see on 1:1).

5. Gk. εἰς τὴν Τρῳάδα. The full name was Ἀλεξάνδρεια ἡ Τρῳάς to distinguish it from other places named Alexandria after the famous Macedonian conqueror. The Troad is a wide promontory that gives its name to the city Troas, which is a few miles to the south of Homeric Troy, overlooking the mouth of the Dardanelles. The city, whose population was estimated as between thirty and forty thousand, became a Roman colony under Augustus, "Colonia Augusta Troas," and was, according to Strabo, "one of the notable cities of the world" (*Geography* 13.1.26). For the view, based on the unusual Pauline use of the article with a city, that εἰς τὴν Τρῳάδα points not to the city Troas but to the whole region of the Troad where the city was located, see Thrall, 1.182-83. Thrall holds that Paul came for ministry to the whole region, not merely to the city. Troas is mentioned elsewhere in the NT (Acts 16:8, 11; 20:5-6; 2 Tim 4:13); see further C. J. Hemer, "Alexandrian Troas," 79-112.

6. Gk. θύρας μοι ἀνεῳγμένης indicates (1) by the passive voice that, ultimately, God opened the door, (2) by the perfect tense that it remained opened, and (3) by the dative of advantage that it was opened "for" Paul's ministry. For similar expressions relating to missionary work see 1 Cor 16:8-9; Col 4:3; Eph 6:14-20; Acts 14:27 (cf. 1 Thess 1:9; Rev 3:8). Thrall, 1:184, reflects on whether the image originally may have had the more literal sense of the availability of lodgings, rooms for preaching, etc., citing the case of the Cynic preacher Crates, who was known as " 'Door-opener' — the caller to whom all doors would fly open — from his habit of entering every house and admonishing those within" (Diogenes Laertius 6.86).

Macedonia. By an arrangement made at the time of his dispatch to Corinth bearing the "Severe Letter," Titus was to come to Troas ahead of, or within the same time frame as, Paul and report on the Corinthians' response.

By his words expressing purpose, "I went to Troas *for the gospel of Christ,*"[7] we infer that Paul had harbored that desire for some time, perhaps from the occasion of the initial visit, which was foreshortened by the "Macedonian call" (Acts 16:8-10). Being near the mouth of the Dardanelles with considerable human traffic passing through, the apostle would not have been slow to notice the strategic possibilities for ministry that Troas presented.[8]

Paul intended to come to Troas "for the gospel of Christ," or, in effect, to establish a church in that city.[9] Church creating was among Paul's goals in evangelism. Paul preached Christ with the intention of gathering a group of people who, together, were *eis Christon,* focused on Christ (see on 1:19, 21-22; 11:2-4). It is reasonable to suppose that in the midst of his distress Paul saw the Corinthian crisis as providential, giving him the occasion to establish a church, or perhaps to strengthen an existing church, in the important entrepôt, Troas.

The phrase "a door was opened for me" expresses Paul's conviction that God was actively responsible for the opportunity to minister that he found on coming to Troas. That it was "in the Lord"[10] specifies the sphere of activity of this God-given opportunity, namely, in relationship to the preaching of the Lord ("we preach Jesus Christ as *Lord*" — 4:5; cf. 8:5).

13 The rest of Paul's sentence is in four parts.[11] Paul (1) makes a negative statement ("I . . . had no peace of mind"[12]), (2) gives the reason

---

7. Gk. εἰς τὸ εὐαγγέλιον τοῦ Χριστοῦ, literally translated; the verb "to preach" does not appear. The noun εὐαγγέλιον appears here for the first time in 2 Corinthians (see also 4:3, 4; 8:18; 9:13; 10:14; 11:4, 7). The verb εὐαγγελίζομαι appears in 10:16; 11:7. The genitive τοῦ Χριστοῦ is an objective genitive, "the gospel *about Christ.*"

8. Paul appears to have chosen Corinth, Ephesus and the Macedonian cities on the *Via Egnatia* as centers for sustained ministry on account of their strategic locations for evangelism. Each was a significant city, with many travelers and traders passing through to more distant parts of the empire, thus facilitating the spread of the gospel and the planting of churches. Though a significantly smaller city, Troas shared with Corinth and Ephesus the status of a Roman city, a center through which a large volume of human traffic passed.

9. Attention is drawn to Rom 15:19, "I have fulfilled *the gospel of Christ*" (πεπληρώκεναι τὸ εὐαγγέλιον τοῦ Χριστοῦ), which appears to mean not merely the initial preaching of the gospel but the further process of establishing congregations. See W. P. Bowers, "Fulfilling the Gospel," 185-98; P. T. O'Brien, *Consumed by Passion,* 38-51.

10. Gk. ἐν κυρίῳ, dative, where "the Lord" signifies (1) the sphere of opportunity ("proclaiming the Lord") rather than (2) agency ("by the Lord").

11. Both the RSV and the NIV render as two sentences.

12. Gk. οὐκ ἔσχηκα ἄνεσιν τῷ πνεύματί μοι. Paul uses a similar expression in 7:5: οὐδεμίαν ἔσχηκεν ἄνεσιν ἡ σάρξ ἡμῶν. For ἄνεσιν see also 8:13. To be noted is the

("because I did not find Titus[13] . . . there"), (3) explains how he responded ("so I said good-bye to them"), and (4) describes what he did next (". . . and went on to Macedonia"[14]).

Evidently Paul expected Titus to reach Troas before him. But Titus was not in Troas, nor even in Macedonia, when Paul arrived there (7:6). The reason for his delay (in Achaia?) is not known. By his revealing personal comment (lit. "I had[15] no relief in my spirit[16]") Paul adds to the picture of deep personal distress in and since the writing of the "Severe Letter" (in Ephesus?[17]) on whose outcome rested Paul's future apostolic relationships with the Corinthians (2:3-4). Once again Paul is telling us — though indirectly — of his deep feelings for this church (cf. 6:11-13; 7:2-4; 11:11, 20-21; 12:11-16).

---

interchange between πνεύματί (2:12) and σάρξ (7:5). Here "spirit" is not pneumatological (i.e., Holy Spirit), but, like "flesh," anthropological (see G. D. Fee, *Presence,* 296). Both effectively stand for the personal pronoun (so Thrall, 1.186).

13. Historically, Titus's earliest appearance within the NT was at the Jerusalem Missionary Meeting, *c.* A.D. 47, as part of the Antiochene delegation. Paul's reference to Titus as his "true child" (Tit 1:4) marks him as a convert to Paul's ministry. Uncircumcised Titus is described as Ἕλλην ὤν (Gal 2:3), making him one of the earliest Gentile Christian leaders. His multiple visits to Corinth (8:6, 10; 9:2; cf. 12:18; 7:6; 8:16, 23) may mean that he was *specifically* a Greek (for Paul Ἕλλην meant no more than a Gentile). Titus is important within the pages of 2 Corinthians: (1) Paul calls him "My partner and fellow worker to you" (κοινωνὸς ἐμὸς καὶ εἰς ὑμᾶς — 8:23), suggestive of a special role as Paul's envoy to the Corinthians, sharing with Paul a God-given "earnestness" for the Corinthians (8:16). (2) Although, not mentioned in the First Letter, Titus was probably the initiator of the collection in Corinth (8:6; cf. 1 Cor 16:1-4), and possibly the bearer of the "Previous Letter" (1 Cor 5:9-10). (3) Titus was probably the bearer of both the (lost) "Severe Letter" (7:8-15) and canonical 2 Corinthians (8:6, 16, 23); the latter letter is Paul's response to Titus's account of affairs in Corinth at the time he rejoined the apostle in Macedonia (7:6, 7, 13, 15). As letter bearer, Titus was probably also expected to explain and justify the letters he carried. (4) Titus enjoyed a special place in Paul's estimations (Τίτον τὸν ἀδελφόν μου), who brought him great comfort at a time of personal anxiety (7:5-6).

14. Paul next picks up his travel narrative in 7:5, thus making 2:14–7:4 a "long digression." See J. Murphy-O'Connor, "Paul and Macedonia," 99-103.

15. Gk. ἔσχηκα (cf. on 1:9). NIV, "I still had. . . ." The perfect tense may point to the duration of Paul's distress from the time of Titus's dispatch from Ephesus, which had not ended until he met with Paul in Macedonia (7:5-16). Some, however, regard ἔσχηκα as an "aoristic" rather than a "true" perfect (for discussion see Thrall, 1.185 n. 401).

16. Gk. τῷ πνεύματί μοι is dative of advantage, "for my spirit" (see LXX Gen 8:9).

17. Since Paul feels it necessary to refer to his ordeal in Asia (1:8-11) and explain why he did not return directly to Corinth (1:23), but traveled north to Troas and then to Macedonia (2:12-13), it is reasonable to conclude that Titus left Ephesus for Corinth with the "Severe Letter," while Paul was still in Ephesus, presumably after the ordeal.

Not finding Titus there, Paul did not remain in Troas but set out for Macedonia. It is possible that his arrival in Troas coincided with that season of the year when the winter squalls closed the seas to shipping. If Titus had not by that time come to Troas, then he would not be coming before the spring, thus signaling the need for Paul to move to the next rendezvous. Paul's route[18] would have taken him across the mouth of the Dardanelles, to, or past, the island of Samothrace, and to Neapolis, the northernmost port of Macedonia. From there he would have traveled by the Egnatian Way to whichever city (Philippi?) he had next arranged to meet Titus.

That Paul bade "them" farewell (in a final sense?[19]) points to the existence of believers in Troas,[20] despite Paul's lack of opportunity to exercise a ministry on that occasion. When Paul visited Troas many months later, he remained for seven days and, according to the Acts, taught believers on the first day of the week in an upper chamber (Acts 20:7-12). It appears that, despite his own view that he would not return to Troas, God kept the door open.

III. DEFENSE OF THE MINISTRY OF THE NEW COVENANT (2:14–7:4)

The passage that follows (2:14–7:4) is the longest coherent section within 2 Corinthians and is, arguably, the centerpiece of the entire letter. Nonetheless, it is not freestanding, but continuous with what precedes it. To this point Paul has offered an apologia for his conduct, both as to his motives (1:12-14) and to his actions (1:15–2:4). Some of this apologia is picked up[1] in his defense of the ministry of the new covenant that follows.

18. The previous Troas-Neapolis voyage took two days, with an overnight stay at Samothrace (Acts 16:11). Paul's subsequent reverse journey, however, took five days (Acts 20:6).

19. The formal-sounding ἀποταξάμενος may indicate a final farewell (as in Mark 6:46; Luke 9:61; 14:33; but cf. Acts 18:18, 21), expressive of Paul's hope that the Corinthians had responded positively to the "Severe Letter." On that scenario he expected finally to withdraw by ship from the Aegean region with the collection from Corinth, and to head directly for Jerusalem (Acts 20:3). It is probable that he did not expect to return to Troas.

20. It was at the time of Paul's first visit to Troas that the anonymous diarist (Luke?) — apparently already a believer — first attached himself to Paul's group, though only from Troas to Philippi, where he seems to have remained from A.D. 49 to 56 (Acts 16:10, 40; 20:5-6). Were the believers Paul found in Troas in c. A.D. 55 connected with the anonymous believer who seven years earlier left Troas with Paul for Philippi?

1. See, e.g., (1) the repetition of εἰλικρίνεια in 1:12 and 2:17, and (2) his defense of his probity in 1:12-17 and 4:2; 6:6-10.

In particular, however, it is the theme of his sufferings and God's comfort in and deliverance from those sufferings (1:3-11) that is immediately reintroduced in the striking triumphal/antitriumphal metaphor in which God leads the apostle as conquered captive (2:14-16). This metaphor, with its paradoxical power-in-weakness elements, may have been chosen to answer to those who suggest that such sufferings somehow disqualify or invalidate his ministry.[2] On this hypothesis, this metaphor, combining elements of both suffering and triumph and appearing as it does at the beginning[3] of this defensive excursus, establishes its underlying theme of power in weakness (see on 4:8–5:10; 6:4-13).

Paul's exposition, however, is not merely apologetic. A polemical element is quickly introduced, in which Paul contrasts his ministry with that of those "who peddle the word of God" (2:17–3:1 — "not . . . as . . . but as . . . but as . . . as . . .").

This contrast is then expanded and elaborated upon. Through Paul's ministry the Spirit of the living God has been mediated to the Corinthians (3:3), as Paul had earlier reminded them (1:18-22). Paul is preparing the ground for his claim to be a God-enabled minister of the new covenant (3:6).

A line of thought appears to have been begun by the "letters of commendation" (3:1). This is picked up as "written in ink" (3:3), as such letters would have been. The immediately paralleled "written . . . in tables of stone" suggests a connection between the ink-written letters borne by the peddlers (2:17–3:1) and that ministry associated with "tablets of stone . . . the letter," that is, the ministry of Moses.

By contrast, Paul's ministry mediates "the Spirit of the living God" in "tablets of hearts of flesh," making the Corinthians themselves Paul's letter of commendation from *Christ,* known and read by all in Corinth (3:2-3).

This polemical contrast between Paul and the "peddlers" continues in the following contrasts between (1) the permanent and surpassing glory of the ministry of the Spirit and the transitory and inferior glory of the ministry of "the letter" (3:7-11), and (2) the unveiledness of those who turn to Christ and who see and are transformed into this ultimate glory of God and the veiledness to the glory of those who remain under the old covenant (3:12-18). With this passage (3:12-18) Paul introduces the theme of the hope of glory, which he will reintroduce later in 4:14, 14–5:10.

---

2. See Introduction, 36-38, for the suggestion that the newcomers in Corinth point to Paul's sufferings as evidence that he lacked "glory," thereby invalidating his claims that his gospel fulfilled the Mosaic dispensation, Moses being popularly regarded as a still-glorious figure.

3. This excursus begins with a thanksgiving, which has been seen as a second introduction to the letter, in parallel with the benediction (1:3-7); see Thrall, 1.188.

The apologetic-polemical line continues. Against the charge that his debility disqualifies his ministry as lacking glory, Paul asserts that in his pursuit of "this ministry" he has not lost heart, has not conducted himself improperly, and does not veil the gospel (from Jews?), but, to the contrary, as he proclaims the gospel that Jesus is Lord, he deflects the knowledge of the glory of God to others (4:1-6).

Nonetheless, returning to the theme of power in weakness, he acknowledges his own frailty and thereby his utter dependence on the power of God (4:7-8). Indeed, the bearer of the light of the gospel reproduces the dying and the life of the One from whom the glory passes into human hearts. He dies that the Corinthians may live (4:9-15). The death and resurrection of the proclaimed are replicated in the proclaimer.

The exposition of the theme of his power in weakness leads Paul into a brief statement about the universal experience of power in weakness through aging and death (4:16–5:10) in the epoch between the resurrection of Christ and the general resurrection and judgment (4:15; 5:10). The unseen future aeon is laden with glory, and death will not deprive the believer of his "house eternal in the heavens" (5:1). Nonetheless, while in the body he is not yet with the Lord, and he is burdened as he faces the nakedness of death, should that precede the onset of God's future age (5:2-4).

This in turn lays the foundation for the climax of the entire passage, Paul's exposition of the apostolic office of reconciliation. Doubtless, mindful of others who seek acceptance as ministers in Corinth, Paul declares that the Corinthians should take pride in his ministry, which he exercises in a right mind through which he seeks to persuade people to be reconciled to God. This is the day of God's salvation: Christ has died and been raised for all, and God has given Paul the ministry and word of reconciliation (5:11–6:2).

That Paul's pursuit of this ministry — which is exercised in great suffering — places no stumbling block before people (6:3-10) resumes the defensive theme. By inference the minister of God suffers and is misunderstood like the One whose ambassador he is. Nonetheless, weak though outwardly he is, he bears the power of God. This apologia for his ministry reaches its climax in Paul's impassioned plea that the Corinthians as his children open wide their hearts to him and his ministry; his father's heart is wide open to them (6:11-13).

A powerful exhortation now follows. Having reminded them that he is God's mouthpiece calling on them to be reconciled to God and to be open to his ministry (5:20–6:2; 6:11-13), he demands that they separate themselves from the religious cults of Corinth (6:14–7:1).

The entire exposition concludes with a short summary, assuring them that he has wronged no one. Let the Corinthians make room in their hearts for him. Basing his judgment on the good news from Corinth brought by

139

Titus, which is the subject of the next passage, Paul expresses great confidence in them (7:2-4).

The controlling theme throughout is Paul's defense of his ministry in the new covenant; the vocabulary of ministry[4] appears frequently within these chapters. Nonetheless, it must be made clear that the subject is not ministry per se, but *Paul's* ministry. As such, the ministry of the new covenant is an eschatological ministry. The theme of God's time having come, in fulfillment of (1:20) — yet discontinuous with (3:6) — the old covenant, is powerfully stated (see 3:3; 5:14–6:2). History is now split into "no longer" and "now" aeons. Paul is claiming nothing less than to be the mouthpiece and yokefellow of God, heralding the long-awaited, newly arrived *new covenant* (see on 5:20; 6:1; 4:5). The now-illuminated — but formerly darkened — heart of the apostle is the source of light for the blind (4:6).

At the moment of eschatological fulfillment God has reconciled the world to himself. God has also given the ministry of reconciliation, or entrusted the word of reconciliation to the apostles (5:18-19). The climax of the passage is Paul's call to the Corinthians, "Be reconciled to God . . . wide[n] your hearts [to us]" (5:20; 6:11-13). This call is followed immediately by his impassioned exhortation to separate themselves from the Gentile cults (6:14–7:1).

In his presentation of himself as a minister of the new covenant, Paul employs the rich vocabulary of Isaiah 40–66 for the restoration of exiled Israel. Indeed, Paul portrays his relationships with the Corinthians in terms analogous to the relationships of the Isaianic Servant of the Lord with captive Israel (see on 5:20; 6:1).[5] Paul sees himself as the ambassador-delegate of Christ, his apostle (5:20; cf. 1:1; 12:12), and — by analogy with the Isaianic Servant — the spokesman of God, in this the "day of [God's] salvation" (6:2). Hence the new covenant, the "now"-fulfilled eschatology, and Paul's apostleship are inextricably connected.

For this reason Paul generally employs the first person "we"/"us" throughout this lengthy defense of his apostolic office.[6] This is what we may

4. Gk. διακονία, διάκονος and διακονέω.

5. See G. K. Beale, "Reconciliation," 550-81.

6. For general discussion on Paul's use of singular and plural pronouns within 2 Corinthians, see on 1:1. Throughout the extended passage on the new covenant (2:14–7:1) he will mostly employ the plural first personal pronouns (but see 6:13). This appears to be a literary plural, to emphasize primarily Paul's unique role in the ministry of the new covenant. By way of exception, however, in 3:12-18 and 4:14, 16-5:10; 5:18a, 21 the plurals refer to the new covenant people for whom Paul writes representatively.

That Paul is actually referring to himself, while using the plural, emerges in his emotional appeal, "*We* have spoken freely to you, Corinthians, and opened wide *our* hearts . . . *I* speak as to *my* children" (6:11, 13). Paul's use of first person plural pronouns within

call "the apostolic plural." By "we"/"us" Paul is not referring to himself and Timothy, the cowriter (1:1), nor even to himself, Silvanus, and Timothy, heralds of the gospel in Corinth (1:19), but to Paul as apostle. In this regard we should note the several places where Paul addresses his readers as "you."[7] Thus, implicit throughout this extended passage is Paul over against the Corinthian church. Paul's "we"/"us" does not ordinarily include them;[8] rather, by using this plural pronoun of himself as Christ's apostle, he addresses them, the church of God in that place.

These characteristics give this passage a special place within Paul's writings, as a number of scholars have observed. W. H. Bates called it "the most intricate and profound exposition of Paul's apostolic ministry to be found anywhere in his letters,"[9] and G. Bornkamm regarded it as "the great apology of the apostolic office."[10]

What, then, gave rise to this important exposition? Broadly, three views have been held. One is that Paul's defense is conditioned by objections to his apostleship that have been raised by newly arrived intruders, whoever they are deemed to be — Judaizers, "divine men," or gnostics. Another view is that Paul is responding to breaches — some of them of long-standing — between the Corinthians and him. On this view the intruders hypothesis has been overstated; Paul is seeking the Corinthians' reconciliation with himself chiefly as a prerequisite to their proper reconciliation with God (6:11-13; 5:20).[11] A further opinion is that Paul's teaching — especially 2:14–3:18 — is unconditioned by specific concerns, but is a general statement of his ministry.[12]

---

this extended passage is, in most cases, in reference to himself — not to his person but to his office as an apostle, not inclusive of the Corinthians but over against them (but see the exceptions noted above).

Other explanations are less likely. One possibility is that the "we"/"us" stands for Paul and Timothy from whom this letter comes (1:1). But this is doubtful on the grounds that in that case we would have expected to find "we"/"us" *throughout* the letter. Another possibility — that "we"/"us" refers to Paul, Silvanus and Timothy, the heralds of the gospel in Corinth (1:19) — suffers from the same objection.

7. E.g., 6:1, 11-13.

8. But see 3:12-18; 4:14, 16–5:10, 18a, 21, where he writes representatively and inclusively.

9. W. H. Bates, "Integrity," 56-69.

10. G. Bornkamm, "History of the Origin," *NTS* 8 (1962), 260.

11. See J. L. Sumney, *Identifying Paul's Opponents,* who sees the issues of 2 Corinthians to be (1) establishing criteria to evaluate ministry, (2) receiving money as evidence of genuine apostolicity, (3) that an unimpressive demeanor is exclusive of genuineness, and (4) whether divine power has been revealed in ministers' lives. P. Marshall, *Enmity,* argues that the refusal of Paul to receive patronage from the Corinthians lies at the heart of their difficulties with him.

12. See C. J. Hickling, "Sequence," 380-95.

In my view the apologetic and polemical elements in this section arise both from local and newly arrived sources. Those apologetic and polemical elements are reflected in (1) Paul's recognition of his own physical deficiencies,[13] along with his assertion of perseverance in spite of them (2:14; 4:1, 7–5:10; 6:3-10); as a sufferer he replicates, as he spreads, the knowledge of the glory of the Sufferer, the Crucified; (2) his denial that he is self-commended (3:1; 4:2; 5:12; 6:4; 7:11); (3) his assertions — direct and oblique — of the insincerity of "many who peddle the word of God" (2:17; 4:2); and (4) his admonition to those who remain enmeshed in the cults of Corinth to "come out from them and be separate" (6:14–7:1).

Two obstacles stand in the way of clear identification of Paul's critics and opponents in this passage. One is that Paul's remarks are so fragmentary as to make precision difficult. Second, there is little from the Corinthian side, apart from phrases where Paul appears to be quoting their words (e.g., 10:10, which is from a later part of the letter), and even these stand within Paul's text, not theirs. The second is that Paul here chooses to allow the present situation to give him the opportunity to make broader theological statements that transcend — and therefore, to a degree, mask — the original situation.[14]

Mindful of these inherent limitations, the following suggestions are offered as to the criticisms and opposition Paul may have been addressing at that time.

First, Paul stood criticized for inadequacy in ministry. This criticism, which was along superspiritual lines.[15] Paul appears to have addressed in the preceding major section of the letter (1:1–2:13; see especially 1:12, 17; cf. 10:2-7). In that section Paul does not deny or even play down his personal difficulties in the period since the unsuccessful second visit. Is this because Paul wished not only to defend himself from misunderstanding and misinformation but also to lay a foundation for the theology of glory in suffering — both of the minister of God and of the people of God, based on the glory of the Crucified — in this and later sections of the letter? Thus, so much of what he now writes — his use of the captive image (2:14-16), his argument for

---

13. Which he has already acknowledged in the First Letter (e.g., 1 Cor 4:8-13).

14. A parallel may be seen in the first canonical letter, where Paul responds to matters of an "occasional" kind — by reports from Corinth (1:11; 5:1) and questions from Corinth (7:1, 25; 8:1; 12:1; 16:1) — while also expanding topically in related areas (e.g., chaps. 1–4, cf. 1:11; chaps. 8–11, cf. 8:1). Paul is not content merely to respond; he takes the opportunity to teach as well. This appears to be true also for 2 Corinthians 2:14–7:4.

15. Paul's clarifying statements that being at home in the body means absence from the Lord (5:6b-7) appears to be addressed to an overrealized eschatology (cf. 1 Cor 4:8; 14:36-37; 15:12?). His defense of his ministry against a perceived inadequacy in paranormal behavior (5:11-13) could be in response to the Judaizers or the superspiritual or both.

God-given competency in ministry (2:16; 3:5-6), his admission as one who is subject to aging and death (4:8-12, 16–5:10) to being a mere "jar of clay" (4:7), in whom, nonetheless, may be seen great endurance (6:4) in the face of adversity (6:3-10) as the the sign of the new aeon and the mark of true apostleship (12:12) — follows directly as an expansion upon the sufferings mentioned in the preceding passage (1:1–2:13). Just as suffering and the mind of the servant were fundamental to Jesus (cf. 5:21; 8:9; 10:1), so, too, suffering and serving were fundamental to his true minister — as opposed to the false apostle (1:24; 4:5; cf. 11:13, 23).

Second, Paul was responding to the intruders' (probable) claim that there was but one covenant and Jesus belonged within that still-effective covenant of the still-glorious Moses.[16] In their view Peter had come earlier to Corinth, establishing this very point, and they were continuing his work (see on 10:13-15). From their perspective Paul was promoting a schism by Jews (and Gentiles?) from the historic people of God, the evidence for which was his failure to promote "righteousness" in acceptable terms. Such a scenario would make sense of Paul's reference to those who bring letters of commendation and who peddle the word of God (2:17–3:1), which is followed immediately by his dramatic dismissal of the old covenant as having been abolished and therefore obsolete (3:7-15) in light of the eschatologically fulfilling arrival of the new covenant of righteousness and the Spirit (3:3-9, 18). Moreover, it would go some distance to explain Paul's exposition of Christ's death as universally applicable — that is, not merely for the people of Israel — as the means of reconciliation with God (5:14-21). It is from these newly arrived, letter-commended ministers, apparently, that the telling complaint was made that Paul was merely self-commended (see on 3:1).[17]

Third, Paul was acutely sensitive to the failure of certain Gentile elements within the community of believers to separate themselves from the cultic life of the community of unbelievers (6:14–7:1; cf. I Cor 8–10 passim). It is quite likely that the intractable involvement in sexually promiscuous behavior was connected with the local cults (see on 12:20–13:2). The obduracy of particular Corinthians in such matters was, of course, deeply offensive to Paul. Beyond that, Paul's critics — whether local or newly arrived — could point to such ongoing idolatry (and immorality?) as proof-positive of Paul's incompetence and indeed inauthenticity as an apostle.

Such may have been the painful issues Paul felt driven to address; though — we repeat — our reconstructions are of necessity conjectural.

Whatever the truth about the currents of thought in Corinth at the time — and we are unlikely ever to know them with confidence — Paul appears

---

16. See Introduction, 37-38.
17. See S. J. Hafemann, " 'Self-Commendation,' " 66-88.

to have constructed this powerful defense as a statement in its own right. Its applicability is not finally dependent upon our ability to reconstruct the historical situation. As in the First Letter, Paul appears to have allowed the problems of the moment to stimulate a Spirit-led response of breadth and depth that profoundly transcends the immediate and now long-forgotten circumstances in Corinth, providing believers and churches from every generation with godly instruction and inspiration.

What, then, is the abiding significance of Paul's exposition? In sum, three matters arise from our text.

First, in Christ God has eschatologically divided history. There is a new covenant and a new creation (3:6; 5:17), both of which were anticipated in the prophetic aeon (Jer 31:31-34; Isa 43:18-19; 65:17). The net result of being under the old covenant was condemnation and death; under the new there is righteousness, reconciliation with God, freedom, and spiritual transformation. Under the existing order of creation there is decay and death; under the new there is the hope of the permanent glory of God (3:12), that is, of ultimate re-creation (3:18; 4:16-18).

Because all will be raised from the dead (4:14) and judged (5:10), Paul pursues his ministry with great seriousness (5:11). Meanwhile all have the Spirit (5:5), who inspires longing for the onset of the coming age (5:2-4). Clearly there are great benefits to those who align themselves with God's saving purposes in Christ. Paul's exhortation to his original readers in light of the eschatological moment that has now come (6:1-2) — "be reconciled to God" — still stands.

In consequence — and this is the second teaching of continuing significance — Paul's ministry should be seen as eschatologically unique and therefore unrepeatable. It stood right next to the history-splitting, universally applicable (5:14-17), reconciling death and resurrection of Christ (5:18-19). Paul was God's chosen pioneer in a God-given diaconate to the Gentiles. God's provision of the diaconate and the word of reconciliation were integrally connected with that reconciling event at the first Easter.

Because of God's call to him to be an apostle, Paul was the bringer of light (4:6), the very mouth of God and the yokefellow of God in his ministry to the churches at the turning of the aeons (5:20–6:2). As such, Paul's boldly uttered words (3:12) were God's revelation to a church like Corinth (4:2), just as Isaiah the prophet's words had been to captive Israel under the epoch of the old covenant. The signs, wonders, and miracles wrought in patient endurance by Paul marked him out as an apostle of Christ in the face of the self-proclaimed apostles who had recently come to Corinth (12:12; 11:13-15).

In other words, this defensive excursus serves to undergird the authority of Paul, through his words spoken and written, as Christ's apostle to the

Gentiles, then and now (cf. 10:8; 13:10). Paul was and remains the mouth of God (cf. 5:20), one to whom the churches, in obedience to God, must submit. Resistance to that was and remains the "Corinthian" problem.

Third, Paul's ministry stands as a model for the ministry of other missionaries and pastors who would come after him throughout history down to the present time. To be sure, in some respects — as we have noted above — Paul was unique as the instrument of God's revelation; his signs, wonders, and miracles wrought in patient endurance were evidence of that uniqueness. Nonetheless, Paul's fidelity to God's circumscribed, "given" word, the gospel, his exaltation of Christ, his demands for holiness, his obediently transparent lifestyle, and his embodiment of Christ's own sacrifice in his service of the churches — in the face of their fickleness, even perfidiousness — provide a paradigm for ministers in every generation and in every culture. As such, 2 Cor 2:14–7:4 may be included with Paul's other "pastoral letters" in their applicability to ministers of the gospel.

A. PAUL DEFENDS HIS MINISTRY (2:14–4:6)

1. God's Victory Procession (2:14-17)

This passage is very important within the structure of the letter. As noted earlier,[1] there is a significant continuity with the preceding section. At the same time the thanksgiving with which it opens may be seen as a second beginning to the letter, parallel with the initial benediction.[2] The passage bears an important relation to the subsection 2:14–4:6, in particular to 4:1-6. There is significant repetition of vocabulary and ideas between 2:14-17 and 4:1-6,[3] so that those passages "frame" the subsection.

> 14 But thanks be to God, who always leads us in triumphal procession in Christ and through us spreads everywhere the fragrance of the knowledge of him. 15 For we are to God the aroma of Christ among those who are being saved and those who are perishing. 16 To the one we are the smell of death; to the other, the fragrance of life. And who

---

1. See above, 137-38 (following III).

2. See J. Lambrecht, "Structure," 345-46, and Thrall, 1.188-89, for analyses of the structure of 2:14–7:4. It is clear that, whereas this section can be subdivided in various ways, 2:14–4:6 is a discrete subsection, with many repetitions occurring in the "framing" passages 2:14-17 and 4:1-6; see Thrall, 1.189 n. 6.

3. E.g., τοῖς ἀπολλυμένοις (2:15); τοῖς ἀπολλυμένοις (4:3); τῆς γνώσεως αὐτοῦ (2:14); τῆς γνώσεως . . . τοῦ θεοῦ (4:6); καπηλεύοντες τὸν λόγον τοῦ θεοῦ (2:17); δολοῦντες τὸν λόγον τοῦ θεοῦ (4:2); κατέναντι τοῦ θεοῦ (2:17); ἐνώπιον τοῦ θεοῦ (4:2).

is equal to such a task? 17 Unlike so many,[4] we do not peddle the word of God for profit. On the contrary, in Christ we speak before God with sincerity, like men sent from God.

In the immediately preceding passage Paul described his sufferings in Troas (vv. 12-13), after which he moved on to Macedonia,[5] where further pain awaited him (7:5). But Paul has also been alluding to other suffering in the recent past — the deadly peril in Asia (1:8-11) and the anguish (there?) in writing to the Corinthians (2:4). Joined to the suffering motif, however, is the triumph of the power of God, expressed earlier as God's comfort and deliverance of Paul (1:3-11). This power-in-weakness theme, which will reappear at other points within the defensive excursus on new covenant ministry (cf. 4:7–5:10; 6:3-10), appears at the beginning of the excursus in the paradoxical triumphal but antitriumphal metaphor (2:14-16).[6]

For the moment Paul lays aside the other major theme to this point in the letter, namely, his defense of the charge that in not returning to Corinth but sending a letter instead he made his plans "lightly" and "according to the flesh" (1:12–2:2). Paul now rests his defense of his travel decision to give an account of his ministry under the new covenant.

The opening metaphor is a complex combination of a victory procession (v. 14) and the impact of fragrance and aroma on God and people (vv. 15-16). As God leads Paul in his victory procession through Paul's preaching and life, the apostle spreads the fragrance of the knowledge of Christ wherever he goes (v. 14). Yet, the bearer of this fragrance to people suffers in the course of his apostleship, whether in Ephesus or Troas. Hence Paul sees himself — in continuity with "the sufferings of Christ"[7] — as the aroma of an acceptable sacrifice ascending to God (v. 15a).

The paradoxical nature of the metaphor may be conditioned by the circumstances then prevailing in Corinth. The arrival of the "peddlers" (v. 17) may have cast Paul in a different light in the eyes of the Corinthians, at least so

---

4. Gk. οἱ πόλλοι, "the many," is to be preferred to οἱ λοίποι (as in p[46] and Marcion).

5. See generally J. Murphy-O'Connor, "Paul and Macedonia"; A. C. Perriman, "Between Troas and Macedonia," 39-41; J. I. H. McDonald, "Paul and the Preaching Ministry," 35-50.

6. We agree with Perriman, 39, insofar as he argues (against, e.g., Hughes and Barrett) for the continuity of this passage with the preceding material. However, we disagree with his preference for an interpretation of the metaphor along exclusively positive lines (with Barrett — "glory of the triumph"), rather than along paradoxical lines ("strength-in-weakness"). In our view the triumph metaphor of 2:14 paradoxically expresses the power of God in the apostolic weakness, a theme that Paul has already introduced within the letter (1:3-11; 2:4, 12-13) and which will ofter reappear (4:7-15; 6:3-10; 12:4-4, 7-9).

7. Cf. 1:5.

146

it appears to Paul. Paul's word to characterize their self-presentation is *hyper,* "above," "superior." He calls them "superlative" *(hyperlian)* apostles and is sensitive to the inference that he is, thereby, "inferior" (11:5; 12:11). They are, indeed, triumphalists, whose "boasting" of superiority has forced Paul to the "foolishness" of "boasting" — in his case, by contrast, in his "weaknesses" (see on 11:1–12:13). His catalogue of privations and suffering in ministry in the "Fool's Speech" proper (11:23–12:10; see also 4:7-12; 6:3-10) serves as commentary on the antitriumphalist element in the victory parade metaphor.

This triumphal yet antitriumphal image points to Paul's effectiveness in ministry (see also on 10:3-6). As God leads Paul in triumphal parade, his hearers are divided into those who are being saved and those who are perishing (v. 15b, c). For some Paul is the fragrance of death (v. 16a), to others of life (v. 16b), depending on their response to the apostolic message of the death and resurrection of Christ. Their response to Paul confirms them either in death (those who are perishing) or life (those who are being saved), causing him to cry, "Who is equal to such a task?" (v. 16c).

Paul's apologetic for his ministry under the triumph–fragrance–aroma–fragrance imagery (vv. 14-16) then gives way to a polemical note. Unlike the many who peddle the word of God, Paul exercises his ministry out of sincere motives, as called by and accountable to God (v. 17). This negative contrast prepares the ground for the extended contrasts of new and old covenant ministries — their glories and their peoples — that will unfold in the next chapter.

14 The sudden[8] and unheralded introduction[9] of triumphal imagery[10]

---

8. The contrastive but usually untranslated δέ indicates both (1) a new section (as at v. 12) and (2) the greatness of God in contrast to the human predicament; ὁ δὲ θεός — or similar words — are very common — see, e.g., Luke 16:15; 18:7; Acts 3:18; 13:30; Rom 15:5, 13; 16:20; 1 Cor 6:14; 15:57; Gal 3:20; Eph 2:4; Phil 4:19; Heb 13:20; 1 Pet 5:10. Paul is indeed giving deliberate thanks to God in contrast to listing the difficulties in Troas (vv. 12-13) and Asia (1:8-10), but in so doing he introduces a metaphor that will establish the power-in-weakness character of the new covenant ministry set out in the excursus following (2:14–7:4).

9. See P. B. Duff, "Metaphor, Motif and Meaning," 79-92, who holds 2:14–6:13; 7:2-4 to be "an independent letter fragment," for the suggestion that the striking triumph vocabulary was carefully chosen by Paul to attract the attention of the various groups in Corinth.

10. Gk. θριαμβεύοντι, "leads in triumph"; NIV, "leads . . . in triumphal procession." For comprehensive analysis of the lexical background of θριαμβεύω (which appears in the NT elsewhere only at Col 2:15 and not at all in the LXX) and historical references to Roman victory processions see S. Hafemann, *Suffering and Ministry,* 16-34 (also Furnish, 174-75; Thrall, 1.191-95). Among the various views of the meaning of the metaphor we note: (1) Hafemann, 18-19, who rejects ten meanings canvassed by others in favor of this definition: ". . . all the evidence points to the conclusion that there is only one basic and common meaning for this term available in the time of Paul, namely, that of the triumphal procession in which the conquered enemies were usually led as slaves to death,

147

is striking. To be sure, Paul has spoken of God's comfort and deliverance of him (1:3-11), but nothing has prepared the reader — then or now — for the

---

being spared this death only by an act of grace on the part of the one celebrating the triumph" (33). Because a military triumph must precede a triumphant procession Hafemann concludes that the imagery points to God's triumph over Paul on the Damascus road and then to his leading the apostle to his death as a minister of the gospel. But against Hafemann it is to be noted that Paul declared that God had delivered him from "deadly peril" (1:10). Indeed, 2 Corinthians is more about Paul's suffering and the *process* of dying (see 4:7-12) than summary death as by execution in the Roman triumph. Moreover, to see in this one word the whole story of God's triumph over Paul in his conversion and God's subsequent leadership of him as his minister may be to prove too much from that single word. In any case, it is doubtful whether the readers would have read all this into θριαμβεύω.

(2) Furnish, 175, who observes that the notion of the apostle being put on display is the essence of the metaphor and that it is by no means certain that a Roman triumph is in mind. He sees as the main point that the gospel of Christ is effectively proclaimed through Paul's ministry. But this minimizes the contrastive note of thanksgiving in the face of suffering, which is so important in this passage.

(3) P. B. Duff, "Metaphor, Motif and Meaning," 79-92, who suggests that in this image Paul uses a calculated ambivalence, which his various readers may interpret either as a Roman victory triumph or a Hellenistic royal epiphany procession, depending on their opposition or support of Paul.

(4) Hughes, 76-79, who views this image as indicating "victorious progress," and Barrett, 98, who regards "Paul . . . [as] represent[ing] himself as one of the victorious general's soldiers sharing in the glory of the triumph."

In our view θριαμβεύοντι should be regarded as a passing allusion to a Roman victory procession intended to express both (1) the reality of God's sovereignty in Paul's ministry as a preacher of Christ (cf. Paul's prayer ἵνα ὁ λόγος τοῦ κυρίου τρέχῃ καὶ δοξάζεται — 2 Thess 3:1), and (2) the itinerant apostle's suffering in that ministry.

In regard to (2), P. Marshall, "Metaphor of Social Shame," 302-17, has argued plausibly that to be "led in triumph" is a metaphor of humiliation. Marshall finds evidence of the humiliation of the captives in Seneca's comments: they are "placed upon a foreign barrow to grace the procession of a proud and brutal victor" and "driven in front of the chariot of another" (*On the Happy Life* 25.4). A culturally vivid picture of apostolic humiliation drawn from the Roman triumph but not using the present vocabulary is to be seen in 1 Cor 4:9 — ὁ θεὸς ἡμᾶς τοὺς ἀποστόλους ἐσχάτους ἀπέδειξιν ὡς ἐπιθανατίους, ὅτι θέατρον ἐγενήθημεν τῷ κόσμῳ καὶ ἀγγέλοις καὶ ἀνθρώποις, "God has put us apostles on display at the end of the procession, like men condemned to die in the arena . . . a spectacle to the whole universe, to angels as well as to men," which G. D. Fee, *1 Corinthians,* 174-75, takes to refer to the Roman triumph, as in 2 Cor 2:14.

That *God* leads Paul *in triumph* is a paradox. It is at the same time both triumphal (God is the leader) and antitriumphal ("led in triumph" meant suffering).

Further, in our view θριαμβεύω must be regarded as integral with the two connected images of fragrance and aroma; it does not stand alone. On the one hand, God's sovereignty is seen in the impact of the ministry ("a fragrance from death to death" and "from life to life" — v. 16). On the other hand, "the aroma of Christ to God" (v. 15a) speaks of sacrificial suffering. Among many other views see, e.g., S. B. Heiny, "The Motive for the Metaphor," 1-21.

148

remarkable thanksgiving[11] with which he begins the section on the ministry of the new covenant (2:14–7:4).[12]

There is a natural structure[13] to this powerfully metaphorical verse. A brief thanksgiving ("But thanks be to God"[14]) is followed by two participles, one that God "always *leads* us in *triumphal procession,*" the other — which amplifies the first — that God "*spreads*[15] the fragrance of the knowledge of [Christ[16]] through us in every place." Each participle is qualified by a universal: God "*always* leads us . . . spreads *in every place*[17] the . . . knowledge of [Christ] through us."

> Thanks be to God,
>> who always
>> leads   us in triumph in Christ
> and through us
>> spreads the fragrance of the knowledge of [Christ]
>> in every place.

Set against the barely escaped deadly perils of Asia (1:8-10), the writing of the emotion-wrought letter (2:4), and the deep disappointment in Troas (1:12-13), Paul gives thanks to God that, despite everything, he leads his minister, Paul,[18] in triumph.

---

11. Gk. τῷ δὲ θεῷ χάρις.

12. Only after this defense is completed will he resume his travel narrative, describing his coming to Macedonia and his eventual reunion with Titus (7:5-6).

13. Gk.   τῷ δὲ θεῷ χάρις
             τῷ πάντοτε θριαμβεύοντι   ἡμᾶς ἐν τῷ Χριστῷ
             καὶ τὴν ὀσμὴν   τῆς γνώσεως αὐτοῦ
                  φανεροῦντι δι' ἡμῶν
       ἐν παντὶ τόπῳ.

14. Man of faith that he is, Paul gives thanks to his God through it all. As God has delivered him from danger (1:10) and God makes him "sufficient" for the ministry of the new covenant (2:16; 3:6), so *God* also leads him in triumph in the midst of suffering.

15. Gk. φανεροῦντι. The verb φανερόω means to make visible an invisible reality (important within 2 Corinthians — 2:14; 4:10, 11; 5:10, 11; 7:12; 11:6; cf. the adverb φανερῶς in 4:2). The suggestion noted in Furnish, 175, that Paul is here using the vocabulary of his opponents, is questionable given its use in 1 Cor 4:5 and Rom 1:19; 3:21; 16:26.

16. Gk. τῆς γνώσεως αὐτοῦ. Whose "knowledge" does Paul make known? Does αὐτοῦ have God (so, e.g., Furnish) or Christ (so, e.g., Plummer) as its antecedent? Because αὐτοῦ lies between ἐν τῷ Χριστῷ and Χριστοῦ εὐωδία, it is more probably the "knowledge *of Christ*" rather than the "knowledge of God" that is in Paul's mind. Nonetheless, the "knowledge of [Christ]" is the means to the "knowledge of [God]" (see 4:4, 6).

17. The phrase ἐν παντὶ τόπῳ specifies that in *each* place Paul goes, he spreads the fragrance of the knowledge of Christ (cf. ἐν ὅλῳ τῷ κόσμῳ — 1 Thess 1:8; Rom 1:8).

18. Paul here reverts to the plural "we"/"us," following a passage cast in the singular "I"/"me" setting out his feelings at the writing of the "Severe Letter" (2:3, 4, 9)

It is, indeed, the triumph of God, here accentuated by the universals "always . . . in every place"; if Paul triumphs, it is not of himself but only of God, and that through weakness. There is paradox here, as implied by the metaphor "lead [captive] in triumph," which points at the same moment to the victory of a conquering general *and* the humiliation of his captives marching to execution. The metaphor is at the same time triumphal and antitriumphal. It is as God leads his servants as *prisoners of war* in a victory parade that God spreads the knowledge of Christ everywhere through them. Whereas in such victory processions the prisoners would be dejected and embittered, from this captive's lips comes only thanksgiving to God, his captor. Here is restated the power-in-weakness theme (cf. 1:3-11) that pervades the letter.[19]

It is quite possible that Paul's use of the "triumph" metaphor is calculated to answer those Corinthians who, we infer, regard him as physically and spiritually debilitated (10:3-4, 7, 10; 13:3). To be sure, his ministry is marked by suffering, but so far from that disqualifying him as a minister, God's leading him *in Christ* as a suffering servant thereby legitimates his ministry. Christ's humiliation in crucifixion is reproduced in the life of his servant. All that he endures as a preacher is in continuity with the crucified Christ he preaches (5:21; cf. 6:4-10). There is no hiatus between the sufferings of Christ and the sufferings of the apostle in a world blinded to God and alienated from God (4:4; 5:18-20). The "sufferings of Christ" do indeed flow over into the apostle's life (1:5). His "weaknesses" are "on behalf of" Christ (12:10). It is "for Jesus' sake" that he is their "slave" (4:5), that he is continually being given over to death (4:11).

The image of the captive-slave in a military procession is critical both to the sovereignty of God and to his servants' sufferings "in Christ" as they proclaim him; it is *"in Christ"* that God leads him.

The continuity of suffering shared by the obedient Christ and his faithful servant forms a point of contrast with newly arrived "superlative" apostles (11:5; 12:11). These "false apostles" (11:13) corrupt the message of Christ to their own advantage (2:17; cf. 4:2), possibly avoiding some of the opprobrium of the world by so doing. It appears that they compound that sin by pointing to the apostle's distress as evidence of his inferiority in contrast to their various gifts, which are evidence of their supposed superiority to him (see on 10:12–12:13 passim).[20]

---

and the difficult experience at Troas (2:12-13). For Paul's use of singular and plural pronouns within this letter see generally on 1:1.

19. As the letter unfolds, Paul will refer at length, though in more general terms, to his *life* of suffering as a minister of the gospel (4:7-12; 6:4-10: 11:23–12:13).

20. To be noted is Duff's view, "Metaphor, Motif and Meaning," 90-92, that Paul's metaphor "led in triumph" is directed apologetically to those who say that God is taking

Powerful as the triumphal but antitriumphal image is, however, it must not be separated from that of the fragrance-aroma[21] image employed in the third section of this verse and which reappears with different vocabulary in v. 15 and the same vocabulary in v. 16,[22] but transmuted in those verses to a new image, that of the Levitical sacrifices. In this verse as "God . . . spreads . . . the fragrance of the knowledge [of Christ] through us," it is probably connected with the image of the Roman triumph, in which the prisoners in the captivity procession strew incense as they walk.[23]

God makes manifest the fragrance of the knowledge of Christ everywhere through "us." But this manifestation of Christ is not located in Paul's *person* — as if by some kind of incarnation[24] — but *in his gospel ministry*. This is clear from the immediate context, which shows that Paul is referring to his reason for coming to Troas, namely, "for the gospel of Christ" (v. 12). It is by Paul, as herald of Christ, that God manifests the knowledge of Christ. It is not in his person alone, but through Christ crucified and risen whom he proclaims and whose sufferings he replicates, that Paul manifests the knowl-

---

vengeance on Paul for embezzlement. But (1) there is no clear evidence in the passages quoted (2:17; 4:2; 7:2) that Paul was accused of embezzlement, and (2) it is more likely that he was here accused of "inadequacy" (cf. 2:16; 3:5, 6), and that the imagery of God's prisoner of war in his victory parade is well accounted for on this basis.

21. The vocabulary is ὀσμήν (v. 14) . . . εὐωδία (v. 15) . . . ὀσμὴ . . . ὀσμή (v. 16), on which see S. Hafemann, *Suffering and Ministry,* 35-49. It should be noted (a) that the two words often occur together in the LXX (ὀσμὴ εὐωδίας τῷ κυρίῳ) in sacrificial contexts (e.g., Lev 1:9, 13, 17; 2:2), where they have the sense of *"terminus technicus* meaning 'a soothing, tranquillizing odor of sacrifices acceptable to YHWH' " (so BDB, 629, 926); (b) that ὀσμὴ εὐωδίας is found twice elsewhere in Paul's letters (Eph 5:2; Phil 4:18); in both cases θυσία appears in the context; and (c) that where the LXX metonymy is employed, but the words are separated as in 2 Cor 2:14-16, ὀσμή and εὐωδία are virtual synonyms for the odor of acceptable sacrifice (so Sir 24:15).

22. Gk. ὀσμή (v. 14), εὐωδία (v. 15), and ὀσμή (v. 16).

23. The strewing of incense as part of the victory ceremonial is mentioned at the triumph of Scipio Africanus minor (Appian, *Punic Wars* 66). The use in context of θριαμβεύω with ὀσμή appears to demand some allusive connection of this kind, despite the Levitical/cultic use of ὀσμή in the LXX and elsewhere in Paul (see above, n. 38). Bultmann, 64, rejects the association of ὀσμή both with incense and with sacrifice, preferring "the ancient idea that fragrance is a sign of the divine presence and the divine life." But this is to introduce a complicating and extraneous image into the discussion.

24. *Contra* Hafemann, *Suffering and Ministry,* 17: ". . . Paul views himself in his apostolic calling not only as one who *preaches* the message of good news to the world, but equally important, as one ordained by God to be an *embodiment* of that gospel, called to reveal the knowledge of God by and through his very life. It is this identification of the message with the messenger, first seen in Christ and then carried on in his apostles, that Paul develops in 2:14-16a." It is better, however, to emphasize that the sufferings of the apostle replicate the sufferings of the Lord as a *consequence* of Paul's preaching of Christ.

151

edge of Christ. The proclamation of Christ is like a strong fragrance, unseen but yet powerful, impinging on all who encounter Paul in his sufferings as he preaches Christ wherever he goes.[25] In the victory parade metaphor of this verse, the apostle is God's captive, whom God leads about spreading the knowledge of Christ — incense-like — by means of the proclamation of Christ.

15 Paul's initial "for"[26] immediately picks up the "fragrance" of the previous verse, which is now given as "aroma." Paul is the "aroma of Christ" that impacts concurrently[27] both (1) vertically ("to God") and (2) horizontally among people ("among those who are being saved and among those who are perishing").

Thus part (c) of the previous verse ("God . . . spreads . . . the fragrance . . . of [Christ] through *us*") is the logical basis for part (a) of this verse ("*for we* are to God the aroma of Christ . . ."), and parts (b) and (c) represent the two groups for whom this is true ("those who are being saved" and "those who are perishing"). These in turn form the first two parts of the chiasmus that will be completed in v. 16. The Greek word order of v. 15a ("because *of Christ* an aroma we are to God") points to the significance of Christ in this passage.[28]

One aspect of the metaphor of v. 15 is that the suffering apostle, like the Christ he preaches, is analogous to the aroma of the sacrificial victim that, as in the Levitical picture, ascends to the nostrils of God.[29] Strikingly, Paul asserts that "*we* are the aroma of Christ to God." This suffering arises because the world to which Christ came and in which the apostle preaches Christ is hostile to God. Paul implies that his sacrifice, like that of Christ himself, is one with which God is well pleased, as with those sacrifices acceptable to God under the old order. In the previous verse the fragrance of Christ was the knowledge of him conveyed by the apostle's preaching. But in this verse the

---

25. Thrall, 1.196-99, gives alternative connotations of ὀσμή in this context. In addition to the above, these include ὀσμή as signifying (1) the imperfect nature of revelation, (2) the presence of divinity, (3) an association with OT Wisdom, and (4) the Levitical imagery of acceptable sacrifice. None of these suggestions is likely to be what Paul had in mind. In our view the ὀσμή imagery (1) is continuous with the Roman victory parade, in particular the use of incense, and (2) refers to the all-pervasive, irresistible impact of that powerful odor. The word of God, like a strong odor, is invisible yet powerfully effective.

26. Gk. ὅτι, expressing a "causal" relationship between the previous verse and this verse.

27. Gk. τῷ θεῷ ἐν τοῖς σῳζομένοις καὶ ἐν τοῖς ἀπολλυμένοις.

28. This significance also emerges from Paul's repetition of Christ within vv. 12-15: "gospel of *Christ*" (v. 12). . . . God . . . leads us . . . in *Christ*. . . . [God] . . . spreads . . . the knowledge of [*Christ*] (v. 14). . . . of *Christ* an aroma we are . . ." (v. 15).

29. E.g., Lev 1:9, 13, 17; 2:2.

aroma of Christ, insofar as it impinges on God, is the apostle's sacrificial sufferings, which rise, odorlike, to God.[30]

The apostle as this aroma, however, also impinges on humankind, "among those who are being saved and those who are perishing." Reference to the earlier letter shows that Paul's "*we* are the aroma" should not be taken as if he himself, as distinct from his preaching of the cross, is that aroma:

1 Corinthians 1:18	2 Corinthians 2:15
For the *message of the cross*	For *we* are to God the aroma of Christ
is foolishness to *those who are perishing,*	among *those who are being saved*
but to us *who are being saved* it is the power of God.	and *those who are perishing.*

It is Paul as the *proclaimer* of Christ crucified, and who as a consequence suffers, who is the aroma of Christ. The personally powerful fragrance-aroma imagery of vv. 14-16 is controlled by the immediate context, which began with his reference to coming to Troas "for the gospel of Christ."

Paul divides those among whom he moves into one of two classes — "those who are being saved" and "those who are perishing."[31] There is no third group. Here we are reminded of the eschatological character of the gospel;[32] the apostle's hearers are either those who, through the word of God, are now reconciled to God — those who are being saved — or those who remain alienated from God, perishing (cf. 2 Thess 1:7-10). The "day of Christ" will reveal who are saved and who are lost (cf. 1:14; 4:14; 5:10; 1 Thess 5:2; 1 Cor 1:8; 5:5).

The present tenses for "being saved" and "perishing" — used in identical terms as in 1 Cor 1:18 above — point to the dynamic character of the gospel of Christ, the word of God. It is not that "being saved" or "perishing" are themselves processes but that the *message* borne by the apostle as he is led about by God *dynamically divides* the hearers into one of two groups.

---

30. *Contra* S. J. Hafemann, *Suffering and Ministry,* 45: "the two images" (i.e., "triumphal procession" and "sacrificial aroma") . . . "form a coherent picture of Paul as the medium of the revelation of the knowledge of God manifested in Christ." In our reading of vv. 12-16 this is only true of Paul, who suffers as a herald of Christ. The sacrificial Paul in himself is no revelation of God.

31. Cf. 2 Thess 2:10. Only "those who are perishing" are mentioned in 4:3, who are there identified as "unbelievers" in 4:4.

32. Bultmann comments: "The gospel is . . . not equivocal, and hearing spells decision (cf. 4:2). In the separation which it brings about between the σῳζόμενοι and the ἀπολλύμενοι there occurs the eschatological event, the judgement" (68).

It is probably not fortuitous that the stress in the chiasmus (vv. 15b, c, 16 a, b), that is, on the first and last line, is on "being saved" and "life." God's intention is positive, that is, to save, to give life. John Calvin noted that we must "distinguish between the proper office of the gospel, and the accidental one (so to speak) which must be imputed to the depravity of mankind, to which it is owing, that life is turned into death."[33] God's "proper" work is "to save" and "give life," whereas his "accidental" work is to cause to "perish." In this regard, the apostolic word, like the prophetic, if proclaimed in uncorrupted form (cf. 2:17; 4:2), is invariably powerful, leaving no hearer unaffected (see, e.g., Isa 55:10-11).

16 The previous verse is now further elaborated. The untranslated particle *men* immediately picks up the "aroma of Christ . . . among those perishing" as "to some a fragrance of death to death." The balancing particle *de* picks up "aroma of Christ . . . among those who are being saved" as "to others a fragrance of life."

Structurally in this three-part verse, parts (a) and (b) complete the chiasmus begun in v. 15b and v. 15c. Part (c) of v. 16 is a question (lit. "who is sufficient to these things?") that arises either from the aroma image (vv. 15-16) alone or more probably — since the pronoun ("these things") is plural — from both it and its predecessor, the fragrance image (v. 14).

The chiasmus (vv. 15b, c, 16a, b) may be set out as follows:

We are . . .
> the aroma of Christ

A		among those	being saved
B	and	those	perishing
B		to some the fragrance of death to death	
A		to others the fragrance of life to life.	

The references to "death" and "life"[34] point to the death and resurrection of Christ, as in "the gospel of Christ" that Paul proclaims wherever he goes (v. 12; cf. v. 14). The "fragrance" of the death of Christ smelled in the apostolic herald by those who reject Christ crucified is "unto death," a sign of their own eternal "death." The "fragrance" of the risen Christ smelled in the apostle by those who turn to Christ is "unto life," a sign of their own eternal "life."[35] This

---

33. John Calvin, *Romans–Galatians,* 1764.

34. The rabbis compared the various effects of the Torah on those who read it: "since he busies himself with the Torah, it becomes the medicine of life . . . but for everyone who does not busy himself with the Torah for its own sake, it becomes the medicine of death" (Str-B 3.498ff., quoted in Bultmann, 68).

35. Phrases such as ἐκ θανάτου εἰς θάνατον . . . ἐκ ζωῆς εἰς ζωήν suggest a Semitic idiom expressing superlatives, namely, "the stench of *ultimate* death . . . the fragrance of *ultimate* life" (Furnish, 177); for a similar construction see 3:18; 4:17; Rom 1:17.

"death" and "life" are encountered in Christ's physical absence in the persona of the apostolic messenger.

Are we to give a positive or a negative answer to Paul's question, "Who is sufficient. . . ?"[36] Perhaps in favor of a negative is his reference to "those who peddle the word of God" (v. 17), who might have suggested that they were, indeed, adequate for such a task.[37] In this case Paul would be saying that neither they nor he is sufficient for this ministry. Had not Joel asked, "Who is *sufficient* for this?" (i.e., the "Day of the Lord" — Joel 2:11), expecting the reply, "No one." But given his confident statements in the verses following, it is more likely that Paul's question is actually an assertion of his adequacy for the ministry of an apostle. Unlike these other preachers Paul's ministry originates in God (2:17), and he is made adequate for it by God (3:6).[38]

Paul, therefore, is making a stupendous claim — Barrett called it "the horrifying truth"[39] — that people encounter (the aroma of) Christ crucified and risen in the one who preaches Christ crucified and risen, and that eternal destinies are determined by that encounter.[40] Small wonder, therefore, that he cries out: "Who is sufficient[41] for these things?" Rudolf Bultmann asks: "Who can be a bearer of such a word. . . ?"[42] Who indeed? Paul will give his answer to that question a few verses later: "[God] has made us sufficient as ministers of a new covenant" (3:6). Paul's question masks an assertion; he is "sufficient" in ministry, despite what his detractors say.[43]

For this reason, Paul's movements — associated as they often were with difficulty and suffering — should be viewed aright. So far from being a

36. See Thrall, 1.208-10, for extended discussion of this question.

37. Thrall, 1.208, notes, with references, that Paul's τίς questions usually expect a negative reply.

38. It is possible that the Corinthians have taken out of context his words ὃς οὐκ εἰμὶ ἱκανὸς καλεῖσθαι ἀπόστολος (1 Cor 15:9), to which Paul must now reply.

39. Barrett, 102.

40. See Thrall, 1.207-08, for discussion of the question why Paul would offer thanks to God (v. 14) and then proceed with so much emphasis on "the perishing"/"death." Attractive is her suggestion that Paul is anticipating criticism of a lack of response from Jewish hearers. How, then, would Paul's ministry be from God? Such a consideration might explain Paul's "from death to death" and "from life to life." The Torah, the prime document of Judaism, had the same effect; it becomes "the medicine of life" to him who "busies . . . himself with it," otherwise it is "the medicine of death" (see p. 154 above — n. 34).

41. Gk. ἱκανός, which, according to K. Rengstorf, *TDNT* 3.293-96, means "to be sufficient," "large enough," "qualified," "competent." See further F. T. Fallon, "Self-Sufficiency or God's Sufficiency," 369-74, for linguistic background for ἱκανός and possible connections with the "divine man."

42. Bultmann, 69. Plummer asks, "What kind of a minister ought he be who preaches a gospel which may prove fatal to those who come in contact with it?" (72).

43. In view of the contrast with Moses that follows (3:12-18), it may be significant that Moses says οὐχ ἱκανός εἰμι (LXX Exod 4:10); Paul is ἱκανός, but it is from God (3:4-6).

sad, defeated figure — therefore disqualified from recognition in ministry by his sufferings, as some appear to have been saying — let the Corinthians understand that in preaching the gospel of Christ crucified and risen, the sovereign God was leading his suffering apostle in triumph, spreading the odor of the knowledge of Christ through his preaching wherever he went (v. 14) and dividing humanity into those being saved and those perishing.

17 Paul's "for"[44] implies an answer to the question, "Who is sufficient for these things?" with which the previous verse ended. The whole opening phrase, "*for* we are not" (RSV), implies that Paul and his associates are, by God's strength, "sufficient" for that task, but that those about whom he will now speak are not. Moreover, whereas Paul's "we are the aroma of Christ to God" spoke of close identification of the apostle with his Lord in acceptable sacrificial ministry, the contrastive "peddling" image now introduced points to tawdriness on the part of these letter-bearing ministers.

Thus a polemical theme is now introduced to the letter, to be developed at greater length and intensity later (cf. 5:11-13; 10:12–12:13). Rhetorically speaking, we are now faced with the language of contrast as Paul introduces the newly arrived ministers in Corinth,[45] setting his ministry against theirs.

Paul achieves this contrast by a two-part sentence that begins, "We are not as[46] the many,[47] peddling the word of God,"[48] whereas the second part reads, "but as men of sincerity, indeed as from God, before God, in Christ we speak."[49] Unlike them he does not "peddle the word of God"; rather, he "speak[s the word of God] with sincerity."

---

44. Gk. γάρ, untranslated in the NIV.

45. Who are they? From 2:17–3:3 important information may be gleaned about them, namely, that they are (1) a *group* ("the many . . . some" — cf. 10:12-18; 11:5, 12-15, 22-23a; 12:11) who have (2) *come* to Corinth from elsewhere ("letters of recommendation"). Since there is no reference to them in 1 Corinthians, it is likely that they have arrived recently in Corinth, within a year or so since the writing of that letter. Paul's careful designation of himself as a "minister of a new covenant" (3:5) and his conclusion that Moses' glory has now been superseded (3:7-11) make it likely that these newly arrived ones are Jews, ministers of a covenant of Moses. This is confirmed by his questions "Are they Hebrews . . . Israelites . . . Abraham's descendants?" (11:22) and his designation of them as "ministers of righteousness" (11:15).

46. Gk. οὐ . . . ὡς.

47. The "many" (οἱ πολλοί) of this verse, repeated as "some people" (τινες) in the next, suggests that "the many" is rhetorical (and disparaging) rather than numerical.

48. The first part of the sentence could also be taken as, "We are not peddling the word of God as many do." The meaning is unaffected either way.

49. Gk. ἀλλ[ά ἐσμεν] ὡς ἐκ θεοῦ κατέναντι θεοῦ ἐν Χριστῷ λαλοῦμεν. Note (1) that the repetition of ἀλλά is ascensive, "but . . . indeed . . . ," and (2) the end location of λαλοῦμεν, "we speak,"is emphatic, in contrast to their "peddling," which is also present tense.

For we are not as the many

                                      peddling the word of God

    but as from sincerity

    but as from God

      before God

               in Christ we speak.

How is Paul able confidently to attribute such negative motives to these men, while expecting his own claim "of sincerity"[50] to be accepted? It appears that he is appealing to the known fact that these men have received some material benefit from the Corinthians (cf. 11:20), whereas Paul deliberately refused payment from them (11:7-12; 12:13-16). It is sufficient to apply the verb "peddle"[51] to them — a pejorative word implying adulterating a product for improper gains — and "sincerity" to himself to signal that the whole subject of financial benefit is being raised, even though the Corinthians may not accept his view of things (4:2; 7:2; 12:17-18).

What Paul "speak[s]" — and the newcomers "adulterate" — is "the word of God,"[52] the "word of reconciliation" (5:19), which is synonymous with the "gospel"[53] of Christ crucified, God's message of "good news" for

---

50. He has already pointed to his sincerity in 1:12.

51. Gk. καπηλεύω; NIV, "peddle for profit"; see the extended note in Furnish, 178; Thrall, 1.212-15. The verb is found only here in the NT and not at all in the OT. The cognate noun κάπηλος, which is found in the OT and the Apocrypha (LXX Isa 1:22; Sir 26:29), is virtually synonymous with ἔμπορος, "merchant." Merchants were routinely regarded as cheats who would adulterate their products for improper gain.

According to Plato, "Knowledge is the food of the soul; we must take care that the sophist does not deceive us when he praises what he sells, like those who sell the food of the body, the merchant and the hawker (κάπηλος), for they praise all their wares, without knowing what is good or bad for the body. In like manner those who carry about items of knowledge, to sell and hawk (καπηλεύειν) them to any one who is in want of them, praise them, all alike, though neither they nor their customers know their effect upon the soul" (Plato, *Protagoras* 313D).

In the Hellenistic era καπηλεύω was used metaphorically of itinerant teachers and philosophers. Philostratus, e.g., criticizes Euphrates, a teacher, "huckstering his wisdom" (τὴν σοφίαν καπηλεύειν — *Life of Apollonius* 1.13). Plummer, 74, notes that κάπηλος was often associated with wine selling, making the imagery allusively consistent between 2:17 and 4:2.

52. A phrase occurring forty times within the NT, including twelve times in Acts and frequently in Paul's letters (4:2; 1 Cor 14:36; Rom 9:6; Col 1:25; 1 Thess 2:13; 2 Tim 2:9; Tit 2:5). Often where "the word" is used alone (e.g., 1 Cor 2:2), "the word of God" is clearly implied. The phrase refers to the spoken message about Christ, the gospel of God, as the various usages indicate.

53. Cf. 2:12; 4:3, 4; 8:18; 9:13; 10:14; 11:4, 7 (τὸ εὐαγγέλιον); 10:16; 11:7 (εὐαγγελίζομαι).

the world, which God has entrusted to Paul (cf. 5:18). That this "word" is able to be "adulterated" by others (cf. 4:2) implies its existence in a standard, pure form (cf. Rom 6:17; 2 Tim 1:13), which Paul claims to declare in its purity. A "pure" gospel makes possible "sincere and pure devotion to Christ" (cf. 11:2-4). The objectively measurable character — the "thatness" — of the "word of God/the gospel" is implied in the important formulalike statement recorded in the First Letter.[54]

Within the second part of the sentence Paul gives a valuable summary of his ministry, which, brief as it is, has overtones of the Damascus Road call. This segment — indeed the whole sentence — is controlled by the verb "we speak."[55] This *speaking* is characterized by four qualities that are true of Paul but, by implication, not of the "peddlers." (1) Paul speaks "with sincerity"[56] from pure motives, as we have already noted. (2) He speaks "as from God";[57] what he says originates with God. As he will say later, "God gave us the ministry of reconciliation. . . . [God] committed to us the word of reconciliation" (5:18-19). The "word" spoken by Paul was given to him by God, as at his Damascus road call (cf. Gal 1:15-17). (3) He speaks the word, "before God," "in the presence of God,"[58] mindful that the all-knowing God hears what he speaks in his name and will hold him accountable on the day of judgment (4:2; 5:10; 12:19). (4) That Paul speaks "in Christ"[59] also points back to his incorporation "in Christ" as at the Damascus event (5:17; cf. Acts 9:18; 22:16); his present speaking flows from that unique event (cf. 4:13-14).

This verse is linked with the passages on either side.[60] In regard to what has preceded, those preachers "who peddle the word of God" stand in contrast with Paul, who went to Troas "for the gospel of Christ," whom God "leads in triumphal procession," and through whom God "spreads every-

---

54. The gospel by which Paul established the church in Corinth and which he now repeats by way of reminder (1 Cor 15:1-7) consists of four statements about Christ — Christ died for our sins according to the scriptures, he was buried, he was raised the third day, and he appeared to the people listed — each introduced by "that," ὅτι.

55. Gk. λαλοῦμεν.

56. Gk. ἐξ εἰλικρινείας. See also 1:12; 1 Cor 5:8.

57. Gk. ἐκ θεοῦ.

58. Gk. κατέναντι θεοῦ. See further D. A. Renwick, *Paul, the Temple and the Presence of God*, 49-50, for an explanation as to how Paul lived in the presence of God and yet *suffered*.

59. Gk. ἐν Χριστῷ.

60. This verse provides an example of Paul's pastoral method in which he moves from the *occasional* to the *theological* (see on 3:6). What begins as a defense of his ministry (concurrent with an attack on the newcomers — 2:17–3:1) will soon become an exposition of the new covenant (3:4–4:6), the bridge to which is "written on our hearts" (3:2), a direct allusion to the OT promise of the new covenant (Jer 31:33).

where" the "knowledge of [Christ]" (2:12, 14). On the other hand, "the *many* [who] peddl[e] the word of God" of this verse is repeated in the next as "*some . . . who need letters of recommendation.*"

While Paul's words represent an apologetic for his apostolate then, they have application for the pastorate now. To be sure, there are differences. The origin in God of Paul's Damascus call, when he saw the risen and glorified Lord uniquely, conferred on him the office of apostle and revelator (see on 4:6). Nonetheless, in this verse Paul sets certain standards for missionaries and ministers who come after him in succeeding generations. There is a givenness, a thatness, to the word of God that must not be reduced or distorted. All ministers must be as committed to the canon of the gospel as Paul was. That this verbal message is the word of God demands that those who speak it incarnate the integrity of God in their lives, mindful that they do so in the sight of the God before whose tribunal they must stand (see on 5:10). And, like Paul, they speak out of the fullness of a relationship with Christ, that is, as those "in Christ."

2. Commendation of Ministry (3:1-3)

> 1 *Are we beginning to commend ourselves again? Or do we need, like some people, letters of recommendation to you or from you?* 2 *You yourselves are our letter, written on our*[1] *hearts, known and read by everybody.* 3 *You show that you are a letter from Christ, the result of our ministry, written not with ink but with the Spirit of the living God, not on tablets of stone but on tablets of human hearts.*

Mindful of the "peddlers," their jibes against Paul, and their own mode of achieving acceptance in Corinth, Paul asks rhetorically — expecting negative replies — is he commending himself again or needing letters of recommendation to the Corinthians? On the contrary, they are his letter in Corinth, resulting from his ministry, written on their hearts by the Spirit of God, not on stone tablets.

These verses spring from 2:17, the verse that concluded the previous passage. The *"many"* of that verse reappear here as *"some people"* (3:1). In turn, Paul's question about *"letters* of recommendation" (3:1) is carried forward to the next verse as *"you . . . are our letter"* (3:2) and *"you are a letter"*

---

1. The reading "our" is better attested by far (p[46] A B C D etc vg syr[p,h] cop[sa,bo] goth arm) than "your" (ℵ 33 88 eth[ro]). So Metzger, 577, as followed by the majority of translations (but not the RSV or the NAB). Some commentators, e.g., Barrett (96 n. 3), Martin (51), and Thrall (1.223), prefer "your" as making better sense of the context.

(3:3). That such a "letter" is "*written* on our hearts" (3:2) repeats as "*written* . . . on tablets of human hearts" (3:3). These repetitions, carrying from one verse to the next, bind vv. 1-3 together and tie this passage back into 2:17. In turn, the language "written with the *Spirit* of the *living* God" of v. 3 forms the foundation for the momentous declaration "[we are] . . . ministers of a new covenant . . . of the *Spirit* [who] gives *life*" of v. 6.

But, not to run too far ahead of Paul's argument,[2] this new covenant ministry is not spoken of in the abstract. Rather, Paul will set this ministry of the Spirit in positive contrast with another (vv. 7-11), to which he now draws preliminary attention by "written . . . in tablets of stone" (3:3), a reference to the tablets of stone God gave to Moses on Mount Sinai,[3] the commandment-based covenant with the people of Israel.[4]

However, the ministry that had been historically given to Moses has a contemporary expression through the newly arrived letter-bearing ministers in Corinth, those who "peddle the word of God" (2:17).[5] By referring to their "letters of recommendation," which are "*written* . . . in ink" (3:1, 3), and by adding immediately "*written* . . . in tablets of stone" (3:3), Paul points to the continuity of these ministers with Moses.[6] Paul again contrasts himself, first with the newly arrived ones ("we are not as *[hōs]* . . ."; "we [do not] need as *[hōs]* . . ." — 2:17; 3:1[7]), and then with the commandment-based covenant ministry that they seek to perpetuate ("our letter you [Corinthians] are . . . written *not* on tablets of stone *but* on tablets of hearts of flesh" — 3:3). The

2. Within the extensive literature on this passage see, e.g., C. J. Hickling, "Sequence," 380-95; E. Richard, "Polemics," 340-67; T. E. Provence, "Who Is Sufficient?" 54-81; J. Lambrecht, "Structure," 344-80; J. B. Pohill, "Comfort and Power," 325-45. Of interest is the view of D. Georgi, *Opponents,* 258-82, and others that 2 Corinthians 3 is Paul's refutation of his opponents' midrash on Exodus 34. For arguments against this hypothesis see, e.g., Hickling and Provence, above. Whereas we doubt the existence of an extant exegesis as the target for Paul's rebuttal, it appears likely that the peddlers saw Paul as an inglorious suffering figure, a living denial of the fulfillment eschatology he had preached in Corinth. By contrast, Moses' glory was popularly viewed as undimmed. See Introduction, 37-38.

3. See Exod 34:1, 4, 28, 29; cf. 31:18; 32:15, 16, 19.

4. See Exod 34:27-28.

5. The polemical historical context may be seen in Paul's series of "not . . . but" contrasts (Gk. οὐ . . . ἀλλά) in 2:17; 3:3, 6 and the "if . . . how much more" comparisons (Gk. εἰ . . . πῶς μᾶλλον/πολλῷ μᾶλλον) in 3:7-8, 9, 11.

6. Overlapping vocabulary (ἐνγράφομαι . . . γράμμα) should be noted. Those "peddling the word of God" need συστατικῶν ἐπιστολῶν . . . ἐγγεγραμμένη . . . μέλανι (vv. 1, 3); Moses/the old covenant, which is still being read (vv. 14, 15), was originally ἐγγεγραμμένη . . . ἐν πλαξὶν λιθίναις . . . γράμματος . . . τὸ γὰρ γράμμα . . . ἐν γράμμασιν ἐντετυπωμένη λίθοις.

7. Gk. οὐ ἐσμεν ὡς . . . μὴ χρῄομεν ὡς (2:17; 3:1).

countermissionaries in Corinth are, in some significant way, exponents of the Mosaic ministry. They are, to use the term imprecisely, "Judaizers."[8]

This passage, therefore, points to the marks of authentic as opposed to inauthentic ministry. These newcomers bring "letters of recommendation to [the Corinthians]," as well as seeking such letters *from* them (v. 1). Paul, however, has no need of such letters but points, instead, to the Corinthian church as Christ's "letter of recommendation" of him. Their lives are "known and read by everybody" (v. 2).

The church, then, was Christ's "letter" to Corinth, commending its bearer, Paul. Because of the church Paul has no need of self-commendation (v. 1); he is commended by the Lord (10:18), as he ought also to have been by the Corinthians (12:11).

But what is outwardly manifest about them to others results from the operation of the Spirit of the living God within their hearts (v. 3). This, in turn, signals that the long-awaited new covenant, prophesied by Jeremiah and Ezekiel, has come. Since these effects — visible outwardly because real inwardly — have come as a result of Paul's ministry, it is evident (as he will assert in vv. 4-6) that he is a minister of this new covenant.

Earlier in the letter, as defense for his motives in writing rather than returning to Corinth (1:15-17), Paul had indicated that God had given the Spirit to the Corinthians at the time Paul preached the "word of God," the Son of God (1:18-22). Paul picks up that reference to the Spirit in these verses, and beyond them in the chapter as a whole, climaxing in v. 18.[9]

1 This verse is connected to and continuous with its predecessor. In particular "the *many* peddling the word of God" (2:17) are the "*some* people"[10] of this verse, who, we infer, "need[11] letters of recommendation."[12]

---

8. Traditional use justifies the continuing use of "Judaizer," though the verb "to judaize," as used in the NT, means "to live as a Jew" rather than "to promote Judaism" (see Gal 2:14).

9. For a discussion of the role of the Spirit in this passage, see G. D. Fee, *Presence,* 296-320.

10. Paul often uses the impersonal τινες in referring to his opponents (10:2; 1 Cor 4:18; 15:12; Gal 1:7; 1 Tim 3:9).

11. The question, "Do we need. . . ?" introduced by μή, expects a negative answer.

12. Letters of introduction were common in the early church (8:22; 1 Cor 16:10-11; Rom 16:1; Col 4:10; Acts 15:25-26; 2 John 12). Typically, the person commended was the bearer of the letter and would receive an appropriate welcome and hospitality on arrival, with special attention to some detail in the letter. Such letters were then customary in both Jewish and Gentile circles; see further Furnish, 180; C. W. Keyes, "The Greek Letter of Introduction," 28-44; C.-H. Kim, *Letter of Recommendation,* Appendix III; *New Docs.* 1.64-66; 4.250-55; 6.180. The practice, however, was subject to abuse among Christians in the next century (so Lucian, *The Passing of Peregrinus* 13). However, Epictetus held that the intelligent readily recognized genuine people, making such letters unnecessary (*Dissertations* 2.3).

Clearly, Paul is referring to a specific group of missioners who have come to Corinth and who will be readily identified by these words.

Verse 1 consists of two questions — which are answered in v. 2 — underlying which is the more basic question, "What is it that legitimates *Paul's* claim that he speaks [the word of God]" (2:17)?

The first question is: Does his apostolic legitimacy exist because he says it does, that is, because he "commends [himself]?"[13] Significantly, the theme of commendation is prominent throughout the letter (3:1; 4:2; 5:12; 6:4; 7:11; 10:12, 18; 12:11).[14] Clearly this was an issue in Corinth. Verse 2 gives the reply: Paul is not commending himself as an apostle. The Corinthian church is his commendation; he is commended of the Lord and should have been commended by them (10:12; 10:18; 12:11; cf. 1 Cor 9:2).

Why should Paul need to defend himself against the charge of self-commendation?[15] His basic difficulty lay in not having been one of the band of original disciples who followed Jesus. His sensitivity to this may be read between the lines in 1 Corinthians (see 9:1-3; 15:8-11), though the verb "commend" does not appear in that letter. If, as we hold, his newly arrived opponents came from Jerusalem,[16] they would have pointed out Paul's lack of status in this regard. This would neatly explain the appearance of the verb,

---

13. For συνιστάνειν generally see W. Kasch, *TDNT* 7.896-98. Plummer, 77, points out that the verb συνιστάνειν (συνίσταναι) has nuances in Paul's letters, and in 2 Corinthians in particular, not found elsewhere in the NT. It can mean, on the one hand, "to introduce or commend [persons]" (4:2; 5:12; 6:4; 10:12, 18), or, on the other, "to prove by argument or evidence" (7:11). For the apologetic and polemical use within 2 Corinthians see S. J. Hafemann, "Self-Commendation," 66-88.

14. Paul's defensive remarks (3:1; 5:12) imply criticism that he is self-commended. But there is a distinction between verbal self-commendation, which he disclaims (3:1; 5:12), and the impact of his ministry commending him (4:2; 6:4), which he asserts. Later he implicitly charges his opponents with self-commendation (10:12), suggesting a major dispute between Paul and his opponents in Corinth. At the climax of the "Fool's Speech" Paul chides the Corinthians for their failure to commend him as an apostle (12:11).

15. It is not certain whether πάλιν is connected with ἀρχόμεθα or with συνιστάνειν. Either way the πάλιν tells us that Paul is here responding to the criticism of self-commendation. Because two later references to συνιστάνειν (10:12; 12:11) occur in passages where Paul is referring to the newly arrived false apostles, as well as 3:1 (cf. 2:17), it seems likely that they were the chief source of this criticism, the more so because Paul was particularly vulnerable at this point, not having been a disciple of the Lord, nor having been present with the other disciples when the Lord was raised from the dead. Thrall, 1.218, however, claims that Paul is merely rejecting the self-commendation he engaged in when he first came to Corinth. But why does he need to mention this now if no one else is making an issue of it? Rather, there appears to be an apologetic motive.

16. See C. K. Barrett, "Paul's Opponents," 233-54; P. W. Barnett, "Opposition," 3-17. For further discussion, which, however, is inconclusive as to Jerusalem as the source of the letters, see Thrall, 1.219-20.

for the first time, in this letter (i.e., immediately following the first reference to the intruders — 2:17). For his part, the appearance of the Lord to him — even if "last of all" and in a different manner ("as to one abnormally born" — 1 Cor 15:8) — secured his place among the apostles. Paul's problem was that his claim that the Lord appeared to him (and commissioned him, Gal 1:15-16) rested on his own words.

If Paul's ministry does not arise from self-commendation, is it warranted by the commendation of others, as the ministry of the newcomers is? Thus he asks a second question: "Do we need . . . letters of recommendation?" Again, the answer is "No," as he proceeds to explain.[17]

Easily missed is the second part of the second question, "Do we need, like some people, letters of recommendation . . . *from* you?" This implies that the newcomers will spring from Corinth to other churches, probably those established by Paul.[18] It is evident that they sought to establish some kind of network of support, a countermission to Paul (see on 10:12-18; 11:4, 12-15). The opinion that Peter and James, the leaders of Jewish Christianity in Jerusalem, were the instigators of an anti-Pauline mission in Corinth — and therefore the signatories to a letter of recommendation — is rendered unlikely by this question. Why would the newcomers need letters of recommendation from the Corinthians if they possessed letters of recommendation from such weighty persons as Peter or James?[19] Possibly the source of recommendation lay with Greek-speaking members of the Pharisaic brotherhoods who were within the orbit of the churches of Judaea[20] and who were profoundly disturbed by what appeared to be antinomian[21] emphases in Paul's Gentile mission.[22] It is likely that such countermissionaries went with the knowledge of James, but not at his instigation (cf. Acts 15:24).

2 Paul now makes the positive claim that gives the answer "No" to the two rhetorical questions asked in v. 1, picking up the keyword "letter"[23]

---

17. It would not reflect well on the Corinthians' intelligence if they now felt that Paul should have had letters of recommendation. Since he had founded the church, how could he bring letters to it?

18. Plummer's view, 77-78, that the newcomers had already left Corinth when Paul wrote these words, depends on the hypothesis that chapters 10–13 were the "Severe Letter," written prior to the present passage.

19. Perhaps, though, support from a Pauline church like the Corinthian would have been helpful to them; so Thrall, 1.220 n. 224.

20. This was Paul's own background. See M. Hengel, *Pre-Christian Paul*, 54-62.

21. From Romans, the letter written by Paul after 2 Corinthians — and written from Corinth — we are conscious that Paul is replying to charges of antinomianism (3:8; 6:1; cf. 3:1; 9:1; 11:1).

22. Furnish, 192, suggests "other Hellenistic congregations," including those established by Paul, as the source of the letters.

23. Gk. ἐπιστολή.

from "letters of recommendation" in the previous verse (cf. "written . . . with ink" — v. 3). That claim is stated tersely (following his own word order): "Our letter [of commendation] you[24] yourselves are."[25] That letter has an inward as well as an outward aspect; it is written on Paul's heart,[26] and it is known and read by all.

His assertion "our letter you are" is remarkable, given the disloyalty, fickleness, and waywardness evident within the messianic community in Corinth. Nonetheless, Paul carefully addresses them as "the church of God in Corinth . . . [sanctified]" (1:1), assuring them that God, having set them facing Christ, will guarantee their ongoing loyalty to their Lord (1:21-22; cf. 11:3). He will remind them that God is "powerful among [them]" (13:3), through the apostle's disciplinary confrontation of them. Certainly, many long-term sinners had undergone astonishing moral transformation through the power of Christ and the Spirit (cf. 1 Cor 6:11). The signs of grace, together with the continuing marks of sin, are visible in this church, which like all others is both flesh and Spirit because it has one foot in the present evil age (Gal 1:4) and the other in the age to come (cf. 5:1-5).

For the remainder of this verse and into the next Paul amplifies the meaning of "letter of recommendation" through a series of qualifying phrases — one subjective, the other objective. First, the Corinthians, as a "letter," were "written[27] on [Paul's] heart."[28] In the course of his evangelistic, pastoral, and disciplinary ministry, including by letter (cf. 2:4), Paul took the people into his heart (cf. Phil 1:7).[29] Relationships of care and love, perhaps of a paternal kind (see on 6:13; 11:2; 12:14-15; cf. 1 Cor 4:14-15), are implied by this phrase. Such relationships, because not reciprocated by them, brought him pain (6:12; 11:7; 12:13). Possibly the apostle also has in mind the sufferings sustained for them (another paternal image?), conveyed by the words "the death [that] is at work in [him]" for the sake of "the life [that] is at work in [them]" (4:12; cf. 1:7).

The phrase "written on our hearts," though here applied to Paul, calls to mind the promise of a "new covenant" in which God would "write" his

24. Paul had already referred to the Corinthians as the "seal" of his apostleship (1 Cor 9:2).

25. The juxtaposition of the first and second person pronouns "our you" (ἡμῶν ὑμεῖς) is rare and therefore striking.

26. See n. 1 above for comment on the preferred reading "our."

27. Gk. ἐγγεγραμμένη, perfect tense, shows that it was a letter that remained permanently written in his heart. "The compound ἐγγεγρ. implies that this fact cannot slip from our hearts, cannot be forgotten" (Plummer, 80).

28. The "heart" in Semitic thought is the locale of understanding and obedience to God, where the Spirit works (see A. Sand, *EDNT* 2.250-51; J. Behm, *TDNT* 3.609-16).

29. *Contra* Plummer, 80, who here infers Paul's subjective reassurance ("Our own hearts tell us that you are our recommendation . . .").

law "on their hearts" (Jer 31:33; cf. Ezek 11:19; 36:26). This, in turn, sets the contrast with the law written on stone (Exod 31:18; 32:15ff.). Having begun with occasional comments defending his ministry and attacking the newcomers (2:17–3:1), Paul, with this series of fluid metaphors, begins the transition to theology, namely, his major explanation of the new covenant (3:4-18).

The second and objective qualifying phrase expanding upon the Corinthians as Paul's "letter"[30] is that it is "known and read by everybody."[31] This must mean that the messianic community was, by the time of writing, to some extent visible in the wider Corinthian community (cf. 1 Cor 11:18),[32] even though in the latter part of Paul's initial visit to Corinth the Proconsul Gallio did not distinguish the believers from the Jewish community (Acts 18:14-16). Perhaps, as more Gentiles were added to the church its impact upon the wider community increased, as this verse may indicate. Paul's comment is prophetic. Within the next half-century the separate existence of Christians is well established, being referred to in the extant writings of Josephus, Pliny, Tacitus, and Suetonius.[33]

3 This verse repeats, but in reverse order, the outer/inner elements of the previous verse. Paul's words, "You show ["manifest"] that you are a letter," pick up the outward aspect of them as a "letter . . . known and read by all" from the previous verse (but adding [1] "a letter *from Christ,*" and [2] "ministered *by us*"). He then reverts to the inner aspect of the previous verse (but now with reference to them, not himself). This "letter" is written within *them,* not with ink but by the Spirit of the living God, not on tablets of stone but on tablets of hearts of flesh. Here we note rapidly changing imagery (written with ink/tablets of stone/tablets of hearts of flesh).

This verse is explicitly apologetic. Paul can point to a letter of introduction (the Corinthian church) written by a third party (Christ), who is a supernaturally higher authority, in which, however, he (Paul) has played a

---

30. If Paul is drawing an analogy with his own letters — as seems probable — we must conclude that his letters were public and official in character within the churches ("known and read by everybody"). See R. N. Longenecker, "New Testament Letters," 101-14.

31. The participles γινωσκομένη and ἀναγινωσκομένη are present tense in contrast with ἐγγραμμένη, which is perfect. What was written — or better, "inscribed," i.e., *deeply* — when Paul established the church is "continually being known and being read." A similar wordplay occurs at 1:13. Nothing hangs on the unusual order of the words; the second word, a compound, aurally intensifies the first.

32. The existence of the church as an entity separate from the synagogue was not apparent to Gallio the Proconsul (Acts 18:14-16).

33. Josephus (*Ant.* 18.64), Pliny (*Letters* 10.96), Tacitus (*Annals* 15.44.2-8), and Suetonius (*Nero* 16). See, generally, R. L. Wilken, *The Christians.*

critical role. At the same time it is implicitly polemical. The intruders' higher authority is merely that of human signatories on nothing more than a piece of paper.

Structurally, v. 3 is divided into three parts:

You show that you are a letter from Christ,
the result of our ministry,
written not . . . but . . . not . . . but. . . .

Paul uses the first part to repeat and reinforce information from the previous verse ("you are a letter"[34]; cf. v. 2 — "you yourselves are our letter"), but with the addition of the participle "you show"[35] (NIV), with which v. 3 commences. Paul knows of his own integrity in ministry before God, even though others question it (4:2-3); the church at Corinth is the "epiphany," the manifestation of the truth of his claims, for all to see. The "letter" written not on paper but in people[36] — the Corinthian messianic assembly — is Christ's visible commendation of Paul, the church's founder. The church is the Lord's commendation of him (cf. 10:18).

What is "known and read . . . manifest" outwardly is a consequence of what has occurred inwardly, the life-giving activity of the Spirit of the living God within their hearts (v. 3; cf. vv. 6 [twice], 8, 17 [twice], 18). The dramatic change in their lives did not arise from the imposition of a code of morality, but from the Spirit of God arising from Paul's preaching of the Son of God among them (1:18-22; 5:5; 13:14; cf. 11:4).

The flow of Paul's thought from the previous verses to this verse may be seen in the following:

1   Do we need as some [do]
                letters of commendation to you
                                or from you?
2   Our letter   you are,
    written on our hearts,
                        known and read by all men.

---

34. Gk. ἐστὲ ἐπιστολή. Also repeating from v. 2 — ἡ ἐπιστολὴ ἡμῶν ὑμεῖς ἐστὲ . . . ἐγγεγραμμένη . . . καρδίαις.

35. Gk. φανερούμενοι. The verb φανερόω means to make visible an invisible reality (important within 2 Corinthians — 2:14; 4:10, 11; 5:10, 11; 7:12; 11:6), thus repeating the idea "known and read by everybody" of v. 2. φανερούμενοι agrees with ὑμεῖς ἐστέ of the previous verse. It could be either middle ("you show") or passive ("you are shown"); the meaning is relatively unaffected.

36. "Paul's credentials are not on paper but in persons," according to C. F. D. Moule, "2 Cor. 3:18b," 232.

3   You show
                                         that you are
                        a letter from Christ
            ministered by us
                written not with   ink
                        but with the Spirit of the living God,
                        not on tablets of stone
                        but on tablets of hearts of flesh.

Further, to his words "You show that you are a letter" Paul adds "from Christ."[37] The newcomers' letters of recommendation bear the names of their authors; Paul's "letter" — the Corinthians church — comes from Christ. How were the Corinthians "a letter *from Christ*"? In all probability Paul is reflecting on the congregation's focus on Christ in its assembling to confess and praise him, with the members together set toward him, having been anointed by the Spirit (1:21-22; 3:17; cf. 11:3b-4[38]). They are "the temple of the living God" (6:16).

The second part of this verse — "the result of our ministry" (more literally, "ministered by us"[39]) — reiterates the thrust of v. 2, where he claims that they are "[his] letter [of] recommendation." Although all that is visible in them of their Christward orientation has its origin in Christ, it is through Paul's ministry that these spiritual realities are visible in Achaia.[40] The church itself stands as Paul's "letter of recommendation," that he is an authentic minister of Christ. Despite their shortcomings, so obvious from the two extant Corinthian letters, they were by confession — if not always in practice — a Christian body, and as such evidence of the legitimacy of the apostle who had established and nurtured it.

In the third part of the verse Paul points to the marks that identify the Corinthian church as a "letter from Christ," ministered to by a genuine

---

37. The genitive Χριστοῦ is subjective, "from Christ" (authorial), not objective, "about Christ."

38. In both those passages Paul describes the Corinthians as εἰς Χριστόν, a phrase that means both "oriented toward" and "moving toward" Christ.

39. Gk. διακονηθεῖσα ὑφ' ἡμῶν; NIV, "the result of our ministry." The aorist points to a completed event, i.e., the initial creation of the church in Corinth (cf. present tense διακονουμένη ὑφ' ἡμῶν in relation to the collection 8:19, 20). It is not clear whether Paul's use of this phrase in relationship to a letter implies a sustained image, that he sees himself as an amanuensis or a courier (as in W. Baird, "Letters of Recommendation," 166-72). In all probability "ministered" and "letter" are not to be connected at all. According to Plummer, 81, "The words mean that St Paul and his colleagues were Christ's ministers in bringing the letter of recommendation into existence by converting the Corinthians."

40. There is an important balance here. The church owes its origin to Christ, not Paul. Yet Paul is the human instrument by which the church was established. Paul does not commend himself, yet in all humility he will not deny the critical part he has played (cf. 10:18; 12:11).

minister. Here he appeals to the unquestionable reality of the "Spirit of the living God"[41] in their midst,[42] a subject that will dominate the remainder of this chapter. The active presence of the Spirit among them — writing[43] Christ's letter in their hearts (v. 3c), giving them life (v. 6) and freedom (v. 17), and changing them by varying degrees of glory (vv. 8, 18) into the image of the Lord (v. 18) — is the evidence of the onset of the new covenant, that they are "[a letter] of Christ" and that he, Paul, is Christ's faithful minister.

How is this "letter" that is visible to others "written" in them? Paul employs two "not . . . but"[44] statements in the third part of the verse. According to the first, this "letter" is written "not[45] with ink"[46] — as the newcomers' letters of recommendation are (v. 1) — "but with the Spirit of the living God," demonstrating that Paul is a minister of Christ in the new covenant. This positive assertion introduces the note of fulfillment of "promises" made under the old covenant (cf. 1:20), in particular that made in Ezekiel:

> *I* will give you a new heart
> and   *put*   *a new spirit in you;*
> I will remove   from you
>   your heart of stone
>   and give   you
>   a heart of flesh.
> And *I will put*   *my Spirit in you*
> and   move you to follow my decrees
> and   be careful
>   to keep my laws.
>
> Ezek 36:26-27 (cf. 11:19; Prov 7:3).

41. The phrase "the living God" is common in the LXX (e.g., LXX Deut 5:26; LXX Josh 3:10; cf. Matt 16:16) and in Paul (e.g., 1 Thess 1:9; 2 Cor 6:16; Rom 9:26). See further H. E. Everding, "The Living God." It is noteworthy that the hearts of the people were inscribed with "the Spirit of the living God" and that they were also "the temple of the living God" (6:16). It is also to be noted that the Greek philosopher Epicurus (341-271 B.C.) referred to τὸν θεὸν ζῷον (Diogenes Laertius, *Epicurus* 10.123).

42. Only here do we find "the Spirit" connected with "the living God." It is striking that "*stone tablets* written with the *finger* of God" (Exod 31:18) is echoed here as "the *Spirit* of the living God . . . on *tablets* of human *hearts*" inscribed by "the *Spirit* of the living God." For major references to the Spirit outside chapter 3, see 1:21-22; 5:5; 11:4; 13:14.

43. Gk. ἐγγεγραμμένη is perfect tense, indicating the ongoing positive effects of the coming of the Spirit. Compare the perfect tense ἐντετυπωμένη (3:7) for the ongoing negative effects of the inauguration of the old covenant.

44. Gk. οὐ . . . ἀλλά (2:17).

45. Gk. οὐ negates the noun, not the participle; so Turner, 287.

46. Gk. μέλανι. Ink was then made of soot mixed with thin glue; hence it is described as μέλαν, "black." See further *IDB* 4.918-19.

Paul's gloss on Ezekiel's text, whereby in place of a "*heart* of stone" he substitutes "*tablets* of stone," is a clear reference to the tablets of stone on which the commandments were written.[47] According to Paul, under that dispensation the stone tablets of the Law, given outwardly to Moses, were internalized within the people as "tablets of stone." Thus Paul signifies that the Law of God given to Moses became, in the hearts of the covenant people, stonelike, dead. Implicit in Ezekiel's "promise" of a "heart of flesh" in place of a "heart of stone" is the conviction that the people do not "follow" God's "decrees" or "keep" his "laws," which is probably the reason why Paul interprets the prophet's "hearts of stone" as "*tablets* of stone." Disobedience to God's laws[48] has desensitized "hearts of flesh" so as to become "tablets of stone"; the Law of God is as dead within them as their own dead hearts. In the verses following, Paul will expand upon the negative impact of "the letter,"[49] the Law, upon the people of the old covenant; that "letter" both "kills" (v. 6; "a ministry of death" — v. 7) and was, in effect, a "ministry of condemnation" (v. 9).

Matching the reference to "tablets of stone," and to heighten the contrast with the new covenant, however, Paul glosses Ezekiel's words as "tablets of *hearts of flesh*." The hearts of the people have been changed from "tablets of stone" to "tablets of hearts of flesh," that is, to "living hearts." This remarkable transformation of the hearts of the people from "stone" to living hearts of "flesh" is attributable to "the Spirit of the living God," in demonstration of the genuineness of Paul's claims as a minister of the long-awaited new covenant. The Law of God has been internalized in hearts made alive by the Spirit of the living God (see Jer 31:33; cf. v. 6).

In the structure of v. 3c "written . . . with ink" (i.e., the newcomers' letters of recommendation — v. 1) and "tablets of stone" are in tandem, making it likely that Paul is connecting the newcomers' ministry with the Mosaic covenant. With that ministry he is contrasting his own. Paul's ministry — as implied by the alternative matching phrases — expresses and is legitimated by

47. For LXX references to πλάξ λιθίνη see LXX Exod 31:18 (twice); 32:15 (twice); 34:1 (three times); 4 (twice); LXX Deut 4:13; 5:22; 9:9 (twice), 10; and for πλάξ see LXX Exod 32:16 (twice), 19; 34:28, 29; Deut 10:1, 2 (twice), 3 (twice), 4, and 5; 11:11, 15, 17.

48. Paul's reference to a "new covenant" (v. 6) must be in terms of the "promise," which, however, is made by the prophet Jeremiah, who declared that the people had "broken" the existing covenant (Jer 31:32). Paul (as in 1 Cor 10:5-11) and other NT writers (e.g., Heb 3:17-19; Jude 5) are conscious of Israel's disobedience to God, especially within the very period in which the Mosaic covenant was given. This is a common theme within the OT also (e.g., Isa 29:10-11; Ps 106:24, 26; Num 14:29, 37, 40; 26:64, 65; Deut 1:32, 35; 2:15; 9:23).

49. Gk. γράμμα.

"the Spirit of the living God," who has, thereby, created "tablets of hearts of flesh." In this verse Paul is anticipating the statement of v. 6 that he is "a minister of the new covenant," the covenant foreshadowed by another prophet, Jeremiah, in which God will "write [his] law on their hearts" (Jer 31:33).

Verse 3c, therefore, is powerfully eschatological. That "the Spirit of the living God" is now present and active in these people in Corinth is evidence that the long-expected "day of salvation" has arrived, that this is God's "now"-time (5:16), "the time of God's favor" (6:2). The "no longer" epoch, the dispensation of "Moses" — the "old" — has passed; the "new" has come (5:17). God's promise made through Ezekiel (and Jeremiah) is "now" a reality. Consequently, Paul implies that the ministry of those who have newly arrived, who bear "ink-written" letters, and who promote "tablets of stone"[50] is hopelessly anachronistic. Their day has ended; another has dawned. The work of the Spirit is the evidence of that.

3. Paul: A New Covenant Minister (3:4-6)

> 4 Such confidence as this is ours through Christ before God. 5 Not that we are competent in ourselves to claim anything for ourselves, but our competence comes from God. 6 He has made us competent as ministers of a new covenant — not of the letter but of the Spirit; for the letter kills, but the Spirit gives life.

Having rejected the notion of self-commendation (v. 1), Paul nonetheless introduces the theme of "confidence" (v. 4) and reintroduces the theme of "sufficiency" (vv. 5-6; cf. 2:16). Though not self-commended, he has "such confidence," that is, that the Corinthians are his "letter [of recommendation] from Christ . . . known and read by everybody," a letter that is "written . . . by the Spirit of the living God . . . on tablets of human hearts" (v. 3). He has this confidence "through Christ" and "toward God" (v. 4). Confidence is one thing, however; claims to self-sufficiency another. But he will not claim the self-sufficiency even to reckon whether anything comes from him. No; his sufficiency is from God (v. 5), who has indeed made Paul sufficient as a minister of the new covenant (v. 6). Thus Paul answers the question he raised earlier, "Who is sufficient for these things?" (2:16).

---

50. Paul's implied association of them with "tablets of stone" — i.e., the Mosaic covenant — is consistent with his later references to them as "Hebrews . . . Israelites . . . descendants of Abraham" (11:23). As to their mission, regrettably Paul nowhere specifies what they came to Corinth to achieve. However, in view of Paul's insistence in this chapter that "Moses" is now superseded (3:6-16), it seems likely that they were promoting the Mosaic covenant. See P. Barnett, "Opposition," 3-17.

The presence of "the Spirit of the living God . . . [in] human hearts" is evidence of the coming of the day of salvation (6:2), the moment of God's great eschatological action and the fulfilment of all his promises (1:20-22). Such "confidence" as Paul feels, however, should not be understood in modern psychological terms, nor, indeed, in the sense that Paul believed he enjoyed the approval of others; Paul's confidence was directed toward God. The activity of the Spirit in the lives of the Corinthians and others was the basis of his confidence, through Christ, that he was a true minister of God, and that, heaven forbid, he was in any sense a false minister of God (cf. 1 Cor 15:15).

This confidence is entirely God-given; Paul lacks the "sufficiency" from within himself even to make that assessment. The act of making the assessment, as well as the assessment itself that he is a minister of God, is, from start to finish, from God. It is God and no other who has given Paul the resources to become a minister of the "new covenant" as well as the "confidence" that he is such a minister.

> But we have such confidence
> > through Christ
> > to   God.
> Not that we are sufficient
> > > of ourselves
> > to reckon anything as from ourselves,
> > > > but our   sufficiency
> > > is from God,
> > > > who has made us   sufficient
> > > > > as ministers of a new covenant.

It is not that Paul makes this claim *in vacuo*. He is, in fact, continuing the positive contrast of his ministry to the ministry of the "peddlers," "the many who peddle the word of God . . . who need . . . letters of recommendation . . . written in ink" (2:17–3:1). Because of the close connection in Greek of the verb "written" (*engegrammenē* — vv. 2, 3 — applying to Paul's present opponents) with the noun "letters" (*gramma*[1] — vv. 6 [twice], 7 — applying to Moses' tablets of stone), it appears that these opponents are involved in a Moses-type ministry. That ministry *was* "on tablets of stone" (v. 3) and *was and is* "a letter" that "kills" (v. 6). The ministry of the new covenant, is, by contrast, "of the Spirit," as demonstrated by the work of the Spirit in the lives of the Corinthians. Because it is the Spirit of the *living* God, it is this ministry that gives *life*[2] (vv. 3, 4; cf. v. 18).

---

1. Gk. ἐγγεγραμμένη . . . ἐγγεγραμμένη . . . γράμματος . . . γράμμα . . . ἐν γράμμασιν (vv. 2, 3, 6 [twice], 7).
2. Gk. πνεύματι θεοῦ ζῶντος (v. 3) . . . ὁ δὲ πνεῦμα ζῳοποιεῖ (v. 6).

4 While the (untranslated) particle *de*[3] with which the verse begins signals the beginning of a new passage, Paul's "such confidence" points back to an antecedent in the previous verse and so indicates a continuity of thought. Here Paul makes the simple assertion that "we[4] have such confidence," a confidence pointing back to the tangible existence of the Corinthian church as the evidence that Paul is a minister of Christ (vv. 2-3). His confidence does not spring from the commendation of others or from himself (cf. 3:1; see on 10:2), but rather from the presence of the Spirit in the hearts of the Corinthians. This confidence is directed toward God, and is "through Christ."[5] The Corinthians are "a letter from Christ"; Christ is the "author" of Paul's letter of recommendation, and therefore of his confidence.

The nonappearance of "confidence"[6] in letters written earlier than 2 Corinthians (on which see 1:15; 8:22; 10:2;[7] but cf. Eph 3:12; Phil 3:4) suggests that Paul chose it in view of his present opponents' complaint of his self-commendation. For Paul the Godward ("confidence") rather than the humanward ("commendation") is important. Self-"commendation" advertises oneself, whereas "confidence . . . toward God"[8] reflects a deep trust in God arising from Paul's careful reflection about his ministry.

Paul wishes to establish that his "confidence toward God" is "through Christ." Possibly this manner of expression also implies the former Pharisee-persecutor's total inner conversion. Whereas once his "confidence" toward God was on his own account (Phil 3:4-6; cf. Gal 1:13-14), now it is "through Christ," as he loses no opportunity to testify. Such was the radical new direction his life had taken in his service of the God of his fathers.[9] Nonetheless, we could understand Paul periodically asking himself, "Am I right to be serving God as an "apostle of Christ"? His answer is: "through Christ," the Christ who had been crucified but who had confronted him en route to Damascus, Paul has "confidence . . . toward God" of the rightness of his new ministry.[10]

---

3. Gk. δέ.

4. As with almost all first person plural references in the excursus on the ministry of the new covenant (2:14–7:4), Paul is speaking about himself as an apostle. See on 1:1; 2:14.

5. Cf. 1:20 — διὸ καὶ δι' αὐτοῦ τὸ ἀμὴν τῷ θεῷ, "and so *through him* the 'Amen' is spoken . . . to God."

6. Gk. πεποίθησις.

7. An incidental strand of evidence in favor of the unity of the letter is a word (πεποίθησις) previously unused by Paul that appears in parts of the letter that were — it is claimed — originally separate.

8. Gk. πρὸς τὸν θεόν, "toward God," is preferred to "before God" (NIV).

9. Paul's present "zeal" for God should not be mistaken for bigotry (11:2; cf. 10:1 — "By the meekness and gentleness of Christ I appeal to you").

10. Various factors may have contributed, in varying degrees, to Paul's "confidence

5   Paul immediately qualifies his assertion of "confidence" from the previous verse. He must immediately allay any concern that he is, after all, "self-commended" (see on v. 1). This he does by a verse structured in two parts and hinging on a simple "not . . . but."[11] He declares that *from* himself he is not sufficient to reckon anything as *of* himself;[12] he rejects even the capacity to discern that anything could emanate from him. But, he affirms, our sufficiency is from God.

Since he does not regard himself as self-sufficient, he cannot be self-commended. "Confidence" — which he has (v. 4) — is different from "sufficiency,"[13] which "of [himself]" he does not possess enough even to "reckon"[14] whether he has it! No. Such "sufficiency" as he has for apostolic ministry is "from God."[15] It is "toward God" that he has his "confidence," but it is only "from God"[16] that he has his "sufficiency."

This verse qualifies its predecessor. It also serves to give the answer to the question asked in 2:16, "Who is sufficient for these things?" — by which he means that awesome ministry by which the hearers of the word of

---

toward God." (1) The reality of the Christophany on the Damascus Road, which is expressed allusively within his letters (see especially 3:16-18; 4:4-6; 5:16-17). (2) His corroboration about the earthly Jesus based on his inquiries with those who knew him, the apostles Cephas and James (Gal 1:18-20). (3) His confidence in the reality of Christ's resurrection (see 1 Cor 15:3-19). (4) His assurance that the "promises of God" made under the old covenant were indeed fulfilled by the Son of God whom he and his colleagues proclaimed (see 1:18-20). (5) His observation that the Spirit of the living God was at work in the lives of those who accepted his ministry, changing them into the likeness of Christ (see 1:21-22; 3:3, 18; 13:3-5).

11. Gk. οὐκ . . . ἀλλά.

12. Note the prepositions — ἀφ' and ἐξ.

13. Gk. ἱκανότης. See on 2:16 for comments on the word group ἱκανός, ἱκανότης, ἱκανοῦν. As noted there, Paul may be correcting the Corinthians' mis-exegesis of his comment in 1 Cor 15:9 (ὃς οὐκ εἰμὶ ἱκανὸς καλεῖσθαι ἀπόστολος). Moreover, it may be significant, in view of the contrast following with Moses (vv. 12-18), that Moses said: οὐκ ἱκανός εἰμι (LXX Exod 4:10). Paul insists that he is what Moses was not, though it is only from God. Further, it is to be noted that in LXX Ruth 1:21 (twice) and in LXX Job 21:15; 31:2, and 39:32 ἱκανός is used as a divine name. God is "the Sufficient One" ([ὁ] ἱκανός). "Our sufficiency comes from the Sufficient One" (Plummer, 85).

14. λογίσασθαι is rendered as "claim" (NIV, RSV). The word group λογίζομαι-λογισμός is important within 2 Corinthians (5:19; 10:2, 5, 7, 11; 11:5; 12:6), though its appearance in 1 Corinthians suggests that it may not have been distinctive within the current conversations between Paul and the Corinthians (but see on 10:2, 5, 7, 11).

15. A comparable disavowal of self-sufficiency/avowal of God's sufficiency may be seen in 1 Cor 15:9-10: "I . . . do not even deserve (οὐκ εἰμὶ ἱκανός) to be called an apostle. . . . But by the grace of God I am what I am." Cf. Rom 15:18: "I will not venture to speak of anything except what Christ has accomplished through me."

16. Gk. ἐκ τοῦ θεοῦ.

God are either confirmed in eternal "death" or "saved" from it (2:15). His delayed reply to that question is: "Our sufficiency is from God."[17]

Of course it could not be otherwise. Everything is "from God" (5:18)[18] — the "new creation" (5:17), reconciliation to God through Christ (5:18), and the ministry and the message of that reconciliation (2:17; 5:18-19). All this is "from God," and none of it is "from [Paul]" (v. 5; cf. 12:11) or any other human source (cf. Gal 1:11-12, 15-16).

6 The subject of the first part of this three-part verse — "God" — is located in the previous verse; its verb, "to make [someone] sufficient," is closely related to the adjective "sufficient" and the noun "sufficiency," which are also found in the previous verse. The statement Paul makes here, that "God has made [Paul] sufficient[19] to be [a] minister[s] of a new covenant," serves as an interim conclusion to the passage that began in 2:14 with the question: "Who is sufficient for these things?" (2:16).

The noun "ministers"[20] here makes its first appearance in the letter, following close behind the first use of a member of the word group, the verb "to minister" in v. 3. The members of the "ministry" word cluster occur six times within this chapter, serving to contrast the new and the old covenants.

Using the plural (as the apostolic plural[21]), Paul speaks of himself as a "minister of a new covenant."[22] The term "new covenant," as opposed to

---

17. See n. 13 above. Furnish, 196-97, points to the use of ἱκανός in humility language within Hellenistic Judaism — notably in Philo — as an argument against those who assert Paul's opponents to be Hellenistic *theioi andres* ("divine men") claiming "all-sufficiency" over against Paul's weakness.

18. Gk. ἐκ τοῦ θεοῦ.

19. Gk. ἱκάνωσεν is aorist, referring to the occasion of Paul's conversion and commission.

20. Gk. διακόνους. Paul's only use of διάκονος prior to 2 Corinthians is 1 Thess 3:2 and 1 Cor 3:5. Of the thirty-six uses of the word family in Paul's letters, twenty occur within 2 Corinthians. While it is quite possible that the opponents may have made particular use of this vocabulary (see 11:15, 23), it is not true that they initiated such vocabulary; references outside 2 Corinthians are too numerous. J. N. Collins, *Diakonia*, 194, corrects the widespread belief that the *diakonia* words meant "humble activity." Rather, the root idea was "go between." Fundamental is the concept of one who "undertakes actions for another, be that God or man, master or friend." He is an agent who has a "mandate and an obligation." Care must be taken, however, not to read current word use into Paul's, whether of "humble activity" or of "go-between." His own usage in the various contexts must be noted.

21. See on 1:1; 2:14.

22. Gk. καινῆς διαθήκης is anarthrous, reflecting LXX Jer 38:31. Plummer, 85, notes that καινός, as opposed to νεός ("young"), "implies superiority to that which is not καινός, whereas what is νεός may be better or worse than what is not νεός." Thus "the covenant is fresh and effective, with plenty of time to run, in contrast with the old which is worn out and obsolete." While διαθήκη means a binding agreement or covenant between two parties, it is initiated by

the "old covenant" (v. 14),[23] occurs in Paul's writings only in this verse and in 1 Cor 11:25,[24] where it is found in a tradition about the Lord's Supper originally formulated by others and "delivered" to Paul, who in turn "delivered" it to the Corinthians. In all probability that tradition was established soon after the Last Supper within the earliest messianic community in Jerusalem. The term "new covenant" makes its first literary appearance in 1 Corinthians *c.* A.D. 55, appearing at later (?) dates within the Matthean and Markan traditions of the Last Supper as "the covenant" and in the Lukan tradition as "the new covenant" (Matt 26:28; Mark 14:24; Luke 22:20).[25]

These references, which are traceable to Jesus at the Last Supper, represent his affirmation that "in [his] blood" the "new covenant" prophesied by Jeremiah had been inaugurated. The prophet had written:

> "The time is coming," declares the LORD,
>   "when I will make a *new covenant*
> with the house of Israel and
>   with the house of Judah. . . ." (Jer 31:31)[26]

---

one party, in this case by God (see, e.g., Gen 15:18; Jer 31:31). A covenant *mutually* agreed upon is συνθήκη. For discussion in favor of the view that διαθήκη as used in the LXX is unilateral rather than bilateral, and that Paul's use reflects that emphasis, see Thrall, 1.233-34.

23. But perhaps Paul is contrasting two forms of new covenant. Were Paul's opponents advocating a new covenant (along Qumran lines, but now christianized?) that was different from Paul's new covenant? For discussion and rejection of these suggestions see Thrall, 1.236-37. Paul is contesting the Sinai covenant, not "a contemporary christianised concept of a new covenant."

24. Although these are Paul's only references to "new covenant" within the NT, Paul contrasts two covenants in Gal 4:21–5:1, in a manner closely resembling his contrast in this passage between the "new covenant" and the "old covenant." There Paul makes an allegory of two covenants from the two wives of Abraham, Sarah and Hagar, based on the mode of conception of their sons. Because he was born from the word of promise, Sarah's son was "free," whereas because he was born "according to the flesh," Hagar's son was "a slave." The covenant of slavery symbolized by Hagar, which is "from Mount Sinai . . . and corresponds to the present city of Jerusalem," clearly belongs to the old covenant/Moses/the law of 2 Cor 3:7-15. The covenant symbolized by Sarah with its references to "the Spirit" and "freedom" (Gal 4:29; 5:1) is "the Jerusalem that is above," which corresponds to the "new covenant" of 2 Cor 3:3-18 with its references to "the Spirit" and "freedom" (vv. 3, 6, 17, 18).

25. In relationship to the tradition in 1 Corinthians 11 see G. D. Fee, *1 Corinthians,* 546-47.

26. Not so often noted is Jer 32:38-41: "They will be my people, and I will be their God. I will give them singleness of heart and action, so they will always fear me for their own good and the good of their children after them. I will make an everlasting covenant (διαθήκην αἰωνίαν) with them: I will never stop doing good to them, and I will inspire them to fear me, so they will never turn away from me."

Paul is here claiming that God had appointed him a minister in that covenant prophesied by Jeremiah and inaugurated by Jesus at his death ("my blood," as in 1 Cor 11:25; cf. 2 Cor 5:21). The repetition of "sufficient/sufficiency" from 2:16 in this verse ties ministry of the new covenant back into the activities Paul outlined in that passage, where by "the gospel of Christ" (2:12) Paul spread the "knowledge of [Christ] . . . everywhere" he went (2:14), bringing salvation to some and confirming others in perdition (2:15). Paul's ministry in the "new covenant," the apostolic proclamation of the Son of God, affirms that the prophetic promise is now fulfilled (1:20), that the "time of God's favor, the day of salvation" has "now" come (6:2). "Now" is the time to "be reconciled to God," since God has reconciled the world to himself through Christ and given the apostles the ministry and word of reconciliation (5:18-21). The signs of this great eschatological moment are the preaching of Christ (1:20) and the presence of the life-giving Spirit in the hearts of the people (1:21-22; 3:3, 18), as Paul now — in the second part of the verse — proceeds to say.

With an emphatic "not . . . but"[27] Paul goes on to describe the nature of the new covenant. The "new covenant" is not "of the letter,"[28] which after comparison with v. 3 must mean not "engraved (v. 3[29]) . . . on tablets of stone," an allusive reference to the Law of God as given to Moses on Mount Sinai.[30] The new covenant, as prophesied by Jeremiah, will replace the out-

27. Gk. οὐκ . . . ἀλλά, as also in 2:17 and 3:3, indicating a polemical historical context.
28. Gk. οὐ γράμματος. On the question of the contrast between "letter" and "Spirit," see S. Westerholm, " 'Letter' and 'Spirit,' " 229-48.
29. Gk. ἐγγεγραμμένη, noting the similarity with γράμμα.
30. Exod 24:12; 31:18; 32:15, 16; Deut 4:13; 5:22. See T. E. Provence, "Who Is Sufficient?" 62-68, for a survey of three historic interpretations of the meaning of the "letter"/"Spirit" distinction: (1) the "hermeneutical," by which the "Spirit" should be invoked rather than the "letter" in the interpretation of biblical texts (Richardson); (2) the "legal," in which "letter" is a synonym for "law" (Dunn); (3) and the "allusive," in which "letter" equates with the legalists' distorted misunderstanding of the Law (Cranfield). While (3) is Provence's preferred option, the distinction made between the Law as having an inner "good" character and the Law as "letter" (with its specific demands, interpreted legalistically and with consequent distortion of the Law's true intention), while perhaps true of the Sermon on the Mount (see especially Matt 5:17-20), is not the point of the contrast Paul is making here. Provence's second option, the "legal" (as argued by J. D. G. Dunn, "2 Corinthians III.17 — 'The Lord Is the Spirit,' " 310, and Thrall, 1.234-36), is to be preferred. References to "written on stone tablets . . . inscribed in letters on tablets of stone" (vv. 3, 6, 7), to Moses' second reception of the Law (v. 13; cf. Exod 34:29-35), and to "the reading of the old covenant/Moses" (vv. 14, 15) support the notion stated by Dunn: "The antithesis is . . . between the law and the Holy Spirit, the regulating principles of the old and new covenants respectively" (310 n. 2). See G. D. Fee, *Presence*, 305-6, for a modification of this, i.e., that by γράμματος Paul is talking about Law as a demand for obedience but unaccompanied by the empowering Spirit. For a review of scholarly opinion as to the place of Law in Jewish thinking of the time and for Paul's interaction with it, see generally F. Thielman, *From Plight to Solution*, 1-45.

ward imposition of the Law on a people of rebellious heart. Rather, under this covenant, the Law of God will be in the hearts and minds of a forgiven people who, from least to greatest, will "know the LORD" (Jer 31:33-34).[31]

The positive and contrastive "but of the Spirit"[32] now follows. Although Jeremiah made no reference to the Spirit, the covenant prophesied by him, in effect, would be "of the Spirit" since in it the Law of God would be written inwardly. Ezekiel's prophecy, referred to in the closely connected v. 3, does explicitly mention the Spirit in contrast to "[God's] laws":

> I will remove from you your heart of stone
>   and give you a heart of flesh.
> And I will put my *Spirit* in you
>   and move you to follow my decrees
>   and be careful to keep my laws. (Ezek 36:27)

The third part of v. 6 is introduced by an explanatory "for"[33] and repeats in the same order "letter" and "Spirit" of the second part of the verse, both of which are now given a predicate ("the letter *kills*"/"the Spirit *gives life*").

The oracle of Ezekiel just quoted — so similar to that of Jeremiah — explains what Paul has in mind when he writes "*for* the letter kills." "The letter" comes to a people whose hearts are "stone," that is, dead, unable to "follow" God's "decrees" or "keep" his "laws." Thus "the ministry [of the letter]" is a "ministry of death" and a "ministry of condemnation" (vv. 7, 9). By contrast, "but the Spirit gives life"[34] is — to use Ezekiel's words — a replacement of hearts of stone with hearts of flesh, God's own Spirit within the people moving them "to follow [his] decrees."[35]

Paul's line of argument is as follows. The Spirit has changed the inner lives of the Corinthians, making them obedient from the heart to God, which is expressed in their observable behavior (vv. 2-3), giving Paul "confidence" (v. 4) that as an apostle of the Messiah Jesus, the Son of God, whom he has proclaimed to the Corinthians (1:20), he is a minister of the covenant proph-

---

31. Although Paul speaks positively about the Law (Rom 7:12, 14, 16; 8:4; cf. 1:32; 2:26), he does not apply it in an unqualified way to his readers. For comment on the application of Law — as the Law of Christ — under the new covenant, see on v. 17.

32. Gk. ἀλλὰ πνεύματος.

33. Gk. γάρ. See also vv. 9, 10, 11, and 14.

34. Note the contrastive τὸ δὲ πνεῦμα ζῳοποιεῖ.

35. The radically contrastive views of Paul to the rabbis may be seen in *Exod. Rab.* 41-50 on Exod 31:18: "While Israel stood below engraving idols to provoke their creator to anger . . . God sat on high engraving tablets which would *give* them *life*." But Paul here declares, "[the] letter . . . written . . . on tablets of stone . . . *kills* . . . condemns" (vv. 3, 6).

esied by Jeremiah/Ezekiel, in this the long-awaited "day" of God's salvation (6:2; cf. 1:20).

4. Glory of Two Ministries Contrasted (3:7-11)

> 7 Now if the ministry that brought death, which was engraved in letters on stone, came with glory, so that the Israelites could not look steadily at the face of Moses because of its glory, fading though it was, 8 will not the ministry of the Spirit be even more glorious? 9 If the ministry[1] that condemns men is glorious, how much more glorious is the ministry that brings righteousness! 10 For what was glorious has no glory now in comparison with the surpassing glory. 11 And if what was fading away came with glory, how much greater is the glory of that which lasts!

Paul's far-ranging and negative contrasts of the ministry of the new covenant with that of the old covenant (cf. vv. 6, 14), which immediately follows his comparison of the "peddlers' " ministry with his own (2:17–3:1, 3), implies that these newly arrived ministers had been commending the ministry of the old covenant. For them, apparently, the existing Mosaic covenant was still in force, whereas Paul argued that it had been overtaken by the new. Fundamental to Paul's difference with them, insofar as we can apprehend their thought, is eschatology. In Paul's view the "promises" of God now stand fulfilled in the Son of God, whom he and his companions preached (1:18-20), and therefore the long-prophesied "day of salvation" has now come (6:2), as witnessed by the activity of the Spirit in the lives of believers (1:21-22; 3:3, 6, 18; 5:5; cf. 11:4).

The simple (implied) contrast between the ministries of the covenants that Paul made in v. 6, he now expounds (vv. 7-18)[2] in a "Christian midrash"[3]

---

1. Basing his judgment on excellent textual attestation, Metzger, 578, takes "the ministry" as dative (τῇ διαχονίᾳ), though most translations assume the nominative. Either way the meaning is relatively unaffected.

2. According to A. T. Hanson, "Midrash in II Corinthians 3," 12-18, this passage is "the Mount Everest of Pauline texts as far as difficulty is concerned — or should we rather call it the sphinx among texts, since its difficulty lies in its enigmatic quality rather than its complexity?"

3. So J. Lambrecht, "Structure," 345-47, following Windisch, 112. For an opposite view see W. J. Dumbrell, "Paul's Use of Exodus 34 in 2 Corinthians 3," 179-94, who argues against the view of Hooker, Dunn, and Fitzmyer that vv. 7-18 is midrashic in character. To the contrary, Dumbrell holds that Paul has here captured and faithfully reproduced the explicit flow of thought of Exodus overall, and of Exod 34:29-35 in particular.

— an analogical commentary in the rabbinic style — based on Exod 34:29-35.[4] In the first part, vv. 7-11, the keyword is "glory," whereas in the second, vv. 12-18, it is "veil," which are the two interrelated concerns of the Exodus narrative.

In the present paragraph (vv. 7-11) the keyword "glory"[5] appears as a noun and a verb ten times. These verses are dominated by Paul's negative comparison between the "glory" of the old and the "glory" of the new covenant: (1) the antitheses between the two — between death and the life-giving Spirit (vv. 7-8), condemnation and righteousness (v. 9), abolished and permanent (v. 11) — constitute "opposition"[6] between the two; (2) the threefold use of the "lighter to weightier"[7] pattern, "If [relating to the old]

---

4. Scholars are divided as to Paul's intentions in vv. 7-18. Some take these verses to be explicitly and intrinsically in answer to the "peddlers" (2:17), who may have used the same passage (Exod 34:29-35) midrashically against Paul so that by his use of the passage it may be possible to reconstruct their polemical use of it against him (so D. Georgi, *Opponents,* 258-82). Others view the passage as "not . . . fundamentally polemical" but a "theological exposition with a polemical edge" (so Furnish, 243; see also C. J. Hickling, "Sequence," 380-95). The position taken here is that since the overall context from 2:17 to 4:6 is both polemical (against the peddlers' ministry) and apologetic (in defense of his ministry), the passage vv. 7-18 is midrashic of Exod 34:29-35 as a theological contrast between two covenants and two ministries (of Moses and of Paul) and it is therefore implicitly polemical/apologetic. The opinion that Paul's opponents used Exod 34:29-35 against him appears to us to be possible but, in the circumstances, inaccessible to analysis. It is more likely that the "peddlers" in Corinth disparaged Paul's sufferings as evidence of his lack of "glory" and contended that his fulfillment eschatology was necessarily faulty. Moses' glory was undimmed, a sign that his covenant still obtained, as against Paul's claims.

5. Gk. δόξα.

6. So J. Lambrecht, "Structure," 354-55. Based on the extensive table that follows, he calls the comparison of the glory of the old with the new "thoroughly unfavorable . . . the poles of opposition are . . . irreconcilable":

3:7-8	death	life; cf. v. 6, τὸ . . . γράμμα ἀποκτέννει
	stone	hearts
	engraved letters	Spirit
	ἐγενήθη ἐν δόξῃ	ἔσται ἐν δόξῃ
	Sinai event	eschatological event
3:9	κατάκρισις	δικαιοσύνη
3:11	τὸ καταργούμενον	τὸ μένον
	διὰ δόξης	ἐν δόξῃ

7. Paul here uses the method of arguing from "the lesser to the greater" (*ad minori ad maius*), a well-known rhetorical device among the rabbis (Qal Waḥomer — "from the lighter to the weightier"; H. L. Strack and G. Stemberger, *Introduction to the Talmud and Midrash,* 21; Thrall, 1.239-40). Cf. Rom 5:9, 10, 15, 17; 11:2, 24. For parallels to the εἰ . . . μᾶλλον construction see *New Docs.* 6.69-70.

... much more [relating to the new]," sets apart the two "glories," enlarging the latter over the former; and (3) the polarization between the two glories develops progressively: the question "how much more?" (v. 8) becomes the assertion "by how much more" (vv. 9, 11); the "ministry of righteousness overflows" in glory" (v. 9), and the latter is a "surpassing glory" (v. 10). Above all — as stated in the climactic v. 11 — if the former ministry that "was being abolished"[8] had glory, how much greater must be the "glory" of "that which remains"?[9] Thus:

> But
>> *if* the ministry of death
>>> came with glory,
>> *how much more*
> shall the ministry of the Spirit be with glory?
> For
>> *if* the ministry of condemnation
>>> [came with] glory
>> *how much more*
> the ministry of righteousness
>>> shall overflow with glory.
> For
>> *if* that which was being abolished
>>> came through glory,
>> *how much more*
> that which remains
>>> shall be with glory.

Paul appears to be affirming two great, if paradoxical, truths. On the one hand, he upholds the "glory" of the old covenant ("it came with glory" — v. 7), something he repeats twice (vv. 9, 11). The very assertions he makes in regard to the superiority of the new depends on the reality of the "glory" of the old. That it proved to be a "ministry of death ... of condemnation ... [and] was being abolished" (vv. 7, 9, 11) was due not to that covenant in itself, nor to an absence of glory, but to the spiritual incapacity of the people to fulfill its just requirements (cf. Jer 31:32; Ezek 36:16-21). Paul has a high view of that

---

8. Gk. τὸ καταργούμενον. The subject of καταργεῖν (always used in passive forms in this chapter, hence "abolish*ed*" or "annull*ed*" — see on v. 7) is the glory on Moses' face (vv. 7, 11, 13; cf. v. 14 — the veil over the minds of the people of the old covenant). Although the present tense is used (vv. 7, 11, 13), the aorist "came" (ἐγενήθη — v. 7) indicates a past time when the present tense action was occurring; hence "was being abolished" (vv. 7, 11, 13).

9. Gk. τὸ μένον.

covenant; in it are to be found the promises that God has faithfully fulfilled in Jesus Christ, the Son of God (1:18-20; cf. 7:1).

Nonetheless, the "glory" of the new covenant — because it brings the "Spirit [and] righteousness" and because it "overflows . . . surpasses . . . remains" — has the effect of robbing the old of the glory it had (v. 10). The old is deglorified because it is outshone by the new, just as the low wattage light is outshone and superseded by the midday sun. Thus, Paul secures the "glory" of the old while insisting that the new has overtaken it, rendering it — in effect — obsolescent.

The net effect of the apostle's contrast of the new with the old is that, by now, the old, while "glorious" in its own time, is "abolished" and therefore — whatever that past glory — is not applicable once the new has come.[10] Indeed, because it is a "ministry of death [and] of condemnation" now replaced by a "ministry of the Spirit [and] of righteousness," it would be futile to continue in it, as the "peddlers" apparently are proposing.

7-8   In these verses Paul employs the first of his three "if . . . much more" contrasts — in this case a question ("how much more?") — by which he reveals the obsolescence[11] of the old[12] covenant. Basic to the question is the specific contrast between the opposites, "the ministry of *death*" (v. 7) and "the ministry of the *Spirit*" (v. 8). This question (substantially longer than the following two assertions) is amplified by the inclusion of other information, which in turn will be reproduced within this passage[13] (vv. 7-11) and the next passage[14] (vv. 12-15).

"The ministry of death" — which is so because "the letter kills" (v. 6) — was said to have been "engraved in letters on stone"[15] (cf. v. 3), a clear

---

10. *Contra* W. J. Dumbrell, "Paul's Use of Exodus 34," 187, who regards the "old covenant not as having been abolished but as having been subsumed or built upon."

11. *Contra* Thrall, 1.239-40, who understands the Qal Waḥomer device ("lighter to heavier" — see n. 7) as used by Paul to justify the greater glory of the Christian ministry because of the fact, rather than the obsolescence, of the glory of the Mosaic ministry. However, since we take τὴν δόξαν . . . τὴν καταργουμένην to be speaking of a glory that was even then "being abolished," the notion of obsolescence is justified.

12. In 5:15–6:2 Paul is comparing the old creation ("no longer" — 5:15-16) and the new creation ("now" — 5:16 [twice]; 6:2 [twice]). Nonetheless, the comparison of the old covenant with the new covenant may also be implicit in the contrasts between the new and the old creations.

13. δόξα (vv. 8, 9, 10, 11); καταργουμένην (v. 11).

14. μὴ . . . ἀτενίσαι τοὺς υἱοὺς Ἰσραὴλ (v. 13); τὸ πρόσωπον (vv. 13, 18); Μωϋσῆς (v. 15); τὴν καταργουμένην (vv. 13, 14); τὴν δόξαν (v. 18).

15. Gk. ἐντετυπωμένη; NIV, "engraved." Compare the perfect tense used here for the ongoing negative effects of the inauguration of the old covenant with perfect tense ἐγγεγραμμένη (NIV, "written" — 3:3), indicating the ongoing positive effects of the coming of the Spirit.

reference to God's gift of the commandments to the people through Moses.[16] This enigmatic reference is clarified a few verses later where Paul writes of "the ministry of condemnation" (v. 9), implying that the effect of the commandments of God on those whose hearts had not been changed was only to condemn. Thus, spiritually speaking, it "kill[ed]" the people, and rendered the old covenant a "ministry of death."[17] This possibility was recognized even under the old covenant (i.e., Deut 27:26; 30:17-18). The complex "wretched man" passage (Rom 7:7-25) may be, in part, Paul's personalization of the devastating impact of the Law of God on a person sinful of heart, as Paul the Israelite, but now "in Christ" (and thus aware of his sinful character), understood himself to be. That passage from Romans may serve — again, in part — as commentary on the people under the old covenant subjected to a "ministry of death . . . of condemnation" (see Rom 7:8-11).[18]

Nonetheless, such a "ministry," even if it resulted in "death," Paul insists, "came with glory,"[19] the aorist verb suggesting the significance-laden moment when the covenant was instituted ("the ministry . . . came"[20]). Against the dark and godless background of the Gentile world of the time, God's covenant with his elect people was indeed glorious. That he can go on to speak at all of the greater glory of the new depends on the reality of the glory of the old ("if . . . how much more?"), which in any case is central to the Exodus narrative.

Paul is thus reflecting on the splendor with which Moses' face shone when he came down from the mountain (Exod 34:29-30), as a result of which "the Israelites could not look steadily[21] at the face of Moses." The reason

16. Gk. ἐν γράμμασιν ἐντετυπωμένη λίθοις. Paul's echoing of the Exodus language may be seen here and in v. 3 — ἐγγεγραμμένη . . . ἐν πλάξιν λιθίναις when compared with, "The LORD said to Moses, "Chisel out two stone tablets (πλάκας λιθίνας), like the first ones, and I will write (γράψω) on them the words that were on the first tablets. . . . So Moses chiselled out two stone tablets like the first ones . . ." (Exod 34:1, 4).

17. Cf. Ezek 18:4: "The soul who sins is the one who must die." Paul's treatment here is "broad brush" and is not invalidated by the undisputed fact of godly and insightful individuals like the prophets and psalmists, in whom God's Spirit was active for particular purposes within that now superseded dispensation.

18. See generally R. H. Gundry, "Moral Frustration," 228-45.

19. Apart from 1:20 this is the first of many references to δόξα in this letter (3:8, 9, 10, 11, 18; 4:4, 6, 15, 17; 6:8; 8:19, 23). Yet δόξα appears only a few times in 1 and 2 Thessalonians, with rather more references in 1 Corinthians. The reason for a greater emphasis on δόξα in 2 Corinthians is probably due to the strong autobiographical references in this letter to Paul's glorious Damascus Road encounter with Christ (see 3:16-17; 4:4-6; 5:14-17). See further S. Kim, Origin, 3-31.

20. The historic gift of the Law is implied by the aorist ἐγενήθη ἐν δόξῃ.

21. The construction ὥστε + infinitive (μὴ . . . ἀτενίσαι) expresses result. Cf. πρὸς τό + infinitive (μὴ ἀτενίσαι, v. 13), which expresses purpose. The verb ἀτενίζειν occurs in Paul's letters only here and in v. 13.

182

Paul gives for this — which is his own gloss on the Exodus text[22] — is that the glory on Moses' face was "being abolished."[23] According to Paul, that glory was only ever a sign pointing forward to the greater and permanent glory to come; it was not an "end" in itself (cf. v. 13).

How is it that, glorious as the inauguration of the old covenant had been, as symbolized by the shining of Moses' face, the new covenant, being a "ministry of the Spirit," will be[24] "more glorious"? Here we should note that "death" and "Spirit" belong to lists of "opposites."[25] The "letter kills" (v. 6), so that its dispensation, "the old covenant . . . Moses" (vv. 14, 15), is a "ministry of death [and] condemnation" (v. 7), whereas the "Spirit gives life" (v. 6), so that its dispensation, "the new covenant" (v. 6), is a "ministry of righteousness" and, by inference, "of life."

Thus "death," arising from disobedience and its accompanying "condemnation," characterizes the old covenant, whereas "life" accompanying "righteousness" and[26] "the Spirit," enabling and empowering obedience to

---

22. The story in Exod 34:29-35 may be summarized as follows. When Moses came down from Mount Sinai with the stone tables of the Law, his face shone and the people were afraid to approach him (ἐφοβήθησαν ἐγγίσαι αὐτοῦ — LXX Exod 34:30). After he had given them the commandments, he placed a veil on his face. W. J. Dumbrell, however, rather than associating the shining face with fear, sees the glory on Moses' face as a "sign . . . authenticating the commandments" as the "divine will to Israel" ("Paul's Use of Exodus 34," 181). But, to the contrary, Paul's interpretive expansion of the text (διὰ τὴν δόξαν τοῦ προσώπου αὐτοῦ τὴν καταργουμένην) is eschatological in character; the Law had a τέλος that had been reached in Christ (v. 13; Rom 10:4), so that the glory with which the Law was inaugurated was "now" no more, having been "abolished" in principle from the time of its inception. This eschatological demarcation whereby the glory of the old covenant was "abolished" when it reached its appointed "end" (Christ) is supported by the vocabulary of chapters 5–6 (5:15, μηκέτι; 5:16, ἀπὸ τοῦ νῦν . . . νῦν οὐκέτι; 5:17, ἐν Χριστῷ καινὴ κτίσις; 6:2, ἰδοὺ νῦν εὐπρόσδεκτος, ἰδοὺ νὺν ἡμέρα σωτηρίας).

23. "Fading," according to the RSV, TEV, NIV, and most translations. The verb καταργεῖν/καταργεῖσθαι is prominent in chapter 3 (vv. 7, 11, 13, 14). For discussion preferring "abolished" to "fading" as the meaning of the verb, see A. T. Hanson, *Jesus Christ in the Old Testament,* 25-35. A survey of Paul's use of the verb, which is frequent (22 times; e.g., Rom 3:3, 31), supports the notion of something invalidated or replaced (so also BAGD), and especially in light of its usage in the earlier letter (1 Cor 13:8 [twice], 10, 11). The passive form of the verb/participle used throughout the passage suggests that God is the subject of the abolition, while the present tense in this verse indicates that the abolition began at the time of the inauguration (ἐγενήθη — aorist tense) of the glory, upon which the Israelites were not able to gaze (ἀτένισαι — aorist tense infinitive).

24. The future ἔσται is in contrast with the aorist ἐγενήθη (v. 7), signifying that future covenant glory which was then in prospect, which from Paul's perspective was a present reality.

25. See above, n. 6.

26. "Righteousness" (Gk. δικαιοσύνη) is, in its more complete expression, "the righteousness of God" (5:21), which those who are "in" the one "who was made sin"

God, characterizes the new covenant. The "ministry of the Spirit" is more glorious because the Spirit, as the fulfilment of the prophetic promise and the prime blessing of the new covenant (see on v. 6), is able to change otherwise rebellious hearts, inclining them "now" (cf. 5:16 [twice], 6:2) to hearken to the Law of God.

But where is the "glory" of the "ministry of the Spirit" to be seen? In this section (vv. 7-18) Paul's words are allusively autobiographical. The "glory" of the "ministry of the Spirit" is to be seen in him. As an Israelite he had been blinded to the glory on Moses' face. But now on the Damascus Road, having seen the glory to which Moses' glory pointed, that is, toward the glorified Christ, and having turned to that Lord, Paul has come to experience the blessings of freedom and life through the Spirit. How much more glorious, then, is the ministry of the Spirit to the person previously blind?

But there is also a polemical edge to Paul's words. The "peddlers' " ministry (2:17–3:1) is in continuity with the ministry of the old covenant, which is a "ministry of death [and] condemnation" (cf. v. 9).[27] How futile it will be for the readers to embrace that ministry now that they have been blessed by the coming of the Spirit through the preaching of the Son of God, in whom all the promises of the old covenant have been fulfilled (1:18-20).

The "glory" that Paul saw on that one life-changing occasion serves to describe — metaphorically — the experience of those who, through the "light of the gospel" (4:4), have come under the righteousness of the new covenant (cf. 5:21). What Paul saw with his eyes also tells the story of the people in whose hearts the "light of the knowledge of the glory of God" has shone (4:6). It is this "glory," shining in their hearts, arising from the preaching of the gospel, which is greater, infinitely surpassing, and indeed "outpaling" the glory associated with "Moses," the ministry engraved on tablets of stone (v. 7).

9 This is the second of the "if . . . how much more" contrasts within this passage, in this case an assertion, thereby tending to widen the gap between the "glory" of the new over against the "glory" of the old. This contrast is explanatory; the old covenant is a "ministry [of] death" (v. 7)

"become." The new covenant people, i.e., those who are "in Christ," are "righteous" (or "justified"). Through the Messiah's death for them they are forgiven ("justified"), covenantally dedicated to God. The Spirit is the life-giving (3:6), life-changing (3:18) presence of God within their lives, who has come in consequence of the preaching of the Son of God (1:18-21; cf. Gal 3:1-5).

27. Thrall, 1.246-48, is correct in seeing the contrast between non-Christian Judaism and Christianity (both Jewish and Gentile). True, yet those who are mediating the present message appear to be *Christian* Jews (11:22-23), whose ultimate loyalties and insights were Jewish rather than Christian.

because[28] it is a "ministry of condemnation." The meaning of "condemnation"[29] is defined, to a degree, by a nontheological use later in the letter ("I do not say this to condemn you" — 7:3). Nonetheless, the full force of eschatological, forensically based condemnation — the divine rejection — is found in closely related words as used in other Pauline references. The earlier metaphorical statements "the letter kills" and "the ministry of death" (vv. 6, 7) must be seen as anticipating and leading to this reference to "the ministry of condemnation." This was God's just condemnation of his people on account of their failure to uphold the covenant that was based on "letters written in stone" (v. 7), the commandments of God given at Mount Sinai. In echoing Jeremiah's promise of a new covenant (v. 6), Paul is aware of the prophet's assessment of the people. The people have "broken" the covenant of God and have committed "wickedness" and "sins" (Jer 31:32, 34).

As with the previous contrast (vv. 7-8), the former "ministry," that of "condemnation," was "glorious," whereas the latter, that of "righteousness," is much more abundantly "glorious." Again, as with vv. 7-8, the "glory" of the old is the basis for the "glory" of the new.

But what is this "righteousness?" As with the previous question (vv. 7-8), where Paul's rhetorical contrast is between opposites, so here "condemnation" and "righteousness" should be viewed as opposites. "Righteousness," therefore, whatever its nuances as used elsewhere, must in this context carry a forensic meaning like forgiveness, acquittal, or vindication.[30] This is borne out by the covenantal-forensic use of this word group in the earlier letter to the Corinthians — the best hermeneutical tool for understanding 2 Corinthians — even though the references there are few.[31] References

---

28. Gk. γάρ, "for," is untranslated by the NIV.

29. Gk. κατάκρισις. The only two appearances of κατάκρισις in the NT are in 2 Cor 3:9 and 7:3. The verb κατακρινεῖν appears in Paul rather more frequently (1 Cor 11:32; Rom 2:11; 8:3, 24); see also the closely related κατάκριμα (Rom 5:16, 18; 8:1). As a noun ending with -ις, however, where the concrete expression of the verbal idea is implied, Paul's use of κατάκρισις may be deliberately precise.

30. See R. Y.-K. Fung, "Justification by Faith," 247-61. Fung, noting that the counterpart to κατάκρισς is δικαίωσις (as in Rom 5:18), suggests that δικαιοσύνη may include ethical as well as forensic righteousness (253). Ethical righteousness is certainly to be inferred by the Spirit references in this passage (vv. 3, 6, 18), especially when read against Ezek 36:27, but the ethical claim for δικαιοσύνη is problematic. For verses that connect the Spirit (vv. 3, 6, and 8) and righteousness/justification see 1 Cor 6:11; Gal 5:5.

31. To be regarded as covenantal and dedicatory are: ". . . Christ Jesus, whom God made our wisdom, our *righteousness* (δικαιοσύνη) and sanctification and redemption" (1 Cor 1:30) and "you were washed, you were sanctified, you were *justified* (ἐδικαιώθητε) in the name of the Lord Jesus and in the Spirit of our God" (6:11). The forensic element appears gratuitously in "I am not aware of anything against myself, but I am not thereby *acquitted* [δεδικαίωμαι — i.e., by *people!*]. It is the Lord who judges me" (4:4). These

to "righteousness" later in 2 Corinthians support this understanding of the word.[32]

Why is "the ministry of righteousness . . . much more glorious" (lit. "overflows in glory")? As noted regarding v. 8, the greater glory expresses what Paul saw on the Damascus Road, which, in turn, provides the vocabulary to describe the blessings to those who, through the gospel, now enjoy the covenantal and forensic relationship with God mentioned above. Through "this ministry" (see 4:1) believers are "in Christ," dedicated covenantally to God, having the "righteousness of God" from Christ the sinless One in exchange for their unrighteousness (see 5:21).

10 Again, though more intensively,[33] Paul engages in a contrast between the old and the new covenants, specifically the respective degrees of "glory" of the covenants. The contrast is achieved in a paradox by two uses of the verb "to glorify." In reverse order, the second is a participle in the perfect tense ("that which had been endowed with glory"[34]) that is the subject — in the negative — of the first ("is not now endowed with glory"). Once again Paul is thinking of the splendor on Moses' face when he came down from the mountain (see on v. 7). But that which had been glorified is no longer glorious.

Why is the glory associated with Moses not now glorious? It is because of the "surpassing glory,"[35] that is, the glory seen by Paul on the face of Jesus

---

three references — when read together — point to a use of δικαιοσύνη/δικαιοῦν that is covenantal, eschatological, and forensic and that fits well with the use of δικαιοσύνη in 2 Corinthians (3:9), written soon after 1 Corinthians.

32. While some of the references to δικαιοσύνη in 2 Corinthians are moral-ethical (6:7, 14; 9:9, 10), they should generally be seen as expressive of the covenantal-forensic use in the critical text, "For our sake he made him to be sin who knew no sin, so that in him we might become the righteousness of God [δικαιοσύνη θεοῦ — 5:21, RSV]." The people are covenantally dedicated to God, forgiven, in the sinless One who, for their sake, "was made sin." The "ministers of Satan" who masquerade as "ministers of righteousness" (11:15) are promoting "another Jesus, a different gospel" (11:4) in which, so it appears, the believers' ethical and moral fulfillment of commandment-"righteousness" is the fulfillment of the covenant.

33. The initial καὶ γάρ is intensive, "for indeed."

34. Gk. τὸ δεδοξασμένον is neuter gender, pointing not to Moses' face but to the institution of the old covenant. W. J. Dumbrell, "Paul's Use of Exodus 34," 186, argues that the perfect tense τὸ δεδοξασμένον, "what once had splendor" (RSV), supports the proposition of "the continuing glory of the old covenant." But the negative οὐ δεδόξασται, "has come to have no splendor," with which it is in balance, appears to negate this point.

35. The notion of "surpassing," as expressed by the vocabulary ὑπερβάλλειν (3:10; 9:14), ὑπερβολή (1:8; 4:7, 17; 12:7), and ὑπερβαλλόντως (11:23), is critical to and distinctive to 2 Corinthians. This word group is concentrated in 2 Corinthians, with only one reference beforehand (1 Cor 12:31) and few subsequent to it (Rom 7:13; Eph 1:9; 2:7; 3:19). It is possible that the opponents claimed that Jesus belonged to the existing covenant

(4:6), the glory of the new covenant, associated as it is with "the Spirit" and "righteousness" (vv. 8, 9) and expressed in the gospel (4:4). The latter out-glorified the former, thus deglorifying it. The brightness and permanence of the one has outpaled the other, so that whatever glory it had is, in effect, no more.

11 Once again — for the third and last time — Paul asks an "if . . . how much more" question (cf. vv. 7-8, 9), intending to point out the obsolescence of the old, in relationship to the new, covenant. As with v. 9, which explains an earlier verse (v. 7), this verse begins with "for,"[36] explaining earlier verses (i.e., vv. 7, 10). Here the contrast is between "that which was being abolished,"[37] which "came" (v. 7)[38] "*with* glory," and "that which remains," which "will be" (v. 8) "*in* glory."[39] The contrast between impermanence and permanence is the primary concern, to be taken up in the passage following.

Following the previous verse, the focus is on "glory," the "glory" of the dispensation of "letter" represented by the splendor with which Moses' face shone when descending from the mountain (Exod 34:29-30), in contrast with the "surpassing glory" (v. 10) that Paul saw on the face of Jesus Christ on the Damascus Road (4:4, 6). The point of the comparison is the temporariness of the old against the eternity of the new. Indeed, Paul even characterizes the old as "that which was being abolished,"[40] even though it *came*[41] "with glory." Thus the "glory" of the old was "being abolished" in principle from the time of its inauguration. But the glory of the new covenant remains[42]; it

---

and that no new covenant had been inaugurated, requiring Paul to point to the "surpassing" nature of the covenant of Christ and the Spirit.

36. Gk. γάρ, untranslated by the NIV.

37. Gk. τὸ καταργούμενον (NIV, "fading") is neuter, referring to the Mosaic covenant. The words τὸ καταργούμενον pick up τὴν δόξαν . . . τὴν καταργουμένην of v. 7, which point to τὸ δεδοξασμένον of v. 10, which anticipates τὸ καταργούμενον. "Glory," which "had been abolished" (feminine — v. 7), is now "that which had been endowed with glory," which "had been abolished" (neuter — vv. 10, 11).

38. There is no verb governing "with glory" (διὰ δόξης); this (ἐγενήθη) has to be understood from v. 7

39. The former "ministry" came "with glory" (διὰ δόξης), whereas the present "ministry" is "that which remains *in* glory" (ἐν δόξῃ). To be sure, the former "ministry" also was ἐν δόξῃ (v. 7), but this described the circumstances attendant on its coming, rather than its permanence (so Hughes, 106).

40. Gk. τὸ καταργούμενον. See on v. 7, especially the note on καταργεῖν/καταργεῖσθαι. τὸ καταργούμενον is present tense and is applicable as a term ("that which is being abolished") to the old covenant, characterized as it was by condemnation and death (vv. 7, 9). The covenant that "came" (ἐγενήθη — v. 7) with glory (τὸ δεδοξασμένον — v. 10) is now effectively "abolished" by that which is now permanent, never to be abolished or superseded.

41. Gk. ἐγενήθη ἐν δόξῃ . . . τὴν δόξαν . . . τὴν καταργούμενην (v. 7), "it came in glory . . . glory . . . which is being abolished."

42. Gk. τὸ μένον.

is eternal, never to be abolished, never to be outshone. This new covenant glory is incomparable and eternal because it is the glory of God that shines on the face of Christ (4:6), who is the "likeness" *(eikōn)* of God (4:4; cf. 3:18). The believer, although a mere "earthen vessel" (4:7) and an "earthly tent" (5:1), is being transformed into the "likeness" and the perfect glory of the Lord who is glorious (3:18).

5. The People of the Old Covenant: Veiled (3:12-15)

> 12 *Therefore, since we have such a hope, we are very bold.* 13 *We are not like Moses, who would put a veil over his face to keep the Israelites from gazing at it while the radiance was fading away.* 14 *But their minds were made dull, for to this day the same veil remains when the old covenant is read. It has not been removed, because only in Christ is it taken away.* 15 *Even to this day when Moses is read, a veil covers their hearts.*

Paul continues to contrast the old covenant with the new, based on his midrash of Exod 34:29-35. He turns now to the people of the old covenant (vv. 12-15), with whom he will compare the people of the new covenant (vv. 16-18).

If the keyword in vv. 7-11 is "glory," the keyword for vv. 12-18, of which vv. 12-15 form the first part, is "veil";[1] "veil"-related words occur six times in these verses.

The connecting particle, "therefore,"[2] followed by "such a hope," indicates that this passage flows logically out of what has been written. The "hope," which is of the "glory that remains" (v. 11), makes Paul "very bold" (v. 12). This "boldness," or, more probably, "openness," is opposed to the "veiled"ness that was interposed between "Moses" — symbolizing the old covenant — and the people of Israel, which prevented them from seeing the "end" of the "glory which had been abolished" (v. 13). "But"[3] — in contrast with Paul's and others' "opened"ness (v. 12), and consonant with Israel's "veiled"ness (v. 13) over their hardened minds — the same veil remains unlifted at "the reading of the old covenant"; only in Christ is the veil abolished (v. 14). Again he says "but," repeating that the same veil lies upon their hearts at "the reading of Moses" (v. 15), that is, "letters [originally] inscribed in stones" (v. 7; cf. v. 3).

---

1. Gk. τὸ κάλυμμα, which occurs in the NT only in vv. 13, 14, 15, and 16. The first is literal, i.e., the cover with which Moses veiled his face; the others are metaphorical for the "veil" covering the glory of Moses/the Law.

2. Gk. οὖν.

3. Gk. ἀλλά.

The story from Exod 34:29-35 about the "veil" Moses placed on his face to cover the "glory" provides Paul with an elaborate and complex image in vv. 14-18: (1) to explain the blindness — as he saw it to be — of the people of Israel (vv. 14-15), but also (2) to show how the veil is removed (v. 16), and (3) to teach what happens when the veil is removed (v. 18).

In v. 13 Paul introduces the main elements of that narrative which he will expound in the following verses: Moses placed a veil on his face to prevent the Israelites from seeing the glory on his face. Paul uses the narrative detail that Moses veiled the glory on his face to observe that the glory in the old covenant that pointed forward to Christ was veiled to the people whenever the "old covenant ["Moses"] is read." That veil, he says, lies upon their hearts (v. 15). How is it that the Israelites have the veil on their hearts (v. 15)? It is on account of their "hardness" (v. 14). In vv. 14-15 the repeated adversative "but" sets the "veiled" Israelites in contrast to Paul and fellow believers who "have such a hope" (of unending glory — v. 11) and who "are very open" (v. 12 — i.e., now able to see the glory of God), preparing the way for the climax of the passage, "*we all* with unveiled face . . . are being changed" (v. 18).

The "glory" of God was inherent in, but temporary to, the revelation of Moses ("the letter")/the old covenant; it pointed forward to Christ. This "glory" had been, from its inception and in principle, "abolished," temporary, about to be outglorified and thus deglorified by the greater and permanent glory of Christ and the Spirit (vv. 10-11). But a "veil" of "hardness" (v. 14) prevents them from seeing even that "glory." This "veil," however, is lifted "in Christ" (v. 14), that is, as one "turns to the Lord" (v. 16). Paul himself, who had incessantly heard the reading of Moses/the old covenant, had been so "veiled," or blinded. But, having turned to the Lord (Jesus), he had experienced firsthand the openedness, the removal of the veil. He saw the glory of God in the face of Jesus Christ (4:6).

Thus, whereas the contrast between the "glory" of the old and that of the new (vv. 7-11) is rationally and dispassionately argued, the contrast between the peoples of the old and the new covenants — as symbolized by the "veil" — is more personal. "They" — the Israelites — are without hope and blind ("veiled" — vv. 12, 14, 15); "we" — who have "turned to the Lord [Jesus]," as the next passage will declare (v. 16) — are "free," unveiled, able to see (as in a mirror) the glory of God and subject to transformation into the same image, that is, of Christ (vv. 16, 17, 18). In this way Paul introduces his theology of the hope of glory, which will come to the surface again in 3:18, and be further developed in 4:14, 16–5:10.

12-13 Paul now applies the argument of vv. 7-11, that the glory of the new is greater and that the glory of the old was temporary, being now abolished.

189

These verses make an outright contrast between the people of the new covenant for whom Paul — representatively[4] — speaks ("we," v. 12; cf. "we all," v. 18) and the people of the old, "the Israelites"[5] (v. 13). Having the "hope" of the greater and permanent "glory" (vv. 7-11), Paul and fellow believers are, he says, "very bold," or, as we shall suggest, "very open." This first verse in a new passage lays the foundation for what follows, both in this passage and the next, reaching a climax in v. 18. In particular Paul now introduces his theology of the hope of glory, on which he will reflect further in 3:18 and 4:14–5:10.

The new covenant people, "having such a hope . . . are very bold/open," whereas the Israelites were "not able to gaze at the end[6] of" [the glory] that "was being abolished."[7] The present tense of the verbs ("having[8] . . . are"[9]) indicates the permanence of the latter glory (cf. v. 12), while the

---

4. Paul generally uses "we"/"us" in his defensive excursus on new covenant ministry (2:14–7:4) as a literary plural, referring to himself as an apostle (see on 1:1; 2:14). Nonetheless, in vv. 12-18 he uses "we" of himself not in regard to his ministry but representatively, as one who has "turn[ed] to the Lord" (v. 16), and therefore of all who, through Christ, belong to the new covenant. There is another view, however, that Paul is speaking directly of *his* ministry (so, e.g., Thrall, 1.254-55).

5. Gk. τοὺς υἱοὺς Ἰσραήλ, "the sons of Israel," an idiomatic expression, as in v. 7.

6. Gk. τὸ τέλος (untranslated in the NIV) has an important eschatological meaning, "goal" or "end," as in a number of parallel statements by Paul, e.g.,

1 Cor 10:11 — εἰς οὓς τὰ τέλη τῶν αἰώνων κατήντηκεν.
(". . . upon whom the fulfillment of the ages has come.")
Rom 10:4 — τέλος γὰρ νόμου Χριστὸς εἰς δικαιοσύνην παντὶ τῷ πιστεύοντι.
("Christ is the end of the law, so that there may be righteousness to those who believe.")

For arguments in favor of the view that τέλος means (1) *terminus,* see Furnish, 207, or (2) *cessation,* see Thrall, 1.256. In reply, it should be noted that the whole passage vv. 7-13 points to what is to come, not merely in the sense of terminus, but of *fulfillment* by that which is so much greater. Rather, Paul uses "end" in the sense of "goal." Here, too, we differ with Hughes, 109 n. 6, who takes εἰς τὸ τέλος as indicating *duration* rather than end point.

7. Gk. τὸ τέλος τοῦ καταργουμένου; NIV, "while the radiance was fading away." The location in the past of the *process* of abolition (τοῦ καταργουμένου) is determined by the *historic* inauguration (ἐγενήθη) of the old covenant (see on v. 7). Paul's comment here is pointed in view of the rabbinic tradition that declared that the glory on Moses' face continued to shine undiminished till the day of his death (cited in Hughes, 110 n. 6).

8. Gk. ἔχοντες — present indicative, probably used in a causal sense, "since we have . . ." (so NIV).

9. Gk. χρώμεθα from χράομαι, "use" (also 1:17; 13:10; cf. 1 Cor 7:21, 31; 9:12, 15). The context here suggests that it is "are," present indicative (being in parallel with 4:1), rather than a hortatory subjunctive, "let us be. . . ."

aorist (single-action tense — "gazing at"[10]) indicates the completedness, and, therefore, impermanence of the time of the former glory (cf. vv. 10-11).[11] Thus the people of the new covenant have "such a hope," that is, of the glory that remains[12] and is yet in prospect (so v. 11: "the glory . . . which remains"). The people of the old covenant, by contrast, had no hope, but were prevented — throughout its duration — from looking at a glory that "was being abolished" (see vv. 7, 11; cf. v.) because it was to be "ended" or "fulfilled" (see 1:20) by the permanent and greater glory that was to come (vv. 10-11) and to which it pointed.

For this reason, Paul declares, "we are very bold," or, more probably, "very open."[13] By contrast — to continue the midrash on Exod 34:29-35

10. Gk. ἀτένισαι — aorist infinitive of ἀτενίζω, a verb that is used by Paul only here and in v. 7.

11. For the view that Paul's reference to glory is meant to be understood, in the first instance, "within the time-frame of Moses' activity" rather than pointing beyond itself to a fulfilling or "ending" of it in "the future time of Christ," see S. J. Hafemann, "Glory and Veil," 42.

12. *Contra* L. Belleville, *Reflections,* 192-93, who identifies "such a hope" not with the people but with "the superior character" of the gospel ministry and who regards these verses as a contrast between a new covenant *minister* and Moses (and the peddlers).

13. Gk. πολλῇ παρρησία; NIV, "very bold." There are two main options in determining the meaning of παρρησία, one with a Greek background, the other with a Jewish: (1) For freedom/openness of speech in a Greek political context. H. Schlier, *TDNT* 5.871-75 demonstrates that the word παρρησία was very important in Greek political theory and practice at that time, with consequent popular use. Furnish (206) gives evidence for "boldness" as also applied to private speech. The word so understood would have been well known in a politically aware Greco-Roman city like Corinth. (2) For eschatological trust and assurance of future joy with God as used in the OT and other Jewish passages. H. Balz, *EDNT* 3.45, cites examples from the LXX and near contemporary Jewish texts in which παρρησία means "confidence and openness in the presence of God."

Various suggestions have been made as to the meaning of πολλῇ παρρησία in the present context. Plummer, 96, takes it to refer to the clarity and certainty of the apostolic message in contrast to the occasional opaqueness of the prophetic oracles under the old covenant (cf. Matt 13:17; 1 Pet 1:10, 12). Furnish, 205-6, thinks it relates to Paul's forthrightness in addressing the Corinthians, as in the earlier chapters of the letter. Martin, 67, noting a parallelism between 3:12 and 4:1, proposes that "boldness" in 3:12 is in contrast to "faint-heartedness" in 4:1.

The problem with the latter proposal is that in vv. 12-18 Paul is using the plural pronoun not for his apostolic ministry so much as for himself as a representative member of the new covenant, in particular one who had been a "veiled" Israelite, but for whom the veil was now removed.

W. C. van Unnik, "With Unveiled Face," 160-61, suggests that παρρησία derives from an Aramaic loanword signifying to "uncover the head" rather than "shame and mourning." To be sure, the Gentile Corinthians may not have understood this Semitic background, being familiar with the political and popular use (as in 1 above) of the word.

begun in v. 7 — Moses placed a veil on his face with the purpose[14] of preventing the Israelites from seeing the end of the glory on his face that was already, in principle, abolished. The circumstances of Moses' purposive action are given in v. 14 as "their minds were hardened."[15] It is for this reason[16] that "the same veil . . . is unlifted" (v. 14).

Throughout his midrashic treatment of the Exodus story in vv. 7-13 Paul has pointed to the veil on Moses' face as masking an already-being-abolished glory, whose function was to point forward to the greater and permanent glory of the new covenant (vv. 4-13). Paul's exposition, however, was really about the "letters inscribed in stones" (v. 7; cf. v. 3) that God had given the people of Israel through Moses. His point is that, not only did the "letter" kill (i.e., condemn — v. 9) and thus become a "ministry of death" (v. 7), but its glory had no permanence. Its glory, which was eschatologically prospective, was veiled from them (literally) and is now veiled from them (figuratively) due to their "hardness."[17]

14-15 In these verses Paul continues to reflect upon the plight of the old covenant people, which as an Israelite (11:22; cf. vv. 7, 13) he had experienced firsthand. In the previous verse he suggested (by implication) that they had no hope, since whatever "glory" there had been in that covenant, it was veiled from them. Now he will emphasize[18] the dire circumstances of the

---

Nonetheless, option (2), canvassed by Balz and van Unnik, fits the context of Paul's argument. Since he immediately states, "not like Moses, who placed a veil on his face" (v. 12), and concludes the passage with "we all with *un*veiled face" (v. 18), it would appear that πολλῇ παρρησίᾳ means "openness" as opposed to "veiledness," being "sighted" as opposed to being "blinded." As a member of the old covenant, Paul, "a son of Israel," knew what it was to have been "veiled" to the "glory" of God (v. 13). But Paul had "turn[ed] to the Lord" and experienced the lifting of the veil so that he had seen the glory of God (vv. 14, 16, 18). Thus, as one with "unveiled face," he writes as a representative of the new covenant people.

14. In v. 7 the construction ὥστε + infinitive (μὴ . . . ἀτένισαι) expresses result; here πρὸς τό + infinitive (μὴ ἀτενίσαι) expresses (negative) purpose. The verb does not occur within the Exodus text and is thus Paul's gloss upon that text. In Paul's interpretation of the text the Israelites do not "see" the *doxa* adhering to Moses.

15. See on v. 14.

16. Gk. γάρ; NIV, "for."

17. See Thrall, 1.259-61, for an extended review of various understandings of Moses' veiling, one of which, in our view, gives sufficient weight to the veiling as "hardness," as in v. 14.

18. The intial ἀλλά is connected with τοὺς υἱοὺς Ἰσραήλ of the previous verse so as to underline, while explaining, the reality of their blindness to the glory in their covenant: "To keep the Israelites from gazing . . . *but* their minds were hardened. . . ." Furnish (207), however, takes the adversative ἀλλά as *correcting* and interpreting the veiling by Moses of the previous verse. It was not Moses who veiled the glory but the people's minds that were responsible for the blindness. However, the point of ἀλλά is to

people. Their hardened[19] minds were responsible[20] for their blindness to the eschatological glory.

Much of what Paul says in v. 14 is duplicated in v. 15, which in turn serves as a lead-in to the contrast in v. 16:

v. 14	**v. 15**
But their minds were hardened.	
For until this day	But until today
the same veil	
remains at the reading of the old covenant;	whenever Moses is read
not unveiled (i.e., unlifted)[21]	a veil lies upon their hearts.
because in Christ it is abolished.	

In common are (1) until today, (2) when the old covenant/Moses is read, and (3) their minds/hearts are veiled.

Paul had good reason to speak in this dramatic manner. He himself had sat in the synagogue Sabbath after Sabbath listening to the reading[22] of the old

---

contrast those like Paul who now "have such a hope" and are "very open" (v. 12), i.e., "unveiled" (v. 18), with those who remain blinded, without hope under the old covenant (v. 13). An adversative ἀλλά appears also at the beginning of v. 15, repeating and intensifying the essential *contrastive* idea of the previous verse.

19. Gk. ἐπωρώθη; NIV, "made dull." This is probably an ingressive aorist, "became hardened." An ambiguity is implicit in πωροῦν since both the disobedient and God participate in the hardening of the heart. For his part, Paul does not hesitate to say that God is the subject of the hardening of the hearts of the disobedient (see Rom 9:13-18).

20. "Their minds were hardened, *for* (γάρ) to this day the same veil . . . remains unlifted."

21. Gk. μὴ ἀνακαλυπτόμενον; NIV, "not . . . removed." The translation and punctuation are uncertain here. The options include: (1) ". . . the same veil remains unlifted, [the veil] *which* is abolished in Christ" (KJV, RV). Here μὴ ἀνακαλυπτόμενον is the predicate of μένει and ὅτι is taken as ὅ τι, an unusual construction. (2) "The same veil . . . remains; it is not revealed *that* it (the old covenant) is abolished in Christ" (Moffatt). In this case μὴ ἀνακαλυπτόμενον is accusative absolute ("it is not revealed"), ὅτι is declarative, and the "old covenant" is the subject of "abolished." But the participle ἀνακαλυπτόμενον is forced to have a meaning not natural to it. (3) "The same veil . . . remains unlifted, *because* [it is] in Christ that [it is] abolished" (RSV). But here μὴ ἀνακαλυπτόμενον would be redundant. (4) "The same veil . . . remains; unlifted *because* [it is] in Christ [that] it is abolished" (effectively, Furnish, 209, 210). Here μὴ ἀνακαλυπτόμενον is independent of μένει. Although "abolished" had referred earlier to "glory," not "veil," this option is to be preferred.

22. The synagogue inscription in Jerusalem bearing the name of Vettenus, which is believed to date from the NT era, declares that the synagogue was for "the reading of the law and the teaching of the commandments" (C. K. Barrett, *Documents,* 54). For references to the reading of Scripture in the synagogue see Acts 13:15; 15:21; cf. 1 Tim 4:13.

covenant/Moses, but blinded to its glory, which pointed toward Christ. Moreover, as a Christian, he had preached Christ in the synagogues, explaining how the Scriptures (i.e., the Law and the Prophets — cf. Luke 24:44-46) had been fulfilled by the Messiah Jesus (Acts 13:15; 17:2-3), only to be faced with the obduracy of his hearers. Paul is not alone in commenting on the hardness/blindness of God's historic people in their attitude to Jesus; the Evangelists also notice it (Matt 11:25; Mark 3:5; 6:52; 8:17; John 9:39-41; 12:40).

Paul's word "today"[23] (vv. 14, 15) reflects the irony of their blindness. The "day of salvation" has "now" come (6:2), and the light of the glory of God has shone on the face of Christ (4:6). The "peddlers," by their countermission against Paul (2:17–3:1), are actively attempting to bring the people under a covenant whose members historically had been veiled from the glory of God that was to be revealed.

But this "veiled"ness of the covenantal people did not begin with the coming of Christ. Throughout the period of the old covenant from the time the "letters inscribed in stones" were originally given, the people had hardened their hearts. Paul is not dogmatizing from a distance; Moses himself said as much (Deut 29:2-4; cf. Isa 6:9-10; 63:17). As God speaking through Jeremiah tersely stated, "My covenant, which they broke" (Jer 31:32). In Paul's words that hardening of the minds is like a veil that blinds the people.[24] It is a chronic blindness evident from the beginning, when "the old covenant"[25] was given, and is unaffected — even confirmed — Sabbath after Sabbath to that very day as the people hear "Moses"/"the old covenant" read.[26]

---

23. Gk. ἄχρι . . . τῆς σήμερον ἡμέρας; NIV, "for to this day." These words probably derive from LXX Deut 29:3: "Up to this day the Lord (ἕως τῆς ἡμέρας ταύτης) did not give you a heart to know and eyes to see and ears to hear."

24. This verse should be read with Rom 11:7-8, where the verb πωροῦν also occurs (ἐπωρώθησαν). In Rom 11:7-8, where Paul echoes a number of OT passages (LXX Deut 29:3 and LXX Isa 29:10), he writes that, apart from the elect, "the rest were *hardened* . . . to *this very day.*"

25. Gk. τῆς παλαιᾶς διαθήκης, a term not found elsewhere in the NT, prompting Plummer, 99-101, to suggest that Paul may have been the first to speak in this way. It should be noted that Paul quotes the phrase ἡ καινὴ διαθήκη from the tradition he received, ultimately from the Lord (1 Cor 11:25; cf. Luke 22:20). In the Parable of the Unshrunk Cloth, Jesus says that "the new [patch tears] from the old [garment]," using the words found in 2 Corinthians 3, καινός and παλαιός (Mark 2:21). The vocabulary also occurs in the Letter to the Hebrews: "In speaking of a new (καινήν) [covenant] he treats the first as obsolete (πεπαλαίωκεν). And what is becoming obsolete (τὸ . . . παλαιούμενον) and growing old is ready to vanish away" (Heb 8:13, RSV).

26. Verses 3 and 7 — "letters in tablets of stone . . . letters inscribed on stones" and "the reading of the old covenant/Moses" in vv. 14 and 15 must be taken together as referring to that covenant which was overtaken by the new covenant of Christ and the Spirit, in which Paul was a minister (vv. 6, 8, and 9).

Tragic as this blindness is, it, too, was part of God's great plan, as preparation for the ingathering of the Gentiles (Rom 11:25). Yet even this was calculated for Israel's good, that she might ultimately be saved (Rom 11:11-12, 26).

But as Paul well knew from his own experience on the Damascus Road, that Mosaic veil is "abolished in Christ" (v. 14). The careful play on the words for "abolished" should not be missed. The glory on the face of Moses "was being abolished" in principle the moment it "came" (v. 7), pointing toward a glory that would outshine it and remain permanently (vv. 7, 11, 13).[27] The "veil" on Moses' face that covered that "being-abolished glory" remains unlifted. But now, "in Christ,"[28] that veil itself is "abolished," allowing the glory of God to shine brightly and forever "in the face of Christ" (4:6). Paul will repeat this autobiographical allusion in v. 16 with the words, "whenever anyone turns to the Lord, the veil is removed."

Paul is saying, in effect, that only as Israelites turn to Christ, on the basis of the preaching of the gospel, will they discern the inner meaning and glory of the old covenant. Apart from Christ those who remain under that covenant remain veiled to the eschatological glory to which it pointed.

6. The People of the New Covenant: Unveiled (3:16-18)

> 16 *But whenever anyone turns to the Lord, the veil is taken away.* 17 *Now the Lord is the Spirit, and where the Spirit of the Lord is, there[1] is freedom.* 18 *And we, who with unveiled faces all[2] reflect the Lord's glory, are being transformed into his likeness with ever-increasing glory, which comes from the Lord, who is the Spirit.*

In vv. 14-15 Paul had been writing about the "veiled"ness of the Israelites (v. 13). In vv. 16-18, by contrast, he speaks of the "*un*veiled"ness of those who turn to the Lord. He establishes this contrast by the repeated staccato use of the particle, "but"[3] — "*but* whenever . . . *but* we all . . ." (vv. 16, 18).

Critical to this passage, too, is the change from the plural subject "the Israelites" (vv. 7, 13), with plural pronouns "*their* minds . . . *their* hearts"

---

27. Gk. τὴν καταργουμένην . . . τὸ καταργούμενον . . . τοῦ καταργουμένου . . . καταργεῖται (vv. 7, 11, 13, and 14). The only references to this verb in 2 Corinthians occur in chapter 3.

28. As one "turns to the Lord," as in v. 16.

1. Many authorities (e.g., ℵ[c] D[b,c] F G K L it[d,g] vg syr[h] cop[sa] etc.) supply ἐκεῖ as co-relative with οὗ. The shorter reading is "decisively supported" (Metzger, 578) by 𝔭[46] ℵ* A B C D etc. In any case, Paul does not usually balance οὗ with ἐκεῖ.

2. The πάντες is omitted in 𝔭[46].

3. Gk. δέ.

(vv. 14, 15), to the singular, "whenever *anyone* turns to the Lord" (v. 16). This "anyone" is indeed true of *anyone,* that is, in regard to Paul himself, who, on the Damascus Road, "turn[ed] to the Lord [Jesus]." But this is true representatively as well as autobiographically; Paul will conclude the passage, "we *all* with unveiled face . . ." (v. 18).

The flow of these verses and their relationship to what has gone before should be noted. Paul begins with an adapted citation of Exod 34:34, which he then (v. 17) interprets in the light of the Spirit, picking up the argument from vv. 1-8, and concludes (v. 18) by bringing all of the elements together (veil, Spirit, face, glory) to show the greater glory of what God has done (and will do) through Christ and the Spirit, thus making obsolete the old covenant.

That "Lord" he calls "the Spirit" (v. 17). This is a brief way of pointing to the Lord of the new covenant *of the Spirit* of the living God who "gives life" and "freedom"/"unveiling" (vv. 3, 6, 17/18). Here the implied contrast is with the now surpassed, outglorified, deglorified covenant, whose "letter kills" because it "condemns" (vv. 6, 9).

Paul as "minister" of the new covenant (v. 6) presents himself here as a paradigmatic *member* of the new covenant, the Spirit of God having taken away the "tablets of stone" and having given him, instead, "a heart of flesh" (v. 3). In that regard he is able to speak, not merely as an apostle ("we"/"us" — vv. 4-6), but on behalf of the entire people of the new covenant ("we . . . having such a hope . . . are very bold/open . . . we *all* with unveiled face" — vv. 12, 18) as opposed to the "veiled" and darkened ones of the old covenant under which he also once lived (vv. 14-15; cf. 5:16-17). Able now to behold the glory of God — because they are opened and unveiled through Christ — the people of the new covenant are being transformed by the Spirit of God into the image of the Lord Jesus.

16 The initial particle, "but" *(de),* marks the beginning of a new passage, serving also to establish a contrast with the previous verse. Whenever Moses is read, a veil lies upon their hearts (v. 15); *but whenever* "he" (i.e., "anyone"[4]) turns to the Lord (i.e., the Lord Jesus Christ[5]), the veil is removed, making it possible to see the glory of the Lord (v. 18).

---

4. Grammatically, the subject of "whenever *he* . . ." appears to be Moses (v. 15a). But the context demands that "he" be a personalization of "a veil covers *their* heart" (v. 15), noting that "heart" is singular. Hence "he" in v. 16 is "anyone." This was the understanding of Augustine ("a man"). Hughes, 133 n. 16, noting other classical interpretations, such as (1) "Israel" (Tertullian) and (2) "Moses" (Calvin), himself favored (3) "their heart," i.e., those Jewish hearts that turn to the Lord. This latter is not effectively different from "anyone," adopted above. It is very significant that in Paul's citation of Exod 34:34 Moses is expunged, thus opening the removal of the veil to "anyone."

5. Because the veil is abolished *in Christ* (v. 14).

These contrasts appear as the verses are set side by side:

v. 15	v. 16
But to this day	
whenever	But whenever
Moses is read,	he turns to the Lord,
a veil lies on their hearts.	the veil is removed.

Common to both verses are (1) "whenever"[6] and (2) a reference to "veil." The latter verse, however, is powerfully contrastive of the former, as signaled by its opening words "but whenever." In the former the veil remains, *but whenever* one turns to the Lord the veil is removed. Blindness is replaced by sight.

Pauline eschatology is presupposed here. One covenant was begun and continues to be read "to this day," although it was intended to cease with the onset of the new covenant to which it pointed. "Veiledness" was always the mark of the old covenant — in that the people were hard-hearted toward God from the beginning — a blindness that, so far as its members are concerned, continues "to this day." Nonetheless, the new covenant has now come, so that although the blinding effects of the "hardness" continues ("a veil lies on their hearts" — v. 15), the new covenant has now begun to apply ("the veil is removed"[7]). What is it that brings sight, or removes the veil? It is the turning to the Lord.

Here Paul continues to reflect on Exod 34:29-35, on which his midrash is based,[8] in particular Exod 34:34:

> whenever [Moses] entered the Lord's presence
> to speak with him,
> he   removed the veil.[9]

---

6. Gk. ἐνίκα ἄν (v. 15) . . . ἐνίκα δὲ ἐάν (v. 16). Since this particle appears nowhere else in Paul, it is likely that LXX Exod 34:34 (ἐνίκα δ' ἄν) is already in view in v. 15. See G. D. Fee, *Presence,* 310 n. 82.

7. Gk. περιαιρεῖται; NIV, "removed." Paul is citing the LXX here. The compounded verb "removed" is more likely to mean *thorough* removal than removal of a veil that is *around* (περί) the head.

8. See on vv. 7-18.

9. This is an example of Paul's "intertextual" treatment of an OT passage, whereby he "echoes" an OT passage and "refits" it into his own situation. See R. B. Hays, *Echoes of Scripture,* 21-24. A comparison of the texts is instructive:

LXX Exod 34:34	**2 Corinthians 3:16**
ἡνίκα δ' ἂν εἰσεπορεύετο Μωϋσῆς ἔναντι κυρίου λαλεῖν αὐτῷ,	ἡνίκα δὲ ἐὰν ἐπιστρέψῃ πρὸς
περιηρεῖτο τὸ κάλυμμα	περιαιρεῖται τὸ κάλυμμα.

In "echoing" this text, Paul makes a number of changes to it, appropriate to the

But does Paul's "citation" of the words "[Moses] removed the veil" suggest that (1) he thinks Moses is the type of one who now "turns" to the Lord,[10] or (2) does he employ these words to maintain his verbal connection with the Exodus passage. Since "Moses" is a symbol for the "tablets of stone . . . letters inscribed on stones" (vv. 3, 7 — i.e., "the old covenant"), who remains "veiled" throughout Paul's midrash in this chapter, it would be inconsistent now to point to him as the one who "turned" to the Lord. In any case, the Exodus passage does not say Moses "turned" to the Lord, but only that he "entered the Lord's presence"; it was the *people* who "turned toward Moses" (Exod 34:31[11]). In Paul's "citation" the "turning" is "to *the Lord.*" The second option — an evocative "echoing" of the language of an OT text — is preferred.

It is not Moses,[12] then, who "turns" to the Lord. Rather, "anyone" over whose heart a veil of blindness had previously lain (v. 15) has turned to the Lord. Since Paul appears to be speaking representatively of himself in vv. 12-18 ("we . . . we all"), it is reasonable to conclude that he is identifying himself — though not exclusively — with the "he" who turns to the Lord.[13] This Paul did on the Damascus Road when confronted by the glorified Lord Jesus, and so others when confronted by that same Lord in the word of God, the gospel (4:2, 4, 6).

Who, then, is "the Lord" to whom "one" turns? Paul himself answers that question in the verse following with the words, "The Lord is the Spirit." Notwithstanding that clear statement, scholars are divided as to whether "the Lord" of v. 16 is (1) Yahweh, the covenant Lord of Israel, or (2) the Lord *Christ.*[14] Although "Lord" is here frequently taken to mean Yahweh,[15] as in the OT passage referred to, Paul's words in v. 14, "because

---

use he wishes to make: (1) not "Moses" but "he" (= "anyone"; cf. v. 15b) is the subject; (2) the verb εἰσεπορεύετο ("enter") is replaced by ἐπιστρέψῃ ("turn to," i.e., "convert to"); (3) the imperfect middle περιῃρεῖτο ("[Moses] used to remove") is altered to passive περιαιρεῖται ("is being removed" — i.e., *by God;* a divine passive, the present tense indicating an ongoing activity).

10. So Thrall, 1.271.

11. Gk. Καὶ ἐκάλεσαν αὐτοὺς Μωϋσῆς, καὶ ἐπεστράφησαν πρὸς αὐτὸν Ἀαρὼν καὶ πάντες οἱ ἄρχοντες τῆς συναγωγῆς . . . ("And Moses called them, and Aaron and all the rulers of the synagogue turned to him . . .").

12. *Contra* Furnish, 211, who thinks that Paul "wishes to broaden the reference to include more than just Moses." Bultmann, 89, and others take the subject to be the Israelites.

13. G. D. Fee, *Presence* (310 n. 83), doubts whether Paul here sees himself as an example of such, against L. Belleville, *Reflections,* 249-50, who does.

14. For detailed discussion of these options, see, e.g., Furnish, 211-12, and L. Belleville, *Reflections,* 254-55.

15. So, e.g., J. D. G. Dunn, "2 Corinthians III.17," 309-20; Furnish, 211; L. Belle-

in *Christ* [the veil] is abolished" give a christological identification[16] of the "Lord" in this verse. Moreover, it was to the "Lord" *Jesus* that Paul turned on the Damascus Road (Acts 9:5 pars.), and it is *Jesus Christ* as "Lord" whom he preaches (4:5), to whom he turns his hearers (cf. 8:5; 11:2).

But what does he mean by "turn"?[17] The exact phrase "turn to the Lord" occurs many times in the OT (e.g., Deut 4:30; 2 Chron 24:19; 30:9; Isa 19:22) to portray Israel's return in penitence to her God. Within the NT this and similar expressions denoted Christian conversion, a turning to the Lord Jesus (1 Thess 1:9; Acts 9:35; 11:21; 14:15; 15:19; 26:20; 1 Pet 2:25; cf. Gal 4:9). "Turn to the Lord" here means conversion, to the Lord Jesus Christ.

17   In this verse Paul says who is the "Lord" of the previous verse to whom one "turns." That verse was Paul's reformulation of his OT text (Exod 34:34). His opening words, "Now the Lord. . . ," which pick up a keyword from the OT citation, signal that an interpretation of that keyword now follows.[18] The verse is stated in two sentences: (1) "The Lord" — to whom one "turns" (v. 16) — "is the Spirit," and (2) "where the Spirit of the Lord is, [there is] freedom."

Earlier references are repeated here: (1) "Spirit" from an earlier passage about the new covenant (vv. 3-7), (2) "Lord" from the previous verse, and (3) "freedom" (probably) from "boldness"/"openness" (v. 12). On the other hand, key concepts — "Lord" and "Spirit" — reappear in the climactic next verse (as "the Lord who is the Spirit"), along with, in all probability, "freedom," expressed as "with unveiled face." Verse 17, therefore, forms an important transition from the earlier passages of the chapter to its finale, v. 18.

The difficult phrase "the Lord is the Spirit"[19] has been understood in

---

ville, *Reflections,* 255; G. D. Fee, *Presence,* 312. This case rests on several considerations: (1) "LORD" = Yahweh in the text cited (Exod 34:34); (2) the anarthrous κύριος is seen to be consistent with LXX usage and with Paul's quotations of such passages. In response we note: (1) Paul's intertextual method in OT citations significantly qualifies the importance of particular words in the original text; that "LORD" = Yahweh in Exod. 34:34 places no control on the interpretation of Paul's words; only *his* context does that; (2) there are occasions in the NT when the anarthrous κύριος clearly refers to Christ (Rom 10:13; 1 Cor 4:4; 7:22). For his part, G. D. Fee, *Presence,* 310 n. 87, regards the debate as "nearly irrelevant" in light of the identification Lord = Spirit in v. 17a, an identification, however, that we do not make (see on v. 17).

16. So D. Capes, *Yahweh Texts,* 155, and many commentators, e.g., Meyer, Hodge, Plummer, Strachan, Tasker, Wendland, Bruce, Barrett, and Bultmann.

17. Gk. ἐπιστρέψῃ; NIV, "turns." See G. Bertram, *TDNT* 7.722-29.

18. Gk. ὁ δὲ κύριος; for other examples of this construction introducing a "citation," see 1 Cor 10:4; Gal 4:24.

19. See Thrall, 1.278-82.

several ways, including: (1) the pneumatological,[20] which neatly identifies "Lord" = "the Spirit," and (2) the associational,[21] in which "the Spirit" identifies the "Lord" to whom one turns under the new covenant as "Spirit," or "spiritual."

On the face of it, the former understanding appears to be correct: one turns to the Lord; the Lord[22] is the Spirit; therefore, one turns to the Spirit. This seems to be consistent with vv. 3 and 6, where the Spirit is "the essential characteristic of the transforming power of the new covenant."[23] However, there are a number of problems with this view. One is that, in the echoes we hear of apostolic preaching in the NT, it is the Lord Jesus Christ to whom the hearer "turns" (see on v. 16, where "[anyone] turns to" the *Lord* [Jesus Christ]). Moreover, the NT teaches that Christ is the Spirit-giver (e.g., John 4:14; 7:37-39; 15:26; 16:7; 19:30; Acts 2:33) and that the Spirit is given in consequence of hearing a message centered on Christ (e.g., Acts 10:44; 19:2; Gal 3:1-5; Eph 1:13). To be sure, the believer is not to grieve the Spirit once he has been given (see Eph 4:30; but cf. Eph 1:13), but the notion of "conversion to the Spirit" (Thrall's phrase — 1.274) is alien to the thought of the NT.

The latter option, the associational, is to be preferred because, (a) for Paul, Christ is "the last Adam . . . a life-giving Spirit" (1 Cor 15:45),[24] (b) the

---

20. See E. Wong, "The Lord Is the Spirit," 1.48-72, for a pneumatological as opposed to a christological or theological interpretation of "Lord"; also Thrall, 1.274. G. D. Fee, *Presence,* may be correct in saying that "the Spirit . . . is the key to the eschatological experience of God's presence" (312) and that "this is . . . a pneumatological passage, not a christological one" (311 n. 91). Nonetheless, while Fee's assertion (310 n. 87) that "the LORD" in Exod 34:34, as contextualized by Paul, "refers in fact to the Spirit" is indisputable, any inference that one's "turning" is "to the Spirit" would be problematic. The NT emphasis is that "turning" is "*to* Christ," with consequent blessings "by, with or in the Spirit" (cf., e.g., Acts 1:5; 11:16; 1 Cor 12:13; Eph 1:13; 5:18). Paul's gospel is not a pneumatological gospel, though he powerfully affirms the blessing of the Spirit in consequence of his proclamation of the Lord Jesus and the "hearing with faith" (see 1:18-21; Gal 5:1-5).

21. Summarized, though without agreement, by Thrall, 1.280 who cites literature in favor.

22. The κύριον of v. 16 is repeated in v. 17a as ὁ κύριος, i.e., with anaphoric article and introductory δέ.

23. So Thrall, I.274.

24. This terminology is also appropriate for Paul's manner of meeting with the "Lord," i.e., the Lord *Jesus* as the risen and glorified one who gave the Spirit (Acts 9:5, 17). While Paul knows of and is convinced about the historical Jesus (see on 10:1), his practical references to him are as the Risen One, *the Lord.* Paul's encounter with and knowledge of Christ were to the *spiritual* Lord, the post-Easter Lord. Paul's association of the "Lord" with "the Spirit" may have been accentuated by the opponents' location of Jesus within a still operative, quite physical ("fleshly"), commandment-based covenant.

covenant in which *Jesus* is Lord (4:5) is that *new* covenant in which, according to prophecy, the Spirit of God comes (3:3, 6, 8), (c) "the Spirit" comes in consequence of the hearing of the gospel (4:5; 8:5) and turning to the Lord Jesus (1:19-22; 3:16), and (d) the Spirit is associated with that "righteousness" imputed to those who are "in" the sinless one who was "made sin" for them (5:21; cf. 3:8-9).

So understood, Paul's words continue, as from v. 17, his gloss on the original passage (Exod 34:34). Thus restated, the "Lord" in that passage (Yahweh) is to be understood as "the Lord *Christ*" (cf. v. 14), and that Lord "is the Spirit," that is, the Lord of the "new covenant . . . of the Spirit"[25] (v. 3; cf. vv. 6, 8). Had Paul simply reproduced the words "turn[s] to the Lord," "Lord" could have been taken to refer to the "LORD" (= Yahweh) of the old covenant, suggesting that that covenant still applied. To assert that "the Lord is the Spirit," however, points to the Spirit's coming as the fulfillment of the promises of God (1:20-22; 6:2; cf. Ezek 36:27; Jer 31:33). This is an eschatological affirmation that the age of the Spirit has come, the evidence for which is the changed hearts and converted lives of the Corinthians (see on v. 3).

Closely connected is the probability that, as from 2:17, Paul has been responding to the countertheology of his Jewish opponents. It seems likely that they are affirming that there is no *new covenant,* only the one covenant, which is still in force, in which Jesus as an observant Jew was a member (cf. on 11:4). As one who belonged to the "now" time of this the "day" of God's salvation, as part of the "new creation" (5:15-17; 6:2), Paul did not "know Christ according to the flesh," but — by inference — according to the Spirit. But these Jewish missionaries know Christ only "according to the flesh," as if still belonging to the old covenant. Based on this reconstruction of their understanding, they would have had no interpreted conviction about the coming of the Spirit as the fulfillment of the promises and the inauguration of the new covenant (see on vv. 3, 6; 1:20-22; 6:2). On this interpretation, Paul's reference to the Lord as "the Spirit" is quite pointed.

---

25. Elsewhere Paul writes in similar terms of "*two* covenants . . . *one* from *Mount Sinai,* bearing children for *slavery.* . . . [She] corresponds to the *present Jerusalem.* But the *Jerusalem above* is *free,* and she is our mother." He continues, "The *son of the slave* was born according to the *flesh,* the *son of the free* woman through promise. . . . He who was born according to the flesh persecuted him who was *born according to the Spirit*" (Gal 4:23, 24, 29). Here is an allegory that points to Paul's churches in relation to Jerusalem, and which may be applicable to the current situation in Corinth. One covenant, associated with Mount Sinai, is now symbolized by Jerusalem, is expressed in slavery and flesh, and is a persecutor; the other is associated with the Jerusalem that is above, and has children who are begotten according to the Spirit by the word of promise and who are free, though persecuted.

The phrase "the Lord is the Spirit" does not equate that "Lord" with "the Spirit," as is clear from the expression in the second sentence, "the Spirit of the Lord."[26] "The Lord" to whom one "turns" and "the Spirit of the Lord" are separate "persons."[27] Since "the Lord" to whom one "turns" is "the Lord Jesus Christ," it must mean that "the Spirit of the Lord" is his "Spirit," who must in turn be identified with "the Spirit of the living God" referred to earlier in the chapter (v. 3). The Spirit of Christ is the Spirit of God (see Rom 8:9, 10).

References to the Spirit are eschatological, pointing both to the now-realized fulfillment of prophecy and onward to the end time. The earlier references to the Spirit in this chapter (vv. 3, 6) indicate that the "new covenant" prophecies of Jeremiah and Ezekiel have now come to pass (see on those verses). At the same time it is clear that Paul regards the Spirit as anticipatory of the future glory of God. Thus Paul declares, with reference to the future, that "God . . . anointed us (lit. "christed us"), sealed us [and] gave us the Spirit in our hearts as a guarantee" (1:22; cf. 5:5). The Spirit must be linked with eschatology, whether in relationship to the present fulfillment of past prophecy as seen in the changed lives of the new covenant people (v. 2), or in their enjoyment of the blessings of present relationships with God in anticipation of the full realization of those blessings.

What, then, is meant by "where the Spirit of the Lord is, there is freedom"? What is this "freedom"? Since "freedom" and related vocabulary[28] do not appear elsewhere within 2 Corinthians, our most likely source of understanding lies in references to the Spirit earlier in this chapter.[29] In our view[30] it is a "freedom" from "the letter"; "letter" is the antithesis of "the Spirit" (v. 6).

---

26. A phrase that is often found in the LXX (e.g., LXX Judg 3:10; 11:29) and occurs in the NT (e.g., Luke 4:18; Acts 8:39).

27. According to Plummer, 103-4, "It is in the interests of Trinitarian doctrine that the possible, but most improbable translation, 'the Spirit is the Lord,' is sometimes adopted. Grammar allows it, for both terms have the article; but the preceding πρὸς κύριον, which shows that ὁ κύριος means Christ, and the order of the words, forbid it."

28. Gk. ἐλευθερία, ἐλεύθερος, ἐλευθεροῦν.

29. As well as in Gal 4:21–5:1, which should be read in conjunction with 2 Cor 3:3-18. Each passage serves as a partial commentary on the other. Whereas 2 Cor 3:17 is the only verse in the entire letter to use ἐλευθερία or its cognates, this word group is powerfully concentrated in Gal 4:21–5:1 (see 4:22, 23, 26, 30; 5:1). In that passage the "present Jerusalem" (τῇ νῦν Ἰερουλασήμ), those descended by "the flesh" from Abraham's slave wife Hagar, are "in slavery" (4:25; cf. vv. 30, 31). The "slavery" is to be "under law" (ὑπὸ νόμον — v. 21). But, according to an earlier passage in Galatians, "Christ redeemed us from the curse of the law, having become a curse for us, for it is written, 'Cursed be every one who hangs on a tree' " (3:13), a passage that is parallel in meaning to 2 Cor 5:21.

30. Cf. N. T. Wright, "Reflected Glory," in *The Glory of Christ,* 139-50, thinks that Paul is equating "freedom" with "boldness in speech," as in v. 12. G. D. Fee, *Presence,* 313, correctly takes it to refer to "freedom from the 'veil,' " as in v. 16.

"The letter ... inscribed in stones" — the dispensation of law — is "a ministry of death" that "kills" the people bound by covenant to it because it is "a ministry of condemnation" (vv. 3, 6, 7, 9). The new covenant — "a ministry of the Spirit ... and of righteousness" (vv. 8, 9) — brings "life" in place of "death" and "condemnation" (vv. 6, 7, 9). On this basis "freedom" is, in the first instance, from the implied metaphorical "slavery" under God's just condemnation of a people who break his covenant, a freedom achieved by the righteousness of God in the death of the righteous One who "became sin" for his people (5:21). As a consequence, this spells "freedom" from the obligation to observe the covenantal "letter" as the means of righteous acceptance with God.[31]

Nonetheless, this "freedom" is not to be understood as moral or spiritual permissiveness (Gal 5:13-14; 1 Cor 8:9). It is "freedom" from the "condemnation" arising from inability through "the flesh" to keep the Law of God (cf. Rom 7:7-12). Furthermore, it is a Spirit-empowered freedom, arising from the "righteousness" of those dedicated to God "in Christ" (1 Cor 6:11; 2 Cor 3:8; 5:21) to fulfill the "righteous" requirement of the Law (Rom 8:4). The new covenant as promised by the prophets was not a covenant of lawlessness, but a covenant under which the people would be moved by the Spirit to "follow [God's] decrees and be careful to keep [his] laws" (Ezek 36:27), to have "[his] law in their minds ... [written] in their hearts" (Jer 31:33). Jesus, followed by Paul, however, did not interpret the "fulfillment" of the Law under a new covenant as characterized by legalism — as in the legalism of the Judaism of that epoch. Rather, he understood it as observing the true intention of the Law (Matt 5:17-20), in particular, the obligation to love — to love God and neighbor and to forgive one's enemies (Mark 12:29-31; Matt 5:43-48; Rom 12:9-21; 13:8-10; Gal 5:14). This is the "law of Christ" (Gal 6:2), the "royal law ... the law of liberty" (Jas 2:8, 12). Thus Paul can speak of "not being without law toward God but under the law of Christ"[32] (1 Cor 9:21, RSV).[33]

---

31. "Freedom" brought by the Spirit is anticipatory ("the *glorious* freedom of the children of God" — Rom 8:21), just as, elsewhere, the Spirit is anticipatory of the blessings of the end time (see 1:22; 5:5). As with other future blessings, however, they are enjoyed now, even though the "present evil age" continues (cf. Gal 1:4). Paul will set out these blessings in classical terms in a letter to be written in the near future, i.e., his Letter to the Romans (especially Rom 8:1-27). There he will state that "the Spirit of life in Christ Jesus ... set[s us] ... *free* from the law of sin and death," enabling believers to enjoy "life and peace," with "spirits made alive because of righteousness," as those who have been "led out" of "slavery" and "fear," who are now "sons [and daughters] of God," who cry out to God as "Abba, Father," and who, as those who have the "firstfruits of the Spirit," confidently await "the redemption of their bodies ... the glorious *freedom* of the children of God" (Rom 8:2, 6, 10, 14, 15, 21, and 23).

32. Gk. ἔννομος Χριστοῦ.

33. F. F. Bruce, *Paul,* 191, believes that the Spirit takes the place of the Law in the life of the Christian. Insofar as one's access to God is concerned, we may agree; but

18 This verse is an interim and powerful summary of the passage on new covenant ministry that began at 2:14. Whereas Paul generally uses the plural "we"/"us" for *his* ministry, in this verse his "we *all*" clearly includes all the people[34] of the new covenant, of which he is a minister (v. 6). Indeed, his plural pronoun references from v. 12 on ("Having such a hope, *we* are very bold/open") appear to be representative of the new covenant people, who, because "unveiled," are able to "behold the glory of the Lord." These are to be distinguished from "the Israelites," who, because of the "veil" resulting from hardened minds, are unable to see the glory of the old covenant/Moses (vv. 14, 15). By contrast, "we all" who are of "unveiled face" are those who have "turn[ed] to the Lord," that is, "the Lord [Jesus Christ] who is the Spirit[-giving Lord]" (vv. 16-17). Thus v. 18 is, in particular, a contrastive summary and conclusion to the passage begun at v. 12.

We may analyze this complex[35] verse as follows. The subject "we all" has two qualifying phrases — (1) "with unveiled face," and (2) "behold[ing] as in a mirror[36] the glory of the Lord." The predicate of "we all" is "are being transformed," so that the central idea of the verse is: "we all . . . are being transformed," for which there is (1) *an end* — "we all . . . are being transformed into the same image from glory *to* glory," and (2) a *source* — "as *from* the Lord the Spirit."[37]

> But we all
>> with unveiled face,
>> beholding as in a mirror the glory of the Lord,
> are being transformed
>>> into the   same image   *End*
>>> from glory
>>> to glory
>>> as from the   Lord the Spirit   *Source*

---

in regard to the ethical expression of our faith, the exclusion of the principle of Law in any form — as living κατὰ σάρκα — does not fit easily with the ethical passages that are so extensive in Paul's writings and that, generally speaking, express the Law as radically crystalized — and therefore simplified but also, paradoxically, profoundly deepened — by Christ's reinterpretation of the Law.

34. *Contra* L. Belleville, *Reflections,* 275-76, who restricts the meaning to gospel ministers, a view that affects her interpretation of the remainder of the verse.

35. This verse is helpfully analyzed by Furnish, 238-39.

36. Gk. κατοπτριζόμενοι — my translation; NIV, "reflect." NRSV has "seeing . . . as though reflected in a mirror." See further n. 38 below.

37. The verb tense and voice are significant — ἀνακεκαλυμμένῳ is perfect tense, indicating that the veil, once lifted, remains lifted, while κατοπτριζόμενοι and μεταμορφούμαι, being present tense (participle and indicative), point to a continuing "beholding" (by those with now unveiled face) and a continuing "being transformed," i.e., *"by God."*

Having "turn[ed] to the Lord," God has removed the veil (v. 16) so that "we all" are now able to "behold as in a mirror the glory of the Lord." Of great interest is the meaning of the verb,[38] which occurs only here in the NT and which has been much discussed. It is one of three "optical" verbs in the passage 2:17–4:6,[39] but unlike the others it has the distinctive idea of seeing indirectly, *as by reflection.* In this case the verb may have been chosen by Paul because of its applicability to its object, "image."[40] It is instructive to compare this verse with two others that will soon appear (4:4, 6):

3:18	4:4	4:6
beholding as in a mirror	that they might not *see*	
the *glory* of the Lord	the . . . *glory* of Christ,	the *glory* of God
are being transformed		
into the same *image.*	who is the *image* of God	in the *face* of Christ

In common are (1) the use of optical verbs ("beholding as in a mirror," "see"), and (2) the object of the optical verbs, "glory." Moreover, it is clear (1) that "the Lord" (3:18), that is, "Christ" (4:4), is the "image of God" (4:4; cf. 3:18), and (2) that the "image of God" (4:4) is found in "the face of Christ" (4:6). When these verses are read together, it emerges that what "we all behold as in a mirror" is the "face of Christ," who is "the image of God," radiant with the glory of the God.

What, then, does Paul mean by his carefully chosen words "beholding as in a mirror"? Here we should not make a connection with "seeing in a mirror dimly," that is, indistinctly, where the present is contrasted with the eschatological future "when the perfect comes," as in 1 Cor 13:12.[41] Rather,

---

38. Gk. κατοπτρίζεσθαι (cf. κάτοπτρον = "mirror") has been understood in three ways: (1) "to behold as in a mirror" (so, e.g., Hughes, Furnish, Martin, Thrall, NASB, and NRSV), (2) "to reflect like a mirror" (so Chrysostom, Plummer, KJV, RV, NEB, JB, NIV, and as argued, e.g., by J. Dupont, "Le Chrétien, miroir," 393-411; and L. Belleville 279-81), and (3) "to behold" or "gaze," with no association with a mirror (so RSV, NAB). In favor of (1) are (a) a verb of seeing for the "we all" is required by the context, where the contrast is with "the Israelites," who because of the "veil" of hardness could not see (vv. 13-14), and (b) an apt parallel in Philo, where the verb means "see . . . as in a looking glass" (κατοπτρισαίμην — *Allegorical Interpretation* 3.101). See Furnish, 214, for extended discussion of this passage from Philo and also *New Docs.* 4.149-50 for further cultural background.

39. Also used are ἀτενίζειν (3:7, 13), and αὐγάζειν (4:4). Outside this passage, but significantly in parallel with κατοπτρίζεσθαι, is σκοπεῖν (4:18).

40. Gk. εἰκών. Comparison of Wis 7:26 with *Odes Sol.* 13:1 shows that "image" and "mirror" are synonyms. See further on 4:4.

41. Corinth was famous for its bronze mirrors (see *Corinth, A Brief History of the City and a Guide to the Excavations* [American Schools of Classical Studies in Athens],

Paul's "mirror" analogy suggests that we see the "glory of the Lord" *indirectly,*[42] "mirrored," as it were, in "the face of Jesus Christ," "the image of God."[43] Thus, Paul's language transcends a local dispute between Paul and the Corinthian church. Here is the revelation of the glory of God to humankind, in the human face — glorified, to be sure, but human nonetheless — of Jesus Christ, the image of God.

There may be a further inference, a "seeing" that is, as it were, image to image. "We all" who "see" the glorified image of God are ourselves also the image of God, so created by God, but now an image marred and defaced through disobedience to God (Gen 1:27; 3:22-24; cf. 2 Cor 5:19-21). The One "we all" see mirrored from God, though different from us, yet corresponds with us who see him. It is a vision of who we shall be (cf. 1 John 3:2). Through the gospel the One whom we see as in a mirror is the glorified human, the Lord Jesus Christ, who is the glorified, reflected image of God.[44] As "we behold [him] as in a mirror," we are transformed into "the same image." It would appear that Paul has chosen his verb "beholding as in a mirror" with care.

Where is that glory beheld?[45] Paul saw the glory of God "in the face of Christ . . . the image of God" (4:6, 4) on the Damascus Road "in the glory of that light . . . above the brightness of the sun" (Acts 22:11; 26:13, RV; cf. 9:3-4). In 2 Corinthians, however, Paul speaks representatively as one who saw the glory of God *not with his eyes* but "in [his] heart" (4:6; cf. Gal 1:16[46]). But God shone in Paul's heart for a purpose, namely, that "the light of the glory of God in the face of Christ" might be deflected so as to shine in the hearts of others (see on 4:6[47]). What will be Paul's torch to shine the glory of that light into the hearts of others? It is "the gospel," the word of God," by which the "knowledge of God" lights up the hearts of Paul's hearers (4:4, 6; cf. Gal 1:16). Paradoxically, therefore, Paul's readers *see* the glory of Christ as they *hear* the gospel, which in turn gives the knowledge of God.

1972, 5). Ancient mirrors were relatively distorted and unclear in relationship to modern mirrors, something that lent itself to Paul's contrast between the imperfection of our knowledge of God in the temporal "now" and its perfection in the eschatological "then" (1 Cor 13:12). But this does not appear to be the point here.

42. Paul may be rebutting a pro-Moses inference drawn from Num 12:7: "With [Moses] I speak face to face . . . he sees the form of God." Paul is saying that "we all" who have turned to the Lord (Jesus Christ) see the glory of the Lord, but *indirectly,* "mirrorlike."

43. The closeness of "image" and "glory" is seen in the words "the glory of the Lord" and "the *same* image." See also 1 Cor 11:7: "man is the *image* and *glory* of God."

44. N. T. Wright, "Reflected Glory," 145, argues that the glory of Christ is mirrored in fellow Christians.

45. See, generally, S. Kim, *Origin,* 3-31.

46. Gk. ἐν ἐμοί.

47. Gk. ἐν ταῖς καρδίαις πρός. . . . Cf. Gal 1:16: ἐν ἐμοὶ ἵνα. . . .

Closely connected with this "beholding as in a mirror" is the major affirmation of this verse, "we all . . . are being transformed." Paul and "all" who have "turn[ed] to the Lord [Jesus Christ]" (v. 16) and who, "unveiled," now "behold as in a mirror the glory of the Lord," are in the process of "being transformed."[48] Significantly, the verbs "behold" and "transformed" are both present tense, suggesting that the second occurs at the same time as — and as the result of — the first. As we behold, so we are transformed.

The goal of our transformation is "the same image." Here Paul is drawing upon the language of the early chapters of Genesis, where man is created in the image of God (Gen 1:26-27; 5:1; cf. Wis 2:23; Sir 17:3). Paul's meaning is amplified by his use of the "image" vocabulary in 1 Corinthians and Romans,[49] the letters written immediately before and after 2 Corinthians. In the former, he declared that "as we have borne the *image* of the man of dust [i.e., Adam], we shall also bear the *image* of the man from heaven [i.e., Christ]" (1 Cor 15:49, RSV; cf. 11:7). In the latter he wrote that "God . . . predestined . . . [us] to be conformed to the *image* of his Son" (Rom 8:29, RSV),[50] the

48. Gk. μεταμορφούμεθα. The same verb is used of the transfigured Christ (Mark 9:2; Matt 17:2). There is an important cross reference in Rom 12:2, where, because συσχηματίζεσθε means "outward conformity with," μεταμόρφουσθε must mean "transformation of the inner or real being." Hence μεταμορφούμεθα carries the idea of the "transformation of the essential person." With this we contrast μετασχηματίζεσθαι (referring to the "false apostles" in 11:13), where a superficial change in implied ("masquerade," "disguise").

See Furnish, 240-41, for a helpful discussion of the similarities between and differences from Paul's reference here and (1) the Hellenistic mystery cults (e.g., the passage in Apuleius's *Metamorphoses,* where the author describes the consequences of his initiation into the Isis cult in Corinth — he was in brightly colored clothing "like unto the sun . . . beholding the image of the goddess" (11.24), and (2) apocalyptic Judaism (e.g., 2 *Apoc. Bar.* 51:1, where it is said of the righteous, "they will be changed into any shape which they wished, from beauty to loveliness, and from light to the splendor of glory").

In the case of the Hellenistic cults the transformation was in the nature of a present material/physical apotheosis through mystery cult initiation, whereas for Paul the "glorification" belongs in the end time. For apocalyptic Judaism the perspective — like Paul's — was eschatological, but unlike Paul's it had little reference to the the present reality of suffering. Whereas apocalyptic Judaism envisaged ecstatic experience as the means of transformation, for Paul it is by the "beholding as in a mirror" (Christ, the glorified image of God), which is metaphorical for hearing the gospel (4:4, 6). Paul's christological goal of transformation ("to be conformed to the image of [God's] Son" — Rom 8:29) is unparalleled. See further J. A. Fitzmyer, "Glory Reflected," 630-44; J. Lambrecht, "Transformation in 2 Cor 3:18," 243-49.

49. For other references to εἰκών, see "he is the *image* of the invisible God" (Col 1:15); "the *image* of him who created him" (Col 3:10).

50. The combination of "metamorphosis" and "image" vocabulary in 2 Cor 3:18 (τὴν αὐτὴν εἰκόνα μεταμορφούμεθα) and Rom 8:29 (συμμόρφους τῆς εἰκόνος τοῦ υἱοῦ αὐτοῦ) should be noted.

outcome of which Paul gives by the single word "glorified" (Rom 8:30).[51] This
is the goal God has for those who "turn to the Lord."

Paul, however, envisages no merely "biological" or automatic process
of transformation. The now-exalted Lord into whose glorious likeness we are in
process of being conformed (Rom 8:29) is the Jesus of whom we hear in the
gospel, the Son of God whose moral and spiritual perfection is seen in the face
of adversity, rejection, suffering, and death at the hands of "the rulers of this
age" (1 Cor 2:8). According to Romans 8, the womb of our transformation is
that world-aeon which in "the present time" is characterized by "suffering" for
the "children of God," whether the sufferings shared with the "whole creation"
or those afflictions arising from direct involvement in the ministry of the gospel
(Rom 8:18, 21, 22, 35-36). Paul makes it clear that we must understand our
transformation to be the will of God for us and that we should actively cooperate
with him in bringing to reality the eternal destiny for which we were predestined
(Rom 12:1-2, 28-30). Our transformation is nothing else than a transformation
into the moral and spiritual likeness of the now glorified Christ. It is transformation into that Christ-likeness which will be ours in the end time, when he will be
the "firstborn among many brothers" (Rom 8:29).

This transformation is said to be "from glory to glory." The first
"glory" is that "seen" (in our hearts — 4:4, 6) when, through the gospel, we
"turn[ed] to the Lord" and our "faces [were] unveiled." It is likely that Paul
here includes the "glory" in the old covenant/Moses, which was hitherto
veiled, which is seen only when one turns to the Lord (Jesus). The ultimate[52]
"glory" is the glory of the glorified Lord, whose glory we will behold on the
last day. Unlike the glory of Moses, which was veiled because it was eschatologically circumscribed ("abolished"), the glory from the Lord is endless and
ultimately infinite, as glorious as God himself.[53]

The *source* of this eschatological transformation is "even as from the
Lord, the Spirit."[54] The One who is the *end* of our transformation ("the Lord")

---

51. Some, however, suggest that Paul and the Corinthians together participate in
the "same likeness," since they are "in Christ" (so Dunn, "2 Corinthians III.17," 320;
Wright, "Reflected Glory," 148-50).

52. The phrase ἀπὸ δόξης εἰς δόξαν is idiomatic for a glory "seen" initially in
the world, within history, in and through the gospel, in relationship with that "glory" which
will be revealed eschatologically and which will be infinite and eternal (see on 3:16).

53. According to Plummer, 107, "It is a continual and gradual progress, 'from
strength to strength' (Ps 84:7), 'shining more and more unto the perfect day' (Prov 4:18)."

54. Gk. καθάπερ ἀπὸ κυρίου πνεύματος raises a number of questions: (1) Are
the genitives appositional ("from the Lord who is the Spirit")? (2) Is the article to be
supplied in one case, both cases, or neither case? (3) Is it possible that κυρίου is adjectival
(" 'sovereign' Spirit")?

Critical to any solution is καθάπερ, which means, in relationship to what Paul has

is also its means and provider (through "the Spirit"). As if in a final reply to his Jewish opponents, Paul is saying that not the "letters inscribed in stones," but "the Spirit" as promised by the prophets, who is "now" a life-changing reality in the new covenant, is the only possible means of spiritual growth for God's people. Under Moses they are blind and immobile; through the Spirit, they see, are set free, and are being transformed into the ultimate glory of God (see 4:16-18).

Whether intentionally or not, in this summary comment about the new covenant, Paul has given his readers what will prove to be one of his most potent theological declarations. It spans the covenants, implying the blindness under the old covenant while affirming the brightness of sight of those within the new. Moreover, it spans from the creation of humanity as *imago dei* and the fall with its rebellion and death, to conversion-illumination and from there through metamorphosis to glorification. It teaches that "we all" in whom the image of God is defaced are able through the gospel to "see" that image in its perfection, in the face of Jesus Christ. And we are enabled not only to see that image but to be progressively transformed into it by the sovereign Spirit.

Second Corinthians 3:18 teaches us about the goodness and power of God who brings good out of our evil, and brightness out of our darkness; such is his grace. If Paul taught elsewhere that the righteousness of God is imputed to the unrighteous through the death of the righteous one (5:21), his point here is that this righteousness is, in consequence, progressively imparted to believers through to its perfection in them. This world is passing away and believers with it as they wither and die (4:16–5:1); but Paul here teaches them about the triumph of the glory of God. It is not, however, unqualified triumphalism but power *in weakness,* as will be made clear in the chapters following (4:7–5:10).

---

just written, "as one would expect," namely, that the transformation into the image of the Lord must derive "as·one would expect — from the Lord." Because κυρίου is anarthrous here (as it was anarthrous in the first part of the verse), πνεύματος is matchingly anarthrous. In relationship to πνεύματος Paul appears to be saying both (1) that "the Lord" is the glorified Lord Jesus Christ who gives "the Spirit" (cf. John 16:7), and (2) that "the Lord" is the Risen One, whose covenant is characterized by the Spirit and not by "letter." The latter emphasis, if correct, would be an indirect rebuttal of the Jewish countermissionaries in Corinth who advocate an earthbound Jesus circumscribed within a still operative Sinai-based and unfulfilled covenant and for whom the Spirit is unknown (see on 11:4; cf. Acts 19:2). To be rejected is Hughes, 120, who finds "[no] direct mention here of the Third Person of the Trinity" but rather the notion of "spirit" as "transforming power," which he identifies as "the Lord Jesus Christ." If the Spirit of the living God earlier in this chapter (vv. 3, 6, and 8) is the Holy Spirit, so, too, by association (cf. v. 17), the Spirit in this verse must be the Holy Spirit.

7. This Ministry (4:1-6)

1 *Therefore, since through God's mercy we have this ministry, we do not lose heart.* 2 *Rather, we have renounced secret and shameful ways; we do not use deception, nor do we distort the word of God. On the contrary, by setting forth the truth plainly we commend ourselves to every man's conscience in the sight of God.* 3 *And even if our gospel is veiled, it is veiled to those who are perishing.* 4 *The god of this age has blinded the minds of unbelievers, so that they cannot see the light of the gospel of the glory of Christ, who is the image of God.* 5 *For we do not preach ourselves, but Jesus Christ as Lord, and ourselves as your servants for Jesus' sake.*[1] 6 *For God, who said, "Let light shine out of darkness," made his light shine in our hearts to give us the light of the knowledge of the glory of God in the face of Christ.*[2]

This passage continues Paul's defensive excursus (2:14–7:4) on his new covenant ministry (cf. "this ministry" — v. 1). It is especially linked with the opening paragraph (2:14-17) by means of "ring composition," a literary device that "complete[s] the circle of ideas."[3]

At the same time, it provides a recapitulation and summary of material in 3:7-18[4] and serves to intensify the contrast between the apostolic office of Paul and the corrupt ministry of the "peddlers." Of particular interest is the apostolic boldness/openness ("we are very bold" — 3:12) that Paul now expresses as determination ("we do not lose heart" — 4:1). In so doing he reaffirms that God leads him in the "triumphal procession" of spreading everywhere the knowledge of Christ (2:14; cf. 2:12).

1. The reading διὰ Ἰησοῦν ("for Jesus' sake"), read by the majority (incl. A* and B) and adopted by most translations and commentaries, is probably to be preferred to διὰ Ἰησοῦ ("through Jesus"), read by mostly Egyptian texts (p46 ℵ* C 0243 33 1739 1881 pc cop). Paul does not elsewhere use "Jesus" absolutely when he has agency in mind.

2. There are three possible readings: (1) Ἰησοῦ Χριστοῦ (p46 ℵ C H K etc.); (2) Χριστοῦ (A B 33 etc.); (3) Χριστοῦ Ἰησοῦ (D F G etc.). Although the stronger external support favors (1), reading (2) best explains how the others emerged ("Jesus" was added before or after "Christ"). The UBS committee was divided; thus "Jesus" appears in brackets.

3. So Martin, 75, who notes the repetitions: ἐν τοῖς ἀπολλυμένοις (4:3; cf. οἱ ἀπολλύμενοι, 2:15), Paul's claim to live ἐνώπιον τοῦ θεοῦ (4:2; cf. κατέναντι θεοῦ, 2:17), and his reference to τῆς γνώσεως τῆς δόξης τοῦ θεοῦ (4:6; cf. τῆς δόξης αὐτοῦ, 2:14).

4. We may agree with Plummer, 109, that "the division of the chapters [between chaps. 3 and 4] is unintelligently made." Bultmann, 99, notes the following correspondence between 4:1-6 and 3:7-16 based on the repetition of ἔχοντες (4:1; cf. 3:12); (1) διακονία (4:1; cf. 3:7), (2) the similarity of καθὼς ἐλεήθημεν (4:1) to διὰ Χριστοῦ (3:4), and (3) the similarity of κεκαλυμμένον . . . νοήματα (4:3ff.) to νοήματα . . . κάλυμμα (3:14).

In the present paragraph Paul's own story can be traced. He had been an unbeliever, blinded to the light of the gospel (v. 4). On the road to Damascus, however, Paul had seen the glory of God in the face of Jesus Christ, who is the image of God (vv. 4, 6). Having given him the ministry of the new covenant, God showed him mercy, illuminating his heart that he might give the light of the knowledge of God to others (vv. 1, 6). In proclaiming the word of God, the gospel that "Jesus Christ is Lord," Paul "sets forth the truth" (vv. 2, 4, and 5), and he does so as their "slave" for Jesus' sake.

Here Paul appears to be answering those who criticize him on a number of counts — of fading in his ministry (v. 1), of chicanery in financial matters, of corrupting the message of God, of being self-commended (v. 2), and of obscuring the gospel (v. 3 — from Jews?). Against those who oppose and criticize him Paul declares that God's act of mercy toward him has been matched by his apostolic renunciation of secretive shameful behavior. Moreover, he contends that his lifestyle is marked by determined perseverance (v. 1), and the avoidance of craftiness and of corrupting the word of God (v. 2). In setting forth the truth he commends himself — as it were indirectly — to the conscience of all in the sight of God (v. 2). But Paul's defense may be, at the same time, an oblique polemic against the "peddlers" who, in insincerity and guile, hawk the word of God, corrupting its message (2:17; 4:2).

He concedes the possibility that his gospel is "veiled" (v. 4), perhaps from those Jews who find it unacceptable. Those from whom the gospel is veiled are "perishing" (i.e., not being "saved" — 2:15). The god of this age, Satan, has blinded their eyes. But by proclaiming Jesus Christ as Lord Paul is deflecting the light God shone in his heart into the lives of others.

1 Paul now affirms that because he has "*this* ministry," about which he has said so much in the previous chapter, and which he has on the basis of God's mercy to him, he does not give up.

The initial "Therefore,"[5] with which both the opening sentence and the whole passage begin, ties what follows with what has just been stated. Indeed, each word or affirmation of v. 1 has an antecedent in the previous chapter.[6] "This ministry," that is, the ministry of the "new covenant"[7] (3:6)

---

5. Gk. διὰ τοῦτο, which is stronger than the merely conjunctive οὖν, expressing literally, "for *this* reason," on the basis of what has just been said.

6. Gk. ἔχοντες (cf. 3:12); τὴν διακονίαν ταύτην (cf. 3:5-6 — θεοῦ . . . ἱκάνωσεν ἡμᾶς διακόνους καινῆς διαθήκης); καθὼς ἐλεήθημεν (cf. 3:4 — πεποίθησιν . . . διὰ Χριστοῦ); οὐκ ἐγκακοῦμεν (cf. 3:12 — πολλῇ παρρησίᾳ χρώμεθα).

7. His reference to "this ministry" also implies a negative contrast with the ministry of the old covenant (3:14) — a ministry of death and condemnation (3:7, 9) — which has already been the subject of sustained contrast (3:7-11).

that brings the Spirit and righteousness (3:8, 9, 17-18), is "from God" (2:17), who has made Paul "sufficient" for it (3:6).

Such ministry flowed from and was given to Paul at the same moment as he "received mercy,"[8] that is, when he "turn[ed] to the Lord [Jesus]" (3:16). That he does "not lose heart"[9] — or, better, does "not despair" — is to be taken with the earlier declaration of openness[10] (3:12), which, along with perseverance, expresses the revelational and saving character of the apostolic office. Indeed, since the glory of the new covenant ministry "remains" (3:11), as opposed to the old that is "abolished" (3:11), it is appropriate that the new covenant minister "remains," that is, "perseveres," "does not give up."[11]

A note of pathos is probably sounded by his denial of despair, implying that the burdens of ministry — not least to the Corinthians — may have tempted him to abandon his apostolic calling (see on 11:28). Quite possibly he is obliquely answering criticism that, since his ministry is characterized by such difficulty and reversal, his legitimacy as a minister is, to say the least, problematic. Paul will argue that, on the contrary, his endurance[12] in the sufferings of ministry (hinted at here but made explicit elsewhere in the letter[13]) mark the apostle out as a genuine servant of Christ, whose own sufferings are now reproduced in the ministry of the one who represents him (5:20; 12:10; see on 6:3-10).

2 Paul continues to spell out the consequences of "having this ministry" (v. 1a). God's call to the new covenant ministry has meant the acceptance of patterns of behavior[14] consistent with that ministry: (1) determined

---

8. Gk. ἐλεήθημεν; NIV, "through God's mercy." Paul's past life as a persecutor and his deep appreciation of God's mercy (note the divine passive, "received mercy") are implied by this expression. See also 1 Cor 7:25; 1 Tim 1:13, 16.

9. Gk. οὐκ ἐγκακοῦμεν, "we are not weary," as supported by other Pauline uses, which are always with a negative (v. 16; 2 Thess 3:13; Gal 6:9; Eph 3:13; cf. Luke 18:1, the only non-Pauline use in the NT). Not all take this view, however; see, e.g., (1) Thrall, 1.298-300, who takes it as "behave remissly in . . . duty"; (2) Bultmann, 99, who argues that οὐκ ἐγκακοῦμεν = οὐκ ἐπαισχύνομαι ("I am not ashamed" — Rom 1:16) and that the antonym of ἐγκακοῦμεν is θαρροῦμεν (5:8); and (3) Furnish, 217, who takes it as "having confidence," based on the contrast it provides to 3:12. In parallel with οὐκ ἐγκακοῦμεν in the letter is the apostolic "endurance" (ὑπομονή — 1:6; 6:4; 12:12), "courage" (θαρροῦμεν — 5:6-8), and "confidence" (πεποίθησις — 3:4; 10:1-2).

10. Cf. Eph 3:12-13, where μὴ ἐνκακεῖν and παρρησία are found in connected contrast.

11. This assertion — "we do not lose heart" — launches the sequence of opposite statements that runs on into the next verse: "not (v. 1) . . . but . . . not . . . nor . . . but" (v. 2).

12. Gk. ὑπομονή, as in 1:6; 6:4; and 12:12.

13. 1:5-11; 2:1-4, 12; 4:7-15; 6:3-13; 7:5-8; 11:23–12:10.

14. The verb usage should be noted. Because ἀπειτάμεθα is, with ἠλεήθημεν

212

perseverance (v. 1b), (2) renunciation of (a) secretive disgraceful behavior, (b) craftiness, and (c) corrupting the word of God, in contrast with which (3) he sets forth its truth, thus commending himself to others, in the sight of God.

The principal statement of the preceding verse, "we do not lose heart," provides the foil for the initial "but"[15] of this sentence, which is followed by "not . . . nor . . . but."

> . . . we do *not* lose heart.
> *But* we have renounced the hidden things of shame,
>> *not* walking in guile
>> *nor* corrupting the word of God,
>
> *but*
>> by the manifestation of the truth
>> commending ourselves
>>> to the conscience of every man
>>> in the sight of God.

Paul adopts an apologetic stance in regard to accusations that (1) he engages in secretive disgraceful behavior,[16] that is, practicing guile[17] (that, while rejecting payment for ministry, he has received the Corinthians' money indirectly, through his delegates?[18]), (2) tampering with the word of God, the

---

(v. 1), an aorist, we may infer with Hughes, 122, and Thrall, 1.300 (*contra* Furnish, 217), that Paul's "renunciation" occurred at the time of his conversion and call. The present tenses οὐκ ἐγκακοῦμεν . . . μὴ περιπατοῦντες . . . συνιστάνοντες appear to indicate ongoing behaviors in contrast to the completeness of the renunciation implied by the aorist ἀπειτάμεθα. The middle voice ἀπειτάμεθα is taken by some in its full meaning, i.e., "As far as we are concerned" (so C. K. Barrett, 128).

15. Gk. οὐκ . . . ἀλλά.

16. Gk. τὰ κρυπτὰ τῆς αἰσχύνης; NIV, "secret and shameful ways." According to Thrall, 1.300-303, following extensive discussion: "the secretive practices of disgraceful behavior." While τῆς αἰσχύνης could mean the attitude of "shame," the context of observable behavior in what follows suggests that "disgrace" is to be preferred. Given the context of the letter in which Paul is accused of underhanded ways of pursuing ministry related to money (12:16-18; cf. 7:2), this, rather than pagan vices (as in Eph 5:12; cf. 1 Cor 4:5), is more likely to be intended.

17. Gk. πανουργία; NIV, "deception." The derivation of the word (παν + ουργια — "every work") may, in this case, give a clue to a Machiavellian meaning whereby "the end justifies" whatever "means" employed. As with "secret shameful things," Paul may be responding to efforts to discredit him in matters related to money. It appears that they accused Paul of "guile" in *not* receiving payment for his ministry (12:16; cf. 11:7-9), while receiving it by the "back door" from his envoys (12:16-18). They may have suspected that he loftily declined payment (11:7-11) with a view to some kind of moral manipulation, or perhaps because he was too proud to be paid.

18. See 11:7-12; 12:13-15, 16-18.

gospel (in not requiring Gentiles to submit to the Mosaic covenant?[19]), and (3) commending himself[20] (because he lacks dominical and apostolic accreditation for his ministry?[21]).

Because of echoes of 2:17, it is possible that this verse is obliquely polemical as well as more directly apologetic. Both texts (1) refer to an inappropriate ministry of the word of God[22] ("peddling the word of God" — 2:17; "corrupting the word of God" — 4:2), and (2) speak of ministry "in the sight of God." It would appear that Paul is here contrasting his ministry with that of the "peddlers" so that his words are also an indirect criticism of them. Whereas Paul does not turn aside from his apostolic calling (v. 1), it is these men — he may be implying — who are guilty of (1) secretive disgraceful behavior and crafty practices (cf. "these men are . . . deceitful workmen masquerading as apostles of Christ" — 11:13), and (2) corrupting the word of God (cf. they "preach *another* Jesus . . . a *different* gospel" — 11:4).

Having defended his own ministry, as well perhaps as having criticized the "peddlers" in the first three parts of the verse, Paul speaks positively in the fourth about his own ministry, which he introduces with "but." The apostle makes the astonishing claim that he is an instrument of the revelation ("a setting forth"[23]) of "the truth." Here it is not primarily the truth in some abstract sense, as if incarnated by Paul (see on 2:14). Rather, the emphasis is on the truth of "the word of God" mentioned in the previous clause, "our gospel" in the next verse, and the proclamation of "Jesus Christ as Lord" in v. 5.[24] This "manifestation of the truth" (RV) (of the word of God) is in line with Paul's assertion of the openness and determination of his apostolic office (3:12; 4:1). The light God shone in Paul's heart on the Damascus Road is, by means of Paul's preaching of Jesus Christ as Lord, deflected toward the hearts of others, glorifying "the face of Jesus Christ."

According to the second and subsidiary half of this final part of the

---

19. So Barrett, 128. Cf. Thrall, 1.301, who takes it to refer to discreditable missionary methods in seeking success as an evangelist.

20. See on 3:1.

21. See on 3:1.

22. Gk. ὁ λόγος τοῦ θεοῦ, which, it should be noted, refers to the preached gospel, not the written scriptures. See, e.g., 1 Thess 2:13 (cf. 1:5-6); 1 Cor 14:36; Rom 9:6; Acts 8:4, 14; 11:1; 13:5, 7, 44, 46, 48; 16:32; 17:13; 18:11. Phrases in parallel include "the word of the Lord" (1 Thess 1:8; 4:15), "the word of the cross" (1 Cor 1:18), and "the word of truth" (2 Cor 6:7).

23. Gk. φανερώσει, which occurs only here and at 1 Cor 12:7, with the adjective φανερῶς occurring only at 1 Cor 14:5 and Rom 2:28. The verb φανεροῦν, however, is important in 2 Corinthians (2:14; 4:10, 11; 5:10, 11; 7:12; 11:6).

24. Cf. 6:7: "by the word of truth" (my translation); Eph 1:13; Col 1:5: "the word of truth, the gospel . . ."; 2 Tim 2:15: "the word of truth"; Gal 2:5, 14: "the truth of the gospel."

sentence, Paul's revelation "commends" him.[25] Although that revelation of the truth is primarily "of the word of God," Paul's own person cannot be separated from that word. Thus the gospel that Paul preaches, as uttered by its messenger, "commends" Paul — not as in his opponents' "letters of recommendation" to the Corinthian church (3:1) — to "each and every[26] conscience." He is not commending himself as his critics maintain (see on 3:1), at least not directly and actively. Nonetheless, he is confident that his ministry and life impact the "conscience[s]" — the total understanding, moral and intellectual[27] — of others (see also 5:11). There is an eschatological dimension to this confidence; what is now "open" in Paul's apostolic ministry and person to "the conscience" of "each and every person" is also "open" before God,[28] as it will be "before the judgment seat of Christ" (5:10). Paul is confident that through Christ (3:4) the revelation he makes before others in the gospel he preaches and the life he lives is, and will be, acceptable and pleasing to Christ his judge.

3 Paul now qualifies[29] the previous verse, where, through his ministry, he claims to "set forth the truth plainly." Nonetheless, his words "and even[30] if our gospel is veiled" concede that not all discern a revelation in Paul's ministry. Evidently some find his message obscure.[31] In that case, however, it is veiled among those who are perishing.

---

25. The participle συνιστάνοντες is in consequence of the instrumental τῇ φανερώσει τῆς ἀληθείας. The manifestation of the truth in his life serves to commend him to the consciences of others (cf. 5:11).

26. So Barrett, 129; the Gk. has πᾶσαν συνείδησιν ἀνθρώπων. Cf. NIV, "every man's conscience."

27. According to Furnish (219), "conscience" must not be restricted to a personal sense of guilt in regard to one's past actions, but should "include the function of assessing the actions of others." In 1:12 Paul appealed to his own conscience in regard to his sincerity; now he appeals to the consciences of others.

28. Prominent in 2 Corinthians is Paul's notion that he exercises his ministry "before God" (κατέναντι θεοῦ, 2:17; 12:19; ἐνώπιον θεοῦ, 4:2; 7:12) and that — however or on what basis others will be judged — he will be "open" and judged on the basis of his ministry (τοὺς γὰρ πάντας ἡμᾶς φανερωθῆναι δεῖ ἔμπροσθεν τοῦ βήματος τοῦ Χριστοῦ — 5:10). Furnish, 219, plausibly suggests that "before God" is an oath-formula.

29. As by the introductory Gk. particle δέ.

30. Gk. εἰ . . . καί, a concessive construction (for other examples of εἰ καί, see 4:16; 5:16; 7:8; 12:11). Plummer, 113, comments that "the use of εἰ καί . . . and the emphatic position of ἐστίν . . . show that St Paul concedes what is stated as hypothetically to be actually a fact." Less likely is the explanation of Thrall, 1.303 n. 792, who suggests that "the εἰ may be separated from the καί and the καί may be seen to be strengthening what follows: '(But) if our gospel is veiled. . . .'"

31. To be noted is the contrast between φανέρωσις τῆς ἀληθείας (v. 2) and ἐστὶν κεκαλυμμένον τὸ εὐαγγέλιον ἡμῶν; the truth (of the gospel) is revealed, but the gospel is veiled.

A literal translation of v. 3 reveals the centrality of the phrase "it —
the gospel — is veiled"[32]:

> And even if it is veiled
>
> > our gospel
> >
> > among those who are perishing
>
> it is veiled.

Apparently, Paul is responding to criticism that, to some, his gospel is no
revelation at all; in other words, it is "veiled." From whom would such
criticism come? According to the context, a likely source would be the newly
arrived Jewish "peddlers" in Corinth, whose ministry Paul is contrasting with
his own (vv. 1-2; cf. 2:17–3:3).[33] From whom, according to them, would his
gospel be "veiled"? Their reply would be, "It is veiled from fellow Jews[34]
because Paul's message is unacceptable to them."[35]

Various reasons for this might be advanced. The most probable is that
Paul preached "Christ crucified, a stumbling block to Jews" (1 Cor 1:23).[36]
Related to this might have been Paul's assertion that through the crucified
Messiah the promised Spirit had come (cf. Gal 3:1-5), signaling the arrival
of the new covenant, and ending the former dispensation (2 Cor 3:3-11). Such
a message would readily be seen as a threat to the people of that dispensation.
The obligations of that dispensation would now be a matter of merely cultural
choice.[37]

32. Gk. ἐστὶν κεκαλυμμένον, a periphrastic perfect construction, might suggest
an existing state: "is and remains veiled." Most commentators, however, follow Moule,
18, in regarding the periphrastic perfect as "virtually an adjective."

33. *Contra* Thrall, 1.305, who sees the "unbelieving Jews of Corinth" as the source
of the complaint that Paul's gospel is obscure.

34. Other views are (1) that Paul is recognizing a general lack of perception of
his message (Hughes, 125), and (2) that Paul is replying to the charge that "his preaching
was obscure and shifty" (Plummer, 113). To be rejected is the thesis of D. Georgi, *Opponents,* 261-62, that Paul is here countering the newcomers' own positive exegesis of the
Exodus 34 passage in which the veil was an essential part of the Mosaic ministry.

35. The complaint of Paul's opponents may have been that Paul's ministry was
ineffective among Jews because it was offensive to them. Such ineffectiveness arising from
hostility may be inferred from the many places in the Acts where Paul's attempts at ministry
in the synagogues of the Diaspora met with opposition (Acts 13:45, 50; 14:2, 19; 17:5,
13; 18:12; 19:9; 20:3, 19; 21:17; cf. 2 Cor 11:26), and indeed violence (2 Cor 11:24).

36. According to D. A. Renwick, *Presence of God,* 47-48, Paul's opponents may
have regarded his suffering and unimpressive style as uncharacteristic of apostolic life.
Based on Exodus 32–34, the glorified Moses was their paradigm for apostleship. On this
hypothesis the sufferings of Paul would veil his gospel. However, the assumption that the
newcomers used Exodus 32–34 in their polemic against Paul remains conjectural.

37. The attitudes of James/the Elders in Jerusalem at the time of Paul's final

According to Paul's exposition in the previous chapter, the "veil" over the glory on Moses' face turned out to be a veil over "the end" or goal of that glory, namely, Christ (see on 3:13). Thus Moses had, as it were, veiled the gospel ahead of its time on account of the Israelites' hardness of mind (3:14). Thus, whenever Paul preached to Jewish audiences, his message came to a people already "veiled," blinded to the glory of God anticipated in the old covenant, something he knew to his cost. Thus the concessive part of the sentence ("even if our gospel is veiled") should probably be understood to mean something like ". . . veiled *among the Israelites*."

In the apodosis (the "then" part of the conditional sentence) Paul goes on to indicate to whom his gospel is veiled. "It is veiled," he says, "among[38] those who are perishing," who in v. 4 are designated as "unbelievers," including even God's historic people, the Israelites (cf. 3:7, 13). Implicit here, perhaps, is a warning to Paul's Gentile readers in Corinth not to follow the pro-Moses teaching of the "peddlers." If God's historic covenant people can be veiled and, in consequence, lost, so, too, can they.

By this language Paul picks up his earlier reference to "the perishing" (i.e., those who are not being saved — 2:15) in the opening sentences (2:15) of this excursus on apostolic ministry (2:14–7:4). To "the perishing" the gospel borne by its apostolic messenger is "the stench of death" and confirms the hearers in ultimate or eternal death (see on 2:15). As noted above, the repetition of "perishing" rounds off what was said earlier (2:14-17) by the rhetorical method known as "ring composition."

Earlier Paul raised the awesome question that, since human beings are "perishing" or "being saved" according to their response to the gospel of Christ, who can be "sufficient" to bear that message (2:16)? Here he touches another aspect of this dreadful reality, the great care that needs to be taken that the gospel is not by any means veiled, whether by its bearer corrupting the message itself or by ethical and moral failures on his own part undermining it. Only the gospel can "save"; only the gospel can bring the light of God to the blind. Let it not be veiled by those who bring it.

---

visit implies that, whereas a large number of believing Jews were "zealous for the law" as a result of their ministry, this — it is implied — could not be said of Paul's ministry. Rather, it was reported that his ministry had undermined fundamental tenets of Judaism (Acts 21:20-21). Moreover, it is hinted that Paul had not required the Gentiles to uphold the terms of the Jerusalem Decree in deference to Diaspora Jews (Acts 21:25; cf. 15:19-21).

38. *Contra* N. Turner, *Grammatical Insights,* 264, who takes ἐν with the dative here as indicating a sphere of disadvantage, hence "to those who are perishing" rather than "among. . . ."

4 With an introductory "among whom"[39] Paul continues his (now very long) sentence (vv. 3-4) by explaining how "the perishing" come to be "veiled." It is because the "god of this age," Satan, has "blinded . . . unbelievers" to prevent[40] them from "seeing[41] the light."[42] Three genitives qualify that "light"; it is "the light *of* the gospel *of* the glory *of* Christ."[43] "Christ" is declared to be "the image of God."[44]

---

39. Gk. ἐν οἷς, untranslated in the NIV in the interest of shortening Paul's long sentence (vv. 3-4). In terms of strict translation ἐν οἷς should be rendered "among whom." This, however, would imply that "unbelievers" were a subgroup of "the perishing" of v. 3, which is clearly not the intention of the writer. Furnish, 220, explains the irregularity as due to Paul's "dictation style," in which he has lost track of his own syntax. "The veiled perishing" are "the unbelievers."

40. Gk. εἰς τὸ μή could be "either final or consecutive" (Moule, 143 n. 2). However, given Satan's negative purposes, it is probably a final or purpose construction.

41. The verb αὐγάζειν is not found elsewhere in the NT and is rare in the LXX. In classical literature it means either (1) "to see clearly," or (2) "to beam upon, as by the sun." The difficulty is to decide whether the verb is transitive or intransitive. If intransitive, the subject of the infinitive αὐγάσαι would be the accusative φωτισμόν. The option taken by most modern translators, however, is transitive, in which case the subject would be αὐτούς (understood), taken with meaning (1) above. For references to other "optical" verbs (ἀτενίζειν, κατοπτρίζεσθαι, σκοποῦν) in this part of the letter, see on 3:18.

42. Gk. τὸν φωτισμόν; cf. φωτισμόν (v. 6).

43. Gk. τὸν φωτισμὸν τοῦ εὐαγγελίου is taken to mean "light emanating from the gospel" (genitive of origin). According to N. Turner, *Grammatical Insights,* 218, where several genitives are joined together, the governing genitive usually precedes the dependent one. Thus both δόξης and Χριστοῦ are governed by εὐαγγελίου. According to Barrett, 131-32: "Light streams from the Gospel that Paul preaches because the theme of the Gospel is Christ . . . and Christ . . . is himself a glorious figure."

44. Gk. εἰκὼν τοῦ θεοῦ. The εἰκών vocabulary as applied to Christ (1 Cor 11:7; 15:49; Rom 1:23; 8:29; Col 1:15) is limited to Paul in the NT, and its use here without explanation suggests that Paul had already introduced it to the Corinthians in regard to *Christ* (cf. 1 Cor 11:7). Furnish thinks the concept did not originate with Paul but with the pre-Pauline church, whereas Thrall, 1.309-10, attributes it to Paul himself. See Thrall, 1.309-11, for the view that Paul's usage originates, in part, from Hellenistic Judaism, and particularly from the Wisdom of Solomon and Philo, where "wisdom" approximates "the image of God," because wisdom mediates the knowledge of God. It is to be noted that Philo referred to humankind as εἰκὼν εἰκόνος, "the image of the image" (*Creation of the World* 25). According to A. M. Ramsey, *The Glory of God,* 150, "The word εἰκών means 'that which resembles' . . . in particular the resemblance of something to a prototype from which it is derived. Christ . . . shares in God's real being and hence can be a perfect manifestation of that being."

This complex verse may be laid out as follows

[The perishing . . . — v. 3]

```
                    . . . among whom                          A
the god of this age
        has blinded the minds of unbelievers
            that                    they                      B
        might not see the light of the gospel
                            of the glory
                        of      Christ,
                            who is the image of God.
```

The two constituent parts this verse, when taken together, are a paradox. Whereas in the first (A) the "god of this age"[45] blinds unbelievers so that they cannot see, the second (B) states that "light" is to be seen, that is, "the light of the gospel," which, however, unbelievers do not see. This light comes from the "glory" radiated by Christ, who is "the image of God." It will be remembered that those who turn to the Lord (3:16) see the "glory of the Lord" and are transformed into "the same image" (see on 3:18).[46]

The Exodus narrative forms the background to this passage. In response to Moses' request God revealed his glory to him, but he was not permitted to see the face of God (Exod 32:18-23; cf. v. 6). On the Damascus Road, Paul, too, saw the glory of God. But there was a shape to it. Paul beheld "the image (*eikōn*) of God," the glorified Christ. In the heavenly Christ the invisible God, who cannot be seen, has perfectly and fully revealed himself (cf. Col 1:15). The glorified Christ is the ultimate and eschatological revelation of God. There is nothing more that can or will be seen of God.

What Paul saw with his eyes in that unique moment he now "sets forth" by means of "the truth" of the gospel (v. 2) addressed to the ears of his hearers (cf. Gal 3:2, 5), by means of which the light of God comes into darkened hearts (v. 6). Light from the glorified Christ streams into the heart through hearing the gospel. God's revelatory "image," the heavenly Christ,

---

45. Gk. ὁ θεὸς τοῦ αἰῶνος τούτου, a reference to Satan (so Thrall, 1.306-8), for whom elsewhere in this letter see 2:11; 11:14; 12:7. The striking term ὁ θεὸς τοῦ αἰῶνος τούτου is not found elsewhere in the NT; but see ὁ ἄρχων τοῦ κόσμου τουτου (John 12:31). This "god" is the master of this age, the "god" behind every idol, yet subject to the decree of God. "The unregenerate serve Satan as though he were their God" (Hughes, 127). Nonetheless, there is no dualism here, as if God and Satan were equals.

46. For other references to εἰκών and δόξα together, see 1 Cor 11:7 ("a man . . . is the image and glory of God"); 2 Cor 3:18 ("beholding . . . the glory of the Lord . . . transformed into the same image"); Rom 8:29-30 ("conformed to the image of his Son . . . glorified").

shown to the apostle, becomes the revelation of God for those who hear and receive the gospel.[47]

In broadening his reference of blindness from the "veiled" Israelites (3:15) to "unbelievers" generally, Paul is declaring what is the eschatological reality of "this age."[48] On the one hand, people generally, Jews and Gentiles alike, if they are "unbelievers,"[49] are and remain "veiled" (v. 3), having been "blinded" by "the god of this age." Such blindness is not merely the historic incapacity of the people of Israel under the old covenant (3:13-15). The darkness is universal, demonic and cosmic. Yet into the darkness of these blinded minds,[50] light — God's own glory now manifested in Christ — shines forth from the gospel Paul proclaims (cf. v. 6). Here, once again, is the apostolic openness/boldness (3:12), the eschatological disclosure of the truth of the word of God (v. 2), by means of which these are enabled to see whose blindness has been overcome by God's light.

Such "seeing" of "the light . . . of the glory" is, of course, metaphorical for *hearing*. The gospel of Christ comes first not as an optical but as an aural reality (see, e.g., Rom 10:17; Gal 3:2, 5; cf. 3:1). Nonetheless, his words are not merely figurative. The intensity of Paul's language suggests that he is appealing to shared spiritual experience, his own and his readers'. When the gospel is heard and the hearer turns to the Lord, the veil is removed so that he now "sees" the glory of the Lord (see on 3:16, 18). Light does shine in darkness (cf. v. 6).

5 With an explanatory "For"[51] Paul now sets forth to explain his

47. Consonant with the language of vv. 3-4 is Christ's commission to Paul recorded in the Acts: "to open [Gentile] eyes and turn them from darkness to light and from the power of Satan to God" (Acts 26:18).

48. Gk. ὁ αἰῶνος οὗτος — a temporal concept that is in contrast with ὁ αἰῶνος ὁ μέλλων (cf. Eph 1:21), representing an eschatological dualism of contemporary Judaism that is common to Paul's thought (e.g., 1 Cor 1:20; 2:6; Rom 12:2). The present age is characterized by "evil" (Gal 1:4). According to *2 Clement* 6: "This age and the coming one are two enemies." Nonetheless, in NT thinking "the coming one" has already become present in "this one."

49. Gk. ἄπιστοι are found earlier in Paul only in 1 Cor 6:6; 7:12-16; 10:24; 14:22-25, where the word is used only of Gentiles. Paul's inclusion of Jews as "unbelievers" may be seen as very pointed, and indeed offensive, since the ἄπιστοι of 2 Cor 6:14, 15 are worshipers in Gentile temples, where people would be defiled through contact with food offered to idols (cf. Acts 15:29; 21:25)!

50. The parallel references to "minds" (v. 4), along with "hearts" (v. 6), remind us that these words are really interchangeable (cf. 3:14, 15). Yet, νόημα may have a special place in 2 Corinthians, given the negative references elsewhere to "reasonings" (2:11; 3:14; 10:5; 11:3), which is the more striking since Paul has only one other use, and that a later one (Phil 4:7). See also on λογίζομαι . . . λογισμούς (10:2).

51. Gk. γάρ. So Plummer, 118. Less probably, γάρ could point to "ourselves" and pick up but qualify "we commend ourselves" of v. 2 in answer to Paul's critics ("we commend *ourselves* . . ." [v. 2]; . . . "we do not preach *ourselves*").

own role in what he has said about the gospel in v. 4b. At the same time his "we proclaim" not only picks up immediate references to "not distorting the word of God . . . but setting forth the truth plainly" (vv. 2-3), "our gospel" (v. 3), and "the light of the gospel" (v. 4), but also the more distant motif at the beginning of the excursus: "God . . . leads us in triumphal procession and through us spreads . . . the knowledge of [Christ]" (2:14). Since the "light" of God (v. 4) is found in the gospel, Paul does not proclaim himself but the Lord, from whom gospel "light" comes (see on 3:16).[52]

Paul's is a proverblike statement, based on a "Lord" and "slave" antithesis that is structured around "not . . . but . . . and."[53] Thus he declares, "*not* . . . ourselves we proclaim, *but* Jesus Christ as Lord"; and, having initially dismissed "ourselves" as the content of what is proclaimed, he adds, "*and* ourselves your slaves on account of Jesus," in terms of his pioneer role in the proclamation. Paul's deliberate antitriumphalism (see on 2:14) may be tilted against those who claim to be "superior" to Paul (see on 11:5-6), but who "make slaves" of the Corinthians (see on 11:20). Paul's sufferings in ministry — his "weaknesses" (11:23–12:10) — are incurred as their "slave" on account of Jesus.

This verse also prepares the way for the next, in which he states how he gives light to others. It is by proclaiming Jesus Christ as Lord.

> For we do not preach ourselves   A
>   but
> [we]   [preach[54]] Jesus Christ as Lord
>   and   ourselves your slaves   B
>   for Jesus' sake.

According to C. K. Barrett (134), "It would be hard to describe the Christian ministry more comprehensively in so few words."

In this gnomic saying Paul gives the means, content, and manner of new covenant ministry ("this ministry" — 4:1). Paul expresses the *means* of his ministry as "we preach,"[55] one of his two preferred words for his declaration of the gospel.

---

52. For the argument that Paul is here defending himself from the charge of preaching his own Damascus Road experience for some kind of egotistical control over others, see Thrall, 1.313.

53. Gk. οὐκ . . . ἀλλά . . . δέ. . . .

54. The verb in part (A), "we do not *preach* ourselves," is to be understood in part (B), "but [we *preach*] Jesus Christ. . . ."

55. Gk. κηρύσσομεν. Within 2 Corinthians Paul's key gospel preaching words are (1) κηρύσσειν, where the object is "the Son of God, Jesus Christ" — 1:19; "Jesus" — 11:4; (2) εὐαγγελίζεσθαι, with the object (10:16, intransitive) "the gospel of God" — 11:7; (3) λαλεῖν, where the object explicit or implicit is "the word of God" — 2:17; 4:2,

The *content* of Paul's *kērygma,* as stated here ("Jesus Christ as Lord"[56]), is echoed on a number of occasions elsewhere in Paul's writings as a summary of Christian belief (e.g., 1 Cor 12:3; Rom 10:9; Phil 2:10-11). Implicit in this brief statement is the conviction that the crucified Christ has been exalted through resurrection as the heavenly Lord; God's suffering servant, the agent of atonement, is now the ruler of the world. Personal conviction as expressed by open confession that "Jesus is Lord"[57] issues in the salvation of God (Rom 10:9). The implication here is that lordship equates with deity. "LORD" regularly translates "Yahweh" in the LXX, and there are numerous NT references to Jesus as "Lord" that echo OT (LXX) passages that refer to Yahweh.[58]

As to *manner,* as a "slave for Jesus' sake,"[59] the apostle models himself on the ministry of Christ, to whose "meekness and gentleness" he will refer later (10:1). If Paul, a "good minister of Christ" — as he exhorts Timothy to be (1 Tim 4:6) — is a "slave,"[60] it is "on account of Jesus"[61] whom he serves and whom he proclaims, because Jesus was the "slave" who, by his death, came "to minister" (Mark 10:44[62]; Rom 15:8). Unstated,

---

"our" or "the gospel" — 4:3, 4. The keywords εὐαγγελίζεσθαι and κηρύσσειν, with cognates εὐαγγέλιον and κῆρυξ, had important cultic associations in the Greco-Roman world at that time, as well as a significant history of use within the Greek translations of the OT. See G. Friedrich, *TDNT* 2.707-37, for εὐαγγελίζεσθαι/εὐαγγέλιον, and G. Friedrich, *TDNT* 3.683-718, for κηρύσσειν/κῆρυξ. The LXX, in particular, is the chief quarry for these words.

56. Similar to v. 5 is 1 Cor 1:23: "We preach *Christ crucified. . . .*" Both statements summarize a critical aspect of Paul's *kērygma.*

57. Gk. Ἰησοῦν Χριστὸν κύριον. The response of the people of Macedonia who "first gave themselves to the Lord" (8:5) was, in all likelihood, because Paul proclaimed Jesus Christ as *Lord.*

58. See, e.g., 1 Thess 4:16/Ps 46:5; Rom 10:9-13/Joel 2:32; Phil 2:10-11/Isa 45:22-24).

59. It is possible that Paul is here either pointedly apologetic (answering the charge that he rates his authority as an apostle more highly than preaching the gospel — cf. 1:24) or obliquely polemical (against the newcomers whom he is presently criticizing, and whom he will accuse of insincerity and harshness — cf. 2:17–3:1; 4:2; 11:20). Paul is also restating his long-understood servant's role; cf. 1 Cor 3:5 (διάκονος); 4:1 (ὑπηρέτης); Rom 1:1; Phil 1:1 (δοῦλος).

60. Gk. δοῦλος.

61. Gk. διὰ Ἰησοῦν. Also 4:11 — "we are always being handed over to death *on account of Jesus. . . .*"

62. Whereas Paul speaks of himself as δοῦλος, as does Jesus in Mark 10:44, it is παῖς that occurs in the LXX version of the Servant passages in Isaiah (see, e.g., Isa 52:13–53:12), as echoed in Matthew (cf. Matt 8:17; 12:18-21). There are hints in Paul's writings that he understands his own role in terms of the Servant of Yahweh, as in Isaiah's Servant Songs (e.g., Rom 15:21). For a discussion of *Paul* as Servant of Yahweh in 2 Corinthians, see G. K. Beale, "Reconciliation," 562-66. But it must be noted that Paul does not refer to himself as παῖς nor, indeed, use the word in his letters.

but perhaps understood, is the inference that the One who is now "Lord" had first been the "slave."[63] A more antitriumphalist statement is difficult to conceive.

6 The reason ("For"[64]) Paul the apostle gives for being a "slave" (v. 5) is now stated. It is because God has shone in Paul's heart[65] to give the light of the knowledge of God to others. Whereas, earlier, the god of this world blinds minds to the light of the gospel (v. 4), by response, in this verse, the God who called forth the light of creation has illuminated Paul that he might bring the glory of God to darkened human hearts.

This verse is tripartite. The subject of the first part (A) — "the God . . ."[66] — is the subject (understood) of the second (B). Thus "the God who said, 'Let light shine out of darkness,' " is[67] ["the God] who[68] has shone in our hearts." The third part (C) gives expression to God's purpose latent in the second, namely, "to give the light[69] of the knowledge[70] of the glory of God."[71]

63. The exaltation of the humble Servant as Lord is classically stated in Phil 2:7, 9, 11 — μορφὴν δούλου λαβών . . . ὁ θεὸς ὑπερύψωσεν . . . πᾶσα γλῶσσα ἐξομολογήσηται ὅτι κύριος Ἰησοῦς Χριστός.

64. Gk. ὅτι, which is here equivalent to γάρ (A. T. Robertson, *Grammar,* 962) and gives the basis for v. 5, just as the γάρ of v. 5 had given the grounds for v. 4.

65. Gk. καρδίαις ἡμῶν, "our hearts." With Thrall, 1:316-17, this is taken as singular (as at 7:3-4), i.e., as Paul's *heart,* because (1) his first person plural pronouns ("we"/"us") throughout the excursus on new covenant ministry (2:14–7:4) generally refer to his apostolate (see on 1:1; 2:14), and (2) the immediate context (vv. 1-4) relates to Paul's ministry. Nonetheless, the illumination of the heart is by no means limited to Paul. Paul is a paradigm for and representative of all believers.

66. I have followed the RSV in this verse. Alternatively, but less probably, ὁ θεός could be taken as a predicate: "it is God who said. . . ."

67. Gk. ἐστιν supplied; so Plummer, 119.

68. Gk. ὅς, which some authorities omit (e.g., D* G 81 Marcion).

69. Gk. πρὸς φωτισμόν (cf. τὸν φωτισμόν — v. 4). Whereas ἔλαμψεν points to Paul's conversion, πρὸς φωτισμόν points to that ministry of shedding forth God's light as an evangelist, which was the purpose of his conversion. Cf. Gal 1:16 — ἀποκαλύψαι τὸν υἱὸν αὐτοῦ ἐν ἐμοὶ ἵνα εὐαγγελίζωμαι αὐτὸν ἐν τοῖς ἔθνεσιν. . . . Less probably, however, Thrall, 1.318, treats φωτισμόν as parallel to ἔλαμψεν, pointing only to the illumination of Christ to Paul, with no evangelistic intention expressed at this point.

70. While Bultmann, 108, takes γνῶσις here in the sense of gnostic enlightenment, the reference to γνῶσις in the context of evangelism (2:14; cf. 2:17; 4:2-5) excludes such a view, as does the OT use of "the knowledge of God." See also R. Bultmann, *TDNT* 1.696-701.

71. The "glory of God in the face of [Jesus] Christ" (v. 6) is the same thing as the "glory of Christ" (v. 4), implying a close identification between God and Christ. Barrett comments (132), "In God's Son God is himself encountered, yet at the same time remains the Invisible One."

For   A

the God who said,

              "Light shall shine out of darkness,"

    has   shone in our hearts   B

    to give

      [the] light   C

             of the knowledge

             of the glory of God

             in the face of Christ.

There is an outward as well as an inward aspect here.[72] Outwardly, on the way to Damascus, Paul saw "the glory of God in the face of Christ"; inwardly, and as a consequence, "God has shone in our hearts" (cf. "God revealed his Son *in* me" — Gal 1:16). Whereas God's outward revelation of his glory to Paul was unique, his inner enlightenment of the heart also describes the illumination of all[73] who receive the gospel message (cf. "see the light of the gospel" — v. 4). "The gospel is now 'the fundamental re-presentative agency for the splendor of God'; God's glory is present in the proclamation."[74]

The statement of purpose "to give" (C) explains how Paul is a "slave" (v. 5), as demanded by the connective "for" with which v. 6 begins. Paul's apostolic role as "slave" is to beam forth to others the light that God has shone in his heart. This he does by preaching "Jesus Christ as Lord" (v. 5), so that his hearers may "see" the "glory of God" in "the face of Christ, who is the image of God." (The "face"[75] that his hearers see figuratively Paul had

---

72. There are parallels between the Acts accounts of the Damascus event and this verse. The present φωτισμός appears as φῶς (Acts 9:3; 22:6, 11; 26:13) and the λάμπ-group words occur in this verse and in Acts 26:13.

73. According to Thrall, 1.319, "... could [Paul] really speak of both the Corinthians and himself (ἡμεῖς πάντες, 3:18) as beholding the Lord's glory, unless there was in some way a real identity of experience between them?" See further G. Theissen, *Psychological Aspects,* 117-58.

74. So Thrall, 1.319; see generally her Excursus V — 4:4, 6: *Christophany.*

75. Gk. πρόσωπον, while taken literally here, is often taken figuratively as "person," or "presence." The "face of Christ," which is now "glorious" (see also 3:18), had previously, and in continuity, been the person of the incarnate Jesus of Nazareth (cf. 8:9). In relationship to the latter, A. McGrath observes, "Without incarnation, we are left in the realm of ideas. We are left unable to put a human face to God. We are left in a world of ideas and ideals — a chilly world, in which no words are spoken, and the tenderness of love is unknown. The incarnation allows us to speak with authority of God being personal. It speaks of God entering our history, and allows us to abandon the cold and unfeeling world of ideals in favour of a world charged with the thrilling presence of God" (*Bridge Building,* 169). McGrath's comments about the incarnate One hold true as well for the glorified One.

seen literally on the Damascus Road.) Under the old covenant the glory on the face of Moses was veiled from the people (see on 3:7, 13). But by the ministry of the new covenant those who hear the gospel "see" the "glory of God" in "the face of Christ" (see on 3:18). This giving forth of the light of God by preaching Jesus Christ *is* the "boldness/openness" (3:12), the "setting forth" of the truth (v. 2), that is the very essence of the apostolic office, from which he will not recoil (v. 1).[76]

The language of vv. 5-6 resonates with key vocabulary used of the creation in the opening chapter of Genesis ("image of God," "God . . . said, 'Let there be light' ").[77] God, who addressed the primeval darkness with his word that brought day in place of night, now addresses the darkness of human sin and chaos. That darkness, according to v. 4, is attributable to the god of this world, who blinds the minds of unbelievers. This verse gives the answer to that; God — the true God, the creator and giver of light as opposed to the false god — illuminates the inner lives of those previously blinded by Satan.[78] From the hitherto darkened heart of the apostle, in whom God had shone his light, now streams forth light for those who will hear the word of God — that Jesus Christ is Lord — from him. To them God shines in his light, dispelling the darkness of ignorance, fear, and guilt, removing the veil.

Paul's use of such language from Genesis 1 anticipates his reference to "a new creation" (5:17). If there is a *"new* covenant" (3:6), there is also

---

76. Paul's language in v. 6 evocatively describes universally the experience of Christian conversion. At the same time his words (3:16–4:6) reflect, autobiographically, his own life-changing encounter with Christ on the road to Damascus, and the effects of his ministry since that time. Paul's meditates retrospectively on his own sense of having been "veiled" from the glory of God during the Sabbath-day reading of Moses (3:14-15). When confronted by the glory of God on the Damascus Road, he "turned" to the Lord — the Lord Jesus Christ, whose face he then saw — that veil was removed, and the Spirit came, bringing "freedom" (3:16-17) from condemnation and death (3:7, 9). He saw the glorified "face" of Jesus Christ, who is "the image of God" (3:18; 4:4, 6). Conscious of having been shown the "mercy" of God at the same moment as receiving his apostolic commission to new covenant ministry (4:1; 3:7), Paul "renounced" his previous life (4:2). From that time, as he preached the gospel — namely, "Jesus Christ as Lord" (4:4-5) — God beamed the light that Paul had seen into the darkened minds of all who would receive the word of God, so that they, too, might "see" the "face of Christ," who is the "image of God" (3:18; 4:5-6). Thus, through Paul's ministry as apostle to the Gentiles there was the open and bold declaration of the day of salvation (6:2), the *phanerōsis* of God's truth (3:12; 4:2), an activity from which he would not turn aside (4:1).

77. There may also be echoes of Isa 9:1 (φῶς λάμψει ἐφ' ὑμᾶς; cf. ὁ θεός . . . λάμψει) as well as of the light-giving role of the Servant of Yahweh (Isa 49:6). Paul may be making some oblique reference to himself as the Servant of Yahweh (see on v. 5).

78. The language of darkness/light as of the creation narrative is used of Christian conversion elsewhere (cf. Acts 26:18; 1 Pet 2:9).

a "*new* creation," reminding us once more of the deeply eschatological nature of the apostle's thought. The old has passed, and the new has come in fulfillment of it (see on 1:20-22; 3:3; 5:15-17; 6:1-2).

Paul's words in vv. 1-6, which are redolent of his Damascus Road encounter with the glorified Christ, are given in defense of his ministry. Possibly, too, there is concurrently an oblique polemic against the "peddlers" (see on v. 2). In particular, Paul here claims to be a revelator to others of the glory God shone in his heart, that is, to set forth the truth plainly (see on vv. 2, 6). In terms of his intention in writing, this author is seeking to defend, so as to confirm, his authority as a minister of the new covenant. He has not written to secure emulation from others but recognition of his apostolic task by the Corinthians.

What application, then, do these words have for others, in particular those who are missionaries and pastors? Despite the particular and historic context of Paul's apologetic for his ministry, the applicability of these words to others beyond Paul and that distant situation is clear enough. A pioneer of that new covenant ministry Paul certainly was, and with a unique revelatory role, accompanied by the signs, wonders, and miracles of an apostle (12:12). Nonetheless, that new covenant continues, and with it a new covenant ministry, until the closure of the age.

Significant for such ministry is Paul's statement that God has "shone in" his heart (4:6). This is deliberately representational. God shines into the hearts of all who respond to the gospel; they also "see the light of the glory of God" (4:4). As ministers under the continuing new covenant, missionaries and pastors themselves need to have "seen" that "light" from the gospel, and, on that basis, so to preach the gospel that God will shine his light into the hearts of others.

Acceptance of and involvement in new covenant ministry as a life calling require the same ethical qualities as those stated by the apostle in v. 2 — determined perseverance, and a renunciation of the shamefully secretive and of craftiness (especially in matters relating to money). The minister will not corrupt the gospel by adding to it, but rather commend himself to others before God, by an open declaration of it from a godly life.

Clearly, too, Paul's words in v. 5 stand as a rebuke to any minister of the gospel, then or since, who aspires to worldly greatness or recognition. Whoever fails either (1) to preach "Jesus Christ as Lord" or (2) to be "slave for Jesus' sake" fails at the most fundamental point of ministry that has any claim to be apostolic.

B. THE MINISTRY: LIFE AND DEATH (4:7-15)

Throughout his apologia on new covenant ministry to this point (2:14–4:6), Paul has spoken of the gifts of God to the Corinthians, including (1) the Spirit of the living God (3:3), and (2) the light God has shone in their hearts (4:4, 6). These blessings have come through "the word of God" (2:17), "the gospel" (4:4) by which they have the knowledge of Christ/of God (2:14; 4:6). But there is this problem: How could such glory be mediated by so inglorious an instrument, the suffering Paul?

The motif of the death and life of Jesus is prominent within this passage (vv. 10-12; cf. 2:16), in two closely connected respects. Within himself in the course of his ministry Paul experiences the death but also the life, or deliverance of Jesus (vv. 10-11). At the same time the death that is at work in Paul brings life to the Corinthians (v. 12).

Unpalatable as it may have been in Corinth,[1] the truth was that God was leading his minister from place to place in humiliating suffering, replicating Golgotha wherever he went (2:14-15a). The message of Christ crucified, which brought them life, was, and must be (cf. 4:5), borne by one whose own existence was cruciform. Because the glory is God's glory, the bearer must be dependent on God, which, indeed, Paul's missionary sufferings caused him to be.

1. The Minister: Handed Over to Death (4:7-12)

> 7 *But we have this treasure in jars of clay to show that this all-surpassing power is from God and not from us.* 8 *We are hard pressed on every side, but not crushed; perplexed, but not in despair;* 9 *persecuted, but not abandoned; struck down, but not destroyed.* 10 *We always carry around in our body the death of Jesus, so that the life of Jesus may also be revealed in our body.* 11 *For we who are alive are always being given over to death for Jesus' sake, so that his life may be revealed in our mortal body.* 12 *So then, death is at work in us, but life is at work in you.*

This passage, which is about suffering and death (vv. 7-12), stands in stark contrast with the theme of "glory" so brilliantly developed by Paul in 3:7–4:6, to which he also will return in vv. 16-18. Paul, God's slave, the transmitter

---

1. See Introduction, 37-38, for the view that the "peddlers" may have seen in Paul's sufferings a lack of "glory" that served to discount his claims of an eschatology that fulfilled and superseded the old covenant. By contrast, its founder, Moses, was of undimmed glory, a sign of the ongoing applicability of the Mosaic covenant.

of the life-transforming, saving glory of God, is himself nothing more than a fragile "jar of clay" (v. 7). He is subject to afflictions, bewilderment, persecution, and being struck down (vv. 8-9). As mere "mortal flesh" who is constantly being "handed over to death," his body is the bearer of "the dying of Jesus" (v. 10). "Death is at work" in him (vv. 1-12). Paul's sufferings are "on account of Jesus" (v. 11), so that "life" may be "at work" among the Corinthians (v. 11). God's apostolic "slave" models himself upon God's ultimate slave, Christ Jesus himself (cf. Phil 2:7-8).

However, as we see the weakness of the apostle we also see the power of God. Here once more is the theme of power in weakness (1:3-4, 8-10; 2:12-15; cf. 11:29; 12:7-10). If Paul is a fragile jar of clay, he is also subject to the surpassing power of God, so that he is "not crushed . . . not in despair . . . not abandoned . . . not destroyed" (vv. 8-9). The resurrected "life" of Jesus is also "at work" in him (vv. 10-12).

Indeed, weakness in the apostle is precisely according to the purposes of God. Such power as may be at work in him must not be his own, but only from God (v. 7). Thus, in the midst of the his continuous difficulties of his ministry (vv. 8-9), the apostle is constantly subject to the "life of Jesus," in anticipation of his resurrection (v. 14).

This passage thus includes the first of the so-called *peristasis*[1] cata-

---

1. A term meaning "catalogues of circumstances" and applied to the numerous lists of "good" and "bad" — but chiefly "bad" — circumstances affecting people as found in the literature of the Hellenistic period, including the literature of Hellenistic Judaism. Though the word *peristasis* does not appear in the NT, the term may be appropriately applied to lists of sufferings such as are found in vv. 8-9. See J. T. Fitzgerald, *Earthen Vessels*, 166-80, who notes parallels to *peristasis* catalogues in the Hellenistic moralists in which the sage is revealed to be composed and serene in the face of adversity. Fitzgerald cites Seneca,

> If you see a man who is unterrified in the midst of dangers, untouched by desires, happy in adversity, peaceful amid the storm, . . . will not a feeling of reverence for him steal over you? "This quality is too great and lofty to be regarded as resembling this petty body in which it dwells? A divine power has descended upon that man. . . . A thing like this cannot stand upright unless it be propped by the divine." (*Epistle* 41.4-5)

Fitzgerald regards Paul's "we do not lose heart" (4:1, 16 — οὐκ ἐγκακοῦμεν) with the four οὐκ statements (4:8-9) as indicative of Paul's similarity with the "suffering sage who is triumphant over his hardships" (166). Nonetheless, there are differences. Whereas the sage is self-confident, Paul's utter confidence is in God (v. 7; cf. 1:9). Even so, according to Fitzgerald, Paul has an apologetic concern to establish his legitimacy as a minister of God. The format and content of this *peristasis* is to that end.

Fundamental to Fitzgerald's thesis is the assumption that Paul was aware of the *peristasis* literary convention. While it is unlikely that Paul was familiar with specific

logues within this letter (cf. 6:3-10; 11:23b-33; 12:9-10; but see also 1:5-11; 2:14-17).

Since these verses belong to Paul's defense of his new covenant ministry, a critical hermeneutical question is: Do they apply only to the apostle or may a more general application be seen in them? The latter must be allowed because (1) these verses serve as a foundation for Paul's universally applicable words about dying, death, and judgment that follow (4:16–5:10), and (2) Paul will refer to his apostolic sufferings in other letters, but representatively, as if such sufferings are endured by believers generally[2] (see Rom 8:35-39; Phil 3:4-11).

7   In this new passage[3] Paul sets out to explain the paradox stated first in 2:14-16. Although his ministry imparts life (2:16), and brings the Spirit of God (3:3) and the glory of God (4:4, 6), in himself he suffers humiliation in God's triumphal procession (2:14) and the basis of his ministry is that of a slave, the crucified Christ (4:5). Those things that the Corinthians and their new teachers disdain in him, that is, his missionary sufferings, he now declares to be fundamental to ministry that faithfully represents the Crucified One.

The human vessel bearing "this treasure" (= "the light of the knowledge of the glory of God," v. 6)[4] is a mere "jar of clay." But this is for a divine purpose — stated positively and negatively[5] — that the "all-surpassing power might be (1) "from God," and (2) "not from us." This "all-surpassing power of God" probably picks up — but so as to reverse — a reference to his sense of overwhelming debility that he made near the beginning of the letter (1:8).

His verb ("we have") in the first part of the verse occurs a number of times in the immediate context of the letter, where Paul is reflecting upon the new covenant ministry.[6] Paul is deeply conscious of the "treasure"[7] that he carries within him.

The previous passage (3:18–4:6) powerfully celebrated the glory of

---

writers like Seneca, insofar as the *peristasis* existed in popular culture as a vehicle for Stoic thought, it is likely that Paul expressed himself in these terms. See also S. J. Hafemann, *Suffering and Ministry,* 62ff.

2. So, too, Bultmann, 116; Barrett, 140.

3. Introduced by δέ.

4. Other interpretations of τὸν θησαυρὸν τοῦτον, "this treasure," include (1) the gospel (v. 4; so Barrett, 138), and (2) the ministry of the gospel (v. 1; so Bultmann, 114).

5. Gk. ἵνα . . . καὶ μή.

6. Whether as a finite or participial version of ἔχω. Thus: "we have such confidence" (3:4), "having such a hope" (3:12), "having this ministry" (4:1), "we have this treasure" (4:7), "having the same spirit of faith" (4:13), and "we have a building" (5:1).

7. Gk. θησαυρός, "treasure," elsewhere in the NT only at Col 2:3.

God/of Christ as it is mediated to human lives by the apostolic word. But now there is reintroduced the somber note of the suffering of the one who bears that word,[8] which will run through the entire passage 4:7–5:10. Each part of this verse expresses the antithesis between the power of God and weakness of the apostle (treasure/in clay jars, on the one hand; power from God/not from us, on the other). Such antitheses will characterize the entire passage 4:7–5:10.[9]

Striking is the contrast between the radiant treasure of the knowledge of God/Christ in the heart (4:4, 6)[10] and the inexpensive and easily breakable receptacle[11] that bears it, an earthen pot.[12] Such vessels are both cheap and fragile,[13] thus having no enduring value in their own right.[14] Only their contents give them worth.

The immediately following references to his sufferings in ministry (vv. 8-9) and the workings of death within the apostle's life (vv. 10-12) spring from this understanding of the vulnerability of the bearer who carries the treasure. Indeed, the general statement made by this verse should be seen as

8. See on 2:13.

9. A similar paradox is expressed in the antithesis between triumph and antitriumph, "God leads us in triumph [as prisoners-of-war]" (2:14).

10. Contrary to prevailing Hellenistic thought, Paul does not here imply that the body is a temporal vessel bearing an immortal soul. As a Jew, Paul would regard the body-soul as an integrated unity.

11. Both elements, "treasure" and "vessel," taken *together,* appear to underlie Paul's image. See generally Thrall, 1.322-24, who cites the story of an emperor's daughter who mocked a learned but ugly rabbi with the words, "glorious wisdom in a repulsive vessel" (*b. Ta'an.* 7a), along with the rabbinic observation that the necessity that wine be kept in earthenware containers illustrated the truth that only a humble person could keep the Torah.

12. Gk. ὀστράκινος σκεῦος. The cheapness of the ὀστράκινος σκεῦος is well illustrated by the contrasts in 2 Tim 2:20 (cf. Lam 4:2). For reference to the expendability of broken pots see Jer 19:11; LXX Ps 30:12. There may be a connection between the earthenware pot and God's formation of humankind from the dust (Gen 2:7; cf. Isa 29:16; 45:9; 64:8). Less secure are the views of (1) Barrett, 138, who stresses the unimportance of the vessel; (2) T. W. Manson ("2 Corinthians 2:14-17," *Studia Paulina,* 156), who suggests that the contrast is between "small pottery lamps" and "the flame of God's glory" that they bear; (3) Hughes, 136, who contends that the image points to the booty of silver coins carried in earthen vessels after the Roman conquest of Macedonia in 167 B.C.; and (4) C. Spicq ("L'Image spotive," 210), who argues that Paul has in mind an elect vessel. Paul's own intent with this imagery is spelled out in the verses that follow.

13. J. T. Fitzgerald, *Earthen Vessels,* 167, calls such vessels "the disposable bottles of antiquity." But Paul is pointing to their fragility rather than to their disposability.

14. According to Seneca, the body is "a vessel that the slightest shaking, the slightest toss will break. . . . A body weak and fragile, naked, in its natural state defenceless . . . exposed to all the affronts of Fortune; . . . doomed to decay" (*To Marcia* 11.3).

an introduction to the whole section 4:7–5:10, which becomes universal in its application (4:13–5:10).[15]

Similarly imposing is the juxtaposition of the power of God, which is "all-surpassing,"[16] and human power, which is feeble. This is a recurring theme within 2 Corinthians. Earlier, Paul wrote of being "under great pressure, far beyond our ability to endure" (see on 1:8). Now, in exact answer, he points to God's power, which surpasses the weakness of his mortal body. Later, Paul will recall Jesus' words to him, "My power is made perfect in weakness" (12:9).[17]

This is no merely pious acknowledgment of his limitations as compared to the greatness of God. Rather — as the syntax (purpose construction[18] shows) — it is divinely ordained that the human bearer of the divine revelation should be an earthenware vessel. The enabling — indeed, the surpassing — power for that ministry cannot, must not, arise from the bearer of the message, but only from God. But this is to reiterate Paul's earlier conviction, "Our sufficiency comes from God, who has made us sufficient as ministers of a new covenant" (3:5-6).

Why should Paul teach this? Is it because it happens to be true and worth saying, or is there also a special point to be made? In all probability Paul is giving this emphasis because the newly arrived "peddlers" claim to be *superior* in ministry to Paul, and even to possess special powers. Indeed, Paul's word that characterizes their self-presentation is *hyper*, "above"; they are "superlative" apostles (see on 10:12-18; 11:5). It is as if they claim that power for ministry arises from within them; they have more of it than Paul. In response Paul will often point to the sufferings in apostolic ministry within the letter,[19] and — as here — he will insist that it is only by God's power that the revelation of the glory of God in the gospel can be given (vv. 2, 4, and 6) and that such power can only be seen where its human vessel is "clay." Paul is not the powerhouse but only the place where the power is exhibited.[20] It is not the power inherent in the minister, but only the word he bears, and which he bears in mortal frailty, that brings light and salvation.

---

15. Just as Paul's specific reference to himself as a minister of the new covenant (2:14–3:11) broadens to include all believers (3:12-18), so, too, a subsequent passage about his ministry (4:1-15) merges into a statement about all believers (4:13–5:10).

16. Gk. ὑπερβολή (lit. "a throwing beyond"), "excess," "extraordinary quality or character" (BAGD). See further, G. Schneider, *EDNT* 3.398.

17. The theme of power-in-weakness runs through the entire letter: καθ᾽ ὑπερ-βολὴν ὑπὲρ δύναμιν ἐβαρήθημεν (1:8); ἡ ὑπερβολὴ τῆς δυνάμεως ᾖ τοῦ θεοῦ (4:7); δύναμις ἐν ἀσθενείᾳ (12:9).

18. Gk. ἵνα . . . ᾖ.

19. See on 1:5-6. Apostolic sufferings are also referred to in 1 Cor 4:9-13; Rom 8:35-39.

20. So J. T. Fitzgerald, *Earthen Vessels,* 170.

Nonetheless, although Paul's comments seem to be conditioned by the particular circumstances then prevailing in Corinth, similar views can be found elsewhere in his writings (e.g., 1 Cor 4:8-13; Phil 3:10). In Paul's mind the proclaimer must reflect the proclaimed. He who proclaims a crucified Messiah must himself live cruciform. Let the Corinthians and their current teachers know that the glory of God does not reside on the face of Moses but on the face of the Christ who was crucified. This truth is reflected in the missionary sufferings of the ambassador, the apostle Paul (cf. 5:20; 12:10).

Moreover, it is doubtful whether such remarks are to be confined in their application to him. Although they begin with him, they do not end with him. The present section (4:7–5:10) has, at a number of points, a degree of applicability to all members of the new covenant and not merely to the apostolic leader (see especially 4:16–5:10). Although Paul is referring in the first instance to himself as an apostle, there is a real sense in which Paul here writes representatively for all fellow members of the new covenant, including the Corinthians (3:18; 5:10; but cf. 12:19).[21] Paul's sufferings as an apostle, when considered against the claims of the triumphalists who oppose him (2:14-17), have caused him to reflect more generally on what might be called "the human condition." Thus he reminds readers of these words — then and now — that the power to lift humans out of their power-lessness in the face of suffering, decay, and death does not come from within themselves; it comes only from God. Indeed, these words teach that it is not God's plan — apparently — that the power for revelation or redemption should arise from within a man or woman. Had the priceless treasure of the knowledge of God been contained in a strong and permanent body, it could have proved fatal, given the fact of human pride. This is true even of an apostle.

8-9 These sentences are framed by "in every way,"[22] a phrase that governs the four statements following, as well as "always" in v. 10. These universals also appear in the paradoxical triumph/antitriumph metaphor, with which the excursus on new covenant ministry began (2:14). Verses 8-9 represent the first of the "tribulation lists" (*peristaseis*[23]) found within 2 Corinthians (see also 6:3-10; 11:23b-33; 12:7-10; cf. 1:5-11; 2:14-17).

---

21. Of interest is Rom 8:35-39, where the sufferings listed are chiefly apostle related but clearly apply to all believers.

22. Gk. ἐν παντί — a phrase common in this letter (6:4; 7:5, 11, 16; 8:7; 9:8, 11; 11:6, 9). Along with "always" (Gk. πάντοτε — vv. 10, 11), this phrase serves to accentuate the intensity of Paul's sufferings.

23. For further comment, including reference to specialist literature, see J. T. Fitzgerald, *Earthen Vessels,* 166-80; S. J. Hafemann, *Suffering and Ministry,* 52ff.; Thrall, 1.329-31.

What follows is one of the more powerful rhetorical moments in the Pauline corpus,[24] although comparable to similar antitheses in 1 Cor 4:10, 12-13 and 2 Cor 6:9-10. Each clause follows the same pattern: a passive participle expressing an aspect of suffering is contrasted by "but not,"[25] followed by another passive participle cognate with, but more severe than, the first (e.g., *"hard pressed* but not *crushed"*). At the same time each of the two paired participles expresses a suffering more extreme than the corresponding participle in the line preceding it. Thus:

1. The first pair, "hard pressed" and "crushed,"[26] are virtual synonyms in contemporary Greek. The former ("hard pressed") is probably used first because of its significant and early use in 2 Corinthians (see on 1:4); the latter ("in a narrow space," "constricted") is found in the NT only in 6:12.[27] The rhetorical context determines that the latter has the more severe meaning.

2. The next pair are a wordplay (paronomasia) impossible to reproduce in translation (*aporoumenoi* and *exaporoumenoi,*[28] the second word an intensification of the first). Literally rendered it is: "at a loss but not absolutely at a loss."

3. In the third pair,[29] the first participle, "persecuted," is used elsewhere by Paul for the specific assault on Christians, whether his prior hounding of believers (Gal 1:13, 23; Phil 3:6) or his own sufferings at the

---

24. Thrall, 1.326, comments that "the vocabulary is noticeably biblical and has a particular affinity with the Psalms," but considers Paul's antithetical structure to be "more akin to the style of the hellenistic 'diatribe.' " She notes a parallel with Plutarch, *Moralia* 1057 D-E:

	confined is not impeded
and	thrown from a precipice is not subject to force
and	stretched on the rack is not tortured
and	being mutilated is not injured
and	taking a fall in wrestling is unconquerable
and	being sold into slavery by his enemies is not taken captive.

Paul, however, is comparing a lesser with a greater suffering, whereas Plutarch is declaring that outward adversity is not necessarily inward adversity.

25. The appearance of οὐ, rather than μή, with the participles is explained as due either to (1) the connection of the participles with the indicative ἔχομεν (v. 7), or, more probably, to (2) the participles being used in an absolute sense, as if they were indicatives (see also 5:12; 7:5; 8:19, 20, 24; 9:11, 13; 10:5, 15; 11:6). See further Hughes, 141.

26. Gk. θλιβόμενοι . . . στενοχωρούμενοι.

27. According to J. T. Fitzgerald, *Earthen Vessels,* 174, ". . . although Paul is 'hard pressed,' he is not pressed to the extent that he has little (στενός) or no room (χῶρος) to breathe."

28. Gk. ἀπορούμενοι . . . ἐξαπορούμενοι. Paul's οὐκ ἐξαπορούμενοι is not in contradiction with "we despaired" of 1:8; the discrepancy is formal, not real.

29. Gk. διωκόμενοι . . . ἐγκαταλειπόμενοι.

hands of others.[30] The second, "forsaken," has a rich background in the OT (LXX) for Yahweh's determination not to forsake his people (e.g., Gen 28:15; Deut 31:6, 8; Josh 5:1).[31] This is the word from the mouth of the Crucified, quoting Ps 22:1 (Mark 15:34). Here the word implies an eschatological intent; God will not abandon his chosen ones whom he has redeemed.[32]

4. The final pair[33] reflect an extremity of suffering. The first passive — "struck down" — employs a verb not used elsewhere by Paul, but in contemporary literature it means "laid low" (as by a weapon), "bullied" or "stricken." With it is contrasted "but not destroyed," which like its corresponding predecessor ("but not forsaken") has an eschatological thrust, "perishing" (cf. 2:15; 4:3). The suffering apostle will not be forsaken by God, nor "lost" from him.

The trend toward intensified suffering may be seen in the following table (my translation):

afflicted	but not	trapped
bewildered	but not	in despair
persecuted	but not	forsaken
felled	but not	destroyed

These words must be read against the background of the benediction at the beginning of the letter. While the first word in each line expresses vividly the "sufferings of Christ," which "overflow into our [i.e., the apostles'] lives" (1:5), the "but not" followed by words for even more dire circumstances expresses the "deliverance" from distress by "the God who raises the dead" (1:10).[34] This is the "comfort" God gives to his suffering messengers, which overflows from them to the people of God (1:6).

---

30. See 1 Cor 4:12, part of an earlier *peristasis* — "when persecuted, we endure."

31. This is more likely than the athletic metaphor "pursued but not overtaken," favored by Plummer, 129.

32. Is Paul hinting that, although God did "forsake" his Son for the redemption of humankind (cf. 5:21), he will not "forsake" any of his elect people, redeemed by his Son?

33. Gk. καταβαλλόμενοι . . . ἀπολλύμενοι, perhaps a military image: a soldier felled but rising up to continue the struggle, or, alternatively, struck down but not given the death blow. Thrall 1.329, suggests a possible reference to Paul's own circumstances of persecution, in which he was literally subject to physical violence, though not deterred from continuing his ministry.

34. While there are formal similarities between Paul's words and Stoic statements, there is a fundamental difference. The Stoic sage is self-sufficient, immune to outward assault. For Paul, however, it is the power of God alone that sustains. See further Thrall, 1.329-31.

234

10 To these antitheses a further antithesis is added,[35] transmuted from the specific apostolic sufferings listed (vv. 8-9) to the absolute categories of "death" and "life," thereby tying Paul's sufferings to the death and resurrection of Christ. Whereas the previous verses (8-9) were governed by "in everything," this verse is governed by "always," creating an alliterative link between v. 8 and v. 10.[36] The unrelieved nature of Paul's sufferings — "always[37] bearing about"[38] — is taken up in v. 11 by the emphatic "at all times."[39]

The sentence is divided into two parts, the latter expressing the purpose[40] of the former. The apostle always carries about in his body "the dying of Jesus"[41] in order that "the life of Jesus"[42] might also be revealed[43] in his body. The "dying of Jesus" that takes place "in [Paul's] body" is the affliction, bewilderment, persecution, and humiliation mentioned in vv. 8-9.[44] The "life

---

35. It should be noted that v. 10 continues and concludes the one sentence begun at v. 8.

36. Gk. ἐν παντί . . . πάντοτε.

37. Gk. πάντοτε, which, like ἀεί in the next verse, occurs first in the sentence for emphasis.

38. The present tense περιφέροντες with πάντοτε appears to match 2:14, πάντοτε θριαμβεύοντι, where the participle is also present tense.

39. See also 1 Cor 15:30, 31; Rom 8:36. But contrast 6:10: "sorrowful, yet always (ἀεί) rejoicing."

40. Gk. ἵνα καί. The καί is probably intensive (NIV, "so that"); cf. the identical construction in v. 11.

41. Gk. τὴν νέκρωσιν τοῦ Ἰησοῦ. It is not clear whether the word νέκρωσις — found elsewhere only at Rom 4:19 — means the process of dying (so, e.g., Plummer) or the state of death (so, e.g., R. Tannehill, *Dying and Rising with Jesus*, 85ff.). The term was used by physicians of the period for the dying of the human body (see Bultmann, 117; J. T. Fitzgerald, *Earthen Vessels*, 178-79). The context is one of suffering, suggesting that νέκρωσις is the process of dying.

42. Gk. ἡ ζωὴ τοῦ Ἰησοῦ. The repetition "of Jesus" in regard to his dying and his (risen) life serves to rebut the so-called hiatus between "the Jesus of history" and "the Christ of faith." The same Jesus who died now lives (cf. "this Jesus" — Acts 1:11; 2:23, 32, 36). The name "Jesus" occurs six times in vv. 10-14. In our view, based on the distance separating the texts, it is unlikely that Paul is here polemically anticipating the "[an]other Jesus" preached in Corinth by the "superlative" apostles (cf. 11:4).

43. Gk. φανερώθη (cf. φανέρωσις — v. 2). The manifestation of what is invisible is implied by φανερώθη, an important word in 2 Corinthians (see on 2:14; cf. v. 12). The divine passive tells us that God manifests the life of Jesus in his servants. In dispute in Corinth, apparently, was the question, Where is the φανέρωσις of divine power? The countermissionaries appealed to charismatic powers as evidence (5:12-13; 12:1-6; 12:12?), whereas Paul discerned the power of God in his weakness, i.e., in his sufferings as an apostle and in God's deliverance from them.

44. J. Denney commented on this passage: "The sufferings which come upon [Paul] daily in his work for Jesus are gradually killing him," adding "these repeated escapes of the Apostle . . . are, so to speak, a series of resurrections."

of Jesus," on the other hand, is the deliverance represented by the four "but nots" of those verses. The former (the "dying of Jesus") were endured precisely in order that rescue from them (the "life of Jesus") might be experienced.[45] There is a divine purpose for apostolic suffering, namely, that Paul might testify to God's deliverance (1:11; 4:12-15). Paul sees God's mercy in these present difficulties as of a piece with the eschatological deliverance of resurrection (cf. v. 14; see also 1:10).

This striking antithesis is derived from the center point of the Christian gospel, the "dying" and the "life" of Jesus, by which salvation was achieved (see also 2:15-16). It is not merely an analogy, however; the very "dying" and "life" of Jesus continue and are extended in time in the missionary sufferings,[46] and deliverances from those sufferings, in the experience of the apostles. It is by this twin reality of suffering and deliverance in the lives of the slaves of the Slave (v. 5), and only by means of it, that the true character of Christ's unique salvation was and continues to be manifested in the world and extended into history until the appearing of Christ. Paul's words concerning power in weakness appear quite pointed in the light of the — as he saw it — naked triumphalism of the "peddlers" (2:14-17; cf. 11:5; 12:11).

11 With a concluding sentence, connected by a "for" (*gar*) to what precedes, Paul explains v. 10 by basically recapitulating what is said there.[47] Corresponding to its immediate predecessor, this sentence, too, is in two parts, connected by words expressing purpose.[48] We who live are always being handed over to death on account of Jesus in order *that* the life of Jesus may be made manifest in our mortal bodies.

---

45. Hughes, 142, comments, "But this perpetual dying is not solely the expression of the earthen vessel's frailty. It is taken up into and transformed by the divine power and purpose, so that it becomes precisely the opportunity for the display of the life of Jesus in that same body which carries about the dying of Jesus."

46. In parallel to these apostolic sufferings is 1 Cor 4:9-13, which, however, does not have a deliverance motif, as here. See Thrall, 1.332-34, for alternative views, namely, (1) that Paul suffered as Christ suffered, in imitation of the Master, (2) that Paul suffered through union with Christ's death in baptism, and (3) that bearing the dying of Jesus is primarily revelational of the Messiah who was crucified. While in our view (3) is the only option to consider further, it does not emphasize the unity of the dying *and* the life of Jesus. Rather, Paul is saying that Paul's missionary sufferings and God's deliverances from them replicate the death and resurrection of Jesus, which he both proclaimed and experienced.

47. In effect, the final clause of the preceding sentence (v. 10) and both clauses in v. 11 in various ways make the same points: Paul's sufferings are in keeping with the death of Christ, so that the (resurrection) life of Jesus might be the more evident. And all of this is the theological ground for the opening statement of v. 7 (clay jar/God's power).

48. Gk. ἵνα καί, as in v. 10.

In the first part, the antithesis is between "we who live" (the apostles, i.e., Paul) and "death," to which the apostle is "always"[49] "being handed over"[50] in his missionary sufferings (vv. 8-9). This "handing over" calls to mind the Lord, whose "handing over" dominates the gospel narrative (Mark 9:31; 10:33; 14:10, 11, 18, 21, 41, 42, 44; 15:1, 10) and is found in the pre-formed tradition Paul "received" and cited in 1 Cor 11:23. Paul's being "handed over" to death "on account of Jesus"[51] indicates that in his ministry the apostle replicates the sufferings of his Master, "on his behalf" (12:10). For him it is "like Master, like servant." Once again, Paul is at pains to emphasize the nontriumphalist nature of apostolic ministry (see on 2:14).

The second part of the verse — as with v. 10, and in similar terms — expresses the intention of the first. It is that the "life of Jesus" — for whose sake he is "handed over to death" — might be "revealed"[52] in his mortal flesh.[53] Thus the living apostle is, by his missionary labor and affliction (vv. 8-9), "always being handed over to death on account of Jesus"[54] in order that he might experience the "life of Jesus," the day-to-day as well as the eschatological deliverance of God.

12 The initial "So then"[55] introduces the conclusion of his "death . . . life" line of thought (vv. 10-11), but there is an unexpected twist. He begins by saying that "death is at work in us," meaning "always carrying about the dying of Jesus" (v. 10) and "always being handed over to death" (v. 11). But, to our surprise,[56] the life side of the equation is no longer "in us" as before (in vv. 10-11), but "in *you* [Corinthians]." Paul dies to give life to the Corinthians.

---

49. Gk. ἀεί, matching πάντοτε in v. 10.

50. Gk. παραδιδόμεθα (NIV, "given over"), an important word in Paul's vocabulary, and used of the Lord Jesus on the night he was "handed over" (1 Cor 11:23). The servant of the Lord is being continually "handed over" to death — for Jesus' sake. "As Jesus' herald he not only told [the story of Jesus' passion], he experienced it too" (A. Schlatter, quoted by Barrett, 141).

51. Gk. διὰ 'Ιησοῦν; see also 4:5 ("your slaves διὰ 'Ιησοῦν — *on account of Jesus*").

52. Gk. φανερωθῇ, once again; see on v. 10.

53. Gk. ἐν τῇ θνητῇ σαρκὶ ἡμῶν; NIV, "mortal body." While σῶμα and σάρξ have different connotations in the NT — the former positive, the latter negative — they are used interchangeably in vv. 10-11. Nonetheless, the use of τῇ θνητῇ with σαρκὶ serves to heighten the vulnerability of the bearer of the gospel as an earthen vessel (cf. v. 7).

54. Gk. διὰ 'Ιησοῦν is rendered "for Jesus' sake" by the NIV, RSV, and NRSV. Furnish, 257, however, plausibly argues that the prepositional phrase is causal, "on account of Jesus."

55. Gk. ὥστε, which is here taken as an inferential particle, introducing the consequences of what has been said in vv. 10-12.

56. The more so since Paul does not use a μέν . . . δέ construction, which we might have expected him to do in making such a contrast.

The first clause, "death is at work," is quite paradoxical. Death is, by definition, the absence of life and activity. Yet Paul states that "death is working[57] in us," adding in the second clause, "but life [is working] in you."[58] The latter arises from the former.

"Death"[59] retains its metaphorical meaning, as in v. 11 (cf. "dying" in v. 10), for the specific sufferings of the ministry set out in vv. 8-9. "Life," however, is now to be understood differently, namely, as the "grace" of God that has reached the Corinthians through Paul's apostolic ministry (v. 15). Thus he turns the focus once again from himself and his ministry on their behalf (cf. 3:1-3) to the Corinthians themselves, for whose sake such "dying and living" on his part is carried out.

Here, once more, is the extension of the vicarious sufferings of Christ in the missionary labors of Paul (see on 2:14-15). Such sufferings, while real and serving the purposes of the gospel, are nonetheless of a different order from those of Christ and for a different purpose. Christ was "made sin" that sinners might be given righteousness (5:21), and, in consequence, reconciled to God (see on 5:18-21). Paul suffered as a messenger of that good news, that those to whom he came might have the "life" that Christ's death made possible for them to have.

While the primary reference here is to Paul as an apostle in the ministry of the new covenant, there is a consistent broader application that flows from the spirit of sacrifice of Jesus. Only by dying, seedlike, is there "much fruit," a principle that applies not only to Jesus but also to all who follow him as servants in his great missionary enterprise (cf. John 12:24-26). Although Paul writes as an apostle, it is not apostleship as such that he is here describing. Rather, it is the essential nature of his ministry as the slave of Christ, which is applicable to all believers and which Paul models before the people to that very end, that they might understand it and do it (see on 12:19).

2. The Result: Life for the Corinthians (4:13-15)

13 *It is written: "I believed; therefore I have spoken." With that same spirit of faith we also believe and therefore speak,* 14 *because we know*

---

57. Gk. ἐνεργεῖται, an intransitive deponent with an active meaning, "is at work." Furnish, 257, however, takes it as a passive, which would make God the subject, as with the (divine) passives of vv. 10 and 11.

58. Gk. ὑμᾶς, "you," anticipates "raise and present us with *you*" (v. 14) and "everything is on account of *you*" (v. 15), and echoes "if we are distressed, it is for *your* comfort; if we are comforted, it is for *your* comfort" (1:6).

59. Gk. θάνατος.

*that the one who raised the Lord Jesus[1] from the dead will also raise
us with Jesus and present us with you in his presence. 15 All this is for
your benefit, so that the grace that is reaching more and more people
may cause thanksgiving to overflow to the glory of God.*

The "So then" with which Paul began v. 12 indicates that he intended to finalize
the argument of vv. 7-12. But his twist at the end of v. 12 redirected the focus
toward the Corinthians and the "life" his ministry had brought to them. Given
the tensions between him and them over the very matter of the *nature* of his
apostolic ministry, Paul pauses for a moment to reinforce this final point.

The unity of vv. 13-15 is indicated by the conjunctions "but . . . that
. . . for."[2] These indicate (1) a new point of departure ("*But* having . . . we
believe" — v. 13), (2) whose content, "knowing *that . . .*" (v. 14), (3) leads
him to conclude, "*for* all things are yours" (v. 15).

Nonetheless, this passage is closely connected with its immediate predecessor, explaining how "life — the life of Jesus — is at work" in the Corinthians as a result of the apostle's being "handed over to death" (vv. 10-12). At the
same time v. 13 ("but *having*") also brings to a conclusion the line of thought
begun in v. 1 ("Therefore, *having . . .*") Beyond that, however, Paul's "we
speak" (v. 13) goes back to the first paragraph in the excursus on new covenant
ministry in which he contrasts his "speaking" with that of those who "peddle
the word of God" (2:17). These elements from 2:17 and 4:1, which are repeated
in v. 13, serve to "round off" the excursus at this point as an interim conclusion.

Man of faith (like the psalmist) that he is, Paul "*speaks* [the word of
God]" (v. 13; see also 2:17; 12:19; cf. 4:2-6). Such "speaking" arises from
what he "believes" (v. 13). What he believes rests on his "knowing" that the
One who raised Jesus from the dead will also raise Paul and present him with
the Corinthians to Jesus at the general resurrection (v. 14), when Jesus' universal judgment will occur (5:10). Thus "knowing" issues in "believing,"
which is expressed in "speaking."

But "everything" (v. 15) Paul does — both his "speaking" (v. 13) and
the accompanying suffering (vv. 8-12) — is "for you [Corinthians]." This is
not meant to be limited to them, however; theirs is the church he is currently
addressing. This apostolic "everything" is to the end that ever-increasing
grace might overflow through the thanksgiving of *many* to the glory of God.

---

1. This phrase is expressed by a shorter reading (τὸν Ἰησοῦν — e.g., p⁴⁶ B itᵈ·ᵉ·ᶠ
vg copˢᵃ·ᵇᵒ arm Tertullian Origen) and a longer reading (τὸν κύριον Ἰησοῦν — e.g., ℵ C
D G K L P ψ). The longer reading is marginally preferable due to the diversity of authorities;
the shorter may be due to assimilation to Rom 8:11. On the other hand, the shorter reading
is supported by p⁴⁶ B and Origen. Further variations τὸν κύριον ἡμῶν Ἰησοῦν/τὸν κύριον
Ἰησοῦν Χριστόν are relatively weakly supported.

2. Gk. ἔχοντες δέ (v. 13) . . . εἰδότες ὅτι (v. 14) . . . τὰ γὰρ πάντα (v. 15).

Thus Paul here implies two motives for his "speaking" the word of God, the one in the light of the eschatological judgment at the general resurrection (v. 14), the other for the glory of God, that an increasing number may glorify God in thankfulness for his grace to them in salvation (v. 15).

13 Paul now begins a new section[3] explaining how "life is at work in *you* [Corinthians]" (v. 12), that is, by his *speaking,*[4] an explanation he will amplify in v. 14 (God "will raise . . . *you*") and conclude in v. 15 ("everything is for *you*").

But the verse also resumes the theme of the revelatory character of the apostolic office, which had been expressed in positive terms as "setting forth the truth" (v. 2) and in negative terms as nonresignation from "this [new covenant] ministry" (4:1). By commencing the verse with "having," Paul specifically picks up these themes, in particular v. 1, which also commences with "having" (cf. also 3:12; 4:7).

The opening words, "But having,"[5] are causal in intent, and connect with the key phrase in the sentence "therefore also *we speak.*"[6] Such *speaking,* however, issues from *faith,* a linkage he finds echoed in the sentiment of the psalm that he quotes.

Thus his introductory participial phrase ("having the same spirit of faith . . .")[7] issues in the citation from the psalm introduced by "it is written."[8]

---

3. Signaled by δέ.

4. Not to put too fine a point on verbal *speech,* as though present with them; Paul probably includes what he *writes* for the benefit of the Corinthians, as in the present letter to them.

5. Gk. ἔχοντες δέ. We take this to be the force of the present participle with the (unemphatic) particle δέ. Others, however, e.g., J. F. Collange, *Enigmes,* 162, take δέ as an adversative, "Yet, because we have."

6. Gk. λαλοῦμεν, which, in critical contrast to the "peddlers" (2:17), he "speaks" κατέναντι θεοῦ ἐν Χριστῷ.

7. Gk. τὸ αὐτὸ πνεῦμα τῆς πίστεως, a probable reference to the Holy Spirit, through whom faith comes (see, e.g., 1 Cor 12:3). Despite his emphasis on the eschatological coming of the Spirit in the new covenant, Paul nonetheless acknowledges the work of the Spirit in the life of the psalmist. *Contra* Hughes, 147 n. 15, who doubts direct reference to the Holy Spirit, citing "a spirit of meekness" (1 Cor 4:21; Gal 6:1) as parallel to πνεῦμα τῆς πίστεως.

8. Gk. κατὰ τὸ γεγραμμένον, strictly speaking, is "according to what is written," a citation formula that, though Paul uses nowhere else, is not dissimilar to the standard citation introduction καθὼς γέγραπται (e.g., 8:15; 9:9). The voice and tense of these introductory phrases of citations are instructive. The passive voice implies that God is the source of what is written (divine passive), and the perfect tense that what was written is still operative. Such is the character of Scripture that God is its ultimate source (so 2 Tim 3:16), and the word written continues to speak. See further B. B. Warfield, *Inspiration and Authority,* 299-348; E. E. Ellis, *Paul's Use of the OT,* 22-25.

This is followed by the quotation from LXX Ps 116:10,[9] "I believed; therefore I have spoken." David, the writer of the psalm, had been critically ill, but God delivered him from death and to this he bears testimony. He "believed" God had done this, and therefore he "spoke" of it (see LXX Ps 116:12-19).[10]

Basing himself on the psalmist's example, but in different circumstances,[11] Paul the apostle declares, "we,[12] too, believe and therefore also speak." That the apostle "speaks" is, of course, fundamental to the apostolic ministry, as witnessed by the frequency of the verb "speak."[13] The implied object of his "speaking" is "the word of God" (2:17; 4:2), "the gospel" (4:4), "Jesus Christ as Lord" (4:5).[14]

But what did Paul first "believe"? In the sentence following, Paul will give the content of what he believes. It is "knowing that" the God who raised Jesus will raise Paul and other believers. As Paul stated earlier, God is the "God who comforts . . . who raises the dead" (1:4, 9). Like the psalmist, Paul speaks because he believes in God, and the God in whom he believes rescued Paul from "deadly peril" (1:8-10), "leads him in triumph" (2:14), and delivers him from the sufferings sustained in ministry (vv. 7-11). Above all, God has "saved" Paul from "perishing" (cf. 4:3).

It is to be noted that Paul's "we speak" rests on "therefore,"[15] which in turn springs from "we believe." In this terse statement Paul summarizes his apostolic ministry as it flowed out of the Damascus event. It is because he came to "believe" particular things about God based on that revelation to

---

9. The reader of the English Bible will find Paul's quotation in Ps 116:10, which is a translation of the Hebrew (MT). Paul, however, was quoting the Greek OT, the Septuagint (LXX), where the words appear in Ps 115:1. Psalms 114 and 115 from the LXX are combined in the Masoretic Text as Ps 116. A further complication is that the Greek (ἐπιστεύσα διὸ ἐλάλησα) as a translation of MT 116:10 is problematic because the original Hebrew is quite obscure.

10. Less likely in our view is the proposal of A. T. Hanson, *Paradox,* 51-53, that the speaker is Christ in his sufferings and triumph.

11. It is likely that Paul saw in this short Psalm (LXX Ps 115) more than a convenient form of words that he could echo. It was an apt parallel to his own circumstances. God delivered the psalmist from affliction and death, whereupon he "believed and therefore [have] spoke[n]." Paul, too, had been delivered from death (1:8-10), as well as in an eschatological sense on the Damascus Road (see on v. 6), so that he, too, "believes and therefore speaks."

12. Here, as generally throughout the apologetic excursus on apostolic ministry (2:14–7:4, with the exception of 3:12-18 and 4:14, 16–5:10; 5:18a, 21), the plural applies to Paul alone. See on 1:1; 2:14.

13. In 2 Corinthians note especially 2:17; 12:19. But the verb is used in 1 Corinthians with a similar meaning (2:6, 7, 13; 9:8).

14. See 1 Thess 2:2 — "to *speak* to you the gospel of God."

15. Gk. διό, as in the citation.

him that he "speaks"[16] in the course of his ministry. However, this pattern is not to be limited to the apostle Paul. Missionaries and pastors must, like the apostle and the psalmist before him, *first* be believers in God's saving actions for them, and *then,* on that basis, speak. Those who speak must have a firsthand, not a secondhand, faith in the God who delivers his servants.

Paul now gives two motives for what he "speaks," one eschatological (v. 14) and the other doxological (v. 15).

14 The introductory phrase "knowing that"[17] gives the basis for the apostle's "believing . . . speaking" of the previous verse. It is because of what the apostle "knows" that he "believes" and "speaks." This verse supplies a reason — an *eschatological* reason — for Paul's verbal ministry; the verse following will yield a further reason.

This eschatological note is immediately sounded in the first part of what follows (A), "He who raised the Lord Jesus." Significantly, the participle "raised"[18] is in the aorist tense, indicating a completed act, in this context occurring in the past.[19]

A second part (B) uses the same verb "raise," but in the future tense, with its object "us" (Paul, but speaking representatively). It is striking that to the words God "will raise us," Paul adds "with Jesus," as if to suggest the closeness in principle, if not in time, of the future resurrection of believers and the past resurrection of Jesus.[20] This connectedness in resurrection of

---

16. Unlike the LXX citation, where the two verbs are aorist, both verbs as applied by Paul to his ministry are in the present tense, signifying the continuous and incessant character of apostolic ministry. Moreover, in the psalm the writer spoke to *God,* whereas Paul is speaking the gospel to people.

17. The verb εἰδότες, in the perfect tense, means "come to know, hence, continues to know" and is suggestive of the moment of revelation on the Damascus Road (see on v. 6). The content of Paul's "knowing" in this context, however, is anticipatory of the eschatological judgement. The ὅτι often, as here, introduces something quoted, in this case information of a credal or semicredal character (cf. 1 Cor 15:3-5). The phrase εἰδότες ὅτι often introduces a formulation the writer assumes is known to his readers (1:7; 5:6; 1 Cor 15:58; Gal 2:16; Jas 3:1; 1 Pet 1:18), in this example the specific doctrine of the general resurrection.

18. Gk. ἐγείρας.

19. Cf. 1:9, where, however, it is "God who raises [*present* tense] the dead." The present tense indicates that it is God's character to raise the dead. In passing, we are more confident to regard the resurrection of Jesus as historically true since what Paul says about the resurrection is introduced in 1:9 and 4:14 so inconspicuously and gratuitously, as an undisputed reality.

20. Paul's interest in the general resurrection in this verse, which forms the eschatological hinge for the turning of the present and the future ages, cautions us against the popular view that Paul was preoccupied with the Parousia and its appearance before his own demise. Paul is preoccupied, not with the Parousia of Christ (unmentioned in 2 Corinthians), but with resurrection. See A. C. Perriman, "Paul and the Parousia," 512-21.

believers and Jesus may touch on the teaching in the first letter, where Paul sees the resurrection of Jesus and the resurrection of believers as belonging to the one eschatological event (a harvest), the former being the "first-fruits" of the latter (1 Cor 15:20).

Knowing that				A
	he who	raised	the Lord Jesus	
also		will raise	us	B
			with Jesus	
and		present	[us]	C
			with you	
			[to Jesus].	

The critical element in v. 14 comes in the third segment (C) with the use of the verb "to present," which, like "raise" in the second, is in the future tense. Resurrection will be accompanied by presentation. To whom will God "present" Paul (representing other believers) and "you [Corinthians],"[21] and for what purpose?

The only other use of this verb[22] in 2 Corinthians establishes that it is *to Christ* that God will "present" them, eschatologically (11:2). As to the purpose, the statement "we must all appear before the judgment seat of Christ" (5:10) suggests that it is especially for judgment, since 5:10 is followed immediately by "knowing the fear of the Lord, we persuade men" (5:11). The "knowing" followed by "persuading" of 5:11, used in a context of judgment (5:10), is parallel with and explanatory of "knowing" as a basis for "speaking" in 4:13-14,[23] where what is "known" is strongly eschatological. We conclude that the basis and motive for Paul's "speaking" are eschatological, specifically in reference to judgment.

This verse is important in the flow of Paul's argument. Whereas in 3:12, 18 he wrote representatively of the hope and transformation of *all* believers, between that latter verse and this he has written "we"/"us" as a

21. In this verse Paul's twofold σύν joins himself ("us") (1) with Jesus, and (2) with "you [Corinthians]." God has raised Jesus, and he will raise Paul; God will present Paul and the Corinthians to Christ (and, by implication, he will present all believers past, present, and future). This coupling of Jesus/Paul and Paul/Corinthians is suggestive, on the one hand, of a high view of the apostolic office and, on the other, of the mutuality between apostle and people (see also 1:14; Phil 2:14-18; 4:1). Elsewhere σύν signifies the note of eschatological reunion (1 Thess 4:17).

22. Gk. παρίστημι, which has an eschatological meaning elsewhere (Rom 14:10; Eph 5:27; Col 1:22, 28).

23. Cf. 4:13-14 (λαλοῦμεν . . . εἰδότες) with 5:11 (εἰδότες . . . πείθομεν), noting that the verbs are both present tense. What the apostle "knows" about judgment issues in continuous "speaking"/"persuading."

literary plural, referring to himself as a minister of the new covenant. Now, however, he uses the first person plural pronoun for believers in general, a universality that is picked up in 4:16, dominating the passage 4:16–5:10, and in particular 5:10. That universality here relates to the future moment of the general resurrection with, by implication, universal judgment. This, in turn, establishes the critical moment of demarcation between the end of the present age and the beginning of the new upon which the antithetical eschatological dualism of 4:16–5:10 depends.

15 The initial "For"[24] leads into a summary explanation of the passage vv. 13-14, and beyond that, of vv. 7-12. Thus various elements of this verse reiterate words and ideas from earlier verses in this passage. The *"you [for whom] all things [are]"* looks back to "life is at work in *you*" (v. 12) and to "[God] will present *you*" (v. 14). The Corinthians, as the church currently addressed, are in mind. As for the *"all things"* that are "for you," we would include (1) Paul's "speaking [the word of God]" (v. 13), and (2) the apostolic sufferings listed (vv. 8-9), which he calls the "dying of Jesus" (v. 10), "death" that is "working in him" (v. 12).

Thus Paul is saying that his speaking and suffering are for the Corinthians, in order that the increasing grace of God, of which the speaking and suffering are an evidence, may overflow to the Corinthians through the thanksgiving of an increased number of people, to the glory of God.

> For all things
> are for you
>> *in order that* the increasing grace may overflow   PURPOSE
>> *through* the thanksgiving of more [people]   MEANS
>> *to* the glory of God.[25]   GOAL

In the difficult[26] latter part of the sentence Paul explains how "all things are for you." He sets out the complex relationship between (1) his *purpose* in giving

---

24. Gk. γάρ.

25. There is a play on words, χάρις . . . εὐχαριστία, and an alliteration, πλεονάσασα . . . πλειόνων.

26. Furnish, 259, calls this half-verse "a syntactical thicket." Critical questions are: (1) Does διὰ τῶν πλειόνων belong with πλεονάσασα or περισσεύσῃ? and (2) Are πλεονάσασα and περισσεύσῃ transitive or intransitive? The complexity is underlined by the alternatives noted by Plummer, 135: (1) "In order that the grace (χάρις), being made more (πλεονάσασα) by means of the more (πλειόνων), may cause the thanksgiving (εὐχαριστία) to abound to the glory of God." (2) "In order that grace, having abounded, may, through the greater number of converts, make thanksgivings to abound." (3) "In order that grace, having abounded, may, through the thanksgivings of the greater number, superabound." (4) "That grace, having increased the thanksgiving by means of the greater number, may abound, etc." Plummer's option (1) makes best sense.

himself for them ("in order that[27] increasing grace may overflow [to you]"), (2) the *means* by which that grace becomes a reality ("through[28] the thanksgiving of more people"), and (3) the *goal* of that overflowing grace ("to[29] the glory of God"). Paul sees both his speaking and his suffering as, concretely, the grace of God.[30] In its increasing impact on them this grace overflows through the thanksgiving of a growing number of people, giving glory to God.

In other words, Paul's speaking and suffering (vv. 7-13) for them embody, but also give access to, the grace of God, in order that a greater number of the Corinthians[31] will overflow in their thanksgiving to the glory of God.[32] Critical here are Paul's words *grace* and *thanksgiving,* which are probably to be understood "vertically." Paul saw himself given for them in speaking and suffering as God's grace *down* to and among them, that theirs might be a growing thanksgiving *up* to God.

Paul longed that men and women who "neither glorified [God] as God nor gave thanks to him" (Rom 1:21) would, in ever-growing numbers, "turn to the Lord [Jesus Christ]" (3:16) and express thankfulness to God, and so glorify him. The glorification of God is the apostolic aim, but it is also the privilege and duty of every believer.[33]

This is the *doxological* motive, which must be added to the *eschatological* (v. 14) motive, for Paul "speaking [the word of God]" (v. 13), as well as the *sacrificial* — "dying" that they might "live" (v. 12). Paul now picks up again the theme of glory that had been so dominant in 3:7–4:6, which he will further elaborate in vv. 16-18.

C. HOPE IN THE FACE OF DYING AND DEATH (4:16–5:10)

While encapsulated within Paul's excursus on his apostolic ministry (2:14–7:4), this passage broadens the reference from himself as an apostle to believ-

---

27. Gk. ἵνα.

28. Gk. διά.

29. Gk. εἰς.

30. Gk. ἡ χάρις πλεονάσασα, which is here taken as both (1) that increasing grace enabling Paul to act as an apostle, including under his sufferings (cf. 1:12; 4:8-12), and (2) that grace of God, unconditioned by human worth, which underlies the salvation of God (8:9; 6:1). The verse hardly makes sense unless (1) is understood, yet so powerful is (2) in Paul's thinking that it is probably also included.

31. *Contra* Barrett, 144-45, who takes τῶν πλειόνων to refer to the majority — as compared with the minority — of the Corinthians.

32. For passages elsewhere in 2 Corinthians relating to thanksgiving to God, see 1:11; 9:11, 12.

33. 1 Cor 6:20; 10:31; Gal 1:24; Rom 3:7; 4:20; 15:6, 7, 9; Phil 1:11.

ers in general.[1] It flows out of his description of his suffering and ministry for the Corinthians' "life" now and their resurrection then (4:7-15) into the suffering and hope of all members of the new covenant (4:16-18).

Paul began to develop his teaching on the believers' hope of glory at 3:12, as amplified in the "we all . . . are being transformed" in 3:18. This universal transformation of the messianic people is picked up in their general resurrection (4:14) at which "we all" must be made manifest at the tribunal of Christ (5:10). In a word, 4:16–5:10 engages in theological reflection on his and their present and future.

Paul sets this out as an overarching eschatological contrast between this age, which is temporary and whose elements are visible, and that age which is to come, which is eternal and whose elements are as yet invisible (4:17-18).[2] The present age ends and the coming age begins at that point when God "raises us . . . and presents us" to Jesus (4:14), when we will be "made manifest" at his seat of judgment (5:10). The general resurrection/judgment is the point at which the present age ends and the coming age begins. That moment is the hinge around which those eschatological ages turn.

Corresponding to and contingent upon this eschatological dualism is an anthropological dualism. The outer person (exō anthrōpos), who belongs to the present age, is wasting away, while the inner person (esō anthrōpos), who belongs to the coming age, is being renewed (4:16). The contrast between the two ages, present and coming, and between the outer and the inner person, is the source of powerful antitheses that characterize the majority of the verses in this passage. Whereas the eschatological dualism hinges on the general resurrection, the anthropological dualism is created by the eschatological Spirit, whom God gives now as a "deposit, guaranteeing what is to come" (5:5). It is the Spirit who creates the sense that the "outer person" is "wasting away" and the "inner person" is "being renewed."

The eschatological passage 4:16–5:10 is followed closely by another, 5:14–6:2. The former passage fixes the reader's eyes on the onset of the new age, to be ushered in by the general resurrection and the universal judgment (4:14; 5:10). Meanwhile the Spirit of the future age (5:5) stirs up longing in the believer for all that God's glorious end time will bring (5:2-5); at the same time the believer is painfully aware that the "outer person" in his life in this age is withering away (4:16–5:1). The latter passage (5:14–6:2), however, has little to say about the future; its great emphasis is on the "now"

---

1. *Contra* A. C. Perriman, "Paul and the Parousia," 519, who regards the passage as relating exclusively to Paul.

2. For the affirmation of the importance of the apocalyptic idiom in Paul, against various proposals to existentialize it, see V. P. Branick, "Apocalyptic Paul," 664-75; B. Lindars, "Sound of the Trumpet," 766-82.

(5:16 [twice]; 6:2) of the cosmic reconciliation, the new creation realized through the one who died and was raised for *all*, reconciling the world to God. Here the center of history is located in the death and resurrection of Jesus, with no explicit reference to the eschatological future. Clearly the two passages must be held in creative tension if we are to retain the balance between the "not yet" and the "now," between future eschatology and realized eschatology.

It has been argued that in 5:1-9 Paul's earlier eschatology, centered in the future resurrection of all people, has been replaced by an individualized eschatology, whereby at death a deceased believer goes to heaven.[3] According to this view, which springs from the belief that Paul now expected to die before the Parousia, the Hebraic "horizontal" expectation is replaced by the Hellenized "vertical" expectation.

But that view reads too much into too little. Two responses are offered:

First, several passages within 2 Corinthians, establish that Paul had not abandoned his belief in the future resurrection of all believers. Near the beginning of the letter Paul sets his hope on "the God who raises the dead" and asserts that he "will deliver us again," which in context must refer to the general resurrection (1:9-10). Immediately before the present passage Paul declared that the God who raised Jesus "will also raise us with Jesus" (4:14). It is evident that in 2 Corinthians Paul's future resurrection eschatology remains intact.

Second, Paul is not giving a systematic exposition of his eschatology. Rather, he is — in all probability — responding dialectically to unhelpful emphases among certain elements in Corinth.[4] In what appears to be a polemical corrective of those who claim that the blessings of the future are ours already (i.e., an overrealized eschatology — see on 5:6b-7),[5] Paul insists that we are not yet "away from the body and at home with the Lord" (v. 8) but rather that, so long as this age continues, "we walk by faith, not by sight" (v. 7).[6] Therefore, to the superspiritual who say that we are with the Lord "already" (cf. 1 Cor 4:8), Paul replies that we live in the in-between times,

---

3. Notably by C. H. Dodd, "The Mind of Paul," 110.

4. For examples of othe places where Paul is responding to other concerns regarding eschatology, see (1) 1 Thess 4:13-18 (How should the Thessalonians think about deceased believers?), (2) 2 Thess 2:2 (Has the day of the Lord already come?), and (3) 1 Cor 15:12 (Is there no future resurrection of the dead?).

5. See Furnish, 299-301, for discussion of other possible false options then canvassed at Corinth: (1) gnostic longing for nakedness (Bultmann, W. Schmithals, *Gnosticism in Corinth*), (2) a bodiless existence as in Hellenistic immortality of the soul (P. J. von Osten-Sacken, "Apologie").

6. What J. P. M. Sweet, "A House Not Made with Hands," 383, has called Paul's "customary 'eschatological reservation.' "

between "now" and "not yet." "Now" we have the promise of a heavenly dwelling (expressed as "we have" — 5:1), and God has given "the deposit of the Spirit" as a pledge guaranteeing the fullness of the Spirit in the coming age (5:5); we do "not yet" have the fulfillment and realization. Furthermore, let the superspiritual who hold to an overrealized eschatology understand in all sobriety that the arrival of the new age will be marked by our manifestation in the presence of Christ, in terms of the good or evil we have practiced in this age (5:10).

Consistent with his insistence that, as yet, "we are at home in the body" and therefore "are away from the Lord," Paul canvasses the possibility that death, with its nakedness and bodily divestiture (5:1, 3, 4), could precede the arrival of the new age,[7] though this is not his preference (5:8). It would be "far better" to be "clothed upon" with a heavenly dwelling at the onset of the end time than to be found naked — bodiless — at death, "far better" to be "away from the body" and present "with the Lord." If the dead will be "changed" by resurrection (cf. 1 Cor 15:52), the living — Paul's concern in this passage — will also be changed at the resurrection by transfiguration, by the superimposition of a dwelling/garment from heaven. Thus while "we have a building from God," as God's sure promise to be fulfilled at the general resurrection, we do "not yet" have it in our present experience within this age.

How do we live in the time between "now" and "not yet"? Against possible romantic or ethically minimal attitudes from a superspiritual world-view Paul's attitude toward this "in-between" time is carefully balanced. On the one hand, there is to be confidence, based on the certainty of God's purposes for those who are "in Christ" (5:1, 6, 8). Of particular interest are the resumptives[8] in this passage — "*therefore* we do not lose heart" (4:16), "*for* we know . . ." (5:1), "*therefore* we are always confident" (5:6), "*therefore* we make it our goal" — which maintain the trajectory of hope.

On the other hand, there is the sober recognition that we "groan" with hope mingled with pain, like a woman in the pain of childbirth (5:2, 4); at the same time, however, God has given the Spirit as a "deposit, guaranteeing what is to come" (5:5). Moreover, Paul sounds the strong ethical note that believers must seek to please the Lord, in light of his judgment tribunal at which all that they have done — whether good or evil — will be brought to light (5:9-10).

---

7. The death of a member of a church was then by no means unprecedented. Already at Thessalonica and Corinth some had died since the coming of the gospel (1 Thess 4:13; 1 Cor 15:18, 29). Moreover, Paul's own sense of mortal danger was not a new experience; he had "often" been "near death" (11:23; cf. 1 Cor 15:32).

8. Gk. διό (4:16); [οἴδαμεν] γὰρ ὅτι (5:1); οὖν (5:6); διό (5:9).

1. An Eternal Weight of Glory[1] (4:16-18)

16 *Therefore we do not lose heart. Though outwardly we are wasting away, yet inwardly we are being renewed day by day.* 17 *For our[2] light and momentary troubles are achieving for us an eternal glory that far outweighs them all.* 18 *So we fix our eyes not on what is seen, but on what is unseen. For what is seen is temporary, but what is unseen is eternal.*

These highly rhetorical verses considered together form a closely argued unit, drawing together threads from previous verses in chapter 4 and beyond that from within chapter 3. Thus the rejection of despair (v. 16a) explicitly repeats v. 1, while the decay of the outer and the re-creation of the inner person (v. 16) summarizes — as well as extends — the thought of vv. 7, 10-12. The suffering (v. 17) echoes abstractly the listed specific hardships of vv. 8-9, though not now limiting them to the apostle[3] but rather applying them to all believers, while the glory (v. 17) picks up that great theme from 3:11, 12, 18; 4:4, 6. The re-creation of the inner person is in prospect of the coming age of eternal, weighty glory, which the suffering of the present time is preparing for him, provided he does not focus on what may be seen but on what is not seen.

16   The initial "Therefore"[4] signals that what follows depends on what has gone before. The earlier (and only) use of the phrase "we do not despair"[5] (see on v. 1) sets a border within which the previous ideas on which this verse depends may be sought. Thus his words, "if the outer person is wasting away," refer to the hardships of vv. 8-9 and the "dying" of vv. 10-12, while his contrastive, "our inner person is being renewed," picks up references to the surpassing power of God (v. 7), the "life of Jesus" (vv.

---

1. To preserve the force of the antitheses in vv. 16-18 I have used my own translation of these verses in the text of the commentary.

2. The pronoun ἡμῶν is included by Nestle-Aland, although missing from A, Peshitta, and 𝔭46.

3. Thrall, 1.347-56, takes vv. 16-18 as applying primarily to the apostle Paul, in defense of the claim that he lacks the glory that might be expected of the minister of a covenant more glorious than Moses'. To be sure, Paul is making a personal response to some kind of "glory theology" current in Corinth in relation to his ministry. But as he bears the treasure, the light of the gospel, in a "clay jar," so, too, do all believers. Likewise his experience of constant and progressive inner renewal accompanying outer decay is true of all who belong to this decaying aeon yet fix their hope on God's glorious future.

4. Gk. διό, which ties what follows with what has gone before in vv. 1-15, also occurs in v. 13, quoting LXX Ps 115:1, which, perhaps, Paul is here echoing.

5. Gk. οὐκ ἐγκακοῦμεν. Plummer, 135, comments that the "rhythmic swing," apparent at the end of chapter 3, is easily felt here.

10-11), and God's past resurrection of Jesus and coming resurrection of believers (v. 14).

At the same time Paul may be responding to or anticipating Corinthian criticism that the minister of a covenant more glorious than Moses' covenant could be expected to be a glorious figure, which Paul clearly is not, as witnessed by his sufferings (vv. 7-13).[6] Thus, bearer and bringer of light through the gospel though he may be (vv. 4-6), yet, in common with everyone else in the present age, Paul in his "outer person" is withering away; nonetheless, like *all* who belong to Christ, in his "inner person" he is subject to incessant renewal in prospect of the hope of glory in the coming age.

What is said in this verse — and the two following — is built on the arguments in vv. 1-15, in particular the knowledge of the future resurrection set out immediately before (vv. 14-15). Whereas, however, the rejection of despair of v. 1 was in regard to his ministry in the new covenant, in this verse it is of universal application to believers. Paul continues to speak as a minister of the new covenant, but now he also speaks representatively for all members of the new covenant. All are being transformed by the Spirit (3:18); all will be raised in the coming resurrection (4:14); all will be made manifest at the judgment (5:10); all are encouraged "not to lose heart."

This is expressed as an anthropological antithesis (cf. death/life — vv. 10-12). "The outer 'person,'"[7] which is "wasting away," is contrasted with "the inner [person],"[8] which is "being renewed." The first clause is concessive ("*even if*[9] our outer person is wasting away"), and is powerfully answered

---

6. See further, Thrall, 1.349-51.

7. The expression ὁ ἔξω ἡμῶν ἄνθρωπος (NIV, "outwardly we") is unique, describing the human being who belongs physically to the age (world) that is passing away (1 Cor 7:31). (It is not the same as ὁ παλαιὸς ἡμῶν ἄνθρωπος — Rom 6:6; Col 3:9; Eph 4:22, which is an ethical-moral concept applying to the old, unregenerate nature.) While parallels to Paul's inner/outer person are common in both Greek and Hellenistic Jewish thought (e.g., τὸ ἐντὸς ἄνθρωπος . . . τὸ ἔξω (Plato, *Republic* 9.588Dff.; see further Barrett, 146-47), Paul's categories are not in terms of psychological dualism. Rather, the dualism is eschatological, between this age and the coming age (see further on 5:1-5), and represents the reality that the believer lives in both simultaneously. According to Kümmel, "The contrast is not the Hellenistic one between the visible world without and the invisible world within, but that between the transient present age and the abiding age to come, which in hope is already present; it is in 'not yet' and in the certain hope of the eschatological fulfilment that faith lives" (quoted by Barrett, 148).

8. Gk. ὁ ἔσω ἡμῶν [ἄνθρωπος]; NIV, "inwardly we"; "person" is to be understood in the second part of the antithesis.

9. Gk. εἰ καί; NIV, "though." When taken with the indicative — as in 4:3 — it asserts the *fact* of the matter (see also Phil 2:17). The decay of Paul's outer person was obvious to him, brought home by the sufferings of vv. 7-8, which he characterizes as being "handed over to death" (v. 11). See further *New Docs.* 6.69.

by the affirmation in the second (*"yet*[10] our inner person is being renewed day by day"[11]). This is not renewal in the sense of mere replacement; it is ever-increasing renewal.[12]

Both of these antithetical elements match and develop further the antitheses of vv. 7-12. Thus, on the one hand, the "jar of clay" (v. 7), the "dying of Jesus" (v. 10), "handed over to death" (v. 11), and "death at work in us" (v. 12) are now expressed as "our *outer* person is wasting away." By contrast, the "treasure" (v. 7), the "life of Jesus" (vv. 10, 11), and "life" (v. 12) are now expressed as "our *inner* person is being renewed day by day," a theme that will be caught up in God's gift of the "deposit of the Spirit, guaranteeing what is to come" (5:5). Such daily renewal of the inner person points forward to the hope of being "raised" and "presented" to Christ (v. 14) as well as anticipating the "eternal weight of glory" of the next verse.

17 In this verse Paul turns from an anthropological/eschatological dualism to a more purely eschatological dualism, between the "affliction"[13] of this age and the "glory" of the coming age, which is to be the realm of our now remade "inner person." The initial "For" *(gar)* explains the paradox of the previous verse whereby destruction and renewal are occurring at the same time. In particular, it serves as an explanatory bridge between the re-creation of the "inner person" (v. 16) and the glorious new age that the re-created "person" will inhabit.

The sentence not only matchingly contrasts the temporary and light afflictions of this present age with the "eternal weight of glory" in the age to come, but states that these afflictions are preparing that glory for us.

Few verses from the pen of the apostle Paul come with such spiritual impact as this antithesis in which he contrasts the present age with the coming age. In the first part "suffering" is qualified by "momentary"[14] (referring to

---

10. Each part of the antithesis is introduced by ἀλλά, the first followed by and intensifying the concessive εἰ καί ("even if") and the second stated absolutely: "*but* (ἀλλά) even if (εἰ καί) . . . *yet* (ἀλλά)."

11. Gk. ἡμέρᾳ καὶ ἡμέρᾳ: "day by day" — not so much a Hebraism (*contra* Bultmann, 124) as a Greek colloquialism, though the phrase does not occur in the LXX. It implies the incessant process of remaking the "inner person" for the new age of the glory of God, as in v. 17. Cf. "I die every day" (καθ᾽ ἡμέραν ἀποθνῄσκω — 1 Cor 15:31).

12. Parallel with ἀνακαινοῦται (cf. Col. 3:10) is ἀνακαίνωσις (Rom 12:2; Tit 3:5). The force of the present tenses "is being destroyed . . . is being renewed" must be preserved. It is "a progressive process" (so Thrall, 1.351 n. 1116) rather than repeated renewal (as argued by Furnish, 261). Paul's "we are being renewed" (ἀνακαινοῦται) probably matches his "we are being changed" (μεταμορφούμεθα — 3:18); both are present tense, and both are (divine) passive: "renewed by God . . . changed by God."

13. Gk. θλῖψις, a keyword within the letter. See on 1:4.

14. Gk. παραυτίκα is used only here in the NT, but it is common in classical references; e.g., "no man among them would have given up for all the world the immediate

time) and "light" (referring to weight).[15] "Momentary, light suffering" is then contrasted in the second part with "eternal weight of glory,"[16] which is "utterly beyond description."[17] This is not to say that Paul minimizes the pain of suffering. Rather, it is a matter of perspective. Suffering, real though it is, is ephemeral because it belongs to this age, in contrast with the age to come, which is eternal.

Paul connects the "suffering" in this age and the "glory" of the coming age. The suffering "prepares"[18] the glory "for us." This, however, is not a complete statement. For that we must await the next verse's "not looking to things seen but to the things unseen." The point here is that, evil as it is, "suffering" does not overturn the purposes of God in an age that is characterized by pain and injustice. God's purposes for his people are not thwarted in the "present evil age," as Paul calls it (Gal 1:4). Indeed, under his loving hand every evil thing works together for the good — that is, the *end-time* good

---

hope (τὴν παραυτίκα ἐλπίδα) of deliverance" (Thucydides, *The Peloponnesian War* 2.62). Furnish, 262, takes it as "for the present."

15. Gk. ἐλαφρόν. Cf. Jesus' "My burden is light" (ἐλαφρός — Matt 11:30), and Paul's earlier sharp question, "When I planned this, did I do it *lightly*?" (τῇ ἐλαφρίᾳ — 1:17).

16. Gk. δόξα, "brightness," "splendor," "radiance" (BAGD). In nonbiblical Greek δόξα means "opinion" or "reputation," but these have had little impact on Paul (as in 3:7-11, 18; 4:4, 6). The background to his usage is to be sought in the OT; δόξα is the LXX rendering of Heb. *kābôd* (= "heavy"), where the manifestation of "brightness" expresses the deity and sovereignty of Yahweh (e.g., Exod 24:16, 17; Num 14:10; Deut 5:24). In this verse Paul points to δόξα as the domain of God's end time, which the redeemed of the Lord will share. See further H. Hegermann, *EDNT* 1.344-48. Paul's βάρος, "weight," is not connected philologically with Heb. *kābôd;* rather, it is set in intentional contrast to ἐλαφρόν, "light."

17. Compare καθ' ὑπερβολὴν εἰς ὑπερβολὴν αἰώνιον βάρος here with καθ' ὑπερβολὴν ὑπὲρ δύναμιν ἐβαρήθημεν (1:8). In the earlier passage Paul used ὑπερβολή to convey the extent to which he was "weighed down" (ἐβαρήθημεν). In 4:17 Paul takes up the idea of "weight" (βάρος) and uses ὑπερβολή with it twice, applying it not to suffering as in the earlier verse, but to "glory." The doubling of ὑπερβολήν is Hebraic idiom, and is used for emphasis (so Hughes, 158 n. 10). Commenting on this verse, Calvin noted, "This comparison makes that light which previously seemed heavy and makes that brief and momentary which seemed of boundless duration."

18. Gk. κατεργάζεται (NIV, "achieving"), a verb that occurs frequently in this letter (5:5; 7:10, 11; 9:11; 12:12) and in Romans, but earlier than 2 Corinthians only in 1 Cor 5:3. It implies a long process, a "working *out*" (so Plummer, 138). It should be noted that κατεργάζεσθαι appears in a "chain syllogism" (so Furnish, 262) in Rom 5:3 ("suffering brings about endurance") and Jas 1:2-3 ("the testing of your faith brings about endurance"), suggesting an earlier tradition accessible to Paul and James. This verse does not support the argument of the Council of Trent that suffering "earns" some kind of merit in the divine dispensation (Session vi. *De Justificatione* 16); the verb means "working out," not "working for," and will not allow that interpretation.

— of those who love him (cf. Rom 8:28). Only those who have no genuine vision of eternity think otherwise.

Such "suffering" has been referred to at the beginning of the letter, and denotes the pressure upon the apostle arising out of his ministry (see on 1:4). The verbal form of such "suffering" appears earlier in this chapter as the first in the list of apostolic hardships, "afflicted."[19] Nonetheless, as we have suggested, Paul is not here speaking solely in defense of his own apparent lack of glory, but he writes representatively for all members of the people of the new covenant. They, too, share with the apostle the pain of identification with the Crucified One in his sufferings (cf. 1:6; 2:15), sufferings that, however, are momentary and light in contrast with the eternal weight of glory that will be theirs.

18 The flow of the argument from v. 17 continues, with particular emphasis on the first person plural pronoun (v. 17 — "*our* suffering . . . prepares for *us*"; v. 18 — "since *we* do not look at . . .").[20] In our view, the pronoun "we," as used here, is not narrowly apostolic but applicable to the generality of believers (so also throughout 4:16–5:10; also 3:18). As with v. 17, the dualism is eschatological (v. 17 — "suffering . . . glory"; v. 18 — "things not seen" . . . "things seen").

The concluding part of the verse is introduced by yet another explanatory "for" *(gar),* which declares "things seen" to be "temporary" in contrast with "things not seen," which are "eternal." "Momentary" and "eternal" carry over from the previous verse as "temporary" and "eternal," being reinforced by alliteration, on the one hand (v. 17 — *parautika*: "momentary"; v. 18 — *proskaira*: "temporary") and repetition, on the other (v. 17 — *aiō-nion*: "eternal"; v. 18 — *aiōnia*: "eternal"). Moreover, the transference from "*not* looking at what is seen" in the first half to "looking at what is *not* seen"[21] in the second reinforces the strong sense of the rhetorical in this verse.

But v. 18 also springs from v. 16: "our inner person is being renewed . . . as we look . . . to the things that are unseen." The process of personal renewal occurs as the believer looks to things as yet unseen. In turn, vv. 16

---

19. Gk. θλίψις; cf. θλιβόμενοι (v. 8).

20. As indicated by μὴ σκοπούντων ἡμῶν, a genitive absolute construction. To be questioned is Furnish's observation, 263, that (1) the genitive absolute construction sets this verse apart, (2) so that it merely explicates its predecessor, and (3) that it is not to be taken as, e.g., causal, conditional, or consecutive. On the contrary, v. 18 should be seen as closely connected with v. 17, but so as to qualify it, e.g., in a causal sense ("since we do not look"). The NT writers are not so strict in their application of the genitive absolute construction (see BDF #423).

21. Gk. μὴ σκοπούντων . . . τὰ βλεπόμενα ἀλλὰ [σκοπούντων . . .] τὰ μὴ βλεπό-μενα; NIV, "so we fix our eyes not on what is seen but on what is unseen." Σκοπούντων . . . τὰ μὴ βλεπόμενα ("looking at what is not seen") is a paradox.

and 18 stand in parallel with "we all . . . beholding as in a mirror the glory of the Lord, are being transformed . . ." (3:18). Both passages have in common (1) an optical verb in the present tense (3:18 — "beholding . . ."; 4:16-18 — "we look"), (2) an eschatological object (3:18 — "the glory of the Lord"; 4:16-18 — "glory . . . things not seen"), and (3) a present tense verb, indicating a process, which, because it is in the passive voice, indicates that God is responsible for that process (3:18 — "are *being* transformed"; 4:16-18 — "are *being* renewed").

Comparison of this verse with its predecessor and successor reveals the following:

v. 17	v. 18	5:1
momentary slight suffering =	what is seen	= earthly tent-house
eternal weight of glory =	what is not seen	= a building from God

"What is seen," therefore, relates to our anthropological existence in the present age, in which we — along with Paul — inhabit an earthly tent-house and in which we — again with Paul — are subject to "suffering." By contrast, "what is not seen" is the yet-to-be-revealed "building from God" that will belong to the coming age, the incomparable, weighty, and eternal glory of God.

Thus, we do not focus[22] on the present time, including its suffering and disappointment. Rather, we fix our gaze — metaphorically speaking — on the glorious hope that will be realized in the age to come. As we do so, God will re-create our "inner person," even though our "outer person" is decaying.

The participial construction "not looking at" of this verse carries the idea "since we do not look at," or even, "provided we do not look at."[23] It must be read with "suffering that prepares" of the previous verse. The "preparation for us" of an "eternal weight of glory" in the coming age does not occur by a merely mechanical process through our "suffering" in this age. Rather, two activities of this age — the "suffering" and the "[not] looking to things that are [not] seen" — must be regarded as inseparable. The "suffering" of this age "prepares . . . glory . . . for us," *provided* "we do not look to the things that are seen but to the things that are not seen."

Many years have passed since Paul wrote these words to the believers in Corinth. Despite those years and the technological changes they have brought — or perhaps because of them! — men and women still face the melancholy reality

---

22. The verb σκοπεῖν means a "mark to aim at" (J. Denney, *The Death of Christ*), "keeping-in-view" (Bultmann), and "concentration of one's attention" (Hughes); cf. Gal 6:1; Phil 2:4.

23. So Plummer, 139.

of aging and dying, with the accompanying sense of purposelessness and alienation. The Greek world in Paul's general era had no positive response to the reality of death. Funerary inscriptions of the period bear abundant testimony to questioning and despair on the part of the living toward the deceased and in regard to themselves.[24] But, based on the hope of resurrection, on account of the resurrection of Jesus (4:14) and the knowledge of progressive and ever increasing inner transformation and renewal, believers — then and now — are able to say with the apostle, "having such a hope . . . we do not despair" (3:12; 4:16).[25]

2. Living in the In-Between Time: Groaning[1] (5:1-5)

> 1 Now we know that if the earthly tent we live in is destroyed, we have a building from God, an eternal house in heaven, not built by human hands. 2 Meanwhile we groan, longing to be clothed with our heavenly dwelling, 3 because when we are clothed,[2] we will not be found naked. 4 For while we are in this tent, we groan and are burdened, because we do not wish to be unclothed but to be clothed with our heavenly dwelling, so that what is mortal may be swallowed up by life. 5 Now it is God who has made us for this very purpose and has given us the Spirit as a deposit, guaranteeing what is to come.

The notion of death appeared early in the letter in relationship to the dire circumstances in Asia (1:9-10) and is repeated in Paul's account of its activity within his life in ministry (4:10-12), so that his body is wasting away (4:16-18). But, as these verses teach, death does not have the last word.

Moreover, beyond that, Paul continues the theme of the believers' hope of glory, first introduced in 3:12 and 3:18 and reintroduced in 4:14, 16.[3] He

---

24. See B. Petrakos, *National Museum*, 96-102, for funerary reliefs and inscriptions from the Hellenistic era that reflect a love for natural beauty and physical strength along with despair at the separation of death.

25. A. McGrath comments, "Suffering is not pointless, but leads to glory. Those who share in the sufferings of Christ, know what awaits them at the end of history. . . . The New Testament is unequivocal. Suffering and glorification are part of, but represent different stages within, the same process of growth in the Christian life. We are adopted into the family of God, we suffer and are glorified . . ." (*Bridge Building*, 144, 146).

1. To preserve the force of the antitheses in vv. 1-5, I have used my own translation of these verses in the text of the commentary.

2. While there is some support for ἐκδύσασθαι (D F it), the better evidence is for ἐνδύσασθαι (p⁴⁶ ℵ B C).

3. Note the structure of this paragraph:

v. 1 — γάρ, explaining 4:16-18, followed by
v. 2 — καὶ γάρ, elaborating v. 1.

expresses the strong confidence ("we know") that even though death should intervene ("our earthly tent-house should be pulled down") before the general resurrection (4:14), "we have" (v. 1) a permanent dwelling in heaven.[4] At present believers inhabit an earthly house. However, they prefer to have the overcloths of their heavenly house, a resurrected body (v. 2). Otherwise, they would be found in the nakedness of bodilessness (v. 3). For this reason those who live in tent-houses long to be clothed upon, swallowed up by the life of the coming age (v. 4). But God is the author of this longing, having given the Spirit as a deposit of their glorious future (v. 5).

Here Paul gives little guidance as to the circumstances of the believer between his death and the historical onset of the coming age at the general resurrection, though he will address this in the next passage (vv. 6-10). Rather, Paul contrasts the present anthropological mode of existence with that which is to come, and in such terms as to lift the eyes of hope toward all that God has prepared for his people (v. 1). Yet he frankly acknowledges the tension of life in this aeon, as his people long for God's future blessings rather than being found naked (vv. 2-4). Such longings are themselves God's work within them, his deposit of the Spirit, preparing them for their new mode of existence (v. 5).

1 The initial "For"[5] points to the explanation this verse will provide for the implications of the previous two verses, with which it is closely connected. In those verses Paul had referred to the eschatological dualism between this age and the coming age, hinged on the general resurrection (4:14). Paul concluded these contrasts by the antitheses "what is seen [is] temporary" and "what is not seen [is] permanent." This dualism is now picked up in the antithesis "our earthly tent-house" (corresponding with "what is seen . . . temporary") and "a dwelling from God, a house made without hands, eternal in the heavens" (corresponding with "what is not seen . . . eternal").

The strong confidence of hope characterizing the entire passage (4:16–5:10) may be seen in the firmly expressed resumptive, "*for* we know that. . . ,"[6] which echoes, "*therefore* we do not lose heart" (4:16), and anticipates, "*therefore* we are always confident" (v. 6).[7]

---

v. 3 — εἴ γε καί, giving the consequence of v. 2.

v. 4 — καὶ γάρ, elaborating v. 3, with

v. 5 — ὁ δὲ . . . θεός, declaring a final divine affirmation.

4. Cf. 3:12 — "since we have such a hope."

5. Gk. γάρ; NIV, "now."

6. Gk. οἴδαμεν . . . ὅτι suggests an introduction to a Christian teaching already known. The plural "we know" must be applicable to believers in general (see on 3:18; 4:14; 5:10); it is not a literary plural particular to Paul as an apostle (*contra* Thrall, 1.359).

7. Gk. διὸ οὐκ ἐγκακοῦμεν . . . οἴδαμεν γὰρ ὅτι . . . θαρροῦντες οὖν πάντοτε.

This is a conditional sentence ("*If*[8] our earthly[9] tent[10]-house is pulled down"[11]), whose fulfillment, however, is certain ("we *have*[12] building from God . . ."). The conditional element applies to whether or not the believer will die before the general resurrection (4:14), not to the possession of "a house . . . eternal in the heavens," which is assured.

This condition dictates a two-part structure to the sentence, each part giving expression to an aspect of the controlling antithesis. The contrasts are between (1) a "house" that is "earthly . . . tent"like and a "building from God" that is "eternal in the heavens," and between (2) the former, which is "pulled down," and the latter, which "we have."[13]

What did Paul mean by "a building from God, a house not made with hands,[14] eternal in the heavens"? The contrast with the "earthly house" in the first part of the verse indicates that it must be a *heavenly* "house." When read alongside the nearby 4:14, it appears that it is a *resurrected* "house." The "clothed upon" and "swallowed up by life" imagery (vv. 2-4), when

---

8. Gk. ἐάν. According to Furnish, 265, where "if" is taken with the aorist subjunctive ("our tent is pulled down") followed by the present indicative ("we have a house"), that present tense seems to be "the sign of an axiomatic formulation." This is a "present general" condition — i.e., whenever one condition prevails, so will the second. See further BDF #371. For other examples see 1 Cor 7:39; 8:8; 14:23; 15:36; Rom 7:2-3.

9. Paul's ἡ ἐπίγειος ἡμῶν οἰκία may echo LXX Job 3:19: "As for them that dwell in houses of clay (τοὺς δὲ κατοικοῦντας οἰκίας πηλίνας), of whom we are formed of the same clay. . . ."

10. Gk. σκῆνος. "Tent" was often used metaphorically of the human body (e.g., Wis 9:15; 2 Pet 1:13-15).

11. Gk. καταλύθῃ; NIV, "destroyed." The aorist points to the moment of death. The tent metaphor, "pulled down," is extended by the verb, which can mean "dismantling a tent," "breaking camp." The verb ἀναλύειν is synonymous with καταλύειν and appears to be used metaphorically by Paul for death (2 Tim 4:6; Phil 1:23).

12. Gk. ἔχομεν, present tense, "we have," is taken by Hughes, 163 n. 19, as ". . . a future possession which is so real and assured in the apostle's perspective that it is appropriately spoken of in the present tense." A. T. Robertson, *Grammar,* 1019, notes that "the condition is future in conception, but the conclusion is a present reality."

13. Although there is an intentional contrast between the completed action aorist καταλυθῇ ("pulled down") and the present tense ἔχομεν ("we have"), the point of the contrast is not self-evident and could refer to (1) the fact, (2) the permanency, or (3) the immediacy of having. See the text for further discussion.

14. The contrasting elements of the antithesis of v. 1 match neatly, with one exception, namely, the striking phrase, "a building from God . . . *a house made without hands*" (Gk. οἰκίαν ἀχειροποίητον). This denotes the entirely divine origin of the "house"; it is made by God. It is a biblical truth that God does not dwell in temples "made with hands" (Acts 17:24; cf. 7:48; 1 Kings 8:27-30); Christ does not enter a sanctuary "made with hands" but through a tent "not made with hands" (Heb 9:11).

We should note the interesting parallel between this phrase and the reported

read alongside 1 Cor 15:53-54, leaves little doubt that this "house" is the individual's[15] resurrection *body*.[16]

When the tent-house[17] is pulled down in death, we — each of us — will have from God a "house not made with hands," that is, a new body. This, certainly, was Paul's understanding, as he expresses it elsewhere, "the Lord Jesus Christ . . . will transform our lowly bodies so that they will be like his glorified body" (Phil 3:21).

Does this "we have" (present tense) point to (1) the *fact* of having, (2) the *permanency* of having, or (3) the *immediacy* of having in the event that death

---

accusation of the trial witnesses against Jesus: "We heard him say, 'I will destroy this temple made with hands, and in three days I will raise another, *not made with hands*' " (Mark 14:58, RSV). These allegations are sufficiently close to Jesus' own words (John 2:17-21) to suggest that Jesus did prophesy that a new temple would be raised up, even if he did not actually say that he would destroy the existing temple. See J. P. M. Sweet, "A House Not Made with Hands," 372. Mark 14:58 has a number of echoes in v. 1, suggesting that Paul was familiar with this text (or, more probably, the tradition underlying it). The repeated elements in these texts are as follows:

Mark 14:58	2 Cor 5:1
καταλύσω	καταλύθη
οἰκοδομήσω	οἰκοδομή
ἀχειροποίητον	ἀχειροποίητον

Furnish, 294, however, regards it as more likely that the similarities are better explained by a common dependence on the apocalyptic tradition of the house from God = new Jerusalem, a view we do not share.

15. Views to be rejected are that the house/building is (1) the body of Christ, the church (so J. A. T. Robinson, *The Body,* 96; E. Ellis, "II Corinthians v.1-10," 211-24; for replies see Martin, 103-4, J. Osei-Bonsu, "Resurrection Body," 81-101); (2) the new Jerusalem (so Furnish, 294, based on *2 Apoc. Bar.* 4:3 and 2 Esdr 10:40-57, which appears quite conjectural); (3) the heavenly temple of the Lord's presence (so K. Hanhart, *Intermediate State,* 160-61; for a response see J. Osei-Bonsu, "Resurrection Body," 81-101); and (4) the mansionlike abode to which the Lord's people go after death (so Thomas Aquinas, Hodge, and Tasker, who base their views on John 14:2ff.). A problem with this view is that it requires the word "house" to be used in two quite different senses in one sentence.

16. According to other references in the NT the present earthly body will be replaced by a new body (Rom 8:11; 1 Cor 15:51-54; Phil 3:20-21). By way of parallel we note John's gloss on Jesus' prophecy of the new temple, "[Jesus] spoke of the temple of his *body*" (John 2:21).

17. The source of Paul's tent imagery is debated. Possibly Paul is reflecting upon the OT relationship between the temporary tabernacle and the permanent temple building that replaced it. The writer to the Hebrews speaks in eschatological terms of Abraham as a sojourner "in a land not his own, dwelling in *tents*" who was looking for a city that has foundations, whose "builder and maker is God" (Heb 11:8ff.). As a tentmaker (Acts 18:3), as well as, we assume, on occasions a tent user, Paul had good reason to use tent imagery for the vulnerability and impermanence of the human body (cf. 4:7).

should occur prior to the Parousia.[18] In our view Paul is thinking of the fact and the permanency of having,[19] rather than the immediacy of the having. To be sure, immediacy of "having" may be implied by his "for . . . longing to be clothed upon" in the following verse. Nonetheless, immediacy would raise the whole matter of the body ("the intermediate state") between death and the general resurrection, which he does not discuss here.

Since the general resurrection has not yet come, it follows that Paul's "we have" is the language of hope. It is certain hope, yet it remains hope; it is yet to be fulfilled (v. 6; cf. 3:12; 4:14).[20] We walk by faith, not by sight (see on v. 7).

It seems unlikely that the personal, death-related eschatology, as set out in this verse, would have been new to the Corinthians, who had been taught about the believers' resurrection at the return of Christ (1 Cor 15:12-57). It is equally unlikely that Paul is here developing a new eschatology. Despite some opinion to the contrary, there are several reasons for affirming this point of view. First, the words "we know that" imply that the apostle is rehearsing a doctrine that had been taught,[21] with which his readers would have been familiar, rather than something new.[22] Second, Paul has already — a few verses earlier — acknowledged his belief in the general resurrection (4:14; cf. 1:9-10). Third, the tension between the now-deceased believer and the as yet unarrived universal resurrection is not new to this verse, but is faced in the Thessalonian letters (1 Thess 4:13; 2 Thess 2:1ff.).[23] Fourth, 1 and 2 Corinthians have a number of keywords

18. So M. J. Harris, "2 Corinthians 5:1-10," 32-57; Thrall, 1.368-70.

19. See J. Osei-Bonsu, "Resurrection Body," 81-101. Cf. Barrett, 102-3, who thinks that Paul is referring here both to his death and to the Parousia of Jesus. But the reference in context to "taking off" (5:3b) suggests death.

20. If death precedes the coming of the Lord, is the believer now "asleep" (1 Thess 4:14, 17) or "with Christ" (Phil 1:21-23)? Paul does not set a timetable of personal eschatology, so that any reconstruction is to a degree speculative. It appears to be true both that (1) the deceased believer is "with the Lord" at his coming (1 Thess 4:17), and that (2) at death he/she has "depart[ed]" to be "with Christ" (Phil 1:23). It would seem to follow, therefore, that some kind of "independent state" exists between a person's death and the general resurrection. This appears to be what Paul is stating in v. 8, "to be away from the body" is to be "with the Lord," and in Col 3:3, "our life is hid with Christ in God" so that "when Christ appears you will appear with him in glory."

21. Gk. οἴδαμεν ὅτι. *Contra* Thrall, 1.359, who finds no allusion here to earlier teaching.

22. See 1:7; 4:14; 5:11, [16]. Generally speaking, οἶδα implies something revealed, whereas γινώσκειν implies something learned through human knowledge. Where Paul is introducing new information he customarily writes, "We do not want you to be uninformed. . . ." See on 1:8.

23. According to Hughes, 161: "It is fitting that, so long as he is alive, the apostle should associate himself with the expectation of those who will still be living when Christ

in common. In both passages we find the word "unclothed," "earthly" as opposed to "heavenly" existence, and the mortality and death of the present age being, respectively, "clothed" and "swallowed up."[24] The recurrent use of such words, carrying similar meanings in the two letters, is evidence that Paul's teaching on the character of the Christian hope is fundamentally unchanged.

Death, the grim reaper, leaves none unharvested (except, of course, those who are alive at the Parousia). Everyone — believers included and with no exceptions — faces his inexorable scythe. But, thanks be to God, the believer, confident of the certainty of Christ's resurrection as founded on the apostolic word, "knows" that beyond death lies the sure prospect of "a house not made with hands, eternal in the heavens," which "we have." The God who raised his Son from the dead will raise us also (4:14).

2 A new note is struck in this verse that serves to qualify its joyous predecessor. To be sure, there is the prospect of receiving "our dwelling from heaven," which will be superimposed upon us. But meanwhile "in this," that is, our present mode of existence, we groan, longing for what the future will bring.

For indeed	A
in this we groan,	
longing to put on our dwelling	B
that is from heaven.	

The eschatological dualism of 4:16–5:1 continues, and, as with those earlier verses, uses vivid antitheses. In this case, however, the first half (A) of the antithesis repeats the corresponding half of the previous verse by using the pronoun "in this,"[25] that is, "in this earthly tent-house."

The change of tone is signaled by the intensified opening words ("For indeed"[26]) and made explicit by "we groan . . . longing." The two main verbs

---

returns rather than with the prospect of those who have died, without in any way presupposing that he would not be overtaken by death."

24. Gk. γυμνός (1 Cor 15:37; 2 Cor 5:3); ἐπουράνια . . . ἐπίγεια (1 Cor 15:40); ἐπίγειος . . . ἐν τοῖς οὐρανοῖς (2 Cor 5:1); τὸ φθάρτον τοῦτο ἐνδύσασθαι ἀθανασίαν (1 Cor 15:54); τὸ οἰκητήριον ἡμῶν τὸ ἐξ οὐρανοῦ ἐπενδύσασθαι ἐπιποθοῦντες (2 Cor 5:2); κατεπόθη ὁ θάνατος εἰς νῖκος (1 Cor 15:54); τὸ οἰκητήριον ἡμῶν τὸ ἐξ οὐρανοῦ ἐπενδύσασθαι ἐπιποθοῦντες (2 Cor 5:2).

25. Gk. ἐν τούτῳ, "in this," referring back to his "tent-house" of v. 1 and on to "tent" (v. 4). This is to be preferred to other possibilities, e.g., (1) "meanwhile" (Hughes, 167 n. 27), or (2) "because of" (Furnish, 266)

26. Gk. καὶ γάρ. According to Plummer, 144, the καί of the introductory καὶ γάρ is either (1) intensive (e.g., "For, indeed"), or (2) argumentative (e.g., "For, moreover"). Either way, the beginning of the verse qualifies what has been said in v. 1. Thrall, 1.373, however, prefers to see καὶ γάρ as a simple connective, making v. 2 parallel to but not logically dependent on v. 1. For a similar construction see 1 Cor 12:12-14.

of vv. 1 and 2 ("we have . . . we groan") convey the tension of Christian hope. As believers "we have" *now* — by God's promise — "a house not made with hands," in prospect of which, however, because we do *not yet* actually have it, "we groan." This is not the "groaning" of doubt or fear, or even of mortality,[27] but of hopeful "longing,"[28] as of a woman in prospect of child-birth (cf. Rom 8:23-25).[29]

The reason for the "groaning" in the first half of the antithesis is given in the second (B). It is because "we long to *put on over* . . ."[30] that "we groan." What is it that "we long to put on over"? It is "our heavenly[31] dwelling,"[32] the individual's resurrection body, as we argued in v. 1. This being "clothed over" with the resurrection body will occur at the Parousia, and it is for this, as opposed to the intervention of death, that Paul actually "longs for" (see 1 Cor 15:50ff.).

While this architectural image is similar to that in v. 1 ("a . . . house in heaven"), the clause "we are clothed over" alters the imagery from the architectural to the sartorial.[33] If in v. 1 we have one form of dwelling in place of another, namely, a house for a tent, here our longing is that new clothing will be superimposed on the old. According to Plummer, "The more per-manent dwelling is to be drawn over the less permanent one, as one garment is drawn over another, and is to take its place. . . ."[34]

27. *Contra* Furnish, 296: "Here the issue is mortality, and in particular the meaning of apostolic sufferings." Rather, Paul is speaking representatively for all believers, but out of his explanation of his physical vulnerability (4:7).

28. The participle ἐπιποθοῦντες explains and gives the reason for στενάζομεν: "we groan *because* we long. . . ." Paul uses the verb ἐπιποθεῖν elsewhere to express longing for absent friends (e.g., 1 Thess 3:6; Rom 1:11; Phil 1:8; 2:26; 2 Tim 1:4); the use here is analogous.

29. Parallel with στενάζειν of this text is συστενάζει καὶ συνωδίνει (Rom 8:22). Furnish, 266, notes, "it is not the sighing of unrelieved distress . . . but the sighing of pain charged with hope."

30. Gk. ἐπενδύσασθαι; NIV, "be clothed with." This verb, which is not found elsewhere in the NT or the LXX, is a double compound ἐπ(ι) + ἐν of the verb δύομαι, which is the core of related or similar compounds ἐνδύομαι (v. 3), ἐκδύομαι . . . ἐπεδύομαι (v. 4). The prefix indicates the putting on of *additional* or *outer* garments. The double compound is significant and not merely a synonym for the uncompounded word. See Hughes, 168, for examples from Herodotus, Josephus, and Plutarch. The cognate ἐπενδύτης, "outer garment," is found in John 21:7 and LXX 1 Kgdms 18:4; 2 Kgdms 13:18.

31. Gk. ἐξ οὐρανοῦ should be matched with ἐκ θεοῦ (v. 1). The dwelling is "from heaven" because it is "from God."

32. Gk. τὸ οἰκτήριον. The difference between οἰκία (v. 1) and οἰκητήριον is that the latter implies an οἰκητήρ, an inhabitant, a dweller for a dwelling.

33. According to Plummer, 145, "The body may be regarded either as a dwelling or as a garment, and here we have the two ideas combined."

34. Plummer, 145.

3 The imagery of being "clothed over" from v. 2 is repeated[35] and treated as a premise or presupposition for this verse. That is the effect of the opening phrase, "presupposing, of course."[36] Should believers be "clothed over" — as they will be at the onset of the coming age — then, of course, they will not be "found[37] naked."[38] But unless and until that "clothing over" occurs (at the general resurrection — 4:14), they will continue to groan, longing for that "new clothing." Perhaps Gentile readers within Greek culture need to be told that the disembodied state is incomplete until the general resurrection, however secure the soul of the righteous beyond death.

Once more a verse in the sequence begun at 4:16 is antithetical in character, arising from the eschatological dualism. The "outer person" (4:16) belongs to this "temporary" age, in which, however, he or she does not wish to be "found naked." Rather, they wish to be "clothed over" at the onset of the coming age.

The context dictates that "nakedness" means the intervention of death — with subsequent bodilessness — before the inception of the end time at the general resurrection (4:14),[39] when God's people will be "clothed over" with their dwellings from heaven. To be "clothed over" with such a dwelling at the arrival of the universal resurrection in the midst of our years is to be preferred to the state of "nakedness" resulting from the prior arrival of one's death. This verse establishes that Paul envisaged a state of disembodiment[40]

---

35. Except that there the verb was ἐπενδύσασθαι, and here ἐνδύσασθαι. The preposition in a compound verb may be omitted without weakening the sense, when the verb is repeated (ἐπενδύσασθαι . . . ἐνδύσασθαι).

36. Gk. εἴ γε καί; NIV, "because when." Furnish, 267, thinks that this should not be regarded as one expression; the γε strengthens εἴ, and the καί emphasizes what follows. Plummer, 147, renders it so as to express assurance, "Of course, on the supposition that. . . ." The alternative, expressing limitation, "at least if," is less likely. See further Thrall, *Greek Particles,* 85-91. The phrase is also found in Gal 3:4.

37. Gk. εὑρεθησόμεθα — future passive. While the verb "found" occurs in forensic contexts (e.g., 1 Cor 4:2, 4; 15:15; Gal 2:17), those contexts do not support Furnish, 268, who claims that "found" here refers to the last judgment per se (as in 5:10). Rather, it points to the circumstances one is in when God's critical moment intervenes, in this case the onset of the coming age.

38. Gk. γυμνός. Philo speaks of the disembodied soul as naked, "The body, the shell-like growth which encased him, was being stripped away and the soul laid bare (ἀπογυμνουμένης) and yearning for its natural removal hence" (*On the Virtues* 76).

39. So, e.g., Plummer, 148; Barrett, 154-55; Furnish, 268. *Contra* (1) E. E. Ellis, *Paul's Use of the Old Testament,* 220-21, who takes nakedness as being exposed to God's judgment; (2) R. V. G. Tasker, 79, who thinks that nakedness is homelessness.

40. There is some evidence even within the Hebraic tradition for a disembodied existence of the soul (*1 Enoch* 39:4; 71:14ff.; see further J. Osei-Bonsu, "Soul and Body in Life after Death," 101-8).

between death and the universal resurrection (so too "unclothed" — v. 4), though he does not elaborate further until vv. 6-9.[41]

Not that the "naked" are not "with Christ" (cf. Phil 2:21-23). Indeed, their lives are "hidden with Christ in God" and will appear in glory when he reappears (Col 3:3-4). The deceased believer is secure in God, awaiting the blast of God's trumpet to awaken him for the general resurrection (1 Thess 4:14-17).[42] Nonetheless, we sense that Paul shrinks somewhat from "naked-ness"; to be "clothed over" with the dwelling from heaven, to be "away from the body and at home with the Lord" (v. 8), is to be "preferred."

Paul's frankness about the undesirability of nakedness may have been conditioned by romanticism associated with a superspirituality arising from overrealized eschatology in Corinth (see on vv. 6-7).[43] To be sure, the entire passage is full of hope (3:12; 4:14, 16; 5:1, 6, 9). Nonetheless, there is also a sober balance. While the general resurrection is for the believer a joyous prospect, death of itself is viewed ambivalently. Paul's words realistically reflect that tension.[44]

4 Paul now repeats and summarizes his thought in the previous two verses. The opening words — "For truly"[45] — serve to concentrate or inten-sify his argument. We who inhabit the tent-houses in this temporary aeon do, indeed, groan in anticipation, not to be unclothed, that is, in the nakedness of death, but to be "clothed over," that the mortal (in this age) may be swallowed by life (in the age to come).

> For truly   A
>   while we are in the tent
>   we groan
>   being burdened

---

41. See J. Osei-Bonsu, "Resurrection Body," 81-101; W. L. Craig, "Dilemma," 145-47; T. F. Glasson, "2 Corinthians v.1-10," 145-55. In support of the "intermediate state" see, e.g., B. Witherington, *End of the World,* 202-7.

42. Nonetheless, the martyrs of Revelation cry, "How long, O Lord?" (Rev 6:9).

43. Thrall, 1.379-80, sees a possible continuing contrast from chapter 3 between Paul and Moses. In popular thought Moses' glory remained undimmed until his death. Moreover, according to Philo, Moses' death was "a dignified process" (so Thrall) as the soul prepared to leave his body. In face of the belief that Paul's sufferings and death are humiliating, he might be asserting the certainty and orderliness of his hope. Against this, however, Paul's exposition of hope (4:16–5:10) is not so much personal as representative of the people of God; these verses are not specifically apologetic.

44. G. E. Ladd, *Pattern,* 163, asks whether this is not "precisely the kind of psychologically sound tension that a man could express when caught in the grasp of strong ambivalent feelings? Death is an enemy; disembodiment is to be abhorred . . . but mean-while, if he must die . . . it will be all right, indeed for better, for it will mean to be with the Lord even without resurrection."

45. Gk. καὶ γάρ, repeating from v. 2. NIV has "For while."

> not that we wish to be unclothed[46]   B
> but   [we wish] to be clothed over
>   that what is mortal   C
>   may be swallowed up by life.

In the first part (A), Paul catches up once more the "tent"[47] vocabulary of v. 1 to depict the insubstantiality and temporariness of the "outer person" in the present age (4:16). Believers, though they share with all others the frailty of humanity in this aeon, unlike others, "groan" and "are burdened."[48]

Why is this? In the second part (B) Paul gives the reason,[49] stated negatively and positively. It is *not* that "we wish"[50] to be "unclothed" (i.e., in the "nakedness" of disembodiment following death — v. 3), *but* that "we wish" (unstated but understood) to be "clothed over."

It is not that such "groaning" is a merely existential, creaturely anxiety or a sense of hopelessness. Quite to the contrary, it is eschatological and full of sure hope (so 4:16). Nonetheless, the joyful eschatological "groaning" is "burdened," that is, "weighed down" by "suffering" (see on 1:8; 4:17). This points to being "unclothed" in this part of the verse, that is, subject to the "nakedness" of death. Thus bright hope is in tension with the dark reality of mortal suffering.

In the third part (C) Paul gives the reason[51] why the believer wishes to be "clothed over." Here the imagery changes from his being "clothed over" to being "swallowed."[52] The believer — for whom Paul continues to speak

---

46. Gk. ἐκδύσασθαι (cf. on ἐνδυσάμενοι — v. 3). See *New Docs.* 4.176 for a rare pre-Pauline use of a cognate.

47. The article in ἐν τῷ σκήνει is used in an anaphoric or repetitive sense ("*this* tent"), picking up "tent" in v. 1.

48. Gk. στενάζομεν βαρούμενοι, which should not be taken as causal ("we are sighing because we are burdened"), but as circumstantial ("we are sighing being burdened").

49. Gk. ἐφ' ᾧ is found in the NT only in Rom 5:12 and Phil 3:12; 4:10. Though its meaning is disputed, most interpreters take it as equivalent to ἐπὶ τούτῳ ὅτι and therefore causal in meaning. For detailed discussion see Furnish, 269.

50. Gk. θέλομεν — present tense, "we wish," agreeing with στενάζομεν — present tense, "we groan." These words are to be contrasted with the aorists ἐκδύσασθαι . . . ἐπενδύσασθαι, which point to the coming eschatological moment in which we "put off" and "put on."

51. Gk. ἵνα.

52. Gk. καταποθῇ, the compounded verb indicating a complete swallowing (see on 2:7), as in 1 Cor 15:54 — "death is swallowed up (καταποθῇ) in victory." Furnish, 270, less plausibly, takes it to mean "engulfed."

— wishes that "what is mortal"[53] (his mortal existence in this age) will be "swallowed" by "life"[54] (in the coming age).

In this verse — and its two predecessors — Paul declares his great confidence that in place of his frail human existence ("jar of clay," "outer person wasting away" — 4:7, 16) in this temporary age God will give him a substantial and eternal existence in the next.[55] Nonetheless, Paul frankly faces the possibility that the present insubstantial mode of life will end in death before the end time can superimpose on him its eternal blessings, on which he has fixed his hope.

In these verses our mode of life in the coming age is contrasted with our mode of life in the present age by three overlapping images: (1) an eternal, heavenly building in place of an earthly tent-house, (2) being "clothed over" in place of "nakedness," and (3) having "what is mortal" "swallowed up by life." Again, Paul's decided preference ("we groan . . . longing . . . are burdened . . . we wish") is that God's good future will descend upon him while he is still alive; that is preferable to the "nakedness" of death.

5 The apostle now moves to correct a possible misunderstanding of these remarks, hence his opening "but."[56] The words "this very purpose" refer immediately to the objective "what is mortal may be swallowed up by life" of the previous verse. More fundamentally, however, they point to the subjective — the groaning, the longing, the being burdened (vv. 2-4) — which gladly anticipates all that awaits us in the coming age. Such inner yearnings do not arise from within us; rather, it is *God* who has prepared us for these stirrings of hope, having given us the Spirit as a deposit. This deep eschatological longing is itself from God, mediated to us by the eschatological Spirit he has given to us at the hearing of the gospel (1:19, 21-22).

Thus it must not be thought that God is present with us only in the glorious end time, that he is somehow not present in the evil age in which believers — along with all others — now live. On the contrary, it is God

53. Gk. τὸ θνητόν. Only Paul uses the adjective θνητός — with "body" (Rom 6:12; 8:11) or "flesh" (2 Cor 4:11), where it is associated with suffering (2 Cor 4:11), sin (Rom 6:12), and death (Rom 8:11). τὸ θνητόν belongs with "things that are seen" (4:18).

54. Gk. ὑπὸ τῆς ζωῆς, noting that this construction is *personal* (ὑπό + the genitive), not impersonal. " 'Life' . . . is an action of God" (Hughes, 170 n. 35).

55. I.e., as a *body* that belongs to the present age and, as clothed over, will belong to the coming age; there is no reference here to an *interim* body. To be sure, there appears to be an intermediate state, but this is not the same as an interim body.

56. Gk. ὁ δέ. *Contra* Furnish, 270, who takes the construction as merely "continuitive."

himself "who has prepared us"[57] for[58] "this very purpose,"[59] that is, "to be clothed over . . . swallowed up by life" (v. 4), by giving us the longing and the desire for it.[60] The eschatological "groaning" — as of a woman soon to deliver her child, who is at the same time full of hope and afflicted with pain — comes from God, inspired by the Spirit, here described as a "deposit"[61] or down payment (see on 1:22).[62]

The now/not yet tension in both eschatology and anthropology is well represented by this commercial image for the Spirit. Eschatologically, Paul's reference to the Spirit as a "deposit" reminds us how emphatic he is that "the time of God's favor, the day of salvation" has come (see on 1:19-22; 3:3; 5:15–6:2). Nonetheless, that the Spirit is a "deposit" signals that the coming age has not yet physically arrived.

Anthropologically, Paul's reference to the Holy Spirit as a "deposit" appeals to the Corinthians' experience of the Spirit as a radical, life-changing power (see on 3:3), for which, remarkably, no further elaboration is necessary. Nonetheless, it is incomplete, pointing forward to the infinitely greater experience of the Spirit — to payment in full, not merely a deposit — with the onset of the end time.[63]

The passage 4:14, 16–5:5 indicates that believers are in a double but related tension between (1) existence in this crumbling age and their expectations for the coming age ushered in by the universal resurrection, and (2) the decay of the "outer person" in this age and the progressive, growing renewal — by the Spirit-deposit — of the "inner person" that points to the coming age. The Holy Spirit as a "deposit" tellingly captures this twofold tension.

57. Gk. κατεργασάμενος; NIV, "has made [us] for." On this matter see W. Trilling, *EDNT* 2.271. The aorists κατεργασάμενος . . . δούς, in context with the present-tense οἱ ὄντες . . . στενάζομεν βαρούμενοι, suggest completed action. Thus when God "gave" them the Spirit, upon hearing the Son of God preached (see also on 1:21-22), he also "prepared" them for their future by giving them — through the Spirit-"deposit" — a yearning for all the future would hold for them. The verb κατεργάζεσθαι, "is preparing," is also used, though in the present tense in 4:17, where, however, the object is "eternal weight of glory," with the indirect object "us." Such is his kindness that God prepares "glory" for us, and prepares "us" for glory.

58. Gk. εἰς.

59. Gk. αὐτὸ τοῦτο.

60. The word order, in which the subject, God, is delayed until the end of the clause (see also 1:21), emphasizes that God is the source of this blessing: "He who has prepared us for this very thing — God, who gave us the deposit of the Spirit" (literal translation).

61. Gk. τὸν ἀρραβῶνα.

62. The genitive τοῦ πνεύματος is appositional to τὸν ἀρραβῶνα and means "the pledge consisting of the Spirit."

63. "[God] has placed himself in the position of a debtor who has paid an instalment; and He is a debtor who is sure to pay the remainder in full" (Plummer, 150).

At the same time the Spirit as a "deposit" points to the faithfulness of God. Having begun his work in us, he will assuredly complete that work. The presence of the Spirit is a source of hope.

Although the precise context in Corinth into which Paul's words in vv. 1-5 are written must remain blurred to us, we sense that it was somewhat romantic, whether due to Corinthian superspirituality, or the "peddlers' " triumphalism, or some kind of union between the two. Had they faced up to the reality of death? To be sure, Paul reaffirms the certainty of the believer's hope in the coming age, of which the Spirit, given by God, is a foretaste of our Spirit-controlled bodies subsequent to the general resurrection (4:14). Nonetheless, the intervention of death must be recognized as a distinct possibility, and with it a period of nakedness, a not-yet-embodied state, prior to the advent of the general resurrection. Far better that the superimposition of the resurrection body on this decaying frame occur first. In the meantime Paul testifies to a burdened longing, as inspired by the activity within of the anticipatory Spirit, a longing that mingles the joy of hope with the tension of waiting.

3. Living in the In-Between Time: Confidence and Commitment[1] (5:6-10)

> 6 Therefore we are always confident and know that as long as we are at home in the body we are away from the Lord. 7 For we live by faith, not by sight. 8 We are confident, I say, and would prefer to be away from the body and at home with the Lord. 9 So we make it our goal to please him, whether we are at home in the body or away from it. 10 For we must all appear before the judgment seat of Christ, that each one may receive what is due him for the things done while in[2] the body, whether good or bad.[3]

With these verses Paul brings to a conclusion a passage relating to believers in general (4:16–5:10), which, however, flowed out of his personal defense of his own frailty (4:7-15). Paul's apologia for his sufferings against those

---

1. To preserve the force of the antitheses in vv. 6-10, I have used my own translation of these verses in the text of the commentary.

2. There is strong manuscript evidence for ἴδια (p[46] goth arm Origen, Ambrosiaster, Cyprian, Theodoret), a reading favored by Hughes (181) since it strengthens the retributive understanding of κομίζεσθαι, thus "in order that each may receive back his own things of the body." However, διά, as read in the greater majority of authorities, is to be preferred.

3. The reading φαῦλον (א C 048 0243 33 81 326 365 630 1739) is preferred to κακόν (p[46] B D F G Ψ); φαῦλον is a less usual word. Moreover, in Rom 9:11 φαῦλον and ἀγαθόν also occur.

who point to his lack of "glory" in ministry has merged into this powerful statement about the dark realities of this age — aging, death, and judgment — which affect not only him but all who belong to the new covenant people of God. What is true for apostle is true also for the people.

The preceding passage contrasted the present and the coming ages, while introducing the possibility that the nakedness of death may intervene before the general resurrection. In this passage Paul develops further the theme of our existence now (at home in the body and away from the Lord — v. 6) in contrast with life *postmortem* (away, out of the body, and at home with the Lord — v. 8). But if we are at home in the body — as he and the Corinthians presently are — then we truly are still apart from the Lord; we walk by faith, not by sight (v. 7). Wherever we are — at home with the Lord or still apart from him — we have one goal, to please the Lord (v. 9). As all will be raised from the dead (4:14), so, too, all must be made manifest before Christ's judgment bench, in order that each will receive back what he has done, according to his practices (v. 10).

If in vv. 1-5 the in-between time was characterized by the Spirit-inspired "groaning" of "longing" for resurrection, the emphasis in these verses is ethical. Even while yearning for the future we must still live righteously. In this hope-laden passage, where Paul expresses "confidence" that the believer will be away from the body so as to be "with the Lord," his goal is to "please the Lord." The passage ends with the sober declaration that all people — believers in particular — must be revealed before the judgment seat of Christ.

With this passage Paul brings to a conclusion his subsidiary theme of the believers' hope of glory that he introduced at 3:12 and 3:18 and that he reintroduced at 4:14, 16. Paul is powerfully hopeful about the future glory of God but realistic about the fragility of the human frame (v. 1), the pain of present sufferings (4:16-18), the nakedness of death (vv. 2-4), and the seriousness of the tribunal of Christ (v. 10). Against those who hold to a lofty and unrealistic spirituality in Corinth, so it appears, Paul brings the sober reminder that while we are yet in the body (vv. 6, 8) we are not with the Lord, and that we walk by faith, not sight (v. 7).

6-7 Paul now affirms the confidence[4] of believers as they live in the in-between time but face the real possibility of death. His affirmation "we

---

4. Gk. θαρροῦντες. Paul's use of θάρρειν is limited to 2 Corinthians (5:8; 7:16; 10:1, 2); see also Heb 13:6 (but for θαρσεῖν see Matt 9:2, 22; Mark 6:50; 10:49; John 16:33; Acts 23:11). The Stoics used the language of confidence in regard to death; see, e.g., Epictetus (c. A.D. 50-120), who declared that one's confidence "should be turned to death" (ἔδει οὖν πρὸς μὲν τὸν θάνατον τὸ θάρσος ἔστραφθαι — *Dissertations* 2.1.14). Perhaps Paul was familiar with a theme that had become popularized in contemporary culture. It should be noted, moreover, that Epictetus uses both θάρρειν and πεποίθησις (*Dissertations* 2.1.38-39), related words that also occur in this letter (πεποίθησις — 1:15; 3:4; 8:22; 10:2).

are always[5] confident" corresponds with his rejection of despair, on the one hand, and expression of hope, on the other, occurring at the beginning of the previous passages within this section — "we do not lose heart" (4:16) and "we know that . . ." (5:1). Within this section he speaks generally for believers and not only as an apostle (4:16–5:10; also 3:12, 18; cf. 4:1).

Paul gives two reasons for believers' confidence. The first, signaled by "Therefore,"[6] relates back to the previous verse,[7] to the blessed future to which the Holy Spirit as "deposit" points. The evident presence of the eschatological Spirit is a source of confidence during the present age. The second[8] is introduced by "knowing that,"[9] but, as it happens, is not followed[10] by any reason for confidence. After all, the statement following, "being at home in the body[11] we are away from the Lord,"[12] is hardly grounds for confidence. On the contrary, it is a painful, if obvious, statement of fact that "life in this world means life in exile, life apart from the Lord."[13] For that second reason we must wait until v. 8, where once again Paul uses the vocabulary of confidence.

It seems, rather, that vv. 6b-7 are a short digression. Before proceeding Paul must pause to correct what may have been a misunderstanding then current in Corinth. On this hypothesis it was written to dampen an overrealized eschatology,[14] whereby some believed that they were *already* "with the Lord" (because of pneumatic powers evident in Corinth?[15]). Paul may be saying, in

5. Gk. πάντοτε. See also 2:14; 4:10. Cf. ἀεί, "always" (4:11; 6:10).

6. Gk. οὖν.

7. *Contra* Furnish, 271, who sees this verse as picking up everything affirmed in 4:16–5:5.

8. Signaled by καί, which implies that *knowing* is coordinate to *having confidence* ("being confident . . . *and* knowing that"); so Furnish, 272. Less probably, however, καί could be concessive, "even though we know that. . . ."

9. Gk. εἰδότες ὅτι.

10. In v. 8 there is a break in Paul's construction (anacolouthon); the participle θαρροῦντες would normally be followed by a finite verb, but for that we have to await εὐδοκοῦμεν in v. 8. Meanwhile Paul addresses a tangential matter in vv. 6b-7.

11. "At home *in the body*" approximates *"in the tent"* (v. 4; cf. v. 1).

12. The verbs ἐκδημεῖν and ἐνδημεῖν are found only here in the NT and not at all in the LXX. The former, ἐκδημεῖν, is common in classical authors for "to emigrate" (e.g., Herodotus, *Histories* 1.30); ἐνδημεῖν is rare in classical authors. The antithesis here is between "at home" and "in exile." In v. 9 the verbs are used without qualifiers ("at home . . . in exile"), whereas in vv. 6 and 8 each verb has an appositional qualifier that gives meaning to the verb. Thus v. 6: ἐνδημοῦντες ἐν τῷ σώματι ("at home *in the body*"); ἐκδημοῦμεν ἀπὸ τοῦ κυρίου ("in exile *away from the Lord*"); v. 8: ἐκδημῆσαι ἐκ τοῦ σώματος ("in exile *away from the body*"); ἐνδημῆσαι πρὸς τὸν κύριον ("at home *with the Lord*"). See further W. Grundmann, *TDNT* 2.63-64; J. Murphy-O'Connor, "Home in the Body," 214-21.

13. Thrall, 1.386.

14. See on 10:7; cf. 1 Cor 4:8; 15:12.

15. See 1 Cor 14:36; cf. 1:7; 2 Cor 8:7.

correction of such views, that our present existence in the body of itself is a denial of that proposition. If we are at home in the body in this mode of being — as we undeniably are — then we cannot yet be at home with the risen Lord. Both cannot be true.

To clinch the point of v. 6b he adds, "For[16] we walk[17] by[18] faith[19]; [we do not walk] by sight."[20] The life of faith means looking not to the things that are seen (i.e., in the present existence), but to the things that are unseen (i.e., in the coming age); see 4:18. Let the Corinthians understand that in the tension of the now/not yet dispensation in which we live, believers are *now* in this age "at home in the body," "walking by faith"; they are *not yet* in the coming age, "at home with the Lord," "walking by sight."

Having (hopefully) cleared up this misunderstanding, Paul is now prepared to give a further reason for confidence in this age.

8 After the corrective digression vv. 6b-7, Paul now resumes[21] his line of argument from v. 6a, to give his second reason for the believers' confidence. This he does by repeating the verb from v. 6a, though not as a participle, "being confident," but as the finite "we are confident."[22] It is a confidence arising from the presence of the eschatological Spirit (see on v. 5). This "confidence" he expresses as his preference ("we are content rather . . ."[23]) to be (literally)

---

16. Gk. γάρ introduces a clarification of the previous statement.

17. Gk. περιπατοῦμεν is a Hebrew idiom for personal conduct (see on 4:2). The present tense indicates our "walk" during the present age.

18. Gk. διά with the genitive πίστεως here is debated; most likely it means the *manner* of one's walk ("by faith . . . not by sight").

19. Gk. πίστεως. "Faith" (see on 1:24) here must have a passive meaning, "that which is believed" (also Rom 10:8; Gal 1:23).

20. Gk. διὰ εἴδους. The meaning is debated, depending on whether the phrase is taken as (1) active ("sight") or (2) passive ("what is seen"), either of which is possible. The context suggests the need for a symmetry with "faith," noting the matching διὰ πίστεως . . . διὰ εἴδους. Hence ". . . faith, not sight," i.e., option (1); *contra* Hughes, 176. Somewhat against the flow of the argument is the proposal of Thrall, 1.387-88, who on linguistic grounds takes εἶδος to be ". . . the form of the glorious exalted Christ who dwells in heaven, not visible to believers who still dwell on earth. . . ."

21. Gk. δέ is resumptive. So Furnish, 273, against Bultmann, 143-44, who takes it as adversative.

22. Gk. θαρροῦμεν, a present indicative — possibly influenced by the finite verb περιπατοῦμεν of v. 7 — and not the present participle θαρροῦντες, as in v. 6.

23. Gk. εὐδοκοῦμεν μᾶλλον; NIV, "prefer." The meaning of the verb εὐδοκεῖν is debated. Following Plummer, 152, it is taken to mean "be content with." Thus, "it is possible to long for one thing, and yet be content with, or even prefer another, because one knows the latter is well worth having, and perhaps better for one. . . . It was better to see the Lord than to be deprived of this bliss through being in the body" (153; see also Martin, 112). Less likely in the context is "resolves" (Furnish, 273).

"away from home, out of the body" so as to be "at home, with the Lord."[24] This preference he expresses elsewhere in a context about his death, "I desire to depart and be with Christ, which is better by far" (Phil 1:23).

Both the verbs ("to be away from . . . to be at home with") are in the aorist (completed action) tense, as is the case with verbs in earlier verses ("pulled down" — v. 1; "put on" — v. 2; "put off" — vv. 3, 4; "swallowed" — v. 4). These aorist verbs point to a single moment in the future when the end time descends upon the present (cf. 1 Cor 15:52).[25] While these future references in the earlier verses are about a future, impersonal *mode* of existence ("a building from God" — v. 1; "a dwelling from heaven" — v. 2; "life" — v. 4), this verse portrays the future in *personal* terms. We will be "at home with[26] the Lord."

There is nothing indefinite or conditional about the believers' future hope. Just as Paul can say, "we have a building from God" (v. 1), so now he is confident that when the time comes for us to be "away from the body," we will be "at home with the Lord." But when would Paul have us understand this to be — at the general resurrection (4:14), or at death (5:3, 4)?

He is now referring to that state of being between death and the general resurrection.[27] To die — when the tent is pulled down (v. 1), when one is

---

24. Gk. ἐκδημῆσαι ἐκ τοῦ σώματος . . . ἐνδημῆσαι πρὸς κύριον. See above, n. 12. The meanings of the verbs ἐκδημεῖν and ἐνδημεῖν are explained by their appositional qualifiers. To be "away from home" (ἐκδημῆσαι) means being "out of the body" (ἐκ τοῦ σώματος). To be "at home" (ἐνδημῆσαι) means to be "with the Lord" (πρὸς κύριον; see on v. 6). Thus "to be away," "out of the body" means being "at home with the Lord." Here Paul is speaking of the believer's intermediate state between death and the general resurrection. To die, expressed as "away, out of the body," also means to be "at home with the Lord."

25. *Contra* Furnish, 274, who takes the aorists ἐκδημῆσαι and ἐνδημῆσαι in an ingressive sense, emphazing the beginning of the action, "leaving home . . . to get on home." The context, however, points to a new state of being rather than movement toward.

26. Gk. πρὸς τὸν κύριον means "face-to-face converse with" the Lord (so John 1:1, 2); less likely is "moving toward" the Lord (so Furnish, 274). Plummer, 152, comments, "Even the possibility of being left 'naked' *(gymnos)* for a time loses its terrors, when it is remembered that getting away from the temporary shelter means getting home to closer converse with the Lord."

27. Thrall, 1.389-92, while accepting the fact that ἐκδημῆσαι ἐκ τοῦ σώματος points to death, argues that ἐνδημῆσαι πρὸς τὸν κύριον follows immediately upon it. In her view Paul's "we have a house not made with hands" follows immediately upon the moment when the "tent is pulled down" (5:1). But in her view this is not a disembodied state ("nakedness"), but perhaps some kind of "spiritual body" that is subject to postmortem transformation, in anticipation of the resurrection body at the Parousia. Paul, indeed, affirms that upon death the believer is "at home with the Lord,"/"with Christ" (Phil 1:23) and that "our life is hid with Christ in God" (Col 3:3). However, he is silent as to the mode of our existence between death and the general resurrection. A postmortem view of transformation could lead to some theory of purgatory.

found naked (v. 3) — is expressed here as being "away, out of the body," which, however, means to be "at home with the Lord." Until the general resurrection it is a body-less state (lit. "out of the body"[28]). Here is a tension of some magnitude. On the one hand, death means being "found naked . . . unclothed" (vv. 3, 4); yet it also means "being at home with the Lord." Death, therefore, while being shrunk from on account of its "nakedness," is also able to be embraced with great anticipation, for it will mean being "with the Lord," or, as he will say elsewhere, "with Christ" (Phil 1:23).[29]

Two factors give the believer an immediate and urgent hope, notwithstanding the real possibility of death preceding the onset of the coming age. One is that God, who "has raised the Lord Jesus from the dead . . . will also raise us . . . present us [at the judgment seat]" (4:14; 5:10). The dead will not remain dead: "The trumpet will sound, and the dead will be raised imperishable" (1 Cor 15:52). The other is that God has given us his Spirit as a deposit, guaranteeing the fullness of the blessings of the coming age (v. 5).

Nonetheless, the passage vv. 2-9, in which Paul frankly faces the real possibility of death intervening before the resurrection, expresses some ambivalence. On the one hand, there is a sense of burden in prospect of the nakedness of disembodiment (vv. 3-4). But on the other, there is a confident preference to be "out of the body" so as to be "at home with the Lord." By analogy, a chronically ill person may be apprehensive of the surgery that is in prospect, yet full of hope for the restoration of health that will result from it.

9 In this verse Paul concludes his discussion about the two modes of existence, "whether at home" (with the Lord) or "whether[30] away" (here in the body) that he began in the previous verse. How is the believer to live in these modes of being?

Verses 6-8 began with "Therefore," and introduced the note of "confidence." This verse begins with "Accordingly,"[31] but speaks of "pleasing [the Lord]," and runs on into the universal judgment mentioned in the next verse.

The verbs in v. 9 have no appositional qualifiers, unlike vv. 6 and 8. Thus the precise meaning of "at home" and "away from home" can only be inferred from a previous verse, whether v. 6 or v. 8. Since the flow of the argument reached a conclusion in the previous verse, it is reasonable to take that verse as the key to this one. In v. 8 Paul's preference was to be "away,

---

28. Gk. ἐκ τοῦ σώματος.

29. Gk. εἰς τὸ ἀναλῦσαι καὶ εἶναι σὺν Χριστόν.

30. Gk. εἴτε . . . εἴτε, a construction used to conclude a point (e.g., 1 Cor 12:26; 15:11).

31. Gk. διὸ καί, springing from v. 8, an inference that is self-evident.

out of the body" so as to be "at home with the Lord." Thus to be "at home"[32] in v. 9 means to be at home "with the Lord" — the believer's true destiny — while to be "away from home"[33] would mean "away from the Lord" (cf. v. 6), that is, still here in the present mode of existence.[34] Nonetheless, wherever we are, whether there or here, "we make it our goal[35] to please [the Lord]."

Paul does not say how we "please the Lord" while "at home with" him.[36] Perhaps this is stated for rhetorical reasons, to preserve the symmetry begun in v. 6. But we are in no doubt how to please him while we are away from him, that is, in the present mode of being. The determination to "please [the Lord]" here and now is in light of the next verse, where the eschatological judgment is according to what we "practice" whether "good" or "evil." To "please the Lord" well summarizes the Christian's life, and is to be understood as doing good and avoiding evil.[37] There is no hint, however, that the believers' motive in pleasing the Lord is to accumulate merit or dominical favor. Such an idea would be at odds with the "confidence" already expressed (vv. 6, 8; cf. v. 1). Rather, it is a desire that springs from the joyous prospect of being "with the Lord" (v. 8) and reflects true conversion; one always wishes to please the one he or she loves.

10 This notable verse, while serving as a climax to the sequence of verses begun at 4:16, beyond that also echoes the "we all" of 3:18.[38] More immediately, however, it is connected with the previous verse, to which it is joined by "for" *(gar);* it supplies the reason why believers aim "to please the Lord" (v. 9). This is because "we all" must be revealed before[39] the

32. Gk. ἐνδημοῦντες.

33. Gk. ἐκδημοῦντες.

34. The verbs ἐνδημοῦντες and ἐκδημοῦντες are in the present tense as in v. 6, as opposed to the aorist forms in v. 8. They are not ingressive, "staying" or "leaving" (i.e., *dying*), but point to states of being (so Plummer, 155).

35. Gk. φιλοτιμούμεθα. The verb literally means "love honor," and is found elsewhere in the NT only at 1 Thess 4:11 and Rom 15:20. It is helpful to see this verb as the positive counterfoil to "not focusing our attention on the things seen" (4:18); rather, we set our sight on pleasing him in light of the coming age when we will be "at home with" him.

36. Since the judgment (v. 10) is in light of one's life, whether good or evil, so that the motive for this life is "to please the Lord," it is inconceivable that we would seek to, or, indeed, have the need to, please the Lord after the judgment, since it would be in the past.

37. For the notion εὐάρεστος τῷ θεῷ/τῷ κυρίῳ, see LXX Gen 6:9; 17:1; Rom 12:1-2; 14:18; Phil 4:18; Col 3:20; Eph 5:10; Heb 13:21.

38. Gk. τοὺς . . . πάντας ἡμᾶς here means "the sum total of us all." Cf. ἡμεῖς . . . πάντας (3:18).

39. Gk. ἔμπροσθεν, a synonym for κατέναντι (see 2:17; 12:19).

Messiah's tribunal. The second part of the verse (B), introduced by "that,"[40] gives the reason for the first part (A). It is that "each" may receive (back) from the Lord whatever is appropriate, according to the good or evil practiced during one's lifetime.

> A For
>   we all
>   must be revealed
>   before the judgment seat of Christ
> B *that*
>   each may receive the things [he has done]
>   through his body
>   according the things he has done,
>   whether good
>   or   evil.

The tenses of the matching verbs in each half of the verse ("revealed . . . receive") are aorists, corresponding with other aorists — or single action verbs — from this passage (vv. 1, 2, 3, 4, and 8[41]), and point to the future eschatological moment, which will bring the present aeon to an end. That moment is the occasion of the general resurrection of the dead, to which Paul referred at the threshold of this passage, at which God will present those he has raised to Jesus (see on 4:14). Although both 4:14 and 5:10 imply the universality, respectively, of resurrection and judgment — and so point on to the universal application of God's salvation ("all . . . the world" — 5:14, 19) — the focus of these verses is on the resurrection and judgment of *believers* ("raise *us* with *you* [Corinthians] . . . *we all* . . . before . . . the judgment seat"). All the new covenant people are being glorified; all will be raised; all will be judged.

In the first part of this verse we have the important verb "to be revealed," or "to be made visible," the passive form implying[42] "be revealed *by God,*" suggesting the revelation of what had previously been hidden. Specifically, what must be revealed are "the things [each has done] through his body," as in the second part of the verse. Believers not only have a divinely made appointment with Christ as judge,[43] but it is one at which each will be

---

40. Gk. ἵνα.

41. Gk. καταλυθῇ (v. 1); ἐπενδύσασθαι (v. 2); ἐνδυσάμενοι (v. 3); ἐκδύσασθαι . . . ἐπενδύσασθαι . . . καταπόθη (v. 4); ἐκδημῆσαι . . . ἐνδημῆσαι (v. 8).

42. The verb φανερωθῆναι, "to be made manifest," is a divine passive; God is the subject. For other references to φανεροῦν within 2 Corinthians see 2:14; 3:3, 4; 4:10, 11; 5:11; 7:12; 11:6 (cf. φανέρωσις — 4:2); see also 1 Cor 4:5.

43. Cf. John 5:22, 27; 9:39; Acts 10:42; 17:31.

carefully scrutinized and his deeds revealed to him. The word "must"[44] is regularly used for actions decreed by God, powerfully strengthening the divinely ordained and unavoidable character of the occasion.

The imagery used here for the future moment of eschatological revelation is that of the forensic process whereby the Roman governor sat on his tribunal[45] to hear accusation and defense of an accused person standing before him. If he judged the accused guilty, the governor would order immediate punishment.[46] Paul's use of this language to the Corinthians may have been calculated; he himself had stood accused before the Roman governor Gallio in the Corinthian *agora* some years earlier (Acts 18:12, 16-17), as the original members of the Corinthian church doubtless remembered.

In the second part of the verse, Paul speaks of what "each" will "receive," or, more accurately, "receive back as his due."[47] What will be revealed, and for which reward and punishment will be given, relates to "the things [each has done[48]] through the body,"[49] that is, during his lifetime during the present "now . . . not yet" dispensation. "The things [done]" is expanded upon and qualified by "in proportion to[50] what he has done, whether good or evil." The very things that we do, these we receive back.

Christ's judgment will be universal and dispassionate, including, in the first instance, the totality of his own people ("we all . . . each"). It is not, however, a judgment "*en masse,* or in classes, but one by one, in accordance with individual merit."[51]

---

44. Gk. δεῖ. See, e.g., 1 Cor 15:25, 53. "A divine decree which cannot be evaded" (Plummer, 156).

45. Gk. βῆμα. A parallel passage — "we shall all stand before the judgment seat of God" (Rom 14:10) — implies an identity of function of Christ and God; God judges and Christ judges. The NT often refers to Christ as God's appointed judge, appropriate to his role as Son of Man, as in Dan 7:13, 14, 26-27 (e.g., John 5:22, 27; 9:39; Matt 25:31-32; Acts 10:42; 17:31; cf. Rev 20:11-15).

46. Jesus stood before the βῆμα of Pilate (Matt 27:19; John 19:13).

47. Gk. κομίσηται, "receive back"; NIV, "receive." The middle voice carries the idea of reward or recompense (so BAGD). For similar judgment usage see Eph 6:8; Col 3:25. Examples of this meaning of κομίζεσθαι from the papyri are set out in MM 2.a.

48. Gk. ἃ ἔπραξεν, "with reference to what he did"; NIV, "what is due . . . for." The aorist or completed action tense points to what each *did* during his or her lifetime, summed up as a total.

49. Gk. διὰ τοῦ σώματος, "through the body" (cf. NIV, "while in the the body"), may be temporal ("during his bodily lifetime" — Plummer, 158), equivalent to the whole of one's life in the present "now . . . not yet" eschatological dispensation.

50. Gk. πρὸς ἃ ἔπραξεν. Citing Wis 1:1-6, 8, 11; 4:20-21; 6:7 in particular, K. R. Snodgrass, "Romans 2," 72-83, argues that judgment according to works was a doctrine basic to Judaism. Snodgrass finds this doctrine echoed at many places within the NT, including elsewhere in Paul (see below, n. 52).

51. Plummer, 157.

But in view of Paul's confidence (1) that those "in Christ" are reconciled to God as forgiven and "righteous" in him (5:19, 21; cf. 3:9), and (2) that they are assured that they "have a building from God" at the onset of the end time (v. 1), how is it that "each [will] receive the things [he has done] through his body according the things he has done, whether good *or evil*"? Clearly, the two positions — God-given salvation (see, e.g., Rom 3:21-31; 5:1-11; Gal 5:4) and the judgment of each according to his works (see, e.g., Rom 2:6-11; 14:10; 1 Cor 14:13; Eph 6:8; Col 3:25; cf. Matt 16:27; 1 Pet 1:17; Rev 2:23; 20:12; 22:12) — were reconcilable to Paul.

One resolution that is to be rejected is that believers are saved through Christ at the time of their incorporation into him but are kept "in" that salvation by their works.[52] Logically this means that they will be excluded at the judgment if they do not fulfill the law well enough.[53] But this would be to suggest that believers enjoy the justification of God only at the point of initial faith in Christ, after which they must, by their own efforts, secure salvation, an outcome that must therefore remain uncertain until the judgment. This view is at odds with the main lines of Paul's thought (see, e.g., Rom 8:1; Gal 3:1-5; 5:3; 6:13; Eph 2:8-9), not least in the next passage, where the apostle writes so conclusively about God's reconciliation of "all"/"the world" to himself through the one who died for all to enable believers to become the righteousness of God in him (5:14-21).

A more consistent explanation would be that believers do not face condemnation at Christ's tribunal (see Rom 5:16, 18; 8:1) but rather *evaluation* with a view to the Master's commendation given or withheld (1 Cor 3:10-15; 4:5; cf. Luke 12:42-48). Perhaps, too, they will receive back within themselves

---

52. Classically stated by E. P. Sanders, *Paul and Palestinian Judaism:* "at the point at which many have found decisive contrast between Paul and Judaism — grace and works — Paul is in agreement with Palestinian Judaism . . . salvation is by grace but judgment is according to works; works are the condition of remaining 'in,' but they do not earn salvation" (543; cf. 112). Also N. T. Wright, "Paul of History," 82-83. See, in reply, R. H. Gundry, "Grace": "Sanders' bisection of getting in and staying in cuts a line through Paul's religion where the pattern shows a whole piece of cloth" (12). For a review of attempts to reconcile justification by faith/judgment by works — by K. Donfried (salvation lost by gross abuse), E. P. Sanders (works a condition of "staying in"), N. M. Watson (warnings of judgment contextually addressed to those who needed to hear it at the time) and K. R. Snodgrass (God does not require perfection; the justified who are obedient will be saved) — see P. T. O'Brien, "Justification in Paul," 69-95.

53. According to Thrall, 1.395, "one cannot rule out the possibility that Paul envisaged an adverse, punitive recompense for sinful Christians which might conceivably threaten their salvation. Salvation is a matter of grace, not to be secured by good works, but grace may be received in vain" (6:1). However, one does not have to go beyond the First Letter to find an assurance of the God-given perseverance of the saints (see 1 Cor 1:8; cf. 1 Thess 3:13; Phil 1:6).

elements of what they had practiced in the body (so 5:10), as eternal reminders that they had been saved through God's mercy, and not by their own efforts. Those "outside Christ" face the sinners' judgment; on the other hand, those "in Christ" face his judgment bench as saints.

The teaching about the judgment seat before which all believers must come reminds us that we have been saved, not for a life of aimlessness or indifference, but to live as to the Lord (see 5:15). This doctrine of the universality of the judgment of believers preserves the moral seriousness of God. It is quite possible that some at Corinth held to a superspirituality associated with an overrealized eschatology leading to a less than earnest approach to their responsibilities during the present age. Paul may be reminding them that so long as they are in this body, they are not yet with the Lord (v. 6). Further, he is emphasizing that while they are in the body it should be their aim to please the Lord. The sure prospect of the judgment seat reminds the Corinthians — and all believers — that while they are righteous in Christ by faith alone, the faith that justifies is to be expressed by love and obedience (Gal 5:6; Rom 1:5), and by pleasing the Lord (v. 9). Our "confidence" that we will be "with the Lord" (v. 8) is to be held in tension with the "fear of the Lord" (v. 11), from which we serve him. Confidence, while real, does not empty service of sobriety (see on 5:14-15).

D. MINISTERS OF GOD (5:11–7:1)

1. Paul's Ministry: A Basis of Pride (5:11-13)

> 11 *Since, then, we know what it is to fear the Lord, we try to persuade men. What we are is plain to God, and I hope it is also plain to your conscience.* 12 *We are not trying to commend ourselves to you again, but are giving you an opportunity to take pride in us, so that you can answer those who take pride in what is seen rather than in what is in the heart.* 13 *If we are out of our mind, it is for the sake of God; if we are in our right mind, it is for you.*

This short passage serves to reintroduce the major theme of new covenant ministry (2:14–7:4) that Paul broke off in 4:14 and 16 to speak also about the circumstances of believers in general. From now until the end of the excursus on his apostolic office, however, Paul will focus on his ministry as an apostle. These verses lay the foundation for all that will follow.

The dominant idea in the previous verse, "the judgment seat of Christ," is carried forward by the transitional "since, then," to this statement, "we know what it is to fear the Lord." Beyond that, however, the words "we persuade men" echo a number of earlier "speaking" passages: "through us [God] spreads . . . the knowledge [of Christ]" (2:14); "in Christ we speak" (2:17; cf. 12:19); and "we also believe and therefore speak" (4:13).

Because he knows what it means to fear the Lord — based on the Lord's coming judgment of all — Paul actively seeks to persuade people[1] to turn to Christ. But he does this aware that he is known by God, and, he hopes, also to the consciences of the Corinthians. Not, he hastens to add, that he is commending himself to them. Rather, by reminding them of this ministry, he is giving them an opportunity for rightful pride in him so that they might have something to say to those who, he says, boast in appearances rather than inner reality. For this reason, let them understand that if he is "beside himself," it is for God, whereas if he is "self-controlled," it is for them.

Three things are happening in this short passage.

First, Paul is defending himself to the Corinthians ("to you") against outsiders ("those who take pride in what is seen rather than in what is in the heart" — v. 12c). These shadowy opponents, we infer, are claiming (1) that Paul is self-commended (v. 12a), and (2) that his ministry is in some way inadequate or inferior (v. 12b).

Second, Paul sets out his ministry in relationship with God. He is known to God (v. 11). His ecstatic behavior (v. 13a) is for the God who knows the heart (v. 12c).

Third, Paul is arguing for the legitimacy of his ministry, not directly, as it were — for that would be self-commendation — but indirectly, in terms of the character of his ministry. He devotes himself to the persuasion of people in view of the fear of the Lord's judgment; and he does so in a self-controlled way, for the benefit of the Corinthians.

But who are "those" who must be answered at this time? For two reasons it seems likely that he is referring to the "peddlers," introduced in 2:17–3:1: (1) his present denial of self-commendation points back to his original denial, which occurred in the passage where the "peddlers" appear in the letter (3:1; cf. 4:2); (2) his confident tone regarding his ministry resembles his assertion of his "sufficiency" in ministry, which also occurs first in a passage where the "peddlers" appear (2:16; 3:6). This, in turn, may relate to his rejection of the proposition that he is "inferior" to the "superlative" apostles (11:5; 12:11). (In our view the "superlative" apostles *are* the "peddlers.")

There is an important message here for the Corinthians. They must not get their bases of assessment mixed. The evaluation of ministry is to be sought in the public realm, not the private. If in private he is "beside himself," this

---

1. Gk. ἀνθρώπους is inclusive, "men and women."

is "for God" and does not bear on his legitimacy as an apostolic minister. In any case, he stands as revealed and open to God now as he will on the day of judgment, before the bench of Christ. Let the Corinthians understand that in the public realm — where judgments about ministry are properly made — his ministry can sustain their scrutiny.

The centerpiece of these verses is the claim "we persuade men [and women]." In these words the fundamental evangelistic and revelatory character of the apostolic office is once more in view. Paul's "we persuade" must be seen as repeating such notions as "setting forth the truth plainly" (4:2), "God . . . made his light shine in our hearts to shine forth [for others] the light of the knowledge of the glory of God . . ." (4:6), and "we . . . speak" (4:13; cf. 2:17; 12:19), and anticipates his "God . . . making his appeal through us" (5:20). Given the divine origin of the apostolic revelation and ministry (2:17; 4:2; 5:20), it is appropriately given in public with a right mind, intelligibly, and not in esoteric and bizarre language.

11 The initial "Since, then"[2] introduces "knowing the fear of the Lord,"[3] which follows directly from judgment by Christ in the previous verse. It also signals a resumption of Paul's excursus of apostolic ministry begun at 2:14, broken off at 4:16, and which will now continue through to the end of the entire passage (7:4). Thus v. 11 lays the foundation for the tightly argued exposition, as he now takes it up again.

The verse is expressed in two sentences, of which the the first (A) serves as the basis for the "hope" he expresses in the second (B).

A Knowing, therefore,
   the fear of the Lord

                  we persuade   men,
                  but we are manifest   to God.

B   And I hope [we are] manifested also to your consciences.

The first sentence commences with "knowing,"[4] which usually signifies an element of well-understood Christian "knowledge" in his readers to which the apostle is now appealing (see on 5:1; cf. 1:7; 4:14; 5:6). This "knowledge" Paul now states as "the fear of the Lord" (cf. v. 8), that is, of Christ's judgment

---

2. Gk. οὖν.

3. Gk. τὸν φόβον τοῦ κυρίου is the objective genitive: "the fear directed towards the Lord." Furnish, 306, takes "the Lord" here to be God, not the Lord Jesus. To be sure, the phrase "the fear of the Lord" relates to that "fear" often referred to in OT Wisdom literature (cf. Job 28:28; Eccl 12:13; Prov 9:10). But this does not necessarily define the use in this context. The οὖν that follows immediately the judicial bench of Christ in v. 10 demands that the "fear" relate to Christ.

4. Gk. εἰδότες.

of his servants, like the apostle Paul. With this "fear"[5] as a motive, Paul declares that he[6] "persuades,"[7] that is, evangelizes,[8] "men" (see v. 14, "the love of Christ compels us," for a related motive for evangelism). Here Paul is alluding to his sense of accountability[9] to the Lord, who called him to be the apostle to the Gentiles and entrusted him with that "stewardship" (cf. 1 Cor 4:1; 9:16-17; Col 1:25; Eph 1:10; 3:2, 9).[10] He then declares, "but we are manifest to *God,*"[11] in contrast with "we persuade *men.*"

The message of the first sentence is clear. If Paul's apostolicity will be revealed before the judgment bench of Christ (v. 10), he also understands

5. Such "fear" does not relate to condemnation, which is abolished for those "in Christ" (Rom 8:1), but to commendation, or, rather, to the absence of it. See on v. 10.

6. As he does in the entire passage about apostolic ministry, Paul uses the apostolic plural, but it is in reference to his own ministry (see on 1:1; 2:14).

7. Gk. πείθομεν, a present tense perhaps understood as a conative, "attempts to persuade," signifying the incompleteness of the persuading.

8. The view taken here that πείθειν = εὐαγγελίζεσθαι is not shared by the majority of commentators. They argue that Paul does not use the word elsewhere in this sense (see, e.g., Gal 1:10). Plummer (169-70), Hughes (186), and Bultmann (147) view Paul's πείθομεν ἀνθρώπους as answering a Corinthian criticism that Paul is adept at persuading people but that he cannot deceive God. Furnish, 306, proposes that Paul is answering those who accuse him of devious persuasion. On this view Paul must here "persuade" others of his sincerity as an apostle, and to that end he points out that he is already open to God.

In favor of πείθειν = εὐαγγελίζεσθαι we note that (1) such an understanding is consistent with the declaratory character of the pioneer minister of the new covenant as expressed earlier: τῇ φανερώσει τῆς ἀληθείας (4:2); θεὸς . . . ἔλαμψεν ἐν ταῖς καρδίαις πρὸς φωτισμόν (4:6); (2) πείθειν, though not used by Paul for evangelism, is used of Paul evangelizing in the Acts of the Apostles (Acts 17:4; 18:4; 19:8, 26; 26:28; 28:23); (3) the flow of the argument from "judgment seat" (v. 10) to "fear of the Lord" makes it more likely that he is speaking about evangelism and less likely that he is defending his integrity, especially when he devotes the second part of the verse to that end ("I hope [we are] manifested also to your consciences . . ."), and (4) a mere assertion of the defense of his sincerity is not of itself "an answer" to his detractors as in the next verse; some concrete activity — most cogently evangelism — is implied there.

It should be noted that Martin, 121, following Denney, regards πείθομεν ἀνθρώπους as a nuanced reference to both evangelism and Paul's personal defense.

9. A "consciousness of responsibility" (so Bultmann, 146). However, Christ's judgment of *sinners* ("objects of wrath" — Eph 2:3), in addition to his judgment of his servants, is probably also intended.

10. As paralleled in 2 Cor 5:18-19: "God gave us the ministry of reconciliation . . . entrusted to us the word of reconciliation."

11. Gk. θεῷ δὲ πεθανερώμεθα. The rhetorical character of the first sentence should be noted: (1) there is an antinomy — ἄνθρωποι and θεός are juxtaposed; "If we persuade [= evangelize] *men,* we are revealed to *God,*" and (2) there is alliteration — πείθομεν . . . πεφανερώμεθα. The perfect tense πεφανερώμεθα is variously understood, whether as a present (Héring, 41) or, more probably, as a true perfect (Plummer, 168): "his character has been, and still is, laid bare."

that his ministry stands revealed to God now (cf. 2:17; 4:2; 12:19). Let the Corinthians understand that Paul exercises his evangelistic ministry knowing that all he is and all he does is "open" to the omniscient One. "As a man is in his conscience, so is he before God."[12] Every day in the life of the apostolic minister is judgment day.

In the second sentence (B) Paul carries forward the idea of "being revealed." Now, however, it not to God but to the "consciences" — the moral understanding[13] — of the Corinthians that he "hopes"[14] he will be revealed. Implicit here is a defense of criticism against him, that he used questionable methods of ministry when present with them.[15] In this regard Paul is here, in effect, making the plea that they call to mind the character of his ministry when he was present with them, that is, that he "persuaded men" to "turn to the Lord" (cf 3:16; 4:5; cf. 8:5), or to be "reconciled to God" (5:20), and that he did so with sincerity and integrity (2:17; 4:2; cf. 1:12-14). Perhaps, too, Paul is expressing the hope that even now some of the Corinthians will, by accepting the truth of the gospel, come to recognize his genuineness in their own consciences. Such a plea is not made *in vacuo,* however, but in the present painful situation in Corinth, where his own ministry is under criticism and threat, as the next verse suggests.

12 Sensitive to those in Corinth who are critical of him, Paul now qualifies the previous verse. In saying that he "persuades men," he is not commending himself (as some evidently say he is — see on 3:1). Rather, he is giving the Corinthians ("you") something about him in which they can be validly proud so as to reply to the outsiders ("those"). These people find their pride in externals (lit. "face") rather than in reality (lit. "heart").

In this three-part [16] verse we have (A) a part introduced by "not" ("we are *not* trying to commend ourselves to you again"), (B) a contrasting part begun by "but" ("*but* are giving[17] you an opportunity to take pride in us"), and (C) a purpose clause introduced by "so that" ("*so that* you can answer those who take pride in what is seen rather than what is in the heart").

---

12. Hughes, 187.

13. Gk. συνειδήσεσιν. See on 1:12; 4:2. Nowhere else in the NT does the plural occur. Here it emphasizes the conscience of *every* one of the Corinthians.

14. Gk. ἐλπίζω is one of the rare examples in the excursus about the apostolic office (2:14–7:4), where Paul writes in the first person *singular.* Is this to express deep personal concern? See further Martin, 122-23. Most commentators take "hope" as used here in a positive and optimistic sense; Paul expects that they will render a favorable verdict on his motives.

15. See Thrall, 1.402-3, for the interesting suggestion that Paul was responding to criticism that since he lacked Moses' splendor in ministry he must have "cajoled them in some devious fashion."

16. Gk. οὐ . . . ἀλλὰ . . . ἵνα.

17. Gk. διδόντες, an absolute participle used as an indicative.

A We are not commending ourselves to you again,
B   but giving you   an opportunity to take pride in us
C   so that you
             might have [an answer?] for those
                                      who take pride in appearance
                                      and not in the heart.

Having asserted that "we persuade men and are revealed to God" (v. 11
— my translation), Paul must backtrack to deal once again with their inevitable
criticism that he is "commending" himself to them "again." His anomalous
position as an apostle who was called directly by Christ and who did not
belong to the college of the twelve disciples meant that he had no option but
to appeal to that call. But this laid him open to the accusation that he was
self-commended. In consequence, whenever he affirms his ministry — in this
case that he evangelizes ("we persuade men") — he must disclaim self-
commendation (see on 3:1 and 6:4). Nonetheless, his ministry did commend
him, as the Corinthians should have recognized (12:11; cf. 4:2; 10:18).

Quite to the contrary ("but"), however, as Paul explains in part B of
the verse, he is giving the Corinthians a "reason"[18] (lit. "a point"; NIV,
"opportunity") for "pride"[19] in his ministry, namely, that he "persuades,"
that is, evangelizes people.[20] His fidelity to the divinely given word (2:17;
4:3) should be regarded as evidence of his genuineness.

The purpose statement following in part C ("that *you* may have[21] . . .
against[22] *those* . . .") reflects the polemical environment implicit throughout
2 Corinthians. Apparently, there are insiders ("you") and outsiders ("those").
In our view the outsiders are the newly arrived, letter-bearing "peddlers" of
the word of God, whom Paul introduced earlier (2:17–3:1).[23]

---

18. Gk. ἀφορμή (11:12 [twice]; Gal 5:13; Rom 7:8; 1 Tim 5:14) was originally a
military term for a strategic place for a camp, or for a good location for attack or defense.

19. The cognates καυχᾶσθαι, καύχησις, and καύχημα are very important within
2 Corinthians (see on 1:12). Although Paul uses the words in a positive sense here and in
1:14; 9:3, in chapters 10–13 their use is mainly negative, in regard of his opponents.
Evidently "boasting" — legitimate and illegitimate — was part of the vocabulary of dispute between Paul and his opponents. See on 1:12-14.

20. According to Martin (124), following B. Holmberg (*Paul and Power*) and
others, Paul is here implying a parental relationship with the Corinthians. While such a
relationship is evident in other passages (see on 1:9; 6:13; 7:15; 10:6; 11:1-4), it is not so
clear in this passage.

21. Uncertain is the object (understood) of ἵνα ἔχητε. Most likely possibilities are
τι or λέγειν τι or καύχημα, or even ἀφορμή, with a slightly different nuance, "answer."

22. Gk. πρός here effectively means "against," i.e., "a rejoinder *against* those
who, etc."

23. In Thrall's view (1:405), however, these are non-Christian Jews who compare

These opponents, who are to be "answered," are now spoken of as "those who take pride in what is seen" (lit. "in face") rather than "what is in [the] heart."[24] This "pride" in externals is explained in the next verse as ecstatic behavior, in all probability ecstatic speech.[25] Such "pride" is not merely an expression of personal preference for Paul's ministry style. The next verse will not allow that view. Rather, their "pride" is their attempt to *legitimate* their ministry with the Corinthians based on the "ecstatic," while at the same time casting serious doubts on Paul's ministry precisely because of his apparent inferiority in such things.

The "answer" to this "pride" is not at all something esoteric or bizarre on Paul's part; his ministry, being public, is, he trusts, "manifest" to the Corinthians, just as Paul himself is "manifest" to God (v. 11). By these few words, therefore, Paul reminds the Corinthians of his work as an evangelist so that they may indeed take legitimate pride in him and have something to say to his detractors.

13 The initial "For" *(gar)* with which this sentence begins serves to explain the two previous verses, while at the same time depending on them to cast light on its meaning. In words that are clearly apologetic, Paul points to two aspects of his behavior: he is "beside himself" and he is "self-controlled." The former is for God, the latter for the Corinthians.

The verse is neatly symmetrical: each part (1) is introduced by "if,"[26] (2) has an antonym — "out of our mind"/"self-controlled,"[27] and (3) has contrasting indirect objects — "for *God* . . . for *you.*"[28]

Paul disadvantageously with the glorious figure of Moses, whose *face* was transfigured. According to this hypothesis, the boast of these people is in the glorious *face* of Moses rather than that to which it pointed, the actualization of the promised new covenant in the *hearts* of the people. Against this hypothesis, however, we note that (1) the "face" of v. 12 corresponds to the ecstasy ("we are beside ourselves") of v. 12, and (2) having introduced the "peddlers," it is more likely that they are the antecedents of "those who . . ." rather than completely new referents, the local Corinthian Jews. It is probable, however, that the newly arrived Christian Jews (the "peddlers") had contact with the Corinthian non-Christian Jews.

24. Gk. ἐν προσώπῳ καὶ μὴ ἐν καρδίᾳ. Yahweh's words to Samuel are probably in Paul's mind: ἄνθρωπος ὄψεται εἰς πρόσωπον, ὁ δὲ θεὸς ὄψεται εἰς καρδίαν (LXX 1 Kgdms 16:7). The Lord told Samuel that the outward appearance of Eliab did not mark him as the Lord's anointed.

25. Thrall, 1.409, draws attention to the view, which she does not share, that Paul is here referring to *faces* transformed in religious ecstasy.

26. Gk. εἴτε.

27. Gk. ἐξέστημεν . . . σωφρονοῦμεν.

28. Gk. θεῷ . . . ὑμῖν. Both are datives of advantage: "for God's sake . . . in your interest." Cf. 1 Cor 14:2, 8, where Paul's glossolalia is *for* God, and 14:3, where prophesying — in contrast to glossolalia — is *for* men (i.e., people), for their upbuilding. Paul's actions are either for God or for others; neither is for him.

In regard to the first part, Paul reminds them that he is an ecstatic ("if we are out of our mind"[29]), something he appears to echo later in the letter (12:1-6). The point, however, is that such ecstasy is "for God." It is a "vertical" and private matter between Paul and God, to whom, in any case, he stands permanently "revealed" (v. 11).

There are other interpretations of "if we are out of our mind." Easily dismissed as improbable options are (1) epilepsy (supposedly Paul's "thorn in the flesh" — 12:7), and (2) excessive self-commendation amounting to mania. A more serious alternative[30] is that Paul's zeal for ministry, like that of Jesus (as in Mark 3:21), laid him open to the charge that he was mad. The procurator Festus made that very accusation against Paul (Acts 26:24). Against this explanation,[31] we note that (1) the verb used in Acts is different from v. 13,[32] and (2) the antitheses in Paul's text (vv. 11-13) are against it:

we persuade	men	11
we are . . . open to	God	

those who	take pride in face	12
and [those who do] not	[take pride] in heart	

beside ourselves . . .	for God	13
self-controlled . . .	for you	

29. Gk. ἐξέστημεν. The aorist is here taken to be a timeless aorist, indicating ongoing activity (so J. H. Moulton, *Grammar,* 1.134). The verb ἐξίστημι is not used elsewhere by Paul, though it is used of Jesus (see Mark 3:21). It is often used in the NT as an expression of amazement (Matt 12:23; Mark 2:12; Luke 8:56; Acts 2:7, 12; 8:13; 9:21; 10:45; 12:16). Its counterbalance σωφρονοῦμεν helps define it as paranormal behavior, and it is so used in LXX Isa 28:7 and in Philo, *On Drunkenness* 146-47. According to Bultmann, 149, the verb "can only mean a 'being-outside-oneself' in pneumatic ecstasy." (Bultmann correctly dismisses the suggestion that "out of the body" [v. 8] is connected with the ecstasy of v. 13.) Ecstatic behavior would have been well known to the Corinthians through the cultic practices at Delphi. Lucian, *The Civil War* 5.67ff., describes the frenzied ecstasy of the Pythian priestess at Delphi: "the wild frenzy overflowed through her foaming lips; she groaned and uttered loud inarticulate cries with panting breath . . . and at last . . . the sound of articulate speech. . . . The frenzy abides; and the god whom she has not shaken off, still controls her . . ." (LCL). In *Phaedrus* 244.A-B, Plato sets σωφρονοῦμεν in contrast with μαίνομεν, which is a synonym for ἐξίστημεν; see further Thrall, 1.406. In the Greek world religious madness was seen as divine inspiration.

30. As argued by Hughes, 191.

31. For a detailed reply see Martin, 126-27.

32. In Acts 26:24-25 Festus accuses Paul of being mad, which Paul denies; the verb is μαίνεσθαι. Paul uses this verb in 1 Cor 14:23 for the outsider's reaction to glossolalia within the assembly, which may support the view that ἐξίστημι here relates to paranormal behavior; see n. 29 above.

From the flow of Paul's text it appears that *persuade* and *self-controlled* are for people ("men . . . you"), specifically the Corinthians in this context. On the other hand, the field of reference of *openness,* the *heart,* and *beside ourselves* is God, not people. We conclude that Paul persuaded (evangelized) people, with a self-controlled manner; but from the heart, to the God to whom he was open, he was "beside himself." Because it is to God and not human beings that Paul was "beside himself," we are able to exclude the explanation that Paul was "beside himself" in evangelism. Paul did not evangelize God.

What is this ecstatic behavior? The options include (1) his own glossolalic speech, as referred to in 1 Cor 14:18 (cf. Rom 8:26), and (2) Paul's experience fourteen years before when he was "caught up to paradise" and "heard inexpressible things that man is not permitted to tell" (12:4).

Option (2) is to be preferred as better suited to the context of 2 Corinthians. These verses suggest that "those who take pride in appearances," whom Paul invites the Corinthians to answer, are — like Paul — "beside themselves." He says that they take pride in externals. Why would he mention his ecstatic behavior unless their ecstatic (outward) behavior was in some way critical? Paranormal speech appears to have accompanied "visions and revelations" (12:1, 4), to which, we infer, Paul's opponents were appealing to legitimate their ministry, as against Paul's, in Corinth (see on 12:1). But Paul, who does not deny such speech, will not point to it in support of his ministry. He will make no "horizontal" or public appeal to legitimacy as a minister based on "vertical" ecstatic behavior.

In the balancing part of this short, symmetrical verse, Paul declares what is for the Corinthians the appropriate commendation legitimizing his ministry. It is that for them he is "right-minded." In the public arena he "persuades men" to turn to the Lord Jesus Christ through his ministry of preaching (1:19; 3:16; 4:5; 8:5), and he does so with self-control. These are matters of public knowledge, and they commend the apostolic minister. It is not, therefore, ecstasy or any other form of religious phenomena of an outward kind that legitimates his ministry. Such things belong to a private realm; they are "for God."

The message Paul brings is from God (2:17; 4:2; 5:20), heralding the day of salvation (6:2) and persuading people to be reconciled to God (5:18-20). It is a divinely given revelation, whose audience is the world (see 5:19), declared appropriately in intelligible and not esoteric terms.

Important and abiding principles are to be discerned in these verses. On the one hand, freedom is to be allowed to the minister or the believer to be ecstatic or nonecstatic; it is a matter of divine gift.[33] On the other hand, in regard to

---

33. 1 Cor 14:4-11.

the recognition of genuineness in ministers, the practice of ecstatic speech or behavior in itself has no bearing. Fundamental to the discernment of the authentic minister, however, is the minister's commitment to persuading people to "turn to the Lord," to "be reconciled to God." If the example of Paul is to be regarded as a yardstick, it should be noted that his life is centered on God and on others, but not on himself. All that he does is "for God" and "for you." His is an other-centered, love-controlled life, as he now explains (v. 14).

Further, since (1) the world that is subject to God's reconciliation (5:19) is the audience of the apostolic ministry, and since (2) such ministry is, therefore, appropriately, public so that Paul places no reliance on the ecstatic for legitimization, it would follow that the public life of the church should not be thought to be "beside itself" by the wider world (cf. 1 Cor 14:23). If public self-control is appropriate to the apostle, it is also appropriate in the life of the church.

2. The Scope of Apostolic Ministry: All People (5:14-17)

14 *For Christ's love compels us, because we are convinced that one died for all, and therefore all died.* 15 *And he died for all, that those who live should no longer live for themselves but for him who died for them and was raised again.* 16 *So from now on we regard no one from a worldly point of view. Though we once regarded Christ in this way, we do so no longer.* 17 *Therefore, if anyone is in Christ, he is a new creation; the old has gone, the new[1] has come!*

Continuing his explanation to the Corinthians of his apostolic office and ministry under the new covenant, Paul now draws attention to Christ's love as the motive for the two priorities in his ministry, namely, that he evangelizes ("persuades men") and that he does this with a "right mind" (vv. 11, 12). The evidence of Christ's love is to be seen in his death and resurrection for all, in consequence of which all "die" (to self-centered living). The purpose for which Christ died and was raised is that those who live, as by spiritual resurrection, now live for him.

This "one" is the center of humanity ("one died for *all*") but also of history ("those who live . . . *no longer* live for themselves but for him"). In

---

1. The shorter reading καινά has stronger support (p[46] ℵ B C D* G 1739 it[d.g.r] vg syr[(p) pal] cop[sa,boh] arm eth[ro]) than the longer reading καινὰ τὰ πάντα (D[c] K P Ψ etc.). The longer reading probably arose by assimilation from the opening words of the next sentence τὰ δὲ πάντα. καινά without the article, as opposed to with the article, is attested in the best texts (ℵ, p[46] B C D*); see further Metzger, 580.

having died and been raised he has divided history into two aeons, the "no longer" aeon and the "now" aeon — although the two overlap until the Parousia. In consequence, in the "now" aeon it is possible "no longer" to "know" people and Christ "according the flesh," but, by inference, "according to the Spirit." Paul testifies representatively to the new way of knowing that is "now" possible (v. 16). Christ is thus the divider of history; the one who is "in Christ," who has died and been raised, belongs to the "new creation" and in consequence is a "new creation" (v. 17).

Although this is an allusively autobiographical passage (the Damascus Road experience is never far from his thoughts), Paul nonetheless speaks representatively for all believers caught up in the overarching purposes of God. Paul and believers generally are encapsulated within the two great elements in the gospel, Christ's death and resurrection. Therefore, anyone who is "in Christ" is "now" part of the "new creation." Christ has overwhelming universal and eschatological significance for those who are "in him," providing Paul with a foundation for all that he will say in the passage following (5:18–6:2).

14 The explanatory "For" relates back to Paul's selflessness in ministry, as in v. 13. If he has been "beside himself," it has been for God; and if he has been "self-controlled," it has been for the Corinthians. Nothing was for Paul. It is, he asserts, a life controlled by Christ's own love. That love is discerned in Christ's death for all, in consequence of which all have potentially died — as Paul has — to self-centered living.

Structurally, then, Paul (1) gives the *reason* "for" *(gar)* his method of ministry set out in vv. 11-13 ("for Christ's love[2] controls[3] us"), (2) he states the *basis* for such an assertion ("because[4] we are convinced that one died for all"), and (3) he draws a logical *conclusion* from that statement ("therefore[5] all died").

It is worth noting that in his former existence as a Pharisee, the compel-

---

2. Gk. ἡ . . . ἀγάπη τοῦ Χριστοῦ is capable of being interpreted either as an objective genitive ("love for Christ") or as a subjective genitive ("Christ's love [for us]"), a love that was directed to both Paul and the Corinthians (cf. 4:11). The context indicates that the latter is uppermost in the writer's mind, and most grammarians and commentators take it as a subjective genitive (e.g., A. T. Robertson, *Grammar,* 539; Plummer, 173; but cf. Héring, 41-42).

3. Gk. συνέχει. The verb implies that which confines and restricts (Luke 8:45; 12:50; 19:43; Acts 18:5; "hold in custody," BAGD), rather than that which "compels" (NIV). "Christ's self-sacrificing love restrains Paul from self-seeking" (so Thrall, 1.408, reflecting on v. 14 in the context of vv. 11-13). Christ's love controls the direction of the apostle's ministry.

4. Gk. ὅτι. It must be allowed, however, that ὅτι may be epexegetic to τοῦτο, meaning "namely that."

5. Gk. ἄρα.

ling force in Paul's life had been his zeal (or jealousy) for the name of Yahweh (see on 11:2), a zeal that drove him to destroy the followers of — as he then saw him — the blasphemer Jesus (cf. Gal 1:13, 23; Acts 22:8; 26:19). Now love has taken the place of that zeal as the controlling force at the center of his being.

Thus there emerge from v. 11 and v. 14 two motives for apostolic evangelism, the "fear of the Lord" and the "love of Christ." Both motives are christological (cf. the doxological motive in 4:15) and, despite appearances to the contrary, reconcilable. The one relates to Jesus' role as Judge, the other to his role as Savior. The "fear of the Lord" is not cringing terror, but profound, awe-filled respect for the Lord as Judge (see on v. 10); the "love of Christ" is no sentimental thing, but his unconditional burden for those lost from God that he expressed in his gift of himself in sacrificial death for them (see Gal 2:20). The love of the Savior who is also the Judge is both profound and serious.[6]

In the second part of the verse Paul explains that he knows of, and is controlled by, "the love of Christ," because he became "convinced"[7] that "one died for all."[8] In other words, Paul's sense of ongoing compulsion to evangelize ("controls") arose from his considered judgment ("we are convinced") when he understood that "[Christ had] died for all."

Most probably these words are autobiographical, reflecting that comprehension at or soon after the Damascus event when the despised crucified One addressed Paul out of the heavenly glory. Since glory could come only from God, the glorified Crucified clearly had the stamp of divine approval. At that time and in the course of reflection subsequent to it, Paul reversed his opinions about the Crucified, whose followers he had persecuted. So far from viewing Christ as an object of hate because of his accursed heretic's death "on a tree" (Deut 21:23), the persecutor concluded instead that he, Paul, was the object of Christ's love. Christ had indeed died as the accursed of God, but in the utterly unexpected sense that he had died under God's curse, not for his own sins but "for"[9] the sins of others (Gal 3:13; Acts 13:29), but especially that he had died for him, Paul (cf.

6. See E. Brunner, *The Christian Doctrine of God* (London, 1962), 183-99.

7. Gk. κρίναντας, aorist tense.

8. *Contra* Furnish (310), who regards κρίνειν here as applicable to all believers and not directly to Paul. The context, however, points to Paul in the first instance.

9. Paul now introduces ὑπέρ into this passage. Earlier he had used the preposition in regard to his own sufferings "for" the Corinthians (see on 1:6). Now he begins to use the preposition for Christ's vicarious death (vv. 14, 15 [twice], 21). Apart from 1 Thess 5:10, ὑπέρ is used in passages earlier than the present one where Paul is quoting traditions going back either to Jesus or to the Jerusalem apostles (1 Cor 11:23; 15:3 — see G. D. Fee, *1 Corinthians*, 551; also Gal 1:4; 2:20; 3:13, where the usage appears to be tradition-influenced, though the dating of Galatians remains problematic). See L. A. Belleville, "Gospel and Kerygma," 146-47, for exploration of the theory that Paul here interprets the ὑπέρ-tradition in terms of his own convictions.

Gal 2:20; 1 Tim 1:12-16). Paul's understanding that Jesus, in his death, loved *him* was now the controlling force in the apostle's life.

The universality of the statement "one died for all" is implicitly both eschatological and christological (cf. 1:19-20). It is eschatological in that this was the central event, along with the resurrection mentioned next, that divided history into the time before and after it. This brief paradox lays the foundation for the "no longer"/"now" hiatus that will be made explicit in the next verse, thereafter dominating the passage following (5:15–6:2). That "one died for all" declares, in effect, that God's eschatological midpoint has been reached and now lies in the past. Equally, the statement is implicitly christological. If *"one* died for all," then such a "one" must be uniquely significant. Inevitably, this theme — implicit in this verse — will soon become altogether predominant (vv. 18-21).

In the third part — "therefore all died," the enigmatic corollary of "one died for all" — the significance of the epoch-dividing intervention by a critical eschatological event is reinforced. But what do these words mean? Of the various explanations proposed by scholars[10] the most likely, in our view, is that

---

It should be noted that Isa 52:13–53:12, on which Paul significantly depends, does not use ὑπέρ but either περί (cf. v. 4 — περὶ ἡμῶν; cf. v. 10 — ἐὰν δῶτε περὶ ἁμαρτίας) or, more generally, διά (cf. διὰ τὰς ἀνομίας αὐτῶν παρεδόθη — 53:12). Someone earlier than Paul has changed περί and/or διά to ὑπέρ, reflecting the probable influence of Jesus or the Jerusalem apostles on the interpretation of Isa 52:13–53:12. Moreover, in both traditions of the Eucharist ὑπέρ appears — ὑπὲρ ὑμῶν (Luke 22:19, 20; 1 Cor 11:24), and ὑπὲρ πολλῶν (Mark 14:24). For a non-Pauline use that may support a pre-Pauline use and therefore a pre-Pauline origin of ὑπέρ related to the death of Christ, see 1 Pet 2:21-24, a passage that echoes Isa 53:4, 5, 6, 12.

Scholars debate whether ὑπέρ means (1) the equivalent of ἄντι = "instead of" (see Mark 10:45; cf. 1 Tim 2:6); so A. T. Robertson, *Grammar,* 631; J. H. Moulton, *Grammar,* 3.358, or (2) "for the benefit of" (so, e.g., Barrett, 168-69; Thrall, 1.409). Meaning (1) demands meaning (2), but the reverse does not hold. The debate centers on whether Christ in his death was *substitute* or *representative* (see J. D. G. Dunn, "Death of Jesus," 140-41, who argues that Jesus died as representative, "as Adam"). The problem is complicated by various uses of ὑπέρ within the wider passage 5:14–6:2. It should be noted that ὑπέρ is used in nonatonement senses in v. 20, as *representative* ("ambassadors *for* Christ") but also as *substitute* ("we implore you *on* Christ's *behalf*"). Two difficulties with ὑπέρ as substitute are (1) that one can represent, but not substitute for, *many,* and (2) the depersonalized associations that are connected with it. These problems are mitigated (1) if the death of one *for* all is seen primarily in qualitative as opposed to quantitative terms, so that one represents one, acts for one, and (2) if we replace "proxy" with "substitute," thus personalizing the notion of substitution (as in Martin, 130-31; see also L. A. Belleville, "Gospel and Kerygma," 148).

10. See Thrall, 1.409-11, for a review of various opinions of scholars, including: (1) the juridical: all are regarded by God as having died in Christ to the penalty of sin, (2) the representational: in the death of Christ all actually underwent death to their sinful selves, and (3) the potential: in Christ's death is the possibility of death to self. Thrall views

"all have died" is to be seen in parallel with that primal sin of Adam, in which "all have sinned" and from which, in consequence, "death through sin" has come into "the world" (Rom 5:12).[11] However, through the death and resurrection of the "one," Christ, the deathly effects to "all" of the sin of the "one," Adam, are overturned, at least potentially. The death and resurrection of Christ is the potential reversal of the death on account of the sin of Adam. In the death of Christ, however, they die to death as the penalty of sin; in his resurrection, through the Spirit, they are made alive (Rom 8:10-11).

In regard to "all" — "one died for *all* . . . *all* died" — a distinction is to be made between "all" who are "in Adam" and "all" who are "in Christ." "All" who are "in Adam," that is, all people regardless, do actually die as a result of Adam's sin (Rom 5:12, 18a, 19a). But the "all" for whom Christ died, who also have "died" in him, while potentially inclusive of "all" who are "in Adam," is in actuality limited to those who are "in Christ," through faith-commitment to him. The "all" who have died "in Christ" are not coextensive with the "all" who sin and die "in Adam." The end of death and the beginning of life in Christ's death and resurrection are only for those who are "in" Jesus Christ.

As in part two of the verse, these words, as well as those of the next verse into which they lead, are autobiographical. From the time he understood that Christ died for him, Paul also "died," that is, to a mode of life in which he was the center; Christ now occupied that place (". . . in the cross of our Lord Jesus Christ . . . I [have been crucified] to the world" — Gal 6:14; 2:20). While Christ's death is vicarious ("for us"), it is no less intended to procure "death"

---

these words as a "counterstatement" to Rom 5:12 and argues for a combination of views, with some connection with baptism. While the connection with baptism is problematic, the echoes of v. 14c (οἱ πάντες ἀπέθανον) with Rom 5:12 (ἐφ᾽ ᾧ πάντες ἥμαρτον; see also Rom 5:18; 1 Cor 15:22) are clear enough. All have participated collectively in Adam's sin, and therefore in his death. In response, Christ's death and resurrection is for all, canceling the effects of sin and death and thus providing the potentiality, objectively and subjectively, of the end of death and the beginning of life for all.

11. Paul's enigmatic remark, "all died," may be illuminated by the following apocalyptic comment on Genesis 2–3:

> ". . . better had it been that the earth had not produced Adam, or else, having once produced him, (for thee [God]) to have restrained him from sinning. For how does it profit us all that in the present we must live in grief and after death look for punishment? O thou Adam, what hast thou done! For though it was thou who sinned, the fall was not thine alone, but also ours, who are your descendants! For how does it profit us that the eternal age is promised to us, whereas we have done the works that bring death?" (4 Ezra 7:116-20).

Paul may be saying that, by Christ's death "for all," there has been a reversal of Adam's action that brought such loss to his descendants.

to living for oneself. The "one" — Christ — has indeed "died for all"; in consequence "all" are intended to die to living to self as the center of reference as a result of his death for them. Paul's living *for* God, *for* the Corinthians, and not for himself (as in v. 13) illustrates the impact on him of Christ's love-motivated death for him. There is no room here for "cheap grace."

Thus there is a double dying; *one* has died that all might be reconciled to God, and *all* are to die to themselves. The meaning of the death of the "one" will be developed in vv. 18-21. But the meaning of the death of "all" is to be explained in the next verse, into which it flows. Suffice it to observe now that to the double death — Christ's and ours — there is added a double rising from the dead, his and ours.[12]

Therefore, the "all" in parts two and three of the verse clearly emphasize the universal, inclusive nature of Christ's death; none is excluded from the sphere of God's saving purposes in Christ.

15 The close connection with the previous verse is indicated by the initial "And,"[13] followed by the repetition of "[he] died for all." The reason is that believers should no longer live for themselves but *live* for the one who died and was raised "for them,"[14] the positive side to "that all might *die*" of the previous verse.

Again we find a threefold structure: the first clause (A) repeats the middle part of the previous verse, with one alteration ("and *he* died for all"), followed by a twofold purpose clause regarding "those who live" (i.e., those raised to life following their death in Christ): (B) stated negatively,[15] "that those who live[16] should no longer live for themselves,"[17] but (C) stated positively, "but[18] [that they should live] for him."

---

12. In brief, vv. 14-15 give a preliminary sketch of the picture which the apostle will paint in full in his next letter, that to the Romans. There the believer is depicted as having died to the old self within and being raised alive for obedience to God. Christ's death and resurrection — into which the believer is incorporated through faith-commitment at baptism — symbolize and make possible the believer's death to the old self within and his resurrection to the new life of obedience to God (Rom 6:3-10). However, in vv. 14-15, in contrast to Rom 6:3-10, (1) there is no hint of baptism, and (2) the "resurrected" person lives to Christ, not to God.

13. Gk. καί is explicative, giving a further explanation of what has preceded.

14. Gk. ὑπὲρ αὐτῶν. Christ not only died but was also *raised* "for them," i.e., ὑπὲρ αὐτῶν should be connected with both ἀποθανόντι and ἐγερθέντι. While ὑπὲρ αὐτῶν is closer to ἀποθανόντι, there is no reason to think that it does not also relate to ἐγερθεντί.

15. Gk. ἵνα . . . μηκέτι.

16. Plummer's view of this verse as meaning, literally, "those who are alive in the body and still in the world" (175), is untenable and shared by few others.

17. Gk. ἑαυτοῖς ζῶσιν is dative of advantage.

18. Gk. ἀλλά, with ἵνα understood.

Because	one died for all		14
	therefore all died		
A	and	he died for all	15
B		in order that those who live	
		should no longer live	for themselves
C		but [that they should live]	for him
		who died [for them]	
		and was raised [for them].	

To the single reference to Christ's vicarious death ("[one] died *for*"[19]) in the previous verse, two others are added in this verse. With the second of these is bracketed[20] Christ's vicarious resurrection "for" his people ("he . . . was raised for [them]"). They are caught up into his death and resurrection, though here Paul does not say how this occurs.[21] On account of his death for them, they die; on account of his resurrection for them, they live. From the time of their incorporation "in him" (see v. 17), having "died" (v. 14), they "no longer" live for themselves, but for the one crucified and raised for them (v. 15).

As with the previous verse, Paul's words here, with which they are closely linked, are autobiographical. The Damascus encounter has turned Paul's life inside out. Formerly he lived for himself, even in zeal for Yahweh expressed in the persecution of Jesus' followers;[22] now he has died to all that and lives for the one who — as he now understands — died and was raised for him. Equally, however, Paul also speaks representatively for all believers, including the Corinthians. This theological statement, which is applicable to all believers, is forged out of and expressed in terms of his own particular experience.

The vocabulary and syntax of this verse declare the inextricably connected universal and eschatological centrality of Christ. His universal centrality is revealed in that "he died for *all*," and his eschatological centrality in that, from the moment of his death, those for whom he died *"no longer"* live for themselves but for him. The "no longer" signals the turning point of the

19. Gk. ὑπέρ. See on v. 14.

20. The bracketing of Christ's resurrection with his death is fundamental to the apostles' proclamation of the gospel and the confession of the churches (1 Cor 15:3-5, 11; 1 Thess 4:13; Luke 24:46; Acts 17:3; cf. Mark 8:31 pars.). The tenses of the verbs may be significant. As an aorist active participle ἀποθανόντι implies both the factuality and the voluntariness of Jesus' death, while the aorist passive ἐγερθέντι implies — again — the factuality of the resurrection as well as that he was raised *by God*.

21. But see Rom 6:3-10, where the faith-commitment at baptism, based on ethical instruction, is implied.

22. See especially Phil 3:6, where he refers to his former privileges and exemplary zeal in Judaism as "putting confidence in the flesh"; cf. Gal 1:13-14; Acts 22:3-4; cf. 2 Cor 11:2.

aeons from the "former" to the "new" creation (cf. Isa 43:18) and from the "old" to the "new" covenant (see 3:3-6).

Thus the solidarity of humankind with Adam in his sin (cf. Rom 5:10), that is, his self-centeredness, is broken. Those who belong to Christ *no longer* live for themselves but for him. Because Paul lives for Christ, not himself, he lives and dies for the Corinthians (v. 13; 4:12, 15).

16 As a result of that moment from which we "no longer" live for ourselves but for the One crucified and risen for us, "from now on" we believers do not "know" anyone, Christ in particular, "according to the flesh."

This enigmatic-sounding verse consists of two closely connected sentences.[23] In the first, the words "we, from now on . . ." are located for emphasis immediately following the initial "so" ("so, accordingly"[24] — which springs from "we are convinced" of v. 14); the verb "we know"[25] is that used in the immediate context for matters of a confessional kind (4:14; 5:1, 6, 11); and the negative ("from now on we know *no one* according to the *flesh*") by its very nature implies something positive and opposite (i.e., "from now on we know *others* according to the *Spirit*").

In the second sentence Paul uses a different verb "know,"[26] which, however, is here virtually synonymous with the verb in the first sentence. The sentence is in two parts, of which the first is concessive conditional ("*even if*[27] we knew Christ according to the flesh"). In the balancing second part the strong contrast is achieved by the opening "but" buttressed by the temporals "now," "no longer"[28] ("*but now no longer* we know [him thus]"). As in the first sentence of the verse, the negative ("no longer") really implies something positive and opposite (i.e., ". . . *now* . . . we know Christ according to the *Spirit*").

A   So from now on

           we know no one according to the flesh.

B   Even if   we knew Christ   according to the flesh,

           yet now   we know [him   thus]

                no longer.

---

23. Linking the two sentences are (1) the effectively synonymous verbs οἴδαμεν . . . ἐγνώκαμεν . . . γινώσκομεν, used with nuanced tenses (present . . . perfect . . . present), (2) the temporals ἀπὸ τοῦ νῦν and νῦν οὐκέτι, (3) the alliterative negatives οὐδένα and οὐκέτι, and (4) κατὰ σάρκα repeated in both, though qualifying the verb in the first and both the substantive and the verb in the second.

24. Gk. ὥστε.

25. Gk. οἴδαμεν.

26. Gk. ἐγνώκαμεν . . . γινώσκομεν, meaning "we know," or "we recognize," or "we evaluate."

27. Gk. εἰ καί; NIV, "though." This phrase is not uncommon in this letter. See earlier 4:3, 16; 5:3. Here it implies a real situation ("an admitted fact of the past" — Thrall, 1.415).

28. Gk. ἀλλὰ νῦν οὐκέτι.

The reader must address three questions: (1) Whom does the "we" represent, Paul, or Paul and the Corinthians in particular?[29] (2) Do the temporals "from now on" and "now . . . no longer" refer to the conversion of Paul or to the new eschatological aeon? (3) Does the twice-used phrase "according to the flesh"[30] qualify the verbs ("we know") or the objects of the verbs ("no one" . . . "Christ") in their respective clauses?

As to (1), the context from vv. 14-15 ("one died for all . . . all died") suggests that Paul is writing universally. Nonetheless, vv. 14-17 are written from the perspective of Paul's own experience at and since the Damascus Road encounter, yet in such a way as to be true of all believers.

Likewise (2), the temporal references ("from now on . . . now . . . no longer") in the first instance point to the time of Christ's death and resurrection for all,[31] while at the same time expressing Paul's personal revolution. The moment of Paul's personal change lies within, and is made possible by, the moment of eschatological/universal change, when Christ died and was raised for all (vv. 14-15).

In regard to (3), the understanding of the subtly nuanced use of the phrase "according to the flesh" in the two sentences is critical to the understanding of the verse.[32] Because "now" is the "day of salvation" (6:2), the age of fulfillment and proclamation (1:18-20) and of the long-awaited Spirit (1:21-22; 3:3), we "no longer" know Christ[33] "according to the flesh," but, we infer, "according to the Spirit."

In the first sentence "according to the flesh" qualifies the verb "know." Who is intended by the words "no one"? In all probability Paul has in mind "those who take pride in what is seen" of a few verses earlier (v. 12). These are the newcomers who are mere "peddlers" of the word of God (2:17), false

29. According to H. Lietzmann (*An die Korinther*, 126) it is Paul, but according to Bultmann (156) it is believers.

30. Gk. κατὰ σάρκα; NIV, "from a worldly point of view."

31. See in particular τὰ καινὰ ἀπὸ τοῦ νῦν (Isa 48:6). According to R. C. Tannehill, *Dying and Rising*, 67, it "is the decisive event through which the believer has entered the new life . . . the time of God's decisive act which changed the situation of men in the world."

32. Most commentators take both uses of the phrase in the adverbial sense. See Furnish, 312-13, and Thrall, 1.418-20, for surveys of the use of the phrase in the NT and for a summary of scholarly opinion as to the application.

33. Paul may have had in mind his failure to discern not only the Lord's identity but also the spiritual reality about those followers of Christ whom he had been persecuting. Thrall, 1.420, sees a connection with v. 12 in her understanding of that verse in terms of the Samuel narrative; Paul had formerly failed to recognize the *Christos* (looking only on the outward aspect), just as Samuel had not initially recognized David as the Lord's anointed (see on v. 12). Conversion (ἀπὸ τοῦ νῦν . . . νῦν οὐκέτι) brings a new set of evaluative insights.

apostles who masquerade as apostles of Christ (11:13).[34] Others, including the Corinthians, may be duped by such people; Paul, a man of apostolic insight, is not deceived. Indeed, not only have the Corinthians been wrong in welcoming the newcomers; correspondingly, they have also been wrong in their coolness toward Paul. "From now on," that is, from the time of his incorporation "in Christ," he has been able to discern the truth about such people, though he would not have been able to do so beforehand. Perhaps there is a barb here. Should not the Corinthians, as a Spirit-anointed community (1:21-22), have had the insight to recognize these men as peddlers of a now superseded dispensation?

In the second sentence, however, "according to the flesh" appears to qualify both the substantive ("Christ") and the verb "we knew." Introducing the sentence by "even if,"[35] Paul is suggesting that he knew, or knew of, the historical Jesus, the Jesus "according to the flesh." Historically speaking, this is quite probable.[36] Jesus was prominent in Jerusalem during his years of public ministry, especially in his last year from the Feast of Tabernacles to the Feast of Dedication (October to December) and at the time of the Feast of Passover (April),[37] when the observant young rabbi,[38] Saul of Tarsus, converted within a year or two of the first Easter,[39] would (probably) have been in Jerusalem. Grammatically, Paul's "we knew"[40] suggests that he continued to remember Jesus as he had then noticed him.

But Paul does not set too much store by such knowledge of the historical Jesus because Paul's "knowing" of Christ was — the phrase now qualifying the verb — "according to the flesh," superficial and misguided. Here Paul is alluding to his former view of Jesus as a blasphemer, whose following he had sought to destroy (Acts 22:3-4; 26:9-11).

In the final part of the verse ("but we know [him thus] no longer") Paul speaks for all believers, but again in terms of his own personal intellectual/spiritual revolution, which he began to do in v. 14. These words turn on that moment of judgment ("we *became* convinced" — v. 14). Before then he "knew" Christ superficially and falsely, but afterward he "knows" Christ, we infer, according to the Spirit. Since his Damascus Road encounter Paul "now"

---

34. Different views are taken, e.g., by Hughes, 197, who views this as a general spiritual insight subsequent to conversion.

35. Gk. εἰ καί; NIV, "though." According to Furnish, 313, the εἰ with the indicative refers to "a real case," something "hypothetically real."

36. Cf. M. Hengel, *Pre-Christian Paul*, 64, who regards this as no more than possible, and Thrall, 1.416, who finds no exegetical basis for it in this verse.

37. See John 7:2, 14; 10:22; 12:1.

38. Gal 1:14; Acts 22:3; 26:4-5.

39. See M. Hengel, *Between Jesus and Paul*, 47.

40. Gk. ἐγνώκαμεν — perfect tense: "we came to know and *continue* to know."

knows Christ as he really is, according to the Spirit, as the one who, by having been crucified and raised for him, thereby demonstrated his love for him (v. 14). For this one Paul, having "died" to his former life, now lives, in obedience to his apostolic calling. This is the One he "now knows" and whom, by inference, he calls upon his readers to know.

The newly arrived Jewish countermissionaries appear to have no such apprehension of Jesus (see 2:17–3:1; 5:11-13). To them he is a merely Jewish Jesus circumscribed within the existing physical and Sinai-based covenant of Israel. By the present-nuanced use of the same phrase in the last part of the verse Paul may also be targeting the countermissionaries who proclaimed "another Jesus" (11:4), in all probability a Christ "according to the flesh," whom Paul "no longer" knows. The Christ Paul and his readers "know" is the cosmic and eschatological figure who "died and was raised for all."

17 Again Paul states a consequence, "so that,"[41] which flows from the spiritual death and resurrection of those (vv. 14-15) whom he now characterizes in the singular as "anyone [who is] in Christ," who is "a new creation." For that person the things of the former times, and especially the worldview, are in the past. "Look," he says, "the new has come."

Thus the first of the two sentences in this verse is brief and proverblike, and the second is subsidiary to and dependent upon it. In the first, the words "so then" (with which the previous verse also begins) introduce the pithy sentence of six words that sums up the entire passage vv. 14-16. In this conditional sentence the "if"-clause is "if any [one is] in Christ,"[42] and the "then"-clause is, tersely,[43] "new creation."[44] The result is a memorable text of unsurpassed power in the writings of Paul.[45]

---

41. Gk. ὥστε, as in v. 16. The two ὥστε sentences are parallel, springing independently from vv. 14-15. ὥστε, "so then," is much used by Paul in 1 Corinthians, and states the consequences of what has just been said.

42. Gk. ἐν Χριστῷ, which also occurs elsewhere in this letter (2:14, 17; 3:14; 5:19; 12:2, 19). In our view this much-discussed phrase refers to one who (1) has responded in faith to the gospel of Jesus Christ crucified and risen (cf. vv. 14-15), who (2) is ἐν σώματι Χριστοῦ (cf. Gal 3:27-28), belonging to a community of the baptized that confesses Christ, and who (3) is, therefore, ἐν πνεύματι (cf. Rom 8:1, 9), within the sphere of the Spirit's activity. See Thrall, 1.425-26, for a review of other possibilities and her inclination to regard a person ἐν Χριστῷ as one incorporated through baptism into Christ as an "inclusive" or "corporate" person.

43. Although the NIV and most translations have "he is a . . . ," the context as well as the cosmological understanding ("creation"), as opposed to the anthropological ("creature") meaning of κτίσις, tilts the translation toward "there is." Nonetheless, the anthropological, personal, and subjective interpretation ("he is a new creature") clearly follows from the prior interpretation ("there is a new creation").

44. The phrase καινὴ κτίσις is taken by the RSV, NEB, JB, NIV, and the overwhelming majority of translations and commentaries as "new creation." The only other

In the second sentence the subject of both parts is "the old [things]."[46]
The verbs in the two parts are significant. In the first "passed away"[47] (NIV,
"gone") is aorist, indicating a single action, now completed, pointing (1) to
the end of the former dispensation, and (2) to the end of the former life of
the person who is now in Christ. In the second "become"[48] (NIV, "come")
is perfect tense, indicating a past action with continuing effects. The triumphant "look,"[49] followed by the perfect tense ("become") and the antonym
"new," combines to make the impressive statement, "behold, the old things
have become and *are* new."

A   So that, if any[one is] in Christ,
        [there is]   a new creation.
B   The old [things] have passed;
            behold,   they   have become
                        new.

---

exact parallel is Gal 6:15, suggesting that the phrase was introduced into Christian use by
Paul (but see 2 Pet 3:13; Rev 21:1-5). The phrase, however, is found in Apocalyptic Judaism
(e.g., *Jos. and As.* 8:10-11; *1 Enoch* 72:1; *2 Apoc. Bar.* 32:6; 1QS 4:25), but more particularly beyond that it has its roots in the OT, especially τὰ καινὰ ἀπὸ τοῦ νῦν (LXX Isa
48:6) and μὴ μνημόνευτε τὰ πρῶτα. καὶ τὰ ἀρχαῖα μὴ συλλογίζεσθε. Ἰδοὺ ποιῶ καινά
(LXX Isa 43:18-19; cf. Isa 42:9; 65:17-25; 66:22). For general discussion of the phrase
see Furnish, 314-15; G. K. Beale, "Reconciliation," 550-81. Argument in favor of the less
commonly held alternative understanding of "new creature" is set out in J. Reumann et
al., *Righteousness in the New Testament*, 51.

   If, as seems likely, the vocabulary of "new creation" was current in the Judaism
of Paul's day, when was it thought to apply — at the end of, or within, history? Thrall,
1.420-22, concludes that this terminology was thought to apply only to the end of history.

   45. Another example of a "gnomic" saying introduced by "if anyone" is "If
anyone loves God, he is known by him" (1 Cor 8:3; see also, e.g., 1 Cor 3:12; 7:12, 13;
16:22).

   46. In the OT (LXX) τὰ ἀρχαῖα is synonymous with τὰ πρῶτα (Isa 43:18-19) and
is contrasted with τὰ ἔσχατα (Ps 139:5). In the apocalyptic tradition, by which Paul would
have also been influenced, τὰ ἀρχαῖα signified the totality of creation.

   47. Gk. παρῆλθεν; NIV, "gone." The verb is used elsewhere in the NT in end-time
contexts and the passing away of the old order and its replacement by the new (Matt 24:35;
2 Pet 3:10; cf. Rev 21:4).

   48. Gk. γέγονεν; NIV, "has come." Hughes, 201, correctly takes τὰ ἀρχαῖα
(understood) as the subject of γέγονεν, with καινά as the predicative adjective, seeing
therefore a "radical continuity" between the "old" and the "new." This is opposed to the
discontinuity implied by Furnish's view (316), based on Jewish apocalyptic thought, that
γέγονεν is to be translated absolutely, indicating a "total replacement." On Hughes's view,
which we share, the cosmos is renewed and transformed, not replaced.

   49. In the OT (LXX) ἰδού is used frequently for "see!" or "look!" especially in
contexts of end-time announcements (Isa 42:9; 43:19; 65:17-18). See Paul's use in 6:2
(twice); 6:9; 7:11; 12:14; and 1 Cor 15:51.

297

The two sentences together emphasize the eschatological centrality of Christ. "In Christ" the old ends and the new — a new creation — begins. But this eschatological centrality is tightly connected with the soteriological centrality of Christ. Christ is the "one" who "died and was raised for all," the "one" in and for whom "all" who have "died" now "live" (vv. 14-15). The crucified and risen Christ is the divine agent of universal salvation, the divider of history into two aeons, the "no longer" aeon when all things were "old" and the "now" aeon when all things have become, and are, "new."

But this "new creation" is coterminous with the "new covenant" mentioned earlier (3:6); together they divide history into two epochs. The "old" things of creation and of the "old covenant" (3:14) coincide, as do the "new" things of the "new covenant" and the "new creation." The inauguration of both the "new covenant" and the "new creation" occurs "in Christ," and at the same time, that is, when he died and was raised for all, bringing to their respective ends the "old" in the former creation and in the "old covenant." The "old" in the former creation are the things to which those who are "in Christ" have "died," that is, to the godless, self-centered living, "according to the flesh," of those "in Adam" (v. 15; cf. Rom 5:12). The "old" in the "old covenant" relates to law-keeping as the method of relational acceptance with God, which Paul also characterizes as "according to the flesh" (Rom 8:4). Both the "old" in the former creation and the "old" in the "old covenant" have "now" passed and "no longer" govern those who are "in Christ." Those who are "in Christ" are — and are to be — governed by the Spirit (cf. Eph 5:18).

While the blessings of both the "new covenant" and the "new creation" have "come" in Christ, as proclaimed by his apostolic servant Paul, they remain hidden until the universal resurrection (4:14); they are not yet "by sight" (5:7). Nonetheless, the "new creation" may be entered now, through the word of God, the gospel, "by faith" (5:7). This openness to all is indicated by the "if anyone . . ."[50] with which the verse begins.

Who is this *"anyone"*? As with the entire passage (vv. 14-17), Paul is speaking in the first instance of himself. These few words are Paul's spiritual autobiography and testimony in a nutshell. The very openness and brevity of the expression "if anyone . . ." are eloquent expressions of Paul's sense of the love and mercy of Christ toward *him,* the persecutor of Christ's people (4:1; 5:14). The words "if anyone" mean "yes, even such a one as me" (see 1 Tim 1:12-16).

Thus, this verse may be understood in both an objective and a subjective sense.[51] Objectively, it is Paul's declaration that "in Christ," by faith, he

---

50. Gk. εἴ τις.

51. Martin (152), following Bultmann, W. G. Kümmel *(Introduction)* and R. Tannehill *(Dying and Rising),* contends that καινὴ κτίσις should be taken only in the objective

has entered the "new creation" in which the "old" things have "passed away" and have become "new." Work on the "building from God," which will be his at the general resurrection, has already been begun (4:17). This process of "edification," which began at the moment of incorporation "in Christ," will continue quietly and unseen throughout life until the final moment of revelation and glorification (see 3:18; Rom 8:19).

Subjectively, this verse summarizes the changes in Paul's own life. Love for others is now his controlling motive in place of self-interest (v. 14), which he had expressed in zealous persecution. Serving the one who had died and been raised for him has taken the place of self-centered living (v. 15). True understanding of Christ and of his people has replaced ignorance and error (v. 16). The Creator who once said, "Let there be light," has more recently shone his light into Paul's darkened heart, making *him* a new creation (4:6). The subjective personal revelation, experienced "now," is the sign of the objective "new creation" to be revealed then.

Nonetheless, as throughout this passage, Paul is also speaking representatively for all. Implicit in the words "if anyone" is the gracious evangelical invitation and summons to "all" for whom the "one" died and was raised (vv. 14-15) to enter "into" Christ by faith-commitment, to enjoy the benefits, objective and subjective, that will "now" hold true for "anyone" who responds. The invitation and summons, which are implicit in v. 17, will soon be made explicit, though in the different terms, "be reconciled to God" (v. 20).

3. God's Appeal through His Minister (5:18–6:2)

18 *All this is from God, who reconciled us to himself through Christ and gave us the ministry of reconciliation:* 19 *that God was reconciling the world to himself in Christ, not counting men's sins against them. And he has committed to us the message of reconciliation.* 20 *We are therefore Christ's ambassadors, as though God were making his appeal through us. We implore you on Christ's behalf: Be reconciled to God.* 21 *God made him who had no sin to be sin for us, so that in him we might become the righteousness of God.* 1 *As God's fellow workers we urge you not to receive God's grace in vain.* 2 *For he says, "In the time of my favor I heard you, and in the day of salvation I helped you." I tell you, now is the time of God's favor, now is the day of salvation.*

---

and eschatological sense. But this does not do justice to the subjective revolution implied by dying in the one who died and living in the one who has been raised (vv. 14-15). It is simply a false dichotomy that Paul would not have understood.

This passage is the crux of the exposition of the apostolic office (2:14–7:4) and of the entire letter. It is a message on a grand scale. The God of the cosmos and of history has reconciled rebellious humankind to himself through the "one" (v. 14) whom he "made sin," on account of whom trespasses are no longer reckoned (vv. 19, 21). The "righteousness of God" imputed to those who are "in Christ" is the basis of their reconciliation to God.

These verses are in continuation of the apostolic apocalypse that began with reference to the universal resurrection (4:14) and ended with the universal judgment (5:10), into which was interjected the "deposit" of the Spirit in anticipation of the blessings of the eschaton (5:5).[1] Reconciliation and righteousness must be bracketed with the resurrection, the judgment, and the Spirit as forming the cluster of blessings of the end time. Fundamental to the gospel, however, is the astonishing reality that these blessings, which had been thought to belong exclusively to the future, are "now" — in principle and by anticipation, if not in finality — the possession of those who are "in Christ."

God's "gift" of a "ministry *(diakonia)* of reconciliation," to whom he has entrusted his "word of reconciliation," must be seen as part of God's gift to the world and to history, along with reconciliation, righteousness, and the Spirit.[2] God himself addresses the world through the mouths of his apostles, who speak the word of reconciliation, "Be reconciled to God." Hence the apostle is God's partner and fellow worker, empowered by God, through whom

---

1. See Thrall, 1.445-49, for decisive argument rejecting various theories as to a prior existence of vv. 18-21, e.g., that it was "a pre-Pauline hymnic fragment" (E. Käsemann, "Die Legitimatät") or "a confessional statement" (Martin).

2. As will be noted in the exegesis of vv. 18 and 19, the ἡμῖν ("to us") in Paul's phrases τοῦ θεοῦ . . . δόντος ἡμῖν τὴν διακονίαν τῆς καταλλαγῆς and θεὸς . . . θέμενος ἐν ἡμῖν τὸν λόγον τῆς καταλλαγῆς are here taken to refer to *Paul* in his apostleship. While some commentators take this view in a full or modified way (e.g., Windisch, Barrett, Harris, Martin, and Plummer), a majority (e.g., Furnish, Thrall; see also S. E. Porter, Καταλλάσσω, 130-44) think that Paul is referring to the believing community. Among other reasons, they argue that since the first use of "us" in this verse refers to the believing community, the second "us" must also refer to the believing community.

Our view that Paul is here referring to himself in his apostolic office is based on the following reasons: (1) the passage overall (2:14–7:4) is an apologia to the Corinthians for Paul's apostolate, with the latter part (5:11–6:13) implicitly or explicitly autobiographical. (2) Throughout 5:20–6:13 (passim), Paul specifically and directly appeals to the Corinthians ("you") (a) to be reconciled to God, and (b) to be open to him as their "father." We suggest that his basis for this is his assertion that to him has been "given"/"entrusted" the "ministry"/"word" of reconciliation, as in 5:18-19. Paul distinguishes carefully between himself ("we"/"us") and the Corinthians ("you"). They are not included with him in ministry, but rather are those *to whom* his ministry is directed. This is the intention of the excursus as a whole (2:14–7:4), but particularly its latter part (5:11–6:13). See further notes to the exegesis of vv. 18 and 19.

God speaks and who, as such, shares the dignity of the OT prophet who declared, "Thus says Yahweh."

This entire apologia (2:14–7:4) has been necessitated by Corinthian doubts about Paul's apostolicity in view of serious opposition and criticism of him in Corinth.[3] Paul's twofold appeal ("Be [you] reconciled to God. . . . [You] do not receive the grace of God in vain" — 5:21; 6:1) is directed specifically to the Corinthians. Their doubts about Paul as an apostle are tending to place them outside God's saving purposes. Hence Paul's powerful reminder, "Behold, now is the time of [God's] favor . . . the day of salvation." To align themselves with the eschatological purposes of God, they must first accept Paul's place in the divine scheme of things (see, too, on 6:11-13).

18 The unemphatic particle *(de)* at the head of this sentence marks a further development in the writer's line of thought. Paul begins by affirming that God is the source of all things ("All things[4] [are] from God"). He then declares God to be the subject of two acts:[5] (1) his action by which he "reconciled us to himself through Christ," and (2) his gift to "us" of "the ministry of reconciliation."

> But all things are from God,
> who reconciled us to himself
>   through Christ
> and gave   us the ministry of
>   reconciliation.

Whereas verses 14-17 were christocentric, v. 18, with v. 19, is theocentric. God is the subject of the verbs in these verses, most strikingly of the verb "reconcile," which has "the world" as its object in v. 19. The assertion "All things [are] from God" (cf. 1 Cor 8:6; 11:12b) appears to apply particularly to God's action in reconciling "the world" to himself. "All things" also picks up the "all" for whom Christ died in vv. 14, and 15, as well as the cosmological "new creation" of v. 17.

Christ, however, is the agent of the reconciling work that emanates from God.[6] In vv. 14-17 are clustered *universal* ("all" — vv. 14, 15) and *cosmological* ("new creation" — v. 17) categories in consequence of the *eschatological* action ("no longer . . . now" — vv. 15-17) in which Christ

---

3. See the introduction to 2:14-17.

4. Gk. τὰ . . . πάντα, referring to vv. 14-17 (cf. NIV, "all this").

5. Gk. καταλλάξαντος . . . δόντος; the participles are both aorists, suggesting completed actions.

6. Note the prepositions Gk. ἐκ θεοῦ . . . διὰ Χριστοῦ. These also occur in passages relating to creation. See John 1:2; Heb 1:2, where God is the *source (ek)* and Christ the *means (dia).*

died and was raised (vv. 14-15). In 5:18–6:2 Paul declares that *cosmological* reconciliation ("of the *world*" — v. 19) has been achieved "through Christ" (v. 18), signaling a new *eschatological* and *soteriological* moment (*"now"* is the day of *salvation*").[7] Nothing could be clearer than that Christ — crucified and risen (vv. 14-15) — is the locus and the means of fulfilling God's purposes for history, humanity, and the world and creation.[8]

Since "all things" flow "from God" and are brought to pass "though Christ," it follows that God and Christ are in perfect agreement, sharing the same mind as to the needs of humanity and the world, and what should be done to meet those needs.

The phrase "through Christ" is explained by the wider context as "through Christ's *death*" (vv. 14, 15, 21; cf. "we were reconciled to God through the death of his Son" — Rom 5:10). This is supported by the parallel phrase in the next verse, namely, "not counting their sins against them." It is through Christ's death, by which he does not count sins against people, that God has reconciled the world to himself. This is made clear in the climactic text, v. 21, where, on account of the sinless one being "made . . . sin, we become the righteousness of God." The relational blessing ("reconciliation with God") rests on forensic forgiveness ("righteousness"), as in the parallel passage in Romans where "being reconciled to God" (5:10) depends on "being justified" (5:1, 9).[9] Here the aorist tense, "reconciled," is significant, pointing to the completed character of the divine action. God has effected reconciliation objectively, prior to and

---

7. Gk. κόσμον καταλλάσσων . . . ἰδοὺ νῦν ἡμέρα σωτηρίας (5:19; 6:2).

8. The overlapping eschatological schemas of 4:16–5:10 and 5:14–6:2 should be noted:

4:16–5:10 —— present —————————— "not yet" ————————— **X** ———— coming
                  age   general   age
                                                      resurrection

5:14–6:2 ———— no —————— **X** —————— "now" ———→ **[X]**
              longer   death/
                    resurrection of Christ/
                    Spirit/New Creation/
                    Ministry of Reconciliation

In the first, the turning point from the present to the coming age is the general resurrection (4:14), and the emphasis is "not yet." In the second, the turning point is the death/resurrection of Christ/Holy Spirit/"gift" of ministry of reconciliation, and the emphasis is "no longer . . . now."

9. Gk. δικαιωθέντες . . . καταλλάγεντες, as noted by Bultmann, 158. *Contra*, e.g., T. W. Manson, *On Paul and John,* 38, who also asserted that reconciliation "denotes a change in relations between God and man and more particularly a change in man himself" (52). In fact, God reconciles the world to himself as he declares its members to be forgiven through Christ.

independent of subsequent human response, and, indeed, in the face of human hostility (see Rom 5:8, 10). By his initiative God has dealt with the trespasses that alienated humankind from him, removing from his side the obstacle to peace with him, his settled displeasure ("wrath") aroused by human sin.

With v. 18 is introduced into this letter — and indeed into Paul's epistolary corpus — the theme of "reconciliation,"[10] whose most extensive treatment occurs here (but see also Rom 5:10-11; cf. Rom 11:15; Eph 2:16; Col 1:20, 22). In vv. 18-21 the verb "reconcile" or the noun "reconciliation" occurs no less than five times.

Reconciliation, one of the blessings of the end time, is, like all the eschatological blessings of God, "realized" in Christ "now." This cosmic restoration (cf. Rom 11:15), while pointing ultimately to the reordering of all that is chaotic and distorted in the created world alienated from God and hostile to him, here applies specifically to human alienation from God.[11] It is *"their* trespasses" that are "not reckoned to *them."* Reconciliation with God, however, implies reconciliation among God's people (cf. Eph 2:16), something Paul later

10. See I. H. Marshall, "Meaning of Reconciliation," 119-20; G. K. Beale, "Reconciliation," and the literature cited there (550 n. 2); S. E. Porter, Καταλλάσσω, 125-44.

Scholars debate the influences upon Paul's use of the "reconciliation" vocabulary. G. K. Beale, "Reconciliation," 554-55, sees the theme of Israel's *restoration* to the land in terms of *creation* in Isaiah 40–55 as the primary source of Paul's words in 2 Cor 5:17-21 (see Isa 40:28-31; 41:17-20; 42:5-9; 44:21-23, 24-28; 45:1-8, 9-13, 18-20; 49:8-13; 51:1-3, 9-11, 12-16; 54:1-10; 55:6-13; cf. Isa 60:15-22; 65:15-17). It should be noted, however, that precise "reconciliation" vocabulary is not found in these Isaianic passages.

The only major parallel closer to NT times is in various texts in 2 Maccabees, where, however, God is simply the subject of reconciliation, e.g., "[God] might hear your requests and be reconciled to you" (καταλλαγείη ὑμῖν — 2 Macc 1:5; cf. 5:20; 7:33; 8:29; Josephus, *Ant.* 6.143). In 2 Cor 5:18-20, however, the divine act of reconciliation is complete, certain, and unconditionally available. God himself is the source of reconciliation, "us"/"the world" the object, God himself the indirect object, and Christ the agent of reconciliation. Apart from 2 Maccabees the notion of "reconciliation" is relatively undeveloped within Judaism contemporary with Paul, whether the LXX, the intertestamental literature, Josephus, or the rabbis; see F. Büchsel, *TDNT* 1.251-59.

The "reconciliation" vocabulary is found in no other NT writer. In Paul it is καταλλαγή (Rom 5:11; 11:15; 2 Cor 5:18, 19), καταλλάσσειν (Rom 5:10 [twice]; 1 Cor 7:11; 2 Cor 5:18, 19, 20). The only extant NT occurrence prior to 2 Cor 5:18-20 is 1 Cor 7:11, a marriage reference (τῷ ἀνδρὶ καταλλαγήτω). A few related "reconciliation" cognates are found in the NT — see διαλλαγῆναι (Matt 5:24) and ἀποκαταλλάσσειν (Eph 2:16; Col 1:20, 22). For the view (which we do not share on account of the paucity of references to it) that reconciliation is the "chief theme" in Paul's theology, see generally R. P. Martin, *Reconciliation,* an evaluation of which is offered by P. T. O'Brien, "Justification in Paul," 83-85.

11. The suggestion of, e.g., Barrett, 177, that κόσμον includes demonic forces is not warranted by 2 Cor 5:18–6:2, nor by Col 1:19-22, to which he refers.

calls "your mending" or restoration[12] (13:9, 11). There is a close connection between "new creation" (v. 17) and "reconciliation"; both are cosmic and end-time blessings, and both impact humans, to be accepted and given expression "now." Astonishingly, this cosmic reconciliation arises from a *death,* the death of that One (vv. 14-15) who, although without sin, was "made sin" by God to impute the "righteousness of God" to all who believe (5:21). The "righteousness of God," too, appears to be a blessing of God belonging to the end time, which, however, has "now" been brought into the present "in Christ."

Who, then, is the "us" whom God has reconciled to himself and to whom he has given the ministry of reconciliation? Is the second "us" to be, or not to be, identified with the first? Here there is no consensus among commentators. It is widely held that both references to "us" are to the community of believers.[13] Some hold that the first "us" refers to Paul, with the second referring to believers.[14] But most who do not equate the two references see the first pointing to the believing community, with the second pointing to the apostles.[15]

In our view both references to "us" apply in the first instance to Paul, with the first reference also inclusive of all believers (as in 3:18; 4:14, 16–5:10). This verse belongs to a wider passage (5:11–6:13), that is implicitly or explicitly autobiographical and that brings to a climax Paul's extended apologia for his apostolic office (2:14–7:4).[16] As the passage moves on to its conclusion, the "we"/"us" references are unambiguously apostolic and personal (5:20–6:13). Paul the writer ("we"/"us"), who is defending himself to the Corinthians, also appeals directly to the Corinthians ("you" — 5:20; 6:1, 11; cf. 5:12-13). The Corinthians are not those to whom the ministry and word of reconciliation have been given. Rather, they are to submit to that ministry and word, given to God's minister, Paul (6:3-4), which is directed to them.

In short, Paul is here saying, autobiographically, "God reconciled me . . . gave to me the ministry of reconciliation." But his words "reconciling the world" in the next verse immediately indicate that his words "reconciling us" are not narrowly autobiographical; he is speaking representatively for all believers (as also in vv. 14-17) and for "the world." However, the clause,

---

12. Gk. κατάρτισις.

13. So, e.g., Furnish, 317; Bultmann, 161.

14. So, e.g., Thrall, 1.430.

15. So, e.g., Barrett, 176; Harris, 354; Plummer, 182; and Windisch, 194.

16. Paul's defensiveness is apparent in 2:16b; 3:5-6 (his "sufficiency"); 2:17–3:3 (his divine call); 4:1-3 (his probity); and 4:7-13 (his sufferings). Consistent with his use of "us"/"we" for the apostolic office throughout this lengthy excursus (2:14–7:4), the "us" is here used for the apostle Paul (see on 2:14). Exceptions are where "we"/"all" is explicitly inclusive of believers in general, as in 3:12, 18 and between 4:16 and 5:10, or where the context demands it, as in v. 18a and v. 21.

"and entrusted to us the word of reconciliation" (v. 19), balancing "and gave us the ministry of reconciliation," suggests that this ministry/word is to be understood rather more narrowly, that is, as relating to Paul in his apostolic office. Paul, to whom God has given this ministry and word, will immediately address the Corinthians, calling directly on them to be reconciled to God and to his apostle (5:20–6:2, 11-13).

Consistent with the profoundly eschatological character of the passage 5:14–6:2 ("no longer . . . now"), God's gift of this "ministry" *(diakonia)* must likewise be seen as eschatological. By means of the "one" who died for "all," Christ, through whom God reconciled his enemies, God established his eschatological midpoint, his moment of "new creation" (v. 17). At that point he also established the ministry of reconciliation, which Paul earlier referred to as the ministry of a "new covenant" (3:6), a ministry of "the Spirit" and of "righteousness" (3:8, 9). As an apostle, Paul is "minister" in "this ministry" (4:1; cf. 6:3).

19 Paul now replays in essence what he asserted in v. 18. The sentence thus has the effect of reinforcing and explicating the ministry of reconciliation — both Christ's and Paul's — that was set forth there. Once again God is the subject and source of two acts that, with important differences, correspond to the previous verse: (1) God *is reconciling* (present tense) the *world* to himself, *not counting*[17] their trespasses to them, and (2) God has *entrusted* to us the *word (logos)* of reconciliation.

> That is,
> in Christ God was reconciling
> > > the world to himself,
> > not reckoning to them their trespasses.
> And he
> > has entrusted to us the word of reconciliation.

Verse 19 commences with an unusual phrase[18] that, broadly speaking, is interpreted[19] (1) "as it is said," introducing a quotation of traditional material,[20] (2) "as it is said," allusively introducing Paul's own material that he

---

17. Gk. λογιζόμενος, present participle, matching the imperfect periphrastic ἦν . . . καταλλάσσων.

18. Gk. ὡς ὅτι (NIV, "that"), an expression found also in 11:21 and 2 Thess 2:2. T. Muraoka, "The Use of ὡς in the Greek Bible," *NovT* 7 (1964), 65, based on analysis of the LXX and other koine literature, finds no clear solution to the meaning there.

19. Thrall, 1.431-32, suggests that ὡς ὅτι introduces direct or indirect speech, i.e., some form of quotation. If the words do not introduce a quotation, the remaining possibilities are that they are to be understood in a comparative, causal, or epexegetical sense. For a review of these see S. E. Porter, Καταλλάσσω, 132, who favors the epexegetic.

20. Furnish, 334, views it as "a citation formula."

had previously taught in Corinth,[21] or, (3) "that is," introducing an explanation of the previous verse.[22] We note that if a quotation is being signaled, it would probably end with the christological "in Christ God was reconciling the world" (v. 19a) rather than with v. 19b, v. 19c, or v. 20, each of which would add an extraneous element inconsistent with the coherence of a hymn, creed, or received teaching. In our view, option (1) is unlikely, given that the language of reconciliation is confined to Paul, and option (2), while possible, is conjectural. Option (3) appears to be the most unproblematic. The verse as it stands serves to restate v. 18, in particular picking up the "reconciliation" vocabulary, which Paul had not previously used in any (extant) letter. In all likelihood, therefore, by these opening words Paul appears to be introducing an explanation and expansion of the previous verse rather than rehearsing traditional or his own pre-Corinthian material. Whatever the case, however, the point of the verse is clear enough: God is bringing the world back into forgiven relationship with himself, and he is doing this by means of a "word" entrusted to the apostles.

There is a degree of ambiguity to the words following,[23] which, in broad terms, have been taken either as "God was in Christ reconciling the world to himself" (RV) or, preferably, as "in Christ God was reconciling the world to himself" (RSV).[24] The former would emphasize the incarnation, which, though mentioned in the letter (8:9), is not the burden of this passage. Rather, the death of Christ, which dominates the passage (vv. 14-15 and v. 21) and which overarches vv. 18-19, provides the key to the interpretation. The phrase "in Christ" repeats from v. 17, which in turn points to the "one" who died and was raised "for all" (vv. 14-15). Moreover, "in Christ" in this verse equates with "through Christ" (see on v. 18), that is, through that *death* by means of which God reconciled the world to himself. Further, the second part of the verse ("not reckoning their trespasses to them") firmly anchors the meaning in the death of Christ. The focus of this passage is the death and resurrection of Christ, in particular his death; the incarnation is not prominently in view.

21. So L. A. Belleville, "Gospel and Kerygma," 157-58.

22. As argued by S. E. Porter, Καταλλάσσω, 132.

23. Gk. θεὸς ἦν ἐν Χριστῷ κόσμον καταλλάσσων ἑαυτῷ. For extensive analysis and review of the meaning of these words see Martin, 153-55; S. E. Porter, Καταλλάσσω, 132-39.

24. While the former has few advocates (e.g., Allo, Bachmann, Collange), the latter is supported by most commentators (e.g., Plummer, Hughes, Barrett, Bultmann, Furnish, Martin, and Thrall). Because of the word order the text as it stands could be taken either way, and, indeed, in other ways beyond these (see S. E. Porter, Καταλλάσσω, 133; Thrall, 1.432-35). The context of vv. 14-21 must determine the more likely alternative, which in our view is the latter.

Whereas the primary referent ("us") of God's reconciliation in the previous verse was the apostle, this verse explains that such reconciliation is actually universal in scope ("the world"). Here the "world"[25] picks up the "all" from vv. 14-15 and points on to *their* trespasses to *them*."[26] God's reconciliation applies to "all . . . the world" and its members, since God does "not reckon[27] their trespasses[28] to them." God does not post to their account debts that are rightfully theirs.

What, then, is the significance of the change of tense of "God . . . reconcil*ing*" from "God . . . reconcil*ed*" of the previous verse.[29] Is reconciliation complete or incomplete?[30] It is held that the mere use of a present tense does not determine the sense that something is ongoing or incomplete. The flow of the passage must also be evaluated. Thus, when taken with the completed action "God . . . reconciled . . . through Christ['s death]" (v. 18), the words "God was . . . reconciling . . . not counting their trespasses against them," serve to emphasize that God's work of reconciliation stands finished and complete.[31]

Implicit in God's reconciliation of the world to himself is the fact of human alienation or estrangement from God. This is explicit in the parallel Rom 5:10: "For if, when we were God's *enemies*, we were reconciled to him through the death of his Son." Such enmity is due to human sin, as the reference to "sins" in this verse and to "sin" in v. 21 makes clear (see also Isa 59:2; Gen 6:5-6). Few have put so clearly as Denney the need and the consequence of reconcilia-

25. Cf. Rom 11:12, 15, where "the reconciliation of the world" means the Gentiles, and Eph 2:16, where both Jews and Gentiles are reconciled to God through Christ crucified, as expressed in the one body of fellowship.

26. Here the allusion is to the "blessed" man who is forgiven by God (Ps 32:1-2), a passage that Paul will quote and expand on in Rom 4:6-9. Cf. 2 Sam 19:19.

27. Gk. λογιζόμενος; NIV, "count[ing]." The verb λογίζομαι is commercial, referring to the calculation of a debt (see H. W. Heidland, *TDNT* 4.284-85).

28. Gk. παραπτώματα = "trespasses," but as the parallelism with Rom 4:25 shows, it is interchangeable with "sins." For Greeks παραπτώματα are errors made in innocence, whereas for Jews they are willful acts against God (e.g., LXX Job 36:9; Ps 19:12; Ezek 14:11). See W. Michaelis, *TDNT* 6.172.

29. Gk. καταλλάσσων . . . μὴ λογιζόμενος; cf. v. 18, καταλλάξαντος . . . δόντος.

30. In favor of reconciliation in v. 19 as ongoing, see Plummer, 183; Bruce, 209. For his part, Martin, 154, believes that the periphrastic imperfect (ἦν + participles καταλλάσσων . . . μὴ λογιζόμενος, "was reconciling . . . not reckoning") denotes an element of contingency. Although the the reconciliation is complete from God's side, there is the possibility that some people may not accept it. However, Thrall, 1.434, would have expected a periphrastic *present* construction had Paul intended "reconciling . . . not count-ing" to be understood as a continuous process. Thrall suggests that it is " 'a disguised aorist,' employed for reasons of style and rhythm."

31. See S. E. Porter, Καταλλάσσω, 138-39, who argues that on aspectual grounds v. 19 should be taken as "God's *act* of reconciliation" (emphasis added), with the peri-phrastic construction used for emphasis.

tion: "'Reconciliation' in the New Testament sense is not something which we accomplish when we lay aside our enmity to God; it is something which God accomplished when in the death of Christ he put away everything that on his side meant estrangement. . . ."[32] However, the imperative in v. 20 indicates that human response is required for it to be subjectively effective.

Remarkably, God is the initiator of the process by which those who have alienated themselves from God are reconciled to God. The notion of mediation is well known in modern culture; the mediator is usually an impartial third party. In this reconciliation, however, the aggrieved party is God, and it is God who initiates and secures the means of reconciling the self alienated from him back to him. Historically, certain attempts at explaining the atonement have used analogies of an impersonal kind.[33] In this passage, however, grammatically speaking, we have a subject, an object, an indirect object, an agent, and a verb. Each is personal. Both the subject and the indirect object are God ("God . . . to himself"), the object is fellow humans ("the world . . . their . . . to them"), the agent is Christ, and the verb "reconcile" is relational. It was "through Christ," the Son of God" (1:19), that "God . . . reconcil[ed] the world to himself." The personal/relational character of God's saving action must be kept uppermost.

Balancing the words "God . . . has given us the ministry of reconciliation" of the previous verse are the words "God . . . has entrusted to us[34] the word of reconciliation." The similarity of the form of the words and the use of the aorist or completed action verb suggest a close relationship between the two. Having reconciled the world to himself through Christ, God has provided for the communication and application of this knowledge, in the first instance, in the institution of the apostolate.[35] The "message *(logos)* of reconciliation" that God entrusted to the apostles ("us"), Paul included, is quoted in the next verse, namely, "Be reconciled to God." There it is made clear that God himself speaks this word through his human ambassador. This is nothing else than "the word of God" (see on 2:17; 4:2), the "gospel of Christ" (2:14; cf. 4:4), or the

32. J. Denney, *Death of Christ,* 211.

33. E.g., a set of scales, with Christ's righteousness outweighing human sins; an object — symbolizing sins — transferred from one hand to the other, illustrating the notion of exchange. The deeply personal character of both alienation and reconciliation is diminished by such examples.

34. Gk. θέμενος ἐν ἡμῖν; NIV, "committed to us" (lit., "having deposited in us"). Mindful of the contrast between Moses and Paul in chapter 3, Thrall, 1.436, sees here a pointed reminiscence of LXX Ps 104:27: ἔθετο ἐν αὐτοῖς τοὺς λόγους τῶν σημείων? God entrusted to Moses and Aaron (αὐτοῖς) only the message about the plagues to Pharaoh, but he has entrusted to Paul the word of reconciliation for the world. Cf. "For this I was *appointed* (ἐτέθην) a herald and apostle . . . a teacher of the Gentiles" (1 Tim 2:7; cf. 2 Tim 1:11).

35. *Contra* Furnish, 320, who takes ἐν ἡμῖν as the community of faith as the receptors of this word (see also S. E. Porter, Καταλλάσσω, 139). Paul generally uses "we"/"us" of himself as an apostle throughout the excursus on new covenant ministry (see on 1:1; 2:14).

· "preaching of the Son of God"/"Jesus Christ as Lord" (1:19; 4:5), to which Paul has already referred within the letter, through which reconciliation occurs.[36]

20 Paul is Christ's envoy, God's spokesman. Let the Corinthians heed his word to them. His use of "therefore"[37] signals that he is about to make a statement whose basis is in what he has already written. Paul's assertion is based not only on the two previous verses, however, but on the entire passage about the apostolic office that began in 2:14. In the two previous verses he wrote of (1) God's gift to him of the ministry of reconciliation (v. 18b), and (2) of God's entrusting to him of the message of reconciliation (v. 19c). Based on this authority to address them, Paul now begins a passage in which he challenges the Corinthians to be, in reality, what they profess to be, the new covenant people of God. Specifically, he calls on them (1) to be reconciled to God, (2) to widen their hearts to him, their "father" in the gospel (6:11-13), and (3) to withdraw from the temple cults of Corinth (6:14–7:1).

As it unfolds, the verse is in three parts: (1) Paul's assertion of apostolicity ("we are Christ's ambassadors"), (2) his claim that God speaks through him ("as though God were making his appeal through us"), and (3) his appeal to the Corinthians, the "word of reconciliation" ("We implore you, on Christ's behalf, 'Be reconciled to God' ").

This verse has a special place within the extended section in which Paul defends his apostolic office to the Corinthians (2:14–7:4). The defensive tone at certain points within this passage probably reflects a degree of doubt among Paul's readers regarding the validity of his claim to apostleship (e.g., 2:17–3:3; 5:12-13, 16; 6:3-13; 7:2-4). Paul, however, implies that their attitude to him and their relationship with him cannot be separated from their relationship with God and his salvation (6:11-13). Let the Corinthians understand that it was through Paul's apostolic ministry that they have been caught up in God's eschatological-reconciling purposes; therefore, let them continue to be subject to Paul's ministry so as to confirm and continue in God's good purposes for them.

Thus Paul begins by stating a fundamental aspect of apostleship, namely, "we represent, on Christ's behalf. . . ."[38] Here Paul expresses the well-known

---

36. G. Bornkamm, *TDNT* 6.682, notes that, "The preaching . . . is not just a later imparting of the news of the act of salvation; it is an essential part of it."

37. Gk. οὖν.

38. Gk. ὑπὲρ Χριστοῦ . . . πρεσβεύομεν, which, it should be noted, matches δεόμεθα ὑπὲρ Χριστοῦ. Paul, however, not only "represents . . . implores on behalf and in the place of" Christ; he also sustains "weaknesses . . . on behalf of Christ" (12:10). As Christ's envoy Paul not only speaks for the One he represents; he also replicates his sufferings.

The use of ὑπέρ in culturally identifiable terms relative to the ancient envoy or delegate, and with such a clear meaning as "on behalf of," "in the place of," is very significant for the meaning of the word in more controversial passages relating to the death of Christ. The clear substitutionary/representational meaning in v. 20 must also apply in vv. 14, 15, and 21.

role of the "apostle" within Judaism (the *shaliaḥ*[39] — see on 1:1), whereby an envoy from the Sanhedrin or High Priest would "represent" to a distant synagogue decrees and judgments of the sender, with the authority of the sender. Appropriate to a Greco-Roman readership, Paul states this in the culturally familiar terms of a group of envoys representing a nation[40] or of a legate representing the emperor.[41] Such delegates — Jewish or Greco-Roman — came with the authority of the sender, in his place, to secure his interests. It is this role that Paul is reasserting to the Corinthians (see on 1:1). He is an envoy of Christ, the Messiah of God; Paul is his apostle.[42] In that period, to reject the representations of an envoy was to reject the one who sent him.[43] To ignore Paul at this point would have been to ignore the Christ on whose behalf he spoke.[44]

Paul adds to this credential the closely related claim that "God makes his appeal through us,"[45] that is, God speaks through apostles (which in this context means Paul himself). This is a claim Paul has made earlier in the letter (see on 2:17[46]). God's "appeal" *(parakalountos)* through the apostle reminds

39. According to Mishnah *Berakoth* 5.5, "A man's agent is as himself."

40. E.g., Thucydides, *The Peloponnesian War* 8.45.4; 1 Macc 14:21-22. See, generally, G. Bornkamm, *TDNT* 6.681-83; D. Kienast, "Presbeia," *PWSup* 13.546-52; M. M. Mitchell, "New Testament Envoys," 641-62. For a connection between "ambassador" and "minister" in the Hellenistic sources — as a possible background to Paul's vocabulary — see J. T. Fitzgerald, *Earthen Vessels,* 186.

41. For evidence see Bultmann, 163; Furnish, 339.

42. Cf. 1 Cor 1:17: . . . ἀπέστειλέν με Χριστὸς . . . εὐαγγελίζεσθαι.

43. Philo, who represented the Jewish community in Alexandria to Emperor Gaius and who knew firsthand what it was like to be an envoy, commented, "for the sufferings of envoys recoil on those who sent them" *(Embassy to Gaius,* 369).

44. *Contra* S. E. Porter, Καταλλάσσω, 139-40, who argues that πρεσβεύομεν includes Paul's Christian readers with himself, calling on them to be ambassadors on behalf of Christ, because (1) the "us" references in vv. 18 and 19 should not be limited to the apostles, (2) ὡς with the genitive absolute τοῦ παρακαλοῦντος in v. 20, is best taken as "with the thought that God appeals through us," and (3) καταλλάγητε τῷ θεῷ is addressed to those to whom the Corinthians are ambassadors. Porter's case, however, fails to account adequately for (1) the otherwise consistent use of "we"/"us" by Paul throughout the excursus on new covenant ministry (see on 2:14), (2) the direct appeal Paul makes to the Corinthians (ὑμᾶς) in "not to receive the grace of God in vain" in 6:1, and (3) the closely related appeal to the Corinthians for restored relationships with Paul himself (6:11-13); reconciliation to God and restoration to Paul are inseparable, and Paul is appealing to *the Corinthians* about these things.

45. The genitive absolute construction τοῦ θεοῦ παρακαλοῦντος preceded by ὡς expresses a subjective judgment that may represent a view that is either (1) correct (e.g., 2 Pet 1:3) or (2) incorrect (e.g., 1 Cor 4:18; 1 Pet 4:12). The context indicates that (1) is here intended. Thus Paul is expressing the conviction that God is, indeed, making his appeal through Paul.

46. See 2:17: ὡς . . . ἐκ θεοῦ . . . λαλοῦμεν (cf. 4:2). ". . . in the proclamation of the message God was himself present" (Martin, 156).

us of God's call to Isaiah to "comfort, comfort" his exiled people in view of his coming deliverance and restoration of them to their land (Isa 40:1 — *parakaleite;* see also on 1:4). Its use here is evocative of God's kindness to his people at that time, calling on them in this the day of salvation (6:2) to accept his merciful action toward them. Paul's is a momentous assertion, analogous to the declaration of the OT prophet, "Thus says Yahweh."[47] He is claiming for the apostle the same authority as a prophet like Isaiah. Paul's appeal — which is God's appeal — expresses in its own way the apostolic nonresignation, the revelation, the breaking forth of light referred to earlier (4:1, 2, 6). This is appropriate given the reality of the "no longer . . . now" aeon inaugurated by the death and resurrection of Christ. The ministry and the message of reconciliation are inextricably part of the inception of that aeon of the "new creation."

Then — as an apostle representing Christ and an eschatological spokesman of God — in tender and compassionate terms he "implores"[48] them once more "on Christ's behalf."[49] But what do the words "Be reconciled to God"[50] mean? Taken broadly, Paul is admonishing the Corinthians to be restored in their relationships with God. At this time they are all too easily tolerating heterodox teaching about Jesus (11:4) under the influence of the newly arrived "peddlers of God's word" (2:17). Moreover, Paul's defensive tone throughout the excursus indicates significant disapproval of his role and ministry in Corinth (3:5-6; 4:2, 7, 12; 5:11-13; 6:3-10; 7:2-4). In consequence, this church has drifted some distance from God and his spokesman, Paul. Paul is encouraging them to return to their God and to the word spoken by Paul, the apostle of Christ (see on 6:11-13).

Paul's words, however, must also be taken in a narrower sense, as dictated by the verses on either side. Paul is appealing to the Corinthians to confirm their acceptance of the forgiveness of God (v. 19) and the "righteousness of God" given them in the death of the Sinless One (v. 21). The passive injunction "Be reconciled" means "Be reconciled *by God*," that is, allow God to reconcile you, bring you back to himself, by means of his forgiveness. The parallel statement "through [Christ] we have now receiv*ed* our reconciliation" (Rom 5:11) shows that reconciliation is God's gift to be "received." Here Paul is facing the Corinthians with the very fundamentals of the word

---

47. So Plummer, 185.

48. The verb δεῖσθαι introduces earnest and tender exhortations: 10:2; cf. 1 Thess 3:10; Rom 1:10.

49. Gk. ὑπὲρ Χριστοῦ is repeated so as to reinforce "the official and authoritative capacity in which Paul writes" (Furnish, 339).

50. Gk. καταλλάγητε τῷ θεῷ. The aorist, while referring to the moment of conversion of the Corinthians (see also 1:19; 12:12), may also point to a critical moment of obedience to the apostolic word; the closely related πλατύνθητε (6:14) is also aorist.

of God on which the church is founded (cf. 1 Cor 15:1-5). In God's own appeal to them, spoken by the apostle of Christ, is the call to continue in what they have begun to be, a people forgiven by God, reconciled to God through Christ's sacrificial death for them.

21 This justly famous verse is one of the most critical in this letter and, indeed, within the writings of the apostle Paul. It comes near the end of the passage to which it belongs (5:14–6:2) and is the theological foundation ("a delayed conclusion"[51]) for the entire passage, including the theme of reconciliation that dominates the earlier verses (vv. 18-20). Nonetheless, the sentence lacks any connective linking it with what has gone before;[52] it stands as an impressively absolute statement.

Structurally, v. 21 is in two parts: (1) the first, in which God is the subject (understood[53]) and "him who knew no sin" (Christ) the object, and (2) the second, introduced by the purposive "that,"[54] in which "we" is the subject and "might become the righteousness of God" the complement. The sentence derives its rhetorical power from the paradoxical chiasm in the first part (lit. "the one who knew not sin . . . sin [God] made"[55]), and the antithesis between the first and second parts ("[God] made him *sin* that we might become the *righteousness* of God in him"). Juxtaposed in the first are "no[t] sin" and "sin," and between the first and the second are "sin" and "righteousness." Here, stated succinctly and with power, is the heart of the gospel.

```
A    The one who knew not sin
            for us
                        sin                   [God] made,
B                 that we might become
                        the righteousness   of God
      in him.
```

Given its striking, proverblike, free-standing character, it is not surprising that many scholars have sought the origin of this verse in an earlier creed, hymn, or teaching.[56] More probably, however, it is Paul's own adaptation

---

51. So N. Dahl, quoted by Furnish, 351.

52. Grammatically, the construction that lacks a connective particle is called asyndeton. Failing to appreciate the power of the verse in a freestanding sense, some copyists have inserted γάρ, "for."

53. From the final words of the previous verse: τῷ θεῷ.

54. Gk. ἵνα.

55. Gk. τὸν μὴ γνόντα ἁμαρτίαν . . . ἁμαρτίαν ἐποίησεν; NIV, "God made him who had no sin to be sin."

56. See, e.g., Martin, 156-57, who notes (1) that ἁμαρτία is here used in an un-Pauline way for the punishment rather than the power of sin, and (2) that δικαιοσύνη is here imparted rather than imputed. Judgments based on linguistic tendency, however,

of an earlier *hyper*-tradition[57] that he "received" (from the apostolic community in Jerusalem?) and "handed over" to the churches, as is evident in the First Letter (see, e.g., "This is my body, which is *for* you" — 11:24; "Christ died *for* our sins" — 15:3). As such, the adaptation of the tradition in this verse[58] may be bracketed with Gal 3:13: "Christ . . . became a curse *for* us."[59] Underlying both of Paul's adaptations of the pre-Pauline *hyper*-tradition — if these assumptions are correct — are a number of OT texts by which he was apparently influenced: (1) the deuteronomic "a hanged man is accursed by God" (21:23, RSV),[60] and, more directly, (2) the vicarious, sin-bearing sufferings of the Servant of Yahweh in Isa 52:13–53:12.[61]

This verse makes powerful assertions about Christ, his life and death.

---

tend to be inconclusive, especially in so brief a passage as this. "Made sin" is a metonymy whereby this abstraction stands for something concrete, the crucifixion (see also on 8:9).

57. Gk. ὑπὲρ ἡμῶν. See on v. 14.

58. For a possible parallel to the ἁμαρτία/δικαιοσύνη adaptation of the ὑπέρ-tradition in this verse see 1 Pet 3:18: δίκαιος ὑπὲρ ἀδίκων.

59. Gk. Χριστὸς . . . γενόμενος ὑπὲρ ἡμῶν κατάρα. For an analogous parallel see Rom 9:3: ηὐχόμην γὰρ ἀνάθεμα . . . ἀπὸ τοῦ Χριστοῦ ὑπὲρ τῶν ἀδελφῶν μου. . . .

60. Gk. κεκατηράμενος ὑπὸ τοῦ θεοῦ πᾶς κρεμάμενος ἐπὶ ξύλου (LXX Deut 21:23). This text was very influential within the NT as an apologetic-theological interpretation of the death of the Messiah (Acts 5:30; 10:39; 13:29; Gal 3:13; 1 Pet 2:24; Rev 2:7; 22:2 [twice], 14, 19). While Gal 3:13 (Χριστὸς . . . γενόμενος ὑπὲρ ἡμῶν κατάρα) is linguistically dependent on and indeed quotes — with alteration — Deut 21:23, the same cannot be said for 2 Cor 5:21, where ἁμαρτίαν ἐποίησεν only notionally resembles κεκατηράμενος ὑπὸ τοῦ θεοῦ.

61. Note the many references to the Servant as sin-bearer in this passage: v. 4, οὗτος τὰς ἁμαρτίας ἡμῶν φέρει ("he bears our *sins*"); v. 5, ἐτραυματίσθη διὰ τὰς ἁμαρτίας ἡμῶν καὶ μεμαλάκισται διὰ τὰς ἀνομίας ἡμῶν ("he was wounded on account of our *sins,* and was bruised because of our *iniquities*"); v. 6, Κύριος παρέδωκεν αὐτὸν ταῖς ἁμαρτίας ἡμῶν ("the Lord gave him up for our *sins*"); v. 8, ἀπὸ τῶν ἀνομιῶν τοῦ λαοῦ μου ἤχθη εἰς θάνατον ("because of the *iniquities* of my people he was led to death"); v. 10, ἐὰν δῶτε περὶ ἁμαρτίας ("if you can give an offering for *sin*"); v. 11, καὶ τὰς ἁμαρτίας αὐτῶν αὐτὸς ἀνοίσει ("and he shall bear their *sins*"); v. 12, καὶ ἐν τοῖς ἀνόμοις ἐλογίσθη καὶ αὐτὸς ἁμαρτίας πολλῶν ἀνήνεγκε καὶ διὰ τὰς ἀνομίας αὐτῶν παρεδόθη ("and he was numbered among the transgressors; and he bore the *sins* of many, and was delivered because of their *iniquities*").

On the basis of these references we can readily understand Paul's terse ἁμαρτίαν ἐποίησεν [θεός], "God made him . . . sin" as an apt summary of the entire chapter, especially vv. 10, 11, and 13. See also Rom 8:3: περὶ ἁμαρτίας κατέκρινεν τὴν ἁμαρτίαν ἐν τῇ σαρκί (i.e., God condemned sin in the flesh of Christ). For the argument that 2 Cor 5:21 is profoundly influenced by Isaiah 53, see G. K. Beale, "Reconciliation," 559-60. For the opposite view see B. H. McLean, "The Absence of Atoning Sacrifice," 531-53.

It points first to the sinlessness of his incarnate[62] life ("he knew no sin"[63]) and then to his sin-laden death ("[God] made him sin"). It is to be inferred that the efficacy of his death arises from the sinlessness of his life. Because in his death God "made"[64] *this* sinless man sin for us,[65] those who are "in him" by faith commitment "became[66] the righteousness of God."

The term "righteousness of God"[67] is located in a passage in which

62. Some, however, view these words as applying to his preincarnate existence; see, e.g., Plummer 187; Furnish, 340. Against this view and in favor of the above, we note (1) that the temporal "he *knew* no sin" points to a moment when he did, i.e., at crucifixion, and (2) that the efficacy of Christ's redemption logically rests on a demonstrated sinlessness during his *earthly* ministry.

63. The Greek verb "know" gives expression to the Hebraic "know" of the OT, which implies comprehensive, not merely intellectual, knowledge (cf. Gen 4:1: "Adam *knew* Eve his wife and she conceived," RSV). Here it means that Christ did not practice sin, but was blameless and innocent in life and motive before God. The sinlessness of Christ is attested by several NT writers (see 1 Pet 2:22; 1 John 3:5; Heb 4:15; 7:26; cf. John 8:46). It is probable that the NT writers are influenced by the apostolic perception of the historical Jesus and by reflection on Isa 53:9 — ἀνομίαν οὐκ ἐποίησεν, οὐδὲ δόλον ἐν τῷ στόματι αὐτοῦ ("he practiced no iniquity, nor craft with his mouth"); 53:11 — δικαιῶσαι δίκαιον εὖ δουλεύοντα πολλοῖς ("to justify the just one who serves many well").

64. Gk. ἐποίησεν is aorist — completed action — tense.

65. From the patristic era on, two main lines of interpretation for ὑπὲρ ἡμῶν ἁμαρτίαν ἐποίησεν have been pursued: (1) that Christ suffered as though he was himself a sinner (αὐτοαμαρτία — "sin itself"), that he was "sin personified." But this is to contradict the verse itself; Christ "did not know sin." (2) That he was a "sin offering" (as argued by L. A. Belleville, "Gospel and Kerygma," 152). The basis for this view is (a) that Heb. *hatta't,* "sin offering," is rendered as ἁμαρτία on several occasions in LXX Leviticus 4. This viewpoint is supported by Rom 8:3, where περὶ ἁμαρτίας echoes Isaiah's Servant, who makes himself "an offering for sin" (περὶ ἁμαρτίας — Isa 53:10). (b) His sinlessness reminds us of the unblemished offering of the sacrifice. To be sure, Paul's reference in this verse to sinlessness *and* "justification" is consistent with Isaiah's Servant, who committed no sin and justified many (Isa 53:9-11). However, the consideration that ἁμαρτία in τὸν μὴ γνόντα ἁμαρτίαν in the first part of the verse cannot mean "sin offering" remains a strong reason to exclude "made sin" = "sin offering" in the second. Rather, Paul's words summarize without explaining Isa 52:13–53:12.

66. Gk. ἐποίησεν . . . γενόμενος are aorists, here signifying completed actions. The aorist "we *became* the righteousness of God" matches, and is on account of, the aorist "[God] *made* him sin."

67. Gk. δικαιοσύνη θεοῦ; see also Rom 1:17; 3:5, 21, 22, 25, 26; 10:3 (twice); Phil 3:9. See K. Kertelge, *EDNT* 1.325-30. Chronologically this is the first known use of this phrase. It should be noted that δικαιοσύνη may be translated "righteousness" or "justification." Although δικαιοσύνη and its cognates are relatively infrequent to this point in Paul's letters, their use will expand dramatically in the Letter to the Romans, beginning with the affirmation that in the gospel is revealed δικαιοσύνη . . . θεοῦ (1:17-18). It may be significant that Isaiah 53, Paul's major intellectual quarry for this verse, speaks of God's justification of the righteous servant (δικαιῶσαι δίκαιον εὖ δουλεύοντα πολλοῖς —

both soteriology and eschatology are powerfully asserted (*"now* is the day of *salvation"* — 6:2). The long-awaited "day" has dawned. The "former" times are concluded; they are "no longer" (5:14-17). The salvation of God "now" stands revealed "in Christ," ahead of the coming ages when it was formerly expected that the blessings of God for his people would be manifested.[68] Because of their proximity a close parallel exists between the statements "become the righteousness of God" and "not reckoning their trespasses to them" (v. 19). As indicated earlier, "righteousness" is the opposite of "condemnation," the divine rejection (see on 3:9). The words "become the righteousness of God in him" point to forgiveness, the reversal of condemnation. Here, then, is the objective, forensic "justification" of God to those who are covenantally dedicated to God "in Christ,"[69] whom God "made sin." This theme is touched on in the First Letter (1 Cor 1:30; 6:11) and expressed in the present letter (cf. 3:9), possibly in response to a works-righteousness schema of the false apostles (see 11:15).

As noted above, this verse, though coming near the the end of its passage, is effectively the foundation of that passage; statements unexplained in earlier verses are now made clear.[70] The resolution of the divine displeasure at sin in the One who knew no sin being made sin is the basis of the divine reconciliation of those alienated from God by their sins.

This verse explains how the "one"/"he" effectively "died for all," how he revealed his "love" for them (vv. 14-15), how eschatologically and personally a "new creation" occurs "in Christ" (v. 17), and how God reconciled the apostle/his people/the world to himself (vv. 18-19). Above all, the vicarious death of Christ in v. 21 provides the emotional and spiritual basis for the heart-rending appeal of the previous verse. That God made the Sinless One sin for us leaves sinful ones like the Corinthians, and all readers since, with no real alternative but to heed the apostolic call, "Be reconciled to God."

1 Paul now speaks directly to the Corinthians ("you"). The opening connectives[71] introduce an amplification of what has preceded, and may be

---

53:11). Is Paul implying that our justification is *in* the just one whom God justified on account of his "good" service? (See Furnish, 341.)

68. See Furnish, 340, for discussion whether or not Paul was dependent on apocalyptic Judaism for the phrase "the righteousness of God." In all likelihood he was.

69. To be rejected is N. T. Wright, "Righteousness of God," 206, who identifies "we" as the covenant minister, Paul himself. (". . . [He] represents the one for whom he speaks in such a full and thorough way that he actually *becomes* the living embodiment of his sovereign — or perhaps . . . the *dying* embodiment." In that case Paul would need to preach himself, which, of course, he says he does not (4:5).

70. In support of the case that justification is "foundational to Paul's gospel," see P. T. O'Brien, "Justification in Paul," 84-85.

71. Gk. δὲ καί.

paraphrased as "but there is more to be said. . . ."[72] His next statement "we *appeal*" clearly echoes "as though God were making his *appeal* through us" from v. 20.[73] Thus Paul's undefined "working together with,"[74] with which the sentence begins, must point to God as the One with whom Paul works.[75] Paul works together with God because God, through Paul, makes his appeal to the Corinthians (v. 20).

The second part of the sentence gives the content of God's appeal through Paul to the readers ("you — do not receive the grace of God in vain"). Having inferentially admonished the Corinthians ("Be [you] reconciled to God," RV), Paul now addresses them directly with the pronoun *"you,"* which, for further emphasis, comes at the end of the sentence. However the "world" may respond to God's reconciling activity toward its members through the word of reconciliation he has entrusted to the apostles (vv. 18-19), let the Corinthians clearly demonstrate their positive response.

The aorist "receive"[76] in "not to *receive* God's grace in vain" (i.e., "to no profit"[77]) is capable of several interpretations: (1) in the timeless sense (i.e., "having received and continuing to receive"), and (2) in the past sense (i.e., "not to have received . . ."). The latter is more probable, pointing to the moment the Corinthians submitted to the eschatological proclamation of the Son of God, as the fulfillment of the promises of the old covenant and the inauguration of the new covenant, when they were reconciled, justified to God (5:18-21), and, in consequence, received the long-awaited Spirit of God (1:19, 22; 3:3, 6; 5:5; 12:12; cf. 11:4). Paul is saying, in effect, "You have been caught up in God's eschatological and saving purposes; do not let that have been in vain."

But what is this "grace of God" that they are in danger of having "received in vain"? It must be noted that these words come at a critical point

---

72. Plummer, 189.

73. Gk. παρακαλοῦντος . . . παρακαλοῦμεν.

74. Gk. συνεργοῦντες; NIV, "as God's fellow workers."

75. Plummer, 189-90, lists five possibilities cited by scholars as to the one with whom Paul is a fellow worker: (1) with God, based on vv. 18 and 21; (2) with Christ, as inferred by ὑπὲρ Χριστοῦ in v. 20; (3) with the Corinthians; (4) with other teachers; and (5) with Paul's exhortations. Plummer correctly favors (1). While (2) is less likely, options (3) and (4) are improbable. Clearly option (1) is correct.

In a private communication R. H. Saunders notes that the use of the noun συνεργός in classical and Hellenistic literature and within the NT suggests that one "partner" is subordinate to the other. Thus Paul would be God's junior partner. But see 1 Cor 3:9, where Paul and Apollos are equals as coworkers.

76. Gk. δέξασθαι. Note that the same verb in the aorist tense is used for "receiving" the gospel (11:4).

77. Gk. εἰς κενόν. LXX Lev 26:20; Job 39:16; Isa 29:8; Jer 6:29; 28:58; also 1 Thess 3:5; Gal 2:2; Phil 2:16.

within Paul's long apologia for the apostolic office (2:14–7:4). The answer to the question now asked must be connected with the answer to the question: Why did Paul write this apologia to the Corinthians? Surely it was because of the challenge to his apostleship being raised at that time in a number of quarters in Corinth.[78] These include the newly arrived opponents (2:17–3:1; 5:11-13; 11:13-23), his superspiritual critics in Corinth (10:3-7), and those who remain perilously involved with the cults of Corinth (see on 6:14–7:1).[79] By this understanding the "grace of God" is Paul's terse caption for the grand vista that he has just painted portraying God's eschatological salvation by which God reconciled the guilty to himself through the death of the Innocent One (vv. 18-21; cf. 8:9). Intrinsic to God's gracious reconciliation of the world to himself is God's appointment of his yokefellows, the apostles to whom God entrusted the word of reconciliation.[80]

Thus the apostolic herald of that new aeon now stands before the Corinthians. As God raised up Isaiah[81] as his prophet to speak through him to "comfort, comfort" God's people (Isa 40:1), so within this new eschatological aeon God has called Paul to be his coworker and instrument to reconcile the world to God, and to "appeal" to those already reconciled to remain so. This statement, therefore, must take its place with others within the letter through which Paul makes the highest claims for his apostleship. By his use of the vocabulary of "appeal"[82] (5:20; 6:1; cf. LXX Isa 40:1, where it may be rendered "comfort" or "appeal") and the text from Isaiah in the verse following, Paul is claiming an authority analogous to that of the OT prophets, who spoke for God. God made one "appeal" through his prophet; now he makes another "appeal" through his apostle (see on v. 20). The authority of the apostolic office has come to the surface on a number of occasions so far (1:1; 3:12; 4:1, 2, 6) and, indeed, will do so again before the letter is concluded (10:8; 12:12; 13:10).

Paul's authority in ministry, however, is not freestanding, but rather is

---

78. Martin, 166-67, focuses on Paul's unnamed adversary in Corinth (7:12) and the reconciliation with him achieved by Paul's actions (2:5-11). However, the differences between Paul and this man may have been rather more personal than in relation to Paul's standing as an apostle. The length and intensity of the passage on his apostleship (2:14–7:4) imply that it was now under renewed assault, in all probability through the arrival of the newly arrived "peddlers" (see on 2:17).

79. Barrett, 183, understands these words as addressed to all believers, all of whom run the risk of continuing to live for themselves and not for Christ (cf. 5:15), thus receiving the grace of God "in vain." But more probably Paul is addressing the critical challenge posed by particular parties in Corinth at that time.

80. See G. K. Beale, "Reconciliation," 560-61.

81. See Introduction, 46-47.

82. Gk. παρακαλεῖν.

inextricably connected with and dependent upon the word of the gospel entrusted to Paul (vv. 18-19). In turn, that gospel demands that its bearer embody its central truths of death and resurrection. Thus the moral authority for Paul's ministry, which he repeatedly defends to the Corinthians, is that the death of Jesus is replicated, as it were, in "death"like sufferings incurred in ministry, and in "resurrection" deliverance from those sufferings by the power of God (1:8-10; 4:7-12; 6:3-10; 7:5-6; 12:7-9). To this he will turn in the passage 6:3-10.

2 This verse is arguably the key verse of the apostolic excursus (2:14–7:4) and, indeed, of the entire letter.[83] Quoting God's words to Isaiah (Isa 49:8), and applying them to the Corinthians, Paul declares that, with the death and resurrection of Jesus Christ (5:14-15), the very day of God's salvation has dawned. This is the eschatological grace of God (v. 1).

The opening words flow directly from v. 1, "as God's fellow workers. . . . For *he* [God[84]] says." There follows a citation of God's words to Isaiah that he had heard and, in consequence, helped the prophet in the day of salvation. But to whom do the words, as quoted by Paul, apply? To himself or to the Corinthians? Given that the previous verse ended with "you" (Corinthians), the most likely answer is that Paul is addressing the Corinthians in this citation.[85]

Powerfully and explicitly Paul declares that the world and history have been overtaken by God, that God's "time,"[86] his "day of salvation," has "now" arrived. Everything that Christ has done as the cosmic, soteriological, and eschatological centerpoint is now affirmed by the word that covers all the ground of vv. 14-21 — salvation. Paul writes these words conscious that he and his readers belong on this side of the historic inauguration of both "new covenant" and "new creation" (3:3; 5:17).[87] Through the gospel the grace of God has come to them; that is, in terms of the citation, God has "heard" and "helped" them. Let them not turn their backs on this "grace."

---

83. *Contra* Plummer, 190, who regards this verse as a "footnote."

84. Is Gk. λέγει ("he says") in reference: (1) to Yahweh, who is being quoted in Isa 49:8, or (2) to Scripture, which, as it were, still "speaks" (so Hughes, 219). In favor of (2) it should be noted that λέγει is used in other Pauline citations of Scripture (Rom 15:10; Eph 4:8). More probably, however, it is God who speaks, since the antecedent of λέγει is τοῦ θεοῦ.

85. So Thrall, 1.453; *contra* G. K. Beale, "Reconciliation," 561-62.

86. Gk. καιρός, God's "special moment," the time of eschatological opportunity, when God summons to repentance and obedience. See the classic statement in O. Cullmann, *Christ and Time*, 37-59.

87. The accent in 5:14–6:2 is on the "now" of salvation; but this emphasis must be kept in tension with 4:16–5:10, where the emphasis was on "not yet." The present thus includes Paul's weaknesses, even though the present gift of the Spirit guarantees the realization of what is "not yet."

The OT citation, LXX Isa 49:8a, is Yahweh's word to his "servant," Isaiah the prophet, for the captive people of Israel in Babylonian exile. It is in the form of "synonymous parallelism":

At the right time[88] I gave heed to you;
on the day of salvation I helped you."

Paul glosses[89] this oracle by repeating Isaiah's statements, introducing both with the dramatic and joyful "Behold, now."[90] He intensifies the first[91] ("the *welcomed* time") and repeats exactly the second ("the day of salvation"). Paul's twofold refrain "Behold, now" here picks up and emphasizes what he has written in the previous passage ("behold" — v. 17; "now" — v. 16 [twice]). In all probability Paul is seeking the attention of the Corinthians by his repeated, "Behold now. . . ."

Paul's appeal is not to be taken primarily in the sense of urgency, as if delay is dangerous. Rather, the twice-repeated "Behold, now" points to the final phase that salvation history has now entered, ushered in by God's reconciliation of the world and his appointment of preachers of reconciliation (vv. 18-19). This is the "grace of God." The eschatological reality of the now-arrived "day of salvation" is the bedrock for God's twice-given "appeal" through Paul to them, (1) that they "be reconciled to God" (v. 20), and (2) that they do not "receive the grace of God in vain" (v. 1). As such, this soteriological-eschatological basis for Paul's "appeal" is — we take it — directed to the present confusion and crisis within the Corinthian church. Let them bring their beliefs and behavior in line with God's saving purposes, now revealed.

A major hermeneutical question is raised by the exegesis we have adopted for 5:18–6:2. In our view Paul is speaking about himself as an apostle. The ministry God gave to Paul, the word God entrusted to him, this Paul exercises as an ambassador or apostle (vv. 18-20). Paul is Christ's representative, his surrogate, and it is through Paul as an apostle that God appeals to his hearers, "Be reconciled to God" (v. 20). He is God's coworker (6:1), words Paul wrote

88. Martin, 168, points out (against Plummer, 190-91) that the "right" or "acceptable" time means the time when, through his grace, humankind is "acceptable" *with God* (see Isa 61:2).

89. Martin, 168-69, suggests that this is an example of an interpretative method known as *pesher,* whereby Paul "analyzes the OT quotation and makes contemporary fulfillment the point to be grasped."

90. Gk. ἰδοὺ νῦν.

91. Isaiah has δεκτῷ, which Paul intensifies (so Plummer, 191) as εὐπρόσδεκτος, a word that is not found in the LXX but which Paul uses elsewhere (8:12; Rom 15:16, 31).

319

being conscious that this is the dawn of the "day of salvation." Moreover, Paul establishes this significant point, as a basis from which to launch his climactic appeals to the Corinthians (1) to be reconciled to God (5:20; 6:1), (2) to widen their hearts to Paul their "father" (6:11-13), and (3) to withdraw from all that is unclean in Corinth (6:14–7:1).

The question is: Do these words apply beyond the apostolic generation to persons who are not apostles? As to their initial and primary intent, as from the pen of Paul to this wayward church, we note that Paul was offering a defense for his ministry rather than giving a pattern for believers. This passage belongs to the excursus on apostolic ministry in which Paul is a source of revelation (see, e.g., 4:2, 6), through whom — as he will say later — God worked the signs of an apostle (12:12). He has been given the Lord's authority (10:8; 13:10). The point Paul is making is that, as an apostle of Christ, he exercises religious authority over the Corinthians, an authority that cannot — by its nature — be shared with, for example, members of the church in Corinth. He expects to be heeded (2:9; 10:5; 13:11). Thus understood, these verses cannot be applied without qualification to others outside the apostolic circle beyond the apostolic age. Such persons do not bear the direct authority of Christ, as his ambassadors, in the way Paul did.

Paul's authority as an apostle of Christ, however, cannot be separated from the faithful exercise of that ministry in proclaiming the gospel of the death and resurrection of Christ. It is one thing to claim that authority — as, indeed, Paul does (1:1; 10:8; 12:10). Such authority, however, is not legitimated merely by claiming it. Rather, it is authenticated in the ministry itself, as the central gospel affirmations about Christ's death and resurrection may be discerned in the life of the minister. This, surely, is the major reason for Paul's repeated references to his sufferings and the deliverances from those sufferings that punctuate this letter (1:8-10; 4:7-12; 6:3-10; 7:5-6; 12:7-9).

Moreover, Paul's manner of ministry in other respects should be noted. He did not pursue this ministry in a triumphalist (2:14) or lordly manner (1:24). On the contrary, he is their slave for Jesus' sake (4:5). His ministry is exercised in sincerity and with integrity (2:17; 7:2-4; 12:17-8), in repudiation of all that is morally inappropriate (4:2). Nor is he coldly and impersonally authoritarian. He appeals to them as a "father" to wayward and unresponsive children in deeply personal tones (6:11-13; 11:2; 12:13-17).

However, the apostolate is not the only ministry that has been "given." In addition to apostles, the ascended Christ also "gave" prophets, evangelists, and pastor-teachers (Eph 4:11),[92] whose ministry in the churches is not circumscribed within the apostolic circle or confined to apostolic times. Presumably the moral authority legitimating Paul's ministry, noted above, is the

---

92. Note the aorists δόντος . . . θέμενος in 2 Cor 5:18-19 and ἔδωκεν in Eph 4:11.

same for all other ministries — "official" and "unofficial" — engaged in by believers to this day.

Paul words (5:18–6:2), therefore, have application beyond the apostle and beyond his time. The sun has not set in this the day of salvation. The world remains effectively alienated from God. God's servants in this and every generation, like Paul the apostle, will continue to implore people, "Be reconciled to God." Although our ministries, relative to his, may be secondary and derivative, insofar as we faithfully give expression to the apostolic admonition, as legitimated by faithfulness in the face of suffering, and with Christ-likeness of character and probity of life, we do speak with real authority.

4. Credentials of God's Ministers (6:3-10)

This passage is in close relation with its predecessor, in which God makes his appeal by his minister, Paul (5:18–6:2).[1] Thus, (1) "the ministry" (v. 3) and "ministers of God" (v. 4) pick up "the ministry of reconciliation" (5:18); (2) the participles "giving" (v. 3) and "commending" (v. 4) must be bracketed with the participle "working together with" as expressing Paul's "appeal" (v. 1); and (3) "in anything" refers back to the manner of the ministry of reconciliation in 5:20 and 6:1.

In vv. 3-10 Paul (1) denies giving offense in anything, lest the ministry be "discredited" (v. 3), but on the contrary (2) commends himself as a minister of God, in particular in "endurance," which is the mark of apostolicity (v. 4a, b; see on 1:5; 12:12). This endurance is shown (a) "in" the face of various sufferings in the course of ministry (vv. 4c-5), (b) as expressed "in" manifestations of the Spirit of God (vv. 6e-8b), and (c) in victory despite the appearance of defeat (vv. 8c-10).

Thus, once more, the theme of "death" (i.e., apostolic sufferings — vv. 4c-5) and "resurrection" (i.e., divine deliverance, in this case by "the Holy Spirit . . . the power of God" — vv. 6-7b) may be seen; the twofold motif of the gospel's content is apparent in the death and life of its bearer. This serves to legitimate Paul's assertion of apostolic authority both retrospectively (referring back to 5:20) and prospectively (referring on to 6:11-13).

This rhetorically powerful sequence,[2] which has been called Paul's

1. Technically Martin, 167, is correct in regarding v. 2 as parenthetical. That verse, however, makes such an important eschatological statement in the exposition of the apostolic office and indeed in regard to the whole letter that one hesitates to classify it as a parenthesis in the usually understood meaning of that word.

2. Martin, 161-62, following Collange and others, argues that Paul has used a "preexisting text." Reference is made to the careful structure of the passage and to parallels

"apostolic identification card,"[3] derives its impact from its structure and repetitions. The antithetical statements of vv. 3-4a (lit. "*not* giving a stumbling block in *anything/but* commending ourselves in *everything*"), followed by "in great endurance" (v. 4b[4]), stand at the head of what will follow, in the first instance the list of hardships. These elements are introduced by a variety of prepositions, perhaps to break the potential monotony of a long list.[5]

(1) A series of nine hardships in ministry is introduced by "in" (*en* — vv. 4c-5), under the general heading of "in great endurance":

> in great endurance
>> in troubles
>> in hardships
>> in distresses
>>
>> in beatings
>> in imprisonments
>> in riots
>>
>> in hard work
>> in sleepless nights
>> in hunger

(2) A series of eight graces in ministry, associated inferentially with "the Holy Spirit . . . the power of God," is also introduced by "in" (*en* — vv. 6-7b):

---

in, e.g., *2 Enoch* 66:6. While it is agreed that texts parallel to 2 Cor 6:3-10 existed both in Jewish apocalyptic literature and in the Hellenistic moralists, it should not be doubted that Paul had the literary skill freely to compose this passage. In any case, the strongly autobiographical section (vv. 4b-5) and the polemical responses (vv. 7-10), which together make up the greater part of the passage, militate against that view. For an extensive survey of points of contact with other *peristaseis* ("tribulation lists") in the literature of the Hellenistic, including the Jewish Hellenistic, world contemporary with Paul, see J. T. Fitzgerald, *Earthen Vessels,* 184-201.

3. K. Prümm, cited by S. J. Hafemann, *Suffering and Ministry,* 73. 2 Cor 6:3-10 may be compared with 1 Corinthians 13 for rhetorical intensity.

4. Although "in great endurance" is joined to "in everything" in v. 4a (despite the anacolouthon), it does not follow that the sufferings phrases following are unconnected with it. The sufferings listed are the embodiments and occasions of the "great endurance." *Contra* S. J. Hafemann, *Suffering and Ministry,* 73-74, who sees "in great endurance" connected with "in everything" and not so directly connected with the list of sufferings following.

5. So Hughes, 231 n. 73.

in purity
in understanding
in patience
in kindness

in the Holy Spirit
in sincere love
in the word of truth
in the power of God

(3) A series of three antitheses set out the circumstances "through" *(dia)* which Paul conducted his ministry (vv. 7c-8b):

through the weapons of righteousness on the right hand and the left
through honor and dishonor
through bad report and good report

(4) A series of seven antitheses is introduced by "as," contrasting how Paul appeared in the eyes of some against the inner reality (*hōs* — vv. 8c-10):

as deceivers and yet true
as unknown and yet well known
as dying and behold we live
as chastened but not dying
as sorrowful yet always rejoicing
as poor but making many rich
as having nothing yet possessing all things.

Ultimately, the force of these words lies in their transparent integrity in the face of physical and emotional suffering, reference to which is progressively heightened within the passage.[6] According to Hughes, "This movingly beautiful hymn-like passage flows from the deep heart of the Apostle's knowledge and experience. . . . It challenges every serious reader to re-examine as before God his own relationship to the crucified, risen, and ascended Lord and with redoubled earnestness to dedicate his life and talents afresh to the single-minded prosecution of the cause of Christ."[7]

---

6. Suffering is intrinsic to this passage, which is one of a number of "tribulation lists" (so-called *peristaseis*) found within 2 Corinthians (see 4:8-12; 11:23–12:10; cf. 1:5-11; 2:14-17). See on 4:8-12.
7. Hughes, 238.

a. Ministers of God (6:3-4a)

3 We put no stumbling block in anyone's path, so that our ministry will not be discredited. 4 Rather, as servants of God we commend ourselves in every way: in great endurance.

Since God has "given the ministry of reconciliation . . . entrusted the message of reconciliation" to Paul (5:18-19), the apostle is concerned that he cause no offense, lest that ministry be censured. On the contrary, he positively commends himself as a minister of God — in particular, in great endurance. But this passage is also prospective. Paul here begins to lay a foundation from which to make his appeal that they widen their hearts to him as their "father" (6:11-13).

3-4a These verses carry forward Paul's "appeal" to the Corinthians from v. 1. Structurally, their two parts turn on the contrast between "not" (lit. "to no one in *nothing*[1] giving a cause of stumbling" — v. 3) and "but" ("but in *everything*[2] commending ourselves" — v. 4). Balancing each part is a subsidiary clause relating to the ministry: (1) "lest the *ministry*[3] be discredited," and (2) "we, as *ministers* of God in great endurance."

The verses, literally translated, are as follows:

To no one in nothing giving a cause of stumbling
                              lest the ministry be discredited
but in   everything
                         commending ourselves
                         we, as ministers of God
         in great endurance. . . .

Paul's words "in nothing" (v. 3) embrace, negatively, the whole gamut of his apostolic ministry — as ambassador, as mouthpiece of God appealing for reconciliation to God, and as yoked to God as his fellow worker — set out in 5:20 and 6:1. Paul denies giving offense to anyone in these wide-ranging

---

1. Gk. μηδεμίαν ἐν μηδενί. Note Paul's emphasis here through (1) the appearance of the words first in the sentence, (2) the use of alliteration (cf. 8:22; 9:5, 8; 10:6 for examples of alliteration in 2 Corinthians), and (3) the double negative "no one in nothing" (μηδενί is here taken as neuter; some take it as masculine).

2. Gk. ἐν παντί could be taken (1) adverbially ("in every respect"), or (2) temporally ("on every occasion"). Because it stands in contrast with ἐν μηδενί, option (1) is preferred.

3. Gk. ἡ διακονία, correctly translated as "the ministry," referring to "the ministry of reconciliation" (5:18; cf. "ministry of the Spirit . . . ministry of righteousness" — 3:7, 9). There are no textual or exegetical grounds for supplying the pronoun "our" (as, e.g., in the RSV and the NIV).

aspects of ministry. The "giving" of a "cause of offense"[4] relates to failings in Paul that would deflect people from their reconciliation with God.

The defensive note struck here reflects a number of criticisms of Paul by the Corinthians. The most important — the moral — he does not accept, whether in the realm of vacillation in travel arrangements (1:12–2:4) or of craftiness in money-related matters (4:2; 7:2; 12:16-18). Another area of criticism, apparently, was in regard to inadequacy in gifts of verbal ministry, which Paul does not deny, and indeed accepts (10:10; 11:6). A third, which we infer from this and other "tribulation lists" (4:7-12; 11:23–12:10), was in relationship to his sufferings and setbacks, which were seen as evidence of his inadequacies in ministry. This, too, Paul accepts and, indeed, perhaps elaborates further, as in this and other such lists within the letter. Paul's great concern was that "the ministry" — the apostolic ministry, as in 5:20 — should not be discredited,[5] as it would be if he was in fact guilty of moral failure, which he here denies.

In v. 4a Paul turns from defense to positive affirmation. Here his "in nothing" of v. 3 is reversed by "in everything" and his denial of "giving offense" is reversed by his "commendation"[6] of himself. The nominative "ministers" suggests a translation such as, "we, as ministers of God,[7] commend ourselves . . ." rather than "as servants of God we . . ." (NIV). The difference in nuance suggests that Paul is assured that he is a minister of God; it is not something he has to prove. The minister of God commends himself in a range of circumstances, such as those that now follow, which demonstrate the mind of one who is the servant of God and of the people of God.

It should be noted that Paul does here (and in 4:2) what he says he does not do in 5:12, and what he implies he does not do in 3:1, that is, "commends" himself. Our difficulty is that we are tuned in to only one side of an argument. It appears that Paul was being criticized for self-commendation (3:1; 5:12), but also that the newly arrived opponents do actively commend themselves, over against him (10:12). While Paul rejects *active*

---

4. Gk. προσκοπή is found only here within the LXX and the NT; the usual NT nouns for this meaning are πρόσκομμα (1 Cor 8:9; Rom 9:32, 33; 14:13, 20; 1 Pet 2:8) and σκάνδαλον (see, e.g., 1 Cor 1:23; Gal 5:11; Rom 9:33; 11:9; 14:13; 16:17; 1 Pet 2:8; 1 John 2:10).

5. Gk. μωμάομαι, used of human but not divine censure. It is found in the NT only here and at 8:20 (q.v.) and is rare in the LXX. Hughes, 221, notes that Momus (μῶμος) was the Greek god of mockery and ridicule.

6. Gk. συνιστάνοντες. On συνίστημι see W. Kasch, *TDNT* 7.896-98, and specifically for its use within 2 Corinthians, S. J. Hafemann, "Self-Commendation," 66-88.

7. Gk. ὡς θεοῦ διάκονοι; NIV, "as servants of God." The word order probably emphasizes that God is the source of ministry (cf. 2:17 — ἐκ θεοῦ . . . λαλοῦμεν).

self-commendation, he expects and hopes that the quality of his servant ministry, as he now describes it, will commend him to them as a minister of God (4:2; 12:11; cf. 5:11). The implicit paradigm of true ministry of the verses following, by which Paul measures himself, and by whom the Corinthians should measure him and other ministers, is the suffering servant, Jesus.

The negative phrase "lest the ministry be discredited" (v. 3) is reversed by its now-completed parallel "we, as ministers of God, *in*[8] *great endurance.*" This latter phrase picks up "in everything" and anticipates the nine examples of suffering that follow, each of which expresses and is the embodiment of "great endurance." Through these Paul "commends" himself to the Corinthians as a minister of God. Earlier he identified God as the energizing source of his "patient endurance" (1:6); later, that same "patient endurance" will be cited as the primary mark of an apostle (12:12). Appropriately, therefore, this "patient endurance," as the chief credential of genuine apostleship, stands at the head of the sufferings that will now be listed, as their explanation.[9]

b. Paul's Commendation: Patient Endurance Embodied in Examples of Suffering, Sustained by God-Given Power (6:4b-7a)

4b *in troubles, hardships and distresses;* 5 *in beatings, imprisonments and riots; in hard work, sleepless nights and hunger;* 6 *in purity, understanding, patience and kindness; in the Holy Spirit and in sincere love;* 7a *in truthful speech and in the power of God.*

Paul gives several examples of "in great endurance" (v. 4a) by means of which he commends his ministry "in every way."

4b-7a Now follow seventeen words or phrases, each introduced by "in" (*en*[1]). These are in three triplets, followed by two tetrads.

The first group of three has "in troubles, in hardships, in distresses,"[2] though the NIV does not bring out the intensity of these sufferings. These are "generic tribulations" (so von Hodgson[3]), reflecting the end-time nature of apostolic ministry. The first ("in inner pressures") speaks of the sense of

---

8. Gk. ἐν, used here, is instrumental.

9. Thrall, 1.457, calls it "a kind of title for what follows."

1. Gk. ἐν; the next ten uses appear to be local, "in troubles," etc.

2. Gk. ἐν θλίψεσιν (see also 1:4, 8; 2:4; 4:17; 7:4; 8:2), ἐν ἀνάγκαις (see also 9:7; 12:10), ἐν στενοχωρίαις (see also 12:10). It should be noted (1) that θλῖψις appears early and is a major term within 2 Corinthians — see on 1:4; (2) that the three words are repeated from the "tribulation list" in 4:8; and (3) that ἀνάγκη and στενοχωρία are repeated in the brief "tribulation list" in 12:10.

3. Quoted in Martin, 161.

oppression arising from constant opposition from this world order. The second ("in necessities") implies both the inevitability of suffering in the service of Christ and the "necessity" laid on Paul to preach the gospel ("woe to me if I do not preach the gospel" — 1 Cor 9:16). The third ("in constraints") means a confined place ("straits") from which there can be no escape, illustrating Paul's feeling of being trapped by circumstances over which he had no control (but see 4:8). Each of these words arises out of the grave difficulties of bringing God's message to a culture hostile to God and to people alienated from God.

The second triplet ("in beatings, in imprisonments, in riots"[4]) consists of specific and concrete examples of suffering at the hands of others. Paul later speaks of receiving the thirty-nine lashes on five occasions and the Roman beating with rods three times (11:23-25; cf. Acts 16:23). Similarly he will speak of being imprisoned "frequently" (11:23; cf. Acts 16:23-40). As to "riots," according to the Acts of the Apostles there was scarcely a major center visited by Paul that did not sustain some social upheaval in the course of his ministry there.[5] This triplet serves to remind us of the eventful and painful career of the apostle, as he made his way from city to city bearing the message of the gospel.

The third triplet ("in hard work, in sleepless nights, in hunger"[6]) expresses difficulties of a more voluntary nature and related to his itinerant ministry. "Hard work" probably refers in its first instance to the arduous labor of tent-making,[7] by which he provided for himself and his companions (1 Thess 2:9; 2 Thess 3:8; 1 Cor 4:11-12; 9:12, 15; Acts 18:2-3; 21:34). But it may also include the "labors" associated with ministry (cf. 10:15; 1 Cor 15:58). "Sleepless nights" probably means tent-making by night (1 Thess 2:9; 2 Thess 3:8) or, less probably, sleepless vigils in prayer (cf. Eph 6:18). "In hunger" refers more to the lack of food because of privations in travel (11:27) and to his desire not to be burden to anyone (11:7, 9; 12:13-16; 1 Cor 9:12-14) than to fasting, which Paul nowhere else mentions (cf. Acts 13:2-3; 14:23).

---

4. The first two — ἐν πληγαῖς, ἐν φυλακαῖς — reappear (with elaboration) in 11:23-25a, and the third — ἐν ἀκαταστίαις — in 12:20.

5. Acts notes civil disturbances attending Paul's ministry in Pisidian Antioch (13:50), Iconium (14:5-6), Lystra (14:19), Philippi (16:22), Thessalonica (17:5-9), Beroea (17:13), Corinth (18:12-17), Ephesus (19:21-23), and Jerusalem (21:27-36).

6. Gk. ἐν κόποις (see 10:15; 11:23, 27), ἐν ἀγρυπνίαις (see 11:27), and ἐν νηστείαις (see 11:27). Note that each of the three in this triplet reappears in the same order in a later "tribulation list" (11:22-33). While Hughes, 225, takes ἐν κόποις to refer to missionary labors, it is preferable to follow R. F. Hock, Social Context, 34-35, in seeing this as a reference to Paul's self-support in tent-making, especially in light of 1 Cor 4:11-13.

7. It is generally accepted that tents were then made from leather and that "tent-making" was a general description for leather-working, as e.g., "saddlery" today means more than saddle-making (see "Tent-making," DPL). Difficult, indeed, were the parallel circumstances of Micyllus the Shoemaker, hungry and poorly clothed and at his workbench by dawn (referred to by Lucian, The Cock 1, cited in Hock, Social Context, 34-35).

In the tetrads that follow Paul leaves behind the physical sufferings set forth in the three triplets. He turns now to God-given qualities cognate with "great endurance" at the head of the "tribulations list." It is "by"[8] these that he also commends himself to the Corinthians. If hardships were seen by his critics as evidence of his weakness and, therefore, of his basic ineligibility for ministry, his reminder about his actions and qualities in the face of those difficulties is a sign of the power of God (cf. 10:3-4).

Lack of cross-references to "purity"[9] makes it difficult to be sure precisely what Paul meant. Purity in sexual matters (cf. 12:20-21), because it is raised late in the letter (12:20–13:2), appears less likely than "sincerity" (2:17) or integrity in financial matters (cf. 4:2), to which Paul has already referred (cf. 7:2; 12:16-18).

"Understanding"[10] is common in both 1 and 2 Corinthians, with varying emphases; his nuance here is not altogether clear. Most probably Paul is referring to his ministry of disseminating the "knowledge of God" through the gospel (cf. 2:14; 4:6; 10:5; 11:6), whose message he has just rehearsed (5:14–6:2).

"In patience"[11] continues Paul's affirmation of spiritual and moral qualities by which he commends his ministry to his readers. Along with "patience," "kindness"[12] is a quality of God himself (Rom 2:4) and a fruit of the Spirit (Gal 2:22).[13] Whereas "patience" is reactive, "kindness" is proactive and positive. Both are God-given evidences of the "new creation" to which Paul belonged in consequence of his incorporation "in Christ" (5:17). Indeed, such belong to the cluster of qualities associated with the historical Jesus (cf. 10:1).

The second tetrad is really an *inclusio* formed by "in the Holy Spirit" and "by the power of God," which are virtually synonymous. Enclosed within the two phrases are "in unhypocritical love"[14] and "by the word of truth." Each element in this tetrad, unlike those in its predecessor, is given in three words.

---

8. Gk. ἐν, with which these qualities are also prefixed, carries the instrumental nuance "with" or "by," as with other uses of ἐν in this passage.

9. Gk. ἐν ἁγνότητι (see 11:3; cf. ἁγνός — 7:11).

10. Gk. ἐν γνώσει.

11. Gk. ἐν μακροθυμίᾳ (which relates more to people than does ὑπομονή — v. 4).

12. Gk. ἐν χρηστότητι. Neither word is found elsewhere in 2 Corinthians, though both are found elsewhere in Paul.

13. Hughes's suggestion, 227, that "endurance" (v. 4) is in reference to unbelievers and "patience" has to do with fellow believers is difficult to prove in the light of the available evidence. More probably they are synonyms. Both "patience" and "kindness" express "love" (cf. 1 Cor 13:4), which, in any case, is found in v. 6.

14. "Love" and "the Holy Spirit" are often bracketed together in Paul (Gal 5:22; Rom 5:5; 15:30; Phil 2:1-2).

Despite the opinions of various commentators to the contrary, *en pneumati hagiō* should be understood as "by the Holy Spirit."[15] Is the emphasis here on the Holy Spirit as power or on his personhood?[16] While the matching "by the power of God" would support the former, the reference immediately following to "unhypocritical love" supports the latter. It is reasonable to argue that there is no conflict between the two. The Holy Spirit, being both personal and powerful, is the agency by whom Paul is enabled to fulfill his ministry.

"Love" is a supernatural and eschatological quality (cf. Gal 5:6), the "fruit" of the Spirit of God (Gal 5:22). "Love" that is "*un*hypocritical"[17] is enjoined upon believers in general (Rom 12:9). Unhypocritical love is no empty profession but thoroughly genuine, without pretense. It may be included here to point up the falsehood of the newly arrived countermissionaries, whom he calls *pseudo*-apostles and (probably also) *pseudo*-brothers (11:13; 11:26).

The NIV rendering "in truthful speech" perpetuates the false impression that Paul is here listing virtues. But the evangelical and soteriological context (5:20; 6:2), together with parallel phrases elsewhere for, literally, "word of truth,"[18] indicates that Paul's words here point to the gospel (Eph 1:13; Col 1:5; cf. 2 Cor 2:17; 4:2).

By the "power of God" completes the Holy Spirit *inclusio,* indicating the divine source of power by which Paul exercises his ministry "in great endurance." At the same time, Paul may be replying to those who claim that he is a man of "flesh," powerless (see on 4:7-12). On the contrary, his effectiveness in capturing proud minds for the obedience of Christ is evidence of the "power of God" in his ministry (see on 10:3-10).

To be sure, Paul suffers in the course of his apostolic ministry, as the nine evocative words make clear. But by the Holy Spirit and the power of God he displays unhypocritical love and he speaks the word of truth, the

---

15. Gk. ἐν πνευματὶ ἁγιῷ, which Plummer, 196-97, takes to mean "a [human] spirit that is holy" (cf. also Barrett, 186-87). But (1) various cross-references point to the meaning "the Holy Spirit" (e.g., 13:13; cf. 1 Thess 1:5, 6; 4:8; 1 Cor 6:19; 12:3; Rom 5:5; 9:1; 14:17; 15:13); and (2) the qualities listed in vv. 6-7 are of supernatural origin; it is misleading to call them "human" qualities.

16. D. P. Francis, "Statistical Enquiry," 136ff., argues for the former, while G. D. Fee, *Presence,* 333, suggests the latter.

17. Gk. ἐν ἀγάπη ἀνυποκρίτῳ, where ἀν + ὑποκριτῷ is, literally, "unmasked." The NIV translation "sincere love" unhelpfully conveys the idea of a virtue or human quality. The call for unhypocritical behavior is found also in 1 Tim 1:5 (faith); 2 Tim 1:5 (faith); Jas 3:17 (wisdom); and 1 Pet 1:22 (love of the brethren).

18. Gk. ἐν λογῷ ἀληθείας. NIV's "in truthful speech" fails to catch Paul's reference to the gospel, as in references above.

gospel. His life bears the stamp of the message of the death and resurrection of Christ that he proclaims, thus undergirding his claims to apostolic authority with moral authority.

c. Apostolic Persistence in the Face of Both Praise and Blame (6:7b-8)

7b *with weapons of righteousness in the right hand and in the left;*
8a, b *through glory and dishonor, bad report and good report.*

Paul's "tribulation list" continues with a series of three antitheses introduced by "through,"[1] indicating the manner or way Paul commends his ministry (v. 4).

7b-8b The first ("with weapons of righteousness in the right hand and in the left") uses military imagery, something common to Paul (10:3-4; Rom 6:13; 13:12; Eph 6:13-18). "In the right hand and in the left" probably means "thoroughly equipped" (so Barrett), perhaps in the sense of offense (the sword for the right hand) and defense (the shield in the left).

But to what is Paul alluding by the words "weapons of righteousness"? What is the nature of such "righteousness"? Two options are: (1) righteousness before God through Christ (5:21) as a mark of true, as opposed to false ministry (3:9; 11:13-14), or (2) ethical righteousness, as suggested by the context of Paul's use of the phrase "weapons of righteousness" in Rom 6:13. In favor of (1) is the close parallel "weapons of our warfare" in this letter (10:4), whereas (2) is supported by the exactness of the parallel in Rom 6:13. On balance (2) is to be preferred, especially in the immediate context.

As such, it is probable that "weapons of righteousness" serves (1) to rebut those who raise questions about Paul's probity (4:2; 7:2; 12:16-18), and (2) to introduce the apologetic elements that will now follow (vv. 8c-10).

The second and third of these antitheses, also introduced by "through," but separated by "and,"[2] reflect the widely varying reactions to Paul's ministry just outlined (vv. 6-7). Thus, in the eyes of some Paul is "honored,"[3] that is, held in high regard (Gal 4:14), whereas to others he is repudiated[4] (cf. 7:2; 10:10; 12:16; cf. 1 Cor 4:10, 13). The third antithesis ("[through] bad report and good") is really an aural device (*dysphēmias* . . .

---

1. Gk. διά, usually expressing secondary agency. His commendation is thus mediated "through" these contrasts as well.

2. Gk. καί, introducing something unexpected — "and, yet."

3. Gk. διὰ δόξης; NIV, "through glory." However, δόξα here conveys a classical meaning, "good opinion," as also in John 5:44; 12:43; "popularity," according to Hughes, 231 n. 74.

4. Gk. διὰ ἀτιμίας; NIV, "dishonor."

euphēmias[5]) in which the second does little more than repeat the first. The apostolic minister is the object of praise and calumny. Either way, the minister is not deflected from his task.

d. Human Appearance and Divine Reality (6:8c-10)

8c *genuine, yet regarded as impostors;* 9 *known, yet regarded as unknown; dying, and yet we live on; beaten, and yet not killed;* 10 *sorrowful, yet always rejoicing; poor, yet making many rich; having nothing, and yet possessing everything.*

Seven antitheses[1] follow in which the first element is introduced by "as if" (*hōs*[2]), and the second by the contrastive "yet."[3] Thus in the first part of each Paul declares the perception of him that many hold. One of these is incorrect as to fact (impostor[s]), the others in varying degrees correct ("unknown . . . dying . . . beaten . . . poor . . . having nothing"). In the second part, Paul declares — antithetically — the divine reality ("yet . . .").

8c-9a   Here are two antitheses that have in common that both result from varying perceptions of Paul, thus picking up the two preceding antitheses. The first ("impostors," NIV; but more probably "deceivers"[4]) he rebuts with the words "yet genuine." Whatever his critics and opponents say of him — for example, that he failed to honor his travel undertakings (1:15-18) — Paul knows before God, and with a good conscience, that his apostolic call and ministry are from God and are true (2:17; 3:4; 4:2).

In the second ("as if unknown but well known"[5]) we encounter another aural assonance (*agnooumenoi . . . epiginōskomenoi*[6] — cf. v. 8b), which serves to heighten the mounting pathos as this passage reaches its climax. It

---

5. Gk. δυσφημίας . . . εὐφημίας.

1. See 1 Cor 4:12b-13a and 2 Cor 4:8-9 for other examples of Paul's use of antitheses.

2. According to E. D. W. Burton, *Syntax*, 446, ὡς + adjectival participles introduces the notion of manner, "as if." *Contra* Martin, 180, who takes ὡς in an adversative sense ("yet").

3. As expressed by καί in antitheses 1, 2, 3, 4, and 7 and by δέ in 5 and 6.

4. Gk. πλάνοι, "deceivers" (cf. the verb πλανᾶν, "to lead astray"), as found elsewhere in the NT (e.g., 1 Tim 4:1; 2 John 7) and in Josephus (e.g., *J.W.* 2.273). This may reflect an anti-Pauline polemic (from a Jewish quarter? Cf. Rom 3:8; 3:1; 6:1; 9:1; 11:1). In modern times Paul is sometimes portrayed as a deceiver, one who, in his presentation of the gospel, willfully distorted the historical Jesus.

5. My translation.

6. Gk. ἀγνοούμενοι . . . ἐπιγινωσκόμενοι; NIV, "unknown yet regarded as well known." We note the intensification of the compounded ἐπιγινωσκόμενοι, "fully known."

may be significant that both participles are passives, indicating that he had been and was the object of scrutiny leading either to lack of recognition or to recognition. In regard to the one, it appears that Paul was unrecognized by some (many?) in his apostolic vocation.[7] As to the other, it seems likely that he is now pointing to God as the one by whom he was recognized as an apostle. There were, however, many in Corinth who recognized the ministry of Paul (see on 2:5-11; 7:11-13a). On this basis the fundamental contrast is between human lack of recognition and divine recognition. Because of the reality of the latter Paul can cope with the appearance of the former.

9b-10   In the third antithesis ("as dying and, behold, we live"[8]) Paul is picking up the themes of death and life that are so important within this letter. The references to death appeared early in the letter and repeatedly come to the surface (1:8-9; 4:7–5:10; 11:23-26). Matching these, however, is the triumph of resurrection and life (1:10; 4:10, 11, 14; 5:1-9), as indicated by the joyful and triumphant "behold"[9] (5:17; 6:2 [twice]).

Once again the contrast is between the human perception and the divine reality. To outward appearance Paul is subject to a barrage of sufferings, and is in seeming defeat. But "behold," the "all-surpassing power of God" is at work within him (see on 4:7). Though "dying," nonetheless he "lives" (see on 4:8-12). As with other aspects, the pattern of Paul's experience serves to disclose Jesus, in this case the death and the life of Jesus (see 6:10b).

The fourth antithesis ("as chastised, but not put to death"[10]) contrasts divine correction with death, and serves to amplify the third antithesis. His "chastised" corresponds with "dying," and "not put to death" with "we live." Perhaps, too, Paul is reflecting upon his assault on Stephen and the early Christians, for which he deserved to be put to death. But thanks to the divine mercy (see on 4:1), he was spared. The present verse may reflect his sense of the Lord's hand of chastisement upon him in the midst of his various apostolic trials (cf. 1:9; 4:11; 11:23-33). To be sure, he testified to God's empowerment in the midst of the weakness of suffering (12:9).

The fifth antithesis is: "as sorrowful, yet always rejoicing." In the first half the verb "sorrowful," when taken with its cognate noun (which can also

---

7. Thrall, 1.464, raises the possibility that Paul is thinking of his lack of recognition in the public world of learning and politics. However, it does not seem likely that Paul was exercised by this consideration!

8. Paul's words appear to echo LXX Ps 117:17 — οὐκ ἀποθανοῦμαι, ἀλλὰ ζή-σομαι, "I shall not die, but I shall live. . . ."

9. Gk. ἰδού.

10. Gk. παιδευόμενοι καὶ μὴ θανατούμενοι; NIV, "beaten, and yet not killed." NIV's "beaten" is unsatisfactory. The background to Paul's words appears to be LXX Ps 117:18: παιδεύων ἐπαίδευσέ με ὁ Κύριος, καὶ τῷ θανάτῳ οὐ παρέδωκέ με, "with discipline the Lord disciplined me, and has not handed me over to death."

mean "grief"[11]), occurs no less than eighteen times within this letter. His life of travail, as listed in the three sets of triplets (vv. 4-5) as well as in the longer "tribulation list "(11:23–12:10), reminds us of the causes of such sorrow. The Corinthians themselves contributed substantially to his "grief" (e.g., 2:4; cf. 11:28-29). Nonetheless, he may be echoing the critical observation of those who pointed to his difficulties as proof of his ineligibility for the apostolate. Given the tone of much of the letter, such a view is plausible; it is also consistent with the pattern in vv. 8c-10, where the first part of each antithesis appears to reflect the views that others had of Paul, most of which were, in their own way, true.

But if "sorrow" was the human opinion of Paul, "joy" was the divine reality. Once again Paul is not referring to some inherent quality or virtue. Such "rejoicing" is entirely God-given and eschatological, a "fruit of the Spirit" in this the "day" of God's salvation (3:3; 6:2), a reality to which Paul bears frequent testimony in this letter and elsewhere (2:3; 7:4, 7, 9, 13; 13:9;[12] cf. 1 Thess 2:19-20; 3:9; 5:16; 1 Cor 16:17; Rom 12:12, 15; 14:17; 15:13, 32; 16:19; Phil 1:4; 2:17; 3:1). As in the third antithesis, where "behold" heightens the contrast, so here the adverb "always"[13] with "rejoicing" gives the sense of exultation, which can only be from God (cf. "Rejoice in the Lord *always*"[14]; Phil 4:4).

The sixth antithesis ("poor but making many rich") has been variously interpreted. Some deny the reality of the "poverty," interpreting it spiritually;[15] others suggest that the "riches" are literal and relate, for example, to the benefits of the collection to those who will receive it.[16] It is more likely, however, that the poverty is literal and the riches are spiritual, as they are in the case of the preincarnate and the incarnate Christ upon whom Paul appears to pattern his lifestyle (cf. 8:9). Of course, any such resemblance between Christ and the apostle must be entirely a matter of outward analogy, not inner reality.[17] By this allusion Paul is identifying himself as the *imitatio* of the Servant (4:5, 12). As Christ lowered himself (to raise others), so did Paul (11:7; cf. Phil 2:6-8). As Christ impoverished himself to make others rich (8:9), so did his servant. This Paul did through his free gift to them of his

---

11. Gk. λύπη . . . λυπούμενοι. This letter contains eighteen of the twenty-three Pauline uses of this word group.

12. Members of the χαρά-χαίρειν word group occur twenty-three times within the letter.

13. Gk. ἀεί.

14. Gk. πάντοτε.

15. So Martin, 184.

16. So Chrysostom, quoted by Martin, 184.

17. A parallel to Paul as outwardly analogous to Christ is his application to himself of ὑπέρ in relationship to the churches (see on 1:6; 12:15).

ministry (11:7), by which at no charge to them he brought the treasure of the grace of God, which, ironically, the Corinthians were in danger of repudiating (6:1).

In the seventh antithesis ("as having nothing but possessing all things") there is a wordplay on the two participles *(echontes . . . kate-chontes).*[18] The second is a compounded version of the first, indicating a more intense ownership. The first part is, in effect, a repetition of the the corresponding part of the previous antithesis ("as poor . . ."), reflecting Paul's indigent lifestyle.[19] In the second part, by contrast, Paul asserts his possession of "all things," a shorthand term for the totality of eschatological and soteriological blessings.[20] Once again we note the difference between the human perception, true as it was in this case, and the divine reality. Here is strong rhetoric, powerfully summarizing what has preceded, and thus climaxing the whole.

5. O Corinthians, Reciprocate My Affections (6:11-13)

> 11 *We have spoken freely to you, Corinthians, and opened wide our hearts to you.* 12 *We are not withholding our affection from you, but you are withholding yours from us.* 13 *As a fair exchange — I speak as to my children — open wide your hearts also.*

Paul, the minister of God (6:4), has stated, with rhetorical and emotional power, his supernatural credentials, which are revealed in the face of sufferings sustained through apostolic ministry. Included among those sufferings is the Corinthians' superficial appraisal of him (vv. 8c-10).

Now, once more, he addresses them directly; twice in this short passage Paul uses the pronoun "you" (vv. 11, 13), as he had done at 6:1. The earlier appeal relates to the Corinthians' relationship to God (5:20; 6:1); this one relates to the Corinthians' relationship to Paul. The two are clearly interconnected. To be reconciled to God means to be reconciled to Paul, his minister, since it is through such ministry that the former happened at all.[1] It is as if Paul stands blocking the pathway to perdition that they appear willfully determined to tread. To proceed further toward apostasy from Christ, they must brush him aside.

18. Gk. ἔχοντες . . . κατέχοντες.
19. As such Paul stands in contrast with many wealthy church leaders, past and present.
20. See 5:18; cf. 1 Cor 3:21-22.
1. As Paul is accustomed to remind them (1 Cor 2:1-5; 4:16-17; 9:1-2, and especially 2 Cor 1:18-22).

His address to them is painfully emotional ("our mouth is open . . . our heart is wide"), as indeed was the catalogue of his credentials in suffering that he felt compelled to give them (6:3-10). These words, with those, form the climax to the entire apologia for his apostolic office that began at 2:14. Paradoxically, they are at once office-related *and* emotional. Here we hear Paul in his most human self-disclosure. The apostolic office, which is to a significant degree a model for subsequent pastoral and missionary ministry, is a human ministry; it can never be a mere institution.

11   Paul's is a doubly direct address. It is to "you," picking up 6:1,[2] to which he adds the vocative, "Corinthians." Only rarely does Paul address his readers by name ("you foolish *Galatians*" — Gal 3:1; "as you *Philippians* know" — Phil 4:15).

In making this direct appeal Paul mentions his mouth and his heart. These organs represent the natural two-part division of the sentence. By the one he speaks to them; by the other he thinks and feels about them. His mouth was and is still "open" (as signified by the Greek perfect tense "opened"[3]). Some commentators and translations[4] here opt for the idiomatic "we have spoken freely" (NIV), as if in reference only to the powerful rhetoric of the preceding passage (6:3-10). Yet it is equally likely that Paul is thinking of the whole letter to this point, in particular the sustained apostolic apologia, which began at 2:14 and reached a great height in 6:3-10. In this case, the nuance would be, "We have spoken a word to you, a word that continues to speak. Listen!"

Paul's other organ here mentioned, the "heart" — then understood as an organ of thought as well as of feeling — is, he declares, "wide." This verb is also perfect tense ("widened"[5]), matching its counterpart, "opened," in the first part of the verse. Perhaps Paul is here reflecting more broadly than is sometimes suggested. It quite likely that Paul is now recalling the crisis of the "painful" second visit to Corinth a year earlier, when he might easily have turned his back on the Corinthians. Does the present reference point instead to his "widened" heart as expressed by his writing first of one letter (now lost), followed by another (this letter), with the determination to visit them one more time? Paul's word "heart" symbolizes the pastor's love he feels

2. See also 3:2; 4:5, 12, 14, 15; 5:11-13.

3. Gk. ἀνέῳγεν. According to Plummer, 203, "ἀνέῳγα is almost always intransitive . . . with the meaning of 'standing open.' " The open mouth is a biblical idiom for someone speaking (Judg 11:35-36; Job 3:1; Matt 5:1).

4. E.g., Hughes, 239; NIV.

5. Gk. πεπλάτυνται. The verb πλατύνω is used with καρδία in LXX Deut 11:16 and Ps 118:32, but neither reference suits the present context. See G. K. Beale, "Reconciliation," 569, 576-77, who finds a captivity "restoration" motif here, based on a verbal connection between LXX Ps 118:32 and Isa 60:5.

and shows toward his churches (see on 3:2; 12:14-15; also 1:7). His reference to the "widened" heart controls his thinking in the next two verses.

12 Continuing his painfully direct address to the Corinthians,[6] Paul now expands upon the "wide . . . heart" of the previous verse, though with different vocabulary. Instead of "heart[s]" Paul now uses the synonym "affections,"[7] and in place of "wide," referring to himself, the antonym "constrict," referring to their misconceptions (NIV, "withhold"). Thus Paul states that the Corinthians are "not constricted," or "narrowed,"[8] "in us." By contrast,[9] the Corinthians are "narrow" "in their affections" toward him (cf. 12:15). Perhaps, they felt that he did not love them (11:11).

Paul knows himself, and he knows the Corinthians. He knows of the wide, expansive love he has for them (12:15). They are in his heart (3:2), his spiritual "children," as he will remind them in the next verse (cf. 11:2). But these Corinthians have proved to be fickle and disloyal to him both as a person and as an apostle. Some have been intractably involved in promiscuous sexuality from the beginning (12:20–13:2; cf. 1 Cor 5:9, 11; 6:12-20), most probably through ongoing involvement in the Greco-Roman and mystery cults that flourished in Corinth (see on 6:14–7:1). Others appear to have portrayed him as a man of "flesh," lacking the power of God (see on 10:3-7), powerful only from a distance, by letter (10:10-11). Yet others (the Jews among them?) have given a welcome to Jewish missionaries (who have come on Cephas's coattails? — see on 10:15) and are bent on "stealing" the Corinthians — or at least the Jewish Corinthians — from Paul for their version of messianism. Others accuse him of craftiness in purporting not to accept their emoluments, all the while receiving the Corinthians' gifts via Titus and other delegates (11:7-12; 12:16-18; cf. 4:2; 7:2).

In rejecting Paul's ministry, however, they are rejecting Paul's person; the two are inseparable. His call to be reconciled to God in this the "day of salvation" (5:20; 6:2) is, in effect, a call to be reconciled to him, Paul. Only he and his gospel can prosper them on their way to salvation and deflect them from a pathway to eternal dereliction (2:15-16; 4:3), which they are in serious danger of choosing (see on 11:2-4).

---

6. With asyndeton, i.e., without a connecting particle.

7. Gk. σπλάγχνοις literally means the upper part of the intestines, heart, liver, and lungs and is interchangeable with καρδία.

8. Gk. στενοχωρεῖσθε (NIV, "witholding") appears in both parts of the verse. The first is passive, indicating that the Corinthians are not "narrowed" by Paul in his affections toward them, but the second is middle and effectively active voice; the Corinthians are "narrow" in their affections toward Paul. The verb derives from στένος (= narrow) and χωροῦν (= to make room — cf. 7:2), hence "to cramp" or "to constrict" (see further H. Kraft, *EDNT* 3.373).

9. Gk. δέ, "but . . . ," indicating contrast.

13   Paul drives home his appeal to them. Picking up the reference to his "wide heart" (v. 11), he calls for reciprocation, by way of fair exchange, addressing them in personal terms[10] as his "children" and concluding with the emphatic words, "you also."

The first basis of his appeal is equality; the key term "exchange"[11] means a *"quid pro quo,* something given in fair exchange."[12] The second is paternal; the Corinthians are his "children" through the gospel (see on 3:2; 11:2; 12:14-15; cf. 1 Cor 4:14-15; Gal 4:19; 1 Tim 1:2, 18); they owe their own relationship to God as his children to Paul (see on 1:2-3, 18-21). Paul's address to them here as "children" does not imply spiritual immaturity on the part of the Corinthians (cf. 1 Cor 3:1-2). Rather, it is an assertion of spiritual paternity expressive of his apostolic relationship with them, and a call for recognition and response.

The appeal — "as a fair exchange" — picks up his language of v. 11. As his heart is "wide" toward them, so let their "affections" (v. 12) be "wide" toward him. Here we are again reminded that the apostle-to-church relationships, though ordained by God as part of the eschatological dispensation (5:18–6:2), are genuinely *human,* reciprocal relationships.

But how will the Corinthians respond to Paul's plea? They will recognize that, notwithstanding his sufferings, and indeed on account of them and his deliverances from them, his ministry is shaped by the death and resurrection of Jesus, thus giving his ministry dominical legitimacy. Let them recognize that, in being influenced by the "peddlers" (2:17), they have strayed from the path of apostolic truth and need to "be reconciled" to their God (5:20) through the forgiveness of sins in the death of Christ (5:18-19, 21). They will demonstrate this reconciliation to God by separating themselves from the temple cults of the city in which they live.

6. A Call for Separation (6:14–7:1)

With this powerful appeal Paul now brings the apostolic excursus, begun at 2:14, to its climax. More immediately it relates to the passage begun at 5:18. God has given to Paul the ministry of reconciliation and entrusted to him the message of reconciliation (5:18-19). On that basis he has exhorted the

---

10. Only rarely has Paul used the singular "I" in his excursus on apostolic ministry (5:11; 7:3-4; see on 1:1; 2:14).

11. Gk. τὴν . . . αὐτὴν ἀντιμισθίαν, lit. "recompense in kind," "the same recompense." It should be noted that Paul has not used a verb in this sentence. It has been suggested that the present words are to be added to others, e.g., τὸ δὲ αὐτό (so Moule, 34-36), yielding "and accordingly, by way of recompense on your part." As Paul's heart is "wide," so, as a corresponding "recompense," let theirs be "wide," too.

12. Quoted in Martin, 186.

Corinthians to be reconciled to God (5:20–6:2). His exposition of his sufferings, in which the power of God is nonetheless active (6:3-10), provides moral authority for his appeal that the Corinthians be reconciled to God, and, in the passage following (6:11-13), to him also. Now follows the strong exhortation to which all this has been leading and for which it has served as the foundation. The Corinthians must separate from all that is unclean in Corinth.

Many scholars and commentators, however, believe the passage following to have been written by a hand other than Paul's[1] and to have been inserted subsequently into this letter. They have given two basic reasons for this view:[2]

1. The transition from the emotional appeal "Widen your hearts also" (v. 13) to the harsh passage beginning "Do not be yoked together with unbelievers" (v. 14), which is followed by the emotional appeal "Make room for us" (7:2), is so uneven as to be best explained by an interpolation hypothesis. It is argued that this "jerk" (as Barrett called it) between the two passages is so great that the latter cannot have been written by Paul.

2. The passage 6:14–7:1 is non-Pauline, evidence for which is its un-Pauline character in (a) *vocabulary:* it has no less than six *hapax legomena;*[3] in (b) *style:* the dualistic contrasts — along with a Qumran word, "Belial"[4] — are said to give the text a close affinity with the literature of Qumran[5] ("a meteor fallen from the heaven of Qumran into Paul's epistle"[6]); and in (c) *doctrine:* the extreme sense of exclusiveness expressed in the passage by the "flesh"/"Spirit" dualism (7:1). The elements (a), (b), and (c), it is claimed, demand a verdict of non-Pauline authorship.[7]

---

1. Two leading theories as to the origin of the passage are (1) that it came from the Qumran community (J. A. Fitzmyer, "Interpolated Paragraph," 271-80), and (2) that it originated in Jewish Christianity (H. D. Betz, "Anti-Pauline Fragment?" 88-108). For arguments in favor of the integrity of this passage in regard to Pauline authorship see G. D. Fee, "Idols," 140-61; J. M. Scott, *Adoption,* 189-95, 215-17; and Thrall, 1.25-36.

2. For further discussion see the Introduction, 23-24.

3. Gk. ἑτεροζυγεῖν, μετοχή, συμφώνησις, Βελίαλ, συγκατάθεσις, and μολυσμός.

4. It is true that "Belial" is found in the Qumran literature (e.g., 1QM 13:1-4; cf. 1QS 1:18, 24; 2:19; 1QH 6:21); but it is also to be found within Jewish apocalyptic literature (*Jub.* 1:20; *T. Reub.* 4:11; *T. Sim.* 5:3; *T. Levi* 19:1; *T. Dan* 4:7; 5:1; *T. Naph.* 2:6; 3:1; *Asc. Isa.* 3:11). Paul's use, though unusual — it appears nowhere else in the OT or the NT — does not of itself point to a Qumranian provenance of this passage. See further Martin, 199-201; G. D. Fee, "Idols," 146-47; M. E. Thrall, "The Problem of II Cor. VI.14–VII.1," 132-38.

5. So, e.g., J. A. Fitzmyer, "Interpolated Paragraph," with other literature noted in Martin, 189.

6. P. Benoit, "Qûmran," 258-64.

7. Some scholars argue that Paul has reworked a preexisting text. See, e.g., Martin, 193-95.

But there are practical questions that raise difficulties for the "interpolation" hypothesis: (1) Why would Paul, or anybody else, insert this supposedly *discrete* non-Pauline passage into a Pauline writing?[8] (2) Why would it be inserted at this precise point? (3) Would the early Christians have felt free to insert an extraneous text into an apostolic writing? Practical answers to these questions are either lacking or unconvincing.[9]

Apart from these unanswered questions, a number of objections raised against the integrity and Pauline authorship of the passage may be met, in part, as follows:

1. An overall continuity within 6:11–7:4 is perceptible. The directness of appeal, "Our mouth is open *to you*" (6:11), may be seen also in the succeeding verse: "Do not [*you*][10] be yoked, etc." Direct appeals to the readers are uncommon in the section about the apostolic office (2:14–7:4) to which these passages belong.[11] The appearance of relatively rare direct appeals in consecutive verses suggests continuity, not discontinuity, between those passages.

Moreover, the proposed original continuation (7:2-4) has only one explicit element in common with the passage it is supposed to succeed (6:11-13), namely, "You are in our hearts" (7:3; cf. "Our hearts are wide" — 6:11). But Paul specifically introduces this by, "for I have said *before*,"[12] which he would not otherwise need to say. The opening words in the passage 7:2-4, "Make room for us," are well understood as resumptive of 6:13, but with different vocabulary.[13] In view of these considerations it is unlikely that 6:14–7:1 is a non-Pauline interpolation.

2. The claim that *hapax legomena* are evidence of non-Pauline authorship is difficult to sustain. Second Corinthians alone contains no less than fifty *hapaxes*;[14] there are only six in this passage. Further, it is characteristic

---

8. See G. D. Fee, "Idols," 140-61.

9. Explanations for the various theories tend to be unconvincing. On the one hand, G. D. Fee, "Idols," 141, mentions Collange's suggestion that *Paul* wrote *two different editions* of this letter, one ending at 6:13 and the other at 7:4; and, on the other hand, H. D. Betz, "Anti-Pauline Fragment?" argues that the fragment is *anti*-Pauline. Such is the diversity and antithetical nature of some of the theories. Betz acknowledges that he does not know the reasons for an anti-Pauline interpolation.

10. Gk. μὴ γίνεσθε, noting, however, the absence of the pronoun "you."

11. Only at 6:1, 11; 7:4 does ὑμᾶς appear within the passage 2:14–7:4.

12. Gk. προείρηκα γάρ.

13. So G. D. Fee, "Idols," 161. 7:2, χωρήσατε ἡμᾶς; cf. 6:13, πλατύνθητε καὶ ὑμεῖς. It should be noted that 7:2-4 is one of a number of transitional or bridge passages within 2 Corinthians that repeat words or ideas from earlier passages (here "heart," from 6:11) and that introduce words or ideas that will carry forward into passages following ("encouraged" is carried forward to 7:6-7). For similar "bridge" passages see 2:12-13; 2:17; and 12:11-13.

14. So Hughes, 242.

of Paul that rhetorically powerful passages such as this tend to be *hapax*-laden.[15] Of the so-called *hapaxes* in 6:14–7:1 it has been demonstrated that at least three repeat closely cognate words from 1 Corinthians; this passage is pointedly directed at the unacceptability of local temple attendance, an important issue in the earlier letter.[16]

3. It is true that the passage contains a number of dualisms (6:11-14). But antitheses are common in Paul, as, for example, in the passage a few verses earlier (6:7-10). Dualisms or antitheses of themselves do not point away from Pauline authorship, especially since much of that vocabulary is unquestionably Pauline.[17]

4. The theme of purity or separation — based on the purification of "flesh and Spirit" (7:1) — so far from being extraneous is, in fact, Pauline.[18]

Positively speaking, on the basis of the comparison between vv. 16d-18b and Rom 3:10-18, it has been argued that the threefold structure of OT citations is demonstrably Pauline in style and not at all Qumranian.[19] Moreover, the question form of vv. 14b-16a does not at all derive from Qumran, but from the Hellenistic-Jewish wisdom tradition.[20] This passage does not stem from a sectarian backwater, but from mainstream Hellenistic-Jewish thought with a pattern of OT citations that is entirely Pauline.

15. So Martin, 192. The passage 6:3-10, e.g., has four *hapaxes* as well as two other words found only in Paul. See G. D. Fee, "Idols," 144.

16. Gk. μετοχή (v. 14) — μετέχομεν . . . μετέχειν (1 Cor 10:17, 21); μολυσμοῦ (7:1) — μολύνεται (1 Cor 8:7). In regard to κοινωνία (v. 14), we note a sustained use in the earlier letter: κοινωνία . . . κοινωνία . . . κοινωνός . . . κοινωνός (1 Cor 10:16 [twice], 18, 20). See further G. D. Fee, "Idols," 144-45.

17. G. D. Fee, "Idols," 147, has listed, among others, the following, showing the parallels in Paul: Μὴ γίνεσθε . . . ἀπίστοις . . . δικαιοσύνη . . . ἀνομία . . . κοινωνία . . . φωτὶ . . . σκότος (6:14); ναὸς θεοῦ . . . ζῶντος (6:16); λέγει Κύριος (6:17); ταύτας οὖν ἔχοντες τὰς ἐπαγγελίας ἀγαπητοί . . . ἐπιτελοῦντες . . . ἐν φόβῳ θεοῦ (7:1).

18. It has been held that "flesh" (σάρξ) is negative for Paul, that the Spirit (πνεῦμα), being the Holy Spirit, is hardly in need of purification, and that the use of these terms here is proof of non-Pauline authorship. However, there are nontheological uses of these words within this letter: "our flesh found no relief . . . I had no relief for my spirit" (7:5; 2:13; cf. 1 Cor 7:34; 1 Thess 5:23). According to G. D. Fee, "Idols," 161, the words merely mean "outwardly" and "inwardly."

19. See J. M. Scott, *Adoption,* 191-95.

20. J. M. Scott, *Adoption,* 190 refers to Sir 13:2, 17-18:

How (τί) can the clay pot associate (κοινωσήσει) with the iron kettle?
What (τί) fellowship (κοινωσήσει) has a wolf with a lamb?
No more has a sinner with a godly man.
What (τίς) peace is there between a hyena and a dog?
And what (τίς) peace between a rich man and a poor man?

The repeated τί . . . τίς and the use of κοινωσήσει provide significant contact with 2 Cor 6:14b-16a.

If the passage is Pauline, a remaining question is, Why does it appear in this position, as the climax of the entire apologia for Paul's new covenant ministry, which he began 2:14? His call for separation from the temple cults of Corinth and probable associated sexual activities was not new. It dominated the center section of the First Letter (1 Cor 6:12-20; 8:1–11:1) and was probably the occasion of his emergency second visit and followup "Severe Letter" (see on 2:1-4; 10:1-6; 12:20–13:2). Paul's exhortation is that the Corinthians must separate themselves from the cults of the city, assuring them that they are the temple of the living God, the sons and daughters of the Lord God almighty, their Father. The presence of the Spirit is the evidence of the divine legitimacy of Paul's ministry under the new covenant (3:3, 6).[21] To capitulate to the cults will not only distance the Corinthians from their God; equally, it will distance them from Paul since it will deny the reality of the activity of the Spirit among them. Seen in this light, this passage is not anomalously located, but forms a fitting conclusion to the whole excursus on Paul as minister of a new covenant.[22]

This passage is a specific call for separation from the temple cults of Corinth, in direct continuity with the holiness-separation theme of 1 Corinthians,[23] and is located here as the climax of the apologia for Paul's apostolate. In the immediately prior passage (6:11-13) Paul had called on the Corinthians to widen their hearts to him. Withdrawal from the Gentile cults will be their way of responding to his call to them, demonstrating that they truly are an apostolic church.

> 14 *Do not be yoked together with unbelievers. For what do righteousness and wickedness have in common? Or what fellowship can light have with darkness?* 15 *What harmony is there between Christ*

---

21. Although Paul insists that there is no route to the righteousness of God through law (Rom 7:4-6; 10:4; Gal 2:19), the believer is not law-free (Rom 6:12-19; Gal 5:13-25). Paul insists on holiness of life (Rom 12:1-2).

22. It should be noted that 6:14–7:1 is an extraordinarily tight-knit unit. J. M. Scott, *Adoption*, 218, suggests it "might represent catechetical material from the classroom of the Apostle."

23. Much of 1 Corinthians is devoted to the nature of the separation of a Christian congregation from the world. In the former (canonical) letter Paul had canvassed the holiness of the congregation in regard to (1) the gross sin of one of the members (5:6-13), (2) the call to holiness to those whose former lifestyle had been unholy (6:9-11), (3) the bodily separation from sexual immorality (6:16-20), (4) the consecration of the unbelieving spouse and child through the believer as spouse and parent (7:14), and (5) the necessary separation from Gentile cults (10:14-22). Implicit is Israel's separation from the nations (= Gentiles) as the pattern for a congregation's separation from its Gentile environment (see, e.g., Deut 17–25 passim).

and Belial?[1] *What does a believer have in common with an unbeliever?*
16 *What agreement is there between the temple of God and idols? For*
we are the temple of the living God.[2] *As God has said: "I will live with*
them and walk among them, and I will be their God, and they will be
my people."
    17 *"Therefore come out from them*
        and be separate,
                                    says the Lord.
    Touch no unclean thing,
        and I will receive you."
    18 *"I will be a Father to you,*
        and you will be my sons and daughters,
                says the Lord Almighty."
    1 *Since we have these promises, dear friends, let us purify ourselves*
from everything that contaminates body and spirit, perfecting holiness
out of reverence for God.

Here now is the climax of the apostolic excursus. Paul claimed to have been
given the ministry and message of reconciliation, and on that basis he had
appealed to them to be reconciled to God (5:18–6:2). Then he defended his
ministry from criticism, pointing out that it was marked by both suffering and
the power of God (6:3-10). Operating out of this moral authority, he urged
the Corinthians, as his children, to widen their hearts for him (6:11-13). This
leads into the great ethical imperative with which the excursus comes to its
climax. Let the Corinthians separate themselves from the local temple cults.

Critical to this admonition is Paul's question, "What does a believer
have in common with an unbeliever?" Who are these "unbelievers"? We will
argue that they are the unconverted Gentiles of Corinth. They are not, however,
"unbelievers" per se, but as the rhetorical questions (vv. 14b-16) imply,
unbelievers at worship in the Greco-Roman and mystery cults of Corinth.[3] In

---

1. Although βελιάρ is better attested than βελιάλ, the latter is to be preferred since
it renders Heb. *beliyy 'al.* In this case there has been a scribal interchange from λ to ρ,
which is not uncommon. (See further, Hughes, 248 n. 12.)

2. The reading ὑμεῖς . . . ἐστε, though supported by p[46] C D[c] G K Y 614 Byz.
Lect it[g,61] vg syr[p,h] goth arm, probably assimilates from 1 Cor 3:16. The reading ἡμεῖς . . .
ἐσμεν is preferred because it is supported by both Alexandrian and Western witnesses (א*
B D* 33 81* it[d] cop[sa,bo]).

3. Less probably are these "unbelievers" to be identified with Paul's recently
arrived judaizing opponents; the rhetorical antitheses (vv. 12-15) make that unlikely. Paul
would hardly charge *Jewish* opponents with "wickedness" as opposed to "righteousness,"
"darkness" as opposed to "light," "Belial" as opposed to "Christ," or "idols" as opposed
to "the temple of God." See further W. J. Webb, "Who Are the Unbelievers?" 27-44.

our view Paul is here addressing the circumstances that precipitated his emergency visit and the writing of the "Severe Letter," namely, the Corinthians' accelerated slide toward idolatry and sexual immorality that were endemic in the community within the Achaian capital. The Corinthians have set some of those matters right (see on 2:5-11 and 7:5-16), though not others (see on 12:20–13:2). The apostle wants the Corinthians to know that, in the light of his pending final visit, his heart is open to them as he hopes theirs will be to him. But this means that they must not be joined to the unbelievers in their cultic worship. They cannot have it both ways. To choose Paul is to reject them; to choose "unbelievers" is to reject him.

Here, then, Paul is commanding the Corinthians not to be "yoked" with "unbelievers." These he identifies by a series of rhetorical questions, in particular the last question, "What agreement is there between the temple of God and *idols?*" For that "temple of the living God," he says, "we are." On that account, he commands the Corinthians, "Come out from them [i.e., the idolaters] and be separate." God has promised to "receive" and "be a "Father" to those who thus "separate" themselves. Therefore, he encourages — reverting to the first person — "let us purify ourselves from everything that contaminates."

Structurally, 6:14–7:1 consists of the following:[4]

(a) A prohibition ("Do not be yoked together with unbelievers"; 6:14a).
(b) Five antithetical rhetorical questions (6:14b-16a).
(c) The basic assertion ("we are the temple of the living God"), supported by an OT citation (6:16b-e).
(d) A direct command, supported by two promises (6:17-18).
(e) An encouragement to purity and holiness (7:1).

This passage is an *inclusio,* begun and ended by similar-style exhortations (6:14a; 7:1). Between these exhortations are two substantiations, one introduced by "for" (*gar* — v. 14b), the other by "therefore" (*dio* — v. 17a). The former consists of a series of rhetorical questions expecting a negative answer and stating in proverbial form the truth that believers may have nothing to do with wickedness, darkness, Belial, unbelievers, and idols. The second line of substantiation springs from the assertion that believers are the temple of the living God, and affirms, by a series of subtly linked OT citations, that God dwells among his people. Based on the "promises" of God in the citations, that the covenant God has received them as his children, the Corinthians are exhorted to "come out . . . be separate."

---

4. Adapted from G. D. Fee, "Idols," 156.

a. A Prohibition (6:14a)

14a The passage commences without any connectives to link what is now stated with what has gone before. Paul sometimes uses this grammatical method (asyndeton) to make freestanding statements and thus to heighten the impact of his words.[5] The prohibition in the form of a negative present imperative, "Do not get into,"[6] suggests that the readers were on the brink of doing what Paul here forbids. Such a view of the grammatical intention is consistent with the view that Paul is addressing once more the issues and circumstances that necessitated his unscheduled visit to the Corinthians followed by his "Severe Letter."

The prohibition is in the form of a metaphor based on two OT texts, one that banned cross-breeding of animals (LXX Lev 19:19), and the other that forbade the yoking together of an ox and an ass for plowing (Deut 22:10).[7] The force of the metaphor lies in the recognition that the "unbelievers" are of a different "breed" and that care must be taken as to the nature of the relationships one might enter with them. Some scholars have suggested that the notion of *incongruity* catches the idea of the image; believers must not be *incongruously* joined to unbelievers;[8] they must selectively disengage from them.[9]

Historically, the meaning of "unbelievers" has often been taken as a call for separation of Christian from Christian, based on the context (1) "come out from them," (2) "touch no unclean thing," and (3) "let us purify ourselves from everything that contaminates body and spirit." On this interpretation "unbelievers" are seen as *false* believers, apostates who give expression to "unrighteousness" (v. 14), "idols" (v. 15), and "unclean[ness]" (v. 17). Some interpreters regard the "peddlers" (2:17) as these false believers. But nothing in the passage suggests that "unbelievers" are false believers; the OT quotations are used in a way analogous to the call for Israel's separation from the idolatry of Babylon. Care must be taken not to press the exegesis of these OT citations beyond their original intention.

Rather, the meaning of "unbelievers" must be determined by other uses

---

5. 5:21 is another example.

6. Gk. μὴ γίνεσθε ἑτεροζυγοῦντες is present imperative with a present participle, making a periphrastic construction (see BDF #354). It is taken as a warning not to *become* involved by Martin, 196, and by Furnish, 361. Less probably Hughes takes it as "Do not go on becoming unequally yoked with unbelievers, as you are already doing" (245 n. 8).

7. Paul's verb ἑτεροζυγοῦν occurs nowhere else in the NT. It does not spring from Deut 22:10, where we might have expected to find it, but from the adjective ἑτερόζυγος, which is used in the LXX only at Lev 19:19.

8. So, e.g., Hughes, 196.

9. So W. J. Webb, "What Is the Unequal Yoke?" 162-79.

of that word where it chiefly occurs, namely, within Paul's two Corinthian letters.[10] Such uses make it clear that "unbelievers" are unconverted Gentiles who inhabit the dark world of idolatry and immorality in such a city as Corinth, blinded people who are under the sway of the "god of this world" (see on 4:4).

Nonetheless, Paul does not ban social interaction with "unbelievers" (1 Cor 5:9-10; 10:27), even envisaging them entering the assembly of believers (1 Cor 14:22-24). Nor does Paul discourage believers from remaining in the bonds of marriage with unbelievers (1 Cor 7:12-15). The question, therefore, is what is meant by being "yoked together" with "unbelievers"? What kinds of relationships should not be entered into with "unbelievers"? The rhetorical questions that follow give the answer. The Corinthian believers must not be joined with Corinthian "unbelievers" in the cultic life of the city, but rather "come out" from among them.[11]

b. Five Antithetical Rhetorical Questions (6:14b-16a)[12]

The five rhetorical questions which now follow should be considered as a unit: (1) the connective "for" *(gar)* is found in the first line and again only after the fifth question has been put, (2) each question after the first begins alternatively with "or what"[13] and "but what,"[14] (3) each question then uses a word for likeness or agreement that is followed by balanced opposites,

10. Paul's use of "unbeliever" (ἄπιστος) is confined to 1 and 2 Corinthians and the Pastorals. For a discussion of the Christian's sense of separation from unbelievers in the subsequent centuries see *New Docs.* 3.151.

11. So, G. D. Fee, "Idols," 158. Other views are listed in Martin (196-97) and include the hypothesis that ἄπιστοι = Paul's judaizing opponents (D. Rensberger, "Fresh Examination"; Collange). Against this Paul would not speak of *Jewish* opponents as associated with "wickedness," or "idols" (as opposed to "the temple of God"). Hughes, 246, thinks Paul is speaking broadly against any action that might compromise the integrity of the faith, including intermarriage. While Paul did prohibit a believer from entering into a marriage with an unbeliever (1 Cor 7:39 — "a woman/wife . . . is free to be married . . . only in the Lord" — ἐλευθέρα ἐστὶν . . . γαμηθῆναι, μόνον ἐν κυρίῳ), this is not to be read directly out of this passage. Thrall, 1.473, suggests that the passage may be adapted from a baptismal catechesis to correct his earlier and more liberal teaching in 1 Cor 7:1-16 so as now to prohibit entry into marriage or business partnership, with its inevitable involvement in cultic activity. But we might have expected Paul to make some reference to that earlier teaching had he now been correcting it.

12. Hughes, 246, comments: "It is almost as though we can in this passage catch an echo of Paul the preacher; the series of rhetorical questions, the notable variety of vocabulary and construction, the quotation from the Old Testament Scriptures and the application of the biblical promises to those he is addressing (7:1) — all these conjure up a vivid picture of the power and effect of the apostle's preaching."

13. Gk. ἢ τίς.

14. Gk. τὶς δέ.

345

expressing in each case an exact antithesis, (4) there is no verb in any of the questions, and (5) the second part of the antithesis is introduced in turn by "and . . . to . . . to . . . with . . . with." Literally,

For				
what	in common		righteousness	and	wickedness?
Or what	fellowship	with	light	to	darkness?
But what	harmony	of	Christ	to	Belial?
Or what	portion	by a	believer	with an	unbeliever?
But what	union	by the	temple of God	with	idols?

His initial prohibition ("Do not be yoked together with unbelievers") is amplified by these five balanced rhetorical questions, of which the fifth ("What agreement is there between the temple of God and idols?") is climactic, and thus the most important.[15] Considered separately or together, they express in proverbial form the utter incongruity of godliness and ungodliness.

14b The explanatory connective, "for," introduces not only the first, but, we infer, each of the self-answering questions belonging to the unit. With this question, as with the others, the very asking of the question gives the negative answer, "none," thus reinforcing the prohibition not to be misyoked with unbelievers (v. 14a).

In Paul's original word order "in common"[16] comes after the interrogative "what," and before the antithesis "righteousness and wickedness." Thus his question, which has no verb, reads literally, "For what in common righteousness and wickedness?"

The meaning of "righteousness" is determined by its matching opposite, "wickedness."[17] It is the same contrast often made in the Psalms between "the righteous" and "the wicked" (e.g., Pss 1, 11, 34). Paul does not here mean God's gracious gift of righteousness for those "in Christ" (cf. 3:9; 5:21). Rather, he has in mind that ethical righteousness which gives expression to the will of God as discerned in the Law of God set out under the old covenant. By contrast, "wickedness" literally means "without law," "lawless"[18] and describes — in

15. According to G. D. Fee, "Idols," 158: "[It] is the great question to which others lead."

16. Gk. μετοχή, meaning "partnership." Cf. n. 19 below.

17. Gk. δικαιοσύνη καὶ ἀνομία. For δικαιοσύνη see on 6:7.

18. See Rom 6:19 as a conclusion to a sustained contrast between "righteousness" and "wickedness" (cf. Rom 6:13-19). The discovery of these antitheses in the literature of Qumran (1QH 14) does not necessarily imply Paul's present dependence on that literature; more probably Paul and Qumran are each directly dependent upon the OT (see Barrett, 197). It is possible that Paul is obliquely addressing the "peddlers" and their Jewish supporters in Corinth, who may have felt that Paul's doctrine of grace blurred the distinction between righteousness and wickedness (cf. Rom 3:8; 6:1).

general terms — Paul's perception of "unbelievers" (i.e., unconverted Gentiles), particularly in their characteristic cultic life[19] that involved both idolatry and temple prostitution. Despite rumors to the contrary, and indeed misinformation,[20] Paul is no antinomian.

14c The second rhetorical question — also verbless — is (literally): "Or what fellowship[21] with light[22] to darkness." "Light" and darkness," the daily experience of humankind, stands as a common spiritual and moral antithesis in the writings of Paul[23] and elsewhere in the NT.[24] Nonetheless, its appearance here is probably dictated by 2 Cor 4:3-6, where God's light in the gospel shines in the darkened minds of unbelievers who are blinded by the "god of this world." Nowhere is that darkness due to blindness more evident than in the unbeliever's participation in cultic worship of the gods and the sharing of cultic meals in Gentile temples.

In the First Letter, by a sustained use of the vocabulary of "fellowship" (1 Cor 10:16 [twice], 18, 20), Paul pointed out the impossibility of the believer's idol worship, including eating and drinking food offered to the gods. To be present and to share in such food is to fellowship with demons (1 Cor 10:20). It is precisely for this reason that Paul employs the word "fellowship" in this context. Believers can have no "fellowship" with "unbelievers" at that most characteristic moment of unbelief, the worship of other gods. It seems likely that by his use of this vocabulary Paul is calling to mind his earlier teaching to the Corinthians (1 Cor 10:20). The "god of this world"/"demons" are the source of darkness; there can be no "fellowship" with them by participation in Gentile cultic activity.

15a The third rhetorical question — also verbless — is (literally): "But what harmony[25] of Christ to Belial?" The significant question here is why Paul employed the otherwise unused word "Belial"[26] over against the familiar "Satan" (see 2:11; 11:14; 12:7; this is the only occurrence of Belial in the entire NT). As to its background, the Hebrew word *beliyy 'al*

---

19. This is supported by the use of the cognate μετέχειν in the passage in the First Letter, where Paul teaches the impossibility of the believer sharing in cultic meals in Gentile temples (1 Cor 10:17, 21). It is significant that μετέχειν and the κοινωνία group of words are used both in 1 Cor 10:14-22 and the present passage. See G. D. Fee, "Idols," 158-59.

20. Rom 3:8.

21. Gk. κοινωνία. See n. 19 above.

22. Gk. φωτί. The dative here is repeated in vv. 15a and 16a and appears to be used in three of the five rhetorical questions for stylistic variety. Of itself it is no evidence for non-Pauline authorship.

23. E.g., Rom 13:12; 1 Thess 5:5; Eph 5:11-14.

24. E.g., Matt 8:12; 22:13; 25:30; Luke 16:8; John 1:4-9; 12:36; 1 Pet 2:9.

25. Gk. συμφώνησις, from which our word "symphony" is derived.

26. Gk. βελιάλ. See further Hughes, 248 n. 12.

appears in the OT with the meaning "worthlessness" (e.g., Deut 13:13; 15:9; 2 Sam 22:5; Ps 18:4), but there is no evidence of its being used of a person. Nonetheless, in the intertestamental literature (e.g., *Jub.* 1:20; *T. Reub.* 4:11) it has a personal use, and means an opponent of God. The same may be seen in the Qumran beatitude ("Blessed be the God of Israel . . . but cursed be Belial with his hostile purpose . . ." [1QM 13:1-4; cf., e.g., 1QS 1:18, 24; 2:19])[27] and in the rabbinic literature, as, for example, noted below.

In the latter the similar-sounding word *beli Jol* = "having no yoke" is used (*Sifre Deut.* 117; *Sanh.* 111b).[28] It looks as if the rabbinically trained Paul may be engaging in a typically rabbinic pun, springing from his initial "Do not be yoked . . ." (v. 14a). Whatever the source of the word to Paul, it remains a mystery why he would have used a word so unfamiliar to Gentiles. Doubtless "Belial" was well known to the Jewish members of the Corinthian church. Perhaps Paul wanted the Jewish believers in the first instance to understand and agree with his rigorous stance and then to explain it to those Gentiles who stood in spiritual danger at that time. Was it Paul's oblique way of defending himself before the Jewish component of the Corinthian church, who were under pressure from the Judaizing intruders?

As with the first and second rhetorical questions, the background to this question is to be found in Paul's earlier ban on participation in cultic meals in the temples of Corinth (1 Cor 10:14-22). There Paul sets against each other "Christ"/"the Lord" and "demons." The Corinthians cannot have "fellowship" with both. Significantly, in this passage Paul sets in antithesis "Christ" and "Belial," the prince of demons (cf. Mark 4:22). By this question, as with the others, the Corinthians are called upon to separate themselves from the local cults.

15b The fourth rhetorical question — also verbless — is (literally): "Or what portion by a believer with an unbeliever?" Here, logically following the third question, "the believer" is starkly contrasted with "the unbeliever," the only occasion in the NT where the two are found in the one verse *(pistos . . . apistos).* The "believer" is one who belongs to Christ and enjoys the fellowship of the community of believers in the congregation;[29] the "unbeliever" has no attachment to Christ or to the congregation, but is domiciled outside in the world of "wickedness" and "darkness," living for "Belial."

---

27. This is the chief evidence in the case for a Qumranian provenance of this passage. But it should be noted that Belial is usually the enemy of God and rarely of the Messiah (= Christ").

28. For further documentation and discussion see Barrett, 198; Martin, 200.

29. Less probable is the view that πιστός here refers to God, who is faithful and reliable (as in 1:18), and hence by extrapolation to someone who is faithful and reliable (see, e.g., 1 Cor 1:9 and 4:17).

Paul's question does not demand or imply the severance of social relationships by the believer from the unbeliever (see 1 Cor 5:9-10; 7:12-15; 10:27; 14:22-24). Rather, it is to reinforce the juxtaposition of the previous three antithetical questions and to lay the ground for the absolute separation expected in the climactic final question. It is in the cultic sense that the "believer" has no "portion" with the "unbeliever."

16a The fifth and critical rhetorical question — also verbless — is (literally): "But what union by the temple of God with idols?" The utter incompatibility of the elements of the antithesis — "temple of God"[30] and "idols" — is signaled by the bridge word "union,"[31] preceded by the interrogative "But what?" There is no possible *union* between these entities. This rhetorical antithesis is the climax of the four preceding questions, making clear their meaning and explaining the nature of the forbidden "yoke" with "unbelievers" (v. 14a).[32]

Under the old covenant the temple of God was that sanctuary of Yahweh, the God of Israel, who by his very name and commandment forbade the making and worshiping of idols.[33] Under the new covenant, however, the temple of God is the congregation of holy ones, those set apart to God in Jesus Christ and made so by God's indwelling presence, the Holy Spirit (1 Cor 3:16-17; cf. John 2:19-21).[34] Just as it was inconceivable that idols could be brought into the temple of Yahweh, so under the new dispensation it is impossible for the temple of God, the members of the holy congregation of God (1 Cor 1:2),[35] to go to or share in the cultic

---

30. Gk. ναὸς θεοῦ. Paul here uses the term ναός, which generally, but not universally, points to the shrine of a temple (see, e.g., Mark 14:58; 15:29; John 2:19, 20; 2 Thess 2:4), rather than ἱερόν, the more general structure in which the ναός was located (see, e.g., Mark 11:11, 15, 16, 27; 12:35; 13:1; 14:44). See further O. Michel, *TDNT* 4.880-90. The word ναός, however, was not confined to the temple in Jerusalem but was also applied to the shrines of Gentile cults (see, e.g., Acts 17:24). For possible eschatological inferences associated with "temple," as well as for possible connections with the Qumran literature and practice, see B. Gärtner, *Temple,* 57.

31. Gk. συγκατάθεσις; NIV, "agreement." This word is not found elsewhere in the NT, but is common in Hellenistic writers for "union," "agreement" (e.g., Philo, *The Sacrifices of Cain and Abel* 175). The verb συγκατατίθημι, "I agree with," however, is found in the LXX (e.g., Exod 23:1; 2 Kings 21:7; 23:6; Ezek 8:3-18).

32. G. D. Fee, "Idols," 159, states appositely, "The church is not to 'come out from among' unbelievers *per se,* but rather, as the temple of God, it cannot associate with unbelievers in the temple of demons."

33. See Ezek 8:3-13; cf., e.g., Exod 20:4; 23:24; Lev 26:1; Deut 5:7-10; 4:16, 23; 27:15; 32:16, 21; Josh 23:7.

34. See also G. D. Fee, *Presence,* 336-38.

35. It is held that "temple" is a congregational rather than a distributive image ("people of God"). For preference for the latter nuance see G. D. Fee, "Idols," 146-47.

worship of idols in Gentile Corinth (1 Cor 10:14-22; cf. 8:10-13). Idolatry (1 Cor 5:10, 11; 6:9; 12:2; Gal 4:8; 5:20; Col 3:5; 1 Thess 1:9), and the fornication — casual or cultic — with which it was often associated (1 Cor 10:7-8; 6:15, 18[36]), were utterly abhorrent to Paul; believers can have no direct association with them.

Paul's call to turn from idols was fundamental to his proclamation of the gospel (1 Thess 1:9; cf. 1 Cor 5:10, 11, 20; 6:9; Rom 1:22-25). To return to idolatry, or to fail to disengage from it, would be to receive the grace of God in vain (6:1).

c. The Basic Assertion Supported by an OT Citation (6:16b-e)

16b The immediately prior question is now restated as an emphatic assertion: (1) the connective "for" *(gar)* draws a conclusion from the five rhetorical questions, especially the one immediately preceding, (2) the pronoun "we," which occurs first, is used for emphasis,[37] and (3) the word order "temple of God we are" is to be taken as "we are *the* temple of the living God."[38]

Paul's attributive "the *living* God" serves to create an antithesis between a "temple," which is ordinarily lifeless, and one that — because *"we"*[39] are that temple — must be *alive*.[40] That temple must be living because it is "the temple of the *living* God."[41]

It is unlikely to be coincidental that the other reference to "the living

---

36. Paul applies the same imperative φεύγετε to both fornication and idolatry (1 Cor 6:18; 10:14), suggesting both (1) the moral seriousness of these activities, and (2) their cultural connectedness. According to Wis 14:12: "the idea of making idols was the beginning of fornication, and the invention of them the corruption of life."

37. Gk. ἡμεῖς. According to Plummer, 208, the "we" is "very emphatic."

38. Gk. ναὸς θεοῦ ἐσμεν. G. D. Fee, "Idols," 147 n. 11, commenting on the similar word order of 1 Cor 3:16 (ναὸς θεοῦ ἐστε) draws attention to "Colwell's rule," namely, "that predicate nouns that precede the verb are usually definite, even if they do not have the definite article."

39. It is significant that Paul declares that *"you* are the temple . . ." in the First Letter (1 Cor 3:16), whereas here *"we* are the temple." Moreover, a few verses earlier he has addressed his readers as *"you* Corinthians" (6:11-13; cf. 5:20–6:2). Is Paul here affirming the closeness of relationship between himself as apostle and them ("you . . . we")? See, e.g., 1:6-7, 11, 14, 24; 2:10-11. Martin's suggestion, 202-3, that Paul is extending the plea of 5:20 is not convincing.

40. There is a similar paradox in 1 Pet 2:5 — ". . . like living stones . . . built into a spiritual house."

41. See LXX Dan 5:23 for a probable parallel: "the house of the living God," referring to the Jerusalem temple. Here, however, "temple" is metaphorical for the people of God assembled.

God" is to "the *Spirit* of the living God" (see on 3:3).[42] There Paul speaks of the long-awaited promise of a new covenant in which the Spirit will create a people with hearts responsive to God. Corporately the people whose hearts have been changed by the Spirit are the "temple of the living God." Their life comes from the "living" God through his life-giving Spirit who dwells in them. Corporately they are a living temple of God, indwelt by his Spirit because individually they are temples of God, indwelt by his Spirit (cf. 1 Cor 3:16-17; 6:19).[43]

Fundamental to this interpretation is the fulfillment motif, which dominates the apostle's thought within 2 Corinthians. In the proclamation of the Son of God by Paul and his companions may be seen the fidelity of God to his covenantal promises, which are inwardly confirmed to the recipients of that message through the coming of the Spirit of God, anointing them as a messianic people (see on 1:18-22). This heart-changing Spirit is nothing else than the God-given blessing of the new covenant long promised by the prophets (see on 3:3, 6, and 18). All this is attributable to the arrival in history of "the time of God's favor, the day of salvation" (6:2). With the completion of the reconciling work of God in the death and resurrection of Jesus Christ and the institution of the ministry and word of reconciliation in the apostles, that "day" has "now" arrived. The "no longer" time has passed; the "new," "now" time has arrived (5:14–6:2).

It is for reasons of eschatological fulfillment that gathered believers in a church like Corinth are deemed to be the people of the Spirit, "the temple of the living God." But it is precisely at the point where that "temple" meets the culture of "idols" in the Gentile metropolis of Corinth that the challenge to compromise and syncretism becomes most painful, and to which the Corinthians are in danger of succumbing. This is the reason for Paul's present challenge to the Christians of Corinth. They are "the temple of the living God" in a city given to the worship of idols in Gentile temples (see 1 Cor 8:5; cf. Acts 17:16).

16c, d, e That eschatological fulfillment has now occurred in the

---

42. This is supported by the parallel between 1 Cor 3:16 and this verse:

1 Cor 3:16   **2 Cor 6:16b**

you . . . are God's temple . . .   we are the temple
God's Spirit lives (οἰκεῖ) in you.   of the living (ζῶντος) God.

The "living God" gives life to his human temple by his Spirit.
43. Compare ναὸς τοῦ θεοῦ ἐστε καὶ τὸ πνεῦμα τοῦ θεοῦ οἰκεῖ ἐν ὑμῖν (1 Cor 3:16) with τὸ σῶμα ὑμῶν ναὸς τοῦ ἐν ὑμῖν ἁγίου πνεύματός ἐστιν (1 Cor 6:19). The gathered people are a Spirit-indwelt temple, an assembling of Spirit-indwelt individual temples.

Corinthian assembly is established by Paul's adapted quotation of a threefold "promise" of God (cf. 1:20; 7:1) made under the old covenant, based on LXX Lev 26:11-12.[44] Paul's adaptation of that scripture may be seen by a comparison of the OT text with his:[45]

LXX Lev 26:11-12	2 Cor 6:16c, d, e
	As God has said,[46]
"I will set my tabernacle in you,	"I will live with them
and my soul will not abhor you.	
I will walk among you	and I will walk [among them],
and I will be your God,	and I will be their God,
and you will be my people."	and they will be my people."

Adapting the words of Lev 26:11-12, Paul discerns this threefold personal promise in the mouth of God: (1) "*I* will live with[47] them," (2) "*I* will walk [among them]," and (3) "*I* will be their God."[48] In the light of the Corinthians' reception of the word of God and God's anointing of them with his Spirit (see on 1:18-22), it is evident that God's words of promise have now been kept; they are a present reality. God *does* dwell in them, *does* walk among them; he *is* their God, and they *are* his people. Thus the Corinthians are, indeed, "the temple of the living God" (v. 16b).

44. Thrall, 1.477, and J. M. Scott, *Adoption,* 195-201, see Paul here conflating two texts, Ezek 37:27 and Lev 26:12, both of which have covenantal contexts. In our view, however, there is no need to propose Paul's citation of Ezek 37:27 in this passage. Paul's use of the third person plural pronouns could as easily have been his own alteration.

45. This is an example of the so-called pesher method whereby an OT text is restated so as to apply to the present context. According to E. E. Ellis, "A Note on Pauline Hermeneutics," the adaptations are "evidently designed for a messianic age interpretation of the prophecies" (130). It is likely that Paul's opponents had their own line of OT exegesis (on which see D. Georgi, *Opponents,* 265-82).

46. Gk. καθὼς εἶπεν ὁ θεός, a citation formula not found elsewhere in Paul (but cf. 4:6 — ὅτι ὁ θεὸς ὁ εἰπών). A roughly similar parallel in Qumran (CD 4:13-14) is no argument that the formula is more typically Qumranian than Pauline (for further discussion see Martin, 203).

47. Gk. ἐνοικήσω ἐν αὐτοῖς, words not to be found in the LXX but which dynamically paraphrase θήσω τὴν σκηνήν μου ἐν ὑμῖν (Lev 26:11).

48. To achieve this, Paul has (1) paraphrased "I will set my tabernacle in you" as "I will live with them," (2) imported "I will be their God" to complete and introduce the well-known refrain "I will be their God, and they will be my people," and (3) altered the pronoun "you" to "they." As noted above, some scholars argue that Paul also had in mind Ezek 37:26-27: "I will make a covenant of peace with them; it will be an everlasting covenant. . . . I will put my sanctuary among them for ever. My dwelling place shall be with them; I will be their God, and they will be my people."

These powerful verses teach (1) the fidelity of God to his word of promise, (2) the continuity in the world of the people of God, though under a new covenant (see on 3:3-6), and (3) the necessity of separation of God's people-temple from the defilement of idols, as he now proceeds to declare.

d. A Direct Command Supported by Two Promises (6:17-18)

17-18   God has domiciled among them, his people, as their God (v. 16b-d). From this great reality ("therefore"[49]) he makes two exhortations to separate themselves from the pollution of the Gentile world, followed by two divine "promises" as they do this.

The two exhortations — (1) "come out from *them* and be separate," and (2) "touch no unclean thing" — are drawn from Isa 52:11 ("Go out from there and touch no unclean thing. Go out from the midst of *her,*[50] be separate").[51] It appears that the parallel is not merely verbal but situational. Isaiah is addressing the people of God exiled in Gentile Babylon. The prophet exhorts Israel as those who "bear the [sacred] vessels of the LORD" to leave the idolatrous city, touching no unclean thing as they go out of her. Using the prophet's words, the apostle Paul warns God's "temple-people" in Gentile Corinth to have no part in the cults of the city; they are to come out and be separate, touching no defiled thing.[52]

Now follows the first of the two promises, "and I[53] will receive you," which is based on Yahweh's word given to the people in exile through another prophet of the exile, Ezekiel (LXX Ezek 20:34; cf. 20:41; 11:17). Through Ezekiel God promised to welcome home and receive his people from the nations (i.e., the Gentiles) in which they are dispersed. Through the words of the apostle Paul — who is citing Ezekiel — God is summoning his people out of the cultic uncleanness of the Gentiles; he promises to welcome them as they come out. One prophet, Isaiah, has just been cited, exhorting them, "Come out and be separate." Here another, Ezekiel, is cited, promising in God's name, "I will receive you."

---

49. Gk. διό.

50. In Paul's hands the αὐτῆς, Babylon, of LXX Isa 52:11 has become αὐτῶν, "them," an implicit allusion to the "unbelievers" of Corinth.

51. Cf. Jer 51:45; Ezek 20:34.

52. Paul omits from his quotation of LXX Isa 52:11 the cultic οἱ φέροντες τὰ σκεύη Κυρίου, suggesting to some that the citation is ethically and morally rather than cultically directed (see Martin, 205). In terms of the cultic tone of v. 17b ("touch no unclean thing") and 7:1a ("let us purify ourselves"), however, this view is not exegetically warranted.

53. Gk. κἀγώ formed by crasis of the καί from LXX Ezek 20:34b and the ἐγώ from LXX 2 Kgdms 7:14a, cited next. See J. M. Scott, *Adoption,* 207, for argument that Paul has by the use of κἀγώ welded the texts Ezek 20:34b and 2 Kgdms 7:14a together.

The second promise, "I will be a Father to you, and you will be my sons and daughters," is based on Yahweh's word through Nathan to David about David's coming son, "I will be a father to *him,* and *he* will be my son" (2 Sam 7:14). Whereas Heb 1:5 cites this text as applying to Christ,[54] Paul applies it to Christ's *people.* Paul here makes some alterations[55] to the original text: (1) he changes "him . . . he" to *"you . . . you,"* and (2) he expands "my son" to "my son*s*[56] *and daughters."* The effect of these changes is to intensify a specific and direct focus on the readers, now including the women in the messianic assembly in Corinth. It would be anachronistic, however, to see in this adaptation of 2 Sam 7:14 an anticipation of modern views on women's rights.[57] Rather, Paul has amalgamated 2 Sam 7:14 with another text, Isa 43:6, where God said, "Bring my son*s* from afar, and my *daughters* from the ends of the earth." This verse, like "come out from among them and be separate," quoted above, speaks of the second exodus. The impact of Paul's citation of 2 Sam 7:14 plus Isa 43:6 is primarily eschatological, to remind readers that the second exodus has come to pass and that God, their Father, has received them as his children. In turn this is closely connected with the now-fulfilled new covenant of the Spirit and righteousness (3:7, 9), in which Paul is a God-appointed minister (see on 3:6).

The manner of address is, of course, fundamental to the relationship of the covenant people with God. He is their "Father" (1:2); they are his "sons and daughters." But the Corinthians — and all God's children at every time and in every place — must live consistently as God's sons and daughters. They can have no part of the cultic worship of other gods. They must "come out" and "be received" by their heavenly Father. Otherwise their behavior would be a practical denial of his paternity and their covenantal relationship with him.

54. In the interpretation of 4QFlor 1:2 this person was the "branch of David" who would arise at the end of time to save Israel.

55. It is a characteristic of the pesher style of interpretation of scriptural texts to expand or alter the text to reflect the insight of the interpreter into the current situation.

56. Paul may be connecting the concept of "sons" (υἱοί) with that of "adoption" (υἱοθεσία — Rom 8:15, 24; 9:4; Gal 4:5; Eph 1:5). It should be noted that 2 Sam 7:14, as cited by Paul, spoke of the "son" of God, which, however, Paul here cites as "son*s*." Is Paul inferring that through the Son of God, Jesus Christ, preached among them (1:19), the Corinthians are now "sons," having received the divine adoption (υἱοθεσία) in *the* Son of God (see Gal 4:4-6)?

57. By discerning in the reference to "daughters" per se a particular and high view of women, as the spiritual equals of men — true as that view was for Paul (cf. Gal 3:28) — is perhaps to deduce more from Paul's gloss in 2 Sam 7:14 than is warranted. For positive argument see Martin, 206, with many references.

Just as the exhortation "come out . . . and be separate" is stated in the words of the formulaic, "says the Lord"[58] (v. 17), so this promise is followed by, "says the Lord almighty." The addition of "almighty,"[59] though common to the LXX,[60] is found only here in the writings of Paul. This is the last of the promises, and indeed the end of the parenesis beginning at v. 14; the declaration that this is the word of "the Lord almighty" is appropriate. The "living God" (v. 16a) is the "almighty Lord"; he has spoken. Again, as noted above, the apostle is his instrument for the upbuilding of the church (see on 10:8; 13:10), through the pesher-type application of the OT scriptures as cited here and throughout the letter.[61]

e. An Encouragement to Purity and Holiness (7:1)

1 Paul now concludes the exhortation begun at v. 14. He here addresses his readers by the affectionate term "beloved,"[62] rather than by more direct words, as in vv. 14a, 17a, b. Moreover, he adopts a cohortative form of address ("let us . . ."),[63] consistent perhaps with his earlier identification with them ("*we* are the temple of the living God" — v. 16). Though absent from them, he identifies himself as though present by his use of the reflexive "ourselves" ("let us purify *ourselves* . . ."). This exhortation should be taken with the warmly pastoral appeals made earlier (5:20; 6:1, 11-14). Indeed, the whole parenesis 6:14–7:1 is the end point and climax of the appeal he began at 5:20.

The opening connective "therefore"[64] refers specifically to "having these promises," that is, to the promises in this passage (vv. 16, 17, and 18).[65]

---

58. Gk. λέγει κύριος, which is common in the OT (LXX), and found as a citation introduction in Paul (1 Cor 14:21; Rom 12:19). Here "Lord" is "God," not Christ (so D. Capes, *Yahweh Texts,* 111).

59. Gk. παντοκράτωρ, "almighty," appears in the NT only here and in Revelation, where it is a frequent attributive of God (Rev 1:8; 4:8; 11:17; 15:3; 16:7, 14; 19:6, 15; 21:22).

60. Including at 2 Sam 7:8, a few verses earlier than 2 Sam 7:14, which he has just quoted. See further Hughes, 256 n. 19.

61. See also, e.g., on 3:3, 16; 4:6, 13; 6:2; 9:9; 10:8; 13:10.

62. Gk. ἀγαπητοί. Paul is sparing in the use of this word (12:19; 1 Cor 10:14; 15:58; Rom 12:19; Phil 2:12; 4:1), though it is not uncommon elsewhere in the NT (Heb 6:9; Jas 1:16, 19; 2:5; 1 Pet 2:11; 4:12; 2 Pet 3:1, 8, 14; 1 John 2:7; 3:2, 21; 4:1, 7, 11; Jude 3, 17). This pastoral address is entirely congruent with his earlier appeals to them, "Be reconciled to God. . . . Do not receive the grace of God in vain" (5:20; 6:1); see further Martin, 208.

63. A hortatory subjunctive: καθαρίσωμεν, "let us purify. . . ."

64. Gk. οὖν.

65. The character of these "promises" (τὰς ἐπαγγελίας) here may help us understand what Paul meant by his earlier reference: "No matter how many promises

Paul's exhortation to cultic separation is based on the gracious actions of God arising from his promises now fulfilled ("having[66] these promises"), a principle that applies when Paul presses the demands of Christian living on his readers (see, e.g., Rom 12:1). Imperative rests on indicative, "ought" upon "is." The doctrine of grace is not abandoned or compromised.

What follows is a single exhortation ("let us purify ourselves . . ."), followed by the attendant consequence ("perfecting holiness . . ."). Specifically, Paul exhorts "let us purify[67] [or *cleanse*] ourselves. . . ," language that specifically picks up "touch no *unclean* thing" a few verses earlier (v. 17). This is the vocabulary of ritual[68] and is entirely consistent with the thesis we are following, namely, that Paul is here calling on his readers to separate themselves from the temple cults of Corinth. This is confirmed by his words "from everything that contaminates. . . ." Although the noun ("stain, defilement"[69]) occurs nowhere else in the NT, the verb[70] is to be found in the passage in the First Letter where Paul speaks of the defilement of conscience through a believer's eating in an idol temple (1 Cor 8:7; cf. v. 10). The combination of "cleanse" and "defilement" appears to clinch the case that this whole passage is directed to the Corinthians' involvement in the various Greco-Roman and mystery cults of the region. That the totality of one's being must be preserved undefiled is indicated by Paul's "of body and spirit"; no part physical or emotional is exempt from Paul's call for cleansing.[71]

God [Gk. ὅσαι ἐπαγγελίαι θεοῦ] has made, they are 'Yes' in Christ" (see on 1:20). The "promises" in vv. 16, 17, and 18, taken together, are OT *testimonia* that outline God's relationship with people under the new covenant. God will live in them, welcome them, and be their Father. These "promises," however, are latent in the OT, receiving definition and resolution by the Son of God whom the apostle proclaimed (1:18-20). Other "promises" that were appealed to were doubtless more specific in character (cf. Rom 15:8).

66. Gk. ἔχοντες. To be noted is Paul's use of present tense indicatives and present tense participles of the verb "to have" (ἔχειν) in this letter — 3:3, 12; 4:1, 7, 13; 5:1. "We have" these various blessings, as from God.

67. Gk. καθαρίσωμεν, "let us *cleanse*"; cf. ἀκαθάρτου (v. 17), "*unclean* thing."

68. So Martin, 209, citing 1 Esdr 8:20; 2 Macc 5:27; cf. LXX Jer 23:15.

69. Gk. μολυσμός, which appears in LXX OT passages relating to the defilement of idols (Jer 23:13; cf. 1 Esdr 8:80; 2 Macc 5:27). It is synonymous with ἀκαθαρσία, a word found elsewhere in Paul (Rom 1:24; 6:19; Gal 5:19).

70. Gk. μολύνειν, which, apart from 1 Cor 8:7, occurs elsewhere in the NT only at Rev 3:4; 14:4; the noun occurs only at 2 Cor 7:1.

71. Paul's technical use elsewhere of the terms "body and spirit" (σαρκὸς καὶ πνεύματος) has been used to reject Pauline authorship of this verse, as part of the argument that 6:14–7:1 is a non-Pauline fragment. But within this letter these words are used in a nontechnical sense (2:13; 7:5; cf. 1 Cor 7:34; 1 Thess 5:23). G. D. Fee, "Idols," 161, thinks that Paul means only the idiomatic "inwardly" and "outwardly."

The consequence of that "cleansing" is now stated, namely, "perfecting holiness." Although the noun "holiness"[72] is rare (1 Thess 3:13; Rom 1:4), the members of the word family are often found within Paul's writings, including 2 Corinthians.[73] A church is the incorporation of Spirit-indwelt individuals and is itself "the temple of the living God," as Paul has just observed (see on v. 16a; cf. 1 Cor 12:12-13; 3:16; 6:19). According to his definition in the First Letter, "a church of God" is a body "*sanctified* in Christ Jesus," whose members are "called to be *saints.*"[74] By God's grace the church enjoys this holy status in the eyes of God who is holy, a status, however, that it is to fulfill in obedience to the will of God (see 1 Thess 4:3). This it cannot do, however, since its members are "unclean" through their participation in the wickedness of idolatry through which they are in fellowship with Belial (vv. 14-16a).

The verb "perfect,"[75] meaning "complete" or "fulfill," is a present participle that, however, probably does not imply a process of perfection in moral holiness. The holiness that is to be perfected is covenantal rather than developmental or processive in character.[76] On the contrary, the action of separation from the idol-worshiping cults (v. 17), which is tantamount to the act of self-cleansing from defilement (v. 1a), should be seen as a prerequisite to the perfection of the church's calling to be God's holy temple (v. 16); without this separation the Corinthians cannot be what they are called to be. To infer a theology of moral and spiritual development at this point, although taught elsewhere (see on 3:18), would be to import a theme that is foreign to the present context.

Let the Corinthians respond to Paul's admonition, literally, "in fear of God."[77] While his exhortation to them to withdraw from cultic involvement arises from the gracious "promises" of God, let them understand that not to do so would be to invoke the profound displeasure of God their Father, whose temple and people they are (vv. 16-18; cf. 1 Cor 10:22).

Paul has now reached the climax of his excursus on apostolic ministry, calling the Corinthians out of cultic uncleanness. That call is based on God's appoint-

---

72. Gk. ἁγιωσύνη.

73. ἅγιος (1:1; 6:6; 8:4; 9:1, 12; 13:12); ἁγιότης (1:12).

74. Gk. ἡγιασμένοις . . . κλητοῖς ἁγίοις (1 Cor 1:2; cf. 2 Cor 1:1; 13:12).

75. Gk. ἐπιτελοῦντες. This is also used of the collection (8:6, 11 [twice]; Rom 15:28).

76. *Contra,* e.g., Martin, 210, and Hughes, 258. The latter takes the present participle (Gk. ἐπιτελοῦντες) as "advance constantly in holiness."

77. Gk. ἐν φόβῳ θεοῦ; NIV, "out of reverence for God." There is a background in the Wisdom literature to "the fear of God" (e.g., Ps 2:11; 5:7; Prov 1:7, 29; 8:13). Paul, too, invokes the "fear" of the Lord/Christ/God (5:11; Eph 5:21; 6:5; Phil 2:12).

ment to the ministry of reconciliation (5:18–6:2), undergirded by the moral authority of a life lived out in replication of the death and resurrection of Jesus (6:3-10), and, finally, expressed as a direct appeal to the Corinthians to widen their hearts to their "father" in the gospel (6:11-13).

But is this of merely historical interest, with no application beyond those times? The view taken here is that Paul, the apostle to the Gentiles, continues to have authority in the consciences of Christians and churches through his letters, which are now part of the church's canon of Scripture.

How, then, might these words apply? Insofar as Christians live in interface with modern counterparts to the cults of Corinth, which through multiculturalism are also increasing in traditionally "Christian" countries, his admonition has immediate applicability. But there are also implications for cases, for example, in which through entering a marriage or a business partnership a Christian would be brought into overly close association with those who engage in the cultic practices of other religions. Moreover, Christian involvement in non-Christian religious services would appear to be in conflict with the apostle's teaching in this passage. However, Paul is careful not to encourage wholesale separation from human affairs (cf. 1 Cor 5:9-10), which would involve, for example, situations of employment, neighborhood location, buying, and selling. Nor does he encourage a Christian to withdraw from an existing marriage with a non-Christian (1 Cor 7:12-15).

There is no exegetical basis here for separation from fellow Christians who, in our opinion, may have deviated from biblical norms,[78] though such a basis may be found elsewhere.[79] The "unbelievers" in these verses are not Christians but outright pagans.

E. EPILOGUE: WORDS OF ENCOURAGEMENT (7:2-4)

> 2 *Make room for us in your hearts. We have wronged no one, we have corrupted no one, we have exploited no one. 3 I do not say this to condemn you; I have said before that you have such a place in our hearts that we would live or die with you. 4 I have great confidence in you; I take great pride in you. I am greatly encouraged; in all our troubles my joy knows no bounds.*

These three verses are important to the structure of 2 Corinthians. They resume and bring to completion the appeal made in 6:11-13. More broadly, they serve as a conclusion to the lengthy excursus on apostolic ministry in 2:14–7:4,

---

78. Unless those deviations were grossly heretical or immoral.
79. See, e.g., 1 Cor 5:11; 1 Thess 5:14; Tit 3:10-11; 2 John 10-11; cf. 1 John 2:19.

which is the longest and most important section within the entire letter. Yet vv. 2-4 — especially v. 4 — are both the end of the excursus and — at the same time — the beginning of the passage that will follow (7:5-16).[1]

More broadly still, the positive note sounded in v. 4 is the basis for the major admonitions that form the latter part of the letter, that is, chapters 8–13. The optimism of vv. 2-4, especially v. 4, is foundational to Paul's appeals regarding the collection (chaps. 8–9), in regard to those who question his spiritual effectiveness (10:1-8), to those who receive the judaizing intruders (11:1-4) and to the intractably immoral (12:20–13:2). Although these final four chapters are ironical and reflect Paul's personal hurt, nonetheless, when taken with chapters 8 and 9, they end on a positive and optimistic note (see 12:19; 13:5-10).

Thus vv. 2-4 are a hinge on which the two main parts of the letter turn. They bring to an end the apologetic first part of the letter, where Paul has been defending his actions (1:12–2:13) and his ministry (2:14–7:4). At the same time they lay an admonitory foundation for the second part, where Paul will prepare the Corinthians for his final visit to them.

Apart from v. 3b the sentences represented by these verses lack connectives (asyndeton), which is suggestive of the pace at which Paul is now operating, whether by dictation or by his own hand.

One of the puzzling elements of this letter comes into view in these verses, namely, Paul's use of singular and plural first person pronouns. From 2:14 to this point Paul has fairly consistently used the first person plural "we"/"us" in regard to his apostolic office as minister of the new covenant (see on 2:14). Paul's use of the singular pronoun "I"/"me," both inside[2] and outside[3] this frame of reference, usually occurs when he is writing in more personal and emotional terms. But in the present passage he mixes the plurals and singulars, ending with the singular.[4] The passage following (7:5-16) is dominated by singular pronouns, supporting the idea that these verses are structurally transitional.

---

1. 7:2-4 is one of a number of transitional or bridge passages within 2 Corinthians that repeat words or ideas from earlier passages (καρδία — 6:11; 7:3) and that introduce words or ideas that will carry forward (παράκλησις — 7:4, 7, 13; 8:4, 17) into passages following. See also 2:12-13, 17; 12:11-13.

2. However, this is a rough-and-ready rule. See, e.g., 6:12; 7:2, where, by this formula, Paul might have been expected to use the more personal singular, "I . . . me."

3. As, e.g., 2:11-12; 7:5-16 and throughout the "Fool's Speech" (11:1–12:13).

4. "We" occurs in v. 2; "I" in v. 3a; "we" in v. 3b; "I"/"me" in v. 4. The singular also occurs at 5:11 and 6:13. Less convincing to our mind is the view of M. Carrez, "Le 'nous,' " 474-86 (see on 2:14) that "we" includes the "you" of the people to whom he wrote, including local church ministers. Carrez holds that Paul uses "we" in positive and affirming contexts. But 6:11-13; 7:2-4 surely qualify that assertion. It is more likely that "we"/"us" is used as an apostolic plural, and "I"/"me" in more personal contexts.

2 After his powerfully rhetorical call for separation from the ritual uncleanness incurred through participation in the local cults (6:14–7:1), Paul resumes his appeal for the Corinthians' reconciliation, both to him personally and to his ministry. Implicit in this appeal, followed by his apologia, is the fact of his prospective and final visit to them.[5]

This verse begins, literally, "Make room for us," which appears to pick up "We have . . . opened wide our hearts" (6:11), though the vocabulary is different.[6] This plea is followed immediately by three apologetic disclaimers of identical pattern — "We have wronged no one, we have corrupted no one, we have exploited no one."[7] Each disclaimer has a verb in the first person plural aorist tense — indicating the comprehensiveness of the rejection[8] of allegations? — followed by the subject "no one." At no point within the verse is there a connective. This construction (asyndeton), as it appears here, is taken to indicate the rapidity of Paul's thought as he wrote or dictated this part of the letter.[9]

Because of their location together, there appears to be some connection between Paul's restated appeal ("Make room for us . . .") and the three protestations ("We have wronged no one," etc.). Most probably Paul is defending himself along the lines, "Make room for us; *we* have done you no harm. There is no need to exclude us."

Against which accusations is Paul defending himself? The first, "We have wronged[10] no one," points to one who had "done wrong," in all likelihood to Paul as the wronged party (see on 7:12). Whatever wrong another has done, this is not true of Paul. The second, "we have corrupted[11] no one," points beyond that to the false apostles, who, we are meant to infer, are "corrupting" Corinthian minds away from pure devotion to Christ (11:3).[12] The third, "we have exploited[13] no one," is Paul's defense against the charge that he has by guileful means "got the better" of the Corinthians (12:16). This relates to the suspicion that, although he declines financial support (11:7-11;

---

5. See 2:1; 9:4-5; 10:2, 6; 12:14, 20, 21; 13:1, 2, 10.

6. Gk. ἡ καρδία ἡμῶν πεπλάτυνται (6:11); χωρήσατε (7:2).

7. Cf. 2:17; 4:2-4; 5:11-12; 12:17-18.

8. Hughes takes the aorists to point back to a definite occasion when Paul was in Corinth.

9. So Plummer, 213.

10. Gk. ἠδικήσαμεν. This verb appears in this letter only here and at 7:12.

11. Gk. ἐφθείραμεν. This verb appears in this letter only here and at 11:2. Furnish, 366, however, takes this as a rather general statement, rather than — as we see it — a specific and pointed reference to the false apostles.

12. Thrall, 1.481, suggests that Paul may be defending himself from the charge of preaching a law-free gospel that has corrupted the morals of the Corinthians.

13. Gk. ἐπλεονεκτήσαμεν, "exploit, get the better of [someone]." This verb appears in this letter only here and at 2:11; 12:17-18.

12:13-15), he has received it indirectly through Titus and other delegates (12:16-19). He is answering the charge of having lied to gain a moral advantage over them. He will say, however, that the false apostles are guilty of financial exploitation of the Corinthians, as well as of other forms of abuse (11:20; cf. 2:17).

Paul's purpose, however, is not to condemn others — as he will say in the next verse — but rather to imply that, by contrast with others, he is fit for their affections and loyalty. There appears to be an implied protest that the Corinthians make room in their hearts for those who misuse them, but they barely tolerate him, even though he has done them no wrong (see on 11:1, 4, 19, and 20).

If this understanding of Paul's intention is correct, this verse may contribute significantly to our apprehension of the historical circumstances underlying the writing of 2 Corinthians. The references to "wrongdoing," "corrupting," and "exploiting" appear to be case-specific and suggest that v. 2 is a good point to enter the letter and trace the complex web of relationships between certain elements within the Corinthian church and the apostle Paul.

3   Paul is now approaching the end of the extended passage about his apostolic ministry (2:14–7:4). In the first sentence of the verse, and for one of the few times within the entire passage, he leaves the use of the plural "we"/"us" for the singular "I"/"me" (cf. 5:11; 6:13), though he will reintroduce the plural in the second sentence. Perhaps the change signals the approaching end of the passage. In the next verse — the last in the passage — he will use "I"/"me," and this singular pattern will dominate in the passage following (7:5-16; but see 7:13).

The first sentence qualifies the previous verse. As with v. 2, we note here the absence of any connective (asyndeton — but see v. 3b), suggestive perhaps of Paul's quickened pace in writing or dictating.

Paul wants no misunderstanding. While his defensive words point obliquely to wrong behavior in others, he is not now writing to condemn. What, then, is his intention? Is he (1) disclaiming something as severe as condemnation, implying a lesser negative reaction, or (2) limiting his targets to those responsible and not to the Corinthian church as a whole? The absence of an object suggests that the former may have been in his mind, true though the latter may have been. Nonetheless, despite all that he has suffered from their actions and attitudes toward him, he still has them in his heart, as he proceeds to say in the second sentence of the verse. Historically, few ministers can have suffered at the hands of their congregations as much as Paul had from the behavior of the Corinthians. Yet he continued to hold them in his heart.

Critical to the second sentence is the explanatory connective "for" *(gar)*, with which it begins. He does "not condemn" them *because,* as he said before,[14] "You are in our hearts." By this statement Paul returns to the point he made earlier (see on 6:11-12), and from which he departed to make his appeal for separation from unbelievers (6:14–7:1).

The second part of this sentence gives the purpose of the first. The Corinthians are in "our hearts"[15] *that*[16] they might "die with and live with" Paul.[17] Once again Paul uses the death/life motif of the gospel of the death and resurrection of Jesus (see, e.g., 2:16; 4:10-12; 5:14-15; 6:3-10).[18]

Here Paul appears to write at two levels of meaning: (1) literally, the ever-present possibility of his death through persecution, followed by resurrection, which the apostle faced on their behalf in the pursuit of his ministry for them (see on 1:9-10; 4:11, 14; 5:1), and (2) spiritually, the "death" to oneself, followed by a "life" lived for Christ, to which as fellow believers Paul and the Corinthians were committed (see on 5:14-15). It is likely that Paul has both possibilities in mind. The point is that, through Paul's ministry, the Corinthians (his "children" through the gospel — see on 6:12) shared with him the prospect of his death and life, whether considered in a literal or a spiritual sense. In either or both senses their destiny is encapsulated in the apostle,[19] just as he and they together are encapsulated "in Christ"[20] — such is the unity that Paul and the Corinthians shared (see on 1:3-7). Implicit here is a subtle call (as in 1 Cor 4:16) for them to imitate his cruciform lifestyle.

4 This is the final verse in Paul's long excursus on the new covenant ministry (2:14–7:4). Whereas he had used the plural "we"/"us" throughout, he now uses the singular "I"/"me" (see also v. 3a; 5:11; 6:13), as he will continue to do in the passage following (7:5-16; but see 7:12). This suggests

---

14. Gk. προείρηκα (see also 13:2). However, "I have said before" has been interpreted differently by others, as referring to the time of, e.g., (1) an earlier visit, or (2) an earlier letter (as 2:4, 9; 7:8, 12), or (3) as referring to a statement made earlier in this letter (i.e., 3:2).

15. The plural (ἐν ταῖς καρδίαις ἡμῶν) may indicate that here Paul is specifically associating his colleagues Timothy (1:1) and Titus (7:6) with him and that he is not speaking only in an "apostolic plural" (see on 2:14). Had he referred only to himself, he would most likely have written in the singular, as in 6:11. But see 3:2, where the plural "hearts" is used in a context where Paul alone is in view.

16. Gk. εἰς τό.

17. My translation. See 2 Sam 15:21; Rom 8:38, 39.

18. See R. Tannehill, *Dying and Rising,* 93. With less probability, some interpreters take dying and living with as a formula of abiding friendship based on classical allusions (for references see Furnish, 367).

19. By analogy with Christ — but only by analogy — Paul suffers for the people. In this sense, the apostle is a Christ-figure. See on 1:6; 6:10; 11:7; 12:15.

20. Paul's frequent "in Christ" (ἐν Χριστῷ) is not so common in 2 Corinthians as in other letters (but see 2:14, 17; 3:14; 5:17, 19; 12:2, 19). See further C. F. D. Moule, *Phenomenon,* 21-42; *The Origin of Christology,* 47-96.

that v. 4 serves as a point of transition, an overlap verse; it ends the one passage and begins the next.[21]

As with vv. 2-4 generally, this verse is without connectives (asyndeton — but see v. 3b), a probable sign of the speed of writing or dictating (see on v. 2). Cast in two staccato sentences, this verse is powerfully rhetorical, especially aurally. The first sentence is verbless; the second has two verbs — one in the perfect tense, and the other in the present tense. Alliteration[22] and assonance[23] are prominent in the original, whose force a literal translation can barely convey:

> 4a Much to me boldness   to you;
>   Much to me confidence for you.
> 4b I am filled   with encouragement;
>   I   overflow with joy
>   in the face of all our afflictions.

This verse proves to be an intersection for significant vocabulary ("confidence" . . . "pride" . . . "encouragement" . . . "joy") found in other parts of the letter.[24] Here we see Paul expressing an optimism about the Corinthians that reflects both his faith in God's good purposes for this people and — flowing from that — Paul's own godly leadership of them. To be sure, major problems remained, including the as-yet-uncompleted collection (chaps. 8–9). Moreover, Paul was all too conscious that some — at least — appear to have looked down on him as spiritually ineffective (1:12, 17; 10:1-7; 13:3). Even more worrying was the persistent sexual immorality of some Corinthians (12:20–13:2; with their failure to be separate from the local cults? — 6:14–7:1). Most serious of all, however, was the welcome given (by Jewish members?) to the false apostles who have now come to Corinth to undermine the influence of the apostle (cf. 2:17–3:1; 10:12-18; 11:4, 13-15, 18-20, 22-23).

One of Paul's remarkable God-given abilities, apparently, was a pastoral objectivity that enabled him to separate the various areas of difficulty in a church from his involvement personally. Thus, while there were such unresolved problems as those listed above, there was also the matter that had been

---

21. It should be noted that three of the four words found in v. 4 are repeated in the next section: pride (καύχησις — 7:14), encouragement (παράκλησις — 7:7, 13), and joy (χαρά — 7:13).

22. Gk. πολλή . . . παρρησία . . . πολλή . . . πεπλήρωμαι . . . παρακλήσει . . . ὑπερπερισσεύομαι. Paul has a fondness for words beginning with π (see 8:22; 9:5, 8; 10:3-6; 13:2; cf. Plummer, 215).

23. Gk. καύχησις . . . παρακλήσει . . . χαρᾷ.

24. "Confidence" (παρρησία — 3:12), "pride" (καύχησις — 1:12; 7:14; 8:24; 11:10, 17), "encouragement" (παράκλησις — 1:3, 4, 5, 6 [twice], 7; 7:7, 13; 8:4, 17), "joy" (χαρά — 1:15, 24; 2:3; 7:13; 8:2). For the pastorally reinforcing nature of such vocabulary see on 2:4.

settled, for which he gave hearty thanks, namely, the disciplining of the wrongdoer whom he had mentioned earlier (2:5-11) and whom he is about to discuss once more (7:5-16). In the midst of so many problems Paul is able to rejoice that this one difficulty — admittedly a major one — had been satisfactorily dealt with. Paul's spiritual enthusiasm at evidences of the grace of God working in the Corinthians reflects the simplicity of his own relationship with God, as well as of his deep concern for them. If he is filled with encouragement, he is overfilled with joy.[25] Ever the realist, Paul's spiritual excitement is experienced "in the face all our affliction" (see on 1:5). The sufferings of ministry to a world alienated from God is constant (see on 7:5 — "this body . . . had no rest . . . harassed at every turn . . . conflicts on the outside, fears within").

The confidence, pride, encouragement, and joy that he here expresses — upon which he will now expand (7:5-16) — are on account (so it seems) of that matter. This pastoral skill, expressed in encouragement — even when there were other matters to redress — is a quality of ministry worth pondering. Others may have been overwhelmed by the difficulties; Paul was overwhelmed by the one matter for thanksgiving. His admonitions in other matters — the collection (chaps. 8–9), criticisms of his inadequacy (10:1-7), the false apostles (10:12–12:12) — sprang from that thankfulness.

Thus v. 4 is not only a transition from the apostolic excursus (2:14–7:4) to thankfulness for the repentance of the Corinthians (7:5-16), but it also serves as a bridge to the other major issues in Corinth to which Paul will soon turn and which will dominate the remainder of the letter (8:1–12:12).

IV. PAUL IN MACEDONIA:
TITUS BRINGS NEWS FROM CORINTH (7:5–9:15)

The location of this section in the structure of the letter should be noted. These verses pick up the personal apologia broken off at Troas (2:12-13) to develop Paul's lengthy excursus on his new covenant ministry (2:14–7:4[1]). It is likely that Paul delayed the expression of confidence in 7:5-16 until he had completed the defense of his ministry in the extended excursus.

---

25. Gk. πεπλήρωμαι, "filled," is perfect tense and probably points back to the time Titus brought the good news of the positive Corinthian response to the "Severe Letter" (see 7:11). In the other verb, Gk. ὑπερπερισσεύομαι, the preposition prefixed to the verb suggests an intensified overflowing, a "superabounding."

1. See on 7:4, especially the vocabulary used (confidence, pride, encouragement, and joy), which serves to introduce 7:5-16.

This passage resumes that personal apologia from Macedonia (2:12-13). It is not merely resumptive, however, but serves to lead into the remainder of the letter. In the latter part of the letter (chaps. 8–13) he repeatedly speaks of his intention to come to Corinth (9:4; 10:2, 6; 12:14, 20, 21; 13:1, 2, 10; cf. 11:9). The joyous confidence Paul expresses (7:5-16) at the Corinthians' positive response to Paul and to Titus lays the pastoral foundation from which to address matters that the Corinthians must rectify (chaps. 8–13), regarding which he also expects and hopes for positive responses. The first of these is the collection, to which Titus, the bearer of this letter, must attend. Presumably it is for this reason that Paul's references to Titus dominate the latter part of this section (vv. 13b-15), leading immediately into the subject of the collection, which Titus had come to Corinth to secure, as bearer of the present letter.

A. THE EFFECTS OF THE "SEVERE LETTER" (7:5-16)

Titus's purpose in visiting Corinth had been to deliver the critical "Severe Letter," now lost to us. From the earlier and parallel passage (2:1-11) it appears that Paul was not prepared to return to Corinth until the congregation had resolved their relationship with him. He would not make "another painful visit" to them (2:1).

During that visit the apostle had been "wronged" by an unnamed man (7:12; 2:5), who apparently had the ongoing support of a minority of the Corinthians (cf. 2:6). We conclude that the majority, while not disagreeing with Paul, had not actively supported him by taking disciplinary action against the offender, which the "Severe Letter" called upon them to do (2:9; 7:12). At stake, therefore, was the future of his apostolic relationships with this church. From the earlier passage we learn of their effective discipline of the man (2:6). From the present passage we discover the dramatic effects of the letter that led to their decisive action (vv. 7, 11).

That letter raised at least two problems for the Corinthians. The first, that he had written rather than come in person according to his previous arrangement with them, he answered earlier (1:12-24; see also 10:9-11). The second, that the letter was hurtful to them (v. 8), he answers within this section (vv. 8-12).

Paul begins by telling them of the difficulties he encountered upon coming to Macedonia (v. 5), in which, however, he was comforted by God at the arrival of Titus (v. 6), but more particularly by his announcement of their desire for restoration of relationships with Paul (v. 7).

He diplomatically acknowledges the hurtful effect of that letter upon them, revealing that, until now, he had regrets about writing it (v. 8). Now, however, he rejoices, not that they were "grieved" by the letter, but that, arising from it, their godly grief issued in repentance (v. 9). Godly grief brings repentance unto salvation, whereas the worldly kind produces death (v. 10). In that regard he points to the dramatic outcome of godly grief among them as expressed in such eagerness toward him (v. 11). Indeed, his real purpose in writing that letter was not to reckon with the wrongdoer or the wronged man (himself), but that by it the Corinthians might have revealed to them their true commitment to Paul (v. 12).

Besides his encouragement at the Corinthians' reassurances toward him, Paul rejoices still more at Titus's joy — such was his relief at their response to him (v. 13). Paul had expressed confidence to Titus about them beforehand (v. 14), and this had been vindicated by the positive response of the Corinthians to him (v. 15). Paul concludes by declaring his joyous confidence in them (v. 16).

Joy dominates this section. The last verse of the previous passage (v. 4) introduced joy, and it appears again at the end (v. 16) to form an *inclusio*. In each constituent passage joy is the dominant element — joy at the arrival and reports of Titus (vv. 5-7), joy that the Corinthians have repented (vv. 8-13a), and joy at Titus's joy (vv. 13b-15).

1. Paul's Joy at the Arrival of Titus (7:5-7)

> 5 For when we came into Macedonia, this body of ours had no rest, but we were harassed at every turn — conflicts on the outside, fears within. 6 But God, who comforts the downcast, comforted us by the coming of Titus, 7 and not only by his coming but also by the comfort you had given him. He told us about your longing for me, your deep sorrow, your ardent concern for me, so that my joy was greater than ever.

Paul's reference to "afflicted" (v. 5) immediately repeats his generalized "in all our affliction" of the previous verse, now indicating the problems he encountered upon arrival in Macedonia. But, as in the benediction (1:3-7), the God of comfort, true to his character, again comforted his servant, in this case by the return of Titus (v. 6). It was not merely his arrival, however. Titus brought news of the Corinthians' encouragement of him from which Paul himself drew great encouragement. Paul rejoiced to hear of their longing for him, their regrets over what had happened, and their expression of loyalty to him (v. 7).

Although Paul had used the singular pronoun in the transitional passage 7:2-4, in 7:5-16 he reverts (with few exceptions) to the first person plural, the practice he had generally followed in 2:14–7:4.

5 The explanatory opening words, "for even,"[1] which lead into his account of sufferings in Macedonia, catch up (1) the last words of the previous

1. Gk. καὶ γάρ.

verse ("in all our affliction"), and beyond that — and more particularly — (2) the remote words "when I came to Troas . . . I still had no peace of mind" (2:12-13). His words in that distant verse are now almost precisely echoed.[2] The lengthy excursus on new covenant ministry (2:14–7:4) is completed; Paul will now pick up the threads of his personal apologia begun at 1:12, which he broke off at 2:13.

Paul's use of the word "afflicted"[3] picks up the general reference "in all our afflictions" in the benediction (1:4), a concrete example of which is immediately given as occurring in Asia (1:8). Paul also writes of "much affliction" at the time he wrote the "Severe Letter" (2:4), which we think also occurred in Asia. Very significantly, the words "in all our afflictions"[4] in the previous verse (7:4) exactly echo those of 1:4, thus forming an *inclusio* (1:4–7:4),[5] independent of and overarching his excursus on the apostolic ministry of the new covenant (2:14–7:4).

It might be thought that the problems on the eastern side of the Aegean, whether the "afflictions" in Asia, the anguish in writing the "Severe Letter," or the "mind" that could find "no peace" in Troas (1:8-10; 2:1-4, 12-13), would be left behind with the crossing of the waters. But difficulties also awaited Paul at Macedonia; Titus was not there either! Paul speaks of finding "no peace" and being "afflicted."

The verse is in two parts. The first is introduced by an explanatory concessive clause ("for even[6] when we came to Macedonia"), followed by a "no[t] . . . but"[7] contrast ("our flesh found *no* rest, *but*[7] we were afflicted in every way"). Paul's sense of pain cries out through his text as follows: (1) the use of "flesh"[8] signifying frailty, (2) the perfect tense verb "have"[9] implying

---

2. Compare 2:13 — οὐκ ἔσχηκα ἄνεσιν with 7:5 — οὐδεμίαν ἔσχηκεν ἄνεσιν. There are differences: (1) the former reference is singular whereas the latter is plural, and (2) the former reference is to πνεῦμα, the latter to σάρξ.

3. Gk. θλιβόμενοι (NIV, "harassed"). The nominative case of the participle is surprising ("irregular, but intelligible and not rare" — Plummer, 218). Nonetheless, Paul's meaning is clear; Furnish, 385-86, calls it "a kind of anacolouthon"; cf. BDF #468. The θλίβειν/θλίψις word group is very important in this letter, as introduced in the benediction (see on 1:4) and cited at the head of the apostolic sufferings, in the face of which he commends his ministry "through great endurance" (6:4).

4. Gk. ἐπὶ πάσῃ τῇ θλίψει ἡμῶν; NIV, "in all our troubles."

5. Paul does not employ this vocabulary of himself in this letter beyond this verse. However, he does use it subsequently in reference to the Macedonians and the Corinthians (8:2, 13).

6. Gk. καὶ γάρ.

7. Gk. οὐδεμίαν . . . ἀλλ[ά].

8. Gk. σάρξ. As used in the context of this verse, σάρξ also means the whole person as equivalent to "we."

9. Gk. ἔσχηκεν (see on 1:9).

ongoing suffering from his arrival in Macedonia, (3) the intensive negative "not even any[10] rest," and (4) his verb "afflicted," evocative of deep emotional suffering (see on 1:4, 8; 2:4, 12).

The second part, although composed of only four words, is powerfully rhetorical. Contrasted are the opposites "without . . . within,"[11] and juxtaposed are "fightings . . . fears."[12] The problems Paul faced, both external to him and internal within him, supply the reason for the statement in the first sentence. As to his meaning, we can only speculate whether "fightings without" refers to a persecution of the church in Macedonia — from a Gentile or Jewish quarter[13] — or to quarrels among the Macedonian believers. The balance of probability suggests that persecution may be in mind.[14] The Macedonian churches of the Philippians and Thessalonians, insofar as we know them from Paul's letters, appear relatively united (but see, e.g., Phil 1:27–2:5; 4:2-3), though they did face hostility externally (see, e.g., 1 Thess 2:14-16; Phil 1:27-30).

Likewise, "fears within" is problematic. These could have arisen from "fightings without," stated symmetrically and without specific additional content. More probably, however, they point to his as yet unresolved anxiety about the Corinthians' reaction to the "Severe Letter." Paul's "fears within" in Macedonia appears to correspond with his "no peace of mind" in Troas and the nonreturn of Titus reassuring him of the Corinthians' response (see on 2:13). Titus's delay surely suggested a further deterioration in Corinth.

To which place in Macedonia did Paul now come? The strongest possibility is Philippi, just a few miles along the Egnatian way from Neapolis, the most probable port for arrival from northern Asia (see Acts 16:11-12). Three reasons make Philippi Paul's likely[15] place of sojourn in Macedonia: (1) the most probable rendezvous point with Titus, once the time to come to

10. Gk. οὐδεμίαν.

11. Gk. ἔξωθεν . . . ἔσωθεν (cf. 4:16).

12. Gk. μάχαι . . . φόβοι: "cases of fightings . . . fears. . . ." Possibly an allusion to LXX Deut 32:25.

13. See Acts 16:11–17:15.

14. Furnish, 386, argues that μάχαι is used in the NT only for quarrels (2 Tim 2:23; Tit 3:9; Jas 4:1), not for armed conflict. Thus it would refer not to persecution but to church disputation. Based on the suggestion that Philippians was written during an Ephesian imprisonment, Furnish, 394, proposes that the conflict mentioned here by Paul may be related to quarrels with "dogs . . . evil workers" (Phil 3:2). But this is conjectural, as he concedes.

15. Against the Philippi hypothesis is the consideration that, apart from their recent kindness involving Epaphroditus, Paul's reminiscences about the Philippians relate back to his earliest time with them (see, e.g., 4:14-18). If Paul had been there at the time of writing 2 Corinthians, we might have expected his letter to the Philippians to refer to it, unless, of course, Philippians had been written earlier, during an Ephesian imprisonment.

Troas had passed, was Philippi/Neapolis; (2) the church, which he established about six years earlier, had been especially caring toward him (Phil 4:14-16); and (3) given the problems of his initial visit, it would have been more difficult for Paul at Thessalonica, the other strategic possibility (Acts 16:35-40; 17:9; 1 Thess 2:18). If Philippi was the city in Macedonia to which Paul came, it is likely that he wrote this letter from that place. Nonetheless, it is evident that Paul had extensive contact with the Macedonian churches during this period (see on 8:1-6, 16-24; 9:2).

6 The grim words of suffering from the previous verse — focused on the word "afflicted" — are summed up here by one word, "downcast."[16] The opening contrastive "but" serves to set Paul's disclosure in that verse as a somber backdrop for the bright words of deliverance that now follow. Paul reinforces this contrast by his word order: "but he who comforts the downcast . . . God,"[17] which must be rendered: "but God,[18] who comforts the downcast."[19]

The pattern of teaching here replicates that of 1:3-11. There God "comforted" Paul "in all his afflictions" (1:4), specifically delivering him from the "affliction" in Asia, where he faced death (1:8-10). In the present verses God "comforts" Paul in Macedonia in his anguish through the arrival of Titus and the encouraging news of the Corinthians' reaffirmation of their loyalty to him (v. 7).

God as the source of "comfort" for his people is critical within 2 Corinthians, appearing in the opening benediction and in many other places throughout the letter (see on 1:3). The vocabulary calls to mind God's comfort of his people through the prophet Isaiah[20] (LXX Isa 40:1; 49:13; 51:3, 12, 19; 52:9; 61:2; 66:13); the "consolation [i.e., comforting] of Israel" (Luke 2:25) described the long-awaited messianic age. Paul's extensive use of such

---

16. Gk. ταπεινός, which, although bearing the meaning "humble" elsewhere (e.g., 10:1), is required by the present context to be understood as "depressed," "downcast."

17. A parallel example where Paul placed "God" last for emphasis is: ὁ δὲ βεβαιῶν ἡμᾶς . . . θεός (1:21). Paul's use of a present participle with God conveys a divine attribute, or characteristic activity: 1:4 — θεὸς . . . ὁ παρακαλῶν; 1:9 — τῷ θεῷ ἐγείροντι τοὺς νέκρους; 1:21 — ὁ . . . βεβαιῶν . . . θεός; 2:14 — τῷ . . . θεῷ . . . θριαμβεύοντι; 5:19 — θεὸς ἦν . . . καταλλάσσων; 5:20 — θεοῦ παρακαλοῦντος.

18. Gk. ἀλλὰ . . . ὁ θεός. For parallel contrastive statements involving God see on 2:14.

19. Paul's words ὁ παρακαλῶν τοὺς ταπεινοὺς παρεκάλεσαν ἡμᾶς echo LXX Isa 49:13: καὶ τοὺς ταπεινοὺς τοῦ λαοῦ αὐτοῦ παρεκάλεσαν. It should be noted, however, that Isaiah's ταπεινούς carries the meaning "humble," whereas Paul uses it to mean "downcast." For the significance of Isaiah 40–55 for Paul's exposition in 2 Corinthians see G. K. Beale, "Reconciliation," 550-81.

20. For Paul's awareness of his role in Isaianic terms as the mouthpiece of God for the comfort of God's people, see on 5:20; 6:1.

language within 2 Corinthians is taken to imply that this age has arrived, a view that is explicit elsewhere within the letter (see on 3:3, 6; 6:2). Thus the statement "God . . . comforts the downcast" is not merely an edifying reflection on the gracious character of God expressed in this action; it also symbolizes God's action toward his people under the new covenant.

God's instrument in his comfort of Paul was "the coming[21] of Titus."[22] Titus was a regular delegate[23] of Paul's with the Corinthians.[24] Loyal Titus ("my brother Titus" — 2:13), Paul's "partner and fellow-worker" (8:23), who was like-minded with the apostle (8:16), stood in welcome relief to the fickle, not to say capricious, Corinthians. Titus also appears to have been a man of some influence, as well as of affection for the Corinthians, who — to a significant degree — secured the Corinthians' obedience to the "Severe Letter" (v. 15).

Titus's reunion with Paul, at which various reports from Corinth were conveyed to the apostle, must have been critical to the writing of the present letter. Second Corinthians should be regarded as Paul's response to the mixed reports Titus brought to Paul. To be sure, there is the good news of the positive response to the "Severe Letter" (2:5-10; 7:12). But along with that — apparently — Titus related the failure of the Corinthians to finalize the collection. Moreover, he relayed to Paul the negative attitudes and behavior of various factions in Corinth — whether in accusing Paul of being spiritually ineffective (10:1-7), or in regard to a continuing involvement of some in promiscuous (12:20–13:2) and cultic activities (6:14–7:1), or, paradoxically, in relation to others who had readily welcomed the newly arrived Jewish missionaries (11:1-4).

7 Two leading ideas of the previous verse — "comfort" and Titus's "coming" — are now brought forward, so as to be qualified and elaborated upon.

---

21. Gk. τῇ παρουσίᾳ Τίτου. Although παρουσία often signifies an official arrival, here it means no more than that Titus's coming was important to Paul (so Plummer, 218; cf. *New Docs.* 4:167). See, too, 10:10 for a reference to Paul's Parousia to them. *Parousia* is not used of Christ in this letter.

22. For an approximately parallel expression we should note: "Timothy has just now come to us from you [Thessalonians] . . ." (1 Thess 3:6).

23. See further M. M. Mitchell, "NT Envoys," 641-62, for the view that Paul dispatched his envoy to Corinth because he thought a visit by Titus would be more effective than his own coming.

24. Evidently Titus had gone to Corinth on account of the collection in the previous calendar year (8:6, 10; 9:2; 12:17, 18?) and then, more recently, as the bearer of the "Severe Letter" (7:8-13). Paul would send him — with others — to finalize the collection ahead of Paul's arrival and presumably to deliver 2 Corinthians to the Corinthians (8:17). It is interesting, however, that Titus, although like-minded with Paul, was to a degree autonomous, acting independently of Paul (8:17). See further on 2:13.

The verse has a fourfold structure — (1) a negative clause ("not only by [Titus'] coming"), (2) a contrastive echo ("but also by the comfort with which he was comforted among you[25] [Corinthians]"), followed by (3) an explanatory clause ("as [Titus] told[26] us of your longing, your deep sorrow, your zeal for me"), and (4) a result clause ("so that[27] I rejoiced still more"[28]).

Taken together, vv. 6 and 7 reflect Paul's heartfelt relief that the Corinthians have become reconciled to the apostle as a result of Paul's "Severe Letter," as delivered and ministered by Titus. God has comforted Paul by the return of Titus, who was able to report on the Corinthians'[29] "longing" (to see Paul again?), their "grief" (at their treatment of him during his recent visit?), and their "zeal"[30] for him (as opposed to the "wrongdoer" — 7:12).

These verses reveal (1) Paul's approach to ministry, and (2) his temperament. In regard to (1), we observe a certain objectivity in Paul. Although — as the greater part of the letter indicates — the Corinthian church remained beset by problems of some magnitude, Paul is able to isolate this particular matter for rejoicing. Quite possibly such objectivity resulted from Paul's theological perspective, whereby he is able to see this still-sinful church in its eschatological perfection, while being thankful at whatever signs of grace were to be seen. Paradoxically, however, and at the same time, we note, in regard to (2), Paul's very human desire for warm personal relationships with this church (see 6:11-13; 7:2). In its relationships with people, the pastoral ministry can never be merely "objective." Pastors, too, have feelings, and their ministry is exercised in the context of relationships.

2. Paul's Joy at Their Reception of the Letter (7:8-12)

8 *Even if I caused you sorrow by my letter, I do not regret it. Though I did regret it — I see[1] that my letter hurt you, but only for a little while*

---

25. Our understanding of ἐφ' ὑμῖν; so Furnish, 386.

26. Gk. ἀναγγέλλων. Apart from Rom 15:21, where it is quoted from the LXX, this is Paul's only use of ἀναγγέλλειν. In a parallel passage Paul uses εὐαγγελίζεσθαι (1 Thess 3:6).

27. Gk. ὥστε.

28. So Plummer's reading of ὥστε με μᾶλλον χαρῆναι (219); NIV, "so that my joy was greater than ever."

29. To be noted is his "your . . . your . . . your," following "among *you*." The repeated "you" emphasizes the global response of the church to the apostle. Paul expands upon this response in v. 11.

30. Gk. ζῆλος, here meaning their loyalty to Paul. Later Paul speaks of his godly "zeal" for the Corinthians in regard to their fidelity to Jesus (see on 11:2).

1. Gk. βλέπω [γάρ] (א C D1* F G Y 0243 vg mss*) is to be retained against

— 9 yet now I am happy, not because you were made sorry, but because your sorrow led you to repentance. For you became sorrowful as God intended and so were not harmed in any way by us. 10 Godly sorrow brings repentance that leads to salvation and leaves no regret, but worldly sorrow brings death. 11 See what this godly sorrow has produced in you: what earnestness, what eagerness to clear yourselves, what indignation, what alarm, what longing, what concern, what readiness to see justice done. At every point you have proved yourselves to be innocent in this matter. 12 So even though I wrote to you, it was not on account of the one who did the wrong or of the injured party, but rather that before God you could see for yourselves how devoted to us you are.

The now-lost "Severe Letter" arose from Paul's second visit to Corinth when, so it appears, he suffered an act of injustice at the hands of another man (v. 12). In all probability Paul had been attempting to rectify a moral crisis in the congregation, perhaps connected with ongoing sexual and cultic involvement by some of the members (see on 6:14–7:1; 12:21–13:2). The failure of the church to support Paul the apostle in disciplining the offender meant that Paul's future apostolic relationship with the church was in question. Paul's "Severe Letter" sought to focus the attention of the Corinthians on this issue.

Although Paul's "Severe Letter" caused them pain in the short term, something Paul diplomatically admits as a source of regret on his part (v. 8), he does not ultimately regret that letter because it has provoked "godly repentance" (vv. 9-10) as expressed in their desire for reconciliation with Paul (v. 11). Significantly, the Corinthians' reaction to Paul in this matter is inextricably connected with their relationship with God and his salvation. To have rejected Paul's authority in this matter would have been, in an ultimate sense, to have rejected their salvation. Their godly grief in response to the letter had immediate and dramatic effect upon their declaration of "eagerness" for the apostle (v. 11). Indeed, it was not on account of either wrongdoer or wronged that Paul wrote, but that the Corinthians' genuine loyalty to Paul might be revealed to them (v. 12).

The passage that follows is deeply personal and revelatory of Paul's inner feelings. He did regret the "grief" to them incurred by his letter, but in the light

---

βλέπων (p⁴⁶* vg) following "preponderant attestation" (Metzger, 581). Although γάρ is bracketed as doubtful and viewed as explicable as a copyist's desire to relieve Paul's syntax from anacolouthon, it probably should be retained to make sense of this statement in relation to what went before. As against the NIV text above, a better reconstruction is: "Although I grieved you, I do not regret it, though I did regret it. For I see that . . ." (so Thrall, 1.490-91).

of Titus's report of its good outcome, he no longer regrets it. Indeed, he rejoices, not that they were grieved but that their grief issued in repentance. Finally, he assures them that uppermost in his mind was the question of their "eagerness" toward him. A measure of the relational character of the passage may be seen in Paul's use of pronouns: (1) alongside his more customary use (in the letter to this point) of the plural pronoun "we"/"us" (as in vv. 9 and 12), he employs the more personal singular "I"/"me"[2] (vv. 8 [four times], 9, 12), and (2) he concentrates on "you" (Corinthians) pronouns (vv. 8 [twice], 11, 12 [three times]).

8 Paul now amplifies[3] the joy he expressed at the end of the previous verse. In a problematic sentence[4] he concedes that he may[5] have grieved them by his letter, something he does not now regret, though he did regret it after he wrote it. As he explains,[6] as a result of Titus's report back to him, he realizes that the letter did grieve them, if only for a short time. Hints of apology may, perhaps, be heard here.

Paul now reintroduces the vocabulary of "grief"[7] from an earlier passage (2:1-11 passim). Paul's earlier visit had been characterized by the "grief" that the Corinthians suffered (2:1). Ultimately, however, the "grief" to the congregation had been caused by the wrongdoer himself, not by Paul (2:2, 5). Knowing through Titus's report that the man had come to a better mind, the Corinthians were to restore the man lest he be overcome by "grief" (2:7). The follow-up letter was not written to incur more "grief," but so that a further visit would not involve "grief" as the second visit had (2:3).

Paul declares outright that he does not now "regret"[8] sending the letter

---

2. Furnish, 397, suggests that Paul did this to exempt his associates from any involvement, noting that he reverts to the plural pronoun only when he had left behind the matter of the "tearful letter" (v. 13aff.).

3. As indicated by the initial ὅτι.

4. (1) The correct reading (see n. 1 above) and (2) the awkward syntax make it difficult to know whether "even if I did regret it" belongs to the tail of the preceding sentence (as we believe, following Thrall, 1.490-91) or begins a new sentence (as NIV).

5. This verse has a threefold concessive εἰ καί, "even if" (see Moule, 167). "Even if I grieved you . . . even if I did have regrets . . . even if for a little while."

6. We take the explanatory γάρ (for comment on its inclusion see n. 1) as commencing a second sentence. Otherwise Paul is saying that he hurt them by the letter, for he sees he hurt them by that letter, which would be tautological. Following Furnish, 387, the words introduced by "for I see" to the end of the sentence are best understood as a parenthesis. They probably reflect a degree of embarrassment on Paul's part in regard to the "grief" produced by the "Severe Letter."

7. Gk. λύπειν (verb); λύπη (noun).

8. Gk. μεταμέλομαι also means "change one's mind" and so approximates μετανοεῖν (see v. 7), though there is no semantic connection. His first usage, μεταμέλομαι, is present tense, while the second, μετεμελόμην — in contrast — is durative imperfect, signifying that Paul did have regrets over a period of time.

because, as stated in the previous verse, it has resulted in restored relationships with him ("your longing for us, your deep sorrow, your zeal [for Paul]"). This is not because he is insensitive, nor because he enjoyed imposing "grief," as some of them may have supposed (see 10:9-10; cf. 1:13-14). The fact is that after he dispatched the letter, he did regret sending it because he knew it would bring pain. But now he does not regret it because he is aware that the letter "grieved" them "only for a little while," that is, relatively speaking.[9] The outcome of their "grief," as he has learned of it from Titus's report, brought his regrets to an end.[10] The letter — whose impact may have been intensified by the ministry of its bearer, Titus (v. 15) — has produced a dramatic and instant effect.

9 The net result, despite the momentary grief caused by this letter, is that *now,* at the writing of this letter, Paul rejoices — a note he picks up from the end of v. 7 and now sets out to explain vis-à-vis their sorrow. His present joy is not that they were "grieved"[11] per se, but that they were "grieved" to repentance. For theirs was a "godly grief" (NIV, "godly sorrow"); they suffered no loss, only gain, from Paul's imposition of it.

Thus Paul "rejoices *now,*" that is, in contrast with his sense of "regret" experienced during the period between sending the letter and hearing the Corinthians' positive response to it. But in keeping with the delicate nature of their past relationships, he quickly qualifies that rejoicing. It was not because the Corinthians were "grieved" by his letter, but because their "grief" issued in "repentance." Thus theirs was "grief" as "God intended," or "a godlike grief,"[12] in contrast with another form of "grief," worldly grief, which he will mention in the next verse. Although they had been "grieved" by his pastoral discipline, they were not "harmed in any way"[13]

9. Gk. πρὸς ὥραν, lit. "for an hour," but to be understood as "for a little while" (so NIV). The phrase can mean a shorter (Gal 2:5) or longer (Phlm 15) period. It probably represents the time between their original hearing of the letter, which gave way to their repentance, and their longing for Paul.

10. Hughes, 268-69, suggests that a father-son metaphor is here implied, especially when taken with the earlier requirement for "proof" of their obedience in all things (2:9; cf. 6:13). Paul may be implying that like paternal punishment, which has issued in a child's "better mind," there is the sense in which the punishment was useful, even though it was grievous at the time — not just for the child but also for the father.

11. The threefold ἐλυπήθητε is aorist, with an inceptive sense, "you became grieved"; NIV, "you were made sorry."

12. Gk. κατὰ θεόν, which he repeats in vv. 10 and 11 (cf. Rom 8:27; *T. Gad* 5:7), means "grief" that "is according to God's will." This points to the quality, rather than the fact, of this sorrow.

13. Gk. ἐν μηδενὶ ζημιωθῆτε is probably an example of litotes. Paul makes his point ironically by stating it as a negative. Thus, far from harming them, Paul's action has led to "repentance" that will issue in "salvation." See Hughes, 269-70, for the view that failure to have written as he did would have amounted to spiritual negligence on his part.

by Paul.[14] On the contrary, as he will explain, the "repentance" arising out of their "grief" is the kind that leads to "salvation."

Significantly, by his use of "repentance,"[15] Paul employs one of the great biblical words for God's call that humankind "turn" to him. The messengers of this repentance were first the prophets of the old covenant, but then more recently the Son of Man himself (Mark 1:15 pars.; cf., e.g., Amos 4:6, 8, 9, 10, and 11). Here, however, the messenger is Christ's apostle, Paul. But the "repentance" called for by Paul in the "Severe Letter" is not directed to God but to Paul himself, specifically in regard to the Corinthians' attitudes toward his authority (cf. vv. 7 and 11).

Striking as this focusing on Paul's own ministry is,[16] it is consistent with the teaching of the apostle elsewhere in 2 Corinthians. As an ambassador of Christ, as a fellow worker with God, and as one given the ministry/message of reconciliation to the world, the apostle called on the Corinthians not to receive the grace of God in vain in this the day of God's favor, his day of salvation (5:18–6:2). But this is virtually equivalent to Paul's closely connected call to them to "open wide [their] hearts to [Paul]" (6:13) himself — such is the closeness of relationship between God and his apostolic minister. Repentance toward God, like reconciliation with God, cannot be separated from reconciliation with and repentance toward his apostle. Nonetheless, Paul is not their "lord" (1:24) but their "slave" (4:5), whose lifestyle of sacrifice and suffering consistently reproduces and embodies the sacrifice and suffering of the Christ whose apostle Paul is (6:3-10). He exercises his ministry "by the meekness and gentleness of Christ" (10:1).

Hermeneutically, however, it is to be doubted whether Paul's authority (10:8; 13:10) carries over in quite the same way to subsequent generations of ministers of the gospel. To be sure, a rejection of the word of God may involve rejection of the bearer of that message, as appears to be the case with the

14. Gk. ἐξ ἡμῶν — a loss to them originating in Paul, which he denies.

15. Gk. μετάνοια. While Paul uses the term and its verb only infrequently (cf. v. 10; 12:21; Rom 2:4; 2 Tim 2:25), preferring his concept of "faith," he can scarcely have been unaware of the historical usage of the word. Martin, 230, noting that the Hebrew root for "repentance" (šûb) signifies a "turning" to God, suggests that the Corinthians have now followed Moses' example in "turning" to the Lord (3:16), an exegetical presupposition we question (see on 3:16). Furnish's suggestion, 387, that μετάνοια should be rendered as "contrition" fails to recognize the closeness of the relationship between the Corinthians' relationship with God and with Paul; repentance and reconciliation in regard to Paul cannot be separated from their restoration to God.

16. So also Bultmann, 149: "The decision for the Gospel and for Paul are one and the same. When the Corinthians do not understand him, they do not understand the Gospel as well...." Less helpfully, Strachan, 127-28, portrays Paul as a "great religious psychologist," whose recent letter has repaired the broken relationships between the Corinthians and Paul.

Corinthians. Let ministers and pastors be careful, however, that it is the word that is being rejected and not, in reality, some fault in them. Such rationalization is not unknown. In any case, Paul was an apostle of Christ (12:12), a revelator of the glory of God (4:2, 6), in a way that cannot be true of others outside that generation. A pastor's authority is derived from the apostles, and qualified to that extent. Nor must a great Protestant insight be forgotten: the people, too, can read the word of God. Pastors are not infallible exegetes or interpreters.

10 The previous verse is now amplified, as signaled by the initial explanatory "For" *(gar),* followed by Paul's much-quoted two-sentence proverb in which he contrasts "godly grief" with "worldly grief." The one brings about repentance leading to salvation and brings no regrets; the other brings about death.

The first sentence gathers up the references from the previous two verses to "godly grief," "repentance," and "regret," climaxing with a new phrase, "which leads to salvation." The second sentence introduces the notion of "worldly" grief (in contrast with "godly" grief — v. 9), "which brings death." The structure of Paul's verse is:

> For
>> the grief
>>> that is according to God
>>>> works repentance
>
>>>> [that] leads to salvation,
>>> [which]   is without regret.
> But
>> the grief
>>> that is   of the world
>>>> works
>>>>> death.

Looking closely at the second sentence, one can see that Paul omits certain elements from the first (in reverse form) that are nonetheless implied. Thus it is to be inferred that "grief that is of the world works [*un*repentance, which leads to] death [and is *with* regret]."

Critical to this verse is the word *ametameleton*,[17] meaning "without

---

17. Gk. ἀμεταμέλητον; NIV, "no regret." Probably a further example of litotes (see also on v. 9) whereby something of great value, namely "salvation," is stated negatively (i.e., "with no regrets"). In this case ἀμεταμέλητον should be taken with σωτηρίαν, not μετάνοια (*contra* Martin, 232). Nonetheless, the juxtaposition of the antithetical words μετάνοια ("repentance") and ἀμεταμέλητον ("unregretted") forms "a striking oxymoron" (so Furnish, 388).

regret" ("unregretted"),[18] which deliberately reverses the twice-repeated verb "regret" *(metamelomai)* of v. 8, which contrasted how Paul felt when he first dispatched the letter with his present positive feelings in the light of their reported "repentance."

"Repentance," which issues from "godly grief" — not the kind that is "of the world,"[19] a superficial kind — leads to and is a prerequisite to "salvation."[20] Continuance in unrepentance, characterized by nothing more than shallow remorse unaccompanied by positive action in disciplining the offender, could have spelled the end of Paul's ministry to them and led, in time, to their spiritual "death."[21] But "godly grief," expressed in "repentance" toward God — as declared practically in the reaffirmation of Paul's authority in their disciplining of the offender — would mean their "salvation."[22]

To be noted is Paul's verb "works"[23] (NIV, "brings"). The "Severe Letter," as ministered by Titus, aroused "godly grief," which "works repentance to salvation." In the next verse he will write, "See what this godly grief has *worked* in you." The Corinthians were a body in whom the Spirit of God was present (1:21-22; 3:2-3); Christ Jesus is "in" them (13:5). They have "received the grace of God" (6:1). Paul's words remind us that God does "work" in such people (cf. Phil 4:13), despite their evident shortcomings.

Once again we are confronted with the closeness of relationship between the gospel and the apostle who proclaimed it (see on v. 9). Intrinsic to that gospel declared by the apostle was the eschatological reality that in the Son of God, whom Paul and his companions proclaimed in Corinth, the "day of salvation" had dawned, in fulfillment of the promises of God (1:18-20; 6:1-2; cf. 1:6).[24] To

---

18. Furnish, 388.

19. Gk. τοῦ κόσμου, "the sphere in which life is lived without God and in opposition to God" (Thrall, 1.493).

20. Paul may have in mind the examples of David's genuine sorrow of heart over his sin in contrast with Esau's shallow remorse (Ps 51:1-11; Gen 27:38, 41; cf. Heb 12:16-17).

21. To take "repentance" and "salvation" as nothing more than existential or relational entities — so J. Murphy-O'Connor, *Theology,* 71 — would be seriously to underestimate Paul's eschatological meaning here. See 2:16: "To those [who are perishing] we are the smell of death, to those [who are being saved] the fragrance of life."

22. Gk. σωτηρία. According to Thrall (1.492), it is "final deliverance from divine wrath and final deliverance to divine glory."

23. Gk. ἐργάζεται . . . κατεργάζεται; NIV, "brings . . . produces." The former (occurring only here in this letter) refers to the outworking of "godly grief," the latter of "worldly grief." It is doubtful whether the latter intensifies the former; the usage is more probably stylistic. But the next verse picks up κατεργάζεσθαι.

24. It is held that Paul's reference to the "day of salvation" (see on 6:2) is the key text of 2 Corinthians. It is a quotation from Isaiah 40–55, upon which Paul is deeply dependent for much of his thinking in this letter (see the Introduction, 46-47).

reject the apostle — as the Corinthians were effectively doing by their passivity toward the offender — was nothing less than to live as if the "day of salvation" had not come. But repentance toward Paul, God's coworker and Christ's ambassador (5:20; 6:1), and therefore repentance toward God, confirmed the Corinthians in their salvation. In line with his pastoral method employed in this and other letters, Paul is, by this statement, reinforcing his readers in appropriate attitudes, in this case "godly grief."

11 As with the previous verse, which amplified its predecessor, this verse commences with an explanatory "For" *(gar)*. This is followed by the interjection, "look,"[25] pointing to the very thing in question, their godly grieving, which has produced in them such a response, as in the seven reactions he lists. They have now commended themselves as blameless in this matter.

For the third time in successive verses Paul writes of "godly grief" (vv. 9, 10, and 11). Equally striking, for the second time in consecutive verses, "godly grief" is the subject of the same verb "worked," which is translated in the NIV as "brings" (v. 10) and in this verse as "produced."[26] Such "godly grief," so Titus had reported to Paul, had worked "earnestness . . . eagerness to clear [themselves] . . . indignation . . . alarm . . . longing . . . concern . . . readiness to see justice done." The seven Greek words represent the specific expression of the Corinthians' "repentance that leads to salvation," more generally referred to in the previous verse.

Paul here conveys the powerful impression of a rapid and dramatic reaction in Corinth to his "Severe Letter," as brought by Titus (cf. vv. 13-15). His interjection, "look," suggests the liveliness of the imagined scene in the church. Then the first of the seven words is preceded by "what[27] [earnestness],"[28] the following six by "not only so but . . ." (on each occasion translating the single word "but,"[29] thus creating an ascending climactic effect from the initial word. The significance of the word "earnestness," or "eagerness," is seen not only from its appearance as first in the list but also from its repetition in the next verse. Furthermore, each subsequent word is strong and vivid, painting its own picture of animated reactions among the Corinthians, whose force the NIV tends to blur.[30]

---

25. Gk. ἰδού; see also 5:17; 6:2, 9; 12:14.

26. Gk. κατειργάσατο; NIV, "produces."

27. Gk. πόσην.

28. Gk. σπουδήν. Members of the σπουδ- word group occur eight times in chapters 7–8, more often than other Pauline references combined.

29. Gk. ἀλλά. Cf. A. T. Robertson, *Grammar,* 1185, who states that the six uses of ἀλλά are "confirmatory and continuative."

30. The NIV understates the rhetorical force of Paul's words: σπουδήν (= "eagerness" — to deal quickly with the problem?), ἀπολογίαν (= "defense" — for their failure to deal with the man, or, alternatively, that he was not really one of their number?),

It appears that until the arrival of Titus and the "Severe Letter," the Corinthians had not understood how serious the matter was from Paul's perspective. Either he had not made the point at the time of his recent visit, or the Corinthians did not at that time apprehend it. While it is not altogether clear from this verse whether the offender was a member of the assembly or an outsider, the balance of probability is that he was a member of the church.[31]

By their response the Corinthians have now "commended"[32] themselves "in every way" to be "innocent in this matter."[33] This is not to say that they protested innocence when they had been guilty, but rather that by their repentance they were now effectively blameless.[34] Clearly, the Corinthian repentance was not so much for the wrong directly committed by them, but for their failure to rectify the wrong committed by the offending man against Paul (see 2:9; 7:12). By this powerfully stated verse Paul has reinforced the Corinthians in the stand that they have taken for him.

12 Paul now concludes his line of thought, begun at v. 8, with a sentence beginning with the inferential, "So then."[35] His following words, "even though I wrote to you," appear to concede that the letter had caused "grief" among them (vv. 8-9), though that is at most implied, not stated. In any case, he did not write for the sake of either the wrongdoer or his victim (probably Paul), but for the sake of the relationship between the Corinthian church and Paul, that is, the revelation to them of their "eagerness" toward him in the presence of God.

ἀγανάκτησιν (= "indignation" — toward the man or toward Paul for blaming them for what he, but not they, had done?), φόβον (= "fear"; cf. v. 15 — their end as a Pauline church?), ἐπιπόθησιν (= "longing"; cf. v. 7 — for their desire see Paul again?), ζῆλον (= "zeal"; cf. v. 7 — a godly passion to be reconciled to Paul as apostle?), ἐκδίκησιν (= "vindication" — either their felt need to vindicate Paul against the wrongdoer or to vindicate themselves in his sight from direct blame for the offense?).

31. *Contra* Barrett, 211-12, who thinks that the man was a visitor to Corinth associated with, but not a member of, the church. The presence of ἀπολογία in this list may suggest that the Corinthians are defending themselves by distancing themselves from someone who was not a true member. On the other hand, the report of "repentance leading to salvation" would seem inappropriate if the offender were an outsider, since it would not then intrinsically be a Corinthian problem. Moreover, the call for his restoration (2:5-11) would scarcely be warranted if he were an outsider.

32. Gk. συνεστήσατε; NIV, "proved." This is one of the keywords of the letter (3:1; 4:2; 5:12; 6:4; 10:12, 18; 12:11). The aorist points to the Corinthians' effective demonstration in this "matter" during Titus's recent visit to the church.

33. Gk. πρᾶγμα, "matter," has a quasilegal meaning (cf. 1 Cor 6:1). Paul's use of a rather vague word may indicate his desire to put the issue behind him (so Plummer, 223).

34. So Hughes, 275. Thrall, 1.495, suggests the possibility that Paul is exaggerating a little, or perhaps that their "repentance" in this "matter" has restored their relationship to its former state.

35. Gk. ἄρα. See also 1:17; 5:14.

Thus, for the last time in the present context, Paul refers to the "Severe Letter" (see on 2:5-11; cf. 1:13; 2:3; 10:9-11). His introductory syntax ("so then even though"[36]) serves to concede something to their criticism of (the severe tone of?) that letter.[37] Three times he employs the word "on account of,"[38] preceded diplomatically[39] by the negatives "not . . . not even"[40] before the positive adversative "but,"[41] which introduces his purpose in writing: "that before God you could see for yourselves how devoted to us you are." Here the writer brings into this verse the keyword "earnestness"[42] of the previous verse.

Along with 2:5, this verse is critical in revealing the occasion of the "Severe Letter," which was necessitated by the visit that had preceded it. By referring to "the [man] who did the wrong" and "the [man — probably Paul (see 2:5, 10)[43] —] who suffered the wrong," Paul implies that at the time of the second visit to Corinth a man had acted unjustly against him.[44]

Many opinions have been expressed as to the identity of the wrongdoer and the nature of his act of injustice toward Paul.[45] Most likely, in our view,

36. Gk. ἄρα εἰ καί.

37. Cf. Gk. εἰ καὶ μετεμελόμην, βλέπω γὰρ ὅτι ἡ ἐπιστολὴ . . . ἐλύπησεν ὑμᾶς (v. 8).

38. Gk. ἕνεκεν. Although ἕνεκεν plus infinitive is generally used for purpose, here it is causal.

39. Paul's cautious and diplomatic qualification of his statement here and elsewhere (e.g., 1:24), together with a winsome pastoral tone where the letter is referred to (2:1-11; 7:8-12), suggests that he may have been chastened by their critical reaction to that letter.

40. Gk. οὐχ . . . οὐδέ. Hebraic idiom (so Plummer, 224) meaning, "less because of . . . still less because of."

41. Gk. ἀλλ᾿.

42. Gk. σπουδή.

43. So most commentators; but see W. G. Kümmel (*Introduction,* 206), Thrall (1.496), who argue that the victim is not Paul.

44. The Greek τοῦ ἀδικήσαντος . . . τοῦ ἀδικηθέντος is instructive, (1) the gender indicating that both persons were males and (2) the aorists that an *act* of injustice (ἀ + δικ-) occurred. Although Paul earlier generalizes that the whole congregation and not just one person suffered (2:5), it is apparent that one individual was the focus of the wrong, and that in all probability that individual was Paul.

45. See comments on 2:5 and the Introduction, 29. The traditional view that the offender was the "incestuous man" of 1 Cor 5:1-5 (as in, e.g., Hughes, 59-65) is rebutted at length by Furnish, 164-66. This view requires that the man "wronged" was the offender's father, who, however, is not mentioned directly in 1 Corinthians and not at all in 2 Corinthians. On the other hand, it appears that Paul was the injured party (2:5). What wrong did the man do to Paul? Furnish, 166-68, 396, following Barrett, 212, argues that the man's offense was slander, for which, however, unambiguous evidence is lacking. A more likely suggestion may be that the man publicly opposed Paul's attempts at church discipline during his second visit at a time of disturbance in Corinth over sexual matters, as set out in the text above (see on 10:1-6; 12:20–13:2). *Contra* F. T. Fallon, "Sufficiency," 65-66, and Barrett, 256, 258, the view taken here is that Paul keeps the problem of the "false apostles" separate from matters relating to his second visit and the "Severe Letter." It

is the suggestion that this event should be linked with a public disturbance during the second visit (12:20) when Paul confronted those who had not relinquished their former sexual practices (12:21–13:2), connected as these probably were with ongoing temple attendance (6:14–7:1). The most consistent reconstruction of Paul's scattered remarks on the subject throughout 2 Corinthians is that this man publicly opposed, and to some degree thwarted, Paul's attempt at discipline during that fateful visit. While the man was not actively supported by a majority of the Corinthians,[46] nonetheless, he was not directly opposed by them nor subject to any expression of displeasure on their part, nor, least of all, the congregational discipline appropriate to the circumstances. In effect, so long as the Corinthians failed to act, the man's continuing full participation in the life of their assembly stood as a symbol of the Corinthians' failure to acknowledge the leadership of Paul the apostle. Paul's position, therefore, was rendered impossible. He had no option but to withdraw from Corinth and communicate to the Corinthians by the now-lost letter that a further visit to the city could not occur unless and until they demonstrated their loyalty to him by taking appropriate disciplinary action against the man. This they have now done (2:5-11), though the tone of Paul's "Severe Letter" has remained a point of criticism (vv. 8-11; cf. 10:9-10).

Paul labors the point that he did not write on account of the offending man, even less on his own account (see on 2:5). In any case, they have now dealt with the matter (2:6). What, above all, they must understand is that his real purpose in securing their action against the man was so that *they* might know, what he himself did know, namely, "how *devoted* to [him they] are." This "earnestness" (so NIV, v. 11) now shown toward Paul is equivalent to the "[obedience] in everything" in the earlier, parallel passage (2:9), which the "Severe Letter" really sought to prove.

Lest this be seen as a form of authoritarianism, as Paul's need to hold onto the leadership in Corinth at all costs, we should note the vital phrase "made known[47] . . . *before God*[48]" (NRSV), which occurs at the end of the sentence for emphasis. This is one of a number of phrases used in 2 Corinthians that calls for appropriate actions in the present in the light of the great eschatological moment when all things will be revealed,[49] including the true

---

appears likely that these opponents were newly arrived at the time of Titus's recent visit. Problems created by them may have intensified in Corinth after Paul began to write 2 Corinthians. See the comments on chapters 10–13, passim.

46. Cf. 2:6: "The punishment inflicted on him by the *majority*. . . ."

47. Gk. φανερωθῆναι; NIV, "see for yourselves."

48. Gk. ἐνώπιον τοῦ θεοῦ.

49. Gk. τοῦ φανερωθῆναι . . . ἐνώπιον τοῦ θεοῦ; cf. τῇ φανερώσει . . . ἐνώπιον τοῦ θεοῦ (4:2; cf. 8:21); ἡμᾶς φανερωθῆναι δεῖ ἔμπροσθεν τοῦ βήματος τοῦ Χριστοῦ . . . θεῷ δὲ πεφανερῶσθαι (5:10, 11); κατέναντι θεοῦ ἐν Χριστῷ λαλοῦμεν (2:17; 12:19).

relationship between the apostle and his people (see comment on 1:14). At that time each will take pride in the other. The Corinthians (and other churches) will boast of his sacrificial ministry on their account, while Paul will boast of their obedience to his apostolic word. But this eschatological reality, which was in danger of being obscured in Corinth, is to be revealed to the Corinthians now, and it was to that end that Paul wrote the "Severe Letter."

Paul's actions have shown him to be a "paradigm" of the word of reconciliation[50] proclaimed by him (5:18-20; see on 13:9). By his letter Paul has provoked the Corinthians to "turn back" to God as well as to Paul, their apostle (vv. 7-10). His forgiveness of the man who wronged him and his appeal that the Corinthians restore the man to the messianic fellowship (2:7-11) are a practical and pastoral demonstration of reconciliation.

3. Paul's Confidence in Them (7:13-16)

> 13 *By all this we are encouraged. In addition to our own encouragement, we were especially delighted to see how happy Titus was, because his spirit has been refreshed by all of you.* 14 *I had boasted to him about you, and you have not embarrassed me. But just as everything we said to you was true, so our boasting about you to Titus has proved to be true as well.* 15 *And his affection for you is all the greater when he remembers that you were all obedient, receiving him with fear and trembling.* 16 *I am glad I can have complete confidence in you.*

Beyond his own encouragement at the outcome, Paul rejoices at the joy of Titus, refreshed as he was by the Corinthians ("from you all" — v. 13). Although, we infer, Titus had certain misgivings as he set out for Corinth as the bearer of Paul's "Severe Letter," Paul had been able to reassure him that the Corinthians would receive him favorably. On his return Paul was struck by the degree to which this conviction had proved to be true (v. 14). Titus's affection for the Corinthians is the greater as he remembers their obedience, how with reverence they received him (v. 15). Thus Paul rejoices in his confidence in them (v. 16).

The Corinthian reassurances of loyalty to Paul in response to the "Severe Letter" and their evident welcome of Titus brought great joy and confidence to the apostle. To be sure, there were other and weighty matters to resolve in advance of the return of Titus, as bearer of this letter, and soon afterward of the apostle himself. Thus the collection with which Titus has a direct involvement must be dealt with immediately. For this reason Paul

---

50. Helpfully suggested by Martin, 238-39.

concludes the section by highlighting Titus's positive relationships with the Corinthians (vv. 13-15).

Whereas the letter to this point sets out his apologia (1) for his actions (1:3–2:13) and (2) for his apostolic ministry (2:14–7:4), the remainder of the letter (chaps. 8–13) is focused on matters the Corinthians must set right before his return.

13 The first part of v. 13 is a short sentence ("For this reason[1] we are encouraged") that properly belongs to the previous verse as a concluding remark to that passage (vv. 8-13). Titus has brought a report of a positive response to the "Severe Letter," and as a result Paul was and continues to be encouraged.[2]

The longer second sentence is in three parts: (1) A recapitulation of the previous sentence ("besides[3] our encouragement"[4]), (2) a principal clause stated as a comparative ("we rejoiced still more[5] at the joy of Titus"), and (3) its basis ("because[6] [Titus's] spirit[7] was refreshed by all of you").

This last phrase is quite revealing. That Titus was "refreshed[8] by all of you[9]" expresses the deep sense of relief felt by Titus, which he has conveyed to Paul (see on vv. 6-7). The present letter is witness to the confirmed confidence Paul now feels toward them, arising out of Titus's evident relief felt at the time and shown to Paul on his return to him.

Is there something to be read between these lines? Is Paul implying that Titus has been overwhelmingly well received by the Corinthians (see also v. 7),[10] whereas Paul's letter has been somewhat less well-received (v. 8),

---

1. Gk. διὰ τοῦτο.

2. Gk. παρακεκλήμεθα; NIV, "we are encouraged." The force of the perfect tense passive voice (divine passive) is that *God* has encouraged Paul and that he continues to be encouraged (cf. ὁ παρακαλῶν τοὺς ταπεινοὺς . . . ὁ θεός — "God who encourages [present tense] the downcast" — v. 6).

3. Gk. ἐπὶ δέ.

4. Now stated as a noun — παράκλησις.

5. Gk. περισσοτέρως μᾶλλον ἐχάρημεν; NIV, "we were especially delighted." A double comparative; literally, "still much more."

6. Gk. ὅτι.

7. Gk. πνεῦμα, his human spirit.

8. Gk. ἀναπέπαυται. A perfect passive indicating (1) that the sense of relief was ongoing (*contra* Plummer, 226, "a temporary relief," suggesting, perhaps, that the problems of Corinth were not now finally resolved), and (2) possibly that God was the source of the relief (if a divine passive). For other uses of the verb ἀναπαύειν by Paul see 1 Cor 16:18; Phlm 7, 20.

9. Gk. ἀπὸ πάντων ὑμῶν. When it came to the implementation of the disciplining of the offending man, however, only "a majority" (τῶν πλειόνων) were of that mind (2:6).

10. We may speculate that Titus had a better reception in Corinth than Timothy, the bearer of canonical 1 Corinthians (1 Cor 16:10), whose return to Ephesus precipitated Paul's "Painful Visit." The present passage speaks glowingly of Titus's achievement; Titus — not Timothy — was the bearer of the "Severe Letter" and of canonical 2 Corinthians.

though he is thankful enough for its effects? Perhaps Titus's person was better received than the letter of Paul that he had come to deliver (cf. 10:9-11). Certainly Titus's recent visit had been more successful than Paul's second visit, which provoked contempt for him (10:10); but Paul reveals only thankfulness for Titus, with no trace of jealousy.

14 Paul now expands[11] upon the joy he experienced at the joy of Titus. He had expressed pride to Titus about the Corinthians beforehand, and thus he was not embarrassed by what had happened. On the contrary,[12] just as everything he had said to them was true, so too[13] his pride[14] in them to Titus has proved true.

Paul's "if *(ei)* I had boasted about you to him . . ." continues the rather conditional tone evident in v. 8 (twice) and v. 12, suggesting that, although he mentions it, Paul does not want to make too much of it. Some tentativeness beforehand on Titus's part is also to be inferred. Was Titus far less confident than Paul about the Corinthian prospective attitude to the "Severe Letter"? Nonetheless, because of the good result of the visit, Paul is not ashamed at having expressed this confidence to Titus. Rather, as everything he said[15] to the Corinthians was true — a probable rebuttal of their questioning of his integrity relating to declared travel arrangements (see on 1:12, 15-18) — so his pride about them in the presence of Titus[16] also had proved true.[17]

Thus the refreshment of spirit Titus recently experienced from the Corinthians (v. 13) is entirely in line with what Paul had led Titus to expect from them. Although, as it appears, Titus had undertaken this visit with misgivings, Paul had been confident that Titus would be well received by the Corinthians. This has, indeed, proved to be true. Paul's assertion that he has in all things spoken the truth to them serves as a reminder how deeply they felt about his apparent vacillation over his travel plans.

How is Paul able to be confident about the Corinthian response to Titus's visit? In our view it is because he knew that, because they had received the word of God, the Spirit of God was active in them (1:18-22; 3:2-3, 18),

---

11. As indicated by the initial ὅτι.

12. Gk. ἀλλά.

13. Note the contrast, "just as . . . so too" (ὡς . . . οὕτως καί).

14. Gk. κεκαύχημαι, perfect tense, indicating Paul's ongoing pride in them (see on 9:2).

15. Gk. ἐλαλήσαμεν, referring, in all likelihood, to his altered travel arrangements, whether during the second visit, the "Severe Letter," or within the present letter (1:15-18). Furnish (390), however, ponders the possibility of an epistolary aorist, confining the matter to the present letter.

16. Gk. ἐπί with the genitive Τίτου means "in the presence of." See 1 Cor 6:1, 6; Mark 13:9; Acts 25:9.

17. Gk. ἀλήθεια ἐγένετο, "it became true," for Titus.

and that Christ Jesus was "in" them (13:5). They had "received the grace of God" (6:1). Paul's confidence, then, was not in the Corinthians, but in God who was so evidently at work in their lives through the Spirit.

15 Paul continues[18] to rehearse Titus's account of his recent visit to the Corinthians, in particular — as from the previous verse — Titus's own experiences among the Corinthians. His affection for them is all the greater as he remembers their obedience, how with fear and trembling they received him.

This verse has (1) a principal clause ("[Titus] feels the most abundant[19] affection for you [Corinthians]," (2) a statement of attendant circumstances ("as he remembers the obedience of you all"), and (3) a further explanation ("how with[20] fear and trembling you received him").

Evidently Paul's "Severe Letter" had been precise in its demands for the obedience of the Corinthians in regard to their disciplinary action against the wrongdoer (2:9; 7:12). As Paul had confidently predicted to Titus (v. 14), the Corinthians did, indeed, heed what was, apparently, his insistence that he would not return in the face of their failure to acknowledge his apostolic authority in this matter. This will account for their "fear and trembling," a phrase derived from the OT (Exod 15:16; Deut 2:25; Isa 19:16) and used elsewhere by Paul in what are arguably contexts relating to eschatological salvation (1 Cor 2:3; Phil 2:12; Eph 6:5).

The phrase may imply an eschatological dread as the Corinthians heard the "Severe Letter" and faced the possibility of a final separation from Paul's apostleship. It is clear enough that, though he was their "servant" (4:5) and one who did not "lord it over" them (1:24), nonetheless he expected obedience from the congregation in the face of apostolic ministry (2:9; 5:20–6:2; 6:11-13; 10:8; 13:10).

It seems likely that this "fear and trembling" is connected with earlier references to their "longing . . . mourning . . . zeal" (v. 7) and their "godly grief" that "worked repentance unto salvation" (v. 10), expressed as "earnestness . . . eagerness to clear [themselves] . . . indignation . . . alarm . . . longing . . . concern . . . readiness to see justice done" (v. 11). Paul, however, felt the need to acknowledge that his letter did impart "grief" (v. 8) and to explain that he did not intend to "frighten" them by sending it (10:9).

Once again Paul observes that "all" the Corinthians responded positively to Titus (see also v. 13). How, then, do we account for the indication made earlier that a "majority" took disciplinary action against the offender

---

18. As indicated by the initial καί.

19. Gk. περρισοτέρως is a strong expression, equivalent to ὑπερβαλλόντως (11:23).

20. Gk. μέτα implies accompaniment, "You received him along with fear and trembling."

(2:6)? Has Paul's enthusiasm at the broad thrust of Titus's report overstated their response, something quite understandable in the circumstances? Or did the initial impulse of the whole congregation to the "Severe Letter" fail to translate into universal action against the wrongdoer? If Titus's presence was more effective than Paul's letter alone had been (see on v. 13; also vv. 8-12), the latter suggestion may be the more likely of the two.[21]

16 Paul rounds off the section (vv. 5-16) with this brief sentence of simple structure ("I rejoice that I have confidence in you[22] in everything"). Syntactically, the sentence lacks any particle giving continuity with its predecessor (asyndeton), thus giving it the force of a freestanding statement.[23]

The "joy" expressed here by Paul has been much in evidence within this passage, whether as a verb (vv. 7, 9, 13) or as a noun (vv. 4,[24] 13). Beyond that, the expressions of "joy" earlier in the letter in a passage relating to the "Severe Letter" appear to have eschatological connotations (see on 2:3). As a consequence of the Corinthians' positive response to Paul's recent letter, as delivered and ministered by Titus, Paul is now able to return to Corinth in the confidence of a joyful reunion. It seems that, just as the eschatological reunion of apostle and people will be a matter of mutual pride (see on 1:14), so, too, Paul had hoped that his proposed reunion with the Corinthians in the near future — his final visit to them — would also be a time of "joy." Paul's "Severe Letter" held out the possibility of not returning to them and, therefore, of being cut off from them, unless he could envisage that his final visit with them would be joyous.

The "joy" introduced in v. 4 has now come full circle, forming an *inclusio*. Each of the three passages of which the section vv. 5-15 is composed is characterized by "joy": (1) joy at the arrival and reports of Titus (vv. 5-7), (2) joy that the Corinthians have repented (vv. 8-12), and (3) joy at Titus's joy (vv. 13-15).

Thankfully the Corinthians have heeded his admonitions and he is able to return in confidence.[25] More immediately, Paul's references to their positive response to Titus (vv. 13-15) create the context for Titus's return visit, bearing the present letter (8:16-24). Thus he is able confidently to press the claims for the completion of the collection at the hand of Titus (8:6), the topic that follows next.

---

21. When Paul later echoes the Corinthian complaint that "his letters are weighty and forceful, but in person he is unimpressive and his speaking amounts to nothing" (10:10), he may be reflecting the Corinthians' contrast between Titus's presence and Paul's disappointing second visit followed by his frightening (10:9) and hurtful (7:8) "Severe Letter" at the time of Titus's delivery of it.

22. Gk. ἐν ὑμῖν, "in respect of you" (cf. Gal 4:20).

23. Other examples include 5:21; 7:2, 3, 4.

24. Verse 4 serves as a bridge into the passage vv. 5-16 (see on v. 4).

25. See earlier at 2:1, 3, as well as subsequently at 9:4; 10–13 passim.

B. CALL TO COMPLETE THE COLLECTION (8:1–9:15)

In the previous major section (7:5-16) Paul described his arrival in Macedonia and the eventual return of Titus from Corinth for his reunion there with Paul. That section is dominated by Paul's relief at Titus's enthusiastic report of the positive reaction of the Corinthians to his delivery of Paul's "Severe Letter" (7:7, 13b, 15, 16). Paul's portrayal of Titus's enthusiasm for the Corinthians in the immediately prior passage (7:13-15) prepares the ground for Paul's admonitions about the collection, which he is now to make, and in which Titus will play a significant part now that he has arrived back in Corinth.

Titus's report to Paul in Macedonia on the progress of the Corinthians' collection for the Judaean believers was not encouraging. (Titus had initiated the collection in Corinth on Paul's behalf during the previous calendar year — 8:6, 10; 9:2; cf. 1 Cor 16:1-4.) Although Titus must have been the source of Paul's knowledge of the collapse of the collection, Paul does not attribute this understanding to a report by Titus. This supposition has to be inferred. Paul's silence about Titus at this point is probably diplomatic.

In the passage immediately following, Paul again retraces his steps to his arrival in Macedonia (cf. 7:5-6), now recounting the unexpected interest in and support for the collection from the Macedonian churches (8:1, 3, and 5a).

This turn of events has provided Paul with a point to make to the Corinthians over their failure with the collection. He will devote two chapters[1]

---

1. In 1776 J. S. Semler argued that chapters 8 and 9 were originally separate compositions. This view is followed by many commentators, including Martin, 249-51, and, most conspicuously of all, H. D. Betz, *2 Corinthians 8 and 9*, 25-36, who dismisses the methodologies used on both sides of the unity debate, preferring a literary analysis of each chapter. Thrall, 1.36-40, discusses Betz's literary analyses of chapters 8 and 9, and rejects the various classifications (exordium, narratio, etc.) that he has applied to the text.

Furnish, 428-33, after carefully weighing arguments *pro* and *contra,* sees no serious obstacle to regarding these chapters as an integrated unity, an opinion followed here. The chief points in favor of partition are (1) that in 9:1 Paul appears to be introducing the topic of "ministry to the saints" *de novo,* whereas he has been discussing it in the previous chapter, and (2) that the Macedonian brothers Paul is sending in the earlier chapter have a passive role (8:18-24) whereas those in the latter chapter (9:3) have an active role in regard to the collection.

The case for unity is compelling: (1) the keyword χάρις (see also 8:4, 6, 7, 9, 16, 19; 9:8, 14) appears in 8:1 and 9:15 as in "ring composition" (other repeated vocabulary includes ἁπλότης [8:2; 9:13] and περισσεύειν [8:2; 9:12]), (2) the repetition of critical phrases in the so-called separated sections (διακονίας τῆς εἰς τοὺς ἁγίους in 8:4 and 9:1; cf. 9:12, 13) virtually demands a resumption of earlier argument, and (3) Paul's περὶ μὲν γὰρ τῆς διακονίας τῆς εἰς τοὺς ἁγίους περισσόν μοί ἐστιν τὸ γραφεῖν ὑμῖν (9:1) is better seen as pastorally reinforcive (so J. Denney, *Second Epistle to the Corinthians,* 279-80) than as introductory to an entirely different document (see on 2:3; 7:4). See further Hughes, 321-22; S. K. Stowers, *"Peri men gar,"* 340-48; and C. H. Talbert, "Money Management," 359-70.

to the respective responses of the Macedonians and the Corinthians to this fund. Let the arrival of Titus, the bearer of the present letter to Corinth, with the two delegates from the Macedonian churches be the catalyst to bring the Corinthian collection to its conclusion. Indeed, he is sending them ahead that they "might rectify in advance"[2] (9:5; 8:16-24) the problem. These "apostles," specifically the renowned — but unnamed — brother, but in all probability the lesser delegate also, will later accompany Paul to Jerusalem with the collection after he, too, has come to Corinth (8:18-19, 23; Acts 20:3-4).

We assume Paul's decision to send Titus back to Corinth to ensure the finalization of the collection (8:6, 16-9:5), along with that envoy's good news of their positive response to the "Severe Letter" (7:7, 11-13), created the context in which Paul decided upon the writing of 2 Corinthians. This letter is the carefully written precursor to the apostle's own visit (9:4), which he can now proceed with in the reasonable confidence of a broadly favorable response to him in Corinth. We view chapters 1–6 and 10–13 as fitting in with the central decisions that are reflected in chapters 7–9.

In our view, chapters 8–9 can be consistently viewed as having a coherent and consecutive argument.[3] Based on the voluntariness of the Macedonians' involvement in the collection and their sacrificial generosity, Paul calls on the Corinthians to complete their participation in it (8:1-7). These words, however, may lead to misunderstandings: (1) This is "advice," not "command"; "grace" and "readiness" are their appropriate responses (8:8-11); (2) it is not a call to give more than they have, but for the completion of what was both desired and begun (8:11-12); and (3) the Jerusalemites' relief is not at Corinthian impoverishment; it is for "equality" between the Jerusalemites and the Corinthians (8:13-15). In the light of the coming of Titus and two highly regarded Macedonians, let the Corinthians give proof of their love and of Paul's pride in them (8:16-24). In particular, when Paul himself comes, with other Macedonians, let the Corinthians spare him and themselves the humiliation of being "unprepared" (9:1-5). Finally, as a theological consideration, let them note that God further blesses the generous giver and unites givers and receivers in spiritual fellowship (9:6-15).

Thus it is abundantly clear that Paul wants the Corinthians to complete the collection. But it is at least as clear that the doctrine of grace is to be upheld as they do so. Indeed, the most powerful impression these chapters have upon us is the centrality to the apostle of that doctrine. This emerges

---

2. Gk. προκαταρτίσωσιν.

3. See also Stowers, *"Peri men gar,"* 346. For the argument that Paul is here employing an ABA structure in chapters 8–9, see Talbert, "Money Management," 369 nn. 8, 9, and 10, *contra* the rhetorical patterns noted by H. D. Betz, *2 Corinthians 8 and 9,* 38-39.

very strongly from the vocabulary he uses throughout these chapters, for example, (1) the keyword "grace" — *charis*[4] — whose overall impact is not softened by its use with different nuances (though it is not always translatable as "grace"); (2) a cluster of words pointing to the nature of acceptable response consistent with the principle of "grace" — "overflowing,"[5] "generosity,"[6] "voluntariness,"[7] "willingness,"[8] "eagerness,"[9] and (3) contrastive references relative to the collection — not a "command" but "advice" (8:8, 10); "not an exaction but a willing gift" (9:5); "not reluctantly nor under compulsion but . . . cheerful[ly]" (9:7). Paul ends his exposition in keeping with this: "Thanks be to God for his inexpressible *gift* [of grace]!"[10]

1. The Grace of God Shown to the Macedonian Churches: A Basis of Appeal to the Corinthians (8:1-7)

> 1 *And now, brothers, we want you to know about the grace that God has given the Macedonian churches.* 2 *Out of the most severe trial, their overflowing joy and their extreme*[1] *poverty welled up in rich generosity.* 3 *For I testify that they gave as much as they were able, and even beyond their ability. Entirely on their own,* 4 *they urgently pleaded with us for the privilege of sharing in this service to the saints.* 5 *And they did not do as we expected, but they gave themselves first to the Lord and then to us in keeping with God's will.* 6 *So we urged Titus, since he had earlier made a beginning, to bring also to completion this act of grace on your part.* 7 *But just as you excel in everything — in faith, in speech, in knowledge, in complete earnestness and in your*[2] *love for us — see that you also excel in this grace of giving.*

4. Gk. χάρις — 8:1, 4, 6, 7, 9, 16, 19; 9:8, 14, 15. The word χάρις was also used in relation to the collection in 1 Cor 16:3.

5. Gk. περισσεύειν — 8:3, 7 (twice); 9:8, 12; περίσσευμα — 8:14; περισσεία — 8:2.

6. Gk. ἁπλότης — 8:2; 9:11, 13.

7. Gk. αὐθαίρετος — 8:3, 17.

8. Gk. ἡ προθυμία — 8:11, 12, 19; 9:2.

9. Gk. ἡ σπουδή — 8:7, 8, 16; σπουδαῖος — 8:17-22.

10. Gk. δωρεά.

1. The reading followed here (κατὰ βάθους — so most MSS) is more pointed and is to be preferred to κατὰ βάθος (p[46]).

2. The reading ἡμῶν ἐν ὑμῖν, supported by p[46] B 1739 it[r] cop[sa, bo] Origen, is the harder reading and is supported by Metzger, 581 (also Barrett, Hughes). Though difficult to translate, it is preferred to the more straightforward alternative — ὑμῶν ἐν ἡμῖν, which, however, is more widely attested (e.g., ℵ C D G K P ψ) and is followed by the RSV, NEB, and NIV. (Cf. G. D. Fee, "ΧΑΡΙΣ," 533-38, who calls ὑμῶν ἐν ἡμῖν the more difficult reading.)

It appears that when the collection was first mooted, Paul had not thought to include the churches of Macedonia in this "ministry" for the poor believers in Judaea, presumably on account of their own hardships. In consequence of gospel ministry among them since his return to Macedonia (7:5), the members of the Macedonians have given themselves to the Lord, and, in consequence, to Paul (v. 5).

As a result, despite their "rock bottom" poverty, they have begged Paul to allow them to be included in participation in the collection (v. 4). The grace of God has been given to them; they overflow in generosity (vv. 1-2). Paul has witnessed their generosity, which has been beyond their capacity (v. 3). Because of (1) their initiative (vv. 3b, 4a) and (2) their unexpected and sacrificial openhandedness (vv. 2, 3, 5a), Paul has urged Titus to go back to Corinth to bring to completion the collection that he had initiated earlier (v. 6). The point of appeal in the passage is found in its final verse: as the Corinthians overflow in other "graces," let them overflow also in this "grace" (v. 7), generosity in regard to the collection.

These verses are dominated by the notion of "grace" *(charis)* (vv. 1, 4, 6, and 7). The primary meaning is that "grace" given by God in the afflicted and poverty-stricken Macedonian churches has overflowed in their generosity for the collection (vv. 1-2). The same word is repeated as the Macedonians beg Paul "for the favor" *(charis)* of sharing in this ministry (v. 4). In addressing the Corinthians Paul has urged Titus to return to complete among them this "grace," that is, the now-lapsed collection (v. 6; cf. v. 4), which, however, is a proof of love, not a command — v. 8. Nonetheless, as they overflow in other "graces" — faith, speech, knowledge, eagerness, and Paul's love for them — let them also over flow in this "grace" (v. 7).

1 A new subject is signaled[3] by Paul's address to his Corinthian readers as "Brothers [and sisters], we want you to know. . . ."[4] The "knowledge" Paul wishes to convey to the Corinthians is that "the grace of God has been given among the churches[5] of Macedonia."[6] This is an

3. The particle δέ and the address ἀδελφοί mark a point of transition (cf. 1 Cor 1:10; 4:6; 7:29; 12:1; Rom 15:14; 16:17).

4. Gk. γνωρίζομεν ὑμῖν suggests that something important is about to be communicated (Gal 1:11; 1 Cor 12:3; 15:1; cf. 1:8: "We do not want you to be uninformed, brothers . . .").

5. Gk. ἐν ταῖς ἐκκλησίαις, which is taken as (1) "among the churches" (A. T. Robertson, *Grammar,* #587; Plummer, 233; RV) rather than (2) "to the churches" (Furnish, 400; RSV; NIV). In context, the churches' overflowing generosity (v. 2) supports (1), the notion of God's grace as dynamically active.

6. Paul refers to "churches" of a particular region — "of Galatia" (1 Cor 16:1; Gal 1:2), "of Asia" (1 Cor 16:19), and "of" — or "in" — "Judaea" (Gal 1:22; 1 Thess 2:14), which, with "Macedonia," appear to be a Roman provincial association. Specifically

introductory verse; Paul will explain what he means by "the grace of God" in vv. 2-4.

The grace of God[7] is his attitude of unconditioned kindness *shown* toward us. This was manifested (1) in the incarnation of our Lord Jesus Christ (8:9), whom Paul also thinks of as God's "gift" (*dōrea* — 9:15; cf. Rom 5:15, 17), and (2) in the hearing of that word from God which reconciles men and women to God (6:1; cf. 5:20; see also 4:15). God's invisible "grace" *(charis)*, however, is also made visible and concrete in the "grace" God *gives* to members of churches, specifically their "faith," "utterance," "knowledge," and "love" (v. 7). The "grace" that has been given to the Macedonian churches, and that Paul seeks in the church in Corinth, is sacrificial, freely given, generosity. "Grace" as meaning that graciousness which God shows *toward* us, as well those attitudes and ministries which, as a consequence, he produces *in* us, is roughly paralleled by Paul's use elsewhere of *charis/charisma* (Rom 12:6).

The verb "given"[8] is significant: (1) the passive voice (divine passive) indicates that God is the giver, and (2) the perfect tense is suggestive of a gift that, although given at a point in the past, continues to be given.

Paul's words imply that, although he may have been primarily domiciled in one place (Philippi? — see on 7:5), nonetheless he was well aware of the circumstances of the Macedonian churches, through direct contact with them.[9] This is to be inferred from his knowledge that "the grace of God" had been "given" and continued to be evident in these churches of northern Greece (cf. v. 3 — "I testify"). Paul's words give no clear indication as to the time this grace began to be manifest, but it is probable that it occurred in the period since he had returned to that region (cf. 7:5).[10]

Paul's present words allow a hope of renewal or revival within congregations after they have been established for some time. These churches were and had been genuinely Christian for a number of years, as is evident from Paul's letters to the Thessalonians and Philippians. Yet in the recent past God had "given" these believers his "grace," which, in their case, was manifested in a remarkable and unanticipated generosity.

Paul has in mind the Macedonian churches of Philippi, Thessalonica, and Beroea, and any other churches established in the period since (cf. 1 Thess 1:8).

7. Gk. τὴν χάριν τοῦ θεοῦ. See further K. Berger, *EDNT* 3.457-60; A. B. Luter, *DPL,* 372-74.

8. δεδομένην.

9. That the Macedonian churches "gave themselves to . . . us" (i.e., Paul), as in 8:5, and that he had expressed pride to the Macedonians (9:2) suggest that Paul had been involved in ministry to them prior to the writing of this letter.

10. However, Paul had earlier sent Timothy and Erastus from Ephesus ahead of him to Macedonia (Acts 19:22). It is possible that their ministry played some part in the Macedonians' interest in the collection.

2 The initial "that"[11] (untranslated) is a bridge from the previous verse introducing an explanation of "the grace of God given the Macedonian churches." God's grace to them is now revealed in their grace to others, shown in the midst of great affliction. Their overflowing joy and their rock-bottom poverty overflow in a wealth of generosity.

This two-part sentence is characterized by the antonyms affliction/joy and poverty/riches:[12]

> in great testing of *affliction*[13]
> their overflowing[14] *joy*[15]

and   the depth of their *poverty*[16]
>   overflowed
>   in the *riches* of their generosity.

Generosity has flowed out of poverty and joy. Critical to the present verse are the words "overflowing . . . overflowed" ("their *overflowing* joy . . . their deep poverty *overflowed*"). Thus "the grace of God," now "given" in the Macedonian churches, may be seen in "their overflowing joy" in the midst of a "great trial of affliction," a joy that, out of "their profound poverty," has "overflowed" in "their rich generosity."

Since the Macedonians were so poor, it is evident that their "generosity"[17]

---

11. Gk. ὅτι, which is clearly epexegetic in this case. (See BAGD 1.)

12. Poverty overflowing into wealth is an oxymoron, the combination of contradictory ideas.

13. Gk. ἐν πολλῇ δοκιμῇ θλίψεως; NIV, "out of the most severe trial." See on v. 8 for comment on δοκιμή, "trial," or, better, "proof" or "testing" (cf. 2:9; 9:13; 13:3), and 1:3-7 for comment on θλίψις, "affliction," which here points to the pressure of suffering arising from the profession of Christ in a hostile environment. The whole phrase here means "in great testing shown in affliction."

14. Gk. περισσεία; cf. περισσεύειν in the same verse. This word cluster is important within these chapters — περισσεία (8:2), περίσσευμα (8:8), περισσεύειν (8:2, 7 [twice], 9:8, 12).

15. Gk. χαρά. Despite their suffering Paul refers to "their overflowing joy." "Joy" is regularly noted in the NT in those who have received the gospel, whether from the lips of angels, Jesus, or the apostles (Luke 2:10; 8:13; 15:7, 10; Acts 8:8; 13:52; 15:3). Joy in affliction is a strong theme within 2 Corinthians (e.g., 1:24; 2:3; 6:10; 7:4, 7, 9, 13, 16). See generally W. G. Morrice, *Joy,* 111-33.

16. ἡ κατὰ βάθους πτωχεία αὐτῶν; NIV, "their extreme poverty." More literally it is their "down-to-the-depth poverty" (Furnish) or, more imaginatively, their "rock bottom" poverty (Barrett).

17. Gk. τῆς ἁπλότητος, genitive, is explanatory of τὸ πλοῦτος. The Macedonians' "wealth" is their generosity. Although ἁπλότητος, which is used only by Paul in the NT, usually means "simplicity" or "single-mindedness," the most likely meaning here, based

must have been — like that of the poor widow[18] whom Jesus commended — primarily qualitative rather than quantitative. In implied contrast with the laggardly Corinthians Paul is commending the Macedonians' spirit of determination and sacrifice.

The present passage suggests that the Macedonian churches were poorer than the assembly in Corinth. This is understandable given the wealth of the Achaian capital, which was proverbial.[19] Yet the northern cities of Philippi, Thessalonica, and Beroea where the Macedonian churches were located, though exploited by their Roman masters,[20] were by no means indigent. This raises the question why Paul should speak of the "deep poverty" of these churches. The most likely explanation is probably to be found in the words "in great testing of [their] affliction," which point to persecution of the believers in the the Macedonian churches.[21] Local social ostracism with its accompanying economic disadvantages to believers perhaps best explains Paul's reference to the Macedonians' "great testing of affliction."[22]

It is worth reflecting on the generosity of these Macedonian believers, as compared to their laggardly Achaian counterparts. It is quite likely that those who are poor on account of persecution will identify with and relate to others in similar circumstances. Perhaps the Macedonians who knew firsthand the pain of poverty through persecution felt a deep fraternal affinity with the persecuted Jewish believers in Judaea.[23]

3 As with v. 2, the initial "that"[24] (NIV — "For") introduces Paul's explanation of the previous verse. Having declared that God's grace was "given" in the churches of Macedonia (v. 1), that is, the members have overflowed in generosity despite their poverty (v. 2), Paul now explains that they have given not only according to, but beyond, their ability, and they have done so spontaneously.

---

on its use in 9:11 and Rom 12:8, is "generosity." Although the context of chapters 8–9 implies "generosity" as the meaning, the more basic idea of single-mindedness may also be inferred; a "channeled generosity."

18. According to Mark 12:44, the "poor widow . . . contributed . . . out of her poverty . . . her whole living" (RSV).

19. See the Introduction, 2-4.

20. Since their conquest of the region 168 B.C. the Romans had seized the gold, silver, and copper mines of the region as well as the rights to mill the forests. The Macedonians felt like a lacerated animal (Livy, *History* 45.30).

21. For the sufferings of persecution of the Thessalonians and the Philippians, see respectively 1 Thess 1:6; 2:14 and Phil 1:27-30.

22. See generally S. D. Cuss, *The Imperial Cult,* for the social circumstances of believers in Macedonia in light of local developments in the imperial cult.

23. Paul tells the Thessalonians that they became imitators of the Judaean churches, suffering the "same things from their countrymen as they did from the Jews" (1 Thess 2:14).

24. Gk. ὅτι. It is more likely that ὅτι is linked to v. 2 than to γνωρίζομεν in v. 1.

Lacking any connecting particle, this verse is really in continuation of v. 2. Needing to be supplied is a verb (e.g., "they gave") for the statements "according to [their] power" and "beyond [their] power."[25] Having asserted that [they gave] according to their power, Paul interjects a mild oath ("I testify") followed by an intensifying, "*even*[26] beyond [their] power," which is then explained by "voluntarily."

> that
>
>   according to [their]   power,
>   I testify[27]
>   even beyond   [their]   power,
>   [they gave]   voluntarily.[28]

This grace of God given in the Macedonian churches is expressed in their sacrificial and voluntary participation in the collection. This voluntariness mirrors (1) the grace of Christ toward humankind in his unconditioned impoverishment of himself in incarnation (v. 9), and (2) the grace of God in this the day of salvation, which has come to them in Paul's ministry (6:1-2; cf. 5:20). Rather bluntly Paul is citing the Macedonian voluntariness to admonish the Corinthians voluntarily to renew their involvement in the collection.

Let the Corinthians note from this passage that the grace of God is (1) shown "voluntarily" by God (implied in v. 3), (2) works dynamically in those to whom it is shown (vv. 1-2), who (3) respond voluntarily in ministry to others (v. 4), and (4) is characterized by generous oversupply ("[they gave] beyond . . ." — v. 3).

The appropriate course of action open to the Corinthians is implicit in these none-too-subtle words of the apostle.

4 Paul's words obliquely give an impression of what happened after Paul's arrival in Macedonia. Evidently the churches raised with Paul the subject of the collection. It is not clear how or when this occurred. It seems

25. Gk. κατὰ δύναμιν . . . παρὰ δύναμιν; NIV, "as much as they were able . . . even beyond their ability." Note Paul's similar-sounding but antithetical κατά ("according to") and παρά ("beyond"); for a parallel see Rom 11:24 — κατὰ φύσιν . . . παρὰ φύσιν, "naturally . . . unnaturally."

26. Gk. καί.

27. Gk. μαρτυρῶ, a singular pronoun, interrupting a pattern of plurals. Furnish, 400, translates "I swear," i.e., as an oath.

28. Gk. αὐθαίρετοι; NIV, "entirely on their own." This word occurs only here and in v. 17 within the NT. Cognates used elsewhere (2 Macc 6:19; 3 Macc 6:6; 7:10) suggest a present meaning "voluntary," "spontaneous." See further *New Docs.* 4.127-28. According to Rom 15:26, εὐδόκησαν γὰρ Μακεδονία καὶ Ἀχαΐα κοινωνίαν τινὰ ποιήσασθαι εἰς τοὺς πτωχοὺς τῶν ἁγίων τῶν ἐν Ἰερουσαλήμ, where εὐδόκησαν implies the voluntary nature of the action.

likely that (1) Paul visited the churches (as we might conclude from 9:2; also 8:1, 4), and (2) that he met with delegates elected by those churches (as we might infer from 8:18-23).[29] His opening words (lit. "with great appeal [= considerable urgency] they begged[30] us . . .") reflect animated conversation by Macedonian believers with Paul (cf. 9:2-3).

The Macedonians sought from Paul a "favor" (RSV, JB) or "privilege" (NIV). These words translate the keyword of the passage, *charis* (cf. vv. 1, 6, 7), which, although not bearing the meaning "grace," here is used to reinforce the "grace"/"graciousness" behind their action. This "favor" he now specifies[31] as

> the participation
> > in the ministry
> > > that is to the saints.

Each word here is important.

"Participation"[32] (see also 9:13) relates to the sharing of the churches of various provinces in the "collection for the saints,"[33] as Paul calls it in the First

---

29. While we know of Paul's coming to Macedonia (2:13; 7:5) and of Titus's eventual reunion with Paul there (2:12; 7:6), we do not whether Paul's involvement with and knowledge of the Macedonian churches occurred before or after Titus's arrival in Macedonia. The reference in 9:2, 4 favors the former.

30. Gk. δεόμενοι; NIV, "they urgently pleaded." The participle is dependent on the unexpressed "they gave" of the previous verse. Moule, however, takes it as a finite verb, "they begged" (179).

31. In τὴν χάριν καὶ τὴν κοινωνίαν the καί is epexegetic, "the favor, that is, the participation. . . ." The construction is known as hendiadys, the joining by καί of two different nouns to express one complex idea, so as to avoid a repetition of genitives ("the favor *of* the participation *of* the ministry . . .").

32. Gk. κοινωνία; NIV, "sharing." Such "sharing" is applied to this "ministry" also in Rom 15:26 (cf. κοινωνεῖν — Rom 15:27).

33. Gk. τῆς λογείας τῆς εἰς τοὺς ἁγίους. For useful analyses of the references to the collection across the Pauline corpus, see G. D. Fee, *1 Corinthians,* 809-17; Furnish, 408-13. The origins of the collection referred to in 2 Corinthians 8–9 are to be found in the διακονία of famine relief sent to the Jerusalem church from the church of Antioch *c.* A.D. 47 (Acts 11:29-30; 12:25). It is possible that the famine of the mid-forties exacerbated an existing problem caused by the large component of dependent widows in the Jerusalem church (cf. Acts 6:1-7). At the private meeting of the Jerusalem leaders (James, Cephas, and John) with the Antioch delegates (Barnabas and Saul), who had brought the relief (cf. Gal 2:1), Paul's gospel and apostolate to the Gentiles were formally recognized but with the request that, as reported by Saul, μόνον τῶν πτωχῶν ἵνα μνημονεύωμεν (Gal 2:10). Paul's brief rejoinder was that he had been eager to do this very thing (ὃ καὶ ἐσπούδασα αὐτὸ τοῦτο ποιῆσαι), as witnessed by the relief recently brought (Gal 2:10). The Antiochene church's relief for Jerusalem finds a parallel in the action of Queen Helena of Adiabene in Mesopotamia, a proselyte

Letter (1 Cor 16:1). The failure of the Corinthians to complete the collection forms the background to the writing of chapters 8–9 in the present letter. These chapters are written in the expectation that the collection at Corinth will be completed in time for Paul's impending final visit (8:11, 24; 9:4).

---

to Judaism, who also sent aid to Judaea at the time of the famine (Josephus, *Ant.* 20.49, 51; 101).

In *c.* A.D. 55-56, when the end of Paul's Gentile mission to the eastern provinces was in sight, this earlier, general agreement, that Gentile believers should help the poor believers of Jerusalem, was formalized as Paul's special appeal, marking the conclusion of this phase of his ministry (see Rom 15:25-26; 1 Cor 16:1-2; 2 Cor 8–9; Acts 20:4). Henceforth Paul decided to move his base of operations to the western province of Spain after a period of transitional ministry in Rome (Rom 15:18-24; Acts 19:21). Meanwhile churches from Macedonia, Achaia, Galatia, and Asia offered, or agreed, to participate in this appeal for the poor among the saints of Jerusalem. Whether the initiative for this appeal lay with Jerusalem, signifying that church's primacy, or whether it lay with, e.g., the Corinthians, signifying that church's patronage, is a point debated by scholars. From the text of Paul's letters the initiative appears to have lain with the apostle, as sparked by his decision to move to the west (cf. 1 Cor 16:6; Rom 15:24-29).

As to the rationale for this appeal to charity, Paul declares it to be the "debt" the Gentiles owed to the saints of Jerusalem for the "spiritual blessings" that have flowed out from them to the Gentiles (Rom 15:27). As reported in Acts, Paul called these gifts "alms and offerings," which he had brought after some years "to my nation" (Acts 24:17). This resembles Queen Helena's "desire to go to the city of Jerusalem and to worship at the Temple of God . . . and to make thank offerings there" (Josephus, *Ant.* 20.49). Also to be noted is the possibility that the Gentiles sent such gifts to secure a place in the covenant in lieu of circumcision (for evidence see Martin, 258).

The appeal is characterized by its own vocabulary: λογεία (1 Cor 16:1); εὐλογία (2 Cor 9:5); χάρις (1 Cor 16:3; 2 Cor 8:6, 7, 9; 9:14); λειτουργία (2 Cor 9:12; cf. Rom 15:27), and κοινωνία (2 Cor 8:4; 9:13; Rom 15:26). It may be significant that as Peter expressed κοινωνία in the gospel to Saul/Paul (Gal 2:9), so, reciprocally, Paul called for κοινωνία between the Gentile and Jewish churches.

Various views have been advanced as to Paul's underlying motivation in mounting this appeal (for a review see Martin, 256-58). The most probable, based on 2 Corinthians 8–9, are that he sought by this means (1) to relieve a genuine and ongoing need in Jerusalem (8:14) by a method that would, in consequence, (2) deepen a sense of fellowship and unity from the Jewish to the Gentile branch of Christianity (9:12-14).

Perhaps Paul also hoped that the money from the Gentiles, and more particularly the presence of the large contingent of Gentiles who brought the money (Acts 20:4), would be a potent sign of the success of the gospel among the uncircumcised. It is possible that such a strategy was Paul's practical embodiment of his teaching in Romans 9–11, which he formulated immediately prior to his return to Jerusalem, namely, that Jews would be provoked to become believers on account of the ingathering of the Gentiles (Rom 11:14; so J. Munck, followed by K. Nickle, *The Collection*). Certainly Paul surrounded himself with a large number of Gentiles when bringing the collection from the Aegean region to Judaea (Acts 20:4). Doubtless this was to protect the money and to secure Paul's integrity in financial matters from calumny, but perhaps also to make an impact in Jerusalem with such a powerful Gentile presence along the lines of

"The ministry[34] for the saints"[35] has a semiofficial ring to it (the phrase is reproduced exactly in 9:1 and in similar terms outside this letter[36]). A later reference will explain it as an activity that "supplies the needs of the saints" (9:12-13). It is that "service," initiated by Paul, in which the members[37] of the churches of Achaia, Galatia, Asia, and Macedonia[38] participate by their contributions, for the sake of their brothers and sisters in Judaea, which will be taken by the delegates of the churches of these provinces to Jerusalem.[39] Is this Paul's "ministry" in which the people of the churches "participate," or is it more generally a "ministry" of both Paul the initiator *and* those churches who are involved? In our view the various references to "ministry" in these chapters indicate that Paul is referring to *his* "ministry" and that the churches contribute toward it (see 9:1, 12, 13; in Rom 15:31 it is "*my* ministry for Jerusalem").[40]

Rom 11:14. If this is correct — and it is an open question — it would follow that the Gentiles' delivery of the collection in Jerusalem, accompanied by the conversion of Israel, would be quickly followed by the Parousia (cf. Isa 2:2-3; 60:5-6; Mic 4:1-2). One difficulty with this suggestion is that Paul would hardly have planned to go to Spain if he had expected the Parousia to occur as a result of the coming of these Gentile converts in Jerusalem. However, R. Aus, "Paul's Travel Plans to Spain," 232-62, identifies Spain with the "Tarshish" of Isa 66:19-20, from where "brothers . . . from all the nations" will come to God's holy mountain in Jerusalem as "an offering to the Lord" (cf. Jer 3:14). But Paul makes no explicit connection between the collection for the saints and the bringing of the Gentiles to Jerusalem as an offering to the Lord, whether in 2 Corinthians 8–9 or in Rom 15:15-33.

There is no way of knowing how successful the collection may have been in fulfilling such hypothetical intentions. His frosty reception in the Jerusalem church suggests that, initially at least, Paul's hopes for a fellowship-strengthening outcome between Jews and Gentiles were not realized (Acts 21:17-26). James and the Jerusalem elders made it clear that they did not need any help from Paul or his Gentiles for the conversion of Israel (Acts 21:20)! Moreover, the presence of a Gentile companion of Paul's in the temple precincts was to have disastrous consequences for Paul in Jerusalem (Acts 21:29; cf. 20:4). Whether or not it provoked the conversion of Jews is not known.

34. Gk. διακονία is important in this letter for Paul's apostolic service in the new covenant; see 3:7, 8, 9; 4:1; 5:18; 6:3; cf. 11:8. However, διακονία carrying the meaning of charitable service is found in Acts: (1) local assistance for widows (Acts 6:1), and (2) the Antiochene church members' famine relief for the Jerusalem church (Acts 11:29; 12:25). As noted in the text above, it is *Paul's* ministry that is now referred to.

35. Gk. τῆς διακονίας τῆς εἰς τοὺς ἁγίους; NIV, "this service to the saints."

36. As in Romans 15 — πορεύομαι εἰς Ἰερουσαλὴμ διακονῶν τοῖς ἁγίοις (25), ἡ διακονία μου ἡ εἰς Ἰερουσαλήμ (31). "Ministry to the saints," however, could also be applied to the local "saints," as in 1 Cor 16:15 (see Fee, 829).

37. The contributions were made by individuals in the churches, not — apparently — by the churches (1 Cor 16:2 — "each of you . . ."; cf. Acts 11:29).

38. 1 Cor 16:1; Rom 15:26; Acts 20:4.

39. 8:16-24; 9:3; Rom 15:25-28; Acts 20:3-4.

40. So, too, Furnish, 401.

The "saints"[41] (see on 1:1), though not further defined here (but see 9:1, 12), are identified more closely in Paul's next letter as "the poor among the saints at Jerusalem" (Rom 15:26, RSV). This latter expression suggests that not all the "saints at Jerusalem" were "poor."[42] Nonetheless, that the collection is generally designated for the "saints" suggests that as a group they were for all practical purposes "poor." It is likely that their poverty, like that of the Macedonians, was primarily caused by local social ostracism and its consequent financial disadvantage and difficulty.

5   The writer now expresses his surprise at the level of the Macedonians' contribution to the collection. He notes, however, that first of all they had given themselves, that is, given themselves once more, to the Lord, and to his apostle, Paul.

Words must be supplied near the beginning of this sentence to complete its meaning. To "and" we add "they did so," that is, participated in "the ministry to the saints" (as in the previous verse). Paul expresses this now-supplemented statement as a "not . . . but"[43] contrast:

> And [they did so]
>
> > > *not* as we expected,
> > > *but*
> >
> > themselves[44]
> > they   gave
> > > first to the Lord
> > > also to   us
> > >
> > > > through the will of God.

The first part of the contrast ("not as we expected") picks up "they [gave] beyond their power" (v. 3). Their generosity exceeded Paul's expectations. Evidently, the members of the Macedonian churches (or "most of them" — 9:2) had begun to make their contributions at the time of writing, though it appears that these would not be completed until Paul finally left Macedonia for Corinth (9:4). These words imply a greater duration of ministry by Paul among the Macedonian churches than might be inferred by his earlier terse statement about his arrival in Macedonia (7:5).

---

41. Gk. ἅγιοι.

42. C. E. B. Cranfield, *Romans:* "the collection is intended for the benefit of those of the Jerusalem brethren who are particularly poor" (772). It is striking that Paul does not mention Jerusalem as the destination of the collection, in contrast to 1 Cor 16:1-4; Rom 15:26-31.

43. Gk. οὐ . . . ἀλλ[ά].

44. Gk. ἐαυτούς, "themselves," located at the beginning of the clause for emphasis.

The second part of the contrast is tangential[45] ("but themselves they gave . . .") to its predecessor. The surprisingly high level of their contribution *and* their gift of themselves to the Lord and to Paul appear to be unconnected. In reality, however, the two statements are connected; their surprising generosity is a direct result of their dedication of themselves to the Lord.

Paul earlier summarized his proclamation as "Jesus Christ as Lord" (4:5); here we are allowed to see the response of the Macedonians: "themselves they gave first[46] to the Lord." That earlier verse, when taken with this, gives a complete, if terse, picture of apostolic ministry, both as to message and to response.

What, then, is meant by "themselves they gave . . . also[47] to us,[48] through the will of God"? This could mean either (1) a general acknowledgment that all response to the Lord, with accompanying graciousness to others, is "through the will of God," or (2) that the Macedonians specifically recognized Paul's apostleship to them as being "through the will of God." While option (1) fits in with the Macedonians' generosity as in vv. 1-4, option (2) could point on to vv. 6-7, where Paul is calling for a Corinthian response of generosity. Moreover, option (2) is possible because the phrase "through the will of God"[49] is generally restricted elsewhere to Paul's apostleship, including the opening words of this letter (1:1). Here it would be a statement of some importance in the context of this letter, implying that, in giving themselves to the Lord, in response to Paul's ministry, the Macedonians effectively reaffirmed Paul's authority as an apostle to the Gentile churches, as "through the will of God" (cf. 10:8; 13:10).[50] Given the ambiguity of the Achaian believers' attitude to Paul in recent times, in regard to the collection (v. 6) as well as in their welcome to the false apostles (11:4, 13), Paul's comment here for the benefit of the Corinthians may be quite pointed.

Paul's office, however, is not separated from his person, as the words

---

45. A more direct contrast to the first part would have been, e.g., "but beyond what we expected."

46. Gk. πρῶτον does not mean (1) a temporal priority (as if commitment to Paul came later), but rather (2) a relative priority of self-giving, first to the Lord, appropriate because of his greatness, but also to Paul, his apostle. See the next note.

47. Gk. καὶ ἡμῖν is best understood as "[first to the Lord] also to us" (so Furnish, 402), appropriately widening the gap between the Lord and the apostle. "Also" is to be preferred to (1) "and" (RSV), which unhelpfully closes the gap between the Lord and the apostle, or (2) "then" (NIV), which suggests consecutive sequence of action (in which case ἔπειτα would have been expected).

48. I.e., Paul; a literary plural. See on 1:1; 2:14.

49. Gk. διὰ θελήματος θεοῦ, a phrase Paul also uses to introduce himself as "an apostle . . . through the will of God" (1 Cor 1:1; Eph 1:1; Col 1:1; 2 Tim 1:1; but Rom 15:32 is an exception to this).

50. See, e.g., Gal 1:16; Rom 1:5; 15:16; Eph 3:1-6.

"themselves they gave . . . also to *us"* indicate (see also 6:11-13; 12:14). Gospel ministry is very personal, establishing a bond between the bearer of that word and those who respond to the Lord through it. Moreover, Paul's words "they gave *themselves"* ward off in advance those Corinthians who suspect that, through the collection, he is really seeking their money (see also 12:14-18).

If the words "themselves they gave . . . also to us" relate to the recognition of Paul's apostolicity, it is a point that should not be lost on modern (Gentile) Christian readers. Paul expected that recognition of the Lord's authority meant, thereby, a recognition of his own apostleship. Many today — like the Corinthians then — are uncertain about the role of Paul's letters in their consciences. In their gift of themselves "to the Lord *also* to" his apostle "through the will of God," the Macedonians recognized Paul's God-given authority over their attitudes and actions, specifically here in regard to the collection. Paradoxically, however, Paul's high claims for his office and person are validated by his servant ministry (4:5), in imitation of the "meekness and gentleness of Christ" (cf. 10:1). Paul's present comments support the canonical status of his writings in the lives of believers and churches (10:9-11). But they provide no basis for prelacy in ministers, whether Protestant or Roman Catholic.

6 This is an important statement in the flow of the letter. Now (at last!) Paul explains to the church in Corinth why he has sent Titus back to them. He had prepared the readers for this moment by his joyful account of Titus's affection for the Corinthians when he was recently with them, which he gave at the close of the previous passage (7:13-15). Titus's return to the Achaian capital was prompted by the Macedonian churches' unanticipated interest in, and, indeed, their unexpected generosity toward, the collection (vv. 1-5). So, mindful that Titus had initiated the collection, Paul has urged[51] him to return to Corinth to bring it to completion. In this verse Paul lays the foundation for his pointed appeal to them, which he will make in the next verse.

Paul spells out the content of his appeal to Titus

that[52]
> just as he previously began   [this grace],
> so, too, he should   finalize this grace
> > > among you.

---

51. Gk. εἰς τὸ παρακαλέσαι ἡμᾶς, "In consideration of this, we have urged" (Furnish, 402). Paul's dispatch of Titus to Corinth resulted from (εἰς τό) the unanticipated generosity of the Macedonians (v. 5).

52. Gk. ἵνα is epexegetical, "that is."

Once again Paul uses his keyword from this passage, *charis* (cf. vv. 1, 4, and 7), here translated "act of grace" (NIV) or "gracious work" (RSV). Although Paul had taken the initiative in establishing the collection in various places, he regarded it as a free and gracious action on the part of those who responded. Paul, through Titus's action during the previous year (see on v. 10), called upon the Corinthians to support the appeal; but they remain free to participate or not participate in it (cf. vv. 3, 8). Thus it remains (literally) "a grace."

Now that Titus has returned from Corinth with good news of the discipline of the offender (7:6-12), Paul, further encouraged by Macedonian interest in the collection, but aware of the difficulties in Corinth on account of it, urges Titus to return to Achaia to bring it to finality. Titus would be the bearer of the present letter (cf. 8:16-17; 12:17-18), whose chapters 8–9 were devoted to the exhortation that the Corinthians bring it to completion. Let the Corinthians resolve this matter before the Macedonian representatives arrive, so as to be spared embarrassment (cf. 9:4).

Titus was eminently qualified for this task because (1) during the prior year (see on v. 10) he "began"[53] the appeal in Corinth, (2) he knew the current

---

53. Gk. προενήρξατο; NIV, "earlier made a beginning" (lit. "begin earlier"). This verb appears in the NT only in the two references in 2 Corinthians 8 (vv. 6 and 10). The latter reference pinpoints what the *Corinthians* "began to do earlier," to "a year ago" (ἀπὸ πέρυσι — cf. 9:2), whereas the former relates to *Titus's* institution of this "act of grace." The proximity of references of this rare verb, separated by only a few verses, although having different subjects, indicates that it must refer to the one event, namely, Titus's inauguration of the appeal in Corinth a year ago (i.e., during the previous calendar year — see on v. 10; 9:2). Although Titus is not mentioned in the First Letter, these verses make it likely that Titus's/the Corinthians' "earlier" action during the "previous year" underlies the inquiries from the Corinthians that Paul answers in the First Letter (1 Cor 16:1-2). Almost certainly the collection had been begun (by Titus) before the writing of 1 Corinthians.

Thus Titus is known to have gone to Corinth on at least three occasions: (1) during the previous year when he began the collection (8:6, 10; 9:2; cf. 1 Cor 16:1-2 — as bearer of the "Previous Letter"?); (2) as bearer of the "Severe Letter," when he observed the shortfall in the collection; and (3) as bearer of 2 Corinthians, with the "brief" to revive the collection, in the company of two brothers (8:6, 18, 22).

Titus's prospective third (known) visit (8:6, 16-17) touches on two related questions:

(1) Is the visit in 12:17-18 the same as, or subsequent to, the visit in prospect in 8:6, 16-17? Paul's later questions in 12:17-18 ("Did I exploit you through any of the men I sent — ἀπέσταλκα — perfect tense — to you? I urged Titus and sent with him the brother" — παρεκάλεσα . . . συναπέστειλα — aorists) are here taken to refer to Titus's third visit to Corinth that is in prospect in 8:6, 17, 24. Two reasons for this view are: (1) the coincidental mention of "*the* brother" whom Paul will send with Titus (8:18; 12:18), and (2) the proximity of παρεκάλεσα and συναπέστειλα regarding Titus (12:17-18), which reminds us of τὴν . . . παράκλησιν ἐδέξατο and συνεπέμψαμεν also regarding Titus (8:17-18).

A barrier to the identification of these visits is the reference to "our brother" (8:22) in addition to Titus and "the brother" (8:18), whereas 12:18 mentions only Titus and "the

situation, having just returned from Corinth, and (3) at that recent visit to Corinth Titus had been refreshed by and was affectionate toward the Corinthians (7:13-15). The "just as . . ." points to Titus's initial visit to Corinth, when he "began" the collection, and the balancing "so, too" to a forthcoming visit in regard to which Paul had "urged" Titus to "finalize" the collection. This was, almost certainly, the occasion when Titus was to come to Corinth bearing the present letter, in company with "the brother" and "our brother" (8:18, 22; 9:3; cf. 12:18).[54]

7 This verse is the climax of vv. 1-6; Paul now faces the Corinthians, in effect, with the challenge to complete the collection. At v. 1 he introduced the "grace of God," which, he said, had been "given in the Macedonian churches" (v. 1) and from whom it had "overflowed . . . in generosity" (v. 2). Now he addresses the gift-laden church in Corinth, where, however, the "grace" of generosity in the collection was not in evidence, calling on them to "overflow" in the same "grace" (i.e., as in v. 6).

The sentence (1) begins on a hortatory note, "but[55] just as you overflow . . . ," (2) lists some evidences of the grace of God among them,[56] and

---

brother." However, Titus and "the brother" are mentioned in the one verse in both 8:18 and 12:18, suggesting their association, independently, of "our brother."

(2) Does 12:17-18 belong to a letter subsequent to and separate from the letter to which 8:6, 16-17 belonged? Since, as argued in (1), 8:6, 18 and 12:17-18 refer to the same visit to Corinth by Titus, there is no necessity to regard 12:17-18 as belonging to a separate letter written subsequently to 8:6, 18. The aorist used for the prospective sending of "the brother" with Titus appears to be epistolary in meaning ("we are sending" — συνεπέμ-ψαμεν — 8:18; cf. 8:22). The aorist in the latter reference (12:18 — συναπέστειλα), however, when understood aspectively ("we have sent with"), may refer to the now accomplished dispatch of Titus and "the brother" with the current Letter to Corinth. In our view the unity of the letter — chapters 1–9 with chapters 10–13 — is not threatened by the aorist συναπέστειλα in 12:18. See the Introduction, 21-22.

54. The matching aorists παρακαλέσαι . . . ἐπιτελέσῃ refer to Paul's "appeal" to Titus to "complete" the collection at some point after its institution. This reference points either (1) to an interim visit to Corinth, as, e.g., when he delivered the "Severe Letter," or (2) to Titus's prospective visit to Corinth (8:17-18). Option (2) is almost certain to be correct because the flow of the argument from vv. 4-5 leads into a result clause at the beginning of v. 6. Thus Paul's surprise about the Macedonians' level of interest in the collection when impacted by Titus's arrival in Macedonia with bad news about the progress of the collection in Corinth has led Paul to write, "so that we appealed to Titus." Logically this points Titus's prospective return to Corinth (with this letter accompanied by "the brother" and "our brother" — 8:17; 9:3) in advance of Paul to reinstate the collection in Corinth.

55. Gk. ἀλλά is not a contrastive adversative here, but serves to lead into and to strengthen the exhortation that follows (see also Matt 9:18; Mark 9:22; 16:7; Luke 7:7; Acts 9:6; 10:20; 26:16).

56. This verse — one of the few in 2 Corinthians to echo the First Letter — finds parallels in 1 Cor 1:5 ("in *every* way you were enriched in [Christ Jesus] in all *speech* and

(3) concludes "[may you][57] also overflow in this grace"[58]:

> But just as
> > in everything
>
> you   overflow —
> > [in] faith,
> > and [in] speech,
> > and [in] knowledge,
> > and [in] all earnestness,
> > and [in] our love for you —
>
> [may you] also overflow in this grace.

Critical to the verse is the verb "overflow,"[59] which picks up the Macedonians' *overflowing* joy, "which has *overflowed* in the riches of their generosity" (v. 2). In the present verse it occurs first as a present indicative (what is happening) among the Corinthians and then as a present subjunctive (what should happen). This verb is written to encourage and admonish the Corinthians. They *overflow* in other "graces"; let them also *overflow* in this.

The various catalogues of charismata in the First Letter[60] do not appear to follow any logical system. This is not the case here. The first three — "faith" (to work miracles of healing?[61]), "speech" (teaching, glossolalia, and prophecy?[62]), and "knowledge" (an understanding of God and his ways?[63]) — relate to activities that are prized within the Corinthian assembly. To these he pointedly adds "all earnestness," which in the context of this letter means "all earnestness" *for Paul* (so 7:12), something that has only now been shown. The last in the list is "in our love to you,"[64] that is, the love that Paul has for them (see 6:11-12; 11:11; 12:15); there is no mention of their love for him.

The Corinthians were strong in activities that are local to and centered upon them (miracle-working faith, charismatic speech, and theological understanding), but weak on those that are for the benefit of those outside, in this

---

in all *knowledge*"), 1 Cor 1:7 ("you are not lacking in any spiritual gift"), and 1 Cor 12:8, 9 ("to another . . . the *word* of *knowledge* . . . to another *faith*").

57. Gk. ἵνα is elliptical and effectively introduces an imperative construction, "may you."

58. Gk. χάριτι, the keyword (χάρις) of chapters 8–9; see on vv. 1, 4, and 6.

59. Gk. περισσεύειν.

60. 1 Cor 1:4-7; 12:4-11; 13:1-3, 8; 14:6-7.

61. See 1 Cor 12:9-10.

62. See 1 Cor 12:10.

63. See 1 Cor 12:8; 8:1-7.

64. For discussion of variant readings see n. 2 above. To be preferred is the more difficult reading, "the love from us among you" (see Hughes, 297), rather than "the love from you in us." The latter would not sit well with 6:12.

case the "saints of Jerusalem." As they overflow in other "graces," let them also overflow in this.

Significantly, the grace of God is both (1) "given," that is, by God (see on v. 1), and, (2) at the same time, actively overflowing from believers. This can only mean that believers are not passive in the experience and ministry of the gifts of God. Indeed, the apostle designates certain gifts that believers are to desire (1 Cor 14:5, 12-19) and for which they are to pray (1 Cor 14:13). Clearly the grace of giving is among these, and in this case the climactic point to which the previous six verses have been leading.

2. Possible Misunderstandings Anticipated (8:8-15)

> 8 *I am not commanding you, but I want to test the sincerity of your love by comparing it with the earnestness of others.* 9 *For you know the grace of our Lord Jesus Christ, that though he was rich, yet for your sakes he became poor, so that you through his poverty might become rich.*
>
> 10 *And here is my advice about what is best for you in this matter: Last year you were the first not only to give but also to have the desire to do so.* 11 *Now finish the work, so that your eager willingness to do it may be matched by your completion of it, according to your means.* 12 *For if the willingness is there, the gift is acceptable according to what one has, not according to what he does not have.*
>
> 13 *Our desire is not that others might be relieved while you are hard pressed, but that there might be equality.* 14 *At the present time your plenty will supply what they need, so that in turn their plenty will supply what you need. Then there will be equality,* 15 *as it is written: "He who gathered much did not have too much, and he who gathered little did not have too little."*

Paul has appealed to the Corinthians, on the basis of the "overflow" of generosity on the part of the Macedonian churches, to "overflow" in this grace of generous giving, that is, to renew their participation in the collection (vv. 1-7). In the verses following he reminds them of the desire they had demonstrated "last year" when the collection was initiated (v. 10), exhorting them to complete "now" what they had begun (v. 11). But at the same time he offers them theological (christological) and biblical reasons for it (vv. 9, 13-15).

Throughout this passage Paul is responding to three possible misunderstandings of his words. First, he is giving "advice," not a "command"; their appropriate responses are "grace" and "willingness" (vv. 8-11). His method has been to point to the "eagerness of others" — the Macedonians (vv. 1-5), but now also the "grace of our Lord Jesus Christ" (v. 9) — to prove the genuineness of the Corinthians' love (v. 8). Second, his words are not a call to give more than they have, but to complete from their existing resources what they have desired a year earlier and, indeed, had begun to do (vv. 12-13). Third, the relief of the Jerusalemites is not at the cost of Corinthian impoverishment; it is for "equality" between the Jerusalemites and the Corinthians (vv. 13-15), a case in which Paul reflects his own deep roots in the OT. The net result is a cluster of reasons for the Corinthians' getting on with the collection.

8 Having exhorted the Corinthians to "overflow" also in the "grace" of generosity, Paul is quick to establish that his words are not given "as a command." Rather, "through" the Macedonians' "eagerness" the Corinthians would "prove the genuineness" of their own "love."

Thus Paul secures this correct understanding of his meaning by a careful "not . . . but"[1] statement.

> *Not* by a command
>
> I[2] speak,
>
> > *but* . . . to prove the genuineness of your love.

Paul's exhortation to the Corinthians in this matter is "not by a command."[3] By this Paul means (1) a "command" that issued from Christ to Paul as an apostle, which (2) Paul is to lay upon the churches. Paul uses this term in two ways. First, there is the command of the risen Christ that the gospel be proclaimed and obeyed.[4] In this case the apostolic "command" should be seen as closely connected with "the will of God," mentioned a few verses earlier, "through" which the Macedonians "gave themselves first to the Lord and to [his apostle]" (v. 5). The Macedonians obeyed the gospel that Christ commanded Paul to preach.[5] Second, there are "commands"[6] that emanated from the Lord, such as those relating to marriage (1 Cor 7:6, 25).

---

1. Gk. οὐκ . . . ἀλλά.

2. Paul's use of pronouns in this passage — whether singular (v. 3) or plural (vv. 1, 5, 6) — varies, lacking the broader consistency of plural in the apologia for the apostolic office (2:14–7:1) and of the singular in the "Fool's Speech" (11:1–12:13).

3. Gk. οὐ κατ' ἐπιταγήν; NIV, "I am not commanding you." See *New Docs.* 2.86 for evidence of usage for a divine command.

4. Paul himself was subject to just such a "command" (1 Tim 1:1; Tit 1:3).

5. A parallel may be seen in Rom 16:25-26 (RSV):

> . . . according to my gospel
> > and the preaching of Jesus Christ . . .
> > > [which] is now made known to all nations,
> > according to the *command* of the eternal God
> > > > to bring about the obedience of faith.

6. See Phlm 8, ". . . though I am bold enough in Christ to command you (ἐπιτάσσειν σοι) . . . ," referring to Paul's apostolic authority, which in the case of Phile-mon he did not then invoke.

But Paul has no such "command" from the Lord in regard to the collection. Rather, his exhortation is for their sakes: the collection is "to prove"[7] the genuineness[8] of the Corinthians' love. Such a "proving" has a positive intent, with the confident expectation of a good result. Although sharing in the collection is not a dominical command, it will serve to confirm and reinforce the reality of their love.

The instrument by which their love is "proved" is "the earnestness[9] [cf. v. 7] of others." Here Paul is referring — none too obliquely — to the earnestness and generosity of the Macedonians (vv. 2-5a).

Whereas obedience to a "command" of the Lord would be obligatory, participation in the collection is not. Rather, it is a free and spontaneous response (v. 3) to a situation of need, in demonstration of genuine love, an evidence of the "grace of God" toward and within the givers (vv. 1, 7).

9 The initial "For"[10] (1) explains why the collection is not a "command" (v. 8a) but a "grace" (cf. vv. 1, 4, 6, 7), a "voluntary" action (v. 3), and (2) points to the "grace . . . of Christ" as the example of "genuine love" (v. 8b). That "grace of . . . Christ"[11] the Corinthians already "know."[12] Paul states it as:

> that
>
>   for you   he became poor[13]   being rich
>
> in order that
>
>   you by his   poverty might become rich.

7. Gk. δοκιμάζων; NIV, "test." This is an iron forger's term and is common in Paul's letters as encouraging a practical expression of Christian behavior as the outworking of the principles of Christian belief. As such it is unlegalistic, calling for a godly "proving" of God's will in decision making and action (cf. 13:5; 1 Cor 11:28; Rom 2:18; 12:2; 14:22; Gal 6:4; Eph 5:10). Δοκιμάζειν should be contrasted with πειράζειν, which generally means testing intended to produce failure. This vocabulary cluster is important within these chapters (8:2, 22; 9:13; cf. 8:24, τὴν . . . ἔνδειξιν . . . ἐνδεικνύμενοι).

8. τὸ . . . γνήσιον; NIV, "sincerity." This is a substantive formed from the neuter singular adjective γνήσιον, which literally meant "true born," hence metaphorically "legitimate" or "genuine."

9. Gk. σπουδή; cf. the use of this word regarding the Corinthians in v. 7 (and back to 7:11, 12).

10. Gk. γάρ.

11. This is the first part of the famous "grace" with which 2 Corinthians concludes (13:14) and a liturgical benediction in its own right — hence its use of "our" in a context where Paul addresses the Corinthians as "you" (see also 1 Thess 5:28; 2 Thess 3:18; 1 Cor 16:23; Rom 16:20; Gal 6:18; Phil 4:23; Phlm 25).

12. Gk. γινώσκετε. Paul sometimes uses οἶδα in 2 Corinthians in contexts expressing the "knowledge" of Christian readers, e.g., 4:14; 5:1, 6, 11 (16). In this case, as so often, Paul presumes on the knowledge of his readers in the churches about the life and character of Christ (see on 10:1; cf. Gal 1:19; 3:16; 1 Thess 2:14-15; 4:4; 1 Cor 11:23-25; 15:4-8; Rom 1:3; 15:3, 5, 7; Phil 2:7-8; 1 Tim 6:13).

13. Gk. ἐπτώχευσεν, though taken by Furnish (404) as an ingressive aorist (i.e.,

The power of this highly figurative[14] statement derives from Paul's use of the antonyms poor/rich and from the exchange of Christ's circumstances for the Corinthians' (Christ's poverty/your rich[es]).[15] The result is that he picks up the theme of "grace" shown by the Macedonians in their poverty (vv. 1-5), but applies it to Christ's incarnation and crucifixion, as the climax of his appeal to the Corinthians likewise to exhibit such grace.

Paul's syntax is significant: (1) The word order gives priority to "for *you*" and juxtaposes "*you* by *his* poverty," and thus is pointed toward the ungenerous Corinthians whom Christ, by his voluntary impoverishment, has made rich. The sentence taken as a whole is bracketed by "you know" and "you become rich." (2) The verb tenses are expressive of both Christology and soteriology: "*being* rich"[16] (present participle) indicates Christ's "un-begun" preexistence,[17] whereas the temporally contrastive "he *became* poor"[18] (aorist) emphasizes his historic act of incarnation and — similarly — "that you might *become* rich"[19] (aorist) stresses the benefits of his historic act of atonement.[20]

"he began to become poor"), more probably refers to "the *event* of Christ's incarnation" (Hughes, 300 n. 24 — emphasis added).

14. This verse is expressed by the rhetorical device known as metonymy, whereby an abstract term (poverty) is used for a more concrete one (Christ's birth, life, and death). See also 5:21.

15. Although in 5:21 the subjects are God and "we" and in 8:9 the subjects are Christ and ("you") both texts use antonyms and the notion of Christ's exchange of situation purposefully for our benefit:

5:21	8:9
τὸν μὴ γνόντα ἁμαρτίαν . . .	πλούσιος ὤν . . .
ἁμαρτίαν ἐποίησεν . . .	ἐπτώχευσεν
ἵνα γενώμεθα	ἵνα
δικαιοσύνη θεοῦ	πλουτήσητε.

When 5:21 and 8:9 are amalgamated, an important Christology-soteriology emerges:

	5:21	8:9
Preexistence		πλούσιος ὤν
Incarnation/life		ἐπτώχευσεν
Sinlessness	τὸν μὴ γνόντα ἁμαρτίαν	
Death/Atonement	[θεὸς] ἁμαρτίαν ἐποίησεν	
Justification	γενώμεθα δικαιοσύνη θεοῦ	πλουτήσητε

16. Gk. πλούσιος ὤν; NIV, "though he was rich." Here used in a concessive sense.

17. J. D. G. Dunn, *Christology*, 121-23, disputes the pretemporal existence of Jesus; against this view see A. T. Hanson, *Image*, 64-66.

18. Gk. ἐπτώχευσεν.

19. Gk. πλουτήσητε.

20. An analogous connection between Christ's sacrificial ministry and that of apostles and pastors in continuity with his sacrifice are to be found in this verse. If Christ's poverty makes believers rich, so, too, does the apostolic ministry (cf. 6:10 — "poor, yet making many rich"; cf. 11:7).

(3) The active voice *"he* became poor" teaches the Corinthians that Christ *voluntarily* — that is, by grace — impoverished himself to enrich them. Let them do likewise — for others!

If the poor Macedonians provided one canon by which the rich Corinthians could measure their lack of grace (vv. 1-7), they should know that there is an even greater one, the Lord Jesus Christ. By pointing the ungracious Corinthians to the "grace of our Lord Jesus Christ" in that rather mundane, now long-forgotten situation, Paul has given a statement about Jesus that has been treasured by readers in every generation since. By these words Paul teaches us that Jesus' personal existence did not begin with his birth in Bethlehem in the last years of Herod the Great. Paul's words "he *was* rich" indicate Jesus' eternal preexistence, while the contrastive words "he *became* poor" speak of his entry into the stream of history at a particular time and place. The juxtaposition of his riches with his poverty is calculated to set in sharp relief[21] the greatness of his wealth in that former existence with the depth of poverty in his incarnate life.[22] Jesus' poverty is apparent at every point — whether at his birth in Bethlehem, as the Son of Man with nowhere to lay his head, or, in particular, in his death by crucifixion when God "made him sin."[23] The poverty of his birth, life, and death is "an indissoluble unity."[24]

What are these "riches" that Christ gives to his people? Two possibilities are suggested, one from an earlier passage, the other from this passage. In an earlier passage Paul also mentioned "grace," namely:

in [Christ] we . . . become the righteousness of God . . .
do not receive the *grace* of God in vain. . . . (5:21–6:1)

Most probably Paul would have the Corinthians and other readers understand that believers are "rich" in the "righteousness[25] of God" through Jesus' death

---

21. Hughes states: "From highest heaven He descended to Calvary and the grave. None was richer than He; none became poorer than He" (299).

22. The best commentary on this text is Philippians 2. There Paul amplifies Jesus' "riches" by noting that he was "in very nature God" and that he possessed "equality with God" (v. 6). He expanded upon Jesus' poverty as he "made himself nothing," he "took the nature of a slave," and he "humbled himself and became obedient to death — even death on a cross" (Phil 2:7, 8).

23. Luke 2:7; 9:5; 2 Cor 5:21. According to J. Denney, *Death,* 179, "The New Testament knows nothing of an incarnation which can be defined apart from its relation to the atonement. . . . Not Bethlehem but Calvary is the focus of revelation." J. I. Packer, *Knowing God,* 51, declares, "The crucial significance of the cradle at Bethlehem lies in its place in the sequence of steps that led the Son of God to the cross of Calvary."

24. E. Brunner, *The Mediator,* 399.

25. Gk. δικαιοσύνη can be translated "righteousness" or "justification."

for them, as proclaimed by the ministers of reconciliation. The possession of these riches is, by God's promise, "now," although their inheritance is physically entered into at the end time, the gift of the Holy Spirit being the "deposit" in the meantime of what is to come (5:5; cf. Gal 5:5; Rom 8:23-24).

But in the context of the present verse Paul has also referred to the "overflow" of "grace[s]" in regard to the gifts evident within the Corinthian church — speech, knowledge, earnestness, and Paul's love for them (v. 7). There is a connection between the "grace" of God/Christ shown toward humankind and revealed in the saving work of Christ and the "gifts" manifest within the body of believers. As believers receive the one, so also they receive the others. In that sense all congregations of true belief are to be "charismatic."[26]

Since we are made "rich" by Christ's grace — in both salvation and gifts — the appropriate response can only be our generosity to others. This is the message of these two chapters. Grace begets grace!

Beyond that, however, this great text on the incarnation, life, and death of Jesus Christ is in line with Paul's view of ministry as nontriumphalist and "slave"like, which is a major strand running through the entire letter. Christ's sacrificial other-centeredness, as expressed in this verse, tells the story of Christianity itself, a story that was under assault in Corinth at that time through the self-centeredness of the "superlative" apostles.

10 Paul moves directly from the unusually powerful imagery — and thus theology — of v. 9 to a direct application of all of this to the Corinthians themselves. At the same time his opening "And so"[27] sets the words following in contrast with v. 8. There he did not speak to them as by "a command" (v. 8); here he "give[s]" his "advice[28] — not command — in this"[29] matter. This "advice" is, he explains,[30] "helpful for you,"[31] an expression

---

26. See Rom 6:23, where the *charisma* of God is his gift of eternal life.

27. Gk. καί — for this usage see BAGD 1.2-3.

28. The critical words are ἐπιταγή ("command") and γνώμη ("advice"), which are contrasted also in 1 Cor 7:25 (where δίδοναι + γνώμη also occurs). For other examples of γνώμη see 1 Cor 1:10; 7:40; Phlm 14 (cf. Phlm 8). Not that such "advice" is not serious; it arises from one who is guided by God's Spirit (cf. 1 Cor 7:40). It is "serious apostolic counsel" (Furnish, 405). Nonetheless, such "advice" is not obligatory; otherwise their response could not be "of grace."

29. Gk. ἐν τούτῳ is ambiguous. Although it could mean either (1) "in regard to the collection," or (2) "in what I am saying," (2) is more likely.

30. Gk. γάρ.

31. Gk. ὑμῖν συμφέρει; NIV, "what is best for you." The verb συμφέρειν is also found in 12:1 and frequently in Stoic writers (see K. Weiss, *TDNT* 9.72-73). See S. N. Olson, "Confidence," 214, who sees Paul's use of this verb as evidence of the influence on him of Hellenistic rhetorical forms. Paul, however, regards "what is helpful" as that which "builds up" the church (1 Cor 10:23).

that stands in contrast with "what is lawful" in the First Letter (1 Cor 6:12; 10:23). Good ethical behavior in such a matter is responded to freely, in and by grace (see v. 3).[32]

But to what does the word *"this"* that is "helpful" refer? Is it (1) the liberal giving to the collection (vv. 6-7), or is it (2) the giving of "advice" rather than a "command"? The remainder of the verse suggests (2). Their "wanting" in regard to the collection was and is the important factor.

His address to the Corinthians as "you who," followed by "not only . . . but also,"[33] serves to make an ascending contrast between their "doing" and their "wanting."[34] Their *doing* is in abeyance, but their *wanting* to participate in the collection remains and is a point of Paul's appeal to them.

Paul focuses on what happened "last year"[35] when the Corinthians

> previously began[36]
> > not only   to do
> > but rather[37] to want
> > > > [this gracious work] — cf. v. 6).

Clearly Paul puts the *wanting* above the *doing.* Why is this? Most likely the wanting (1) reflected the voluntary manner in which the Corinthians agreed

---

32. See also Phlm 14 (RSV): "I preferred to do nothing without your consent (γνώμη) in order that your goodness might not be by compulsion (κατὰ ἀνάγκην) but of your own free will (κατὰ ἑκούσιον)."

33. Gk. οὐ μόνον . . . ἀλλὰ καί compares something important with something more important (cf. 8:19).

34. Two articular infinitives τὸ ποιῆσαι and τὸ θέλειν are connected. The latter, a present, emphasizes that their *wanting* is still something Paul can count on, though their *doing,* an aorist, is not occurring. The expected order, "both to will and to do," is set forth in Phil 2:13 (cf. Rom 7:15-16).

35. Gk. ἀπὸ πέρυσι means "from last year," i.e., the previous calendar year, not "a year ago" (as the RSV, but now corrected in the NRSV). Depending on when this letter was written, this could have been a matter of only a few months or as many as twenty-three-months earlier. As to which calendar Paul is referring to — whether Roman (which began Jan. 1), Jewish liturgical (which began in the spring), or Macedonian/Jewish civil (which began in the autumn) — there can be no certainty, though there have been many suggestions (see Furnish, 405-6). 1 Cor 16:1-3 presumes that the collection had already been initiated — hence their clarificatory question, which Paul answers in these verses. After their visit to the Achaian capital Timothy returned to Ephesus, precipitating Paul's emergency visit and the writing of the "Severe Letter." This in turn was followed by Paul's flight to Troas and from there to Macedonia, where there was interaction with the Macedonian churches prior to the writing of this letter. It must be concluded, therefore, that a period of many — rather than a few — months is presupposed by "last year."

36. Gk. προενήρξασθε; NIV, "you were the first." This is a rare verb that appears in the NT only at v. 6 *(q.v).*

37. Gk. ἀλλὰ καί; NIV, "but also."

to contribute, and (2) was a present reality, something to appeal to. Their *wanting* was at that time the "proving" of a genuineness of love (see v. 8) that had been present for some time but that is not presently expressed in *doing*.[38] Since participation is not a "command," a willing desire must occur before any tangible action is taken.[39] The point, of course, is that in v. 11 he will pick up these in reverse, appealing to their "willing" to bring the "doing" to completion.

Paul's exhortations to resume the collection must preserve intact the doctrine of grace.

11 Paul's opening words, "But now,"[40] stand in contrast with the Corinthians' known "want[ing] . . . last year" (v. 10). Let the Corinthians *now* complete the collection so that their initial eagerness in wanting to do so is matched by their completion of it, from what they have.

The first part of the verse is an imperative ("But now complete the doing"), while the second part gives the purpose[41] of the first[42]:

> in order that
> > even as there was the readiness in   wanting,
> > so also there [will be readiness] in completing
> > > out of what you have.

Critical to this verse and to those that succeed it (vv. 12, 19; 9:2) is the noun "willingness"[43] (RSV, "readiness"), which is consistent with Paul's emphasis on the need for a "voluntary" response (see vv. 3-4). Only on this basis can their action "prove" or "demonstrate" the "genuineness" of their "love" (v. 8).

Paul's "the completion" in the second part picks up "but now complete" of the first part (cf. v. 6). This, however, is qualified by "out of

---

38. It is reasonable to assume that the difficulties associated with the "Painful Visit" and "the Severe Letter" were major factors in the falling away of the collection in Corinth. It is likely that the support of the collection — or the lack of it — was a measure of Paul's standing with the Corinthians.

39. Plummer, 242, suggests that the Corinthians may have been the first to begin to respond to the collection, hence the significance afforded to their desire for it.

40. Gk. νυνὶ δέ. These initial words, "But now," are quite sharp because (1) they call for action "right now," (2) in the light of the now-arrived "brothers" in Corinth who will soon be followed by Paul himself, with "Macedonians" (8:16–9:4). Following this urgent opening note Paul calls on them to "complete the doing."

41. Gk. ὅπως.

42. The second part, while expressed concessively (Gk. καθάπερ . . . οὕτως), does not effectively diminish the force of the prior "willing," which is to encourage the Corinthians to "do."

43. Gk. ἡ προθυμία.

what you have"[44] (see also vv. 12-15). Although the Macedonians have given beyond their means (vv. 2-3, 5), Paul does not wish to imply that a similar course must be taken by the Corinthians. Possibly he is sensitive to the allegation that, in view of their past misdemeanors toward him, he may be attempting to gain some kind of moral advantage over them by pointing to the Macedonians' sacrificial generosity. Paul is a pastor, not a manipulator. He will be content when their present "doing" matches their earlier "wanting."

12 Having introduced the notion of "willingness,"[45] Paul now explains[46] that if there is "willingness," it is "acceptable"[47] in proportion to what one has, not to what one does not have.

But "acceptable" to whom? The cultic overtones of the word and its associations[48] make it likely that it is to God that such "willingness"[49] is "acceptable." However, it is not the gift — neither the fact of it nor its amount — that is "acceptable" to God, but the sincere motive that inspires it, namely, "willingness." Paul's sentiment here is entirely in line with the OT prophets' teaching that the right attitude to Yahweh is more important than the sacrifice itself.[50]

To reinforce the point that he is not seeking from the Corinthians a heroic sacrifice along the lines of the Macedonians, Paul adds that such contributions[51] should be

---

44. Gk. ἐκ τοῦ ἔχειν, which is comparable to the Macedonians' giving κατὰ δύναμιν (v. 3). In this verse and the next ἔχειν is taken in the sense of "to be able." Other examples of this use are Matt 18:25; Luke 7:42; 14:28; Acts 4:14; 25:26; Eph 4:28; 2 Pet 1:15.

45. Gk. ἡ προθυμία, as in v. 11.

46. Note the initial explanatory γάρ, "For."

47. Gk. εὐπρόσδεκτος (6:2; Rom 15:16; 1 Pet 2:5). But see, too, Rom 15:31, where Paul expresses concern that his service for Jerusalem may be "acceptable" (εὐπρόσδεκτος) to the saints.

48. Rom 12:1 (εὐάρεστον τῷ θεῷ), Phil 4:18 (θυσίαν δεκτήν, εὐάρεστον τῷ θεῷ) and Heb 13:16 (εὐαρεστεῖται ὁ θεός).

49. Cf. LXX 2 Chron 29:31.

50. E.g., 1 Sam 15:22; Ps 40:6-8; 50:8, 9; Isa 1:11-13, 16, 17; Jer 7:22-23; Mic 6:6-8. Nonetheless, this is a call for prudent giving as in 1 Cor 16:2, where the readers were encouraged to give (1) *systematically* ("on the first day of every week, each of you is to put something aside"), (2) *proportionately* ("as he may prosper. . . ," RSV), and (3) *without duress* ("so that contributions need not be made when I come"). A different point is made in the Lord's commendation of the poor widow (Mark 12:42-44); it is for her wholehearted generosity, relative to the gifts of those who could well afford them.

51. This is an elliptical sentence. The "readiness" implies "to contribute" (or such like), and the verb "has" or "has not" implies the impersonal subject "one." Thus the sentence may run: "For if the readiness [to contribute] is there, it is acceptable, in proportion to what [one] has, not in proportion to what [one] does not have."

in proportion to what[52] [one] has,
not in proportion to what   [one] does not have.[53]

Let the Corinthians be quite clear that Paul is not implying that they should give in the way the Macedonians have. That would be to miss his point altogether. Rather, their proper course is to do what they said they would do, but which they have not yet done.[54]

At this point Paul switches his discussion from the Corinthians and the Macedonians (vv. 1-12) to the Corinthians and the Jerusalemites. Whereas the Macedonians had recently been spontaneously gracious and sacrificially generous, the Corinthians had allowed their original intention to participate in the collection to lapse. Now he anticipates[55] a Corinthian question: Is it not unfair that the Jerusalemites should be relieved at the cost of our impoverishment?

13-14   The initial explanatory "For"[56] springs from Paul's assurance of the previous verse that he is not encouraging the Corinthians to give from what they do not have. This leads him to address another possible concern, that others be relieved at the cost of their own suffering.

For
    not that [there is to be] relief   for others
    [and]   hardship[57] for you.

Not only is there not to be "hardship" for them (by giving from what they do not have — v. 12), but the relief that will be sent to "others" will not be at the cost of such "hardship." These "others" in this case refer to the

---

52. Gk. καθό = καθ' ὅ = "in proportion to what."

53. Paul's word here echoes the apocryphal Tob 4:8 (RSV): "If you have many possessions, make your gift from them in proportion; if few, do not be afraid to give according to the little you have." The entire passage (Tob 4:1-11) is devoted to almsgiving.

54. *Contra* Furnish, 419, who infers from this passage that the Corinthians had retained their intention to contribute, but had failed to do so then because they felt the result would be inadequate. The historical context, however, makes it more likely that the rupture of Paul's relationships with them lay behind their discontinuance of the collection. Paul's insistence that the giving be according to their capacity is to guard against any charge of moral manipulation (cf. 4:2; 7:2; 12:16-18), based on the Corinthians' relative affluence over against the Macedonians' poverty.

55. Paul is probably anticipating their questions rather than responding to articulated questions.

56. Gk. γάρ.

57. Gk. ἄνεσις ἄλλοις . . . θλίψις ὑμῖν; NIV, "others relieved . . . you hard pressed." For ἄνεσις see on 2:13, and for θλίψις see on 1:4.

413

"saints" (see on v. 4), the poor among the believers in Jerusalem[58] (cf. Rom 15:26).[59]

Thus, to the question, "Is Paul asking us to give beyond our means," his reply is that they should do what they originally agreed to do (vv. 10-12; cf. 1 Cor 16:1-2). But, they inquire, "Will our relief to the Jerusalemites impoverish us"? Again, no. It will be a matter of "equality," as Paul proceeds to explain by the following chiasmus[60] ("your . . . their . . . their . . . your").

13	. . . but according to equality	
14 At the present time		
	your surplus is	A
	for *their* shortfall,	B
that	*their* surplus might be for	B
	your shortfall,	A
that	there might be equality.	

This chiasmus is introduced by "according to equality" and ended by "equality."[61] What does Paul mean by this principle[62] of "equality"? Does he (1) anticipate that if the economic circumstances were reversed, the Jerusalemites would reciprocally relieve the Corinthians' need,[63] as perhaps the next verse implies? Or (2) will the Corinthians' benefit be in the form of the Jerusalemites' loving and prayerful fellowship[64] with the Corinthians, as 9:14 implies? The most likely answer is that Paul teaches that (2) will definitely occur and that (1) would occur if reversed economic circumstances arose.

Critical to these verses is the phrase "at the present time,"[65] which could

58. Note that Jerusalem is not mentioned in these chapters relating to the collection; but see 1 Cor 16:3.

59. For a response to the view that Paul is thinking of the Macedonians, see Hughes, 306-7.

60. That chiasmus is based on the pronouns. This is not the pattern based on the antithetical nouns — surplus (περίσσευμα) . . . shortfall (ὑστέρημα) . . . surplus (περίσσευμα) . . . shortfall (ὑστέρημα).

61. Gk. ἐξ ἰσότητος . . . ἰσότης. The term ἰσότης is found elsewhere in the NT only at v. 14 and Col 4:1. It is, however, found in Hellenistic writers such as Philo, who praises "equality" as the highest good (*Special Laws* 4.165-66) and who regards "equality" of contributions as "proportionate to the valuation of [an] estate . . ." (*Who Is the Heir?*, 145). The use of ἐκ in ἐξ ἰσότητος, "according to equality," is similar to v. 11, ἐκ τοῦ ἔχειν, "based on ability."

62. The ἐξ is critical. Just as they are to be governed by the principle of giving according to what they have (τὸ ἐπιτελέσαι ἐκ τοῦ ἔχειν), so they are to be governed by the principle of "equality" (ἐξ ἰσότητος).

63. So, e.g., Plummer, 245; Hughes, 306.

64. So, e.g., Harris, 370; Allo, 220.

65. Gk. ἐν τῷ νῦν καιρῷ.

point either to (1) their need to act "now" (v. 11) in contrast to wanting to do so "last year" (v. 10), or, in the light of similar references,[66] could be taken (2) in an eschatological rather than a temporal sense. My preference[67] is for (2). In this case it would refer to the era when the promises of God concerning the new covenant of righteousness and the Spirit and the long-awaited "day of salvation" have been fulfilled (see on 1:18-22; 3:3; 5:14–6:2). This is the "now"-time; the cosmos has been reconciled to God and a new covenant is in place.

As a consequence of this now-fulfilled eschatology there is a world-wide covenant people — "the household of faith," as Paul calls it elsewhere (Gal 6:10; cf. John 21:23; 1 Pet 5:9). Within this international fraternity there is — and there is to be — "equality." This is to be expressed in the first instance in a spiritual fellowship and unity among the ecumenical body of believers, but, where appropriate and necessary, it should issue in material assistance as well, as "each . . . may prosper."[68] Paul's brief reference to "equality" within this fulfillment framework ("in this present time") gives it a significance that is abiding and an application that is universal.[69] The eschatological setting lifts the importance of the collection from the particular to the general, providing the basis for a theology of practical relief among "the Israel of God" (Gal 6:16) that will apply until the Parousia.

15 Paul illustrates the principle of "equality" (vv. 13-14) that is to apply between the churches — Jewish and Gentile, as it happens — by a quotation[70] from the OT (LXX Exod 16:18[71]). In that text the Israelites gathered varying amounts of the manna, but they were to have access to only

66. See Rom 3:26; 8:18 for the use of this phrase in eschatological contexts (cf. 11:5).

67. Following Martin, 267, but *contra* Furnish, 408.

68. 1 Cor 16:2; cf. Gal 6:10 — ". . . as we have opportunity, let us do good . . . to those who are of the household of faith." This is not a rigid and imposed "equality," as in communism; the initiative to give and the dimension of the gift lie with the giver.

69. The view that "in order that their surplus might be for your shortfall" points to the reconciliation of Israel as a prelude to the "final homecoming of the nations" (thus Martin, 267) is unwarranted. By that understanding Paul's words were applicable only to that generation, rather than throughout the entire Christian dispensation.

70. Paul frequently uses the formula καθὼς γέγραπται to introduce an OT citation (see, e.g., 8:9; 1 Cor 1:31; 2:9, and frequently in Romans). The perfect tense indicates that, though written in the past, it still speaks, and the passive voice implies that God is the subject; it was written — ultimately by God — and God continues to speak through it. This is the fourth of five scripture citations in this letter, where, however (apart from 9:9), the introductory words differ — κατὰ τὸν γεγραμμένον (4:13); λέγει γάρ (6:2); καθὼς εἶπεν ὁ θεὸς ὅτι (6:16-18).

71. See also Philo, *Who Is the Heir?*, 191, where the theme is "equality" and where the same text is quoted: "One essential form of equality is the proportional, in which the few are regarded as equal to the many, and the small to the greater. This is often employed by states on special occasions when they order each citizen to make an equal contribution from his property, not of course numerically equal, but equal in the sense that it is proportionate to the valuation of his estate. . . ."

"an omer apiece." Thus the one who had gathered much did not have too much, while the one who had gathered little did not have too little.

By his use of this scripture in a passage relating to Gentile believers helping Jewish believers (see on v. 14), Paul appears to be pointing to an ecumenism among believers. As God imposed "equality" within Israel during the wilderness pilgrimage, so at "the present time" under the "new covenant" (3:2-6; cf. 6:16), when there is, by fulfillment, an "Israel of God" (Gal 6:16), there is also to be "equality." In this the time of God's eschatological fulfillment (v. 14),[72] that "equality" is to be voluntary (vv. 3, 8-9), joyous, and generous (v. 2).

3. Commendation of Three Men Paul Is Sending to Corinth (8:16-24)

16 *I thank God, who put[1] into the heart of Titus the same concern I have for you.* 17 *For Titus not only welcomed our appeal, but he is coming to you with much enthusiasm and on his own initiative.* 18 *And we are sending along with him the brother who is praised by all the churches for his service to the gospel.* 19 *What is more, he was chosen by the churches to accompany us[2] as we carry the offering, which we administer in order to honor the Lord himself[3] and to show our eagerness to help.* 20 *We want to avoid any criticism of the way we administer this liberal gift.* 21 *For we are taking pains to do what is right, not only in the eyes of the Lord but also in the eyes of men.*

22 *In addition, we are sending with them our brother who has often proved to us in many ways that he is zealous, and now even more so because of his great confidence in you.* 23 *As for Titus, he is my partner and fellow worker among you; as for our brothers, they are representatives of the churches and an honor to Christ.* 24 *Therefore show[4]*

---

72. *Contra* Barrett, 227, and Martin, 267, who see this text as purely illustrative, with no christological, eschatological, or ecclesiological overtones.

1. The aorist δόντι ($\aleph^3$ p⁴⁶ D E G L), followed by the NIV, NAB, and NRSV, although the easier reading, is preferred to διδόντι ($\aleph$* B C K P), followed by the RSV, JB, and TEV. The aorist reflects Titus's decision in the (recent) past to return to Corinth.

2. Which is to be preferred: (1) σὺν τῇ χάριτι (B C P 33 1739 vg syrᵖ copᵇᵒ,ˢᵃ), or (2) ἐν τῇ χάριτι (p⁴⁶ $\aleph$ D G K etc.)? (1) is marginally preferable, being the harder reading; a scribe would have difficulty with ... συνέκδημος ἡμῶν σύν. ... There is little difference; either way it means "with this offering."

3. Gk. αὐτοῦ is omitted by B C D* F G L, giving an easier reading. See Barrett, 217 n. 2, for argument in favor of retention.

4. Although ἐνδεικνύμενοι is less well attested (e.g., B D* F G 44) than ἐνδείξασθαι ($\aleph$ C Dᵇ,ᶜ K L P), it is to be preferred as the more difficult reading (grammatically). Possibly it is to be understood as a semitism denoting an imperative.

these men the proof of your love and the reason for our pride in you,
so that the churches can see it.

We sense that a critical point in the letter has now been reached. Having made his appeal to the Corinthians to complete the collection (vv. 1-7) and, further, having anticipated and responded to their misgivings (vv. 8-15), the apostle now — at last! — commends to the church Titus, his chief delegate (vv. 16-17), along with a brother renowned among the Macedonian churches (v. 18), and with them a third brother (v. 22). The three men are — almost certainly — the bearers of the letter.[5] The finalization of the collection among the Corinthians is to be fulfilled prior to Paul's arrival by the impact on the Corinthians of chapters 8–9 of this letter, as well as the ministry of these three men in Corinth.

This short passage serves, in part, as a letter of commendation[6] within the wider letter.[7] Titus and the renowned brother — and with them, the other brother — are well qualified to bring the letter to Corinth. Titus and the lesser brother are "earnest for" the Corinthians (vv. 16, 22); the renowned brother has been appointed by the churches (vv. 18-19).

Paul's commendation of them, however, also provides him with the opportunity to defend himself from possible criticism and misunderstanding in regard to the collection (vv. 19-21): (1) the collection gives expression to Paul's "goodwill," that is, for the needs of the saints in Jerusalem (v. 19); (2) he has taken forethought so as not to be blamed for its administration (v. 20), aiming (3), in particular, to do what is honorable before people (v. 21). Paul was conscious of Corinthian suspicion about him in relationship to money (4:2; 6:3; 7:2; 12:16-18).

The presence in Corinth of these three men, in particular the two Macedonians, will give the Corinthians the opportunity to complete the collection, thus demonstrating their love for the "saints" as well as their worthiness of the confidence Paul has expressed concerning them (v. 23)

---

5. It is noteworthy that Paul leaves it to this advanced point within the letter to introduce and commend the men who have brought the letter that is now being read to the church. Titus, however, was well known in Corinth and needed no introduction. "The brother" whom Paul is sending "with" Titus (also 12:18) presumably needs no introduction, though "our brother" may not have been known in Corinth. It seems that a critical moment in the letter is now being reached. The chief point of the letter — which they are bringing — is that the Corinthians are to prepare themselves for Paul's pending final coming (and, with Paul, other Macedonians — 9:3). The final chapters are dotted with references to Paul's final visit to Corinth.

6. See on 3:1. However, it is not a letter of recommendation pure and simple since v. 24 resumes the appeal to the Corinthians in regard to the men who have been sent.

7. See also Rom 16:1ff.

16 This verse, a thanksgiving for Titus' loyalty to the Corinthians, comes at an important point[8] in Paul's argument. Paul had challenged the Corinthians to "overflow" in regard to the collection (v. 7). Then he had anticipated various objections, that (1) the collection was a "command" (v. 8), (2) they were being asked to give beyond their means (vv. 12-13), and (3) the relief of the Jerusalemites would be at the cost of Corinthian impoverishment (vv. 13-15). Having pointed to Titus's good relationships with the Corinthians during his recent visit (7:13-16), and on noting the Macedonian initiatives to participate in the collection (vv. 4-5), he had urged Titus to return to Corinth to finalize the collection (v. 6).

Now Paul begins a passage commending the three delegates to Corinth by directing his thanks to God for Titus,[9] his "partner and fellow worker" (v. 23). It is a measure of Paul's deep thankfulness for Titus that he uses such a thanksgiving formula[10] for him. Titus will be critical in the success of this project. His special status in relationship to Paul is mentioned at v. 23. Since Titus had come from Corinth in fairly recent times, the Corinthians may have been surprised to see him so soon.

> Thanks be to God,
>> who gave[11] the same earnestness
>>> for you
>>>> in the heart of Titus.

The basis for Paul's thanksgiving is that God has "given" to Titus "the same earnestness"[12] that he has given to Paul. Just as God "gave grace" to the Macedonian churches to enable them to give generously to the collection (v. 1), so, too, God gave "earnest" care both to Paul and Titus, which, he

---

8. The particle δέ in χάρις δέ . . . marks the next point to be introduced. See on 2:14.

9. See on 2:13; 7:6.

10. Gk. χάρις δὲ τῷ θεῷ — an expression of formal thanksgiving Paul uses elsewhere at 2:14 (τῷ δὲ θεῷ χάρις); 9:15 (χάρις τῷ θεῷ); 1 Cor 15:57 (τῷ δὲ θεῷ χάρις); and Rom 6:17 (χάρις δὲ τῷ θεῷ). The keyword of chapters 8–9 is χάρις, here used for "thanks [be to God"], but with different nuances elsewhere (8:1, 4, 6, 7, 9, 19; 9:8, 14, 15).

11. Gk. τῷ θεῷ τῷ δόντι; NIV, "I thank God, who put. . . ." See the note to v. 1 above. Only of the living God, whom people of Hellenistic culture came to know only through the publication of the OT scriptures (LXX) and the proclamation of the gospel, can one say, "Thanks be to God, who gave. . . ." For other examples in which an attribute of God is expressed in terms of what God actively does, see, e.g., 1:4, 9, 21; 2:14; 7:6.

12. Gk. σπουδή. Most commentators interpret "the same earnestness" as referring to Paul, even though Paul has not spoken directly of his "earnestness" toward them. It is possible, but less likely, that he means "the same earnestness . . . you [Corinthians] have for us" (based on 8:7; 7:11, 12) or "the same earnestness [the Macedonians have for us]" (based on 8:8).

pointedly adds, is "for you [Corinthians]." Tactfully, however, Paul does not immediately mention the collection (but see v. 24).

Like immature children who do not perceive their parents' love for them, the Corinthians must be reminded of Christ's "grace" toward them (see on v. 9) and of his servants' "earnestness" toward them (cf. 6:11-13). Beyond that, as Plummer observes, "The Corinthians might think that the zeal of Titus for the relief fund was zeal on behalf of the Jerusalem poor; but it was really on behalf of the Corinthians. They would be the chief losers if a suitable sum was not raised in Corinth."[13] It is doubtful whether the Corinthians understood the word of the Lord, "It is more blessed to give than to receive" (Acts 20:35).

17 The evidence "for"[14] the assertion of the previous verse — that God gave Titus "earnestness for [the Corinthians]" — is now given. It is in two connected parts, as indicated by the "on the one hand . . . on the other" construction.[15]

> For,
>> to be sure, he welcomed[16] our appeal,[17]
>
> but   being very earnest of his own accord
>> he is going forth[18] to you.[19]

Such is his characteristic "earnestness" that Paul did no more than make his appeal to Titus; his response was immediate and voluntary.[20] Thus Titus is, with the Macedonians, an example to the Corinthians of unconditioned and voluntary response in godly behavior, which for them relates to the collection.

---

13. Plummer, 247.

14. Gk. ὅτι, expressing cause.

15. Gk. μὲν . . . δέ.

16. Gk. ἐδέξατο is an epistolary aorist, translated as a present (so Plummer, 247; Moule, 12). Furnish, 421, however, thinks it may be a "real aorist" even though "is going" (v. 17b) and "we are sending" (v. 18) are epistolary aorists. Titus's "welcoming" would be already past for the writer. Either way, the meaning is not affected.

17. Gk. παράκλησιν, which could be "encouragement," but is more likely "appeal" (based on the use of the cognate verb in v. 6 and the use of the same noun with the same meaning in v. 4).

18. Gk. ἐξῆλθεν is an epistolary aorist, translated as a present.

19. The repetition of "you" (Corinthians) in this passage is significant. God gave his "earnestness" to Paul and Titus "for *you*" (v. 16); Titus is Paul's "partner . . . and fellow worker toward *you*" (κοινωνὸς ἐμὸς καὶ εἰς ὑμᾶς συνεργός). Is Paul reassuring them of their place in his affections (cf. 6:11-12; 11:7-8)? Were they jealous of the Macedonians?

20. Gk. αὐθαίρετος; NIV, "on his own initiative." The same word is used of the voluntariness of the Macedonians' response to the collection (see on v. 3). Other words that express the keyword χάρις are περισσεύειν (8:2, 7), σπουδή (8:7, 8), τὸ θέλειν (8:10), and ἡ προθυμία (8:11, 12).

18 Titus does not come alone, however.[21] Paul's "*with* [Titus][22] we are sending[23] . . ." signals (1) that Titus was the preeminent member of Paul's delegation,[24] but (2) another — "the brother,"[25] famed in the work of the gospel among all the churches — has also been sent.

The names of "the brother" and of the other associate, "our brother" (v. 22), are not given (see on v. 19 for comment as to his possible identity); presumably Titus will introduce them in Corinth. As with Titus, Paul is careful to establish the good credentials of those he is sending. As to this first unnamed "brother," his

> praise
>> for proclaiming the gospel
>> rings through all the churches.[26]

Although the purpose of this visit was financial and administrative, Paul sends a man who is noted in the churches "in regard to the gospel." He can think of no higher commendation.

But does Paul mean by "all the churches"[27] (1) all the churches everywhere, (2) all the churches of Judaea (so Nickle), (3) all the churches raised up by his mission in Macedonia, Achaia, and Asia (supported by 11:28; 1 Cor 7:17; Acts 20:3-4[28]), or (4) all the churches in Macedonia (so most commentators, but not Hughes)? The most likely option is (4) because both the antecedent reference (v. 1) and the succeeding (v. 19) reference to "churches" are in regard to Macedonia — the former explicit, the latter implicit.

---

21. The initial unemphatic particle δέ indicates a qualification to the previous verse.

22. Gk. μετ' αὐτοῦ.

23. As with at least the previous verb, συνεπέμψαμεν is an epistolary aorist, translated as a present; cf. v. 22. See on 8:6 and 12:18 and the Introduction, 21-22. Paul is using the apostolic plural "we."

24. Priority of names signifies greater eminence (cf. Gal 2:1, 9).

25. The similarity of συνεπέμψαμεν μετ' αὐτοῦ [Titus] τὸν ἀδελφόν with Τίτον καὶ συναπέστειλα τὸν ἀδελφόν (12:18) suggests that Paul bracketed together with Titus "the brother" whom he sent with him to Corinth and that "our brother," who is sent "*with* them," stood outside them and was junior to them.

26. Plummer's helpful paraphrase of the elliptical ὁ ἔπαινος ἐν τῷ εὐαγγελίῳ διὰ τῶν ἐκκλησιῶν, in which he has supplied the verbs "proclaiming" and "rings." It is possible, however, that ἐν τῷ εὐαγγελίῳ has a more general application (see on 2:12), apart from preaching (so Furnish, 422).

27. Gk. πᾶσων τῶν ἐκκλησιῶν, a phrase used without qualification elsewhere in 11:28; 1 Cor 7:17; Rev 2:23 (see also 1 Cor 14:33; Rom 16:4, 16).

28. It is clear from Acts 20:3-4 that (1) as many as seven representatives chosen by the churches to accompany Paul with the collection converged on Corinth, and (2) that Paul had intended to sail directly to Judaea; the decision to travel to Judaea via Macedonia was not his original plan.

19 Not only this, but[29] "the brother" had also[30] been "elected"[31] by the Macedonian churches[32] as Paul's travel companion in company with the gracious gift that is being administered by[33] Paul to the glory of the Lord and to show Paul's goodwill.

Here we see a similar pattern to that in the First Letter: Paul will send to Jerusalem those whom the local church has approved (1 Cor 16:3[34]). The assemblies will elect their delegates but the apostle will send them, thereby providing external and apostolic sanction of those chosen by the churches.

In the case of "the brother" the mission was not merely the immediate visit to the Achaian capital, nor, as in the case of Titus, is he coming at Paul's urging. Paul is specific. The churches chose this man to be "our [Paul's] traveling companion,"[35] that is, to accompany Paul (and the other unnamed brother — v. 22?) to Jerusalem. This is further amplified by "with this gift which is being ministered by us," a clear reference to the collection destined for Judaea (cf. 8:4, 6, 7; 9:12, 13; cf. 1 Cor 16:3). The visit to Corinth was but the first stage of a much longer journey. In Corinth he (and the other brother — v. 19?) would be joined by Paul and would travel with him by ship "to Syria"; Paul's return to Macedonia was not part of the original plan, being necessitated by a Jewish plot against him.[36] Although Paul is silent about the other "brother" (v. 22) in regard to the collection, we infer that since both are "apostles of the churches," both were chosen not in the first instance to go to Corinth but to go all the way to Jerusalem with the collection, representing the believers of Macedonia (see on v. 23). This suggests that the

29. Gk. οὐ μόνον δὲ ἀλλά, as in v. 10, indicating something important contrasted with something even more important (i.e., his election).

30. Gk. καί, "also," referring back to this brother's fame in all the churches for the gospel (v. 18).

31. Gk. χειροτονηθείς; NIV, "chosen." This word is rare in the NT, being found only at Acts 14:23 for the appointment by Paul and Barnabas of elders in the Galatian churches. According to Furnish, 422, originally it meant elect "by show of hands" but later simply "elect." See Plummer, 249, for a full discussion; also *New Docs.* 1.123.

32. See on v. 18. Based on vv. 1-5 and v. 19, we conclude that Paul must have spent some time in Macedonia prior to the writing of this letter. Evidently Paul had spent sufficient time in ministry there for the response implicit in vv. 1-5 to occur and for the churches to choose these "apostles" (v. 23) to accompany their contributions to Judaea. We do not know by what means the election took place, whether by informal or formal means, or whether by church representatives or plenary gathering.

33. Gk. διακονουμένη ὑφ' ἡμῶν (also v. 20), an identical phrase to that used in 3:3 of the Corinthian congregation as "a letter, administered by us." Paul can use this verb (διακονεῖν) of himself in regard both to new covenant ministry and the collection.

34. "Those whom you accredit by letter to carry your gift to Jerusalem" (RSV).

35. Gk. συνέκδημος ἡμῶν; NIV, "to accompany us." See also Acts 19:29.

36. So Acts 20:3. If, as has been conjectured, a number of Jews were traveling by ship to Jerusalem for a feast, Paul would have been the more vulnerable.

Macedonians' contributions were complete, or at least well advanced, adding considerable moral pressure on the Corinthians (see on 9:3).

Two purposes[37] for "this gracious work"[38] (RSV) are now briefly stated: it is (1) "for the glory of the Lord,"[39] and (2) "[to show] our good-will."[40] The latter states, without elaboration, Paul's motivation in initiating and administering this project. Elsewhere the apostle declares that the Gentile believers are "in debt" to the "saints at Jerusalem" since they have come to "share in their spiritual blessings" (Rom 15:27). Paul's creation of a collection by Gentiles for the Jerusalem believers demonstrates his own "goodwill" toward them. The former purpose — the "glory of the Lord" — relates to that Lord whose "grace" has made all believers, the Corinthians included, rich (v. 9). Their generosity will point to and glorify his. Subsidiary to this, it is possible that Paul's own probity in the matter is an implied source of the glory of the Lord (see v. 21).

Who is this renowned brother? The Acts of the Apostles gives the names of those from the Macedonian churches who traveled with Paul from "Greece" to Jerusalem, after his final visit to Corinth: "Sopater of Berea . . . and of the Thessalonians Aristarchus and Secundus" (Acts 20:4). There is an ancient opinion (going back to Origen) that the renowned but unnamed brother of 2 Cor 8:18-19 is none other than the author of Luke-Acts.[41] To be sure, the anonymous diarist from Troas had apparently spent the past seven (?) years in northern Macedonia (Acts 16:11-17). However, a major problem for this hypothesis is the unlikelihood, based on Acts 20:4-6, that the "we" passage recommences in "Greece" (i.e., Corinth); Philippi is more likely. Thus the renowned brother may have been one of the three persons named

---

37. Gk. πρός. See Hughes, 316 n. 44, who draws attention to the two different orders of ideas introduced here, which, however, have an underlying apologetic intent, i.e., to anticipate and answer fractious comment.

38. Gk. τῇ χάριτι ταύτῃ; NIV, "the offering." Again we see the use of Paul's key word χάρις (8:1, 4, 6, 7, 9, 16; 9:8, 14, 15), here used descriptively of the collection. NIV, "offering," blurs the point; "grace" lies behind all that Paul writes in chapters 8–9.

39. Gk. τὴν . . . τοῦ κυρίου δόξαν; NIV, "honor the Lord." Although "glorify God" appears later (9:12-13), "the glory of the Lord" probably refers to the Lord *Jesus Christ* (v. 9; cf. v. 5), not the Lord God. Furnish, 423, however, takes "Lord" (probably) to mean "God."

40. Gk. προθυμία, "goodwill" — RSV; Furnish, 423. See also 8:11, 12; 9:2, where it means "willingness." NIV takes "willingness" to be the meaning here. By this understanding Paul exemplifies a quality that he calls for in the Corinthians (vv. 11-12) and that is fundamental to this relief mission; it is not a command (v. 8), nor an exaction (9:7).

41. See Martin, 274-75, for a review of the various suggestions that have been made. Hughes, 312-16, makes a sustained case for Luke, whereas Furnish, 435-36, prefers to identify the renowned brother as one of the Macedonians listed in Acts — Sopater, Aristarchus, or Secundus.

above; otherwise we are completely in the dark. If the diarist (Luke) joined the entourage only at Philippi, as appears to be the case, he would be automatically excluded from the reckoning. Because the text of Acts 20:3-5 is inconclusive, further speculation is pointless.

20 Paul now states his purpose in sending[42] Titus and the representatives of the churches. It is

> lest anyone blame[43] us
> > in this lavish [gift][44]
> > > which is being administered
> by us.[45]

Unless his language is exaggerated or ironical, we must infer that the collection was of generous proportions, though details are lacking. When combined, the gifts of the members of the churches of Achaia, Galatia, Asia and Macedonia amounted to no small sum that would make its exit from the wharves of Cenchreae (Acts 20:3-4).

The large dimensions of a fund, which of necessity had to be physically conveyed from places so far away to Jerusalem, inevitably raised questions as to its vulnerability to misuse. Paul was deeply sensitive to any negative inferences in relationship to himself in this matter, as is clear from this verse.[46] His decision that local church delegates must accompany the fund was his way of distancing himself from direct contact with the money and so protecting his own reputation. Indeed, in the First Letter, it was not yet established that he and the Corinthians delegates would even travel together (1 Cor 16:4). As

42. Gk. στελλόμενοι τοῦτο. στέλλεσθαι is used in the NT only here and at 2 Thess 3:6, where it means "to avoid, keep away from" (so R. H. Rengstorf, *TDNT* 7.588-90). It is taken in this sense by the NIV. But it is cognate with ἀπόστολοι, as in v. 23, and congruent with συμπέμπειν, as in vv. 18, 22, and thus has also been taken as "to send," in which sense it is used by Philo (*Embassy to Gaius* 216). The nominative participle is taken in the sense of an indicative. Thus, "we are sending Titus. . . ."

43. Gk. μωμήσηται, found in the NT only here and at 6:3 *(q.v.),* where Paul expresses concern lest "the ministry [of reconciliation] be blamed." Paul may be reinforcing the probity of that ministry by giving assurances in regard to the details of the delivery of the money to Jerusalem.

44. Gk. ἐν τῇ ἁδρότητι ταύτῃ; NIV, "this liberal gift." Plummer, 250, notes that Paul might have used ἐν τῇ χάριτι, as in vv. 7, 19, but prefers the unusual and striking ἡ ἁδρότητος (not found elsewhere in the NT), meaning fullness and strength in the human body — hence "lavish" or "munificent." The cognate ἅδρος appears in the LXX (e.g., "the rich men" — Jer 5:5).

45. Gk. διακονουμένη ὑφ' ἡμῶν, an identical phrase with that in v. 19 *(q.v.).*

46. Paul was doubtless conscious of public scruples in this matter. Cicero noted that "The chief thing in all public administration and public service is to avoid the slightest suspicion of self-seeking" (*On Moral Obligation* 2.21.75).

to the sources of possible blame of Paul, we may only speculate whether he had particular persons in mind. There is no doubt, however, that money matters involving Paul were of deep sensitivity in Corinth (see on 2:17; 4:2; 7:2-4; 11:7-12; 12:14-18; cf. 6:3).

The hypothesis that representatives from the Gentile churches converging on Jerusalem with the collection had an eschatological significance so as to usher in the salvation of God's historic people is not even hinted at in this verse (see on v. 4), where the purpose of such appointments is stated. It was to protect Paul's good name and that of his apostolic ministry[47] that Gentile delegates accompanied Paul with the collection to Jerusalem, as he proceeds to say in the next verse.

21 At the end of this subpassage Paul at last gives the reason[48] for his action in the previous verses (vv. 18-20).

> For
>> we take forethought
>>> for what is good
>>>> not only before the Lord
>>>> but also before men.

Closely basing his words on LXX Prov 3:4,[49] the apostle cites the important principle that his behavior in ministry must be open to the scrutiny of the Lord (i.e., of the Lord Jesus[50]), but particularly[51] of people.[52] He stated this requirement earlier in his own words, "we commend ourselves to every man's conscience in the sight of God" (4:2; cf. 2:17; 5:11). It was Paul's instinct, apparently, that few things would destroy his ministry so effectively as doubts cast about his uprightness in matters relating to financial administration. Hence everything must be "above board," not only in the eyes of the Lord but particularly also before men.

With the citation of this important principle Paul concludes a passage (vv. 18-21) that, along with 1 Cor 16:1-4, as supplemented by Acts 20:4,

---

47. See on 6:3, where the verb μωμᾶσθαι also appears in relation to Paul's ministry.

48. Gk. γάρ.

49. Gk. προνοῦ[μεν γὰρ] καλὰ [οὐ μόνον] ἐνώπιον κυρίου [ἀλλὰ] καὶ ἐνώπιον ἀνθρώπων. Paul here expands the LXX text a little, as indicated by the addition of the words in the square brackets.

50. See on v. 19.

51. As indicated by Gk. οὐ μόνον . . . ἀλλά, an idiom Paul also used at vv. 10 and 18 to emphasize one part of the text above another. In this case the part of Prov 3:4 that is stressed is "before men." This emphasis also emerges in a parallel passage — also alluding to Prov 3:4 — where, however, he omits reference to the Lord: "take forethought to what is good in the sight of men" (Rom 12:17, literally rendered).

52. Gk. ἄνθρωποι, here used generically.

provides illuminating insight into the physical arrangements for the collection as touching "the apostles of the churches" (v. 23).

22 Paul now mentions the third delegate — also unnamed[53] — to Corinth. Like the renowned "brother" (v. 18), he is an "apostle" of the churches,[54] to accompany the collection on their behalf to Jerusalem. His location in the list — Paul "sends" him "with them,"[55] that is, Titus and "the brother" (v. 18) — signifies his lesser seniority. Moreover, unlike that of the renowned brother, this brother's appointment by the churches is not mentioned. He is well known to the apostle Paul, however, who declares that "he has often in many things[56] proved[57] him to be earnest." This man has the same quality — "earnestness"[58] — that Paul finds in himself and in Titus (see on v. 16).

What commended him to the Macedonians, however, was that this "earnestness" was displayed in his considerable "confidence"[59] toward the Corinthians. Possibly a measure of the Macedonians' diplomacy — as well as Paul's — is to be read between these lines. It would not have helped the Corinthians to complete their contributions if the Macedonians and Paul had sent one who was skeptical of even the possibility that the Corinthians might do so. Apparently this man was one of a number who accepted Paul's presentation to the Macedonians that Corinth was, in principle, "eager," "ready," and "enthusiastic" to complete the collection (see on 9:2; 8:10-11).

23 Paul prepares to bring this passage commending these three men to its appropriate conclusion. There will be a strong appeal in the next verse, which is the climax of the passage to that point. But first he will sum up the qualifications of the three men whom he is sending. His manner of doing so suggests that he is replying to anticipated Corinthian questions about these men.

The sentence, which lacks a verb, is in two parts, each introduced by "whether."[60] In the first half the next words, "about Titus,"[61] suggest that

---

53. In all probability one of the three Macedonians sent to Corinth — Sopater, Aristarchus, or Secundus (Acts 20:4). See on v. 19.

54. I.e., the Macedonian churches — see on vv. 18 and 23.

55. Gk. αὐτοῖς. It is possible, but in our opinion unlikely, that "with them" points to this brother's separate visit, subsequent to that of Titus and the renowned brother (vv. 16-17). The next verses suggest that both the brothers, with Titus, formed the one party.

56. Gk. ἐν πολλοῖς πολλάκις; NIV, "often . . . in many ways." This is an example of paronomasia, the use of two words of common stem.

57. Gk. ἐδοκιμάσαμεν, "we have tested, proved." See on v. 8.

58. Gk. σπουδαῖον ὄντα; NIV, "zealous." The vocabulary of "eagerness" is important in 2 Corinthians: see σπουδή (7:11, 12; 8:7, 8, 16); σπουδαῖος (8:17).

59. Gk. πεποίθησις. See also 1:15; 3:4; 10:2. Paul reminded the Corinthians of his pride in them, as expressed to Titus prior to the most recent visit (7:14-16).

60. Gk. εἴτε; see also 1:6.

61. Gk. ὑπὲρ Τίτου.

there should be added, "Whether [anyone asks about] Titus," to be balanced in the second half by "whether our brothers [be asked about]."

>   Whether [anyone asks] about Titus,
>   [he is] my partner
>   and   fellow worker
>   toward you;[62]
>   whether   our brothers
>   [be asked about]
>   [they are] apostles of the churches,
>   the glory of Christ.

In his statement of their various qualifications, the notion of representation is implicit. Titus is *Paul's* "partner and fellow worker toward you [Corinthians]"[63]; the unnamed brothers are "apostles of the [Macedonian] *churches.*"[64] The specific purpose for which these brothers were "elected" as "apostles" was to represent the churches of their province in escorting the collection — "this gift" (v. 19), "this lavish gift" (v. 20) — to Jerusalem (see on 8:19; also Acts 20:3-4).[65] This is not necessarily to imply that the collection from the Macedonian churches had been finalized and was being brought by these "apostles" to Corinth preparatory to being transported to Jerusalem. The Macedonian contributions may have needed some extra time and would be taken to Corinth by the "Macedonians" who will accompany Paul (see 9:4).

It is noteworthy that by this early stage in Christian history such ministry titles were in use. Paul's nomenclature for Titus is in keeping with his mode of reference to such colleagues as Timothy and Apollos (1 Cor 16:10,

---

62. Furnish, 424, suggests the addition of "*in toiling* for you" (based on Gal 4:11; Rom 16:16).

63. Gk. κοινωνὸς ἐμὸς καὶ εἰς ὑμᾶς συνεργός; NIV, "my partner and fellow worker among you." Titus's special status is indicated by Paul's words, "Titus . . . *my* partner . . ."; the two "apostles of the church" are merely "*our* brothers." For references to other "fellow workers" (συνεργοί) of Paul, see 1 Thess 3:2; Rom 16:3, 9, 21; Col 4:11; Phlm 1, 24; Phil 2:25; 4:3.

64. Gk. ἀπόστολοι ἐκκλησιῶν; NIV, "representatives of the churches." For ἀπόστολος see on 1:1.

65. The Jews of the Diaspora chose specially qualified men to escort the temple tax paid annually to Jerusalem. According to Philo, "at stated times there are appointed to carry the sacred tribute envoys selected on their merits, from every city, those of the highest repute . . ." (*Special Laws* 1.78; cf. *Embassy to Gaius* 216). Josephus reports on a Roman edict to the people of Ephesus that Jews dwelling in Asia were "permitted . . . to bring the offerings, which each of them makes of his own free will . . . and travelling together under escort (to Jerusalem) without being impeded in any way" (*Ant.* 16.172). It is probable that Paul modeled the arrangement for the collection on Jewish (synagogue?) practice.

12), who had a special place in his wider ministry to the churches.[66] Titus, "my brother," as Paul calls him, appears to have enjoyed particular esteem (see on 2:13). In the years to come Paul would refer to one Epaphroditus, an "apostle" of the church of Philippi, sent to his side in prison (Phil 2:25).

Paul adds a gratuitous comment about the churches: "[they are] the glory of Christ."[67] Later, Paul will tell one of the Macedonian churches, the Philippian, that its members shone "like lights in the world" (Phil 2:15). Perhaps the moral evil and the harsh intolerance of Christ and his people (see on 8:2; 7:5) in the Gentile cities in which these churches were located provided the dark backdrop against which the churches shone brightly, and so glorified Christ. A similar idea may be found in John's vision of Christ holding in his right hand the "seven stars," a probable reference to the seven churches of the Roman province of Asia (Rev 1:16). If this is a correct line of thought, we are to regard the local church as the source of brightness or glory of Christ (see also on 4:6), serving as a beacon to the truth of God in a darkened world.

24 The word "Therefore"[68] with which this verse commences clinches the argument of the previous verses (vv. 16-23). The appeal Paul makes in this verse should be seen as the climax to this point of his exposition on the collection. Central to the thought here is Paul's play on two words with a common root, which could be rendered "demonstrate the demonstration."[69] His concern, in light of the presence of the envoys from Paul and Macedonia, is that the Corinthians' love will become evident (by their completion of the collection for the saints; thus Paul's boast about them will also become evident.

---

66. See further E. E. Ellis, "Co-Workers," 437-53.

67. Gk. δόξα Χριστοῦ; NIV, "an honor to Christ." This is ambiguous and has been taken to refer, either, (1) to these Macedonian envoys as commended in vv. 16-24 (e.g., by Hughes, 320; Furnish, 425; Martin, 278; NIV), or (2) to the churches (e.g., by Barrett, 230 and the RSV). The general context of vv. 16-24 and the symmetry of v. 23 tend to support (1). However, the question of Paul's intention here cannot be answered by the syntax alone; theological probability must also be weighed. In our view, on theological grounds, it is difficult to understand how these words apply readily to envoys of churches. It could be said that particular "apostles," such as these brothers, were the "glory of Christ." But, as it stands, the words appear to apply to envoys in general, and therein lies the difficulty. On the other hand, as argued in the text above, there are theological grounds for referring to the churches as "the glory of Christ."

68. Gk. οὖν.

69. Gk. ἔνδειξιν . . . ἐνδεικνύμενοι; NIV, "show . . . the proof." Here is another example of paronomasia (see n. 56). Though used only in this verse within this letter, and not appearing in earlier letters, ἐνδείκνυμι and ἔνδειξις are used to some extent in Romans (2:15; 3:25, 26; 9:17, 22). If the parallels δοκιμάζω/δοκιμή (8:2, 8, 22; 9:13) indicate "a working out in practice" (see on 8:8), then ἐνδείκνυμι/ἔνδειξις point to "evidence of what is unseen." The participle ἐνδεικνύμενοι has the force of an imperative.

This "demonstration" will be for the eyes of the Macedonians (lit. "to the face of the churches"[70]). Paul calls on the Corinthians to "demonstrate" before these watching northern congregations (1) "your love," that is, for the saints in their need (8:4, 8, 14; 9:12), and (2) "our pride in you" to them, that is, Paul's pride in the Corinthians expressed to the Macedonian churches (see 9:2-3). This twofold "demonstration" the church in Corinth will give by completing the collection — which is now in abeyance — in the presence of these newly arrived Macedonian "apostles." Here, then, is a strong challenge to the church in Corinth, and there is much at stake if they fail.

The theme of "pride"[71] is now introduced; it will be taken up and elaborated further in the next passage (9:2-3), which will lead into the ultimate challenge of Paul's entire exposition (9:4-5). This is a strong argument in favor of the unity of chapters 8 and 9; the "pride" theme binds together the two parts (see on 9:1).

Paul's qualities in Christian leadership are to be seen in these verses. In addition to his work as evangelist, pastor, and teacher, Paul exercised a significant role in planning and administration, in this case in regard to the collection. Duly concerned at the matter of probity, both real and in perception, Paul has gone to considerable lengths in providing for the appointment of delegates from the churches to accompany the collection on its long and dangerous journey to Judaea. Moreover, these verses indicate his concern that the Corinthians clearly understand how highly commended are the three men who have now come to Corinth to assist in the completion of the collection. Paul has prudently anticipated both their criticisms about the collection (vv. 8-15) and their questions about these men (vv. 16-24). This is instructive. While Paul leaves us in no doubt that new covenant ministry has evangelism, doctrinal teaching, and pastoral prayer as its chief priorities, this passage reveals that Paul also gave careful attention to thoughtful organization and prudent administration as fundamental to the apostolic enterprise.

4. Paul's Own Impending Arrival in Corinth (9:1-5)

1 *There is no need for me to write to you about this service to the saints.* 2 *For I know your eagerness to help, and I have been boasting about it to the Macedonians, telling them that since last year you in Achaia were ready to give; and your enthusiasm has stirred most of them to action.* 3 *But I am sending the brothers in order that our*

---

70. Gk. εἰς πρόσωπον ἐκκλησιῶν. Hughes, 321 n. 59, takes εἰς πρόσωπον as a Semitism, "in the presence of."

71. Gk. καύχησις is widely used in this letter; see on 1:12.

boasting about you in this matter should not prove hollow, but that you may be ready, as I said you would be. 4 For if any Macedonians come with me and find you unprepared, we — not to say[1] anything about you — would be ashamed of having been so confident. 5 So I thought it necessary to urge the brothers to visit you in advance and finish the arrangements for the generous gift you had promised. Then it will be ready as a generous gift, not as one grudgingly given.

Paul's words here follow directly from the previous paragraph (8:16-24), in which he had commended to the Corinthians both Titus and the two envoys from the Macedonian churches. He has enjoined the Corinthians to demonstrate to these men the validity of his "boasting" to them about the Corinthians' support of the collection, a theme he picks up in vv. 2, 3, and 4. The unusual words, "It is superfluous for me to write to you. . . ," with which this passage begins, however, signal the change of tack he is about to make. This is an awkward situation; Paul must choose his words diplomatically, but without loss of impact.[2]

From one viewpoint there is no need to write to them; he knows of their "willingness." And he has been telling the Macedonians with pride since his arrival that the Corinthians have been "prepared" since "last year" (vv. 1-2). He has sent "the brothers" from the Macedonian churches, in order that his pride expressed to the Macedonians may not prove empty, that — even as he had said they were prepared — the Corinthians may, indeed, be prepared (v. 3). If this is not the case, how humiliating it will be for Paul, to say nothing of the Corinthians, if some Macedonians should accompany Paul to Corinth (v. 4), as they most likely will. It was for that reason that he had urged "the brothers" to go on ahead of Paul to "arrange in advance" this "gift" so that it would be the "free gift" it was meant to be, not as it would be if left to the time of Paul's (and the other Macedonians') coming, an "exaction" (v. 5).

1 Only for the second time in this letter (see 1:8) does Paul introduce a topic by "about,"[3] though he often employs this method in the First Letter (cf. 1 Cor 7:1, 25; 8:1; 12:1; 16:1, 12). Although it is often thought to represent the beginning of an independent fragment,[4] several matters make it more likely that Paul is now expanding upon his previous argument:[5] (1) the explanatory

---

1. The reading λέγω, as supported by e.g., p⁴⁶ ℵ Cᶜ D G etc., is to be preferred to λέγωμεν, which may be due to scribal assimilation from καταισχυνθῶμεν (v. 4).

2. We note, too, the predominance of the first person singular pronoun in vv. 1-5, though the plural appears in vv. 3 and 4.

3. Gk. περί.

4. See the extended note on p. 387.

5. See S. K. Stowers, *"Peri men gar,"* 340-48, who points out that 8:24 is the climactic exhortation to that point and that the περὶ μὲν γάρ of the next verse provides the resumptive warrant to explain it.

resumptive "for";[6] (2) the exact reproduction of the words "the ministry to the saints" (from 8:4); (3) the repetition of his certainty about their "willingness" (from 8:11); (4) the picking up of such "willingness" from "last year" (8:10); (5) the further mention of the sending of *the* brothers;[7] together with (6) the elaboration of the theme of "pride"[8] from 8:24 in vv. 2-3.

The introductory (usually untranslated) particle introduces a note of contrast, which is picked up in v. 3 by an answering particle[9]:

> For, on the one hand, concerning the ministry to the saints,
>> it is superfluous for me to write to you
>> (for I know your willingness,
>>> which I boast about to the people of Macedonia);
> yet, on the other hand, I am sending the brothers. . . .

The next verse explains why it is superfluous for Paul to write to the Corinthians about "the ministry to the saints" by reminding them what he has just said to them in 8:10-12.

2 The opening words "For I know"[10] now supply the reason Paul does not need to write to them about this matter (v. 1). It is that

> I know
>> your willingness,
>>> about which
> I have been proud[11] to the Macedonians,
>> that[12]Achaia has been prepared since last year.[13]

---

6. Gk. γάρ.

7. An anaphoric use relating to 8:23.

8. Gk. καύχησις, καυχᾶσθαι.

9. Gk. μὲν . . . δέ.

10. Gk. οἶδα γάρ. The word γάρ of this verse explains why it is superfluous for him to write.

11. Gk. καυχῶμαι is present tense, suggesting that Paul was engaged in ministry to the Macedonians at the time of writing this letter.

12. Gk. ὅτι, introducing Paul's words to the Macedonians.

13. Gk. ἀπὸ πέρυσι. The chronology here may be important. During the previous calendar year (ἀπὸ πέρυσι — see on 8:10) Titus had initiated the collection (see on 8:6, 10; cf. 1 Cor 16:1-4), and the Achaians — i.e., not just the Corinthians, but the nearby churches as well (see on 1:1) — had demonstrated "willingness" (8:11-12). But then Paul had made his second, "Painful Visit" to Corinth, after which, apparently, the collection languished. Meanwhile Paul, having dispatched the "Severe Letter" from Asia, traveled on to Macedónia, where the matter of the collection had been raised. Unaware that the collection in Corinth had fallen on hard times, in all honesty he had pointed to the Corinthians' "willingness" to contribute.

As a result, he adds,

and your zeal has stirred[14] most of them.[15]

Here, then, is a situation of some sensitivity. During his period of ministry among the Macedonians,[16] Paul had pointed with "pride" to the Corinthians' "willingness" (8:11-12) in regard to the collection. He had told them that Achaia[17] had been "prepared since last year." "Your zeal," he tells them, has "stirred" the Macedonians to respond generously, beyond his expectations (8:2, 5). But now Titus has come from Corinth with the discouraging report that the collection is in the doldrums. This, as he points out in vv. 3-5, could now be a cause of some embarassment to both him and them. This also now puts into perspective several matters in chapter 8.

Critical to this text is the phrase "prepared [since last year]," that is, from the time Titus initiated the collection. Paul picks up this word in the next two verses. He is sending "the brothers" on ahead from Macedonia (8:18, 22-23) so that the Corinthians will be "prepared" (v. 3) lest the Macedonians who will come with Paul find the Corinthians "*un*prepared" (v. 4).[18]

Thus, from one point of view it is unnecessary to write to them; he himself does know of their "willingness," as he has just told them. Why, then, does Paul need to write these chapters, devoted as they are to this very subject? The answer is to be sought in Paul's pastoral method. In that regard, Paul seeks to encourage them for their right attitudes, insofar as he is able to do so, but, then, from that plateau, to urge them on to greater heights to complete what they have begun (8:10-11).

3 Having reassured them that in terms of his own confidence in them he has no need to write about the collection, nonetheless he has written and now goes on to explain why. It has to do with boasting about them to Macedonia in light of Titus's report as to present realities in Corinth. Thus

---

14. Gk. ἐρεθίζειν, meaning "irritate" or "provoke"; here it means "stir up" in a positive sense.

15. Gk. τοὺς πλείονας, the "majority," as in 2:6. This detail amplifies his account of the Macedonian response set forth earlier (8:1-5), indicating that "most — but not all — of them" had been "stirred" to contribute.

16. See on 8:4 for comments about Paul's ministry among the Macedonians subsequent to his arrival there.

17. See 1:1 — "the saints throughout Achaia," i.e., not just the Corinthians. The reference to Achaia is the basis for the theory that chapter 9 was originally a circular letter to churches of that province, which was later grafted onto this letter (so, e.g., Windisch, D. Georgi, *Opponents,* but especially H. D. Betz, *Paul's Apology*). But the case for the unity of chapters 8 and 9 is compelling (see on v. 1).

18. There is a wordplay (paronomasia) here between "prepared" (παρεσκεύασται, παρεσκευασμένοι) and "unprepared" (ἀπαρασκευάστους).

the particle with which the verse begins[19] answers that with which the passage began in v. 1.[20] He is saying, "Yes, it is unnecessary for me to write . . . ; *but* I am sending the brothers. . . ."[21] Now, therefore — and we sense the delicacy of the situation — Paul must give his reason (as signaled by the purposive "that"[22]) for sending[23] "the brothers" (8:18-24) to Corinth. It is

> lest in this matter[24]
> > our pride in you
> > > might be made empty,
> that
> > you may be prepared,
> > > as I repeatedly said.[25]

Paul's "pride" in the Corinthians — often expressed — was that "the Achaians are prepared" (see on v. 2). But now the revelation of "*un*preparedness" (v. 4) in the face of "the brothers" (vv. 18, 22) from the Macedonian churches, where the collection was complete, or at least well advanced, would make vacuous the apostle's "pride" in them. The very thing that had "stirred" the Macedonians to respond, namely, the Corinthians' "willingness" and "preparedness" — of which he had repeatedly told them — would have been "made empty."[26]

4 With this verse, and the one following, Paul's appeal to the Corinthians, begun at 8:1, reaches its climax.[27] Paul now gives the further and ultimate reason for sending "the brothers" on ahead to Corinth.

Paul himself is coming to Corinth.[28]

It would be one thing for his "pride" to be revealed to be unfounded

19. Gk. δέ.

20. Gk. μέν — see v. 1.

21. Although Titus was not called "brother" in the previous passage (8:16-24), it is likely that he is now included in the "brothers" mentioned here (cf. 2:13).

22. Gk. ἵνα.

23. Gk. ἔπεμψα is epistolary aorist, rendered as a present (so also 8:18, 22).

24. Gk. ἐν τῷ μέρει τούτῳ, "in this respect," or, more literally, "in this part of the whole" (cf. Col 2:16).

25. The probable force of the imperfect ἔλεγον.

26. Gk. κενωθῇ, "may not be in vain," lit. "empty." Elsewhere Paul often uses the corresponding adjective out of concern that his labors in the gospel may have been "in vain" (e.g., 6:1; 1 Cor 15:14; Gal 2:2; Phil 2:16).

27. 8:24 is an interim climax, forming a launching pad for his final thrust (9:1-5), of which the peak is 9:4-5.

28. Paul had hinted at this near the beginning of the letter (2:3) and in the previous chapter (8:19). His impending return to Corinth is a dominant theme in chapters 10–13.

by the arrival in Corinth of the "brothers" he is now "sending" (8:18, 22). How much worse it will be when he, who had so often expressed his "pride" to the Macedonians (8:24; 9:2), must himself, perhaps[29] with Macedonians by his side, arrive in Achaia to find the Corinthians "unprepared." Thus he is sending the "brothers" (v. 3) on ahead (v. 5) that such an eventuality might not occur, "lest we be put to shame."[30] Then, to make the point even more painfully, he adds,

> *we,* to say nothing of *you,*[31]
> in this undertaking.[32]

Who are these "Macedonians" who may accompany Paul to Corinth? Does the juxtaposition "brothers" (v. 3) with "Macedonians" in this verse imply that the "brothers . . . apostles of the churches" (8:18, 22, 23b; 9:3) were not Macedonians? Since in the previous chapter "the churches" appear to be *Macedonian* churches,[33] it is preferable to regard the unnamed "brothers" (8:18, 22; 9:3) as "apostles" of the Macedonian churches chosen to go to Corinth, but beyond there to Jerusalem with Paul, accompanying the collection. Because there is no evidence that the Macedonian collection was finalized at the time of writing this letter, the "Macedonians" of this verse may have included other "apostles" who would be "elected" to accompany the collection to Jerusalem (8:19; 23; cf. Acts 20:3-4). These had heard Paul say, "the Achaians have been prepared since last year . . . they are prepared" (vv. 2, 3). In the presence of Paul let not these Macedonians find the Corinthians "unprepared," bringing "shame" to Paul and to them.[34]

5 Here, finally, Paul explains the motives ("therefore I thought it

29. Gk. μή πως ἐάν; NIV, "For if any. . . ." Despite the conditional note Paul expects these Macedonians to accompany him to Corinth.

30. For an important study on the social nature of "shame" in the world of that time, see generally P. Marshall, "A Metaphor of Social Shame," 302-17.

31. The repetition of the pronouns ἡμεῖς . . . ὑμεῖς is pointed. Literally, ἵνα μὴ λέγω ὑμεῖς = "in order that I might not say *you*" and is an example of paralipsis, i.e., where one person (Paul) makes the point for others (the Corinthians — ὑμεῖς); see A. T. Robertson, *Grammar,* 1199.

32. Gk. ἐν τῇ ὑποστάσει ταύτῃ; NIV, "so confident"; "ground of confidence" (Plummer, 255). Furnish, 427-28, however, argues that ὑπόστασις nowhere carries this meaning in the NT (see 11:17; Heb 1:3; 3:14; 11:1) and prefers "undertaking" or "project," for which there is support elsewhere, e.g., LXX Jer 23:32; Ezek 19:5.

33. Explicitly in 8:1, almost certainly in 8:24 (cf. 9:2), and therefore in all probability in 8:18 (see on 8:18).

34. Given the Corinthian unhappiness that Paul had declined to receive their patronage, but that the Macedonians had sent him money to support his ministry serving the Corinthians (see on 11:8-9), his present challenge that the Corinthians not lose face in the presence of poor Macedonians is very pointed.

necessary . . .") to "urge"[35] "the brothers" to go ahead of his own coming to Corinth, where they would "rectify in advance"[36] the "blessing"[37] that they had "previously promised."[38] This is the practical end point of his entire argument to the Corinthians about the collection, begun at 8:1.

The arrival of the advance party of "the brothers" would give the Corinthians time freely to make their preparations so as to complete the collection before the arrival of Paul and the Macedonians. Paul's coming with some Macedonians would, by contrast, create an impossible situation in Corinth. They would both lose face. Although Paul has applied a degree of moral pressure on the Corinthians by (1) holding up the example of the Macedonians (8:1-5), (2) by urgently reminding them of their own initial "desire" and "willingness" in the previous year (8:10-12), and (3) by telling them he had used their example of "willingness" and "preparedness" in promoting the appeal to the Macedonians (8:24; 9:2-3), nonetheless it was important that their response was "voluntary" (8:3), as appropriate to the "grace of God/Christ" (8:2, 9); Paul's words are not "command" but "advice" (8:8, 10). Thus Paul wants their response to be "a free gift," not "an exaction."[39] Let the Corinthians respond now, in

---

35. Paul here uses the verb παρακαλεῖν, which he had also used in relationship to Titus's coming to Corinth (8:6, 17). Paul also uses the vocabulary of "sending" [συν]πέμπειν in regard to Titus and these "brothers" (8:18, 22; 9:3). Apparently, Paul both "urges" them and "sends" them.

36. Gk. προκαταρτίζειν; NIV, "finish the arrangements," lit. "to mend in advance." This is the only use of the compounded verb in the NT. For the uncompounded verb καταρτίζειν see on 13:11. The preposition πρό dominates the compound verbs here — προέλθωσιν . . . προκαταρτίσωσιν . . . προεπηγγελμένην. The entry of outsiders (delegates from the Macedonian churches) into the church of Corinth to make whatever arrangements were necessary is a remarkable indication of qualified autonomy in a NT church and of the overriding authority of the apostle. Hughes, 327 n. 58, interprets these three verbs as indicating that the Corinthian problem was lack of organization rather than unwillingness. It would be more consistent, however, to view the strained relationships with Paul as the cause of the problem. Moreover, the contributions were set aside by the *members* of the church (1 Cor 16:2).

37. Gk. εὐλογία (NIV, "generous gift"), used twice in this verse. Although with varying meanings in the NT — e.g., "blessing," "fine speaking" (see 1 Cor 10:16; Rom 15:29; 16:18) — it appears to be used here as "gift," as in LXX Josh 15:19; 4 Kgdms 5:15. It is possible that εὐλογία is a wordplay on λογεία, "collection" (1 Cor 16:1).

38. Gk. προεπαγγέλλομαι, "I promise in advance, I pledge." A powerful moral obligation is implied.

39. Gk. ὡς εὐλογίαν καὶ μὴ ὡς πλεονεξίαν; NIV, "a generous gift not grudgingly given." We note the assonance — ίαν . . . ίαν. Elsewhere πλεονεξία is used for "fraud" or "extortion" (e.g., 1 Cor 5:10, 11; 6:10; Rom 1:29); the use is metaphorical here. The corresponding verb πλεονέκτειν is used in this letter for "to cheat," "to get the better of" (2:11; 7:2; 12:17-18).

freedom, in the presence of advance party of "the brothers," not later when he comes, when it would be, in effect, "an exaction."

Having given this specific and practical, not to say painful, "advice" to the Corinthians, the apostle turns now to give a lyrical account of the blessings associated with free and generous giving (vv. 6-15).

So far from opportunistically playing off one church against another, as is often concluded from this passage, Paul is, rather, seeking to preserve the reputation of the Corinthians in a situation of potential misunderstanding in which they would have lost face. Father-like (6:11-13; 11:2; 12:14-15), he expresses confidence in them, a confidence, he tells them, that he has expressed to others (8:24; 9:2, 3, 4). Moreover, he is aware of the interprovincial sensitivities that are likely to have existed between the Achaians and Macedonians. Shame in Corinth would do nothing to strengthen the bonds between them and the northern churches, but rather the contrary.

5. The Blessings of Generous Giving (9:6-15)

> 6 Remember this: Whoever sows sparingly will also reap sparingly, and whoever sows generously will also reap generously. 7 Each man should give what he has decided in his heart to give, not reluctantly or under compulsion, for God loves a cheerful giver. 8 And God is able to make all grace abound to you, so that in all things at all times, having all that you need, you will abound in every good work. 9 As it is written: "He has scattered abroad his gifts to the poor; his righteousness endures forever." 10 Now he who supplies seed to the sower and bread for food will also supply and increase[1] your store of seed and will enlarge[2] the harvest of your righteousness. 11 You will be made rich in every way so that you can be generous on every occasion, and through us your generosity will result in thanksgiving to God. 12 This service that you perform is not only supplying the needs of God's people but is also overflowing in many expressions of thanks[3] to God. 13 Because of the service by which you have proved yourselves, men will praise God for the obedience that accompanies your confession of the gospel of Christ, and for your generosity in sharing with them and

---

1. The verbs χορηγήσει and πληθυνεῖ are taken as futures, following ℵ* B C D* p⁴⁶.

2. The verb αὐξήσει is, with the two preceding verbs, taken as a future as in ℵ* B C D*; p⁴⁶, however, takes it as optative, "may he increase."

3. The reading of the accusative case εὐχαριστίαν (supported by p⁴⁶) is by scribal assimilation from v. 11. The weight of evidence supports εὐχαριστιῶν (ℵ A B C D G K P Ψ etc.).

with everyone else. 14 *And in their prayers for you their hearts will go
out to you, because of the surpassing grace God has given . you.*
15 *Thanks be to God for his indescribable gift!*

Having urged the Corinthians not to bring embarrassment to him — or them
— over his confidence in their completion of the collection by the time he
comes to Corinth (v. 4), Paul turns now — positively — to encourage their
joyful and generous giving. He places two motives before them. (1) Using
the analogy of generous sowing bringing a bountiful harvest (vv. 6-7), he
points out that God is able amply to provide for those who give generously.
As a result they lack nothing, but rather have further means of giving (vv.
8-10). By "blessing" (v. 5), they are "blessed" by God, so as to "bless"
further. (2) Their generosity will relieve the needs of the "saints" in Jerusalem
but more particularly inspire their thanksgiving to God. Thus they will long
for and pray for the Corinthians, strengthening the bonds of the worldwide
fellowship (vv. 11-15).

6 Paul's initial emphatic "But this [I say[4]]" draws attention to what
follows as a well-established and important principle. His proverblike statement is in the form of a complex double chiasmus:[5]

I	Whoever sows		A
	sparingly		B
	sparingly		B
		will reap	C
II	and whoever sows		A
	generously		D
	generously		D
		will reap.	C

Although the Corinthians were set in the major metropolis of the Aegean
provinces, theirs was nonetheless an agricultural environment. Paul's sowing-
reaping image, with which he commences the new passage and which will control
vv. 6-10, will have been readily comprehended by his readers. The lesser the
sowing, the lesser the reaping; the greater the sowing, the greater the reaping.[6]

4. Gk. τοῦτο δέ. An ellipsis. Although in the Greek of this period τοῦτο could
stand without a verb, it is likely that λέγω, or such like, should be added, "But I am saying
this. . . ."

5. The layout of the passage shows that these are not symmetrical chiasms. Line
4 in both parts ("reap") does not repeat line 1 ("sow"), but is its opposite. Lines 2 and 3
have antithetical adverbs in part I ("sparingly") and part II ("generously"). Other examples
of chiasmus may be found at 1:3; 1:4; 2:16; 8:6; 8:14; 10:11-12; 13:3.

6. The Jewish Wisdom literature has many references to sowing and reaping. See,
e.g., LXX Prov 11:21, 24, 26, 30; 22:8; Job 4:8. Paul also uses the imagery at Gal 6:7-9.

Critical to this verse are the contrastive adverbs "sparingly" and "generously."[7] While the former is found only here in the NT, the latter is deliberately repeated from the previous verse ("free gift"). There the meaning was to indicate that the contributions were "a free gift," whereas here the nuance is that where contributing is done "generously" or "bountifully,"[8] there will be a bountiful outcome. The one word maintains the symbolic continuity of the thought; the differing contexts of each verse give a different, yet closely connected flow of thought. Freely given, generous contributions produce a bountiful yield.

7   The challenge to the *individual* ("whoever sows . . .") implicit in the previous verse is now made explicit: "*Each* [should give][9] as *he* [or she] has decided in [*his or her*] heart." Paul's advice is consistent with and in continuity with his instruction given in the First Letter: ". . . *each* of you is to put something aside . . . as *he* may prosper" (1 Cor 16:3, RSV).[10] Careful prior deliberation by the giver is implied by these instructions.

But what criteria does Paul give to assist the Corinthian contributor in deciding the level of his gifts? Paul's guiding principle is that such giving is not made "reluctantly or under compulsion."[11] Here the latter element would contribute to the former; contributions given "under compulsion" would be made "reluctantly." (This would be to "sow reluctantly," as in v. 6.) Such a compulsory contribution would indeed be an "exaction" (v. 5), which to preserve the precious doctrine of grace is the very thing Paul seeks to avoid. God's grace is to be reciprocated "voluntarily" (8:3), "freely" (9:5), and "generously (9:6)"; any legalistic impost is inimical to this principle.[12]

The OT scripture (LXX Prov 22:8) now quoted ("for God loves[13] a

---

7. Gk. φειδομένως . . . ἐπ᾽ εὐλογίαις. φειδομένως nowhere appears in biblical Greek and is very rare in nonbiblical literature. Hughes, 328, who points to an early use of the verb φείδεσθαι = "to be miserly," suggests φειδομένως = "in a miserly manner," and its opposite, ἐπ᾽ εὐλογίαις = "generously," "bountifully."

8. So Plummer, 258.

9. The ellipse (i.e., words omitted) strengthens the force of the statement.

10. See also the Antiochenes' *individual* giving for the believers of Jerusalem (Acts 11:29).

11. Gk. ἐκ λύπης . . . ἐξ ἀνάγκης, lit. "out of sorrow . . . out of coercion." There is an echo here of LXX Deut 15:10 — "You shall most certainly give to [the poor man] and lend him as much as he lacks, according to his need; and you shall not be grudging in your heart as you are giving to him, because on account of this the LORD God will bless you in all your works."

12. Apart from the call to "sow generously" in the previous verse, Paul gives no other guidelines, as, e.g., that such contributing should be by a proportion (e.g., tithe) of one's "prosperity."

13. Gk. ἀγαπᾷ, "loves," in the sense of "approves" (so Barrett, 236). Similar affirmations are found in other Wisdom literature, e.g., Wis 7:28 ("For God loves nothing as much as the man who lives with wisdom").

cheerful giver"[14]) is no merely pious adjunct to the above, but a solid reinforcement ("for"[15]) of the principle that giving, if it is to be true to "the grace of God," can only be offered "graciously." Giving that is "cheerful" or "glad," which gives expression to the "generous sowing" from v. 6, is the opposite of that which is "reluctant or compulsory."

In his strategic assault on their dilatoriness in giving Paul has, in these chapters, subjected the Corinthians to disadvantageous comparison, given them encouragement, and finally applied considerable moral pressure on them (see on 9:5). Nonetheless, through all this he has tenaciously upheld the doctrine that the grace of God can only be responded to in freedom and in grace.

8 Having exhorted the Corinthians to free and liberal giving (vv. 6-7), the apostle now allays their fears that such generosity will leave them impoverished (cf. 8:12-14). God is greater than either their needs or their fears. Paul's word order is telling: "Able is God. . . ."[16] God's power is seen not merely in providing, as if the provision narrowly met the need. Rather, God is powerful to make his grace[17] overflow[18] toward the Corinthians, so that they will have ample sufficiency.[19] But even this, as good as it may be for the giver, is not an end in itself, but rather "that"[20]

> having[21] . . . sufficient[22]
>> you may overflow
>>> in every good work.

14. Gk. ἱλαρὸν . . . δότην. Paul's words are adapted (from memory; so Plummer, 259) from Prov 22:8: "God blesses a cheerful and liberal man." The adjective ἱλαρόν is found only here in the NT; our word "exhilarating" is a derivative, and, as it happens, is suggestive of the right attitudes in giving. In Rom 12:8, Paul calls for "acts of mercy with cheerfulness" (ἱλαρότητι). For other references to "cheerful" giving see Sir 35:8 ("with every gift show a cheerful face") and Philo, *Special Laws* 4.74 ("Let not the rich man collect great store of gold and silver . . . but bring it out . . . that he may soften the hard lot of the needy with the unction of his cheerfully given liberality").

15. Gk. γάρ.

16. Gk. δυνατεῖ δὲ ὁ θεός; NIV, "God is able." As in the previous verse, "God loves a cheerful giver," ὁ θεός comes at the end of the phrase for emphasis. For other references to the power of God, see 4:7; 6:7; 12:9; 13:4; Rom 14:4.

17. Gk. χάρις, but used here in the sense of "benefit," or, perhaps, even "blessing."

18. Gk. περισσεύειν, "to overflow, abound," is an important word in these chapters (see on 8:2).

19. As conveyed by ἐν παντὶ πάντοτε πᾶσαν αὐτάρκειαν ἔχοντες, lit. "having in all things at all times all sufficiency."

20. Gk. ἵνα, expressing purpose.

21. Gk. ἔχοντες is the first of three nominative participles (cf. πλουτιζόμενοι — see on v. 11; δοξάζοντες — see on v. 13), which should probably be translated not as imperatives but as indicatives: "You have [enough] . . . you are enriched . . . you glorify [God]."

22. Gk. αὐτάρκεια, "self-sufficiency," appears only here and at 1 Tim 6:6 (for

By his power, God makes his grace overflow abundantly toward them so that, in turn, they may overflow in good works, such as in the collection for the poor saints of Jerusalem. The overflowing grace of God to them overflows from them to others (see on 1:5). It is one thing for God's power to provide amply what is needed to his servants, but perhaps a greater outpouring of divine power is needed to impel those servants to overflow in generosity to others, as witnessed by the resistance of the Corinthians to be open-handed to others. There are few evidences of God's power so impelling as the transformation from tightfisted meanness to openhanded generosity.

This great power of God is expressed in a string of universals: "God is able to make *all* grace overflow toward you so that, having sufficient in *all* things at *all* times, you might overflow for *every* good work."[23] This latter ("every good work"[24]) points primarily to what he refers to as the "sharing in this service to the saints" (8:4; cf. 9:1, 12, 13) or as "this liberal gift" (8:20; cf. 8:6) that "we administer" (8:19). The purpose underlying this considerable project was to observe the principle of "equality" among the international community of the churches (see on 8:13-15; 9:13).

It is worth noting that Paul wrote these words about God's power to provide from Macedonia, where the people in the churches were characterized by "rock bottom" poverty. In our view, this poverty was in consequence of persecution (see on 8:2). In his power and faithfulness God was both providing for them and enabling them to give generously for the needs of other believers, whom they did not know and whom they would probably never meet (cf. Phil 4:18-19).

9 With this verse and the next Paul introduces the important vocabulary of "righteousness" into these chapters (see also 3:9; 5:21; 6:7; 11:15). First, God's lavish provision of v. 8 is picked up here from LXX Ps 111:9, which he cites; God's own righteousness is revealed in his giving to the poor. Second, in v. 10 Paul declares God to be the generous supplier of "seed" for *their* giving, thus enlarging the harvest of *their* righteousness.

The OT citation (LXX Ps 111:9) is introduced by "As it is written."[25]

---

the adjective see Phil 4:11), but is found in Plato (*Menexenus* 347A) and in various Hellenistic authors (see further G. Kittel, *TDNT* 1.466). The Hellenistic ideal was one of independence from others, a detached "self-sufficiency." For Paul, however, it meant enough so that one could share with others (cf. Eph 4:28).

23. Along with the double use of the verb "overflow" (περισσεῦσαι ... περισσεύητε), Paul uses these universals: πᾶσαν χάραν περισσεῦσαι ... παντὶ πάντοτε ... περισσεύητε ... πᾶν ἔργον. His repeated use of the stem πας is an example of paronomasia (wordplay).

24. Gk. πᾶν ἔργον ἀγαθόν, "every good work," as a singular appears in 1 Tim 2:21; 3:17; Tit 1:16; 3:1; cf. 2 Thess 1:11). The plural "good works" is found in Eph 2:10; 1 Tim 2:10; 5:10, 25; 6:18; Tit 2:7, 14; 3:8.

25. Gk. καθὼς γέγραπται. For the differing formulas in Paul see n. 70 on 8:15.

> He has scattered abroad his gifts to the poor;
> his righteousness endures forever.

But to whom do these words refer, (1) the righteous man of LXX Psalm 111 as originally written, or (2) God, who is the subject of the previous verse ("God is able . . . *he* scatters . . . *he* gives . . . *his* righteousness") to which this quotation refers? Since the first part of the next verse, which gives a gloss on the citation, clearly has God as its subject ("*He* who supplies . . ."), we conclude that Paul intends us to understand that it is *God* who gives to the poor and that his righteousness endures forever.[26]

This "righteousness" of God is here taken to mean his covenantal loyalty,[27] his faithfulness to his people ("God is faithful" — 1:18), as evidenced in his watchful care over them and active generosity toward them. If the previous verse taught that God is powerful enough to make them overflow in generosity, this verse teaches that God will not abandon them, but remain true to them. Because God is both powerful and faithful, they are set free to be generous to others.

10 Paul now applies the citation directly to the present argument, that is, to the Corinthians' need to follow through on their prior commitments, but to do so generously — in light of God's own character. In some ways this verse repeats what is said in v. 8, but does so now by way of the citation in v. 9, so that the end result is God's supply producing the same kind of righteousness in them.

God is the subject of this verse in terms of (1) what he characteristically *does* in nature ("who supplies seed to the sower and bread for food"[28]) and, therefore, (2) what he *will*[29] do for readers ("who . . . will

---

26. In the previous psalm (LXX Ps 110) it is the righteousness of *the Lord* that endures forever (v. 3), and he provides food for those who fear him (v. 5). Paul appears to have bracketed together these two psalms, taking the language from LXX Psalm 111 and the content from LXX Psalm 110.

27. So Furnish, 448, based on LXX Psalms 110 and 111. The phrase "his righteousness endures forever" is found in LXX Ps 110:3 and Ps 111:3. Furnish, 448-49, dismisses other explanations of "righteousness": (1) general moral uprightness, (2) specific righteous acts, especially almsgiving, or (3) christological righteousness (as in Hanson's "Christ's righteousness in Christians").

28. Based on LXX Isa 55:10, where Paul replaces σπέρμα with σπόρον. What the prophet sees rain producing Paul attributes directly to God's gift. God's twofold supply of "seed for sowing" and "bread for food" is parallel with the twofold motif of v. 6 ("sow . . . reap") and v. 9 ("[God] scatters abroad, gives to the poor").

29. In the first part of the verse the verb tense is present (ἐπιχορηγῶν — "supplies"), whereas in the second the tenses are future (χορηγήσει . . . πληθυνεῖ . . . αὐξήσει — "will supply . . . will increase . . . will enlarge").

supply[30] and increase your store of seed and will enlarge the harvest of your righteousness"[31]).

In regard to (2), Paul is really reinforcing the teaching of a previous verse. Thus

v. 8	**v. 10**
God is able	He . . .
to make every grace	
overflow to you	
that . . . having enough	will supply and
you may overflow	increase your store of seed and
to every good work.	will enlarge the harvest of your righteousness.

God gives "enough" (He "will supply . . . your store of seed") so that "you may overflow" (He "will increase your store of seed") "for every good work" (He "will . . . enlarge the harvest of your righteousness").

Out of the provision God makes to him the recipient has the means of generous giving to those in need, that is, "for every good work." In the process, God "will enlarge the harvest"[32] of their "righteousness." If "righteousness" in v. 9 referred to God's covenantal faithfulness to his people, "righteousness" here is attributed to the people of God ("*your* righteousness").

But what is this "righteousness"? Is it (1) the moral goodness of the godly man expressed in his almsgiving,[33] or (2) "Christ's righteousness in Christians"?[34] In our view it not a matter of either/or, but of one thing issuing in another.[35] God's covenantal "righteousness" (as in v. 9) has bestowed his

---

30. There is probably no difference between ἐπιχορηγεῖν and the uncompounded χορηγεῖν, both of which derive from the vocabulary of the Hellenistic theater (originally "lead the chorus" but later "supply the chorus," a costly exercise). Likewise λειτουργία (see on v. 12) has its origins in Hellenistic culture, one example of which was to "supply the chorus."

31. The phrase τὰ γενήματα τῆς δικαιοσύνης is quoted from LXX Hos 10:12, ". . . seek the LORD until the yield of righteousness comes to you."

32. Gk. τὰ γενήματα. The term γένημα is used of the harvest in general, but also more particularly of the fruit of the grapevine (LXX Isa 32:12; Mark 14:25 pars.). For a parallel between καρπός and δικαιοσύνη cf. Heb 12:11. See also *New Docs.* 2.79.

33. As in LXX Ps 111:9, quoted in v. 9.

34. As in 5:21; cf. 3:9. This evocative phrase derives from A. T. Hanson, *Technique*, 179-80.

35. It is unlikely that Paul would employ this meaning of the word "righteousness" in a manner consistent with that of the "peddlers" (2:17), who appear to have been promoting a "righteousness" based on "the letter" of the Mosaic covenant (3:6-9). In our view the "superlative apostles" and "false apostles" of chapters 11–12 are to be identified

forensic righteousness upon his people in Christ (5:21; cf. 3:9), which in turn. is to be expressed in the righteousness of generosity ("sow[ing] generously" — v. 6; "giv[ing] cheerful[ly]" — v. 7; "abound[ing] in every good work" — v. 8). In the people of the new covenant, to whom God has bound himself, whom God deems righteous in Christ, there is to be, as a demonstration of that "righteousness," the generous sharing of goods in times of need so that there might be "equality" among God's covenantal people (8:13-15).

Thus this "righteousness" is no merely nominal thing. Picking up *God's* "righteousness" from v. 9, Paul here writes of "the harvest of *your* righteousness." This harvest language echoes that of LXX Hos 10:12 ("Sow to yourselves for righteousness, gather in for the fruit of life. . . . Seek the LORD till the fruits of righteousness come upon you"). Clearly the "righteousness" Paul calls for from Christians is dynamic and active, characterized by generosity. We take it that "the harvest of your righteousness" is the fruit of God's justification of his people in Christ (5:21), expressed in their generosity toward needy saints. For Paul their participation in the collection is a "proof" of "love" (8:8; cf. a "demonstration" — 8:24) and of "the obedience that accompanies your confession of the gospel" (9:13).

11 This verse is transitional as Paul moves from the assurance that God will both provide for the givers and enable them to be generous to those in need (vv. 6-10). Paul turns now to his second reason for contributing, the eucharistic (vv. 11b, 12)[36] or the doxological (v. 13). Thus, the first part of the verse focuses on the Corinthians ("*you* are enriched"), whereas the second points to the Jerusalemites (i.e., their "thanksgiving to God"):

> In everything
> [you are] being enriched
>> unto all generosity,
>>> which is being worked through us
>>> for thanksgiving to God.

As in vv. 8 and 10 there are the connected themes of (1) God's provision ("in everything you are being enrich*ed*"[37] — i.e., by God) and (2) "all generos-

---

with the "peddlers" of 2:17. These were "ministers of [a] righteousness" (11:15) inimical to that proclaimed by Paul (3:9; 5:21). Paul is so insistent on the place of "grace" in chapters 8–9, and therefore to a "righteousness" arising from grace, that a shift to a "righteousness" of another basis would be quite inconsistent to his carefully developed argument.

36. Not as in the sacrament (1 Cor 11:24), but as in thanksgiving: εὐχαριστία (vv. 11, 12).

37. Gk. πλουτιζόμενοι, a divine passive. As a nominative it could be taken (1) as an imperative ("be enriched") or (2) as an indicative ("being enriched"). Option (2) is preferable because of the flow of the argument; God is the lavish supplier (vv. 9-10).

ity"[38] (see on 8:2). To these is added (3), for "thanksgiving to God,"[39] that is, on the part of the recipients in Jerusalem. Again, as in v. 8, we note the universals "in *everything . . . all* generosity."

Here Paul is the go-between. The Corinthian generosity, which is "for" the Jerusalemites' thanksgiving, is "being worked *through (dia)* us," that is, through Paul.[40] Paul initiated this ministry and is now engaged in reinvigorating it, and he will oversee its fruits to Judaea (cf. 8:19-20).

There is no hint here of a "prosperity theology." Enrichment, like "overflowing" (v. 8), is metaphorical, and is not at all motivated by self-interest. This "ministry" is for the purpose of generosity, and that with a view to thanksgiving to God. All things are from God and for God: God enriches for generosity, which results in thanksgiving to God. Paul was devout toward his God. He preached the gospel that men and women might glorify him (4:15); his arrangements for the collection were to the same lofty end.

12   Paul immediately gives the basis for "thanksgiving to God," taken from the previous verse and signaled by his introductory word "because" *(hoti)*. He explains that "the ministry of this service," as initiated by him and as participated in by them (8:4), not only meets the needs of the believers in Jerusalem, but also overflows "through many thanksgivings to God."[41] Thus Paul shifts the focus from the Corinthians in the first part of the verse to the Jerusalemites in the second. By structure the sentence turns on a "not only . . . but also" axis, giving two complementary rationales for the collection, the second even more important than the first[42]:

Because
the ministry
of this service

---

38. Gk. εἰς πᾶσαν ἁπλότητα; NIV, "that [you can be] generous on every occasion."

39. Gk. εὐχαριστίαν τῷ θεῷ.

40. Gk. δι' ἡμῶν. This could mean, either (1) Paul, using a literary plural pointing to himself, as he has generally done to this point in the letter (see on 1:1), or (2) Paul and his entourage who will depart from Corinth with the collection from the churches of various provinces en route to Jerusalem. For consistency of usage we prefer (1), even though the singular pronoun has dominated vv. 1-5.

41. Gk. διὰ πολλῶν εὐχαριστιῶν could be taken as either (1) "through thanksgivings of many to God" (so, approximately, the NIV), or (2) "through many thanksgivings to God" (RSV). On balance (2) is preferred. The reading διά followed by genitive πολλῶν εὐχαριστιῶν is well attested (see note above), and is probably to be understood as signifying attendant circumstances: this service overflows, i.e., "in many thanksgivings. . . ." The plural "thanksgivings" occurs in the NT only here and at 1 Tim 2:1.

42. Gk. οὐ μόνον . . . ἀλλὰ καί, an idiom in which something important is contrasted with something more important, i.e., the thanksgiving to God (see also 8:19, 21).

> not only supplies[43] the needs of the saints
> but also overflows in many thanksgivings to God.

The first, the supply of the "needs of the saints,"[44] had been signaled earlier when Paul referred to the "needs" of the recipients (8:14) and the desirability of "equality" among the people of God (8:13-15). Paul was concerned lest there be significant shortfall among the people of God (see on v. 13). The second, the theme of thanksgiving, had been introduced in the previous verse (see also on 1:11; 4:15). As he will go on to teach, the basis of this thanksgiving to God is the sense of "participation" or "sharing"[45] (v. 13; cf. 8:4), that is, with Paul in his "ministry of service" for the one community of the world-wide fraternity of faith, spanning the gulfs of geography and culture between the Gentile churches and the church of Jerusalem.

As indicated in v. 12, Paul is the one through *(dia)* whom Corinthian generosity meets Jerusalem's needs; he is the mediator. Here Paul portrays his role in initiating and completing this collection as "a ministry of priestly service."[46] This language has been understood by some in cultic terms, whether Jewish of Greco-Roman. The more literal understanding, however, appears improbable, whether Jewish or Gentile. On the one hand, having argued for the obsolescence of the old covenant (3:6-11), Paul would be

---

43. Gk. προσαναπληροῦσα. πρός + ανα + πληροῦν, "to fill up in addition," thus "supplying." See also 11:9 (the only other NT use), where the Macedonian churches supplied Paul's needs.

44. Gk. τὰ ὑστερήματα τῶν ἁγίων, "the 'shortfall' among the saints" (NIV, "God's people"). "The saints" are the believers in Jerusalem (see 8:4; 9:1; Rom 15:25, 26, 31). See also 11:9, where the Macedonian churches supplied Paul's "shortfall" in Corinth.

45. Gk. κοινωνία.

46. Gk. ἡ διακονία τῆς λειτουργίας ταύτης. A justifiable rendering since δια-κονία, "ministry," should be retained for consistency (see on 8:4; cf. 9:1); the NIV has "this service," which is quite inadequate. For λειτουργία (cf. λειτουργεῖν — Rom 16:27) see H. Strathmann, *TDNT* 4.226-31. This vocabulary had a long history in Greek and Hellenistic culture. In a society without sophisticated methods of tax collecting a "liturgy" was an obligatory public or religious service, performed by citizens with financial means above a particular level. It also had cultic connotations in the LXX (e.g., Num 8:22: "the Levites went in to perform their service" — λειτουργεῖν τὴν λειτουργίαν), raising the possibility that Paul implied a sacral, rather than a profane, meaning in this verse. While Paul sometimes uses this vocabulary in a profane way (e.g., Rom 13:6; Phil 2:30 — but see Phil 4:18), he also appears to use it in a religious sense (λειτουργὸν Χριστοῦ Ἰησοῦ εἰς τὰ ἔθνη ἱερουργοῦντα τὸ εὐαγγέλιον τοῦ θεοῦ — Rom 15:16; see C. E. B. Cranfield, *Romans,* 2.755-56, who sees Paul's language as casting him in a Levitical role). Moreover, the other terminology for the collection may have theological overtones (χάρις — 8:4, 6, 7, 19; 9:8; εὐλογία — 9:5). In all probability, however, because it is infrequently used, Paul's references should be seen as allusive and metaphorical and not systematic and theological (so H. Strathmann, *TDNT* 4.227-28, but *contra* Furnish, 443).

unlikely now approvingly to reintroduce key elements of that covenant. On the other hand, it would be quite inconsistent for him to call for separation from the local Gentile cults (6:14–7:1) while endorsing the priestly activities of those cults. In our view Paul's language is allusive and metaphorical.

13 Paul now turns his attention from the recipients of the collection in Palestine, who give thanks to God (vv. 11-12), back to the donors in Corinth. Having indicated earlier (8:8; cf. 8:24) that he was writing in this way so as to "prove" the sincerity of their love, he now returns to that theme, looking at it from the perspective of their expected resumption of "sharing" in the collection. The Corinthians will have "passed the test" not only through their own obedience but more particularly as that results in the Jerusalemites' praise of God.

By their involvement in "this ministry"[47] (an abbreviation of the longer title in v. 12) the Corinthians provide "proof" (see on 8:8, 24; cf. 2:9), "proof through which"[48] they glorify God.[49] He spells out this "proof" as occurring (1) *"at"*[50] the obedience of their confession of the gospel of Christ,[51] and (2) *"at"* the generosity of their sharing in this ministry.

47. Gk. τῆς διακονίας ταύτης, returning once more to this vocabulary (see 8:4; 9:1, 12).

48. Gk. διὰ τῆς δοκιμῆς; NIV, "by which you have proved."

49. The nominative participle δοξάζοντες, like πλουτιζόμενοι in v. 11, could be taken as (1) imperatival ("glorify God") or (2) indicative ("you glorify God"), the latter being preferred. The subject of this participle, as with ἔχοντες (v. 8) and πλουτιζόμενοι (v. 11), is here taken to be the Corinthians. See further Martin, 294. The Corinthians "have enough . . . are enriched . . . glorify God" (see on v. 8). NIV's "men will praise God," however, could be taken to mean the Jerusalemites.

50. The preposition ἐπί, translated "at [the] obedience . . ." and understood as also governing the dative ἁπλότητι, "and [at the] generosity. . . ."

51. Gk. τῇ ὑποταγῇ τῆς ὁμολογίας ὑμῶν; NIV, "for the obedience that accompanies your confession of the gospel of Christ." This is a difficult phrase because (1) this is Paul's only use of ὁμολογία outside the pastorals (1 Tim 6:12, 13), (2) ὑποταγή is rarely used (Gal 2:5; 1 Tim 2:11; 3:4), and (3) the genitive τῆς ὁμολογίας ὑμῶν is ambiguous and could be understood as (a) a subjective genitive — "[obedience] arising from your confession," (b) an objective genitive — "[obedience] to your confession" (Hughes, 339 n. 75), or (3) an epexegetical genitive — "that of which obedience consists, namely one's confession of the faith contained in the gospel" (Furnish, 444-45). In our view (a) is to be preferred to (b) and (c); otherwise Paul would be contradicting his earlier remark that the collection was not a "command" (8:10), i.e., a matter of direct "obedience."

Although ὑποκοὴν πίστεως (Rom 1:5) is formally in parallel with the above, its context suggests an epexegetical (or appositional) nuance, "the faith which consists in obedience" (so C. E. B. Cranfield, *Romans* 1.66). Against those who doubt that the above phrase is genuinely Pauline, we note that the noun ὑποταγή is used in Gal 2:5 as well as in the Pastorals (cf. Heb 3:1; 4:14; 10:23), and that the verb ὁμολογεῖν appears in an important passage in Romans, where the object of the confession is κύριον Ἰησοῦν (Rom 10:9-10).

445

Their "confession" — which is in regard to "the gospel of Christ" — calls for "obedience." But to what is this obedience directed? The context suggests that it is their obedience in the "generosity of sharing" in the collection. Does this mean Paul has moved off his earlier point, that the collection is not a matter of "command," that is, something to be *obeyed* (see on 8:10)? No, rather, Paul appears to be saying that their obedience, arising from a confession of Christ, which in turn arises from the gospel of Christ, is directed to Christ. Their generous sharing in the collection is an outcome of that obedience,[52] which, however, is a matter of indirect rather than direct obedience. Contributing to "this ministry" is a God-glorifying "proof" that, therefore, expresses practical "obedience" to the believers' gospel-inspired "confession" of Christ. Thus their gifts are "a harvest of righteousness" (see v. 9).[53] Paul does not relinquish the doctrine of grace.

In the latter part of the verse Paul sets forth a second expression by which the Corinthians "glorify God":

and at[54] the generosity[55] of [your] sharing with them
and everyone else.

Such "sharing"[56] (see on 8:4), which is expressed by the gifts of money, implies commonality of an entity and the existence of bonds of relationship. This sharing is stated as being "to them [i.e., the Jerusalem "saints"] and to everyone else,"[57] that is, "all believers" ("the household of faith" — Gal. 6:10).[58] This latter phrase is easily missed; it points to a sharing with others, not only the saints in Judaea.[59] Just as believers were to "participate in the needs of the saints"[60] *within* a congregation, so these Gentiles were to "share" with "saints" *elsewhere,* especially at this time in Jerusalem.

52. Such "confession" is suggestive of a formal or overt act at the incorporation of the believer into the community (see Rom 10:9-10; cf. 1 Tim 6:12).

53. Implicit in Paul's words is the divine vindication of his ministry; the Gentiles have confessed the gospel as proclaimed in truth by him, i.e., according to grace; their gifts are the tangible evidence of that grace to the mother church (cf. Rom 15:27).

54. The ἐπί is understood; see the note above.

55. Gk. ἁπλότης, "channeled generosity" (see on 8:2; cf. 9:11).

56. Gk. κοινωνία, "sharing." The root is κοινός, "common" (cf. Acts 2:44, "They — the Jerusalem community — had everything *in common*").

57. Gk. καὶ εἰς πάντας.

58. So Furnish, 445.

59. The broadening of the scope of sharing stated here is a point against the theory that the collection was motivated by a theological motif whereby, through the collection brought to Jerusalem, Paul is offering the Gentiles to God, so as to provoke a Jewish response to the Messiah Jesus.

60. As in ταῖς χρείας τῶν ἁγίων κοινωνοῦντες (Rom 12:13).

The vehicle of this sharing was the collection that Paul had established and that he is committed to bringing to Jerusalem. Thus Paul gives expression to his belief in a worldwide covenant fraternity, for which the constituent members had obligations of reciprocity (see on 8:12-14). Paul is not narrowly congregationalist nor individualistic in his outlook.

14 Paul's phrase "the generosity of your sharing with [the Jerusalemites]" from the previous verse is completed by the opening words of this verse, *"and* [the Jerusalemites'] prayers for you, longing for you." The recipients of the Corinthians' "sharing" will in turn pray for the Corinthians with deep longing for them because of the abundant grace shown to them. With his use of the word "grace" *(charis)* Paul begins to round off the passage begun at 8:1, and which has been, despite various nuances, the keyword throughout these two chapters (8:1, 4, 6, 7, 9, 16, 19; 9:8, 15). These Jerusalem believers will pray for and long for the Corinthians on account of the surpassing grace of God that — he hopes and expects — will be shown to the Corinthians.

The worldwide commonality expressed by the pronouns, as in "[*your*] generosity toward *them* and everyone else" (v. 13), is now stated reciprocally as *"their* prayer for *you,* longing for *you."*[61] But the catalyst[62] of this reciprocity will be "the surpassing[63] grace God has given *you* [Corinthians[64]]," if only they will receive it (cf. on 6:1) and give expression to it as the Macedonians have (8:1)!

By this phrase Paul evokes the whole free and gracious movement of God toward humanity in its poverty before him by which, through the death and resurrection of Jesus and the dispatch of his apostolic herald, these Corinthians have been evangelized, declared righteous before God, reconciled to God, given the Spirit, and enabled to make their "confession" that "Jesus is Lord."[65] This "grace of God to [them]" is to stir up in them gracious and free generosity toward their brothers and sisters in distant places, expressed through the collection instituted by Paul. That bond, having been strengthened

---

61. Gk. καὶ αὐτῶν . . . ἐπιποθούντων, "while they [the Jerusalemites], too [i.e., along with Paul] are longing." A genitive absolute construction. The dative δεήσει ὑπὲρ ὑμῶν, "in their prayer for you," expresses the circumstances in which the longing occurred, i.e., "in their prayers they longed. . . ."

62. As expressed by διά, "on account of."

63. Gk. τὴν ὑπερβάλλουσαν χάριν. The ὑπερβολή word cluster is important within this letter (see on 1:8)

64. Gk. χάριν τοῦ θεοῦ ἐφ᾽ ὑμῖν. See on 8:9. God had shown his grace to both the Macedonians (enabling them to give generously) and, if they would receive it, to the the Corinthians, enabling them in turn to be generous.

65. 6:1 (cf. 5:14-21); 8:9; 1:18-21; 4:5.

by the "fellowship" of money, is reciprocated by the Jerusalemites' prayer and longing for these Gentiles in faraway Achaia.[66]

Clearly, Paul is deeply moved in spirit as he reflects upon this vision of the unity of God's covenant people as he prepares to make the great exclamation of praise in the verse following.

15 And so Paul himself ends this appeal in the very way he indicates their response will be received in Jerusalem, with praise to God for his indescribable gift. Here, then, is the conclusion to the exposition of chapters 8–9. The word "grace" (*charis* — 8:1), with which Paul began, he now uses symbolically in this final statement. To be sure, the meanings are different; at the beginning it means "grace," while here it means "thanks." Indeed, the word *charis,* although used with different nuances and meanings throughout this long passage,[67] has served to give an overarching unity to the whole, thus forming an "elaborate *inclusio.*"[68]

It is, of course, "God" to whom the apostle expresses his "thanks"[69] (see on 8:16; cf. 2:14). Thanksgiving — first by the "saints" of Jerusalem (vv. 11-12) and now by the apostle — has dominated these final verses of his exposition.[70]

What is "[God's] indescribable[71] gift" (*dōrea*[72]) for which Paul offers his thanks to God? It is "the surpassing grace of God to you," as stated in the previous verse, which has sparked a chain reaction. What began in free, unconditioned generosity has issued in thankfulness and longing in the fellowship within the "household of faith . . . the Israel of God," in which there can be "neither Jew nor Greek" because "all are one in Christ Jesus" (Gal 6:10, 16; 3:28). While the immediate context demands such an answer, a broader sweep of this passage hints that, ultimately, "God's indescribable gift" can only be gracious Jesus himself, who, though rich, impoverished

---

66. By contrast with the confidence expressed in vv. 11-15, in his next written letter Paul sounds a note of uncertainty as to the Jerusalemites' reception of this ministry (Rom 15:31).

67. "Grace" (8:1), "favor" (8:4), "benevolence" (8:6), "grace" (8:7, 9), "thanks" (8:16), "benevolence" (8:19), "grace" (9:8, 14).

68. So Martin, 295.

69. Gk. χάρις τῷ θεῷ.

70. It should be noted that Paul uses different vocabulary for thanks(giving) to God. In vv. 11-12 by the Jerusalemites it is εὐχαριστία τῷ θεῷ, here by Paul it is χάρις τῷ θεῷ.

71. Gk. ἀνεκδιήγητος. By derivation ἀν + εκ + δι-ηγέομαι (= "describe"), thus "indescribable," not found elsewhere in the NT or the LXX. The "indescribable" in this verse matches the "surpassing" of the previous verse.

72. As used elsewhere by Paul, δωρεά is sometimes in apposition to χάρις, and approximates it in meaning (see Rom 5:15; Eph 3:7; 4:7). So here, the use of δωρεά following the use of χάρις suggests that the words are very closely related in meaning.

himself to make the poor rich (see on 8:9).[73] Jesus Christ is "the divine gift which inspires all gifts" (so Tasker).

So conclude chapters 8–9, a remarkable and sustained exposition of the "grace of God" as applied to the historic situation in Corinth where the members of the church had allowed their contributions to Paul's collection to fall into abeyance. Despite his powerful desire that the Corinthians complete the collection, at no point does Paul weaken his grip on this great truth of the gospel. As he began, so he ends, with "grace," God's "indescribable gift," as he calls it, or rather *him,* Jesus Christ.

Paul's words stand as a rebuke to the Corinthians' myopic individualism and congregationalism (8:7). Paul's emphasis is upon "equality" within the worldwide people of the new covenant and the mutual responsibility each member is to show to others, regardless of geographic separation or ethnic difference (8:13-15). The Corinthians displayed a lack of practical commitment to this reality as compared with the zeal and generosity of the very poor Macedonians. Paul presents these northern Greek believers, in whom the grace of God was at work, as a shining example of loving generosity to others in time of need, beyond their immediate circle.

Moreover, *God's* righteousness, in covenantal fidelity (9:9) to the people to whom he has given his forensic righteousness (5:21), is to be expressed by them in the bountiful fruits of *their* righteousness (9:10), that is, in generous "sharing" with others (9:6-10) within the worldwide covenant people (9:13). God's grace does not terminate in the recipient, but is to be reproduced in generosity. This is the "proof of love" (8:8, 24) and of obedience to the confession of Christ through the gospel (9:12). Sharing with others beyond the immediate congregation glorifies God and will be reciprocated by the recipients' prayers for and longing toward the givers (9:13-14), the distant brothers and sisters in congregations beyond. Against Corinthian fears that their own needs would be unmet should they "share" in the collection (8:13-15), Paul gives assurances as to the power and faithfulness of God in providing for their own ongoing needs and for their own ongoing generosity toward others (9:6-10).

Various views have been expressed regarding Paul's theological motivation in activating the collection. Prominent among these is that, in fulfillment of the promises of the prophets, the collection represents the ingathering of the Gentiles, which, in Paul's view, would provoke a Jewish acceptance of

---

73. For a *contra* view see Furnish, 452, who thinks that it must relate to something in the immediate context, which is Paul's pattern when he breaks forth in thanksgiving. In this case it is God's "grace" of the previous verse, which in turn relates back to 8:1, the "grace of God given in the Macedonian churches."

the Messiah (as in Rom 9–11), thus hastening the Parousia. As noted earlier, we do not subscribe to this interesting view; Paul sets forth his own reasons for the collection, and the above hypothesis is not found among them (see Rom 15:15-33). Significantly, too, Paul states that the "sharing" is also for "everyone else" (v. 13), not only for the "saints" in Judaea.

Whatever the case, the collection was *Paul's*. It was his "ministry of service . . . for the saints" (8:4; 9:1, 12, 13), in which the churches were asked to "share." As such it was a merciful "ministry" *(diakonia)*, which should be bracketed with the "ministry of reconciliation" that God had "given" him (5:18). Edifyingly, Paul's exercise of the "ministry of service . . . for the saints" was conducted with careful forward planning (8:10; 1 Cor 16:1-4), with prudent attention to detail (8:16-24), with sensitivity to matters of probity (8:20), with perseverance in face of difficulty and disappointment (8:6-12), and, not least, in unswerving devotion of the doctrine to the grace of God (8:1–9:15 passim).

These chapters tell us that Paul was a visionary leader and statesman with a worldwide sphere of ministry.

V. CORINTHIANS: PREPARE FOR PAUL'S THIRD VISIT (10:1–13:14)

Many scholars believe chapters 1–9 (so-called Letter "D") and chapters 10–13 (so-called Letter "E") originated as separate letters. In brief, there are two main reasons for this opinion. First, the change of tone from the joy of the previous chapters (see especially 7:13, 16) to the admonitory, often bitter, character of chapters 10–13 is regarded as otherwise inexplicable in the one letter. Second, in these latter chapters Paul appears to be commenting on Titus's return visit to Corinth as an accomplished fact (12:18), whereas in the earlier chapters that visit is still in prospect (8:18, 22, 24; cf. 8:6).

The view taken in this commentary, however, is that our canonical 2 Corinthians did not originate as two separate letters that were subsequently joined as the one we have today. The letter as we have it is the letter as written by Paul in the first place.[1]

---

1. It may be asked whether chapters 10–13, with their admittedly different style, were in Paul's mind as he planned his letter. It is held that Paul generally envisaged a powerful finale to the letter to provoke the Corinthians to set matters aright before he arrived. But it is possible that further negative communication from Corinth reached Paul during the writing and that he may have warmed to the task with unanticipated fervor once he began to dictate the final chapters, particularly the "Fool's Speech" (11:1–12:13).

Arguments in favor of the unity of 2 Corinthians have been set forth at greater length in the Introduction, some of which, however, are briefly re-stated because of the almost universal belief that a new letter now begins. In our opinion a new letter does not now commence, for the following reasons.

First, in chapter 10 we immediately encounter words or combinations of words rarely used outside this letter but which occurred earlier within the letter. The combination "I appeal . . . I beg"[2] (vv. 1, 2) matches closely his exhortation in 5:20, although not found elsewhere in Paul's writings. Likewise, the word "confidence"[3] (RSV), which occurs in v. 2, is found earlier in the letter (1:15; 3:4; 8:22) but not in any letter earlier than 2 Corinthians (but see Eph 3:12; Phil 3:4). The immediate appearance of this combination and this word is a ground for believing that what now follows is in continuation of chapters 1–9 of the letter rather than the beginning of an entirely separate letter.

Second, the joy and confidence Paul expressed at the end of chapter 7 needs to be understood in terms of his pastoral method.[4] His positive expressions about the Corinthians are not absolute but relative, circumscribed by (1) his thankfulness that the "Severe Letter" has been effective in achieving its major objective, their expression of loyalty to Paul in disciplining the wrongdoer (7:12), and (2) his preparation of the Corinthians' minds for his appeal that the Corinthians complete the collection by the hand of Titus, whom Paul is sending back to them for that very purpose (8:6; cf. 7:13b-16).

Third, Paul's pastoral method is to organize the material in the letter so as to make important theological comments within the various discrete sections (see on 12:19). He treats issues under discussion as opportunities to teach his readers important principles of theology.[5] We propose that chapters 10–13 of 2 Corinthians, with their teachings about apostolic power-in-weakness as opposed to the triumphalism of the "superlative" apostles, follow naturally from the immediately preceding section in which he urged that the collection be completed before his arrival and in which the theme of divine grace is dominant.[6] (1) Having cleared the ground of the issue of their loyalty to Paul as opposed to the wrongdoer (7:7-12), and (2) having appealed for the restoration of the collection by the hand of Titus, Paul is able to make his final impassioned plea to the church to resolve their other difficulties before his final visit (13:10).

2. Gk. παρακαλῶ . . . δέομαι.

3. Gk. ἡ πεποίθησις.

4. See S. N. Olson, "Confidence," 282-95.

5. See the Introduction, 40-46.

6. Doubt that Paul would precede his final appeal (chaps, 10–13) by a request for money (see Martin, 298) is met when Paul's pastoral technique in chapters 8–9 is noted. His exposition of divine grace in those chapters forms a fitting prelude to his exposition of power in weakness as opposed to triumphalism in 10:12–12:13.

451

Fourth, it appears that, as the letter draws to its conclusion, Paul's appeal to the Corinthians becomes more intense emotionally. Like many an orator (and preacher!), he has kept the most urgent and controversial matters until the end and dealt with them passionately so that his last words make their greatest impact on the Corinthians. In this regard, Paul may be observing an existing rhetorical convention in (written) speeches from the Hellenistic era that conclude with a powerful peroration calculated to stir the hearers to appropriate attitudinal and behavioral change.[7]

Nonetheless, it is not often noted — as it deserves to be — that chapters 10–13 do not maintain a passionate intensity throughout. Paul begins to moderate his tone at 12:19, where he corrects a possible misapprehension that he has been merely offering a personal apologia. Indeed, from 13:5 to the conclusion of the letter Paul adopts more confident and encouraging tones, so that the latter part of the letter is little different in intensity from the preceding chapters 7–9. If this is true, the argument for a separate letter, on grounds that it is so emotionally different from what precedes it, is weakened.

Fifth, it is far from clear that the early Christians would have felt free to eliminate the ending of one apostolic letter (letter "D") and the beginning of another (letter "E") so as to unite into one two originally separate letters. For a scribe to emend an obscure or embarrassing word in an apostolic text is one thing, but for a church to excise whole sections from two letters is another.[8] Critical to exegesis is the question of the identity of persons or groups who are addressed or referred to in these chapters. To this end it is helpful to analyze the apostle's use of pronouns. It emerges from such a study that these chapters are dominated by "I/we . . . you" references. Apart from the "Fool's Speech" proper (11:21b–12:10), where only the first person "I/me" is found, chapters 10–13 are characterized by Paul's direct address to the Corinthians globally ("you"). By this means the apostle appears to be rebuilding the bridges between him and them, perhaps the more so in light of his prospective final visit with them.

At the same time there are fewer, though possibly equally significant, occurrences of third person pronouns and other third person references.[9] It appears from a close study of these third person references that Paul, while

---

7. See the Introduction, 17-19.

8. Even if the hypothetical Letter "E" lacked thanksgiving or benediction — as in the case of the heated opening of Galatians — it would involve the arbitrary elimination of some verses for a salutation, introductory prayer, and possibly a connecting passage leading to the present hypothetical beginning.

9. "Some" — 10:2; "anyone" — 10:7; "some" — 10:10; "such a one" — 10:11; "some of those" — 10:12; "other [men]" — 10:15; "[an]other man" — 10:16; "the one who" — 10:18; "someone" — 11:4; "those 'superlative' apostles" — 11:5; "those who" — 11:12; "many" — 11:18; "anyone who" — 11:20; "Hebrews, etc." — 11:22; "superlative" apostles — 12:12; "many who" — 12:21; "those who" — 13:2.

addressing the Corinthians directly and referring to others indirectly, is either speaking to the Corinthians *about* these persons or speaking obliquely *to* them. It would appear that these persons referred to indirectly have an importance beyond the number or nature of references to them. Who are these persons referred to in this indirect way?

The contexts in which such references occur go some way toward answering that question. In 10:1-11 and 12:20–13:2, the conjunction of "you . . . some" (10:2), "you . . . anyone" (10:7), "you . . . many of those" (12:21), and "you . . . those who" (13:2) suggests that "some . . . anyone . . . many . . . those who" are *insiders,* existing members of the Corinthian fellowship. Nonetheless, the two passages do not refer to the *same* insiders.

In the former passage Paul is pointing to insiders who regard him as "walking according to the flesh"[10] (10:2), who, while confident that they are "of Christ,"[11] appear to doubt that Paul is "of Christ," based apparently on his bodily weakness and contemptible speech[12] exhibited during the second visit (10:10). Here Paul appears to be addressing a lofty and superspiritual attitude among the Corinthians toward him that was already painfully evident at the time of writing the First Letter.[13]

In the latter passage the insiders are "those who have sinned earlier and have not repented" (12:21; cf. 13:2). In our view Paul has in mind those Gentile Corinthians who remain enmeshed in the web of sexual immorality of the local cults and whom he had admonished earlier in the letter (6:14–7:1). Paul is calling on them to break with their sins once and for all.

Thus the insiders who belong to the whole body and who are being addressed indirectly throughout these chapters are (1) those who regard Paul as unspiritual and fleshly, and (2) the persistently immoral. It is not possible to say how these related to each other or to the faith community as a whole, only that their respective attitudes and behaviors were of concern to the apostle. It does seem likely, however, that the former were critical of Paul's efforts in dealing with the moral problems associated with the latter during the Second Visit.

Outsiders may also be detected within these chapters. The flow of the passage 10:12–12:13 makes it clear that Paul is referring to newcomers, the "superlative" apostles who have "come" to Corinth (11:5, 4; cf. 12:11), whom he addresses later as "false apostles" (11:13). Whereas he is prepared to show

---

10. Gk. ὡς κατὰ σάρκα περιπατοῦντας; NIV, "by the standards of the world."

11. Gk. Χριστοῦ.

12. Gk. ἡ . . . παρουσία τοῦ σώματος ἀσθενὴς καὶ ὁ λόγος ἐξουθενημένος; NIV, "in person he is unimpressive and his speech amounts to nothing."

13. Note the "we . . . you" juxtaposition in 1 Cor 4:8-13; cf. also 14:36, suggesting that the whole congregation, not merely a faction within it, felt this way about Paul.

boldness toward insiders who deprecate his spirituality (10:2), he declares —
with the heaviest of irony — that he would not be so bold[14] as to "classify
or compare" himself with the outsiders who "commend" themselves and who
"boast" of their ministry (10:12-13). By these ironic statements Paul is introducing the signature themes that will soon be developed in the "Fool's
Speech" (11:1–12:13), reaching its plaintive climax, "I ought to have been
commended by you (Corinthians)" (12:11). Paul is here addressing the
Corinthians — in particular those (Jewish members?) who have received
(given hospitality to?) the newly arrived emissaries. But he has in mind the
newcomers, too.

However, we do not meet these attitudes and persons for the first time
in these climactic final chapters. Criticism of Paul's spirituality may be detected earlier (1:12-14, 17). The judaizing opponents are introduced in 2:17–
3:1 (5:11-13?) and the unrepentant sinners — probably but not certainly — in
6:14–7:1. Moreover, in addressing the Corinthians in general over his failure
to accept their financial patronage and answering their suspicions of his
motives for doing so (11:7-12; 12:13-18), he is expanding on matters that had
been hinted at earlier in the letter (4:2; 7:2; cf. 6:3). Thus this latter part of
the letter focuses on important issues between him and them, so that the
problems they have with him, and, indeed, the problems he has with them,
will be set right by the time of his arrival (13:10; cf. 12:19).

The dominant passage in these final chapters is 11:1–12:13, the so-
called "Fool's Speech." In this rhetorically striking passage the apostle
develops further the apologetic theme that was so prominent in the early
chapters, in particular (1) his rebuttal of triumphalism in ministry (2:14-16),
(2) his response to the charge that he is "insufficient" for the task of ministry
(2:16; 3:5, 6), and (3) his reply to those who felt that he "commended" himself
(3:1; 5:12). These criticisms appear to have arisen from the lofty attitudes of
the Corinthians toward Paul, as intensified by the arrival of the "superlative
apostles."

What, then, are we able to say about the triangular relationship between
Paul, the outsiders, and the Corinthians? To be sure, the newcomers appear
to be comparing Paul disadvantageously with themselves. Clearly they present
themselves as "superior"[15] (see, e.g., 10:12-16; 11:5-6, 23; 12:1, 11). Reintroduced in 10:12-18, they become the counterpoint to his sustained comparison in the "Fool's Speech" that follows. But what did the Corinthians
think of these newcomers? For several reasons it seems likely that the
Corinthian church was impressed with these outsiders: (1) The extent and
rhetorical power of the "Fool's Speech" were made necessary by their pres-

14. The verb τολμᾶν occurs in 10:2 and, ironically, in 10:12.
15. Gk. ὑπέρ.

ence in Corinth. (2) The frequency of the "you" references within the "Speech," beginning with "I am jealous for *you*" and concluding with the heart-rending "I ought to have been commended by *you*. . . . How were *you* inferior to other churches?" (11:1; 12:11, 13), points to the seriousness of the threat posed by them.

With chapter 10, therefore, a critical point in the letter is reached. From now on it is dominated by references to Paul's pending return to them, in light of which he begins to exhort them to rectify the problems in the church beforehand.

In 10:1-11 he admonishes those Corinthians who, based on the perceived problems of the recent visit and their resentment of the "Severe Letter," discount Paul as ineffectual when present, and only powerful when absent, by letter.

He turns, then, to the outsiders, who commend themselves by "classifying and comparing" themselves with Paul, into whose field of missionary labor assigned to him by God they have trespassed (10:12-18).

Now follows the beginning of the "Fool's Speech." Paul expresses grave fears for them (11:1-2). Father-like, he has betrothed them to Christ, but they are flirting with "another Jesus," as preached by the "superlative" apostles who have come to Corinth (11:3-4). Paul will concede no inferiority to them in knowledge, though he does in speech (11:5-6).

To be sure, he "lowered" himself in manual labor to preach the gospel to them "free of charge," even receiving support from the Macedonians (11:7-9). But this was an expression of love and of service to them (11:10-11). To accept payment for ministry, as the Corinthians desire to provide and, indeed, the newcomers seek, will only reduce Paul to their level and thereby authenticate their claim to an apostleship equal with his (11:12).

But these men are false apostles, who come disguised as true apostles of Christ (11:13). Since Satan disguises himself as an angel of light, it should come as no surprise if his ministers disguise themselves as ministers of righteousness (11:14-15).

In 11:16-21a Paul reintroduces the theme of "foolishness" from 11:1. Though he is not a "fool," let them receive him as a "fool," so that he, like "many" (the false apostles), may also "boast." The real "fools," however, are the Corinthians themselves (who think they are "wise"), since they put up with the abuse and exploitation of the "false apostles."

So Paul begins the "Fool's Speech" proper (11:21b–12:10). "Fool"-like, he, too, will "boast," which he will do by "classifying and comparing" himself with the "false apostles" (cf. 10:12). After insisting on his equality with them as a Hebrew, a son of Abraham, and an Israelite, he proceeds, through a catalogue of sufferings climaxing with the "thorn in the flesh," to point to his "weaknesses" by which he claims "superiority" over them as a

455

"minister of Christ." Paul's integrity as a true minister of Christ as opposed to their falsity is to be seen in his "weaknesses," which replicate those of the one whose minister he is.

In the epilogue to the "Fool's Speech" (12:11-13), Paul exclaims that they have forced him to speak as a "fool," whereas he should have been "commended" by them. In no way is he "inferior" to the "super apostles," and in no way are they "inferior" to other churches through his ministry, except that he has not burdened them financially.

The "Fool's Speech" concluded, the apostle proceeds to lay to rest the accusation that his refusal to accept payment is inspired by guile. He does not accept recompense; but his coworkers do (12:13-19)!

Then, after admonishing the sexually wayward among them (12:20–13:4), the apostle expresses confidence that because they pass the test that Christ is "in" them, they may be confident that Paul, too, passes the test; they are the "proof" of his labors (13:5-7). Nonetheless, there is the need for their congregational "mending," something that Paul prays for and admonishes (13:8-14).

A. PAUL'S PLEA NOT TO HAVE TO BE BOLD WHEN HE COMES (10:1-11)

1. Paul Defends His Discipline (10:1-6)

> 1 By the meekness and gentleness of Christ, I appeal to you — I, Paul, who am "timid" when face to face with you, but "bold" when away! 2 I beg you that when I come I may not have to be as bold as I expect to be toward some people who think that we live by the standards of this world. 3 For though we live in the world, we do not wage war as the world does. 4 The weapons we fight with are not the weapons of the world. On the contrary, they have divine power to demolish strongholds. 5 We demolish arguments and every pretension that sets itself up against the knowledge of God, and we take captive every thought to make it obedient to Christ. 6 And we will be ready to punish every act of disobedience, once your obedience is complete.

The opening verses of this passage are similar in tone and vocabulary to 5:20–6:2 ("I appeal . . . I beg"). We stand on the threshold of a significant exhortation (see on 13:11).

Paul seeks to correct their misconception of his ministry, past and future. In their view he is "timid" when face to face with them (i.e., during his second visit), and only "bold" when absent (i.e., in his "Severe Letter").

But they mistake timidity for what it really is, "the meekness and gentleness of Christ," through which he now exhorts them, that is, *by letter* (v. 1)! He pleads with them that when present among them (in the forthcoming visit) he may not have to be "bold," as he counts on being toward those who think that he merely lives "according to the flesh" (v. 2). While he lives "in the flesh" he does not conduct his warfare "according to the flesh" (v. 3). Under the metaphor of a siege, Paul declares that his weapons are empowered by God, for (1) throwing down the strongholds of human reason raised up against the knowledge of God, and (2) taking captive every thought to make it obedient to Christ (vv. 4-5). He is ready to punish every disobedience when he comes, once their obedience is complete (v. 6).

1 This extraordinarily emphatic opening to a new section of the letter is consistent with the view expressed above, namely, that with it Paul is now beginning the final, heightened, climactic part of his letter. It commences with the emphatic "myself,"[1] followed by the rare "I Paul,"[2] who expresses himself by the confident verb "appeal"[3] (also in the first person singular[4]), an appeal that is made through no less than Christ[5] himself, his "meekness and gentleness."

These striking terms, "meekness and gentleness," are clearly related to the loaded phrases " 'timid' when face to face . . . 'bold' when away,"[6] each of which stands in symmetrical counterbalance to the other.[7] The face-to-face "timidity" with which he is charged is as unacceptable to his accusers as the "boldness" when absent with which he is also charged. As these categories are developed and illustrated within the passage (vv. 1-11), it

---

1. Gk. αὐτός — untranslated in the NIV, but found in other translations, e.g., the RSV. The authoritative tone is achieved both by αὐτὸς . . . ἐγώ and ἐγὼ Παῦλος, the ἐγώ strengthening both αὐτός (cf. 12:13) and Παῦλος.

2. Gk. ἐγὼ Παῦλος — cf. Gal 5:1; Eph 3:1; Col 1:23. As used in 1 Thess 2:18, the expression distinguishes Paul in a letter written by all three companions. The other uses of this rhetorical phrase *within* the body of Paul's letters argues against the proposition that a new letter begins here.

3. Gk. παρακαλῶ. According to Martin, 302, παρακαλεῖν is used by Paul "when the question of [his] authority is unproblematic." For a full study of this verb see B. J. Bjerkelund, "*Parakalō* Form," 164-67. *New Docs.* 6.145-46 compares the weighting of various verbs of petition in the NT — παρακαλεῖν in v. 1 and δεῖσθαι in v. 2; see on 5:20; 6:1.

4. Out of 239 uses of "I" in 2 Corinthians, 147 are found in chapters 10–13 (cf. M. Carrez, "Le 'nous,' " 275). In v. 2 Paul reverts to the first person plural. See generally on 1:1; 2:14.

5. Gk. διὰ . . . Χριστοῦ.

6. Gk. κατὰ πρόσωπον . . . ταπεινός; ἀπὼν δὲ θαρρῶ.

7. Gk. κατὰ πρόσωπον . . . ἐν ὑμῖν, "face to face with you," is counterbalanced by ἀπὼν . . . εἰς ὑμᾶς, "away."

emerges that Paul is answering a current criticism that he is only "bold" when absent, that is, by letter,[8] but that in his physical presence he is "timid" (v. 1) and "unimpressive" (v. 10). Paul is responding to criticisms of (1) his preceding visit, when he was perceived to be "timid," and (2) his followup letter, (now lost) when he was perceived to be "bold."

Thus in v. 2, using their word — though ironically — he pleads that he should not have to be "bold" when he comes,[9] while in v. 11 he specifically warns a (presumed?) critic that in his impending presence he will be no less "bold" than he is perceived to be when absent as a letter writer. Despite their perceptions of "boldness," however, Paul the letter writer appeals to them "through the meekness and gentleness of Christ."

Significantly, "timid" (better, "humble") is a word both Paul and his critics use of him, though with different nuances.[10] Its importance in the argument that follows (vv. 1-11) is demonstrated by its appearance at this early stage. Paul characterizes himself this way in various contexts within 2 Corinthians — as "downcast" in his sufferings as an apostle (7:6), as a manual laborer "lowering" himself in self-support to "elevate" the Corinthians in salvation (11:7), and — as applicable in this setting — as one who is "humbled" as he "mourns" for unrepentant sinners in the congregation (see on 12:21). But in this criticism by the Corinthians,[11] accustomed as they doubtless were to ruthless methods of discipline in the Greco-Roman cities,[12] Paul's "humbleness" when present is seen as "feeble"[13] (10:10).

By the phrase he uses in the first half of the verse — "through the meekness and gentleness of Christ" — Paul both anticipates and answers his critics' interpretation of him as "timid." However the Corinthians may per-

---

8. Paul's defense for the "Severe Letter" may be heard at a number of points within 2 Corinthians (1:13; 2:3-4, 9; 7:8, 12; 10:9-10).

9. See 12:21–13:2, which, in our view, serves as commentary on 10:1-11. It should be noted that ἀπών/παρών of 10:1-2 is found also in the later passage, as well as ταπεινός, which, however, is repeated as the verb in that reference.

10. Gk. ταπεινός generally has negative connotations of "servile," "humiliated," or "despised" in the Greek literature of the period. See W. Grundmann, *TDNT* 8.1-5.

11. Although the singular is used — τις (v. 7); ὁ τοιοῦτος (v. 11), it is probable that this is the notional individualization of the Corinthians as a whole or of a significant group of the Corinthians.

12. There are also hints that the intruders were severe in their dealings with members of the congregation (cf. 11:20, 21).

13. Gk. ἀσθενής; NIV, "unimpressive." Martin, 300, takes their accusation to mean that Paul was seen as "servile" or even "obsequious" when present in contrast to his arrogance in absence. In my opinion, however, based on the combination of passages relating to immorality and discipline (12:20–13:3), these references are colored by their perception that his discipline was ineffective because it lacked the toughness of other disciplinarians with whom they would have been familiar.

ceive him, let them know that he presents himself to them in ministry as the model[14] of "Christ" himself.[15]

The members of the word cluster used here — "meekness . . . gentleness . . . humble" (RSV)[16] — are echoed in many places in the exhortations to Christian living set forth in the letters of Paul and other writers (Phil 2:8; 4:8, 12; Col 3:12; Tit 3:2; Jas 3:13, 17; 1 Pet 2:18; 3:4, 15; 5:5-6). In all probability these streams of thought emanate from Christ himself, who, by his own words, revealed himself to be "gentle and humble of heart" (Matt 11:29)[17] and who pronounced the blessing of God on "the meek" (Matt 5:5) and the promise of exaltation to the humble (Luke 18:14; cf. Matt 18:4).[18] Jesus' words were abundantly embodied in his meek servanthood as recorded in various incidents in the Gospels (Mark 9:33 pars.; John 13:14-17), in particular the accounts of his demeanor in the face of hostility and death, so extensively recorded in the passion narratives.[19] These, too, have left their mark in hortatory passages in the early letters (cf. 1 Pet 2:23; Heb 2:9-11; 5:7-10).[20] Christ's character, apparently, was the subject of instruction by Paul

14. Gk. διὰ . . . Χριστοῦ is here taken to mean "by the model of Christ" rather than "on the authority of Christ."

15. Paul refers to "Christ" four times in vv. 1-7, and to "Jesus" not at all. The "superlative" apostles appear to have proclaimed "[another] Jesus" (11:4), whereas Paul declares, "I betrothed you to Christ" (11:2). Although 11:4, in contrast to 11:2, suggests (factional?) support for the "Jesus" preached by the "superlative" apostles, the references to "Christ" in vv. 1-7, where both Paul (vv. 1, 5, 7) and his detractors (10:7; cf. 13:3) make claim to "Christ," make it difficult to discern, e.g., a "Christ"-party (cf. 1 Cor 1:12). Martin, 302, however, is more confident.

16. Gk. τῆς πραΰτητος . . . ἐπιεικείας . . . ταπεινός; NIV, "meekness . . . gentleness . . . 'timid.' " The first two words, which Paul positively claims, are virtually synonymous and are sometimes bracketed in writers of the period (e.g., Philo, Creation of the World 103; Plutarch, Pericles 39.1; Sertorius 35.44; Lucian, The Dream 10). On the other hand, ταπεινός appears to be used against Paul, though he is content to apply it to himself. It has a generally negative connotation in contemporary usage and here carries the meaning of "obsequious." (See P. Marshall, "Invective," 359-73.) All three words, however, appear in the LXX. See LXX Ps 44:5 for πραΰτης (cf. Num 12:3), LXX Ps 85:5 for ἐπιεικής, and, e.g., LXX Ps 9:39; 17:28; 33:19; 81:3; 101:18; 112:6; 137:6 for ταπεινός.

17. Contra Furnish, 455-60, who thinks that Paul is influenced not by traditions about Jesus so much as by the Jewish wisdom tradition and by OT passages prophetic of the Messiah.

18. Matthew's account of Jesus' entry to Jerusalem is in terms of Zech 9:9 — "See, your king comes to you, gentle (πραΰς) and riding on a donkey" (Matt 21:4-5).

19. See further J. Murphy-O'Connor, "What Paul Knew of Jesus," 35-40. Furnish, 460, does not think that Paul is here referring to the "character" of the earthly Jesus.

20. See G. D. Fee, 1 Corinthians, 186, for comment on 1 Cor 4:16, an important passage setting forth how Paul, as their father in the gospel, exemplified the ways of Christ before them.

in the churches when he had been present with them so that — as on this occasion — he merely has to point to it without any elaboration.[21]

This important phrase — "through the meekness and gentleness of Christ" — must also be considered next to other statements by Paul about Christ — notably his incarnation and death — as used elsewhere in 2 Corinthians. Although Paul proclaimed Jesus to be "Lord" (4:5), from whose "face" the "glory of God" is reflected into the heart (4:6), this glory crowned One who had, for the sake of others, forsaken "riches" and embraced "poverty" in humble birth (8:9) and sacrificial death (5:21). Sustaining much suffering in the course of his work as an apostle (6:3-10), Paul says that he carries in his body "the death of Jesus" (4:10). By such a ministry, which is the reverse of any notion of triumphalism (see on 2:14) — physical or spiritual — Paul exemplifies in a concrete and visible way a lifestyle that was both heard from and seen in Christ himself, and by it he now appeals to the Corinthians.

2 This verse carries forward the "bold when absent" accusation implicit in the previous verse. Now, however, he turns it back on the Corinthians. He "begs" them not to have to be "bold *when present.*" His words "I beg" spell out the content of his "I appeal"[22] of v. 1.

When "present" may he not have to be "bold" as they claim he is toward them when "absent," as in the writing of the "Severe Letter" (10:9-10; cf. 7:8).[23] That is, given what he has just said about the "meekness and gentleness of Christ," it is clear that "boldness" is not what he prefers. Nonetheless, given the nature of the opposition, he fears that he may have to step out of character in resolving the problems in Corinth. He "reckons" on being bold toward those who "reckon"[24] that he walks according to the flesh. Significantly, however, he immediately softens that "boldness" with "by the confidence. . . ."[25] This perhaps indicates his preference to be seen as relating to them in pastorally more positive ways than by their portrayal of him as "bold" (or "arrogant").

---

21. See further L. A. Belleville, "Gospel and Kerygma," 140-41.

22. Gk. δέομαι is more deferential than παρακαλῶ in v. 1.

23. Fee, *First Corinthians,* 205, suggests that Paul implies that he is present in spirit/Spirit with them in the prophetic word, namely, his letter.

24. Gk. λογίζομαι . . . τοὺς λογιζομένους, "I reckon . . . those who reckon," a play on words, i.e., his play on their word. The repetition of λογίζομαι within this verse, its recurrence in vv. 7 and 11, and the appearance of the cognate λογισμός in v. 4 suggest that this word is used by those who were critical of Paul, which he now turns back against them. λογίζομαι is a middle ("I reckon"), not a passive ("I am reckoned").

25. Gk. τῇ πεποιθήσει, translated as "expect to be" by the NIV. See Furnish, 456, for the view that τῇ πεποιθήσει means Paul's "self-confidence" in conflict with his opponents. The usage of ἡ πεποίθησις (1:15; 3:4; 8:22), however, and its cognate πείθω (1:9; 2:3; 5:11; 10:7) within 2 Corinthians is generally warmly pastoral, i.e., "confident."

This verse is particularly important in the overall structure of 2 Corinthians, for two reasons. First, Paul now begins strongly to establish in the minds of the Corinthians that he is in fact coming back to them and that they must prepare for his coming. It is true that he referred earlier to his coming (9:4-6; cf. 2:1, 3), but this is now stated in strong terms that he will repeat many times before the letter reaches its end (10:6; 12:14, 20, 21; 13:1, 2, 10).

Second, Paul now refers to "certain"[26] detractors among the Corinthians,[27] whose charges against him are implicit in vv. 1-2 and that become explicit in vv. 9-10, namely, that in person Paul is "feeble" and in speech "beneath contempt," and that only from a distance, "by word, not deed" (v. 11) — that is, by a letter that "frightens" (v. 9) — is he anything. These critics appear to be contrasting the ineffectual discipline attempted by Paul during the second ("painful") visit with the success of the "Severe Letter" written afterward in place of the expected return visit. Thus, they see him as ". . . at once a coward and a bully."[28]

In v. 2 Paul gives the probable clue to his critics' basis of opposition to him. Judging his attempted discipline of moral offenders in Corinth to have been ineffectual, they "reckon" that Paul must be a man who "walks according to the flesh."[29] Here we see a connection with 1:12-24, where he defends himself against charges that he acted by "fleshly wisdom . . . made his plans

26. Gk. τινας; NIV, "some people."

27. *Contra* Furnish, 464, who regards those referred to as outsiders, not members of the congregation (also Martin, 304). But this makes less sense of vv. 7-11. It should be noted that although Paul does not elsewhere address the newcomers directly ("you"), he often addresses the Corinthians directly. Nor does he elsewhere exhort the newcomers indirectly (e.g., "let them/him do x"). These opponents are simply there (e.g., "some," "them," "they"). But in 10:1-11 Paul writes "you . . . ," "if any . . . let him . . . of himself" (v. 7), "he/they say[s]" (v. 10), "let such a one" (v. 11), i.e., moving from direct address to indirect reference. Therefore it is held that for consistency of understanding these detractors are more probably Corinthians, who, expressing a lofty attitude in regard to Paul's perceived weakness, are critical of Paul's unimpressive timidity when present as opposed to his arrogance when absent, which probably refer, respectively, to the second ("painful") visit and the "Severe Letter."

28. Plummer, 275.

29. Unhelpfully, the NIV translates κατὰ σάρκα περιπατοῦντας as "[who] live by the standards of the world" (cf. the critique in Fee, 124). Following OT idiom ("walking" in the ways of Yahweh — *halakah*), the verb περιπατοῦν is regularly used in the NT for one's manner of life, in the sense of behaving in a certain way, as in 4:2; 5:7. Martin, 305, suggests that the specific Corinthian complaint was that Paul "walked" in "cunning" and "tampered with the word of God" (4:2). The view taken here is that Paul's ineffectiveness in disciplining moral offenders in Corinth marked him in their eyes as one who "walked according to the flesh," i.e., as one who manifestly lacked the power of the Spirit.

according to the flesh"[30] in not returning to Corinth but writing to them instead. The earlier criticisms (1:12, 17), which otherwise might have been regarded as general within the Corinthian community (cf. 1 Cor 4:8-13; 14:36), appear to be associated with a group within the church (compare "you" in v. 1 with "certain people"[31] in v. 2) who think that "[Paul] walks according to the flesh."[32] By claiming this, his detractors may be saying, in effect, that he lacks the empowering Spirit in his ministry.[33]

Typical of his pastoral method, Paul has kept this issue and the critics in question separate within the letter (vv. 1-2) in order that he may reflect theologically upon it for the sake of his readers; this he now proceeds to do (vv. 3-6).

3 Paul has appealed to the Corinthians that he may not have to display "boldness" when he comes, but that he will against "certain" who diminish him. Paul digresses in vv. 3-6 to give the Corinthians a truer interpretation of his ministry than they (or his detractors among them) appear to hold. The specific ministry that he hopes not to exercise ("boldness" — v. 2) most likely relates to his capacity to discipline the morally wayward, a capacity that his critics are questioning (cf. 12:21–13:3). Nonetheless, Paul's language in these verses suggests that he is taking the opportunity to defend his ministry in rather broader terms, not confining his ministry to moral discipline.

The explanatory connective "For"[34] introduces the first half of the

---

30. My translation of 1:12 — ἐν σοφίᾳ σαρκικῇ — and 1:17 — βουλεύομαι κατὰ σάρκα.

31. Gk. ἐπί τινας; NIV, "some people" (cf. ὑμᾶς, v. 1). Possibly these are to be thought of as "superspiritual" detractors by his reference to them in v. 7: "if any one thinks he *of Christ . . . ,*" and 13:3, "since you seek proof that *Christ* is speaking in me." It is possible, but no more than that, that these critics of Paul were associated with a "Christ" party referred to in the First Letter (1 Cor 1:12; cf. 4:18-21; 14:36). For a rejection of this hypothesis see Fee, *First Corinthians,* 59 n. 55.

32. Nonetheless, it is probable that the congregation as a whole was influenced by such criticisms; otherwise Paul would not give them such prominence in the early passage 1:12-24.

33. However, we must note that there is no reference to the Spirit in this passage. Nor does Paul elaborate on the σάρξ and πνεῦμα antithesis so much in evidence in Galatians and Romans. In 7:1 σάρξ and πνεῦμα are not set in antithesis. However, the reference to σάρξ in 5:16 may imply an antithesis with πνεῦμα. Paul's declaration that "from now on . . . [he does] not know . . . Christ . . . according to the flesh" seems to imply that in the new creation that has "now" come (5:17), he knows Christ with the insight of the "Spirit" (cf. 1:22; 3:3; 5:5). Although Paul juxtaposes σάρξ against πνεῦμα somewhat infrequently in passages earlier than 2 Corinthians (cf. 1 Cor 3:1-4; 5:5), the connection is so intrinsic in classical passages (Gal 5:16-24; Rom 8:2-13) that it would be perilous to argue that this juxtaposition developed only subsequent to the writing of 2 Corinthians.

34. Gk. γάρ appears to be explanatory, introducing the whole passage (vv. 3-6) to demonstrate that their charge of "fleshliness" in ministry cannot hold true.

sentence ("For though we walk in the flesh"[35]), with which the second is contrasted ("we do not wage war according to the flesh"[36]). In the first part Paul concedes their criticism, effectively making the point that he (and, by implication, all believers) is "in the flesh," that is, in this nonpejorative sense. But he does not conduct his ministry "according to the flesh," as "some" appear to be saying.

In conceding that he "walks *in* the flesh" but asserting that he does not wage war "*according to* the flesh," Paul establishes two important and related truths about his ministry. On the one hand, he disclaims any special powers that might imply that he is *in himself* the instrument of God; quite to the contrary, he is "in the flesh." On the other hand, he denies any personal ineffectiveness in ministry, but implies effectiveness in that ministry.

Here once more is an expression of the power-in-weakness paradox of apostolic ministry. Like all other people who "live in the flesh," Paul is a mere "jar of clay" (4:7), who "outwardly" is "wasting away" (4:16), a "thorn"-afflicted man (12:7). Yet he is in the midst of such weakness an effective bearer of the word of God (2:17; 3:2-3; 4:1-6; 5:11-12; 11:2; 12:19; 13:3-4). But because he is "in the flesh," it can only be the gospel-word, the "treasure" itself (4:7), not its frail, ever debilitating, human bearer, that is powerful in achieving God's purposes. Paul's catalogues of personal suffering in obedience to apostolic ministry (4:7-10; 6:4-10; 11:23–12:10) mark him out as one who "walks *in* the flesh," in implicit denial that the triumph of God could ever be attributable to him *in himself*. His power, that is, *Christ's* power, for both living and serving, is perfected in weakness (12:9).

The general martial allusion "wages war" will lead into the imagery of the ministry as siege warfare that he expresses elaborately in vv. 4-6.[37] The metaphor develops logically in line with military process from beginning to end. Paul "wages war" (v. 3) and has "weapons of warfare" by which he "demolishes fortresses" (v. 4), whereupon he takes "captives" and "punishes" any unyielding defenders (v. 5).[38] Within this siege and captivity picture in vv. 4-6,

---

35. Gk. ἐν σαρκὶ γὰρ περιπατοῦντες is unhelpfully translated "we live in the world" by the NIV, missing the repetition of σάρξ (v. 2) and σαρκικός (v. 4) and the attendant implication that Paul is not a man of πνεῦμα. "In the flesh" here refers to "the laws and limitations which are common to human flesh" and, as used here, has a "neutral sense to denote the medium of man's present corporeal existence" (Hughes, 349).

36. Gk. οὐ κατὰ σάρκα στρατευόμεθα.

37. Along with Eph 6:10-17, vv. 3-6 represent Paul's most extensive use of military imagery (cf. 6:7; 1 Cor 9:7; Rom 13:12, 13; 1 Thess 5:8; Eph 6:10-17; 1 Tim 1:18; 2 Tim 2:3). See further Malherbe, "Paul at War," 143-73; *New Docs.* 4.28.

38. 2 Corinthians is rich in images of apostolic ministry. The minister is God's captive (2:14), Christ's "aroma" (2:15-16), Christ's letter courier or amanuensis (3:2-3), Christ's diplomatic representative or ambassador (5:20), Christ's matchmaker (11:2), and here Christ's military conqueror (10:4-6).

Paul uses language in a rhetorically deliberate manner. His words "wages war" are repeated as "warfare,"[39] his "pulled *down*" as "pulling down" that which is "lifted *up*."[40] Their "disobedience" is made "obedient to Christ."[41] Moreover, running through these verses, though not obvious in translation, is a sustained alliteration.[42]

4 Paul has declared that he does not "wage war according to the flesh" (v. 3). The initial "For"[43] introduces his explanation that the "weapons of his warfare"[44] are "not fleshly,"[45] but, on the contrary, have "divine power"[46] for (1) "the casting down of strongholds,"[47] and (2) the capturing of minds in obedience to Christ (v. 5). In this verse he mentions "reckonings," and in the next "every high pretension raised up against the knowledge of God."

But what are these "weapons" about which Paul seems defensive (cf. 10:7; 13:3)? We infer from the context (vv. 1-2) that Paul is referring to his disciplinary ministry to them at the time of the second visit and through the "Severe Letter," in regard to whose effectiveness, however, he and his detractors have different opinions. What Paul considers as "being humbled" in that he "mourned"[48] for the unrepentant during the second visit (12:21), they

---

39. Gk. στρατευόμεθα . . . τῆς στρατείας.

40. Gk. καθαίρεσιν . . . καθαιροῦντες . . . ἐπαιρόμενον.

41. Gk. ὑπακοὴν . . . παρακοὴν . . . τὴν ὑπακοὴν τοῦ Χριστοῦ.

42. Gk. πᾶν ὕψωμα ἐπαιρόμενον . . . πᾶν νόημα . . . πᾶσαν παρακοήν (pan hypsoma epairomenon . . . pan noēma . . . pasan parakoēn).

43. Gk. γάρ.

44. The repetition στρατευόμεθα . . . τὰ γὰρ ὅπλα τῆς στρατείας ἡμῶν, "we wage war . . . weapons of our warfare," is obscured by the NIV: ". . . wage war . . . weapons we fight with." Cf. "weapons of righteousness" (6:7).

45. Gk. οὐ σαρκικά, which Furnish, 457, takes as "inadequate." However, this does not take into account the strong eschatological element running through the letter (1:18-22; 3:2-3; 5:14–6:2). The antithesis of σάρξ/σαρκικός in the present context is δυνατὰ τῷ θεῷ, which implies power from the Holy Spirit (see on 6:6-7 — ἐν πνεύματι ἁγίῳ . . . ἐν δυνάμει θεοῦ). The opinion that Paul here rebuts, that he "walks according to the flesh . . . wages war according to the flesh," is tantamount to saying that "he does not have the Spirit of God." For discussion on Paul's adjectives σαρκινός and σαρκικός, see Fee, *First Corinthians,* 124-26.

46. Gk. δυνατὰ τῷ θεῷ could be (1) a dative of advantage, "powerful for God's cause," or more probably (2) a semitism, "divinely powerful," as in LXX Jonah 3:3 (Moule, 184). A superlative sense may be implied by δυνατὰ τῷ θεω, "powerful to God, therefore exceedingly powerful" (cf. LXX Jonah 3:3).

47. Gk. πρὸς καθαίρεσιν ὀχυρωμάτων; NIV, "to demolish strongholds." Along with Paul, Philo (*Confusion of Tongues* 128-31) also employs this siege imagery, which these authors could derive from Prov 21:22, but which more probably comes through the Hellenistic literary tradition, as in, e.g., 1 Macc 5:65; 8:10 (so Malherbe, "Paul at War," 143-73). See also Luke 19:43-44.

48. Gk. ταπεινώσῃ — 12:21; cf. ταπεινός — 10:1.

regard as his "timidity" since his efforts seemed to them so relatively ineffective (10:1, 10). Paul also appears to be thinking of his followup action, the
"Severe Letter," which he regarded as achieving a "godly sorrow . . . repentance that leads to salvation" (7:10), but which his detractors dismiss as
"arrogant toward them, but only from a distance"[49] (v. 1; cf. v. 10), which
was also partly obscure (1:13-14), "hurtful" (7:8), and written so as to
"frighten" them (v. 9). On this view he and they have differing appreciations
of his recent ministry among them.

Twice in this verse he states that his weapons "demolish," a compound
verb meaning "pull *down*,"[50] which he also uses in v. 5 in regard to things
that are "lifted up."[51] The "strongholds" Paul "pulls down" are "reckonings"[52] that he appears to apply to "those who reckon[53] that he walks according to the flesh" (v. 2). These "reckonings" that need to be "pulled down"
are expanded upon in broad terms in vv. 5-6. His immediate application in
this verse, however, may be to his detractors among the Corinthians.

5 Continuing the siege metaphor, Paul adds[54] that the "reckonings"
that he is divinely empowered to "pull *down*" include every "high thing"
that is "lifted *up* against the knowledge of God."[55] As a second consequence
of the divine empowerment of v. 4 he points to his "capture of every mind
obedient to Christ."

Perhaps Paul has in mind here both (1) the self-elevated Corinthian
critics in the immediate past and (2) a more generalized reflection about his
ministry. In regard to the former it is quite likely that he is thinking of the

49. Gk. ἀπὼν . . . θαρρῶ εἰς ὑμᾶς; NIV, "bold when away."
50. Gk. καθαιροῦντες — cf. v. 8.
51. Gk. ἐπαιρομένον.
52. Gk. λογισμούς; NIV, "arguments." It is more likely that Paul's language has
been influenced by LXX Prov 21:22 — πόλεις ὀχυρὰς ἐπέβη σόφος καὶ καθεῖλεν τὸ
ὀχύρωμα ἐφ’ ᾧ ἐπεποίθεισαν οἱ ἀσεβεῖς, "a wise man scales the strong cities and brings
down the stronghold in which the ungodly trust" — than by descriptions of Hellenistic
battles, as argued by Malherbe, "Paul at War," 143ff. But see 1 Macc 8:10, where both
αἰχμαλωτίζομαι and ὀχύρωμα are used. It is possible that Paul's language has also been
influenced by the account of the rebellious builders of Babel who declared: "Let us build
ourselves a city, with a tower that reaches to the heavens, so that we may make a name
for ourselves . . ." (Gen 11:4).
53. Gk. τινας τοὺς λογιζομένους; NIV, "some people who think."
54. The initial καί is almost certainly epexegetic, whereby "reckonings" is
amplified by the next phrase, "arguments and every proud obstacle to the knowledge of
God" (RSV). Note that vv. 4-5 are one sentence, and complex at that.
55. Gk. πᾶν ὕψωμα ἐπαιρόμενον κατὰ τῆς γνώσεως τοῦ θεοῦ. The "knowledge
of God" probably refers to the gospel (so Furnish, 458). See 2:14, "knowledge of him,"
which we take as "knowledge of Christ." While "knowledge," used absolutely, was
common in 1 Corinthians, in this letter it appears less frequently (see 4:6; 6:6; 8:7; 11:6).

effectiveness of the "Severe Letter" in "pulling *down*" both the wrongdoer (2:6; 7:12) and the greater majority of the congregation who had failed actively to support him against the wrongdoer during the second visit (7:12), but who have now fallen into line (2:5-9).

But it seems likely that Paul is also commenting in general on the "high bulwarks against his gospel"[56] thrown up by learned scribes in the synagogues (cf. 1 Cor 1:20) and Gentile intellectuals such as those he addressed in the Agora and Areopagus in Athens prior to his first visit to Corinth (Acts 17:17-34). In his mind may be the preaching of Christ crucified, which "pulled *down*" Jews for whom that message was a "stumbling block" and Gentiles for whom it was "foolishness" (1 Cor 1:23). From such ministry to Jews and Gentiles, however, have issued the very tangible messianic assemblies in the major cities of the Greco-Roman world, not least at Corinth (3:2-3).

Following through with the siege metaphor, the conqueror having "pulled *down*" the high rampart of the fortress, he proceeds to take prisoners into captivity.[57] With this image Paul the victor takes "every thought" captive and brings it in obedience to Christ. The "capture" of "every thought" appears to be closely related to the "reckonings" (of his local detractors?) that he "pulls *down*."[58]

This captive-taking stage of the siege metaphor is a striking image for the apostle-minister as a military general who takes fortified rebels captive and brings them into submissive obedience to[59] Christ. This is a highly figurative way of saying, "We . . . preach Jesus Christ *as Lord*" (4:5) as well as — and with no contradiction — "We preach Christ *crucified*" (1 Cor 1:23), the other side of the paradox of Christ. In v. 1 Christ is "meek . . . gentle . . . [humble]"; here Christ is a conquering king to whom prisoners are brought.

Although this is capable of application to his ministry in general, Paul probably has in mind his prospective relationships with the Corinthians in particular. This emerges from the next verse, where the image of obedience is pursued but in a context referring to Paul's planned return to Corinth and the discipline that he hopes he will not have to exercise (v. 2; cf. 12:20-21).

6 This final clause, which concludes a line of thought begun in v. 2,

---

56. Furnish's phrase, 462.

57. Cf. 1 Macc 8:10; Luke 21:24.

58. Gk. λογισμοὺς καθαιροῦντες . . . καὶ αἰχμαλωτίζοντες πᾶν νόημα. Here we note a series of nominative absolute participles λογισμοὺς καθαιροῦντες (v. 4) . . . αἰχμαλωτίζοντες (v. 5) . . . ἐν ἑτοίμῳ ἔχοντες (v. 6), which are to be taken as indicatives: "we pull down . . . we take captive . . . we are ready."

59. Gk. εἰς τὴν ὑπακοὴν τοῦ Χριστοῦ. Hughes, 353 n. 9, takes εἰς as signifying "as though *into* the victor's territory" (emphasis added).

also serves as commentary on that verse. In v. 2 Paul pleaded that he would not have to be "bold" when "present" with the Corinthians by the application of discipline at the impending third visit. It is now made clear that the "boldness" in question would be displayed in "punish[ing] every act of disobedience." He will hint at the unusual nature of his discipline later (see on 12:21). The present verse is also the climax and conclusion of the siege metaphor, begun in v. 3. The ramparts of the fortress having been pulled down and prisoners captured, vengeance is now wrought on those defenders who have finally surrendered. Hence, "we are ready to punish every disobedience when your[60] obedience is complete."

Once again rhetorical expression plays a significant role in this final clause, as with the passage as a whole, though again this tends to be lost in translation. First of all, there is a severity conveyed by (1) the repetition "every" continued from v. 5 (where it occurs twice), (2) some complex alliterations based on the Greek letters *e* and *p*,[61] and (3), aurally, the inversion of "disobedience" *(parakoē)* and "obedience" *(hypakoē)*. Powerful rhetoric and the strong military imagery combine to make vv. 3-6 among the more memorable passages in 2 Corinthians, and indeed within the Pauline writings.

But what situation is Paul addressing in this verse? Who are those whom he is "ready"[62] "to punish"[63]? What is their offense? Three possibilities are (1) those Corinthians who "reckon" that Paul "walks according to the flesh" (v. 2), (2) those unrepentant of sexual misdemeanors to whom he will refer later (12:21; 13:2), or (3) the "superlative" apostles/false apostles[64] who are corrupting the Corinthians' understanding of and loyalty toward Christ (11:4-5, 13).

We may eliminate (3) on the grounds that those Paul has in mind appear to be insiders, not newcomers.[65] On balance, we prefer option (1). In the context of this passage he has been referring to "some" who regard him as "walking according to the flesh" (v. 2), that is, in regard to Paul's perceived ineffectiveness regarding the sexually unrepentant. Paul reserves his comments about these until considerably later in the letter (12:21; 13:2).

---

60. In the phrase ὅταν πληρωθῇ ὑμῶν ἡ ὑπακοή the location of ὑμῶν is for emphasis, i.e., relating to the disciplining of the Corinthians.

61. Gk. πᾶν νόημα . . . πᾶσαν παρακοὴν . . . ὅταν πληρωθῇ, and καὶ ἐν ἑτοίμῳ ἔχοντες ἐκδικῆσαι. It is not pssible to convey the alliteration in English.

62. Gk. ἐν ἑτοίμῳ ἔχοντες, a common Classical Greek construction (see also 12:14).

63. Gk. ἐκδικῆσαι, lit. "do justice," which should perhaps be read alongside other legal terms like ἐπιτιμία and κυρόω (2:6, 8) and ὁ ἀδίκησας and ὁ ἀδικήθεις (7:12).

64. So Martin, 306.

65. See 453-55 above.

The theological teaching on ministry in vv. 3-6 is a good example of Paul's pastoral method. Arising from a mundane situation — and one that is impossible for us to reconstruct at this distance — Paul gives his readers an important teaching that does not ultimately depend on whatever historical context existed, but stands — even today — in its own right. This is not the only occasion within 2 Corinthians when the attitudes of the Corinthians have forced him to offer an apologia for the worth of his ministry in general (3:4-6; 4:1-6; 5:11-13). Beyond that, Paul's account of the effectiveness of his ministry is applicable to all who speak the word of God, past and present. Paul's stirring words in vv. 3-6 serve to encourage ministers of the gospel to remain faithful to that gospel, and to believe their ministry to be powerfully effective, even though there are detractors — as there were with Paul — who find little to encourage them that a work of the Spirit is occurring.

2. Paul's Rebuke of His Critics (10:7-11)

7 *You are looking only on the surface of things. If anyone is confident that he belongs to Christ,*[1] *he should consider again*[2] *that we belong to Christ just as much as he. 8 For even if*[3] *I boast somewhat freely about the authority the Lord gave us for building you up rather than pulling you down, I will not be ashamed of it. 9 I do not want to seem to be trying to frighten you with my letters. 10 For some say,*[4] *"His letters are weighty and forceful, but in person he is unimpressive and his speaking amounts to nothing." 11 Such people should realize that what we are in our letters when we are absent, we will be in our actions when we are present.*

After his important theological statement about his divinely empowered ministry (vv. 3-6), Paul resumes his interaction with his local detractors. In vv. 2-3 he pointed to "some[5] who "reckon" that [Paul] walks according to the flesh" (my translation), that is, who reckon him to be an unempowered man. In this new passage he begins by addressing the Corinthian believers collec-

---

1. Some authorities (D* E* F G, d e f g) add δοῦλος before Χριστοῦ, possibly in anticipation of διάκονοι in 11:23.

2. NIV apparently omits ἐφ᾽ ἑαυτοῦ, which occurs in ℵ B L and is preferred to some MSS, which read ἀφ᾽ ἑαυτοῦ.

3. There is a little more support for the inclusion of τε rather than for its exclusion, in which case it should be rendered "even if," as by the NIV and the RSV.

4. The verb φησίν is third person singular (φημί), "he says" (so Barrett, 260; Martin, 311), though most commentators take it in an impersonal sense, "it is said"; hence NIV, "some say." A small number of lesser MSS (e.g., B^{f.g.r} vg. Syr.) have φασίν plural, "they say."

5. Gk. τινας.

tively ("*you* look . . ."), but immediately refers to an individual ("if *anyone* . . . let *him*").[6] The oscillation between Paul's address to the church and to an individual continues through to the end of the passage (vv. 9, 11).[7] While it is possible that a particular individual is in mind (the spokesman of a group critical of Paul?), it appears more likely that the individual references are only notional and that he is addressing the Corinthians as a whole, or a group within the church.

In particular Paul urges his critic(s) to look at what is before them, that is, at the church that owes its existence to Paul's powerful ministry (v. 7; cf. vv. 3-6). Here is evidence that Paul is "Christ's" (see on 3:2-3), and that his actions arise from the Lord's authorization of his ministry, which, however, is not primarily to "pull down" (i.e., by harsh discipline) but to "build . . . up" the church (v. 8). Despite their views to the contrary, he had not written the "Severe Letter" to frighten them (v. 9). For they are saying that only his letters are powerful; in person he is weak and his speech contemptible (v. 10). When he returns he will be no less powerful in person than they judge him to be when absent by letter (v. 11), though, to be sure, he appeals to them to change their attitudes and ways so that this will not be necessary (v. 2).

7   This verse consists of two sentences that repeat vocabulary[8] from earlier in the passage. The first sentence, which has only four words, is capable of several interpretations depending chiefly whether the verb, "look,"[9] is taken (1) as an indicative ("you look" — so the ASV, TEV, and NIV), or (2) as an imperative ("look" — so the RSV, NEB, and JB).[10] Moreover, the object[11] could be understood as (1) "what is before your eyes" (RSV), that is, evident, or (2) as "on the surface of things" (NIV), that is, superficially. If the verb is an imperative, it follows that the object cannot be option (2). Paul would scarcely command them to be superficial!

6. εἴ τις . . . ἑαυτῷ . . . λογιζέσθω . . . ἐφ' ἑαυτοῦ . . . αὐτὸς Χριστοῦ. The reference εἴ τις is probably a generic singular and might refer to any or all who held such a view (cf. 1 Cor 3:18; 8:2; 14:37, where the use of εἴ τις signifies key points at which Paul and the Corinthians are at odds and where no particular person is intended). Less probably, Paul's use of ὁ τοιοῦτος (v. 11), with which v. 7 could be connected, may point to a specific person. Most likely both εἴ τις and ὁ τοιοῦτος are generic singulars, with no particular individuals in mind. Against this, however, there are instances where τοιοῦτος refers to a particular person (e.g., 1 Cor 5:5, 11; 2 Cor 2:6, 7, but cf. Gal 6:1).

7. Gk. ἐκφοβεῖν ὑμᾶς (v. 9); φησίν? (v. 10); λογιζέσθω ὁ τοιοῦτος (v. 11).

8. Gk. κατὰ πρόσωπον (v. 1); πείθω, cf. πεποίθησις (v. 2); λογίζομαι (v. 2 [twice]); cf. λογισμός (v. 4).

9. Gk. βλέπετε.

10. The KJV takes βλέπετε as interrogative, "Do you look?" This is, effectively, a variation of (1) the indicative, "you look," which in this case would be either a rhetorical or a direct question, neither of which would call forth the statement following.

11. Gk. τὰ κατὰ πρόσωπον.

The interpretation adopted here is that the verb is an imperative,[12] based on Paul's usage elsewhere. Once the meaning "look" is established, the object can only be option (1), "[at] what is before your eyes."[13] But, again, there is ambiguity. Does he mean, "look at" (a) the fact of the church in Corinth, or (b) the problems of the church and those who cause them? Because Paul goes on to assert defensively that he is "of Christ," option (a) is preferable. On this basis Paul is pointing to the fact of the church to support his claims that his ministry is "of Christ." Earlier he had stated that the Corinthian church is "a letter from Christ, ministered by [Paul]" (3:2-3; cf. 10:18; 12:12).

In the second sentence "a certain one,"[14] real or more probably notional,[15] is exhorted to "reckon again"[16] what he had previously been "confident" about, suggesting that his former perception had been incorrect. Since Paul now mentions himself, it appears that he is calling on the Corinthian church, or, more probably, a group within it (as in v. 2 — "some"), to reconsider *him*.

Their question was whether Paul was "of Christ."[17] In our view,[18] this means that they doubted that he was a Spirit-empowered minister.[19] This

---

12. So Furnish, 465. The verb form βλέπετε is almost always used by Paul in an imperatival sense (1 Cor 8:9; 10:18; 16:10; Gal 5:15; Eph 5:15; Phil 3:2; Col 2:8; 4:17; only 1 Cor 1:26 is unclear). That the word appears at the end of the phrase is not a problem for this view. It is not so apparent, however, as Furnish, 465, proposes (based on 1 Cor 8:9; Gal 5:15; Phil 3:2; Col 2:8) that βλέπετε carries the meaning, "be alert to."

13. This understanding of Gk. τὰ κατὰ πρόσωπον would sever any connection with 5:12, where this phrase is also used but in a context where it means "outwardly," "superficially," i.e., as opposed to ἐν καρδίᾳ.

14. Gk. τις . . . ἑαυτῷ . . . τοῦτο . . . ἐφ' ἑαυτοῦ . . . αὐτός.

15. Barrett, 260, argues for an individual as against Martin, 307, who argues for a group "personalized as a single number."

16. Gk. λογιζέσθω πάλιν; NIV, "consider again."

17. Gk. Χριστοῦ, "of Christ," or "Christ's."

18. Options for the meaning of Χριστοῦ εἶναι with their scholarly advocates and arguments are conveniently listed in Furnish, 476, and, Martin, 308-9. In brief, they are: 1. A Christian. 2. A personal disciple of the earthly Jesus. 3. Either one who had been authorized for apostolic ministry directly by Jesus (Martin, 309) and/or one who was authorized indirectly by someone of apostolic rank (so, e.g., Furnish, 476). 4. A *pneumatikos,* a Spirit-filled person (Schmithals, *Gnosticism,* 197-99, views the *pneumatikoi* as linked with Christ in a gnostic-mythical relationship).

We eliminate (2) and (3) since this passage vv. 1-10 is directed toward Corinthians, "insiders" who are critical of him in relation to his feeble previous visit and his frightening followup letter. Only when we reach 10:12 and read the wider passage 10:12–12:13 does Paul begin to discuss "outsiders," the "superlative" apostles (11:5; 12:11) who are to be equated with the "false apostles" (11:13) who have "come" (11:4) to Corinth. Option (4) is discounted since it is dubious that Gnosticism was at that time a definable reality.

19. The words Χριστοῦ εἶναι in this passage may have meant different things to Paul, on the one hand, and (some of) the Corinthians, on the other. To Paul it meant a Christian, someone who "belonged to Christ" (see 1 Cor 3:23; Gal 3:29 [ἡμεῖς [δὲ]

opinion is based on Paul's rebuttal of their judgment (1) that he "walked according to the flesh" (v. 2), (2) that he employed "weapons . . . of flesh" (v. 4), and (3) that he must assert that his "weapons" have "divine power" (v. 4) and are effective in ministry (vv. 3-6).[20]

What is the basis for their negative judgment of him? Their conclusion has been arrived at, apparently, on account of what they regarded as his ineffectual attempt at church discipline when "present" during the second visit, followed by his "bold" (arrogant?) "Severe Letter" when "absent."[21]

But Paul has a different understanding of "of Christ," which is, simply, one who belongs to Christ, a Christian (1 Cor 3:23; 15:23; Gal 3:29; 5:24). Paul exhorts the (notional) individual "again" to "reckon" — the detractors' word by which they reached negative conclusions about him?[22] — "within himself." Is *he* "of Christ"? Then so, too, is Paul. If this "one" is confident that he is "of Christ" — a Christian — then Paul does not raise doubts about his spiritual standing. But let the same recognition be extended to Paul!

But there is a barb in Paul's challenge. If this "certain one" is a Christian, then let Paul's role in that be recognized, both for the inner life of the individual and for the objective reality of the congregation. The "one" needs to look both (1) "within himself," to the reality of the Spirit's presence,[23] and (2) without, at "what is before your eyes," the fact of the con-

---

Χριστοῦ]; cf. Rom 8:9b; 14:8 and 1 Cor 15:23; Gal 5:24 (οἱ [δὲ] τοῦ Χριστοῦ). But perhaps certain of Paul's detractors among the Corinthians thought Χριστοῦ εἶναι was a spiritually empowered person, something they "reckoned" Paul was not (see 13:3)!

20. It is a problem for exegetes that Paul is interacting with those who "reckon" that he is not "of Christ." Paul portrays his detractors (vv. 2, 4) in terms of what they question in him, rather than what they claim for themselves or even what he sees them to be. Their primary criticism appears to be in the area of disciplining moral offenders when present face to face (10:1-2; 12:21; 13:2a). They appear to doubt that Paul will achieve any better result when he makes yet another visit to them (10:2; 12:20) since they question whether Christ is "speaking though" Paul (13:4).

21. The present/absent pattern is fundamental to the passage, where Paul is also accused of "walking according to the flesh" (vv. 1-2, 6; cf. 13:2). Moreover, the words echoed by Paul indicating their view of his "presence" are negative (ταπεινός, v. 1; cf. ταπεινώσῃ, 12:21; ἀσθενής . . . ἐξουθενημένος, v. 10), and of his "absence" — as a letter writer — are no less negative (θαρρῶ — vv. 1, 2; ἐκφοβεῖν ὑμᾶς — v. 9; βαρεῖαι καὶ ἰσχυραί — v. 10). Most likely their estimate of Paul as "walking by the flesh" — and therefore not by the Spirit? — was aroused, in part at least, by their perception of his actions first when present and subsequently when absent. In line with this is their estimate that his decision not to return directly after the second visit was based on "*fleshly* wisdom" (ἐν σοφίᾳ σαρκικῇ, 1:12; cf. 1:17).

22. Gk. λογίζεσθαι (NIV, "consider") is used four times in vv. 1-11 (v. 2 [twice], v. 7, and v. 11); cf. its cognate λογισμός in v. 4.

23. He will later encourage the Corinthians to submit to a test by which they can be assured that "Christ Jesus is *in* [them]" (13:5). A recurring theme of the letter has been

gregation (cf. 3:2). Not only is Paul like this "certain one," "of Christ," a fellow Christian, but he is, as an apostle, a "divinely empowered" minister (v. 4) who does not "walk according to the flesh" (vv. 2-4). His ministry is powerfully effective; the evidence is to be found both within their lives and in the existence of a Christ-confessing congregation.

8 The flow of Paul's argument in vv. 1-11 is continued by the repetition from v. 4 of the word "pulled down." In v. 4 he answered his detractors' complaint of inadequacy in disciplining offenders by asserting that by "divine power" he "pulled down" all that was "raised up" against the knowledge of God. Now he urges that "the authority the Lord gave [him]" was not for "pulling you[24] down." The Lord did not commission Paul to be a demolisher (i.e., engaged in disciplining offenders in churches) but to be a builder of congregations.[25] He is asking them, "Why do you criticize me for failing to do what the Lord has not called me to do?"

Rather, let these detractors understand that "the Lord gave [Paul] authority for building . . . up." Paul's comments here are of considerable importance. Although they are, in effect, Jeremiah's words echoing Yahweh's long-term relationship with Israel,[26] Paul uses the prophet's vocabulary to refer to the "authority" the Lord uniquely "gave" him on the road to Damascus.[27] The Damascus event underlies much of Paul's teaching throughout 2 Corinthians,[28] though at no point does he refer directly to it.

Moreover, it is significant that it is the "Lord" — the ascended, glorious One (cf. 4:5-6)[29] — that Paul speaks of, not, for example, "Christ," although that is the term used elsewhere in vv. 1-11. Paul's manner of reference to the person — Christ, Son of God, Lord, Jesus — often implies something about his function. It is appropriate that, in respect to his Damas-

---

his reminder to them of the presence and activity of the Spirit among them (1:19-22; 3:3, 6, 8, 18; 5:5; cf. 11:4).

24. His use here of ὑμῶν, which is not found in the almost identical 13:10, supports our argument that Paul in vv. 1-11 is addressing a situation domestic to (a group within?) the Corinthian church, namely, those who complained that Paul "walks according to *the flesh*," as demonstrated both by his ineptness in church discipline when present and his bullying when absent, by letter.

25. *Contra*, e.g., Furnish, 477, who suggests that Paul may be answering charges that his influence was destructive or that he is referring to the newcomers' destruction of the church in Corinth. These and other suggestions appear less likely in the flow of the argument of vv. 1-11, where, as we have argued, Paul is addressing "insiders," not newcomers.

26. The keywords "build" (οἰκοδομοῦν) and "pull down" (καθαιροῦν) occur in LXX Jer 24:6; 38:27-28; 51:54.

27. Gk. ἔδωκεν. The aorist "gave" implies a single action. Paul's Damascus Road experience was historical and unrepeatable.

28. See further S. Kim, *Origin*, 5-20.

29. Paul's favorite mode of reference to Jesus. See comments on 1:2.

cus call, Paul should say, "the authority the *Lord* gave. . . ." This is not an absolute, but a derived "authority" from the Lord that is exercised "over" (cf. 1:24) the churches, by one who saw himself not as a "Lord" but as a "slave" (4:5).

Furthermore, in regard to the "authority"[30] given to Paul we should note the use of this word in the Gospels. "Authority" is something God delegates to the Son of Man to execute eschatological actions on his behalf — to dominate the unclean spirits (Mark 1:27 pars.), to forgive sins (Mark 2:10), to lay down and take up his own life (John 10:18), and to pass the final judgment on humankind (John 5:27). In turn Jesus delegated his "authority" to the Twelve "to have authority over unclean spirits" during their mission to the towns of Galilee (Mark 3:15; 6:7). In Paul's use of the word in letters prior to 2 Corinthians we note in particular a concentration of references in 1 Corinthians 9, where Paul is writing about his "authority" as an apostle that gave him the right to be supported as he preached the gospel (1 Cor 9:1, 4, 5, 6, 12, 18). These references from the First Letter form the immediate linguistic, historical, and theological background for Paul's dual references to "authority" in the Second Letter (i.e., 10:8 and 13:10). Implicit throughout 2 Corinthians is Paul's assumption that he is their apostle, whose authority is to be acknowledged by them.[31]

That Paul "boast[s]" — takes pride in[32] — "somewhat freely"[33] or abundantly of this "authority" is something of which, he says, "I will not be ashamed."[34] This is probably an eschatological allusion. When he is revealed before the judgment seat of Christ (5:10), he will not be ashamed to have claimed the "authority" of an apostle of Christ in whose name he has come (cf. 1:14).

---

30. Gk. ἐξουσία.

31. This is pointedly established at the commencement of the letter (1:1), evident where he refers to their "obedience" to him (2:9; 10:5, 6; cf. 7:15), implicit in passages alluding to his Damascus call (3:4–4:6; 5:16–6:13; 10:8; 13:10; cf. 2:17), and assumed in the strong and confident tone adopted as he concludes his letter in preparation to coming to them (12:14–13:14). It is hinted at in passages referring to the eschatological reunion of apostle and people (1:12-14; 1:23–2:3; 7:12).

32. See on 1:12.

33. Gk. περισσότερόν τι is generally understood idiomatically rather than comparatively. However, Hughes, 359 n. 14, may be correct in taking it comparatively, taking pride "somewhat more," i.e., than he ordinarily does. Paul's use of the comparative adjective περισσότερος (2:7; 10:8) and the adverb περισσοτέρως (1:12; 2:4; 7:13, 15; 11:23; 12:15) is important in 2 Corinthians, being found often in contexts of emotion such as pride, love, or grief.

34. An example of litotes, or deliberate understatement. He is actually proud to be exercising the Lord's authority. It should be noted that while "I boast" is subjunctive mood and therefore indefinite, "I am [not] ashamed" is indicative and certain.

The Lord gave his authority to the apostle "for upbuilding."[35] This is a common term used by Paul for strengthening in faith and Christian conduct within congregations (12:19; 1 Cor 3:9; 14:3, 5, 12, 26; cf. 1 Cor 3:10, 12, 14; Rom 15:20), in particular, love (1 Thess 5:11; 1 Cor 8:1; Rom 14:19; 15:2). Paul's reference here, however, appears to include his apostolic "building" of the churches, as at Corinth (1:18-22; 12:12).

By this deliberately understated pride in his exercise of the Lord's "authority" Paul seeks to achieve two results. First, he seeks to reinforce the Corinthians' understanding of his apostolic rule at this critical final stage in the letter that is preparing them for his coming (see 13:10). The Corinthians must rectify the problems he now addresses in this letter so that he will not have to do so when he comes, with attendant "grief" and "humility" (see the comments on 2:1; 10:1; 12:21). Second, he wants them to understand that church discipline ("pulling down") — wherein his detractors deem him to have "walked according to the flesh" — is not primary to the Lord's call. The Lord has commissioned him to be a builder, not a demolisher (cf. 12:19). In their criticisms they have made the secondary primary.

9 Paul now[36] pauses to reassure the Corinthians of his motives in exercising the "authority" given him by the Lord (v. 8). The Lord's "authority" was granted for "building up" and not for "pulling [them] down" (i.e., by discipline), he has just told them. Thus under no circumstances, he now adds, was he commissioned to "frighten" them, though that is precisely what he is accused[37] of having done, by "his letters."

By "letters" he is referring, in particular, to the "Severe Letter" of the recent past.[38] To be sure, the "Severe Letter" appears to have been, in effect, an ultimatum that the Corinthians declare actively — not merely passively —

---

35. Gk. εἰς οἰκοδομήν; NIV, "for building you up." Whereas οἰκοδομήν is used absolutely, καθαίρεσιν is qualified by ὑμῶν. However, ὑμῶν should probably be applied also to οἰκοδομήν, for balance.

36. This verse presents the translator with several problems because (1) the transition from v. 8 to v. 9 is unclear, and (2) the text itself is capable of different interpretations, depending on one's view of the opening words ἵνα μὴ δόξω. These could be taken as, e.g., (a) prohibitive: "Do not think of me as frightening you. . . ," or (b) negative purposive: "*lest* I appear to be frightening you. . . ," or (c) an apodosis answering the previous verse: "If I boast . . . I would not seem to be frightening you. . . ," or (d) a protasis that is answered in v. 11 (with v. 10 in parenthesis): "lest I should appear to be frightening you . . . [I say]: let that man consider what we are through our letters. . . ," or (e) introducing a new, unattached sentence of imperatival meaning: "Let me not appear to be frightening you. . . ." On balance (e) is to be preferred (so Moule, 145).

37. The Gk. δόξω ὡς ἄν, "I appear, as it were . . ."; NIV, "I do not want to seem. . . ." This suggests that Paul is countering an accusation.

38. Possibly in mind also are the (lost) "Previous Letter" (1 Cor 5:9), our canonical 1 Corinthians (cf. 1 Cor 4:18-21), and the present letter.

their loyalty to him (2:8; 7:12). This they had effectively done by their discipline of the man who had wronged Paul (2:6, 7; 7:11-13a). Nonetheless, the Corinthians ("you"), now in view, remain critical of that letter, asserting that it was intimidatory, sent to "frighten[39] them."

Unstated here, but implied, is his concern that his letters be seen to "build up," not "pull down," the congregation. He will pointedly comment later that the present letter is for their "upbuilding" (12:19). If Paul's letters are to have an ongoing authority with the Corinthians — and with the churches subsequently — it is important that they are seen to have the positive intention to "build up" the churches. Paul's letters, written in his absence from the churches, should be seen as as much a part of his exercise of the "authority" the Lord gave him for their upbuilding as his ministry when physically present with them. These detractors seek to drive a wedge between Paul as absent and Paul as present, asserting that he is useless in both situations, as he reports in the verse following. Paul, however, does not ultimately distinguish between his letters and his person (v. 11).

10 Paul now amplifies the meaning of the previous verse. "I do not want to seem to be frightening you with my letters *because*. . . ."[40] Remarkably, the explicit and scathing criticism of Paul by his detractors (among them) is now set before us, almost certainly in their own terms.[41] With his quotation of their words the whole passage vv. 1-11 reaches its climax and is made coherent. Now we are explicitly told why they regarded him ("they say"[42])

39. Gk. ἐκφοβεῖν, "to terrify" (cf. LXX Job 7:14; 33:16), is not found elsewhere in the NT (but cf. Mark 9:6; Heb 12:21).

40. Gk. ὅτι.

41. Elsewhere in this passage (vv. 1-11) their criticisms of Paul have to be reconstructed, as best we are able, from his rebuttals of his detractors. It is part of Paul's epistolary method to keep both his detractors (insiders) and opponents (outsiders) at arm's length, so that they are not named nor their views given too much credence by overly explicit reference. His quotation of their damning criticism of him in this verse is noteworthy. For a culturally parallel example of innuendo see *New Docs.* 4.65.

42. Gk. φησίν is third person singular (φημί), "he says" (so Barrett, 260; Martin, 311), though most interpreters take it in an impersonal sense, "it is said," hence NIV, "some say." A small number of lesser MSS (B[f,g,r] vulg. Syr.) have φασίν plural, "they say." Paul here provides us with the earliest external comment about his letters (cf. 2 Pet 3:16). The remark, as quoted, is primarily in regard to the "Severe Letter," though probably applicable also to the "Previous Letter" and canonical 1 Corinthians. It should be noted, however, that their reaction is not freestanding, but in contrast with — as they saw it — an unimpressive personal presence. In the first part of the next century Polycarp wrote to the Philippians, "For neither am I, nor is any other like me, able to follow (κατακολου-θῆσαι) the wisdom of the blessed and glorious Paul, who when he was among you in the presence of the men of that time taught accurately and steadfastly the word of truth, and also when he was absent wrote letters to you, from the study of which you will be able to build yourselves up in the faith given you" (*Phil.* 3:2).

as "walking according to the flesh" (v. 2) and why he felt they needed to "look at what is before them" (v. 7). One may presume that their criticisms were brought to Paul in Macedonia by Titus (cf. 7:5-7).

Their sentence as quoted by Paul is in two parts,[43] which correspond to the "absent" (letter writer) versus "present" (visitor) pattern so evident within vv. 1-11, as well as in related passages.[44] As "absent," they say, "his letters are weighty and forceful." By itself this might serve as a compliment, but when read against the balancing second half of the sentence it is a damning sarcasm. When "present" — that is, "in person"[45] — they say, "he is unimpressive, and his speaking amounts to nothing." What he should be when present — "weighty and forceful"[46] — he is only when absent; what he should be when "absent" — "[physically] unimpressive[47] and with speech [of no account]" — which by definition, as it were, a letter is — he is when present. At both points he is the opposite of what they expect him to be. In their eyes he is a total failure, a man of "flesh" (see on v. 2).

While their negative views of his "person" and "speech," broadly speaking, probably have overtones of disappointment in his lack of expertise in rhetorical skills[48] and lack of physical "presence,"[49] the context of vv. 1-11

43. Their verdict on Paul, as quoted by him, has a rhetorical ring to it: (1) It is in two parts, balanced by μὲν . . . δέ; (2) the twofold character of his letters ("weighty and forceful") in the first part is balanced in the second by (a) his "presence," which is "feeble," and (b) his "speech," which is "beneath contempt." Perhaps their very rebuke was crafted to show up his lack of rhetorical skill (see on 11:6).

44. V. 1, κατὰ πρόσωπον . . . ταπεινὸς . . . ἀπὼν . . . θαρρῶ; v. 2, παρὼν [μὴ] θαρρῶ; v. 11, τῷ λόγῳ δι᾽ ἐπιστολῶν ἀπόντες . . . παρόντες τῷ ἔργῳ; cf. 13:2, ὡς παρὼν τὸ δεύτερον καὶ ἀπὼν νῦν; 13:10, ἀπὼν γράφω ἵνα παρὼν μὴ ἀποτόμως χρήσωμαι.

45. Gk. ἡ δὲ παρουσία τοῦ σώματος; NIV, "in person"; lit. "the presence of [his] body." It should be noted that παρουσία is related to παρών (cf. vv. 2, 11; 13:2, 10), both of which derive from πάρειμι (cf. ἀπών from ἄπειμι). Since παρουσία was used of the "arrival" of official visitors and notable people, with appropriate pomp and circumstance, their words ἡ δὲ παρουσία τοῦ σώματος may be quite sarcastic. His παρουσία should have been what his letters were, βαρεῖαι καὶ ἰσχυραί, but it was ἀσθενής, "feeble." *His* "arrival" was a distinct anticlimax.

46. Gk. βαρεῖαι καὶ ἰσχυραί. The former, βαρεῖαι, implies "burdensome" (1 John 5:3); and the latter, ἰσχυραί, implies "forceful" (cf. "confident" — v. 1).

47. Gk. ἀσθηνής, with cognates ἀσθενεῖν, ἀσθένεια, is critical in Paul's dialectic with the Corinthians, whose self-estimation was one of strength upon which they placed great store (cf. 1 Cor 2:3; 4:10; 2 Cor 11:21, 29, 30; 12:5, 9, 10). It is likely that the Corinthians were generally influenced by the traditional Greek veneration for gods and heroes, as portrayed by statues emphasizing physical perfection and power.

48. It is clear from his defensive tones in 1 Corinthians that Paul has been made to feel inadequate in rhetorical speech (1 Cor 2:1-5; cf. 1:18-31). Possibly the arrival of the verbally gifted Apollos between Paul's first visit and the writing of the (extant) First Letter created some sense of dissatisfaction with Paul's capacity as a public speaker (cf.

makes it probable that their primary criticisms were directed at his unimpressive attempts to discipline the morally wayward during the recent visit (cf. 13:2; 12:21; 10:1-2), and the dispatch, instead, of a letter when they were expecting a return visit (1:15–2:3).

11 Using earlier vocabulary — "absent . . . present [vv. 1-2] . . . reckon [vv. 2 (twice), 4, 7] . . . letters" (v. 10) — Paul now rounds off vv. 1-11[50] by addressing his detractors in the *persona* of a notional individual.[51] Paul directly contradicts the devastating complaint reported in v. 10. "Let such a one 'reckon' " — Paul advises his detractor — "that what we are when 'absent' by *word (logō)* through our letters we are also by *work (ergō)* when present."[52]

Here Paul may be reiterating his own complaint, made earlier (v. 7), that in judging Paul these persons have "not looked at what is before their eyes," that is, the undeniable fact of the Corinthian church. We can only speculate what Paul is referring to in speaking of his effectiveness when present with them. Perhaps he is saying that, despite their criticism that his recent visit accomplished little, it should not be forgotten that he managed to retain the loyalty of the greater majority of the church, even though they

---

Acts 18:24-28 in regard to Apollos — ἀνὴρ λόγιος . . . δυνατὸς ὢν ἐν ταῖς γραφαῖς . . . ζέων τῷ πνεύματι ἐλάλει . . . εὐτόνως γὰρ τοῖς Ἰουδαίοις διακατηλέγχετο δημοσία ἐπιδεικνὺς διὰ τῶν γραφῶν εἶναι τὸν Χριστὸν Ἰησοῦν). See on 11:6.

49. Although the Corinth of Paul's day had a Roman foundation, the Greek cultural influence should not be underestimated. For centuries Greek art and sculpture had expressed evident appreciation for outward form, both of buildings and of people, in particular athletes and warriors who were customarily presented "heroically." Consistent with this the public orator was judged for the excellence of his rhetoric as well as for his physical presence, both the power of his voice and an imposing bearing (cf. Epictetus, *Dissertations* 3.22.86-89; Lucian, *Lover of Lies* 34, *Dream* 13; Dio Chrysostom, *Discourses* 8.2; Theon, 2.112-15. See generally C. B. Forbes, "Comparison," 1-30). According to an oft-quoted second-century work *The Acts of Paul and Thecla,* Paul was unpromising in this regard: "A man of middling size, and his hair was scanty, and his legs were a little crooked, and his knees were projecting; and he had large eyes and his eyebrows met, and his nose was somewhat long . . ." (quoted in Plummer, 283; see further E. M. Howe, "Interpretations of Paul," 33-49). This description, if authentic, though unflattering, hardly justifies the description of Paul as ἀσθενής. It is possible that a long-term illness or disability ("the thorn in the flesh" — 12:7) is intended by ἀσθενής (see on 12:7).

50. By this repetition of vocabulary (ring composition or *inclusio*) Paul rounds off the section.

51. It remains possible that Paul is employing the singular to address the leader of a group (see also v. 7).

52. My translation of τῷ λόγῳ δι᾽ ἐπιστολῶν ἀπόντες/παρόντες τῷ ἔργῳ. The NIV has "what we are in our letters when we are absent . . . we will be by our actions when we are present." Paul's nicely balanced rhetoric may have been provoked here by the jibe that his speech (λόγος) is "beneath contempt" (v. 10).

needed to be more demonstrative in their support (2:6; 6:11-13; 7:12). But Paul is not only defending himself against the widely held view of his ineffectiveness in the recent past. More particularly he is preparing the way for the third visit. If they hold a healthy opinion of him only, and ironically, as a letter writer, let them understand that Paul will be no less powerful in person, as he plans to come to them soon, prepared to discipline those who persist in sexual immorality (10:2; 12:20; 13:2).[53]

Paul is here defending his effectiveness when "present," not merely his effectiveness when "absent," as a letter writer. Nonetheless, it should be noted that Paul does not disclaim, but tacitly endorses, the effectiveness of his letters, undergirding their importance to this church and to other churches.[54] Such letters, which, in the nature of things, come to churches in his absence, are no less an expression of "the authority the Lord gave" for "building up" (v. 8) believers and churches than his own immediate physical presence (cf. 1 Thess 5:27; 2 Thess 2:15; 3:14). In the physical absence of the apostle then — as well as now — his letters express the Lord's "authority" to his apostle *in absentia*.

In the previous passage (vv. 1-11) Paul began in earnest to confront the Corinthians with the reality of his impending final visit. Against their misconception of his ineffectiveness in person — as opposed to his perceived, sarcastically affirmed strength as an absent writer of "frightening" letters (vv. 9-11) — Paul assures them of a firmness of approach when he comes, though he hopes a change of heart about him will make that unnecessary (vv. 2, 11).

The passage reflects Paul's sense of being adjudged spiritually unempowered by (some of?) them, a man of "flesh" (v. 2). But let them look at what is before their eyes (the church) as well as what is within (the Spirit). If they are "of Christ," Christians, then so, too, is he, and, indeed, more. He is an apostle; what is before their eyes, as well as within them, should tell them that (v. 7). Let them understand that his ministry is modeled on Christ — his "meekness and gentleness" (v. 1) — as authorized by the Lord to build up his church (v. 8). Despite their low view of his effectiveness, his ministry is divinely empowered to humble proud rebels against God in obedience to Christ (vv. 3-6).

Throughout 2 Corinthians Paul portrays the conversion of believers in

---

53. So Martin, 313. Identification of τῷ ἔργῳ — as opposed to τῷ λόγῳ — with "signs, wonders . . . miracles" (12:12) is unlikely since these are phenomena that occurred when Paul established the church in Corinth. The ἔργον that is in prospect relates to his effective discipline of sinners.

54. As a measure of the importance of his letters in his eyes, Paul urged that they be copied and shared with other churches, even though the occasion of writing may have been specific to the church to whom it was directed (Col 4:16; cf. Rev 1:4, 11).

general in terms of his own specific and unique experience.[55] It is also likely that in describing his unique ministry as an apostle he is describing pastoral and evangelistic ministry in general.

Several implications may be drawn from Paul's pastoral method in the writing of this letter. First, those engaged in Christian ministry should, like Paul, model themselves on Christ — his "meekness and gentleness" — using the weapons of the Spirit, not the flesh, confident that God will achieve his purposes through such a ministry. Second, let those who are tempted to be dismissive of the ministry of others take heed lest they pass judgment by outward and secular criteria such as the numerical growth of a congregation. The Lord judges his ministers (1 Cor 4:4-5; cf. 2 Cor 5:10).

B. "SUPERLATIVE" APOSTLES (10:12–12:13)

1. Intruders (10:12-18)

> 12 *We do not dare to classify or compare ourselves with some who commend themselves. When they measure themselves by themselves and compare themselves with themselves, they are not wise.* 13 *We,[1] however, will not boast beyond proper limits, but will confine our boasting to the field God has assigned to us, a field that reaches even to you.* 14 *We are not going too far in our boasting, as would be the case if we had not come to you, for we did get as far as you with the gospel of Christ.* 15 *Neither do we go beyond our limits by boasting of work done by others. Our hope is that, as your faith continues to grow, our area of activity among you will greatly expand,* 16 *so that we can preach the gospel in the regions beyond you. For we do not want to boast about work already done in another man's territory.* 17 *But, "Let him who boasts boast in the Lord."* 18 *For it is not the one who commends himself who is approved, but the one whom the Lord commends.*

Chapters 10–13 are Paul's emotionally charged admonition to the Corinthians to set certain matters right so as to relieve Paul of that task when he will make his final visit to them. In these chapters various groups — those who

---

55. E.g., 3:16; 4:6; 5:14-17.

1. The omission from D*, G, the Old Latin, and in part the Vulgate of the last words of v. 12 and the first of v. 13 (οὐ συνιᾶσιν. ἡμεῖς δέ) is attributable to the copyist's eye passing from οὐ to οὐκ (so Metzger, 583). For arguments in favor of the shorter reading, which, however, he rejects, see Furnish, 470.

regard him as spiritually powerless (10:1-11), the "superlative" apostles (10:12–12:13), and the morally wayward (12:20–13:3) — come more clearly into view, though he had made reference to them briefly in earlier parts of the letter. Thus, in the previous eleven verses he had admonished his detractors, who are indigenous to Corinth. Now, although he continues to address the Corinthians, he is really directing his attention — obliquely — to his major opponents, the outsiders, the "superlative" apostles, whom he is contrasting with himself. He had already briefly referred to their arrival (2:17–3:1[2]; cf. 5:11-13); now he deals with them at considerable length, devoting the greater part of chapters 10–12 to their damaging influence in Corinth (10:12–12:13).

In this passage he declares — with heavy irony — that he will not dare compare himself with those who commend themselves. Because Paul is outside their circle and cannot be compared with them, their comparison of him reveals a lack of understanding (v. 12). Referring to the respective spheres of missionary labor allocated to the newcomers and to him, he does take pride ("boasts") in the "field" God has assigned to him, and he has come as far as Corinth (v. 13). But he does not "boast" in what is "off limits" to him. For — unlike the newcomers — he has not overreached himself; indeed, he has reached even to them with the gospel of Christ (v. 14). So — again unlike the newcomers — he does not take pride in what is "off limits," that is, in the "labors of others." But he hopes that, as the faith of the Corinthians grows, his ministry among them will increase and overflow so that he is able to evangelize in regions beyond them, not in another person's field, taking pride in work already done (vv. 15-16). It is only in the Lord that one can take pride; for it is not the one who commends himself who is "proven," but the one whom the Lord commends (vv. 17-18).

This passage, while appearing to be about Paul, is also about those who "classify or compare" themselves with him, with those who, thereby, "commend" themselves. Only once does he refer to them, and then only in an impersonal manner ("*some* who commend *themselves . . . they*"[3] — v. 12). It should be noted that he does not address them directly nor exhort them even indirectly. They are simply there, offstage — as it were — not dignified by direct reference. Their method is to "commend" themselves (vv. 12, 18), as they rhetorically "classify" and "compare" themselves with him (v. 12[4]),

2. In our view the peddlers (2:17) = the "superlative" apostles (11:5; 12:11) = the false apostles (11:13).

3. Gk. τισιν . . . ἑαυτοὺς . . . αὐτοί.

4. The main part of Paul's "Fool's Speech" (11:22–12:10) is Paul's parody of their rhetorical comparison of themselves with him.

thus seeking to undermine Paul's position in Corinth. Paul's repeated use of the negative in this passage[5] reveals the extent to which he must reply to their polemic against him.

Critical to this passage is Paul's denial that he has evangelized "in the field of another man"[6] (v. 16). Who is this "other man" who had "already" ministered in Corinth? One possible answer is Cephas, who had visited Corinth between the time Paul founded the church and his writing of the First Letter (i.e., between *c.* A.D. 52 and 55).[7] On this hypothesis the newcomers may be arguing that by his coming to Corinth Cephas had staked the claim for the present (Jewish) mission, which they are now exploiting in a way Cephas may not have foreseen or intended. Quite possibly they argued that *Paul* was the interloper in a field of mission that was properly theirs on account of Cephas,[8] to the exclusion of Paul (see the comments on vv. 13, 14, 15, and 16). From Paul's position, given the place of Cephas in early Christianity, this would be an extremely sensitive matter, perhaps explaining the obliqueness of the passage. This reconstruction, while possible, remains conjectural. It is equally possible, and perhaps simpler, to say that this "another" is a notional self-reference to Paul himself, as if to say, "these men have come into *my* field."

Paul's is a two-edged approach. In addition to defending himself against this assault, he is able to make his own criticism of the newcomers, who are guilty of trespassing into Paul's "field" of labor. The pattern of negatives in this passage serves both purposes. The succession of negative statements, by stating what is *not* true of him, serves — indirectly — to accuse them.

12 The initial explanatory "For,"[9] followed by the verb "dare,"[10] sets up a contrast with v. 2, and with vv. 1-11 overall, where Paul "dares" those Corinthians who "reckon" that he "walks according to the flesh." With outsiders now in view, he states, ironically, that he does *not* "dare" to "classify

---

5. It is striking that, apart from the citation of Jer 9:23 in v. 17, every sentence in the paragraph contains the negative particle, which is sometimes repeated (v. 12 [twice], 13, 14-16 [four times], 18).

6. Gk. ἐν ἀλλοτρίῳ κανόνι; NIV, "in another man's teritory."

7. See Barrett, *Essays,* 35-39; Martin, 323. However, Fee, *First Corinthians,* 57-58, is quite doubtful of this hypothesis.

8. Barrett, 38, comments: "Peter, in the hands of those who made use of him, was on his way to ruining Paul's work in Corinth."

9. Gk. γάρ. There is no need to posit a hiatus between v. 11 and v. 12 due to, e.g., "a pause in dictation" (so Windisch, 308). It should be noted that Paul continues with the first person plural pronoun to which he had reverted in v. 11 and which continues through to v. 18.

10. Gk. τολμῶμεν (see also 10:2; 11:21).

or compare" (*enkrinai . . . synkrinai*[11]) himself with those who "commend themselves." Indeed,[12] such persons are "without understanding" because they "measure themselves by themselves and compare[13] themselves with themselves."

"Commend,"[14] which appears again at v. 18 (thus framing the paragraph), occurred earlier in the letter (3:1) when Paul's newly arrived opponents (2:17–3:1) first appear. In all probability the reappearance here of "commend" signals that these "peddlers" are now reintroduced. Here is a brief recall of that sentence. In 3:1 Paul denies that he is commending himself, but especially contrasts himself to these interlopers who need letters of commendation to give them access to the churches. Paul needs no such thing. Now, and with not-too-subtle irony, Paul declares that "commend[ing]" is something he would not "dare" to do. Only the Lord can commend his servants; they cannot commend themselves (10:18; cf. 3:2-3). Paul is the apostle of Christ, not of men (Gal 1:1), and he is commended by Christ, not men.[15]

---

11. Gk. ἐγκρῖναι ἢ συγκρῖναι. There is a play on words (the spelling is supported by B* and D*), something in which Paul evidently takes some pleasure. The one — ἐγκρῖναι — means to judge within a class (as, e.g., among of group of enlisted soldiers or athletes in a contest — see Furnish, 469); the other — συγκρῖναι — means to contrast or compete with something outside its class (see Furnish, 481). Various efforts have been made to point up the pun (paronomasia): Plummer, 286, "pair or compare"; RSV, "class or compare"; NIV, "classify or compare"; and, less probably, Hughes, noting the use of ἐγκρῖναι in athletic imagery (365 n. 21), "compete or compare."

12. Gk. ἀλλά, emphasizing contrast with and opposition to "those who commend themselves."

13. The verb συγκρίνειν appears in both sentences, in the first paired as a wordplay with ἐγκρίνειν and in the second with μετροῦν. Μετροῦν is carried on into the passage in its cognates τὸ μέτρον (v. 13) and τὰ ἄθμετρα (vv. 13, 15). Forbes, "Comparison," 1-30, shows that σύγκρισις was used in formal rhetorical education (Hermogenes, *Progymnasmata*, e.g., "for we compare city with city . . . race with race, nurture with nurture, pursuits, affairs, external relations" — cited on 7-8). Nonetheless, there are vulgar examples of its use by poorly qualified but pretentious teachers who are overreaching their capacities. If Paul is using συγκρίνειν in this sense, the irony already so evident in the verse is intensified.

14. Gk. συνιστανόντων. The verb συνιστάνειν does not occur in 1 Corinthians and apart from two references (6:4; 7:11) occurs in 2 Corinthians in passages that appear to relate to the newcomers (3:1; 4:2; 5:12; 10:12, 18; 12:11).

15. Martin, 316-317, correctly understands this passage to be Paul's response to the opponents' rejection of Paul's jurisdiction in that "territory." He notes four responses of Paul to this challenge: (1) Paul has the "power to deal effectively with the situation," whether by letter or in person; (2) his "measure" for legitimacy of ministry is what had been "apportioned" him by God; his opponents are self-authorized, pointing to "charismatic powers" as accrediting "signs"; (3) he appeals to his prior arrival in Corinth, staking a claim based on the missionary concordat (Gal 2:6-10); and (4) Corinth is his "home base," from which he will launch forth to further regions of missionary work.

However, this reconstruction does not place sufficient weight, on the one hand,

In any case, their self-commendation is futile. Unlike Paul, to whom the Lord gave his authority (v. 8), their commendation issues from within their own circle, from no one higher than themselves. Through his apostolic call, however, Paul is unique, not able to be "classified" or "compared" with them (see also on 11:12). He is outside such comparisons, in a class by himself.

For the reason that he will give at the end of the paragraph — that not the self-commended but only those the Lord commends are "proven" — Paul in this opening verse is dismissive of those who "classify" or "compare" themselves so as to seek "commendation" or legitimacy for their ministry. Such comparing and contrasting is, he says, "without understanding" (RSV).[16] The creation in Corinth of a new covenant community directed to Christ and Spirit-anointed (1:21-22; 3:2-3; 11:3-4) was the "proof," the Lord's own commendation of Paul's ministry (v. 18). Those who seek accreditation from earthbound others do not begin to understand the Lord's ways.

The point of their "classification and comparison" of themselves with him, which emerges as 10:12–12:13 unfolds, was to establish their *superiority* to Paul in ministry,[17] in two areas in particular — in rhetoric (11:5-6) and in "visions and revelations" (12:1; cf. 5:12-13). Although Paul says he will not "classify and compare [himself]," he does precisely that, but in a radically different and surprising manner (11:21–12:13). He points to his superiority in ministry through a display of *weaknesses*.

We do not know how many persons were involved or what the complete range of comparison might have been. What does emerge from this verse and from the paragraph as a whole is that a significant mission existed, as we infer from the sixfold repetition of "themselves" within the verse. This impression is reinforced from 3:1, where we learn that these newcomers arrived with "letters of recommendation" *from* another place or places and that they sought letters from the Corinthians *to* other places to secure a "field" of ministry

---

on Paul's apostolicity (1:1) and the authority delegated to him by the Lord (10:8; 13:10), nor, on the other, to the significance of the Jerusalem missionary concordat for mission work in the apostolic era (Gal 2:6-10). Paul rejects human "recommendation" precisely because the *Lord* has called him en route to Damascus and "commends" the reality of that call by the creation of congregations that are εἰς Χριστόν (1:21; 11:2-3; cf. 3:2). The considerations mentioned by Martin, while true enough, do not appear to coincide with the apostle's scale of importance.

16. Furnish, 480, argues that their lack of understanding is their "lack of self-knowledge," and that they have "exceeded the boundaries of what is true and proper," criticisms others have have made of Paul, which he now turns back on them.

17. The preposition ὑπέρ, including its use in compound verbs, is very important in 10:12–12:13 — ὑπέρ, 11:23; ὑπερεκτείνειν, 10:14; ὑπερέκεινα, 10:16; ὑπερλίαν, 11:5; ὑπερβαλλόντως, 11:23; ὑπεραίρομαι, 12:7; and ὑπερβολή, 12:7. Paul's denial of inferiority to the "superlative" apostles (ὑπερλίαν ἀπόστολοι) — except in speech (11:5-6; cf. 12:11) — is his reply to their negative comparison of him to themselves.

elsewhere (cf. v. 15). It is almost certainly a Jewish network — a Jewish *Christian* network (see on 11:23) — extending from Jerusalem (?) and other places (?), and which — to Paul's chagrin — is now establishing itself in Corinth.

13 Paul's opening words, "But we,"[18] establish an immediate contrast between himself and those who "commend" their ministry to the Corinthians as they "classify"/"compare"/"measure" themselves with him (v. 12). Unlike them, he does not[19] "boast" in regions that are "beyond proper limits,"[20] but only according to the "measure of the field" (*kanōn*[21]) that God has "allocated" to him as "his measure."[22] In keeping with this "measure" he has reached "even"[23] as far as the Corinthians. In other words, Paul asserts that in having come to Corinth he is operating within the "field" God has

18. Gk. ἡμεῖς δέ.

19. This is the first example in this passage of the negative οὐκ by which Paul appears both to defend himself and to attack his opponents. This verse, in two parts of unequal length, is a "not . . . but" (Gk. οὐκ . . . ἀλλά) contrast.

20. Gk. εἰς τὰ ἄμετρα (exactly as in v. 15), i.e, as relating to Paul's assigned sphere of ministry. Less probably, however, it could mean "excessively" or "inappropriately," as in, e.g., Epictetus, *Encheiridion* 33.14.

21. Gk. κανών. This word is critical to the meaning of this verse and the paragraph (cf. vv. 15, 16). Paul had used it previously (Gal 6:16) in a quite different sense. The uncertainty of understanding it here is illustrated by Lightfoot, who took the image to be from the surveying and allocation of land, and by Hughes, who thought it meant the runners' lanes in an athletic contest (see Hughes, 366-67).

An inscription from Sagalassos (Pisidia) on which the word is found indicates that κανών is used for "the imposition of transport and billeting services upon local communities" by the Roman authorities. E. A. Judge, *New Docs.* 1.36-45, commenting on κανών in the Sagalassos inscription, notes: "It means . . . the official schedule, in this case of transport services to be supplied by the local community. . . . The κανών is not in itself a a geographical concept, but the services it formulates are in this case geographically partitioned. . . . [Paul] reflects the older spirit of the liturgical system (i.e., of civic duties) as a competition in honour through duty fulfilled. To go beyond one's limit would deprive the next man of his turn." See also *New Docs.* 2.88. Furnish's translation, 471, "jurisdiction," captures the idea of "sphere" and "right," but it may impose a specifically legal meaning not altogether present with κανών. "Field," a geographic category, is less satisfactory but difficult to improve on as a translation.

22. The verse is dominated by the vocabulary of measurement: Τὰ ἄμετρα . . . τὸ μέτρον τοῦ κανόνος . . . ἐμέρισεν . . . μέτρου. Much depends on whether the vocabulary of measurement in this verse and in vv. 12-16 is taken metaphorically or literally. Barrett, 263, regards the comparison as related to "apostolic status," boasting in which is inappropriate for the newcomers since Christ himself is the only possible instrument of measurement. The geographical language, however, is sustained throughout the passage, suggesting that Paul's basic point of reference is to geographical missionary demarcation (so Furnish, 471; Martin, 320; *contra* Barrett, 265).

23. Gk. καὶ ὑμῶν is emphatic, "even to you."

demarcated to him; but, by implication, the outsiders, in coming there, have trespassed into a sphere established by God for Paul.

> We will not boast beyond limits,
> > but
> [we will   boast]
> > > according to the measure of the field
> > > that God has allocated to us
> > > > as our measure
> > > > > to reach even as far as you.

The meaning of this verse, although not clear in itself nor from its immediate or broader contexts, must — by the confident manner he expresses it — have been obvious to the Corinthians. We, however, are forced to look elsewhere to make sense of it. Most probably the apostle is alluding to the missionary concordat in Jerusalem in c. A.D. 47 between the "pillars" of the mother church and the delegates from the church of Antioch (Gal 2:7-10).[24] It was then agreed that, since Paul had been entrusted with "the gospel to the uncircumcised . . . [a mission] for the Gentiles," he should "go" to them,[25] on the understanding that he would "remember the poor," that is, the "poor among the saints in Jerusalem" (Rom 15:26, RSV; cf. 1 Cor 16:4; 2 Cor 8:4; 9:1, 12).

This missionary agreement, however, was dependent upon God's anterior commission to Paul on the Damascus Road that he "preach his [Son] among the Gentiles" (Gal 1:16), a commission that owed nothing to human intermediaries (Gal 1:1, 10-12). Paul's present reference to "the field God . . . assigned to [him]" probably has in mind both the divine commission and its endorsement by the missionary accord in Jerusalem in c. A.D. 47.[26] Deliberate missionary work among the Gentiles followed, including that within major

24. Furnish, 481, rejects this interpretation on the ground that there is no direct reference to the Jerusalem meeting in this passage but an allusion to God's commission to Paul to take the gospel to the Gentiles. It is likely, however, that any reference Paul makes to the Jerusalem concordat rests on the more basic reality of the Damascus Road call. He could not refer to the one without thinking about the other.

25. The "pillar" apostles, in agreeing that (Barnabas and) Saul should "go" to the Gentiles, confirmed as acceptable the gospel he preached to the Gentiles (Gal 2:2) and that he had been "entrusted" (i.e., by God — en route to Damascus?) with the "mission" (ἀποστολή, "apostolate") to the Gentiles (Gal 2:7-9). Paul's dominical commission was direct and unmediated; the Jerusalem accord recognized and confirmed that mission, but did not initiate it.

26. That God's Damascus Road commission of him and the Jerusalem missionary accord dovetailed in Paul's mind may be seen that both are recorded in the one letter and in the appropriate sequence (Gal 1:11-17; 2:7-10).

cities of the Aegean provinces. In accordance with God's commission and the missionary accord, Paul had "reach[ed][27] even to [them]" in Achaia.

Thus Paul does "not boast beyond proper limits," unlike his opponents who have trespassed into his missionary "field," the Gentiles. To be sure, there was a synagogue in Corinth, and Jews were among the believers in the church of Corinth (Acts 18:8). The newly arrived Jewish missionaries probably had been received into their homes, as Cephas had doubtless also been (the same houses?). Nonetheless, it was essentially a Gentile church in a Gentile region. Not least, Paul had arrived first (see on v. 14). Paul is pointing out that Corinth is his rightful sphere of missionary labor and that the "superlative" apostles have intruded into it "beyond proper limits." Corinth is a "field" assigned to him by God.[28]

In this verse Paul introduces to the paragraph the "boasting"[29] vocabulary that will reappear significantly toward its end (in vv. 15-17), as well as in later paragraphs in 10:12–12:13 and that relates to the claims of the newcomers. Paul's opponents use the vocabulary to make capital in their competition with him; for him "boasting" means, in the good sense, "taking pride in"[30] something.

We infer from Paul's reference to "boasting" that his opponents "boasted." But in what? As we reconstruct it, their "boast" consists in those ministry-related matters in which, after classifying, comparing, and measuring themselves with Paul, they declare themselves to be "superior" (see on 11:5, 23). In the present case the newcomers may have "boasted" of coming as far as they have — even to Corinth — perhaps a distance greater than Paul had traveled to come to them.[31] Be that as it may, they have certainly intruded

27. Gk. ἐφίκεσθαι, though common in Classical Greek, is found only here in the NT.

28. Unless, following Barrett and Martin (see n. 7), we identify "another" in v. 16 with Cephas. Cephas appears to have visited Corinth between Paul's first visit and the writing of 1 Corinthians (cf. 1 Cor 1:12; 3:22; 9:5; cf. 15:5). On this hypothesis the newcomers would have pointed to a synagogue ministry in Corinth by Cephas, seeking now, on that basis, to expand a work among the Jews as well as some kind of penetration into the wider community of believers in the city. Such claims, if they were in fact made, could not be upheld; Paul arrived before Cephas and had a sustained relationship with the Corinthians over a seven-year period. See further on v. 16.

29. Gk. καυχησόμεθα, "we will boast." By immediately referring to "boasting," which he denies doing, Paul appears to be drawing a close connection with classifying/comparing of v. 12. The verb ("boast") from the first part of the sentence must be understood in the second.

30. See on 1:12. "Boasting," although culturally unusual to modern readers, was unexceptional then. The great Roman politicians and generals unself-consciously "boasted" of their civic and military deeds, as did Jews of their piety (Luke 18:11-12).

31. The distance from Jerusalem to Corinth is further than from Antioch to Corinth, i.e., on the presumption that the "superlative" apostles have come from Jerusalem.

into a field that does not belong to them. As the passage develops, Paul will, in fact, "boast" — he has been forced to ("I must boast" — 11:30; 12:1) by his opponents' "boasting" (11:16-18) — but it will be "boasting" that is "foolish" because it will be "boasting in weakness" (11:30; 12:5, 9). The "measuring" of themselves with him and their "boasting" of "superiority" over him will compel him to "boast — but of weaknesses" — and "force" him "to become a fool" (12:11).

14 Having stated[32] in the previous verse that he reached even as far as Corinth, Paul repeats that assertion, adding "for[33] . . . we are not over-extending ourselves," obliquely inferring that the newcomers have over-reached themselves. He repeats his "for," explaining, "we reached even as far as you with the gospel of Christ."

> For we are not[34] overextending ourselves
> as [we should be doing[35]] if
>   we did not reach   even to you.
> For we   reached even as far as you
> with the gospel of Christ.

Paul's opponents appear to be claiming that Corinth was their rightful "field," though we can only guess at the basis for their claim.[36] Whatever it was, for Paul they were the ones who had "overreached" in coming to Corinth.

The sentence is dominated by vocabulary of distance and space, consistent with the theme of measurement of the previous verse.[37] Specifically, Paul has not "overreached"[38] himself in "reaching even to you"[39] (Corinthi-

---

32. Following Plummer, 288, we take v. 14 as leading into v. 15 and not a parenthesis of v. 13.

33. Gk. γάρ.

34. Gk. οὐ. Once again Paul employs a negative as the first word of a sentence (as also in vv. 12, 15), by which he is able to defend himself while indirectly accusing his opponents.

35. Plummer, 288, proposed the addition of certain words to make sense of the sentence.

36. Were they pointing, perhaps, to Cephas's sojourn in Corinth (see on vv. 13, 16) as having staked a claim for a Jewish mission there, arguing that it was Paul who was the intruder in his planned return to the city? See above, n. 7.

37. Gk. ἐφικνούμενοι ("reach") . . . ὑπερεκτείνομεν ("overextend") . . . ἐφθάσαμεν ("reach").

38. Gk. ὑπερεκτείνομεν, "overreach" (RSV), "going too far" (NIV, which unhelpfully makes "boasting" the object). On the importance of ὑπέρ to the vocabulary of the opponents, who saw Paul as ὕστερ-, "inferior," see the notes to v. 12 and the comment on 11:5. The proliferation of verbs compounded with ὑπέρ in 10:12–12:13 makes it almost certain that these words originate with Paul as his ironic response to opponents who present themselves — by various modes of *comparison* (cf. v. 12) — as "superior" to (ὑπέρ) Paul.

ans) with the gospel of Christ. This would be true had Paul not ventured beyond his base, Antioch. It is no less true because Paul has come as far even as to them. Gentile Corinth is as much part of the gospel "field" demarcated by God to Paul as Gentile Antioch.

But what is Paul implying about the movements of the intruders?[40] In reaching Corinth they have "overextended" themselves. The "field" of mission God has assigned to them is either in Judaea or with the Jews of the Diaspora living among the Gentiles. We may conjecture that had they come to Corinth and confined their ministry to the synagogue (as Cephas had?), there would have been no problem. The difficulty appears to be that these newcomers are not content with that; they wish to move into Paul's God-assigned "field" of ministry, the Gentiles.

Paul loses no opportunity to remind the Corinthians — and other readers as well — that the "gospel of Christ/of God" was the prime reason for the distance traveled. Paul is reflecting here on the two dovetailing realities: the Lord's commission to be his apostle to the Gentiles, and the missionary concordat of Jerusalem of *c.* A.D. 47 that recognized that commission, agreeing that Paul should "go" to the Gentiles (see on v. 13). Thus understood, it was for "the gospel"[41] — the mission to the Gentiles — that Paul came originally to Corinth (11:7; cf. 1:19; 2:17; 4:5; 5:11, 20), as it had been also to Troas (2:12). His complaint against the newcomers was not only that they had intruded into a "field" of mission divinely assigned to him, but also that the message they brought was "heterodox" (11:4; cf. 3:7-11).

15-16 As Paul's sentence proceeds, he returns to the theme of boasting (v. 13), but now in terms of having reached even Corinth in proclaiming the gospel about Christ. He now sets out to explain what "boasting within

---

Thus, against Martin, 321, ὑπερεκτείνειν is Paul's word for them, not their word for him. Martin's attempt (following those of H. D. Betz and P. Marshall) to find traces of "over-weening pride" (ὕβρις) in the opponents' accusation of Paul seems tenuous.

39. Gk. καὶ ὑμῶν ἐφθάσαμεν; NIV, "We came as far as you." Here the καί is emphatic: "We came *even* to you." Scholars are divided over the translation of φθάνειν, whether, e.g., with Hughes (366 n. 24) and Barrett (266), it should be regarded as "come first, precede" (so 1 Thess 4:15 and in classical use), or (as, e.g., with Furnish, 472) simply as "come" (so 1 Thess 2:16; Rom 9:31; Phil 3:16). Since Paul does not "want to boast about work done in another man's territory" (v. 16; cf. Rom 15:20), it seems that *prior* arrival was one of the principles by which rightful access to a mission field was determined.

40. If Paul is defending himself from the opponents' accusation that he is in some way "overextending himself," it would be interesting to know where they thought he should have remained. Possibly they claimed that he should have confined himself to the region of Coele-Syria and not embarked on his missionary journeys, including that to Corinth (cf. Acts 15:23; D. R. Catchpole, "Apostolic Decree," 436-39).

41. Gk. τὸ εὐαγγέλιον τοῦ Χριστοῦ — an objective genitive: the gospel that is about Christ.

proper limits" means. Repeating that phrase, he now adds — in light of v. 14 — "in work done by others." Rather,[42] he hopes that, as their faith grows, his ministry among them within his "field"[43] may be increased and overflow so as to evangelize regions beyond them, so as not to boast in work already in another's field (as the intruders are doing).

The text is complex and the verse divisions unhelpful. The conclusion of the previous verse ("For we reached even as far as you with the gospel of Christ") carries over to the first part of this verse ("not[44] boasting beyond limits"[45]). The second part of v. 15 ("we hope[46] that as your faith grows,[47] our ministry among you within our field might be increased to overflowing"[48]) continues into the first part of v. 16 ("to evangelize in regions beyond you").

Verse 15a repeats in almost identical terms the phrase from v. 13,[49] except that now, by the phrase he adds, he amplifies its meaning. Thus, his words "in the labors[50] of others" explain the meaning of "beyond limits" from v. 13. The territory that is "beyond limits" is one in which "the labors of others" occur.

As in vv. 13 and 14, Paul is here obliquely accusing the newcomers of encroaching into the "labors of others," that is, into *his* missionary and pastoral labors in Corinth. He will not evangelize "in the field of another man," nor should they. These are *Paul's* own missionary labors — his

---

42. Gk. δέ.

43. See on v. 13.

44. Gk. οὐκ. Once again a negative appears at the beginning of the sentence (see also vv. 12, 14, and 18).

45. Gk. οὐκ εἰς τὰ ἄμετρα καυχώμενοι, literally rendered, is "we do not boast in[to] the unmeasured," which probably means that he does not take pride in regions of ministry that have not been allocated to him.

46. The participles καυχώμενοι and ἔχοντες are used in an absolute sense (Plummer, 289), "we boast . . . we hope," noting the first person plural verb ἐφθάσαμεν ("we reached") in v. 14 and the first person plural pronoun ἡμῶν later in this verse.

47. Gk. αὐξανομένης τῆς πίστεως ὑμῶν (NIV, "as your faith continues to grow"), a genitive absolute construction.

48. Gk. ἐν ὑμῖν μεγαλυνθῆναι . . . εἰς περισσείαν, "[our ministry] among you . . . might be increased to overflowing." Whereas Furnish, 473, takes ἐν ὑμῖν with the previous τῆς πίστεως ὑμῶν, "as your faith grows among you," it is preferable to take it with the verb μεγαλυνθῆναι. Furnish translates μεγαλυνθῆναι . . . περισσείαν as "that . . . we may be abundantly praised." The passage, however, is consistently marked by the vocabulary of measurement, and should be so understood.

49. Gk. οὐκ εἰς τὰ ἄμετρα καυχησόμεθα (v. 13); οὐκ εἰς τὰ ἄμετρα καυχώμενοι (v. 15).

50. Gk. κόποι is used of "labors" in ministry, whether by Paul (1 Cor 3:8; 15:10b; Gal 4:11; Phil 2:16) or by others (Rom 16:6, 12; 1 Cor 15:58; 16:16; 1 Thess 5:12). But it is also used of the "labor" of self-support to make his ministry "free of charge" possible (6:5; 11:23; cf. 11:7).

measured mission "field," his pride — in which, however, the newcomers now boast.

Once again the Damascus Road commission/the missionary concordat of Jerusalem (see on v. 13) appear to be in mind. Working within the limits set — that he should go to the Gentiles/the uncircumcised — Paul has come to Achaia and established a ministry there. Thus Corinth is part of the "field" God assigned to him. But these newcomers, in setting up ministry in Corinth, are actually "boasting" of work done where they have no right to be. The Gentiles of Corinth are "out of bounds" to them; they have trespassed into his sphere of labor.

In v. 15b Paul sets forth positively his aspirations for ministry in Corinth. He appears to be alluding to his forthcoming visit to Corinth and the gospel ministry he wishes to enjoy when he comes. In direct denial of a space for ministry to the intruders, Paul "hopes" that, "as the faith [of the Corinthians][51] grows" — in response to the gospel[52] that, we infer, he will preach once more when he comes (cf. v. 14) — his ministry[53] will be greatly "increased" among them. The repetition of the critical word "field" *(kanōn)* from v. 13, but set within the phrase "according to *our* field," pointedly reminds the Corinthians that what Paul does "among [the Corinthians]" is within the limits set by God, but "off limits" for the newly arrived ministers.

In passing, it is important to note the confidence and hope expressed in v. 15b. A majority of exegetes portray chapters 10–13 as defensive, ironic, and embittered and therefore necessarily a letter separate from chapters 1–9. This opinion, however, needs to be qualified by the optimism of this verse as well as the rather genial final part of the letter (13:5-14).

Verse 16a gives the reason Paul hoped for an enlarged influence in Corinth, namely, "*that* we can preach the gospel[54] in regions beyond[55] you." The brevity of this part of the verse is such — five words in the original — that Paul's rationale is not altogether clear. Most probably he means that an

51. Gk. τῆς πίστεως ὑμῶν. For other references to the Corinthians' "faith" expressed elsewhere in this letter, see 1:24; 8:7; 13:5.

52. J. H. Schütz, *Anatomy,* 39, notes that "in almost every instance the verb εὐαγγελίζεσθαι seems to presuppose the definition of its cognate noun."

53. M. Zerwick, *Grammatical Analysis,* 556, regards the subject — which is not stated — as "we," i.e., Paul. But it is clear that it is not Paul per se who is increased, but his "labors" or "ministry."

54. Gk. εὐαγγελίσασθαι, an aorist infinitive expressing purpose.

55. Gk. τὰ ὑπερέκεινα, "regions beyond," is the substantive version of the verb appearing in v. 14. It is closely connected to, if not synonymous with, τὰ ἄμετρα (vv. 13, 15). Plummer, 289, regards this term as coined by Paul, not being found elsewhere. Some believe that τὰ ὑπερέκεινα demands a westward trajectory beyond Corinth, which would mean that these words could not have been written from Macedonia, the evident provenance of chapters 1–9. But it is to be doubted that Paul had such precise geography in mind.

expanded ministry in Gentile Corinth will give him greater confidence as he moves on to other places of ministry, in particular to Spain[56] and the western extremities of the empire (Rom 15:24, 28-29). From Paul's viewpoint it would be helpful if he left behind a strong center of faith in the Achaian capital. The bonds of fellowship and the support in prayer would be of great benefit as he moved out of that region toward the west.

But just as Paul looked "beyond" Corinth for further mission work, so, too, the newcomers looked "beyond" Corinth, as indicated by "letters of recommendation . . . *from* you" (3:1). We may discern two mission groups with competing aims, the one associated with Paul, the other with his opponents, each seeking to spring from a secure base of ministry to other places. The one was concerned with proclaiming Christ and winning allegiance to him, whereas the other was concerned with judaizing Gentiles who had already been evangelized.

Having declared his hope that the gospel should be proclaimed in "regions beyond" them, he immediately returns in v. 16b to his defense of himself as an oblique attack on the opponents. This second half of v. 16 is, in effect, a new sentence that significantly also commences with a negative (see vv. 12, 14, 15; cf. v. 13). That Paul will not take pride in *"another man's* field" is a restatement — now in the singular — of v. 15, where he would not take pride in the labors of *other men.* Paul will not — as they should not — "boast in the field of another," that is, "in regions already[57] evangelized" by *him.*

From these verses emerges a principle of missionary demarcation among the apostles. God had assigned to Paul a "field" (vv. 13, 14)[58] — the Gentiles — into which the Jewish mission may not intrude. He would not intrude into a "field" in which another apostle was already working. This appears to be confirmed by his attitude toward ministry in Rome, where the foundation had been laid by someone else (Cephas?) and upon which he would not build, even though Rome was the capital of the *Gentile* world (Rom 15:20).[59] It is a credit to Paul's breadth of vision that he can uphold the

---

56. 1 Clement, *Corinthians* 5, states that Paul traveled to the farthest limit of the west, a reference to Spain.

57. Gk. εἰς τὰ ἕτοιμα, "work already done" (RSV and NIV). This second phrase is appositional to ἐν ἀλλοτρίῳ κανόνι, "in another's field," and is in contrast to τὰ ὑπερέκεινα, "regions beyond."

58. By means of the Damascus Road commission as recognized by the missionary concordat at Jerusalem *c.* A.D. 47. See on v. 13.

59. Clearly Paul does not feel free to establish a base in Rome, through which he is passing en route to Spain (Rom 15:20-24). Someone else — probably Peter — had arrived before him, just as Paul had preceded his opponents to Corinth (cf. v. 14: ἐφθάσαμεν — "we arrived first"). Nonetheless, he does seek to impart to, and receive some benefit from, the believers there and reap a harvest among the Gentiles (Rom 1:11-15). Yet Paul will not attempt to do in Rome, on the foundation laid by someone else, what his opponents are attempting to do in Corinth, i.e., capture the ministry for themselves.

missionary rights of another apostle in circumstances where unacceptable representatives of the other mission were in the process of destroying his work in Corinth.

This apostolic principle should serve to caution missionaries and ministers beyond the apostolic age. It is no light thing to set up ministry when an acceptable and effective gospel ministry to the same people group is already in place.

17 Paul's introductory particle[60] (untranslated) serves to stop the flow of thought of the previous few verses and to introduce the biblical citation. With this verse — adapted from LXX Jer 9:24[61] (see also 1 Cor 1:31) — Paul prepares to conclude the paragraph, which he does in the verse following. The theme of "boasting," introduced in v. 13, has been very important, being repeated in vv. 15 and 16. Pointedly referring to the newcomers, Paul declares that he will not boast where he should not — "beyond proper limits" (v. 13), "in the work done by others" (v. 15), in "another's field," in "regions already evangelized" (v. 16). Unlike them, Paul will not boast where he should not.

Nonetheless, the implication from vv. 13, 15, and 16 is that Paul does boast, by which he means something rather different, namely, "takes pride in,"[62] or even "puts confidence in."[63] His opponents have given him no option but to defend and explain himself, which he has done in the previous verses of this passage. But now Paul makes it quite clear that anything that has been achieved has been only through the Lord, not by Paul his servant.[64] This is no mere passing sentiment, but a clear reference to a concrete reality, the church of Corinth, as the next verse shows.

18 With his initial explanatory "For,"[65] Paul now concludes this important paragraph begun at v. 12, clinching his arguments by referring again to the notion of "commending" with which it began.[66] In a proverblike "not . . . but" saying, the apostle declares that it is not the one who commends himself who is "proven," but the one whom the Lord commends.

---

60. Gk. δέ.

61. Cf. LXX 1 Kgdms 2:10, which is similar. Paul also alludes to LXX Jer 9:24 in Rom 2:29. Although D. Capes, *Yahweh Texts,* 135, takes "Lord" here as Christ, as indeed it must be in the verse following, the straightforward citation here of Jer 9:24 is against this.

62. See on 1:12-14, where "boasting" is ultimately eschatological; therefore, its basis in truth, or otherwise, will be revealed.

63. Jer 9:23-24, as cited by Paul in 1 Cor 1:31, and repeated here, carries this nuance.

64. See 12:11; 1 Cor 15:10; Rom 15:17; Eph 3:7; Gal 2:8 for other instances where Paul disclaims merit for what has been accomplished.

65. Gk. γάρ.

66. This is an example of "ring composition," by which an *inclusio* is formed. See also on v. 11.

As with the other sentences of the paragraph (except v. 17), a negative[67] again appears at the beginning. By this device Paul is able both to defend himself and to point to his opponents without referring directly to them. Unlike him — casting the group in the persona of an individual — these opponents commend themselves. Let them understand that it is "the one whom the Lord [Jesus[68]] commends" who is "approved." How does the Lord Jesus commend his servants? Clearly, by the concrete reality of a new covenant church, a group of people focused on Christ (*eis Christon*[69]), where the Spirit of God is concretely present to change the hearts of the people (1:21-22; 3:3; 5:5; 6:16). For all its shortcomings the assembly at Corinth is such a church, and by that church the Lord Jesus commends Paul. That church is a "letter of recommendation . . . from Christ," ministered by Paul (3:2-3), "proof"[70] of his claim to have been called by Christ to be his apostle.

Near the end of the long passage dealing with the newcomers (10:12–12:13) Paul sadly comments, "I ought to have been commended by you" (12:11). The Lord's commendation of his minister on account of effective church planting (1:18-20; 11:2-3; 12:12) ought to be echoed by the members of the church so established. Poignantly, in the case of the Corinthians, it was not.

The references to "commendation" in vv. 12 and 18 clearly tie this passage to 2:17–3:3, where Paul writes of those who bring "letters of commendation." This paragraph — linked as it is with that earlier one — lays a foundation for the strong words that follow and that are directed to those who have "received" the intruders (11:1-11) and, though expressed obliquely, to the intruders themselves (11:12-23a). These passages will form part of the "Fool's Speech," which becomes rhetorically more intense thereafter (11:23b–12:13). The passage just completed leads into the emotional climax of the letter.

The import of this passage is threefold.[71] First, Paul establishes that

---

67. Gk. οὐ.

68. The "Lord," repeated from the previous verse quoted from Jer 9:22-23, must refer in that verse to Yahweh but in this verse to the Lord Jesus. For other examples where the NT writers transfer references to Yahweh to Jesus see 1 Cor 1:31; 2:16; 10:22; Rom 10:13; Phil 2:11.

69. Gk. εἰς Χριστόν (1:21; 11:3).

70. Gk. δόκιμος, "proven," "approved." The "prove" word cluster is important within this letter: δοκιμάζειν — 8:8, 22; 13:5; δοκιμή — 2:9; 8:2; 9:13; 13:3; δόκιμος — 13:7. It should be noticed that 13:3-7 uses all three words. It is reasonable to infer that Paul's ministry was being "put to the proof" at that time.

71. J. Denney comments that "two feelings are compounded all through this passage: an intense sympathy with the purpose of God that the gospel should be preached to every creature; and an intense scorn for the spirit that sneaks and poaches on another's ground, and is more anxious that some men should be good sectarians than that all men should be good disciples" (*Second Epistle to the Corinthians*, 309).

the spreading of the gospel is the priority of Christian ministry. In Paul's case this meant the mission to the Gentiles to which he was called by God on the road to Damascus, as recognized by the missionary concordat of Jerusalem c. A.D. 47. Second, because the existence of another mission — that to the Jews — brought its own complications and tensions, accepted principles of cooperation were needed, as they continue to be in comparable situations. Third, self-commendation in Christian ministry is excluded. The Lord commends his servants for ministry by the fruits of their ministry.

2. The Fool's Speech (11:1–12:13)

The "Fool's Speech" — as it is called[1] — that follows (11:1–12:13) may be analyzed as (1) Introduction (11:1-21a), (2) the "Fool's Speech" proper (11:21b–12:10), and (3) Epilogue (12:11-13).

1. A term attributed to H. Windisch *(Narrenrede)* and justifiable by the recurring vocabulary of "foolishness" (ἀφροσύνη, ἄφρων, παράφρων) within this passage (11:1, 16 [twice], 17, 19, 23; 12:16, 11). But is there a cultural context for such a "speech"? J. McCant, "Paul's Thorn," 550-72, following — but modifying — H. D. Betz's *Paul's Apology* views the "speech" as an εἰρωνεία in "parody of self-praise," a "philosopher's apology" directed at the Corinthians (not the opponents) whereby Paul becomes an "ἄφρων because καυχᾶσθαι (12:1, 11) is forced on him. His καυχᾶσθαι is ironical because he boasts only in ἀσθενείᾳ (11:30)." Accordingly, McCant distinguishes in these chapters (1) a *prodiorthosis* (advance justification — 1:1–11:21a), (2) a "Fool's Speech" proper (11:21b–12:10), and (3) an *epidiorthosis* (subsequent justification — 12:11-18).

An obstacle to the acceptance of such analysis is the presumption that Paul had read widely in Hellenistic authors going back several centuries and was familiar with such rhetorical forms as περιαυτολογία ("self-commendation," as in Plutarch), περίστασεις ("catalogue of trials," as in Cynic-Stoic writers), and "aretalogy" (Hellenistic praise devoted to gods, heroes, and famous people). We do not find *direct* corroboration of such forms in this letter. To be sure, Paul uses some of the rhetorical vocabulary — e.g., ἐγκρῖναι . . . συγκρῖναι (10:12), ἀπολογοῦσθαι (12:19) — but this is more probably due to his increased everyday awareness of a culture that had been long influenced by rhetorical conventions in past authors. In any case, McCant concedes that Paul's boasting is "unsystematized" (560), listing no less than eight of Paul's own principles for its exercise. This appears to weaken the case that Paul was literarily dependent on Hellenistic authors in favor of a hypothesis wherein he was broadly influenced by his cultural context, which, however, he rather freely adapted. See Martin, 328-31, 358-60, for a review of scholarly opinion on Paul's dependence or otherwise on rhetorical forms. Basing his judgments on the analysis of J. Zmijewski, Martin notes, on the one hand, irony, sarcasm, mock humility, wordplay, diatribe, and rhetorical comparison, but, on the other, many Semitic elements, e.g., Hebraic couplets (12:2-4), "light to heavy" argument (11:13, 14), the divine passive (12:7), and so on, reflecting "an OT-rabbinic cast of mind."

Is the "boasting" that gives the "Fool's Speech" its "foolishness" (1) an *example* of the perceived offensiveness of promoting one's own importance (so Plutarch: "It is agreed that to speak to others of one's own importance or power is offensive, but . . . not many even

But who is the "Fool" and to whom is the "Speech" directed? The "Fool" who speaks is Paul (11:1, 16 [twice], 17, 19, 23; 12:6, 11), though he suggests that both the Corinthians and the opponents are also "fools" (11:16; 19:20). It is significant that, although he mostly uses the first person pronoun in 2 Corinthians, within the "Fool's Speech" — with the exception of 11:4, 6, 21 — he employs the first person singular, "I."[2] The hearers of the "Speech" are the Corinthians, whom he often addressed directly as "you" (11:4, 7, 8, 9, 11, 19, 20; 12:11, 13). Nonetheless, the unnamed opponents are being addressed indirectly as well (11:4-5, 12-15, 19-23a, 26, 28?); indeed, the "Speech" is necessitated by their behavior in Corinth. That Paul's only references to them are indirect may be calculated; direct reference might serve to dignify them.

While the "Fool's Speech" appears to be a discrete literary unit, it cannot be divorced from the previous passage (10:12-18), with which it is in continuity both in style and content.[3] In style, the "Speech" is an elaborate, if ironic, "comparison" between Paul and the "superlative" apostles (cf. 11:5). This "comparison" *(synkrisis)* springs from 10:12, where, to be sure, Paul declines to "classify or compare" himself with others. Nonetheless, within the "Fool's Speech" proper (11:21b–12:10) Paul proceeds to do precisely this, though it will be an utterly surprising form of "comparison" — boasting of weaknesses — which appears to be without literary precedent.[4] In content,

---

of those who condemn such conduct avoid the odium of it" — *On Praising Oneself Inoffensively* 1), as suggested by McCant, 558-59, or (2) a *parody* of the convention of self-advertisement, whether Hellenistic (so E. A. Judge, "Paul's Boasting," 37-50; "St Paul and Classical Society," 36) or Jewish (so S. Travis, "Paul's Boasting," 527-32)? Fundamental to the "Fool's Speech" is Paul's theology, or, to be precise, *Christology* of "weakness" ("Christ . . . was crucified in weakness" — 13:3, 4), which is reproduced in the weakness of his apostle (especially in the "Fool's Speech" proper — 11:23b–12:10). His boasting, which is of "weakness[es]" (11:30; 12:5, 9), is no mere rhetorical exercise in politeness consonant with, e.g., Plutarch, as above; it is christological in intent. In Judge's words, Paul was "in violent reaction to much that was central to the classical way of life" ("St Paul and Classical Society," 36), and this from the standpoint of the one "crucified in weakness."

2. For discussion on Paul's use of singular and plural first person pronouns within 2 Corinthians, see on 1:1.

3. Scholars debate the analysis of this passage and its relationship with what precedes and follows. Martin, who surveys opinions (328-29, 360-61), regards 11:1-15 as "a diversion from the chief theme begun in 10:13-18 (361). The persistent use of the "fool" vocabulary in 11:1–12:13, however, suggests that we should regard this as a coherent unit. To be sure, however, it is in continuity with 10:12-18.

4. See C. A. Barton, *Sorrows of the Ancient Romans,* 107-44, and literature cited, for the ritualized role of the *derisor,* whereby various emperors and other notables of the period provided for themselves to be mocked and pilloried by a "fool" — the *fatuus,* the *morio,* or the *sannio* — whether by buffoons, dwarfs, or the deformed, both in private and in public (including at the Saturnalia). Paul mocked *himself* as "fool," and, in the event, the Corinthians and the newcomers also.

Paul will refer to those who have "come" to Corinth (11:4). This, too, is implicit in the immediately preceding passage (cf. 10:13) as well as, of course, in 2:17–3:1, where the newcomers are first referred to in the letter.

a. The "Fool's Speech": Introduction (11:1-21a)

(1) The Corinthians "Bear with" Deceivers (11:1-4)

> 1 *I hope*[1] *you will put up with a little of my foolishness;*[2] *but you are already doing that.* 2 *I am jealous for you with a godly jealousy. I promised you to one husband, to Christ, so that I might present you as a pure virgin to him.* 3 *But I am afraid that just as Eve was deceived by the serpent's cunning, your minds may somehow be led astray from your sincere and pure*[3] *devotion to Christ.* 4 *For if someone comes to you and preaches a Jesus*[4] *other than the Jesus we preached, or if you receive a different spirit from the one you received, or a different gospel from the one you accepted, you put up with*[5] *it easily enough.*

Since we have alluded to the arrival of the newcomers in the preceding passage (10:12-18), their mission now comes into even clearer view, especially in v. 4.

Structurally this passage is framed by "bear with" (v. 1 [twice], v. 4), used in an ironic sense. The constituent parts of the closely connected passage are joined by "for . . . for . . . but . . . for. . . ."

If only they will "bear with" him in a little "foolishness." Do let them "bear with" him (v. 1). *For* he has "the jealousy of God" for them. *For* he "betrothed" them to "one husband," to "present" them as a "pure virgin," to Christ (v. 2). *But* he is afraid that as the serpent in his "cunning" deceived Eve

---

1. Gk. ὄφελον (א B M P) is to be preferred to ὤφελον (D F G K L).

2. The NIV, with some commentators, takes μου with ἀφροσύνης. It is preferable to construe μου with the verb, as in the next sentence. Thus "bear with me . . . you do bear with me."

3. Gk. καὶ τῆς ἁγνότητος is found in p⁴⁶ א* B G syrʰ copˢᵃ,ᵇᵒ but not in אᶜ Dᶜ H K P. Barrett, 270, thinks that ἁγνότητος should be omitted on the principle of *lectio brevior potior* because it copies ἁγνὴν of v. 2. Hughes, 376, however, argues for its inclusion on the ground of haplography rather than its omission on account of dittography. Metzger, 583-84, retains the longer reading but in brackets in deference to MSS that omit it. The longer reading is found in the RSV, TEV, NIV, and NAB; the shorter in the JB and the NEB.

4. A few MSS have Χριστόν.

5. Many MSS have the imperfect ἀνείχεσθε, which implies less certainty: "If he comes . . . you would bear well with him" (so Plummer, 297). But the context — as seen by the threefold repetition of γάρ — suggests a real situation supporting the retention of ἀνέχεσθε.

their "minds" may be "corrupted" from the "single-mindedness" and "purity" appropriately directed to Christ (v. 3). *For* if, indeed, someone "comes" proclaiming "another Jesus," or if they receive a "different Spirit," or if they accept a "different gospel," they "bear well with" him (v. 4).

The irony is clear. He must urge them to "bear with" him, the one who has joined them to their one true husband, Christ, but they "bear *well* with" one who proclaims "another Jesus," an alien. They have positively welcomed those[6] who are intent on destroying Paul's authority with the Corinthians. They are "bearing with" newcomers who are diverting them away from their one true husband, to whom the apostle has joined them.

These verses, therefore, along with 10:12-18, serve to contrast these "ministers" with Paul. Although he said that he would not "classify or compare" himself with them, this is what he now proceeds to do in the "Fool's Speech" as it unfolds.

1 Having dismissed his opponents' attempts to "commend" themselves (10:12-18), Paul now sets forth their folly by joining in their exercise. A note of irony is immediately introduced by Paul's initial word, "if only,"[7] which points to a wish that is impossible to fulfill, namely, that the Corinthians would "bear with" him[8] in "a little foolishness." The second sentence — "but,"[9] followed by the indicative, "you do bear with me" (NIV, "you are already doing that") — intensifies the irony.

Because two words that are continually repeated in what follows — "foolishness"[10] and "bear with"[11] (RSV) — are now introduced, this verse serves as a heading for the "Fool's Speech" (although the "Speech" proper does not begin until v. 21b).

Paul had earlier characterized his speech as "right-minded" (5:13), the very opposite of the "foolishness" of which he now speaks.[12] But speak "as

---

6. See the note following for the argument that the singular "he who comes" is generic, pointing to a group.

7. Gk. ὄφελον. The particle ὄφελον, when used with the imperfect, as here, expresses a pious hope, which, however, is unlikely to be fulfilled, an unattainable wish (BDF #359). The irony implied by ὄφελον is intensified by ἀλλὰ καί in the sentence following: "O, that you would bear with me in a little foolishness. *But* you are already doing that."

8. Gk. ἀνείχεσθέ μου . . . ἀφροσύνης could be taken as (1) "bear with me," or (2) "bear with my foolishness." The commentators are divided. Option (1) is preferred because of the proximity of ἀνείχεσθε and μου.

9. Gk. ἀλλὰ καί.

10. Gk. ἀφροσύνη, "foolishness," reappears in vv. 17 and 21 (cf. ἄφρων, "fool" — vv. 16 [twice], 19; 12:6, 11; παραφρονεῖν, "to be mad" — v. 23).

11. Gk. ἀνέχεσθαι, "bear with" (vv. 4, 19, 20).

12. The opposite of ἀφροσύνη is σωφροσύνη, "self-controlled," which, however, does not occur within this letter (see 1 Tim 2:9, 15; Acts 26:25). For the verb σωφρονεῖν, "to be self-controlled," see 5:13.

a fool" he must, to avoid the charge of self-commendation and "boasting," which he had just repudiated in others (10:12, 17, 18). It appears likely that it is being bandied about in Corinth that Paul is a "fool" whom the Corinthians must "bear with," that is, "humor" or "tolerate."

The next sentence may be understood as (1) "You are already [bearing with me]" (indicative; cf. NIV, "you are already doing that"), or (2) "Do bear with me" (imperative — RSV).[13] While we prefer (1), either way Paul expresses his pain that a church that he has established and for whom he had suffered so much feels it must "bear with" him, and that "as a fool." It is quite likely that by these words Paul is throwing back at them a line being spread either by his local detractors or by the newly arrived "superlative" apostles (11:5). But — as he will now remind them — it was he, Paul, who first joined them to Christ, and it is his calling to present them, uncorrupted, to Christ.

2 The word "For"[14] (untranslated by the NIV) is dominant in v. 2, appearing in both of its unequal sentences, providing the link between Paul's three ideas in vv. 1b-2: "You do bear with . . . me. *For* I am jealous for you . . . *for* I betrothed[15] you . . . to Christ."[16] These ideas are given in reverse order of ministry sequence of his relationship with them. First, he joined them to Christ; second, therefore, he cares about their fidelity to Christ; third, they do, ironically speaking, "bear with" — barely tolerate — him.

Critical to this verse and the next is the apostle's portrayal of his ministry by the metaphor of betrothal,[17] a practice alien to modern Western culture.[18] It

13. Gk. ἀνέχεσθε is taken as (1) indicative by e.g., Plummer, 293, and (2) imperative by, e.g., BDF #448.6; Furnish, 485. If ἀλλὰ καί is a strong adversative ("but indeed"), it would tip the scales in favor of the indicative (so Hughes, 373 n. 31). Moreover, the explanatory γάρ, "for," following immediately, makes better sense with option (1): "You do bear with me. *For* I am jealous for you. . . . *For* I betrothed you . . . to . . . Christ." Either way, however, the sense is unaffected.

14. Gk. γάρ.

15. Gk. ἡρμοσάμην; NIV, "I promised [you]." The middle voice of ἁρμόζειν (not used elsewhere in the NT) is used here with an active meaning; cf. classical usage, "I betroth myself."

16. Gk. τῷ Χριστῷ. As in v. 3, "Christ" comes last in the sentence for emphasis.

17. 2 Corinthians is rich in images of apostolic ministry. Here the minister is a father-betrother (11:2). For other examples see on 10:3.

18. Paul will be referring to Jewish marriage customs whereby the father was responsible for his daughter's virginity until the marriage (Gen 29:23; Deut 22:13-21). In the OT, Israel is often spoken of as the Lord's betrothed (e.g., Isa 54:5-6; Hos 2:19-20) or as his spouse, jealous of her fidelity (Isa 54:5-6; 62:5; Jer 3:1; Ezek 16:23-33). According to the later rabbis, Moses presented Israel to the Lord (Bruce, 234). For Greco-Roman practices with which the Corinthians will have been familiar, see J. Carcopino, *Daily Life in Ancient Rome*, 93-94; and for the lordship of Christ over his bride the church, see generally R. A. Batey, *Nuptial Imagery*, 12, 20, 62.

is, in all probability, a paternal image[19] whereby a father pledges a daughter in marriage to a prospective husband, taking responsibility for her virginal fidelity to her betrothed in the period between the betrothal and the marriage. The apostle's pride in his people "on the day of the Lord Jesus" (1:14) is consistent with the marriage imagery used here whereby a father would finally present his betrothed daughter with pride to her husband on the long-awaited wedding day.

By this elaborate metaphor Paul neatly describes the eschatological nature of apostolic evangelism. As the result of evangelism (1:19) a church ("a betrothed") comes into being, related by "faith" (cf. 5:7) to her physically absent "husband"-to-be, whom she will not see until his appearing, when the marriage is consummated. In the meantime the father-betrother is responsible for the virginal purity of the betrothed until he "presents"[20] her "as a pure virgin"[21] to her "one husband."[22] How outrageous, therefore, that outsiders should come to Corinth and sully their purity, preaching "*another* Jesus" (v. 4).

Contrary to the practice of much evangelism where the greater effort tends to be concentrated on and limited to proclamation-response,[23] Paul as an apostle operates within a distinct eschatological framework, regarding himself as responsible for the fidelity of the church to her Lord in the period between proclamation and consummation. The ongoing fidelity of the church in prospect of the end time is his concern. But what of the congregation already founded? It is to be inferred from this verse that the pastor of a congregation evangelized beforehand by others enters into the eschatological sweep of the "ministry" *(diakonia)* of the new covenant, confirming and constantly repeating the gospel by which the church was created, as well as exhorting the believers to remain focused on Christ, as Paul does here with the Corinthians (see, e.g., Col 2:6-7).

Appropriate to this view of his *diakonia*, Paul declares at the outset, "I am jealous for you with a godly [RSV, "divine"] jealousy." This sentiment should not be confused with the petty possessiveness that mars human rela-

---

19. This is consistent with the paternal picture of Paul's relationships with his churches and converts (1 Cor 4:14-17; 1 Thess 2:11; Gal 4:19; 2 Cor 6:13; 12:13-15; Phlm 10; 1 Tim 1:2; 2 Tim 1:2).

20. Gk. παραστῆσαι, an aorist infinitive, pointing to a single eschatological act of presentation (cf. 4:14; 1 Cor 8:8; Rom 14:10; Eph 5:27).

21. Gk. παρθένον ἁγνήν. According to *New Docs.* 1.71-72, there are various cultic references to ἱερὰ παρθένος. While the notion of a woman dedicated to a god in cultic circumstances is not uncommon, there is "no analogy to a group of people being regarded collectively as a παρθένος" (71).

22. Gk. ἑνὶ ἀνδρί. Paul insists on a woman's commitment to her "own husband" (Eph 5:22; cf. 1 Cor 7:2). As in Rom 7:4, the community of believers belongs to the risen Christ.

23. For a critique see generally W. J. Abraham, *Evangelism,* 92-116, 164-84.

tionships. His words — which could also be rendered "I am zealous for you with God's own zeal"[24] — reflect an important theme in the (LXX) OT. Yahweh, Israel's covenantal God, in *zeal* for his holy name, binds his people to him in a relationship that excludes the worship of other gods (LXX Exod 20:5; 34:14; Deut 4:24; 6:15). The theme of "zeal" also reflects God's covenantal care for his people (LXX Isa 9:6; 37:32; 63:15-16). The inter-testamental tradition[25] looked back on individuals like Phinehas and Elijah, who took violent action against idolatry and apostasy, as having acted in *zeal* for their God. Inspired by *zeal* for Yahweh, the pre-Christian Saul of Tarsus, as a persecutor of the church, stood in the same tradition (Gal 1:13-14; Phil 3:6; Acts 22:3-4).[26] The Christian Paul's zeal, however, is a *converted* zeal, free of the violence that characterized his pre-converted days and zealots before him, a zeal now driven by love (see on 5:14).

The Corinthians are not yet in outright apostasy, though there are danger-ous possibilities in that regard (see v. 4). Since he is the initiator of the betrothal, it is his responsibility to safeguard the rights of the divine husband, Christ.[27] The apostle bears the responsibility to ensure that the betrothed is kept faithful to the One she will marry, not diverted nor seduced by an interloper to "another" husband. Let the Corinthians and the would-be seducers understand that the apostle has "betrothed" this bride-to-be to "*one* husband," to "present" the Corinthians "as a pure[28] virgin" to Christ. The *one* Christ, as preached by the apostle, was, and is to remain, the focus of ministry and of faith.

3 In v. 2 Paul stated his formal relationship as the betrother of the church to Christ, emphasizing their purity, which he now takes up. Signaling contrast,[29] the apostle states his deep concern lest the Corinthians be turned aside from the relationship with Christ into which he had established them. He "fears lest somehow" their "minds" should be "corrupted away" from a "single-minded"[30] and "pure"[31] focus toward Christ. Implicit here is the

---

24. Gk. ζηλῶ γὰρ ὑμᾶς θεοῦ ζήλῳ; NIV, "I am jealous for you with a godly jealousy," a genitive of quality or of origin. The zeal, or jealousy, comes from God.

25. For references and details see W. R. Farmer, "Zealot," *IDB* 4.936-39.

26. See S. Kim, *Origin*, 32-50; M. Hengel, *Pre-Christian Paul*, 63-86.

27. That Christ is the husband of a bride — who is God's Israel (cf. Gal 6:16) — ascribes deity to Christ (cf. Isa 54:5-6; 62:5; Jer 3:1; Ezek 16:23-33; Hos 2:19-20). See also on 10:17.

28. See 7:11; Phil 4:8; 1 Tim 5:22.

29. Gk. δέ, used in adversative sense to establish contrast with the previous verse.

30. Gk. ἁπλότης (NIV, "sincere") is not used in a letter by Paul before this letter, where, however, it has different nuances — see 1:12 (integrity); 8:2; 9:11, 13 (generosity).

31. Gk. ἁγνότης (NIV, "pure"), omitted by some MSS (see the note on the text above). See 6:6, the only other reference in the NT, where it is used for "probity." It is a word appropriate for a bride's prenuptial "purity" (see v. 2).

possibility that the purity of the Corinthians is capable of being sullied. This is an important verse in the "Fool's Speech" as well as within the entire letter. The very future of the Corinthians as an apostolic church is in jeopardy.

The metaphor from v. 2, that betrothal is for the purity of the betrothed woman for her husband, is now transmuted in the first half of the verse into the biblical story[32] about the circumstances that overtook another woman, Eve,[33] who had been deceived[34] by the serpent (Gen 3:1-7). Under the symbolism of this allegory, Eve represents the church at Corinth and the serpent those "ministers of Satan,"[35] the "superlative" apostles (v. 5), who have come preaching "another Jesus," to divert the Corinthians from the Christ to whom Paul had joined them.

The sole characteristic of the serpent mentioned by Paul is "cunning"[36] (cf. Gen 3:1 — "The serpent was more crafty than any of the wild animals the LORD God had made"). But how was that "cunning" brought to bear on Eve? It was by his *words* that the serpent deceived her in the Genesis account, a point Paul probably implies in that it is by what the interlopers *preach* that the Corinthians are led astray (v. 4). It may also be for that reason that he is content to be regarded as "not a trained speaker" (v. 6). This viewpoint is supported in a closely parallel passage where Paul writes of "those who cause divisions and put obstacles in your way that are contrary to the teaching you have learned. . . . By smooth *talk* and flattery they *deceive* the minds of naive people. . . . The God of peace will soon *crush Satan* under your feet" (Rom 16:17-18, 20). The references in 2 Cor 11:3 and Rom 16:18, 20 to (1) "the serpent" (i.e., Satan —

32. In all probability Paul's allusions arise from LXX Genesis. Eve's words — ὁ ὄφις ἠπάτησέν με, καὶ ἔφαγον (3:14) — are almost certainly the basis of Paul's words ὡς ὁ ὄφις ἐξηπάτησεν Εὕαν. Less certain is the suggestion, based on the probable linking of v. 3 with v. 14, that Paul was acquainted with pious legends arising from the biblical story whose existence is posited by fragmentary references in various Jewish apocalypses (e.g., *1 Enoch* 69:6; *2 Enoch* 31:6), as well as in later rabbinical literature (e.g., *Yebam.* 103b; *'Abod. Zar.* 22b; *Šabb.* 146a).

33. Eve is mentioned elsewhere in the NT only in 1 Tim 2:13, where the verb ἐξαπατεῖν is also used, prompting A. T. Hanson, *Pastoral Epistles,* 71-72, to argue that 1 Tim 2:13 is derived from 2 Cor 11:3.

34. Gk. ἐξηπάτησεν; NIV, "led astray." Whereas LXX Gen 3:13 has ἠπάτησεν, "deceived," Paul intensifies it as a compound verb carrying the meaning "*utterly* deceived" (cf. 1 Tim 2:13).

35. Satan's influence in Corinth was a matter of concern to Paul. See 2:11; 11:14; 12:7; 1 Cor 5:5; 7:5.

36. Gk. ἐν τῇ πανουργίᾳ αὐτοῦ, an accusation from which Paul must defend himself in Corinth (cf. 4:2; cf. 12:16) but which he now lays at the door of the newcomers. It should be noted that the "craftiness" of the serpent (Gen 3:1) is expressed in the LXX by φρονιμώτατος, which, however, appears in Aquila and Symmachus as πανοῦργος, a possible source — but in our opinion a less likely one — of Paul's present use of ἐν πανουργίᾳ.

v. 14), (2) "crush Satan," and (3) "deceive" tie both passages back to Genesis 2–3 and to each other. Paul sees *words* — erroneous in content but smooth of delivery — as Satan's instrument to seduce the church from her loyalty to Christ.

In the second half of the verse the apostle directly expresses his "fear" for the Corinthians. It is that "[their] minds"[37] — the receptors of the word of God, but corruptible by deceptive words — "may somehow be led astray."[38] But from what did Paul fear their minds might be led astray? In this part of v. 3 we are very close to the heart of Christianity as understood and proclaimed by the apostle Paul. The minds of the Corinthians — and all believers — are to be directed to Christ, minds that in their focus on him — as with the betrothed woman in her time of waiting for her marriage — are to be "sincere" (i.e., undivided — see Eph 6:5; Col 3:22) and "pure."[39]

This teaching about "the minds directed *toward* Christ,"[40] followed as it is by references to "preaching Jesus" — even though in a negative context — is closely parallel with 1:19-22. In that earlier passage — as with this — the preaching of the Son of God is matched by "God anointed [lit. "christed"] us *toward* Christ."[41] It is by the apostolic word about Christ that God sets the minds of believers — together in the messianic assembly as well as individually — "toward" Christ.

But who is the Christ toward whom the Corinthians are to be directed? Is he *Paul's* Christ, a messianic figure of his making? In the first letter Paul quotes the faith-formula — centered on the "that-ness" of the death, the burial, the resurrection, and the appearances of the risen Christ — that had been the foundation on which the church of Corinth had been established (1 Cor 15:3-7). But, Paul insists, this was not a message created by him; rather, it was "received" by him from those who stood between him and the historical Jesus (1 Cor 15:3). Moreover, it was the message of "the apostles," not just Paul. Writing of the apostles collectively, he declares, "so *we* preach, and so you [Corinthians] believed" (1 Cor 15:11, RSV; cf. 15:9). In other words, the Christ to whose minds Paul kept directing the Corinthians was not a Pauline Christ, but the apostolic Christ. It is from this Christ that the Corinthians are in danger of being diverted.

---

37. See also 3:14; 4:4.

38. The preposition ἀπό with the verb φθαρῇ stresses the notion of separation. Paul uses the verb φθείρειν for moral ruin or corruption (1 Cor 15:33; cf. 1 Cor 3:17; LXX Gen 6:11; Hos 9:9). His denial that he has corrupted the Corinthians (2 Cor 7:2) may reflect a pattern of charge and countercharge (as with πανουργία in the same verse?). Less likely is φθείρειν to be understood as "to seduce" (see BAGD).

39. Gk. τὰ νοήματα ὑμῶν ἀπὸ τῆς ἁπλότητος [καὶ τῆς ἁγνότητος] τῆς εἰς τὸν Χριστόν. See *New Docs*. 3.24 for cultural background to betrothal and marriage.

40. Gk. τὰ νοήματα ὑμῶν . . . τῆς εἰς τὸν Χριστόν; NIV, ". . . to Christ." Note that as in v. 2 "Christ" comes last in the sentence, for emphasis.

41. Gk. εἰς Χριστὸν καὶ χρίσας ἡμᾶς θεός.

4 In vv. 1-3 Paul has (1) declared, ironically, that the Corinthians "bear with" him (v. 1), and (2) expressed his fear lest their minds be led astray from a single-minded and pure loyalty to Christ (v. 3). The opening words, "For if indeed,"[42] point to the statement that follows, where his fear for them is currently being realized; the Corinthians are "bearing *well*"[43] with one who preaches *"another Jesus."*

For the third time vv. 1-4 Paul employs the explanatory "for" (cf. v. 2 [twice]),[44] reflecting the connectedness of the argument within those verses, which, with due abbreviation, we may paraphrase as:

> If only you would
> bear with me. . . .
> You do bear with me,
> *for* I have God's jealousy toward you,
> *for* I betrothed   you   to Christ.
> I am afraid that you will be led astray from Christ,
> *for* if someone preaches   another Jesus, . . .
> you   bear it *easily*.

This closely argued passage is (1) framed by "bear with," used ironically,[45] and (2) the threefold "for" serves to link the points of the argument.

The verse commences with "if" and is followed by "or" twice repeated, thus giving a hypothetical tripartite situation: *"If* someone comes . . . *or* you receive . . . *or* you accept. . . ."[46] Nonetheless, these words are directed to a painfully real situation now existing in Corinth.[47]

> For if indeed
> one comes preaching another Jesus,
> whom we[48] did not preach,

---

42. Gk. εἰ μὲν γάρ; NIV, "For if."

43. The untranslated particle μέν prepares the reader for καλῶς ἀνέχεσθε, ". . . indeed . . . you bear well [with him]." The point of καλῶς, "well," is ironic: "You put up [with the one who comes] *easily*" (cf. Mark 7:9).

44. Gk. γάρ.

45. The irony of "bear with" is intensified as bitterness in vv. 19-20: "For you gladly bear with fools. . . . For you bear it if a man makes slaves of you, etc."

46. Gk. εἰ . . . ἤ . . . ἤ.

47. See J. Murphy-O'Connor, "Another Jesus," 238-51; G. D. Fee, " 'Another Gospel," 111-33.

48. Gk. ἐκηρύξαμεν, "we preached." Having used the singular, "I," in vv. 1-3, Paul slips back into the plural, here used in an apostolic sense, typical of his practice in the excursus on the new covenant ministry (2:14–7:4); see on 1:1. The singular, however, predominates throughout the "Fool's Speech."

or if   you are   receiving
                              a different[49] Spirit
                              that   you did not receive,

or if   a different gospel
                              that   you did not accept,

                              you bear[50] it [him[51]] easily.

Apart from the heterodoxy[52] of the anonymous "one who comes" — almost certainly a *group* of newcomers[53] — this verse stands as an impressive description of the preliminary stages of Paul's own gospel penetration, which could not fail to have reminded the initial converts in Corinth what had happened a few years earlier when he arrived. First, there was his *coming* ("he who comes"). It was followed, second, by the *proclaiming* ("he preached . . . Jesus"). That, in turn, was marked, third, by the *receiving of the Spirit* ("you received . . . the Spirit"[54]). The threefold aorists "preached . . . received

49. Paul changes the sequence from ἄλλον το ἕτερον . . . ἕτερον. Although ἕτερον means "the other [of two]," in this context ἄλλον and ἕτερον are effectively synonyms (so Hughes, 378), as they are in 1 Cor 12:8-10.

50. Gk. ἀνέχεσθε (NIV, "you put up with"), present tense, the reading preferred to ἀνείχεσθε, an imperfect (so some MSS), which might suggest that Paul is dealing with a hypothetical rather than a real situation.

51. The object of "bear with" has to be inferred as (1) "it" (so Furnish, 489, and most translations), or (2) "him," i.e., "he who comes." Contrasted would be "[you] bear with me" (v. 1 [twice]) and, here, "you bear with *him*." It should be noted that the object is personal in vv. 19-20.

52. Gk. ἄλλος . . . ἕτερον . . . ἕτερον, "other . . . different . . . different . . . ," which here are roughly synonymous, declare that Paul viewed the message of the newcomers as *heterodox,* specifically in relation to Jesus. "Another Jesus" must mean a "different gospel." See also vv. 2-3, which imply that Christ is the "one husband," from whose loyalty Paul is concerned the Corinthians may be seduced in favor of "another" who is preached by the "one who" now "comes."

53. Gk. ὁ ἐρχόμενος. "Someone" has indeed "come" to Corinth (as implied also by 3:1). But what is meant? (1) Is the singular a generic use, a rhetorical device to diminish the significance of the group (cf. τινες, 3:1; 10:12, 16) that had arrived (so Furnish, 488, and most others)? Or (2) is it an individual, a ringleader who now comes into view (so Martin, 335, who, however, identifies him — wrongly in our view — with the individual of 10:7, 10, 11)? On balance, option (1) is preferred for the sake of consistency; the earlier singular references appear to be generic.

54. Gk. πνεῦμα . . . λαμβάνετε. Paul uses this verb "receive" with the "Spirit" in other places (see 1 Cor 2:12; Rom 8:15; Gal 3:2). This verb and this noun typically go together elsewhere in the NT (John 7:39; 14:17; 20:22; Acts 2:38; 8:15-17; 10:47; 19:2). Paul's "you received . . . the Spirit" appeals to the Corinthians' sure recollection of inner spiritual transformation (3:3) and the coming of eschatological hope (1:22; 5:5). Elsewhere

. . . accepted"[55] point to the moment when Paul established the church at Corinth.

This initial proclamation in Corinth, and the church's experience at that time, may also be inferred at a number of other points within this letter. Paul reminds the Corinthians that he and his associates proclaimed "the Son of God, Jesus Christ, among [them]," in fulfillment of "the promises of God" (1:19-20). It is "Jesus Christ" as "Lord" whom he "proclaim[s]" (4:5); in response, the Corinthians, typical of others, have "turn[ed] to the Lord [Jesus]" (see on 3:16; cf. 8:5). For his part, God set the Corinthians Christward *(eis Christon),* having anointed ("christed") them, sealed them, and given them the down payment of the Holy Spirit (1:21-22), thus confirming them to be a congregation of the new covenant (3:3-5). The entire process — his proclamation of Christ and their reception of the Spirit — is summarized by the word *gospel* ("you received the gospel"). Moreover, it was by Paul's coming to Corinth, when he proclaimed Christ and they received the Spirit, that he betrothed them as brides-to-be to Christ (v. 2), in prospect of the consummation at the Parousia.

But what is meant by *"another* Jesus . . . a *different* Spirit . . . a different* gospel"? Who is this "[an]other Jesus" whom Paul "did not preach"[56]? That Paul calls him "Jesus," having twice referred to him in the previous two verses as "Christ," may be significant. In our view, it points to a preaching of Jesus the Nazarene, whose historic Jewish persona was being emphasized at the expense of his risen Lordship by the newly arrived "Hebrew" missioners in Corinth (11:13, 22-23a). Such a "Jesus" may have been proclaimed as circumscribed within the continuing Mosaic covenant (3:3-6). This would explain why Paul, as a minister of the new covenant of the Spirit and righteousness (3:6, 8-9), which had overtaken and made obsolete the old covenant, would refer to the current preaching of a "gospel" as "different" from that which the Corinthians "received" from the apostle.

Paul can refer confidently to the readers' new, Spirit-given, "Abba"-attitude (Gal 4:6; Rom 8:15) and to such concrete external realities as miracles accompanying the hearing with faith (Gal 3:5; cf. 1 Cor 12:9-10).

55. Gk. ἐκηρύξαμεν, ἐλάβετε, ἐδέξασθε. In regard to "you accepted the gospel," it should be noted that the verb δέχεσθαι is nowhere else used with "gospel," though it is with "the word" (Luke 8:13; Acts 17:11; 1 Thess 1:6; Jas 1:21) and with "the word of God" (Acts 8:14; 11:1; 1 Thess 2:13). The approximate synonym of λαμβάνειν and δέχεσθαι is παραλαμβάνειν, which is also used with "gospel" (1 Cor 15:1; Gal 1:9, 11-12).

56. Various proposals have been made as to those who preached this "[an]other Jesus" — (1) Judaizers (e.g., Barrett), (2) gnostics (e.g., W. Schmithals), (3) divine men (e.g., D. Georgi), or (4) pneumatics (e.g., E. Käsemann). For an extensive survey of these and other views, see Martin, 336-42. As noted above, our preference is for option (1).

How, then, are we to understand "a different Spirit, which you did not receive [as a result of my preaching]"? The words are probably to be taken as ironic. To be sure, the newcomers may have proclaimed "Jesus . . . a gospel." But if they were advocating a ministry based on "tablets of stone . . . letter" (3:3, 6) that is, some kind of Torah observance, the Corinthians cannot have received the Spirit thereby. The Spirit was not given in response to Torah-keeping (3:15-18; Gal 3:1-5), but in response to the preaching of Jesus Christ as the Son of God (1:18-22), in whom the covenant people are dedicated, forgiven by God (5:19-21).[57] So powerfully solemn is the description of Paul's own gospel ministry in this verse that he is unlikely to attribute the reception of the Spirit[58] directly to the deceivers who have come to Corinth, turning the believers away from their "pure" relationship to Christ (cf. v. 3). It is more likely that he is parodying their ministry. By saying they "preached another Jesus" and that "you receive a different spirit . . . a different gospel," he may be pointing up the very absurdity of the idea (cf. Gal 1:6-7).[59]

Who "received" — "bore well with" — these newcomers, the whole church, or only a section of the church? In an assembly apparently based on households it is probable that the hospitality afforded to the newcomers was limited to a section of the congregation. Since the newcomers were "Hebrews . . . Israelites . . . Abraham's descendants" (11:22), it is almost certain that their hosts were Jews,[60] in all probability those who had given hospitality to Cephas a few years earlier (1 Cor 1:12; 3:22; 9:5). Gentile households within the Corinthian assembly are not likely to have welcomed them because of traditional dietary and cultic differences. Those who had not broken with sexual immorality (12:20–13:2) nor temple worship (6:14–7:1), in all probability being Gentiles, are quite unlikely to have welcomed ministers whose route to righteousness was via the Law of Moses (11:15; cf. 3:6) with its uncompromising prohibition of immorality and idolatry.

(2) Paul and the "Superlative" Apostles (11:5-6)

5 *But I do not think I am in the least inferior to those "super-apostles."* 6 *I may not be a trained speaker, but I do have knowledge. We have made this perfectly clear to you in every way.*

57. See G. D. Fee, *Presence,* 286-311; S. Westerholm, "Letter and Spirit," 229-48.

58. For the unlikely view that not the Holy Spirit but a spiritual "attitude" is in mind here, see Plummer, 297; Hughes, 378; and Martin, 33, and, for a rebuttal, G. D. Fee, "Another Gospel," 11.

59. Plummer, 296, however, conjectures that Ἰησοῦς, πνεῦμα, and εὐαγγέλιον are a triplet of leading terms of the newcomers.

60. Martin, 336, speaks of "wayward hospitality," noting that δέχεσθαι also appears in v. 16.

In this short passage of two verses, which follows logically on the previous verse, Paul begins to respond to the comparisons of the newcomers by which he is said to be "inferior." These newcomers he calls by the ironic title "superlative" apostles. While he denies any inferiority to them (v. 5), he immediately concedes that he is "nonprofessional" in speech (v. 6a). This may be a calculated concession, since it was by "preaching" that the newcomers were deceiving the Corinthians, corrupting their relationship with Christ. By contrast, in "knowledge," that is, of Christ and the gospel, Paul is thoroughly equipped.

5 Once again Paul uses the word "For"[1] (see comment on v. 4), in this case to tie his thinking back through v. 4 to v. 2 and ultimately to v. 1. The Corinthians should "bear with" Paul, *for* he is not inferior to those who have now come, the "superlative" apostles.[2]

His "reckon[ing]"[3] that he is not inferior — the one point of this brief verse — implies that it is in this light that his opponents both regard him and portray him. "Inferior"[4] was apparently their word of comparison (12:11; cf. 10:12): he was inferior, they superior. This is confirmed by his ironic reference to them as "superlative"[5] (lit. "over," "very much" — cf. 12:11) apostles. But in what did they classify him as inferior to them? From his replies scattered throughout the extended passage relating to them (10:12–12:13), we may discern in particular two claims to superiority over Paul — superiority as a trained speaker (11:5-6), and superiority in "visions and revelations" (12:1; cf. 5:13).[6]

His designation of them as "superlative" apostles is both ironic and

---

1. Gk. γάρ, "for," "because." In our view Furnish, 489, is incorrect in denying that the argument is related to that in v. 4. The "but" of the NIV seems unjustifiable.

2. The "superlative" apostles are those "who have come" to Corinth "preaching another Jesus" (v. 4). Although many argue that they are different from the "false apostles" of v. 13, in our view they are the same. For further discussion see on vv. 13-15.

3. Gk. λογίζομαι; NIV, "I think." The verb has been prominent in 10:2, 7 and 11, possibly suggesting contempt for Paul, which he now throws back at them.

4. Gk. ὑστερηκέναι; NIV, "I am [not] inferior." The verb ὑστερεῖν is also found in 12:11, where it is also used in relation to ὑπερλίαν ἀπόστολοι (cf. 11:9). Here ὑσερη-κέναι is perfect tense, indicating that Paul is not, and was not, inferior to them.

5. Gk. ὑπερλίαν is not found in Greek earlier than Paul, and may have been coined by him. Fifteen of the thirty-four words compounded with ὑπέρ and used by Paul are found in this letter. For a list of ὑπέρ compounds see Furnish, 490.

6. There is no reason to believe that the "superlative" apostles pointed to "signs, wonders and miracles" in their claims to superiority over Paul (see 12:12). Paul, having denied any "inferiority" to them (12:11), merely refers to his apostolic miracles at the time he first came to Corinth to clinch outright, and, without further argument, his claim to apostolicity. On this understanding, Paul's miracles — and the "superlative" apostles' lack of them — were an unarguable demonstration of his authentic apostleship.

factual. It is probably factual, in part at least, because of their claim to be "apostles . . . ministers . . . workmen" (11:15) who were "superior" to Paul in important areas of ministry. It is also ironic because he designates them "*very* superior." Throughout the "Fool's Speech" where he catalogues his sufferings and privations in ministry, he exposes and parodies their boastfulness. They attempt to legitimate their ministry at the expense of his by marks of superiority (see above). For his part, Paul seeks recognition of his ministry as authentically "of Christ" by demonstrating that the "sufferings of Christ" do "flow over" into his life (1:5). The catalogues of privation (4:7-8; 6:3-10; 11:23–12:10), not unconnected from sufferings arising from offering the gospel "free of charge" (see on vv. 7-11), indicate that the message of the crucified Messiah — the center of his message (5:14-21) — was incarnated in his life and ministry. It is here, rather than in marks of "superiority" through power, that Paul sought recognition of the legitimacy of his ministry.

6 Having denied any inferiority to the "superlative" apostles (v. 5), Paul makes an immediate qualification, "even though I am. . . ."[7] In response to an apparent jibe Paul concedes that he is "not a trained speaker" (more precisely, "unskilled in speaking" — RSV[8]). But, emphatically, he is not inferior in "knowledge," as he has demonstrated to them in everything.

By the structure of v. 6 Paul sets himself in a double comparison with them[9] — in "speech" and in "knowledge." In the first of the two sentences of the verse, the first clause is concessive ("even if I am a layman in speech")

---

7. Gk. εἰ δὲ καί; NIV, "Even if." The words "I am" are absent from the text and must be understood.

8. Gk. ἰδιώτης τῷ λόγῳ; NIV, "not a trained speaker." The word ἰδιώτης was used of an "amateur," an "untrained" person (see Acts 4:13; H. Schlier, *TDNT* 3.216-17). Paul's disclaimer finds an echo in Dio Chrysostom (*Discourses* 42.3): "in speaking (τοὺς λόγους) . . . I am only a layman (ἰδιώτης)."

Josephus affords several examples of professional public speakers among the retinue of Herod the Great. Herod's court historian Nicolas of Damascus publicly presented the case for Archelaus to Augustus in Rome (in Greek?) 4 B.C. when Herod's will was in dispute (*J.W.* 2.14, 21, 34-37; cf. *Ant.* 16.335-55; 17.54, 106-21). Antipas's case was argued "eloquently" by Irenaeus the ῥήτωρ (*J.W.* 2.20-22). Later, the advocacy against Paul in Caesarea on behalf of the high priest was articulated by the ῥήτωρ Tertullus (Acts 24:1). It is evident that there were rhetoricians in Jerusalem during this general era; therefore, it is conceivable that Jews from Jerusalem educated in Greek, as many were, might find acceptance in faraway Corinth on account of their rhetorical skills. This is more likely to have been the milieu of the newly arrived ministers than the florid "Asian" style of rhetoric of the sophists of the day, as referred to by Furnish, 490.

9. It is possible, but unlikely, that "unskilled in speech but not in knowledge" is unrelated to the "superlative" apostles but is stated for the benefit of the Corinthians independently of the challenge to Paul of the newcomers. His portrayal of them as "superlative" apostles, however, followed immediately by statements about himself, militates against that possibility.

508

while the second is strongly adversative ("but [I am] not in knowledge"[10]). This adversative is carried into the second sentence by the repetition of "but"[11] ("*but* in all things and in every way we have made this clear to you"). By his grammatical structure Paul declares what was truly important in ministry, namely, knowledge.

Inadequacy in speech was a long-standing, perceived weakness in Paul, one to which he displayed sensitivity in the First Letter (1 Cor 2:1-4). It is likely that the arrival in Corinth after Paul of the rhetorically gifted Apollos (Acts 18:24-28) led the Corinthians to reflect negatively about the apostle's capacities as a public speaker. Rhetoric was a long-established, highly esteemed profession in the Greco-Roman cities. Paul realistically declared immediately that in this he was "unskilled" (*idiōtēs* — lit. "a layman," "non-professional"[12]).

This was obvious to the Corinthians, and it would have been foolish for Paul to pretend otherwise. But he is comparing himself specifically with the newcomers who were fellow Jews in this regard. Since Paul was a *Hellenistic* Jew, for whom Greek would have been his primary and Aramaic his secondary language, we may reasonably assume this to have been true of the newcomers also. Paul's fluency in Greek would have been formed as a child in Hellenistic Tarsus[13] and developed as a young rabbi in the Hellenistic synagogues of Jerusalem.[14] These newcomers — whoever they were — must have excelled Paul in the public speaking of *Greek*. Such a concession is consistent with a criticism echoed by him earlier that "in person he is unimpressive and his speaking amounts to nothing," even though this detraction applied specifically to Paul's perceived weaknesses in imposing discipline during his second visit (see on 10:10).

Nonetheless, it ought not be concluded that Paul was a poor speaker. That he was inferior to them (and Apollos?) does not logically require that he was without gifts in that respect. Paul's dialectic in this verse should not lead

---

10. Gk. . . . ἀλλ᾽ οὐ τῇ γνώσει . . . ; NIV, ". . . but I do have knowledge." For comment on the juxtaposition of "speech" and "knowledge" in 1 Corinthians, see G. D. Fee, *1 Corinthians,* 366. See also on 2 Cor 8:7.

11. Gk. ἀλλ᾽ οὐ . . . ἀλλ᾽.

12. His critics readily, if ironically, acknowledge Paul's skills as a writer (10:10), which, however, are different from those of a rhetorician, and which, in their opinion, he lacked.

13. According to Strabo: "The people of Tarsus have devoted themselves so eagerly, not only to philosophy, but also to the whole round of education in general, that they have surpassed Athens, Alexandria or any other place that can be named where there have been schools and lectures of philosophers" (*Geography* 14.5.12-13). Strabo adds, however, that few foreigners came to study at Tarsus, and that most Tarsians completed their education abroad.

14. Cf. M. Hengel, *Pre-Christian Paul,* 54-61.

us to draw wrong conclusions. It is to be noted that the statement "Eve was deceived by the serpent's cunning" (v. 3) is followed immediately by "if one comes *preaching* another Jesus" (v. 4). The newcomers' deception and cunning were expressed in preaching, an area in which Paul is said to be inferior. He is happy to infer that the newcomers are strong in speech because by it the Corinthians were "corrupted . . . from Christ" (v. 3; cf. Rom 16:17-20). Thus, in the context of Hellenistic rhetoric, it quite suits Paul to confess to being "inferior" to the newcomers, a mere "layman." But it does not necessarily follow that Paul was an ill-equipped or ineffective preacher. Few places he visited did not appear to lack a messianic assembly as a result of his ministry. His verbal skills must have been, at the very least, adequate, and, quite possibly, considerable, even though he lacked the high professionalism of the trained rhetorician.

In the second area of comparison — "knowledge" — Paul will not concede to being "nonprofessional" and therefore to inferiority to his opponents. "Speech" and "knowledge"[15] may have been the two focal points of a synagogue teacher's competence, which, presumably, were true also of a teacher in the Christian assemblies. In the subtleties of his interaction with these outsiders, Paul will agree to "nonprofessionalism" in "speech," but, by comparison, assert his expertise in the realm of "knowledge." What is this "knowledge"? While the immediate context suggests that "knowledge" is closely associated with "Jesus" and "the gospel" (v. 4), the broader context points to that "knowledge of God" which Paul defends against pretentious opposition to it (see on 10:5). Judging from other references in this letter, we conclude that "knowledge"[16] is that correct understanding of the gospel which directs the minds to Christ, something that Paul claims to have done when, by preaching the true Jesus in the true gospel, he betrothed the Corinthians to Christ (vv. 2, 4; cf. 1:19, 21).

In regard to his competence in "knowledge" the apostle has "made this perfectly clear[17] to [them] in every way."[18] There may be a touch of

---

15. "Speech" (λόγος) and "knowledge" (γνῶσις).

16. See 2:14, where the words τῆς γνώσεως αὐτοῦ mean "the knowledge of Christ," and 4:6, where "the knowledge of [the glory of] God" is found "in the face of Christ." "Knowledge" is significant in 1 Corinthians especially in chapter 8, where — along with the verb "to know" — it means truth about God; see 1 Cor 8:4-7. Although many interpreters have attempted to tie the word group — the verb is more common than the noun — to gnosticism, it is far from certain that there is any connection at this early stage in Christian history. See G. D. Fee, *1 Corinthians,* 365 n. 32.

17. Gk. φανερώσαντες; NIV, "we have made this perfectly clear." The absolute participle is used as an indicative, "we have, etc."

18. Gk. ἐν παντὶ . . . ἐν πᾶσιν εἰς ὑμᾶς is difficult because the gender is indeterminate. Plummer, 300, suggests: "in every particular . . . among all men."

irony here; mere "layman in speech" though he is, he has, nonetheless, made everything quite clear. His associations with the Corinthians now go back six or seven years to the foundation of the church, when he "betrothed" them to Christ (vv. 2-3). He has visited them once since then, and he proposes to do so once more in the near future. This is now the fourth letter he has written to them. Truly Paul has repeatedly demonstrated the adequacy of his "knowledge" of the gospel, which he has "made clear" to them during this period.

(3) Undercutting His Opponents' Claims (11:7-12)

7 *Was it a sin for me to lower myself in order to elevate you by preaching the gospel of God to you free of charge?* 8 *I robbed other churches by receiving support from them so as to serve you.* 9 *And when I was with you and needed something, I was not a burden to anyone, for the brothers who came from Macedonia supplied what I needed. I have kept myself from being a burden to you in any way, and will continue to do so.* 10 *As surely as the truth of Christ is in me, nobody in the regions of Achaia will stop this boasting of mine.* 11 *Why? Because I do not love you? God knows I do!* 12 *And I will keep on doing what I am doing in order to cut the ground from under those who want an opportunity to be considered equal with us in the things they boast about.*

Once again Paul raises matters related to money (see on 2:17; 4:2; 7:2-4), a subject he will also pick up later (see 12:13-18). Here he is defending himself from the criticism that he supported himself so as to preach the gospel to the Corinthians at no cost to them, not wishing to "burden" them. The Corinthians think that he does not love them. The newcomers, who do accept payment, would like Paul to do so also, since this would put them on the same footing as him. Nonetheless, although under pressure to reverse this policy, Paul will not do so.

Paul begins by asking the rhetorical question, "Did I 'sin' in bringing the gospel to the Corinthians 'free of charge' "? He even "robbed" other churches to minister to them! When in need he did not burden them; brothers from Macedonian provided for him. As a fundamental part of his apostolicity, Paul's of evangelism "free of charge" will not be silenced in Achaia. Contrary to their view, this is not because he does not love them; emphatically he does. Indeed, he will continue this policy of nonpayment when he returns to undercut those new ministers who want to stand on the same ground of apostleship as Paul.

At first sight this passage appears to interrupt the flow of the apostle's argument. He has referred to the "superlative" apostles (vv. 5-6), and he will refer next to the "false apostles" (vv. 13-15). Why, then, does he digress (vv. 7-12) to answer the Corinthians' complaint that he has declined to receive *their* financial support?

Did his opponents argue that failure to accept money was a *de facto* admission that he was no true apostle. Surely a true apostle would accept payment; failure to do so could only represent a fatal admission of nonapostolicity. Since they present themselves as "apostles" (v. 13) while at the same time seeking to be regarded as "equal with [him]" (v. 12), it does not appear that they were disputing his apostolicity per se. It would appear that it is his *inferiority* to them in apostolicity (see on v. 5), not his nonapostolicity, that sets his ministry at a lower level than theirs.

Paul locates this passage as part of his attack on the "superlative" apostles (vv. 5-6), who are the "false apostles" (vv. 13-15). His studied financial independence from the Corinthians had been a sore point since he first came to Corinth (1 Cor 9:12-18), and it may have called for further comment anyway. But since these newcomers evidently sought or at least accepted financial support in Corinth (v. 20), Paul seizes the opportunity both to reply to the Corinthians' criticism (vv. 7-9) and to undermine his opponents' claims to authentic ministry (vv. 10-12).

Moreover, these verses reflect Paul's deep sense of hurt that the Corinthians prefer these heterodox outsiders to him. Although it was he who had "betrothed" them to Christ by preaching the gospel to them, in their eyes he is just a "fool" to be "put up with" (11:1-3). But those who preach "another Jesus" are "put up with . . . easily enough" (11:4). In the passage under review he cannot forbear reminding them what it cost him to preach the gospel "free of charge" to the Corinthians. He "lower[ed himself]" in arduous self-support, though in need at the time, to serve them (vv. 7-8). But they have gladly welcomed these new ministers even though they prey on them and violate them (v. 20). Thus, although on the face of it Paul is reflecting on his own relationships with the Corinthians, the context in which the passage is set reveals the sadness he feels in being rejected by the Corinthians in favor of such men.

This passage should be seen as belonging to a broader context of "boasting" begun in the previous chapter (10:12-18). His opponents appear to have "boasted" that Paul's "field" of ministry in the "regions of Achaia" is rightfully theirs, a claim that Paul emphatically rejects (see on 10:15-16; vv. 10, 12). Unlike that of the newcomers (see v. 20), Paul's ministry in his divinely allocated "field" was offered "free of charge," a policy he is again under pressure to abandon. But when he comes again to Corinth he will continue his ministry without charge, precisely because by so doing he will undercut the claims of these intruders.

512

7 Paul asks[1] a rhetorical and ironic question, "Did I commit a sin[2] . . . because I preached the gospel of God to you free of charge?" In evangelizing them without cost, Paul "lowered" himself so as to[3] "elevate [them]."[4] Paul's "sin" was that he did not accept financial support from the Corinthians while preaching the gospel of God to them.

To be sure, from their viewpoint Paul had painfully breached social conventions in rejecting their patronage of money, gifts, and hospitality, which were at that time conventionally given to those who taught and lectured.[5] Perhaps Paul gave the impression of pride.[6] It is probable, however, that "sin" is Paul's word rather than theirs, reflecting his deep pain in response to their criticism.

> Did I[7] commit a sin[8]
>   myself   lowering
>   that you might be elevated
> because I preached the gospel of God[9]
>   to you   free of charge?

Although in two parts of unequal length, the verse is kept symmetrical by the antonyms "lower" and "elevate"[10] found in the first and second parts respec-

---

1. The ἤ with which the verse begins signals a rhetorical question.

2. Gk. ἁμαρτίαν ἐποίησα; NIV, "Was it a sin for me. . . ?" (Cf. RSV, "Did I commit a sin?") For another example of irony in this matter see 12:13 — ". . . I was never a burden to you. Forgive me this wrong (τὴν ἀδικίαν)."

3. Gk. ἵνα.

4. Gk. ὑμεῖς ὑψωθῆτε. The pronoun is for emphasis, "that you indeed might be elevated."

5. Paul's practice of self-support in teaching by manual labor created three problems in a Greco-Roman culture like Corinth: (1) teachers at that time expected to be paid, (2) those to whom they came expected to pay them, and (3) those who worked with their hands were generally held in low esteem. See further R. F. Hock, *Social Context,* 59-65, and Martin, 344-45.

6. This impression would have been compounded by his acceptance of assistance from Macedonia, inviting the criticism that he favored the Macedonians. The view that the newcomers used the Jesus tradition about the support of ministers (Matt 10:8-10/Luke 10:7) to prove Paul's inferiority, as repeated in Martin, 345, is speculative.

7. Paul speaks here of his pioneer ministry in Corinth in the singular, although Silas and Timothy were also present (see also 1:19; 12:12; Acts 18:1-5).

8. Gk. ἁμαρτίαν ἐποίησα (NIV, "Was it a sin for me?") closely resembles his terminology in an important passage occurring earlier (5:21) and is therefore more likely to be a Pauline than a Corinthian expression. The aorist is complexive, reviewing the apostle's conduct overall.

9. Gk. τὸ τοῦ θεοῦ εὐαγγέλιον εὐηγγελισάμην, "I gospelled the gospel of God." For the appearance together of verb and noun see also 1 Cor 9:18; 15:1; Gal 1:11.

10. Gk. ταπεινῶν . . . ὑψωθῆτε. God exalts the lowly (see 1 Sam 2:7; Job 5:11; Ezek

tively. Not to be missed is the painful interaction between "myself" and "you" (twice). Lowering *himself* he elevated *them,* evangelizing *them,* free of charge.

The meaning of "lowering" himself is expanded upon in v. 9, where he reminds them that he did not burden them in providing for his needs at the time he established the church a few years earlier. Significantly, "lowering" is a present participle, in contrast to the aorists "elevate" and "preaching." Thus "lowering" is a *process* that began when he first came to Corinth supporting himself by exhausting manual labor[11] — "preaching the gospel to [them] . . . free of charge"[12] (cf. 1 Cor 9:18[13]) — but that continued through the humiliation he suffered at their hands during the second visit and through their attitudes to him since.[14]

How, then, did Paul "elevate" the Corinthians? The second half of the verse declares that it was by preaching the gospel (cf. v. 4) to them that he joined them — as it were, by "betrothal" (v. 2) — to Christ (v. 3; cf. 1:21), in prospect of their "elevation" in a heavenly marriage with their "one husband" (v. 2) at his eschatological coming. Through Paul's ministry the "day of salvation" had come; they were a messianic congregation, sanctified to God, participating in the new covenant of righteousness and the Spirit (3:3-9, 16-18). But the Corinthians did not enjoy these benefits independently of the one who had been and was still their "minister" *(diakonos),* Paul. It was because he "lowered" himself that they had been and would be "elevated."[15]

In another metaphor of reversal, they owed their eschatological "riches" to *Christ's* "poverty" (8:9). In other words, their "enrichment," their "eleva-tion," was the direct result, first of the "poverty" of Christ and then of the "lowering" of his minister, Paul. Paul's self-"lowering" in the sufferings of

---

17:24; 21:26; Matt 23:12; Luke 1:52; 14:11; 18:14; Jas 4:12). Ταπεινός and ταπεινοῦν are important within 2 Corinthians (see on 7:6; 12:21; but in particular 10:1, where the word appears to be used by the Corinthians against him, with the nuance "timid" or even "despised").

11. Cf. 1 Thess 2:9; 2 Thess 3:7-8; 1 Cor 4:12; 9:18; 2 Cor 6:5; 11:23, 27; Acts 20:34-35. It is now widely believed that tents were made of leather, making tentmaking both arduous and unclean. See P. W. Barnett, "Tentmaking," *DPL,* 925-27.

12. Gk. δωρεάν . . . εὐηγγελισάμην ὑμῖν. The words of Jesus to the Twelve in Matt 10:8 — δωρεὰν ἐλάβετε, δωρεὰν δότε — are reflected in 2 Thess 3:8; cf. Rev 21:6; 22:17; LXX Exod 21:11 (δωρεὰν ἄνευ ἀργυρίου, "free without money"). Plummer, 303, speaks of this phrase as: "Emphatic juxtaposition. 'God's gospel, that most precious thing, — *for nothing!'* " The word translated "without charge" is also used for the manner of God's vindication of sinners — δικαιούμενοι δωρεὰν τῇ αὐτοῦ χάριτι . . . (Rom 3:24). See, too, 9:15, "[God's] inexpressible gift (δωρεα)."

13. Gk. ἀδάπανον θήσω τὸ εὐαγγέλιον. Whereas 1 Cor 9:18 uses ἀδάπανον with gospel preaching, 2 Cor 11:7 uses δωρεάν. The two appear to be close in meaning.

14. As reported by Titus (cf. 6:11-13)?

15. The vocabulary of "lowering"/"elevating" is used of Jesus himself in Phil 2:8 (ἐταπείνωσεν ἑαυτόν) and 2:9 (ὁ θεὸς αὐτὸν ὑπερύψωσεν).

ministry for the Corinthians was the continuation of the "poverty" of Christ in his incarnation and death. Along with Christ, through whom God reconciled the world to himself, God also "gave" the "ministry" *(diakonia)* and the "word" *(logos)* of reconciliation (5:18-19) in this the promised "day of salvation" (6:2).

Suffering for others motivated by love for them lies at the heart of God's work of reconciliation. Although Christ's sufferings are unique in their redemptive quality, the sufferings for others by his ministers and missionaries extends the same vicarious principle into the "day of salvation" (1:6; 4:12, 15).

8 Continuing his defense of his affection for them — which they are questioning (v. 11) — the apostle declares that, in addition to his own sacrifices for them (v. 7), he "robbed[16] other churches." Paul amplifies this vivid image in the words "by receiving support from [these churches]." The purpose[17] of this action was "so as to serve you [Corinthians]."

Paul's ironic and exaggerated language — such as, "was it a sin?" (v. 7; cf. 12:13) — reflects back to the Corinthians their sense of affront that he would not receive what was appropriate from them as their teacher but that he would receive what was inappropriate from other churches (thus "he robbed" those churches).

This "support[18] from [other churches]" is further expanded upon in the next verse, namely, that brothers from Macedonia brought him relief in Corinth. Paul was determined that the Corinthians should contribute nothing toward the ministry they received. On the one hand he "lowered" himself (by self-support) to preach the gospel "free of charge" to them (v. 7), and on the other he received support from the Macedonian[19] churches.[20]

---

16. Gk. συλᾶν, "to rob," is not found elsewhere in the NT (but cf. Rom 2:22; Col 2:8 for compounded forms of the verb), though it is used in Classical Greek for stripping an enemy of his armor or plundering a defeated city.

17. Expressed as Gk. πρός.

18. Gk. ὀψώνιον is used of a soldier's rations (so 1 Cor 9:7; cf. Luke 3:14) — implying the bare necessities and perhaps continuing the military image commenced with στρατευόμεθα (10:3) and συλᾶν (cf. note 16 above). *New Docs.* 2.65 points to evidence of allowances that were minimal and "in kind," while *New Docs.* 4.98 shows the generally paltry level of recompense for hired labor.

19. It is probable that the Corinthians from educated and affluent Corinth would have bristled at the very idea that the poor northerners of Macedonia would support someone who was ministering to them! In any case, racially mixed Macedon's genuineness as a Greek civilization was doubted, especially in the light of Philip's conquest of the southern city-states in the fourth century.

20. There is an apparent contradiction between the words "I robbed *other churches* . . . the brothers came from Macedonia," and Paul's comment to the Philippians, "when I left Macedonia, *no church* entered into partnership with me in giving and receiving *except you only*" (Phil 4:15 — RSV). G. D. Fee, *Philippians,* 442 n. 17, rejects the explanation that "at the beginning" (Phil 4:15) refers to the time before the letter was written, proposing

His purpose in this is given as "so as to serve you" (NIV) or, more literally, "for the ministry to you."[21] The single word "ministry" *(diakonia)* of this verse sums up the phrase "the gospel of God I preached to you" of the previous verse.[22] From this is clear that apostolic "ministry" is "gospel" ministry. Let the Corinthians be reminded — however painful it might have been for *them* — that it was Paul who preached the gospel to them, or brought the ministry to them, and that he did so "free of charge." His reason for his continuing policy in this will be given in vv. 10-12.

9 Continuing his review of his initial period of ministry in Corinth, Paul explains that when he had been in need he did not burden them; the brothers from Macedonia supplied that need. As he had kept himself from being a burden to them, so he would continue to do so.

This verse is in three parts, the first two explaining the previous two verses. Thus v. 9a elaborates on what it meant for Paul to "lower" himself (v. 7). When he was "present[23] with them" and "needed[24] something" — he does not say what those needs may have been — he did not "burden"[25] anyone. In this regard, it is curious that Paul makes no mention of his specific labors as a tentmaker, though he does mention "labors" in the "Fool's Speech" proper (vv. 23, 27). Perhaps he knew how offended they had always been that when ministering to them he supported himself by such menial — and, indeed, unclean — physical work as tentmaking (Acts 18:3; cf. Acts

---

instead that "other churches" in 2 Cor 11:8 means "other believers." A better solution may be that the "partnership in giving and receiving" between Paul and the Philippians described something more technically formal than the support "from other churches," which may have been rather more ad hoc support. For a discussion of Paul's special relationships with the Philippians, see further P. T. O'Brien, *Philippians,* 533-35.

21. Gk. πρὸς τὴν ὑμῶν διακονίαν. Note the emphatic repetition "you" (ὑμῶν) in this verse from the previous verse ("elevate *you* . . . preached to *you* . . . serve *you*"). "The Corinthians got his services, and he allowed other Christians to pay for them" (Plummer, 303).

22. Gk. πρὸς τὴν ὑμῶν διακονίαν (NIV, "so as to serve you") is clearly parallel with if not equivalent to τὸ τοῦ θεοῦ εὐαγγέλιον εὐηγγελισάμην ὑμῖν (v. 7). Once more we note the importance of διακονία in referring to the gospel ministry in Corinth. (The word cluster διακονία, διάκονος, διακονεῖν occurs twenty times in 2 Corinthians.)

23. Gk. παρών usually describes an earlier visit to Corinth — either the first, as here, or the second (cf. 10:2, 11; 13:2). The third visit is indicated by 13:10.

24. Gk. ὑστερηθείς. Paul's use of ὑστερ — in ὑστερηθεὶς . . . τὸ γὰρ ὑστέρημα — is probably deliberate in the light of the Judaizers' vocabulary of ὑπέρ and ὑστερ — as applied by them in comparison to him (see 10:12, 14, 15; 11:5, 23).

25. Gk. κατεναρκεῖν is found in the NT only here and in 12:13, 14. The uncompounded ναρκεῖν means to cramp or numb a joint (hence *narcotic*). Plummer, 304-5 regards it as a medical term perhaps meaning "to cripple," while Martin, 347, sees "an insidious nuance" suggesting a Corinthian accusation that Paul "pressured" them to support him by devious means.

20:34-35; 1 Thess 2:9; 2 Thess 3:8; 1 Cor 4:12; 9:18; 2 Cor 6:5; 11:23, 27). Tents were made of leather.

In v. 9b Paul repeats "I needed . . . something" as "what I needed," expanding on the stark reference of v. 8 that he "robbed other churches" to make possible his "ministry" *(diakonia)* to the Corinthians. That "robbery" occurred as "the brothers . . . came from Macedonia,"[26] who, having heard of his circumstances, "supplied"[27] whatever the bereft apostle lacked. This reference points to one such visit from Macedonia, not many.[28] Was Paul inconsistent in receiving assistance from the Macedonian churches but not from the Corinthians? Against that possibility it appears that Paul did not receive ongoing support from the Macedonian churches while he was present ministering in them, but only once he had moved on and special circumstances were applied.

In v. 9c Paul summarizes his determination that "in all things"[29] (NIV, "in any way") — by whatever means, whether by his own labors or by help from Macedonia — he will be financially independent of the Corinthians. So far he has "kept"[30] (lit. "guarded") himself from being a "burden," and he will continue to do so (cf. 12:13, 14). Paul's careful use of the future "will continue to do so" points again to his forthcoming visit to Corinth (see on 10:2). There will be no change in his policy, as he will explain in v. 12. Doubtless, this statement was a bitter pill for the Corinthians to swallow,[31] and Paul must have had substantial reasons for it.[32]

---

26. It is probable that the Macedonians were from the church at Philippi (Phil 4:14).

27. Gk. προσανεπλήρωσαν. The verb προσ + αν + επλήρωσαν, interpreted as thorough fulfillment or replenishment of Paul's needs, may be at odds with the more Spartan provision of needs (Gk. ὀψώνιον) implied by the military image of the previous verse. Alternatively, and more probably, the verb points to a Macedonian gift that *added to* or supplemented what he had been able to earn by working.

28. Gk. ἐλθόντες, aorist or completed action tense — as used of other verbs in this verse — supports one, not a number of visits.

29. Gk. ἐν παντί; NIV, "in any way."

30. Gk. ἐτήρησα.

31. Hughes, 388-89, points out that both Chrysostom and Calvin took Paul's point to be that the Corinthians failed financially to support Paul rather than that they were upset that Paul declined it.

32. There are three reasons in particular why Paul worked to support himself, of which the third was the weightiest.

a. Paul was conscious that he may have been perceived as just one of many itinerant lecturers or philosophers who were common in Greco-Roman culture, who would be paid a fee for their efforts or, alternatively, given hospitality and other benefits by wealthy patrons. It was not uncommon for itinerant lecturers to suffer an evil reputation (Philostratus, *Life of Apollonius,* 1.13; Lucian, *Hermotimus* 59; Dio Chrysostom, *Discourses* 8.9). Paul may have worked to support himself out of concern lest his ministry and the message of the gospel be associated with traveling philosophers (cf. 1 Thess 1:5; 2:3-6; 1 Cor 9:12b; Acts 20:33-35). In contrast to the newly arrived opponents in Corinth "who peddle (οἱ

While Paul insists that the local and permanent teacher in the church be paid,[33] it may be that his apostolic ministry, "free of charge," provides a useful paradigm for pioneer missionaries in subsequent generations. The minister engaged in groundbreaking evangelism, who expects remuneration from those he evangelizes, runs the risk of portraying his ministry as venal.

10 Having reminded the Corinthians of his basic policy — past and continuing — in conducting his ministry to them "free of charge" (vv. 7-9), Paul now reaffirms his determination to continue in the same vein (vv. 10-12). This he immediately does by what is in effect a Christian oath.[34] First he declares the oath ("as the truth of Christ is in me"); then he gives its content[35] ("this boast of mine will not be silenced[36] in the regions of Achaia"[37]).

καπηλεύοντες) the word of God," Paul refuses to "tamper with (δολοῦντες) God's word" (2:17; 4:2). These newcomers "prey upon" (lit. "devour") the Corinthians (11:20). This vocabulary implies the receipt of improper payment, the watering down of the message, and the exploitation of the hearers. Paul was true to the message, declined payment for his ministry by *working,* and cared for his congregations (cf. 1 Thess 2:5-10). Much of Paul's suffering arose from the fact that he worked to support himself (vv. 23, 27; cf. 6:5).

b. Paul regarded idleness, which was endemic in Greco-Roman society, as inappropriate for the Christian. So he deliberately set the example of hard work to support himself and called upon his converts to imitate him (1 Thess 5:14; 2 Thess 3:6-13). The practical values of life in Christ were concretely exemplified in his own deliberate lifestyle in which he supported himself by work (Eph 4:28; cf. Acts 20:35).

c. As one called to be the apostle to the Gentiles, Paul had no option but to obey God's call to preach the gospel. Because it was *God* who called him, Paul made "the gospel free of charge" to the people to whom he came (1 Cor 9:16-18; 2 Cor 11:7). His obedience to God would have been diminished by receiving payment from others. His pay was to receive no pay. His work was between himself and God; he would not be paid for it. Gifts from the Macedonians were just that, *gifts,* not payment for work done. While Paul expects the indigenous teacher in the congregation to be paid (1 Cor 9:3-14; Gal 6:6; 1 Tim 5:17-18), he steadfastly declined this in his own case. Paul the worker, who supported himself at such personal cost (see vv. 23-27), was a sign of his unique apostolicity; because God had called him, he could not be paid.

33. See 1 Cor 9:3-14; Gal 6:6; 1 Tim 5:17-18.

34. See also 1:18, 23; 2:10; 11:11, 31; Rom 9:1, and for further comment, Furnish, 493.

35. Introduced by Gk. ὅτι.

36. Gk. φρασσεῖν, "to cut off or obstruct" (as of a road or a river — LXX Job 38:8; Hos 2:6 — hence "restrict, silence"); NIV has "nobody . . . will *stop*"). Once more Paul's use of a verb in the future tense (φραγήσεται) points to his impending (and final) visit to Corinth (cf. vv. 9, 12). Let the Corinthians be assured that there will be no change of policy when he comes.

37. RSV. It is noteworthy that in referring in succeeding verses to Macedonia and Achaia Paul chooses to place his emphasis on the (Roman) provinces, not the cities in which the churches were located (see 1:1; 9:2 [Achaia]; 1:16; 2:13; 7:5; 8:1 [Macedonia]). Possibly Paul wishes to take the Corinthians' spotlight off themselves so as to think in a less "parochial" manner in the awareness that there are Christians elsewhere in proximity to themselves (see on 1:1).

The oath appears to be a reference to Christ's encounter with him on the road to Damascus, when he was "called" to be an apostle[38] in consequence of which "Christ's truth"[39] was "in" *(en)* Paul. Later he will assert that "Christ is speaking *in (en)* me" (13:3), just as he had stated earlier that "God [is] making his appeal *through (dia)* us" (5:20). This oath is an affirmation of apostolicity and of apostolic authority (see also 10:8; 13:10).

What, then, is "this boast"[40] which, he adjures, will not be muted in the regions of Achaia[41]? Clearly, it is that he has "preached the gospel of God" to the Corinthians *"free of charge"* (v. 7; cf. 12:13; see also 1 Cor 9:12-18). These "regions" are part of the "field" allocated to him by God as apostle to the Gentiles (see on 10:15-16; cf. v. 12). Paul's "boast" is the divinely given sphere of ministry among the Gentiles, which he exercises freely, without payment from them.

Paul's sufferings are inextricably connected with his "labor" in support of himself (see vv. 23-27). Such labor in self-support, by which he "lowered" himself (v. 7), was a sign legitimating his unique apostolicity. God had called him, and to this specific "field" of ministry (10:15-16); since it was a matter of obedience, he could not be paid. He will neither concede to his opponents their right to be in his "field" nor resile from his determination that his proclamation of the gospel will be at no cost to the hearers. For so doing he would have conceded that his ministry was on the same basis as theirs (see v. 12).

This oath expresses the depth of Paul's commitment to his apostolic ministry, free of charge, and to the concomitant necessity that he "labor" in self-support. Significantly, this truth-oath is later echoed by a lying-denial oath (v. 31), asserting the reality of "weaknesses," which, as we have argued, in a measure flow from his determination to "labor and toil" so as to offer the gospel without payment.

11 Paul now interjects the rhetorical question: "Why? Because I do not love you?" This, in all probability, was their complaint against him. "He

---

38. This is pointedly established at the commencement of the letter (1:1), implicit in passages alluding to his Damascus call (3:4–4:6; 5:16–6:13; 10:8; 13:10; cf. 2:17), and assumed in the strong and confident tone adopted as he concludes his letter in preparation to coming to them (12:14–13:14). It is also hinted at in passages referring to the eschatological reunion of apostle and people (1:12-14; 1:23–2:3; 7:12).

39. Gk. ἀλήθεια Χριστοῦ; NIV, "the truth of Christ." Because the truth of Christ is "in" Paul, i.e., personally apprehended, it is more probably subjective genitive ("truth from Christ") than objective genitive ("truth about Christ").

40. Gk. ἡ καύχησις αὕτη; NIV, "this boasting." According to Martin, 347, "boasting" is the "decisive watchword of the entire 'Fool's Speech.'" See, e.g., 11:12, 16, 17, 18, 30; 12:1, 5, 9.

41. See on 1:1.

received support from Macedonia; therefore he loved them. He declined support from us in Corinth; he does not love us."[42] Fundamental to vv. 7-10 is Paul's desire to reassure the Corinthians that he did, in fact, love them.

Paul's assurance, supported by yet another oath, "God knows, I do,"[43] probably has a a hidden depth to it. On the surface — as he will explain in the next verse — his actions do not in any way arise from favoritism to others or lack of love for them. More profoundly — though with a sense of pain — he gives emphatic if ironic expression to a depth of love, patience, and sacrifice that the Corinthians' willful fickleness has demanded over a long period and will continue to demand. If the truth be known, the one thing the Corinthians should never question is Paul's love to *them* (cf. 2:4; 5:14; 6:6; 8:7; 12:15).

It is remarkable that the Corinthians should complain that the apostle did not love them. In neither of the two extant letters is Paul able unambiguously to acknowledge (1) their love for him (see on 8:7), or (2) for congregations beyond their own (cf. 8:8, 24), or even (3) their love for one another. It was on account of their signal lovelessness[44] that Paul must write his famous words about love to admonish them (1 Cor 12:31b–14:1; cf. 16:14).[45]

12 At this the conclusion[46] of the paragraph vv. 7-12, the apostle at last makes explicit his reason for continuing his policy not to accept financial support from the Corinthians. Evidently he felt he might be put under pressure to accept the Corinthians' payment when he next came to Corinth.

The sentence[47] is in three parts: (1) his statement ("What I do I will also do"), followed by (2) an expression of purpose ("that I might undercut

---

42. It is possible that Paul's reflection back to them, "He does not love us," graciously masks their actual complaint, "He despises us."

43. Gk. ὁ θεὸς οἶδεν needs to have "I do [love you]" or something similar supplied. The words "God knows" reappear in 12:2, 3 but with quite a different meaning.

44. In contrast to the Macedonian churches of the Thessalonians and the Philippians, whom he repeatedly commends for their love (1 Thess 1:3; 3:6, 4:9; 2 Thess 1:3; Phil 1:9; cf. 4:14-16). The First Letter reveals a community racked with divisions (1 Cor 1:10-17; 3:1-4), thankless for Paul's ministry (4:8-15), internally litigious (6:1-6), thoughtless about the new convert (8:1-13), culturally insensitive toward the unsaved (10:23–11:1), selfish at the communal meal (11:17-22), and proudly displaying the *pneumatika* at their meetings (14:1-4). This willful individualism is manifest also in the Second Letter, which reveals an uncharitable zeal to write him off as spiritually tepid, vacillating, and defeated (6:11-13; cf. 1:12, 17, 23; 2:16; 3:6; 10:1-3, 7-10; 13:3) while they — or one of their factions — have extended welcome and comfort to outsiders who have intruded into his proper field of labor (10:12-17). Here they proclaim a heterodox gospel (11:4) and are taking pecuniary advantage of the people (11:19-20).

45. See, too, P. D. Gardner, *Gifts of God,* for the significance of love in another passage (8-11:1) within the First Letter.

46. Gk. δέ, untranslated, points to a conclusion now to be stated.

47. The complex repetition of words — ποιῶ . . . ποιήσω . . . ἵνα . . . ἀφορμὴν . . . ἀφορμὴν . . . ἵνα — does not appear in the translations.

the ground from those who seek a basis"[48]), followed by (3) a phrase that expands[49] upon its predecessor (namely, "that in what they boast about, they may be found even as we [are"]). What is meant by this difficult sentence? Apparently Paul is asserting that he will continue to decline payment in order to cut the ground under those (intruders) who seek to stand as equals with him in ministry.

He will continue to reject the Corinthians' financial assistance because by so doing he will remove the claim of those who now seek to preach in Corinth, that they do so on the same basis as Paul.[50] It appears that these persons received support from the Corinthians, thus creating pressure on Paul to do likewise when he comes. But his determination to offer the gospel "free of charge" was fundamental to his ministry in the "field" God assigned to him, as apostle to the Gentiles (cf. v. 10; 10:15-16).

Who are these people, and what is the basis of ministry that, they claim, is the same as Paul's but whose claim he rejects?[51] These questions are answered in the verses immediately following. So far from being ministers on the same basis as Paul, these men are "*false* apostles" (see on v. 13) who seek to be recognized in Corinth as "apostles of Christ," "workmen," and "ministers" (vv. 14-15), that is, on the same terms Paul applied to himself. But they have been given financial support (v. 20), at the very least hospitality (by Jewish members of the church?). Such support is probably implied also by his earlier reference to "pedd[ling] the word of God" (2:17; cf. 4:2), which implies payment.

Paul, however, has not received and will not receive payment from churches where he ministers the gospel. On the Damascus road God called Paul to become his apostle to the Gentiles (Gal 1:15-16; Rom 1:5; 15:14-16; Acts 26:16-18). That Paul proclaimed the word of God "free of charge" (v. 7; cf. 1 Cor 9:18) was his badge of apostleship together with the sufferings arising from his nonpayment and self-support (see especially vv. 23,

---

48. Gk. ἀφορμή (NIV, "opportunity") is a military term for a base from which to launch a military operation (so Hughes, 392 n. 54). It thus means "occasion," "opportunity," or "pretext" (see also 5:12).

49. The second ἵνα is not dependent on the first, but on the immediately preceding τῶν θελόντων ἀφορμήν.

50. Hughes's suggestion, 390, that these ministers were attempting directly to induce Paul to accept payment, is unsubstantiated. But indirect pressure is possible. It is likely that the Corinthians have urged Paul in this direction, as communicated to him by Titus on his return to Paul.

51. Martin, 348-49, summarizes the options, giving preference to their pride in laying claim to the same territory as the point of Paul's objection. While this is true of 10:12-18, it does not reflect the drift of Paul's argument in vv. 7-12. Remuneration is in view here.

27). To have received payment for his ministry — apart from unsolicited supplementation from the Macedonians once he had left them (see on vv. 8-9) — would have compromised his obedience to God's call. His payment was to receive no payment. By not deviating from this policy Paul continued to wear the badge inscribed "apostle to the Gentiles," which his opponents — because they received payment — could not wear. Thus Paul will "cut the ground *from under*"[52] his opponents, who claim, mistakenly, to have the same basis of ministry as his, namely, that of apostleship, which they "boast" of having.

(4) The "False Apostles" (11:13-15)

13 *For such men are false apostles, deceitful workmen, masquerading as apostles of Christ.* 14 *And no wonder, for Satan himself masquerades as an angel of light.* 15 *It is not surprising, then, if his servants masquerade as servants of righteousness. Their end will be what their actions deserve.*

Paul has previously referred to the intruders as "peddlers" (2:17–3:1) and as "superlative" apostles (11:5; cf. 12:11). Now he directs his guns at them with a barrage that calls their very relationship to Christ into question. They are now styled "false apostles . . . deceitful workmen," who fashion themselves into "apostles of Christ." Since Satan fashions himself into an angel of light, it is no surprise that Satan's ministers fashion themselves as "ministers of righteousness." Their end will be according to their works. The "false apostles" are "false" *(pseudo)* because they claim to be — what Paul (by inference) is, but which they are not — "true workmen, apostles of Christ, ministers of righteousness." To the contrary, they merely "masquerade" as such.

There is a major disagreement about their identity. Many scholars argue that the "false apostles" are to be distinguished from those whom Paul earlier calls "superlative" apostles (11:5), the former being identified with the newly arrived emissaries, the latter with "high officials"[1] in the Jerusalem church from whom they have come.

But this distinction is artificial. The two groups are found in the one continuous passage (10:12–12:13), beginning with the paragraph that refers to those who have come to Corinth as having trespassed into Paul's "field." As the passage continues, these trespassers are called "superlative" apostles (11:5) and spoken of as those who "want an opportunity to be considered

---

52. Gk. ἐκκοπτεῖν.
1. Notably distinguished by F. C. Baur, on which see C. K. Barrett, "Opponents," 78-83.

equal with [Paul]" (11:12). But in the next verse (11:13) they are immediately called "false apostles" because they claim to be "apostles of Christ." Thus, rather than distinguish "superlative" apostles from "false apostles," it is preferable to regard them as the same group referred to by different terms; they are at once "superlative" apostles and "false apostles."

Moreover, the "false apostles" are lodged within the one prolonged passage (10:12–12:13) where Paul is rejecting the claim that he is "inferior" to these newcomers. It is significant that within this extended passage where the "false apostles" are mentioned, words prefixed with *"hyper"*[2] are common (see comment on 10:12). The use of numerous *hyper-* words in the passage that surrounds the mention of "false apostles" makes it probable that the *hyperlian* apostles are to be identified with the *pseud[o]*-apostles. It is, therefore, unlikely that Paul is referring to two separate groups.

Structurally speaking, vv. 13-15 are united by the appearance in each verse of the verb "fashion," or "transform."[3]

v. 13   "such men" fashion themselves as apostles of Christ.
v. 14   "Satan" fashions himself into an angel of light.
v. 15   "[Satan's] ministers" fashion themselves as ministers of righteousness.

The connectives "for" and "therefore"[4] are important in the flow of the argument:

> Such men   fashion themselves as apostles of Christ,
> *for* Satan   fashions himself   as an angel of light;
> *therefore* it is no surprise that
> Satan's ministers fashion themselves as ministers of righteousness.

The transformation of "Satan's ministers" into "ministers of righteousness" springs from, and is analogous to, Satan's transformation "as an angel of light." It appears that Paul would have us understand that "such men," that

---

2. Gk. ὑπέρ (11:23); ὑπερεκτείνειν (10:14); ὑπερέκεινα (10:16); ὑπερλίαν (11:5); ὑπερβαλλόντως (11:23); ὑπεραίρομαι (12:7); ὑπερβολή (12:7).

3. Gk. μετασχηματίζεσθαι; NIV, "masquerades." This verb is repeated in vv. 13, 14, and 15. It appears in the LXX only at 4 Macc 9:22, and elsewhere in the NT only at 1 Cor 4:6 and Phil 3:21, none of which references gives a clear idea of the meaning here. The core of the verb is σχῆμα = an object's form or shape; μετα- implies change, hence "transform." The usual translations are "masquerading" or "disguising." The middle voice present tense μετασχηματίζεται followed by εἰς suggests (1) the reflexive, "[Satan] fashioning *himself*" (so BAGD), and (2) an ongoing or habitual activity. On this understanding Satan continually appears to the church as an angel of light.

4. Gk. γάρ and οὖν respectively.

is, the "false apostles," are "Satan's ministers" who transform themselves into "apostles of Christ," that is, as "ministers of righteousness."

13 The explanatory "For" and the demonstrative pronoun "such men"[5] point back to those of the previous verse who wish to be considered equal with Paul in ministry. In reality, however, they are "false apostles" and "deceitful workmen," who fashion themselves into, so as to pass themselves off as, "apostles of Christ."

Paul now begins to speak in his frankest terms about the newcomers in Corinth (see 2:17–3:1; 5:12-13; 10:12ff.). The pointedness of his invective reflects the grave and scandalous nature of their challenge to Paul's position as an apostle to the Corinthians. These men "seek an opportunity to be considered equal with [Paul]" in ministry in Corinth. But the truth is quite otherwise. Dramatically and emotionally he now exposes them as, first, "false apostles"[6] and, second, as "deceitful workmen."[7] When he adds immediately, "fashioning themselves as apostles of Christ," it is clear that their falsity and their deceitfulness lie in the deviant gospel they preached (see on 11:4) and their pretense in the measures they took to present themselves as "apostles of Christ," that is, in the same terms Paul had applied to himself (v. 12). In contrast to Paul, who is commended by the Lord, these men are self-commended, self-advertised (see on 10:18). His oath a few verses earlier, "As . . . the *truth* of Christ is in me" (v. 10), serves as a foil to their pretense and deception.

Although Paul does not say how these men sought to gain acceptance in Corinth as "apostles of Christ," they appear to have adopted two related strategies. First, that they clothed themselves in works of ministry in which, after negatively "classify[ing] and compar[ing]" Paul with themselves (10:12), they emerged as "superior" to Paul (cf. v. 23 — *hyper,* "better") — in speaking ability (11:5-6) and in "visions and revelations" (12:1; cf. on 5:13). If these expressions of ministry, contrived to gain acceptance in Corinth,

---

5. Gk. οἱ γὰρ τοιοῦτοι. . . . Once again γάρ serves to link what now follows with the previous verse. The word τοιοῦτος occurs in the Corinthian letters to refer to individuals and groups whom Paul calculatedly does not name (1 Cor 5:5; 2 Cor 2:6, 7; 10:11), even though in one passage it is clearly himself (12:2, 3, 5).

6. Gk. ψευδαπόστολοι is probably coined by Paul; it does not appear elsewhere in the NT. False apostles are ὑπερλίαν ἀπόστολοι ("superlative apostles"), preach ἄλλον Ἰησοῦν, ("another Jesus"), and bring εὐαγγέλιον ἕτερον ("a different gospel" — v. 4). The prefix ψευδ- speaks of falsity based on pretense (cf. ψευδομάρτυρες — 1 Cor 15:15; ψευδάδελφοι — Gal 2:4; 2 Cor 11:26).

7. Gk. ὁ ἐργάτης appears elsewhere as a term for a teaching elder (1 Tim 5:18) and for Paul's coworker, Timothy (2 Tim 2:15). Clearly it belongs to vocabulary used of Christian ministers (cf. Matt 9:37-38), a view confirmed by Paul's negative qualification *"deceitful* workmen" (see also Phil 3:2).

were the various parts of their disguise, we have some understanding of the intensity of Paul's speech in these verses.

A further strategy may be revealed in the two verses following, where Paul states that Satan's ministers "fashion" themselves as "ministers of righteousness," suggesting that — as Paul saw it — "righteousness" was a mask worn by these men to win recognition in Corinth as "apostles of Christ." As we shall argue, such "righteousness" was not only "righteous" behavior but more particularly an ideology of "righteousness" that they promoted. Their manner and message of "righteousness" were a garment in which they masqueraded as "apostles of Christ," and their claims to superiority over Paul, mentioned above, were the accessories of that clothing.

14 Beginning with an exclamation ("And no wonder!"), Paul continues this assault on the intruders with an explanation that ties their ministry to Satan, not Christ ("for[8] Satan himself fashions himself as an angel of light").

This verse is structurally central to the passage (vv. 13-15). The appearance of "for" in the second sentence flows out of the preceding exclamation, which in turn springs from "such men . . . fashioning themselves as apostles of Christ" in the previous verse; the "therefore" in the next verse points back to it as its basis also. The linked phrases from vv. 14 and 15 — "And no wonder . . . it is not surprising, then"[9] — further serves to clamp the passage together around v. 14.

Paul's argument is that, if Satan himself — the very archetype of evil — is capable of habitually "fashioning himself into[10] an angel of light," then it is no matter for surprise if "these men" are able to transform themselves into "apostles of Christ," that is, that "Satan's ministers" are able to transform themselves into "ministers of righteousness" (v. 15).[11] We conclude from this verse that "ministers of righteousness" is a term closely related to "apostles of Christ."

There is a connection between "Satan fashioning himself into an angel[12] of light"[13] and "Eve . . . deceived by the serpent's cunning" earlier

---

8. Gk. γάρ.

9. Gk. καὶ οὐ θαῦμα . . . οὐ μέγα οὖν, which is quite classical in idiom.

10. Gk. μετασχηματίζεται; see n. 3 above.

11. See 4:4, where Satan is styled "the god of this world," who in the case of unbelievers "blinds" them so that they cannot see the light of the gospel of the glory of Christ.

12. Gk. ἄγγελος is applied elsewhere to a preacher, whether false or true (Gal 1:8; 4:14).

13. Gk. ἄγγελος φωτός, a descriptive genitive, "an angel of bright appearance," or so it seemed.

in the chapter (v. 3).[14] Common to both references is (1) the activity of deception, and (2) the object of deception, the church. Verses 3 and 14 are to be read together. The serpent's (Satan's) deception of Eve (the church [of Corinth]) is achieved by these men who "preach another Jesus" ("fashioning themselves" into something they are not, namely, "apostles of Christ"), so as to lead the people astray from their loyalty to Christ (v. 4).

What, then, is the "light" of this "angel" into which Satan has disguised himself in coming to Corinth? The next verse provides the answer, namely, the "light" of the "righteousness" that these "ministers" both attempt to embody and proclaim.

15 Paul's introductory "therefore"[15] leads into the climax of this short passage (vv. 13-15), which is the most devastating comment of all. Thus he begins with an understatement, "It is no great surprise[16] if. . . ." Although given in conditional terms ("if"[17]), this apocalyptic statement is not hypothetical but actual: "If indeed [Satan's] ministers fashion themselves as ministers of righteousness. . . ." Paul concludes with a dire warning, "whose end will be according to their works."

Set up by v. 14, Paul now dismisses these "superlative" apostles as no apostles at all; rather, they are "ministers [of Satan]." True, by an outward change of form, they present themselves as "ministers of righteousness," but that is by deception. The term "ministers of righteousness" must now be added to the earlier ones, "workmen . . . apostles of Christ" (v. 13). Herein lies their pretense and deception. Paul was a "workman . . . an apostle of Christ" and, though he does not apply the exact term to himself here, a "minister of righteousness" (but see 3:9; 5:20-21). These men, however, in fashioning themselves in the guise of "workmen, apostles, ministers of righteousness," are, in effect — though probably not in intention — "ministers of Satan."

Along with the Spirit, "righteousness" is one of the signs of the new covenant of which Paul was a "minister" (3:6, 8, 9). The apostolic appeal to "be

14. Whereas in v. 3 Paul appeals to the serpent's deception of Eve from Genesis 3, his appeal here to Satan's transmutation of himself into "an angel of light" appears to arise from intertestamental tradition (*contra* Plummer, 309; Martin, 352). Examples (as cited in Furnish, 495) include "Satan appeared in the form of an angel . . ." (*Apoc. Moses* 17:1-2); "Satan . . . transformed himself into the brightness of angels, and went away to the river Tigris to Eve, and found her weeping, and the devil himself pretended to grieve with her . . ." (Latin version of *Adam and Eve* 9:1).

15. Gk. οὖν.

16. Gk. οὐ μέγα; NIV, "and no wonder," lit. "nothing so great." This is an example of litotes or understatement made for emphasis. The phrase should be read with οὐ θαῦμα, "no wonder" (v. 14).

17. Gk. εἰ καί, "if indeed." While this expression is usually a concessive, the context here demands that καί be an intensive (as also in 1 Cor 4:7; 7:11; 2 Cor 4:3; Phil 4:17; 2 Tim 2:5).

reconciled to God," based on the "righteousness of God" arising from Christ's sacrificial death (5:21), is a "ministry" that God gave Paul as an apostle (5:18). Paul as an apostle of Christ was, indeed, a "minister of righteousness."

The use of "righteousness" in this context suggests that "righteousness" was also fundamental to their "ministry" and therefore to their message.[18] But "righteousness" is most likely expressive of the Law of Moses, or at least an attempt to predicate "righteousness" in Torah observance, for two reasons: (1) Those who purport to be "ministers of righteousness" were "Hebrews, Israelites, descendants of Abraham" (v. 22), and (2), as those "peddlers" who "need[ed] letters of recommendation" to legitimate their coming to Corinth, they were "ministers" of a now overtaken "old covenant," which was "[written] on tablets of stone" (see on 3:3, 14, 3, 6). "Righteousness" associated with such men appears to have been Mosaic and Torah-based.[19] Since they proclaimed "another Jesus . . . a different gospel," it seems likely that they advocated a *different* "righteousness," a "righteousness" arising out of the Mosaic law[20] rather than from Messiah Jesus' reconciliatory death. As "ministers of righteousness" — so defined — they are effectively, even if unintentionally, "ministers of Satan."[21]

In parallel with the ancient serpent who first compromised the word of God (Gen 3:1, 4), before alienating Adam and Eve from the Lord (Gen 3:7-8), these "ministers of Satan," by their corruption of the apostolic word of God (2:17; cf. 4:2), effectively divert the Corinthians away from their "sincere and pure devotion to Christ" (v. 3). As agents of Satan — even if unintended on their part — these newcomers were as capable of causing believers at Corinth to fall away from God as the serpent who caused Adam and Eve to fall away from God in the garden. The word of God, when heeded, unites the hearers to God, but when corrupted, it cuts men and women off from God.

So serious is their pretense and dangerous their alternative message that Paul declares, solemnly, that "their end will correspond to their works."[22] Elsewhere Paul calls the Judaizers "enemies of the cross," whose "end is

---

18. This view is not shared, e.g., by Bultmann, Barrett, Furnish, and Martin, who argue that "righteousness" is unrelated to the message of these newcomers. They see no evidence that "righteousness" is here connected with the Law of God.

19. See, too, Phil 3:2, 6, where he appears to connect "evil workmen" with "righteousness under the Law."

20. See R. H. Gundry, "Grace," 37, for a discussion of the nature and relationship of faith and works in salvation.

21. Cf. Mark 8:33, where Jesus calls Peter "Satan," which, however, was not in reference to the intention, but the effect, of Peter's words.

22. Gk. ὧν τὸ τέλος ἔσται κατὰ τὰ ἔργα αὐτῶν; NIV, "Their end will be what their actions deserve." The NT often speaks of judgment according to works (see, e.g., 5:10; 1 Cor 3:13-15; Rom 2:6; Gal 6:7-9; Eph 6:8; Col 3:24).

perdition" (Phil 3:18-19[23]). So too, here, those who mask the true righteousness of God in the crucified One (5:21), peddling instead a Torah-righteousness that brings only condemnation (2:17; 3:9), face the same dreadful "end." Perhaps Paul implies a pointedly deeper meaning here.[24] As "ministers of righteousness," they have preached "the law" and, therefore, "its works" (cf. Gal 3:10-14); their end — perdition — issues from their "works," that is, their "works"-righteousness.

Here, then, Paul sets forth a clear warning to those engaged in ministry, especially missionaries and church pastors. The righteousness of God is located only in the vicarious death of Christ and not in the works of the Law. Those who preach and teach must direct their hearers to the message of the cross so that no one is in doubt as to the means of divine acceptance. Let those who preach otherwise take note of the consequences set forth here by the apostle.

(5) A Fool Boasts (11:16-21a)

16 *I repeat: Let no one take me for a fool. But if you do, then receive me just as you would a fool, so that I may do a little boasting.* 17 *In this self-confident boasting I am not talking as the Lord would, but as a fool.* 18 *Since many are boasting in the way the world does, I too will boast.* 19 *You gladly put up with fools since you are so wise!* 20 *In fact, you even put up with anyone who enslaves you or exploits you or takes advantage of you or pushes himself forward or slaps you in the face.* 21 *To my shame I admit that we were too weak for that!*

Having directed such strong attention to the "false apostles" (vv. 13-15), Paul now moves to the subtle triangular interplay between them ("anyone" — vv. 16, 20; "many" — v. 18; "fools" — v. 19), the Corinthians ("you" — vv. 16, 19, 20), and himself ("me" — v. 16; "I" — vv. 17, 18, 21a; "we" — v. 21a). He does so by picking up the "fool" theme from v. 1. Paul tells the Corinthians not to take him for a "fool." Nonetheless, if they prefer to do so, let them receive him just as they would any "fool," so that he, *too,* can "boast" (v. 16), a reference back to the "false apostles" (vv. 13-15) who are characterized by "boasting" (10:12-13).

What proceeds now is full of biting irony. Since "boasting" is what "fools" do, we are meant to infer that Paul is imitating and parodying these men as "fools." Yet — let the Corinthians understand — he is not speaking "according to the Lord," but "as in foolishness," in this mode of "boasting" (i.e., as the

---

23. Cf. Rom 3:8; 2 Tim 4:14.
24. So Hughes, 396.

"false apostles" are doing — v. 17; cf. 10:12-13, 17-18). Since they are "boasting according to the flesh," so, "too," Paul will "boast" (v. 18).

Having asked them to "receive" him "as a fool" (v. 16), Paul comments ironically that the Corinthians, being so "wise," gladly "bear with fools" — that is, himself, but also the "false apostles" (see v. 20). Again, ironically, he notes that the Corinthians "bear with" those who exploit and abuse them (v. 20). The Corinthians, too, must be "fools" to put up with that! He rounds off the passage with an expression of irony tinged with pain, "to my shame, we were too weak for that" (i.e., to exploit and abuse others — v. 21).

This is, indeed, the language of pain. If he speaks as "a fool" or as "weak," it is because, in all probability, some at Corinth — probably the newcomers ("anyone" — v. 16; cf. "anyone" — v. 20) — have spoken of him in those ways. If he "boasts," it is because others — almost certainly the newcomers — are "boasting" of their achievements, while comparing Paul disadvantageously with themselves (see on 10:12-13). But Paul's irony is biting; the Corinthians, too, will feel pain at his words.

Here we see, even at this distance in time, the suffering of a minister of the gospel, the founder of a church, whom that church is perilously close to rejecting in favor of other teachers who claimed to be superior but whose doctrines are capable of corrupting the church. Although the rhetorical terms in which Paul expresses himself are strange to us today, they would have provoked considerable comment in his day. The "Fool's Speech," as it will develop, is, in fact, a daring countercultural exercise. At that time one boasted of achievements, not of weaknesses.

16 Paul now picks up again the threads of his "Fool's Speech" introduced in v. 1 ("I repeat: Let no one take me for a fool"; cf. v. 1 — "my foolishness"), a "speech" that will itself begin in v. 21b.

The words "fool" (vv. 17, 18, 21; 12:6, 11) and "madman" (v. 23 — RSV),[1] are very important in the extended passage 11:16–12:13. But who is calling Paul a "fool"? His injunction, "Let not *anyone* regard me as a fool," points to the "false apostles" as his accusers; in v. 20 the fivefold "anyone" is in clear reference to them.

But this leads on to something else. In the first half of a second sentence he adds, ironically, "Otherwise, if you must"[2] — that is, *you Corinthians —* take me for a "fool," then "receive me as you would any 'fool.'" The

---

1. In 1 Corinthians a member of the ἄφρων-ἀφροσύνη word group appears only once (1 Cor 15:36), whereas μωρός-μωρία appears repeatedly there but not in 2 Corinthians. The appearance of ἄφρων-ἀφροσύνη in 2 Corinthians suggests that these words are current as criticisms of Paul in Corinth.

2. Gk. εἰ δὲ μή γε (NIV, "but if you do") is found only here in Paul, but is common in Luke.

Corinthians have "borne with" those who have preached "another Jesus" (v. 4); let them "receive" (and "bear with" — v. 1) the "fool," Paul. This is for the purpose stated in the second part of that sentence, namely, "that"[3] he, "too,"[4] can "do a little boasting."[5]

If there are others who "boast" — who likewise must be "fools" — then Paul, too, will "boast." By accepting their tag "fool" in the way he has, Paul has at the same time pinned it on those who call him "fool." By boasting — though of an inverted, mocking kind — he will show who is really foolish. In the speech following he will boast like other fools to show how foolish those who call him foolish are.

17 He hastens to correct any possible misunderstanding. Let them not think he is "speaking according to the Lord."[6] No, this is another way of speaking — not an apostle's way, but a "fool's" way. If they call him a fool, let them hear what a fool has to say.

Nor is it merely "boasting"; it is "boasting" in a "self-confident"[7] way, which, as v. 18 goes on to say, is "boasting according to the flesh."

v. 17   What I speak
              I speak not according to the Lord
                    but as in foolishness,
                        in this self-confident boasting.
v. 18   Since many are
                              boasting
             according to the flesh. . . .

For the sake of this rhetorical exercise Paul casts himself in the role of his opponents. What they do he will do. If they "boast in . . . self-confidence, in the flesh," then so, too, will he. "But," he declares, it is "as in foolishness."[8] This is a two-edged comment. It is "foolish" for him; but since he is playing *their* part, it is "foolish" for them, too. By his parody Paul reveals their "foolishness" while at the same time positively expounding the authentic "foolishness" of God's ways, which he, Paul, is following.

3. Gk. ἵνα.
4. Gk. κἀγώ, "I, too"; Paul did not start this foolish boasting.
5. Paul has already declared that "only in the Lord" may one "boast" (10:17-18). He will boast only "a little," presumably in contrast with the newcomers, whose boasting is extensive and the basis of their acceptance in Corinth.
6. Gk. οὐ κατὰ κύριον λαλῶ; NIV, "not talking as the Lord would"; RSV: "not with the Lord's authority" (cf. 1 Cor 7:10; 9:8).
7. Gk. ἐν ταύτῃ τῇ ὑποστάσει, which Furnish, 496, representing many, takes to mean "in this matter" or "project." NIV's "self-confident," which is followed here, fits well the flow of the text.
8. Gk. ὡς ἐν ἀφροσύνῃ; NIV, "as a fool."

What others — Paul's opponents — "boast" of, and their "self-confidence" in doing so, is open to question (but see on v. 18). But — by implication — Paul's "boasting" is securely based in reality. By exposing their "foolishness" in such self-confident boasting, let them see his sanity.

18 Since "many," indeed, do "boast according to the flesh,"[9] so, too, will Paul. It is probable that the apostle is here pointing to the "many" newcomers (cf. "so many" — 2:17; "some" — 3:1; "some . . . they" — 10:12) and their "boasting." He may be thinking of their distinctive route to "righteousness" (v. 15) by means of the moral and ceremonial observances of the Mosaic dispensation (see on v. 15), which would be a ground for "boasting" (cf. Rom 3:27; Eph 2:9). On the other hand — and this would not exclude the previous consideration — he may be referring to their "boasting" in regard to the elements of ministry in which they regard themselves as "superior" to Paul as they "classify and compare" themselves with him (see on 10:12; 11:5).[10]

Now it is precisely because these people "boast" — for the reasons suggested — that Paul, too, "boasts." Because they "boast," he "must boast" (11:30; 12:1). Such "boasting" is, of course, "foolish" (see on v. 16). Their "foolishness" in "boasting" has "forced" Paul also "to be a fool" (12:11), forced him "to boast" (11:30; 12:1).

If such people can boast "according to the flesh," so, too, can Paul (cf. "For if I wish to boast, I will not be a fool" — 12:6). But his "fleshly" boasting will take a surprising turn; it will be of his "weakness[es]" (see on 11:30; 12:9).

19 The connective "For"[11] introduces the basis — delayed by some verses — on which he has made the original statement (v. 16). "Receive me as a fool," he says, *"for* you gladly[12] put up with[13] fools." "Put up with" (vv. 1, 4, 20), along with the "fool" vocabulary (v. 1), again picks up the threads of the "Fool's Speech" introduced earlier (v. 16; cf. v. 1).

---

9. Gk. πολλοὶ καυχῶνται κατὰ σάρκα is taken by the NIV (also the RSV) — unhelpfully — as "in the way the world does." A better rendering would be: "according to the flesh" since this brings out the notion of self-effort, as opposed to the empowering Spirit of the new covenant in the day of salvation (1:17; 5:16; 10:2, 3). Κατὰ σάρκα is to be preferred to κατὰ τὴν σάρκα. Both have equal textual support, but the latter would convey the improbable meaning: "from their human point of view."

10. Possibly, too, they were boasting of the one — Cephas? — who, in their opinion, staked the claim on their behalf for their mission in Corinth (see on 10:16).

11. Gk. γάρ.

12. Gk. ἡδέως, which comes first for emphasis. The adverb καλῶς, "easily," is used with this verb in 11:4.

13. Gk. ἀνέχεσθε, "you put up with, bear with," is one of the keywords of this passage, used with irony and pain (11:1, 4, 20).

On the face of it he is speaking of himself, as indeed he is, but with irony. The "Fool's Speech," especially as it intensifies in 11:21b–12:13, is focused on the "foolishness," even "madness," of the apostolic life. Yes, he is the "fool" (i.e., "the unwise"), whom these "wise,"[14] these theologically gifted Corinthians (8:7; cf. 1 Cor 4:10; 10:15), "put up with."

But are these who "put up with" the "unwise" Paul "wise" in fact? By a subtle twist Paul proceeds to say that they — the "wise" Corinthians — "put up with" dreadful abuse (v. 20). So are they not "unwise," "fools"?

20 With one more explanatory "For,"[15] Paul introduces the climax of vv. 16-21a. Once more Paul uses the keyword "put up with," which, as we have seen, is capable of several nuances (see on vv. 1, 4, 19). The Corinthians are the subject of the verb "put up with," and the object, understood, is "it."[16] When, however, he lists five situations in which the Corinthians ("you") are the object of abusive behavior by "anyone," it is clear that the "false apostles" are the subject and the Corinthians the object of their actions.

Instead of "putting up with" a "fool" like Paul, he cleverly reverses the object. The Corinthians themselves are "fools" who put up with (it) when the newcomers inflict indignities on them.

Again, he speaks of the newcomer*s* (i.e., plural, as in 10:12; 11:5, 12, 13, 15, 18) in the singular, and in an impersonal manner "anyone" (so also 10:16, 18; 11:4). Five times he uses the rhetorical "if anyone."[17] Now follow the five evil actions[18] of the newcomers that the "foolish" Corinthians have "put up with." The intruders "enslave" the Corinthians, that is, subject them to the kind of domineering leadership Paul himself was careful not to impose (cf. 1:24; 12:14; cf. 4:5). Second, they "exploit" them, or, more literally, "devour"[19] them, a probable reference to securing financial support from the Corinthians. Third, the newcomers "take advantage of" them, in all probability amplifying the first action, "enslave." This speaks of exerting complete control over the Corinthians. The word "catch"[20] is sometimes used of snaring a bird or catching

---

14. The combination here of ἀφρόνων and φρόνιμοι adds to the rhetorical impact. The ironic "foolish"/"wise" contrast between himself and them is found also in 1 Corinthians, except that a different word for foolishness is used there: ἡμεῖς μωροὶ . . . ὑμεῖς φρόνιμοι (1 Cor 4:10).

15. Gk. γάρ.

16. For a parallel see Josephus, "When plundered, you put up with it (ἀνέχεσθε), when beaten you are silent . . ." (*J.W.* 4.165).

17. Gk. εἴ τις.

18. Gk. καταδουλοῖ . . . κατεσθίει . . . λαμβάνει . . . ἐπαίρεται . . . δέρει. . . . The first two verbs are compounded, signifying intensified meaning.

19. Gk. κατεσθίει. Cf. "The scribes . . . who devour (κατεσθίοντες) widows' houses" (Mark 12:40).

20. Gk. λαμβάνει.

fish (cf. 12:16; Luke 5:5). Fourth, they "push themselves forward," again, more literally, "lift themselves up" in a superior way (cf. 10:5). Fifth, these men "have slapped [the Corinthians] in the face." While many commentators regard this as metaphorical for "humiliate,"[21] it may point more literally to some physical violence against the Corinthians.[22] Of the five actions listed, this alone is specific in character, adding weight to the possibility that Paul is referring to a well-known incident in Corinth in the recent past.

Whatever the exact meaning of these five elements they represent the antithesis of the godly minister of the new covenant modeled on the "meekness and gentleness of Christ" (10:1). Such a minister gives himself to and for the people — as Christ did — in a spirit of self-sacrifice. The contrast is the more pointed because Paul will immediately relate how he has fulfilled such a ministry, and at considerable personal cost (11:21–12:13). This evil description serves as a dark backdrop against which the bright goodness of Paul's own ministry may be seen. The exploitative and manipulative actions listed here have become all too familiar in the treatment by leaders of both adults and children in a number of highly publicized modern cults.

Paul's subtle use of "foolish" (i.e., "unwise") and "wise" in vv. 16-20 should be noted as applying (1) to his opponents, who, because they "boast," show themselves to be "fools" (v. 16), whom the Corinthians also "put up with" (v. 19); (2) to Paul, who, because he, "too," "boasts," shows himself to be a "fool" (v. 16), and whom the Corinthians "put up with"; and (3) to the "wise" Corinthians, who are "fools" to "put up with" the "fools" who misuse them (v. 20).

21a Paul's irony now reaches its most biting expression. If the opponents say[23] he is "weak," as apparently they do (see on 10:1), let them know that it is just as they say: "we are [too] weak[24] [for that]." That is, he was too weak to treat the Corinthians as the newcomers have (v. 20). It is "to [his] shame"[25] to admit it, but he does.

This ironical admission of "weakness" signals the introduction proper of the "Fool's Speech" in the next verse, reaching its climax in the famous "power-in-weakness" passage (12:7-10). The vocabulary of "weak-

---

21. So Furnish, 497, citing others.

22. Both Christ and Paul were struck in the Sanhedrin (Mark 14:65; Acts 23:2). Paul exhorts that a bishop/elder should not be violent (1 Tim 3:3; Tit 1:7).

23. The phrase ὡς ὅτι introduces a quotation (of theirs!), as in 5:19. Furnish, 497, however, thinks that ὡς is Paul's ironic judgment whereas ὅτι is dependent on λέγω.

24. Gk. ἡμεῖς ἠσθενήκαμεν. Note that (1) ἡμεῖς is emphatic and contrastive with the false apostles in v. 20, (2) something (e.g., "for that") has to be supplied to give the sense, and (3) the perfect tense indicates "we were and *are* weak."

25. Gk. κατὰ ἀτιμίαν λέγω, lit. "I speak with respect to shame. . . ." Clearly, Paul is speaking about himself.

ness[es],"[26] which has been employed only once to this point in the letter
(10:10), will be used constantly from this point to the end of the "Fool's
Speech" (11:21b–12:13). Because "many" have "boasted" (11:18), Paul,
too, "must boast" (11:30; 12:1), but it will be in his "weakness" (11:30;
12:9); hence the importance of the introduction here of the vocabulary of
"weakness." He has been forced to be a "fool" (12:11; cf. 11:16).

b. The "Fool's Speech" Proper (11:21b–12:10)

It is probable that this "Speech" mirrors, but so as to parody and also correct,
the claims of the newly arrived false apostles. From what appear to be his
responses to them, his opponents "boasted of": (1) their Jewish heritage
(11:22), (2) their accomplishments that accredited them as ministers of Christ
(11:23), and (3) extraordinary "visions and revelations" (12:1-4). It is quite
likely that they pointed to Paul's evident misfortunes and humiliations in the
pursuit of his ministry as signs of inferiority and incompetence. Paul will not
attempt to match them in their favorable comparisons of themselves with him.
Rather, he will daringly boast of "weaknesses," the very weaknesses they
deplore, so as to mock his opponents' crassness in boasting while at the same
time establishing that it is *his* ministry that authentically replicates the suffering ministry of Christ. The true trajectory of Christ's ministry is to be seen
as continued in Paul and his ministry and not in the ministry of these men.

In the "Fool's Speech" proper Paul (1) exposes the triumphalism of
the "false apostles," whose keyword is *hyper* (they have "more" to offer than
Paul, whom they are "above," or "better" than), but also (2) "boasts" of his
"weaknesses," that is, of those sufferings incurred in the course of ministry
in replication of the sufferings of Christ. This is Paul's "foolishness," his
"madness," which is the "foolishness" and "madness" of Christ himself. As
such this part of the "Speech" is profoundly antitriumphalist and must be
read with the antitriumphalism of the striking prisoner-of-war image at the
beginning of the excursus on new covenant ministry (see on 2:14).

(1) Comparison: The Opponents and Paul (11:21b-23a)

21b *What anyone else dares to boast about — I am speaking as a
fool — I also dare to boast about.* 22 *Are they Hebrews? So am I. Are
they Israelites? So am I. Are they Abraham's descendants? So am I.*
23 *Are they servants of Christ? (I am out of my mind to talk like this.)
I am more.*

---

26. Gk. ἀσθενεῖν also occurs in 11:29; 12:10; 13:3, 4, 9; ἀσθένεια in 11:30; 12:5,
9, 10; 13:4; and ἀσθενής in 10:10.

This "speech" is Paul's "daring" (v. 21b) reply to the apparent jibes that he is "weak" and a "fool," as contrasted with them, who are are strong and wise! So, remarkably, he not only accepts their labels but expands and elaborates upon them in an astonishing catalogue of "weaknesses" and "foolishnesses."

This, however, is not merely an ingenious disarming rhetorical device. Profound theology lies at its base. Such weaknesses and foolishnesses demonstrated in suffering in gospel ministry reveal him to be a genuine minister of Christ ("a *better* [minister] of Christ" — 11:23) and, indeed, to be identified with Christ, who was "crucified" in weakness (13:4). If Christ is seen most definitively in his suffering on the cross, then his minister is seen most definitively in foolish weakness, not in power. In these sufferings Paul had identified with the weak as no one else had. Grimly he will ask, "Who is weak and I am not weak"? (11:29, RSV). But, then, he is able to go on, climactically, to share his experience of the power of God resting on him in his most profound experience of weakness, the "stake/thorn" (12:8; cf. 13:4).

Thus the "Speech" proper has elements of antitriumphalism as well as of triumph, characteristics that inexactly replicate those in the remarkable victory parade metaphor set out in 2:14.

21b In this brief sentence Paul begins the "Fool's Speech" proper. It is cast in the first person singular ("I"/"me"), unlike much of the first nine chapters of this letter, which is in the first person plural ("we"/"us"). The first two verses establish this intensely personal presentation by his fourfold "I also"[1] (vv. 21b-22):

> In whatever anyone is bold
> — I am speaking in foolishness —
> I also   am bold.

Paul's vocabulary — "boldness" and "foolishness"[2] — appears to echo a polemic against him in Corinth — the former from the Corinthians (see 10:2), the latter from the "false apostles" (see on v. 16). His own manner of life and speech as a man "in Christ" is disciplined, circumscribed by the "meekness and gentleness of Christ" (10:1, RSV). This, however, together with his well-known sufferings, appears to have led to the interpretation of him as "weak"[3] (i.e., lacking "boldness") and "foolish," suggestive of slogans used against him.

His assertion "I am bold" — in the face of whatever it is that "anyone is bold" [about] — takes us back to a denial made earlier, "*Not* that we are

---

1. Gk. κἀγώ = καὶ ἐγώ, an example of crasis, lit. "and I am."
2. Cf. Gk. τολμᾶν (NIV, "dare" — 10:2, 12); ἀφροσύνη (NIV, "foolishness" — 11:1, 17); ἄφρων (NIV, "Fool" — 11:16 [twice], 19; 12:6, 11); παραφρονεῖν ("NIV, "out of my mind" — 11:23).
3. See 10:10; 11:19, 30.

bold to class or compare ourselves with those who commend themselves" (see on 10:12). In spite of that denial, in the catalogue following (11:22–12:10), he is indeed bold "to class and compare" himself with those who deem themselves "superior" to (*hyper* — lit. "over" — see on 11:5) him. But his comparisons, unlike theirs, are a tragic-comic parody of self-commendation, Paul's "fool-speak." So far from listing achievements that might commend and legitimate him as a minister of Christ, as the newcomers apparently have, he lists his sufferings and humiliations.

Who are these persons? Based on information scattered throughout the previous chapters, it appears they are the "self-commended" ones (10:12, 18), the "superlative" apostles (11:5), who have "come" to Corinth preaching "another Jesus . . . a different gospel" (11:4), those "false apostles" who as "ministers of Satan" have "fashioned themselves as ministers of righteousness" (11:13-15) and who have captured and abused the Corinthians (11:20). But in the next verses Paul will supply the piece of the jigsaw that, more than any other to this point in the letter, will assist in establishing the profile of these opponents.

22, 23a These verses are critical in the exposition of Paul's "Fool's Speech" (11:21b–12:13). By means of these four rhetorical questions he "classes and compares" himself with the "false apostles" (see on v. 21b; cf. 10:12).

Hebrews	are they?	So am I.
Israelites	are they?	So am I.
Seed of Abraham	are they?	So am I.
Ministers of Christ	are they?	I am better.

This fourfold "comparison"[4] (see on 10:12) yields critical data as to (1) the identity and (2) the mission of these newly arrived opponents of the apostle. By *identity* these men are "Hebrews"[5] and "Israelites,"[6] pure members of

4. Paul's comparisons ("So am I . . . I am better") appear to follow the Hellenistic σύγκρισις that appealed to "good breeding" (εὐγένεια), as seen, e.g., from a contemporary inscription to one Tiberius Claudius Zopas by his son as "son of his city, lover of his country, both on account of the gravity of his manners and of his *good breeding* (he inherits) from his ancestors" (cited in E. A. Judge, "St Paul and Classical Society," 9-36).

5. Gk. Ἑβραῖοι. Paul's self-description "Hebrew" here and at Phil 3:5 implies race. Eusebius describes Philo, the aristocratic Alexandrian Jew contemporary of Paul, as "descended from Hebrew stock" (*Hist. Eccl.* 2.4.2). By contrast Luke's reference (Acts 6:1) — the only other reference in the NT — implies language. In terms of Acts 6 we should probably think of the pre-Christian Paul as Ἑλληνιστής, a rabbi teaching the Greek-speaking synagogues in Jerusalem. (See M. Hengel, *Pre-Christian Paul,* 54-61.) Quite possibly these "Hebrews" who have now come to Corinth were drawn from the same "Hellenist" group as Paul, who first bitterly opposed Stephen and then Paul himself (cf. Acts 6:9-11; 9:29).

6. Gk. Ἰσραηλῖται, one who belongs to the people of Israel. Note the more Semitic

that race descended from its patriarchal fountainhead, Abraham,[7] whose "seed"[8] they are.[9] Of such persons (of "the people of Israel") he writes elsewhere,

> Theirs is the adoption as sons; theirs the divine glory, the covenants, the receiving of the law, the temple worship and the promises. Theirs are the patriarchs, and from them is traced the human ancestry of Christ. (Rom 9:4-5)

These men — like Paul — belong to God's unique people, whom he chose and redeemed, with whom he made covenant, to whom he sent his prophets, and from whom the Messiah would come.[10] They are clearly Jews.

The designation "Hebrews," as contrasted with "Hellenists" in the Acts of the Apostles (Acts 6:1), is usually taken to imply people of Aramaic speech.[11] Does Paul's present racial reference "Hebrews" (cf. Phil 3:5) also carry that linguistic import here? To the contrary, that these "Hebrews . . . Israelites" have come to Corinth, a Greco-Roman metropolis, makes it almost certain that they were Greek-speaking, as Paul was, even though he, too, was "of the people of Israel . . . a Hebrew" (Phil 3:5). For them, a significant level of competence in the Greek language is implied.[12] Paul will not concede inferiority to these men in the fundamentals of apostleship, but he does in speech (11:5-6; cf. 10:10).

So these men are Jews, Greek-speaking Jews, who have "come" (see on 10:13-15; 11:4), bearing "letters of commendation" (3:1), to Corinth. But what was their purpose, their *mission?* Paul's question, "Ministers of Christ[13]

---

term υἱοὶ Ἰσραήλ in 3:7, 13. The speeches of both Peter and Paul to Jewish audiences, as recorded in the Acts, are addressed to, "Men, *Israelites . . .*" (Acts 2:22; 3:12; 5:35; 13:16; 21:28).

7. Rom 11:1; Matt 1:1-2, 17; 3:9; 22:32; Luke 1:55, 73; 19:9; John 8:33, 37, 39, 53, 56; cf. Gen 12:2-3; Isa 51:1-2.

8. Gk. σπέρμα Ἀβραάμ, (NIV, "Abraham's descendants") is hardly distinguishable from Ἰσραηλῖται (see Rom 11:1; 4 Macc 18:1).

9. Paul's "comparison" with these persons in this verse must be interpreted by his outright statements about himself in (1) Phil 3:5, where as a "Hebrew" he is "of Hebrews" (Ἑβραῖος ἐξ Ἑβραίων), i.e., by physical descent (cf. John 1:12 — "born of bloods") and "by race, Israel" (ἐκ γένους Ἰσραήλ), and in (2) Rom 11:1, where he declares himself to be "an Israelite, a descendant of Abraham" (ἐγὼ Ἰσραηλίτης εἰμί, ἐκ σπέρματος Ἀβραάμ). Martin's suggestion, 374, that "Hebrews . . . Israelites . . . Seed of Abraham" marks these men out as Jewish *Christians* is unlikely; this verse, along with Phil 3:5; Rom 11:1, is a reference to Jewishness, pure and simple.

10. See on 2:17-3:3.

11. So M. Hengel, *Between Jesus and Paul,* 1-29.

12. So M. Hengel, *Pre-Christian Paul,* 60.

13. "Ministers of Christ" should be set alongside a later reference to those who

are they?" when read alongside "such men are false apostles . . . fashioning themselves as apostles of Christ" (see on v. 13), supplies the answer. These men come on a "Christian" mission; their representation of themselves, apparently, was as "ministers of Christ." But Paul saw them as *"pseudo,"* as *"false* apostles . . . ministers of [Satan]" (v. 13) and as *"false* brothers" who put his life in danger (see on v. 26).

Thus from the data scattered throughout this letter it emerges that these opponents of Paul who have come to Corinth are Jewish Christian — from their point of view, if not from Paul's — "ministers." What was their mission, their "ministry"? A few verses earlier Paul called them "ministers of righteousness." When read with the contrast between the "ministries" *(diakoniai*[14]) of the "old covenant" (i.e., of Moses) and the "new covenant" (i.e., of righteousness and the Spirit), this suggests that their purpose in coming to Corinth was to "minister" that "righteousness" associated with Moses/the Law ("on tablets of stone . . . the letter" — 3:3, 6), as opposed to that "righteousness" issuing in "reconciliation with God" based on Christ's death (3:9; 5:21), which was the "ministry" of Paul (3:6; cf. 2:17–3:4; 5:18, 19, 20).

Paul does not here deny outright that they are "ministers of Christ";[15] rather, he claims to be "better," which he proceeds to argue by the catalogue of his greater sufferings in the "Fool's Speech" following. Indeed, his "I am better"[16] controls the list of weaknesses following, including the climax, the "thorn in the flesh" (12:9).

It is noteworthy that while he condemns them as "false apostles, evil workmen . . . ministers [of Satan]" a few verses earlier (11:13-15), in this verse he calls them "ministers of Christ." What is the explanation of this apparent contradiction?

"preach Christ . . . proclaim Christ," yet who did so out of malice to Paul (Phil 1:15, 17) and who advocated the circumcision of Gentiles (Phil 3:2). Paul uses their high qualifications within Judaism as a comparative basis for his own standing as "a Hebrew of Hebrews, as to Law a Pharisee, as to zeal a persecutor of the church" (Phil 3:5-6). Do the references in Philippians indicate a deepening of enmity toward Paul from this quarter?

14. Gk. διακόνιαι. See 3:3, 7, 8, 9.

15. Gk. διάκονοι Χριστοῦ (NIV, "servants of Christ"), the only parallel to which in the NT is Col 1:7 — Ἐπαφρᾶ . . . διάκονος τοῦ Χριστοῦ. But see 2 Cor 6:4 — "ministers of God."

16. Gk. ὑπὲρ ἐγώ; NIV, "I am more." An elliptical phrase, which stated fully could be (1) a comparative — "I [am] even more [a minister of Christ]," or (2) a superlative, "I [am] the very best [minister of Christ]." Given the comparatives in v. 23, option (1) is preferred. Paul's reference to ὑπερλίαν ἀπόστολοι (11:5; 12:11) is ironic; only they say they are "superlative." According to Hughes, 405 n. 71, this is the only use of ὑπέρ as an adverb in the NT.

Two comments are offered. First, from their viewpoint they were "ministers of Christ." They presented themselves as "apostles of Christ" (v. 13), "preaching Jesus . . . a gospel" (11:4), and they came bearing "letters of recommendation" (presumably) from Christians elsewhere. Yet from Paul's perspective as a pioneer minister of the new covenant theirs was "*another* Jesus . . . a *different* gospel*," belonging to a now-superseded dispensation (see on 3:6-11). The content of their doctrine found no approval in Paul's eyes.

Second, their self-presentation was triumphalist (see on 2:14), the foil for which was Paul himself in his "foolishness" and "weakness." They sought to legitimate their ministry by comparing themselves with Paul, pointing to their superiority and his inferiority. Paul, however, by implication, sees his ministry in its sufferings as an authentic extension of the sufferings of the crucified One. Hence his weaknesses, as listed in the passage following, point to his "superiority" as a "minister of Christ," that is, the Christ who was "meek and gentle" (10:1), and who was crucified (13:3). Quite possibly the sufferings incurred in his own ministry as set forth in the "speech" as it unfolds were, in themselves, sufficient to discredit the ministry of these triumphalists without further comment.[17]

(2) Paul's Catalogue of Weaknesses (11:23b-33)

23b *I have worked much harder, been in prison more frequently, been flogged more severely, and been exposed to death again and again.* 24 *Five times I received from the Jews the forty lashes minus one.* 25 *Three times I was beaten with rods, once I was stoned, three times I was shipwrecked, I spent a night and a day in the open sea,* 26 *I have been constantly on the move. I have been in danger from rivers, in danger from bandits, in danger from my own countrymen, in danger from Gentiles; in danger in the city, in danger in the country, in danger at sea; and in danger from false brothers.* 27 *I have labored and toiled*[1] *and have often gone without sleep; I have known hunger and thirst and have often gone without food; I have been cold and naked.* 28 *Besides everything else, I face daily the pressure of my concern for all*

---

17. Paul's advantageous contrast of the new covenant with the old served effectively to invalidate and thus overturn the latter, though not in as many words. It should be noted that the vocabulary of comparison used there appears here also — μᾶλλον (3:8; 12:9); περισσεύειν (3:9), περισσοτέρως (11:23); ὑπερβάλλειν (3:10); and ὑπερβαλλόντως (11:23).

1. The MSS are divided over the inclusion/exclusion of ἐν with the datives κόπῳ . . . μόχθῳ. Because of the probability that ἐν was added to match the remainder of the verse, exclusion is preferable.

the churches. 29 Who is weak, and I do not feel weak? Who is led into sin, and I do not inwardly burn?

30 If I must boast, I will boast of the things that show my weakness. 31 The God and Father of the Lord Jesus, who is to be praised forever, knows that I am not lying. 32 In Damascus the governor under King Aretas had the city of the Damascenes guarded in order to arrest me.[2] 33 But I was lowered in a basket from a window in the wall and slipped through his hands.

Paul's catalogue of his sufferings,[3] many of them related directly or indirectly to his travels,[4] is his daring response to the intruders' "classification and comparison" (cf. 10:12) of themselves as superior *(hyper)* to him. Such greater sufferings are not sufferings per se; they arise directly from the foolishness/madness of Paul's missionary travels and accompanying labors. Above all, he is impacted daily by the pressure of anxiety from the churches.

The exposition of his "weaknesses" set forth here should be read with "God, who leads us in triumph in Christ" in the stunning metaphor of the Roman military triumph (see on 2:14). The details of his sufferings in the "Fool's Speech" proper (11:23b–12:10) serve as commentary on that metaphor.

This list of Paul's sufferings, extensive though it is, represents only part of Paul's total story. It tells us nothing of Paul before he was a Christian. Insofar as the Acts of the Apostles relates to Paul's life as "a man in Christ," from the time of his call/conversion to the time of writing 2 Cor 11:23a–12:9 (i.e., Acts 8:1–20:1), a span of only twenty-five years is represented. Moreover, there would have been much more to Paul's life than even the amalgamation of details from his letters and the Acts would suggest.

23b Paul's elaboration of his "foolishness" (v. 21b) now begins as he "class[es] . . . compare[s] . . . measures" his ministry with that of his opponents (see on 10:12-13; v. 21a). Contrast with these "ministers of Christ" (v. 23a) is implied by the comparative "more abundantly"[5] used with "labors" and "imprisonments," by the comparative "surpassingly"[6] used

---

2. The insertion of θέλων, either before or following πίασαι με, is explained as for stylistic improvement.

3. Technically known as περίστασεις, as found in Cynic-Stoic authors (see Martin, 160-61). Paul, however, does not use this word. See generally the major study J. T. Fitzgerald, *Earthen Vessels,* which, however, does not deal with the *peristasis* following. For an elaborate analysis of the structure of vv. 21-29, see Martin, 368-72.

4. See *New Docs.* 3.58-59 for examples of risks associated with travel and the practice of giving thanks to the gods for safe arrival.

5. Gk. περισσοτέρως; NIV, "much harder . . . more frequently."

6. Gk. ὑπερβαλλόντως; NIV, "more severely."

with "floggings," and by the adverb "frequently"[7] with "[exposed to] death."[8]

This list of four sufferings — "labors . . . imprisonments . . . floggings . . . [exposed to] death" — summarizes in advance the matters on which he will elaborate.[9] Thus he picks up "labors" in v. 27a (see on 6:5), "imprisonments" (by inference) and "floggings" in vv. 24-25a (see on 6:5), and "[exposure to] death" in vv. 24b-26. Whether on the road traveling from place to place or operating from a particular base of ministry, Paul faced suffering and danger to a greater degree, by implication, than those interlopers who have encroached into his "field" of ministry and taken advantage of his "labors" (see on 10:14-15). That they have come a considerable distance may not be denied, but at nothing like the personal cost incurred by the apostle.

It is significant that "labors" is the first-mentioned suffering (cf. v. 27). "Labors" were necessary because Paul steadfastly refused payment from the churches, offering the gospel freely (see on v. 7). This was the badge of his apostolate to the Gentiles as exercised, for example, in Achaia, which the intruders — because they accepted payment — could not wear (see on vv. 10, 12, 20). There is little doubt that had Paul accepted the patronage[10] of the members of the churches — protection, payment, and gifts — many of the sufferings now listed would not have occurred. Thus refusal to accept such patronage and its concomitant, the necessity to "labor," was not only a sign of his divine apostolate but also a significant instrument of his sufferings. But accepting such patronage would have reduced his ministry to their level, thus removing his distinctiveness (see on v. 11).

Unlike the verses preceding and succeeding, which use the generalized references "more abundantly" (v. 23), surpassingly" (v. 23), and "frequently" (vv. 23, 26, 27), vv. 24-25 give specific numbers — "five times," "once," and "three times." In their statements of their exploits the great Romans appealed to statistics; for example, in his *Res Gestae* Augustus declared, "*Twice* I received triumphal ovations. *Three* times I received curule triumphs. *Twenty* times and one did I receive the appellation of imperator" (*Res Gestae*

---

7. Gk. πολλάκις; NIV, "again and again."

8. Gk. ἐν θανάτοις, "in deaths," i.e., "exposed to death" (NIV); less probably, "mortal danger." See 4:12 — "death is at work in us," which refers back to hardships in 4:8-9.

9. Since there is no verb, but only a fourfold sequence ἐν + dative plurals, we should perhaps understand διάκονος Χριστοῦ ἐγενόμην . . . (so Bultmann, 216).

10. There are, however, examples where Paul is known to have accepted hospitality — e.g., in Jerusalem (Gal 1:18-19), in Philippi (Acts 16:15), in Thessalonica(?) (Acts 17:5), in Corinth, first with Priscilla and Aquila (Acts 18:3) and later with Gaius (Rom 16:23), in Ptolemais (Acts 21:7), in Caesarea (Acts 21:8), and in Jerusalem (Acts 21:16).

4).[11] The numerical details given here by Paul probably belong to that tradition, except that Paul's catalogue points to his suffering and defeat.

24-25a Paul first expands upon the two kinds of "flogging" introduced in the previous verse: (1) "under Jews"[12] (the "forty lashes minus one"[13]) and (2) at Roman hands ("beaten with rods").

The former punishment arose from Deut 25:1-5, which provided for the flogging of an offender after being found guilty by judges in a court. In no case was the beating to exceed forty, administered to the man or woman bending down. The Mishnah tractate *Makkoth,* which corroborates Paul's "forty lashes minus one," nominates false witness (e.g., about a priest, that he was the son of a divorced mother — *Mak.* 1:1) as an offense for which this punishment was administered. The minister of the synagogue was to stand on a raised stone inflicting the blows "with all his might," using a redoubled calf strap, to which two other straps were attached. Thirteen blows were delivered to the chest and twenty-six to the back. The severity of this beating can be inferred from the provisions made in the event the offender defecated, urinated, or even died as a result of their blows.

On no less than five occasions the apostle "received" this the most severe beating permitted by the Jewish scriptures, which Josephus called "a most disgraceful penalty."[14] Neither the Acts of the Apostles nor Paul's letters refer elsewhere to these five synagogue floggings, so that we do not know the basis of these punishments that were inflicted on him. Perhaps they arose from false charges and were designed to deter his ongoing presence in a particular town or city.

The other kind of beating Paul received — the Roman — is set in balance with the Jewish. Such "beating with rods"[15] must have occurred within those cities known to have been visited by the apostle that were Roman colonies, that is, Antioch of Pisidia, Lystra, Troas, Philippi, or Corinth.[16] Clearly Philippi was one such (Acts 16:22, 23, 35, 37, 38); we can only guess the location of other two. In Roman *colonia* the praetors *(stratēgoi)* were

---

11. For other examples of such citations of achievements, see Pliny, *Natural History* 7.26.98; Julius Caesar, *Civil Wars* 2.32.

12. Gk. ὑπὸ Ἰουδαίων, "at the hands of the Jews" (NIV, "from the Jews"), for emphasis given at the head of the verse. Cf. ὑπὸ τῶν Ἰουδαίων (1 Thess 2:14).

13. Gk. τεσσεράκοντα παρὰ μίαν, lit. "forty less one," is suggestive of a well-known punishment among Jews. "Lashes" is to be understood (cf. v. 23b). The "less one" was to prevent overflogging. If the victim died as a result of the beating the administrator was not culpable, but he was to be exiled if the victim died where more than one lash beyond the prescribed thirty-nine lashes was applied (m. *Mak.* 3:14).

14. *Ant.* 4.231-32.

15. Gk. ἐραβδίσθην.

16. T. Cornell and J. Matthews, *Atlas,* 72-73.

preceded in public by lictors *(rabdouchoi)* who bore, as symbols of authority, bundles of elm or birch rods bound together (Latin *fasces*) as instruments of punishment. At the instruction of the praetor, the lictors would publicly beat malefactors to inflict summary and deterrent chastisement (Latin *coercitio*). As a Roman citizen Paul ought not to have suffered this indignity (cf. 1 Thess 2:2), though there are examples where the rights of Roman citizens were disregarded in this matter.[17] The provocative nature of Paul's ministry created public scenes, such as that recorded in Philippi, and resulted in the rough treatment described there (Acts 16:16-23).

25b, c, d   In addition to the numerous "beatings" (vv. 23, 24, 25a), which might easily have proved fatal, Paul enumerates other occasions when he was "exposed to death" (v. 23).

The "once" he was "stoned"[18] must be that occasion in Lystra (so Acts 14:19[19]), though an attempt was contemplated in Iconium beforehand (Acts 14:5). Jews inflicted stoning as a capital punishment on adulterers, apostates, and blasphemers (Deut 17:5; 22:22-24; m. *Sanh.* 7:6-7). Ironically, Paul himself had collaborated in the stoning of Stephen (Acts 7:58-59). When we add this stoning to the five synagogue beatings (v. 24), we are able to gauge the sufferings of the apostle at the hands of his "countrymen" (v. 26; cf., e.g., 1 Thess 2:15; Rom 15:31; Acts 9:23, 29; 13:50; 17:5, 13; 18:6; 19:9; 21:30-31).

Neither Paul's letters nor the Acts of the Apostles casts light on Paul's "three times I was shipwrecked"[20]; the famous shipwreck en route to Rome (Acts 27:12-44) occurred subsequent to the writing of 2 Corinthians. Nonetheless, Paul often traveled by sea in the course of his ministry before that journey,[21] providing many opportunities for shipwreck. The leaky wooden vessels of antiquity had no life rafts nor meteorological early warning facilities. With good reason travelers faced sea voyages with trepidation. Maritime disasters were frequent.[22]

---

17. A Roman citizen declared *ciuis Romanus sum* and was thus spared public beating. Cicero, *Against Verres* 2.5.161ff., gives an example in which this was disregarded (cf. Josephus, *J.W.* 2.308). See further A. N. Sherwin-White, *Roman Society*, 73-74.

18. Gk. ἐλιθάσθην.

19. Cf. 1 Clement, *Corinthians* 5.

20. Gk. ἐναυάγησα; ναυ-αγεῖν derived from ναῦς (ship) + ἄγνυμι (break). The verb is found elsewhere in the NT only at 1 Tim 1:19, where it is used metaphorically.

21. Thus, e.g., Acts 13:4 (Seleucia to Cyprus); 13:13 (Paphos to Perga); 14:25-26 (Attalia to Antioch); 16:11 (Troas to Neapolis via Samothrace); 17:14-15 (Macedonia to Athens); 18:18-22 (Corinth to Caesarea via Ephesus); 2 Cor 2:1 (Ephesus to Corinth to Ephesus); 2 Cor 2:13; 7:5 (Troas to Neapolis?).

22. Augustus's prosecution of the Sicilian war was twice delayed by the loss of his entire fleet through shipwreck (Suetonius, *Augustus* 2.16.1-2; see Furnish, 516, for further examples). Regarding the perils of sea travel, see *New Docs.* 4.115.

Finally, he specifies that he "spent[23] a night and a day[24] in the open sea,"[25] doubtless the most desperate of the three experiences of shipwreck just mentioned. From this terse description it is likely that Paul then felt all hope was gone.

When the events of vv. 24-25 are added — the five synagogue beatings, the three Roman floggings, the stoning, the three shipwrecks, one involving twenty-four hours in the open sea — we find that on at least eleven occasions Paul was indeed "exposed to death" (v. 23). This list, however, is only by way of example; it is probably not complete. Within this very letter he mentions the near-death experience in Asia (1:8-10), which finds no reference here.

26 To the four extremities listed in v. 23 — "labors . . . imprisonments . . . floggings . . . [exposed to] death" — he now adds a fifth, "journeyings frequent."[26] Such travels were implicit in God's commissioning of Paul as his "apostle to the Gentiles" (Rom 11:13); he did not go as a tourist! From *c.* A.D. 34-47[27] his movements were restricted to the eastern Mediterranean (Damascus — Jerusalem — Syria and Cilicia — Antioch — Jerusalem — Antioch), but thereafter the will of God bore him further afield, to the towns and cities of the provinces of Pamphylia, Galatia, Macedonia, Achaia and Asia.

Implicit in such "journeyings" were "dangers,"[28] eight of which he now recalls, the first four of which appear to be grouped in pairs, all of which climax with an indirect reference to the false apostles.

The first pair of "dangers" — "of rivers . . . of robbers" — is an example of the hazards the traveler of those times might encounter along the way. Bridges in remote regions were rare; many "rivers" would need to be forded, which in times of flooding — including "flash flooding" — would

---

23. Gk. πεποίηκα, perfect tense, which here means "spend time," suggesting the horror of the constantly remembered experience.

24. Gk. νυχθήμερον, a compound (νυχ + θήμερον) means a full twenty-four-hour period, lit. "a night-day," emphasizing the duration of the experience. This term, found only here in the NT and in literature subsequent to it, may be a peculiarly Jewish reference. Jews reckoned days from sunset to sunset (cf. Gen 1:5ff.; Lev 23:32).

25. Gk. ἐν τῷ βυθῷ (lit. "in the deep") meaning "in the open sea" (clinging to wreckage?). The interpretation that Paul was submerged beneath the water for twenty-four hours and that a Jonah-like miracle occurred is fanciful.

26. Gk. ὁδοιπορίαις πολλάκις; NIV, "constantly on the move." The dative ὁδοπορίαις is to be understood with ἐν, as in ἐν κόποις . . . ἐν φυλακαῖς . . . ἐν πληγαῖς . . . ἐν θανάτοις . . . (v. 23).

27. The suggested date of the Jerusalem concordat (Gal 2:1-10), "fourteen years" from Paul's Damascus Road call in *c.* A.D. 34, which is based on the hypothesis of A.D. 33 as the date of the crucifixion.

28. Gk. κινδύνοις, dative plural, agrees with ὁδοπορίαις and bears the modal sense "risking" or "experiencing" dangers (NIV, "in danger"). Paul achieves rhetorical variation by the use of the genitive plural in the first pair, followed by ἐκ + the genitive plural in the next pair, followed by ἐν + the dative plural in the final two sets of pairs.

have presented acute difficulties. The apostle does not indicate the names of the rivers, but, with their tributaries, they will have included the Jordan in Judaea and Trachonitis, the Orontes in Syria, the Cydnus in Cilicia, the Meander and Cayster in Asia, and the Strimon and Axios in Macedonia.

Once out in the country away from urbanized regions private travelers, as opposed to escorted official parties, were vulnerable to the depredations of "robbers." This was true even in the era of greater stability provided by the *Pax Romanum.*[29] The poverty of life drove many to join groups of brigands who ranged unchecked in many rural regions. Where times of acute food shortage coincided with times of political turmoil — as they did in Palestine during and after the late forties on account of the great famine — the ranks of the brigand bands were swollen dramatically, assuming a political significance, especially if there was a "charismatic" leader.[30]

By contrast with the preceding pair, the next — "dangers from my own countrymen,[31] dangers from Gentiles" — reflect problems faced by the apostle in towns and cities. Not uncommonly such "dangers" to Paul arose from a combination of Jewish and Gentile forces against him, as, for example, in Pisidian Antioch, Iconium, Lystra, Thessalonica, and Corinth, where Jews stirred up, or attempted to stir up, Gentile action (Acts 13:50; 14:2, 5, 19; 17:5-6; 18:12). However, Paul was also endangered by Gentiles independently of any Jewish action, as, for example, at the time of the uprising of the silversmiths of Ephesus, which forms the immediate background to this letter (Acts 19:23-41; cf. 2 Cor 1:8-11).

At this point the classification of the "dangers" in pairs breaks down. Paul now introduces a triad — "dangers in the city, dangers in the country, dangers at sea" — thus giving an expansive impression of the breadth of his missionary travels. Of these "dangers" those of the "city . . . country" make explicit — in reverse order — what was implied in the first and second grouping ("rivers . . . robbers . . . my countrymen . . . Gentiles"). Whether in "the city" or "the country," Paul the missionary traveler faced distinctive perils. Added to that, however, was the danger he had faced from the "sea" ("three times shipwrecked, a night and a day in the open sea" — v. 25).

Anomalously, "dangers from false brothers"[32] stands alone and unpaired at the foot of the list, thus giving it preeminence in this catalogue of hazards to Paul's life.

29. Although Epictetus, *Dissertations* 3.13.9, declares that there was "no brigandage on a large scale" under the *Pax Romanum,* travelers in isolated regions were vulnerable (see, e.g., Tacitus, *Annals* 6.41; 11.15).

30. See Josephus, *J.W.* 2.228-40.

31. While the Gk. ἐκ γένους means "from [the] people," Paul means his fellow Israelites (Gal 1:14; Phil 3:5).

32. Gk. ψευδαδέλφοις.

Paul's reference here to "false brothers" *(pseudadelphoi)* and to "false apostles" *(pseudapostoloi)* earlier in this passage (v. 13) is striking; he rarely uses words with the prefix *pseud-*.[33] Some connection between the two is implied. In regard to "false brothers" the context of the only other reference (Gal 2:4) identifies them as believers (they were in some sense "brothers") in Jerusalem who were revealed to be "false" by their attempt to make obligatory the rite of circumcision on the Gentile believer Titus, thus over-turning "the truth of the gospel" (Gal 2:5; cf. 2:14). These same "false brothers" came from Jerusalem to Antioch, attempting to compel Gentiles "to live like Jews," thus compromising the "truth of the gospel" (Gal 2:11-14).

Paul's sole reference to "false apostles" is within this passage and points to those newly arrived persons who have sought to pass themselves off as "apostles of Christ" (see on v. 13). These "false apostles" are "Hebrews . . . Israelites . . . seed of Abraham . . . ministers of Christ" (v. 22) and are, in all probability, to be identified with the "false brothers" of v. 26 (and Gal 2:4). "False brothers" who are "false apostles" have — in some sense — been welcomed by believers in Corinth (11:4), and bring "danger" to the apostle. Paul's life may have been indirectly imperiled by the action of mem-bers of the Corinthian assembly.

We can only speculate how such "false brothers" posed "danger" to Paul. Since they were observant Jews (from Jerusalem?) who had come to the cities in the Jewish Diaspora where Paul had established his Gentile-dominated assemblies devoted to the Messiah Jesus, their "danger" to him may have arisen indirectly from their contact with the synagogues that effectively put in negative contrast Paul's insistence that no demands be imposed on Gentiles touching the ordinances of Judaism (cf. Gal 5:1). The presence locally of such Jewish Christian "brothers" may have sparked off a chain reaction[34] whereby first Jews and then, in consequence, Gentiles[35] opposed Paul, thus putting his life at risk.

27 Having indicated the various sources of hardship — "labors . . . imprisonments . . . floggings . . . [exposed to] death . . . journeyings" (vv. 23, 26), Paul now reflects on these from the perspective of their personal impact on him.[36]

---

33. Cf. "false witness" (1 Cor 15:15 — ψευδόμαρτυς); "liar" (1 Tim 4:2 — ψευδόλογος).

34. Based on Gal 6:12 (cf. 1:7), it appears that non-Christian Jews persecuted Christian Jews, who in turn "agitated" that Gentile believers submit to circumcision. In a later letter Paul attributes direct malice to Judaizing Christian Jews who "preach Christ" (Phil 1:15, 17; cf. 3:2-6).

35. See the comment above on "dangers of my own people, dangers from Gentiles."

36. The sentence is without a verb, the instrumental datives without and with ἐν naturally translating themselves as "[I have] labor[ed] and toil[ed and have] often [gone] without sleep; [I have known] hunger and thirst [and have] often [gone] without food; [I have been] cold and naked" (so NIV).

Structurally, Paul sets forth three doublets that are separated by two examples of "frequently" experienced (see vv. 23, 26) privations.[37]

> By labor and toil,
> in sleepless nights frequently,
> in hunger and thirst,
> without food frequently,
> in cold and nakedness

The apostle's determination not to burden the churches — a point of dispute in Corinth (see on 11:7-12; cf. 1 Cor 9:12, 15) — is captured by his doublet "by labor and toil,"[38] a phrase he uses elsewhere in relation to his work in supporting himself (1 Thess 2:9; 2 Thess 3:8). Night and day in place after place Paul labored at the exhausting and filthy task of making and repairing leather tents[39] (see on v. 7).

This is followed logically by the punctuating privation "in sleepless nights *frequently*"; much of Paul's "labor and toil" was done at night in order to permit his preaching the gospel by day (1 Thess 2:9; 2 Thess 3:8; see on 6:5, where "labor" and "sleepless nights" are paired).

The second doublet, "hunger and thirst," probably evokes memories of sufferings associated with vast distances Paul traveled through the inhospitable and barren terrain of the eastern provinces. It was his lot to experience the extremes of flooded rivers on the one hand (v. 26) and, in all probability, dry creekbeds on the other. Moreover, many miles separated the towns along the way where the apostolic traveler might find work to do and food to purchase.

The second punctuating doublet, "without food *frequently*" is repeated from the earlier list, where it is also joined with "labor" and "sleepless nights" (6:5). It is probably to be associated with involuntary lack of food rather than with fasting, which finds no clear reference in Paul's letters (see on 6:5).

The concluding doublet, "in cold and nakedness,"[40] an illogical sequence, perhaps evokes memories of shipwreck, capture by robbers, or imprisonment.

So concludes the apostle's list of his physical sufferings begun at v. 23b. He will turn now to speak of his emotional pain (vv. 28-30).

---

37. With this part of the list Paul moves closer to hardships catalogued elsewhere (1 Cor 4:11-13; 2 Cor 4:7-8; 6:4-5; cf. Rom 8:35-36).

38. Gk. κόπῳ καὶ μόχθῳ; NIV, "I have labored and toiled." The order κόπῳ ... μόχθῳ is not logical; κόπῳ implies fatigue, μόχθῳ hard labor.

39. Gk. σχηνοποι[ός] τῇ τέχνῃ, "by trade they were tentmakers" (Acts 18:3, RSV; cf. 20:33-35).

40. From this passage κίνδυνος, λιμός, and γυμνότης are repeated in Rom 8:35.

28   The opening words, "apart from everything else,"[41] serve to tail off the sufferings listed in vv. 23b-27. They signal that the list is illustrative, not complete. Nonetheless, logically they belong with and introduce the two phrases following: (1) "the daily pressure on me,"[42] that is, (2) "my anxiety for all the churches." The location of this verse at the end of the list of privations suggests that his concern for the churches was the source of his deepest suffering. The questions of the next verse, "Who is weak, and I am not weak? Who is made to fall, and I do not burn?" clinch the point.

By "all the churches" Paul means the churches established by his apostolic mission and for which he bore an ongoing sense of "anxiety." This sense of "anxiety" was fed by the daily "assault" *(epistasis)* of the reports about those churches that came to him, whether by letter or by personal contact. Paul's letters are his response to the succession of communications that impacted him and provoked deep concerns for his fragile missionary assemblies. The extant letters to the Corinthians, for example, objectify and "freeze" for all time the "anxiety" he felt for them at the time in response to the news about them as it came to him.

Given the alienation of the world from God and its treatment of the One who came from God (cf. 5:18-21), it is no surprise that the apostle of Christ to the Gentiles should encounter the opposition and difficulties listed above in the course of his journeys proclaiming the word of God (cf. 2:14-17). However, we might have expected that, by contrast, the assemblies of believers called into being by that word would have been a source of unalloyed pleasure to him. To be sure, he acknowledges great joy arising from, for example, the Philippians and the Thessalonians (Phil 4:1; 1 Thess 2:19), and he refers to the churches generally as "the glory of Christ" (see on 8:23). Nonetheless, not even those churches that brought him joy were without their shortcomings, to say nothing of the Corinthians! Thus he speaks of "pressure" on him with its resulting "anxiety" for these communities of faith, thus serving as a reminder that although the "day of salvation" has arrived (6:2), it is not yet perfected. The churches of God were and remain a source of joy, but also of anxiety, to those who are their pastors.

---

41. Gk. χωρὶς τῶν παρεκτός; NIV, "besides everything else." The genitive τῶν is probably neuter, "things," not "people" (which would have been τῶν ἔξωθεν — cf. 1 Tim 3:7). The phrase χωρὶς τῶν παρεκτός is taken as (1) "apart from the things that are without," i.e., the external hardships previously listed (so RV), or, more probably, (2) "apart from the things that are omitted" (so, effectively, RSV, NIV, and most commentators). This suggests that the privations listed are illustrative, not exhaustive, and that his anxiety for the churches was the greatest suffering of all.

42. Gk. ἡ ἐπίστασίς μοι; NIV, "I face daily the pressures." In its Hellenistic use ἡ ἐπίστασις meant "attack" or "onset" (2 Macc 6:3). Although BAGD gives "supervision" as a possible meaning, more probably it should be taken as "that which presses or rushes"; hence ἡ ἐπίστασίς μοι ἡ καθ᾽ ἡμέραν would mean "the daily pressure — or onset — on me."

Thus Paul completes his list of sufferings. Under the general headings of "labors . . . imprisonments . . . floggings . . . [exposed to] death . . . journeyings" (vv. 23b, 26a),[43] he has given numerous examples of grim events that impacted on him and that he sustained in the course of his mission work. But coming at the end of the list, as if to reach a climax, he cites "the daily impact on me, my anxiety for all the churches." According to Chrysostom, "This was the chief thing of all, that his soul was distracted, and his thoughts divided."[44]

The catalogue of hardships — general and specific, objective and emotional, physical and spiritual — that he has supplied provides an indelible image of Paul's apostolic ministry. But Paul does not paint a freestanding picture of his apostolate; he intends it as a paradigm for the comparison of his ministry with those "ministers of Christ" who claim to be "better" (*hyper* — cf. v. 23a). If he is a "better" minister of Christ (v. 23), it is precisely because by this list of "weaknesses" he follows the paradigm of Christ. By their self-presentation the "false apostles" measured themselves as "superior" and Paul "inferior," so as to disenfranchise him (see on vv. 4-6). But he will not engage in those comparisons, except to point to sufferings that surpass theirs. In an insight of modern applicability, Chrysostom noted long ago that Paul says nothing here about results, about the number of his converts; he counts only the sufferings incurred in missionary labor to prove the reality of his calling.[45]

29 Finally, and in direct response to v. 28, he asks rhetorically:

Who[46] is weak,   and I am not weak?
Who   is made to fall, and I am not indignant?

By these two questions, "am I not weak? . . . am I not indignant?" Paul spells out the "anxiety" of the previous verse. It is the "anxiety" of the pastor's compassionate identification with "the weak" and with "those who have been made to fall." Here is the greatest suffering of the apostle Paul.

But there is another level of understanding.[47] Paul's question effectively completes his "comparison" of v. 21b and establishes that he is a "*better . . .* minister of Christ" (v. 23), a "comparison" that he proceeded to

---

43. These sufferings were no isolated or recent thing. Earlier he wrote, "To this very hour we go hungry and thirsty, we are in rags, we are brutally treated, we are homeless" (1 Cor 4:11). Later he would write, "Shall trouble or hardship or persecution or famine or nakedness or danger or sword [separate us from the love of Christ]?" (Rom 8:35).

44. Quoted in Plummer, 330.

45. Observed by Plummer, 328.

46. Gk. τίς, "Who"? a rhetorical interrogative (as in 2:2, 16; 5:7; Rom 8:35a), not a generic pointing to a particular opponent or opponents (as in v. 21b).

47. Plummer's identification of Paul's "weakness" with his "anxiety for the churches" (331) of the previous verse is too restricted.

illustrate by catalogues of "labors . . . imprisonments . . . floggings . . . [exposed to] death . . . journeyings" (vv. 23b, 26a; cf. vv. 23b-28). Thus the answer implicit in his question is: "No one compares with Paul in the 'weakness' of privations suffered in the pursuit of his ministry. The 'false-apostles' claim 'superiority,' but if the marks of true Christian ministry are suffering in Christ's service, Paul is 'better.' "

Paul's question takes us back to his biting attack on their exploitation and violation of the Corinthians (v. 20), in which he bitterly asserts, "To my shame we were too *weak* for that" (v. 21a). Thus Paul's question, "Who is weak, and I am not weak?" declares his pastoral identification with and care for the "weak" in the churches, something that he elaborated in the First Letter (1 Cor 8:9-13; cf. Rom 14:1-23). Paul identifies with the oppressed and abused in the church against those intruding false shepherds who exploit them.

This identification is restated and painfully reemphasized in the second rhetorical question, "Who is made to fall, and I am not indignant?" Paul's concern lest the "weak" among the Corinthians are "made to fall"[48] reflects his burden expressed elsewhere (1 Cor 8:13; Rom 14:21) and takes up the warning of the Lord, "Whoever *causes* one of these little ones who believe in me to *sin* . . ." (Mark 9:42 pars.; cf. Matt 18:7; Luke 17:1). Here, paradoxically, Paul combines gentle pastoral identification with fiery indignation[49] for the abused "weak" among God's people. This combination of loving identification with and hot indignation for the misused among the people of God may be seen earlier in Jesus' teaching (as above) and example (the expulsion of the merchants from the temple — John 2:16), and beyond that to the prophets' denunciation of the false ministers of Israel for their assault upon the vulnerable members of the covenant people (e.g., Isa 28:7-9; Jer 23:9ff.; Ezek 12:21–14:11). Such passionate care is of a piece with the apostle's "godly jealousy" for Christ's bride-to-be, the (Corinthian) church, vulnerable to deflection from loyalty to her Lord (see on vv. 2-4).

Thus, this verse is very important within the structure of the "Fool's Speech" because (1) it drives home to the Corinthians his greatest pain of all, his "anxiety" for the churches (v. 28), including the Corinthian church, and (2) it reintroduces the "weakness" theme of v. 21, so that "weakness" can

---

48. Gk. σκανδαλίζεται; NIV, "led into sin." While Paul employs the verb elsewhere only in 1 Cor 8:13, the noun σκάνδαλον, "stumbling stone," occurs in 1 Cor 1:23; Rom 14:13; 16:17; Gal 5:11 as well as in various citations, e.g., Rom 9:33 (quoting LXX Isa 28:16 and 8:14). Paul's usage may derive from Jesus (Matt 13:41; 16:23; 18:7; Luke 17:1); see H. Giesen, *EDNT* 3.249-50.

49. Gk. ἐγὼ πυροῦμαι; NIV, "I inwardly burn." Note the emphatic pronoun. Although the verb πυροῦσθαι is set in eschatological contexts elsewhere (e.g., 1 Cor 7:9; Eph 6:16; 2 Pet 3:12; Rev 1:15; 3:18), it is here used metaphorically (cf. 1 Cor 7:9); the present context does not demand an eschatological understanding.

be repeated in the next verse, but now as the object of another keyword, "boasting" (vv. 10, 12, 16, 17, 18). These two words provide the link to the great climax of the "Fool's Speech," Paul's "boasting in weakness" (see 12:1, 5, 6, 9, 10).

30 As noted in v. 29, this verse — together with that verse — forms the base from which springs the climax of the "Fool's Speech," where Paul "boasts" of his "weaknesses" (12:7-10). Retrospectively, it goes back to the previous chapter, where Paul refers to those who would "classify or compare" Paul with themselves so as to "commend" and "boast" of their ministry (10:12-13) as "superior" to his (11:5, 23).

"If," or, better, "since," he "must boast,"[50] he "will boast[51] of [his] weaknesses."[52] In the struggle between the intruders and Paul, the founder of the church in Corinth, "boasting" by means of "classification and comparison" was employed to establish superiority ("better" — *hyper* — v. 23) and therefore legitimacy in ministry. Paul's opponents, whom he calls "superlative" apostles (v. 5; 12:11), "boasted" of their superiority — but "according to the flesh" (v. 18), in professionalism in speech (11:5-6), and in "visions and revelations" (12:1).

But Paul will "boast" only of "weaknesses," of those privations that arose from traveling from place to place, in "labor and toil" so as to offer the gospel "without charge," the badge of his apostleship (see on vv. 10, 12). To "boast" of "weaknesses" and to "boast" of "not being paid" (v. 10) are closely related.

The rhetorical question ("Who is weak, and I am not weak?") in the the previous verse demands the answer that Paul excelled all others in "weakness," making him — in their terms — a "better" minister of Christ (v. 23). This is not the way Paul would have ordinarily expressed it. It is "fool's speak" (vv. 1, 16 [twice], 17, 19; 12:6, 11), the talk of a "madman" (v. 23), by which he mocks and parodies their manner of seeking superiority over him. But because "many" have "boasted" (11:18) as a result of their "comparison" and "classification" of Paul with themselves, they have forced him to become a "fool" (12:11). Thus, he "must boast" (cf. 12:1), and so be a "fool." As such he is the poor, stumbling, suffering prisoner-of-war led about by God in his victory triumph (see on 2:14).

---

50. The initial εἰ, "if," carries the meaning of ἐπεί, "since." The pronominal subject ("I") of καυχᾶσθαι is understood.

51. Gk. καυχήσομαι, although a future, is given as a summary of his reasons for "boasting" in the manner of a "fool."

52. Gk. ἀσθενείας, which, with its cognates, is one of the keywords in the latter part of this letter (see 12:5, 9, 10; 13:4). Note the use of the plural here and in 12:5, 9, 10, where concrete examples of experienced weakness are probably in mind.

31 "Foolish" though this speech is, it is nonetheless true, as he now proceeds to declare by this oath:[53]

The God and Father of the Lord Jesus,
who is blessed forever,
knows that I do not lie.

Here Paul speaks as both a Christian and a Hebrew. As a devoted Israelite (v. 22), he acknowledges the "God . . . who is blessed forever." This devout ascription to God finds many parallels in the synagogue benedictions of that period (e.g., "Blessed art thou, O Lord our God and God of our fathers. . . . Blessed art thou, O Lord, the shield of Abraham"[54]).

But as a Christian believer he now "blesses" the God of his fathers as "The God and Father of the Lord Jesus" (see on 1:3).[55] This brief benediction testifies (1) to the conviction of Jesus of Nazareth that he was "son" of his *abba*-God (see, e.g., Mark 12:6; 14:36; Matt 11:25-27), and (2) to the remarkable conversion of the persecutor Saul of Tarsus in acknowledging that the crucified Nazarene was the "Lord," the "son" of the God of Israel (1:19; 4:5; cf. Gal 1:15-16), whom he must now "bless" as the "Father of the Lord Jesus."

In what he has been saying about his "weaknesses" (vv. 23-28) — and what he will yet say about them (12:5-10) — Paul adjures that "God . . . knows that I do not lie."[56] The oath asserting his truthfulness earlier in the chapter ("the truth of Christ is in me" — v. 10) must be seen as echoed, though inverted, in this oath denying deceit. These oaths are connected (see on v. 10). The former oath supports his "boast" in offering the gospel "free of charge," while the latter oath sustains his "boast" of "weaknesses" (v. 30; cf. vv. 23-28). These "weaknesses," however, significantly flow from his "labors" (v. 23; cf. v. 27), the direct consequence of insisting on a ministry without payment.

By his asseveration "God . . . knows" Paul is profoundly aware of God's knowledge of his inner life ("what we are is known to God" — 5:11, *q.v.;* cf. 2:17; 4:2; 12:19). The force of Paul's denial of duplicity ("I do not

---

53. Other oaths in this letter are found at 1:18, 23; 2:10; 11:11 (cf. Gal 1:20; Rom 9:1).

54. Benediction 1, quoted in E. Schürer, *Jewish People,* 2.456. There are occasions when Paul simply "blesses" God, as a Hebrew might (see, e.g., Rom 1:25; 9:5).

55. This is a briefer version of the benediction found near the beginning of the letter — "Blessed be the God and Father of *our* Lord Jesus *Christ*" (1:3; cf. Eph 1:3, 17; 1 Pet 1:3; John 20:17).

56. For similar oaths denying deceit so as to assert his truthfulness — i.e., by the rhetorical device litotes — see Gal 1:20; Rom 9:1.

lie" — *ou pseudomai*) is very pointed in regard to those whom he has called "false apostles" *(pseudapostoloi)* . . . deceitful workers . . . false brothers *(pseudadelphoi* — vv. 13, 26). Paul's truthfulness before God serves to emphasize their deceitfulness and falsity.

32-33   These verses strike even the casual reader as odd. Having given this list of grim privations, why does Paul now relate his being lowered down the city wall of Damascus and his escape from the Ethnarch who had set guard on that city to seize him? Numerous explanations have been offered for the description of this event, which appears so out of place in Paul's argument.[57]

Two connected reasons that may best explain these verses[58] and account for their location in relation to the passage following[59] are (1) that being "lowered *down*" in these verses symmetrically counterpoises his description of the man who was "caught *up*" into the "third heaven/Paradise" (12:2, 4), and (2) that taken together his being "lowered *down*" and "caught *up*" form a comic-tragic parody of his opponents' "boast" of "superiority" arising from their "visions and revelations" (12:1). By this hypothesis vv. 32-33 establish an ironic counterbalance ("lowered down") that will be exploited in the passage following ("caught up").

---

57. E. F. F. Bishop, "Aretas," 188-89, declared these verses to be "out of context, out of style, quite out of connection" (189). It has been regarded as misplaced from Gal 1 (so Bishop) or as an interpolation, suggestions for which there is no textual support.

58. The explanation following, broadly speaking, is the view of Martin (384, following J. Zmijewski, 289), to which he adds the suggestion of E. A. Judge, "The Conflict of Educational Aims in NT Thought," 32-45, that the readership of *Roman* Corinth would have been familiar with the "wall crown" (Latin *corona muralis;* στέφανος τείχιχος — see Furnish Plate VIII) awarded to brave soldiers who were first over the wall during the siege of an enemy city (see, e.g., Polybius, *Histories* 6.39.5; Livy, *History* 6.20.8; 10.46.3; 26.48.5). According to A. Gellius, "The 'mural crown' is that which is awarded by a commander to a man who is first to mount the wall and force his way into an enemy town . . ." (*Attic Nights* 5.6.16). On this view, Paul's being lowered *down* a wall points to his humiliation. Although this would be a reversal of his earlier conquest imagery (10:3-6), it is by no means unlikely that Paul could employ both triumphalist and antitriumphalist language (see on 2:14). Martin's further suggestion that Paul is alluding here to Prov 21:22 ("A wise man scales the cities of the mighty and brings down the stronghold in which the godless trust") appears to be too oblique.

59. It is quite likely that (1) the events in Damascus (11:32-33), (2) his being "caught up" to Paradise fourteen years ago (12:1-6), and (3) his being staked "in the flesh" (12:7-10) were sequential. Nonetheless, verses that relate his lowering "down" appear to be juxtaposed deliberately next to verses where he is "caught up." Unconvincing are the suggestions that these verses are (1) "an afterthought" (so Tasker), or (2) illustrative of problems Paul faced in cities — v. 26 (so Plummer), or (3) an elaborate postscript to his other sufferings on account of the ill repute the Damascus flight brought to Paul (so Menzies).

These verses primarily serve Paul's rhetorical purpose as part of his "Fool's Speech" against his opponents' claims to superiority. Nonetheless, they also supply, firsthand, valuable historical detail that supplements the account of Paul's ministry in Damascus found in the Acts of the Apostles (Acts 9:8-25, especially 9:23-25).

After Christ's encounter with him en route to Damascus, Paul entered the city; then, after an indeterminate period, he went to "Arabia," before returning to Damascus (Gal 1:17). It is uncertain whether Damascus was under Nabataean (i.e., "Arabian") or Roman control during the thirties.[60] Either way the Nabataean king, Aretas IV,[61] had an "Ethnarch"[62] in the city, either as his governor (in the less likely case that Damascus was then under direct Nabataean rule) or as Aretas's appointed leader to the Nabataean community within Roman jurisdiction (in the more probable case that the city was then under direct Roman rule).

Although Paul was sought by Nabataean authorities in the city, the historical uncertainty about the control of Damascus at that time leaves open the question whether his misdemeanors were committed inside Damascus or in "Arabia," that is, within the Nabataean kingdom. Whatever the case, at some time after his return to Damascus, the Damascene Ethnarch of a Nabataean king set guards[63] at the city gates in order to seize Paul. But Paul

---

60. Nabataean rule of Damascus during the thirties is urged because (1) there is an absence of Roman coins A.D. 34-62, and (2) Caligula (A.D. 37-41) was known to have reinstated a number of eastern client kings. To advocate Nabataean rule in that period on those grounds, however, is to argue from silence.

61. Gk. Ἀρέτας. Possibly a Hellenized version of *Haritha,* or similar to the Greek word ἀρέτη, "excellence," but especially of manly qualities, "valor," or "prowess." Aretas IV ruled the vast desert kingdom of Nabataea, whose capital was Petra, from 9 B.C. to A.D. 40. Herod Antipas, Tetrarch of Galilee/Peraea from 4 B.C. to A.D. 39, had married Aretas's daughter (to resolve endemic border disputes?), only to divorce her to marry Herodias. Sometime later Aretas inflicted a crushing defeat on Antipas's armies. Antipas complained to Tiberius, who dispatched Vitellius, Legate of Syria, against Aretas. Only the death of Tiberius (A.D. 37) prevented Vitellius from pushing on to Petra, thus sparing Aretas (Josephus, *Ant.* 18.109-26). Aretas's Ethnarch in Damascus knew of Paul's activities; it is possible but not certain that the Nabataean king had heard of the apostle. See further Furnish, 521-22.

62. Gk. ὁ ἐθνάρχης (NIV, "governor"), literally means "ruler of a nation" (ἐθν + ἀρχης). Augustus applied it as a conveniently lesser title than king to Archelaus in 4 B.C., as probationary ruler of Judaea. It was also used as a title for the leader of a self-contained ethnic community, as, e.g., of the Jewish enclave in Alexandria (Josephus, *Ant.* 14.117). Strabo, *Geography* 17.798, helpfully comments that an ethnarch "governs the nation, and distributes justice to them and takes care of their contracts and of the laws pertaining to them, as if he were the ruler of a free republic."

63. Gk. ἐφρούρει (NIV, "guarded"), an imperfect, suggesting that watch was kept for a considerable period.

eluded the Ethnarch's guards[64] and made his escape through a window in the city wall[65] from which he was lowered[66] (by Paul's "disciples" — Acts 9:25) in a "basket,"[67] and so escaped his clutches.[68] It is difficult to escape a note of ignominy here. No scaler of the wall bringing victory he; no crown of gold for his crowning victory. Rather, like a coward in battle, he "escapes" through the wall and is lowered to the ground in what may have been a fish basket! After Paul's escape from the Nabataean Ethnarch of Damascus he went to Jerusalem (Gal. 1:18).

The incident described in these verses impinges on our chronological reconstructions of Paul's ministry. The death of Aretas IV in A.D. 40 establishes the latest date possible for Paul's escape from Damascus, and therefore a latest possible date A.D. 37/38 for Paul's conversion two to three years earlier (see Gal 1:15-18). It is quite likely, however, that, given A.D. 33 as the year of the crucifixion of Jesus,[69] Paul's Damascus Road encounter would have occurred in A.D. 34/35, and the flight from Damascus in A.D. 36/37.

(3) The Climax of Weakness (12:1-10)

Now we come to the climax of Paul's "Fool's Speech," the point where he "boasts" of his most extreme "weakness," the "thorn in the flesh . . . a messenger of Satan" (12:7-9). But here, too, we arrive at the climax of his exposure of the religious pride of the "superlative" apostles.

Through "visions and revelations" from the Lord, Paul had been transported to Paradise, where he had heard words that he was not permitted to utter (12:1-6). But God's "gift" to him of a protracted and debilitating "weakness" pinned him to the earth in humility and dependence on the Lord. Notwithstanding repeated prayer, the "weakness" was not removed; Paul had to be content with Christ's power to endure this suffering. The message is

---

64. According to Acts 9:23-24, the Jews in Damascus were watching to apprehend Paul, which is not necessarily at odds with 2 Cor 11:31-33; Paul may have been in trouble with Arabs *and* Jews!

65. Gk. διὰ τοῦ τείχους, lit. "through the [city] wall." Cf. Josh 2:15-18 for the prostitute Rahab's help in the escape of the Hebrew spies through (a window in her house in) the wall of the city of Jericho. For examples of other escapes over and through walls and windows in biblical and other literature, see Furnish, 523.

66. Gk. ἐχαλάσθην, used elsewhere of the lowering of fishing nets (Luke 5:4) or of ship's gear into the water (Acts 27:17). The passive voice indicates that Paul had assistance; Acts 9:25 says "his disciples" lowered him.

67. Gk. ἐν σαργάνῃ, a flexible basket; cf. σπυρίς (Acts 9:25).

68. Gk. ἐξέφυγον τὰς χεῖρας αὐτοῦ, lit. "I escaped out of his hands."

69. So C. J. Humphreys and W. G. Waddington, "Dating the Crucifixion," 743-46.

clear. Through their "visions and revelations" the newcomers are uplifted in religious pride; they are, indeed, "superlative" apostles. In the unremoved "thorn" Paul exercises his ministry in humility and patience, lacking power of his own, utterly dependent on the Lord. *God's* power is made perfect in weakness.

(a) Visions and Revelations (12:1-6)

1 *I must[1] go on boasting.[2] Although there is nothing to be gained,[3] I will go on to visions and revelations from the Lord. 2 I know a man in Christ who fourteen years ago was caught up to the third heaven. Whether it was in the body or out of the body I do not know — God knows. 3 And I know that this man — whether in the body or apart from the body I do not know, but God knows — 4 was caught up to Paradise. He heard inexpressible things, things that man is not permitted to tell. 5 I will boast about a man like that, but I will not boast about myself, except about my weaknesses. 6 Even if I should choose to boast, I would not be a fool, because I would be speaking the truth. But I refrain, so no one will think more of me than is warranted by what[4] I do or say.*

Paul's "boasting" is an unprofitable exercise, something that the "boasting" of his opponents has forced upon him (vv. 1, 11). Indeed, much that follows appears to "mirror," but so as to correct, the claims of these men. Thus he will come to "visions and revelations from the Lord" (v. 1), specifically the rapture of a man in Christ, some fourteen years ago, in which, however, the man "caught up" brought nothing back that he was free to tell (vv. 2-4). Should he choose to boast of that man, it would not be foolish; all that he says is true (v. 5). But he will boast of weaknesses, that is, about himself, lest they think "more" than they should of the man they have seen and heard (v. 6). Thus Paul does not deny the substance (that he had such experiences), but their significance! Contrary to the intruders' hopes, such phenomena do not authenticate ministry.

1. To be retained is δεῖ, "must," over against the connective δέ (as in ℵ* D); see Metzger, 584.
2. The reading καυχᾶσθαι δεῖ is well supported (e.g. p⁴⁶ B Dᶜ G P itᵈ·ᵍ syrᵖ·ʰ goth). Καυχᾶσθαι δή has only marginal support.
3. Gk. οὐ συμφέρον μέν is to be retained (as in p⁴⁶ ℵ*) over against various other alternatives inserted to improve the difficult syntax; see Metzger, 584.
4. Metzger, 585, supports ἀκούει [τι] because of balanced evidence for (ℵ* B Dc Fᵍʳ G 33 424 itᵍ vg syrᵖ copˢᵃ·ᵇᵒ) and against (p⁴⁶ ℵᶜ D* K L P Ψ 104 itᵈ) the inclusion of τι.

1a Paul's "I must go on[5] boasting"[6] serves as a reminder of the daring rhetorical exercise in which he has been engaged (as from 11:1, the formal beginning of the "Fool's Speech"), in which "boasting" has played a critical role (see 11:16, 17, 18, 30).

But "boasting" is (1) the action of a "fool" (cf. 11:16), (2) is not speaking "according to the Lord" but "in foolishness" (11:17), and (3), by inference, "is not helpful"[7] (NIV, "nothing [is] to be gained"). Why, then, does Paul "boast"? Because "many" — that is, Paul's opponents, the false apostles — "boast" (11:18), Paul, "too, . . . must boast" (cf. 11:30). He has been "forced" to be "a fool" (12:11), given no alternative but to "boast."

Thus this short opening statement serves (1) to remind us of the important "boasting" theme, as used to this point, and (2) as a platform from which will spring his remarks about "boasting" to bring the "Fool's Speech" to its climax (v. 9).

1b Despite its questionable helpfulness Paul will speak about his visions and revelations. His use of the balancing particles[8] sets in contrast the two phrases:

> Although it is unhelpful,
> nonetheless
> I will come to visions and revelations from the Lord.

While on the one hand there is no benefit in it, yet on the other he will proceed to "visions and revelations." Thus Paul signals immediately that such things are irrelevant in the present discussion on legitimacy in apostleship ("It is not

---

5. Gk. ἐλεύσομαι, "I will come," indicates moving on to a new subject.

6. Gk. καυχᾶσθαι δεῖ, present tense infinitive, with the pronoun "I" understood.

7. Gk. οὐ συμφέρον (cf. 8:10) are part of a μὲν . . . δέ construction, requiring the juxtaposition

> Although it is not helpful,
> nonetheless I will come to visions and revelations from the Lord.

At the same time, it seems likely that Paul also wants to connect οὐ συφέρον μέν with the preceding καυχᾶσθαι δεῖ; hence the overall sense might be

> I must go on boasting —
> it is not helpful —
> but I will come to visions and revelations from the Lord.

The grammar is awkward; Plummer (337) suggests that the text may have been emended. Paul may want to say (1) that "visions and revelations from the Lord" are "unhelpful," and (2) that because the "boasting" in question is of "visions and revelations from the Lord," it is also "unhelpful."

8. Gk. μὲν . . . δέ.

557

helpful, but . . ."). It is only because the Corinthians have forced him to become a "fool," that is, "to boast" (12:11; cf. 11:16), that he does so. But, as we shall see, boast of "visions and revelations" he will not, but of "weaknesses" (v. 9). Such matters as "visions and revelations" are private, between Paul and God; they are "for God," not "for the Corinthians" (see on 5:13).

Did these "visions and revelations"9 emanate "*from* the Lord," or were they "*of* the Lord," that is, did they have the Lord as their object? Paul's genitive *(kyriou)* could mean either "from the Lord" or "of the Lord," or both. The view we have taken is that "visions and revelations" are "*from* the Lord"10 because (1) "Lord" is more likely to be subject than object since both nouns are connected to it, because (2) in vv. 2-4 no appearing of the Lord to Paul is involved, and because, (3) given the centrality of Paul's Damascus road call (Gal 1:16, 18; 2:1), we would have expected a different form of words; "revelation" would have been singular, and it would have preceded "visions."

That God gave Paul "visions and revelations from the Lord" is well attested within his own letters and by the Acts of the Apostles.11 However, the terminology is curious: (1) "visions" precedes "revelations,"12 and (2) both are plural. We suggest that the expression is offhand, and perhaps dismissive in intent.13 If, as seems likely, his opponents are claiming paranor-

---

9. Gk. ὀπτασίας καὶ ἀποκαλύψεις κυρίου. The use of plurals without articles signifies that Paul is taking up a general topic for discussion rather than that Paul has experienced multiple "visions and revelations." This is Paul's only use of ὀπτασία (but see Acts 26:19); and although he uses ἀποκάλυψις elsewhere — of the end time (1 Cor 1:7; Rom 2:5), of his apostolic call (Gal 1:12), of God's instruction to him (Gal 2:2), and of God's "revelation" to the NT prophets (1 Cor 14:6, 26) — only here and in v. 7 does the plural ἀποκαλύψεις appear.

10. This is the view of most commentators (e.g., Plummer, 338; Bruce, 246; and Furnish, 524). However, Martin, 397, warns of "too sharp a distinction," and Hughes, 428 n. 97, argues that Paul intends both an objective and a subjective sense. Nonetheless, it is noteworthy that his parallel reference, "revelation of Jesus Christ" (Gal 1:12), in its context makes "Jesus Christ" the object and God the revealer (Gal 1:16).

11. To the point at which Paul wrote 2 Corinthians, apart from the ἀποκαλύψεις of 12:2-4, 7, we know of such phenomena at *Damascus* (Acts 9:3-9 — φῶς ἐκ τοῦ οὐρανοῦ; 26:19 — τῇ οὐρανίῳ ὀπτασίᾳ; Gal. 1:12 — ἀποκαλύψεως Ἰησοῦ Χριστοῦ); at *Jerusalem* (Acts 22:17-21 — ἰδεῖν αὐτὸν λέγοντά μοι); at *Antioch* (Gal. 2:1 — κατὰ ἀποκάλυψιν); at *Corinth* (Acts 18:9-10 — δι᾽ ὁράματος) and subsequent to 2 Corinthians at *Jerusalem* (Acts 23:11 — ἐπιστὰς αὐτῷ ὁ κύριος); and *at sea* en route to Rome (Acts 27:23-24 — παρέστη . . . μοι . . . ἄγγελος). Cf. Paul's vision in Troas of the man from Macedonia (Acts 16:9, 10 — ὅραμα), and Ananias's vision in Damascus (Acts 9:12 — ἐν ὁράματι).

12. W. Michaelis, *TDNT* 5.352-53, regards ὀπτασίαι and ἀποκαλύψεις as interchangeable, noting that at v. 7 Paul speaks only of ἀποκάλυψις.

13. See Martin, 396, who thinks that Paul seeks to avoid drawing too much attention to himself.

mal experiences[14] to validate their apostolate (cf. on 5:12-13), the very vagueness of Paul's reference may be his way of asserting the uniqueness of his apostolate. Having urged his apostolicity upon them in the First Letter (1 Cor 9:1; 15:8) on the basis of having seen the risen Lord, Paul may not wish to repeat such validation, or enter into "comparison" with them as if they were on equal terms with him (10:12; 11:12), as if he needed to reestablish his dominical calling. Rather, it appears that Paul wants that office to be accepted as a given, without further dispute.[15]

2-4 Since these verses have a delicate, integrated structure, they cannot be easily separated. It is best to treat them as a unit[16] and comment on them together.

> 2 I   know a man[17] in Christ
> > who, fourteen years ago,
> > > whether in   the body
> >
> > I do not know,
> > > whether out of the body
> >
> > I do not know.
> > God   knows.
> > > Such a one
> > > > [was] caught up to the third heaven.
>
> 3 And I   know
> > such a man,
> > > whether in   the body
> > > whether out of the body
> >
> > I do not know,
> > God   knows,

---

14. Comparison appears fundamental to the "Fool's Speech": "they — I too; they — I more" (11:22-23; see on 10:12).

15. His opening sentence asserts his apostolicity: "Paul an apostle of Christ, by the will of God" (1:1; cf. 8:5), who is "sent from God" (2:17, ὡς ἐκ θεοῦ), "God making his appeal through him" (5:20), whose "fellow worker" he is (6:1). This assertion indirectly recurs throughout the letter by his use of the aorist tense to point to the *moment* of his apostolic call. In a probable reference to the Damascus event, he says that "God made his light *shine* (ἔλαμψεν) in our hearts . . ." (4:6). Twice he writes of "The authority that the Lord *gave* . . ." (10:8; 13:10 — ἔδωκεν). He speaks of "the field that God *assigned* (ἐμέρισεν) to us" (10:13), and of having "been *convinced*" (5:14 — κρίναντας), and says that "God *gave* (δόντος) us the ministry of reconciliation . . . *committed* (θέμενος) to us the message of reconciliation" (5:18, 19).

16. R. Spittler, "The Limits of Ecstasy," 259-66, called these verses "the paradise pericope."

17. Gk. ἄνθρωπος, "person," rather than the gender-specific ἀνήρ, "male."

```
     4      that        he was caught up to Paradise
                and he      heard unutterable words,
                                which are not lawful
                for a man                              to speak.[18]
```

In these verses Paul narrates[19] the ascent of "a man in Christ" to the "third heaven/Paradise." The tripartite structure — (1) introductory, (2) repetitive, and (3) climactic — corresponds approximately with these three verses.

In the *Introduction* (v. 2) Paul supplies the basic information that (1) he "know[s]" this "man," (2) who was "caught up"[20] to the third heaven fourteen years ago, and (3) that he does "not know" whether or not this rapture was bodily; only "God knows." In the *Repetition* (v. 3[21]) Paul repeats the previous three elements, except that (1) he now refers to "such a man," and (2) he omits the first "I do not know." In the *Climax* (v. 4) he completes the narrative of "a man in Christ . . . such a man" (vv. 2, 3), who was "caught up to Paradise,"[22] where he heard "unutterable utterances,"[23] words "not lawful" to speak.[24]

---

18. My translation.

19. See Martin, 392, for tabular comparison of vv. 3-4 with v. 2. Martin sees "Semitic" synthetic parallelism in a two-part structure ("caught up . . . caught up"). Be that as it may, a three-part narrative, with a climax ("a man in Christ . . . such a man . . . caught up to Paradise," where "he heard unutterable words . . . not lawful . . . to speak"), appears to be a useful description of the text. For general discussion, see further C. Rowland, *The Open Heaven,* 381.

20. Gk. ἁρπαγέντα, accusative passive participle of the verb ἁρπάζειν, which reappears as a passive indicative in v. 4 (ἡρπάγη). This verb is found elsewhere in Paul only at 1 Thess 4:17 (ἁρπαγησόμεθα). Acts 8:39 states that "the Spirit of the Lord caught up (ἥρπασεν) Philip," and Rev 12:5 describes the rapture of Christ (ἡρπάσθη τὸ τέκνον αὐτῆς πρὸς τὸν θεόν). For references in apocalyptic literature to the rapture of a person, see, e.g., *1 Enoch* 39:3-4; 52:1; *Apoc. Moses* 37:3, and in rabbinic literature *Ḥag.* 14b.

21. The initial καί has been taken by some (e.g., Plummer, 344) to point to a second experience, and was so taken by a number of patristic writers (e.g., Clement of Alexandria, Irenaeus, and Tertullian); the one date "fourteen years ago" militates against this view. Rather, the καί is ascensive (BAGD 1.3), signaling that more information is to be given about this "man," namely, that "he was caught up to Paradise" and "heard" speech that he was not allowed to utter.

22. Gk. παράδεισος, "Paradise," occurs in two other places in the NT (Luke 23:43; Rev 2:7) and arises from (1) LXX references to "the garden of Eden," planted by God, "the garden of God/the LORD," etc. (e.g., Gen 2:8, 9, 10, 15, 16; 3:1, 2, 3, 8 [twice], 10, 23, 24; 13:10; Num 24:6; Isa 51:3; Jer 36:5; Ezek 28:13; 33:8 [twice], 9; Joel 2:3), and (2) apocalyptic references that project "paradise" in eschatological terms as the "heavenly garden" (e.g., *T. Abraham* 20; *T. Levi* 28:10; *1 Enoch* 60:7-8; 61:12; *2 Enoch* 9:1–42:3; *Apoc. Abraham* 21:6-7; *4 Ezra* 4:7-8).

23. Gk. ἄρρητα ῥήματα — a paradoxical juxtaposition, "unutterable utterances." R. Spittler, "Ecstasy," 263, notes that, "While *arrētos* doubtlessly comes from the vocabu-

Paul's "fourteen years ago"[25] must be calculated (by internal reckoning) from the time of writing this letter (c. A.D. 55), suggesting that this vision/revelation occurred c. A.D. 42, at which time Paul would have been in his native Syria-Cilicia (Gal 1:18, 21; 2:1; Acts 9:29-30; 11:25).[26] The nearest known supernatural parallels — (1) his visit from Antioch to Jerusalem "by revelation" (Gal 2:2), and (2) the missionary call from Antioch (Acts 13:1-3) — occurred c. A.D. 47, less than "fourteen years ago," apart from the unlikelihood that those events were connected with this experience. In reality, no other occurrence in Paul's life can be readily identified with his narrative in these verses.

As we have noted above (see on v. 1b), Paul was by no means unfamiliar with "visions and revelations from the Lord." One such vision had occurred in Corinth during his initial visit (Acts 18:9-10). Why does he not refer to that? The answer may be that he placed so much importance on the Lord's words spoken to him when the stake/thorn was given to him (v. 9). The experience of being "caught up" to the third heaven in apparent power was the necessary prelude to being brought down to earth in the weakness of the stake/thorn, where the dominical revelation of real power was given to

---

lary of mystery cults, the compound expression *arrēta rhēmata* appears to be unique to Paul." That they are ἃ οὐκ ἐξόν (ἐστίν should be understood, making this a periphrastic construction) indicates that they are more probably (1) "not lawful" than (2) "not able to be translated" (so Martin, 405-6). Various backgrounds — gnostic, rabbinic, and OT — have been sought in Paul's words, which, however, in our view, are written to rebut the newcomers' claims. Since Paul appears to be addressing Jewish "superlative" apostles (11:5; 12:11 = "false apostles"; 11:13, 22, 23), it appears more probable that such persons were influenced by current Palestinian religious phenomena, as reflected in Jewish apocalyptic literature (e.g., "In those days a whirlwind carried me off from the earth and set me down at the end of the heavens. And there I saw another vision . . ." — *1 Enoch* 39:3ff.) and in the behavior of contemporary "sign-prophets" ("under the pretense of divine inspiration . . . persuaded the multitude to act like madmen" — θειασμοῦ . . . δαιμονᾶν τὸ πλῆθος ἔπειθον — Josephus, *J.W.* 2.259-60). See P. W. Barnett, "Opposition," 3-17; *New Docs.* 3.45 has a reference to a "secret to be kept from the uninitiated."

24. Gk. οὐκ ἐξὸν . . . λαλῆσαι; NIV, "not permitted to tell."

25. Gk. πρὸ ἐτῶν δεκατεσσάρων. Specific information of this kind is found in the prophetic and apocalyptic writings (e.g., Ezek 1:1-3; Amos 1:1; Hos 1:1; Isa 6:1; Jer 1:1-3; 26:1; 42:7; Zech 1:1; 2 Esdr 3:1, 2; *2 Apoc. Bar.* 1:1). It is a coincidence that Gal 2:1 refers to δεκατεσσάρων ἐτῶν, which points back to Paul's apostolic call in c. A.D. 34, whereas this reference is to be located c. A.D. 42 (see the note following).

26. Based on an A.D. 33 date of the first Easter and the supposition that his Damascus road revelation occurred within two years of it (c. A.D. 34/35), we calculate that Paul came back to Jerusalem from Damascus (Gal 1:18) c. A.D. 36/37 and to Jerusalem from Antioch (Gal 2:1) c. A.D. 47/48. By this calculation his estimated time span in Cilicia would have been c. A.D. 37-46. The visionary experience "fourteen years ago," c. A.D. 42, appears to have occurred in Cilicia.

him. Despite the grandeur of the experience, it was useless in authenticating his ministry; nothing he heard in Paradise was allowed to be told to others! Like the escape from Damascus, this event served to highlight his weaknesses. As it happens, the events reflected in 11:32–12:9 appear to have occurred in chronological sequence: *Damascus* (the escape down the wall), then *Tarsus* ("caught up to Paradise").

By his brief story about "visions and revelations of the Lord" (v. 1; cf. "these surpassingly great revelations" — v. 7), Paul the narrator is attempting to establish the following: First, by his faintly humorous tone he is ridiculing his opponents' attempt to achieve acceptance in Corinth by claims to paranormal experience. Paul the narrator knows this "man" because he is the man, yet he puts him at arm's length from himself (v. 5);[27] his rivals may have been quite person-specific and detail-specific. Loftily he disdains to "know" whether this man's journey to the third heaven — the highest heaven[28] — was in or out of the body,[29] a detail about which the counterclaimants may have made much capital. In any case, as he well knows, an event as distant as "fourteen years ago" is unlikely to compete with their more up-to-date claims. Rollercoaster-like, he has been "lowered down," sharply "caught up," then, finally and painfully, brought down and "buffeted." He had been humiliatingly let down the Damascus wall in a net like so much merchandise (11:33), only to be powerfully whisked up to the heights of Paradise to hear the voice of God — the whole point of the experience[30]

27. Paul uses the third person because of his unwillingness to boast about what he has done. As a "man ἐν Χριστῷ" Paul was one in whom *God* had wrought a new creation (5:17); therefore, Paul could not boast. So Furnish, 542-44; Martin, 398. Various forms of "arm's-length" self-reference occur in both Jewish classical sources (see Bultmann, 220). Suggestions that Paul is actually referring to another person (e.g., Apollos) are to be rejected; vv. 6b-7a clearly refer to Paul.

28. There is some debate as to the number of heavens currently believed in; some sources suggest five, others ten, though seven heavens are referred to in both Jewish and later Christian writings (*Apoc. Moses* 35:2; *2 Enoch* 3–20; *Ascension of Isaiah* 3:11; *Apoc. Paul* 29. See further C. Rowland, *Open Heaven,* 381). For two reasons, however, Paul is thinking here of the highest heaven: (1) the preposition ἕως implies "up to," "the ultimate," and (2) the supernal connotations of "Paradise" (v. 4), which is a synonym for "third heaven."

29. In Jewish tradition those "caught up" were usually "in the body" — so Enoch (*1 Enoch* 12:1; 14:8; 39:3-4), Abraham (*T. Abr.* 8[B]), Seth (*Adam and Eve* 37:1), and Baruch (*3 Apoc. Bar.* 11:1-2). By contrast, in Greek thought, a journey to another realm is the *soul's* flight from the body (see Plato, *Republic* 10.614B), as reflected in Jewish writers in the Hellenistic tradition (see, e.g., Philo, *Dreams* 1.36 and Josephus, *J.W.* 7.337-88).

30. Biblically, the first "ascent" was Enoch's (Gen 5:24), the basis of much Jewish apocalyptic about "visits" to the heavenly realms. See G. Scholem, *Jewish Gnosticism,* 17-18, for reference to the NT period and journeys to heaven by living venerated persons. The point of those journeys was to receive revelations usually available only after death.

562

— where, however, upon his return, the things he heard were unutterable because he was not allowed (by God) to speak.

Though he employs a somewhat grim humor, yet by no means does Paul denigrate this experience; he simply regards it as private and incommunicable. The verse supplies his own elaboration of his earlier remark, "If we are beside ourselves, it is for God" (5:13, RSV). He had not — apparently — ever referred to it. The "foolishness" of the Corinthians (and the opponents?) has "forced"[31] him to talk about it; nonetheless, he does not reveal the "unutterable utterances" he heard, which he was not allowed to speak.

Second, this essentially negative narrative serves as a foil against which he will construct his wholly positive narrative (vv. 7-9) in which he heard words of the Lord, revelatory words that, unlike the ones mentioned above, he *is able* to speak.

Hence, to return to the subject of "boasting" — the point of the whole passage (vv. 1-10; see on v. 1) — he will not "boast" of the powerful man who had been caught up to "Paradise" but of the man brought down in weakness by the "stake/thorn" (vv. 7-9). This may be quite pointed, indeed, in regard to those who "classify and compare" themselves with Paul on these very grounds and find him "inferior."

5-6a Having narrated ironically his revelationless vision, Paul now proceeds to put it into perspective in terms of his "Fool's Speech." Thus he picks up the major themes of the speech (11:1–12:13) — "boasting" (11:10, 12, 16, 17, 18, 30; 12:1), "weakness" (11:21, 29, 30), and "fool[ishness]" (11:1, 16 [twice], 17, 19, 23), using them now to prepare the way for his "boasting in weakness" (v. 9), the climax of this passage and, indeed, of the entire "Fool's Speech."

Using the language of "boasting" from v. 1, Paul now applies it directly to the previous narrative, where he distances himself from the man caught up to Paradise. In nicely balanced clauses he says (ironically), "About *such a person* I will boast," but "About myself I will not boast," to which he adds, "except in my weaknesses," thus echoing 11:30. This is followed by a double explanatory clause that says, in effect — and unexpectedly — that if he were to boast in his revelations, that would not make him a fool, for he would be speaking the sober truth. But "So what?" is his point since, as he will go on to say, the only boasting that counts is the latter — boasting in his weaknesses.

He has narrated the account of the "man in Christ . . . caught up to Paradise" (vv. 2-4); clearly the man is Paul. Now, however, in regard to boasting Paul distinguishes between "this man" and "myself." On behalf of

---

31. Gk. καυχᾶσθαι δεῖ (v. 1); ὑμεῖς με ἠναγκάσατε (v. 11).

(hyper) "such a man"[32] he "will boast,"[33] but on behalf of himself he will not boast, except "in weaknesses."[34] Should he choose to boast on behalf of that man, however, he would not be a "fool" because[35] he would be telling the truth.[36]

Here, then, is another nuance in Paul's use of "fool" — (1) the opponents' mockery of Paul as a "fool," on account of his "weakness" (11:1, 16); (2) Paul's ironic self-reference to the boasting he must do (11:16, 17), which is, however, an inverted boasting in weakness (11:21, 23; 12:11); (3) Paul's reference to the adversaries' ill-treatment of the Corinthians (11:19-20); and (4) Paul's reference to the Corinthians as putting up with such treatment (11:19-20). To these he adds (5) that if ever he were to "boast" about such experiences, he would not be a fool (unlike them), because he tells the truth.

Let the Corinthians know that he was, in "truth," "caught up" in that remarkable vision/revelation of the Lord. But as such it was a private experience between himself and God and was neither to be communicated nor capitalized on in legitimating his ministry; he was not at liberty to divulge what he had heard (v. 4). This was between him and God (5:13).

6b While Paul will not boast of the man "caught up to Paradise," the strong inference is that he will boast of himself in another persona, that is, in the man the Corinthians actually "see" and "hear," namely, the apostle in his "weakness."

Whereas v. 6a is hypothetical ("If I shall wish to boast . . ."), v. 6b is dismissive of the very idea ("But[37] I refrain[38] . . ."). This, in turn, is followed by a negative statement of purpose:

---

32. Gk. τὸν τοιοῦτον could be neuter, "such an experience" (so, e.g., Luther, Moffatt). The context, however, requires the masculine and personal sense.

33. Gk. καυχήσομαι, "I will boast." Paul also uses the future tense in 11:30.

34. Gk. ἐν ταῖς ἀσθενείαις, plural (as in 11:30; vv. 9b, 10 — but not v. 9a) and referring to the various sufferings and privations experienced in the course of ministry narrated in 11:23-33. Paul is not boasting of "weakness" considered in the abstract. The "weakness" of v. 9a relates to the concrete example of the thorn/stake.

35. Gk. γάρ.

36. If Paul "boasts," he will not be a "fool" because he will speak the "truth." His speaking "the *truth*" is a probable side reference to his opponents, who are *pseudo* — *pseudo*-apostles (11:13), *pseudo*-brothers (11:26); unlike them, we infer, he does "not lie" (11:31). "The truth of Christ" is in him (11:10).

37. Gk. δέ.

38. Gk. φείδομαι, quite possibly an ironic reference, given that the Corinthians appear to be quite open to boasting of such experiences and would, perhaps, be glad to have Paul do some boasting, too.

lest anyone reckon   of me[39]
        above what he sees   in me
           or   hears from me.[40]

The "boasting" from which he refrains was in regard to "such a man," the one "caught up to Paradise" (vv. 3-4), not "myself," about whom he will not "boast" except in "weakness" (vv. 5, 9). As such this verse serves as commentary on and elaboration of 5:12: "We are . . . giving you a cause to boast of us ["that we persuade men . . . in our right mind" — 5:11, 13], so that you may be able to answer *those who boast in 'face,' not in 'heart.'*"[41] For Paul to "boast" of "such a man . . . caught up to Paradise" would be to "boast" of "face," to attempt to legitimate his ministry behind the mask of esoteric visions and revelations and their accompanying ecstatic speech.

Rather, let them relate to him (1) by ordinary observation, by what they "see" in him, that is, his "weaknesses," and (2) by what they "hear" from him,[42] that is, by his preaching of Christ (cf. 1:19; 4:5; 5:11; 11:3-4). These two things that they "see" and "hear" — "weaknesses" and his preaching of Christ — are connected.[43] The "weaknesses" result from being the "minister of Christ" who suffers as a consequence of his preaching, as the catalogues of suffering make clear (4:5, 8-12; 6:3-10; 11:23-29).

Critical to this verse is the word "above" (Gk. *hyper*), the keyword to the extended passage in which the "superlative" apostles = the "false apostles" appear (10:12–12:13). *Hyper,* "above," "superior," appears to be their manner of self-presentation; *hyster,* "below," "inferior," their view and presentation of Paul. Ironically Paul turns their "boast" back on them; they are, in his ironic words, "superlative" apostles,[44] to whom, however, he is not "inferior"[45] (11:5; 12:11). Apparently, they boast that they are "superior" *(hyper)* in a number of ministry-related areas — fluency in speech (see on 11:5), and, in particular, in "visions and revelations from the Lord" (see on

39. Gk. εἰς ἐμὲ λογίσηται, "think of me, form an estimate of me," an "unusual construction" according to Plummer, 346. See LXX Hos 7:15 for a close parallel.
40. My translation.
41. Gk. τοὺς ἐν προσώπῳ καυχωμένους καὶ μὴ ἐν καρδίᾳ (5:12). The "face" is known" to man, the "heart" to God (5:11; cf. 2:17; 4:2; 1:12-14, 23).
42. ὃ . . . [τις] ἀκούει . . . ἐξ ἐμοῦ.
43. It should be noted, however, that the pair "see" and "hear" is used elsewhere in an idiomatic sense (e.g., Isa 6:9; 29:18; Jer 5:21; Ezek 12:2; Matt 11:4; 13:14-15; Mark 8:18; Acts 8:6; 28:26-27), as well as by Paul (1 Cor 2:9; Rom 11:8; 15:21; Phil 4:9). However, here the precise objects με . . . ἐξ ἐμοῦ suggest a more intensive and personal use.
44. Gk. ὑπερλίαν ἀπόστολοι; NIV, "super apostles."
45. Except, perhaps, in "speech" (11:6) and, ironically implied, in the exploitative behavior of the Corinthians (11:20-21)!

12:2-4); Paul will "boast" of being "superior" only in suffering as "a minister of Christ" ("Ministers of Christ are they? I am better" — *hyper;* 11:23). Unlike them, he will not portray himself as a receiver of heavenly revelations so as to suggest that he is "above," "more than" *(hyper),* by plain observation he is — a man of "weaknesses" — whose "weaknesses," or sufferings, arise from his faithful preaching of Christ.

This part verse, when taken with 5:11-13, is important in establishing pointers to authentic Christian ministry. While individuals may, in the purposes of God, undergo various religious experiences, those experiences are between the person and God (5:13) and do not of themselves establish fitness for pastoral or missionary ministry. Based on these texts, the legitimating criteria include preaching Christ (5:12), which is not deterred by suffering and weakness (12:5), expressed out of a "right mind" (5:13). No one is to be judged beyond or apart from what one "sees" in or "hears" from that person (12:6b). What one sees in and hears from that minister is critical.

(b) The Thorn in the Flesh (12:7-10)

7 *To keep me from becoming conceited because of these surpassingly great revelations,*[1] *there was given me a thorn in my flesh, a messenger of Satan, to torment me.*[2] 8 *Three times I pleaded with the Lord to take it away from me.* 9 *But he said to me, "My grace is sufficient for you, for my*[3] *power is made perfect in weakness." Therefore I will boast all the more gladly about my weaknesses, so that Christ's power may rest on me.* 10 *That is why, for Christ's sake, I delight in weaknesses, in insults, in hardships, in persecutions, in difficulties. For when I am weak, then I am strong.*

Paul now brings the "Fool's Speech" to a conclusion, spelling out by way of specific narrative *why* he will boast of his weaknesses rather than his (non)-revelatory experience. The latter might exalt the apostle himself; the former serve to exalt Christ. At the same time it is hard not to see in the opening disclaimer ("to keep me from being elated") a final indirect jab at the "superlative" but fraudulent apostles.

---

1. Some authorities (p46 D) omit διό, which, however, should be retained since it is found in ℵ A B and could be regarded as "the more difficult reading."
2. The inclusion of ἵνα μὴ ὑπεραίρωμαι ("to keep me from being elated") is supported by, e.g., p46 B Ψ but not by, e.g., ℵ* A D G. The context suggests retention, to reinforce the point against the "superlative apostles."
3. The best MS evidence (p46 ℵ) omits "my" (so Metzger, 585-86).

Thus he declares that such an "abundance of revelations" (RSV) might have "over-uplifted" Paul in religious pride, as, apparently, they have so exalted his opponents. Against that possibility God has pinned Paul to the earth with the unidentified stake/thorn (*skolops,* v. 7). At that time Paul prayed for its removal and the Lord effectively replied in the negative, nonetheless promising his sustaining grace/power against his weakness (vv. 8-9). Thus having given them a revelatory story without a revelation, he now gives them a healing story without a healing. Finally, in an astonishing and unexpected turn, Paul declares that he boasts of his weaknesses, confident that this is the circumstance when Christ's power will rest upon him; when he is weak, then he is strong (vv. 9-10).

In this passage there is a complete reversal of the religious pride and the religious triumphalism of the "superlative" apostles. Genuinely apostolic ministry sustains "weaknesses . . . on behalf of Christ," replicating his sufferings yet finding power in ministry in dependence on him. There is no place for arrogance in ministry.

7 This complex sentence[4] states (1) that,[5] therefore,[6] lest by an "abundance of revelations" Paul should be "over-uplifted" (in pride), a *skolops* (a "stake" or "thorn") in (or for) the flesh, a messenger of Satan, was given to him, (2) to buffet him, (3) lest he should be "over-uplifted." This verse is powerfully intentional; each of these elements is purposive[7]: the *skolops* was given to Paul *lest* he be "over-uplifted," *to* buffet him, *lest* he be "over-uplifted."[8] It was God's will for Paul.

The "abundance of revelations,"[9] when read with "visions and rev-

---

4. The awkwardly incomplete opening words of the verse have been taken with either (1) v. 5 ("I will not boast except in my weaknesses . . . and in the abundance of revelations"), or with (2) v. 6 ("but I refrain lest anyone should . . . and by reason of the abundance of revelations" — so Furnish, 528). But both options are against the flow of the argument. It is best, with Plummer, 347, to attribute the brokenness to incoherent dictation and to take the meaning to be, "And by reason of the abundance of revelations, wherefore, that I should not be 'over-uplifted,' there was given me a thorn in the flesh. . . ."

5. The initial καί is explicative, and translated, e.g., "That," or, as by Furnish, 528, "Specifically."

6. Gk. διό, "wherefore," which picks up the previous verse: "But I refrain lest anyone reckon of me above what he see in me or hears from me, *wherefore,* lest, by the the abundance of revelations, I be over-uplifted." Paul does not want "the abundance of revelations" to be "above" what the people "see" in him or "hear" from him so as to "over-uplift" Paul, i.e., exalt him in pride.

7. Gk. ἵνα μὴ . . . ἵνα . . . ἵνα μή.

8. The repetition of ἵνα μὴ ὑπεραίρωμαι frames the statement of v. 7b: "*lest I be elated* there was given to me a thorn for the flesh, a messenger of Satan *lest I be elated.*"

9. Gk. τῇ ὑπερβολῇ τῶν ἀποκαλύψεων. RSV, "abundance of revelations," is preferred to NIV, "surpassingly great revelations."

elations of the Lord" (v. 1), indicates a considerable frequency of such exceptional phenomena (see on v. 1 for known examples). It is likely, however, that both references also mirror the claims of his opponents; his generalized exaggerations probably ridicule their boastfulness. Paul will give only one example of his own, which occurred fourteen years ago (v. 2)! That he has not been "over-uplifted" — bodily airborne — appears to reflect their testimony that they have been so "over-uplifted," by which Paul now means "uplifted in pride" (cf. 10:4-5). He is not, in truth, what they say they are!

The rarely used verb *hyperairōsthai* ("over-uplifted"[10]), like *hyperlian* ("very much more," "superlative," used with "apostles"[11] — 11:5; 12:11), is compounded with the preposition *hyper,* "over," "above," which is critical within his sustained and ironic polemic against the intruders (10:11–12:13). Paul takes their word *hyper* and turns it against them to expose both (1) the falsity of their claims, and (2) their superinflated view of themselves.

Paul, indeed, may have been, but did not remain, "over-uplifted." In this "abundance of revelations" — he does not say when (cf. v. 2) — there was also "given"[12] him (i.e., by God — divine passive) the *skolops,* for the very purpose that he might *not* be "over-uplifted." The verb tenses should be noted. The *skolops* was "given" (a completed action — aorist tense) in order that, as a messenger of Satan, it might continue to "buffet" (present tense) Paul lest he continue to be "over-uplifted" (present tense). Like his opponents, he has experienced "visions and revelations from the Lord . . . an abundance of revelations." But unlike them he has not remained "over-uplifted"; God brought him down to earth by his *skolops,* and kept him there, buffeting him. Meekness, gentleness, humility, patience, and endurance — the Christlike marks of an apostle, of which he has much to say in this letter[13] — are connected with God's "gift" to him of the *skolops.*

But what is the *skolops*[14]? Few questions in the NT have excited greater interest. From early times to the present scholars continue to give their answers.[15] A substantial library of opinion as to the nature of Paul's *skolops* has been created. However, two obstacles bar the way to a solution that can be confidently held: (1) the meaning of the word *skolops* itself is uncertain and, equally, (2) we can only guess at who or what Paul had in mind by his application of this word to himself. Indeed, it is possible that the Corinthians themselves did not know what he meant.

10. Gk. ὑπεραίρωσθαι; NIV, "conceited."
11. Gk. ὑπερλίαν ἀπόστολοι.
12. Gk. ἐδόθη, aorist passive.
13. See 10:1; 4:5; 6:4; 12:12.
14. Gk. σκόλοψ.
15. See Hughes, 443-46; K. L. Schmidt, *TDNT* 3.820-21, for historical surveys on the meaning of the "thorn in the flesh."

In regard to the first barrier, the meaning of the word,[16] the difficulty is that *skolops* was used both for a "stake" and for a "thorn." By derivation it meant "what is pointed,"[17] hence a "stake," and was referred to at the time as, for example, an instrument of torture or execution (possibly equivalent to *stauros,* as in crucifixion[18]), or for spikes to impede a siege force. On this basis the word carries connotations of violence. However, the references in the LXX to *skolops* mean only "splinter" or "thorn," as, for example, when Moses warns of the consequences of not driving out the Canaanites: ". . . those you allow to remain will become barbs *(skolopes)* in your eyes" (Num 33:55; cf. Ezek 28:24; Hos 2:6). The context of v. 7 should help us decide between "stake" and "thorn" (or "splinter"), but the context itself is problematic.

Thus the second barrier to confident understanding is the point of the metaphor as used by Paul in this verse. Broadly speaking, Paul's reference has been thought to be either *physical* ([a] an illness, disfigurement, or disability, or [b] moral temptation)[19] or *relational* (opposition to his ministry or persecution). The context of vv. 7-8 marginally favors a relational interpretation of the metaphor: (1) Paul immediately adds "*skolops* for the flesh,"[20] which is explained as "a messenger *(angelos)* of Satan" — *angelos* is generally personal in its use elsewhere by Paul; (2) the verb "buffet,"[21] "beat with a fist," as, for example, by the soldiers of Jesus prior to the crucifixion (Mark 12:65 pars.; cf. 1 Pet 2:20), is generally interpersonal (but see 1 Cor 4:11); and (3) because the verb "take away"[22] (v. 8) is used in the NT of persons, the pronoun (understood) would probably be masculine ("[take] him [away]").

---

16. See G. Delling, *TDNT* 7.409-24.

17. From Gk. σκάλλειν, "to hack."

18. The verbal forms ἀνασκολπίζειν and ἀνασταυροῦσθαι are interchangeable (G. Delling, *TDNT* 7.409-10).

19. Many suggestions have been made, such as (a), e.g., head or ear pain (Tertullian), eye trouble — based on Gal. 4:13, 14; 6:11 (E. Renan), malaria (W. M. Ramsay), epilepsy (J. B. Lightfoot), defective speech (W. K. L. Clarke). Against the "malady" hypothesis — in whatever specific form — is the consideration that Paul must have enjoyed remarkably good health to undertake the punishing regime of ministry mentioned earlier in his catalogue of sufferings (11:23-33). Regarding (b), whereas medieval interpreters favored a theory of sexual temptation, the Reformers favored spiritual temptation.

20. Gk. τῇ σαρκί; NIV, "in my flesh." Difficulties in resolving the meaning of the phrase add to the problems in this text. (1) "Flesh" could be Paul's "mortal existence" (4:11; Phil 1:24) or his body (7:5). (2) Because there is no ἐν, τῇ σαρκί is probably not "*in* the flesh" but "*for* the flesh," which could be a dative of advantage or of disadvantage. A parallel is 1 Cor 7:28 — those who marry will have "affliction *for the flesh.*" On balance, Paul is not referring to his flesh, i.e., his skin, but about his mortal existence. The thorn, whatever it was, impacted on that.

21. Gk. κολαφίζῃ; NIV, "torment."

22. Gk. ἀφίσταναι.

569

If, indeed, the *skolops* is relational, what — specifically — might it have been? Less likely is the suggestion that the *skolops* is the Corinthian church[23] (or a section thereof). More plausibly, Paul's *skolops* is the rise of the Judaizing, anti-Paul movement, such as was then all too obvious in Corinth. In favor of this possibility, we note that (1) such a view would be consistent with the chronological sequence implicit in this passage — the escape from Damascus (11:32-33) *c.* A.D. 34/35, the "Paradise" experience (12:2-4) *c.* A.D. 42, and now, on this hypothesis, the rise of the anti-Pauline mission *c.* A.D. 47 (Gal 2:1, 4-5, 12-14); (2) the *skolops* as a "messenger of Satan" is matched by the false apostles who are "ministers of Satan" (11:15), false brothers who are the source of danger (see on 11:26); and (3) in the LXX, as noted above, *skolops* is used of the enemies of Israel (Num 33:55; Ezek 28:24), making the present opponents the enemies of the true Israel of God and of Paul his minister (cf. Gal 6:16).

On grounds of historical analysis, however, the truth is that we do not have enough unambiguous information to do more than speculate on the nature of Paul's *skolops*. It is hard to choose between the chief options, the *physical* or the *relational;* there are weak points in both (e.g., [a] the difficulty that so robust a man as Paul evidently was (see on 11:23-33) could at the same time be physically debilitated, or [b] understanding that Paul's "messenger of Satan" [singular] could apply to a *group* or *movement*, or [c] that Paul would say that *God* gave him something as evil as the Judaizing movement [see on 11:13-15]). Neither hypothesis is without questions, whichever one favors.

Doubtless speculations will continue to be made. Pastorally, however, it may be to our advantage not to know. The very openness of the identification allows wide possibilities of personal application to a broad range of personal suffering, which precise identification might limit.

This verse expresses a supreme paradox. A painful *skolops* — whatever it actually was — was "given" to Paul, and that by *God!* This is expanded upon as "a messenger of [or from] Satan." The juxtaposition of "was given [by God]" and "messenger of Satan" recalls the early chapters of Job, where God allows Satan to afflict Job's household (Job 1:12), then his person (Job 2:6-7). This language suggests (1) that Satan was the immediate cause of Paul's difficulty — symbolized by the word *skolops;* (2) that, because the *skolops* was given by God, Satan is subject to God, not his equal (as in dualism); and (3) that in a profoundly mysterious way God was the ultimate source of that *skolops*. Paradoxically, *God* is the invisible source of this suffering in the life of Paul, his child and minister.

23. According to J. McCant, "Paul's Thorn," 572, it is "the Corinthian church's rejection of the legitimacy of Paul's apostolate."

Such inferences demand justification and resolution such as have already been given (the twice-stated "that I might not be 'over-uplifted' ") and which Paul now proceeds to elaborate further (vv. 9-10).

8 Now follows Paul's account of his prayer to the Lord; his answer to the prayer will be given in the next verse. Edifyingly for his readers then — and now — Paul reveals that his response to the stake/thorn was to pray.

> Concerning this
> > three times
> > I prayed[24] to the Lord
> > > that
> > > > he might remove [him]
> from me.

Who is the Lord to whom he prayed, the "Lord Christ" or the "Lord God"? His reference to "my power . . . Christ's power" (v. 9) indicates that it was to the Lord Jesus Christ that he turned in prayer. That Paul can make this statement without further comment shows that both he and his readers understood that they could pray to the glorified Jesus as well as to the God and Father of our Lord Jesus Christ;[25] Christ's deity is implied by such a reference (see on 2:12; 3:16; 4:6; cf. 8:5, 19, 21).

His "three times" stands in parallel with Jesus' threefold prayer to the Father in the Garden of Gethsemane (Mark 14:41).[26] Possibly "three times" was a conventional symbol for repeated prayer (so Chrysostom). Threefold actions appear to have been customary in matters relating to piety (cf. John 21:17; Acts 10:16); prayer was offered three times a day (Ps 55:16-17; Dan 6:10, 13). The aorist tense "I prayed" matches the aorist tense "[a thorn] . . . was given"[27]; the singular onset of the stake/thorn was met with Paul's singular (thrice-repeated) prayer to the Lord. That tense may also suggest that, in the light of the Lord's answer, which he continues to hear (v. 9), the time for prayer had passed. It was now a matter of acceptance of the Lord's will.

The content of that prayer was that God should remove "him" (i.e., the "messenger of Satan" — v. 8) from Paul. Given Paul's use elsewhere, the

---

24. Only here in the NT is παρακαλοῦν used in petitionary prayer. It is, however, to be found in Hellenistic contexts (see Furnish, 529).

25. Cf. 1 Thess 3:11-13. See further R. J. Bauckham, "Worship of Jesus in Apocalyptic Christianity," 322-41; R. T. France, "Worship of Jesus," 16-36.

26. J. McCant, "Paul's Thorn," 571, sees a number of parallels between Paul and Jesus, e.g., (1) Jesus faced a σταυρός, Paul a σκόλοψ; (2) both prayed three times; (3) Jesus prayed, "not my will but thine . . ."; Paul heard the Lord say, "My grace is sufficient"; (4) Jesus was crucified; Paul received no healing; and (5) Jesus was rejected — as Messiah — by his "own"; Paul's "own" church rejected him — as an apostle (11:4).

27. Gk. ἐδόθη . . . παρεκάλεσα.

verb "remove" requires a personal object ("him"[28]), not an impersonal object ("it"), supporting the possibility that the stake/thorn was relational in character (see v. 7).

9a Christ's reply to Paul's prayer must be seen as the climax not only of this passage (12:1-10) and of the "Fool's Speech" (11:1–12:13), but in some ways of the entire Second Letter to the Corinthians. Whatever the stake/thorn was, and however great its pain for Paul, he testifies that the "grace" of Christ was "sufficient" in dealing with it. This was the Lord's reply to Paul's prayer.

Earlier Paul related that in Asia he had been "beyond power . . . crushed" (1:8), how, more generally, as a mere "jar of clay," he was dependent on "the all-surpassing power of God" (4:7). Now he declares that "[Christ's] power is made perfect in weakness."[29] Power in weakness, therefore, runs as a thread throughout the letter, reaching its most powerful expression here. Accordingly, we agree with Hughes that Christ's reply to Paul is "the summit of the epistle" (451).

We do not know how, or by what process, that reply came to Paul, except that it was in the context of prayer, and, we suggest, also upon reflection on the central truths of the gospel of the death and resurrection of Christ proclaimed by Paul.

It is likely that Paul knew of and reflected upon the events of the last twenty-four hours of Jesus' life, both his threefold prayer to his Father in Gethsemane (see on v. 8) and his (apparent) powerlessness to save himself as he was dying on the cross. The words spoken at the cross, literally "he *saved* others; himself he is *not powerful* to *save*" (Mark 15:31), resonate in Paul's words that "Christ crucified" is "the *power* of God . . . the *weakness* of God" (1 Cor 1:21, 23-25). The powerful salvation of God had been wrought in the powerless crucified One.

In words evocative of Good Friday and Easter Paul observes that Christ, who was "crucified in *weakness* . . . lives by the *power* of God," and that believers, "by God's *power,* live with [Christ]" (13:4).

Christ's death and life are reproduced in the lives of his people. God's power through Christ's weakness in *death* by crucifixion issues in the "crucifixion" of Paul's inflated pride, by means of the thorn/stake. God's power, which caused Christ to be alive in resurrection and believers with him, issues in the power of Christ experienced in the patience, endurance, meekness, and

---

28. There is no object of the verb "remove." That the object, understood, is "him," i.e., "a messenger of Satan," rather than the "thorn/stake," is the most natural reading given the flow of the text between vv. 7 and 8.

29. Gk. ἡ γὰρ δύναμις ἐν ἀσθενείᾳ τελεῖται, "For power is made perfect in weakness." NIV, "for *my* power. . . ."

gentleness of Christ. Thus the Lord's reply to Paul's prayer for the removal of the thorn/stake is given in terms of the very gospel of the death and resurrection of Christ that the apostles proclaimed (as, e.g., in 1 Cor 15:1-4).

Unlike the earlier and esoteric "revelation" of "fourteen years ago" in which Paul "heard unutterable utterances" that he was "not permitted to speak" (v. 4), the Lord's oracle to him is clear and communicable. And it is nothing else than the given word of God, the gospel of Christ, the death and resurrection of Christ. This was the Lord's answer to Paul, and Paul has told his readers what the Lord said.

The opening words ("And he said to me") tie together Paul's prayer of the previous verse with the Lord's reply in this verse. The verb tenses of both the prayer and the reply are important. Whereas God's "gift" to Paul of the stake/thorn and Paul's plea to the Lord are expressed in the aorist tense ("there was given . . . I prayed"), reflecting the singular nature of both, the Lord's reply is in the perfect tense: "He said to me — and what he said continues to hold good. . . ." Moreover, the content of his words to Paul is in the present tense: his "grace" "is sufficient" (present tense) and his power "is being made perfect" (present tense). The stake/thorn remains, and Paul *continues* to be buffeted. But the Lord's reply *stands:* his grace *is* sufficient, his power *is* being made perfect in the unremoved "weakness" of the stake/thorn.

That reply is in the form of a couplet or parallelism:

> My   grace is sufficient   for you,
> for [my][30] power is made perfect in weakness.[31]

"Grace"[32] here means that "merciful kindness" which is characteristic of God and of Christ particularly in regard to Christ's impoverishment of himself for the sake of the enrichment in salvation of his people (see on 6:1; 8:9; cf. 1:12; 4:15). There is a close association between "grace" and "power," because (1) these words appear in synonymous parallelism in different parts of the couplet, and (2) the explanatory connective, "for,"[33] links the two ("my grace is sufficient, *for* [my] power . . ."). The grace that Christ displays toward

---

30. Although the best MS evidence omits "my" (see note above), it should probably be understood.

31. Gk. ἀσθενείᾳ, "weakness," here is singular, balancing "power." Paul generally uses the plural, "weaknesses," as in the second part of this verse (also 11:30; vv. 5, 10). The "weakness" is the concrete experience of the thorn/stake; Paul is not saying that he is a weak or insipid or generally debilitated person. By "weaknesses" he means the specific sufferings incurred in the course of apostolic ministry (see the examples in 11:23-33).

32. Gk. χάρις.

33. Gk. γάρ.

his people is expressed in, and is inseparable from, his power. To be shown the one is to be given the other. But this power is "perfected," becomes a reality, in *weakness,* of which the thorn/stake "given" to Paul is a concrete example.

The second half of the couplet may well mirror — but so as to correct — the doctrine of the "superlative" apostles, namely, that God's power was brought to completion in the power of ecstatic experience, such as Paul could point to, but which he now discounts (v. 6). By that understanding it would be "power in power." Christ's power — as now imparted to him by the *risen* Lord — only arose out of his powerlessness in crucifixion. In the divine dispensation there had to be weakness (crucifixion) before there was power (resurrection). In the thinking of the triumphalist opponents, however, there is no crucifixion, no weakness, only a valuing of power (see on 2:14; 4:16-17). But the onset of the stake/thorn provoked Paul to pray, and, in all probability, to reflect on the weakness and powerlessness of Christ in crucifixion and the power of Christ in resurrection. In consequence the Lord told Paul that his resurrection power in this age is perfected in weakness, that is, in the weakness of the stake/thorn that is not taken away.

These words of Christ to Paul should not be limited in their application to Paul as an apostle (see on 3:18; 4:16–5:10) but apply to whatever experiences and circumstances of life render powerless the children of God (see on 12:19). The one thing denied to them, which is exactly what most people demand above all, is to control their own destiny. As children of Adam, despite such this-worldly instruments of power as they may wield — intellect, health, wealth, influence, or position — they do, sooner or later, become powerless and vulnerable. Upon such persons, who in their powerlessness — whether bodily, relational, financial, or structural — call out to the Lord, the grace of Christ is shown and the power of Christ rests. The words of the Lord spoken to Paul, then, are universally applicable. They do not, however, call for resignation, which is passive and impersonal, but for acceptance, which is active and obedient to the Lord, who, in response to our prayer, continues to say, "My grace is sufficient for you, for my power is made perfect in weakness."

9b-10 The conjunctions "Therefore . . . wherefore"[34] at the beginning of v. 9b and v. 10 respectively signal Paul's own responses to the Lord's reply to him (v. 9a). Because Christ's power is made perfect in weakness, (1) *therefore* he will all the more gladly boast in weaknesses. (2) *Wherefore* he takes pleasure in weaknesses.

34. Gk. οὖν . . . διό.

It should be noted that Paul does not boast in "weakness," that is, in feebleness. The plural "in my weaknesses" (v. 9b[35]) points to the sufferings "for Christ" listed in 11:23-33, whereas the "weakness," singular, of v. 9a, the stake/thorn "given" to him by God (v. 7), was the climactic example.

The words "I will boast *rather*"[36] of weaknesses sound a comparative note. To what is he preferring this "boasting"? In all probability he is recalling once more his flight to Paradise (vv. 4-5). This experience truly occurred; Paul would be a "fool" to deny it. But that experience did not make Paul "more" *(hyper)* than he is in reality, either as to the "weaknesses" people "see" in him or the word of God they "hear" from him (v. 6). Such an experience, astonishing though it doubtless was, does not accredit his apostleship. He will make nothing of it, that is, "boast of it." "Rather" than boast of his ecstatic, (non)-revelatory experience, he "will most gladly[37] boast" of his "weaknesses."

He then gives the purpose[38] for his preferred boast, namely, that Christ's power "may rest on"[39] him. Remarkably, this is the vocabulary of the tabernacle of the old covenant as applied to God "pitching his tent" with his people (Exod 40:34). In turn, this imagery is employed within the NT to describe (1) the incarnate life of the Word of God ("The Word became flesh and dwelt [i.e., 'pitched his tent'] among us" — John 1:14), and (2) God's future dwelling with his people (Rev 7:14; 12:12; 13:6; 21:3). In what has been described as a "bold metaphor,"[40] Paul teaches that Christ in his power "pitches his tent" with his saints in their weaknesses.[41] Ecstasy has all the appearances of divine power; but the reality is otherwise. Christ draws near to us, and gives his grace and power to us, in weakness.

In v. 10 Paul expresses his "acceptance of"[42] various difficulties, beginning with "in weaknesses," which is repeated from v. 9b and refers

---

35. Gk. ἐν ταῖς ἀσθενείαις μου, noting the ἐν, which is repeated in v. 10, "in weaknesses, in insults, in hardships, [in] difficulties." The use of ἐν + sufferings was prominent in sufferings listed in 6:4-7 and 11:26-27.

36. Gk. μᾶλλον.

37. Gk. ἥδιστα, "most gladly," the superlative of ἡδέως, "gladly."

38. Gk. ἵνα.

39. Gk. ἐπισκηνώσῃ ἐπ' represents a Semitic love of repetition — ἐπὶ . . . ἐπ[ί].

40. Plummer, 355.

41. *Contra* Furnish, 531, who points out that (1) the verb ἐπισκηνοῦν is found only here in the NT and not at all in the LXX, (2) the noun σκηνή is used in OT (LXX) passages, and (3) noting the rarity of ἐπισκηνοῦν may mean that it was taken over from the opponents. In view of the close similarity between ἐπισκηνοῦν and σκηνοῦν and the appearance of the latter in LXX Gen 13:12; Judg 5:17; 8:11; 1 Kings 8:12, it seems reasonable to see Paul's use of the word as evocative of the OT tabernacle imagery.

42. Gk. εὐδοκῶ; NIV, "delight in." According to Furnish, 531, the verb εὐδοκεῖν means "something less than 'take delight in'" but "something more than 'be content with,'" hence my "acceptance of."

specifically to the stake/thorn. Following "weaknesses" are: (1) "in insults"[43] — found only here in Paul's writings (possibly they refer to the scandalous treatment of him as a Roman citizen by Romans and as an Israelite by Jews — see 11:24-25), (2) "in hardships"[44] (lit. "necessities" — see on 6:4), (3) "in persecutions"[45] (as described in 11:24-25; cf. Rom 8:35), and (4) "[in] difficulties"[46] (lit. "tight corners"; cf. 6:4; the verb occurs in 4:8; 6:12).

Critical to v. 10 is the inferential "wherefore,"[47] which picks up from the immediately preceding[48] "I will boast . . . of my weaknesses," which, "on behalf of Christ,"[49] he accepts. The expression "*on behalf of Christ* I accept weaknesses, etc." must be read alongside "we beseech you *on behalf of Christ,* 'be reconciled to God' " (5:20). Because Christ is not physically present, in his place God "has given" the ministry and "entrusted" the word of reconciliation to the apostles (5:18-19). As Christ's ambassador and apostle, Paul "beseeches" in Christ's place and suffers in Christ's place, as this list of sufferings shows (cf. 4:8-9; 6:4-5; cf. 2:16). Christ's sufferings are replicated and historically extended in the sufferings or *weaknesses* of his apostle as he bids humankind "Be reconciled to God," and it is of these — as opposed to triumphalist "visions and revelations" — that Paul "boasts" (v. 9b) and these that he "accepts."

A connection should also be made between "weaknesses . . . *on behalf of* Christ" and his words "be spent *on behalf of* your souls," a few verses later (see on v. 15). In both cases the preposition *hyper* is used. As apostle of divine reconciliation Paul suffers on behalf of the One he represents — though in a qualitatively different way (see on 5:21) — and he does so for the sake of those to whom he ministers. The keyword of the triumphalist "superlative"

---

43. Gk. ἐν ὕβρεσιν. See 1 Thess 2:2 for the verb ὑβρίζειν: "we had . . . been shamefully treated in Philippi."

44. Gk. ἐν ἀνάγκαις.

45. Gk. ἐν διωγμοῖς.

46. Gk. στενοχωρίαις.

47. Gk. διό.

48. *Contra* Martin, 422, who sees διό as connected with the διό of v. 7.

49. Gk. ὑπὲρ Χριστοῦ; NIV, "for Christ's sake." Furnish, 531, places ὑπὲρ Χριστοῦ — although coming at the end of the list — with the verb εὐδοκῶ at the beginning. He takes ὑπὲρ Χριστοῦ with the verb, not with Paul's hardships. In his view, "*because* Christ's power is made present in weakness," Paul is content *for Christ's sake.* However, it is better to connect ὑπὲρ Χριστοῦ with Paul's weaknesses — "I am content, therefore, in weaknesses . . . on behalf of Christ." Moreover, ὑπὲρ Χριστοῦ is representational, i.e., Paul's "weaknesses" in ministry are "on Christ's behalf," "in Christ's place." This important phrase also appears at 5:20, where Paul beseeches, "ὑπὲρ Χριστοῦ, 'be reconciled to God,' " a parallel not noticed by, e.g., Furnish, 531, or Martin, 422. In passing, a distinction should be noticed between διὰ Ἰησοῦν — 4:5, 11 ("on account of Jesus") and ὑπὲρ Χριστοῦ — 5:20; 12:10 ("for," or "in place of Christ").

apostles (11:5; 12:11) is *hyper* ("more than," "above") Paul. It is Paul's keyword, too. Madman that he is, his "weaknesses" are "more than" theirs (11:23), and those "weaknesses" replicate Christ's sufferings, and do so on behalf of the churches. His nontriumphalist, servant ministry is again undergirded. He is their "slave" on account of *(dia)* Jesus (4:5).

Paul concludes the two parts of vv. 9b-10 with an aphorism: "When I am weak, then I am strong."[50] Such strength is not automatic to weakness. Rather, weakness (as of the unremoved stake/thorn — v. 7) creates the human context of helplessness and utter vulnerability in which Paul the minister of Christ pleaded with the risen, powerful Lord — who himself was once utterly "weak," "sin-laden," and "poor" (13:4; 5:21; 8:9) in achieving our reconciliation with God — who is now strong in resurrected power to give his grace and power to the one who calls out to him.

c. The "Fool's Speech": Epilogue (12:11-13)

11 *I have made a fool of myself, but you drove me to it. I ought to have been commended by you, for I am not in the least inferior to the "super-apostles," even though I am nothing.* 12 *The things that mark an apostle — signs, wonders and miracles — were done among you with great perseverance.* 13 *How were you inferior to the other churches, except that I was never a burden to you? Forgive me this wrong!*

In these few verses Paul applies the "Fool's Speech" begun at 11:1. There is a reproachful tone to be heard here, similar to 11:7, 19; the Corinthians, who ought to have commended him, have forced him to speak like a "fool" in praising himself. Nonetheless, he is not inferior to the "superlative" apostles, God having wrought the signs of the apostle through him in Corinth. Because he is not inferior, the Corinthians have been at no disadvantage to other churches in "signs, wonders and miracles" of divine origin, attesting his apostolicity. Only in one respect have they been worse off; he has not been a financial burden to them!

The repetition of aorist tense verbs in the successive verses ("I am [not] inferior. . . . [The signs of the apostle] were wrought. . . . [How] were you inferior?"), each signifying singular action, points strikingly to Paul's historic ministry in the Achaian capital. Paul is focusing the attention of the Corinthians on the fact and manner of the founding of the church in that place.

Here we see through a window into Paul's apostolic ministry in

---

50. A remote parallel may be seen in Philo's comment on what Moses learned at the burning bush: "Your weakness is your power" (*On the Life of Moses* 1.69).

Corinth: (1) God's working "the signs of the apostle" attesting the apostolicity of Paul to the Corinthians, and (2) Paul laboring to support himself that he might not be a "burden" to them (see on 11:12). Both (1) and (2) mark the turning of the aeons, the dawn of the day of salvation (6:2) in which the apostle had a unique and unrepeatable role.

11 Here Paul completes the ring of references to "foolishness," begun at the opening of the "Fool's Speech" (11:1; cf. 11:16 [twice], 17, 19, 23; 12:6). This verse consists of (1) a reproach to the Corinthians ("I have become a fool"), as explained[1] by (2) his reason ("For I ought to have been commended by you"), followed by (3) an amplification ("For in nothing am I less than the "superlative" apostles).

The reproach, which is deeply felt, is specifically directed from Paul to the Corinthians, as the emphatic pronouns indicate: "It was *you* who compelled *me,* for *I* ought to have been commended by *you.*"[2] Poignant is his "I ought — I had a *right*[3] — to have been commended by you." Paul needed no letter of recommendation; the Corinthians were Christ's "letter," known and read by everybody (3:2; 10:7; cf. 6:4). They themselves were the Lord's commendation (cf. 10:18). Paul ought not to have been forced to speak as a fool in demonstrating his apostolate.[4]

Rather, the Corinthians have been drawn aside to these "superlative" apostles in preference to Paul (see on 11:5). In continuing his reproach to the Corinthians, Paul ironically mirrors the "superior"/"inferior" vocabulary of these opponents: "In nothing was I inferior to these 'superlative' apostles."[5] They are *hyper* and Paul *hyster,* a claim that Paul in no way concedes, as he will proceed to demonstrate in the next verse. The aorist tense of the verb "was I inferior," being singular in import, points to the time of Paul's sojourn in Corinth.[6]

---

1. The explanatory γάρ appears twice in this verse.
2. So Plummer, 357; Gk. ὑμεῖς με . . . ἐγώ . . . ὑφ' ὑμῶν.
3. Gk. ὤφειλον.
4. It is possible that Paul's "foolish boasting" has roots in contemporary cultural convention. Appeal is made to Hellenistic authors, e.g., Plutarch, "On Praising Oneself Inoffensively," 1, and Livy, *History* 33.49.6, to locate patterns that might assist in locating Paul's presentation. From these authors it appears that self-praise is justified when the truth must be told in self-defense where false accusations have been made. But it is less likely that Paul had read such authors than that he is reflecting unwritten culture found in them. See further the note to 11:1.
5. Gk. οὐδὲν γὰρ ὑστέρησα τῶν ὑπερλίαν ἀποστόλων.
6. The contrast is meanful only in regard to "superlative" apostles such as those who, like Paul, have visited Corinth. This is relevant to the question whether the "super-lative" apostles and the "false apostles" are to be differentiated or equated. Those who argue for their differentiation propose that the "superlative" apostles are the preeminent, Jerusalem-based apostles. But the inference here is that the "superlative" apostles are now

Nonetheless, Paul must immediately qualify this comment. This he does by repeating the emphatic negative, "in no single thing."[7] He began the sentence, "in *nothing* am I inferior . . . ;" he now concludes, "even though I am nothing." To be sure, he is inferior "in no single thing," yet — in all humility — he is "no single thing." This qualification flows into the next verse, where its real significance is seen. In fact, "the signs of the apostle" mark him out as an apostle, making him in fact superior to those he calls "superlative" apostles. Thus the disclaimer is a veiled claim in the form of litotes (understatement); in saying that he is nothing, at the same time he is saying that he is everything. Nonetheless, he upholds the canons of Christian humility (cf. 10:1), and as he proceeds to infer, it is God, not he, who validates his ministry because God is the source of what he does.

12 Paul proceeds at once to demonstrate how he was simultaneously "in nothing inferior" while he himself was "nothing." He was "in nothing inferior" because, as he now reminds them, the "signs of an apostle" occurred in Corinth. But he is also "nothing" because these were performed by God in the context of Paul's great endurance of weaknesses.

The initial "Truly" or "Indeed"[8] introduces the explanation for the final part of the previous verse. Paul is not inferior in anything to the "super-lative" apostles, though he himself is nothing, precisely because he is the instrument of God, no less. This is made clear by the (divine) passive of the verb "were done"[9]; *God* wrought the "signs" of which Paul speaks. Moreover, the three terms amplifying "the signs of the apostle" are in the dative case, indicating instrumental use, as if to say "*by* signs, *by* wonders, *by* miracles"[10] did *God* attest Paul's apostleship in Corinth. It is because God was the effective means of these "signs" that Paul can say (v. 11), paradoxically, that (1) he is "not inferior," and that (2) he is "nothing."

The carefully chosen words "the signs of the apostle" suggest that there was a class of persons known as "apostles" who were demonstrated to be such by "the signs."[11] Thus "the signs" accredit Paul as truly "an apostle,"[12] one of the apostles, that unique body from the era closest to Christ,

---

in Corinth, in which case they cannot be identified as apostolic leaders in Jerusalem. These men have come to Corinth, and they are the same as the "false apostles" (11:13), under a different name. (See on 11:5.)

7. Gk. οὐδέν.

8. Gk. μέν. For the concessive use μέν of see A. T. Robertson, *Grammar,* 1151.

9. Gk. κατειργάσθη. See also Rom 15:18.

10. Gk. σημείοις . . . τέρασιν . . . δυνάμεσιν.

11. Gk. τὰ σημεῖα.

12. The articular noun ἀποστόλου refers to the whole class of apostles; so A. T. Robertson, *Grammar,* 408. Furnish, 553, renders σημεῖα τοῦ ἀποστόλου as "The Apostolic Signs."

who, along with the prophets, were the foundation of the new covenant people of God (Eph 2:20). "The signs," which are miracles pointing to God as their author,[13] are the demonstration that Paul was precisely that, one of the select group of the apostles. He is exactly what the professed "apostles of Christ" now come to Corinth are not. They are "pseudo," *false* apostles (11:13); he truly is an apostle. "The signs" establish that. His present reference to "signs, wonders and miracles" in Corinth was not, apparently, a point of superiority claimed by the "superlative" apostles. Rather, Paul, having denied any "inferiority" to them (12:11), can merely point to his apostolic miracles at the time he first came to Corinth to clinch outright, and without further argument, his claim to apostolicity. On this understanding, Paul's miracles — and the "superlative" apostles' lack of them — were an indisputable demonstration of his authentic apostleship.

But this claim is incomplete. To it Paul adds the very significant qualification that such "signs" were wrought (by God) "in all — preferably, *utmost* — endurance"[14] (see on 6:4). The divinely wrought miracles occurred in the context of gospel ministry (cf. 1:19) and therefore of "weaknesses" (as listed in 11:23-33; cf. 12:9-10), and thus of "endurance" in the face of affliction. Miracles were one part of the badge of the apostle; endurance was the other. Thus the apostle replicates and continues the pattern of the Master who sent him; he, too, worked "signs" — though to an infinitely greater degree — with "endurance" in circumstances of suffering. Against the "superlative" apostles who may have thought that power alone accredited them as "apostles . . . ministers of Christ" (see on 11:15, 23; 12:2-4), Paul asserts that power — *God's* power — is exercised in weakness.

Such "signs" were wrought . . . among you,"[15] that is, in Corinth. The Corinthians to whom he now writes must have witnessed these,[16] a further reason for his pained disclosure of the previous verse, "I ought to have been commended by you." Thus the contrast between Paul and the "superlative" apostles explicit in vv. 11 and 13 must be between Paul and "apostles" who also have come to Corinth, that is, the "false apostles" (see on 11:13). Clearly, the "superlative" apostles are the "false apostles." The other hypothesis, that

13. See K. H. Rengstorf, *TDNT* 7.258-60. The suggestion that "the signs of the apostle" include, e.g., missionary conversions or a Christlike life (e.g., by Martin, 434-35) is overturned by the explicatory triad that follows: "signs, wonders, miracles."

14. Gk. ἐν πάσῃ ὑπομονῇ (NIV, "with great perseverance").

15. Gk. ἐν ὑμῖν.

16. Here is clear evidence that God used Paul as an instrument of miraculous works. To make this statement in an almost gratuitous manner to readers who were, to say the least, unsympathetic is strong reason for believing that such miracles did occur. No one knew better than Paul that to make claims that were untrue would be a sure way to discredit him as a charlatan.

the "superlative" apostles were the distant apostles of Jerusalem,[17] makes no sense here.

Although Acts 18 records no miracle of Paul during his sojourn in Corinth, the amplifying phrase "signs, wonders and miracles" demands that a significant manifestation of miraculous activity occurred there at the hands of the apostle. The same three terms, "signs, wonders and miracles," are also found together in Acts 2:22; 2 Thess 2:9; and Heb 2:4 (cf. Rom 15:19). "Signs and wonders" is a recurring phrase in the OT, often in connection with the great saving event of the Exodus.[18] To this common OT duo Paul adds "deeds of power," a term he uses elsewhere for miracles (1 Cor 12:10, 28, 29; Gal 3:5). The effect of giving this triad as "the signs of the apostle" is to tie the apostle to God's great redemptive event under the new covenant, focused on Christ's death and resurrection. "Signs and wonders" mark the Exodus; "signs, wonders and miracles" mark the death and resurrection of Jesus as at the first Easter and its apostolic proclamation.

13 Now appealing to their firsthand experience of "the signs of an apostle," Paul asks, "For[19] how were you inferior[20] to the other churches. . . ?" Once more the aorist verb, signifying singular action, points to Paul's historic sojourn in Corinth (cf. other aorists in v. 11 — ". . . was I inferior," and in v. 12 — "were wrought"). "The signs of the apostle" were wrought by God in "the other churches," including, and to no lesser degree, the church of Corinth (cf. 1:19).

His very question makes it clear that in regard to the divine outpouring of supernatural attestation of the apostle, the Corinthians did not come behind the other churches. Paul's line of reason is apparent. "If you were not inferior" in "the signs of the apostle," as clearly you were not, then I am not "inferior" (v. 11) in apostolicity, despite what the "superlative" apostles say and some of you are tending to believe (see on v. 11; 11:5).

Verses 12-13, when read with 1:19; 4:5; 5:20 (and 11:4), give a clear picture of apostolic pioneer evangelism in Corinth, marking the dawn of the day of salvation (6:2). Here, on the one hand, is the apostolic proclamation of the Son of God in fulfillment of all the promises of God accompanied by the anointing of the Holy Spirit (1:19-21; cf. on 3:3; 5:5; 11:4; 13:14); here, on the other, is the attestation from heaven of "the signs of the apostle — signs,

---

17. As, e.g., in Barrett, 320.

18. As, e.g., in Exod 7:3; cf. 1:9, 10; 3:20; 8:23; 10:1, 2; 15:11; Num 14:21; Deut 4:34; 6:22; 7:19; 26:8; 29:3; Josh 3:5; 24:17; Ps 135:9; Neh 9:10; Jer 32:21. See further D. A. Carson, "Signs and Wonders," 89-118.

19. Gk. γάρ.

20. Gk. ἡσσώθητε, from ἡσσόομαι ("I am defeated"); this verb is found only here in the NT. "Less favored" (RSV) indicates that a different verb from v. 11 ("was . . . inferior") is being used.

wonders, miracles." And all the while the apostle works to support himself so as not to burden the Corinthians, to which he now turns with powerful irony.

There is indeed an exception in one area of "inferiority." He concludes his question: "*except* that I myself [stated with emphasis[21]] was not a burden to you?" In regard to financial support Paul is emphatic. He did not "burden"[22] the Corinthians, though others — the "false apostles" (11:13, 20) — we infer, have done that. Here is the one place — or the second (he did not abuse them, either; 11:20-21) — where his ministry is inferior to theirs!

He completes the verse — and, indeed, the entire "Fool's Speech" — with the heavily ironical supplication, "Forgive me this injustice."[23] This is closely parallel with the earlier, "Was it a sin for me to lower myself. . . ?" (see on 11:7). Since he "lowered himself" in self-supporting labor and received assistance from the Macedonian churches, the Corinthians felt that Paul had acted "unjustly" against them. While Paul had his own personal and theological reasons for refusing their support (see on 11:12), the Corinthians felt that it was their place to support him. Perhaps they felt demeaned by the humiliation of his labor. Culturally, the visiting rhetorician would assume a patronizing role, and the Corinthians appear to have been offended that he would not follow such conventions.

As is his method, Paul introduces into the end of a section a theme that he will pick up and expand upon in the new section,[24] in this case that he has not been nor will he be "a burden" to them.

C. PREPARATION FOR THE IMMINENT THIRD VISIT (12:14–13:14)

1. I Will Not Be a Burden to You (12:14-19)

> 14 *Now I am ready to visit you for the third time,*[1] *and I will not be a burden to you, because what I want is not your possessions but you. After all, children should not have to save up for their parents, but*

21. Gk. αὐτὸς ἐγώ (see also on 10:1).
22. Gk. κατενάρκησα — the same verb as in 11:9 (q.v.).
23. Gk. χαρίσασθέ μοι τὴν ἀδικίαν ταύτην. For ἀδικίαν the NIV has "wrong." The irony may be seen in that Paul himself was "wronged" (ἀδικηθέντος) in Corinth by a Corinthian man, and the Corinthians had been slow to redress the injustice (7:12; cf. 2:5, 10, 11). Note that ἀδικία is used elsewhere for moral wickedness (e.g., Rom 1:18, 29).
24. For other examples see how 2:12 leads into 2:14ff.; 7:4 into 7:5; and 7:16 into 8:8-15.
1. Gk. τρῖτον τοῦτο is doubtless right order (so, e.g., ℵ A B F G), though some MSS reverse the order or omit τοῦτο.

parents for their children 15 *So I will very gladly spend for you everything I have and expend myself as well. If[2] I love[3] you more, will you
love me less?* 16 *Be that as it may, I have not been a burden to you.
Yet, crafty fellow that I am, I caught you by trickery!* 17 *Did I exploit
you through any of the men I sent you?* 18 *I urged Titus to go to you
and I sent our brother with him. Titus did not exploit you, did he? Did
we not act in the same spirit and follow the same course?* 19 *Have you
been thinking all along[4] that we have been defending ourselves to you?
We have been speaking in the sight of God as those in Christ; and
everything we do, dear friends, is for your strengthening.*

The subject is now money, that is, payment for Paul's ministry, and two issues
are canvassed. One is his persistent refusal to be paid, which is inappropriate
for him; he is their father and he provides for them, not they him. The other
is the cynical view of some that Paul does receive money, but through the
back door, via his coworkers.

This passage is deeply interpersonal and, indeed, animated (1) with
references to "I . . . you" in every verse, (2) the emphatic "I" appearing in vv.
15-16, and (3) no less than five rhetorical questions (vv. 15, 17, 18 [twice], 19).

It is evident that Paul's policy of self-support by manual labor was
resented by many Corinthians, as is evident from Paul's echoed replies ("Did I
sin?" — 11:7; "Forgive me this wrong" — v. 13; "Do I love you less?" —
v. 15; cf. 11:11). But Paul was their father-provider (v. 14; cf. 11:2; 6:13), who
will spend himself for them (v. 15), not their "client," to "be patronized" in the
conventions of that culture; it was important to follow the appropriate pattern. At
the same time the more cynical opinion was expressed that, in reality, Paul was
cunningly receiving their money *indirectly* through his associates while appearing
to be self-supported (vv. 16b-18). Thus, he (1) reassures them that he does not
seek what is theirs but them (v. 14), and then (2) puts three questions to them (vv.
17-18) that effectively expose the hollowness of their suspicions (vv. 17-18).

The final verse (v. 19) is an interim conclusion, not only of the section,
but of the entire letter. Paul is not merely writing in self-defense, as a contemporary apologist might. Rather, he writes "before God" and "for the sake
of" the "upbuilding" of the Corinthians. That verse, when read with 13:10,
is very helpful in understanding Paul's purpose in writing the present letter.

---

2. There is stronger support for εἰ, "if" (p[46] ℵ*), than for εἰ καί, "even though"
(ℵ[2] D).

3. There is stronger support for the participle ἀγαπῶν (p[46] ℵ[2] B D G) than for
ἀγαπῶ (ℵ* K L), though it is difficult to choose between them.

4. Although the TR reads the easier πάλιν, the more difficult reading πάλαι is
preferred; it is well supported (p[46] ℵ*, etc.).

14 There is an air of finality as well as of anticipation in the formal-sounding opening words, "Behold,[5] I am preparing to come to you for the third[6] [time]." At the same time the sentence flows directly out of v. 13. As he has not burdened them in the past, so he will not burden them during the third visit. Two statements follow, each in explanation[7] of its predecessor. First, "I will not burden [you], *for*" it is you yourself I care about, not your money. Besides, he further explains, *"for* I seek not yours' but you. *For* children ought not lay up treasure for parents, but parents for children."

Paul's single most important reason for writing this letter was to admonish the Corinthians in advance of a prospective third visit, so that he would not have to exercise his God-given authority when he came (cf. 13:10). The letter is dotted with references to this critical final visit, appearing in the early chapters (2:1, 3), in the later chapters (9:4; 10:6), but increasingly from this point to the conclusion of the letter (12:20, 21; 13:1, 2, 10).

In each such reference Paul draws attention to some action or attitude he wishes the Corinthians to address prior to his coming. In this case it is their attitude to Paul and money, especially his not taking their money as support, but now asking for money for the poor in Jerusalem. Here, and in the verses following, we hear again his determination "not to burden [cf. v. 13; see on 11:9] [you]." He would not accept the Corinthians' support. The reasons given earlier are, presumably, still in mind, that (1) he will not "burden" them (vv. 13, 16; cf. 11:9), and that (2) he does not wish to give the opponents — who did receive money from the Corinthians (11:20; cf. 2:17) — the opportunity to claim that they and he operated on the same supported basis (see on 11:12). In regard to the latter, Paul saw his ministry as a matter of simple obedience to God's apostolic call. To make the gospel "free of charge" by his own self-support was fundamental to Paul (see on 11:7); he would not allow self-professed apostles to drag him to their level by accepting payment.

As an explanation of his determination to support himself, he declares:

> For I seek not yours
> but you.

In explaining his earlier policy, Paul appears to be giving a sidelong glance at his opponents, who did, indeed, seek the money of the Corinthians (11:20; cf. 2:17). Instead, unlike the intruders, Paul seeks *the Corinthians* — their own

---

5. Gk. ἰδού (see also 5:17; 6:2, 9; 7:11).

6. Gk. τρίτον τοῦτο. By its position at the head of the sentence, τρίτον is emphatic. τρίτον τοῦτο is preferably taken with (1) ἐλθεῖν rather than with (2) ἑτοίμως ἔχω. The emphasis is on the visit rather than the preparation for the visit.

7. Each introduced by γάρ, "for."

personal allegiance ("your souls" — v. 15) to Christ and to himself (cf. the Macedonians, who "gave themselves first to the Lord, then to us . . ." — 8:5). In his apostolic ministry Paul is a "slave" to those to whom he preaches Jesus as Lord, seeking them, opening wide his heart to them, in order that, having given themselves to the Lord, they will also give themselves to the apostle (3:2; 4:5; 6:11-13).

This verse, like others in this section, is dominated by Paul's address to the Corinthians in the second person plural pronoun ("I am ready to visit *you* . . . I will not burden [*you*] . . . I seek not *yours* but *you*"). By this very form of speech Paul is seeking their reconciliation with him ahead of the pending third visit. Such a sentiment is explained by his homely proverb of parents' obligation[8] to "lay up treasure for"[9] children, not vice versa.[10] We are reminded of the apostle's role as the father-betrother of his daughter (the church) to her husband (the Lord — see on 11:2; cf. 6:13). He has united them to Christ; he will provide for them, not they for him. Such is his unique "paternal" role as apostle in the eschatological schema.

15   Still using the language of money (cf. vv. 12-13), Paul elaborates on his parental relationship with them. By his emphatic beginning, "But I,"[11] he underlines his distinctive role in relationship to them. "On your behalf,"[12] as he assures them, he will "gladly" spend [himself] and be spent.[13] But the pain for Paul lies not only in his being spent for them, but in their lack of reciprocity (see on 6:13). Whereupon he asks, plaintively, "If I love you more, am I loved less?"

Here the conflict of models regarding Paul's financial support comes to the surface. In keeping with cultural norms they have patronage expectations that Paul, by his independence of them, has thwarted (see on 11:7). They conclude that Paul does not love them (cf. 11:11, "Because I do not love you?").[14] But Paul has an eschatological outlook and thus a "paternal" view of his relationship with them. They are his children through the gospel. He,

---

8. Gk. ὀφείλει.

9. Gk. θησαυρίζειν, "to set money aside," as for an inheritance.

10. Nonetheless, the commandment requires children to honor their parents (Exod 20:12), which Jesus interpreted to include making appropriate financial provision (Mark 7:9-13). Paul's appeal to obligation finds many echoes in the ethical writings of that era, e.g., ". . . in the natural order of things (νόμος φυσέως) children are the heirs of their fathers" (Philo, *On the Life of Moses* 2, 245).

11. Gk. ἐγὼ δέ.

12. Gk. ὑπὲρ τῶν ψυχῶν ὑμῶν.

13. Gk. δαπανήσω καὶ ἐκδαπανηθήσομαι. Paul sometimes uses words in pairs like this, where the second word intensifies the first (see also 1:13; 4:8).

14. Paul also expresses his love to them in 2:4 and 8:7, and — emphatically — in 11:11.

the father, has betrothed his daughter to the yet-to-appear Lord (11:2). As father, it is his role to provide "treasure" for them, not they for him (v. 14). It is important that the Corinthians change their way of thinking about their relationship with him. He is not dependent on them; they are dependent on him. Let them think in child-parent — not patron-client — terms. Self-support, making the gospel free of charge, is an insignia of his apostleship.

Here Paul continues with the financial image of the previous verse ("treasure . . . spend . . . be spent"). Speaking metaphorically of the toilsome labors of self-support and in ministry to them (see on 11:7-11), Paul will "spend . . . be spent." As their father — begetter, betrother, provider — he will do this "very gladly"[15]; there is no resentment on his part. Did the Corinthians think there was?

Appropriately, this verse, together with other verses in this section, is very personal in character. Paul commences with the emphatic "I," twice addressing the readers directly ("*I* will very gladly spend and be spent for *your* souls. . . . If I love *you* more, am *I* loved less?"). Let the Corinthians understand that his self-support by manual labor is not motivated by a lack of love, as if to demean them. To the contrary, his sacrifice expresses the depth of his love (cf. 2:4; 8:7; 11:11).

Paul's vicarious note should not be missed: "I will very gladly . . . be spent for *(hyper)* your souls [i.e., 'selves']." As in his ministry Paul suffers *for* ("in place of," "on behalf of") Christ (see on v. 10), so Paul is "spent" *for* them. As an apostle of Christ, on Christ's behalf Paul called on his hearers to "Be reconciled to God" (see also 5:20) and is, thereby, "spent" in "weaknesses" for the people. In his ministry Paul replicates the sufferings of Christ as he gives himself for the people. Paul makes no hint that he saves people, as Christ does; nonetheless, his sufferings, though nonpropitiatory, are in continuity with those of Christ. Such sufferings, indeed, validate his ministry as a ministry of Christ, as opposed to that of the triumphalist "superlative" apostles.

16 One might have expected Paul to let go of this issue with the plaintive question that concluded v. 15. But all has not been said. Apparently some have suggested that the collection is simply his way of getting money from them but deviously. The verse itself is in two sentences. In the first, he points back (v. 15) to the subject of his love for them, on which he comments, "Be that as it may,"[16] adding emphatically[17] that he had not "burdened" them. In the second, he echoes back a different Corinthian criticism regarding money, that, being a crafty fellow, he had taken them by guile, a criticism he will address in the next two verses.

---

15. Gk. ἥδιστα, "most gladly" (cf. v. 9), superlative of ἡδέως.

16. Gk. ἔστω δέ, where δέ is a transitional, not an adversative particle. The idiom is used to express a point on which writer and readers are in at least provisional agreement.

17. As indicated by the emphatic ἐγώ.

Paul's words in the previous verse can only mean that they see his self-support as evidence of his lack of love to them (v. 15; cf. 11:11), the reverse of which, however, is true. Thus Paul responds, "Be that as it may [whatever you may think about my love for you (v. 15), let me say — Paul is emphatic], I have not burdened you." He will not (vv. 13, 14), and he has not. The verb "weigh down,"[18] referring to ships' ballast (cf. 1:8), is even more definite than the verb "burdened"[19] in vv. 13 and 14 (which repeat his earlier words, "I did not burden anyone" — 11:9). Once more the strongly interpersonal, conversational character of this passage is expressed ("*I* [emphatic] have not burdened *you*").

The second sentence changes Paul's tack.[20] He now echoes a cynical view, as opposed to rebuffed feelings over his financial independence, held by some Corinthians. It is "since"[21] Paul is a "crafty fellow" that he has "caught[22] [lit. "taken"] [them] by trickery."

This vocabulary is not new; earlier (4:2) Paul had specifically renounced "deception" and the "corrupting" of the word of God.[23] What is this "cunning"[24] of which some accuse him? The verses following supply the answer, namely, that Paul's delegates received support from the Corinthians ("took advantage" of them — vv. 17, 18). On this view, Paul had stood on the high moral ground of self-support by manual labor, while having money slipped into his back pocket by Titus and others that they had received from the Corinthians. By appearing to be self-supporting he has "taken" them, that is, gained a moral advantage over them.[25] Paul answers this assertion of craftiness over the next two verses, both of which are balancing rhetorical questions about those who have come to them as Pauline envoys.

17 Paul first asks a rhetorical question, stated in general terms (cf.

18. Gk. κατεβάρησα, "weighed down." See ἐβάρη in 11:9.

19. Gk. καταναρκεῖν, "to burden." See on 11:9.

20. The introductory ἀλλά introduces a contrastive statement.

21. Gk. ὑπάρχων πανοῦργος, a participle of causal meaning, "since," "being," which, when taken with πανοῦργος, means "being by constitution crafty" (Hughes, 464). πανοῦργος an adjective, which appears nowhere else in the NT, means "unscrupulous," "cunning." The noun πανουργία appears at 2:2; 11:2.

22. Gk. ἔλαβον, "taking advantage of someone for one's own gain" (as in 11:20).

23. In 4:2 Paul renounced πανουργία and δολοῦντες τὸν λόγον τοῦ θεοῦ. His echoing of the Corinthians' charge of ὑπάρχων πανοῦργος and "taking" them δόλῳ, "by trickery," in 12:16, terms that are so close to those of 4:2, suggest that the earlier reference relates to the matter that is being expanded upon in this context. The unity of the letter is supported by the appearance in different sections of cognates of these two words.

24. It was through the serpent's πανουργία, "cunning," that Eve was deceived (11:3).

25. I see no evidence here that the Corinthians accused Paul of establishing the collection for personal gain. But see on 8:20.

the specific example following — v. 18), but so structured as to expect a negative reply.[26] Thus (literally):

> Any of those whom   I sent to you,
>   through him did I defraud you?

The answer is emphatically "no," as the Corinthians well know. Paul could not frame the question so confidently unless it were so.

Again we note the personal character of the interchange ("I sent to *you* . . . I defraud *you?*"; see generally vv. 14-19). The grammar of the sentence is pointed: (1) The pronominal structure "any of those whom . . . through *him*"[27] focuses the Corinthian readers on *each* person of the number whom Paul sent to them, but on one in particular (Titus). (2) The perfect tense, "sent,"[28] means "I have sent," indicating Paul's initial dispatch of [an] envoy[s], followed by others. (3) The contrastive singular event in the aorist tense "get the better of," "take advantage over,"[29] when combined with the pronouns, asks, in effect, "Of the *many* whom I have sent to you, did *any* one of them on any one occasion *ever* take advantage of you?"

Paul's reply evidently mirrors the charge some are making. "True, he does not receive money from us directly. But what about the money he receives from us indirectly, *through* his envoys who have come here?" On this hypothesis Paul's representatives, unlike him, were provided for by them, but — for his defense to carry weight — their support would have been minimal.

18 Paul now specifies what was expressed more generally in v. 17. The present verse is in three sentences: (1) The generalized question of the previous verse ("any *one* of those . . . through *him?*") is now made a specific statement ("I appealed to *Titus* and am sending with *him* the brother"), as the basis for (2) a rhetorical question expecting a negative reply[30] ("Did Titus take advantage of you?"), and (3) two consequent rhetorical questions expecting positive replies[31] ("Did we not walk in the same spirit, follow the same steps?").

Their questions in the previous and present verses demand replies that

---

26. Introduced by Gk. μή. Likewise the next question, in the first part of v. 18.

27. Gk. τινα ὧν . . . δι' αὐτοῦ. We note that τινα is an accusative of respect and that ὧν is to be interpreted as τουτῶν ὧν, "of those whom." Thus, "with respect to any one of those whom. . . ." The word τινα is emphatically located at the beginning, to challenge the readers to name a single envoy of Paul who took advantage of them.

28. Gk. ἀπέσταλκα. Barrett, 325, "those whom I have from time to time sent," is preferred to Furnish, 559, who sees this as an aoristic perfect, "I have sent."

29. Gk. ἐπλεονέκτησα. See also 2:11; 7:2.

30. Introduced by Gk. μήτι.

31. Each introduced by Gk. οὐ.

(1) Titus did not take advantage of them, and that (2) Paul has behaved as blamelessly toward them as Titus has. Titus is cited because Paul had "sent" him to Corinth on at least two earlier occasions prior[32] to his current visit bearing 2 Corinthians and seeking to complete the collection. There had been ample opportunity for Titus to "take advantage of" the Corinthians. Titus, however, was known to be a man of considerable stature as a Christian leader (see on 7:15).

Both answers to his questions leave the Corinthians with little alternative but to agree that Paul did not abuse his relationship with them, whether indirectly "through" Titus (see on v. 17) or directly on Paul's own account. Paul's care to assert his and Titus's probity in financial matters establishes an important model for pastors for subsequent generations.

Paul's dispatch of the brother "with Titus" to Corinth poses an important question. Upon that answer hangs the question of the unity of chapters 10–13 with chapters 1–9. Specifically, if Paul's dispatch of Titus, referred to here, is the same as that mentioned earlier (8:6, 18), then there are grounds for believing the present verse belongs to a later letter.

In our view the passages in question (8:6, 17-18; 12:18) point to one visit. In both chapters 8 and 12 Paul (1) "appealed" to Titus,[33] and (2) dispatched with him "the brother."[34] Thus there can be little doubt that chapter 8:6, 18 and 12:18 refer to that visit to Corinth of the renowned brother with Titus which Paul initiated, at which they delivered canonical 2 Corinthians and during which they attempted to bring to completion the collection ahead of the arrival of Paul.

Does that mean that 12:18 belongs to a separate and later letter from the passage in which 8:6, 18 appeared? Certainly, the aorist, understood as a completed action tense, "I sent [with[35]] . . . Titus," would readily support such a view. But the earlier aorist reference (8:18) cannot mean "we sent" but "we[36] are sending[37] . . . Titus" (see also 8:22), an epistolary aorist[38] demanded by the context and so rendered by the translations. These earlier references employing the aorists in an epistolary manner point to the prospective "sending" of the brother with Titus to Corinth. The historic use of the

---

32. The first to establish the collection (8:6, 10 — and deliver the "Previous Letter"?), and the second to bear the "Severe Letter" (7:6, 7, 13, 14, 15).

33. Both references are aorist: 8:6, infinitive (παρακαλέσαι); 12:18, indicative (παρεκάλεσα).

34. In 12:18 Paul can omit reference to the second unnamed delegate ("our brother") since (1) the former brother is so "famous," and (2) the "famous" brother is specifically linked "with" Titus, whereas the other brother is not so linked (see on 8:18).

35. Gk. συναπέστειλα.

36. Since Paul regularly — often inconsistently — switches between "I" and "we" throughout this letter (e.g., 7:2-4), nothing should be made of the discrepancy here.

37. Gk. συνεπέμψαμεν.

38. With an epistolary aorist the form is aorist but the meaning is present.

aorists, "I urged" and "I sent [with],"[39] in 12:18, however, when aspectivally understood, suggest the now completed dispatch to and arrival in Corinth of the renowned brother with Titus.[40] On this reading of the contexts of the two passages 8:6, 18, 22 and 12:18, we conclude that they belong to the same letter, which has been delivered and which the Corinthians are now reading.[41]

The rhetorical question about Titus that follows and that is also expressed in the aorist, "Did Titus take advantage[42] of you?" could refer to a past visit (see above) or to the present visit. Either way the answer is that Titus has not taken advantage of them. To that Paul adds a further question, driving the point home, "Did we not walk in the same spirit;[43] follow in the same footsteps?" Titus they know well — better, indeed, than Paul; as Paul's envoy he has made frequent visits to Corinth, including in the immediate past. As he had not taken advantage of them, no more had Paul. The cynical view that Paul is a cunning man who has appeared to be self-supporting while receiving assistance all the while through his associates (v. 16) is thus rebutted.

19 In a rather more personal tone, addressing them as "beloved,"[44] Paul now asks a question and gives an answer. Have *they*[45] been thinking throughout the reading[46] of this letter that Paul has been defending himself to them?[47] Despite their possible impressions to the contrary, Paul assures them that he has not been doing this, at least not solely or ultimately. Solemnly he assures them that he has been speaking "before God," but[48] that everything he has said has been for their "upbuilding."

39. Gk. παρεκάλεσα . . . συναπέστειλα. . . .

40. See on 8:6.

41. *Contra,* e.g., Furnish, 559, who notices that παρακαλεῖν (8:6) is used in regard to a prospective mission to Corinth and thinks that παρεκάλεσα (12:18) looks back to that earlier mission.

42. Gk. ἐπλεονέκτησεν.

43. Gk. τῷ αὐτῷ πνεύματι, "the same spirit," is to be understood anthropologically ("the same mind") because of the parallel in the balancing question ("the same steps"), as argued by Furnish, 560. This is more likely than the theological understanding ("the same [Holy] Spirit"; cf. 1 Cor 12:8, 9, 11; 2 Cor 4:13), as proposed by G. D. Fee, *Presence,* 357-59.

44. Gk. ἀγαπητοί. See on 7:1.

45. Gk. ὑμῖν, "you," located before the verb for emphasis (cf. on 8:9).

46. It should be noted that 2 Corinthians, as with other NT literature and indeed all literature from the period, was written to be read *aloud* to the audience for whom it was destined. See P. Saenger, "Silent Reading," 367-414. Cf. G. L. Hendrickson, "Ancient Reading," 182-96.

47. Does Gk. δοκεῖτε introduce (1) a statement (so, e.g., Furnish, 560), or (2) a question (so, e.g., Martin, 458). While there is a slight preference for (2), the meaning is unaffected either way.

48. Gk. δέ, indicating a contrast. He has not been defending himself to them . . . but speaking for their upbuilding.

This important-sounding verse appears to round off a section. But which section — the present one relating to financial relationships (vv. 13-18) or something more extensive? For a number of reasons it is held that Paul has in mind the entire letter[49] to this point: (1) his reference to "everything"[50]; (2) the question "Have you been thinking for some time?"[51] suggesting a prolonged period; (3) his clarificatory "that we have been defending[52] [ourselves] to you," which calls to mind his defensive tone of the earliest parts of the letter chapters (see 1:3–2:13); and (4) his repetition of the words "before God in Christ we speak" from an early passage (2:17).

Paul is reassuring them that, although from his viewpoint he has, indeed, been writing an "apologetic" letter,[53] he has also crafted it for their benefit. In any case, Paul must be careful not to give them the impression that he is commending himself, lest his detractors seize upon it (see on 3:1). Nonetheless, he has been concerned to explain and defend past actions, for example, (1) the writing of the "Severe Letter" instead of a direct return to them (1:12–2:4; 10:1-11), and (2) his determined commitment to self-support in ministry (11:7-12; 12:13-16; cf. 4:2; 7:2-4). But there is another dimension to what he has written, which raises the letter beyond a mere personal defense.

So far from merely offering a defense about himself to *them,* let them understand that he is speaking *"before God* and *in Christ."*[54] An oath[55] is implied here (cf. on 1:12, 18, 23; 11:10, 31; 12:6). He is not merely a man arguing a case in his own interests, as one of their contemporaries might. He is speaking in the presence of God, as a Christian believer. The omniscient

---

49. So Plummer, 368, *contra* Martin, 458. Barrett, 328, regards Paul as referring to his relationships with Corinth "as a whole," i.e., not limited to the immediate context of this verse.

50. Gk. τὰ . . . πάντα.

51. Gk. πάλαι, "so far," "up to now."

52. Gk. ἀπολογοῦμαι, "speak in one's own defense," "defend oneself" (BAGD). Here ἀπολογούμεθα, the first person plural ("we"), refers to Paul, rather than Paul and Titus, as might be suggested by the proximity of v. 18 (so Martin, 458). The verb ἀπολογεῖν is found in Paul only at Rom 2:15, though the cognate noun ἀπολογία appears in 1 Cor 9:3; 2 Cor 7:11; Phil 1:7, 16.

53. Pseudo-Demetrius, an analyst of ancient letter writing from Paul's general era, lists twenty-one types of letters, of which the eighteenth is described as: "The apologetic . . . one which brings against charges the opposite arguments with proof" (quoted in F. Young and D. F. Ford, *Meaning,* 39-40). These authors draw attention to a letter from Demosthenes (384-322 B.C.) in exile to the people of Athens (*Epistle* 2), which is really a speech in his defense written in epistolary form, whose structural outline broadly resembles 2 Corinthians. See the Introduction, 17-19.

54. Gk. κατέναντι θεοῦ ἐν Χριστῷ λαλοῦμεν, his exact words from 2:17.

55. Plummer, 367-68, calls these four words (in n. 54) a "double oath," i.e., spoken (1) before God, and (2) in Christ.

God is witness to the truth of the words that he has written to them. Paul is conscious that all that he has done will be revealed in the presence of Christ, his judge (see on 5:10).

With that solemn assurance let them know that everything he writes is "for"[56] their "upbuilding,"[57] that is, for the strengthening of their understanding and character in Christ. The risen Lord called and authorized his apostle to bring this great benefit to the churches (see on 10:8; 13:10). Significantly, though he is not yet physically present, the Corinthians will nonetheless enjoy the blessing of "upbuilding," which Paul here attributes to hearing the reading of this letter (so also 13:10; cf. 10:8-10). It is because, as he says, "before God in Christ we speak" that the blessing of "upbuilding" is mediated to the Corinthians. The earlier and identical reference pointed to the *spoken* word as "the word of God" (2:17); here his *written* letter must be regarded as that word.

But how have Paul's words, apart from defending himself and his ministry, been *for* the edification of the Corinthians? In every issue Paul has raised with them throughout this letter, he has given them an undergirding of theological teaching, whether (1) explaining his actions and movements (1:1–2:13; 7:5-16), (2) describing the new covenant ministry (2:14–7:4), (3) appealing for the completion of the collection (chaps 8–9), or (4) admonishing the Corinthians for, on the one hand, welcoming the false apostles (10:12–12:13) and, on the other, continuing in immorality (12:20–13:4). At every point in the letter Paul has provided some theological and pastoral teaching for "upbuilding" the spiritual and moral lives of the believers.

Notwithstanding the generally edifying teachings of the letter in the various passages, it is likely that Paul is, in particular, pointing to passages about himself. Given the triumphalist character of the "superlative" apostles and, indeed, the triumphalist tendencies of the Corinthians, it is likely that Paul has in mind those passages about *himself* in which the *non*triumphalist, "slave"like[58] character of his ministry has been set forth (e.g., 2:14-16; 4:1-15; 6:3-13). Edifying, indeed, is Paul's own example of one who might well have been inflated in pride through his extraordinary visions and revelations, but who learned humbly to depend on the Lord's grace and power in the unremoved thorn (12:7-10).

---

56. Gk. ὑπέρ, "for the sake of." There is a vicarious note here; Paul might have been expected to use the preposition εἰς or πρὸς . . . οἰκοδομήν. Everything Paul has written to this point has been *for the sake of* (the edification of) the Corinthians (see on 1:6; 5:20; 12:10, 15).

57. Gk. τῆς ὑμῶν οἰκοδομῆς. See J. Pfammatter, *EDNT* 2.495-98.

58. See n. 56 above, observing that Paul uses the preposition ὑπέρ in this verse, a preposition that has been used throughout for Christ's sufferings for others, and Paul's sufferings for them.

Closely related is Paul's emphasis throughout the letter on the power of God impinging on his "weaknesses" (i.e., sufferings-in-ministry). Here the motif of the death and resurrection of Jesus is not only central to the gospel message; death and resurrection also carry over into his own experience, and beyond him to other believers. Sufferings are analogous to Christ's death, and deliverance from those sufferings to Christ's resurrection. The God who raises the dead rescued Paul, as he testifies throughout this letter, from peril in Asia (1:8-10), from persecutions in general (4:7-14; 6:4-7), from the powerlessness of the unremoved thorn (12:7-9), and in his discipline of them (13:3-4). But Paul has written about himself not to defend himself so much as to edify his readers — then and now.[59] The God of the gospel of the death and resurrection of Jesus continues to deliver his people.

To be sure, Paul defends himself throughout the letter, but he does so in such a way as to edify the church. The historical particulars are ultimately unrecoverable because of the historical distance and the incompleteness of the records, but the edifying teaching across the main sections of the letter, and about Paul in particular, remains for the people of God in every generation.

2. Warnings in View of Paul's Third Visit (12:20–13:4)

> 20 *For I am afraid that when I come I may not find you as I want you to be, and you may not find me as you want me to be. I fear that there may be quarreling, jealousy,[1] outbursts of anger, factions, slander, gossip, arrogance and disorder.* 21 *I am afraid that when I come again my God will humble me before you, and I will be grieved over many who have sinned earlier and have not repented of the impurity, sexual sin and debauchery in which they have indulged.* 1 *This will be my third visit to you. "Every matter must be established by the testimony of two or three witnesses."* 2 *I already gave you a warning when I was with you the second time. I now[2] repeat it while absent: On my return I will not spare those who sinned earlier or any of the others,*

---

59. An interesting parallel is 1 Cor 4:9-13, where Paul as apostle lists various sufferings, as "a fool for Christ's sake." He writes this not to make the Corinthians ashamed, but to admonish them as his dear children (4:14), adding, "I appeal to you, therefore, *be imitators of me*" (4:16). Paul's mention of his sufferings arising out his gospel ministry is not an end in itself, but that the Corinthians might imitate him in suffering rather than resile from bearing faithful witness to Christ.

1. The singular readings of both ἔρις and ζῆλος are to be preferred to the plural versions; so, e.g., p46 and other authorities.

2. Some authorities (e.g., D E K and many minuscules) add γράφω; the shorter reading is supported by, e.g., p46 ℵ A B etc., and is preferred.

3 *since you are demanding proof that Christ is speaking through me.*
He is not weak in dealing with you, but is powerful among you. 4 *For*
to be sure, he was crucified in weakness, yet he lives by God's power.
Likewise, we are weak in him, yet by God's power we will live with
him to serve you.

In this part of the letter more than in any other, Paul stresses his impending
third visit. This is written from the pain of the unfortunate second visit, whose
echoes may still be heard in Paul's words. These verses are dominated by the
"fear" he feels at unresolved moral problems he may face when he comes.
However, let them be under no misunderstanding: he will exercise his disciplinary powers if the need remains, though he hopes the problems of immorality will at last be behind them. Let those who disdain his spirituality and his
effectiveness — based on observations of the second visit — understand that
Christ — crucified and risen — does and will speak through him as one who
serves in weaknesses, yet who nonetheless ministers in the power of the risen
Christ.

20 In a passage (12:20–13:4) where he severely admonishes (certain
of) his readers in the light of his impending visit, Paul shifts from the "we"
reference of the previous verse to the first person singular, "I." The "upbuilding" (see 10:8; 13:10) of v. 19, which pointed backward, is now carried
forward to v. 20 by the explanatory connective "for."[3] In the verses that
follow, however, it becomes clear that this "upbuilding" is in the nature of
significant moral amendment that must occur within a specific and highly
charged situation, namely, long-standing and unrepented sexual sins among
the Corinthians (12:20, 21; 13:2).

Paul signals by his "I am afraid," with which this verse commences,
a fear that is in no way hypothetical. That fear,[4] as the next verses demonstrate,
is that when he comes he will "not find [them] as [he] want[s them] to be."
But, bent as he is on resolving these divisive sexual and disciplinary problems
(12:21; 13:1),[5] this will mean that the Corinthians will "not find [him] as
[they] want [him] to be." This chiastic (crisscross) expression

```
what I    want
      I    may not    find . . .
      I    may not be found
what you want
```

---

3. Gk. γάρ.
4. As with other verbs of apprehension, φοβοῦμαι is followed by μή πως (cf.
BAGD).
5. Hughes, 471, 472, helpfully discerns a paternal tone in these verses (cf. on 2:9).

would have had particular impact when read aloud in the assembly. In that regard, as the subjunctive mood in "I may not *find* . . . I may not be *found*"[6] suggests, Paul retains the hope that the Corinthians, influenced by his present words, "may" take it upon themselves to deal with their problems, relieving Paul of that unpleasant duty when he comes.

Specifically, he fears that his coming with resolution[7] to rectify the chronic sexual problems,[8] as he will mention in v. 21, will involve him in "quarreling, jealousy, outbursts of anger, factions, slander, gossip [lit. "whisperers"/"conceits"], arrogance and disorder." This descriptive list is so detailed[9] that it seems certain that Paul was convinced these troubles awaited him in Corinth if he came determined to resolve the problems of sexual immorality.[10] But the specific character of the list suggests that these were the very problems Paul faced during his difficult second visit. These words, therefore, are best explained as descriptive of Paul's recent humiliating expe-

---

6. Gk. εὕρω . . . εὑρεθῶ are subjunctives; also ταπεινώσῃ in v. 21.

7. Martin's opinion, 460, that previously Paul had dealt "passively" with the Corinthians — by retreating from the offender, leaving the congregation to deal with him — is less likely, in our view, than that Paul did seek to resolve the problem at the second visit, but unsuccessfully, leaving him with no option but to withdraw. He then sent them, in effect, an ultimatum by means of the "Severe Letter" (1:23; 2:1). It is not that he had been "passive," but that his disciplinary methods — by "the meekness and gentleness of Christ" (10:1) — have not commended Paul to the Corinthians, accustomed as they probably were to more ruthless modes of discipline at the hands of Roman magistrates and local politicians. Certainly, as he ironically states, the Corinthians have tolerated harsh treatment by the intruders as compared with Paul's treatment of them (11:20).

8. C. K. Barrett's suggestion ("Opponents," 74, 75) that v. 20b and v. 21b reflect two different situations — one of social disorder in a divided church arising from the arrival of the false apostles, the other indigenous to Corinth and related to endemic sexual problems — is rendered unlikely on account of the closeness of the references. We agree with Martin, 468-69, who finds the one group, i.e., the church, guilty of both types of sin.

9. Four of the eight words in this list appear in stereotyped vice lists: ἔρις ("strife," "discord"; cf. Rom 1:29), ζῆλος ("jealousy"; cf. Rom 13:13; Gal 5:20; used with ἔρις in 1 Cor 3:3 and with ἐριθεία in Jas 3:14, 16), θυμοί ("anger," "wrath"; cf. Gal 5:20; Col 3:8; Eph 4:31), and ἐριθεῖαι ("self-seeking"; cf. Gal 5:20). The other words — καταλαλιαί ("evil speech," "slander"), ψιθυρισμοί ("whisperers"), φυσιώσεις ("conceited" — a common problem in Corinth; cf. in 1 Cor 4:6, 18, 19; 5:2; 8:1; 13:4); hence ψιθυρισμοί φυσιώσεις = "conceited gossip-mongers"), and ἀκαταστασίαι ("disturbances") — when taken with the more stereotyped vices earlier in the list — portray in specific, not merely general, terms a messianic community deeply divided by small-minded factionalism. Paul's parental tone in v. 20a is understandable in light of the immature behaviors listed in v. 20b.

10. *Contra* Furnish, 567, who treats the list as "quite traditional," found both in NT and Hellenistic vice lists, and who attributes these disorders to the effects of the intruders. However, not all the vices are "traditional." Moreover, the closeness of "the sins of a divided church" in this verse to the sexual sins in the next would appear to exclude the (*Jewish*, therefore sexually scrupulous) intruders as the source of those misdemeanors.

rience in Corinth, which he now fears he may have to relive when he next comes to them.

21 Paul is afraid that on arrival in Corinth he will have to deal with those who are still unrepentant. The initial "that"[11] is dependent on "I fear"[12] from v. 20. As in the previous verse, the "fear" is associated with his "coming" to Corinth, in this case lest (1) his God humble him "again"[13] before them, and (2) he grieve over many who "sinned before," yet have not repented.

In addition to the "fear" of conflict with the unrepentant (as in v. 20), Paul expresses apprehension at the prospect that, as he says, "my God will humble me before you [again]." This enigmatic remark[14] appears to refer to the profound humbling (cf. 10:1) of himself he would sustain — possibly of a deliberate, even public kind — as he "grieve[s][15] over" unrepented sexual sin within the Corinthian church. This may have involved formally excluding unrepentant offenders from the fellowship, that is, "handing [them] over to Satan" (1 Cor 5:5; 1 Tim 1:20). In these circumstances Paul would openly "grieve" for such sinners and, in so doing, would be "humbled" by God.

Paul's comments imply some kind of congregational procedure (1 Cor 5:4; 2 Cor 2:10) to deal with disciplinary matters (see on 2:5-6). Evidence would be heard, with no fewer than two or three witnesses (13:1), perhaps preceding a congregational vote (cf. 2:5 — "the majority"). A judgment would be passed (1 Cor 5:3), followed by "punishment" (cf. 2:5), apparently some kind of separation or exclusion of the erring member (cf. 1 Cor 5:11, 13). Such a procedure, as best we are able to reconstruct it from fragmentary data scattered through 1 and 2 Corinthians, was to provoke the sinner's re-

---

11. Gk. μή.

12. Not stated in v. 21, but clearly to be understood from v. 20 (correctly, as in the NIV).

13. Gk. πάλιν could be taken with either ἐλθόντος (NIV; NEB; RSV; KJV/AV) or ταπεινώσῃ (Barrett, 330; Furnish, 562; Martin, 465). Both are grammatically possible, and the context does not resolve the dilemma. Following Martin we take πάλιν with ταπεινώσῃ, on the basis of 2:1, where Paul said he would not come to them *again* ἐν λύπῃ.

14. Martin, 465, interprets ταπεινώσῃ in the sense of "humiliation," suggesting (with Bultmann, 241) that this would arise as Paul is forced to use ἐξουσία for καθαίρεσις rather than for οἰκοδομή, its God-ordained priority. But while such an exercise of ἐξουσία would be regretted by Paul (10:8; 13:10), it is far from clear that it would involve humiliation for Paul in the eyes of the Corinthians. Based on the words πρὸς ὑμᾶς and the clause following, however, it is more likely that Paul voluntarily humbled himself in the presence of the Corinthians, by mourning publicly over the unrepentant.

15. Gk. πενθεῖν, used transitively only here in the NT, is the same verb as in the disciplinary passage of the earlier Corinthian letter — 1 Cor 5:2. In that passage the Corinthians are rebuked for their lack of "grief."

pentance with a view to his restoration to the community of faith (1 Cor 5:5; 2 Cor 2:10-11; Gal 6:1-2).

Paul's "fear" in "coming" to Corinth was also due to the "many" who must be dealt with, namely, those "who have sinned earlier."[16] On the basis of 1 Cor 6:12-20 (cf. 10:8), this phrase most likely refers to those who sinned prior to Paul's second visit (so also 13:2). Paul specifies their sin in sexual terms, as "the[17] impurity, sexual sin, and debauchery[18] which they practiced." Greek Corinth of classical times was notorious for its sexual license, and it is likely that the new Roman city was no less debauched, though the evidence applicable to the newer city is less clear in that regard.[19]

Promiscuity within the church in Corinth may be traced from the earliest of Paul's correspondence, from the time he left the city after founding the church. The (lost) "Previous Letter" was occasioned by "sexually immoral" members of the church, from whom Paul had called for separation (1 Cor 5:9-11). In our canonical 1 Corinthians Paul challenged the Corinthians' proud toleration of gross sexual sin, for example, incest (5:1), union with prostitutes (6:15), adultery, sodomy, and homosexual prostitution (6:9). Timothy's visit to Corinth at the time of the dispatch of that letter (16:10) was probably related to the problems canvassed in it, including ongoing sexual sins. Moreover, it is probable that a negative report by Timothy on his return to Ephesus necessitated Paul's unscheduled visit to Corinth, when he confronted the long-term, unrepented sexual sin practiced by "many" (also 13:2). It appears, further, that the (lost) "Severe Letter," written from Ephesus on Paul's return from his humiliatingly unsuccessful visit to Corinth, was prompted by disorder in the church (v. 20). Opposition to Paul's attempt to discipline endemic sexual sin appears to have been led by the man Paul refers to as the "wrongdoer" (2 Cor 7:12).

Further definition of these unrepentant ones is difficult. It seems likely, however, that they were Gentiles, not Jews, since the former were characteristically lax in sexual matters and the latter strictly observant of the Law of God. Moreover, it is likely that they belonged to separate, Gentile subgroups

---

16. Gk. τῶν προημαρτηκότων. The tenses of the verbs should be noted. The perfect προημαρτηκότων suggests persistence in sexual sin going back to some point subsequent to their baptism (if their initial repentance was genuine), whereas the aorists μετανοησάντων and ἔπραξαν suggest that they did not repent during Paul's second visit, or, perhaps, even as a result of the "Severe Letter."

17. Gk. τῇ. The use of the one article with the three nouns may suggest that the latter two words amplify the first.

18. Gk. ἀκαθαρσία ("impurity"; cf. 7:1), πορνεία ("fornication"), and ἀσελγεία ("licentiousness"). The same triplet is found in Gal 5:19, with the first and second also in Col 3:5; Eph 5:3, suggesting typical sex-related behavior in Gentile cities.

19. See the Introduction, 4.

based on house churches in Corinth. There were, however, "many who have sinner earlier," whom Paul would have to confront on his pending arrival in the city, and in the face of whom he may be "humbled" by God as he applies godly discipline.

1 For the third time in successive verses — in each case near the beginning of the verse — Paul signals his intention to "come" to them. Here, however, he specifically refers to the "third"[20] visit, mentioned above in 12:19.

Despite his determination not to come to them again in "grief" (2:1), that is, to deal with unrepented sin by sustained discipline, it appears that just such a visit is now in prospect.[21] Reference to "two or three witnesses" (LXX Deut 19:15[22]) indicates that the forensic practices in the Pentateuch are to apply.[23] That "every word[24] must be substantiated"[25] by multiple testimony suggests a congregational hearing, as noted earlier (see on 12:21).[26]

Who are those against whom such "witnesses" will speak? There is no hint that the man who wronged Paul during the second visit (7:12) — and who might since have lapsed — is in view. Rather, the context points to the "many" (12:21) still involved in sexual sin, supported by "all the rest" (see on 13:2).

Nonetheless, this raises the question of why Paul was so elated at the Corinthians' positive response to the "Severe Letter," as reported to Paul by Titus on his return from Corinth (7:7, 9-11, 13-16). One explanation is that, in the period between Titus's return and the writing of this part of 2 Corinthians, Paul has heard of a large-scale relapse into sexual sin by certain members, unanticipated by Paul's earlier words (7:7-16). Such an explanation would

---

20. Gk. τρίτον. For the use of a neuter adjective in place of a noun see BDF #154.

21. This is not to imply that Paul has gone back on his resolution. The earlier decision (2:1) related to the wrongdoer (7:12) and has now been settled (2:5-12).

22. Paul's ἐπὶ στόματος δύο μαρτύρων καὶ τριῶν σταθήσεται πᾶν ῥῆμα abbreviates LXX Deut 19:15 — ἐπὶ στόματος δύο μαρτύρων καὶ ἐπὶ στόματος τριῶν σταθήσεται πᾶν ῥῆμα (cf. Mark 15:56). This principle is to apply in ministry to erring church members (Matt 18:16) and to erring elders (1 Tim 5:19).

23. Multiple testimony was established forensic procedure among the Jews. See H. van Vliet, *No Single Testimony*, 43-62, 96, 98. The allegorical interpretation that Paul's earlier visits are these witnesses (e.g., Calvin, 169) is farfetched, especially since the first visit was to establish the church, not discipline it.

24. Gk. πᾶν ῥῆμα, which could, however, mean "every charge" (RSV), "every matter" (NIV).

25. Gk. σταθήσεται, "shall be substantiated," a future indicative used to express a categorical imperative, "must be substantiated" (so Furnish, 569).

26. So Hughes, 475. Martin, 469, however, argues against this view on the basis that the identity and guilt of these people was already "a matter of record," further inquiry being unnecessary.

bear negatively on the question of the unity of the present letter, suggesting that this passage would belong to a later letter, a view not taken in this commentary.[27] The present passage, however (12:21; 13:2), gives no evidence that these sinners had interrupted their sinning by repentance.

A better explanation is that Paul, as a matter of pastoral method, deals with various issues in the churches by "compartments," keeping different problems separate so as to retain objectivity and perspective. Certainly that is his approach to problems as they are dealt with throughout 1 Corinthians. In this case, he has deliberately deferred addressing this major problem until the end of the letter, perhaps for greater impact, in the light of his imminent arrival, so that he might be spared the disciplinary encounter about which he expresses his concern (10:1-2; 12:20, 21).

It is indeed possible that he had referred earlier to these sinners in the passage calling for separation from pagan temples (6:14–7:1). That admonition had an element also found in his present admonition to the sexual sinners, namely, that of "purity." The earlier passage exhorted the readers to "purity" (7:1 — "let us purify ourselves"; the present one mentions the sin of "impurity" — 12:21).[28] It has been suggested that "the many" who have not repented from sexual sins are to be identified with or are closely associated with those still involved with pagan temple worship. In all probability these are Gentiles connected with one or more house-based subchurches within the wider faith community in Corinth.

2-3a   Paul now concludes[29] what he began in 12:20 (cf. 12:14), foreshadowing his impending visit to Corinth. Once again — for the fourth time in four consecutive verses — Paul declares his intention to "come"[30] to Corinth. The impact of this repetition upon the hearers of the letter would leave no doubt as to Paul's imminent final visit.

This is a powerful statement directed to "those who had sinned before and all the rest." *As* he had forewarned[31] them *when present* during the "second"[32]

---

27. See the Introduction, 17-23.

28. Two possibilities are suggested by these references. One is that sexual and cultic sins represent two different species of "impurity." The other, more likely possibility is that sexual and cultic sins were so closely related in that culture and that the one sin assumes the occurrence of the other.

29. It should be noted that vv. 2-4 is a single, rather convoluted sentence in Greek. For convenience it has been broken at v. 3b.

30. Except that in this case, unlike the others, the verb "come" is placed near the end of the sentence.

31. Gk. προείρηκα, perfect tense, indicating that while given on a specific occasion (the second visit?), the warning had been intended to apply to the Corinthians until he returned (cf. 7:3).

32. Gk. τὸ δεύτερον, "the second time." This points to the visit mentioned in 2:1-2 (*q.v.*).

visit, *so now while absent*[33] he also forewarns[34] them. Thus he draws a contrast between his second visit and his absence from them now. When present with them he had warned them in advance what a future visit would mean, just as absent now he also warns in advance. Perhaps he is rebutting in passing their complaint that he had been ineffectual in discipline when present for that second visit (see on 10:1-2, 10).

That carefully stated warning is directed to "those who sinned earlier" (see 12:21, where the unrepented sins of "impurity, sexual sin and debauchery" are listed[35]). Significantly, Paul adds, "and all the others" (not "*or* any of the others," as in the NIV). Who are these[36]? Paul may be referring darkly to an amorphous group who tacitly supported the habitual sinners over against Paul's strong demands but who themselves were not actively involved in the immorality. Perhaps they are to be equated with the (implied) "minority" who supported the now-penitent wrongdoer against Paul at the time the punishment against him occurred (2:6).[37]

What, then, of the warning — given during the second visit and now repeated — directed to unrepentant and resistant sections of the Corinthian congregation? It is that[38] "when" he comes (the conditional "if" reproduces his exact words of warning declared during his second visit) he will not "spare"[39] the "many" (13:21) unrepentant sinners and their supporters (see on 12:21).

33. Gk. ὡς παρὼν . . . καὶ ἀπὼν νῦν; for this image cf. Phil 2:13, where the nouns occur.

34. Gk. προλέγω, present tense; cf. the similar past/present usage of the verb in Gal 5:21.

35. Paul limits "sinned before" to the sexual sins of 12:21 (where the verb προαμαρτάνειν is also used) and does not, in our view, include the social sins of 12:20 (*contra* Martin, 471).

36. Furnish, 570, identifies them as "all the rest of the congregation." This is less likely, in our view; Paul would probably have addressed them as "you" in that case.

37. The identifying of "all the rest" as sinners of more recent times (favored by Martin, 471), whom he presently "warns" as "now absent," is based on the following structural arrangement (noticed by Hughes, 476). Here three pairs of phrases are each joined by καί. This proposal, though superficially attractive, is probably too neat:

προείρηκα καὶ προλέγω,
ὡς παρὼν τὸ δεύτερον καὶ ἀπὼν νῦν,
τοῖς προημαρτηκόσιν καὶ τοῖς λοιποῖς πᾶσιν.

The identification set forth in the text is to be preferred.

38. The ὅτι recitative suggests that Paul's words ἐὰν . . . οὐ φείσομαι, "When I come I will not spare. . . ," are verbatim, i.e., what he said during his second visit (cf. 2:1). Since the decision to return is not now conditional on any action of the Corinthians, the wrongdoer has been dealt with (2:5-11). The ἐάν reflects indefiniteness regarding the specific time of Paul's coming and is to be translated "whenever."

39. Gk. φείσεσθαι is possibly a military term (cf. LSJ 2.1920). If so, it may be connected with the martial assault language used earlier (10:3-5).

But can he achieve this discipline within the Corinthian church? There must be some doubt in view of the failed second visit, which was not followed by a further visit but by a letter that was, in effect, an ultimatum. A "weak" personal presence followed by nothing more than a "powerful" letter has left doubts in some minds as to Paul's ability to resolve problems endemic to this church (10:9-10). Paul will address this question in the following verses.

In v. 3a — which is here taken as the conclusion of a sentence begun in v. 2[40] — Paul now states the reason[41] why he will "not spare" the unrepentant sexual sinners when he comes "again"[42] to Corinth. It is, he says, that you "desire[43] proof of "the Christ who is speaking through me."[44] His title, "the Christ," is probably intentional here, pointing to the kingly rule of Jesus. God makes his appeal though Paul; the Christ speaks though his ambassador (see on 5:20).

But who are the "you"[45] who seek "proof" of this? In the first instance it is likely that Paul has in mind those detractors who regard him as spiritually ineffective (see on 10:7 in the context of 10:1-11). Nonetheless, it is quite possible that many of the Corinthians have, to some degree, accepted their criticism of the absent apostle as one who "walks by" and exercises his ministry "by *the flesh*" (10:2, 4; cf. 1:12, 17). The present tense of the verbs "desiring . . . speaking" suggests that this was an issue at the time of writing, probably as reported to Paul by Titus on his return from Corinth (7:6-7).

What these detractors seek is "proof"[46] that Christ is speaking "in[47] [Paul]," that he will effectively discipline the moral offenders within the Corinthian fellowship.[48] This they doubt on account of "the weakness of his

---

40. But not, e.g., by Furnish, 568.

41. Gk. ἐπεί.

42. Gk. εἰς τὸ πάλιν, to be taken with "come" rather than "spare."

43. Gk. ζητεῖτε means "demand," according to Furnish, 570.

44. Gk. τοῦ ἐν ἐμοὶ λαλοῦντος Χριστοῦ. Paul "speaks in Christ before God" (2:17; 12:19) and "the Christ . . . speaks in me" (cf. ὡς τοῦ θεοῦ παρακαλοῦντος δι' ἡμῶν — 5:20). Note that the present tense is used, pointing to the Christ's continuing to speak through his apostle.

45. Furnish, 576, takes this to refer in an undifferentiated way to the Corinthians, who are demanding proof in terms of ecstatic speech or miraculous deeds.

46. Gk. δοκιμή, "verification." See also 2:9; 8:2; 9:13. For uses of the verb δοκιμάζειν see 8:8, 22; 13:5.

47. The ἐν is instrumental, "by means of," which, however, could be rendered "through" Paul.

48. Barrett, 335, takes this to refer to Christ speaking in Paul *as an apostle*. The context (12:21–13:2a), however, suggests that they were referring specifically to his speech in disciplining the offenders in Corinth.

physical presence" (10:10), as displayed — according to them — in his poor efforts during the second visit. He will admit to being "weak" in the physical sense through the "stake/thorn in the flesh" and other "weaknesses" (12:7-10), though nonetheless finding strength from God in such "weaknesses." But he will not admit to being "weak" in the spiritual sense, rejecting altogether the jibe that Christ does not speak through him. The reverse, in fact, is true. The power of God is at work in his ministry, as they should well know (see on 1:20-22; 3:2-3; 8:7; 10:4, 7).

This is not the first time the word "proof" has been used in the troubled relationships with the Corinthians. The "Severe Letter" apparently asked for "proof" that the Corinthians were "obedient" to Paul, which was to be demonstrated by their disciplining the man who had wronged Paul during the second visit, "proof" of which they gave by their disciplinary action (2:9; 7:12). In turn, the Corinthians demand "proof" of Paul that Christ does speak "in Paul."[49]

Using the same blacksmith's vocabulary[50] in the next paragraph (vv. 5-10), Paul expresses the hope that in his forthcoming visit he will not be "disproved" in their eyes (v. 6), though he accepts that they may regard him as "disproved." It is more important, he says, that you "prove yourselves . . . understand within yourselves that Christ Jesus is in you" (v. 5). That the Corinthians "prove" themselves to be indwelt by Christ is more important than their opinion whether or not Christ speaks "in Paul." Paul does not doubt this; quite the reverse, in fact (10:3-6). Nor should they.

3b-4 Having mentioned their desire to see proof of Christ's speaking in him, Paul sets out to do that in a most unusual way — with a relative clause setting forth the fact that Christ himself is not weak, but powerful in/among them. This is followed by double explanatory clauses, both of which pick up the "weakness"/"power" contrast — first with regard to Christ, and second as that now applies to Paul. Verses 3b, 4a, 4b, 4c, and 4d[51] are characterized by a threefold repetition of a weak/powerful motif, which may be rendered:

---

49. Hughes, 477-78, suggests a parallel with Moses, who was subject to rebellion by members of the Exodus community. Rebellion against Moses was rebellion against God (Num 16:28). While Exodus typology is used in 1 Cor 10:1-13, the reference here may be too tenuous for such a typology linking Paul with Moses.

50. V. 5, δοκιμάζειν; vv. 5, 6, 7, ἀδόκιμοι; v. 7, δόκιμοι.

51. See J. Lambrecht, "Notes on 2 Cor 1:4," 261-69.

3b	[Christ][52]	is not *weak*	toward you,	1
but		is *powerful*[53]	in you.[54]	
4a For indeed[55]	he was crucified[56]			
	in *weakness*,[57]			2
4b but	lives[58]			
	through the *power* of God.			
4c For indeed	we also are *weak* in him,			3
4d but	shall live[59] with him			
	through the *power* of God			
	toward you.[60]			

This unit is Paul's penultimate juxtaposition of the weak/powerful theme in 2 Corinthians (cf. 13:9).[61] As such it serves as Paul's second-to-the-last word of self-defense against the criticism of his shortcomings in ministerial discipline.

52. See on vv. 2-3a.

53. Gk. δυνατεῖ. The verb is found in the NT only at 9:8 and Rom 14:4.

54. The first two lines are chiastic: "toward you — not weak/powerful — among you." The subtle use of prepositions ὃς εἰς ὑμᾶς οὐκ ἀσθενεῖ ἀλλὰ δυνατεῖ ἐν ὑμῖν should be noted. Paul may be reminding those Corinthians who think they are "strong" and "already reign with Christ" (1 Cor 4:10, 8) that Christ is only powerful *in* them as he has proved not to be weak *toward* them, i.e., that brokenness and heartfelt repentance must precede their experience of the power of God (see on 12:9-10). Paul will manifest that power when he comes.

55. Gk. καὶ γάρ, repeated in v. 4c, "*For even* Christ was crucified through weakness. . . . *For* indeed we *also* are weak in him." See also 3:10.

56. Only here in 2 Corinthians does σταυροῦν occur. But see 1 Cor 1:13, 23; 2:2, 8; Gal 3:1; 5:24; 6:14.

57. Gk. ἐξ ἀσθενείας, lit. "out of weaknesses." The plural "weaknesses" is used by Paul for his concrete "sufferings" sustained through ministry (see 11:30; 12:5, 9, 10). The crucifixion of Christ was characterized by his utter physical helplessness. Yet "out" of such weakness God wrought salvation. Note the ironical yet insightful words of the chief priests, ἄλλους ἔσωθεν, ἑαυτὸν οὐ δύναται σῶσαι (Mark 15:31). In his powerlessness to save himself lay his hidden power to save others. A balancing use of ἐκ appears in the phrase following, "out of [the] power of God."

58. Gk. ζῇ. As a consequence of his resurrection, Christ "lived" and "lives," including "to God" (Rom 6:9-10).

59. Gk. ζήσομεν. Although this could refer to (1) Paul's afterlife (Barrett, 337), more probably it points to (2) Paul's impending visit to Corinth (Furnish, 571) and the outpouring of divine power he expects to see.

60. Gk. εἰς ὑμᾶς is emphatic, coming at the end of the clause and sounding a note of warning to the Corinthians.

61. The "power" words occur without the corresponding "weakness" words in 1:8; 4:7; 6:7; 10:4, and the "weakness" words without the "power" words in 10:10; 11:21, 29, 30. But "power" vocabulary and "weakness" vocabulary occur together in 12:5-10; 13:3-4, and 13:9.

Consistent with his pastoral method, he treats the particular situation — now substantially lost to us — as an opportunity to teach about Christ. It is, however, a pointed teaching, directed at the views about Christ held by the Corinthians (see on 10:3-7). In apparent rebuttal of their view of Christ, Paul declares that "[Christ] is not *weak* in dealing with [them],"[62] adding in the next verse, "[Christ] was crucified in [lit. "out of"] *weaknesses*." Why is Paul so insistent on this point? In all probability it is because they held such a triumphalist view of the risen and ascended Christ that they minimized both the earthly ministry and more particularly the death of Christ, core truths of the gospel that the apostle Paul was committed to uphold (see on 2:14).

Were they saying that both the message "Christ . . . crucified" was "weak" and the messenger who brought it was "weak"? Their rejection of that message would be tantamount to rejecting Paul as well. However, by declaring that "Christ . . . crucified" was not "weak" toward them, Paul is at the same time answering the criticism that the one who preached "Christ . . . crucified" was also "weak" toward them (see on 10:1-4, 7). Quite the reverse; his ministry is empowered by God (see on 10:2-4).

What, then, does Paul mean by "[Christ] . . . crucified out of weakness . . . is not weak toward you"? "Christ . . . crucified" powerfully stands as a rebuke to sin. Those for whose sins Christ has been crucified cannot continue in their sins or personal arrogance or in a lifestyle centered on themselves. Those for whom Christ has died have themselves "now" died to living to themselves; from "now on" they live for him who died and was raised for them (5:14-15). Paul's earlier reference to the "stake/thorn" given him to stop his being — as the "superlative" apostles were — "over-uplifted" in pride is testimony to "Christ not being weak toward" Paul. Indeed, Paul is "weak" in Christ, that is, broken and humbled in him. Let the Corinthians learn from Paul's experience of the stake/thorn not to be arrogant (cf. 12:19); "Christ crucified is not weak."

Closely connected with this is the apostle's own proposed "humbling" of himself, his "grieving" for those professed believers who continue in their sins (12:21). Though they may despise as "weak" the message of "Christ . . . crucified" and the messenger who preached and embodied that message against the willful sinner, the reality was that Christ crucified is not "weak" in his impact on the believer in his sins and pride.

Not that Paul emphasizes "Christ . . . crucified" to the exclusion of the reality that "Christ . . . lives." If the one refers to the death, the other refers to the resurrection. Paul is equally emphatic about both truths, which

---

62. Plummer, 374, comments: "Neither towards the Corinthians nor among them had Christ shown himself to be wanting in power. There was the amazing fact of 'saints' in such a city as Corinth."

he often sets in balance, as here. Thus Christ — the Christ who has been "crucified" (aorist passive) — now "lives" (present tense) through the "power of God"[63] (cf. 1:9; 4:14), and he is "powerful among you." His resurrection "power"[64] had been made perfect in Paul's weakness of the stake/thorn, through which, as it were, Paul had been crucified. The Corinthians, too, will know that power through Paul's ministry among them. The risen, living Christ — living through the power of God — will be powerful "in" this congregation. Paul's imminent coming to Corinth, as he preaches and embodies the crucifixion, will demonstrate that Christ "lives by the power of God."

Paul specifically connects his own ministry to "Christ . . . crucified . . . living" among them in the closest possible way. Paul is "weak in him . . . yet by God's power . . . lives with him." Here Paul reintroduces the power/weakness language of his interaction with his local detractors (see on 10:7). Against the criticism that his bodily presence is "weak" (10:10) — through his perceived ineffectual discipline during the second visit — he asserted that the weapons of his warfare in reality are "empowered by God" (10:4).

Nonetheless, there is no triumphalism here (see on 2:14). Paul immediately concedes that he is "weak in [Christ] . . . crucified." His apostolic ministry is characterized by the "weaknesses" — by extension, as it were — of the sufferings of Christ, as reflected in the catalogues of apostolic suffering (1:8-11; 4:7-12; 6:3-10; 11:23-33; 12:9-10), including the "weakness" of the thorn/stake, through which he was brought "down to earth" (12:7-9a). Yet as "Christ," who had been "crucified in weakness," now "lives," so, too, Paul, who is "weak in him," now "lives with him . . . toward [the Corinthians]."

The Corinthians must not forget that Christ suffered and died. But equally let them not forget that the apostle, whose ministry is marked by "death" (4:7-12), "lives" toward them powerfully to impose gospel-discipline where it is called for (see on 10:2-6). Let the Corinthians get the balance right. Despite their beliefs to the contrary, the living Christ died and the dying apostle lives, though only in the One who died and who now lives.

---

63. Note the balancing ἐσταυρώθη ἐξ ἀσθενείας
ἀλλὰ ζῇ ἐκ δυνάμεως θεοῦ in which the preposition ἐκ suggests, paradoxically, that both weakness and power emanate from God — the one seen in the crucifixion (cf. 1 Cor 1:25), the other in his resurrection. However, Paul is a dialectic, not a systematic theologian; in another place Paul can associate the power of God with the crucifixion (1 Cor 1:18, 24; cf. Mark 15:31).

64. Although Paul does not indicate his precise meaning of "power," reference to related passages may point to the Spirit-inspired powers evident within the life of the congregation (1:20-21; 3:3, 8, 18; 5:5; 8:7 [cf. 11:4]; 1 Cor 12:4-11; Gal 3:5; cf. 1 Thess 5:19-20).

With vv. 3b-4b is ended the very important passage that began at 12:20. More than any other in the entire letter, these verses identify the crisis in Corinth that necessitated the apostle's second visit, namely, endemic and unrepented sin by a section of the messianic community (12:21; 13:2). In this regard the passage should be bracketed with 2:5-11 and 7:5-12 (quite possibly with 6:14–7:1 also).

Moreover, this passage strongly hints that during the second visit his attempts to deal with the sexual problems — by humbling himself, "grieving" over the sinners (cf. 10:1) — provoked serious social dislocation within the church (12:22), helping create the sense that Paul's mission had failed and that Christ did not speak through him (13:3) — in short, that he was a man of flesh, not Spirit (10:2-4). When we read the foregoing passage with 10:1-11, it emerges Paul had a number of detractors in this regard, scorning him as "weak" when present and "powerful" only when absent, as a distant letter-writer.

Finally, in this passage — so close to the end of the letter — Paul reasserts his capability of dealing with the unresolved sexual problems of the Corinthians when he makes his third visit, though he hopes that this letter will rectify the problems before he comes. Pastorally, Paul showed determination addressing the moral problems of the Corinthians. His resurrection power arose out of the "meekness and gentleness" of a man in Christ crucified.

3. Test Yourselves (13:5-10)

> 5 *Examine yourselves to see whether you are in the faith; test your-selves. Do you not realize that Christ Jesus is in you — unless, of course, you fail the test?* 6 *And I trust that you will discover that we have not failed the test.* 7 *Now we pray to God that you will not do anything wrong. Not that people will see that we have stood the test but that you will do what is right even though we may seem to have failed.* 8 *For we cannot do anything against the truth, but only for the truth.* 9 *We are glad whenever we are weak but you are strong; and our prayer is for your perfection.* 10 *This is why I write these things when I am absent, that when I come I may not have to be harsh in my use of authority — the authority the Lord gave me for building you up, not for tearing you down.*

Paul turns from replying to the Corinthians' demand for "proof" that Christ was speaking in Paul (v. 3) to his encouragement that they "prove" to themselves that Christ Jesus is in them. Thus the vocabulary of "proving" — an ironfounder's image — is prominent within this passage (vv. 5-7 — "to prove," "approved," "disproved"; cf. 1 Thess 2:14; 5:21). Evidently the Corinthians have been "proving" Paul's ministry, and some, at least, regard him as "dis-proved." But Paul calls on them to turn their attention away from him to them. (Note the repeated "yourselves" in v. 5.)

While there are serious grounds for concern about their understanding and practice of Christianity, nonetheless he would have them confirm for themselves that they are "in the faith" and that "Christ Jesus is in [them]." Since they are "approved," so, too, is he "approved." Indeed, if he were to be "disproved," so, too, would they be "disproved" (v. 6), that is, unapostolic. What he prays for is that they will not do evil but good, and that they will be "restored" (vv. 7, 9b) — and this even if in their eyes he may be seen to be "disproved." That is more important than whether or not he seems to be approved by them.

In any case he can do nothing against the truth, but only be subject to the truth; others may be false, but he is not (v. 8). He rejoices that his "weakness" is the means to their "power." But he prays, in particular, for their "restoration" (v. 9). Although the Lord's authority over him includes the power to "tear [them] down," it is more appropriately exercised for their "upbuilding," which he now seeks to do, while absent, in writing to them (v. 10). Thus two keywords emerge, their "restoration" and their "upbuilding." He prays for the one and writes this letter to achieve the other.

5 This verse turns on two imperatives, "examine" and "test."[1] Although the former often has the negative intent to provoke to sin (1 Cor 7:5; 10:3; Gal 6:1; 1 Thess 3:5), its use here is probably synonymous with the second word, that is, to "prove so as to approve" (see 8:22; cf. 1 Thess 2:4; 5:21; 1 Cor 11:28; Rom 2:18; 14:22; Eph 5:10). This in turn leads on to the theme of "disproved" and "approved" that dominates vv. 5-7. The Corinthians were demanding "proof" that the Christ was speaking through Paul (v. 3a); Paul now calls on them to "prove" themselves to themselves (cf 7:12).

"Yourselves"[2] is the object of both imperatives, occurring first for emphasis. Rather than "examine"/"approve" (or otherwise) Paul as they have been doing, let the Corinthians' attention be directed instead at *themselves*. He will show them that their verdict about themselves will likewise be their verdict about him. That is, however they fare in their self-examination is how he also fares, because they owe their existence in Christ to him.

The first imperative ("Examine yourselves") is followed by the conditional phrase, "if you are in the faith." Although the Corinthians' behavior has raised serious questions, the conditional "if" does not necessarily imply that Paul doubted their genuineness as believers. Otherwise he would not have

---

1. Gk. πειράζετε . . . δοκιμάζετε. The noun of the latter word (δοκιμή) occurred in v. 3; Paul will now play on this term so that the adjective appears four times in vv. 5-7, once positively (δόκιμος; NIV, "stood the test") and three times negatively (ἀδόκιμοι; NIV, "fail the test"). To keep the wordplay (paronomasia), I have translated these as "approved" and "disproved."

2. Gk. ἑαυτούς, third person plural, "themselves," serves also for the second person plural, "yourselves."

addressed them as "the church of God" or expressed "confidence" about them (1:1; 7:4, 16). On the other hand, he would not minimize the dangers in which they stood (see on 6:1, 11-13; 11:4). His exhortation, therefore, has a positive pastoral intent.

The article in the phrase "in *the* faith" (see on 1:24; cf. 1 Cor 16:13) implies the propositional and theological content of that *message* about Jesus which is to be the object of "faith." The opponents preach "another" Jesus, a gospel "different" from that brought to the Corinthians by Paul (11:4); his is the true faith. Let them confirm that they stand within its structure.

The second imperative ("test yourselves"[3]) repeats the first, but now using the keyword of vv. 5-7, "prove." In a surprising turn, introduced by "or," he leaves aside the possible doubt in the first clause. Thus Paul makes a strong pastoral appeal to them expressed as (1) a rhetorical question requiring a positive reply ("*Or* do you not[4] know that Jesus Christ is in you?"), (2) which repeats the emphatic "yourselves" with which the verse began, (3) the intensified verb "*thoroughly* understand"[5] in the present (i.e., continuous) tense, and (4) which is experiential ("that Christ Jesus is in you[6]"), in contrast to the above, which is propositional ("if you are in the faith"). Such an appeal may be rendered — "Or surely you yourselves thoroughly comprehend that Christ Jesus is in you," reflecting the power of the risen Christ in the lives of these Corinthians (see on 1:22; 3:3-4, 8, 18; 5:5; 8:7; 11:4), which they cannot deny, in this the now-arrived "day of salvation" (5:14–6:2; cf. 1:20; 3:3).

The concluding "unless[7] you fail the test" is ironic and pointed. Although this may appear to return to the suggestion of doubt in the first clause, in effect it is somewhat tongue-in-cheek. Rather than casting doubt on whether they do in fact know Christ, he adds, "unless of course you were to end up failing the test after all" — which, of course, is unthinkable. But with that in mind he turns in v. 6 to point out the consequences. Of course the Corinthians "thoroughly know that Christ Jesus is in [them]." In view of the astonishing and palpable impact on their lives, how could it be otherwise?

But this must mean that Paul has been and is Christ's true minister. To affirm the one demands the other. Their verdict on themselves is their verdict

3. Self-examination was important in the Greek philosophical tradition. According to Dio Chrysostom, *Discourses* 4.57, the foremost of Apollo's commands, as mediated through the Delphic oracle, was "Know yourself."

4. Introduced by οὐκ, expecting the answer "Yes."

5. Gk. ἐπιγινώσκετε. See on 4:14; 5:1; 8:9. The introductory ἢ οὐκ ἐπιγινώσκετε is but a variation of the more familiar οὐκ οἴδατε. . . , "Do you not know?" (as in, e.g., 1 Cor 3:16; 5:6; and 6:2).

6. Gk. ἐν ὑμῖν, "in you," rather than "among you," as dictated by the twice-repeated "yourselves."

7. Gk. εἰ μήτι.

on him. If they are not "disproved" *(adokimoi),* it can only mean that he is "approved" *(dokimos),* that is, *by God,* as he proceeds to say in the verses following (vv. 6, 10; cf. 3:3; 10:18).

6 This verse continues the line of thought of the previous verse, especially the latter phrase. Its future cast, "I hope[8] that you will know," points to Paul's impending third visit (see on 12:14). The repeated "that" ("I hope *that* . . . you will know *that*") emphasizes Paul's hope that the Corinthians will know that he[9] is not "disproved" *(adokimos)* either — hence the irony in v. 5. Paul bears the God-given authority to upbuild the churches (10:8; 13:10; cf. 12:19). If the Corinthians reject Paul as Christ's apostle, they reject themselves as apostolic. If he is "disproved," then, so, too, are they. He hopes that he will not be, so that they will not be.

But these words are ironic rather than pessimistic. Despite the setback experienced at the second ("painful") visit (2:1-3), the persistence by some in sexual/cultic misbehavior (13:2/6:14–7:1), and the welcome by some of the preachers of "another Jesus" (11:4), the Corinthians have nonetheless responded positively to his most recent ministry, the (lost) "Severe Letter" (7:8-16; cf. 7:4). Despite disappointments, evidences of God's gracious "day of salvation" are to be seen in their midst. Ever the positive pastor, Paul looks to his imminent final visit to yield a good outcome for them.

There is very likely, therefore, a subtle twist to these words. Will the Corinthians "approve" themselves (v. 5)? If their answer is "Yes," as he knows it will be, then they will thereby "approve" Paul. Putting it the other way, will they "disprove" Paul? If they answer "No," then let them understand that, thereby, they "disprove" the newly arrived preachers. Thus to "approve" Paul and not to "disprove" him means that they must logically "disprove" his opponents. All of this is the result of examining themselves by recognizing that since Christ is really in them, Paul must himself have passed the test.

7 Using a mild adversative,[10] Paul now tells his readers his prayer to God for the Corinthians ("we pray to God"), doubtless to reinforce his teaching in their consciences. His prayer is simply put — that they will not do what is evil but what is good. But the sentence itself becomes complex on both sides of the "not"/"but" contrast. He plays again on the theme of his not being "approved"/"disproved," urging first that he does not want them to refrain from evil so that he will look good ("Not that people will see that we have stood the test"), and second that he wants them to do what is good even if he may appear to have failed the test.

---

8. See also 1:3; 5:11, where Paul is also optimistic *(contra* Furnish, 572).

9. The pronoun ἡμεῖς, "we," is emphatic. Whereas the emphasis had been on them in v. 5, it is on Paul in this verse.

10. Gk. δέ.

This verse has a complex, four-part structure; parts (1) and (3) are his antithetical prayers ("not do evil," "do good"[11]) for them ("you"), and parts (2) and (4) relate to himself ("we"). His first prayer for them, that the Corinthians ("you") "do no evil," is echoed negatively in regard to his status, "not that we may appear to be approved." Likewise his second prayer, that the Corinthians "do good," is echoed by the concession against himself,[12] "even though we should seem disproved." In the last resort, the Corinthians' moral welfare is more important that their "approval" of Paul. Thus

> We pray to God
> 1   that you[13] would do no evil —
> 2   not that we might appear to be approved,
> 3 but that you would do   good —
> 4   even though we appear to be as if disproved.

God's positive answer to Paul's present prayer in the amendment of the lives of the Corinthians will have an important bearing on how he will present himself when he comes. If the Corinthians hear and obey this letter as they respond to Paul's prayer for them (summed up as "not do evil/but do good"), then his apostolic purpose will have been thoroughly fulfilled. There will be no need for him to do something physical or visible in relation to the various unresolved errors of the Corinthians noted above (v. 6). The "proof" of his apostleship will already have been achieved by this letter in advance of his arrival; he will have been "approved." Those who demand "proof" (see on 13:3) may feel that the absence of such "proof" when he comes is evidence of Paul's "disproof."[14] But no matter. The real "proof" of Paul's apostolate is that the churches are upbuilt by his word, which demonstrates itself by their doing what is good rather than being dramatically torn down at the time of his arrival (see on 10:8; 13:10).

Various closely related doctrines of Paul[15] may be seen in this verse: (1) that he exercises his apostolic ministry as a servant (see on 1:24; 4:5), (2) that his ministry is powerful, though exercised in weakness (see on 12:10), and (3) that his word written in his physical absence is effective in his God-given ministry to upbuild the churches (see on 10:8, 10, 11). Those who see

---

11. Gk. κακὸν . . . καλόν, "evil . . . good" (see also Rom 7:21).

12. Introduced by Gk. δέ.

13. Although ὑμᾶς could be taken as accusative, making the Corinthians suffer evil at the hands of Paul or God or ?, the context and the balancing phrase (3) make the nominative probable. Paul's prayer is that the *Corinthians* not do evil but do good.

14. Gk. ὡς ἀδόκιμοι.

15. Barrett's view, 339, that Paul takes the role of a sin-bearer substitute is speculative.

the "proof" of Paul's apostolicity in some kind of "showdown" on his arrival do not comprehend the fundamentals of the power of God.

8 The initial explanatory "For"[16] in this proverblike[17] verse shows that what follows flows from what has gone before. But it is not immediately clear what exactly Paul is explaining. The use of "we" suggests that the focus is again on Paul. If so, then he is probably reaffirming that his ministry is not predicated on human approval or disapproval. Rather, it is based, as he states, on the fact that he speaks the truth and does not lie (11:10, 31; cf. 12:6). Moreover, his ministry has to do with "the word of truth" (see on 6:7).

The verb "we are able" is probably pointed, being related to a keyword of this letter, "power."[18] Paul's ministry exhibits Christ's power in weakness (12:9-10), but, as he now declares, it is not and cannot be *against* the truth" but only *"on behalf of*[19] the truth." The experiencing of Christ's power in weakness is "on behalf of," or "for the sake of," truth. Only as his life gives expression to truth — in the word of truth [of the gospel] (4:2; 6:7; 11:10) and moral truth (7:14; 11:31; 12:6) — does he experience and exercise the power of God. Controlled by truth as he is, Paul will not express himself in another guise, that of apparent power, in order to gain "approval" when he comes to the city.

As with other verses in this section, we discern an ironic twist, which is polemical in intention. Paul's claim to live "on behalf of" *(hyper)* the truth is probably pointed at those who are "pseudo," *"false* apostles" and *"false* brothers" (11:13, 26), who present themselves as "superlative" apostles (see on 11:5; 12:7, 11). But they are "false" — both as apostles and brothers; they live "against the truth." By contrast Paul speaks the truth and does not lie; truly he is an apostle of Christ (see on 12:12), for whom gospel truth and moral truth are critical.

9 As with v. 8, this verse begins with an explanatory "For,"[20] though it appears to be some sort of further elaboration of v. 7. We are driven to read between the lines here. Paul has taken the discussion back to his treatment of "weaknesses" (12:7-10). He rejoices, antithetically, when he is "weak" and they are "powerful," adding his prayer for their "restoration."

Because he hopes and expects that the Corinthians will set right their ways in response to this letter, that is, by his absence rather than by his presence (see 13:2), it will not be necessary to attend to such matters when he comes. In

---

16. Gk. γάρ.

17. As parallels see, e.g., "The truth is great and stronger than all things . . ." (1 Esdr 4:35); "Never speak against the truth . . ." (Sir 4:25).

18. Gk. δυνάμεθα, "we are [not] able"; NIV, "we cannot." Gk. δύναμαι is related to δύναμις = "power." For references to "power" see 1:8; 4:7; 6:7; 12:9 (twice), 12; 13:3, 4.

19. Gk. κατά, "against" . . . ὑπέρ, "on behalf of."

20. Gk. γάρ.

consequence it may easily appear to some that he is "weak," and thereby, as it were, "disproved" (v. 7), or that Christ does not "speak through [him]" (13:4).

But even if the Corinthians failed to repent beforehand, his manner of dealing with them in his physical presence will, nonetheless, have the character of "weakness" (12:21 — "my God will humble me . . . I will be grieved"; 13:4 — "we are weak in him"). Either way, whether absent by letter or physically present, his ministry — as opposed to those of some who criticize him — will be marked by "weakness."

This he sums up in the antithetical

> For we rejoice whenever we are weak,
> for then
> you are strong.

The Corinthians' strength "not to do evil"/"but to do good" (v. 7) does not spring from their apostle's apparent strength — charisma, eloquence, and "visions and revelations" — but from his "weakness." By this Paul means his carefully chosen modes of ministry: (1) by admonition — written or spoken (see on 12:19), (2) by the "meekness and gentleness of Christ" (10:1) rather than by worldly anger, (3) by "mourning" for the unrepentant (12:21), and, not least, (4) by utter dependence upon Christ in "stake/thorn"-conditioned helplessness for "power" in "weakness" (12:7-9).

A vicarious note is struck here. The apostle's sufferings are analogous to Christ's, though not in any propitiatory sense. Paul's sufferings in ministry are in continuation of and in place of Christ's (see on 5:20; 12:10) and for the sake of the churches (see on 1:6; 12:15). The Corinthians' "power" will be in consequence of and in exchange for Paul's "weakness."

With these two further explanations of the theme of his "approval" and "disapproval," Paul returns to his prayer for them. Before it was that they should do good and not evil, but now "for their restoration"[21] (less satisfactorily RSV, "improvement," or NIV, "perfection"). Originally used for the setting of broken limbs (so LSJ), this noun is found only here in the NT, but appears as a verb for mending nets (Mark 1:19 pars.), hence — metaphorically — for restoring a sinner to the congregation (Gal 6:1), making up what is lacking (1 Thess 3:10; cf. Heb 13:21; 1 Pet 5:10), so as to effect an appropriate and desired unity (1 Cor 1:10). Significantly, this verb appears in v. 11 as a passive imperative, "be restored."

Clearly the Corinthians were in need of "restoration," despite the presence of "Christ Jesus in [them]" (v. 5). Some were spiritually critical of the apostle, others habitually immoral, and still others again flirting with a

---

21. Gk. κατάρτισιν, used only here in the NT.

heterodox Jesus. Such divergences inevitably set them against each other, but more importantly they set them against their apostle and, more importantly still, against their God. Theirs was a profound need for "restoration," or, to use Paul's earlier word, "reconciliation" (5:18-20). Thus he prays for their "restoration," which amplifies his earlier prayer that they "not do evil/but do good" (v. 7). Both sides of that prayer have to do with their attitude toward him and their own need of restoration.

10   Paul now brings his letter to a conclusion by indicating once more his ultimate concern for writing. He began this long argument by reminding them that the goal of his whole ministry had been for "building them up, not tearing them down" (see on 10:8). He repeated this theme more generally at the beginning of this final warning and appeal (in 12:19). Now he brings both the larger argument (chaps. 10–13) and the final appeal to a conclusion by going over that ground one final time — in this case, not surprisingly, by reminding them that his writing in order to build them up is in keeping with the authority the Lord has given him.

The opening words, "For this reason"[22] (4:1; 7:13), could point back to the previous phrase[23] "for your restoration" as providing his reason for writing "when absent." More probably, however, they anticipate what will follow, that is, in order that,[24] "when present," he may not have to "act harshly" (lit. "sharply"[25]) in regard to various moral matters demanding attention in Corinth (see on v. 6; 10:2). As Plummer puts it: "He writes [these things] sharply, that he may not have to act sharply."[26]

He hopes not to have to "act harshly when present," and he writes to that end. Such action, as now stated, is similar to the form of words used earlier (see on 10:8),[27] namely,

> according to the authority
> > that the Lord gave me
> > for upbuilding
> and not for tearing down.

---

22. Gk. διὰ τοῦτο, an inferential prepositional phrase; NIV, "This is why. . . ."
23. And is so taken by, e.g., Plummer, Barrett, and Martin.
24. Gk. διὰ τοῦτο, followed by ἵνα μή, "for this reason . . . lest."
25. Gk. ἀποτόμως, which appears elsewhere in the NT only at Tit 1:13. The NIV has "harsh."
26. Plummer, 378.
27.

10:8	**13:10**
τῆς ἐξουσίας ἡμῶν ἧς ἔδωκεν ὁ κύριος	τὴν ἐξουσίαν ἣν ὁ κύριος ἔδωκεν
εἰς οἰκοδομὴν καὶ οὐκ εἰς καθαίρεσιν ὑμῶν	εἰς οἰκοδομὴν καὶ οὐκ εἰς καθαίρεσιν

Clearly the differences are quite minimal, amounting only to (1) the case of τῆς ἐξουσίας and ἧς, and (2) the location of ἔδωκεν.

Although the Lord gave his authority to Paul "for" "upbuilding" and not "tearing down," and although he is prepared to "tear down," that is, discipline the moral offenders (13:2), his preferred option is to "upbuild."

This understanding does not deny that the Lord had also authorized Paul for "tearing down,"[28] for "act[ing] harshly." Clearly the Lord had so authorized him (see on 10:2-6), and, if necessary, Paul would exercise that authority when he came to Corinth. Not that such "tearing down" would be aggressive or violent; it, too, was by the "meekness and gentleness of Christ" (10:1), as his apostle "humble[d himself]" and "grieved over" the unrepentant (12:21). But how much better it will be if the letter can achieve its purpose in Paul's absence, by his letter before he comes, so that his final sojourn may be one of joy (see on 2:1-4).

But his words "I am writing"[29] (present tense) raise the important question: What is Paul now (finishing) "writing"? While many commentators suggest that "these things" refers only to the last four chapters, a view based on the assumption that chapters 10–13 are a separate letter,[30] the position taken here is that, because the letter is seen as undivided,[31] Paul has in mind the entire letter. One reason for this stance is that the parallel verse ("all along . . . we have been speaking . . . for your upbuilding" — 12:19) appears to refer to the letter as a whole.

Indeed, Paul did not begin to refer to a further visit to Corinth only within the final chapters 10–13. While the references come thick-and-fast in these chapters (10:6; 11:9; 12:20, 21; 13:1, 2), he does speak of a forthcoming visit earlier — within the early chapters (2:1, 3) as well as within the middle chapters (9:4). In my view, the letter from beginning to end has as its main — but not only — purpose to admonish the Corinthians to prepare themselves before he comes so that his final visit, unlike the "painful" second visit, may be a joyful reunion (see on 2:1-4).

4. Final Greetings (13:11-14)

11 *Finally, brothers, good-by. Aim for perfection, listen to my appeal, be of one mind, live in peace. And the God of love and peace will be with you.*

12 *Greet one another with a holy kiss.* 13 *All the saints send their greetings.*

---

28. Gk. εἰς καθαίρεσιν. It must be remembered that Paul is here and in 10:8 adapting an OT text (LXX Jer 24:6), which refers to "tearing down." The original is not Paul's own words.

29. Paul had used the plural "we" in vv. 6-9. Now he reverts to the singular, "I."

30. So, e.g., Furnish, 574; Martin, 485-86, but not Plummer.

31. See on 10:1; 12:17-18.

14 *May the grace of the Lord Jesus Christ, and the love of God, and the fellowship of the Holy Spirit be with you all.*

Within these last verses[1] of the letter — introduced by "Finally"[2] — are found (1) final pithy admonitions, (2) greetings, and (3) a benediction. Many (partial) parallels for these are to be found elsewhere: (a) among Paul's other writings (e.g., 1 Thess 5:16-28; 2 Thess 3:16-18; 1 Cor 16:19-24), (b) in other NT writings (e.g., Heb 13:20-25; 1 Pet 5:12-14), and (c) in the everyday correspondence of the period.[3]

Those who regard chapters 10–13 as separate from chapters 1–9 naturally interpret vv. 11-13 as applicable only to chapters 10–13.[4] Where the letter is seen as undivided, as argued throughout, these verses serve to conclude the entire letter. Nonetheless, granted that the final chapters direct the Corinthians to correct their errors in light of his now-imminent arrival, these last words tend to sum up the emphases of the latter part of the letter.

11 In an almost identical way to 1 Corinthians (16:13-14), and in keeping with other letters (1 Thessalonians, Philippians), Paul begins his conclusion with a series of "staccato" admonitions. As in 1 Corinthians, too, they are adapted to the concerns of this letter, especially the latter chapters. His address "brothers" — but which would include "sisters" — is consonant with and in preparation for the admonitions following (cf. "beloved" — 12:19). There are five such admonitions,[5] each expressed in the present tense as imperatives; appropriately, they are followed by the assurance that "God . . . will be with you."

The first admonition, "Rejoice,"[6] is so understood, rather than as "good-by" (NIV) or "farewell" (RSV), on account (1) of the immediately prior use in v. 9, and (2) of a close parallel in the admonitions list of 1 Thess 5:16, where, as here, it appears first in a list of imperatives (where it can only mean "rejoice"). The "day of salvation," ushered in by the birth, death, and

---

1. Whereas the introductions to letters generally were more or less standardized in the Greco-Roman period, the same was not true of endings. To be sure, certain common elements were present, broadly speaking, e.g., greetings, a health wish, an autograph, and a postscript. As in his earlier letters Paul uses but freely adapts these elements. See further G. D. Fee, *1 Corinthians*, 825-26.

2. Gk. λοιπόν, as in 1 Thess 4:1 but rather "more colloquial" (so Plummer, 380) than τὸ λοιπόν in Phil 3:1; 4:8. However, λοιπόν in 1 Thess 4:1 and τὸ λοιπόν in Phil 3:1 do not mean "finally" so much as "as for what remains to be said."

3. E.g., see *New Docs.* 1.16; 2.20; 3.16.

4. So, e.g., Furnish, 581-88.

5. Parallel admonition lists are found in 1 Thess 5:12-22; 1 Cor 16:13-14; Rom 12:9-13.

6. Gk. χαίρετε.

resurrection of Christ and the coming of the Spirit, is characterized by "joy." Despite the constant reminders of suffering incurred in his ministry as stated throughout this letter, the apostle has repeatedly spoken of his "joy," both in present experience and in prospect (1:24; 2:3; 6:10; 7:4, 13). Thus, first of all in this list of admonitions, he exhorts the Corinthians, "Rejoice."

The second, "Be restored"[7] (here taken as passive rather than middle voice; cf. Rom 12:2), follows closely "I pray for your restoration" (see on v. 9). He admonishes them to fulfill his prayer for them. The Corinthians need to be "restored" — or "mended" — in their relationship to God and to each other in the messianic community. It is an exhortation to a divided church that its members recover theological, spiritual, and practical unity-in-Christ. Paul's injunction "Be reconciled to God" (5:20) has as its essential accompanying counterpart, "Be restored" to one another.

The third, "Be exhorted" or "Be encouraged,"[8] relates to the various exhortations and encouragements the apostle has laid upon the Corinthians during the course of his letter. Using the same language, Paul has "exhorted" them to reaffirm their love for the wrongdoer (2:8), to be reconciled to God (5:20), not to receive the grace of God in vain (6:1), and not to force him to act boldly toward them (10:1). In addition to his explicit use of the language of "exhortation," there are various examples in which, without the use of this vocabulary, he has exhorted them, for example, "widen your hearts . . . do not be mismated" (6:13-14; cf. 7:2); "give proof, before the churches, of your love and of our boasting about you to these men" (8:24, RSV); or coexhorted them, for example, "Let us cleanse ourselves" (6:1). Such "encouragements" are deliberately "pointed" and bring the will of the writer sharply to bear on the readers. Indeed, Paul's purposes in addressing this letter to the Corinthians may be seen at their clearest in such references. Whatever Paul has "encouraged" them to do throughout the letter, let them do it.

The fourth, "Set your mind on the same thing"[9] (also Rom 12:16; 15:5; Phil 2:2; 4:2), does not require the setting aside of individual opinion in matters of indifference. Rather, it calls on them to be united in their understanding of "the faith" (v. 5). The letter has revealed serious differences over definitions of spirituality (see on 10:2-7) and of apostolicity (11:1–12:14), over the covenant of God, whether it stands intact or whether it is now overtaken by the promised new covenant (3:3-18), over the necessity or otherwise to complete the collection (chaps. 8–9), and over the possibility of continuing in a Gentile lifestyle (6:14–7:1; 12:20–13:2). Let them have a

---

7. Gk. καταρτίζεσθε, not NIV, "aim for perfection." See the discussion of this word on v. 9 above.

8. Gk. παρακαλεῖσθε; NIV, "listen to my appeal."

9. Gk. τὸ αὐτὸ φρονεῖτε; NIV, "be of one mind."

common mind on such matters, as the apostle has been instructing them throughout this letter.

The fifth admonition, "Be at peace,"[10] is closely connected with the fourth. The peace between them will arise from their God-given capacity to "think the same thing." One passage specifically speaks of strife among them (12:20–13:2). But the entire letter presupposes major relationship difficulties within their community, creating the need for the present word of encouragement. Believers are caught up in spiritual warfare, both within their own lives and for the hearts and minds of unbelievers; they are not to be at war with one another.

The assurance, "And the God of love and peace will be with you," is cognate with each of the five preceding admonitions about joy, restoration, submission, unity, and peace. The God who is love and peace will bestow these blessings on the Corinthians as they heed the apostle's injunctions. God imparts his unique qualities to his children as they actively do his will. While "the God of peace" occurs frequently (1 Thess 5:23; Rom 15:33; 16:20; Phil 4:9; cf. 1 Cor 14:33), this is the only occasion when "the God of love" is used in the Bible (but cf. v. 13 — "the love of God").

12, 13   As with the conclusions of other letters of the Greco-Roman period, including ordinary correspondence (where the verb "to greet" is also used), various greetings are now encouraged and expressed.

First he exhorts them to "Greet one another with a holy kiss." No parallel for such a "kiss" is known among the synagogues. The "holy kiss," therefore, appears to be an innovation within the churches. A similar injunction occurs in other letters by Paul (1 Thess 5:26; 1 Cor 16:20; Rom 16:16), as well as the first letter by Peter (1 Pet 5:14a). That it is called "holy" may distinguish the "kiss" as nonerotic;[11] it was probably not to the mouth. As such it expressed affection, as between family members ("beloved . . . brothers" — 12:19; 13:11), greeting one another as God's "holy ones," or "saints" (cf. v. 12b). This encouragement to warmhearted fellowship is particularly appropriate to the church in Corinth, whose fragmentation is evident throughout this letter and is reflected in the admonitions of the previous verse ("be restored . . . think the same thing . . . be at peace").[12]

Second, the apostle sends greetings to the Corinthians from "all the saints," which we take to mean the "saints" (see on 1:1) of Macedonia.

---

10. Gk. εἰρηνεύετε.

11. For an extensive survey of the kiss in antiquity, see G. Stählin, *TDNT* 9.119-24.

12. A century later Justin Martyr connects the "kiss" with the Eucharist; his direction "Salute one another with a kiss" occurred between the prayers and the offertory of bread and wine (*Apol.* 1.65). But evidence that the "holy kiss" was part of the NT Eucharist is lacking.

"Saints" are individual believers, reminding us of the distributive as well as of the congregational character of Christianity (see also 1:1; 1 Cor 1:2; 14:33; cf. Phil 1:1). Although the greeting comes from them, however, it might equally have come from the Macedonian churches (cf. Rom 16:16). There was probably some feeling between the churches of these Greek provinces, especially over their respective attitudes (1) toward the apostle (see on 8:5; 11:9), and (2) toward the collection (see on 8:1-6). It was important, therefore, for the greeting to be sent *and* received.

14 With this justly famous benediction[13] the apostle concludes both his farewell words and the entire letter. A few verses earlier he prayed that the "God of love and of peace" be "with" them (v. 11). Now he prays that "the grace of the Lord Jesus Christ, the love of God, and the fellowship of the Holy Spirit" be "with" them.

This prayer reflects the experience of both the believer and the church through the gospel message (1:19), wherein the "grace [i.e., the sheer mercy — see on 1:2] of the Lord Jesus Christ" is understood. This fundamental of the gospel was expressed as a benediction that was often pronounced on its own (1 Thess 5:28; Gal 6:18; 1 Cor 16:23; Rom 16:20b; Phlm 25) and is reflected in the well-known christological passage earlier in the letter (see on 8:9). As a consequence of apprehending "the grace of . . . Christ," there is the knowledge of "the love of God" (so also Rom 5:5; 8:9), that is, of the Father (see on 1:2-3; cf. 1 Thess 1:2-3). Because he is "the God of love" (v. 11), he is the God who "loves" (cf. 9:7) his children (see on 1:3, 9-11, 21; 7:6). As a further consequence of the "grace of . . . Christ," there is the "fellowship of the Holy Spirit," arising from the now-fulfilled "day of salvation" (5:14–6:2; cf. 1:21-22; 3:3, 8, 18; 5:5; 11:4), as a result of which there is both[14] (1) the individual's fellowship with the Spirit (Phil 2:1; cf. "we cry, 'Abba,' Father" — Rom 8:15; Gal 4:6), and (2) the fellowship created by the Spirit in the assembly of Spirit-indwelt ones (6:16; cf. 1 Cor 3:16-17; Eph 2:21-22).

But this benediction, being normative of the experience of those who receive the word of God, also serves to recall the Corinthians to relearn the fundamentals of "the faith" (see on 13:5a), and so be "restored" (or "mend-

---

13. According to Furnish, 587, "No other Pauline letter concludes with a benediction so theologically imposing as this one." G. D. Fee goes further, referring to it as in some ways ". . . the most profound theological moment in the Pauline corpus" (*Presence,* 363). According to Fee (362), this prayer is almost certainly ad hoc, not directly quoted from the church's liturgical tradition.

14. The genitive ἡ κοινωνία τοῦ πνεύματος can be understood both subjectively and objectively, though many argue for either the former (e.g., Plummer, 383-84) or the latter (e.g., Barrett, 344; Furnish, 584). The subjective genitive is to be preferred, given the emphasis on the Spirit within this letter (1:20-22; 3:3, 8, 18; 5:5; 6:16; 11:4).

ed" — vv. 9, 11) in their relationship to God and to each other. Whether they are flirting with the "other Jesus" of the intruders, or enmeshed in a Gentile lifestyle, or loftily critical of Paul — and by those errors distanced from God and divided from one another — let them return to "the grace of . . . Christ," which in turn opens the doors to their experience of "the love of God" and the "fellowship of the Holy Spirit."[15] Here is the key to renewal of both the individual and the church, then and now.

It is clear from this three-part benediction, when read next to "*the* God of love and of peace" (v. 11), that Paul thinks of the one God as in some sense triune. There is (1) the Lord Jesus Christ, (2) God, his Father (1:3; 11:31) — who are in a personal ("Father" and "Son") relationship — and (3) the Holy Spirit, whose "fellowship" with persons implies that he is a person, not a "force" or "influence."

Triune references are quite common in Paul (e.g., Gal 4:4-6; 1 Cor 12:4-6; Eph 1:3, 13-14; 2:18; 3:14-17; 4:4-6), though there, as here, he does not explain either the relative status of the persons or their relationship with one another or with God. Nonetheless, this statement cannot be dismissed as merely "functional." The "grace . . . love . . . fellowship" relate to "personal beings" who are called by different names. It is a small step to believe that the "God of love and of peace" of whom Paul spoke comes to us as three "persons" within the one God. Thus we may agree with H. B. Swete[16] that this verse "suggests beyond doubt that beneath the religious life of the apostolic age there lay a profound, though as yet unformulated, faith in the tri-personality of God." As Karl Barth observed, "Trinity is the Christian name for God."

So the letter ends. As the lector closes the scroll, the minds of the Corinthians will be focused on one thing: Paul's impending arrival for his final visit. In the weeks between their receipt of the letter and his coming, did they heed his admonition? Although we can only speculate, it appears that this letter, like the "Severe Letter," brought a change of heart, for the following reasons: (1) Paul spent three months there soon afterward upon his arrival (Acts 20:2-3), (2) the Achaians participated in the collection (so Rom 15:26, despite the absence of named persons in Acts 20:4), and (3) the Letter to the Romans, which was probably written from Corinth soon after his arrival, has little of the anguish and heat evident in 2 Corinthians.

15. See R. P. Martin, "The Spirit in 2 Corinthians," 112-28, for the view that the triune benediction is especially approropriate to the present ecclesial situation of the Corinthians and that Paul's emphasis falls on the work of the Spirit in the lives of the Corinthians, in the light of other Spirit references throughout this letter.

16. Quoted in Plummer, 384.

Be that as it may, what remains for posterity is this letter. It is remarkable for the patient confidence of its author toward those wayward and fickle believers in Roman Corinth, for its disclosure of Paul's personal hurt, and for his own robust yet subtle exposition of the gospel of Christ in relationship to the matters of current concern in Corinth, matters that are forever lost through the distance of history and the eternal incompleteness of our knowledge. Yet Paul's words — the text — remain, and come to us borne by the Spirit of God, with the authority of the Lord Christ himself, whose devoted minister Paul was.

INDEX OF SUBJECTS

hope, 45, 79, 245-77

idolatry, 349-50, 355-57
incarnation of Christ, 306, 407-9
inclusio, 93, 328, 343, 366-67, 386, 448,
 492, 503
insiders and outsiders, 453-55, 484-85,
 498
intercession and thanksgiving, 89-90
irony, 458, 481-84, 506, 515, 520, 528,
 532-33, 557, 582, 609
Isaiah, 40-66; in Babylon, 353; language
 of, 46-47, 440; parallel to Paul, 309-
 12, 317; servant of God, 319
Israelites, 182, 190, 192, 204, 217

James, leader of Jerusalem Christianity,
 163, 173
Jerusalem, destination for the collection,
 14
Jesus' ministry, 388, 395-98, 405, 412-
 14, 421-26, 436, 439, 442-44, 448
Jesus, "another," 496-507, 613, 619
Jesus Christ: "as Lord," in proclamation
 and baptism, 64, 103-10, 133-37, 220-
 27, 279-81, 398-400, 466, 472; birth,
 death, resurrection, 616; incarnation
 of, 406-9; in them, 607-12; meekness
 and gentleness of, 457-60, 478-79; revelation of God, 71
Jews, 211, 217
joy, 116-20, 333, 363-64, 366-86, 392,
 436, 451, 614, 616
Judaea, 100-101, 421, 443, 488
Judaizers, 35, 161
Judaizing impact, 68, 112, 527
judgment, 239, 243-44, 273, 275-77,
 279, 474, 592
justification/righteousness, 302

labor in self-support, 327, 511-22, 540-
 42, 581
law, the role of (see also Moses), 202-3
letters of: Greco-Roman era, 56; recommendation, 159-67, 482, 527
life, 227-45
literary issues: unity, 15-25
litotes, 374-76, 473, 526, 579
living God, 165-70, 350-51
love, Christ's, 286-321 passim; Corinthians', 406, 428, 520; Macedonian
 churches, 520; Paul's, 404-6 (see also

at 2:4; 8:7; 11:11; 12:15); proof of,
 justification, 442, 445; questioned by
 the Corinthians, 519

Macedonia, 12-14, 16, 23, 133-37, 146,
 364-82, 387, 421, 439
Macedonian: churches, 13, 16, 389-406,
 413, 417-23, 429, 433, 522; delegate,
 including the famous and the less
 famous brother, 387, 400-402, 411,
 417-20, 425-26, 429-30, 433-35
Messianic: fellowship, corporate character of, 73; sufferings, 74
metonymy, 313, 407
midrash, 178, 188, 191, 192, 197-98
military procession, imagery of, 145-52
ministry: associated with the collection,
 397, 421, 423, 430, 442-44
minister, 174-86, 211, 322, 324, 361,
 516, 592; minister of righteousness,
 526; new covenant, 41, 137-45, 211,
 226-27, 231, 279, 281, 286, 341, 359,
 362, 364, 367
mirror exegesis, 27, 34-35, 102, 534,
 556, 568, 574, 588
missionary concordat in Jerusalem, 485,
 488, 490-91, 494
money disputes, 13, 31-32, 156-59, 212-
 15, 360-64, 511-22, 581-90
Moses, 37, 138, 143, 169-71, 173, 179,
 182-83, 187-89, 191-92, 232, 308,
 506, 527, 531, 538

Nabataea, 554-55
nakedness, 260-68, 272
new covenant, the, 165, 168, 171, 174-
 79, 181, 184, 186-92, 194, 196-97,
 209, 211, 232, 298, 309, 318, 539, 616
new creation, 287-321 passim
Nineteen Benedictions, the, 67, 82, 87

oath-taking, 104-5, 114-15, 123-25, 129-
 31, 518-20, 524, 591
old covenant, 168, 174, 178-79, 181,
 184, 186-92, 194, 196, 209, 211, 220,
 527, 539
opponents, newly arrived, also referred
 to as intruders, 141, 143, 277-86, 325-
 26, 336, 343, 348, 359, 481, 485, 488-
 89, 491, 493-96, 504, 512, 521-22,
 524, 529, 531, 533, 536-82, 584, 595,
 609

INDEX OF AUTHORS

626

INDEX OF SCRIPTURE REFERENCES

9:39	459	145:8-9	70	40:1	69, 317, 369
11	346			40:28-31	46, 303
17:28	459	**Proverbs**		41:17-20	46, 303
18:4	348	1:7	357	42:1-4	75
19:12	307	1:29	357	42:5-9	46, 303
22:1	234	3:4	424	42:9	297
25:6	69, 70	4:18	208	43	46
30:12	230	7:3	168	43:3-4	46
32:1-2	307	8:13	357	43:6	354
32:19	87	8:30	131	43:18	293
33:19	459	9:10	279	43:18-19	144, 297
34	346	10:2	87	43:19	297
40:6-8	412	11:21	436	44:21-22	46, 303
40:12	70	11:24	436	44:24-28	46, 303
44:5	459	11:30	436	45:1-8	46, 303
46:5	222	14:5	104	45:9	230
46:6	63	14:25	104	45:9-13	46, 303
50:8	412	21:22	464, 465	45:18-20	303
51:1-11	377	22:8	436, 437, 438	45:22	23
51:2	70	23:14	87	45:22-24	222
55:16-17	571			48:6	297
65:20	65, 68	**Ecclesiastes**		49:1-6	69
69:16	69, 70	12:13	279	49:6	225
77:9	70			49:8	46, 319, 303
79:8	70	**Isaiah**		49:8-13	46, 303
81:3	459	1:11-13	412	49:9	104
84:7	208	1:16	412	49:13	69, 369
85:5	459	1:17	412	51:1-2	537
101:18	459	1:22	157	51:1-3	46, 303
103:2	5, 69	2:2-3	397	51:3	69, 72, 369, 560
103:2-5	72	6:1	561	51:9-11	46, 303
103:4	70	6:9	565	51:12	72, 369
106:24	169	6:9-10	194	51:12-16	46, 303
106:25	169	8:12	319	51:19	72, 369
106:46	70	8:14	550	52:9	369
110	440	9:6	500	52:11	353
110:3	440	11:1	108	52:13–53:12	69, 289,
111	440	18:20	46		313, 314
111:3	440	19:16	385	53:3	289
111:9	439, 441	19:22	199	53:4	289
112:6	459	26:17	74	53:5	289
115:1	249	28:7	284	53:6	289
116:10	241	28:7-9	550	53:9	314
116:12-19	241	28:16	550	53:10	314
117:17	332	29:6	230	53:11	314
117:18	332	29:8	316	53:12	289
118:32	335	29:10	194	54:1-10	46, 303
119:77	70	29:18	565	54:5-6	498, 500
119:156	70	32:12	441	55:6-13	46, 303
135:9	581	37:32	500	55:10	440
137:6	459	40–55	46, 47, 72, 369,	55:10-11	154
139:5	297		377	59:20	108

INDEX OF EARLY
EXTRABIBLICAL LITERATURE